Guide to Gale Literary Criticism Series

For criticism on	Consult these Gale series
Authors now living or who died after December 31, 1999	*CONTEMPORARY LITERARY CRITICISM (CLC)*
Authors who died between 1900 and 1999	*TWENTIETH-CENTURY LITERARY CRITICISM (TCLC)*
Authors who died between 1800 and 1899	*NINETEENTH-CENTURY LITERATURE CRITICISM (NCLC)*
Authors who died between 1400 and 1799	*LITERATURE CRITICISM FROM 1400 TO 1800 (LC)* *SHAKESPEAREAN CRITICISM (SC)*
Authors who died before 1400	*CLASSICAL AND MEDIEVAL LITERATURE CRITICISM (CMLC)*
Authors of books for children and young adults	*CHILDREN'S LITERATURE REVIEW (CLR)*
Dramatists	*DRAMA CRITICISM (DC)*
Poets	*POETRY CRITICISM (PC)*
Short story writers	*SHORT STORY CRITICISM (SSC)*
Black writers of the past two hundred years	*BLACK LITERATURE CRITICISM (BLC)* *BLACK LITERATURE CRITICISM SUPPLEMENT (BLCS)*
Hispanic writers of the late nineteenth and twentieth centuries	*HISPANIC LITERATURE CRITICISM (HLC)* *HISPANIC LITERATURE CRITICISM SUPPLEMENT (HLCS)*
Native North American writers and orators of the eighteenth, nineteenth, and twentieth centuries	*NATIVE NORTH AMERICAN LITERATURE (NNAL)*
Major authors from the Renaissance to the present	*WORLD LITERATURE CRITICISM, 1500 TO THE PRESENT (WLC)* *WORLD LITERATURE CRITICISM SUPPLEMENT (WLCS)*

ISSN 1056-4349

DRAMA CRITICISM

Criticism of the Most Significant and Widely Studied
Dramatic Works from All the World's Literatures

VOLUME 17

Scott T. Darga
Editor

GALE®

THOMSON
—✦—
GALE

Detroit • New York • San Diego • San Francisco • Cleveland • New Haven, Conn. • Waterville, Maine • London • Munich

THOMSON
★
GALE

Drama Criticism, Vol. 17

Project Editor
Janet Witalec

Editorial
Scott Darga, Kathy D. Darrow, Madeline S.
Harris, Ellen McGeagh, Ron Morelli

Research
Nicodemus Ford, Sarah Genik, Tamara C. Nott,
Tracie A. Richardson

Permissions
Lori Hines

Imaging and Multimedia
Lezlie Light, Kelly A. Quin, Luke Rademacher

Product Design
Michael Logusz

Composition and Electronic Capture
Gary Leach

Manufacturing
Stacy L. Melson

LIBRARY OF CONGRESS CATALOG CARD NUMBER 76-46132

ISBN 0-7876-5946-0
ISSN 1056-4349

Printed in the United States of America
10 9 8 7 6 5 4 3 2 1

Contents

Preface vii

Acknowledgments xi

Preface

*D*rama Criticism *(DC)* is principally intended for beginning students of literature and theater as well as the average playgoer. The series is therefore designed to introduce readers to the most frequently studied playwrights of all time periods and nationalities and to present discerning commentary on dramatic works of enduring interest. Furthermore, *DC* seeks to acquaint the reader with the uses and functions of criticism itself. Selected from a diverse body of commentary, the essays in *DC* offer insights into the authors and their works but do not require that the reader possess a wide background in literary studies. Where appropriate, reviews of important productions of the plays discussed are also included to give students a heightened awareness of drama as a dynamic art form, one that many claim is fully realized only in performance.

DC was created in response to suggestions by the staffs of high school, college, and public libraries. These librarians observed a need for a series that assembles critical commentary on the world's most renowned dramatists in the same manner as Gale's *Short Story Criticism (SSC)* and *Poetry Criticism (PC)*, which present material on writers of short fiction and poetry. Although playwrights are covered in such Gale literary criticism series as *Contemporary Literary Criticism (CLC)*, *Twentieth-Century Literary Criticism (TCLC)*, *Nineteenth-Century Literature Criticism (NCLC)*, *Literature Criticism from 1400 to 1800 (LC)*, and *Classical and Medieval Literature Criticism (CMLC)*, *DC* directs more concentrated attention on individual dramatists than is possible in the broader, survey-oriented entries in these Gale series. Commentary on the works of William Shakespeare may be found in *Shakespearean Criticism (SC)*.

Scope of the Series

By collecting and organizing commentary on dramatists, *DC* assists students in their efforts to gain insight into literature, achieve better understanding of the texts, and formulate ideas for papers and assignments. A variety of interpretations and assessments is offered, allowing students to pursue their own interests and promoting awareness that literature is dynamic and responsive to many different opinions.

Approximately five to ten authors are included in each volume, and each entry presents a historical survey of the critical response to that playwright's work. The length of an entry is intended to reflect the amount of critical attention the author has received from critics writing in English and from foreign critics in translation. Every attempt has been made to identify and include the most significant essays on each author's work. In order to provide these important critical pieces, the editors sometimes reprint essays that have appeared elsewhere in Gale's literary criticism series. Such duplication, however, never exceeds twenty percent of a *DC* volume.

Organization of the Book

A *DC* entry consists of the following elements:

- The **Author Heading** consists of the playwright's most commonly used name, followed by birth and death dates. If an author consistently wrote under a pseudonym, the pseudonym is listed in the author heading and the real name given in parentheses on the first line of the introduction. Also located at the beginning of the introduction are any name variations under which the dramatist wrote, including transliterated forms of the names of authors whose languages use nonroman alphabets.

- The **Introduction** contains background information that introduces the reader to the author and the critical debates surrounding his or her work.

- A **Portrait of the Author** is included when available.

- The list of **Principal Works** is divided into two sections. The first section contains the author's dramatic pieces and is organized chronologically by date of first performance. If this has not been conclusively determined, the composition or publication date is used. The second section provides information on the author's major works in other genres.

- Essays offering **overviews and general studies of the dramatist's entire literary career** give the student broad perspectives on the writer's artistic development, themes, and concerns that recur in several of his or her works, the author's place in literary history, and other wide-ranging topics.

- **Criticism** of individual plays offers the reader in-depth discussions of a select number of the author's most important works. In some cases, the criticism is divided into two sections, each arranged chronologically. When a significant performance of a play can be identified (typically, the premier of a twentieth-century work), the first section of criticism will feature **production reviews** of this staging. Most entries include sections devoted to **critical commentary** that assesses the literary merit of the selected plays. When necessary, essays are carefully excerpted to focus on the work under consideration; often, however, essays and reviews are reprinted in their entirety. Footnotes are reprinted at the end of each essay or excerpt. In the case of excerpted criticism, only those footnotes that pertain to the excerpted texts are included.

- Critical essays are prefaced by brief **Annotations** explicating each piece.

- A complete **Bibliographic Citation,** designed to help the interested reader locate the original essay or book, precedes each piece of criticism.

- An annotated bibliography of **Further Reading** appears at the end of each entry and suggests resources for additional study. In some cases, significant essays for which the editors could not obtain reprint rights are included here. Boxed material following the further reading list provides references to other biographical and critical sources on the author in series published by Gale.

Cumulative Indexes

A **Cumulative Author Index** lists all of the authors that appear in a wide variety of reference sources published by the Gale Group, including *DC*. A complete list of these sources is found facing the first page of the Author Index. The index also includes birth and death dates and cross references between pseudonyms and actual names.

A **Cumulative Nationality Index** lists all authors featured in *DC* by nationality, followed by the number of the *DC* volume in which their entry appears.

A **Cumulative Title Index** lists in alphabetical order the individual plays discussed in the criticism contained in *DC*. Each title is followed by the author's last name and corresponding volume and page numbers where commentary on the work is located. English-language translations of original foreign-language titles are cross-referenced to the foreign titles so that all references to discussion of a work are combined in one listing.

Citing *Drama Criticism*

When writing papers, students who quote directly from any volume in *Drama Criticism* may use the following general formats to footnote reprinted criticism. The first example pertains to material drawn from periodicals, the second to materials reprinted from books.

Susan Sontag, "Going to the Theater, Etc.," *Partisan Review* XXXI, no. 3 (Summer 1964), 389-94; excerpted and reprinted in *Drama Criticism,* vol. 1, ed. Lawrence J. Trudeau (Detroit: Gale Research, 1991), 17-20.

Eugene M. Waith, *The Herculean Hero in Marlowe, Chapman, Shakespeare and Dryden* (Chatto & Windus, 1962); excerpted and reprinted in *Drama Criticism,* vol. 1, ed. Lawrence J. Trudeau (Detroit: Gale Research, 1991), 237-47.

Suggestions are Welcome

Readers who wish to suggest new features, topics, or authors to appear in future volumes, or who have other suggestions or comments are cordially invited to call, write, or fax the Project Editor:

Project Editor, Literary Criticism Series
The Gale Group
27500 Drake Road
Farmington Hills, MI 48331-3535
1-800-347-4253 (GALE)
Fax: 248-699-8054

Acknowledgments

The editors wish to thank the copyright holders of the excerpted criticism included in this volume and the permissions managers of many book and magazine publishing companies for assisting us in securing reproduction rights. We are also grateful to the staffs of the Detroit Public Library, the Library of Congress, the University of Detroit Mercy Library, Wayne State University Purdy/Kresge Library Complex, and the University of Michigan Libraries for making their resources available to us. Following is a list of the copyright holders who have granted us permission to reproduce material in this volume of *DC*. Every effort has been made to trace copyright, but if omissions have been made, please let us know.

COPYRIGHTED MATERIAL IN *DC*, VOLUME 17, WAS REPRODUCED FROM THE FOLLOWING PERIODICALS:

American Drama, v. 4, Spring, 1995. Reproduced by permission.—*American Quarterly,* v. 15, Winter, 1963. © The Johns Hopkins University Press. Reproduced by permission.—*Classical and Modern Literature: A Quarterly,* v. 17, Fall, 1996. Reproduced by permission.—*Dance Research Journal,* v. 25, Spring, 1993. Reproduced by permission.—*Essays in Criticism,* v. 26, n. 1, January, 1976, pp. 28-41, for "Serious Bunburyism: The Logic of 'The Importance of Being Earnest'," by Geoffrey Stone. Reproduced by permission of Oxford University Press.—*The Explicator,* v. 54, Fall, 1995; v. 57, Winter, 1999; v. 59, Spring, 2001. Reproduced by permission.—*Forum for Modern Language Studies,* v. 29, n. 1, January, 1993, pp. 31-45, for "Folded Eternity: Time and the Mythic Dimension in Cocteau's 'La machine infernale,'" by Derek F. Connon. Reproduced by permission of Oxford University Press.—*Germanic Review,* v. 37, January, 1962. Reproduced by permission.—*Journal of the Hellenic Diaspora,* v. 26, 2000. Reproduced by permission.—*Literature/Film Quarterly,* v. 26, 1998. Reproduced by permission.—*Los Angeles Times,* v. 104, 1 August, 1985. Reproduced by permission.—*Modern Austrian Literature,* v. 2, Summer, 1969; v. 19, 1986. Reproduced by permission.—*Modern Drama,* v. 6, December, 1964; v. 11, 1968; v. 19, March, 1976; v. 29, September, 1986; v. 33, September, 1990; v. 37, Spring, 1994; v. 39, Winter, 1996; v. 41, Summer, 1998. Reproduced by permission.—*Modern Fiction Studies,* v. 36, Autumn, 1990. Reproduced by permission.—*Modern Language Quarterly,* v. 35, n. 2, June, 1974, pp. 173-86, for "Oscar Wilde's Great Farce: 'The Importance of Being Ernest,'" by David Parker. Copyright University of Washington. Reproduced by permission.—*Modern Language Review,* v. 89, July, 1994, for "The Comedy of Schnitzler's 'Reigen,'" by Ian F. Roe; v. 95, October, 2000, for "Dramaturgies of Sprachkritik: Rainer Werner Fassbinder's 'Blut Am Hals Der Katze' and Peter Handke's 'Kaspar,'" by David Barrett © Modern Humanities Research Association, 1994. Reproduced by permission of the publisher.—*Mosaic,* March, 2000. Reproduced by permission.—*The Nation,* New York, v. 149, October 28, 1939. © 1939 The Nation magazine/The Nation Company, Inc. Reproduced by permission.—*New York Times,* v. 144, 26 December, 1994. Reproduced by permission.—*Nineteenth Century Theatre,* v. 23, Summer-Winter, 1995 for "The Persons of the Play: Some Reflections on Wilde's Choice of Names in 'The Importance of Being Earnest,'" by Peter Raby. Reproduced by permission of publisher and the author.—*Philological Quarterly,* v. 63, Spring, 1984 for "Peter Handke's 'Kaspar': A Study of Linguistic Theory in Modern Drama" by Jeffrey Herrick. Reproduced by permission by the author.—*The Quarterly Journal of Speech,* v. 51, n. 3, October, 1965, pp. 311-25, for "Cocteau's 'Orphee': From Myth to Drama and Film," by Chester Clayton Long. Reproduced by permission of the National Communication Association.—*Raritan,* Winter, 1985. Reproduced by permission.—*Romance Notes,* v. 27, Autumn, 1986. Reproduced by permission.—*Romance Quarterly,* v. 35, November, 1988. Reproduced by permission.—*The Saturday Review,* v. 44, June 24, 1961. © 1961 Saturday Review Magazine, © 1979 General Media International, Inc. Reproduced by permission.—*Spectator,* v. 165, September 13, 1940. © 1940 by *The Spectator.* Reproduced by permission of *The Spectator.*—*Texas Review,* v. 5, 1920. Reproduced by permission.—*Theater,* v. 9, Spring, 1978; v. 24, n.1, Summer, 1993, pp. 87-92, for "Seeing Through the Eyes of the Word," by Gitta Honegger. Copyright © Theater 1978, Copyright Yale School of Drama/Yale Repertory Theater, 1993. Reproduced by permission.—*TriQuarterly,* v. 15, Spring, 1969 for "Overtures to Wilde's 'Salome,'" by Richard Ellman. Copyright 1969 by Richard Ellman. Reproduced by permission of Donadio & Olson, Inc.—*The Victorian Newsletter,* v. 89, Spring, 1996 for "A Source Victorian or Biblical?: The Integration of Biblical Diction and Symbolism in Oscar Wilde's 'Salome,'" by Jason P. Mitchell. Reproduced by permission of author.—*Washington Post,* 9 October, 1998, p. N41, for "The Truth About Lake Constance," by Sarah Kaufman. Reproduced by permission.—*Washington Times,* 27 September, 1998. Copyright © News-World Communications, Inc. Reprinted by permission of *The Washington Times.*—*Word & Image,* v. 4, January-March, 1988. Reproduced by permission of Taylor & Francis Ltd., http://www.tandf.co.uk/journals.—*World Literature Today,* v. 73, Autumn, 1999. Reproduced by permission.

COPYRIGHTED MATERIAL IN *DC*, VOLUME 17, WAS REPRODUCED FROM THE FOLLOWING BOOKS:

Finney, Gail. From "Female Sexuality and Schnitzler's 'La Ronde,'" in ***Women in Modern Drama: Freud, Feminism, and European Theater at the Turn of the Century.*** Cornell University Press, 1989. Copyright © 1989 by Cornell University Press. All rights reserved. Reproduced by permission of the publisher, Cornell University Press.—Firda, Richard Arthur. From "Theatrical Experiments," in ***Peter Handke.*** Twayne Publishers, 1993. Copyright © 1993 by Twayne Publishers. All rights reserved. Reproduced by permission.—Hern, Nicholas. From "Kaspar," in ***Peter Handke: Theatre and Anti-Theatre.*** Oswald Wolff, 1971. Copyright © 1971 by Oswald Wolff. All right reserved. Reproduced by permission.—Hern, Nicholas. From "Offending the Audience," in ***Peter Handke: Theatre and Anti-Theatre.*** Oswald Wolff, 1971. Copyright © 1971 by Oswald Wolff. All rights reserved. Reproduced by permission.—Hern, Nicholas. From "The Ride Over Lake Constance," in ***Peter Handke: Theatre and Anti-Theatre.*** Oswald Wolff, 1971. Copyright © 1971 by Oswald Wolff. All rights reserved. Reproduced by permission.—Mason, Jeffrey D. From ***Farce.*** Cambridge University Press, 1988. © Cambridge University Press 1988. Reproduced by permission Cambridge University Press.—Schlueter, June. From "Kaspar," in ***The Plays and Novels of Peter Handke.*** University of Pittsburgh Press, 1981. Copyright © 1981 by University of Pittsburgh Press. All rights reserved. Reproduced by permission.—Schneider-Halvorson, Brigitte L. From "Der Gang Zum Weiher," in ***The Late Dramatic Works of Arthur Schnitzler.*** Peter Lang, 1983. Copyright © 1983 by Peter Lang. All rights reserved. Reproduced by permission.—Schneider-Halvorson, Brigitte L. From "Die Schwestern oder Casanova in Spa," in ***The Late Dramatic Works of Arthur Schnitzler.*** Peter Lang, 1983. Copyright © 1983 by Peter Lang. All rights reserved. Reproduced by permission.—Schneider-Halvorson, Brigitte L. From "Im Spiel Der Sommerlufte," in ***The Late Dramatic Works of Arthur Schnitzler.*** Peter Lang, 1983. Copyright © 1983 by Peter Lang. All rights reserved. Reproduced by permission.—Swales, Martin. From "Tragedy and Comedy," in ***Arthur Schnitzler: A Critical Study.*** Oxford University Press, 1971. Copyright © 1971 by Oxford University Press. All rights reserved. Reproduced by permission of Oxford University Press.—Urbach, Reinhard. From "Early Full-Length Plays," in ***Arthur Schnitzler.*** Frederick Ungar Publishing Co., 1973. Copyright © 1973 by Frederick Ungar Publishing Co. All rights reserved. Reproduced by permission of the Continuum International Publishing Company.

PHOTOGRAPHS APPEARING IN *DC*, VOLUME 17, WERE RECEIVED FROM THE FOLLOWING SOURCES:

Cocteau, Jean, photograph. AP/Wide World Photos. Reproduced by permission.—Handke, Peter, photograph by Jerry Bauer. © Jerry Bauer. Reproduced by permission.—Kaufman, George S., photograph. The Library of Congress.—Schnitzler, Arthur, photograph. © Bettmann/Corbis. Reproduced by Corbis Corporation.—Wilde, Oscar, photograph.

Literary Criticism Series Advisory Board

The members of the Gale Group Literary Criticism Series Advisory Board—reference librarians and subject specialists from public, academic, and school library systems—represent a cross-section of our customer base and offer a variety of informed perspectives on both the presentation and content of our literature criticism products. Advisory board members assess and define such quality issues as the relevance, currency, and usefulness of the author coverage, critical content, and literary topics included in our series; evaluate the layout, presentation, and general quality of our printed volumes; provide feedback on the criteria used for selecting authors and topics covered in our series; provide suggestions for potential enhancements to our series; identify any gaps in our coverage of authors or literary topics, recommending authors or topics for inclusion; analyze the appropriateness of our content and presentation for various user audiences, such as high school students, undergraduates, graduate students, librarians, and educators; and offer feedback on any proposed changes/enhancements to our series. We wish to thank the following advisors for their advice throughout the year.

Jean Cocteau
1889-1963

(Born Jean Maurice Eugène Clément Cocteau) French playwright, poet, novelist, filmmaker, scriptwriter, critic, essayist, librettist, and autobiographer.

INTRODUCTION

Among the most versatile, innovative, and prolific literary figures of the twentieth century, Cocteau is best known for his dramas and films in which he utilized myth and tragedy in modern contexts to shock and surprise his audiences. Identifying himself as a poet and referring to virtually all of his works as poetry, Cocteau rejected naturalism in favor of lyrical fantasy, through which he sought to create a "poetry of the theatre" consisting not of words but of such stage devices as ballet, music, and pantomime. The fantastic, or *le merveilleux,* is made manifest in Cocteau's plays through inanimate objects and symbolic characters, which embellish one's understanding of "reality" by making the impossible possible.

BIOGRAPHICAL INFORMATION

In 1889 Cocteau was born into a wealthy Parisian family. Although he briefly attended the Lycée Condorcet in Paris, he detested school and left to pursue a writing career. His early poetry and novels attracted the attention of critics and intellectuals. Toward the end of World War I, Cocteau became associated with the avant-garde movement at Montparnasse, which included such poets as Guillaume Apollinaire and Blaise Cendrars. Despite his involvement with these central artistic figures, Cocteau never allied himself with any school or movement. The death of his mentor and lover, Raymond Radiguet, in 1923 devastated Cocteau; grief-stricken, he turned to opium, an addiction that plagued him all of his life and was the subject of many of his writings. While hospitalized for opium poisoning in 1929, Cocteau met the Catholic philosopher Jacques Maritain. Maritain's influence prompted Cocteau to turn briefly to religion. In the 1940s Cocteau became involved in filmmaking, adapting several of his plays to film. He was elected to the prestigious Académie Française in 1956. He died on October 11, 1963 in Milly-la-Foret, Essone, France.

MAJOR WORKS

Cocteau's early ballets, *Parade* (1917) and *Le Dieu bleu* (1912), were inspired by Serge de Diaghilev and his Ballet Russes and featured music by Eric Satie and set designs and costumes by Pablo Picasso. *Parade* depicts a festival

and its bizarre promoters, who attempt to entice an onstage audience to enter a mysterious tent; the ballet ends without the spectators having entered the tent, implying that Cocteau's interest is not in the event itself but in the visual occurrences that surround it. Although a complete failure at its first production, *Parade* is generally regarded as one of the twentieth century's most innovative ballets. *Les Mariés de la tour Eiffel* (1924; *The Eiffel Tower Wedding Party*), an irreverent satire of bourgeois values, centers on a banal wedding party at the base of the Eiffel Tower. In *Antigone* (1922), Cocteau adapted Sophocles's tragedy to what he called "the rhythm of our times," thus initiating a lifelong preoccupation with contemporizing Greek mythologies. *Orphée* (1926; *Orpheus*) is among Cocteau's most innovative adaptations, focusing on the poet as interpreter of the supernatural and the poet's relationship to the source of inspiration. In this drama, objects, animals, and characters become symbols of ritual and acquire startling new associations. Cocteau also attempted several adaptations of the Oedipal myth during his career. The first, *Oedipus-Rex* (1926), is an opera-oratorio on which he collaborated with composer Igor Stravinsky. *Oedipe Roi* (1928), a free adaptation that Cocteau revised in 1962 as an attempt at "total theatre," combines virtually all the performing arts to evoke lyric tragedy. Cocteau's best-regarded reworking of the Oedipal myth is *La machine infernale* (1934; *The Infernal Machine*), a drama exploring the relationship between free will and determinism that makes use of modern vernacular and musical forms.

Of his original dramas, *La voix humaine* (1930; *The Human Voice*) is probably Cocteau's most often-performed work. Written as a "monodrama," a one-act lay for a single character, the drama consists entirely of a woman's one-sided conversation with a boyfriend who has abandoned her. *Les parents terribles* (1938; *Intimate Relations*), a drama about family conflict, jealousy, and manipulation, reveals the influence of Greek tragedy but derives its form from Parisian boulevard theater. Cocteau's plays of the 1940s are generally considered less successful than his earlier works. *L'aigle à deux têtes* (1946; *The Eagle Has Two Heads*), his best-known work of this period, is a melodrama in which a young poet, allegorically representing the angel of death, falls in love with a puppet empress and with tragic results attempts to help her regain her power.

CRITICAL RECEPTION

Evaluations of Cocteau's career often touch on the variety of his work and his prolific creative output. Critics have offered mixed assessments of his oeuvre: some reviewers assert that his efforts were inconsistent and that he was too preoccupied with producing avant-garde works; others maintain that his failures outnumber his successes. Moreover, Cocteau's detractors often questioned his importance as an original and innovative artist. Critics note that alienation is a defining thematic concern in Cocteau's work; other subjects for critical commentary have been his focus on the origin of artistic creation and inspiration, the limitations of free will, and the relationships between such opposing forces as adolescence and adulthood, illusion and reality, and order and disorder. Despite the lack of critical consensus on his work, critics generally agree that Cocteau made a valuable contribution to twentieth-century theatre, particularly with his adaptations of ancient Greek dramas.

PRINCIPAL WORKS

Plays

Le Portrait surnaturel de Dorian Gray [*The Portrait of Dorian Gray*] 1909

Le Patience de Pénélope 1910
Le Boeuf sur le toit 1920
Le Gendarme incompris 1921
Paul et Virginie 1921
Antigone 1922
Les Mariés de la tour Eiffel [*The Eiffel Tower Wedding Party*] 1924
Roméo et Juliette 1924
Oedipus-Rex 1926
Orphée [*Orpheus: A Tragedy in One Act*] 1926
Oedipe Roi 1928
La voix humaine [*The Human Voice*] 1930
La machine infernale [*The Infernal Machine*] 1934
Les Chevaliers de la table ronde 1937
L'Impromtu d'Alice 1937
L'Impromptu des Bouffes-Parisiens 1938
Les parents terribles [*Intimate Relations*] 1938
Les Monstres sacrés 1940
La machine à écrire [*The Typewriter*] 1941
Renaud et Armide 1943
L'aigle à deux têtes [*The Eagle Has Two Heads*] 1946
Un Tramway nommé Désir 1949
Bacchus 1951
L'Impromptu du Palais-Royal 1962

Screenplays

Le sang d'un poete [*Blood of a Poet*] 1930
Le belle et la bête 1945
La voix humaine 1947
L'aigle á deux têtes 1947
Orphée 1951
Le testament d'Orphée 1959

Other Major Works

Le Dieu bleu (ballet) 1912
Parade (ballet) 1917
Le grand écart [*The Grand Ecart*] (novel) 1923
Thomas l'imposteur [*Tomas the Impostor*] (novel) 1923
Opera: Oeuvres poetiques, 1925-1927 (poetry) 1927
Les enfants terribles [*The Children of the Game*] (novel) 1929
Opium: Journal d'une desintoxication [*Opium: The diary of an Addict*] (nonfiction) 1930
The Journals of Jean Cocteau (nonfiction) 1956

GENERAL COMMENTARY

Laura Doyle Gates (essay date November 1988)

SOURCE: Gates, Laura Doyle. "Jean Cocteau and 'La Poésie du Théâtre'". *Romance Quarterly* 35, no. 4 (November 1988): 435-41.

[*In the following essay, Gates considers Cocteau's attitude toward poetry and the physical aspects of theatre, particularly in three of his plays:* Parade, Le Boeuf sur le toit, *and* Les Mariés de la tour Eiffel.]

In his earliest dramatic works, Jean Cocteau concerned himself almost exclusively with plastic and architectural aspects of the theatre as opposed to literary or psychological ones. The importance of the *mise-en-scène* cannot be overestimated for *Parade, Le Boeuf sur le toit,* and *Les Mariés de la Tour Eiffel.* From the beginning, Cocteau classified all of his great variety of work as "poésie." He considered these three theatrical experiments to be poetry as well, although overwhelming emphasis was placed on the physical elements of the sets. For Cocteau during this early period poetry was created by all the plastic elements of the *mise-en-scène,* not only by characters' speech. He envisaged in these three plays what he termed "une poésie du théâtre," which he described in the Preface to *Les Mariés* of 1922: "L'action de ma pièce est imagée tandis que le texte ne l'est pas. J'essaie donc de substituer une "poésie du théâtre" à la "poésie au théâtre". La poésie au théâtre est une dentelle délicate, impossible à voir de loin. La poésie du théâtre serait une grosse dentelle; une dentelle en cordages, un navire sur la mer. *Les Mariés de la Tour Eiffel* peuvent avoir l'aspect terrible d'une goutte de poésie au microscope. Les scènes s'emboîtent comme les mots d'un poème."[1] Cocteau was reacting against the "poésie au théâtre," the verbal poetic theatre of playwrights such as Claudel and Rostand. In his view, such theatre was just an excuse for dramatized poetry. Consequently, it was a misuse of the physical properties of the stage, or rather, a waste of the great potential they contained for becoming poetic too. Poetry "in the theatre" is an excessively subtle lace, small and delicate, associated with literature. Cocteau wanted to overwhelm the spectator not with words but with image-filled, poetic architecture and action, a poetry "of the theatre." The metaphors would be active, dynamic, dramatized—not simply spoken to the audience, but shown to the audience.[2]

Thus, for Cocteau, the term "poésie" had wide application, not necessarily corresponding to a traditional conception of poetry. The process of creating "poésie du théâtre" entailed a new alliance among all the elements of the *mise-en-scène.* The role of the actor as a human diminished and that of the set and stage objects increased until a veritable exchange of roles took place. Actor, stage, decor, costume, music, speech, and gesture functioned in an esthetically unified ensemble. The impact of "poésie du théâtre" was intended to be more visual than dramatic or literary.

The principal means of creating "poésie du théâtre" was what he called in *Le Boeuf* "décor qui bouge"—a living or moving set (*Théâtre II,* p. 597). The idea of a moving set was a new conception of dramatic art where the characters are an integral part of the set and where stage objects play as important a role as the actors. Cocteau's early theatre was a marvelous mixture of dance, pantomime, music, and masks. These together created an atmosphere where the fantastic nature of everyday life could astonish the audience in a poetic process.

Cocteau was particularly influenced by Pablo Picasso and Cubism in his early theatre. Picasso collaborated with him for the set design and production of *Parade,* the ballet which became the starting point for more radical experiments. One characteristic of Picasso's Cubism was the recombination of certain aspects of a familiar object so that the viewer could see it in a new and esthetically revealing way, almost as if seeing it for the first time.

At the time of the production of *Parade,* Picasso was doing experiments with sheet metal constructions. He and Cocteau believed their set should play a more active role than was traditionally given to it. So Picasso literally built it on the backs of the actors. Two of the Managers wore costumes three meters tall and moved around the stage like giant buildings, deprived of most of their human quality. Picasso said he wanted to play with the idea that these enormous superhuman structures could become more "real" to the audience than the dancers who played the part of the Crowd.[3] The people in the Crowd would thus be reduced to the size and importance of small puppets despite their more human appearance.

In *Parade, Le Boeuf sur le toit,* and *Les Mariés de la Tour Eiffel,* Cocteau did not use actors, of course, in the proper sense of the word. The roles of the characters were played by professional dancers and clowns. He was more fascinated by the performance of a dancer than by the interpretation of an actor. The dancer is a set that moves on the stage. He uses his body as an instrument, to create a "poésie de mouvement." Looking at a ballet, we do not necessarily concentrate on the dancer as a human being but rather on his body, movements, and gestures as esthetic objects. In traditional theatre exactly the converse is true. A particular actor's dramatic and psychological representation is often quite divorced from his physical appearance. The use and perception of the body as an object, or even a machine, was attractive to Cocteau. For the expression of his conception of theatre the dancer was a very natural medium to choose. Cocteau's esthetic vision—where characters became objects and stage objects became characters—was better fulfilled by a dancer than an actor. So Cocteau became associated with Diaghilev and the Ballets russes early on, and later with Rolf de Maré and the Ballets suédois.

To examine the phenomenon of "décor qui bouge," we must reconstruct as many elements as possible of the *mises-en-scène* of these first three works. Let us start in 1917, with *Parade.* When Cocteau created the ballet *Parade,* he was under the direct influence of Picasso and Erik Satie. In the beginning he envisioned, to accompany the dance, a series of raw sounds in the "bruitiste" tradition of the Futurists. However, Picasso and Satie refused to agree to this. In the end Satie did incorporate into his score parts for typewriters, horns, helicopters, and other machines. Because of technical problems, few of these could be used in the actual performance (Melzer, p. 121). However, the idea of giving obvious importance to machines in the music was certainly there. They would alienate music from its human orientation and thus complement the dehumanized characters of the play.

Picasso rejected Cocteau's idea of making the characters speak through holes in the set. He was just as deaf to the objections of the dancers, who hated the restrictive costumes he had designed (Melzer, p. 121). According to the script, the Managers were supposed to be in front of their theatre booth, gesticulating at the Crowd to come inside and watch the show, and finally crumpling from exhaustion when no one listens to them. But two of the three Managers were nearly ten feet tall—more like buildings than human beings. The other Manager was a horse played by two dancers. Their dramatic interpretation was not easy under the circumstances.

In spite of this, all the dancers' movements were precisely choreographed. The main characters of *Parade* are stereotyped—the Little American Girl, the Chinese Juggler, and the Acrobats. They are in this sense bigger than life, more real than real. The Juggler and Acrobats perform typical music-hall numbers for the Crowd, and the Little American Girl cranks a car, takes a photograph, rides a bicycle, and imitates Charlie Chaplin. The whole effect of the ballet was one of a parade of visual surprises, a distortion of everyday reality *à la cubiste*. The Crowd is so fascinated by the actions of the three characters mentioned above that it pays no attention to the theatre Managers.

The audience at the first performance was outraged by *Parade* and provoked into a violent reaction against Cocteau, Picasso, and Satie. The reaction of the critics was hardly less violent. They blasted the performance right down to the typewriters in the orchestra (Melzer, p. 122). The spectacle of the "moving set," the "décor qui bouge," threatened the members of the audience. They were shocked by the dehumanized, quasi-architectural or blatantly stereotyped "characters." Evidently Cocteau had proved himself a master of a variety of astonishing stage effects, taking an aspect of everyday life—such as the French idea of an American girl—and changing it into spectacle.

His second dramatic work, *Le Boeuf sur le toit* (1920), was for Cocteau a reaction to the critical reception of *Parade*. A few critics had labelled it a "farce" and Cocteau was very offended. He decided to give the Parisians a true farce which would satirize their poor taste. The characters of *Le Boeuf sur le toit* were inspired by the sterotyped image that the Frenchman had of speakeasies in the United States during Prohibition: "Entrent tour à tour: la dame décolletée, en robe rouge, très maniérée, très commune. La dame rousse, aux cheveux de papier, jolie, d'une allure masculine, un peu voûtée, les mains dan les poches. Le monsieur, en habit de moleskine, qui regarde son bracelet-montre et ne quitte pas son tabouret de bar jusqu'à sa sortie. Un bookmaker écarlate, aux dents d'or qui porte un melon gris et une cravate de chasse maintenue par une perle de la taille d'une boule de jardin" (*Théâtre II,* p. 598). Cocteau uses the stereotyped idea of violent American society as a support for the Guignolesque atmosphere of this pantomime, which is supposed to last only about fifteen minutes. The characters move around like automatons in a completely choreographed manner, as if in a dream. The Brothers Fratellini, famous European clowns, played the roles of the barman, the *dame rousse,* and the *dame décolletée.* Using clowns gave Cocteau the same advantages as did using dancers in *Parade*. They were already a "décor qui bouge," a moving set. The characters were even more dehumanized by their costumes and the huge papier-mâché masks they wore.

In *Le Boeuf* the characters do form a "décor qui bouge" as much by their appearance and their movements as by the way in which other objects or stage situations control them, like the different parts of a complex machine. Cocteau uses an associational logic to organize the action. The action can take on qualities of language, reflecting the way that certain words are always associated with certain other words. In *Le Boeuf,* this sort of association leads to a series of visual jokes. Because the pantomime is set in a New York speakeasy, naturally all the stock characters are represented. It is because there is a ceiling fan that the policeman is decapitated; because there is a severed head on the stage, the woman dances the triumphal dance of Salome with the head of John the Baptist. Cocteau uses the elements of the set to determine the plot. We see the same kind of visual wit or invention as in *Parade*.

The music for *Le Boeuf sur le toit* was composed by Darius Milhaud. He contributed lively Brazilian melodies which were played once before the curtain rose, then again during the performance. The music was to have no relation to what was happening on the stage. Its liveliness formed a jarring contrast to the somnambulant movements of the characters, separated from its normal function of complementing action.

Le Boeuf is an intentionally superficial work. In fact there is nothing but surface. The action is determined by stereotyped objects and situations that are immediately identifiable. We cannot predict the direction that the action will take, but this action is always understandable within the logic of the play. Even the characters have only surface, accessible to vision alone, deprived of human expression by huge masks. They are types, without psychological depth. Moreover, the music reveals nothing. Cocteau's audience was forced to stay on the surface—to look only.

Cocteau's intention to leave the audience there, to fascinate with visual aspects of the performance, is manifested differently in *Le Mariés de la Tour Eiffel* of 1921. The element of a text is added, opening the possibilities of language for his creative intentions. Language becomes a property of the set, not of the characters. Cocteau realized that he had at last achieved his esthetic goal of creating a "poésie du théâtre," for which the other two plays had been experiments. Here he uses the idea that Picasso had rejected during the production of *Parade* Rather than having the actors speak through holes in the set, he encloses the two Narrators in large stationary phonograph costumes and has them deliver their lines through the trumpets at each side of the stage.

Cocteau was fascinated as a boy by the carnival game in France in which the player tries to knock over moving figures representing a wedding party.[4] *Les Mariés de la*

Tour Eiffel, a ballet and mime, contains the same characters and the same violent action. Jean Hugo's costumes were charming and quite elaborate, and they gave the dancers the air of large dolls. Hugo describes how he tackled the problem of designing them: "Le poète a voulu réhabiliter les lieux communs. J'ouvris donc le dictionnaire Larousse aux mots baigneuse, bottine, cycliste, marié, etc. J'y trouvai des baigneuses en jupons, des mariées à taille de guêpe, un lion semblable à celui des magasins du Louvre, une cycliste en culotte, des bottines à boutons, tout un style. . . ."[5] Following Cocteau's intentions, Hugo tried to find the most banal representation possible for the characters, so that their extreme banality might bring the commonplace back to life for the audience.

All the actors' movements were choreographed to be automatic—they had to appear to be controlled by the speech of the two Phonographs. The Phonographs are really the only characters that talk (the Camera does talk once). They speak in turn "très fort, très vite, et prononcent distinctement chaque syllabe" (*Théâtre I,* p. 11). Their dehumanized voices recite the lines of all the characters in a monotone. They seem like automatic machines but they possess the power to control the action of the "human" characters.

Les Mariés de la Tour Eiffel is, on one level, a satire of the bourgeois' sacred institutions. The characters represent all that is banal and ordinary; they "talk" to each other in a hilarious juxtaposition of clichés. At the same time, this play is an attempt to astonish with the potentially fantastic nature of everyday life. The amazing world that comes into contact with the everyday one is the Photographer's Camera, which releases a whole series of strange and wonderful personnages. An Ostrich, a Bather, a Child, and a Lion come, and they disturb the guests since their logic does not correspond to that of the wedding party.

Language and object function together according to this unusual logic, belonging to two different worlds simultaneously and having different meanings in each one. They work together to control and limit the action. For example, when the Photographer says, "Regardez l'objectif; un oiseau va sortir," this signals the Camera to produce another miraculous character. The General does not realize that by merely mentioning the tigers in Africa, a Lion will be produced and will eat him, but that is the way the logic works. The ambiguity of the word "balles" results directly in the massacre of the wedding party by little Justin. Ordinary logic no longer applies in this crazy world of linguistic associations. Cocteau no longer uses objects alone to control stage action, as in *Parade,* but extends the same whimsical determinism to language.

The playwright takes the idea of creating a wholly superficial, visual spectacle as far as possible at the end of this play. A complete exchange of roles has taken place between the set and the actors. The actors are almost totally immobile—only the set can act now. The wedding party freezes into a painting, a kind of backdrop, "created" by the conversation of the two Phonographs.

In Cocteau's dramatic vision, objects play roles like those of actors and vice versa. That which means "actor" is not necessarily an animate object or human being, and that which denotes "set" is not always an inanimate object. There is a kind of subjective/objective continuum through which all the elements of a *mise-en-scène* pass during any theatrical performance.[6]

It is essentially upon this phenomenon—this capacity for exchange—that Cocteau plays to create his "poésie du théâtre" using a "décor qui bouge." Poetry, generally associated with language, a property of characters, becomes associated with the set. The set, traditionally associated with inanimate architecture and objects, is now "played" by people. In sum, the early dramatic works of Cocteau demonstrate the magic of theatre, which allows all these elements to be recombined into a spectacular esthetic ensemble.

Notes

1. *Théâtre 1* (Paris: Grasset, 1957), p. 5.

2. E. Freeman, ed,. *Orphée: The Play and the Film,* by Jean Cocteau (Oxford: Basil Blackwell, 1976), p. xvii.

3. Annabelle Melzer, *Latest Rage the Big Drum: Dada and Surrealist Performance* (Ann Arbor: UMI Research Press, 1976), p. 121.

4. Milorad, "De *La Noce Massacrée* aux *Mariés de la Tour Eiffel,*" *Cahiers Jean Cocteau* 5 (1975), p. 30.

5. "Pages de Journal: *Les Mariés,*" *Cahiers Jean Cocteau* 5 (1975), p. 22.

6. Keir Elam, *The Semiotics of Theatre and Drama* (New York: Methuen, 1980), p. 15.

Carol A. Cujec (essay date fall 1996)

SOURCE: Cujec, Carol A. "Modernizing Antiquity: Jean Cocteau's Early Greek Adaptations." *Classical and Modern Literature: A Quarterly* 17, no. 1 (fall 1996): 45-56.

[*In the following essay, Cujec asserts that Cocteau's early classical adaptations—Antigone, Oedipus-Rex, Oedipe-Roi—are "bold avant-garde experiments reflecting the radical revision of the theater by modernist innovators of the era."*]

Following his initial productions of avant-garde ballet, Jean Cocteau sought to confirm his capabilities as a serious dramatist by turning to classical subject matter. Cocteau's interest in the classics was encouraged by his companion Raymond Radiguet who declared: "Il faut éctire . . . comme tout le monde."[1] By "tout le monde," he was not referring to the popular boulevard authors nor to the overly-fashionable avant-garde, but rather to the celebrated authors of Western civilization. Cocteau agreed that only by seeming to conform to the traditional might one achieve the anarchy sought by the modernists. Paradoxically, he hoped to prove that modernity and novelty could be found even in the most ancient of texts: "J'étais agacé par le machinisme d'avant-garde. J'avais voulu démontrer que . . . n'importe quel chef-d'oeuvre ancien pouvait reprendre une incroyable jeunesse entre les mains d'un artiste" (*OC* 9: 319). While his plays *Orphée* and *La machine infernale* have generated much critical interest and analysis, his earlier classical adaptations, *Antigone, Oedipus Rex* and *Oedipe-Roi,* are ignored by critics or simply dismissed as dry precursors to his more celebrated myth plays.[2] However, close inspection of the text and staging reveals them to be bold avant-garde experiments reflecting the radical revision of the theater by modernist innovators of the era.

Classical works were not absent from European stages prior to Cocteau's production of *Antigone* in 1922.[3] Michael Grant calculates that in France alone: "582 French imitations, translations or adaptations of classical originals sprang from *le rêve hellénique* between 1840 and 1900."[4] However, Cocteau was the first French dramatist to realize that these classical dramas no longer engaged the average spectator, presented as they often were as sacred objects of high culture in highbrow translations and staged according to misguided attempts at historical accuracy. Cocteau announced: "L'*Oedipe* de Sophocle . . . ne marche plus à notre rythme. Il s'imposait de transformer un ennuyeux institut en un institut de beauté."[5] Antonin Artaud echoed this sentiment several years later:

> On doit en finir avec cette idée des chefs-d'oeuvre réservés à une soidisant élite, et que la foule ne comprend pas . . . si, par exemple, la foule actuelle ne comprend plus *Oedipe-Roi,* j'oserai dire que c'est la faute à *Oedipe-Roi* et non à la foule.[6]

To remedy this, Cocteau set out to modernize classical dramas and use them as vehicles to communicate personal themes. In France, his example was followed by others such as Gide, Giraudoux, Anouilh, and Sartre.

Cocteau did not regard classical dramas as historical artifacts but as living works of art which seek to communicate with the living spectator. The primary obstacle to communication lay in the complex rhetoric of previous adaptations. Like other modernist innovators such as E. Gordon Craig and Antonin Artaud, Cocteau sought to revitalize the theater by freeing it from the tyranny of the literary text. He strove to minimize the importance of the text by stripping it down to its bare essentials with very little rhetorical ornamentation. Hence, he eliminated what he considered to be unnecessary dialogue and employed frank, colloquial language as opposed to elevated, poetic language-a relatively new and surprising innovation for a production of a classical drama. Cocteau compared his technique of modernization to photographing Greece by airplane, or making a quick sketch of a famous painting at a museum: "De grandes beautés disparaissent, d'autres

surgissent . . . chacun croit l'entendre pour la première fois" (*OC* 5: 139). Reducing the text to its essential elements, he felt, made the play more powerful for the modern spectator: "J'ôte à un drame immortel la matière morte qui recouvre sa matière vivante. . . . Le drame [est] 'rafraîchi,' rasé, coupé, peigné."[7] To purists indignant at the thought of altering a classical text, he quoted Stravinsky: "Vous respectez, moi j'aime" (*OC* 9: 277). Far more offensive to Cocteau was a traditional performance of *Antigone* by an actress whose advanced age made her walk to the tomb seem rather timely.[8]

By reducing and simplifying the text, he shifted the emphasis away from textual lyricism (dubbed by Cocteau "la poésie au théâtre"), allowing him to experiment with the expressive powers of the many other theatrical resources to create his unique style of "poésie *de* théâtre." While these plays mark a drastic change in subject matter and tone from his previous stage works, aesthetically they are similar:

> Peu m'importe de faire rire ou pleurer. Il s'agit de remplir une scène avec certaines masses vocales et plastiques. *Les Mariés de la tour Eiffel, Parade, Le Boeuf sur le toit, Antigone* sont le même prétexte.[9]

Antigone marked Cocteau's first appropriation of Greek subject matter, a motif which would continue to resonate throughout his oeuvre to the very end. By simplifying and eliminating much of Sophocles' rhetoric, he created a text which communicated more easily with a modern audience. He even allowed for the occasional anachronism, as when Creon calls Antigone an anarchist (*OC* 5: 164).[10] Yet the language is not colloquial, since Cocteau did not seek to domesticate his characters as did Anouilh in his *Antigone.* Rather, Cocteau distances the text with respect to normal speech by reviving two ancient practices: the exclusive use of the informal address (*tu*) among all the characters, and the chorus's reference to itself using the first person singular (*je*). Cocteau further distances the characters by specifying that the dry text be delivered dryly. He instructs the chorus to speak almost mechanically: "Très haut et très vite comme si elle lisait un article de journal" (143). Likewise, he insists that Antigone and Creon speak with minimal inflection and gesticulation so that the emotion arises solely from what they are saying. This understated acting style, in stark contrast to the bravado of the *monstre sacré* who dominated classical drama in the nineteenth century, gave the characters a mysterious, inhuman quality. Their inhumanity was further emphasized by their appearance. Beneath the costumes, the actors wore black tights covering their arms and legs to suggest a royal family of insects. The costumes were created by Chanel because, as Cocteau remarked in a whimsical quip: "Je n'imagine pas les filles d'Oedipe mal vêtues."[11] He did not seek historical accuracy in the costumes but boasted that they were admirably inaccurate. For the 1927 revival, the actors wore masks, as in ancient Greece, yet these masks were transparent with delicate features sewn on, once again blending old and new.

Other aspects of Cocteau's staging are similarly stylized and symbolic. In keeping with the minimal text, the chorus is portrayed as a single disembodied voice emanating through a hole in the back wall of the set. For the 1927 revival, Picasso created five monumental heads of young men to surround the hole. In this way, Cocteau demonstrated directorial prowess by eliminating the problem of a cumbersome chorus of many actors.[12] At the height of the confrontation between Antigone and Creon, their opposing stances are represented visually when the two actors converse face to face with their foreheads touching. As Hugh Dickinson points out, this visually reinforces Cocteau's metaphor of a family of insects because "insects, when they communicate, put their heads together."[13] Later in the play, prior to Antigone's march to her grave, a guard thrusts his lance in front of her to prevent her from approaching Creon; she then grasps it as she utters her final justifications, giving the effect of a woman pleading her case in a modern courtroom.

The action moves swiftly forward, leaving no time for realistic transitions or detailed characterization. Cocteau contended: "Notre vitesse, notre patience, ne sont pas celles d'Athènes en 440 avant Jésus-Christ. . . . Ainsi réduite, concentrée, décapée, l'oeuvre . . . roule vers le dénouement comme un express" (*OC* 9: 319). Creon's exit to rescue Antigone leaves the stage empty (generally a theatrical taboo), bringing the rapid action to a tense halt. The void is filled aurally with an interlude written for the production by Arthur Honegger. This music, like the text, is simple-only two instruments. For the 1927 revival, Cocteau had a strange being, "[une] sorte de statue vivante" (*OC* 5: 176), slowly stride across the empty stage at this time. Given his penchant for anthropomorphizing death in later productions, this being can be considered Cocteau's first dramatic representation of the underworld, death coming to retrieve Antigone.

Because Cocteau was quite faithful to Sophocles' plot, despite the textual reductions, it may appear at first glance that the Frenchman put little of himself into the adaptation; Cocteau asserted this himself: "On a cru me reconnaître dessous. C'est bien de l'honneur."[14] Yet upon closer inspection, one can ascertain a personal message, as in all his works. His choice to recreate *Antigone* was not arbitrary, since she epitomizes Cocteau's spirit of independence and rebellion against established social order in the name of a higher (poetic) law. Her declaration to Ismene: "Je sais que je plais où je dois plaire" (*OC* 5: 148), was Cocteau's own battle cry against his enemies. Antigone's individuality is punished by society, making her the first of many martyred Coctelian protagonists. Cocteau considered himself constantly on trial for his art as well as for his homosexuality. He believed that, like Antigone, he would be condemned to suffering and gain admiration and respect only after death.

Given his attitude toward repressive social order, Cocteau subtly emphasizes the element of persecution in the play by rendering both the chorus and Creon more distasteful than in Sophocles. Cocteau describes the chorus as fickle and opportunistic (*OC* 9: 320), most likely due to its reluctance to defend Antigone. Though he condenses much of the chorus's commentary, he does not omit lines which illustrate their passivity and respect for authority, such as the unhelpful remark made during Haemon's confrontation with Creon: "O roi, s'il a raison, écoute-le. S'il a tort, qu'il t'écoute. Le procès est, de part et d'autre, en excellentes mains" (*OC* 5: 164). Like Sophocles, Cocteau regarded the chorus as a reflection of society, in this case the Parisian public. His reducing it to a single voice was perhaps symbolic of his frustration at the audience's (and society's) homogeneity and adherence to one opinion:

> Comment se fait-il qu'une salle soit bonne ou mauvaise, jamais mixte? Comment se fait-il que les salles successives s'accoutument au relief d'une pensée, comme si ces salles étaient une seule et même personne à laquelle on répète quelque chose? . . . Les individus qui composent un public laissent, en principe, leur individualité au vestiaire.
>
> (*OC* 11: 407-408)

Creon, the symbol of social order to Cocteau, is made to appear villainous in the play through his curt, prosaic speech and ice-cold objectivity. While it is true that Sophocles' Creon displays moments of vindictive tyranny in his insistence to punish Antigone, he also exhibits nobility and pathos, allowing the spectator to alternately admire, admonish, and finally pity him. In contrast, Cocteau's Creon lacks nobility, appearing almost juvenile in his treatment of others, as when he hurls simplistic insults at the chorus ("Assez de sottises, vieillesse" [*OC* 152][15]) and at his son ("Coeur mou! Coeur mou!" [166]). The combination of simple language and unemotional delivery, as specified by Cocteau, renders the character brutish and inhuman. He appears particularly cruel when he sends Antigone to her grave with unsettling indifference: "Hop! Qu'on l'emporte vite. Qu'on l'enferme. Qu'on la laisse là!" (170). Antigone's language, on the other hand, is markedly eloquent at times: "J'ai entendu raconter la mort de la fille de Tantale . . . maintenant la neige la recouvre et ses larmes glaciales coulent du haut en bas. Voilà mon lit, voilà les caresses qui m'attendent" (169). Cocteau's goal is clear—as the authority figure is villainized, the free-thinking and poetic Antigone is canonized by poets across the centuries.

Antigone was first performed in 1922 at Dullin's Théâtre de l'Atelier, with Dullin directing and playing Creon, and Cocteau reading for the chorus. The reaction to the production was quite favorable, and it ran for 100 performances. However, the play did not escape criticism. Ironically, ***Antigone*** was attacked by both modernists and traditionalists. The surrealist leader André Breton was forcibly removed from the theater after shouting disruptive comments during one performance. Similarly, Raymond Duncan, who thought himself a true Greek, came twice clad in Greek garb, yelling, through a bullhorn, protests against the novelties of Cocteau's production.[16] André Gide objected to what he called "la sauce ultra-moderne" in which the drama was steeped, yet he admitted that the play was "belle, plutôt malgré Cocteau qu'à cause de lui."[17]

Antonin Artaud, who played Tiresias in the production, applauded Cocteau's inventiveness in adaptation:

> Il est remonté aux sources, mais aux sources psychologiques, humaines, non aux sources littéraires,—et aussi aux sources mythologiques, dans le drame *réel* qu'elles évoquent. Il a voulu nous donner un équivalent actuel de la substance du vieux drame et que nous puissions y croire à nouveau.[18]

But how does Cocteau give us a modern equivalent of the antique drama as Artaud claims? In a modern, largely secular culture he cannot rekindle the religious awe that this drama once inspired, nor does he strive to tug on our heartstrings with excessive pathos. In fact, it seems as though Cocteau purposefully deemphasizes the dramatic impact of the play via unrhetorical language, unemotional acting, rapidity of action, and symbolic rather than realistic costumes and staging. These elements distance the events and characters and promote a sense of ritual, of conscious reenactment. In this atmosphere, Antigone's death no longer has religious significance—it becomes an empty gesture: "An action unexpected, audacious, gratuitous, having little validity beyond itself."[19] To Cocteau, this was the very essence of his *poésie de théâtre*. However, to say that the theatrical takes precedence over the dramatic does not mean that the play leaves the spectator cold. In a manner not unlike Brecht's alienation effect, the characters' stunning objectivity jolts the spectators' humanity—pity and terror give way to surprise and compassion. Thus, through unconventional means, Cocteau did succeed in communicating with the modern spectator and presenting this familiar drama in a vibrant new light.

Cocteau's second Greek adaptation was a collaboration with Igor Stravinsky who, impressed by Cocteau's adaptation of *Antigone,* requested a libretto for his opera-oratorio *Oedipus Rex.* This production was created as a surprise for Serge de Diaghilev, the formidable impresario of the Ballets Russes, to celebrate twenty years of work in the theater. Even more so than in *Antigone,* Cocteau condenses Sophocles' text, reducing the drama to six simple scenes. Aesthetically, the opera magnifies the distance, objectivity, and theatricality of his *Antigone.* Solemnity and distance were achieved textually by translating most of it into Latin. The Latin libretto certainly limits Cocteau's ability to communicate with the spectator, but he explains that the goal of the opera is to preserve only a certain monumental aspect of the various scenes.[20] He also compensates by adding a narrator in modern dress who briefly describes the action in French prior to each scene. The narrator's direct address to the audience and modern dress add a self-conscious tone to the production which, along with his impassive tone of voice, contributes to the distancing of the spectacle from the spectators' reality. The powerful music, described by one critic as reminiscent of the Orthodox church,[21] combined with the Latin libretto evoke the awe of a religious ritual such as a mass. The staging,

like the music, evokes a frightening grandeur. The inhumanity of the characters in *Antigone* is magnified here as all the characters are masked and immobile: "Sauf Tirésias, le Berger et le Messager, les personnages habitent leurs costumes construits et leurs masques. Ils ne bougent que des bras et de la tête. Ils doivent avoir l'air de statues vivantes."[22] To again emphasize the homogeneity of the chorus, it is portrayed as one massive three-tiered sculpture rather than a group of individuals: "Le choeur, au premier plan, se dissimule derrière une sorte de bas-relief en trois étages de gradins. Ce bas-relief formé de draperies sculpturales ne laisse passer que les figures des choristes."[23] Other characters are elevated as well: Jocasta is situated on a balcony, Creon is set on a high rock, and Oedipus stands on a central platform. This platform slowly descends beneath the floor upon Oedipus' discovery of the truth and then ascends for the final scene, the vertical motion symbolic of his tragic fall at the pinnacle of his power. Tiresias is distinct in that he enters from a cave beneath Creon, his low position in contrast to his powers of divine prophecy. Light is used expressively in the production to create atmosphere as well as to symbolize the familiar metaphor of truth. When Tiresias describes Oedipus' fate, for example, he is lit by a spotlight while the remainder of the stage is dark: "De cette grotte sort Tirésias, vague statue couverte de voiles qui flottent autour d'elle et que les projecteurs suivent partout. Après avoir chanté, Tirésias rentre dans la grotte, le rocher se referme et on redonne la lumière."[24]

The overall effect of the staging and music was the creation of a solemn and grandiose spectacle—a monumental tableau. Though merely a dark shadow of Sophocles' play, this opera perhaps succeeded better than Cocteau's *Antigone* in communicating the awe of the antique drama. Unfortunately, the 1927 debut did not particularly impress the Parisian spectators, and, to make matters worse, Diaghilev found it to be a gruesome gift, declaring: "Everybody knows I dislike sleeping with women, and that includes old hags like Jocasta, even if she should happen to be my mother."[25] However, revivals of the opera have met with great success, and it continues to be performed worldwide.[26] One critic even deems *Oedipus Rex* "one of the finest masterpieces of contemporary music-drama."[27]

From this first seed planted by Stravinsky sprang two more plays and numerous other works devoted to Oedipus.[28] Cocteau's second Oedipal work was his play *Oedipe-Roi,* an expansion of his text for Stravinsky. Although written in 1925, it was first performed much later in 1937. Like his adaptation of *Antigone,* the textual modernization of *Oedipe-Roi* consists of a condensation and transposition into modern prose. In addition to eliminating much of the rhetoric Cocteau also altered the standard divisions of a Greek drama by eliminating most of the choral odes. As in *Antigone,* the characters address each other in the informal *tu,* and the chorus refers to itself in the first person singular. He added his own stylized Prologue, similar to the narrator in *Oedipus Rex,* who directly addresses the spectators and describes the myth informally and with Coctelian images such as the angel as fate.

Cocteau took liberties with the text throughout the play, rendering it descriptive and lyrical in some moments and terse and rhythmic in others. Moments of strong emotion are marked by terse cries rather than lengthy lamentations, yet he gives these lines a somewhat musical quality through repetition and symmetry. This is seen in the chorus's plea to Tiresias: "Nous te supplions, parle, parle. Parle, nous te supplions" (*OC* 5: 111).[29] Similarly, when Oedipus argues with Tiresias, he cries: "Quand la chienne chanta, qui sut répondre? Qui sut répondre quand la chienne chanta?" (112). The use of the literary past tense in the play lends a formality to the text which, along with the repetitions, serve to distance the action, placing it in a stylized, ceremonious realm reminiscent of Stravinsky's opera. The chorus's lamentation of Oedipus upon his discovery of the truth is embellished by Cocteau with poetic imagery: "Cher Oedipe, un ventre de mère ne peut-il devenir bouche terrible et crier halte! La voix du sang n'est-elle donc pas assez forte pour éclairer la nuit du corps humain?" (130). Similarly, the messenger's description of Oedipus' self-mutilation is free and vivid: "Il se frappe les yeux. . . . Et il frappait, frappait, frappait, et un sang noir coulait, coulait . . . et il ne coulait pas des gouttes, mais une grêle, mais une inondation de sang noir" (131).

Cocteau envisioned a striking staging, breaking with the traditional dramatic renditions of Greece. The Prologue announces: "Spectateurs! On se représente toujours la Grèce comme une colonne blanche. Imaginez maintenant un lieu brûlé, aride, sous un ciel farouche" (*OC* 5: 103). The walls of the set were to be mobile: "Lorsque la vérité se devine, le mur du fond s'approche peu à peu jusqu'à rejoindre complètement le practicable sur la dernière réplique de Jocaste" (101). This visual metaphor symbolizes Oedipus' inescapable fate closing in on him. Cocteau specified that the light should slowly increase throughout the play, corresponding with Oedipus' discovery of the truth, at which point he declares: "Lumière est faite" (129). Cocteau visualized the characters in multi-colored, bohemian costumes and with long hair. The chorus was to be portrayed as a single disembodied voice as in *Antigone,* but this time emanating from a statue as in *Oedipus Rex.* The statue is described as that of a young man lying down, leaning on his elbow. An actor was to hide inside this statue and speak through a hole.

For the 1937 performance, however, Cocteau altered his original plans. Although the original lighting plan was used, he eliminated the moving wall. In addition, the chorus was portrayed by three young men posed as statues, as opposed to an actual statue. The central chorus member was Jean Marais, who first met and impressed Cocteau through this production. It is not surprising that Cocteau would prefer to showcase his handsome new protégé rather than hide him inside a piece of scenery. The theater critic Emile Mas described the unique placement of the three

chorus members—each one on a separate platform downstage of the action; two chorus members stood on opposite sides of the stage, while Marais was on the center platform in the reclined pose originally intended for the statue.[30] Their scanty costumes designed by Chanel created a small uproar; clad only in white bandages, Cocteau likened them to "un grand blessé . . . une momie,"[31] suggesting at once classical sculpture and the plague upon Thebes. Their placement on downstage platforms physically separated them from the action on stage, making them intermediaries between the stage and the spectators. This permitted them to exercise a certain control over the occasionally unruly public, as described by Cocteau: "Marais devait sans cesse les rappeler à l'ordre . . . par l'autorité du regard et de la voix."[32] In contrast to his *Antigone,* this chorus does not possess the fickle and opportunistic qualities of the Parisian public. It does not bend to those in power, but at one point even exercises a certain authority over them by crying to Oedipus and Creon: "Taisez-vous princes" (*OC* 5: 116). These strange, inhuman characters perched on the border between reality and fiction contribute to the ritualistic tone of the production.

As before, the persecution of the Coctelian protagonist is a central theme. The malevolence of society is suggested by the image of the characters as a family of underground insects. Whereas this image is presented visually in *Antigone* through the costumes, here it is presented verbally by the Prologue: "Des chambres basses, des portes secrètes, des metamorphoses, la peste. Là s'entre-dévorent de grandes familles . . . dont les moeurs ressemblent beaucoup à celles d'insectes souterrains" (*OC* 5: 103). However, in this case, it is not only society which condemns the hero; Cocteau emphasizes in the Prologue his belief that Oedipus is primarily the victim of divine persecution from heartless gods "qui aiment bâtir et poser des pièges" (103), and who possess "la cruauté de l'enfance et leurs jeux coûtent cher aux mortels" (103). The Prologue continues with a Coctelian image: "Sans le savoir, Oedipe est aux prises avec les forces qui nous surveillent de l'autre côté de la mort" (103). This idea of sadistic, capricious deities corresponds to the portrayal of certain gods of antiquity and becomes central to Cocteau's better known Oedipal drama *La machine infernale.* In this respect, mythology proved an ideal vehicle for the expression of Cocteau's persecution complex and Oedipus the perfect symbol of Cocteau's antisocial heroism. The Prologue contains images duplicated in *La machine infernale,* such as that of the Sphinx as the "chienne qui chante" (104). However, given the considerable differences between the two plays, it is unjust to dismiss *Oedipe-Roi* as merely a first draft of *La machine infernale,* as does the Cocteau critic André Fraigneau.[33] If such were the case, Cocteau would probably not have allowed its performance three years *after* the premiere of *La machine infernale.*

In these early adaptations, critics have found little of interest, supposing that the text is merely a dry, reduced version of the original, and dismissing the visual embellishments as superficial surface glitter. Hugh Dickinson is among the most ardent critics of Cocteau's staging:

> Beyond a certain point, it is neither possible nor desirable to present things by means of dramatic picturization. If total dramatization, in the strict sense of the word, were possible by visual means alone, if it could present all themes at all levels and with all degrees of complexity, then pantomime would long ago have become a major, autonomous art-form.[34]

Not only does Dickinson ignore Cocteau's often eloquent text, he also underestimates the expressiveness of the numerous other theatrical resources. Like Artaud who describes the *mise-en-scène* as "la matérialisation visuelle et plastique de la parole," Cocteau sought to create a visual component capable of expressing what words alone cannot.[35] Artaud continues: "[il y a] dans le domaine de la pensée et de l'intelligence des attitudes que les mots sont incapables de prendre et que les gestes et tout ce qui participe du langage dans l'espace atteignent avec plus de précision qu'eux."[36] By means of décor, costumes, lighting, music, and a symbolic staging, Cocteau succeeded in presenting introspective themes and dramatic images to the spectator in a distanced, ritualistic fashion rather than intellectually through complex rhetoric. In this way, he gave these familiar dramas a new texture and revitalized them for the modern spectator. Cocteau once stated: "Un artiste original ne peut pas copier. Il n'a donc qu'à copier pour être original" (*OC* 9: 37). Although he was unjustly labelled an imitator throughout his career, these productions clearly demonstrate that inspiration was no barrier to innovation.

Notes

1. Jean Cocteau, *Oeuvres complètes,* 11 vols. (Geneva: Marguerat, 1946-1951), 11: 458. Subsequent references to his *Oeuvres complètes* (*OC*) refer to this edition.

2. Hugh Dickinson's forty-page chapter on Cocteau's myth plays in *Myth on the Modern Stage* (Urbana: U of Ill Pr, 1969) devotes less than two pages to these plays. Even Neal Oxenhandler's *Scandal & Parade: The Theatre of Jean Cocteau* (New Brunswick: Rutgers U Pr, 1957), one of the few book-length studies of Cocteau's dramas, briskly describes his *Antigone* in two pages and scarcely mentions Cocteau's treatment of the Oedipus legend prior to *La machine infernale.*

3. Prior to World War I, Max Reinhardt's grandiose adaptations of Greek drama received acclaim throughout Europe.

4. Michael Grant, *Myths of the Greeks and Romans* (London: Weidenfeld and Nicolson, 1962), 232.

5. Cocteau, quoted in Jean Touzot, *Jean Cocteau* (Lyon: La Manufacture, 1989), 283.

6. Antonin Artaud, *Oeuvres complètes,* 9 vols. (Paris: Gallimard, 1956), 4: 89-90.

7. Cocteau, "À propos d'*Antigone*," *Cahiers Jean Cocteau* 10 (1985): 93-94.

8. Francis Steegmuller, "À propos de l'*Antigone* de Cocteau," *Revue des Lettres Modernes* 298-303 (1972): 169.

9. Cocteau, "À propos d'*Antigone* (above, note 7) 95.

10. All page numbers are to Jean Cocteau, *Antigone,* in *Oeuvres complètes* (above, note 1) 5: 137-180.

11. Cocteau, "À propos d'*Antigone*" (above, note 7) 93.

12. This was a problem for Austrian director Max Reinhardt whose cast numbered over six hundred in his 1910 production of *Oedipus Tyrannus* in Munich.

13. Dickinson (above, note 2) 77.

14. Cocteau, "À propos d'*Antigone*" (above, note 7) 94.

15. Andrew Brown (for example), trans., Sophocles, *Antigone* (Warminster: Aris & Phillips, 1987), translates the corresponding lines in Sophocles [Soph. *Ant.* 280-281] as: "Stop before your words quite fill me with wrath, or you will be exposed no less foolish than old" (43).

16. Francis Steegmuller, *Cocteau: A Biography* (Boston: Little, 1970), 299.

17. André Gide quoted in Steegmuller, "À propos de l'*Antigone* de Cocteau" (above, note 8) 167.

18. Artaud (above, note 6) 1: 204.

19. Oxenhandler, *Scandal & Parade* (above, note 2) 112.

20. Igor Stravinsky and Jean Cocteau, *Oedipus Rex* (London: Boosey & Hawkes, 1949), Prologue [vi].

21. Alec Harman, Anthony Melner, Wilfrid Mellers, *Man and His Music: The Story of Musical Experience in the West* (New York: Oxford U Pr, 1962), 1011.

22. Stravinsky and Cocteau (above, note 20) iv.

23. Ibid., v.

24. Ibid.

25. Diaghilev, quoted in Neal Oxenhandler, "The Theater of Jean Cocteau," in J*ean Cocteau and the French Scene,* ed. Alexandra Anderson and Carol Saltus (New York: Abbeville Pr, 1984), 144.

26. The film of a 1992 Japanese production of *Oedipus Rex* directed by Julie Taymor was featured at the prestigious Sundance Film Festival.

27. David Bancroft, "Two Early Oedipus works by Jean Cocteau," *Journal of the Australian Universities Language and Literature Association* 32 (1969): 171.

28. Since Cocteau's own life is vaguely reflected in the myth, critics enjoy writing of his "Oedipal complex." Cocteau's father committed suicide when he was eight, and his mother was always attentive and doting.

29. All page numbers come from Jean Cocteau, *Oeuvres complètes* (above, note 1) 5: 99-135.

30. Emile Mas's description of the staging is quoted in Toni W. Andrus, "Oedipus Revisited: Cocteau's 'Poésie de théâtre,'" *French Review* 48 (1975): 723.

31. Cocteau, *L'Avant-Scène Théâtre* 365-366 [Spécial Cocteau] (1966): 33.

32. Ibid.

33. André Fraigneau, *Cocteau par lui-même* (Paris: Éditions du Seuil, 1957), 51.

34. Dickinson (above, note 2) 75.

35. Artaud (above, note 6) 4: 83. Given that Artaud's theories were not widely known until the fifties, and because Cocteau never mentioned Artaud in his critical writings, it is not likely that the two were aware of their similar goals.

36. Artaud (above, note 6) 4: 85.

Cornelia A. Tsakiridou (essay date 2000)

SOURCE: Tsakiridou, Cornelia A. "Greece in Cocteau; Cocteau in Greece." *Journal of the Hellenic Diaspora* 26, no. 1 (2000): 21-37.

[*In the following essay, Tsakiridou explores the defining characteristics of Cocteau's plays, in particular his interest in Greek mythology and culture.*]

It is the irony of the twentieth century in the West to have been determined pervasively in art and politics by certain myths and mythologies and to have destroyed and deconstructed others. The experiments with which artists like Jean Cocteau (1898-1963) assaulted artistic conventions and social norms are now a commonplace of art practice and discourse, with a historiography that seems to confirm the resilience of the ideology that they set out to undermine or reconfigure. The question of "Cocteau's century"[1] is a challenging one, especially when it is not intended in an honorific sense as a way of reasserting our admiration for the artist and his work. If we are to speak of a century marked by Cocteau, we must also speak of the century that marked the artist. The question of the political and ideological context and character of his work and ideas should not be ignored. One cannot belong to a century in any other way.

Cocteau lived sixty-three years of his life in a continent that witnessed dramatic and often violent confrontations and alignments between art and ideology. Some artists tied their art and destiny to a regime and a state; others used their creativity as an instrument of resistance and subversion. Yet others saw themselves as autonomous creators with only an incidental relationship to the social world that surrounded them. Cocteau belonged to this last category. His insistence that myth is superior to history is

well-known, as is his belief that the artist can exist and function outside the contingencies and necessities of politics. Cocteau's views may be explained as the reaction of a sensitive and timid man to a cruel epoch. Perhaps he sought tranquility and safety in a world of fables and fairy tales. Or, he tried to reassert human goodness and solidarity by evoking the shared and inclusive worlds of fantasy and dream, in an age shatterd by war and designed catastrophe. One may even see in Cocteau the paradigmatic child-artist of a century that traumatized the human imagination in such a profound way that only primitive, stuttering utterances and images were left to evoke a lost order of meaning. Yet art is rarely as passive or pathetic as this view might suggest. Trauma and rebellion may go hand in hand, but they can hardly efface the artist as a social being and an agent in his own right. Cocteau did not live or think in a moral vacuum, even as he often wrote about his work in ways that suggested exactly that. In fact, to many of his critics Cocteau was a restless assimilator of values who easily traded convictions for publicity and self-promotion.

Study of Cocteau's diaries from his Greek trips shows evidence of a sensibility that was deeply influenced by the artistic and moral values of orientalism, especially as these reflected the political culture of the French empire at the turn of the century. Cocteau's orientalism was literary rather than pictorial, and is most evident in his travel notes and in his interpretations of ancient Greek drama. In orientalist practice, objects constituted within the schema of a representational or, as some would say, an imaginary ideal, are removed and dissociated from their indigenous or originative meanings. Various categories are then used to reinvest the objects with significance, of a presumably universal character. In the case of Greece, the category of the *classical* has been a commonplace of occidental, European, representation. Considered in its various denominations, the classical encompassed myth, drama, art, philosophy, literature, architecture, and music. It stood at the core of the civilization in the name of which European nations asserted their superiority over their colonial subjects. To the extent that Greece entered the modern imagination as part of the Ottoman empire, it remained, as Cocteau suggests in one of his notes, a place of disorientation, if not exclusion, for Europe's classical and Hellenic identity. One could not be oriental and be classical or Hellenic at the same time. The "orientalized" inhabitants of Ottoman-ruled Greece were no exception. Their Hellenic identity under question, they too had to be hellenized or at best reminded of their heritage.

For the European imagination of the nineteenth century, the cultural geography of Hellas was to be repossessed and liberated in elaborate projects of discovery and reconstruction, planned and executed by men dedicated to the revival of ancient ideals. The assertion of Europe's superior ancestry encompassed all forms and regimes of representation. Like Gustave Flaubert before him, who translated Egypt into a field of domination, desire, and self-observation, Cocteau saw Greece as an extension of his inner geography. In his plays and travel narratives, Greek myth is eroticized, appropriated, and codified in order to enhance and intensify the pleasures of fantasy and creation. The artist is an animator of ruined texts, voices, and forms, all of which succumb to his regenerative powers. As Edward Said has shown for the orientalist aesthetic, the theater, the tableau, the frame (especially that of the camera and the photograph) and the exhibition are the viewing points from which the antique, whether Egyptian, Greek, or Roman, is reconstructed and revitalized.[2] It is because an epistemological and ontological bias exists in this schema, for the past over the present, for the imaginary over the real, that the ethics of orientalism is an ethics of devaluation of all indigenous culture and society, especially in instances where cultural and political autonomy is asserted. Ironically for modernist Cocteau, it is Greek modernity that is constantly devalued and rejected. When he visits Greece, the present is always a parody and modern Greeks the farcical caricatures of their distant ancestors. Greece is transformed into a stage which must be emptied of all distractions so that "creative" Cocteau can return to the past. Through his acts of magic and somnambulism modern Greece must vanish.

. . . . .

"Each time our sailors land, they are asked if they are Communists. They answer that they live at sea and that at sea there is no politics."[3] Cocteau wrote these lines on June 19, 1952 on the deck of *Orphée II* while sailing toward Crete. He was accompanied by Francine Weisweiller, *Orphée*'s owner, and by Edouard Dermit. The trip, his third to Greece (June 12-27), included visits to archaeological sites on the mainland and stops at the islands of Spetsai, Hydra, Crete, and Santorini. Cocteau spent three days in Crete, returned to Piraeus on June 25, and traveled by car to Delphi, his last archaeological stop. He left Greece by plane two days later, and after a stopover in Rome arrived in Paris on June 29. On the plane, from Rome to Paris, he summarized his impressions. Athens was too dry and full of bones. Rome was fertile and lively.[4] From the air, the ruins of politics, history, and art seemed insignificant and absurd. Those who took them seriously lacked "metaphysical spirit." On the whole, the trip had been disorienting and unsettling. Cocteau was happy to return to France.

Less than three months earlier, on March 30, 1952, after a well-staged trial, the Greek government had executed Nikos Beloyiannis, a member of the Communist Party and the Greek Resistance. Cocteau quotes a statement from Beloyiannis's remarks to the military court that sentenced him to death and calls his execution "the mistake of making martyrs."[5] He then notes that French communist newspapers had credited him with the initiative of a petition to the Greek government to pardon Beloyiannis. The initiative was actually taken by two prominent members of the Communist Party, Louis Aragon and André Kedros. Picasso was contacted by Kedros at the urging of Aragon to help with publicity. By March 9, Picasso had sketched the portrait of Beloyiannis smiling and holding a carnation,

based on a color photograph that became famous. Cocteau signed a petition on March 6 and in so doing joined a list of French intellectuals, academics, and artists that included Jean Paul Sartre and his friends Colette and Maria Casares.[6] According to other sources, he also signed a telegram that was sent to King Paul of Greece urging him to pardon Beloyiannis and his seven comrades.[7] In his book, *L'homme à l'oillet*, Kedros includes Cocteau in a group of French writers and artists whose eagerness to support the Beloyiannis cause came as a total surprise.[8]

Cocteau is most genuine when he is apolitical. In May of 1949 he had spent seven days in Greece on his way back from a French cultural tour of the Middle East. In his diary, published under the title *Maalesh: journal d'une tournée de théâtre*, he rejects the political categories of Greek life, communists, royalists, and democrats, and declares that he is under suspicion for everything, a man whose "papers were burned with the library of Alexandria."[9] That same month, south and north of Athens, Greek national forces, strengthened by massive amounts of American military and economic aid, were defeating communist units as the Civil War was rapidly coming to an end. Cocteau seems unaffected and indifferent. His recorded impressions of Greece hardly suggest a country devastated by a decade of war, occupation, and national division. The painter Yiannis Tsarouhis, his escort in Athens, recalls with surprise his lack of interest in contemporary and traditional Greek art and theater and his preference for the high society parties of the Serpieri family.[10] In 1952, his hosts in Athens are an American couple, friends of Francine Weisweiller, the Fullers (the husband a colonel stationed in Greece). As Cocteau reports in his journal, Dosia Fuller, who also acted as his Greek interpreter, briefed him on the execution of Beloyiannis aboard the *Orphée*. Cocteau mentions the discussion in passing and then turns his attention to the aesthetic qualilies of Greek stones and the fragmented phalloi of the Theater of Dionysus.[11]

On May 16, 1949, on the flight from Istanbul to Athens, Cocteau describes Greece as "a design, a theater of forms . . . gymnasts, runners, and birds," all similar to the spectacles that he creates.[12] Departing for France seven days later, he sees himself flying away "on the carpet of the Orient and the winged horse of Hellas."[13] In Greece and Turkey, he observes, the Orient and the Occident meet and merge. The disputes of their people are family squabbles. They belong to the "great zone of orientation and disorientation, of great prestige, of colors so sweet where Orient and Occident embrace."[14] In orientalism the passenger is always in transit, always arranging and rearranging vision, always building on perspective. Projected on a tableau, history becomes two-dimensional, even cinematic, indistinguishable from its representation. Real bodies and real lives do not count.

In Cocteau's Greece everything solid and real is either aestheticized or overlooked. The compulsion to sketch and reduce is paramount. In a place where the past, with its dispersion in time and space, imposes no restrictions on the imagination, Cocteau feels at home. In *Maalesh* he had confessed: "for two months and many years, I have been an archaeologist of souls . . . I have wandered among the sarcophaghi, the sphinxes, the fountains, the tombs, the mute drums of the columns."[15] Archaeology is a favorite orientalist metaphor used by Cocteau to suggest an esoteric and unique relationship to Greek antiquity.[16] The artist's workshop, either imaginary or real, is a place of discovery and reconstruction, superior to the laboratories of academic archaeology. In his notes on *Antigone* (1922), he presents the play as a "contracted" reconstruction of Sophocles's tragedy that probes into the "silence and void of Greece" in ways unknown to archaeologists.[17] The comparison with archaeology is facile, but for Cocteau the mere utterance of the word fascinates; its effect is almost talismanic.

In May of 1952, shortly before embarking on his third trip to Greece, Cocteau performed the narrator's part in a revival of Stravinsky's opera-oratorio *Oedipus Rex,* for which he had written the libretto and designed the stage sets. On June 2, ten days before his departure, he writes: "Fools admire a pale ruin of Greece; the true Greece is motley. In *Oedipus Rex* I have never been closer to Greece"—he adds in parentheses, "on the level of the myth's monstrosity."[18] The image of Greece as a lively collage of colors and figures suggests a light and playful vision of its myths that is incompatible with anything monstrous and savage. If Greece is motley, colorful in the manner of a painting or a harlequin's costume, then its myths have no reality other than that of their reproduction or representation. They exist as framed impressions, caught on stage, on canvas, or on the screen by the artist who is tuned to their frequency. The rejection of romantic antiquity serves only to exaggerate the artist's authority over its objects and meaning. Prompted by an act of sympathetic magic that recalls the logic of the circus and the sideshow, Cocteau reaches out and restores an emptied, ruined antiquity to its vital powers. Greece is not a real place, certainly not a modern one; it is the *topos* of illusion, reverie, and magic. With *Oedipus Rex* as its ontological extension, Greece becomes a performance and a spectacle contrived by Cocteau.

Oedipus Rex was first performed in Paris in 1927. Two years earlier, Stravinsky, impressed by *Antigone,* had asked Cocteau to write the libretto. To meet the composer's conception of the oratorio as a stylized, monumental, and static structure reflecting archaic rhythms and forms, Sophocles's play had to be foreshortened and cast in a "form of language bearing the tradition of ages."[19] Stravinsky chose ecclesiastical Latin, hardly archaic in its evocation and tonality, but clearly giving the work a sense of ritualistic and erudite religiosity that was in order with the perception of France as the Latinate country par excellence and the guardian of classical culture.

Stravinsky's decision to accept the interruption of the drama by Cocteau's narrator, who constantly reminds the audience that they are witnessing the performance of a

myth (specifically of *une version latine d'Oedipe-Roi*), seems at odds with the idea of evoking forms "already established and consecrated."[20] A compressed and slylized reproduction of the Sophoclean play, the oratorio is dominated by the speaker's episodic appearances, the impact of which is a temporal and dramatic disorientation that reduces the myth to a performance or artistic event. When he takes on the speaker's part, Cocteau intrudes into the tight space of the Theban tragedy and joins its indigenous characters like an alter chorus. The assumption that the play cannot speak for itself makes interpretation an imperative and projects the play into an alien mythology, that of its dramatic interpreter, Cocteau. Inverted and dislocated, the myth now derives its authority not only from the spectacle of its reconstruction but also, and primarily, from those who have orchestrated its revival.

. . . . .

Cocteau's approach to Greek antiquity reflects ideas that dominated the French art scene during and after the Great War. Serving largely the rhetoric of national and cultural superiority (principally over Germany and German culture), the revival of the antique, classical spirit expressed a reactionary call to order and social conformity and at the same time an eagerness to incorporate modernist elements from the century's first decade. Cocteau's 1914 magazine, *Le Mot,* praised France's intellectual and creative resurgence and saw in the war a purging of avant-garde confusions and excesses.[21]

French classicism of the interwar period continued a tradition of intellectual and cultural imperialism that started in the late eighteenth century. In Greece, it confronted a country with an oriental (Ottoman) present and an occidental past. The creation of a modern Greek state was itself a confirmation of French and British cultural hegemony. For the philhellene, "Greece" was the topos of a restoration for which the authority, both intellectual and political, laid west, in the civilizing, humanizing, and liberating capitals of the European powers. A site of textual and visual discovery and speculation primarily for outsiders, Greece became a representation even to itself. Defined, idealized, and homogenized within ideological schemata, the classical (and the Hellenic) entered a process of reproduction and appropriation in which myth and reality were often indistiguishable. The true Greeks were outside Greece. Inside the Ottoman-ruled ruins, the philhellene encountered or imagined the revival of antiquity's lost forms in the faces and manners of its uncertain (if not unworthy) descendants. Illiterate shepherds with classical profiles and village women whose bodies recalled the Karyatides, all ready to be sketched, described and transplanted in the Athens of Paris and London. Cocteau was the true Oedipus just like Napoleon (in his 1798 proclamation to the people of Alexandria) was the true muslim and Le Corbusier the naturally selected successor of Iktinos and Kallikrates, the architects of the Parthenon.[22]

The translation of patriotic sentiment into intellectual and aesthetic maxims put Dante and Latin culture on the side of France when Italy entered the war in 1915. On *Le Mot*'s cover, Cocteau drew Dante with Phrygian cap and laurels and the inscription: *Dante avec nous.*[23] As Kenneth Silver has shown, aesthetic discourse and war propaganda became indistinguishable during that period. The national mood favored Latin antiquity. Greece, entangled in Balkan wars and domestic turmoil, and neutral in the beginning of the war, was deemed unworthy of its heritage. The June 1915 issue of Amédée Ozenfant's magazine, *L'elan* (inspired by Cocteau's *Le Mot*), shows a cover drawing of the Nike of Samothrace with these words: *Un bel'elan mais ni tête ni bras.*[24] In this instance, nationalist rhetoric serves to reaffirm, if not legitimize, the custodial rights of French civilization over Greek antiquity.

Cocteau's identification with wartime classicism is most evident in the 1918 work, *Le Coq et L'Arleqin.* Written largely as a reassuring apology for the modernist experiments of **Parade** and its failure to convince the Parisian public that a marriage between the avant-garde and the classical tradition was possible, the book condemns Romanticism and Impressionism as Germanic deviations from the spirit of order, clarity, and simplicity. Cocteau invokes Ingres (the paradigmatic artist of French classicism), the mysteries of Eleusis, the Protagorean maxim ("our music must also be built to fit men"), praises Satie (he "speaks of Ingres"), rejects Wagner, Debussy, and even Stravinsky (he "does not belong to the race of architects"). He then blames his collaborators for not delivering the spirit of the **Parade** as he had envisioned it and uses racial metaphor to call the avant-garde to order: "NEGROES. It is only by distributing lots of bric-a-brac and by much imitation of the phonograph that you will succeed in taming the Negroes and making yourself understood. Then substitute gradually your own voice for the phonograph and raw metal for the trinkets."[25]

Although poetic licence may explain Cocteau in this instance, it should not obscure the facility with which he embraces the prevailing rhetoric and ideology of his time. One gets the impression that language and ideas have no consequences aside from the consent that they can generate in an audience. Speech serves performance and the performer's transformations. Cocteau's public praise some twenty years later of the racialist art of Arno Breker (1900-1991), the "classical" sculptor of the Third Reich, is a telling example of his tendency to profess the moral autonomy of the artist. In the publicity review of Breker's 1942 art exhibit at the *Orangerie* (May 15 to July 31), published in *Coemedia* (May 12), he wrote: "I salute you Breker. I salute you from the high homeland of poets, a homeland where homelands do not exist, except in the measure that each brings forth the treasures of national labor."[26] In the postwar years, he continued to advocate Breker's genius and moral integrity, and like Breker himself, never saw a connection between the aesthetic of ideal, deified forms and fascist ideology.[27] In 1963, Breker completed a bust of Cocteau and thus included his friend in his pantheon of heroic, monumental figures. The sculpture still stands next to Cocteau's grave in the chapel at Milly-la-Fôret.

The myth of classical ideality and civilization allows Cocteau to ignore political and moral reality. The ideological credentials of the ruling regime do not make a difference. One does not have to be a French patriot any more or a critic of German culture, or for that matter a man of principle. It is the poet's prerogative to have no country and his advantage to evade history. Breker's worldview also embraced the notion of a transnational, universal, and timeless principle of artistic creation in the context of which his Nazi past was only an accident of history amid a failed personal judgment. His art, Breker complained to Cocteau in October of 1952, should never have paid the price of history—in 1945 much of Breker's work was destroyed or confiscated by the Allies.[28] Order, harmony, and the glorification of human form remained at the core of Breker's artistic vision. It was in such terms and in the name of classicism that he defied the critics and protestors of his 1981 exhibition in Berlin.

The idea that antiquity provides a universal language, a sort of inventory of archetypes into which the artist can project his own iconoclastic vision, was a commonplace of classicist rhetoric among the avant-garde well after the interwar period. Stravinsky recalls his conception of **Oedipus Rex** in such terms, and so does Cocteau in his notes during the trip to Greece: "any serious work of art," he writes, ". . . demands a ceremonial, lengthy calculation, an architecture in which the slightest mistake would unbalance the pyramid." But for Cocteau the transparency that one would expect from such a method is only a metaphor. In reality, the artist works alone to produce a work whose logic evades the public's understanding and defies criticism. He tells Stravinsky: "[our spectacles] answer to rules that are ours alone, and cannot furnish proof of excellence."[29] Cocteau's claims to uniqueness and genius are often cast in such terms. They are idiosyncratic and typical of his love for equivocation and facile aphorism. But they are also a logical consequence of a detached, aestheticized view of history, which allows the artist the illusion of total freedom in the practice and discourse of art, and the license to manipulate and ultimately ignore its intersubjective realities and moral implications.

. . . . .

On his first day in Athens (June 13), Cocteau finds the Theater of Dionysus the perfect stage for **Oedipus Rex** "in scale and in style." And he notes: "But alas, the Greeks put on very mediocre productions, in which the great tragic ceremony is lost. The scene of Athena and the men with horses' heads would be sublime on the Acropolis. Today's audiences would think I was making fun of them and of the Greek myths."[30] Cocteau had used seven tableaux vivants for the **Oedipus Rex** performance and the Athena scene refers to the second tableau, "Sadness of Athena." In his "verification" of the scenes during the Greek trip, Cocteau describes Athena with the face of a green grasshopper, ascending on a pedestal supported by two men who bear the heads and tails of black horses. It is difficult to see sublimity in this scene. The tableau's decorative, ornamental style gives it a farcical character more appropriate to the stage of **Parade,** Cocteau's 1918 comic ballet, than to an ancient site of ritual cult. The term "verification" is a mere figure of speech. Neither the ancient theater nor the nature that surrounds it are carefully observed and studied in order to test and correct Cocteau's sensibility. Cocteau has nothing to learn from Greece and his Greek colleagues. Typical to the orientalist vision is the invisibility of its subject; typical to its aesthetic is the belief that what it represents is incapable of generating its own norms and rules of representation. Only the visitor, the one who knows how to see from a distance clearly and in the scale of his own studied spectacle, can see Greek theater and Greek myth in their proper dimensions.

Thus Oedipus never leaves France, or, for that matter, Cocteau's private universe of signification. In the twenties, "Oedipus" was one of the attributes of the American female impersonator and acrobat Barbette (Vander Clyle). "His solitude," Cocteau wrote in a 1928 essay, "is that of Oedipus . . . Barbette gives meaning to the Greek legends about young men who were turned into trees or flowers. He displaces their easy magic . . . and what skill he shows in perfecting this combination of enchantments, emotions, and deceptions of mind and senses."³¹ Like Orpheus, Oedipus is a Cocteau icon. It documents his sexual identity and desire and amplifies (publicizes) its world. *La Machine infernal* (1932), considered by some as Cocteau's best rendition of the Oedipus theme, is filled with echoes of the domesticated, autobiographic "mythology" of his Orphic works—the earlier play **Orphée** and later the two films *Orphée* and *Le Testament d'Orphée.* The interjection of ghosts, of a pathetic and ambivalent Sphinx, of a neurotic Jocasta and an infantile Oedipus trivialize and disarm the myth.³² Thebes recalls the claustrophobic world of **Les Parents Terribles** or the bourgeois stage of **Orphée**'s secret illusions and escapades. Ancient theater is reduced and compressed into a living room farce whose only reality is the author's semi-coded confession of complicity and deviance.

In 1952, Cocteau found Greeks hostile to his interpretation of ancient drama and myth. No names of Greek actors, directors, or particular performances are mentioned. On June 14, he writes: "I have the impression that **Orpheus** would astonish—would scandalize. The keepers of the myths would not understand that myths die if they are not adapted to the times."³³ On June 26, his last day in Greece, he returns to the same theme: "What a performance I could put on in the Theater of Dionysus if I were given a free hand. Unfortunately everyone here suspects us of bad intentions, of lack of respect toward the myths."³⁴ His low opinion of Greek productions is perhaps aimed at the actress Marika Kotopouli, who at the time of his visit was on tour in Istanbul. Cocteau recalls being a guest at an official dinner organized by the actress at the Piraeus yacht club, most probably in 1949, the year he joined a French cultural mission to the Near East.³⁵

According to *Maalesh,* he met with Kotopouli at least three times and seemed then, in 1939, quite impressed by her (he calls their encounter *"folle et touchant . . . digne d'Athenes ou tout s'élance"*). No mention is made of any performances that he might have attended during that visit. Kotopouli and her husband drove Cocteau to Sounion and accompanied him to the airport, where she presented him with a twelfth-century vase from Cyprus, which Cocteau took through customs concealed in a bouquet of roses.³⁶ In his notes, Cocteau regrets not having one of his plays performed at Kotopouli's theater, the *Rex,* a prospect that seems unlikely at a time when the actress's career was in decline and she had turned over her theater to others (she will die less than two years later, in September of 1954).³⁷ It is not clear, then, what performances of Greek theater, if any, Cocteau had in mind in 1952 and where his views of Greek productions are based. It is possible that in May 1949 he had discussed tragedy with Kotopouli, who at that time was preparing the *Oresteia* with the National Greek Theater and found little in common with her realist, populist interpretation of tragedy.³⁸

Greek productions of ancient plays included archaeologically and classically driven revivals, starting with the open-air theater of Delphi in 1927, where masks, archaic music (with Byzantine overtones), and traditionally weaved costumes were first used. The festivals of Herodou Attikou and Epidaurus followed in the thirties, and eventually became a permanent fixture in the repertory of the National Theater. It was in the context of that institution that a modern Greek interpretation of Attic drama emerged. The perception that in that area at least Greek actors and directors could follow more easily their insights and intuitions and the natural assumption of an indigenous advantage—especially through a vital oral tradition—brought distance and perspective to the relationship with European prototypes. The experience of two regional wars, two world wars, and one civil war, all within the first half of the century, created a unique "Greek" sensibility whose impact became visible as Greece moved into a period of relative stability in the 1950s. In that period, the National Theater abandoned purist revivals and emphasized instead the existential force of tragedy. Modernist solutions were viewed with skepticism primarily because they were thought to divert attention from the dramatic qualities inherent in the plays and to reduce tragic performance to spectacle and psychomoral caricature. Cocteau's resistance to a dialogue with his Greek colleagues, and his choice to remain a remote and condescending outsider, betrays a nostalgia for another time and a different world, perhaps that of Gide's Tunis in 1893 or of his own Algiers in 1912.

. . . . .

Cocteau recorded his Greek trip in *Diary of an Unknown* and in *The Past Tense.* As we have seen, he had traveled to Greece on two other occasions, in 1936 and 1949 (May 16 to 23), and kept notes of his impressions. The narrative in his Greek diaries is full of disconnected impressions, some more animated than others, some pictorial in their effect, resembling photographic snapshots. In 1936, Athens had impressed him with its crowded buses, its quarreling citizens, and "that disemboweled little cage," the Parthenon, that leaves Athenians indifferent. "Why don't they leap up, why don't they shout something like the *Thalassa* of their ancestors?" he wonders. In Italian-occupied Rhodes, his companion, Marcel Khill, tries to photograph Muslim women. Cocteau observes: "The shadows in their eyes, around their mouths, make these passing women into death's-heads, lepers."[39]

Throughout the cruise, encounters with Greeks disrupted and frustrated Cocteau. After a visit to Knossos, he notes: "The modern Cretans—cretins—respect these enchanting images only to the extent that they can bring them money."[40] He saw modern Greeks as occupants of a land full of ancient marks and traces the significance of which they could not understand or appreciate. Their presence was a nuisance and a distraction. In less frustrated moments, it filled him with sadness. June 13: "We go at once to the Acropolis, to the theaters, to the Tower of the Winds. The same desire to weep, the same strange anguish. The reason for this overwhelming feeling is that we are visiting the graves of intelligence and of beauty."[41] The image of Greece as a topos of loss recalls a commonplace of orientalist narrative: the theorized and imaginary retrieval of meaning in an alien, hostile, and incoherent environment. Again, on June 13: "Many Athenians have never walked up to the Acropolis. And it annoys them to hear it talked about. *Is the past all we have?* Alas, yes."[42] And on June 24, while sailing from Santorini to Piraeus: "The testiness of the islanders results from the fact that we are visiting their ruins. Yet these shadows of the shades of a dead Greece are very much alive when it comes to refusing us gasoline and then selling it for a fortune . . ."[43]

Like Egypt in the letters of Flaubert, the connection of modern Greece to its past is one of geographic coincidence and superimposition. One can always remove the original layer, what Cocteau calls "the real Greece," and carry it away without disturbing the scene.[44] Particular reasons may vary, from study to preservation to a sense of due appreciation not given to the objects in their native context, but they all assume the disinterested advance of a higher order of civilization. The museum, the university, Cocteau's "workroom" at Milly, serve in that function, as depositories, reconstruction sites and virtual habitats for the transplanted objects. "We were tempted to make off with the phallic column from the Theater of Dionysus; with a car and a yacht, it would have been easy enough."[45] He also recalls with amusement how his friend, the actress Yvonne de Bray, smuggled an ancient vase, intended as a gift for him, out of the Athens airport concealed (as with the Kotopouli gift) in a bouquet of roses.[46]

The romance of salvaging antiquity from the accidents of historical development interests Cocteau only as an instrument of self-portraiture and confession.[47] At Delphi he notes the resemblance of his sandaled feet to those of the Charioteer and in an imaginary adventure joins the guard in caressing and arousing the statue.[48] He describes *Oedipus Rex* as a masterpiece of archaic revival, a proof that his art is superior to archaeology. Edward Said's paradigmatic metaphors of orientalist representation, the text and the tableau, dominate Cocteau's imagination. As if through a camera, still or moving, he lifts a parade of disconnected images from the surrounding landscape. Crete becomes a Minoan fresco just like Egypt in his 1936 tour (named "around the world in eighty days") became a "funerary stele" or a "text for the use of the Gods."[49] In Egypt, Cocteau looks at the Sphinx with Napoleon's eyes ("she is seen as Napoleon must have seen her"). He then returns to his theater: "I am glad this region is closed to tourists and couples. Mosques leave me completety unmoved, but here, where men wrapped in burnous prowl around like scene-shifters round the stage, I am integrated in the play which rises effortlessly before me."[50]

Greece and the orient overlap. Cocteau calls Crete the "oriental Greece" and represents it in sketches of elegant, decorative Minoans posing next to ugly caricatures of contemporary types. All around him fragments of frescoes and sculpture match Greek geography, a dispersion in space and time of islands, ruins, bare hills, and mountains with no internal cohesion. "It is likely that Greece was a continent whose islands are in fragments. What had blossomed on these fragments has been gradually exhausted, like the provisions on a wreck."[51] When the immediate impression fades away, the yacht having sailed past it, only shadows and reflections remain. "The Greek islands are nothing but an idea that one creates for oneself." "Greece is a corpse devoured by myths. A ghost crowned with legends."[52] The viewer here is more transparent than the viewed. The spectacle portrays Cocteau. It mirrors his ideas, his moods and his desires. It vanishes when he wishes it to vanish and transforms with a magical plasticity, to match the world that he wants to construct.

Who, then, is Cocteau, the Greek Cocteau? An archaeologist of intangible and invisible treasures, a magician who animates the past, a true son of Greece and France—the one the country of the classical ideal, the other the country of classical elegance—a nostalgic devotee of the salons and high society whose cosmopolitan imagination carries with it the dreams and theater of the French empire. Cocteau's Greece is a topos of desire and regeneration, of erotic discovery and fantasy and of perpetual youth. Like so many other orientalized lands, it belongs to Europe's childhood, and for that reason it is its child and has to surrender to its authority. This is the paradox of orientalist theater. Greece was Cocteau's playground but on its stage he was always the adult. The irony is obvious to those who are familiar with his life. The following entry from the 1952 diary is in some ways a self-portrait: "This morning the liquid air and the sun show all these Greeks to be children and all their clumsiness at receiving foreigners as child's play."[53]

Notes

1. A shorter version of this paper was presented at Victoria College, University of Toronto, for the International Conference, *Le Siècle de Cocteau/Cocteau's Century,* October 2-4, 1998.

2. Edward Said, *Orientalism.* New York: Vintage, 1978: 181-185.

3. Jean Cocteau, *Past Tense: The Cocteau Diaries Volume One.* Translated by Richard Howard. New York: Harcourt Brace Jovanovich, 1987: 184.

4. *Past Tense,* 215.

5. *Past Tense,* 178.

6. André Kedros, *O Anthropos me to Garyphallo.* Translated by Toula Mastroyianni. Athens: Nea Synora, 1990: 202-204, 204-207; *Nikos Beloyiannis.* Athens: George Papakonstantinou: 370.

7. *Nikos Beloyiannis,* 213.

8. *O Anthropos me to Garyphallo,* 203.

9. Jean Cocteau, *Maalesh.* Paris: Gallimard, 1949: 218.

10. Jean Cocteau, *Ellenikon Hemerologion* (Greek Diary). Translated by Thanasis Th. Niarchos. Athens: Kastaniotis, 1986: i-v.

11. *Past Tense,* 178.

12. *Maalesh,* 205.

13. Ibid., 229.

14. Ibid., 232.

15. Ibid., 229.

16. For a study of the classical in Cocteau, see my "Classical Cocteau," in Cornelia A. Tsakiridou, ed., *Reviewing Orpheus: Essays on the Cinema and Art of Jean Cocteau,* Bucknell Review. Cranbury: Associated University Presses Inc., 1997: 78-102.

17. Jean Cocteau. *Théâtre.* Paris: Gallimard, 1948: 9, 11, 37.

18. *Past Tense,* 152, 158.

19. Igor Stravinsky, *An Autobiography.* New York: W.W. Norton & Company, 1970: 51.

20. Ibid., 152.

21. Kenneth E. Silver, *Esprit de Corps: The Art of the Parisian Avant-Garde and the Firsr World War, 1914-1925.* Princeton: Princeton University Press, 1989: 43-47.

22. *Orientalism,* 82; Charles Harrison, Paul Wood, eds. *Art in Theory 1900-1990.* Cambridge: Blackwell, 1992: 238-240; Le Corbusier, *Towards a New Architecture.* London: Architectural Press, 1927: 101.

23. *Esprit de Corps,* 93-95.

24. Ibid., 97, 106.

25. Margaret Crosland, ed., *Cocteau's World: An Anthology of Writings by Jean Cocteau.* London: Peter Owen, 1972: 310-311, 313, 319.

26. "Cocteau," *Liberation,* Oct. 1983: 69; Jean Cocteau, "Salut à Breker," *Coemedia,* no. 18, 12 Mai 1942.

27. *Past Tense,* 302; John Zavrel, ed., *The Collected Writings of Arno Breker.* Clarence: West-Art, 1990: 112-113; Michele Cone, *Artists under Vichy: A Case of Prejudice and Persecution.* Princeton: Princeton University Press, 1992: 159-169.

28. *The Collected Writings of Arno Breker,* 112.

29. Jean Cocteau, *Diary of an Unknown.* Translated by Jesse Browner. New York: Paragon House, 1988: 216.

30. *Past Tense,* 172.

31. *Cocteau's World,* 222-225; Francis Steegmuller, *Cocteau: A Biography.* Boston: Little, Brown and Company, 1970: 364-368.

32. *Cocteau: A Biography,* 16-17, 430-431.

33. *Past Tense,* 174.

34. Ibid., 212.

35. *Cocteau: A Biography,* 478.

36. *Maalesh,* 208, 210, 225.

37. Ibid., 224.

38. F. Hliadis, *Marika Kotopouli: Biographical Corpus* (in Greek). Athens: Dorikos, 1996: 313-324.

39. Jean Cocteau, Professional Secrets. Translated by Richard Howard. New York: Farrar, Strauss & Giroux Inc., 1970: 149-151.

40. *Past Tense,* 187.

41. Ibid., 170.

42. Ibid., 172.

43. Ibid., 195.

44. Gustave Flaubert, *Flaubert in Egypt: A Sensibility on Tour.* Translated by Francis Steegmuller. Boston: Little, Brown and Company, 1972: 75, 82; Arthur King Peters, *Jean Cocteau and André Gide: An Abrasive Friendship.* New Brunswick: Rutgers University Press, 1973: 24-25; *Cocteau: A Biography,* 81.

45. *Past Tense,* 211.

46. Ibid., 206.

47. Ibid., 182.

48. Ibid., 210.

49. *Professional Secrets,* 152.

50. *Cocteau's World,* 250.

51. *Past Tense,* 204.

52. Ibid., 195, 204.

53. Ibid., 211.

LE PORTRAIT SURNATUREL DE DORIAN GRAY (THE PORTRAIT OF DORIAN GRAY)

CRITICAL COMMENTARY

Peter G. Christensen (essay date autumn 1986)

SOURCE: Christensen, Peter G. "Three Concealments: Jean Cocteau's Adaptation of *The Picture of Dorian Gray. Romance Notes* 27, no. 1 (autumn 1986): 27-35.

[*In the following essay, Christensen evaluates the significance of Cocteau's* Le Portrait surnaturel de Dorian Gray *and discusses the issue of homosexuality in the play.*]

In the twenty-two years since Jean Cocteau's death, interest in his work has risen and then waned. The peak period was 1968-1971, which saw the appearance of three biographies—those of Elizabeth Sprigge and Jean-Jacques Kihm, Frederick Brown, and Francis Steegmuller. Since then much previously unavailable work, both private and public, has been published, but not analyzed in detail. In the private realm, we have the first volume of the journal, *Le Passé défini,* as well as the correspondences with André Gide, Jean Bourgoint, Milorad, and Jean-Marie Magnan. In the public sphere there are collections of poems, such as *Faire-Part, Les Vocalises de Bachir Selim,* "Poèmes pour Raymond Radiguet," and short lyrics for Jean Marais. In addition, six interesting works of theater have come to light. These are, in chronological order, *Le Portrait surnaturel de Dorian Gray* (1909), *La Patience de Pénélope* (1910), *Le Gendarme incompris* (1921), *Paul et Virginie* (1921), *L'Impromtu d'Alice* (1937-1938), and *L'Impromptu des Bouffes-Parisiens* (1938). Although none of these plays is likely to change our estimation of Cocteau as a dramatist, we are fortunate to have the chance to look further into his formative years, as four of the six plays were written before *Orphée* (1925)—the first two in his *pre-Potomok* period and the middle two in his 'Radiguet period.' Although there have been major studies of Cocteau's plays by Neal Oxenhandler, Otto Wirtz, and Juergen Grimm, a reevaluation using all the new material is needed.

The four early plays can all be considered types of adaptations: of Oscar Wilde, Homer, Mallarmé, and Bernardin de Saint-Pierre, respectively. On the surface, *Le Portrait surnaturel de Dorian Gray* (a full-length play in five 'tableaux') appears to be the least original of the four.[1] There is an obvious sense in which Cocteau's play is a dramatization of the most striking instances in Wilde's novel. There is no burlesque, as in *La Patience de Pénélope* and *Le Gendarme incompris,* nor do we see Cocteau revising the ending of his source material to suit his own habitual concerns, as he does in *Paul et Virginie.* By its style of adaptation, *Le Portrait surnaturel* clearly

foreshadows *Romeo et Juliette* (written c. 1916) and *Antigone* (1922) as a fast-paced, stripped down version of a major literary work.

Le Portrait surnaturel, which dates from the time of Cocteau's first collection of poetry, *La Lampe d'Alladin* (1909), is, along with a short play at the close of this collection, Cocteau's earliest surviving play. The manuscript is partially in the handwriting of his friend, Jacques Renaud. The play was first scheduled to appear in *Les Lettres modernes* in 1973, but publication was delayed until 1978 when Olivier Orban brought it out. The following year it was discussed in an essay by Jean-Marie Magnan;[2] however, it had earlier received a brief mention by Jacques de Langlade.[3]

It is unfortunate that *Le Portrait surnaturel* was made public too late to be analyzed by René Galand in his essay, "Cocteau's Sexual Equation."[4] At the end of his article, Galand laments the fact that, unlike Genet, who had Sartre, Cocteau has yet to find his exegete—someone who can discover how his most characteristic myths were formed. He suggests that Magnan's work is an important step in this direction. Because of its early date, *Le Portrait surnaturel* may prove to be of major importance. This is particularly true since the issue of homosexuality is raised here, and there is a continuing tendency for writers on Cocteau to avoid it. When the journal, *Masques,* in a recent special issue on Cocteau did make homosexuality a central consideration, it turned out that little literary criticism was included.

In *Le Portrait surnaturel* we are treated to three concealments, and we must answer the questions they raise. First of all, there is the fact that the play was not performed, and it did not see publication until fifteen years after Cocteau's death. Why did a person like Cocteau, skilled at self-promotion, fail to use his connections to have a play, based on such sound and famous source material, mounted? Second, as an adaptation, Cocteau's play omits narrative, description, and dialogue from Wilde's text. By what criteria has Cocteau concealed the original text from the reader/playgoer unfamiliar with Wilde's novel? Third, the most striking thing about Cocteau's dramaturgy is his never making the picture of Dorian Gray visible to the audience. Only the back of the canvas is shown. Whereas this strategy keeps the audience from becoming overly caught up in comparing the portrait with the person acting the role of Dorian, it, nevertheless, diminishes theatrical effect, and we must inquire if there is an additional reason for the concealment. The answers to these questions can be traced to Cocteau's 'erotic imagination,' especially his homosexuality and its relationship to the concepts of literary influence and narcissism.

Before offering my own ideas about the non-publication of the play, I turn to the research of Langlade and Magnan. Langlade mentions two ways (added stress on the fantastic and the affirmation of art over life) in which Cocteau departs from Wilde's novel (p. 256), but he does not follow through with an interpretation of the play. Instead, agreeing with some points made by Claude Mauriac, he relates Lord Harry's closing remark, "Le voilà, le vrai Dorian, admirablement beau, jeune, pur" (p. 120) to Cocteau's personal life, in essence assuming that Lord Harry is Cocteau's mouthpiece. He finds Cocteau concerned with appearing overly artificial and false. Cocteau could do what Wilde could not—be more open about his homosexuality and employ it as an aristocratic privilege, a social claim, a style (pp. 256-58). Thus Langlade gives us a Wilde confined to the closet and a Cocteau allowed to play outside its door. We may well ask, however, if Cocteau did not have his drama performed simply because he felt afraid of being too closely connected with Wilde's scandal-making homosexuality. Cocteau has apparently left us no journal from this period which might clarify his motives.

Unlike Langlade, Jean-Marie Magnan finds *Le Portrait surnaturel* an attack on the novel and Cocteau's means of exorcising it from his life. He writes:

> Lorsque Jean Cocteau découvrira que l'amour est sans brio et sacrifiera le sien, il se montrera sévère pour une œuvre que son adolescence avait prise pour maladie. Cherchait-il encore à s'en prémunir? L'attraque est un reflexe défensif de jeunesse. Mais ce livre lui avait fait perdre (croyait-il) les plus belles années de sa vie. Pour l'expulser, il s'était lance à écrire cette adaptation qui n'eut pas de lendemain. Elle plaide au moins en faveur d'une empreinte profounde.
>
> (p. 191)

Magnan's thesis is reasonable and provocative, but it does not indicate how the play can be seen as an attack on the novel. In fact, most readers would consider the play more of an homage than an attack. Cocteau has the portrait begin to bleed before Dorian stabs Basil Hallward, the artist, and not afterward. As Magnan says, the blood seems to provoke the murder and make it irresistible. I do not think, however, that this change which stresses the supernatural can be considered an "attack." It is, rather, a striking theatrical moment in its reversal of cause and effect.

Consequently, in response to the question of the first concealment, we need to look more specifically at the dialogue of the play, particularly in the early scenes. As it turns out, the discussion of influence within the novel and references to artists and models take on a new dimension when seen in the context of a literary adaptation.

Early in the play's first scene, we learn that Basil Hallward does not want to expose the painting of Dorian Gray to the public. Lord Henry Watton insists on knowing the reason. The conversation runs as follows:

HARRY:

> Bien je me répète: J'ai besoin que vous m'expliquiez pourquoi vous ne voulez pas exposer le portrait de Dorian Gray. Je désire en connaître la vraie raison.

BASIL:

> Je vous l'ai dite.

HARRY:

> Non. Vous m'avez dit que c'était parce qu'il y avait beaucoup de vous-même dans ce portrait; cela est enfantin.

BASIL:

> Harry, tout portrait peint compréhensivement est un portrait de l'artiste, non du modèle . . . Le modèle est purement l'accident, l'occasion . . . Ce n'est pas lui qui est révélé par le peintre, c'est le peintre qui, sur sa toile, se révèle, lui-même.
>
> (p. 17)

At this point the question remains only partially answered. Harry is not aware of the great attraction that Basil has felt for Dorian, even though Basil has hinted at it. When Harry persists on the topic, Basil replies:

> Parce que, d'instinct. . . . Malgré moi, j'y ai mis l'expression de toute cette étrange attirance dont je vous ai parlé, et si je ne veux pas decouvrir mon âme aux bas regards quêteurs qui voudraient en extraire quelque chose de vil! Un artiste doit créer de belles formes mais ne doit rien mettre de lui-même en elles. Nous vivons dans un siècle où l'on a perdu le sens abstrait de la beauté, où l'on cultive une espèce d'art autobiographique.
>
> (p. 18)

The discussion ends when Harry tells Basil that he thinks he is wrong, but then lets the subject drop. Basil reproaches himself first of all for not having achieved an art of impersonal, pure form. The crowd's desire for autobiographically informed art is only of secondary concern. Both situations must have given Cocteau cause for reflection throughout his career, for autobiography appears not only in 'realistic' works such as *Le Livre blanc* but also in fantastic works, such as the film *Orphée*. Cocteau shares some of Basil's ideas, so we should not think of Harry as his only porte-parole.

The argument of the play becomes more complex in the next two scenes, as the subject of models is dropped and the theme of one person's influence on another is taken up when Basil tells Harry to stay clear of Dorian:

> N'essayez pas de l'influencer. Votre influence serait pernicieuse. Je sais votre plaisir, votre joie de modeler, comme une cire vièrge, un caractère à votre fantaisie. Laissez celui-là: le monde ne manque pas de sujets semblables. Ma vie d'artiste dépend de lui. Prenez garde, Harry, je vous en conjure!
>
> (p. 20)

When Dorian enters, Basil tells him that Harry's influence is bad on everyone. Harry, nevertheless, escapes from this criticism by declaring that there is no such thing as a good influence, and that all influence is immoral from a scientific point of view.

. . . influencer une personne c'est lui donner un peu de sa propre âme. Elle ne pense plus avec ses pensées naturelles, elle ne brûle plus avec ses passions intimes, elle devient l'écho d'une musique étrangère, l'acteur d'une pièce qui n'a pas été écrite pour sa nature.

(p. 25)

Writing his play, Cocteau could not fail to notice that he had to confront a model which was influencing him. He had to ask whether the influence of *The Picture of Dorian Gray* was bad in itself, regardless of its so-called 'doctrines.' In *Opium* and "Eloge des Pléïades" (1934), Cocteau denounces not only the play, but the many "sottises coûteuses accomplies en son nom."[5]

Wilde's novel is both the "model" for Cocteau's play and the "influence" on it. Basil says that the portrait (by analogy, **Le Portrait surnaturel**) reveals the artist (Cocteau), not the model (Wilde). Harry, in effect, tells us the opposite: the influence (Wilde) overpowers the passive recipient (Cocteau). Thus the dialogue leads us to the paradoxical situation whereby Cocteau's play both reveals a true self (perhaps Cocteau's homosexual side) and puts forward a false self (Cocteau as decadent author) simultaneously— surely enough reason to raise doubts about allowing the play's performance, as the novel shows us that both Basil and Harry are correct. However, in the novel, model (Dorian) and influence (Harry) are not united in the same figure. It is Cocteau's writing of the play which combines them in the figure of Wilde's novel itself, for the plot of the play is so similar, it is like a 'tableau vivant' of the novel—yet with just enough variation to be Cocteau's own original work.

In the "Eloge des Pléïades" Cocteau pulls a Borgesian turn on *The Picture of Dorian Gray,* asking it to be reread through a subsequent work of art, in this case, von Sternberg's masterpiece, *Morocco* (1930). Cocteau writes that while seeing one of Dietrich's moments in the film, he remembers an incident from Wilde's novel—only here Dietrich is Dorian when he confronts the sailor:

. . . mais sous l'éclairage de Marlène Dietrich et de Garry [sic] Cooper je découvris un épisode oublié: lorsque le matelot s'excuse auprès de Dorian sous la lanterne d'un bouge. N'est-ce pas Marlène qui arrête son geste de menace, en habit noir, le chapeau de soie sur l'oreille; et, malgré la malaise, peut-être à cause de malaise des travestis, je cherche ce qu'attendent un Sternberg, un Lubitsch, un Mamoulian pour asseoir, côte à côte, quelque Adolphe Menjou plus subtil et Dietrich en jeune homme dans le jardin des paradoxes.

(X, 238)

For Cocteau, *Morocco* has turned Wilde's otherwise unrelated novel into its predecessor, eighteen years before Kafka did the same job in Browning and Lord Dunsany in *Otras Inquisiciones.* The novel, which has nothing to do with transvestism, now stars Marlene Dietrich. Cocteau denies that Wilde's novel can influence his outlook any longer, whereas von Sternberg is conceded as an influence.

Cocteau does not position Wilde's novel in relation to an obvious forerunner such as Huysman's *A Rebours* (mentioned in the novel), but with respect to a set of descendants, three great film stylists.

To confront Wilde truly meant dealing with homosexuality, not transvestism. We might think that at age twenty, Cocteau, anxious for a wide audience, wanted to keep his homosexual side a secret, and, indeed, much of the pointed reference to homosexuality in the novel is dropped by Cocteau. We are now at the second concealment, reminded of Cocteau's deletion of the following confession of Basil to Dorian when he comes midway through the novel to obtain the portrait for exhibition:

. . . Dorian, from the first moment I ment you, your personality had the most extraordinary influence on me. I was dominated, soul, brain, and power by you. You became to me the visible incarnation of the unseen idol whose memory haunts us artists like an exquisite dream. I worshipped you. I grew jealous of everyone to whom you spoke. I wanted to have you all to myself. I was only happy when I was with you. When you were away from me you were still present in my art. . . . Of course, I never let you know anything about this. It would have been impossible.[6]

Although Cocteau excises such major speeches, during the same years he was publishing poems on homosexual themes. So we can not say that he was simply being cautious. For example, in his third collection, *La Danse de Sophocle* (1912), there is a poem on "Les Archers de Saint Sebastian," a perennial theme of gay artists. Even more to the point, in *Le Prince frivole* (1910), the second collection, is a poem "Le Dieu nu," with an epigraph from Lord Alfred Douglas, "I was the love that dare not speak its name." Rather than suspect Cocteau of squeamishness in being associated with Wilde's work, we should look instead at the novel itself—to Dorian's response to Basil's visit after he deflects him from his goal of temporarily regaining the portrait:

As he left the room, Dorian Gray smiled to himself. Poor Basil! How little he knew of the true reason! And how strange it was that, instead of having been forced to reveal his own secret, he had succeeded, almost by chance, in wresting a secret from his friend! How much that strange confession explained to him! The painter's absurd fits of jealousy, his wild devotion, his intransigent panegyrics, his curious reticences—he understood them all now, and he felt sorry. There seemed to him to be something tragic in a friendship so colored by romance.

(p. 442)

The key word here is "tragic." The novel is tragic, because, to use Wilde's own words, Basil kills the thing he loves. It is odd that Cocteau has toned down the tragedy, since we are inclined to associate his stagecraft with this genre. However, despite his early *Romeo and Juliet* adaptation, he did not really turn to tragedy until the early 1920's with **Antigone.**

Through Cocteau's exclusion of half of the dynamism of the Basil-Dorian relationship, we are left with a Dorian who is less sympathetic. He lacks moral fiber, and he allows himself to be destroyed by a painting more external than in the novel to his life's story. Basil is less to blame here. This Dorian, corrupted by the portrait is more like Jean Cocteau corrupted by Wilde's novel, since Wilde did not write the novel for Cocteau (who, after all, was only two years old at the time) in particular. The streamlining of Cocteau's novel brings it closer to a non-ambiguous morality play.

For today's readers, playing down the homosexual motif may seem closely related to Cocteau's decision to conceal the portrait of Dorian from the audience. This is because in Wilde's novel, the portrait is connected with Dorian in the same manner as in Ovid's *Metamorphoses* the reflection of Narcissus is related to Narcissus. In the novel, after Sybil Vane has committed suicide, this parallel is presented most clearly:

> A feeling of pain crept over him, as he thought of the desecration that was in store for the fair face on the canvas. Once, in boyish mockery of Narcissus, he had kissed, or feigned to kiss, those painted lips that now smiled so cruelly at him. Morning after morning he had sat before the portrait, wondering at its beauty, almost enamoured of it, as it seemed to him at times. Was it to alter now with every mood to which he yielded? Was it to become a monstrous and loathsome thing, to be hidden away in a locked room, to be shut out from the sunlight that had so often touched to brighter gold the waving wonder of his hair? the pity of it! The pity of it!

(p. 436).

In the myth Narcissus wastes away in disappointment when he finds out that the image of his beloved is really his own image. In the novel, the opaque portrait replaces the transparent water, but gazing at the self is still the way to ruin. When Cocteau conceals the portrait from our eyes, the Narcissus theme in the novel is blocked. There is no Dorian Gray gazing at himself. With this change another facet of the homosexual theme is lost also. The Narcissus myth has been traditionally associated with homosexuality, an idea which Freud canonized in 1911 in his famous essay, "On Narcissism: An Introduction." In *Le Portrait surnaturel,* with the weakened connections between Dorian and Basil and Dorian and the portrait, homosexuality becomes less accountable for all the unpleasant actions.

Perhaps what bothered Cocteau about his adaptation of Wilde was that he could see that he had resorted to psychological simplification along with his dramatic simplification. Wilde's novel is the model that reveals the playwright just out of his teens, the young man copying the old master. Ironically, the old master was so great, so knowing, that the play had to be put away, its insights denied. Are we not allowed to think of it consigned to a dark upper room with other relics of childhood, lest someday its creator stumble on it and find himself, disfigured, in it?

Notes

1. Jean Cocteau, *Le Portrait surnaturel de Dorian Gray* (Paris: Olivier Orban, 1978).

2. Jean-Marie Magnan, "Jean Cocteau et le double peint de Dorian Gray," *Cahiers Jean Cocteau,* 8 (1979), 185-92.

3. Jacques de Langlade, *Oscar Wilde—écrivain français* (Paris: Stock, 1975).

4. René Galand, "Cocteau's Sexual Equation," in *Homosexualities and French Literature,* ed. George Stambolian and Elaine Marks (Ithaca, NY: Cornell U. Press, 1979), pp. 279-94.

5. Jean Cocteau, *Œuvres complètes* (Lausanne: Marguerat, 1950), vol. X, p. 238.

6. Oscar Wilde, *The Works* (London: Spring Books, 1963), p. 441.

LES MARIÉS DE LA TOUR EIFFEL (THE EIFFEL TOWER WEDDING PARTY)

CRITICAL COMMENTARY

Annette Shandler Levitt (essay date January-March 1988)

SOURCE: Levitt, Annette Shandler. "Breasts, Couples, Children and Other *Clichés*: Visual/Verbal Imagery in Surrealist Drama." *Word & Image* 4, no. 1 (January-March 1988): 292-96.

[*In the following essay, Levitt examines the relationship between art and reality in Cocteau's* Les Mariés de la Tour Eiffel.]

In the first moments of *Les Mystères de l'amour* (1924), his only play labelled "*drame surréaliste,*" Roger Vitrac uses visual imagery to initiate a radical shift from conventional staging. The play opens with a Prologue in which the protagonist is seen "tracing sinuous lines in the mud with a stick." He is, he tells a policeman, "finishing off [the] hair" of a female portrait painted on the wall of a house. According to the stage directions, "He leaves, tracing a sinuous line. The curtain slowly falls" (p. 229)[1]. In this brief Prologue the protagonist by his tracing both adds to (and partially relocates) the set and leads the audience's gaze away from the stage. Appropriately, the play's first tableau begins in "A box overhanging the stage. The proscenium lights are out. The house lights, a chandelier above the audience, are lighted" (p. 230), and the action, a parody of courtship rituals, takes place in the box, with occasional shouts into and from the audience. Thus Vitrac transcends the two-dimensional limitations of set design and controls the audience: initially directing its attention from the conventional locus of action and then destroying the traditional boundaries between actor and audience. The protagonist's initial gesture, reinforcing the visual aspects of theatre, ultimately undermines our basic assumptions about the genre.

Undermining assumptions and conventions—in subject as well as in form—is a basic principle of Surrealist drama. Guillaume Apollinaire does both in *Les Mamelles de Tirésias* (1917). His characters shout at the audience through megaphones, and his chorus, "the people of Zanzibar," is actually one "speechless person" (p. 67). His protagonist, Thérèse, tosses away and ignites her balloon breasts and grows a *mustache,* changing her sex to become Tirésias before our eyes. She leaves her husband—wearing her clothes—to be seduced by a lascivious policeman and to make babies with scissors and glue. Exploding balloon breasts, babies coming to life from cutouts, a "kiosk, an inanimate object, [which] dances and sports a living appendage, an arm, that is mechanical"[2]—these are Apollinaire's transmutations for the stage of the basic issue of art versus reality, of theatre as *sur*(super)*réal* representation of life. A character in *Les Mamelles* describes a Picasso painting as *"un tableau qui bouge"*[3] ("a canvas that moves")—*i.e.,* that has life. In the same vein, in his Preface to the play, Apollinaire offers a graphic example to justify the excesses of theatrical surreality: "When man wanted to imitate walking he created the wheel, which does not resemble the leg. In the same way he has created surrealism unconsciously" (p. 56).

The connection between art and reality is also at the heart of Jean Cocteau's *Les Mariés de la Tour Eiffel* (1921). Like Vitrac and Apollinaire emphasizing the visual, even in the non-dramatic language of his 1922 Preface to this play, Cocteau declares, "I seek to paint more truly than the truth" (p. 95). He constantly juxtaposes the visual and the verbal—if only to distinguish between them: "The action of my text is pictorial, while the text is not" (p. 96). Claiming that he opposes the obscure, he insists, in a less literal juxtaposition, "I illuminate everything, I underline everything" (p. 94). Moving into metaphor and ambiguity, Cocteau connects mirrors and light with illusion and reality: "the chief electrician, by means of his reflections, has often illuminated a piece for me" (p. 94). This sort of punning and its implications are central to Cocteau in *Les Mariés.* Lydia Crowson, in *The Esthetic of Jean Cocteau,* has said, "In Cocteau's earlier pieces, plays on word meanings frequently determine the development of the work; in addition to reflecting an existential stance, liguistic ambiguity functions as a structural device"[4]. In *Les Mariés* one word, bearing visual and verbal denotations and social connotations, structures the entire work. Without ever using the word *cliché* Cocteau bases his play on its meanings and implications, not the least of which is the popular connotative usage as something trite or overused.

But at the heart of the play are the denotations of *cliché*: "(phot) negative; (typ) plate, stereotype; *prendre un cliché* (phot) to make an exposure." To put the term in a context: Georges Potonniée, in his *History of the Discovery of Photography,* states that despite disagreement on the date of its discovery, "no one gives the name photography to anything but an image obtained in the camera on a surface sensitive to light and rendered permanent"[5]. The image is "rendered permanent" on a photographic plate, or *cliché,* also called a "negative" because it shows reality in reverse. "Positives" or prints can then be developed in any number, rereversing the image to convey a reproduction of reality.

This language—even in translation—is rich with possibilities, both intrinsic and acquired: negative, stereotype, exposure. We even say that the image is "trapped" in the camera by means of the plate, as opposed to the action of the early *camera obscura,* whose "images could only be observed while the device was being used, and were never 'trapped'"[6].

The language of photography is naturally related to the visual. But a verbal element, introduced by the photographer—the human factor—adds to the reversals inherent in the process and offers Cocteau a point of departure. To hold his subject's attention the photographer typically says, "Watch the birdie"—at least in English. In the original French (for photography was both invented and popularized in France)[7] the photographer's formula is *"Un oiseau va sortir."* ("A bird is coming out.") Thus to get the image *into* his camera, the photographer speaks of a bird *coming out.* The photographer's phrase—indeed, some would say the photographer himself—is not necessary for the process to take place; if the image enters the camera, the action of light on the metal or glass plate creates the negative. But it is just the sort of "ready-made expression" (p. 94) which Cocteau wants to illuminate and underline. "In my play," he declares in the Preface, "I rejuvenate the commonplace. My concern is to present it from angles which will recapture its teens" (p. 95).

In Cocteau's play the visual and verbal elements interact to create a reversal of the "normal" photographic process. Indeed, the reversal inherent in the *cliché,* or negative, is the *donnée* of the play's multiple, complex pattern of reversals. His Photographer's utterance of the verbal *cliché* unleashes a series of bizarre events, turning upsidedown the expectations of a bourgeois couple come to take their wedding photograph on the Eiffel Tower on July 14.

The Eiffel Tower, once the apogee of technology, had become, by 1921, a toy for poets to mock lovingly. When it was built in 1889 "it was a veritable 'Queen of the Machines' as [Cocteau] put it, and 'did no work'; since then, grown dowdy and with a telegraphic station installed within, it had become a mere 'telegraph operator'"[8]. Cocteau revitalizes the mundane aspects of technology not merely by having several wireless telegrams shot down on the first landing of the Eiffel Tower, his set, but by using a "professional photographer's camera, the height of a man" to focus the action. Its bellows "forms a corridor joining the wings. At the front of the bellows the camera opens like a door to let the characters enter or exit" (p. 101). Moreover, all of the action is narrated by "two actors dressed as phonographs, their bodies the cabinets, horns corresponding to their mouths" (p. 101).

Cocteau thus juxtaposes visual and verbal symbols of technology as well as the human and the inanimate object, following Apollinaire's example in *Les Mamelles* as well as his own *"ballet réaliste,"* *Parade* (employing Picasso's "concept for the Managers . . . carrying sets and costumes as one on their backs, blurring the line between actor and object . . ."⁹. In *Les Mariés* the objects dominate, indeed, appear to control the action. The camera has gone crazy, the Photographer reports. When he had said earlier, *"Un oiseau va sortir,"* no little bird, but a huge ostrich came out, he tells us, and he cannot take a picture until it returns.

The camera thus resists the process which leads to *cliché*—in both senses: no negative can be made, and no bourgeois wedding scene will be immortalized. Instead, a reversal has taken place: the Photographer's words have not resulted in an image going into the camera but in a bird, the actualization of his verbal *cliché*—writ large—coming out. The play thus opens with a Hunter pursuing the huge ostrich which has escaped from the camera. Thereafter, whenever the Photographer tries to take a picture, and repeats his verbal formula, another unexpected creature comes out of the camera. It is clear that the Photographer has no control over his art. When he attempts to photograph the wedding party and recites his formula, "A Trouville Bathing Beauty appears. She wears a bikini, carries a landing net, and has a picnic basket slung over her shoulder. Colored lights flash on. The wedding party lifts its hands in admiration." And the First Phonograph aptly declares, "Oh! It's like a picture postcard" (p. 105).¹⁰

On his next attempt the Photographer's line brings forth "A fat little boy" who wears "a green paper crown" and carries books and a basket. (p. 105) He is described as "the image of the wedding," of "his mother," "his father," "his grandmother" and "grandfather" (p. 106). We are told that he will be a captain, an architect, boxer, poet, President of the Republic and "a beautiful little victim for the next war" (p. 107). The final aspiration breaks the mold for this visual and verbal *cliché,* as do the contents of his basket: *balles* (balls or bullets) can be used for playing or for killing, and the child bombards the wedding party until he runs out of ammunition. He then petulantly declares that he wants "'to live his own life'" (p. 108), an impossibility for this image of an image.

The final product of the Photographer's *appareil détraqué* is a lion which, true to form, devours the General, who had not run off with the rest of the wedding party to escape the lion because of his belief that

> There can be no lion on the Eiffel Tower. Therefore, it is a mirage, a simple mirage. Mirages are, so to speak, the white lies of the desert. This lion is actually in

> Africa, just as the cyclist was on the road to Chatou. The lion sees me, I see him, and yet we each recognize that we are simply reflections.

> (p. 109)

As the Father-in-law says of the eaten General in his eulogy, "You never surrendered, even to evidence" (p. 110). But the General had reason for his misapprehension, for he had experienced a mirage in Africa:

> I was eating a tart with the Duke of Aumale. This tart was covered with wasps. In vain we tried to chase them away. Actually they were tigers. . . . They were prowling around by the thousands. A mirage projected them in miniature above our tart, and we mistook them for wasps.

> (p. 104)

Together the General's speeches convey not only another use of the negative—its projection (the manner in which we show slides or films, both being negatives)—but also the illusionary nature of such projections and their implications for our assumptions about reality and illusion, in theatre and in life. Because the wasps in Africa were only projections (light on the film(?) throwing the reduced image onto the tart), on the Eiffel Tower, where one does not expect to see cyclists or lions, they—and the General himself, he tells us—"are simply reflections" (p. 109). Theatre exists to create illusion; if it is too successful, however, it may create solipsism. And if we don't believe in anything, we may be in danger.

Cocteau works against the suspension of disbelief from the start, with his huge camera and the two Phonographs onstage, narrating the action. When the wedding party first appears, the members go for their wedding breakfast to a "table with plates painted on it," and are instructed to sit "Only on one side of the table, so the audience can see you" (p. 103). At the same time we in the audience are supposed to believe that the bathing beauty, child and lion simply appear from the innards of the camera and that they are convinced to return by the Photographer's uses, as when he makes the bathing beauty "think it's a cabana" (p. 105). When the ostrich finally reappears, the Photographer "remembers that one has only to hide an ostrich's head to make it invisible"; "he hides its head in his hat," and "the ostrich walks invisible, a hat on its head" (p. 111). The Photographer's magic is simultaneously reduced—this trick is no more sophisticated than pulling rabbits out of hats—and expanded into another reversal: if photography can create illusion, it can also create invisibility. Thus the wedding party ultimately disappears into the camera whence it came (pp. 114-15)—when it is clear that the camera functions properly. Once the ostrich returns to the camera, the Photographer's formula works, and a little bird does appear—a dove, naturally, so that "Peace is achieved" (p. 114). (This reference and that to the child as "victim for the next war" are reminders, in 1921, of the debacle just past—of reality, in short.) The play thus ends with the creation of the *cliché*: not merely the images but the physical beings enter the camera, and the bourgeois wedding is at last immortalized.

But in the final moments we are reminded that the Photographer is not in control, as the camera itself moves offstage, "followed by its bellows, like railroad coaches. Through various aperatures one sees the wedding party waving handkerchiefs and beneath, feet walking" (p. 115). This is not the Photographer's doing; moreover, when the Hunter complains of having missed the train, the Photographer responds, "It's not my fault" (p. 115). Indeed, when his misadventures began he had exclaimed, "Does one ever know what's coming next? Since these mysteries are beyond me, let's pretend we're organizing them" (p. 105).

The Photographer can pretend to organize, but he is not—as some might still say—an artist. Cocteau goes further, questioning the role of the artist in general and renewing the conflict between art and reality, for when the wedding party is ready to be photographed, an art Dealer appears with a Collector, to show him "a truly unique piece: 'The Wedding Party' . . . a kind of primitive . . . one of the latest works of God. . . . It's more than a wedding. It's all weddings" (p. 113). We are led to conclude that ultimately reality is more real than art but that it is even more of a *cliché*—that it creates its own *clichés*—more effectively than the artist or even the photographer, presumably the true artist of the technological age, can.

But even this masterpiece—God's work—offers surprises, in the true Surrealist spirit of *hasard* or chance. For the General is vomited up by the camera and joins the wedding party's tableau, leading the Second Phonograph to remark, "Here is a fine surprise for the Collector of masterpieces. In a true masterpiece one never ceases to discover unexpected details" (p. 114).

The unexpected has become so much a part of Surrealist drama that it has itself become a *cliché,* visual image of Cocteau's dramatic enterprise, verbal reminder of its own originality. *Prendre un cliché*: to make an exposure. In *Les Mariés de la Tour Eiffel* Cocteau, more directly than other Surrealist playwrights, exposes the *clichés* of modern life and of dramatic form. Using the photographic process as metaphor, he brings light to dead images—both visual and verbal—enacting and reversing them before our eyes.

Notes

1. Citations to all plays in English translation are from Michael Benedikt and George E. Wellwarth, eds. and trans., *Modern French Theatre: The Avant-Garde, Dada and Surrealism* (New York: Dutton, 1966).

2. David I. Grossvogel, *Twentieth Century French Drama* (New York: Columbia University Press, 1961), p. 40.

3. Guillaume Apollinaire, *Les Mamelles de Tirésias* (Paris: Bélier, 1946), p. 76.

4. Lydia Crowson, *The Esthetics of Jean Cocteau* (Hanover: University Press of New Hampshire, 1978), p. 51.

5. Georges Potonniée, *History of the Discovery of Photography,* trans. Edward Epstean, 1936 (New York: Arno Press, 1973), p. 97.

6. William Welling, *Photography in America: The Formative Years* (New York: Crowell, 1978), p. 1.

7. Potonniée offers a charming testimonial to these events: "The history of photography is essentially French. It was a Frenchman, Niepce, who invented photography and a Frenchman, Daguerre, who made it public. . . . it was in France that its great improvements were achieved; the photomechanical process, colour photography and animated photography. . . . in 1839, having purchased the secret of photography, France refused to draw from it any profit whatever and liberally presented it to the world. It is not just to a accord her the glory?" (Preface x)

8. Francis Steegmuller, *Cocteau: A Biography* (Boston: Little, Brown, 1970), p. 266.

9. Annabelle Henkin Melzer, "The Premiere of Apollinaire's 'The Breasts of Tiresias' in Paris," *Theatre Quarterly* 7 (1977), p. 4.

10. Benedikt commits a solecism in his translation: Cocteau's Trouville *baigneuse* wears a *maillot* and carries *une épuisette,* which can be translated as "landing gear" but is more accurate here as "net bag." *Maillot,* however, could not have meant "bikini" in 1921, since the word was not used until after the United States conducted the post World War II bomb tests on the Bikini atoll in the Marshall Islands in 1946. The usage, according to Merriam Webster's *Third New International Dictionary,* comes "from a comparison of the effects wrought by a scantily clad woman to the effects of the atomic bomb."

Works Cited

Apollinaire, Guillaume. *Les Mamelles de Tirésias.* Paris: Bélier, 1946.

Benedikt, Michael, and George E. Wellwarth, eds. and trans. *Modern French Theatre: The Avant-Garde, Dada and Surrealism.* New York: Dutton, 1966.

Brown, Frederick. *An Impersonation of Angels: A Biography of Jean Cocteau.* New York: Viking, 1968.

Cocteau, Jean. *Les Mariés de la Tour Eiffel.* Paris: Gallimard, 1928.

Crowson, Lydia. *The Esthetic of Jean Cocteau.* Hanover, New Hampshire: University Press of New Hampshire, 1978.

Fowlie, Wallace. *Jean Cocteau: The History of a Poet's Age.* Bloomington: Indiana University Press, 1966.

Grossvogel, David I. *Twentieth Century French Drama.* New York: Columbia University Press, 1961.

Melzer, Annabelle Henkin. "The Premiere of Apollinaire's 'The Breasts of Tiresias' in Paris." *Theatre Quarterly* 7.27 (1977): 3-13.

Oxenhandler, Neal. *Scandal and Parade: The Theater of Jean Cocteau.* New Brunswick: Rutgers University Press, 1957.

Potonniée, Georges. *The History of the Discovery of Photography.* Trans. Edward Epstean. 1936. New York: Arno Press, 1973.

Steegmuller, Francis. *Cocteau: A Biography.* Boston: Little, Brown, 1970.

Vitrac, Roger. *Les Mystères de l'amour.* Théatre. Vol. 2. Paris: Gallimard, 1948.

Welling, William. *Photography in America: The Formative Years.* New York: Crowell, 1978.

ORPHÉE (ORPHEUS)

CRITICAL COMMENTARY

Chester Clayton Long (essay date October 1965)

SOURCE: Long, Chester Clayton. "Cocteau's *Orphée*: From Myth to Drama and Film." *Quarterly Journal of Speech* 51, no. 3 (October 1965): 311-25.

[*In the following essay, Long contrasts the mythical, dramatic, and cinematic versions of* Orphée, *emphasizing Cocteau's versions of the Greek myth.*]

1.

No one should any longer question the "distortion" of myth in a poet's work, especially if the poet is writing for the theatre. The free adaptation of whichever of the many versions of a particular myth a poet happens to have at hand during composition is a long and venerable tradition. The Greeks, and specifically Aristotle, adjured the poet not to sacrifice dramatic excellence in the interest of slavish imitation of his model. And that makes perfectly good sense, for the structures of myth, drama, and film are not the same, nor are their functions.

A current style among some critics is to deal with these three structures as though they are intimately related.[1] One gets the impression that in the beginning was the myth, which *caused* the drama, which *caused* the film. This is the archetype that underlies a great deal of modern criticism.

The intention in this [essay] is to depart from this form of reasoning about the three forms and to treat them as separate identities, separate aesthetic structures. It is the film that will be most difficult to treat in this manner, for the film cannot be adequately studied simply as literature, whereas the myth and the drama can be. The mixture of the two worlds of the language arts and the plastic arts in the film is such a fixed form that an exclusive study of the scenario of a film proves an inadequate way of dealing with it.[2]

The partial synopses of myth, drama, and film included here present only the underlying *structure of incidents,* a small part of any poem's structure. Even with this limited view of the structures, however, it should be immediately apparent that the three structures are radically different.

2. STRUCTURE OF THE ORPHEUS MYTH

Robert Graves suggests that Orpheus was originally a worshipper of the moon-goddess, Diana, not of the sun-god, Apollo. Graves takes his cue from the grammarians who tell us that *Orpheus* is derived from the root *ereph,* meaning to conceal or cover.[3] This will become progressively important in relation to our understanding of Cocteau's rendering of the myth into drama and then into film.

Ovid's version of the Orpheus myth presents us with a plot of action containing seven major events. Orpheus, the young virtuoso of singing and lyre playing, marries Eurydice who is killed by a serpent during the wedding feast. Orpheus descends courageously into the underworld to regain his young bride, and does so by charming the rulers of the underworld with his music. They permit him to return Eurydice to the upper world on the condition Orpheus not look back at her during the upward journey. In his concern for her, he inadvertently does look back at his wife, thus losing her again. Orpheus tries a second time to retrieve her, but fails. He returns to the upper world alone, swearing never to love another woman, and while he is wandering disconsolately about one day, the Maenads, who hate him for not loving women, fall upon him, tear his body to pieces, and fling his head into the Hebrus river. The head floats on the stream saying Eurydice's name, whence it reaches the ocean and floats to the island of Lesbos, where it is protected from the ravages of a serpent by Apollo. Meanwhile, Orpheus's shade has rejoined Eurydice in the nether world, where their union is endless, though Orpheus still is not permitted to look on his wife's face.[4]

In constructing his drama, Cocteau selected elements of the mythic structure and transformed them into dramatic form. He did not use all the elements in Ovid's version, and he added some dramatic elements that do not appear in it. In the film, as we shall see, he departs even further from the original elements of the myth.

In a contemporary press review of the play during its first run in 1926, Gerard Bauer had unfavorable things to say of Cocteau's rendering of the myth into dramatic structure. Bauer insisted that Cocteau's rendering of the myth was wrong because it did not emphasize the solar aspects of the myth which had been emphasized in Stephen Mallarmé's prose interpretation of it. Bauer claimed that Cocteau had essentially stripped Orpheus of all his original symbols and remade him into a poem which was not pure in taste.[5]

Actually, Cocteau did not strip the Orpheus of his play. He simply substituted many current elements for the purposes of his dramatic structure and placed some original parts of the myth in a modern, surrealistic context.[6] The introduction of the solar element and of the serpent of the shadows appears only in late myth, and it is known that in another myth used in certain rites Eurydice's victims die of snake bite, not Eurydice herself.[7]

In the play, Orphée's second attempt to retrieve Eurydice is changed to a willful act of allowing the Bacchantes to kill him so that he might return to death permanently. In the film, his second attempt is changed to an accidental shooting of him by the Bacchantes, and Orphée's death strangles him in the "Zone" in order to turn back time and return him to Eurydice in life.

But now let us look more specifically at the conception of myth, and the conception of mythic structure. The ancient function of classical myth is dead. The function of Christian myth (primarily a reconstruction of classical myth) is in its death throes. Our secular myth as a vital force in human affairs is in the process of being born. The secular myth has always been with us, but is now assuming a dominant position in the world, and its name is THE STATE.[8]

Classical myth in our time functions most vitally as an aesthetic object complete within itself and as a raw material to be transformed and digested into other aesthetic objects. It has lost its ritual function, but not its aesthetic function, as it has lost its religious significance, but not its artistic one. So it is dead in one sense, but very much alive in another. The secular myth, which originally had only a practical function, is now beginning to take on both practical and ritual functions.

Classical myth as ritual necessarily dealt with archetypes. Archetypes were its substance, and in a way they still are; but—and this distinction must be made—when archetypes are transformed into literary or dramatic entities they are no longer simply archetypes; to treat them as such, to fail to recognize their particular nature assumed in the transformation, is to miss an important point. The same may be said of Orpheus as the archetypal hero, poet, man, in the myth as ritual or in the myth as literature, and Orpheus as a dramatic character, famous poet, lover of death, father of his child about to be born, and conqueror of the unknown in the drama and film as performed or in the drama and film as aesthetic objects of art to be studied. Behind the particular Orpheus myth lies the archetypal *monomyth*;[9] behind the particular Cocteau play *Orphée* lies the structure of drama as it is generally conceived. Here we shall look at the monomyth and the Orpheus myth. In the second part of the paper we will proceed to observe the general notion of dramatic structure, and the particular dramatic structure of *Orphée*. The third section will attempt to do the same with a general notion of cinematographic structure and the particular nature of Cocteau's film *Orphée.*

The "rites of passage" according to Campbell are: separation—initiation—return, which might be named the nuclear unit of the monomyth. Certainly the Orpheus myth as it was outlined previously contains all three of these essential elements of structure. They represent basic processes in the normal development of the living human being expressed in their most abstract form: "passage" is to *life in time* as "separation" is to *birth and prepuberty*; and "initiation" is to the *process of maturation* as "return" is to the *final acceptance of social responsibility and organic annihilation in death*. In many myths this monomythic pattern may be altered or expanded in innumerable combinations. In the version of the Orpheus myth referred to in this paper the rite of separation takes place before the myth begins, and most of it concerns the initiation section of myth after the hero, Orpheus, has become a young adult. It includes primarily initiation and return. It is limited to the hero task and to the acceptance of social responsibility and death to life in time. The initiation itself is further subdivided into these main episodes: practice of the magic boon, courtship, marriage, completion of the hero task, but inadvertent loss of achievement, a subsequent hero task, failure. The return section of the myth deals with refusal to return from the magic flight, subsequent dismemberment, spiritual return to the nether regions, and finally, a protection of the remains. We are told who Orpheus's parents were, something about his birth, but the separation element of the monomyth plays only a very slight role in the structure of the Orpheus myth proper.

Enough for the ritual structure of the myth and its significance as it was vitally related to the ancients. Now we must speak of its vital significance in the twentieth century, that is, as literature, and quite clearly, narrative literature. The myth as it has come down to us in separate form is essentially narrative. It is important for our purposes to recognize the myth as a thing in itself.

Narrative "fiction is the imitation in language of experience, so arranged through scene and summary and description as to narrate a *complete action* in a *unique world* which is the world of the story or novel."[10] That world is in no way actualized *in scene*. The narration is unfolded within the beholder's mind. And this is the way most of us experience myth, as imaginative fiction. In this sense, then, the characters in myth become characters in imaginative fiction, experienced within the mind through the specific function of narrative as a literary form. They are not for most of us the imitation of archetypes, but, in so far as the limitations of mythic detail will allow, the characters of myth for us are imitations of *particular* beings. We care about these narratives, structurally, in terms of movement, time, and meaning; and we see that they are sketchy in detail, so that we assume that *movement*, the articulation of plot, the concatenation of events (comparatively isolated from character or significance) is what interests us in them primarily.

Essentially what Cocteau does in his play and his film is to take a bare narrative form and transform many of the narrative elements into dramatic or cinematographic form.

In the process he has not only made narrative elements dramatic, but he has also expanded the dramatic elements into a richness and complexity of detail that is astonishing. He has deleted rather than transformed many of the original elements of the myth. Further, he blends into all this elements from the secular myth. We do not respond to them as archetypes but as dramatic or filmic entities. The ministers of death in the play seem like surgeons' assistants (not all surgeons' assistants either, but rather the particular dramatic characters of this play who serve Death). Death is a fully individuated character in the film, however, and she represents only and singly the death of Orphée. In the film her attempt to take Eurydice is punished, but it is not punished in the play. Especially in the film are we aware of this technique of particularizing detail in connection with the servants of death who now ride motorcycles. They are not intended to represent universal policemen pressed into service from the secular myth. They are the particular policemen of one particular agent of "Death," who is not a universal allegorical character in the film. The Princess (Death) is an individual, not an abstraction. Unless one accepts this dynamism of individuation and particularization what meaning the action of the play and the film may have is lost by default.

The structure of the myth then is narrative, sketchy in detail of action, and almost devoid of character. What made it significant for the Greeks is almost wholly lost to us; and yet, the monolithic proportions of the events and their articulation together into an organic whole, and the great imaginative range of myth as a body of literature will probably continue to attract artists and readers for the millennia to come as it has in the past.

3. STRUCTURE OF *ORPHÉE*, THE DRAMA

"But drama in its pure form imitates solely through the use of characters speaking lines and engaging in actions which advance an articulated plot. . . . A play exists entirely in *scene*. Summary may appear, but only in terms of *scene*."[11] Thus, the mode of existence of the myth for us is not in *scene* but in *narrative*. The narrator is transposed between us and the action of the characters. In a drama the literary speaker is wholly absorbed into the life of his characters as they appear in scene. Narrative may be employed in the drama for exposition, but it is always supplied by a character speaking in scene. In drama we are left to draw our own conclusions about the action of the characters. All we know must come from how they act and what they say about themselves and one another. It is true that all literature, in the sense that it involves a speaker, a situation, and a listener, is dramatic; when this view is carried too far, however, it destroys distinctions and does not adequately take into consideration the particular nature of structures: the parts lose their true identity which must always be controlled by their observable relation to an articulated whole. It is the nature of this interarticulation that makes any part in itself what it is.

This effect can be observed in the three characters we have been concerned with so far. Orpheus as an archetype in the monomyth is a type of "every-musician," perhaps even of that musician who exists as part of all men. The Orpheus we experience in the myth, the narrative Orpheus, becomes even more particularized into that literary phenomenon we call a character, a moral agent, an imitation of human character. Finally, the Orpheus we encounter in Cocteau's drama becomes a character in the fullest sense of the word. As an archetype he has only the most abstract qualities. As a character in narrative he takes on the less abstract quality for us of being a moral agent whose actions and significance remain sketchy for us, but as a character in Cocteau's drama he takes on concrete qualities, he is given "a local habitation and a name." In the latter context, the complexity of his actions as a moral agent and the detailed meaning of his essence are spelled out in such intricacy that he appears to be, or gives the impression of being, a *man*.

In the myth-narrative we are told simply that he loves Eurydice; whereas in the drama of Cocteau we see him in the complex state of acting out his love, of being torn (in imitation of human character) between his love of the horse and his love of Eurydice. We are told in the myth-narrative that he loved Eurydice so much he journeyed to the underworld to reclaim her from the powers of darkness; the details of his journey are only sketchily filled in; we get no sense of the minute-by-minute decisions he must make during this journey into the lower world. But in the drama he reports the strange journey to Heurtebise in naturalistic terms. As we shall see, in the film we watch each detailed stage of the journey into the unknown—and here, in the film, Cocteau substitutes his own conception of the world between life and death for the nether world of the myth. He makes of it "the No-Man's land between death and life," the waste land of human desires, memories, and habits, his own special limbo. Clearly there is a vast gulf separating the meaning of Cocteau's dramatic and cinematographic characters and the archetypes of the monomyth. They are not the same, and we can understand only very little of the dramatic character Orphée by demonstrating his similarities to his archetype.

There is, despite all Cocteau's protestation to the contrary, a certain quality about his drama that tempts one to interpret it allegorically. One does not understand his discomfiture on this score unless, of course, he fears such an approach to his drama would fail to apprehend its full texture:

> *Gratuité,* of which André Gide spoke, is what the public is least prepared to accept. It wants a meaning for everything. Especially for things whose beauty consists in not having any.[12]

And though one is not always inclined to trust what an author says about his own work, one certainly can sympathize with him here. His remark could be interpreted to mean that he wants us to apprehend the implicit dramatic texture, the meaning of the thing in itself, rather than a meaning we may abstract to fit into a universal concept. One feels that his phrase "no meaning" is an exaggeration that expresses his irritation at those critics who insist on looking everywhere but at the special structure he has created. One should not decry seeing the universal, allegorical implications of any piece; but the honest critical work of *explication de texte* in terms of the text itself, i.e., practical criticism, must be performed anterior to that task; otherwise, much error may be the result of sincere intentions.

Indeed, Cocteau's structure moves very close to allegory, but at the same time one is acutely aware of its concrete qualities. There is a kind of structural ambiguity here that is extremely attractive:

EURYDICE:

You are going to quote me again the famous sentence.

ORPHÉE:

[*Gravely*]

Yes. [*He goes toward the Horse and recites.*] Orphée hunts Eurydice's lost life.

EURYDICE:

That sentence doesn't mean anything.

ORPHÉE:

It is indeed a question of meaning. Listen carefully to this sentence, listen to the mystery of it. Eurydice alone might be anybody and so might Orphée, but it is a Eurydice whose lost life Orphée would hunt! "Orphée hunts—" that exciting "hunts"—"Orphée hunts Eurydice's—" mark the possessive! and the close: "Eurydice's lost life." You ought to be pleased I am speaking about you.

EURYDICE:

It's not you who are speaking of me. It's the horse. [*Pointing.*]

ORPHÉE:

Neither he, nor I, nor anyone else. What do we know? Who is speaking? We are knocking against each other in the dark; we are up to our necks in the supernatural. We are playing hide and seek with the gods. We know nothing, absolutely nothing. "Orphée hunts Eurydice's lost life"—that's not a sentence, it is a poem, a poem of vision, a flower deep-rooted in death.[13]

Such a text is heavy with overtones loaded with ambiguity. Is the action an allegory of the duel between the sexes? Is it a burlesque of current notions of the artist? Is this simply an imitation of human character in dramatic terms? It is all of these things at once. Our interest is constantly tugged one way and then the other, and as the Prologue tells us:

[*The actor who plays the part of Orphée appears before the curtain.*]

Ladies and Gentlemen, this prologue is not by the author and I expect he would be surprised to hear it. The tragedy in which we are going to act develops on

very delicate lines. I will ask you, therefore, if you are not satisfied with our work, to wait till the end before you express your feelings. Here is the reason for my request: we are playing at a great height, and without a safety-net. The slightest untimely noise and the lives of my comrades and my own may be imperiled.[14]

"Orphée hunts Eurydice's lost life." This is an acrostic, the first letters of each word spelling out the oath "O, hell." This is the poem Orphée submits to the contest in the play. The members of the "ladies social club," accused of lesbianism, among other things, by Orphée, are incensed when their own pseudoprofundity enables them to pick out the "filth" they find concealed in the poem. The great irony here lies in the fact that Orphée, in the supreme innocence of the poet, does not know that the acrostic is concealed in his poem. The simplicity of the poem's diction, its surface diction, is what so fascinates him. It is at once simple and profound. That is exactly what happens in the play; Eurydice does return from hell, and Orphée brings her back. The poem, in terms of the play's structure, is prophetic. And, despite the seeming detachment of all the characters in Cocteau's *Orphée,* Orphée's death in the context of Cocteau's structure is moving and vital drama. The very nature of the conceit Orphée utters just before his death moves us and causes us to think simultaneously:

ORPHÉE:

What are the thoughts of the marble from which a sculptor shapes a masterpiece? It thinks: I am being struck, ruined, insulted, and broken, I am lost. This marble is stupid. Life is shaping me, Heurtebise. It is making a masterpiece. I must bear its blows without understanding them. I must stand firm. I must be still and accept the inevitable. I must help and bear my part, till the work is ended.[15]

Structurally the play is one long and effective *coup de théâtre*. Everything is done to ruffle us. Conventions are shattered (one of Death's assistants borrows a watch from the audience). The hero, in a fit of pique, breaks the taboo of looking at Eurydice, thus sending her back to the realm of death forever. People walk through mirrors. An angel's wings become multicolored panes of glass strapped to his back as though they were a burden; he is in fact a glazier. Eurydice dies from licking the poisoned flap of an envelope. Orphée's horse has the body of a man (combination Pegasus and Centaur?). Death is a ravishing young beauty dressed in a pink evening gown. One critic writing contemporaneously with an early performance of the play in London saw clearly what Cocteau's purpose was:

M. Cocteau knows . . . that it is in the clinical aspect of Death, who with "his well-worn lean, professional smile" . . .

Comes to your bedside, unannounced and bland, which is terrible to us. But when it comes to symbolizing the soul, the symbol of folk-lore is clearly still the best.[16]

The soul, as Mr. MacCarthy points out, is symbolized by a dove attached to a string, which Death releases from the balcony after one of her assistants cuts the string with a pair of shears. This frontal attack on naturalism did not always please the critics, however:

> His version of the Orpheus myth is meant to be terribly original. But under its odd adornments it impresses one merely as a series of squabbles.[17]

This constant shocking of our sensibility is perhaps Cocteau's most clearly individual trait as a dramatist. It is part and parcel of his technique. Wallace Fowlie tells us it is a theory in itself, "angelism":

> A few years later, in *Le Secret Professionel* (1922), he will define angelism as "disinterestedness, egoism, tender gaiety, cruelty, purity in debauchery." His poem of 1925, "L'Ange Heurtebise," was written under the stimulation of this theory. An angel bearing the same name occurs in the play *Orphée* of 1927, and in the film, of the same title, of 1950.[18]

Each of us has an angel within us we are constantly shocking. But this infinite series of shocks does not lead to dissolution, decay, a state of disorder. It leads to a reintegration, a *new* order within us. The angel within us is a kind of moral censor:

> All this shows that minds and souls live without a syntax, that is to say, without a moral system. This moral system has nothing to do with morality proper, and should be built up by each of us as an inner style, without which no outer style is possible.[19]

Cocteau's *Orphée* presents us with a plot of passion containing thirteen major events. Eurydice and Orpheus, the typically married young couple, quarrel over Orpheus's devotion to his occupation, poet, and his oracle, a horse. Orpheus leaves in a huff to enter his latest poem in a contest. Eurydice conspires with the glazier, Heurtebise, to poison the horse with a lump of sugar sent her by Aglaonice, directress of the Bacchantes' club. They fail to poison the horse. Eurydice, having written a letter to Aglaonice, becomes ill upon licking the flap of the envelope (one she had borrowed from Aglaonice), and Heurtebise rushes off to get Orpheus. Death enters from the mirror and takes Eurydice's soul. Orpheus and Heurtebise return to find Eurydice dead. Orpheus takes Death's forgotten gloves, and goes through the mirror to reclaim his wife in exchange for the gloves. Orpheus and Eurydice return through the mirror to have lunch, but quarrel, and Orpheus looks at her while losing his balance, insisting to Heurtebise he, Orpheus, looked at her on purpose. The Bacchantes, having read Orpheus's supposedly insulting poem, appear outside the house, stone Orpheus to death, at which point the sun eclipses. They fling his head into the room, and Eurydice steps out of the mirror to take the disembodied Orpheus to the land of death with her. The police arrive and investigate, interrogating Heurtebise, who disappears, and then they interrogate the bust of Orpheus which has replaced the horse. An interval occurs after the police leave with Orpheus's bust, and when the curtain rises on a neatened stage, Orpheus and Eurydice step from the mir-

ror into their flat "in heaven" exactly like their earthly one. As they sit down to a now peaceful lunch Orpheus recants, saying the horse was the devil, Eurydice was right, and that God is poetry.

Nothing is "explained"; *les jeux sont faits.* The action is crisp and beautiful; we are never beaten about the ears by interminable explanations. It is a sheer piece of theatrical sleight of hand, but in nowise contemptible. For the philosophical implications raised by the deceptively simple, cynical action are myriad. Our first reaction is to gasp at the "scalpelescent" dexterity with which the mystery of death is laid open. The play does not attempt answers; it dramatizes the mystery; its quiddity, the thing in itself is made concrete and coherent. A program of action is not given; in fact, it is very effectively sneered at. "Who," Cocteau seems to be asking, "would be such a boor as to explain a mystery? See the mystery, experience it, but do not attempt an explanation of the marvelous. That way leads to the hopelessness of the conundrum."

In attempting to compare this structure with the structure of the myth as we know it, the first thing one notices is the comparative and deceptive scaling down that has taken place in the drama. An aura of the comedy of the boulevard hangs over the theatrical structure. Cocteau has created his magic, or wrenched it one might say, out of the ordinary, everyday elements of contemporary life. At every point in the progression of the myth Cocteau has substituted some little detail that has the effect of making what was once a remote structure an immediate, specific, and moving dramatic gesture; and, in terms that are pungently significant for a modern audience:

HEURTEBISE:

> I'm entrusting you with the secret of secrets. Mirrors are the doors through which Death comes and goes. Don't tell anyone. You only have to watch yourself all your life in a mirror, and you'll see Death at work like bees in a glass hive. Good-bye. Good luck![20]

What the myth-narrative leaves to speculation Cocteau makes dramatically, almost painfully, explicit.

Many of the elements of the myth-narrative are left out; Hymen, for instance; but notice that the feast, scaled down to "lunch," is still there but serving an entirely different function:

> His simplicity is very deceptive. *Orphée* should be played with the swiftness and directness and ease of a trick in prestidigitation. But it is a play of condensed richness, a surrealist enactment of the most tender and the most profound myth of mankind: the descent of a living man into the realm of Death and his return from there. Men cannot accept truth directly. Cocteau says in one of his aphorisms that truth is too naked: it has to be at least partially clothed in order to attract or excite men. (*La vérité est trop nue; elle n'excite pas les hommes.*) It is almost in these terms that the surrealists attacked realism.

I know of no more pathetic or moving interpretation of death in French literature than Cocteau's *Orphée*. This may seem like an exaggerated claim, but no other work succeeds so well as *Orphée* does for me in making of the myth of death, or the fantasy of death, something extraordinarily real.[21]

This scaling down seems to produce, paradoxically, a greater intensity of thought and emotion combined. Perhaps Cocteau had Euripides' technique in mind in mounting his last scene up to heaven. And as with Euripides, it is dangerous to assume that Cocteau's anger at the gods who box our ears with never an explanation, and his cynical treatment of social behavior, end only in a blank pessimism.

The whole idea of effective human action requiring a death to self, a partial death at least, is not in any way limited to Western thought, nor to any particular phase of it, Greek or Christian. The Eastern religions and philosophies, many of them, have this basic paradox at the heart of their organization, Buddhism being the prime example. The love-death is a commonplace expressed in the literature of all times. The sexual union has been described as a kind of death for the individuals who merge into one being symbolically as a new unity. Even in contemporary American poetry this Elizabethan notion has been renewed:

The body and the soul know how to play

In that dark world where gods have lost their way.[22]

Death completes the man. It does not destroy him. The symbolic deaths of the poet renew him, Cocteau seems to be saying, in part at least. And this applies not only to the poet, it applies to all men in the mystery of love and procreation. We are born again in our progeny through what we sacrifice of ourselves, both figuratively and literally. We resist the process; it is both frightening and beautiful, not simply a saccharin nonentity in Cocteau's view of it in the character of his Orpheus. "This marble is stupid. Life is shaping me, Heurtebise. It is making a masterpiece." "Watch yourself all your life in a mirror, and you'll see Death at work like bees in a glass hive," Heurtebise tells Orpheus earlier in the play. The dialogue seems almost cheerful in tone, clear and concise, but it effects a union of intellectual comprehension and emotional realization unique in drama. The play has been undervalued by some critics (though not recently, and certainly not by French critics, nor American students of French literature). Whatever Eric Bentley could possible have meant by his neat, irresponsible statement that "the center of his drama . . . is a vacuum,"[23] is not clear.

Cocteau is basically at the business of the celebration of "the mystery of dismemberment, which is life in time,"[24] and not in any nihilistic sense either. His stratagem is to make death significant, not a hopeless accident that bowls us over. What he wants, and what he undeniably gets, is a currently valid, currently significant poem of death wherein his main character is aware of the joy of life, the joy of being shaped by it. He tells us that life, through death, through dismemberment, is shaping a masterpiece.

It must be said here that in the film Cocteau is more effective with this metaphor. He is not clearer. The film is simply larger in stature, in magnitude, more moving.

The play and the film deal with all forms of death: symbolic, actual, imagined, creative. This catalogue is not enough, for these ideas divorced from their dramatic components, and the sense of experiencing character that is imitated for us in the drama and film, lose their richness of texture and meaning. The three major deaths these two works imitate, however, are easily discernible: physical death, love-sex death, and the symbolic death of the creative artist. The love-sex death in the film has greater magnitude because the result of it is a child mentioned twice in the film. The play's love-sex death produces simply domestic harmony in the heaven scene of the play.

In the play Orpheus is a priest of the sun. There is an eclipse at the moment of his death; but if the serpent of the shadows is anywhere in evidence, one does not notice him; and if the myth interprets twilight, night, dawn, and daylight, the drama certainly does not. These things are all said to illustrate from the example of Mr. Bauer quoted at the beginning of this paper that an attempt to interpret Cocteau's drama in strict terms of an interpretation of the myth on which it is based fails to sufficiently illuminate Cocteau's dramatic structure. One cannot reduce dramatic structure to mythic structure because dramatic structure is not only different, it is more complex.

4. STRUCTURE OF *ORPHÉE*, THE FILM

George Bluestone writes: "Like the drama, the film is a visual, verbal, and aural medium presented before a theatre audience. . . . But the ultimate definition of a thing lies in its unique qualities, and no sooner do we attend to the film's specific properties than differentiating characteristics begin to assert themselves."[25] So we are faced in this section of the paper with a problem similar to the one encountered in the previous two sections. Arnheim tells us "there is . . . no difference in principle between the visual action of the theatre and the moving image of the film."[26] However, Mr. Bluestone's position seems more in keeping with the facts: the drama and the film are generically separate forms.

"In cinematic terms, then, the method of connecting the film strips becomes the basic formative function. For the two strips joined together become a *tertium quid*, a third thing which neither of the strips has been independently. This is the essence of that much abused concept of Eisenstein's which we have come to know as montage."[27] Montage seems to be the fundamental ictus of the film structure. Once the final editing has been done in the sound film, all the elements of the film's structure—sound, images, montage sequences, scenes, and finally the total structure of the film itself—usually remain invariable. Its nature is ordinarily fixed, static. Whereas in the drama only the language structure can remain absolutely fixed.

The performance of a drama is an ephemeral thing. In criticizing its structure it is generally a more reliable method to depend on the text rather than on a performance of that text, though certainly performance cannot be altogether ignored. But in the film we generally must criticize one fixed, final performance of the scenario. The scenario can aid us to some extent, but our real criticism must commence and end with an experience of the film as it actually exists in fixed performance. The scenario may be an aid to our study in helping us recall the filmed end product, but we would surely be wrong to base our criticism of a film primarily on the written text from which the recorded performance grew. The film's structure is not fully embodied in the scenario; it actually resides in the strip of celluloid that makes up the finished product in the form of images; this is true even of the sound of the film. The sound track which accompanies the celluloid images is a series of abstract light images that excite an apparatus properly set up into the production of the required sounds through a loud speaker.

"But the camera *is* not a dreamer. We are usually agents in a dream. The camera (and its complement, the microphone) is not itself 'in' the picture. It is the mind's eye and nothing more. Neither is the picture (if it is art) likely to be dreamlike in its structure. It is poetic composition, coherent, organic, governed by a definitely conceived feeling, not dictated by actual emotional pressures."[28] *The film, then, is a composite of plastic images so manipulated as to give the illusion of images in motion. When the illusion of a man in the act of speaking is produced, accompanied by a mechanically produced illusion of speech, the speech is no less an organic part of the illusory visual image. It is a function of the images, as illusory, and as synthetic.*

If we may take Cocteau's word for it, the earlier suggestion about the comparative and deceptive scaling down of structural parts of the myth will apply to the film, too, and particularly in the transition from dramatic to filmic structure. Cocteau writes that "in the film, Orpheus is not the grand priest he was. He is a celebrated poet, whose fame greatly irritates the avant guard."[29] In the play Eurydice says to Orpheus: "You would sing the praises of the sun, you were its high priest. But the horse has put an end to all that."[30] Generalizations are not entirely sage at this point, but it seems, as one observes this metamorphosis from myth to drama and from drama to film, that a structural paradox is constantly occurring. The reduction in the scale of parts does not produce a corresponding reduction in the depth and magnitude of the aesthetic power of Cocteau's play and film. For, as was said earlier, the film, which we now see represents further scaling down, is grander, more universal, and much more powerful in its imaginative sweep. This applies exclusively to the three structures the paper has attempted to expose; it is not intended in any way to indicate that this would apply to other similar structural mutations in world drama and film.

Added to the notion about the play being a poetic creation imitating dramatically the forms and significances of death in which death is demonstrated to be a positively creative experience, not a destructive one; and added to Mr.

Fowlie's opinion quoted earlier, we have Cocteau's statement about the scene in the film where the Princess (Orphée's death), Cégeste, and Heurtebise strangle Orphée in the "Zone" between life and death, in order to send the dead Orphée back through time into life. Cocteau compares this to certain rites of Thibetan religion, in which the dead are revived. He also says that the film does not propose to be simply a paraphrase of the ancient Greek myth; and that there is nothing unusual about this.[31]

In the film, the Princess becomes a more fully individuated character. She is the death of Orphée, and of Orphée alone. Her motivation in taking Cégeste and Eurydice has to do with a purely fabricated destiny. She is a functionary, one of the many functionaries or agents of death, who is seen as a process. She takes them as a strategy in capturing Orphée for herself. Her fault is that she has fallen in love with Orphée as much as he has with her. Cégeste broadcasts his own fragmentary poems from the beyond to Orphée. The Princess wants this so it will draw Orphée closer to her. She then takes Eurydice in order to entice Orphée even more deeply into her mystery. Finally, after she has won Orphée's love, she sacrifices herself and Heurtebise (her chauffeur) to send Orphée back through time into life, where Orphée discovers that Eurydice is to have a child. We have known this all along, but Orphée in his preoccupation with death discovers it only at the end of the picture.

In the play Death is a more abstract character; but in the film she takes on the particularities of an individual personality, a more fully individuated character. The possibilities of filmic structure allow a full exposition in cinematographic terms of the void, the unknown, the Zone. These sequences that occur after the characters have passed from life into the beginning of the process of actual death were filmed outside Paris in the ruins of St. Cyr.[32] "The Zone cannot be looked upon dogmatically. It is one of the fringes of life. A no man's land, between life and death. There one is neither completely dead, nor completely living."[33]

In the play Cocteau tried to present in opposition "to the Wagnerian religion of art, a 'poesie de tous les jours,' something skeptical and French; an art which should subsist side by side with the common sense of daily life instead of denying it and utterly replacing it."[34] This is the greatest point of difference between the play and the film; for in the film the treatment of time, simultaneously contemporaneous and universal, is possible as *un fait accompli*. In the play we see Orphée enter the mirror the first time with the clock pointing the exact time of entry; the postman leaves a letter; the scene changes and the postman is still depositing the letter as Orphée emerges from the mirror. Repeated action is the only visual and physical device employed to give us the sense of timelessness in the world of death. But in the film (due to the possibilities of the filmic structure) we (with the camera) follow Orphée into the mirror, and thence through that strange and timeless world of the unknown between consciousness and death, the Zone. Time is stopped for us by the camera; we experience with Orphée the *illusion* of the timelessness of the world beyond; it is not simply *reported* to us as it is in the play. This exact effect, impossible in any conceivable dramatic structure, is fluidly realized in the montage, the heart of filmic structure. This progressive and illusory distortion of time in the film structure is realized in almost every aspect of the film. It is accomplished in the play, also, but not so convincingly, and not so fully.

In the film a Rolls-Royce is substituted for the horse that appeared in the play. The Rolls becomes the source Orphée taps for his poems, but it is no longer Orphée's property. It belongs to the Princess (Orphée's death). Heurtebise is no longer a glazier, but the chauffeur of Orphée's death. Motorcycle policemen are added to the Princess's staff. Instead of surgeons' assistants, she employs dead poets who broadcast over a magical short-wave radio. The clinical aspect of the Princess's function is shifted from operating-room techniques to the suggested techniques of radiology.

Eurydice, now pregnant, is struck by the motorcycle policemen and killed as she leaves the house on her bicycle. Orphée gets the poem fragment from the Rolls radio; and it is no longer an acrostic, but a mystifying phrase: "L'oiseau chanté avec ses doigts." The poem fragment has no prophetic power in the film's structure, but it is apparently a phrase that had been actually included in a letter Cocteau once received from Guillaume Appolinaire.[35] Orphée is faced in the film with insoluble riddles. Things do not work out neatly as they had in the play. He seems as perplexed as men are in real life. He tries to grapple with this unknown. Just before his first trip into the Zone when asked by Heurtebise which he desires most, the Princess or Eurydice, he answers, "Les deux." His second trip into the Zone in the play is a willed act on Orphée's part to allow the Bacchantes to kill him so that he may return permanently to it. But in the film, he is killed through the machinations of the Bacchantes from Le Café des Poètes who hate him, for they believe he has killed Cégeste, his young rival, in order to steal the poem fragment from him. Ironically, it is the dead Cégeste who broadcasts the fragment to Orphée while Cégeste is in the process of assisting the Princess in taking Eurydice.

The whole significance of Orphée as a character is shifted in the film to his attempt to solve the mysteries of the unknown. Thereby he takes on a more powerful stature as a hero; and Death in the play is transformed into the Princess, only one of the innumerable "agents" of Death, which is seen as a process. The Princess defies the order of things as they are in daring to love Orphée, in daring to take "personal initiative," a feat which must be admired in one who is trapped in an impersonal sphere of existence. The film ends with the symbolic strangling of Orphée in the Zone by the Princess and Heurtebise, so that he may go back through time into life where he joins Eurydice and his child about to be born. The Princess and Heurtebise are led off by their own policemen to a higher tribunal, whose punishment will exceed any horror humanly imaginable. One of death's functionaries sacrifices herself so that her beloved poet, Orphée, may gain immortality and live forever in his work and in his human progeny. Reduced to words, this seems a trifle Gothic, perhaps sentimental, but it does not come off that way at all in the film itself. The above mentioned scene in its proper medium, the film, is one of striking power and beauty.

The general order of the montage sequences in the film is based on an associative nexus of visual metaphor. It is what Cocteau calls his logical illogicality. Any attempt to expose his filmic structure as though it is in any way a dramatic structure is doomed to failure. It leads to the kind of carping against mirrors, motorcycles, and sten-guns Mr. Oxenhandler indulged in. "Distortion of the mythic perspective" is exactly what Cocteau is bent on in both his drama and his film; and if we are to accept the limitations and excellences of the film structure, it does no good to complain that it is not like the structure of a drama. Such questions are not permissible unless we disregard the nature of the film medium. A more proper kind of question would be: Does the dialogue become so important in itself that it detracts from or overloads the basic montage at any point? Pierre Dubourg puts it succinctly when he tells us that the meaning of the film is exactly opposite from the meaning of the play.[36]

Speaking of his film, Cocteau tells us:

> Isn't this clear enough? These characters are as far removed from the Unknown as we are, or nearly. It follows that the motorcyclists of *Orphée* don't know anymore about it than our motorcycle police know about ministerial decisions. The actions of the Princess, which actuate the drama, are taken by her of her own accord and represent free will. A thing must be. It *is,* for what happens to us little by little constitutes in reality one single whole. The entire mystery of free will resides in this, that it seems that the thing that is *need not be,* as is illustrated by the amazing words of Christ: "Abba, Father, all things are possible unto Thee: take away this cup from me." Which implies that the whole of time, which we are able to perceive only in perspective, is composed of unthinkable volumes and a mass of conjoint possibilities. Christ seeks to avert the inevitable. Likewise, the Princess dares to substitute herself for destiny, to decide that a thing *may be,* instead of being, and plays the part of a spy in love with the man she was appointed to watch and whom she saves by losing herself. What is the nature of her loss? What is the punishment to which she exposes herself? This is beyond me, and doesn't concern me anymore than do the rites of the beehive or of the ant's nest, those funeral rites whose mystery no entomologist has ever solved. It was essential that some data be missing in my logic, opening breaches into the inaccessible world which it is man's honour to conceive.[37]

Dubourg tells us that Orphée, in the play of 1926, betrays himself in order to regain Eurydice, and admits that the horse is the devil (Eurydice is right) and that God is poetry; everyone is hoisted to heaven in a blaze of mundane glory. But in the film, says Dubourg, the poet sacrifices himself to gain the key to those agonizing questions that plague us all.[38] In the play he is compromised without gaining tangible immortality. In the film he is compromised, but is rewarded with the immortality death bestows on poets through their work and on all men through their progeny.

The film is a better medium for the picturing of the Zone between life and death. It is also a better medium for utilizing and welding together elements of classical myth and elements of the secular myth into an organically whole imitation of human action. Once the "newly created syntax" of the medium of the film is accepted, and once we cease trying to see this film as myth, or as drama, but attempt to see it for what it is, all our objections to motorcycles, Rolls-Royces, mirrors, sten-guns, gas ranges, and the like fade into mere cavil. The author of this essay does not mean to register a preference here. He means to say that these three forms are separate, individual structures. He enjoys all three; he recognizes their limitations and advantages; but he could never insist that any two must be strict imitations of one. He does hope they are imitations of human actions, and he accepts distortion in such imitations as an aesthetic matter of fact.

Notes

1. I refer here to the critical practice, which is common enough, of explaining the particular work being examined primarily *in terms of* another work which may have formed the creative source for the particular work being examined. Many criticisms of Cocteau's two works being examined in this paper have found them wanting on the ground that they "distorted" or "misinterpreted" the Orpheus myth. An example of this adverse criticism of Cocteau's works may be found in the remarks of Jean Boorsch's article, "The Use of Myths in Cocteau's Theatre," *Yale French Studies,* No. 5 (1950), p. 80. As Ronald S. Crane says in his book, *The Languages of Criticism and the Structure of Poetry* (Toronto, 1953), p. 138: "That would indeed be an instance of the grossest of fallacies in history and criticism, the supposition that the form or import of any developed thing can be inferred from its matter or evolutionary substrate. . . ."

2. Consequently, the author rented the films, *Orphée* (Paris: Films du Palais Royal, 1949), and *Le Sang d'un Poète* (Paris: 1932), under a grant from the Subvention Fund for Research of the Graduate School of the University of Illinois, and examined them thoroughly in conjunction with his examination of the 1950 scenario of the film, *Orphée* (Paris: Éditions André Bonne et Éditions de la Parade), and the 1957 edition of the scenario of the film, *Le Sang d'un Poète* (Monaco: Éditions du Rocher).

3. Robert Graves, *The White Goddess* (New York, 1958), p. 94.

4. Ovid, *The Metamorphoses,* trans. Horace Gregory (New York, 1960), pp. 273-276, 277-301, et passim (Bks. X and XI).

5. Gerard Bauer, "*Orphée,* de M. Jean Cocteau," *Les Annales Politiques et Littéraires,* XXCIV (Juin 27, 1926), 690.

6. Arnold Houser in his book, *The Social History of Art* (New York, 1958), p. 236, presents a clear definition of surrealistic style: "It is also this experience of the double-sidedness of existence, with its home in two different spheres, which makes the surrealists aware of the peculiarity of dreams and induces them to recognize in the mixed reality of dreams their own stylistic ideal. The dream becomes the paradigm of the whole world-picture, in which reality and unreality, logic and fantasy the banality and sublimation of existence, form an indissoluble and inexplicable unity."

7. Robert Graves, *The Greek Myths,* I (Baltimore, 1955), 115, 128.

8. Ernst Cassirer, *The Myth of the State* (New Haven, 1945), pp. 37-49. In this section of his work Cassirer clearly defines the nature of myth in regard to its connections between the individual and society. He states: "In mythical thought and imagination we do not meet with individual confessions. Myth is an objectification of man's social experience, not of his individual experience" (p. 47). Though some aspects of social experience are imitated in Cocteau's play, the greatest emphasis is on individual experience, and this is one of the most important reasons why Cocteau's play seems so different from the myth.

9. Joseph Campbell, *The Hero with a Thousand Faces* (New York, 1953), p. 30*n*.

10. Wallace A. Bacon and Robert S. Breen, *Literature as Experience* (New York, 1959), p. 214.

11. *Ibid.,* pp. 220-222.

12. Jean Cocteau speaking in *Cocteau on the Film: A Conversation Recorded by André Fraigneau,* trans. Vera Traill (New York, 1954), p. 126.

13. Jean Cocteau, *Orphée,* trans. Carl Wildman (New York, 1961), pp. 13-14. For the original French see *Orphée, Oeuvres Complètes de Jean Cocteau,* V (Genève, 1948), 24-25.

14. Jean Cocteau, *Orphée,* trans. Carl Wildman (London, 1933), p. 2.

15. *Ibid.,* p. 34.

16. Desmond MacCarthy, "Orpheus," *New Statesman,* XXXI (April 21, 1928), 46.

17. Richard Jennings, "*Orphée* by Jean Cocteau," *The Spectator,* CXL (April 21, 1928), 594.

18. Wallace Fowlie, "A Note on Jean Cocteau," *Poetry,* XXCIV (May 1954), 86.

19. Cocteau, *Cocteau on the Film,* pp. 123-124.

20. Cocteau, *Orphée,* trans. Wildman, 1933, p. 24.

21. Wallace Fowlie, *Age of Surrealism* (New York, 1950), p. 128.

22. Theodore Roethke, "Four for Sir John Davies, 2: The Partner," *Words for the Wind* (Garden City, N. Y., 1958), p. 121.

23. Eric Bentley, *The Playwright as Thinker* (New York, 1946), p. 231.

24. Campbell, p. 25.

25. George Bluestone, *Novels into Films* (Baltimore, 1957), pp. v-ix.

26. Rudolph Arnheim, *Film as Art* (Berkeley and Los Angeles, 1958), p. 213.

27. Bluestone, p. 25.

28. Susanne K. Langer, *Feeling and Form* (New York, 1953), p. 413.

29. Cocteau, *Orphée,* scenario, no pagination (Preface).

30. Cocteau, *Orphée,* trans. Wildman, 1933, p. 5.

31. Cocteau, *Orphée,* scenario, no pagination (Preface).

32. Neal Oxenhandler, "Poetry in Three Films of Jean Cocteau," *Yale French Studies,* No. 17 (Summer 1956), pp. 18-19. It must be said that my study of the play and film cause me to take a position far different from the view expressed by Mr. Oxenhandler in this article, and in his *Scandal and Parade: The Theatre of Jean Cocteau* (New Brunswick, N. J., 1957). In his article he seems to think the mythic perspective should have been adhered to, and questions Cocteau's use of mirrors, motorcycles, and other elements in the film. And in his book (p. 99) he questions what he seems to think an objectionable ambiguity (which I prefer to call ambivalence) in the symbols Cocteau employs in his play.

33. Cocteau, *Orphée,* scenario, no pagination (Preface).

34. Francis Fergusson, *The Idea of a Theatre* (Garden City, N. Y., 1953), pp. 211-212.

35. Margaret Crosland, *Jean Cocteau: A Biography* (New York, 1956), p. 183.

36. Pierre Dubourg, *Dramaturgie de Jean Cocteau* (Paris, 1954), p. 246.

37. Cocteau, *Cocteau on the Film,* p. 129.

38. Dubourg, p. 259.

LA VOIX HUMAINE (THE HUMAN VOICE)

CRITICAL COMMENTARY

Linda M. Willem (essay date 1998)

SOURCE: Willem, Linda M. "Almodóvar on the Verge of Cocteau's *La Voix humaine.*" *Literature/Film Quarterly* 26, no. 2 (1998): 142-47.

[*In the following essay, Willem judges the influence of Cocteau's* La Voix humaine *on Pedro Almodóvar's film* Women on the Verge of a Nervous Breakdown.]

Jean Cocteau's one-act play, ***La Voix humaine* [*The Human Voice*],** consists entirely of a monologue by a woman engaged in a final phone conversation with her lover. Alone in her room, she desperately clings to the telephone as her only link to the man who has left her for someone else. Although this agonizing portrait of abandonment and despair bears little resemblance to Almodóvar's multi-charactered comedic romp through the streets of Madrid in *Mujeres al borde de un ataque de nervios* [*Women on the Verge of a Nervous Breakdown*], Cocteau's play has been named as the source of inspiration for that film. In various interviews Almodóvar has explained that his original intention had been to adapt the play to the screen, but due to its brevity, he needed to expand the material to feature film length. This led him to devise a story of the forty-eight hours leading up to the phone call. In the process, said Almodóvar, "Cocteau's ***La Voix humaine*** had utterly disappeared from the text—apart from its original concept, of course: a woman sitting next to a suitcase of memories waiting miserably for a phone call from the man she loves" (Strauss 80). Despite this seeming dismissal of Cocteau's work, however, Almodóvar insists that the film "truly is a version of ***La Voix humaine***" [es realmente una versión de ***La Voix humaine***] because the play "remains in a latent form" [permanece de una forma latente] (Vidal 258). Linda Hutcheon's *A Theory of Parody* provides insights into how that latent form operates within Almodóvar's film.

According to Hutcheon, the traditional view of parody as a ridiculing of artistic models through stylistic imitation does not account for the numerous reworkings of earlier texts by twentieth-century artists who do not use parody to deride their original sources. Consequently, Hutcheon proposes an expanded concept of parody as "an integrated structural modeling process of revising, replaying, inventing, and 'trans-contextualizing' previous works of art" (11). In this definition parody continues to be "a form of imitation, but imitation characterized by ironic inversion, not always at the expense of the parodied text . . . [I]t is a stylistic confrontation, a modern recoding which establishes a difference at the heart of similarity. . . . Such parody intends no disrespect, while it does signal ironic difference" (6, 8, 10). Hutcheon stresses that "unlike what is more traditionally regarded as parody, the modern form does not always permit one of the texts to fare any better or any worse than the other. . . . The parodied text is often not at all under attack. It is often respected and used as a model" (31, 103).

Almodóvar engages in this sort of creative reworking in *Mujeres.* He trans-contextualizes material from Cocteau's drama by placing it within a comedy format. But his genre switching does not mock any aspect of *La Voix humaine.* On the contrary, Almodóvar has stated his conviction that "if Cocteau had been able to see the film or read the script, he would have thought that it was absolutely faithful to his idea of the work and to the feelings of this abandoned woman" [si Cocteau la hubiera podido ver o leer el guión, habría pensado que era absolutamente fiel a la idea de la obra y de la soledad de esta mujer abandonada] (Vidal 258). Indeed, Almodóvar never pokes fun at the suffering of his protagonist, Pepa. He fully respects her emotions, but he bases his comedy on an inversion of the trajectory that those same emotions take in *La Voix humaine.* Whereas Cocteau's unnamed woman becomes increasingly dependent upon her lover as the play progresses, Pepa gradually achieves what critics have called an "emancipation from machismo" and an "inner liberation from a phallocentric past," resulting in her ultimate rejection of Iván's renewed interest in her is the penultimate scene (Jessup 299; D'Lugo 65). Although both Pepa and Cocteau's anonymous heroine are on the verge of a nervous breakdown at the beginning of their respective stories, that breakdown is ultimately realized by only one of them.[1] By the end of the film Pepa has disengaged herself emotionally from Iván, while Cocteau's protagonist can only repeat "I love you" [je t'aime] over and over again as her beloved hangs up the phone for the last time while the curtain falls on the play.

In transforming Pepa from a victim to a victor, Almodóvar draws on material from *La Voix humaine,* but he alters it to bring about the change in Pepa's situation. Indeed, far more details from the play are present in the film than Almodóvar has acknowledged in his interviews. The first of these concerns the staging of the initial scene in Pepa's bedroom. The stage directions to *La Voix humaine* indicate that when the curtain rises, the audience should see the body of a woman stretched out on the floor in front of her bed "as if killed" [comme assassinée]. Likewise, Pepa is seen for the first time in the film lying down asleep, and both her face-down position and the absence of covers over her body suggest that she too may be dead. This impression is further strengthened by the cross-cutting that takes place between Pepa's bedroom and the studio where Iván is dubbing a movie. When Iván reaches the line "Tell me you would have died" [Dime que te hubieras muerto], the camera suddenly cuts to a view of Pepa's immobile body. Hours later Pepa's possible demise seems all the more likely when she fails to stir as Iván speaks loudly into her answering machine. Suddenly, however, Pepa does awake, bolts out of bed, and rushes to answer the telephone. This frantic dash to the phone also is seen at the start of *La Voix humaine.* Both Pepa and Cocteau's protagonist are desperate to make contact with their lovers, and both are frustrated in the attempt. The woman in the play must contend with wrong numbers, party line problems, and bad connections during her farewell conversation, while Pepa never actually manages to communicate with Iván by phone at all.[2] She only receives messages from him on her answering machine.

After this introduction of Pepa in close imitation of Cocteau's play, Almodóvar's treatment of *La Voix humaine* becomes less straightforward. The theatrical material is no longer simply reproduced, but rather, it is refashioned into a new form which departs from its original context. Although details from the play appear throughout the film, they undergo a series of inversions which, when taken together, lead to Pepa's gradual assertion of her independence from Iván. Thus, Almodóvar's overall parodic enterprise is achieved through his reshaping of the following individual elements of Cocteau's play.

1. The "Voice"

In *La Voix humaine* the "Voice" is that of the woman. Hers is the only voice heard throughout the play, and only silence accompanies the lines supposedly spoken by the man on the phone. All information is communicated to the audience through her monologue, and her voice expresses the play's entire range of emotions. Since the woman is unnamed and, as Cocteau states in his stage directions, she is just "an unexceptional victim" [une victime médiocre], her voice has a universal human quality, representing that of all such women. But in *Mujeres,* the "Voice" belongs to a man, Iván, who makes his living through the use of that voice. "In contrast to Cocteau," states Almodóvar in the pressbook to this film, "I not only have given voice to the man's absence, but I also have turned him into someone who uses his voice professionally" [Al contrario que Cocteau, no sólo le he dado voz al ausente sino que lo he convertido en un profesional de la voz] (Vidal 383). In highlighting Iván's voice Almodóvar not only wanted to make it audible, but palpable as well: "I have intended to photograph it, not just hear it, moving through Pepa's living room like the smell of cooking in the air. . . . Iván's body is his voice" [He intentado fotografiarla, no sólo oírla, moviéndose por el salón de Pepa, como el olor de un giso transportado por la brisa. . . . El cuerpo de Iván es su voz] (Vidal 383). Indeed, the audience's first exposure to Iván is through his voice. Instead of seeing him, we merely hear him in a voice-over reading aloud the words he had written on a record jacket. Later when he is visually introduced during the black-and-white dream sequence, we see him speaking into a microphone, followed soon afterward by an extreme close-up of his mouth in the dubbing studio. Even the film being dubbed initially features Iván's voice alone because Pepa isn't present to provide her part. Iván's entire character is contained in his voice. Therefore, when Pepa does arrive at the dubbing studio after Iván has left, she responds to his prerecorded voice as if he were still there and speaking directly to her. His aural presence is so strong that it causes Pepa to faint during her rehearsal.[3] An even more powerful reaction to the sound of Iván's voice is later described by Lucía, who actually regained her memory after hearing a television performance by Iván which featured the same words he had spoken to her when they were lovers over twenty years before. Iván is the sum of all the things he has ever said, either on-stage or off. As an actor, he habitually utters words he does not feel, and that pretense also extends into his real life. But Pepa's many years of working professionally with Iván has taught her to recognize the sound of his lies. As Pepa explains to her friends, "he can fool me with anything but his voice" [me puede engañar con todo menos la voz].

2. THE TELEPHONE

In *La Voix humaine* the telephone is of paramount importance, not only because it is the physical link between the woman and her lover, but also because it provides the pretext for the monologue to take place. In *Mujeres* the telephone remains an important prop, but its impact is diminished significantly by the presence of an auxiliary apparatus—the answering machine. The woman in Cocteau's play is afraid to leave her room lest she miss the call from her lover. But Pepa's answering machine frees her to travel around Madrid at will, thereby extending the boundaries of the film beyond the four walls which make up the set of *La Voix humaine*. Furthermore, Almodóvar's use of the answering machine allows him to invert the very structure of Cocteau's play. *La Voix humaine* is a dialogue—a conversation between two people—that takes the form of a monologue by a single woman in front of an audience. This process is reversed, however, when Pepa plays Iván's message on her answering machine after returning from her dubbing session. Here Almodóvar takes a monologue—Iván's message—and turns it into a dialogue, with Pepa responding to Iván during his pauses. This same format is continued for Pepa's subsequent scenes with the answering machine. Each time, Pepa comments on the insincerity of Iván's words, and as the film progresses, she is less and less tolerant of his lies. Indeed, the theme of verbal deception is taken directly from *La Voix humaine*.[4] The most dramatic moment in that play occurs when the woman catches her lover in a lie. The audience does not actually hear him lie, however. Rather, we simply see the woman's reaction to her discovery of the truth. But in *Mujeres* we do hear Iván's lies in blatant opposition to what we see on the screen. For example, just before Iván and his new mistress are about to go to Stockholm together, he calls Pepa and hears her message urging him to tell her how she can get in touch with him. Ignoring the content of Pepa's message and hiding the truth about his activities, Iván first accuses Pepa of trying to avoid him and then says, "I'm not taking a trip or going away with any woman" [no me voy de viaje, ni con ninguna mujer]. When Pepa hears this message, she

knows Iván is lying, but rather than forgive him, as does Cocteau's character, Pepa severs her ties with him by destroying the answering machine.

3. THE SLEEPING PILLS

Midway through *La Voix humaine* the woman confesses to her lover that she had attempted suicide the night before by taking sleeping pills in what she thought was a fatal dosage. Sleeping pills also are featured in *Mujeres,* but Pepa does not use them to try to kill herself. Rather, she puts a handful in a batch of gaspacho—Iván's favorite food—in an attempt to keep Iván from leaving her by putting him to sleep. Over the course of the film, however, the gaspacho is drunk by virtually all of the characters except Iván, and it ultimately plays a role in freeing Pepa to go to the airport to save Iván's life. Thus, in Almodóvar's treatment of the sleeping pills, they cease to be a vehicle for the heroine's self-destruction. Instead they become the means by which Pepa successfully works through her feelings for Iván. Although she first intends to use the pills to keep Iván from leaving her, she eventually uses them to ensure his safe departure with another woman.

4. THE CIGARETTES

Early in Cocteau's play the protagonist assures her lover that she is not smoking, a statement which she immediately qualifies by saying, "I've only smoked three cigarettes" [Je n'ai fumé que trois cigarettes]. Pepa engages in a similar struggle with her smoking habit, trying to quit for the sake of her unborn baby, but tempted to smoke to calm down her nerves. As she lights up a cigarette in her home, she suddenly stops, and declaring "I shouldn't be smoking" [No debería fumar], she throws the lit cigarette on her bed along with the remaining pack and a box of matches, thereby starting the blaze that will reduce her bed to ashes. As she stares into the fire, Pepa holds in her hand a ridiculously phallic flower—a gift from Iván—that comically wilts as the intensity of the fire increases, thereby presaging Iván's ultimate loss of sexual power over her.[5]

5. THE LOVE LETTERS

In *La Voix humaine* the man indicates his desire to distance himself from the woman by telling her that he plans to burn the love letters that she has saved for him in his suitcase. She responds by asking him to make the sentimental gesture of storing the ashes from the letters in the tortoise shell box she had given him as a gift. Thus she shows her continued affection for her lover by treating the ashes as if they were sacred relics. In *Mujeres* Pepa shows no such reverence for the momentos of her past with Iván. After she burns her bed—and the amorous associations attached to it—she angrily stuffs Iván's suitcase with what she refers to as his "shit" [mierda]. Having packed all his possessions, along with the gifts he had given her, she turns her attention to a stack of love letters, which she rips in half. Later in the film Pepa shows no sentimentality whatsoever as she unceremoniously throws a photo from Iván on the ashes of the burnt bed and comments about having to clean up the mess.

6. THE VIGIL AND THE PHOTOGRAPH

Although *La Voix humaine* takes place entirely within a single location—the woman's bedroom—actions occurring off-stage are mentioned during the monologue. Two such incidents become part of the plot of Almodóvar's film. The first involves a plan by the woman to take a taxi to her lover's house during the night in order to sit outside of his windows and wait for him to appear. The second pertains to a photograph which she had seen in a magazine, and which had revealed to her the identity of her lover's fiancée. Almodóvar incorporates both of these elements into the scene where Pepa sits outside the apartment of Iván's former mistress, Lucía.[6] While waiting for Iván, Pepa learns the identity of Carlos—Iván's son—through a photograph of Iván and Carlos which Lucía throws out of the window. Later, Pepa's identity becomes known to Carlos through a photograph of her and Iván which he sees when he comes to rent her apartment. Thus, when Pepa and Carlos meet soon afterward, they are able to recognize one another. The resulting friendship allows Pepa to transfer her affection from Iván to Carlos—she even mistakenly calls him Iván at one point—while encouraging a romance between Carlos and Candela.

7. THE GUN

In *La Voix humaine* the woman's attempted suicide with sleeping pills prompts her lover to ask if she has a gun in the house. Although the audience does not hear the question, it is assumed by the woman's answer: "I wouldn't know how to buy a revolver. You can't see me buying a revolver" [Je ne saurais pas acheter un revolver! Tu ne me vois pas achetant un revolver]. This minor point in the play becomes the vehicle for the film's denouement and for Pepa's final break with Iván. All of the story lines come together when Pepa, Lucía, Carlos, Candela, and two police officers meet in Pepa's apartment. During the police interrogation, Pepa figures out that Iván and Paulina will be leaving for a romantic getaway on the plane to Stockholm that Carlos and Candela have warned the police will be hijacked by Shiite terrorists. After the police become sedated by the gaspacho, the mentally unbalanced Lucía steals their guns so that she can use them to murder Iván. Lucía's actions stem from her inability to come to terms with Iván's abandonment of her decades ago. As she explains to Pepa, she can only forget Iván by killing him. Pepa, however, has already eliminated Iván from her life emotionally, so she has no need for revenge. Indeed, her feelings for Iván have altered to such a degree that she can go to his rescue not out of love, but out of a disinterested impulse to help someone in danger.

All of these elements from *La Voix humaine*—the voice, the telephone, the sleeping pills, the cigarettes, the love letters, the vigil, the photograph, and the gun—are drained of their original meanings and ironically repositioned in *Mujeres* in order to permit the most important reversal of all: Pepa's rejection of Iván. Despite Pepa's similarity to Cocteau's heroine at the beginning of the film, Pepa's final situation is not the same because details from *La Voix humaine* function differently in the film than their counterparts in the play. Taken together, these reworked elements redefine the course which Pepa can take. The ending to Cocteau's drama is sad because the woman loses the man that she loves. The ending to Almodóvar's comedy is happy, not because Pepa gets her man back, but because she realizes that she no longer wants him.

In citing *La Voix humaine* as the source of inspiration for *Mujeres,* scholars have been content to take at face value Almodóvar's statement that little more than the original concept of the play remained by the time he had completed the film.[7] But a close examination of both works yields evidence to the contrary. Ironically transposed elements from the play permeate the film and form a rich intertextual network of connections that goes beyond what Almodóvar has admitted. Despite the extent to which Almodóvar has relied upon Cocteau, however, *Mujeres* is not an adaptation of *La Voix humaine.*[8] Rather, Almodóvar uses parodic imitation—what Hutcheon calls repetition with a difference—to create something new out of that play.[9] As such, Almodóvar pays homage to Cocteau's art while simultaneously displaying his own artistry.

Notes

1. The change in Pepa's attitude toward Iván is reflected in the two songs, *Soy infelíz* [I'm unhappy] and *Puro teatro* [Nothing but pretense], which play over the film's opening and closing credits, respectively. In the first, a woman laments the recent loss of her lover, while in the second, the singer speaks of her lover's "well-rehearsed falseness" [falsedad bien ensayada] and states her refusal to tolerate his lies any longer. The link between the opening song and Pepa's situation is clearly established in an early scene through a close-up on a record jacket listing the song. The title is circled, and Iván's voice-over reads the note he had scribbled in the margin: "Pepa darling, I never want to hear you say, 'I'm unhappy'" [Pepa cariño, no quiero oírte nunca decir, "soy infelíz"]. Significantly, Pepa's decision to throw Iván out of her life is accompanied by her act of throwing the "Soy infelíz" record out the window. For a discussion of Almodóvar's use of this song both diegetically and non-diegetically in the sequence leading up to and including this scene, see Deleyto 57-58. Also, the visual aspects of this entire sequence are examined by Smith 99-110 and Edwards 192-93.

2. Technically, Pepa does speak to Iván while she is in Paulina's office, but no actual communication takes place. When Pepa inadvertently answers a phone call from Iván to Paulina, Iván immediately hangs up, leaving Pepa uncertain as to the identity of the caller.

3. Almodóvar's use of a clip from Nicholas Ray's 1954 film, *Johnny Guitar,* in both dubbing scenes compounds the intertextuality of *Mujeres* by creating an

externally and internally duplicating *mise en abyme*. In the first dubbing session with Iván, the concept of human speech is foregrounded through the contrast between the silence that accompanies Joan Crawford's moving lips and the sound that follows Sterling Hayden's. As in *La Voix humaine*, a conversation is taking place between two characters, but the audience only hears the words of one of them. In the second dubbing scene with Pepa, however, the dialogue is completed through Pepa's reading of Joan Crawford's part. The presence of both Pepa's and Iván's voices establishes a parallel between the characters of *Mujeres* and those of *Johnny Guitar.* Thus, when Pepa says "I've waited for you all these years," "I'd have died without you," and "I love you as much as you love me" [Todos estos años te he esperado; Estaría muerta si no hubieras vuelto; Aun te quiero tanto como tú a mái] she is not merely speaking her lines, but also is expressing her feelings for Iván. Whereas this second dubbing scene uses the *Johnny Guitar* clip as an embedded *mise en abyme* alluding to Pepa's situation in the surrounding narrative, the first dubbing scene uses the *Johnny Guitar* clip to stylistically replicate an external referent—*La Voix humaine*—thereby extending the *mise en abyme* beyond the frame of *Mujeres*. For additional comments concerning the *Johnny Guitar* segments see Deleyto 55-56; Smith 95; Edwards 184-85; Eng 152; and Jessup 308.

4. Mendacity permeates *Mujeres*: Candela's Shiite boyfriend lied to her for political reasons; Lucía thanks her father for being such a good liar when it comes to flattery; the *portera* of Pepa's building is a Jehovah's Witness who reluctantly obeys her religion's proscription against lying; the *Johnny Guitar* film being dubbed by Iván and Pepa features Sterling Hayden asking Joan Crawford to lie to him about her feelings; and a TV commercial advertises a detergent that cleans stains so well that "it seems like a lie" [parece mentira].

5. Jessup 305 misidentifies the music accompanying this scene as Manuel de Falla's "Ritual Fire Dance" from *El amor brujo*. Although Falla's music would have been appropriate in this context due to its themes of obsessive love and magical disenchantment, the music that actually is playing during the bed-burning is Rimsky-Korsakoff's *Capricho español.*

6. For a discussion of the influence of Hitchcock's *Rear Window* on how this scene is staged, see Deleyto 53-54 and Evans 17-18.

7. See Vidal 258-59, Strauss 80-81, Jessup 306, Deleyto 55, Edwards 182, and Evans 14. Although Evans recognizes Cocteau's play as the initial source for the film, he also sees traces of Dorothy Parker's story "A Telephone Call," because it features a female narrator who "becomes increasingly frantic as she awaits her lover's promised but never material-

izing phone-call" (15). Evans's only justification for this assertion, however, rests on Almodóvar's mention of Dorothy Parker in connection with the creation of his Patty Diphusa character. Consequently, it is not clear whether or not Almodóvar is aquatinted with this particular story by Parker.

8. For a true adaptation of *La Voix humaine* see Roberto Rossellini's *Una voce umana,* starring Anna Magnani. Due to its thirty-five minute length, it was coupled with another short film, *Il miracolo,* and released under the title of *L'amore* in 1948.

9. In *Ley de deseo,* the film immediately preceding *Mujeres,* Almodóvar uses *La Voix humaine* more directly. The protagonist, Pablo, is a director who is staging Cocteau's play while Juan, the man he loves, is in the process of leaving him. Thus, *La Voix humaine* serves as an intertextual referent to echo the relationships within the film. Pablo's continued desire for Juan parallels that of Cocteau's heroine in that both prefer their lovers' lies—spoken to her, written to him—rather than the truth.

Works Cited

Deleyto, Celestino. "Postmodernism and Parody in Pedro Almodóvar's *Mujeres al borde de un ataque de nervios* (1980)." *Forum for Modern Language Studies* 31 (1995): 49-63.

D'Lugo, Marvin. "Heterogeneity and Spanish Cinema of the Eighties." *España Contemporánea* 5.1 (1992): 55-66.

Edwards, Gwynne. *Indecent Exposures: Buñel, Saura, Erice & Almodóvar.* London: Marion Boyars, 1995.

Eng, David L. "Fractured by Voices: Technologies of Gender in Pedro Almodóvar's *Mujeres al borde de un ataque de nervios.*" *Cine Lit II: Essays on Hispanic Film and Fiction.* Ed. George Cabello-Castellet, Jaume Martí-Olivella, and Guy H. Wood. Corvallis: Oregon State U, 1995. 146-54.

Evans, Peter William. *Women on the Verge of a Nervous Breakdown (Mujeres al borde de un ataque de nervios).* London: BFI, 1996.

Hutcheon, Linda. *A Theory of Parody: The Teachings of Twentieth-Century Art Forms.* London: Methuen, 1985.

Jessup, Florence Redding. "*Women on the Verge of a Nervous Breakdown*: Sexism or Emancipation from Machismo?" *Look Who's Laughing: Gender and Comedy.* Ed. Gail Finney. Amsterdam: Gordon and Breach, 1994. 299-314.

Smith, Paul Julian. *Desire Unlimited: The Cinema of Pedro Almodóvar.* London: Verso, 1994.

Strauss, Frédéric. *Almodóvar on Almodóvar.* Trans. Yves Baignères. London: Faber and Faber, 1996.

Vidal, Nuria. *El cine de Pedro Almodóvar.* Barcelona: Destino, 1989.

LA MACHINE INFERNALE (*THE INFERNAL MACHINE*)

PRODUCTION REVIEW

John Carter (review date 13 September 1940)

SOURCE: Carter, John. "The Theatre." *Spectator* 165 (13 September 1940): p. 267.

[*In the following review, Carter critiques a production of* The Infernal Machine *performed at the Arts Theatre Club.*]

The name of Mr. Oliver Messel is printed as large as the author's. And however deplorable this may seem in principle, it must be confessed that the most satisfying memory of this performance is the décor. Mr. Messel shares with Berard the wonderful sense of colour and the modish neo-classicism which made *Seventh Symphony* and *Symphonie Fantastique* such a pleasure to the eye. Indeed, Oedipus's scene with the Spinx might have taken place only a few yards from the romantic desert in which Massine set Berlioz's Pastorale, and Jocasta's superb red, white and blue bedroom is surely only up one flight from the Ball.

Mr. Messel's scenery sometimes gets in the way of the actors (they have rather a lot of bounding to do), but it is as appropriate to the play as it is beautiful in itself. For M. Cocteau is here in a very Voguish mood. He has played several tricks with Sophocles-the Sphinx, for instance, must needs be eprise with Oedipus-and like Eugene O'Neill or the movies he takes three acts to reach the point where the Greeks liked to start: but he is mainly concerned with revamping the Oedipus Rex in terms of Freud and Schiaparelli.

There is some good comedy among the soldiers in the first act, with Miss de Casalis making Jocasta a sort of fashionable Marion Lorne. There are possibilities of beauty in the Spinx scene, though Miss Leueen Macgrath is more at home as a flirt than with the poetical denunciation. There are many good moments in the wedding night scene (though it is a little too long), and here both Miss de Casalis and Mr. Peter Glenville (Oedipus) are at their best. But in the fourth act, when M. Cocteau comes up with Sophocles, the play falls to pieces. If you are going to be funny with Greek tragedy, you must be wholeheartedly and consistently funny. Up to this point M. Cocteau has done little more than add witty trimmings, a la Girardoux or Shaw, to the original story; but in the end the Greeks are too much for him. The terrific theme scares away Gallic flippancy and up-to-date psychology, and leaves *The Infernal Machine* on the rocks of a bald, bare, rhetorical and ineffective conclusion.

Mr. Carl Wildman's version admirably catches both the poetry and the slanginess of the original, and the actors make the best of an often entertaining but fundamentally empty and unsatisfactory play. Oedipus is drawn as a caricature of a callow boy, and Mr. Glenville is painfully accurate in his playing of the part. Even in the fourth act, 17 years later, his beard and sudden tragic buskins cannot alter him. Miss de Casalis has a chryselephantine quality which lends dignity to her moving playing of the scene in which a wife's passion is mixed with a mother's love. And Mr. Bromley Davenport, exquisitely gowned as a minor prophet by Domenichino, endows Tiresias with a fragile, sightless menace.

CRITICAL COMMENTARY

Derek F. Connon (essay date January 1993)

SOURCE: Connon, Derek F. "Folded Eternity: Time and the Mythic Dimension in Cocteau's *La machine infernale*." *Forum* 29, no. 1 (January 1993): 31-45.

[*In the following essay, Connon addresses the critical reaction to Cocteau's* La machine infernale *and considers the treatment of time in his play.*]

André Gide, wryly responding to the proliferation of works by Cocteau on the same theme as his *Œdipe,* proclaimed an *œdipémie.*[1] The first performance of *Œdipe-Roi* in 1937, closely following that of *La Machine infernale* in 1934, meant that Cocteau had produced two plays on this subject since Gide's creation of his own version of the Oedipus myth in 1930. Gide was here expressing a prejudice about Cocteau which has still not been entirely revised: that his principal talent lay in jumping on bandwaggons. And yet, to a large extent, the laugh was on Gide: Cocteau wrote three versions of the tale, and it would be difficult to deny that he had staked his claim on the material before Gide, since two had been written before the appearance of Gide's *Œdipe* (*Œdipe-Roi,* written in 1922, was first published in 1928, although it waited fifteen years for its first performance, and 1927 saw the première of the collaboration with Stravinsky, *Oedipus Rex*—this, at least, seems the most plausible chronology, although it is a matter on which Cocteau's biographers are both vague and contradictory). Furthermore, two of those three versions have significantly outstripped Gide's play in both influence and reputation, and if the achievement of *Œdipus Rex* is chiefly attributable to Stravinsky's contribution, the success of *La Machine infernale* is entirely Cocteau's.

The use of myth, of course, becomes a rather monotonous feature of twentieth-century French theatre, and the significance of *La Machine infernale* has perhaps been overshadowed because it lacks the obvious political or philosophical content of later excursions into similar territory, for instance Sartre's *Les Mouches,* Anouilh's *Anti-*

gone, or Giraudoux's *La Guerre de Troie n'aura pas lieu.* Cocteau is seen as a showman, and ***La Machine infernale,*** in the absence of an obvious message, is no more than a piece of theatrically effective showmanship. There is certainly no doubt that much of the success of ***La Machine infernale*** lies in its flamboyant exoticism, and that this is the most immediately obvious aspect of the work, but is it really true to say that there is no more to it than this? Lydia Crowson points out a common problem in Cocteau's *œuvre*: "During a performance or at first reading, Cocteau's work often gives the impression of being merely entertaining or clever."[2] This attitude certainly seems to persist in Karelisa V. Hartigan's constant classification of Cocteau's dramatic technique as "theatricalism", and her conclusion that "Cocteau's mythic strategy in ***La Machine infernale*** has created exciting drama and a vibrant series of scenes, but the play lacks a tragic hero".[3]

The comment that ***La Machine infernale*** has no "tragic hero" also points to another commonplace of contemporary criticism of the work: that Cocteau's play cannot be judged an unqualified success because he has trivialised Sophocles and therefore failed to be truly tragic. Hartigan comments: "In one firm stroke Cocteau has negated the very basis of Oedipus' stature. In ***La Machine infernale,*** Oedipus does not solve the riddle of the Sphinx."[4] In another reference to the Sphinx, Sonya G. Stary, herself committing the sin of trivialising Cocteau, makes a not dissimilar criticism: "In Cocteau's play, Œdipe's fate to marry and commit incest with his mother appears to be caused by the vengeful curse of a rejected female admirer."[5] In a spirited defence of Cocteau, aimed in particular at Hartigan, Lewis W. Leadbeater shows that such an attitude is based on a simplistic misreading of Sophocles, and that Cocteau in fact illuminates aspects of this seminal dramatisation of the myth which have been missed by many of his critics: "It is Cocteau's ability to clarify the ancient through the modern which augments the cathartic nature of the piece."[6] He goes on to write:

> By extending the myth on stage he penetrates to the core of the Oedipus myth and allows us to see what is only verbalized in Sophocles. Quite beyond the questions of parricide and incest Cocteau reveals not only *that* Oedipus is culpable in terms of personal motivation and choice, but *why.*[7]

A further worrying aspect of criticism which attacks Cocteau for his failure to provide an accurate repetition of Sophocles, is the apparent tacit assumption that the latter's dramatisation represents some sort of definitive version, an original, or even that it *is* the myth. There is no doubt that it is the most famous version of the tale, a seminal work which has provided the basis for most subsequent reworkings (including Cocteau's), but it is nevertheless in the nature of a myth to remain in a certain respect independent of its specific retellings. As with the copies of a limited-edition print, there is either no original, or every copy is an original. This is not to deny the validity of comparison; indeed, Cocteau invites it, for variation is part of the system of creative renewal he undertakes, and variation

can be perceived only by comparison. Neither is it to deny the validity of qualitative judgements with regard to the effectiveness of this or that aspect of different versions. It is, however, to suggest that any judgement which takes as its point of departure the assumption that it is the obligation of the author making use of myth to reproduce a previous version, as is implied by Hartigan's contention that Cocteau's task is to "recreate" "Sophocles' character",[8] is based on a false premise. On the contrary, by exploiting the variation which is inevitable in repetition to a creative and artistic end, it could be argued that Cocteau is making a profound comment on the whole nature of myth.

Furthermore, luminous as it is, the surface glitter of ***La Machine infernale*** certainly should not blind us to the presence of issues important enough to engage our philosophical attentions, which are nevertheless handled with a control which prevents their ever interfering with the wider mythic structure of the work, themes such as the nature of personal identity or of individual freedom (existential themes, although not presented in an existentialist manner).

One of the most subtle and interesting elements of Cocteau's exploitation of his source is the treatment of the theme of time, an element which pervades the work on both the thematic and the structural levels, but which is also, and perhaps more importantly, bound up with the very choice of a mythical subject in a manner much more naturally organic than many of the political or philosophical messages present in later adaptations of myth.

Even the most apparently straightforward aspect of the temporal structure, the chronological presentation of events, is of interest. As we have noted, the dramatisation of the myth by Sophocles has generally provided the model for subsequent versions of the tale, and dramatised retellings have usually adopted the same structure as that play, which, conforming to the unity of time, presents only Oedipus' investigation of the murder of Laius, during which the details of his own past are gradually revealed. So although the events that we witness are presented chronologically, the main interest lies in the discovery of past events which are present only as retrospective narrations. Part of Cocteau's innovation lies in opening out the structure so that the events confined to narration in these versions become part of his principal action. So the story is enacted before us, not pieced together retrospectively; the events which constituted the past in Sophocles' dramatisation become part of an ever-changing present; Cocteau's emphasis becomes the telling of a story, rather than the solution of a mystery. The choice of this form of presentation in one respect reveals the presence of Cocteau the entertainer: the myth includes a number of incidents which offer the opportunity for stage spectacle, and which all but the most classical of purists must sometimes have wished to be able to see. Cocteau does not disappoint us. We are party not only to the spectacle of the meeting with the Sphinx, and the intentionally titillating scene of the incestuous wedding night, but to much else besides, including elements which spring not from the familiar tale, but from Cocteau's fertile imagination and his fascination with the mystical and the exotic. But this extended presentation of the myth also allows more subtle effects.

One of the most interesting features of the linear aspect of the chronology is the way that Cocteau paces it. For temporally this work behaves in much the same way as a rock rolling down a hill, or, perhaps, a trap closing: this is how Cocteau describes the action of the trap:

> Pour que les dieux s'amusent beaucoup, il importe que leur victime tombe de haut. Des années s'écoulent, prospères. Deux filles, deux fils compliquent les noces monstrueuses. Le peuple aime son roi. Mais la peste éclate. Les dieux accusent un criminel anonyme d'infecter le pays et ils exigent qu'on le chasse. De recherche en recherche et comme enivré de malheur, Œdipe arrive au pied du mur. Le piège se ferme. Lumière est faite. Avec son écharpe rouge Jocaste se pend. Avec la broche d'or de la femme pendue, Œdipe se crève les yeux.
>
> Regarde, spectateur, remontée à bloc, de telle sorte que le ressort se déroule avec lenteur tout le long d'une vie humaine, une des plus parfaites machines construites par les dieux infernaux pour l'anéntissement mathématique d'un mortel.[9]

Here, in the opening narration, Cocteau describes the extreme slowness with which the trap operates, but in his depiction within the play itself he adds a further refinement: just like the rock rolling down the hill, the jaws of the trap begin to move very slowly, but speed up until the moment when they eventually snap shut. So the first two acts provide a feeling of extreme stasis, being not only simultaneous (a non-chronological element to which we shall return), but also much longer than the other two; the laying of the trap is accompanied by a sense of immobility—time passes, the trumpets and cock-crows remind us of that, but so slowly that we can go back and relive it. By Act Three the events are gathering momentum, for this takes place the evening after the preceding acts, and is shorter than them. And then this momentum is transformed into a sudden rushing on ahead as, before the final act, seventeen years pass, "vite" as La Voix tells us. And not only is this act much the shortest of the four, but the exact moment at which the trap snaps shut, at the words "Lumière est faite . . .", is only a little over half-way through it. The trap is prepared extremely slowly, but a man's life is destroyed in an instant.

Margaret Crosland comments:

> Between the third and fourth acts is a gap of seventeen years, unusual in Cocteau's theatre, since most of his plays represent no longer stretch of time than that taken to act them. Cocteau observed the classical unities in his "contraction" of *Antigone,* but with *La Machine Infernale* he attempted to translate the Greek conception of destiny for the twentieth century, and a series of episodes was obviously the way to present a force that has no equivalent today. This break is perhaps one of the reasons why the play has not the same excellence as *Orphée.*[10]

And yet, by seeing the presence of this gap as a fault, a fault which was somehow forced on Cocteau by his choice of an episodic treatment, she has apparently failed to note both its importance for the sense of acceleration within the text, and the fact that the lapse of seventeen years is Cocteau's own deliberate choice, a period which is, to a certain extent, arbitrary and could have been extended or compressed at will.

The chronological treatment of events over an extended time scale (even though the events of the first three acts do take place within a limited period) also allows an exploitation of character development which is less easy within the confines of the unity of time. Of course part of the essence of mythic characters is their immutability, they are archetypal parts of our culture, and in one sense Cocteau trades on this in the same way that other authors dealing with myth have done, surprising us by overturning the expectations which the archetype arouses, as when we discover that the great solver of enigmas is not able to solve the Sphinx's riddle, or when we see the tragic queen lusting after the young soldier. Hence, we feel a sense of character development when these initially rather comic figures become objects of tragic pity and terror in the final act. And yet, in another sense, Cocteau is true to the mythic ideal, since, for the most part, it is less his characters who develop than our attitude to them. Œdipe's failure to solve the riddle in Act Two is consistent with the fact that in Act Four he is equally slow to see the truth: he solves the mystery of his birth only when the evidence has become so obvious that no-one could fail to understand. In this way Cocteau is faithful to the tradition of the myth, and he very much underlines Œdipe's short-sightedness by making it clear that both Jocaste and Tirésias have understood long before him; Tirésias even tries to save him by dissuading him from pursuing his investigation: "Je vous mettais en garde contre votre habitude néfaste d'interroger, de savoir, de comprendre tout" (p. 117). But then another continuing characteristic of Œdipe is his feeling of threat in the face of the father-figure, and he misinterprets Tirésias' motives here in precisely the same way as in their confrontation in Act Three. Œdipe's impulsiveness, evident both in this habit of jumping to conclusions and in his tendency to rush into situations without thought, is present throughout Cocteau's depiction of the character as it is in the Sophoclean character too, but an impulse which is naïve and almost comic on our first encounter with him becomes tragic in the last act.

Our attitude to Jocaste provides an even clearer indication of a progression in our responses. There is an almost exclusively comic impact in the spectacle of her indulging a lecherous attraction for a boy young enough to be her son in Act One, against the backdrop of the somewhat ludicrous spectre of her husband, whom she is unable, and, perhaps we are intended to assume, subconsciously unwilling, to see. Yet on her next appearance, as she prepares to celebrate her wedding night with a man who is no longer merely young enough to be her son, but who actually *is* her son, the situation has become too sinister to be comic. The atmosphere of heavy sensuality, intensified by the anticipation of the incest about to be committed, combines with a feeling of extreme lassitude to underline this threatening yet erotic and exotic scene. And then the situation turns to tragedy: she finds out the truth of her actions, and, when the excitement at almost committing a taboo crime turns to the horror of having done so, she hangs herself. The fact that we have laughed at her in the first act does not prevent our being moved by her tragedy in the last. This is a progression felt in the whole play—comedy moves to a more sinister sensuality, and then finally to tragedy, and thus Cocteau engages our attention for the characters on different levels.

The character who shows this progression most clearly is Tirésias, and in this sense he may also be the only character who truly develops. Œdipe attains full inner sight only at the moment of his blinding; Tirésias embodies a similar relationship between inner and outer vision, but developing more slowly.[11] He is always the wise man of the drama, but that wisdom moves from a relatively superficial sense of his being Jocaste's advisor in Act One, incapable even of satisfying her curiosity by the use of his inner sight: "Et à quoi sert ton troisième œil, je demande? As-tu trouvé le Sphinx? As-tu trouvé les assassins de Laïus? As-tu clamé le peuple?" (p. 26), to a feeling that he understands the situation much more deeply than the others in Act Three, and finally to his total understanding in Act Four. And this corresponds with an onset of blindness: in Act One he is merely "presque aveugle" (p. 25)—Jocaste's "le papa est aveugle" later in the same act (p. 33) is clearly to be seen as a comic exaggeration, intended to reassure the young soldier who suspects the worst when Tirésias (on Jocaste's insistence) begins feeling his muscles; Tirésias has just confirmed the notion of "presque aveugle" in his previous speech, when, in his embarrassed attempt to avoid making comment on the young man's physique, he says: "J'y vois fort mal . . ." (p. 33). By Act Three, however, the situation has worsened, for although Jocaste is still saying that he is "presque aveugle" (p. 86), Œdipe can now describe his eyes as "vos yeux d'aveugle" (p. 91), implying total blindness; and in Act Four the ambiguity has gone: Œdipe comments simply "Tirésias est aveugle . . ." (p. 125), and being blind, he, like Œdipe, is able to see the ghost of Jocaste. So the gradual onset of Tirésias' blindness corresponds with an increase in his wisdom, just as happens to Œdipe in an instant. There is a reciprocal relationship between actual vision and inner sight, and to make this point, Cocteau has again departed from the tradition of the myth, for the blind seer who appears in Sophocles' and subsequent versions of the myth has his own legend in which he does not lose his sight gradually, but is struck blind by a goddess and recompensed with second sight by a god.

On one level, the device of gaining our sympathy for the characters first through laughter and then through sexual titillation before showing their tragic downfall is rather facile, perhaps even sentimental, Cocteau the showman in action again, but it does have more subtle implications, for

through it Cocteau reveals that the sources of comedy can be the same as those of tragedy; that the same emotions and motivations can produce comic or tragic results; that, in the final analysis, the distinction between the two is merely a question of accident, coincidence, the choice of the author or the choice of the gods. What makes the trap set by the gods at the outset of Cocteau's play so devastating is precisely the fact that it begins by seeming innocent enough and then, in its final minutes, turns to a bloody and violent conclusion. Louis Baladier comments:

> La catégorie esthétique du tragique n'est pas exprimée chez Cocteau—et c'est un trait du modernisme—dans les registres stylistiques du grandiose ou du sublime, mais dans ceux du poétique et de l'humoristique.[12]

A further aspect of Cocteau's treatment which underlines the force of linear time is the importance it has for the characters. They are prisoners of the time-scale in which they live, tormented by the importance of both the isolated moment and the need to achieve things before time runs out. The two soldiers wait for the ghost which must materialise before morning; for the ghost of Laïus itself there is also a race against time, to communicate its message before daybreak on this, the last night on which it will be able to appear—and it runs out of time at the crucial moment, on the point of revealing the identity of the murderer; the Sphinx argues with Anubis over whether the trumpet call is the one which will release her from the obligation to kill; the Matrone rushes to get home before the trumpets tell her it is too late; Œdipe too wants to reach Thebes before the last trumpet call; Jocaste and Œdipe struggle to stay awake because they do not wish to miss the unrepeatable moment of their wedding night, and, of course, the supreme tragic moment on which all of the action turns is that of Œdipe's realisation, for without realisation there is no tragedy.

And yet, throughout the play, as well as stressing and exploiting this conventional linear narrative time, Cocteau undermines it. Indeed, even in discussing his linear treatment of chronology, it has been impossible not to mention two elements which contradict it: the simultaneity of the events of the first two acts, and the audience's preconceptions of the archetypal nature of the characters. It is as if Cocteau were dramatising the conflict between two notions of time, the continuous and the discontinuous. Richard Glasser, in his study of the perception of time in French thought, expresses the conflict as follows, defining the two approaches as Bergsonian and Proustian:

> In the Proustian mode of remembering, scenes as well as moments are isolated; they resemble unconnected vessels. Whereas Bergson attached the highest importance to separating time and space sharply from each other, Proust's novel of time, in the final analysis, comes to reducing the temporal succession of states of consciousness to their spatially ordered co-existence. He opposed the Bergsonian flowing and becoming.[13]

Even within the chronological presentation of the tale, we see in action this idea of moments as unconnected units. For instance, whilst we certainly witness more of the events which make up the mythological story enacted before us than in a version dramatised according to the unity of time, we do not see all of them. In Sophocles' play, past and present are brought together in a single dramatic span which is impressive for its sense of unity. In Cocteau's work the discontinuity of the elements which we witness is stressed every bit as much by the simultaneity of the two incidents presented in the first two acts as it is by the seventeen-year gap between the other pair. And the apparent arbitrariness of the selection of moments we witness is underlined by inclusion as well as omission: why are the childhood of Œdipe and the murder of Laïus omitted in favour of the appearance of the ghost on the battlements, a scene which is completely of Cocteau's invention?

There is little doubt that the simultaneous placing of the events of the first two acts is the most striking of all the explorations of time within **La Machine infernale**. Indeed, so unusual was it in 1934 that Cocteau has to explain it in the speech for La Voix introducing Act Two:

> Spectateurs, nous allons imaginer un recul dans le temps et revivre, ailleurs, les minutes que nous venons de vivre ensemble. En effet, le fantôme de Laïus essaie de prévenir Jocaste, sur une plate-forme des remparts de Thèbes, pendant que le Sphinx et Œdipe se rencontrent sur une éminence qui domine la ville. Mêmes sonneries de trompettes, même lune, mêmes étoiles, mêmes coqs.
>
> (p. 47)

And yet, we must remember that this simultaneity is not something which Cocteau has had forced on him; he has chosen it just as surely as the duration of seventeen years for the time-lapse between Acts Three and Four. And as well as creating the remarkable effect of rapid acceleration from a static opening, these aspects also stress the way in which independent moments can be recapitulated and juxtaposed.

This Proustian universe in which moments can be lived and relived, combined and recombined is explained by Anubis:

ANUBIS:

> *il montre la robe du Sphinx.*—Regardez les plis de cette étoffe. Pressezles les uns contre les autres. Et maintenant, si vous traversez cette masse d'une épingle, si vous enlevez l'épingle, si vous lissez l'étoffe jusqu'à faire disparaître toute trace des anciens plis, pensezvous qu'un nigaud de campagne puisse croire que les innombrables trous qui se répètent de distance en distance résultent d'un seul coup d'épingle?

LE SPHINX:

> Certes non.

ANUBIS:

> Le temps des hommes est de l'éternité pliée. Pour nous, il n'existe pas. De sa naissance à sa mort la vie d'Œdipe s'étale, sous mes yeux, plate, avec sa suite d'épisodes.
>
> (p. 72)

So the material is folded together into a system of gathers or pleats, pierced by the pin, and then unfolded so that the pinpricks can be seen spread out on the flattened surface. This is how Cocteau's gods experience human time, but we, as audience, have precisely this same advantage, and time spreads itself out so that we can see two simultaneous episodes at different times, whilst seventeen years will pass in seconds when we so wish. Events can be juxtaposed in other ways too: the effect of age is seen when Jocaste is compared with her flatteringly out-of-date portrait on a coin and cannot be recognised (pp. 27-8); with the use of stage trickery and modern technology we see simultaneously the old and the new forms of the goddess Nemesis who has been the Sphinx. This non-chronological depiction of time is particularly strikingly illustrated in Act Three, in which both past and future encroach on the present, for not only are the symbols of the past, the cradle and the wounds on Œdipe's feet, there to remind us of what has happened, Œdipe also sees a vision of his future in the sightless eyes of Tirésias and experiences the pain of his own self-mutilation (another link between blindness and clairvoyance). And both the Sphinx and Anubis, whom we have seen transform themselves and leave the world at the end of Act Two, put in appearances in this third act, Anubis in person in Œdipe's dream, and the Sphinx in an incident narrated by Tirésias: she has appeared on the day of Œdipe's coronation to return to him the belt which he gave her during the previous night. Jocaste becomes so confused in this act that non-chronological attitudes to time begin to encroach on her own linear time-scale, and she claims that her attraction to the young soldier was caused because he reminded her of Œdipe even before she had met him (p. 98). And in this same act Œdipe comes close to achieving a feat which a linear perception of chronology would normally render impossible. One of the more clever of Cocteau's jokes is his frequent use of Freudian references in this post-Freudian version of the most Freudian of myths. Although the true father, Laïus, is already dead before the play begins, Tirésias has the role of father-figure within the action; Jocaste's nickname for him, Zizi, may be a rather silly and therefore deflating abbreviation of Tirésias, but its phallic connotations also draw attention to one of the principal attributes of the father in Freudian analysis. As a result, Cocteau's Œdipe, when he attempts to strangle Tirésias, almost contrives to commit parricide twice, an achievement made possible even in the blurred chronology of this act only by the use of post-Freudian symbolism.

But this whole aspect of the temporal structure also has strong links with the choice of a mythical subject: Michel Tournier, that great exploiter of myth, has offered as the simplest of his range of definitions of myth that a myth is a story everybody knows, and has added that by using myth he wishes to give even the first-time reader the feeling of rereading his works.[14] It is to this aspect of Cocteau's use of myth that the notion of expectation is related: we can only be surprised by his thwarting of our expectations concerning the behaviour of the characters because of the use of myth, for without the foreknowledge of events given by our familiarity with the story we could have no such expectations. Additionally, much of the loaded dramatic irony of Cocteau's text, whether humorous or otherwise, depends on our ability to see the entire myth spread out in front of us, like the material of the Sphinx's dress, at the same time that we witness the individual scenes as if we were examining the pinpricks. For he also makes use of jokes which rely on our foreknowledge of the dénouement, a further deformation of the time-scale possible only in a version of myth. Such are Jocaste's scarf "[qui] tout le jour [. . .] m'étrangle" (p. 26), and her brooch "qui crève l'œil de tout le monde" (p. 39). Similar is the exchange between Œdipe and the Sphinx about Jocaste's age: she is old enough to be his mother, but "l'essentiel est qu'elle ne le soit pas" (p. 62). And there is Anubis' much more sinister comment about Œdipe: "Beaucoup d'hommes naissent aveugles et ils ne s'en aperçoivent que le jour où une bonne vérité leur crève les yeux" (p. 77). Lydia Crowson says of such references:

> The ambiguous language (sliding from the literal to the figurative with equal validity on both levels) highlights the crucial position of time, since the spectator has access to Oedipus' perspective in addition to his own: the two horizons of knowledge are juxtaposed before him.[15]

There is certainly a strong element of entertainment in the macabre humour of these anticipations of the dénouement, but to dismiss them as mere "cleverness", or call them "annoying", as does W. L. Hodson, is to misunderstand their role in the wider mythic and temporal perspectives of the work.[16]

And yet, combined with the sense of the action first standing still and then gathering speed and rushing headlong to its conclusion, combined too with the sense that moments in time are experiences which can be moved about, relived and recombined, is yet another feeling: that of absolute timelessness—Neal Oxenhandler comments: "Cocteau's plays have a strange suspended quality."[17] This is part of the very nature of myth, and, although later exploiters of myth in French twentieth-century drama would turn it to polemical use, Cocteau and Gide, in beginning the fashion for a return to mythical subjects, were surely attempting a return to the higher ritualistic aims of theatre which had largely disappeared since the undermining of tragedy in the latter part of the eighteenth century. The sense of endless repetition is a major product of the use of myth; Cocteau reminds us strongly of this in the opening narration, telling the story in full before it is presented to us in the play; and this sense of the myth as story to be retold and re-enacted is further stressed by another retelling by Anubis (pp. 72-3). Such is the repetitive power of the tale that the riddle scene can be enacted twice, once hypothetically couched in the provisional conditional tense, and then as a real event; the two versions differ, but that which accords with the tradition of the myth, in which Œdipe is victor, prevails. Similarly, Œdipe and Jocaste both try to escape the truth of their pasts by reinventing them in their stories to each other in Act Three—Œdipe's meeting with the Sphinx is recreated; it is not Jocaste but her servant

who abandoned an infant with its feet pierced—but the truth of the myth inevitably emerges, and even these failed attempts to deform the story reinforce its repetitive power.

The appearance of the ghost of Jocaste towards the end of the play provides a further example of a circular structure, for the ghost of the mother corresponds to the ghost of the father in the first act, and the image of the blinded Œdipe being encouraged by Jocaste and Antigone to count the steps, just as Jocaste had encouraged the almost blind Tirésias at their very first appearance, will inevitably take us back in our minds to the beginning of the drama.

But, that ghost apart, Cocteau has no surprises in store for us in his final act. This is the only act in which the action corresponds more or less exactly with that of the Sophoclean and subsequent dramatisations of the myth; indeed, in this brief act Cocteau covers the ground which constituted an entire play for his predecessors. Its brevity is in part possible because Cocteau has spent so much time setting up his background, but also owes much to our familiarity with the earlier versions—almost as if Cocteau's act were merely a mnemonic for the *Oedipus Tyrranos* rather than a true dramatisation of the myth in its own right. The possibility of using this sort of shorthand allows the devastating compression of that last act, but it also represents a further way of suggesting the cyclic character of the myth: in the opening narration Cocteau has confirmed that we are going to see a re-enactment of the familiar story, and, although he never leaves that story or its familiarity behind, the first three acts both dramatise parts of the myth less familiar in the theatre, and set out to surprise us; with the fourth act it is as if we have returned home. We are on familiar territory now, for we know the end of the action at the beginning, and the end will return to the beginning, both in the counting of the steps, and in the implication of endless repetition.

The suggestion of the repetitive implications of the myth goes to the heart of its nature, and we find it, not in a literal return to the opening of the action at its conclusion (given the nature of the tale this would hardly be possible), but subtly embedded in an exchange between Créon and Tirésias near the end of the play:

CRÉON:

> —C'est im-pos-si-ble. Je ne laisserai pas un fou sortir en liberté avec Antigone. J'ai le devoir . . .

TIRÉSIAS:

> —Le devoir! Ils ne t'appartiennent plus; ils ne relèvent plus de ta puissance.

CRÉON:

> —Et à qui appartiendraient-ils?

TIRÉSIAS:

> —Au peuple, aux poètes, aux cœurs purs.

(p. 126)

It is that phrase "aux poètes" which reminds us of the cyclic nature of the mythic structure, for telling and retelling is one of the most powerful elements in our use of myth—we are watching one poet's version of a myth which has been repeated down the centuries in numerous versions. And the status of Cocteau's version as simply one in a chain of retellings is further underlined by the way his use of both familiar and unexpected elements means that earlier versions are continually in our minds. (It is, of course, typical of Cocteau's self-image that he should choose the word "poète" rather than "dramaturge".)

We are here very close to Jung's ideas of myth, for if the myth is repeated and reinterpreted so frequently, it is because it speaks to us on a deep emotional level. Coincidentally, just as Cocteau exploits Freud's interpretation of the Oedipus myth in his dramatisation of the story, so Jung too takes Freud and the Oedipus complex as his starting point for discussion of the nature of myth in *Symbols of Transformation*:

> When we follow the paths traced out by Freud we gain a living knowledge of the existence of [the] possibilities [that a man can have an unconscious, all-consuming passion for his mother], which, although too weak to compel actual incest, are yet sufficiently strong to cause very considerable psychic disturbances. We cannot, to begin with, admit such possibilities in ourselves without a feeling of moral revulsion, and without resistances which are only too likely to blind the intellect and render self-knowledge impossible. But if we can succeed in discriminating between objective knowledge and emotional value-judgements, then the gulf that separates our age from antiquity is bridged over, and we realise with astonishment that Oedipus is still alive for us.[18]

Cocteau shuns in this play the most obvious way of giving a sense of contemporary relevance to myth, that is the updating of costumes, settings and attitudes, although he does exploit anachronistic dialogue, particularly in the scene between the soldiers. Most striking though is the subtle blurring of distinctions between the time in which the myth is set and our own time, found in the setting for Act Two: "Derrière les décombres d'un petit temple, un mur en ruine. Au milieu du mur, un socle intact devait marquer l'entrée du temple et porte les vestiges d'une chimère: une aile, une patte, une croupe. Colonnes détruites" (p. 48). No-one would deny the probable existence of ruins in classical Greece, but it is nevertheless true that this setting much more accurately reflects a contemporary experience of the period: we associate ancient Greece with ruins not because it was itself full of them, but because it is all that we now know of it. Cocteau therefore sets his mythic action in a decor which reflects our contemporary experience of the period in which it is set, and thereby bridges the divide between the two ages.

A further ramification of Jung's theory of myth springing from an unconscious and collective experience is his demonstration that similar mythic paradigms reappear in different cultures, and can even be imitated by life (for the Oedipus myth his example is Ninon de Lenclos and her son,[19] what he calls "historical and ethnological parallels").[20]

A number of references, too frequently dismissed as further examples of Cocteau's "cleverness", form illustrations of his universalising of the myth by showing links which cross cultural and temporal limitations. They begin at the very outset with a reference to the mythology of a different culture: La Voix, in the opening narration, compares Œdipe to a Germanic hero: "Comme s'élancera le jeune Siegfried, Œdipe se hâte" (p. 12). The presence of Anubis represents a further example of cultural interchange, one which confuses even the characters, for the Sphinx's question, "Pourquoi en Grèce un dieu d'Égypte" (p. 50), never really receives a satisfactory answer, although one of Anubis' attempted explanations coincides with the Jungian notion that the implications of myth are universal even though the details of its symbols may change—geography is no more an obstacle to its significance than time: "L'Égypte, la Grèce, la mort, le passé, l'avenir n'ont pas de sens chez nous" (pp. 50-1). Intertextual resonances are created in the clear reference to the opening of *Hamlet* in the first act—*Hamlet* has become such a well-known part of world literature that Cocteau is able to draw on it in the same way and to the same end that he exploits the tales of classical mythology.[21] The same may be said of the song of the drunk at the end of Act Three, with its reminiscence of *Madame Bovary*. The proximity of life to myth is illustrated by the reference to the death of Isadora Duncan, as Jocaste, anticipating her own death by strangulation, comments on the various ways in which the very scarf with which she will later kill herself threatens to strangle her: "Une fois, elle s'accroche aux branches, une autre fois, c'est le moyeu d'un char où elle s'enroule, une autre fois tu marches dessus" (p. 26). Isadora Duncan died when the flowing scarf she was wearing became entangled in a wheel of the sports car in which she was riding. This reference has been noted often enough, but it has also been criticised as gratuitous. Its inclusion becomes less problematic when seen as part of a scheme of illustrations of the Jungian theory of mythical transformation, but its integration is further strengthened when we see that it is merely part of a more extended comparison between Jocaste and the famous dancer—a comparison which has not generally been noted. For, if Frederick Brown's description of the ageing Duncan as Cocteau knew her at Villefranche is accurate, it is clear that he borrowed from her more than just her death when creating his version of the queen to Thebes:

> Barefoot, surmounted by a mop of magenta hair and trailing the folds of an orange-scarlet negligee, she carried her ruined majesty along the jetty in quest of sailors, and, quite often, to the Hôtel Welcome. Though nearly fifty, Isadora was still, indeed more than ever, responsive to the appeal of young, sandy-haired men, and not infrequently they repaid her maternal lust with adulation.[22]

The gap between mythic past and actual present is once again bridged to give a sense of the timeless nature of things.

Claude Mauriac has pointed out the importance in the whole of Cocteau's *œuvre* of what he calls "l'angoissante question du temps".[23] By making this a central issue of his treatment of the Oedipus myth in *La Machine infernale* Cocteau strikes at the very essence not only of this myth, but of myth in general. Certainly he is an entertainer and a showman—that aspect of his art neither can nor should be ignored—but he is more. Many of the aspects of this play which have been criticised for being mere entertainment can be seen also to fit into a deeper scheme of mystical and mythical examination. Much more than later writers who have used myth as a pretext for the exposition of a single polemical point, Cocteau in *La Machine infernale* justifies its revival in the modern theatre by exploiting characteristics which are an inherent part of its ritualistic nature. The exploitation of a linear time-scale, presenting the events in a more chronologically coherent order than versions which make copious use of retrospective narration, combined with the narrative closure provided by the dénouement, provide the elements which constitute a good yarn, as well as the possibility of drawing a moral conclusion. Alongside these we find devices suggesting cyclic retelling, which stress the experience of timeless repetition across the centuries. This is a combination which is an essential characteristic of the human instinct to mythologise.

Notes

1. Quoted by Frederick Brown, *An Impersonation of Angels: A Biography of Jean Cocteau* (London, 1969), p. 309, and Bettina L. Knapp, *French Theatre, 1918-1939* (London, 1985), p. 115, although neither gives an original source for the remark.

2. *The Esthetic of Jean Cocteau* (New England, 1978), p. 124.

3. "Oedipus in France: Cocteau's mythic strategy in *La Machine infernale*", in: *Classical and Modern Literature* 6 (1986), pp. 89-95 (p. 95).

4. Hartigan, p. 93.

5. "Cosmic disorder and the poet in Cocteau's *La Machine infernale*", in: *Romance Quarterly* 34 (1987), pp. 43-9 (p. 47).

6. "In defense of Cocteau: another view of *La Machine infernale*", in: *Classical and Modern Literature* 10 (1989-90), pp. 113-25 (p. 118).

7. Leadbeater, p. 124 (Leadbeater's italics).

8. Hartigan, p. 89.

9. Cocteau, *La Machine infernale* (Paris, 1934), p. 12.

10. *Jean Cocteau* (London, 1955), p. 137.

11. For a discussion of the relationship between Cocteau's exploitation of the theme of sight/understanding to Sophocles' text see Leadbeater, pp. 119-24.

12. "Jean Cocteau: *La Machine infernale*", in: *École des lettres* 81, iii (1989), pp. 25-36 (p. 35).

13. *Time in French Life and Thought,* trans. C. G. Pearson (original edition, München, 1936, translation, Manchester, 1972), p. 297.

14. For Tournier's ideas on myth see in particular *Le vent Paraclet* (Paris, 1977).

15. Crowson, p. 70.

16. "Theatricalism and Greek myth in Gide, Cocteau and Giraudoux", in: *The Classical Tradition in French Literature: Essays Presented to R. C. Knight by Colleagues, Pupils and Friends,* ed. H. T. Barnwell and others (London, 1977), pp. 229-37 (p. 234).

17. *Scandal and Parade: The Theatre of Jean Cocteau* (London, 1958), p. 154.

18. *Symbols of Transformation: An Analysis of the Prelude to a Case of Schizophrenia,* trans. R. F. C. Hull, in *The Collected Works of C. G. Jung,* ed. H. Read and others, V (London, 1956), p. 4. Although the first publication of *Symbole der Wandlung* dates only from 1952, this work was simply the final revision of *Wandlungen und Symbole der Libido,* published in 1912. Although the direct influence of Jung on Cocteau here is not certain, his ideas would undoubtedly have been known in the French intellectual circles in which Cocteau moved well before the composition of *La Machine infernale*.

19. Jung, p. 4.

20. Jung, p. 6.

21. For an explanation of Cocteau's choice of *Hamlet,* see Rosalba Guerini, "*La macchina infernale* di Jean Cocteau", in: *Studi di letteratura francese* 15 (1989), pp. 140-67 (p. 157).

22. Brown, p. 254.

23. *Jean Cocteau; ou, La Vérité du mensonge* (Paris, 1945), p. 129.

L'IMPROMPTU DU PALAIS-ROYAL

CRITICAL COMMENTARY

Lydia Crowson (essay date March 1976)

SOURCE: Crowson, Lydia. "Cocteau and 'Le Numéro Barbette'". *Modern Drama* 19, no. 1 (March 1976): 79-87.

[*In the following essay, Crowson investigates the relationship between his essay "Le Numéro Barbette" and L'Impromptu du Palais Royal.*]

One of the accusations most frequently leveled against Jean Cocteau is that there is no continuity in his work, that he created merely for the sake of effect without having any real goal in mind. Yet, if the evidence is fairly examined, it becomes clear that this is not the case, at least in his conception of stage performance. One of his earliest esthetic formulations is an article entitled "Le Numéro Barbette" which appeared in the July 1926 issue of the *Nouvelle Revue Française,* and his last play, **L'Impromptu du Palais Royal,** produced and published in 1962, is a theatrical presentation of his theories of theater. The latter is in fact a refinement, a sophisticated version of the former. However dissimilar Cocteau's plays may appear, they are linked by the same high ideal of the craft of theater: if their likenesses have been obscured, it is because they are united not by a theme or a message but rather by a conception of the art of the stage, of what theater as spectacle means. Cocteau was never interested in a play *qua* text; instead, he strove to create a certain art-object/ spectator relationship based on illusion and enchantment. That this essential aim never changed in the course of his career becomes evident through a comparison of "Le Numéro Barbette" and **L'Impromptu du Palais Royal.**

"Barbette" (the stage name of Vander Clyde) was one of the most highly respected trapeze artists and female impersonators of the 1920s and 30s. Born in Texas, he performed in music halls and circuses throughout Europe, although Paris—where he appeared at the Alhambra, the Casino de Paris, the Moulin Rouge, the Empire and the Medrano Circus—remained his favorite city. It was in the French capital that Cocteau met him, saw his act and became intrigued by what he considered to be an outstanding example of theater craftsmanship. There is no doubt that Cocteau's attraction to Barbette's performance was largely sexual: the transvestite appeal of the act can hardly be overlooked. Cocteau writes, for example, that "[Barbette] is to such an extent the archetypal woman that he overshadows the most beautiful women who precede and follow him on the Program" ("Le Numéro Barbette," p. 35). Moreover, Barbette made him understand why "great countries and civilizations cast men in women's roles not just for decency's sake" (p. 36). However, the subject matter of "Le Numéro Barbette" is ultimately theoretical and oriented around questions of perception and illusion. From the transvestite's performance emerges one of the basic structures of Cocteau's theater.

The strength and uniqueness of Vander Clyde's act lay in the fact that it was composed of (and could not exist without) two skills: the performer had to be not only a female impersonator but, in addition, an accomplished acrobat. When "Barbette" came on stage, he was dressed as a woman. To allay any suspicions the audience might have, he performed a kind of strip tease until he was wearing only a female acrobat's costume. In this way, he pantomimed a fairly erotic scene which "established" his sex. Yet, since "Barbette" was presented to the spectators as a tightrope artist, this sequence was actually only a beginning. As Cocteau remarks, "he throws his magic powder in everyone's eyes. He does it with such force that from now on he will be able to concentrate on his work as an acrobat" (p. 36). At the end of the act, he was ap-

plauded for his tightrope performance, and Cocteau was not the only reviewer to note the many curtain calls he received. Hence, he was an excellent acrobatic artist, enthusiastically praised for that talent alone. It was only after such a response that he took off his wig. From accounts of audience reaction, it seems clear that most people were taken completely by surprise. Cocteau describes the wave of astonishment in the room and many embarrassed, disbelieving faces. Just as Barbette had introduced his act by miming the essence of femininity, he ended it by playing an extremely masculine role. According to Cocteau, his simply being a man was not sufficient in the circumstances. Therefore, he had to continue performing, he had to exaggerate: he flexed his muscles, hopped from one foot to the other, resembled a mischievous street urchin.

Were it not for the virtual impossibility of success in what Barbette attempted, his performance would be of little interest. Miraculously, he was able to convince large numbers of spectators to accept him as a female acrobat. He did not imitate a woman in order that his audience immediately perceive his imitation and react to it as a facet of his art. Rather, for them, his sex in theory was not even supposed to come into question. Yet, Vander Clyde was a trapeze artist. With each motion, his body or his costume should have betrayed him since nothing he did on stage was passive. Obviously, then, he had to learn to suppress all types of movement natural to a man, he had to scrutinize each step of his routine and eliminate everything masculine. Such an attempt would be difficult enough in non-demanding activities like walking, for example, but in strenuous acrobatics even reflex actions would have to be controlled to an almost unattainable extent. Moreover, his brief costume made the task all the more difficult. The two aspects of Barbette's act that distinguish it from all others resembling it, then, are its premise of total illusion or deception and its impeccable craftsmanship. These are precisely the two subjects that form the core of Cocteau's article:

> Don't forget that we are in the theater's magic light, in this 'malice-box' where truth is of no value, where what is natural is worthless, where short people become tall and tall ones short, where only card tricks and sleights of hand whose difficulty the public doesn't even suspect can manage to hold firm
>
> (p. 36).

It is clear that for Cocteau entering an auditorium is tantamount to participating in a reality completely removed from that of everyday. Different rules apply and, most important, the nature of perception changes completely. If the theater has a "magic light" that distorts ordinary objects, then whatever is presented on the stage must first be altered: it must be transposed just as music is transposed from key to key. In most cases, actors realize such a transformation through their make-up or costumes. Yet, they usually retain elements of who they really are, whereas Barbette succeeded in altering who he was as completely as possible.

The basic assumption underlying Cocteau's conception of theater as presented in "Le Numéro Barbette," then, is his tenet that the art of the stage presupposes deception. Acting is a game whose success is measured by the degree to which the audience accepts the game as reality. While modifications of such a position are not uncommon in the history of theater, Cocteau's stand is radical in that it contains such great emphasis on shifting from one type of reality to another. Vander Clyde's being a great acrobat would not have intrigued Cocteau, although he certainly would not have underestimated the skill involved. Rather, his ability to portray a female trapeze artist supplied the trick, the "sleight of hand," necessary to raise his performance to the status of genuine theater. For there to be theater, then, the simple convention of illusion that underlies most acting is not enough: there must be a double order of illusion, a double step from commonplace reality. Just as the female impersonator Vander Clyde exists behind the trapeze artist Barbette, the story of Oedipus and Jocasta in *La Machine infernale* is contained within the play of the gods, for example, and the tale of Renaud and Armide forms only a part of the history of Armide's magic ring.

In a play on the word *trompe-l'oeil*, Cocteau summarizes Barbette's performance as "this machine of witchcraft, of emotions, of *trompe-l'âme* [the soul] and of *trompe-les-sens* [the senses]." (p. 38). One of the key words in his description is evidently, the word "deceive": at every moment, the spectators find themselves surrounded by a web of untruth which they believe, which in the atmosphere of a theater they accept as reality. More interesting, however, and ultimately more important for an understanding of Cocteau's work as a whole is the word "machine," because it underscores the deliberateness and precision that characterize every facet of a production. From Death's mechanized ritual in *Orphée* to Oedipus' calculated destruction in *La Machine infernale,* machines and mechanical devices form one of the constants in Cocteau's theater. However random the action on stage may seem, it is nevertheless controlled by an unalterable order. Nothing Barbette does is left to chance: what appears to be carried out with ease or nonchalance has in fact been planned with attention to the smallest detail. Barbette's act is an example of machine-like perfection, it epitomizes a mechanism that is designed to trick and that is, hence, a metaphor for theater. Therefore, flawless craftmanship emerges as perhaps the primary criterion for judging a work of art.

"When one compares himself with certain specialists, he is ashamed to admit how little he knows his craft" (p. 34). Since most work for the stage is discussed as if it consisted of nothing more than a text, the fact that Cocteau insists upon *métier* is not always self-evident. Yet, he never forgot that an illusion of effortlessness is indeed only an illusion, that behind grace and beauty lie hours of planning. Machine-like precision and success do not result from chance and in "Le Numéro Barbette" he contrasts the apparently unlabored steps of a Pavlova or a Nijinsky during performance with the gasping monsters the dancers became in the wings. In his opinion, all the little details preparatory to entering the stage have the status of a sacred ritual

which entails an awareness "proper to clowns, to Annamese mimes, to Cambodian dancers who are sewn into their costumes every evening" (p. 34). Cocteau has an acute sense of perpetuating a tradition of artistic pride. Hence, his primary concerns are with the means by which a performer succeeds in bewitching his audience.

In Barbette's case, it appears that the arrangement of the auditorium itself as well as meticulous planning of each detail made the "sleight of hand" possible. According to reviewers, in the intimacy of a nightclub illusion was much more easily sustained than in the Medrano Circus, for example, simply because there was less space in which to work. Since traveling greater distances on a trapeze involved more effort, movements tended to become more masculine and muscles more evident. Therefore, a close contact between stage and spectators was essential in luring the audience into Barbette's game. It is as if a "suspension of disbelief" could not be accomplished without the kind of rapport that exists in a small group of people.

However biased Cocteau's judgements about the credibility of Barbette's sexual transformation may seem, the photographs available confirm his opinion and he is not the only critic to mention that Vander Clyde may have appealed to some who believed him a woman and to some who guessed he was a man but that in the final analysis he embodied Beauty which itself has a kind of surnatural sexuality. Although under close scrutiny "Barbette" dressed in his woman's costume and wig does not really look completely like a woman, it is doubtful that someone who did not know his sex would guess it. What is striking about the pictures remaining of him is the refinement which characterizes his wig, make-up and every other accessory. Nothing is garish or exaggerated and, as Cocteau reports in describing steps of the actor's "metamorphosis" before the show, even the smallest features (which would have been judged insignificant by a lesser artisan) were attended to. All in all, Barbette seems to have had the strange androgynous beauty of a countertenor's voice.

While *L'Impromptu du Palais Royal* seems more complex because it is in the form of a play with dialogue, it is nevertheless—with the exception of a discussion on the nature of time—little more than a statement of the concepts that can be deduced from "Le Numéro Barbette." As its title indicates, it falls into the category of plays like Molière's *Impromptu de Versailles* and *La Critique de L'Ecole des femmes* or Giraudoux's *Impromptu de Paris* in which the subject of the work is theater. Both Molière and Giraudoux wrote scripts in which the characters consisted of a troupe of actors supposedly at ease and speaking informally. Obviously, such a device is a convention but it is one that intrigued Cocteau because of its essential ambiguity: in an impromptu actors appear not to be acting. They are therefore playing the role of actors and, hence, the action merely seems to be unpracticed. Therefore, such a form was an ideal vehicle for the expression of ideas on illusion, tricks and machine-like perfection.

Cocteau wrote *L'Impromptu du Palais Royal* as a prologue and divertissement for the *Fourberies de Scapin* that the Comédie Française presented on a tour to Japan. Using the general pretext of rehearsal for a Molière play, he complicated his sketch by making it a sort of impromptu within an impromptu just as Barbette's act is a performance within a performance. In Giraudoux's *Impromptu de Paris,* for example, the cast was composed of Jouvet and his company at the Athénée, and although the "rehearsal" begins with a few lines from Molière's *Impromptu* to set the tone for what is to follow, the actors nevertheless represent only members of the twentieth-century crew. Cocteau, however, confuses matters by a two-fold departure from the spectator's world: his actors play the role not only of actors but, in addition, of actors who on a bare stage are in the process of improvising a sketch about Molière, Louis XIV and the court while they wait for the "real" Molière play to begin. Being about theater, the work is consequently about game, and it depicts a cast "playing" before it starts to work. Therefore, many of Cocteau's own ideas are expressed by such characters as the King, Monsieur, or Molière himself and there is a constant juxtaposition of the production's two levels as the actors slip naturally in and out of their improvisation. At each turn, the spectacle is a conjunction of "truth" and illusion. The audience is always aware that what happens at the "court" of Louis XIV is determined by actors who are "improvising," that in fact every word or gesture was selected by the author. By unmasking dramatic conventions, Cocteau destroys the myth of spontaneity and allows his spectators to glimpse the secrets of dramatic art. However, he does so in such a charming, indirect fashion that the *Impromptu* is probably one of his greatest triumphs in sleight of hand.

At the beginning, in a sort of prologue, a man putting on a marquis' costume as he enters stops to speak to the public as if he were addressing it casually. However, he breaks down one level of illusion by explaining that he is really not a marquis but an actor and that in spite of the "freedom" Cocteau has left the cast the essence of the "improvisation" the spectators are about to see is "a frightful mixture of what we are and what we aren't. A trap! . . . Don't be deceived. The strange things you are about to hear are really by our author and we have learned them" (*L'Impromptu,* p. 14). While he is speaking, a lady in the audience interrupts to correct his pronunciation. She is usually a member of the troupe, she claims, but now she is a spectator and she is going to use the liberty the author has given her by stopping the action and expressing her opinions. Yet, it is obvious that her freedom is only a fiction, that everything she says is in fact a part of a carefully worded script. Likewise, the "Marquise" explains to the "Duke" that "we are playing a double game here . . . You have to dance at the end of strings that our invisible author is pulling above us" (*L'Impromptu,* p. 25). Molière, who is frequently Cocteau's spokesman, states that "our vocation consists of making no distinction between what is true and false" (*L'Impromptu,* p. 27). Often the actors argue among themselves about an interpretation of their roles in such a fashion that the elements of game or play which underlie the whole production become evident through their badinage. They make direct allusion to their improvisation as well as correct each other's mistakes. The tone is light throughout as members of the troupe follow remarks about Molière with comments on Cocteau, and as they mingle the two levels of action. "Saint-Simon" for example is waiting for a propitious moment when he can introduce his actress-girlfriend to the King. At one of the King's statements, the "spectator" bursts out with: "What you just said is a hundred percent Cocteau and Louis XIV would never have thought of having such an idea" (*L'Impromptu,* p. 37). Moreover, at the end of the script, Cocteau indicates that if there are curtain calls, the cast should come out to bow in whatever they happen to have on, whether it be street clothes or costumes for the play following *L'Impromptu.* The atmosphere created by the work is one of effortlessness, informality and gaiety. The spectator certainly does not leave the auditorium with an impression of having heard a treatise on theater, because the "machinery" of the production is carefully hidden and calculated to function only indirectly.

It is interesting to note that one of the sources of **L'Impromptu du Palais Royal** is the type of intimacy between stage and audience so important to Barbette's success. In his introduction, Cocteau explains that after performances at the Comédie Française, he had sometimes seen the actors improvise until dawn. He was impressed with their ability to transform imitations that could very easily have been farcical into drama and with the magical atmosphere of such games: "After these intimate festivities, I always wondered whether it would be possible to give form to something that originally depended on chance, to capture one of the improvisations in flight, to translate one of those ghosts into flesh and blood" (*L'Impromptu,* p. 9). In his own *Impromptu,* then, he strove to create an atmosphere of closeness, he quite clearly attempted to draw the audience into his game in order that it not really be aware of the artifice in spite of his warnings. Thus, there could be few conceptions of theater farther removed from Brecht's than Cocteau's. Cocteau wants nothing more than he wants a suspension of judgement that allows make-believe to come to life.

However many years may separate Barbette's act from **L'Impromptu du Palais Royal,** the formal continuity between the two works is nevertheless unmistakable. To qualify as theater, a performance must surpass the old truism of "realistic representation." A stage is not "the real" as it is defined in daily life. It is another sort of reality that has as its very basis the concept of trickery—and not merely a shoddy make-believe, but a game so convincingly and skillfully formed as to be accepted. The world of the stage should charm the spectator, captivate him so that he falls under its spell. Representation is not sufficient: what is presented must be perceived without question as what it is supposed to be.

The "secret" behind achieving such a goal appears to be a well-constructed machine, in Cocteau's vocabulary. No detail is left to chance. Even in the *Impromptu* whose characters blatantly inform the spectator at every turn that he is being deceived, the cleverness of the dialogue creates an impression of improvisation. The structure of the replies is such that the two planes of game interact in quick ricochets which evoke carefree play. Paradoxically, making a series of actions look unplanned requires the utmost in preparation. Each component of the whole must be properly timed, properly arranged. Therefore, just as in the contrast between Nijinsky on and off stage, appearance and reality have little in common. Underlying every successful work for the stage, Cocteau would argue, whether on the level of choreography, performance, or text, is a guiding mechanism that denies the premise of chance in art. Therefore, perfection in craftsmanship must be the criterion for judging the quality of an artisan.

Although Cocteau had been fascinated by machines and by the new age of technology much earlier than 1926, the word "machine" apparently did not then have the same implications that it acquired in "Le Numéro Barbette" and later in Cocteau's career. It appears that the universe to Cocteau was nothing more than a trick mechanism which deceives humanity by hiding the truth. Therefore, the plot of *La Machine infernale* is a game of the gods that Oedipus and Jocasta do not understand until they have been destroyed by it. Barbette is a woman until the audience finally sees him as a man. The structural elements of *Renaud et Armide*, *Les Parents terribles* and *L'Aigle à deux têtes* resemble components that mechanically, inevitably produce a result that could have been predicted if the forces at work had been known. What is important is that the forces are never evident, that the characters in the play occupy the same position in regard to their world as the spectators do in regard to what is happening on the stage; in each case, so many factors are hidden that the observer can grasp the truth only partially. He is, hence, a victim of illusion. In this light, *L'Impromptu du Palais Royal* emerges indeed as an appropriate summary of Cocteau's work for the theater, because the production appears completely superficial and frivolous. Yet, just as the brooch and scarf in *La Machine infernale* mocked or teased Jocasta, the dialogue of the impromptu teases the spectators (although the element of cruelty that dominated the former play is obviously lacking). Each word, like each object, presents a sort of "warning," a kind of indicator that things are not what they seem. The complexity of the whole

becomes evident only when the mask (in whatever form it may take) is removed: a masculine Barbette, the triumphant gods, and smiling actors all preclude the simple.

A definition of theater suitable for Cocteau must necessarily contain the idea of stage presentation, it must include much more than a text. Without performance, there are no games, no tricks, no interlocking networks of reality and illusion which form the essence of theater. Reading the dialogue of *L'Impromptu du Palais Royal* or an outline of Barbette's act immediately gives the secret away, and secrecy is obviously one of the premises which guide Cocteau. Only in a performance of utmost skill can the sleight of hand succeed and the guiding mechanisms remain hidden. Continuity in Cocteau's theater, then, is to be found in structure rather than in content. Whatever the subject matter of the play may be, whether the tone is light or dark, the work is nevertheless constructed in the dualistic fashion that was prefigured by *le numéro Barbette* and that has become Cocteau's trademark.

FURTHER READING

Criticism

Anderson, Alexandra, and Carol Saltus, eds. *Jean Cocteau and the French Scene.* New York: Abbeville Press Publishers, 1984, 239 p.
    Contains essays on Cocteau's works in various genres and discusses his role in intellectual circles in twentieth-century France.

Knapp, Bettina Liebowitz. *Jean Cocteau.* New York: Twayne Publishers, 1970, 179 p.
    Study of Cocteau's life and works.

Oxenhandler, Neal. *Scandal and Parade: The Theater of Jean Cocteau.* New Brunswick, NJ: Rutgers University Press, 1957, 284 p.
    Important early study of Cocteau's dramas.

Additional coverage of Cocteau's life and career is contained in the following sources published by the Gale Group: *Contemporary Authors,* Vols. 25-28; *Contemporary Authors New Revision Series,* Vol. 40; *Contemporary Authors Permanent Series,* Vol. 2; *Contemporary Literary Criticism,* Vols. 1, 8, 15, 16, 43; *Dictionary of Literary Biography,* Vol. 65; *DISCovering Authors: British Edition; DISCovering Authors: Canadian Edition; DISCovering Authors Modules: Dramatists, Most-studied Authors,* **and** *Novelists; DISCovering Authors 3.0; European Writers; Guide to French Literature, 1789 to the Present; Literature Resource Center; Major 20th-Century Writers,* Eds. 1, 2; *Reference Guide to World Literature;* **and** *World Literature Criticism.*

Peter Handke
1942-

Austrian playwright, novelist, memoirist, scriptwriter, short story writer, essayist, and poet.

INTRODUCTION

Regarded as the most important postmodern writer since Samuel Beckett, Handke has earned European literary acclaim as one of the preeminent German-language writers of his generation. Influenced by the writings of philosopher Ludwig Wittgenstein, Handke's own writings challenge the role and influence that language plays in creating one's identity, questioning the importance of language and the barriers that language creates.

BIOGRAPHICAL INFORMATION

Handke was born on December 6, 1942, in the Austrian village of Griffen. His mother, Maria, married Bruno Handke, a German army sergeant stationed in Austria, out of convenience, as Handke's biological father was married to someone else. Handke won a scholarship to a Jesuit seminary located in Tanzenberg and then transferred to a *gymnasium* (European secondary school) in Klagenfurt. He studied law from 1961 to 1965 at the University of Graz, where he became involved with the *Grazer Gruppe* (Grazer Group). In 1966, while attending a literary convention at Princeton University of the Gruppe 47, the most influential association of German writers at the time, Handke criticized the lecturers and discussions for their "empty descriptiveness." He left law school in 1966, failing to take the final exams to earn his law degree, and went to live in Germany where he married Libgart Schwarz. Also that year he created the *Sprechstücke* (speech plays), a series of five experimental plays based on the concept and power of language.

WORKS

The *Sprechstücke,* a collection of plays Handke wrote early in his career, are known for their play on the power of language and for breaking down the fourth wall between the actors and the audience. *Publikumsbeschimpfung* (1966; *Offending the Audience*) begins with rules for the actors. The actors are told to listen to the litanies of the Catholic church, watch a Beatles' films, listen to "Tell Me" by the Rolling Stones, and observe people pretending to be monkeys and spitting llamas in a zoo. Audience members hear noises from behind the curtains, see scenery being set up, and are greeted by ushers who bar them from "watching" the play because they are dressed "inappropriately." When the stage curtains are lifted, the audience meets four actors who explain to them that they, the audience, are the true actors of *Publikumsbeschimpfung*. This is followed by the four actors, or speakers, repeating themselves, contradicting themselves, and both praising and insulting members of the audience. *Weissagung* (1966; *Prophecy*) begins with a quotation from Osip Mandelstam and proceeds with a long series of prophetic figures of speech. *Selbstbezichtigung* (1966; *Self-Accusation*) is written for a male and female speaker. The actors describe their first movements, sounds, and sights as infants, and later, as they learn language, their first forays into socialization. As the actors continue on their language evolution, the audience becomes aware of how critical language is to society and to social rules. In *Hilferufe* (1967; *Calling for Help*) an unidentified speaker uses sentence fragments to convey or associate to the audience a sense of danger. The play explores the notion of the word "help". The last play of the *Sprechstücke* is *Kaspar* (1968). *Kaspar* is based on a real-life account of Kaspar Haser, who at the age of 16 was discovered in Nümberg, Germany, without the ability to speak, read, or even walk. The play focuses on the direct relationship between "words" and "things." After the *Sprechstücke*, Handke wrote *Das Mündel will Vormund sein* (1969; *My Foot My Tutor*), a play about the relationship between two characters, and the dominant/submissive roles the characters have with each other. *Quodlibet* (1970) consists of several characters from various walks of life. The characters do not communicate through complete sentences, but rather by sentence fragments. There is no plot line to the play, but rather by the sentence fragments uttered the audience pulls together a storyline for the characters. In the 1980s, Handke wrote *Über die Dörfer* (1981; *Through the Villages*), a play similar to the work of Greek playwright Aeschylus. In the play, the protagonist Gregor must decide if he should mortgage the house he owns, displacing his brother Hans who lives in the house, to finance his sister Sophie's interest in opening up a shop. In 1989 Handke wrote *Das Spiel vom Fragen oder Die Reise zum sonoren Land* (*Voyage to the Sonorous Land*; or, *The Art of Asking*) Over four hours long, the play consists of eight characters, seven who are travelling to a magical land, and the eighth character a native of this land. Russian author Anton Chekhov and Austrian author Ferdinand Raimund are two central characters in the play.

CRITICAL RECEPTION

Critics' interest in Handke's work has strengthened over time. While he is consistently praised for his evocative explorations of language, perception, and the limits of expression, some of his more experimental works, though appreciated for their ambition, have been judged overly cerebral and abstract to the point of inaccessibility. His first drama, *Offending the Audience,* not only thrilled the audiences that were the object of Handke's abuse, but also the reviewers. Praised for its attack on conventional notions of the theatre, the play has exerted a significant influence on contemporary drama. *Kaspar,* the last of Handke's *Sprechstücke,* has been cited as one of the most important works of post-World War II German literature. Even when the play's thesis—that socialization through the teaching of language robs a person of his individuality—was rejected, the drama was commended for its intellectual rigor and overall dramatic intensity. The success of *Kaspar* established Handke's international reputation and helped silence critics who questioned his qualifications after he spoke out against Gruppe 47.

PRINCIPAL WORKS

Plays

Publikumsbeschimpfung [*Offending the Audience*] 1966
Selbstbezichtigung [*Self-Accusation*] 1966
Weissagung [*Prophesy*] 1966
Hilferufe [*Calling for Help*] 1967
Kaspar 1968
Das Mündel will Vormund sein [*My Foot My Tutor*] 1969
Quodlibet 1970
Der Ritt über den Bodensee [*The Ride across Lake Constance*] 1970
Die Unvernünftigen sterben aus [*They Are Dying Out*] 1973
Über die Dörfer [*Through the Villages*] 1981
Das Spiel vom Fragen oder Die Reise zum sonoren Land [*Voyage to the Sonorous Land, or, The Art of Asking*] 1990
Die Stunde da wir nichts voneinander der wußten: Ein Schauspiel [*The Hour We Knew Nothing of Each Other*] 1992
Die Theaterstücke 1992
Zuruestungen für die Unsterblichkeit: Ein Koenigsdrama 1997
Die Fahrt im Einbaum oder Das Stuck zum Film vom Krieg [*The Canoe Trip or the Play of the Film of the War*] 1999

Other Major Works

Die Hornissen [*The Hornets*] (novel) 1966
Begrüssung des Aufsichtrats: Prosatexte (short stories) 1967
Der Hausierer [*The Peddler*] (novel) 1967
Die Innenwelt der Auenwelt der Innenwelt [*The Innerworld of the Outerworld of the Innerworld*] (poetry) 1969
Die Angst des Tormanns beim Elfmeter: Erzählung [*The Goalie's Anxiety at the Penalty Kick*] (novel) 1970
Ich bin ein Bewohner des Elfenbeinturms (essays) 1972
Der kurze Brief zum langen Abschied [*Short Letter, Long Farewell*] (novel) 1972
Wunschloses Unglück: Erzählung [*A Sorrow Beyond Dreams*] (memoir) 1972
Als das Wünschen noch geholfen hat [*Nonsense and Happiness*] (poetry and essays) 1974
Die Stunde der wahren Empfindung [*A Moment of True Feeling*] (novel) 1975
Das Ende des Fanlierens: Gedichte Aufsätze, Reden Rezensionern (essays, poetry, and speeches) 1976
Die Linkshändige Frau: Erzählung [*The Left-Handed Woman*] (novel) 1976
Das Gewicht der Welt: Ein Journal [*The Weight of the World*] (journal) 1977
Langsame Heimkehr: Erzählung [*The Long Way Around*] (novel) 1979

Die Lehre der Sainte-Victoire [The Lesson of Sainte Victoire] (novel) 1980
Kindergeschichte [Child Story] (novel) 1981
Über die Dörfer: Dramatisches Gedicht (poem) 1981
Die Geschichte des Bleistifts (journals) 1982
Der Chinese des Schmerzes [Across] (novel) 1983
Phantasien der Wiederholung (journals) 1983
Slow Homecoming [contains *The Long Way Around, The Lesson of Sainte Victoire,* and *Child Story*] (novels) 1983
Gedicht an die Dauer (poetry) 1986
Die Wiederholung [Repetition] (novel) 1986
Die Abwesenheit: Ein Märchen [Absence] (novel) 1987
Der Himmel über Berlin: Ein Filmbuch [with Wim Wenders; released in English as *Wings of Desire,* 1988] (screenplay) 1987
Nachmittag eines Schriftstellers: Erzählung [The Afternoon of a Writer] (novel) 1987
Versuch über die Müdigkeit (essays) 1989
Noch einmal für Thukydides [Once Again for Thucydides] (sketches) 1990
Versuch über die Jukebox (essays) 1990
Versuch über den geglückten Tag: Ein Wintertagtraum (essays) 1991
Die Absesenheit (screenplay) 1992
Langsam im Schatten (essays, speeches, and criticism) 1992
The Jukebox and Other Essays on Storytelling [includes English-translations of *Versuch über die Müdigkeit, Versuch über die Jukebox,* and *Versuch über den geglückten Tag*] (essays) 1994
Mein Jahr in der Niemandsbucht: Ein Märchen aus den neuen Zeiten [My Year in the No-Man's Bay] (novel) 1994
Eine winterliche Reise zu den Flüssen Donau, Save, Morawa und Drina, oder, Gerechtigkeit für Serbien [A Journey to the Rivers: Justice for Serbia] (nonfiction) 1996
Sommerlicher Nachtrag zu einer winterlichen Reise (nonfiction) 1997
In einer dunklen Nacht ging ich aus meinem stillen Haus (novel) 1998

*These plays comprise the collection *Sprechstücke.*

GENERAL COMMENTARY

Richard Arthur Firda (essay date 1993)

SOURCE: Firda, Richard Arthur. "Theatrical Experiments." In *Peter Handke,* pp. 13-40. New York: Twayne Publishers, 1993.

[*In the following essay, Firda examines the techniques Handke uses to explore language in his plays.*]

EARLY THEATER, 1966-1967

Though Peter Handke had published an experimental novel, *Die Hornissen,* in 1966, it was the premiere of his first play, *Publikumsbeschimpfung,* in that same year that

established his name as an innovator in modern German theater.[1] *Publikumsbeschimpfung,* first performed on 8 June 1966 at the leftist-oriented Theater am Turm in Frankfurt under the direction of Claus Peymann, is the first work in a collection of *Sprechstücke* (Language plays). The German word *Sprechstücke* recalls the focus in a language play on words, sentences, and language as primary reasons for writing and viewing a play.[2] The underlying experience for the viewer-reader becomes clear only as he or she confronts the play on the stage or reads it as a printed text. Jerome Klinkowitz and Jerome Knowlton note that "linguistic deconstruction" in this play (as in other *Sprechstücke*) creates a sense of radical familiarity, and that in Handke's subsequent language plays, "a fully formed yet nonillusionistic world is being made on stage" (107). There is little here to which the audience can relate from concrete experience. Other *Sprechstücke* written by Handke from 1964 to 1967 are *Die Weissagung* (1966; *Prophecy*), *Selbstbezichtigung* (1966; *Self-Accusation*), and *Hilferufe* (1967; *Calling for Help*).[3]

In *Publikumsbeschimpfung,* as in the other language plays, Handke is preoccupied with nothing less than a total renewal of German and European contemporary theatrical conventions. His language plays depart from traditional theatrical components of theme, plot, character, and structure. They do not relate to those models of antitheater found in Samuel Beckett's *Waiting for Godot* (1955) or even the parody of surrealism in Eugène Ionesco's *The Bald Soprano.* Nor do Handke's language pieces use Bertolt Brecht's concept of *Verfremdung* (alienation) as a basis for the audience's assessment of reality and political change. Never entirely political in a programmatic way, as Brecht is in *St. Joan of the Stockyards* (1929-30) or even *Mother Courage* (1941), Handke regards his language pieces as "prologues" to drama.[4] In *Publikumsbeschimpfung,* for example, his actors make a point of telling the spectators that the play is only a prologue (*Vorrede*) to what they did in the past and are doing in the present. The audience itself is the topic of the play (*Publikumsbeschimpfung,* 42).

The language plays are short works and reveal Handke's debt to the Austrian post-World War II language and literary renewal associated with Vienna and Graz.[5] He was a follower in his early work of Ludwig Wittgenstein, the linguist-philosopher, and as one of the earliest figures of the Austrian literary scene centered at Graz University in the 1960s, Handke subscribed to the idea that the writer should "manipulate" linguistic structures and in that process reveal the social mores and behavior that govern language consciousness. The *Sprechstücke* question whether theater, any theater, can replicate the reality of the outside world. Handke's answer in the language plays, as well as in his later plays is a resounding "no," since the believes that in drama language is basically an artificial linguistic construct. Further, language and truth in theater must be constructed anew for each play and each performance, so a playwright's claim to reality is a false one. The average theatergoer, Handke asserts, fails to grasp the "lies" of the theater. Hence Handke's startling position that if the theater teaches us anything, its lessons relate to the mendacity of language and the underlying social institutions that govern it. Incorporated into these institutions is society's untrue assumption that drama and theater can be guides to a higher morality. It is interesting that Handke would reject such idealistic tragic dramatists as Goethe, Friedrich von Schiller, Jean Racine, and Pierre Corneille. For Handke, theater only creates language awareness of the present, with the subsequent social awareness. The viewer has no choice but to question traditional modes of language and social thinking as reflected in the art of the past (Hays, 351).

PUBLIKUMSBESCHIMPFUNG

The German director Claus Peymann relates that in the spring of 1966 he was asked to read the script of a work that turned out to be Handke's *Publikumsbeschimpfung*.[6] Peymann admits that both he and his actors at the Frankfurt Theater am Turm were at first skeptical that the play was the right vehicle for his company. They questioned Handke's commitment to leftist revisionist art. The manager of the Suhrkamp Theater Book Company, Karl-Heinz Braun, had been enthusiastic, however, in his support for Handke's play, despite its previous rejection by other German regional and national theaters. The producers and artistic directors of those theaters were not amused by the prospect of mounting a play that promised to offend its audience. Only when the supporters of Experimenta I, the experimental theater project in Frankfurt, came through with a guarantee of funding did Handke's first play get both a hearing and a staging. Peymann concludes sardonically that his company's production turned out to be the theatrical event of the year.

The opening night's German audience was first treated to a clever argument against conventional theater. Four performers attack the audience about the nature of theatergoing. Theater tradition and theater as a private fantasy symbolizing existence are two of the several themes found in the lines directed against the viewers. The actors do not exempt themselves from this criticism.

This "assault" is accomplished by literally reversing the traditional roles of actors and audience. In a one-sided confrontation, the audience is lectured on its naïveté and credulity—that is, its presuppositions about the esthetics and reality of drama are challenged at every step, placed under "review" and "correction." Handke's primary goal is to bring the audience around to his theory that an involved audience has a fundamental role in the coding and decoding of meaning in the theater. If the meaning of Handke's play is found in its language and audience consciousness, then his words at the end of the play are an important component of the lesson for the audience about the meaning or nonmeaning of words themselves. At this point the four figures announce that the audience will be offended and that offensive language is a means of communication. Communication of this kind is direct and vital. Barriers are broken (*Publikumsbeschimpfung*, 44).

The audience is addressed as "thoroughbred actors," "cardiac conditions," "potential dead," and "sadsacks." The theatrical wall being torn down is, of course, the wall of trite words that prevents direct emotional contact and perceptive understanding between actors and audience in conventional theater. The tirade of offending words with which Handke concludes his play, however, is not an arbitrary compilation of insults directed by the playwright against a particular audience. These words are intended as examples of banal and stereotypical language. Their use in the play betrays their banality. Their meanings emerge in an acoustical pattern, and this pattern of sounds, for which Handke has definite instructions, seems to be of more interest than the invective and insult of the words. If the language of this tirade can be misunderstood at first by the audience as street language, it is also unmasked by Handke as the meaningless language of conventional theater, for it is in a play that we first hear them. The listener is tempted to use his or her own experience in decoding their apparent references to recent political German history and allusions to Nazi rhetoric, leftist diatribes, and right-wing propaganda. In a 1970 interview Handke warned that the words in *Publikumsbeschimpfung* are in the nature of artifice and dramaturgy, that his point was to use words to "encircle the audience, so that they would want to free themselves. . . . What is said does not really matter. I reduced the play to words because my words are not descriptions, only quotations."[7]

The insults are least effective in giving the appearance of reality, one engendered from the facts of history, religion, and politics. That the words stand out so strongly for the viewer, however, is the result of Handke's deliberately austere dramatic technique of reducing his play to the essentials. *Publikumsbeschimpfung* has no plot, characterization, or scenes. There are only words whose sounds do not refer to anything seen on the stage. The audience is forced to rely upon those words and their underlying falseness in the tirade. Handke is here close to Brecht in the goal of renewing audience consciousness, yet there is an essential difference between the two dramatists—namely, that while Brecht's theater calls finally for political change, Handke's makes the audience aware that theater is a catalyst for insight into language awareness brought about by deliberate artifice created by the dramatist himself.

DIE WEISSAGUNG

Die Weissagung (*Prophecy*), another language piece, was actualy written in 1964, a year earlier than *Publikumsbeschimpfung*.[8] Four months after the 1966 premiere of his first play, however, *Weissagung* and *Selbstbezichtigung* were given a joint performance by the Städtische Bühne in Oberhausen, Germany, presumably because his first play had demonstrated the popularity of their author. His success came about despite the reservations of many German theatrical critics about Handke's future in the theater. They resented the sensationalism surrounding his name and recalled the arrogance with which he spoke out against Group 47 at that group's meeting on the Princeton campus in 1966. Handke was accused of staging his press conferences and of having written an unreadable novel (*Der Hausierer*). Handke, these critics proclaimed, would never be accepted by the fussy, well-educated German theatergoing public. Time itself has shown that early critics of Handke seriously underestimated both his originality and his talent.

In a short note to *Weissagung,* Handke says that of all his language pieces this one is the most formalistic, that the viewer is directed toward language in a way that shows "every sentence is meaningless in the sense that this sentence is independent of any other. *Weissagung* has no meaning, neither a deep one nor any other. . . . I strove only for a density of sound" (*Weissagung,* 204). Despite Handke's denial of any meaning in *Weissagung,* a viewer will persist in searching for meaning in the work, if only from curiosity about the nature of Handke's theater.

Weissagung consists of sentences that, in their totality, are actually listings or predictions about the future read by several speakers. These prophecies, the listener soon finds out, are predictions bound to be true: nothingness will become nothing, as rain will turn into rain. Handke's tone in the play is apocalyptic, owing to the abundance of biblical imagery: the inevitability of disease, the fires of Hell, people dying, bombs crashing, and the Last Judgment. *Weissagung,* however, offers another source of interest. As a language piece it emerges as a "presentation of metaphors" that purport to describe reality, yet these metaphors mean nothing, as Handke has noted, since the reality to which they refer lacks any definite reference to the truth. Examples of this technique, so common in the text, are the references to the conduct of "average citizens" and the sound of cut trees. Shoes fit the feet for which they were made. The solemn recital of the lines themselves, recited by the speakers out of context, is intended to contrast with audience expectations.

It has been suggested by Schlueter that the listings of prophecies are metaphors of obvious and trite comparisons, whose originality and meaning have long vanished through overuse and familiarity (1981, 28-29). The author has complained about the necessity of making odious comparisons or parallels, for example, between moviegoing and theatergoing, a language choice that he regards as impossible or meaningless, as it is for using banal metaphors in literature.[9] Schlueter has noted that the "prophecy" of Handke's play is actually his fear that the world of reality, found in the underlying meanings of words, will drown in language nausea, the consequence of surrendering oneself to meaningless words and sentences while doing the world's business (1981, 30). This might occur in a future world of words, pointless metaphors and observations portraying a primary intention of Handke's play. *Weissagung,* as another language play, is related to his goal of examining the bases of linguistic structure found in his other early plays, but it restricts itself to a unique examination of the ways in which people alienate themselves from language through hollow metaphors and word comparisons.

Selbstbezichtigung

While Handke's first play focuses on the renewal of theater and audience expectations in that theater, and *Weissagung* on the abuse of language through trivial metaphors, *Selbstbezichtigung* is concerned with the castigation of the self through interiorized domination (Nägele, 331). In this work, often considered a prelude to *Kaspar* (1967), Handke's first full-length play, two speakers alternately recite a list of crimes, sins, and transgressions committed by an "I" against society. This "I" is not a specific individual but a generalized, grammatical identification related to man as a whole. The transgressions "committed" and "confessed" fit the general code of social expectations. A development in time is followed and, as Hern has noted, "the piece falls into three sections of two to three pages each, followed by a final section of some thirteen pages. The first section, consisting of the first thirteen paragraphs, begins with the statement: 'I came into the world.' . . . 'I' as 'I' tells how 'I' was born and then proceeds to recount . . . the various stages of growth to full possession, awareness and enjoyment of the most important of the faculties of mind and body" (45).

Selbstbezichtigung emphasizes that forms of speech and, by extension, the social forms they engender are of paramount importance. Each of the work's four sections follows the "I" through a progression from birth to growth, rules, and language indoctrination between the individual and society—the last item showing Handke in a confessional scenario as he goes through the gestures of "asking forgiveness" from the audience for putting them through the regimen of listening to the play itself.

In an early German staging of *Selbstbezichtigung,* a male and a female presented the accusations and self-criticism in the style of medieval religious ritual. At a Frankfurt performance two actors were nude onstage, with only simple masks on their faces. The nudity was not intended to be sensationalistic but to emphasize the open admission of "sins" before the audience, who were confronted with an unadorned stage and an open curtain (Peymann, 50). This play, like Handke's other language pieces, offers no stage barriers between actors and audience.

Hern has written perceptively on the ending of the play: he notes that the work moves from an attitude of penitence to one of proud individuality—"I went to the theater. I heard this piece. I spoke this piece. I wrote this piece" (*Selbstbezichtigung,* 72). This final tone, Hern says, reflects the speaker's realization that "the original sin referred to so often in the piece itself is hardly the Christian doctrine; it is the original sin borne by every individual in his preordained inability to live within the dictates of society" (49).

If this interpretation has merit, as I think it does, then the real achievement of the play lies, as Hern says further, in Handke's having rendered the familiar theme of the individual versus society on a level of abstraction and universality that is new and original (50). In contrast to the traditional devices of characterization and fable that Brecht relies on to make his point about the need for social change, the featureless context of Handke's "I," according to Hern, is an abstract residue of a rebellion carried out, with ironical overtones. The "I" uses words and phrases with the awareness that written and spoken language lead paradoxically to penitence and concomitant confession before the "authority" of social rule and convention.

Nägele has suggested that the work deviates from the pattern of the Catholic confessional. While it is true that Handke's early training at a Catholic school was a pivotal influence on the confessional aspects of the work, and that in the play offenses against the rules of society and language are recited to an unseen authority with the power to punish the transgressor, the petitioner is never named specifically (Nägele, 331). Handke thus reminds the viewer and the reader that the play is not intended to be the confession of a single individual, and that the German title for the play, *Selbstbezichtigung,* has no definite article before it. The title refers to a general confession of sins, for which anyone might be culpable, especially the audience itself. More important, perhaps, is that in *Selbstbezichtigung* the viewer is forced to become an observer of himself in the sense that what he observes during the confession of the "I" is a mirrored image. The viewer is expected finally to realize that his identity is defined through the image of the other (society).

Hilferufe

Hilferufe (*Calling for Help*), the last of the language pieces, was premiered in 1967 in Stockholm under the direction of Günther Böch with a troupe of actors from the Oberhausen Städtische Bühne. The play lasts about 10 minutes (compared with 35 minutes for the other *Sprechstücke*) and is thus dependent on a good stage performance, for it has even less overt substance than the other language pieces.[10] Despite its brevity, Handke has written detailed instructions for the performers and given some insight into its meaning (*Hilferufe,* 91-92). *Hilferufe* wishes to show the way, by words and sentences and guesses, to the sought-after word *help*. Speakers in the piece first play out the game of a need for the word *help* to their listeners onstage, in a setting devoid of any real need of help. They ask whether the sought-after word *help* might be found in newspaper language, in lines from government regulations, or in everyday German. Other inquiries cite language from school lectures, grammar books, breakfast items, and street noises. The speakers ask their questions out of context and without their usual meaning, yet with the hope that the listeners will respond with a "yes" rather than a loud "no." In the interchange between speakers and listeners, sound is important: "As always, Handke instructs his actors to use words as they would use them in a soccer chant, for acoustic effect rather than for meaning. Aid is not summoned; rather, the speakers create an ovation to the word 'help' and in so doing teach the audience a most compelling lesson in language" (Klinkowitz and Knowlton, 117).

Handke, however, has pointed out that once the speakers have guessed the word *help,* they no longer need the word itself. As soon as the speakers get the word, that word has lost its meaning. Linguistically the play is directed toward abstracting the word *help* from its usual meaning and showing that this process of abstraction terminates when *help* becomes a "pure" word in and of itself, devoid of any concrete reference. This process of abstraction, Handke shows us, is reflected in the listeners' refusal to guess and in the audience's perception that the game onstage is an artifice, since everything offered is only another guess in an apparent game.

Since both audience and speakers prefer a game of useless words, *Hilferufe* offers, through linguistic deconstruction, a pile of words that either contain no meaning whatever or can be stripped of that meaning. The banal chains of words preceding the correct guess of "help"—"one-way street," "insect repellent," "twenty-five cent towels"—all relate to media and "public" language. As Nägele points out, the word *help* and the German title of the play, *Hilferufe,* relate not only to the word game that is the ostensible activity onstage between speakers and listeners; the plea for help reflects back to the writer Handke in his continual search for words and phrases (332). For Handke, *Hilferufe* is a model search for new literary methods and strategies. Writing plays for the stage and novels for the reading public is a linguistic process akin to that found in *Hilferufe.* "Finding" the right word, for Handke, shows ideally the end of a successful search by the author himself.

Further Technical Experimentation, 1968-1974

Kaspar was Handke's first full-length play.[11] It was premiered in Frankfurt and at the Städtische Bühne in Oberhausen at the same time, 11 May 1968, when the West German government was trying to implement its "emergency law" (Peymann, 51). It was a period of political protest by leftist students in both France and Germany. According to Peymann, actors from the Frankfurt troupe rehearsing *Kaspar* were political activists. As a result of the social turmoil, German audience and critical reaction to *Kaspar* was, to some extent, influenced by exterior events and by the author himself. Like the earlier *Sprechstücke,* however, *Kaspar* eschews overt political commentary and shows technical and thematic continuity with Handke's ongoing examination of linguistic and language process.[12]

Kaspar reconstructs the steps by which an "alien figure," Kaspar, is brought into a world structured by language. Movements and gestures are pertinent technical devices in the play, foreshadowing their subsequent use by Handke in later works. The drama critic Günther Rühle noted the mutual activity of language and movement in the play: "Movement appears before language, but it is language that makes movement comprehensible."[13] The text of *Kaspar* is 65 paragraphs divided into two sets of parallel texts with Handke's commentary on stage directions. Actors' lines are often spoken in tandem with each other. Handke punctuates divisions in the play by changes in lighting or blackouts, the latter being the equivalent of scene changes in conventional dramatic structure. The stage setting and props for *Kaspar* are intentionally "theatrical": their inter-relationship does not correspond to their usual arrangement in reality. This is a clue to Handke's audience that *Kaspar* is only a theatrical event and not a "slice" of exterior reality (*Kaspar*, 104-5).

Handke derived the inspiration for the central character from a historical incident: the discovery in 1828 of a child, Kaspar Hauser, in the city of Nuremberg. Hauser's origins, along with his incarceration, had deprived him of human contact and prevented him from learning to speak. His extraordinary background became the focus of several European commentaries, many of them speculative and romantic in temper.[14] For some of these writers, Hauser was a "model" figure and a victim of social injustice; they lamented his fate in a world of burgeoning industrialization. German novelists and poets, such as Jakob Wasserman, Georg Trakl, and Hans Arp, contributed in their writing to the myth of Kaspar Hauser. Feature films on related figures were made by the German director Werner Herzog (*Every Man for Himself and God against All* [1975]) and the French director François Truffaut (*The Wild Child* [1969]).

Handke's play pares away the "story" behind the prehistory and subsequent discovery of a "noble savage." Handke's character, whom he calls only Kaspar, is an abstracted and theatricalized figure brought to "birth" onstage in phases from behind drawn stage curtains (*Kaspar*, 107). Handke notes that Kaspar is not a clownlike figure but is analogous to a movie monster (*Kaspar*, 104). His instructions thus emphasize the artificiality of Kaspar's character; they render Kaspar an object of Handke's analysis and show how a "man" is bound to language and the learning process of that language. In an interview with Arthur Joseph, Handke has indicated other reasons for writing the play: "Kaspar fascinated me from the start. . . . For me this was a model of conduct, building a person into a society's course of conduct by language, by giving him words to repeat. To enable him somehow to get along in life, to function, he is reconstructed by voices, by language models, and instruction regarding the objects on stage" (Joseph, 60).

As a model of language acquisition, Handke's play is intended to show what can be done to someone used by society in its role as a manipulative teacher of language. The starting point for this "instruction" is Kaspar's one line, "I want to be a person like somebody else once was" (*Kaspar*, 118). This abstract sentence, changed by Handke intentionally from Kaspar Hauser's original statement that he wished he could "be a horseman like my father was once," is the center of Kaspar's language education by the *Einsager* (prompters), who appear onstage as voices early on, at the first sign that Kaspar's sentence will fail to mediate between himself and things around him (Hern,

63). The prompters thus give him the words for chair, table, and broom (*Kaspar*, 76-77). He is praised by the prompters for his sentence, yet they disavow the limitations of that sentence itself. As the prompters begin to speak, they help Kaspar begin making sentences and allude to the safety and comfort of words that relate "specifically" and directly to objects. It is apparent that the prompters become not only Kaspar's impersonalized teachers, they also symbolize their advocacy of the social order achieved by language control.

At a central point in the play Kaspar is rendered silent by the "dismantling" of his one sentence and the overwhelming profusion of new words. This silence is intended to indicate the first phase of Kaspar's indoctrination into language making, a necessary correlative and a prelude to the second step of starting to speak independently (Hern, 63). Kaspar is taught by the prompters to use the right sentences and words, the correct language models that help an orderly individual to make his way in life. In addition to delineating the linguistic and social relationships between language and order, the play also reveals the underlying affinity between order and space. Tables and chairs that were earlier thrown about on the stage are now rearranged by Kaspar into an acceptable way of perceiving objects. He thus becomes an individual learning to learn order. The prompters next teach Kaspar that words and sentence composition are a viable means of entry into the safe world of "perfect" human beings and the ultimate key to social responsibility. Social responsibility, through an orderly use and perception of language and objects, is also found, according to the prompters, in short, simple sentences with no questions.

The final parts of the play continue the "training" and "reeducation" of Kaspar into the submissive and schizophrenic world of word and object relationships. Here Handke expresses Kaspar's apotheosis as a social conformist with the appearance onstage of similar, masked Kaspar-like figures, a throng of nonsensical, mimetic characters who vacillate between sense and nonsense (*Kaspar*, 103). These figures portend the eventual collapse of Kaspar's previous personality, which, despite its primitive nature, was still of one piece. The new Kaspars ridicule words, make noise, and scorn objects. One of them, in a cunning rendering of Kaspar's original sentence that he would like to be "as someone once was," reverses this line to state that he now desires to join the "crowd." If Kaspar is thus exposed to the gift of language expressibility, he is also exposed to "a greater terror, a realization of the painful inability of language and reality to achieve the perfect union of Kaspar's earlier world" (Schlueter 1980, 29). Kaspar's final predicament, the catalyst that precipitates his fall into "madness," is his realization, achieved through language education, that there is only a tentative and ambiguous connection between a word and its referent. Language learning, Handke says in the play, ultimately reflects the idiocy of language and the language process. Society in general is a willing accomplice in this process, though Handke denies any reference to or criticism of a particular society or culture. To this end, he has said, "In *Kaspar* I criticize no concrete social model, capitalist or socialist. Instead [of] abstracting from modes of speech their basic grammatical elements, I point out the present forms of linguistic alienation. . . . To put it succinctly, in *Kaspar,* history is conceived as a story of sentences" (Joseph, 61).

Indeed, *Kaspar* is an anarchic play only within the framework of what it states about language negation, not of what it implies about politics or political reform. Handke has expressed his nausea at stupid speechification and its resulting brutalization of people. A pertinent artistic realization in *Kaspar* for viewers and readers is Handke's meticulous insight into the relativity and shifting nature of language and phenomena, as separated from a fixed political context. The language "schizophrenia" of *Kaspar* is related to a use of language as "sense," where language is intended as an instrument of power and control, and as "nonsense," where language is the lesser of two evils. *Kaspar* alludes finally to the underlying, hidden, destructive qualities of words and language, especially the corollary that whoever controls thought controls language, too. Vigilance is required when the limits of language are set by the "wrong people," symbolized by the prompters in *Kaspar.* For Handke, the prompters might be any representatives or advocates of a fixed, deterministic social or political system and of the language with which it is identified.[15]

DAS MÜNDEL WILL VORMUND SEIN

The titles of Handke's next two plays, *Das Mündel will Vormund sein* (1969; *My Foot My Tutor*) and *Quodlibet* (1970; Whatever you say; feel free) bring forth unexpected allusions to Shakespeare's theater.[16] *Mündel's* title comes from *The Tempest,* where Prospero rebukes Miranda with the words, "What, I say, my foot my tutor!" (I.ii), indicating his astonishment that a subordinate should hint of a change in the status of master and servant. *Quodlibet's* Shakespearean "borrowing" comes from the allusion to *As You Like It* in its title, which is Handke's teasing invitation to take *Quodlibet's* half-heard and partially understood words and sentences as facts. Yet the audience must work as hard in decoding the meaning of both *Mündel* and *Quodlibet* as it does with the *Sprechstücke,* which, in contrast to these two pieces, are entirely language-oriented in their dramatic structure.

Both *Mündel* and *Quodlibet* signal vital shifts in Handke's everchanging conception of dramatic theory and language practice.[17] These plays stand technically at an intermediate point in the development of Handke's theater and are among those plays in which "gesture" and "movement" are broadly assimilated into the playwright's dramatic technique. In this sense, the gestic language of *Mündel* and *Quodlibet* anticipates the skillful inclusion of speech as gesture in Handke's second long play, *Der Ritt über den Bodensee* (1972).

Thematically, *Mündel* is allied to *Kaspar*'s message of language as power and control. The play is thus another *Kaspar* in that it is one of Handke's abstract lessons in the politics of submission and dominance. The final outcome in *Kaspar,* one recalls, is a natural consequence of language learning and the articulation of human speech. In *Mündel,* however, Handke has chosen to "articulate" the politics of social dominance in a play without words. The text's theatrical environment is characterized by gestures, sound, and movement. Any meaning that *Mündel* has for the spectator lies not only in his or her skill at "reading" gestures and movement as speech; it lies, too, in a keen sense of visual acuity. As a silent or wordless play, *Mündel* isolates human interchange from any semblance of linguistic or narrative reality. Borrowing a clue from Beckett, Handke's behavioral forms emerge as the main claim on spectator attention: Who is doing "what," and "how" is he doing it? As in Beckett, gesture and movement define character, but most important, Handke's technique in *Mündel* forces the viewer to conclude that the postures of the theatrical stage are identical to those of daily life.[18] The representation of theatrical poses is, among other things, an attempt to present the modes of everyday behavior as poses, too. Carl Weber, who has directed Handke's theater, says that Handke, who has never claimed to replicate reality, nonetheless indicates that theater "has derived its images and conventions from the games played by society, which foots the theater's bill."[19] In Handke's *Mündel* eating food, moving a chair, and tearing paper are simple gestic acts, but they evoke models from the structure of social behavior, even as they might be estranged from general human experience.

Mündel was first performed 31 January 1969 in Frankfurt's Theater am Turm, under the direction of Claus Peymann. It consists of 10 short scenes with very detailed and meticulous directions from the playwright throughout. The opening of the piece, for example, specifies the scenery: the "artistic" (false) facade of a farmhouse with birds flying above fields. In front of the house the audience sees an unidentified object, while next to the reproduction of a farm door a block of wood has a hatchet in it (*Mündel,* 9). There are two characters, a ward (Mündel) and a warden (Vormund), who function as a servant and a master, respectively. Their movements range in the opening scene from the bucolic to the menacing. The warden appears in front of the house and begins to stare at the ward. But the ward only eats his apple, ignoring the warden. Both the staring and the gesture of eating are intentionally drawn out (*Mündel,* 12). The play endeavors to mirror power relationships and through movements and gestures shows the control it is possible to maintain over a person without using words. Seemingly innocent activity, such as the ward's eating an apple, is stopped through the act of "staring down," or "ocular assault," by the warden (Calandra, 35). In *Mündel* trivial activities and gestures abound with the force of spoken and printed words, although a unified meaning linking each scene is elusive. During the second scene, for example, the warden demonstrates his authority over the ward through reading and folding a newspaper at a table. In the fourth scene the warden fills a water kettle with a hose as the ward grinds coffee. At the beginning of a new scene one hears a loud breathing that, at times, is like the breathing of a cornered animal (*Mündel,* 36). Several scenes in the piece can be interpreted as signs of either revolt or submission from the ward: namely, when he throws burrs at the warden's back, or when he stands still as the warden throws bottles, plates, and glasses at him. The conclusion of *Mündel* returns to the farmhouse exterior glimpsed by the audience at the beginning of the play. Now we witness the unveiling of an object, a turnip-chopping machine; the warden provides the ward with instructions in how to use it. Since the previous scenes have been filled with indications of revolt on the one hand and intimidation on the other, what ensues is suspenseful and ambiguous. On the darkening stage we search for a last glimpse of the warden beside the ward. The stage becomes quiet. The viewer does not learn what happens to the warden—he might be dead—after the ward begins to use the machine. In a final moment, the ward, who turns out to be the survivor of this last encounter, is viewed pouring sand into a tub filled with water. He embodies despair and archetypal subservience. June Schlueter offers a convincing interpretation of this final scene when she says that "one thinks of the metaphorical sands of time, recalling the earlier scenes where pages are torn [by the ward] from a calendar, also of Beckett's repeated symbolic use of sand" (1981, 54).

The timelessness symbolized by this final gesture can support the reading of *Mündel* as a political parable, as Hern suggests, or even as a "bleak allegory" of intimidation in the perpetual struggle between one man and another (Hern, 81). German leftist students of the 1960s, furious at having to witness another example of Handke's "dead" theater (a theater of no overt political complaint or ideology), missed the point of Handke's experiment in nonverbal communication. *Mündel* is not only a legitimate exploration of behavioral patterns in the interaction of individuals, it also demonstrates that "the way in which experience is ordered, the way in which daily activities are presented and supervised, defines much of the view we have of ourselves and our relation to the world" (Hays, 358). Handke says that what people do to one another can be found in the multiple and experiential levels of gesture, movement, and sound of which *Mündel* consists. Deprived of dialogue and speech, the spectator is forced to become a primary viewer, confronting images that define surface realities in novel ways to reinterpret the human condition from the entrapment of verbal communication.

QUODLIBET

Handke next explored posture as a theatrical device in *Quodlibet,* a short play that premiered in Basel on 24 January 1970, under the direction of Hans Hollmann.[20] In this play Handke demonstrates his continued evolution as an experimental dramatist, challenging his audience to leave the realm of the familiar and the ordinary. For example, *Quodlibet* adapts the principle of auditory hallucination to theater—a borrowing, perhaps, from Handke's earlier play *Selbstbezichtigung.* In *Quodlibet* 10 costumed characters appear on the stage; among them, a

general, a bishop, a university administrator, a politician, and several women. They are all from the upper levels of society, and they step forward in their own order and inclination. Viewed by Handke as figures of speech, not actors playing the roles of specific characters, they relate to the grammatical forms of language (*Quodlibet,* 157). Their gestures and movements, in fact, relate to the visual and kinetic element of language that endeavors to make its way through the half-heard and misunderstood words coming from the spoken text. The audience hears sundry questions and answers, conversation, allusions, jokes and stories, and euphemisms. The actors, Handke notes in prefatory instructions to the play, are free to talk about what they have read or experienced, or about what they wish to do in the future (*Quodlibet,* 42). The actors use some words that the audience will understand. These are placed among those words the audience merely thinks it understands. Handke's intent, however, is to have the half-heard or barely understood word intentionally agitate and upset the listening audience. This scheme is a part of the esthetic context of the play.

Michael Roloff's English translation of *Quodlibet* is very successful in rendering "content" from Handke's German text. Roloff states that "more than any of Handke's plays to date, *Quodlibet* requires fairly extensive adaptation to an American linguistic, cultural, and historical environment."[21] "No palms" can be misheard by Americans as "napalm," "hero sandwich" as "Hiroshima," "bicycle path" as "psychopath," "hit" as "two-run hit." Handke has conceived the play as a "single living movement of speech" and, as such, a "theatrical ornament" that is "bound" to elements of everyday linguistic reality (*Quodlibet,* 157). Calandra notes, "In some respects, *Quodlibet* is like an abstraction of all those half-heard and hardly understood scraps of small talk which form the basis of Chekhov's theater, a tapestry of Chekhovian murmur" (57).

After stripping these characters of their history and psychology, Handke indicates that only the patterns of talk remain, set within the gestures and movements so visible on the stage. Though conveying the ambiguity of perceived linguistic reality is the ultimate goal theatrically in *Quodlibet*—and the audience is indeed free to do whatever it likes—the sundry meanings assigned by the spectators to the stream of words and phrases are in fact emotionally determined by pity, tenderness, sympathy, and fury. What the audience "hears," however, relies greatly on its cultural sophistication and perceptive acuity.[22] Some allusions and stories can truly remain meaningless and irrelevant for a viewer in a different realm of auditory and cultural accessibility. An untutored mind, as Schlueter connotes, may in truth "hear" nothing at all (1981, 61). For such a viewer, *Quodlibet* remains only an ambitious technical piece and not a consciousness-raising play working in tandem with the forces of language itself.

DER RITT ÜBER DEN BODENSEE

Handke's 1970 play *Der Ritt über den Bodensee (The Ride across Lake Constance),* a longer work, shows structural and thematic affinities with *Mündel* and *Quodlibet*.[23] Like *Mündel*, *Bodensee* is highly dependent on the viewer's perception of the underlying connections between normative and theatrical patterns of everyday behavior. In *Bodensee* gestures are as controlled as words, but the relationship in meaning between the two is one of the least obvious aspects of the text. As in *Quodlibet*, language in *Bodensee* exists in the context of semiconsciousness, moving in the direction of language forms rather than language meaning.[24] The face of "realism" gleaned from the sets of the opening scenes of *Bodensee* is no less deliberately artistic than the stylized and formalized shape of the stage settings Handke requires for *Mündel*. In both *Mündel* and *Bodensee* the stage is a place for theatrical demonstration, an area for showing and teaching. Stage movement in *Bodensee*, like that in *Mündel*, is purposely intended to occur in an unidentifiable space with no claim to outer reality. The theatrical space of *Bodensee* lies within a dream or a nightmare of the mind—or, as Hern has stated, in the "abyss, this innermost world beneath a thin veneer of normality, that opens up beneath our feet when we take *The Ride across Lake Constance*" (94).[25]

Critics of Handke's language plays have noted that these earlier pieces, despite their singular emphasis on language, nevertheless contain an underlying core of "social specificity" in that language structure is related to forms derived from a mediating society: for example, the idea of language as thought control in *Kaspar*, the institutionalization of ideologies in *Selbsbezichtigung*, and the rejection of traditional theatrical esthetics in *Publikumsbeschimpfung*. Yet, as Claus Peymann has indicated, *Bodensee* "makes the theatre its exclusive theme . . . the play's characters are actors, aging stars" (53). Peymann, who directed the first German version of *Bodensee* on 23 January 1971 at the Schaubühne am Halleschen Ufer in Berlin, relates further that, at first, his group of politically conscious actors were hesitant to take on the play "because it was not politically practical" (53). As Peymann notes, a group of actors finally agreed to work on the piece. The director conceived that the cast would study its involvement with the profession of acting, its work as individual actors and actresses, and its fears and difficulties while acting. Peymann's group thus sensed the absence of a plot in the play and realized that, in a work like *Bodensee* where there is no continuous narrative, only remnants of stories, the viewer and the actor are always fearful of being thrown off balance, overwhelmed by "the undercurrent of nonsense, illusions and dream-fantasy indulged in by the characters" (Peymann, 53). Handke's stage in *Bodensee* is not intended to mirror reality. If this stage is a laboratory, as Carl Weber claims, it is not a laboratory for the proverbial naturalistic "slice of life" but rather a background against which, as in *Mündel* or *Quodlibet*, theater—"pure theater"—and the norms of social behavior meet head-on.[26] This bipartite relationship, shown in the play as an awareness (a consciousness) of reality, is actually, as Peymann notes, "a deadly embrace for the characters in the play through the traps and ties of language. With knowledge of the order and hierarchies of language, communication between the characters becomes impossible" (54).

The five actors in *Bodensee* appear in the simulated "roles" of a lover, a boss, a worker, a buyer, and a seller. These roles are not intended to be understood as realistic portrayals. As in a Brecht play, characterization in *Bodensee* lies more in "acting out" a role (*Verfremdung*) than in in-depth analysis of character.[27] In fact, Handke moves freely to alienate the audience from stereotypical character definition in both the stage and print versions of *Bodensee*; the book version of the play assigns the names of German silent-screen stars to the actors—Emil Jannings, Heinrich George, Elizabeth Bergner, and Erich von Stroheim. Readers of the play must grasp Handke's allusion to the similarities in gestic acting style between early film and what is intended for the book version. In the stage performance of *Bodensee*, however, the silent-film names are replaced by the names of the actors themselves—Mary Smith plays "Mary Smith"—so that whatever is happening on the stage is perceived as clearly happening to real people, who are "acting out" the dialogue. My discussion of *Bodensee* refers of necessity to the book version of the play.

As the curtain opens, the audience is first confronted with the disorienting image of a nineteenth-century room whose furniture is covered with white sheets and seemingly glued to the spot (*Bodensee*, 63). One wonders if the room has been abandoned or was never occupied. Handke's actors emerge from a richly appointed set containing a plush carpet and a wine-red runner that leads down a staircase, glimpsed in the background. This staircase, contributing to the operatic quality of the large room, has both a right and left part. Elsewhere there are tapestry-covered doors. The audience is hard put to identify the style of the room; moreover, it is uncertain whether it is meant to react realistically to an image of wealth or artistically to the selected items of interior decoration. Another element of estrangement is the sight of a woman in blackface finishing her job of vacuuming the rug. She turns off a machine and pulls the white cover from under the chair of Jannings, who begins to open his eyes, as if awakening from a deep sleep. George, described by Handke as "someone behind" a screen, steps out in front of Jannings. Both men are physically fat, heavily made up, and wearing clothes that clearly suggest a costumed film actor of the past.

The "action" of the play begins with Jannings's cracked voice stating, "As I said . . . a bad moment" (*Bodensee*, 65). The antecedent of this comment is probably the end of a dream, yet this is never revealed, only assumed. Jannings points to a cigar box lying on the floor beside him, and George misunderstands the gesture, thinking there is something to see on the box itself. Jannings, playing the role momentarily of someone "caught" in the act of wishing to be served by an inferior, masks his real intention by noting the "reality" of the blue sky on the box. At this point in the play Jannings and George begin to act out their "roles" in *Bodensee*; the analogy is the master-servant relationship in *Mündel.* Dialogue between the two offers examples of language that centers carefully on the relationship between words and gestures, between one's perception and one's interpretation. In this dialogue Handke also interweaves major themes and underlying motifs that show how language conveys power and authority. George refuses to pick up the cigar box and asks Jannings whether he was "dreaming," and Jannings tells him a "dream story" about a "misunderstood" gesture, in a restaurant setting, between himself and a friend (*Bodensee,* 66). What "happened" in the story, however, is very much in doubt and seems now to be only a metaphor for winter to Jannings. "Winter kidneys flambé" are mentioned. George questions these "details" and others in Janning's narrative. There follows a scene characterized by gesture and mime between Jannings and George. Jannings casually turns up the palm of his hand. George looks at the hand, which seems to be "directing" him to the cigar box. George goes to the box and hands it to Jannings (*Bodensee,* 69).

Uwe Schultz, focusing an extended analysis on the above passage, has pointed out the complexity and subtlety of the linguistic and psychological game being played out between George and Jannings (82-83). Dominance and control are two major themes in the foregoing episodes, and in the end Jannings wins, since George does indeed put the cigar box into his hand. The sommambulistic state, however, from which both Jannings and George emerge at the beginning of the play seems to undermine the words of their dialogue. With these overall conditions, there is no certainty that anything said by anybody in the play is truly being said in the real world. The audience is especially estranged from the meaning of the "game" it has perceived. Are the men master and servant, rich and poor, or two competing friends? Dialogue between Jannings and George operates on many levels: the intrusion of dreams into our waking life; the impossibility of speaking about something of which one has had no direct experience (kidneys flambé); the borderline between a story and a real event. The encounter between the men suggests, too, that society gives arbitrary assignments of meanings to "action" for the sake of sanity and communication. For example, when Jannings takes the cigar box from George, there is a brief pause, as if Jannings had expected something else, and his hand "is still extended." Jannings notes that he had "meant" to say something else with his extended hand. He offers a cigar to George, who is surprised at the turn of events (*Bodensee,* 69).

As was indicated earlier, the preceding episodes from *Bodensee* are typical of the remainder of the play: scenes of dominance continue to be played out as a language game between two individuals. Yet the mental and perceptive states of the two men intrude, floating as they do between consciousness and sleep. This reminds the viewer and reader of the title of Handke's play, for the rationality of the men can never be taken for granted.

Though other characters in the play, especially the women, experience similar moments of "death" and "consciousness" as they move between the two worlds of dream and reality (linguistic reality and outer reality), certain episodes of the work focus on their release from these "supposedly free and sovereign systems of communication" (Linstead 1988, 75). Such an incident occurs early on when George, viewing the rings on Jannings's hand, is caught up in a moment of realization, a passionate moment of "true" ownership (*Besitzrausch*) centering on the rings. We are intended to appreciate the distinction Handke is making between George's unmediated role as an "owner" and his role as a "buyer." George makes a short speech looking at the rings, which seem to him "as if they were made for me" (*Bodensee,* 72). He hugs the rings sensually and kisses them. The rings reflect his heart. He perceives himself as the possessor of the rings.

Linstead has noted that these are moments of epiphany (direct, unmediated experience), and that the stage characters in *Bodensee* "go through a series of mimes which deal with hearing a pin drop, seeing the sea actually glisten, seeing someone have totally empty pockets" (1988, 77). Every instance of such direct experience, however short-lived, is intended to free the characters from the weight of linguistic prejudgment and to help them discover that words and sentences need not stand for anything other than themselves. A telling episode of this kind occurs when Porten and Bergner work together to free Bergner from a loss of "self" by using a mirror. Bergner does not know in which direction to comb or cut her hair, and as she attempts to do so, she walks in a direction where no one is and asks for help. It is Porten, however, who "frees" Bergner from this alienated state and moves her into another one in which a gesture and its related phenomenon are free of meaning and definition. The cure is nothing more than talking to each other, recounting direct experience as much as possible within an unmediated language system. Here Handke notes simply that the longer they talk, the more sure of themselves and graceful they become. Their talk is trivial, recalling such simple acts as walking down a stairway or even placing a tablecloth (*Bodensee,* 99).

That episodes of "awakening" consciousness are of brief duration, however, is a central theme of the play. The "conformist" behavior of the Kessler sisters—symbols of moribund, joyless normality—causes the actors to revert to the frozen sea of their original dreamlike state. This retreat, however, is ironic, since the sisters are the epitome of nondescriptive individuals: they are dressed identically, and their uninspired conversation is filled with polite phrases and stock answers. Handke has alerted his viewers that in his play the illusion of being liberated from meanings and interpretations, of placing "a block between sign and interpretation is nothing less than a utopian comedy" (*Bodensee,* 58). In *Bodensee* all the players take a ride across the thin ice separating the rational from the irrational and retreat finally into a passive state. As one of them reaches for something, he stops as soon as he starts. Another tries a gesture that dies instantly. In a few seconds all of them grow rigid, as if freezing to death (*Bodensee,* 154). *Bodensee* probes the fragile structures of linguistic and mental consciousness, exposing the schizophrenia, madness, and dreams that lie just beneath the "order" society has imposed on us all (Weber, 54).

DIE UNVERNÜNFTIGEN STERBEN AUS

Die Unvernünftigen sterben aus (*They Are Dying Out*) was first staged by the left-wing Theater am Neumarkt in Zürich on 17 April 1974.[28] Subsequent performances were mounted in Düsseldorf, Wiesbaden, Freiburg, and Berlin, and the Yale Repertory Theater staged it in October 1979.[29] *Unvernünftigen* is not a play in the experimental language style of Handke's earlier theater; it moves in a more conventional direction. The play has two acts and a cast of eight characters, of whom the central figure is Hermann Quitt, a capitalist entrepreneur. Quitt, whose name seems to be a variant spelling of the English word *quit,* is a tycoon and a member of an international cartel. Carl Weber calls Quitt "the last Romantic hero of the business world" (Bly, 83). The reasons behind Quitt's suicide at the end of the play are the focal point of Handke's capitalist tragedy. What happens to Quitt as an individual occurs within the framework and setting of a big city resembling Manhattan. The city, of course, is not specifically New York but could easily be London, Frankfurt or Paris. It is a metropolitan city of the present and of the future (*Unvernünftigen,* 7).

In a newspaper interview with the critic Christian Schulz-Gerstein, Handke stressed the analogy between his working concept of *Unvernünftigen* as a capitalist tragedy and the social structures of betrayal, rejected love, and impotence in Shakespearean theater.[30] Modern-day capitalists, said Handke, can be viewed as the counterparts of those men who commit high treason in Shakespeare's tragedies. In the twentieth century, Handke notes, the love of profit has replaced Elizabethan eroticism. Sublime passion has changed into crassness and manipulation. As a contemporary work, *Unvernünftigen* is a parody of traditional tragedy and depicts emotional crisis over factual details that intentionally mirror modern society's obsession with financial balances, checkbooks, and money-making. The central conflict in the play, however, is also a personal one: the gradual "death" of Hermann Quitt as Handke's symbol of "irrationality" within the rational, capitalist context of modern economics. As a further complication to the theme, *Unvernünftigen* also examines the use of subjectivity, veracity, and especially "poetic thought" as tools of the irrational (life-saving) forces that Quitt tries to employ against the programmatic business world.[31]

Surrounding Quitt are members of his business cartel, all of them symbols of free enterprise: Koerber-Kent, a businessman-priest; Von Wullnow, a symbol of conservative business practice; Paula Tax, a Marxist businesswoman; and Lutz. Each acts according to his or her own principles and is a target of Handke's analysis of corrupt capitalism. A point of conflict among Quitt's friends is their suspicion of him as an erratic business person, never to be entirely trusted. Functioning on the outer rim of this circle is Quitt's wife, truly a "victim" of the capitalist system. Hans, Quitt's confidant and servant, dreams of being rich and enjoying the "freedom" that money can bring him. He is preparing to learn from Quitt's success and would like to have similar social status. Like the minority stockholder Kilb, whose role in the play recalls the wise fool of popular theatrical tradition, Hans's destiny is not without interest. Kilb, on the other hand, is only tolerated by Quitt and his group. His lines are humorous and function as a commentary on the play's picture of corrupt and venal business activity. At the end of the play he is literally strangled in a deadly (comic) embrace by Quitt. Hans, on the other hand, as a symbol of opportunistic social mobility, is a survivor of the "tragedy" that ends Quitt's life. Hans's last words before he exits the stage are significant: "somebody" read his palm and predicted he would change the world. That he will never do so is only ironically evident (*Unvernünftigen,* 95).

The plot of *Unvernünftigen* is simple. In Act 1 Quitt forms a cartel with his business associates. The central idea behind the need for the cartel is Quitt's own: he believes that fighting against one another is pointless; as a cartel they can force lesser businesses into bankruptcy (*Unvernünftigen,* 186). Quitt then enumerates the reasons he and his friends must form a cartel: there are too many products on the market, being sold by too many manufacturers, and the ideal capitalist way is to place consumer demand in the hands of a cartel acting as one manufacturing unit. Quitt also has plans to lower workers' wages (*Unvernünftigen,* 28).

In a perceptive analysis of the play, Joseph Federico shows the ambiguity behind Quitt's proposed plan and refers to his role "as the hapless victim of powerful manipulatory forces beyond his control."[32] As a businessman, Quitt has rational insight into the strategies of the business world, but his insight is countermanded by his quixotic sense of personal outrage at common business practices that drive the average business person into "the forest" to feel human (*Unvernünftigen,* 29). If it is true that Quitt's feelings about himself are often expressed in terms of poetic impulses, then it is possible to say, as Federico does (187), that what happens in the play is often the result of its central metaphorical style. In the narrative evolution of the play Quitt is a chief figure, first as a capitalist and then as a figure longing for simplicity and "natural" behavior. For example, his relationship with Hans, with whom he meets daily, is similar to that of Puntila and Matti in Brecht's play *Herr Puntila und sein Knecht Matti* (1940-41). Matti, Puntila's servant and friend, must endure the effects of Puntila's change from kindness to brutality whenever he becomes drunk. Matti walks out on Puntila as a justified act of independence. During an opening scene of *Unvernünftigen* Quitt relates to Hans his "sadness" when he saw his wife in her dressing gown and her "lacquered" toes, a feeling of genuine loneliness, "objective" and yet otherwise (*Unvernünftigen,* 7).

It is, however, characteristic of Quitt that he should waver between fact and sentiment. As a man in conflict with himself, Quitt's search for unity between those two forces is actually a romantic twist. This is a new element in Handke's work, and it foreshadows related subjective and poetic themes in his subsequent novels. An important aspect of conflict in the play, for example, is the opposition of the language of poetic diction and irrationality to the sterile, nonexpressive language of business and rationality. Whenever Quitt leaves the linguistic jargon of business language and moves toward his inner self, his language changes, too—toward poetic diction, language marked by directness, memory, intimacy, and subjectivity. The richness of this expression is tapped briefly in a short exchange at the end of Act 1 when Quitt, in a moment of emotional directness, asks Hans about his life (i.e., his "story"). Hans refuses to believe that Quitt is truly interested and says that the "real" subject of the inquiry is Quitt himself (*Unvernünftigen,* 49).

Poetic diction and irrationality represent for Quitt (and Handke) personal freedom and individuality, the assertion of the inner self and its growth in the romantic sense of limitless expansion. In a speech delivered in 1973 before the Academy of Language and Literature in Darmstadt on the occasion of receiving a literary award, Handke surprised his audience by offering poetic, irrational thought as an alternative to the brute display of economic and political force in today's world.[33] For Handke, however, one's level of language is always directly expressive of one's thought. The Darmstadt speech relates the function of language to either power politics or poetry, and Handke chooses poetry. Handke's speech and Quitt's language in *Unvernünftigen* both make the same distinction between the regenerative language of "poetic thought" and the destructive language of "rational thought." For these reasons, Quitt desires to be "poetic" or irrational. At the end of Act 1 Handke sets before his hero the possibility of another kind of existence, the poetic world. The healing vision of this world might be a way out of Quitt's materialistic universe.

Nevertheless, the very end of the first act continues to test Quitt's vulnerability to the seductive forces of economics and technocracy. At a decisive point in the play Quitt is in a pensive mood as he sits listening to Hans's reading passages from a story by the mid-nineteenth-century Austrian novelist Adalbert Stifter. These passages describe an old man's grief and regret at the next day's departure of his younger relative. He mentions the specter of life's failed opportunities. Stifter's flowing mid-nineteenth-century style acts briefly as a narcotic on Quitt as he hears the wisdom of the text: the older man's words about old age and the onset of time and life's lost opportunities (*Unvernünftigen,* 51-53).

If Quitt is perceptive and recognizes the affinity between the truth of Stifter's text and his present self, he is still skeptical of Stifter and his immediate reaction is to call him a nineteenth-century "restorer," a writer who was still capable in his time of creating the illusion that what was being written was credible and attainable (*Unvernünftigen,* 53-54). Contrasting himself with Stifter, a spokesman in nineteenth-century social and literary communities, Quitt says that all *he* ever does is "quote" (use words without meaning) and that authentic signs of life from himself "slip out" purely by accident. Further, a fundamental difference between the two is that Stifter could still convince his audience that his writerly illusions rang true, while Quitt, on the other hand, must play a role that does not even exist. This is a crucial admission in the play, and Quitt decides to abandon his plans for the business cartel, for reasons that have much to do with self-preservation. Linstead notes correctly that Quitt's latest decision has a double function: the Stifter passage gives him insight into himself, but his decision to return to the businessman-rationalist role means that he is unable to escape his identity as a capitalist (1988, 146). His decision to act will prove wrong and bring on his death, thus ending his quest for happiness.

The second act of *Unvernünftigen* develops the disastrous consequences of Quitt's decision. On the stage are several artifacts, a shrinking balloon and a gray boulder among them. The stone is covered with clichéd statements from philosophy and business: "Our greatest sin—The impatience of concepts—The worst is over—The last hope" (*Unvernünftigen,* 57). One can read these words as linguistic signs that point to further entanglements for Quitt. First of all, Hans and Quitt resume their relationship on a more antagonistic level. Quitt says to Hans that he will always remain a servant and that he will only ever dream of becoming a capitalist (*Unvernünftigen,* 57). Dreams, Hans responds, are a key to a better life. Through these words, with a tone of bitterness directed at Quitt, Hans reminds Quitt that money is the true realm of the rich and that poetry belongs to the poor. Quitt next has an encounter with members of the cartel, who try to resume the pact that he has abandoned. They wish to minimize their financial losses. Rhetorical manipulation, clever appeals by Paula Tax to Quitt's sexuality, and an attempt by Kilb to kill Quitt all fail to turn him around, to bring him back to the old way of working for the interests of his group. Kilb is murdered by Quitt, but this act, too, is only a gesture of impotence. Quitt commits suicide when he runs his head against the block of gray stone. His suicide can be overtly attributed to his inability to break out of his role as a businessman and into that of a "poet" within the context of capitalism.

Linstead, however, has pointed out that Quitt's suicide is a parody of the idea of tragedy in that the conflict in which Quitt purports to find himself is a false one. Quitt can thus be seen as the creator of the social and personal conditions under which he suffers, and "such is the all-pervading nature of this role and its effects upon [Quitt's] inner world that any resistance to it takes on the ambiguous value of also being an extension of it" (1988, 148).

One could also say that Handke himself is not convinced that Quitt's conflict is a real one, since parody is evident throughout the play. The play shows that within the present-day conditions of capitalism, a figure like Quitt can try to escape his role as a capitalist but has no alternative but suicide. He becomes his own victim. Quitt as a capitalist and Quitt as a would-be poet are finally the product of the same phenomenon, capitalism. The death of Quitt, who wants to speak about himself "without using categories," brings on the last category—the lines of an obituary in the next day's newspaper. In this sense, **Unvernünftigen** can be viewed as portraying "truthfully the conditions of modernism which . . . [Handke] sees as a nearly unbridgeable schism between the individual and the world."[34] In this schism, the meaning and the nonmeaning of language are defined by Handke in a new way, within the capitalist setting of contemporary society.

Notes

1. *Publikumsbeschimpfung,* in *Stücke I* (Frankfurt: Suhrkamp, 1972), 9-47; hereafter cited in text as *Publikumsbeschimpfung.*

2. My discussion of Handke's *Sprechstücke* is based on the following standard critical presentations: Klinkowitz and Knowlton, 104-12; Schlueter 1981, 17-40; Nicholas Hern, *Peter Handke* (New York: Ungar, 1972), 21-51, hereafter cited in text; Ronald Hayman, *Theater and Anti-theater* (New York: Oxford University Press, 1979), 95-104, hereafter cited in text; Michael Hays, "Peter Handke and the End of the 'Modern,'" *Modern Drama* 23, no. 4 (January 1981): 346-66, hereafter cited in text; Rainer Nägele, "Peter Handke: The Staging of Language," *Modern Drama* 23, no. 4 (January 1981): 327-38, hereafter cited in text; Uwe Schultz, *Peter Handke* (Velber bei Hannover: Friedrich, 1973), 25-42, hereafter cited in text.

3. *Die Weissagung,* in *Stücke I,* 49-63; hereafter cited in text as *Weissagung. Selbstbezichtigung,* in *Stücke I,* 65-88; hereafter cited in text as *Selbstbezichtigung. Hilferufe,* in *Stücke I,* 89-97; hereafter cited in text as *Hilferufe.*

4. This can be found in Handke's note to *Offending the Audience* and *Self-Accusation,* in *Kaspar and Other Plays,* trans. Michael Roloff (New York: Farrar, Straus & Giroux, 1969), v. Handke's criticism that Brecht worked within a false theatrical framework is found in Nicholas Hern's translation of Handke's essay, "Brecht, Play, Theatre, Agitation," *Theatre Quarterly* 1 (October-December 1971): 89-90. See also Hayes, 350.

5. On the Vienna Group, see Michael Butler, "From the 'Wiener Gruppe' to Ernst Jandl," in *Modern Austrian Writing,* ed. Alan Best and Hans Wolfschütz (London: Wolff, 1980), 236-51. On the Graz Group (the literary-artistic successor to the Vienna Group), see Hugh Rorrison, "The 'Grazer Gruppe,'" in Best and Wolfschütz, *Modern Austrian Writing,* 252-65; hereafter cited in text.

6. Claus Peymann, "Directing Handke," *Drama Review* 16 (June 1972): 48-49; hereafter cited in text.

7. Arthur Joseph, "Nauseated by Language," *Drama Review* 15, no 1 (Fall 1970): 59; hereafter cited in text.

8. There are outstanding discussions of *Weissagung* in Nägele, 329-31, and Schlueter 1981, 24-30.

9. "Theater and Film: The Misery of Comparison," trans. Donald Vordberg, in *Focus on Film and Theatre,* ed. James Hurt (Englewood Cliffs, NJ: Prentice-Hall, 1974), 165; originally published in German as "Theater und Film: Das Elend der Vergleiches," in *Prosa Gedichte Theaterstücke Horspiel Aufsätze* (Frankfurt: Suhrkamp, 1969), 314-26.

10. "The play may be a demonstration of the spatial and verbal distance between the speakers on stage and the audience—a signal of the need to establish a community of support" (Hays, 356). See also Hern, 52.

11. *Kaspar,* in *Stücke I*; hereafter cited in text as *Kaspar.*

12. I have relied on the following substantial discussions of *Kaspar* in English: Denis Calandra, *New German Dramatists* (London: Macmillan, 1983), 63-74, hereafter cited in text: Hays, 356-58; Hern, 58-72; Hayman, 104-07; Linda Hill, "Obscurantism and Verbal Resistance in Handke's *Kaspar,*" *Germanic Review* 53, no. 4 (1977): 304-15, hereafter cited in text; June Schlueter, "'Goats and Monkeys' and 'Idiocy of Language': Handke's *Kaspar* and Shakespeare's *Othello,*" *Modern Drama* 23, no. 1 (March 1980): 25-31. In German: Christa K. Dixon, "Peter Handkes *Kaspar*: Ein Modellfall," *German Quarterly* 46, no. 1 (January 1973): 31-46; Schultz, 43-59.

13. "Der Jasager und die Einsager," in Scharang, 132.

14. See R. D. Theisz, "Kaspar Hauser im zwanzigsten Jahrhundert," *German Quarterly* 49, no. 2 (March 1976): 168-79.

15. "The play provides no specific answer to the problem of linguistic oppression" (Hays, 357).

16. *Das Mündel will Vormund sein,* in *Stücke II* (Frankfurt: Suhrkamp, 1973), 7-38; hereafter cited in text as *Mündel. Quodlibet,* in *Stücke II,* 39-54; hereafter cited in text as *Quodlibet.*

17. "*My Foot My Tutor* . . . is a play of form, not meaning" (Hays, 358). Other discussions of *Mündel* that I have found helpful are Nägele, 334-35; Calandra, 31-43; Haymann, 110-13; Peymann, 52-53; Bonnie Marranca, "Peter Handke's *My Foot My Tutor*: Aspects of Modernism," *Michigan Quarterly Review* 16 (1977): 272-79, hereafter cited in text; Schultz, 60-72.

18. Hern (84) and Marranca (274) both cite the influence on *Mündel* of Beckett's *Act without Words* (1957).

19. Carl Weber, "Handke's Stage Is a Laboratory," *Drama Review* 162 (June 1972): 56; hereafter cited in text.

20. Helpful to an understanding of *Quodlibet* are Calandra, 56-60; Handke, "Zur Aufführung von *Quodlibet*," in *Stücke II,* 157-59; Peter Hamm, "Handke entdeckt sich selbst," in Scharang, 157-62; Rainer Litten, "Theater der Verstörung: Ein Gespräch mit Peter Handke." in Scharang, 157-58.

21. Translator's note to *Quodlibet,* in *The Ride across Lake Constance and Other Plays,* trans. Michael Roloff (New York: Farrar, Strauss & Giroux, 1976), 55.

22. "The success of the play depends on the audience's predictable association and responses" (Schlueter 1981, 61).

23. *Der Ritt über den Bodensee,* in *Stücke II,* 55-154; hereafter cited in text as *Bodensee.*

24. See Handke's introduction to *Stücke II,* 57-59, and "Aus den Notizen zu *Der Ritt über den Bodensee,*" his outline listing of notes to the writing of the play. These notes are in fact a scenario of actors' movements and gestures; movements are also interpreted (*Stücke II,* 161-77).

25. The title of the play comes from an 1828 German Swabian romantic ballad, "Der Reiter und der Bodensee" (The Rider and Lake Constance), by Gustav Schwab (1792-1850), in which a horseman dies when he hears that his perilous ride across the thin ice of Lake Constance was in fact a chance event of nature. For Handke, this is also an encounter with the "thin ice" of rationality. Recommended discussion of *Bodensee* are June Schlueter, "Handke's *The Ride across Lake Constance,*" in *Metafictional Characters in Modern Drama* (New York: Columbia University Press, 1979), 105-19; Michael Linstead, *Outer World and Inner World: Socialization and Emancipation in the Works of Peter Handke, 1964-1981,* European Literary Studies, German Languages and Literature Series, vol. 1024 (Frankfurt: Lang, 1988), 71-81, hereafter cited in text; Schultz, 77-86.

26. Carl Weber directed the American premiere of *Bodensee* on 13 January 1972 at the Forum Theater at Lincoln Center in New York. His article "Handke's Stage Is a Laboratory" contains his notes relating to that production, which had a bad house. See, however, another analysis of the American premiere in Ira Hauptmann, "Aspects of Handke: A Play," *Partisan Review* 45, no. 3 (1978): 425-30.

27. For example, the characters Jannings and George "act out" the features of a prototypical master-servant relationship. Bergner, Stroheim, and Porten symbolize a destabilized lovers' triangle.

28. *Die Unvernünftigen sterben aus* (Frankfurt: Suhrkamp, 1973); hereafter cited in text as *Unvernünftigen.* The English title of the play omits the German word *Unvernünftigen* ("irrational ones").

29. The Yale production is discussed in Mark Bly, "Theater in New Haven: Weber on Handke," *Theater* 11, no. 2 (Spring 1980): 83-87; hereafter cited in text. Other productions are discussed in Calandra, 83-90; June Schlueter, "Politics and Poetry: Peter Handke's *They Are Dying Out,*" *Modern Drama* 23, no. 4 (January 1981): 339-45; Linstead 1988, 136-48; Schultz, 86-103. Hellmuth Karasek, reviewing the Zürich production in *Der Spiegel* (22 April 1974), said it was ironic that Handke's protagonist, Quitt, should have a precedent in Brecht's drama since Handke professed to despise Brecht's theater.

30. Christian Schulz-Gerstein, "Das Leiden als Geschäfts-Trick: Gespräch mit Peter Handke über sein Stück," *Die Zeit,* 26 April 1974.

31. "As opposed to political engagement, Handke opposes a poetic utopia, in which he sees the possibility of becoming a poetic, i.e., an unnatural man" (Arnold Blumer, "Peter Handkes Romantische Unvernunft," *Acta Germanica* 8 [1973]: 126; hereafter cited in text). A similar discussion is found in Arnold, 29-31.

32. Joseph A. Federico, "The Hero as Playwright in Dramas by Frisch, Dürrenmatt, and Handke," *German Life and Letters,* n.s. 32 (January 1979): 166; hereafter cited in text.

33. The German text of the speech, entitled "Die Geborgenheit unter der Schädeldecke," is found in *Als das Wünschen noch geholfen hat* (Frankfurt: Suhrkamp, 1974), 71.

34. Schlueter, "Politics," 343.

PUBLIKUMSBESCHIMPFUNG (OFFENDING THE AUDIENCE)

CRITICAL COMMENTARY

Nicholas Hern (essay date 1971)

SOURCE: Hern, Nicholas. "*Offending the Audience.*" In *Peter Handke: Theatre and Anti-Theatre,* pp. 30-45. London: Oswald Wolff, 1971.

[*In the following essay, Hern disusses the theatrics involved in* Offending the Audience *and how this play differs from standard theatrical productions of the time.*]

The text of **Offending the Audience** is prefaced by a short list of seventeen 'Rules for the Actors' (this is the only time Handke uses the word 'actor' in connection with his *Sprechstücke,* otherwise they are speakers: the casting for this play is simply 'Four speakers'). These rules are a series of 'look and listen and learn' instructions, directing the actors' attention to various more or less mundane sights and sounds, to be heard emanating from Catholic churches, football crowds, riots, debates, simultaneous translation systems, bicycle wheels, cement mixers, trains, the Rolling Stones, and the Radio Luxembourg Hit Parade, and to be seen demonstrated by layabouts, animals at the zoo, Lee J. Cobb, Gary Cooper and the Beatles. Just as John Cage insists that all sound is music, and Ann Halprin that all movement is dance, so Handke seems to be saying to his actors that the very mundanity of these visual and aural experiences should not invalidate them. They are worth seeing and worth hearing for their own sake and Handke even emphasises certain parts of each experience as particularly noteworthy: for instance the gradually increasing noise a cement mixer makes when it has just been turned on. By forcing his actors' attention on these underestimated sights and sounds, Handke presumably wishes them to make use of their increased sensibility in the acting of his play and, in turn, to make the audience more aware of the richness of the ordinary world around them. This would tally with the final sentence of Handke's 'Note to my *Sprechstücke*', where he says that his *Sprechstücke* are not intended to 'revolutionize, but to make aware'. And this in turn tallies with John Cage's philosophy, shared by many artists engaged in Happenings and similar events, that we should all be 'omni-attentive'.

On a more practical level, it would be possible to incorporate the insights gained by following the instructions in the active presentation of the play. In a play with no specific movement, no role-playing, no scenery and no illusion, speech is obviously at a premium, as Handke intends it to be. It will obviate monotony and will lend force to the words if they are orchestrated into interesting and variegated patterns. Many of the sounds cited by Handke, such as the chanting of slogans in a riot, the response in a litany, the interruptions in a debate, the clicking of a freewheeling bicycle as it comes to rest, or the driving beat of a Rolling Stones number, could clearly provide models for just such speech orchestration, often lending extra meaning to the words spoken (as, for instance, any phrase when chanted to an accelerating rhythm carries excitement whatever its literal meaning). These, though, are the lessons taught by Artaud and effectively practised by his disciples, Peter Brook, The Living Theatre, et al. They should be within the ken of most actors and certainly of all modern directors.

More to the point are the references to pop music which Handke has elaborated on elsewhere: 'I wanted to communicate to others the effect of beat music on me—and it was a revolutionary effect—by creating with words and phrases a structurally similar effect . . .' More recently in an interview with Artur Joseph, Handke has qualified this statement:

> I adopted structures which were particularly noticeable in beat. They exist all over the place, in noises or sequences of sound . . . I had noticed that a frequent bravura phrase in beat is a quite particular sound sequence which one can describe pictorially like this: a

train starts out of the station, gradually leaves the station becoming softer and softer. And at the same moment a second train pulls in becoming louder and louder. And finally it stops dead. This structure, these simple sequences, are often used in beat. A very fast variation of rhythmic patterns is running on and there suddenly comes a break—these patterns go on in a completely different tempo. It is not only in beat one can find this sort of thing, but it's there it becomes quite distinct, and it is there that it attracted my attention.

The first and several subsequent producers of the play, however, have not confined themselves solely to these considerations of speech orchestration. By preparing a script devoid of stage-directions, Handke obviously laid himself open to 'free interpretation', possibly a result of his lack of theatrical experience, which, however, he has rapidly gained so that in his later plays every twitch of the eyebrow is accounted for. Consequently, the first production saw the actors relying 'less on beat rhythms and more on the tried and tested theatrical media such as mime, intonation and choreography . . . They stood, knelt, lay, and spoke over the footlights, in the auditorium, from the wings and on the empty stage (flats stacked haphazardly back to front against the back wall); they crawled into the prompter's box; they carried the lid of the prompter's box around with them; once, almost as if in a farce, their heads appeared round the left side of the stage one above the other.' But Handke has subsequently complained that:

> The play was pepped up out of fear that the audience would perhaps be wearied by the continuous speaking. Of course one must speak the play, but one does not need to stand motionless on the stage; one can walk around, move about casually. But nevertheless hold the audience's attention by changes in the rhythms of speech. There is such an infinite number of possible tempos of speech that one can always draw the audience into the spell so that they listen just because they are curious as to what is coming next.

This last remark—'they are curious as to what is coming next'—explains the care that the author has lavished on the introductory passage which precedes the play proper. A set of extremely detailed instructions explain how, long before the curtain goes up, the theatre should be prepared for the elaborate practical joke that is to be played on the unsuspecting audience. Like all practical jokes it only really works on unsuspecting people and this is a charge which can be levelled against the whole play, that it is a 'once-off' joke that does not bear repetition to those who know it.

This preamble is a thematic foreshadowing of the play itself in another, more important way. The author desires that, from the moment the audience enter the theatre (or, indeed, are turned away for being too informally dressed), the house-manager and his staff shall make every effort to maintain and even slightly heighten the usual ritual associated in the audience's mind with going to the theatre. The co-operation of the stage-manager is sought in having certain noises and movements made behind the curtain so as to whet the audience's appetite for the coming show. And then, after a particularly slow and suspenseful dimming of the house-lights, the curtain goes up and—surprise, surprise!—the stage is totally bare, and on it are four ordinarily dressed people who are apparently rehearsing, lit by the same even light which illuminates the auditorium.

What has happened is that the mumbo-jumbo surrounding conventional theatre-going has been set up as an Aunt Sally and has been knocked flying by a display of *un*conventional theatrical goings-on which negate most of the audience's conventional expectations. The audience have been 'had', and, as if cocking a snook, the four people on the bare stage are rehearsing a crescendo of insults. This pattern, of the audience having their theatrical expectations foiled and then being insulted, is precisely the pattern of the play itself.

The play on the page consists of sixty-six paragraphs of varying lengths, which are neither ascribed to particular speakers nor grouped in any way. During the course of the play Handke has his speakers tell the audience: 'You have recognized the dialectical structure of this play', by which is meant that attention is alternately focused on the audience and the actors, or on the worlds each inhabits.

The progression of the play can be said to be spiral. Most of the main themes are stated simply within the first few paragraphs and these are then reiterated and elaborated in turn perhaps three or four times during the play. These themes include the fact that the play is a prologue which is later elaborated to mean a prologue to, among other things, the audience's future theatre-going; that the play is not a conventional play of any known type, there is no acting, no spectacle and no story-telling; that the audience's theatrical expectations will not be satisfied; that the audience are an orderly group of people who are experiencing certain sensations and thinking certain thoughts; that, because there is no difference between the world experienced by the people on stage and the world experienced by the people in the auditorium, actors and audience can be said to form an undivided unity; that the dimension of time in particular is identical on stage and in the auditorium, as it elapses at the same rate in both areas; that there is no symbolic level to the play or to anything on stage, because everything is what it is in reality and nothing more; that there is no theatrical illusionism or trickery; and that the *audience* are the central theme of the evening's entertainment (1).

These reiterated points build to a passage about two-thirds of the way through the play (the classic position for a dramatic climax) which consists of a frontal assault on the sort of play the audience have supposedly been used to watching hitherto. The passage is marked out from the rest of the play by its reference to past events while the rest of the play is concerned only with the present, by its more coherent and sequent argument, and by its variegated

sentence structure in contrast to the protracted anaphora of most of the play. The object of the onslaught is the dead theatre of pretence and illusion, where things were never what they seemed but something else as well. In favourable contrast to this double-natured nonsense is mentioned 'the pure play,' which is defined as being 'timeless' or having the same dimension of time as exists in real life, and not a false, make-believe time. In this attack is clearly discernible the voice of the upstart at Princeton and subsequent campaigns on all fronts against fictions, metaphors and illusion. Indeed this passage is an epitome of the action of the whole play. Having physically demonstrated the exclusion of all the usual fictive theatrical devices, the actors complete the purification process with an explicit verbal attack on the old forms.

The rest of the play is a sort of coda. First comes a final re-statement that this play has none of the conventional trappings of role-playing, simulated action, symbolic levels of meaning, etc. Then the actors explain how the audience will leave the theatre and make their different ways home. 'Before that, however, you are going to be insulted.' There follows the most notorious section of the play, the section which gives the play its title. And yet it doesn't consist solely of abuse aimed at the audience. The insults are alternated with extravagant praise for the 'performance' the audience have just given. These accolades, which at first far outweigh the abuse and only gradually give way to it, are the sort of clichés used by drama critics to praise naturalistic performances. Throughout the play the actors have been ever more insistent that, since there is no distinction between stage and auditorium, the audience have been giving as much of a performance as the actors: and now critical cant such as 'You were life-like . . . You *lived* your parts . . . You were the ideal cast', when applied to the audience, who could hardly help being life-like, succeeds in casting another ironic slur on the whole business of conventional role-playing. The insults themselves are increasingly polysyllabic, increasingly non-insulting, and often witty, both individually and because of their fantastic profusion (one hundred and sixty-four of them).

The play ends with the actors thanking the audience and wishing them good-night. The curtain falls but is immediately raised again to reveal the actors standing looking expressionlessly into the auditorium. A deafening sound of wild applause comes over the loud speakers and continues until the audience leave. Then the curtain comes down.

It is not surprising that this play was immediately dubbed an 'anti-play' and Handke's form of theatre 'anti-theatre' (a label which Handke himself has rejected). Comparisons were made with the famous self-named 'anti-play' of the previous generation, Ionesco's *Bald Prima Donna*. But it is important to be clear that in these cases (as also with *Ubu Roi,* the daddy of modern anti-plays) the 'anti' is only relative to what has gone before: none of these anti-plays represented an act of total destruction, because each of them could only exist and could only make sense within the structure of the existing theatre against which it was rebelling. **Offending the Audience** is a playgoer's play, and far from being anti, it depends on the theatre as an institution.

The play is also dependent on a number of well-tried theatrical devices. Surprising the audience and deceiving their expectations is one of the oldest. Direct address is as old as the Greeks or medieval religious plays and as modern as Brecht. Making the audience part of the performance is as old as the Court Masques and as new as the Happening. There *is* even a degree of role-playing despite the constant disclaimers. Statements such as 'We have no roles. We are ourselves. We are the mouthpiece of the author' reveal niceties of distinction between illusion and reality which outdo Pirandello. Nevertheless, like the actors in *Six Characters,* Handke's actors *are* actors acting actors and not the ordinary people they are required by the author to say they are. But these are fine points, and it is true to say that, for all the theatricality of the play, Handke has done away with a prodigious number of what are normally considered necessary ingredients for a theatrical piece. For this reason, the same ground could hardly be covered again in subsequent plays. Rather like the minimal painter who has reduced his art to a bare canvas, Handke reached a dead end with his first play and had to strike out in a new direction. Nevertheless the play can be seen as a necessary cleansing procedure, a wiping of the slate prior to a new set of inscriptions; hence, perhaps, the insistence that the play is a prologue—a prologue to his own subsequent plays.

As well as sharing the misused label of anti-play, **Offending the Audience** shows other remarkable similarities of origin and structure with *The Bald Prima Donna.* According to Martin Esslin in *The Theatre of the Absurd,* Ionesco's play had originally ended quite differently from the present version:

> Ionesco had planned to let the maid, at the height of the quarrel, announce 'The Author!', after which the author would appear, the actors would respectfully step aside and applaud him while the author would approach the footlights with sprightly steps, but suddenly raise his fists and shout at the audience, 'You bunch of crooks! I'll get you!'.

The similarity between this and the end of **Offending the Audience** is hardly mere coincidence. Both are born of a distrust, almost a hatred, of conventional theatre and of the audience which patronised it. Ionesco has described his attitude to the theatre at the time he wrote the play:

> For me, going to a public performance meant going to see apparently serious people making a public exhibition of themselves . . . what worried me in the theatre was the presence of characters in flesh and blood on the stage. Their physical presence destroyed the imaginative illusion. It was as though there were two planes of reality, . . . two antagonistic worlds failing to come together and unite.

And it was an uncomfortable awareness of 'two planes of reality' in the theatre that similarly spurred Handke to write his first play. The difference being that Handke had no respect for the fictional or imaginative plane and wished to see it abolished.

He wrote: 'The theatre as it was was for me a relic from a past era. Even Beckett and Brecht had nothing to do with me. Stories on the stage did not work for me; instead of being simple, they were always only simplifications. The possibilities of reality were limited by the impossibilities of the stage . . .'. Like Ionesco, Handke too experienced initial dislike of the theatre:

> On one occasion I arrived at the theatre too late and while I waited in the foyer, I heard, behind the closed doors, the actors acting reality: *what* they were performing I didn't understand, but I heard the tense, quiet, irritated, casually spoken, muffled, mocking, subdued, reflective, soundless sounds; that was good enough, but it hasn't been sufficiently provoking for me to be able to deduce my aversion to the theatre from it alone. I have an aversion, that is clear; I had aversions before I wrote the play *Offending the Audience,* and I tried to put something rational, words, in the place of aversions precisely by writing the play.

In fact, he first thought of writing not a play but an essay, 'a pamphlet against the theatre, but then I recognised that a booklet is not the right place to publish attacks on the theatre. It would probably have been ineffective. And so arose the paradox of doing something in the theatre against the theatre, of using the theatre to protest against the current theatre . . .'.

Handke, and, equally, Ionesco, are not of course alone in their discovery of the impact of using the theatre against the theatre. The Dadaists in Zürich and Paris during and immediately after the First World War had, as usual, done it all before. Their soirées, or, as we might now call them, mixed-media events, were considerably more destructive in intent and more relentlessly opposed to all the recognised canons and categories of art than Handke's or Ionesco's vigorous but comparatively stylish protests. Handke has also invited comparison with the Dadaists on account of his successful self-advertisement, but again there is a constructive purpose and ultimately a restraint which does not accord with Dadaist nihilism. In this respect Handke rather resembles the modern purveyors of Happenings and other crypto-theatrical events, who are often labelled neo-Dadaists. The resemblance is not great and is too easily misleading, but, as far as it goes, both turn their backs on conventional theatre while using basic theatrical devices to give their audiences a new and more immediate contact with reality. The Happening aims to achieve this by the audience's total or partial participation in the event, with a resultant variability in the nature of that event; while, despite the variable element of heckling from the audience (which Handke seems to enjoy), **Offending the Audience** usually adheres closely to the shape given it by the author.

A much nearer resemblance to Handke's play is borne by some of the work of the Vienna Group, five young experimental writers (Bayer, Artmann, Rühm, Wiener, Achleitner) who worked together for about ten years from 1952. As Handke's compatriots and contemporaries, their work and possibly some of the writers themselves were known to him, and his own work now appears in little magazines alongside that of ex-members of the Group. Konrad Bayer, their spokesman, writing in 1964, labelled Rühm and Achleitner 'concrete poets' who 'aimed at constructive, materially-orientated writing (harking back to expressionism and the Bauhaus, drawing inspiration from Wittgenstein's writings . . .)'; and Bayer was particularly interesting on the subject of 'our contributions to a possible theatre of the future—presented under the guise of cabaret sketches . . . (1958, 1959: demonstrations of "facts", public acts of destruction, exercises in awareness, attempts at total theatre).' Even from these slight descriptions the shared concerns of both Handke and the Vienna Group are apparent. Handke's theatre too is interested in the presentation of facts rather than fictions; as for awareness, Handke has said his *Sprechstücke* aim to 'make aware'; and his writing too is 'materially-orientated' and influenced by Wittgenstein, though Handke is not a 'concrete' writer in the generally accepted sense of that term. It is also clear that the Vienna Group has learned from Dada and has something in common with the Happening ('public acts of destruction' etc.).

One of Bayer's published ideas for a theatrical event (it forms a section of *der stein der weisen,* Berlin, 1963) illustrates some of the concerns shared with Handke:

> i will write a play with the title: *the sun burns.* then i will find a building or have one put up which conceals in its ground floor or cellar a space suitably large to be partitioned by a curtain into 2 auditoria each to take about half of all the people. they sit there and look at the curtain from each side . . . each of the two compartments has its own access . . . each of these sections of the space separated by the curtain is a theatre. each of these two theatres has its own box-office at its own entrance. in both theatres the first performance of my play with the title *the sun burns* is being got ready. both theatres open at the same time. a flood of publicity is essential. both announce the première of the play *the sun burns.* the human race sits assembled. the curtain goes up. both halves of all the people stare each other in the face. with that the play *the sun burns* is written.

This piece is undoubtedly funnier in the telling than in any possible execution of the idea. Nevertheless, if one imagines it duly carried out, the effect on the audience of this piece would be strikingly similar to the effect of Handke's *Offending the Audience.* By being confronted by another audience where it was expecting a play, Bayer's audiences would be made uncomfortably aware of the state of being an audience, which exactly tallies with Handke's speakers' nagging insistence that:

> By the fact that we speak to you, you can become aware of yourselves. Because we address you, you gain in

self-awareness. You become aware that you are sitting. You become aware that you are sitting in a theatre.

Both Handke's and Bayer's stratagems could be seen as extensions of the Brechtian desire to prevent the audience from falling willing victims to the hypnotising illusionism of the theatre by jerking them back into reality so that they are better able, mentally and spiritually, to deal with the issues raised on stage. Indeed this is a large part of Handke's avowed purpose, except that he would extend the process to the audience's being better able to deal with life as well:

> The play has not been written so that the usual audience should make way for a different audience, but that the usual audience should become a different audience. The play can serve to make the spectator pleasantly or unpleasantly aware of his presence, to make him aware of himself. It can make him aware that he is there, that he is present, that he exists . . . It can make him attentive, keen of hearing, clear-sighted, and not only as a playgoer.

If Bayer's piece is anything more than a 'public act of destruction' (destruction in this case of an audience's expectations), it is about what Handke's play is about: something that might grandly be called the nature of reality in the theatre. The point that both pieces make is that in the theatre, where fantasy, illusion, make-believe and fiction—in a word, unreality—are the order of the day, one of the few *real* elements in the theatrical experience is the audience.

Unlike other theatrical revolutionaries anxious to change the role of the audience in the theatre, Handke does not worship at the shrine of audience participation. When members of The Living Theatre leave the stage in *Antigone* to scream filthy abuse at the audience, it is not at all the same thing as the 164 scripted insults with which Handke's speakers regale their audience. The Living Theatre and their imitators wish to draw the audience into the vortex of the play by extending emotional involvement beyond the confines of the stage into the auditorium; Handke on the other hand wishes his audience to remain supremely aloof and in control of themselves so that they may resist the feigned yet hypnotic emotional lure of the stage action. The Living Theatre's insults intend to merge actor and audience: Handke insults his audience so as to remind them that they *are* audience.

Offending the Audience, then, is a theatrical event which has done away with almost all of the normal ingredients of theatre, like plot, character, theatrical time, place and action, and even perhaps mimesis or role-playing. It even manages to throw doubt on one of the most accommodating definitions of theatre in existence: 'A impersonates B while C looks on' (Eric Bentley). What remains is a stage, an auditorium, some people who speak, and others who spectate. The speech is used to underline what is already obvious: that most of the elements of conventional theatre are deliberately missing but that there is going to be no attempt to form a play or anything normally accepted as theatre from what is left.

What is exciting and entertaining is both the thoroughness with which this one basic idea of non-theatricality is executed and, complementary to that, the inventiveness with which such thin gruel is made sustaining for 30 pages of text or 60 minutes of performance. It is a very theatrical non-theatricality. It is even frequently witty, for instance in the juxtapositions of the anaphora and in the novelty and variety of the final orgy of abuse.

By depriving his own piece of most of the trappings of conventional theatre and yet producing a viable theatrical event, Handke both acts out his wish to destroy the despised mechanisms of plot and character, illusion and make-believe, and also demonstrates the feasibility of dispensing with them, confining himself instead to the true reality of here and now, the reality in which the audience exists. For the audience are the hope for the future; by making the audience constantly aware of themselves in the theatre, he hopes to make them repudiate the old brand of theatrical unreality and accept only their own reality. Having changed them, having opened their eyes to a new awareness, he considers them ready for a new kind of theatre. *Offending the Audience* is after all 'a prologue'— i.e.: 'a prologue'—a prologue to, among other things, Handke's subsequent plays.

KASPAR

CRITICAL COMMENTARY

Nicholas Hern (essay date 1971)

SOURCE: Hern, Nicholas. "*Kaspar.*" In *Peter Handke: Theatre and Anti-Theatre,* pp. 59-74. London: Oswald Wolff, 1971.

[*In the following essay, Hern discusses* Kaspar, *comparing it to The Living Theatre's production of* Frankenstein, *as well as to* The Bald Prima Donna *by Eugene Ionesco.*]

Even the title of Handke's first full-length play [**Kaspar**] signals a new development. Kaspar is after all a name, the name of the central figure, and no figure with a name has hitherto appeared in Handke's plays. More than this, Kaspar represents an actual historical personage, Kaspar Hauser, who mysteriously turned up from nowhere in Nuremberg in 1828, aged 16, but with the mind of a child. Ernst Jandl's short poem '16 years', chosen by Handke to preface his play, can be seen as referring obliquely to Hauser and his limited powers of speech, as it asks lispingly: 'what thall/he do/the lad/with hith/thickthteen yearth'. But, hardly surprisingly, *Kaspar* is not a dramatised historical biography. 'The play *Kaspar* does not show

how THINGS REALLY ARE or REALLY WERE with Kaspar Hauser', reads the first line of Handke's introduction. 'It shows what is POSSIBLE with someone. It shows how someone can be brought to speech by speech. The play could also be called *Speech-Torture (Sprechfolterung).*' In fact, the play was originally provisionally entitled *Speech (Sprechen),* which makes the link with the *Sprechstücke* even stronger.

It is, of course, the metaphorical implications of Hauser's predicament, rather than the historical details, which have attracted Handke as they have attracted many writers before him: the implications of a near-adult apparently coming into contact with the world for the first time, a human being with the physical and mental potential of a man, but with that potential quite undeveloped—the implications in fact of being born a fully-grown man. As Handke explained to Artur Joseph:

> In *Kaspar Hauser* I discovered the prototype of a kind of linguistic myth. The figure made me curious. A human being who for sixteen or seventeen years has lived in a wooden compartment suddenly comes into the outside world and has to make himself familiar with it, although he cannot speak . . . This Kaspar Hauser appeared interesting to me not merely as a mythical figure, but as a prototype of people who do not get on with themselves and the world around them, who feel themselves isolated.

This myth is presented on stage by means of an abstraction of the central situation from the concrete historical circumstances. Kaspar thus becomes a timeless, background-less Everyman figure, much as the 'I' in *Self-Accusation* was an abstraction of everyone. Indeed the themes and development of the two plays are markedly similar, with one significant difference: in the earlier piece the gradual growth by 'I' to full mental and physical power and the cumulative restrictions placed on him are recounted *in the past tense*; in *Kaspar,* because of the central hypothesis that Kaspar is a new-born adult, the audience can be *shown* his subsequent development as it takes place, which makes for infinitely more theatrical impact.

If Kaspar bears only an abstract relationship to his historical namesake, he might be expected to be more concretely related to his theatrical namesake, the Kaspar of the Punch and Judy show. Indeed there is much of the puppet about Kaspar. His first blundering entrance, his unsteady gait, his tendency to walk into things, his set expression (Handke directs that the actor wear a mask—a mask depicting perpetual astonishment), all are reminiscent of a string puppet, and the actor might well adopt this as his 'style' for the part.

But another aspect of the puppet, its manipulability, is more sinisterly relevant. The play shows Kaspar brought to a state in which he is unable to initiate speech or action of his own free will. If at the beginning of the play he looks like a puppet, by the end of the play he has become one, though he no longer looks like one. This sinister aspect is emphasised by Handke's saying that Kaspar resembles Frankenstein's monster or King Kong, the one a creature made of human parts and artificially imbued with life, which runs amok destroying itself and its creator, the other a giant gorilla brought by man from its natural habitat to the city, where it also runs amok destroying half of New York. Kaspar's life too is crucially dictated by man-made forces outside himself; true, he does not run amok, but there is an inference that Handke is suggesting this (at least to his audience) as an untried alternative to submission.

Handke also states that 'Kaspar has no similarity to a clown (*Spaßmacher*)' which he seems to deny in the description of Kaspar's get-up(5). It is certainly not the costume of a traditional clown, not grotesque enough for the Auguste's, although borrowing his baggy trousers, and not elegant enough for the white-faced Joey's, despite Kaspar's pallid mask. It seems rather (and this is the intention) to have been assembled at random from a theatrical wardrobe. But this after all was how Chaplin made up his legendary outfit. If, in appearance, Kaspar is something of a cross between a clown and a knockabout comic, then the antics he is made to perform heighten this impression. His fumbling effort to find the gap in the curtains through which to enter is a standard music-hall routine, as is the bit where he puts his hand into a crevice in the sofa, gets it stuck, puts in his other hand to help, and gets that stuck too. And just to confuse the issue further, a critic who saw Peymann's production of the play at Frankfurt described Kaspar's first appearance as that of an 'Arlecchino' and a '*commedia dell'arte* figurine.' What all these figures have in common is their theatricality (they do not exist *per se* in real life) and their popular appeal (or else they would not have survived). Both these factors works in Handke's favour: the theatricalisation is part of his abstraction and generalisation of the figure, while remaining within the confines of the 'pure play', which must exist on the same plane of reality as the audience; and the popularity of the figure, showing as it does much of the appeal of the 'under-dog' or 'little man', aids its acceptance as Everyman. Handke's denial of the figure's clownishness presumably stems from a Brechtian fear that recognition of a funny and loveable stereotype (rather than a sinister monster) will prevent the audience from seeing the serious implications of Kaspar's fate and its application to their own society. This problem can only be solved in production, by trying to strike the right balance between the sympathetic figure at the beginning and the horror of what he becomes; and indeed there have been as many different Kaspars as there have been productions of the play, many of them going for a mask-less, more or less ordinary-looking figure.

The play itself is, like the *Sprechstücke*, divided into paragraphs, but there the resemblance ends. For the paragraphs (numbered 1 to 65) disguise a much more conventional structure. For instance, much of the play consists of extremely detailed stage directions, leaving much less to the director and actors than did the previous pieces. (His next play, incidentally, will consist of nothing but stage directions.) There is also apportionment of dialogue between Kaspar and the *Einsager* (a made-up word meaning 'in-sayers' but having something of the force of 'indoctrinators' or 'persuaders'), whose job it is to 'bring Kaspar to speech by speech'. In **Kaspar** the two sets of speeches are printed side by side on a vertically divided page, which serves to indicate exactly how the dialogue should overlap. Furthermore, the play is punctuated by a number of blackouts, which have the effect of dividing the play into short scenes, and it is these, rather than the imperceptible paragraphs, that the audience would take to be the stages by which the play progresses.

The action of the first scene up to the first blackout (paragraphs 1-15) is closest to the historical incidents which gave Handke the idea for the play. Kaspar 'can hardly walk', Handke explained to Artur Joseph:

> He has been lying down for practically seventeen years. That is not discernible from history. I took this situation over and decked it out with historical quotations from Kaspar Hauser's autobiography. He describes there what he felt like on the first evening, after he came out into the world. He had only one sentence at his disposal: 'I would like to become a horseman such as my father once was' ('*A söchener Reiter möcht i wärn, wie mei Voter aner gween is*'). He wakes up suddenly in the middle of the night in a strange room and feels pain because he had never walked before. He sees a green stove in the room, and it glows in the night. And Kaspar wants to unbosom himself to it and goes to it and says to it the only sentence at his disposal: 'I would like to become a horseman such as my father once was'. He doesn't know that things cannot hear or answer him, but he says the sentence when he is hungry, or when he is getting on well. He cannot express himself in any other way.

Handke has theatricalised this course of events by transforming the room into a stage haphazardly set with an assortment of props and stage furniture, by transmuting Hauser's awakening into Kaspar's stumbling and astonished eruption on to it, and by abstracting his only sentence into: 'I would like to become such as someone else once was' ('*Ich möcht ein solcher werden wie einmal ein andrer gewesen ist*'). As Kaspar blunders round the stage, upsetting the furniture and repeating his sentence, he kicks open the wardrobe doors, and at this moment the *Einsager,* three or more disembodied, dispassionate voices, are heard over the loudspeakers, commending the multiple uses to which Kaspar can put his sentence. Their conclusion—that 'with the sentence you learn there is order, and with the sentence you learn to learn order'—is ironically contrasted with the image of Kaspar, now silent and still amidst the chaos he has created.

The *Einsager*'s next step is to destroy Kaspar's one precious sentence, the only intellectual concept that he brought with him into the world(6). In Handke's words: 'Through their speech they eradicate this sentence from him . . . That is the first phase. The *Einsager* have brought him to dumbness'. Now they indoctrinate him, painfully and confusingly, in conventional speech and in the conventional precepts of good order and moral conformity. Thus bombarded, Kaspar sets himself and the stage to rights, his actions according more and more with the *Einsager*'s rhythmic recitation of moral maxims.

There follows a sort of baptism by darkness, by which the *Einsager* demonstrate to Kaspar that his new command of speech can be used to overcome such elemental (and unsocial) emotions as fear of the dark; after which Kaspar is taught a variety of grammatical constructions. His first attempts at imitation are interesting surreal distortions, but gradually he produces the required stereotypes. His final, triumphant use of the verb 'to be': 'I am who I am', with its divine and existential echoes, is followed, however, by a glimpse of the allegedly conquered darkness beneath the brilliant surface: 'Why are there nothing but black serpents flying about?' (a quotation, by way of homage, from the recently rediscovered Austro-Hungarian playwright, Ödön von Horvàth).

Seventeen short scenes follow (paras 32-57), in which a number of identical, masked Kaspar-figures perform little sketches to demonstrate, for Kaspar's benefit, such elementary phenomena as movement, pain, noise, sound. Now fully aware of the world around, him, Kaspar, alone on stage, successfully shuts the wardrobe door and delivers an elegant manifesto of his new persona(7). He is the apotheosis of orderliness. He even begins to speak in rhymed verse. 'The world is actually rhymed for him,' says Handke. 'Now,' affirms Kaspar, 'I would no longer like to be someone else.' He leaves the stage; but, sinisterly, the wardrobe doors swing open again. Blackout. Interval.

Much as Handke suggests that before the play begins his opening stage directions be repeated softly over loudspeakers as the audience enters the auditorium, so for the interval he suggests a sound collage to be beamed at the audience in the foyer, the bars and even in the street outside the theatre! The text he provides seems to allude mainly to violent political action, but near the end it changes to a lucid account of dinner-table etiquette. But the instructions are increasingly interspersed with 'rogue' sentences (like subliminal inserts in a film, or the one thing 'wrong' in a Magritte) which are full of actual or implied violence. 'The soup is served from the right . . . The stranglehold comes from both sides.' It seems to be the very orderliness of the domestic scene (directly related to Kaspar's newly ordered life) which has occasioned the violence by repressing all 'undesirable' expressions of emotion. It is this thread which runs throughout the second half of the play.

The first scene (paras. 60-64) begins with the *Einsager* reciting a paean (in the same irregularly rhymed verse used earlier by Kaspar) in praise of beating people up to bring them to order(8). Meanwhile, five of the duplicate Kaspars, their masks (and Kaspar's) now expressing

contentment not astonishment, seat themselves on the sofa ready to provide a cacophonous accompaniment to Kaspar's speech to the audience listing the restrictions which society imposes on its members and the code of behaviour it exacts from them. With this speech (amplified through the *Einsager*'s loudspeakers) Kaspar turns on the audience, as the *Einsager* had turned on him. But just as his earlier integration was undermined by glimpses of the abyss beneath, so here his confident bullying ends in the thrice repeated '*Jeder Satz ist für die Katz*' (approximately: 'All words are for the birds')—a negation of all that the *Einsager* have taught him.

The complex speeches which follow reveal chiefly the disturbingly arbitrary connection between a phenomenon and the word used to describe it; thus, Kaspar recalls, when he learned the word 'snow', he applied it to everything white and then to anything at all, with the result that both the word and snow itself ceased to have any meaning for him. As Handke told Artur Joseph, the play examines 'the impossibility of *expressing* something with language: that is, to say something which goes beyond the actual sentence into the significant and the meaningful'.

A further crescendo of nerve-jangling noise, with the Kaspars advancing towards the audience, climaxes in Kaspar's cry: 'I am brought to speech. I am transferred into reality'. But he is answered with silence and darkness.

When the lights come on again for the short final scene, Kaspar continues speaking, but his words just fail to make sense(9). At the same time, the other Kaspars busy themselves ridiculing 'an object, perhaps a chair', rendering it 'IMPOSSIBLE' by depriving it of its meaning as a chair; and the *Einsager* are endlessly repeating: 'May be', referring partly to the fluidity of meaning revealed by all the Kaspars, and partly to Kaspar's final words: 'I am I only by chance', a pathetic distortion of his earlier triumphant 'I am who I am'. Kaspar has now realised that, since the *Einsager* (representing environmental and societal pressures) have had so much control over his development, he cannot claim to be an absolute product of his own individual qualities; and, more fundamentally, he has realised that since the meaning of language, the medium through which he has developed perception and personality, is arbitrary and relative, and can be altered by forces outside himself, he too can claim only an arbitrary and contingent egoity. He can define himself only in relation to shifting standards. With this devastating realisation, the curtain jerks closed, knocking over all the Kaspars like tailor's dummies. The play is over.

In the course of the play Handke has invented some neat devices to illustrate his abstract theme. Some of these, such as the use of rhyme to indicate the acme of Kaspar's powers of speech and social integration, can be fully appreciated from the text alone; others, such as the use of multiple Kaspars to demonstrate different areas of perception, are more effective in the theatre, although it is never clear whether they are meant to be the original Kaspar split into several bodies for purposes of theatrical demonstration, or whether they are the mass-produced human beings of a society that moulds every human being into an identical form. But there are also echoes of other men's plays and of other men's philosophies.

The play which is perhaps most like **Kaspar** is Beckett's *Act without Words I,* which Handke saw performed at the same Experimenta which launched his own **Offending the Audience** in 1966. *Act without Words I* shares with **Kaspar** a central, abstract, generalised, Everyman figure (the sole figure on stage in Beckett's play is called 'the man') whose behaviour is ruthlessly shaped by unseen but audible forces off-stage, an amount of almost knockabout physical action and, the educative process completed, a desolate ending. Beckett too has theatricalised a situation which might well have been presented in more concrete, naturalistic terms. Thus 'the man' is repeatedly summoned into the wings by whistles only to be flung back on stage every time until he no longer responds to the whistles. Beckett is less interested than Handke in the nature of the off-stage forces but in both plays similarly Pavlovian methods of instruction are used. And Kaspar too starts by suffering from the Cartesian gap between mind and body, between situation and action which is the bane of so many of Beckett's 'clowns' (Beckett also uses a shorthand of recognisable theatrical stereotypes). 'The time-lapse between the decision and the action is a reminder that the connection between the two isn't necessarily a simple one', as one Beckett critic put it. That Kaspar appears to close this gap, to become integrated, is merely a veneer which society demands that its members acquire. It is true that Beckett's concern is less with the individual *vis-à-vis* society than with the individual faced with the void that is life, but his presentation of a theatricalised typical individual has considerable bearing on Handke's solution of a similar problem in **Kaspar.**

The dramatisation of the conflict between society and the individual in which the one attempts to mould the other is not new, even to Handke, who had tackled this theme in **Self-Accusation.** There would be little point in cataloguing all previous treatments of this conflict in the theatre, but two deserve particular mention. One is the Living Theatre's *Frankenstein,* whose monster Handke had said Kaspar resembles. Jeremy Kingston described the performance in *Punch*:

> The company are shot, beheaded, gassed, racked, hung or otherwise executed all over the huge three-tier scaffolding that forms the bulk of the acting area. Dr. Frankenstein . . . then begins the reconstruction of a new creature. Indoctrination follows, with all the woes attendant on an industrial civilisation, and in the last act the cells in the scaffolding fill with prisoners of the state, each going individually mad.

The parallel to **Kaspar** is close, especially as both plays start with the inhuman process of wiping the slate clean, by mass murder in *Frankenstein* or by obliterating Kaspar's only sentence.

The second interesting treatment of 'the individual cowed into conformism by society and convention' is, inevitably, Ionesco's, and these words are used by Martin Esslin to describe the theme of both *Jacques or Obedience* and *The Lesson.* In *Jacques,* conformist society is represented by calling all the members of one family Jacques, just as 'three-quarters of the inhabitants of the town' in *The Bald Prima Donna* are called Bobby Watson, which relates to Handke's device of multiple Kaspars (Ionesco even states that 'all the characters, except Jacques, can wear masks'). More significantly the metaphor of domination in both Ionesco plays is *language*: Jacques at first refuses to pronounce the words that would confirm his acceptance of his family's standards, but, after exclaiming 'Words! What crimes are committed in your name', he accepts the bourgeois creed: 'I love potatoes in their jackets!' as his own; and *The Lesson* has become one of the classic theatrical demonstrations of the use of language as an instrument of power. In a sense, **Kaspar** combines features from both plays in that the *Einsager* use language as in *The Lesson* to bring an individual into line with conformist standards as in *Jacques.*

Still more interesting is Ionesco's explanation in *Notes and Counter-Notes* of what happened to the ending of *The Bald Prima Donna*:

> Unfortunately the wise and elementary truths [the Smiths and Martins] exchanged, when strung together, had gone mad, the language had become disjointed, the characters distorted . . . For me, what had happened was a kind of collapse of reality. The words had turned into sounding shells devoid of meaning; . . . the world appeared to me in an unearthly, perhaps its true, light, beyond understanding and governed by arbitrary laws.

This applies almost word for word to **Kaspar,** and it is closely matched by what Handke says about that play's ending:

> And then [Kaspar] acts as if broken, then falls more and more into confusion, then his speech suddenly begins to go wrong—until complete schizophrenia sets in, complete tohu bohu, an upside down world governs the stage; in the end, chaos.

Ionesco offers a note of interpretation:

> The text of *The Bald Prima Donna* . . . consisting as it did of ready-made expressions and the most threadbare clichés, revealed to me all that is automatic in the language and behaviour of people: 'talking for the sake of talking', talking because there is nothing personal to say, the absence of any life within, the mechanical routine of everyday life, man sunk in his social background, no longer able to distinguish himself from it.

Kaspar breaks down because the language he has been taught is similarly automatic and tailored to the norms of society.

Philosophically the basis of **Kaspar** is that, as language is necessary for the expression of thought (and may even be a prerequisite for thought itself), he who is in a position to control people's language also controls their thought. The *Einsager* are in just such a position *vis-à-vis* Kaspar. Kaspar comes into the world possessing one sentence. This sentence is all he has but it is uniquely his. But because it fails to impose order on the world around him, and because it is his sentence and not theirs, the *Einsager* systematically destroy it and replace it with a language whose expressive power is limited to the reiteration of social conformism. This means that even if Kaspar were to think non-conformist or just individual thoughts, he would have no language to express them.

This is like a parody of Wittgenstein's thesis in *Tractatus Logico-Philosophicus,* in the Preface to which the author writes:

> The aim of the book is to set a limit to thought, or rather—not to thought, but to the expression of thoughts . . . It will therefore only be in language that the limit can be set, and what lies on the other side of the limit will simply be nonsense.

Handke endorses this view in **Kaspar** but the benevolent philosopher attempting to define the limits of language and, therefore, of the expression of thought is replaced by the tyrannic *Einsager.* This is not to say that Handke is deriding Wittgenstein. On the contrary, much of Handke's writing is a literary counterpart to Wittgenstein's logical positivism in its rejection of the metaphysical and its acceptance only of that reality which can be verified by the physical senses. Ever since his first reading from *The Pedlar* at Gruppe 47, critics have been remarking on the similarity of Handke's style to Wittgenstein's in its tendency to approach a phenomenon over and over again from different angles in an attempt to define its absolute reality.

In **Kaspar** Handke is accepting Wittgenstein's view of the limitability of language but is illustrating what happens when the limits are set by the 'wrong' people. Who actually are the *Einsager*? Handke refuses to say: 'No concrete social system is being criticised in **Kaspar,** neither the capitalist nor the socialist system'. The *Einsager* then are intended to be an abstract representation of any force which attempts control of language and, therefore, of thought. But the language they themselves use is too steeped in bourgeois values to remain entirely abstract.

And when Handke offers a political interpretation of **Kaspar,** it is clearly prejudiced in favour of the Left:

> What upsets me is people's estrangement from their own language . . . People who are estranged from their language and their speech are like the workers estranged from their products, who are also estranged from the world.

The second part of Wittgenstein's statement is also illustrated in the play: 'what lies on the other side of the limit will simply be nonsense'. When Kaspar realises that the language he has been taught is so limited as to be virtually useless ('*Jeder Satz ist für die Katz*'), he gradually slips into nonsense as he tries to transcend those limits and achieve meaningful self-expression.

Kaspar, then, has several levels of meaning. It could be taken simply as a theatricalisation of Everyman's life cycle: birth (on to the stage); growth of awareness and physical integration; acquisition of speech; responsibility for one's own and others' behaviour; finally, decay of one's mental faculties; and death (as the curtain closes). Seen as social comment, the play is an abstract demonstration of the way an individual's individuality is stripped from him by society, specifically by limiting the expressive power of the language it teaches him. 'This neutering of language, at once repressive and cunning, is one dominant tendency of its adversary, language control' (Günter Eich). Politically, this criticism can be applied to any person or group in power, but it is phrased in such a way that middle of the road or right wing governments seem most impeached. Philosophically, **Kaspar** is a dramatisation of the connection between language and thought and an examination of the limits that can be set on both. Handke's achievement is to have invented a dramatic form which succeeds for a large part of the time in conveying all these levels of meaning at once.

June Schlueter (essay date 1981)

SOURCE: Schlueter, June. *"Kaspar."* In *The Plays and Novels of Peter Handke,* pp. 41-50. Pittsburgh: University of Pittsburgh Press, 1981.

[*In the following essay, Schlueter discusses Handke's study of language in the play* Kaspar.]

Kaspar (1967), Handke's first full-length play, premiered simultaneously at the Theater am Turm in Frankfurt (under the direction of Claus Peymann) and the Oberhausen Städtische Bühne (under the direction of Günther Büch) and became the most frequently performed modern play in Germany, Austria, and Switzerland during the 1968-69 season.[1] The same audiences who had smiled wryly at the abuse they endured from Handke's first *Sprechstücke,* along with thousands of others, flocked to the theaters to see the producton which *Theater heute* was to declare "Play of the Year" in 1968, which Peter Brook was later to direct in Paris prisons, and which theaters in New York, London, Paris, and numerous other major cities were to perform in subsequent years. Enthusiastic reviewers praised the play as a major theatrical event, suggesting a greatness akin to that of *Waiting for Godot (En Attendant Godot,* 1952) and predicting a permanent place for **Kaspar** in literary history. Jack Kroll called Handke "the hottest young playwright in Europe" and Clive Barnes referred to him as "one of the most important young playwrights of our time."[2]

The historical Kaspar Hauser, well known in German literature and alluded to in Ernst Jandl's prefatory poem (chosen by Handke), was an autistic young man who appeared in Nuremberg in 1828, after some sixteen years of presumably solitary existence, in possession of only one sentence: "*A söchener Reiter möcht i wärn, wie mei Voter aner gween is*" ("I want to become a horseman like my father once was").[3] Recognizing in the Kaspar Hauser story what he calls "*das modell einer Art von sprachlichem Mythos*"[4] ("the model of a sort of linguistic myth"[5]), Handke alters the sentence but not the situation of his protagonist and turns Kaspar into a universalized character who shows not "*wie ES WIRKLICH IST oder WIRKLICH WAR mit Kaspar Hauser. Es zeigt, was MÖGLICH IST mit jemandem*"[6] ("how IT REALLY IS or REALLY WAS with Kaspar Hauser. It shows what IS POSSIBLE with someone"[7]). Since the play does not pretend to be retelling Kaspar Hauser's story, nor even telling Kaspar's, but offering instead a model of possibility, Handke's preface correctly suggests that what the audience experiences is not a story but a theatrical event.

The sixteen stages of Kaspar's development, delineated by Handke at the beginning of the play, take the representative protagonist from birth to death, from innocence to experience, and from unity to schizophrenia, through speech. Barely able to walk, apparently incapable of reasoning, and obviously in possession of only one sentence, the uninitiated Kaspar stumbles across the boards like an oversized infant wandering in the undifferentiated world of childhood. He appears to learn little from his contacts with objects onstage yet displays a constant need to describe and evaluate those experiences through the statement and restatement of his one sentence. He sticks his hands in the crevice between two sofa cushions, with difficulty removes them, and remarks: "*Ich möcht ein solcher werden wie einmal ein andrer gewesen ist*" ("I want to be a person like somebody else was once"). He pulls out a table drawer, watches as the objects contained in it fall to the floor, and remarks: "*Ich möcht ein solcher werden wie einmal ein andrer gewesen ist.*" He battles with a chair in his path, kicks it, and remarks: "*Ich möcht ein solcher werden wie einmal ein andrer gewesen ist.*"

For an audience that cannot function without language, Kaspar's single sentence is woefully incapable of describing or evaluating even those few experiences he encounters. As far as the audience can see, only when one possesses a multitude of sentences can all things be possible, for only when a person can differentiate among objects and experiences can there be a meaningful relationship between that person and the world.

The *Einsager*, or prompters, who are disembodied loudspeaker voices, support the audience's concern and take it upon themselves to educate Kaspar. Listening intently to the *Einsager*'s paradigms, Kaspar proves to be a model student: he learns to use their grammatical constructions;[8] he learns to generalize, then discovers the faults of his generalizations and begins to particularize. He not only learns everything the *Einsager* teach him about language, he also develops a surprisingly wide-ranging vocabulary, until, finally, he is ready to be weaned.

Convinced that their job is complete, the *Einsager* pronounce Kaspar prepared to function in life:

> Du hast Modellsätze, mit denen du dich durchschlagen kannst: indem du diese Modelle auf deine Sätze anwendest, kannst du alles, was scheinbar in Unordnung ist, in Ordnung setzen: du kannst es für geordnet erklären: jeder Gegenstand kann der sein, als den du ihn bezeichnest.
>
> (P. 57)

> You have model sentences with which you can get through life: by applying these models to your sentences, you can impose order on everything that appears chaotic: you can declare it ordered: every object can be what you designate it to be.
>
> (P. 102)

Such faith in the omnipotence of language has been apparent throughout the *Einsager*'s teaching, suggested especially when they ceased adjusting their sentences to Kaspar's movements and watched him begin to adjust his movements to their sentences. For the *Einsager*, experience is the product of language, which has the unquestionable power of controlling reality. This is precisely what they, who are nothing themselves *but* language, have done with Kaspar.

By this time, however, the audience, who at first applauded the progress of Kaspar's education, recognizes that his enlightenment may perhaps not be so positive an achievement after all. Kaspar's first learned sentence is a lament: "*Damals, als ich noch weg war, habe ich niemals so viele Schmerzen im Kopf gehabt, und man hat mich nicht so gequält wie jetzt, seit ich hier bin*" (p. 29) ("At that time, while I was still away, my head never ached as much, and I was not tortured the way I am now that I am here," p. 77), suggesting the pain his emergence into a language-centered world has created. In moving from his world of innocence into the socialized world of the *Einsager*, Kaspar has acquired a consciousness that demands expression and differentiation. He now knows not only that pain is distinct from other feelings but that his present pain is more intense than the pain he had previously felt. He is tortured by his compulsion to name the pain while at the same time aware that such naming is, under his new circumstances, less adequate than his earlier means of naming the pain, through his sentence. With that sentence, he could perfectly express the sensation, at least for himself. As soon as he subscribes to the convention of language which names this sensation as "pain," he is aware that the relationship has changed, for the word "pain" is not his word, but others'. It is invested with meaning and a range of connotations, none of which offers him the possibility the uneducated Kaspar had.

Kaspar discovers that through following the *Einsager*'s models he can incorporate names into sentences, ostensibly ordering his world. But he also realizes that the necessity of interpretation, to which everyone who has access to language must defer, makes every perception impure.

Despite Wittgenstein's picture theory, which attempts to correlate language and phenomenal reality, individual perceptions remain unique, creating an infinite number of linguistic expressions for any object. Any sentence, then, because it is filtered through the individual's interpretive process, is both an expression and a distortion of the object it seeks to describe. The *Einsager* tell Kaspar that he must be mistaken if he sees an object differently from the way he speaks it, yet within a language system, the two can never coincide.

The problem becomes even more complex when language attempts to describe abstract concepts and when Kaspar considers whether anything can be perceived independently of words. The security of order which Kaspar first feels upon discovering he can name the objects of his world deteriorates into confusion as he contemplates the endless ways of representing phenomenal and experiential reality. He realizes that despite the apparent limitations of his original sentence, it enabled him to contain the diversity of the world. The *Einsager* themselves point out that with his one sentence Kaspar could do anything: make himself noticeable, explain things to himself, name everything that comes in his way and move it out of his way, familiarize himself with all objects, bring order into every disorder.

As soon as Kaspar develops a consciousness of himself as distinct from his environment, however, his sentence fails. This crucial moment, precipitated by the *Einsager*'s steady stream of language, is punctuated by Kaspar's sudden interruption of his sentence; he sits in silence as the voices continue to offer him the last hope of hiding behind it. But the hope is already dead, for Kaspar has experienced the beginnings of self-consciousness. The brightly lit stage falls into darkness, signaling the end, and the irretrievability, of Kaspar's primeval world.

As his education into language progresses, Kaspar becomes increasingly conscious of his estrangement from the very world into which he is being initiated. In torment and despair, he asks, *"warum man mich denn von allem, was zu mir gehörte, abgetrennt habe?"* (p. 93) ("why have I been cut off from everything that belongs to me?" p. 133). By this time, Kaspar—and the audience as well—realizes that in permitting his one sentence to be exorcised and replaced by the established patterns of language and hence of society, he has sacrificed his individuality. Metaphorically expressing this by populating the stage with duplicates of Kaspar, Handke directs that five other clown-like figures roam about, playing a symphony of cacophonous sounds, reflecting Kaspar's internal confusion. Handke's hero, ironically, has had his wish fulfilled, for now he is, visibly, someone like others. In a moment that combines triumph and defeat, Kaspar's voice rises out of the chaos to pronounce final judgment on his learning experience: *"Jeder Satz ist für die Katz"* (p. 92) ("Every sentence is for the birds," p. 132) and *"Ziegen und Affen"* (pp. 101-02) ("Goats and monkeys," p. 140), the cry of Othello, similarly victimized by the power of words.[9]

In one version of the play, Kaspar's final cry, punctuated by the staccato pulls of the closing curtain, is *"Ich/bin/nur/*

zufällig/ich" ("I/am/only/accidentally/I"),[10] a statement which contrasts starkly with his earlier, defensive assertion *"Ich bin, der ich bin"* (p. 56) ("I am the one I am," p. 102), spoken in affirmation of his individuality when he first begins to realize it is endangered. Kaspar's final lament perfectly embodies his plight: the sentences he uses are not his sentences, the morality he supports is not his morality, yet they are the tools and guidelines with and within which he must function. Kaspar realizes that he has achieved expression, but because it is simply a borrowed mode, his identity, like reality itself, is arbitrary.

As he approaches the microphone to deliver his "good citizen" speech, Kaspar appears to be the ideal social creature. He is honest, frugal, conscientious, industrious, reticent, modest, friendly, dutiful, receptive. He loves order, does perfectly everything he is asked to do, has an untarnished record, would like to be a member, would like to cooperate, is proud of what has been achieved so far. Poetically relating the story of his life, Kaspar reaches the epitome of articulateness. But then his monologue deteriorates into didactics. In a voice much like that of the prompters, he begins to speak of conforming actions, of what everyone must do and must not do in relation to others, reciting the same kinds of moral maxims that were fundamental to the *Einsager*'s training: *"Jeder muß sich vor dem Essen die Hände waschen / jeder muß im Gefängnis die Taschen leeren"* (p. 86) ("Everyone must wash his hands before eating / everyone must empty his pockets before a beating," p. 127). The *Einsager*'s—and society's—insistence upon order has given Kaspar not only a language but, along with it, an established moral pattern; while seeming to open up possibilities to him, it has instead imposed limitations of both language and living.

The *Einsager* have proved to be no different from the societal order attacked in more abstract terms in the *Sprechstücke* and no less destructive than Nazi propagandists. Insisting as they do on the necessity of order, they have bombarded their victim with the negative commands of society, the prefabricated patterns of language and behavior which are intended to be assimilated but not understood. But where the abstract "I" of *Self-Accusation* defers to social order, confessing a myriad of sins, Kaspar rebels against the prescriptiveness of the order preached by the *Einsager*, defending, even in defeat, not only his individuality but the basic right of, and need for, self-expression.

Just before the play's chaotic ending, the desperate Kaspar cries, "Was habe ich doch gerade gesagt? Wenn ich nur wüßte, was es ist, was ich gerade gesagt habe!" (p. 90) ("What was it that I said just now? If I only knew what it is that I said just now!" p. 131). Painfully conscious of the arbitrary connection between language and reality, he now sees the loss in his gain. His lesson has been that without language, phenomenal reality can only be sensed; with language it can be named, which, in turn, permits differentiating, valuing, and, ultimately, constructing. But language brings with it a history of predetermined meanings against which Kaspar has no immunity. As Handke's protagonist acknowledges, *"Schon mit meinem ersten Satz bin ich in die Falle gegangen"* (p. 98) ("Already with my first sentence I was trapped," p. 137)—trapped by the repressiveness of a system that makes puppets of men. Individually, as one who has become one of many, Kaspar serves as a forceful indictment of society; but on a higher and, for Handke, more significant level, that is, as a model of what is possible, he serves to dramatize the very process of knowing, to which verbal capability is central.

Dramaturgically, **Kaspar** may appear more traditional than the purely presentational *Sprechstücke,* but, as Handke remarks in the interview with Joseph, the full-length play is no more concerned with characterization or plot than the shorter pieces were:

> Das [**Kaspar**] ist nichts Neues. Das ist eine Entwicklung, zu der ich einmal kam, weil ich mich da wieder in ein automatisches Produzieren von Stücken aus purer Sprache einlassen mußte, wo die Wörter nur sich selbst beleuchten. Die Wörter, die puren Wörter, die vorher in der **Publikumsbeschimpfung** auf der Bühne vor sich gehen, verdichteten sich nun zu einer Figur.[11]

> It [**Kaspar**] was nothing new, it only evolved because I was again forced to produce plays automatically from pure language, in which the words only illuminate themselves. The words, the pure words which first occur onstage in **Offending the Audience,** are condensed into a character.[12]

Over the years, a number of productions of **Kaspar** have emphasized the clown characterization implicit in the name (*Kasper* in German means clown) or the characterization suggested by the similarity of the name to the *Kasperle* of the traditional Viennese puppet show. Handke himself mentions the clown reference in his preface, but maintains that there is no resemblance, that his Kaspar is, rather, like Frankenstein's monster: a newborn adult whose discovery of the world leads to his victimization.

In The Living Theatre's production of *Frankenstein* (which was touring Europe while Handke was writing **Kaspar**), Julian Beck and Judith Malina emphasized the anarchistic portions of Mary Shelley's novel as they brought the monster from creation through the stages of discovery to the destruction of its ego. Working from the company's sketchbooks and staging directions, Pierre Biner, in his book on The Living Theatre, re-creates the European production, quoting the monster's description of his preverbal experience of the world, which is strikingly similar to Kaspar's:

> It is with a considerable difficulty that I remember the original era of my being: all the events of that period appear confused and indistinct. I saw, felt, heard, and smelt, at the same time. By degrees, I remember, a stronger light pressed upon my nerves, so that I was obliged to shut my eyes. Darkness then came over me, and troubled me; but hardly had I felt this, when, by opening my eyes, the light poured in upon me again. I walked. Before, dark and opaque bodies had surrounded me, impervious to my touch or sight; but I now found

> that I could wander on at liberty, with no obstacles which I could not either surmount or avoid. The light became more and more oppressive to me; and, the heat wearying me as I walked, I sought a place where I could receive shade. It was dark when I awoke; I felt cold also and half-frightened. I was a poor, helpless, miserable wretch; I knew, and could distinguish, nothing; but feeling pain invade me on all sides, I sat down and wept.[13]

The monster goes on to speak of his development:

> I obtained a knowledge of the manners, governments, and religions of the different nations of the earth. Was man, at once so powerful, so virtuous and magnificent, yet so vicious and base? To be a great and virtuous man appeared the highest honor that can befall a sensitive being; to be base and vicious appeared the lowest degradation. I could not conceive how one man could go forth to murder his fellow, or even why there were laws and governments; but when I heard details of vice and bloodshed, my wonder ceased, and I turned away with disgust and loathing. The strange system of human society was explained to me. I heard of the division of property, of immense wealth and squalid poverty; of rank, descent, and noble blood. And what was I? Of my creation and creator I was absolutely ignorant; but I knew that I possessed no money, no friends, no kind of property. I was, besides, endued with a figure hideously deformed and loathsome. Was I then a monster, a blot upon the earth, from which all men fled, and whom all men disowned?[14]

In describing the monster's passage from innocence to experience, Biner refers to an "April countryside" passing into "the desolation of winter": "Innocence turns into crime and repression by the police, harmony among the faculties of the mind into cacophony and strife, transforming the faculties into victims and executioners."[15] If, as Christopher Innes suggests, **Kaspar** may be read as an "interior, psychological drama," in which "the table, chair and cupboard are the furniture of Kaspar's mind, the prompters are the stream of sense data that impinges on the consciousness, and the verbal forms represent mental states," then the "projection of complete schizophrenia" in the second act may well parallel the monster's experience, and the multiple Kaspars may be the "victims and executioners" of Kaspar's mind.[16]

Undoubtedly the parallels between the two plays can be pursued further, but not without implying a stronger influence than was probably present. Handke's first full-length play clearly evolved from the *Sprechstücke,* and particularly from **Self-Accusation,** but just as Handke saw in Kaspar Hauser a model for his character, so also did he recognize the affinities between the Frankenstein monster and the dramatic model he himself was creating. If he indeed did see The Living Theatre's production, this may have been responsible for his making the comparison between the monster and Kaspar in his preface.

In addition to the abstract Everyman entrapped by language, the figure of Kaspar may suggest, more specifically, the poet, who, in sacrificing his unique language to one of everyday formulations, relinquishes his distinctive voice and permanently ensures the distance between man and his world. The seeds of this idea will flourish in Handke's later work, beginning with **Short Letter, Long Farewell,** in which he thinks in terms of two languages—everyday and poetic—and mourns the loss of the latter. Even in 1967, though, when Handke was still an angry young man, his work was beginning to look to language as not only the source of chaos but its solution as well.

Notes

1. See Joachim Kaiser, "Schauspiel in der Bundesrepublik," *Theater heute,* 11, 10 (October 1970), p. 9. Kaiser records 508 performances, with a total audience of 54,868. His comparisons deal only with "modern, serious" drama.

2. Jack Kroll, "Mind Bending," *Newsweek,* February 26, 1973, p. 91; Clive Barnes, "Theater: Handke's *Kaspar* Is Staged in Brooklyn," *New York Times,* February 16, 1973, p. 26.

3. For an account of the historical and legendary Kaspar Hauser, see A. F. Bance, "The Kaspar Hauser Legend and Its Literary Survival," *German Life & Letters,* n.s., 28, 3 (April 1975), 199-210.

4. Artur Joseph, *Theater unter vier Augen: Gespräche mit Prominenten* (Cologne: Kiepenheuer und Witsch, 1969), p. 35.

5. Artur Joseph, "Nauseated by Language: From an Interview with Peter Handke," trans. E. B. Ashton, in *The Drama Review,* 15, 1 (Fall 1970), 60.

6. Preface to *Kaspar,* in *Kaspar* (Frankfurt: Suhrkamp, 1967), p. 7. Subsequent citations in German are from this edition and appear parenthetically in the text.

7. Preface to *Kaspar,* in *Kaspar and Other Plays,* trans. Michael Roloff (New York: Farrar, Straus & Giroux, 1969), p. 59. Subsequent citations in English are from this edition and appear parenthetically in the text.

8. Linda Hill, "The Struggle Against Language and Behavior Patterns: Handke's *Kaspar,*" in *Language As Aggression: Studies in the Postwar Drama* (Bonn: Bouvier, 1976), lists these models as "condition contrary to fact, active/passive, aber, correlative conjunctions (sowohl . . . als auch, nicht nur . . . sondern auch, zwar . . . aber), je . . . desto, selbstverständlich, jeder (adjective)/niemand, kein, condition contrary to fact, unwahr/wahr, dich (direct object and reflexive), schon and noch, du, object and adverbial clauses, and modal verbs" (p. 176).

9. For a speculative treatment of the relationship between *Kaspar* and *Othello,* see June Schlueter, "'Goats and Monkeys' and the 'Idiocy of Language': Handke's *Kaspar* and Shakespeare's *Othello,*" *Modern Drama,* 23, 1 (March 1980), pp. 25-32.

10. This ending appears in the play as published in *Theater heute,* 9, 13 (1968 Jahrbuch), 69-88. In *Stücke 1,* the final lines are: "Ich/bin/nur/Ziegen und Affen/Ziegen und Affen."

11. Joseph, *Theater unter vier Augen,* p. 35.

12. Joseph, "Nauseated by Language," p. 59.

13. Pierre Biner, *The Living Theatre: A History without Myths,* trans. Robert Meister (New York: Avon, 1972), pp. 132-33.

14. Ibid., pp. 133-34.

15. Ibid., p. 136.

16. Christopher Innes, *Modern German Drama: A Study in Form* (Cambridge: Cambridge University Press, 1979), pp. 244-45.

Jeffrey Herrick (essay date spring 1984)

SOURCE: Herrick, Jeffrey. "Peter Handke's *Kaspar*: A Study of Linguistic Theory in Modern Drama." *Philological Quarterly* 63, no. 2 (spring 1984): 205-21.

[*In the following essay, Herrick discusses language and its limitations in Handke's* Kaspar *and gives a comparison to* The Chairs *by Eugene Ionesco.*]

Although considerable scholarly effort has recently been given to applying linguistic studies and theories to literary texts, especially in deconstruction, almost none has been given to examining literary works in which the creative use of linguistic theory plays a manifest role. Yet several modern European dramatists have clearly concerned themselves with linguistic theory in their plays. The overt use of linguistic theory in drama has largely been due, it seems, to the epistemological basis of much modern linguistic theorizing, since those modern dramatists who deal with linguistic questions generally have philosophical and psychological matters under study. This is nowhere more apparent than in Peter Handke's **Kaspar,** which is a presentation of a linguistic indoctrination that has tragic dimensions. The subtle and insidious power of unseen prompters to control the development of the protagonist Kaspar's mind has its basis in the idea of the deterministic priority of language structure in thought, an idea labeled the Sapir-Whorf hypothesis by linguists. But **Kaspar** is not merely an enactment of this hypothesis. It is a powerful and affecting play which employs linguistic theory in the service of its dramatic ends. And it is not without precedents in this respect. Critics have noted that Handke stands in a line of other Austrian writers concerned with the powers and inadequacies of language, such as Hugo von Hofmannsthal, Karl Kraus, Fritz Mauthner, and Ludwig Wittgenstein.[1] But it has not been noted that he also stands more prominently in a line of other European dramatists in this regard. Before looking at Handke's work in detail, a brief examination of some other modern plays which employ theoretical linguistic ideas will help not only to establish the dramatic precedents for **Kaspar** but also to introduce, as it happens, some of the specific concepts found in **Kaspar** concerning the powers and inadequacies of language.

In a fairly simple way Jean Genet's *The Balcony* deals with linguistic theory in the emphasis it gives to nominative power. Genet shows his characters deliberately blurring distinctions between proper names and professional titles. The roles of Bishop, Judge, and General which ordinary men come to play in Irma's brothel are titles which carry established functions and stature. The titles and roles are appealing and have power, because of the stature the community grants them. Genet is more concerned with the social than the linguistic point. But the linguistic issue he introduces is a serious one. It is one Wittgenstein also explored as he looked into the theoretical problems underlying nominative power. Wittgenstein observed:

> "What the names in a language signify must be indestructible; for it must be possible to describe the state of affairs in which everything destructible is destroyed. And this description will contain words; and what corresponds to these cannot be destroyed, for otherwise the words have no meaning." I must not saw off the branch on which I am sitting.
>
> One might, of course, object at once that this description would have to except itself from the destruction.— But what corresponds to the separate words of the description and so cannot be destroyed if it is true, is what gives the words their meaning—is without which they would have no meaning.—In a sense, however, this man is surely what corresponds to his name. But he is destructible, and his name does not lose its meaning when the bearer is destroyed.—An example of something corresponding to the name, and without which it would have no meaning, is a paradigm that is used in connection with the name in the language-game.[2]

The paradigm to which Wittgenstein here refers includes the role and the functions concomitant with a name or a title. In Genet's play the idea of the power of a title, both over the particular destructible man who fulfills the function which the word designates and apart from him, is illustrated by the desire of the Chief of Police to attain a stature equal to that of the established nomenclature: the Bishop, the Judge, and the General. The Chief of Police finds that his desire can only be fulfilled, in terms of *The Balcony's* paradigm, when someone assumes his role in one of Irma's studios. And when this finally occurs, his identity is displaced, so that he can refer to himself as "intact," yet "larger than large, stronger than strong, deader than dead."[3] Genet thus suggests how language can serve to define and perpetuate personal illusions and social powers.

Another play, which deals even more obviously with the idea of the power of language, but primarily with political concerns in mind, is Václav Havel's *The Memorandum*. The memorandum of the title is a ploy used by Jan Ballas to usurp the directorship of a vast bureaucracy from Josef Gross. It is written in an artificial language called Ptydepe, a language which is understood only by a small group. Ballas cannot stay in power after he has overthrown Gross because he does not understand Ptydepe himself, and because, by his own orders, the bureaucratic rules which regulate the use of Ptydepe insure that any document using it cannot be translated. Those who know Ptydepe have the real power, and the language is particularly appropriate to their bureaucratic ends: it is an attempt to erase the affective connotatons inherent in the natural language, and to institute orthographic redundancy. The theory, as explained by the teacher, Mark Lear, is not necessarily ridiculous. "Briefly: the greater the redundancy of a language, the more reliable it is, because the smaller is the possibility that by an exchange of a letter, or by an oversight or a typing error, the meaning of a text could be altered."[4] In fact, a noted linguist has argued along similar lines in all seriousness.[5] But Havel emphasizes the peculiar unwieldiness of Ptydepe simply to suggest its power as a language for use by the politically unscrupulous to mystify and belittle. When Lear finally loses his last pupil to the memory-breaking complexity of Ptydepe, he continues addressing an empty classroom. The effect is funny, because of the satire directed at the teacher, but it is also rather frightening, because it marks the point at which Havel makes clear what it means for power to be in the hands of linguistic technocrats. Those who know Ptydepe can control those who do not. And, when necessary, they can develop a second synthetic language, Chorukor, to replace Ptydepe, based on a formulation opposite to maximum redundancy, to allow themselves to stay in control. At the end of the play Havel illustrates the possibilities for such manipulation in the natural language, too, when Gross overpowers the originally adept Maris with a hypocritical barrage of empty abstractions. Havel thus completes his representation of the linguistic resources of political machination and deception, and calls attention to the susceptibilities of those who may be well-intentioned but are ill-prepared to deal with power plays in the language-game.

Unlike Genet and Havel, Eugène Ionesco concentrates on the inadequacies rather than the powers of language. In *The Chairs*, he presents an Old Man and an Old Woman who assemble an invisible group of guests about them to await the appearance of an Orator who is to pronounce the Old Man's message for everyone present. The dramatic questions posed, whether or not the orator will come, and if he does come what he will say, are left suspended throughout the arrival of the guests and the ensuing "conversations." A considerable degree of anticipation is generated by the wait and by reminders that the venerable ninety-five year-old has something significant to offer, though he is not prepared to articulate it himself.

OLD MAN:

> I've got a message, you're right, I must fight for it, a mission, I can give birth to a great idea, a message for all men, for all mankind . . .

OLD WOMAN:

> For all mankind, my dear, your message! . . .

OLD MAN:

It's true, that's really true . . .[6]

When the Orator finally comes, breaking through the suspense and answering the first of the dramatic questions, the suicides of the Old Man and the Old Woman clear the stage for him to present the grand message to both the invisible and the real audience. Everything focuses on him and the message. The great anticlimax that Ionesco offers is that the Orator is a deaf mute, able to utter only guttural sounds. In desperation the Orator "turns to the blackboard, takes a piece of chalk from his pocket, and writes in large capitals:

ANGELBREAD

And he continues:

NNAA NNM NWNWNW V

He turns to the invisible public, the public on the stage, and points to what he has written on the blackboard.

ORATOR:

Mmm, Mmm, Gueu, Gou, Gu, Mmm, Mmm, Mmm, Mmm.

Then dissatisfied, he rubs out the chalk-marks with a series of sharp movements, and puts others in their place: among them the following can be discerned, in large capitals:

AADIEU ADIEU APA[7]

This is funny, and sad, and rich with possible meanings. It is funny in the way of most anticlimax, a sudden upset of expectation evoking laughter. It is sad as an answer to the question of whether there would be a significant message or not. And it offers great latitude for interpretation: the Old Man may have been a simple thinker, or he may have been a profound thinker with a message which could not be conveyed with language, or the Orator may have been unable to convey either a simple or profound message, or the Orator may have offered a profound message in a way surpassing ordinary comprehension. This is a deliberate quandary. Ionesco forces an identification between the real audience and the invisible one, at the end, by having the invisible audience begin to make the same sounds as the real one. Members of the real audience are made to feel as though they too had come expressly to hear something important, and they can conclude only that language is an opaque and inadequate tool in the business of trying to communicate and to understand.

Kaspar develops a similar perspective on the inadequacies of language, but as a more central issue, because Handke focuses on the capacity of language itself to limit communicating and understanding. Where linguistic theory is secondary to social and political themes in *The Balcony* and *The Memorandum,* and to an absurdist perplexity in *The Chairs,* it is primary in *Kaspar* because Handke's theme is radically epistemological. *Kaspar* presents language learning as a drama of destructive education. It is resolutely a play of ideas. But Handke's practice in this form was influenced by Brecht. For Handke takes pains to stress presentation over representation, emphasizing immediacy rather than imagination.[8] He is careful to establish distance between his protagonist and the historical figure Kaspar Hauser, for example, who could be familiar, particularly to German audiences, as a celebrated 19th-century case of arrested linguistic development.[9] He does this by having an introduction read over a microphone, as the audience enters the theater, in which he emphasizes that the play is a single history, and that "the audience will not be able to imagine there is a sequel to the story." ["*weil keine Geschichte vor sich gehen wird, können sich die Zuschauer auch keine Nachgeschichte vorstellen.*"][10] He also refers to the presentation as "an event that plays only on the stage and not in some other reality" (p. 60) ["*einem Vorgang zusehen werden, der nicht in irgendeiner Wirkichkeit, sondern auf der Bühne spielt*" (9)]. He does not, however, abandon dramatic representation. He facilitates the credible introduction of the language-learning experience his protagonist undergoes by opening the play with a representation of Kaspar's birth. A movement behind the backdrop curtain signals the stirring of life, and as Kaspar attempts with greater energy to come forth the curtain bulges out like a swollen womb. Finally he finds a slit in the curtain, and is born onto the stage.

Handke mentions three important things about Kaspar in his stage directions after this birth. First, Kaspar looks theatrical. His appearance indicates the theatrical nature of the events which will ensue, since the audience has been oriented to see theatrical things as simply real. Second, Kaspar is "the incarnation of astonishment" (p. 63). ["*Er is die verkörperte Verwunderung*" (10).] This astonishment reveals the inadequacy or the absence of his understanding, a point illustrated by his inability to coordinate. And, third, Kaspar has one sentence, "I want to be a person like somebody else was once" [*Ich möchte ein solcher werden wie einmal ein andrer gewesen ist*"], which he utters "so that it is obvious that he has no concept of what it means, without expressing anything but that he lacks awareness of the meaning of the sentence" (p. 65). ["*Er sagt den Satz hörbar ohne Begriff von dem Satz, ohne damit etwas auszudrücken als dass er eben noch keinen Begriff von dem Satz hat*" (10).] The sentence does, however, have meaning and that meaning signals a significant, apparently innate element of Kaspar's mental equipment. The sentence is ambiguous, of course, but there can be no doubt that its essential proposition is presupposed in "I want." Kaspar wills, without realizing it, a change involving his identity. Noam Chomsky argues that our ability to grasp meaning "behind" ambiguous sentences, to get past misleading or uninformative surface structure indicates "that our knowledge of language involves properties of a much more abstract nature, not indicated directly in the surface structure."[11] If so, Kaspar's sentence at once abstractly yet also immediately establishes his vulnerability. It makes allowance for what happens when the prompters begin to speak.

The prompters start by stressing the usefulness of Kaspar's portmanteau sentence. They bombard Kaspar with propaganda about the value of the sentence qua sentence. The insinuating nature of their addresses is more apparent in the original German than in English, for they are seen to use the familiar "*du*" rather than the formal "*Sie.*" The import of their effort becomes clear gradually. While they speak, Kaspar moves about, disordering or upsetting tables and chairs. He is terribly at odds with his surroundings. He directs his sentence to each object after each mishap, but no ordering results. Yet the prompters assure him:

> You have a sentence to bring order into every disorder: with which you can designate every disorder in comparison to another disorder as a comparative order: with which you can declare every disorder is an order: can bring yourself into order: can deny every disorder. You have a sentence of which you can make a model of yourself. You have a sentence you can place between yourself and everything else. You are the lucky owner of a sentence which will make every impossible order possible for you and make every possible and real disorder impossible for you: which will exorcise every disorder from you.
>
> (p. 69)
>
> [*Du hast einen Satz, mit dem du jede Unordnung in Ordnung bringen kannst: mit dem du jede Unordnung im Vergleich zu einer anderen Unordnung als verhältnismässige Ordnung bezeichnen kannst: mit dem du jede Unordnung zur Ordnung erklären kannst: dich selber in Ordnung bringen kannst: jede Unordnung wegsprechen kannst. Du hast einen Satz, an dem du dir en Beispiel nehmen kannst. Du hast einen Satz, den du zwischen dich und alles andere stellen kannst. Du bist der glückliche Besitzer eines Satzes, der dir jede unmögliche Ordnung möglich und jede mögliche und wirkliche Unordnung unmöglich machen wird: der dir jede Unordnung austreiben wird.*
>
> (11)]

This is an extremely important speech. Its meaning can be identified in linguistic theory when Edward Sapir, for example, speaks of "the tyrannical hold that linguistic form has upon our orientation in the world,"[12] or when Chomsky refers to the mind's formulation of the deep structure of language as "a highly restrictive schematism that determines both the content of the experience and the nature and knowledge that arises from it."[13] When the prompters speak they are like the natural force of language itself. The forms of language dangerously close Kaspar's mind to all disorder, and by the end of the play this imposition undoes him, as he becomes unable to deal with the consequences of Logos.

The course of the play traces these consequences with constantly increasing force and clarity. The prompters are seen to make Kaspar lose his one sentence. As he listens quietly, they teach him that time is presupposed in grammar, and then introduce the subject of pain. Handke's stage directions, while the prompters talk about how language will enable Kaspar to conceptualize and define "hurt," read:

> The stage becomes bright. Kaspar sits quietly. Nothing indicates that he is listening. He is being taught to speak. He would like to keep his sentence. His sentence is slowly but surely exorcised through the speaking of other sentences. He becomes confused.
>
> (p. 71)
>
> [*Die Bühne wird hell. Kaspar sitzt still. Nichts zeigt, dass er zuhört. Das Sprechen wird ihm beigebracht. Er möchte seinen Satz behalten. Der Satz wird ihm nach und nach durch das Sprechen anderer Sätze ausgetrieben. Er kommt durcheinander.*
>
> (12)]

If Kaspar's existence before his linguistic competence was spastically disordered, it was, nevertheless, not confused, because confusion is a linguistic conceptualization of disorder. So the hurt caused by confusion gives cause for alarm. The prompters use it as a prod to still greater consciousness, that is, to increasing linguistic competence. Kaspar's defenses weaken as they proceed:

> The shoelace hurts you. It does not hurt you because it is a shoelace but because you lack a word for it, and the difference between the tight and the loose shoelace hurts you because you don't know the difference between the tight and the loose shoelace. The coat hurts you, and the hair hurts you. You, although you don't hurt yourself, hurt yourself. You hurt yourself because you don't know what is you.
>
> (p. 72)
>
> [*Das Schuhband tut dir weh. Es tut dir nicht weh, weil es ein Schuhband ist, sondern weil dir das Wort dafür fehlt, und der Unterscheid zwischen dem festen und dem lockeren Schuhband tut dir weh, weil du nicht weisst, was der Unterschied zwischen dem festen und dem lockeren Schuband ist. Der Rock tut dir weh, und die Haare tun dir weh. Du, obwohl du dir nicht weh tust, tust dir weh. Du tust dir weh, weil du nicht weisst, was du ist.*
>
> (12)]

The treachery of this logic is that language precedes pain in the formulation and so, in a sense, creates pain.[14] The prompters are using the idea of nominative power of the sort found in *The Balcony* to make language attractive to Kaspar. And yet for Kaspar pain cannot be denied precisely because of this power.

Neither can development of the power be avoided. As he begins to speak, Kaspar produces single words and disjunctive phrases quite independently from the droning prompters. With this detail Handke again suggests that the prompters have merely tapped a linguistic spring which must be innate, since Kaspar was "born" with one sentence. There is, therefore, a sort of inevitability traced in Kaspar's learning. His initial vulnerability and the apparently inexorable trajectory of his linguistic development give the play a distinctly tragic character. Kaspar's first normal, conscious sentence underscores the terrible quality of the competence he is gaining: "At that time, while I was still away, my head never ached as much, and I was not tortured the way I am now that I am here" (p. 77). ["*Damals, als ich noch weg war, habe ich niemals so viele Schmerzen im Kopf gehabt, und man hat mich nicht so gequält wie jetzt, seit ich hier bin*" (13).]

Kaspar's ensuing speech catalogues his new perception of the props he had earlier encountered, punctuated for each object with "as I see only now" ["*wie ich jetzt erst sehe*"], since now he can name them, then rounds to an expression which reveals the real success of the prompters' indoctrination. He shows that he believes in the ordering power that the prompters have so emphasized, and pronounces:

> Now I have gotten up and noticed at once, not just now, that my shoelace was untied. Because I can speak now I can put my shoelace in order. Ever since I can speak I can bend down to the shoelace in normal fashion. Ever since I can speak I can put everything in order.
>
> (p. 78)
>
> [*Jetzt bin ich aufgestanden und habe gleich bemerkt, nicht erst jetzt, dass mein Schuhband aufgegangen war. Weil ich jetzt sprechen kann, kann ich das Schuhband in Ordnung bringen. Seit ich sprechen kann, kann ich mich ordnungsgemäss nach dem Schuhband bücken. Seit ich sprechen kann, kann ich alles in Ordnung bringen.*
>
> (13)]

He is wrong, for a moment. And when he does manage to tie his shoelace, "he elaborately makes a noose with one lace. He places the other lace around the noose. He pulls it through underneath. He draws the noose tight." ["*Er legt deutlich mit einem Band eine Schlinge. Er legt das andere Band um die Schlinge. Er zieht es unten durch. Er zieht die Schlaufe fest zusammen.*"] With this ominous gesture, the stage directions assure, "the first order is created" (p. 80). ["*Die erste Ordnung is hergestellt*" (14).] And with this order, the threat lurking behind what the prompters are teaching becomes clear. It is one of many signs that Kaspar is in trouble.

In the meantime, the prompters have been broaching the subject of transformational grammar. They explain how a sentence is a model which can be used to generate other sentences: "Ever since you can speak a normal sentence you are beginning to compare everything that you perceive with this normal sentence, so that the sentence becomes a model" (p. 79). ["*Seit du einen ordentlichen Satz sprechen kannst, beginnst du alles, was du wahrnimmst, mit diesem ordentlichen Satz zu vergleichen, so dass der Satz ein Beispeil wird*" (14).] And they specify how sentences are perceptual determinants: "that object is a normal object about which no further questions remain to be asked after a short simple sentence: a normal object is one which is entirely clarified with a short, simple sentence" (p. 79). ["*jener Gegenstand ist ein ordentlicher Gegenstand, bei dem sich nach einem kurzen, einfachen Satz keine Fragen mehre ergeben: einem ordentlicher Gegenstand ist der, bei dem mit einem kurzen, einfachen Satz alles geklärt ist*" (14)]. By extension, abnormal objects, which cannot be dealt with in sentences, are shut out. The prompters press this idea to a conclusion which at once gives a speaker an identity and threatens that identity. They say that "stories only begin with abnormal objects. You yourself are normal once you need to tell no more stories about yourself: you are normal once your story is no longer distinguishable from any other story: when no thesis about you provokes an antithesis" (p. 80). ["*Erst mit einem unordentlichen Gegenstand fangen die Geschichten an. Du selber bist in Ordnung, wenn du von dir selber keine Geschichte mehr zu erzählen brauchst: du bist in Ordnung, wenn sich deine Geschichte von keiner andern Geschichte mehr unterscheidet: wenn kein Satz über dich mehr einen Gegensatz hervorruft*" (14).] This is dangerous because it makes identity subordinate to language, as the prompters reveal in saying "the sentence about your shoelace and the sentence about you must be alike except for one word: in the end they must be alike to the word" (p. 80). ["*Der Satz über dein Schuhband und der Satz über dich müssen einander gleichen bis auf ein Wort: sie müssen einander schliesslich gleichen bis aufs Wort*" (14).] It is at this point that Kaspar ties his shoelace into a noose, completing the idea of the threat in a visual way.

The prompters next begin to time their observations to punctuate Kaspar's attempts to button his jacket correctly. During this subtle reinforcement of orderliness, their remarks become even more insidious:

> The table is not yet a true actual, genuine, right, correct, orderly, normal, pretty, even prettier, spectacularly beautiful table if you yourself do not fit the table. If the table is already a picture of a table, you cannot change it: if you can't change the table you must change yourself: you must become a picture of yourself just as you must make the table into a picture of a table and every possible sentence into a picture of a possible sentence.
>
> (p. 82)
>
> [*Der Tisch ist noch kein wahrer, eigentlicher, echter, richtiger, rechter, ordentlicher, angebrachter, schöner, noch schöner, bildschöner Tisch, wenn du selber nicht zu dem Tisch passt. Wenn der Tisch schon ein Bild von einem Tisch ist, kannst du ihn nicht ändern: wenn du den Tisch nicht ändern kannst, musst du dich selber ändern: du musst ein Bild von dir werden, wie du den Tisch zu einem Bild von einem Tisch machen musst un jeden möglichen Satz su einem Bild von einem möglichen Satz.*"
>
> (16)]

Kaspar is seen to have digested this alienating lesson as he begins to put the stage props in order. Then the prompters produce a long barrage of platitudes. These platitudes seem ordinary enough, yet they keep returning to the themes of suffering and order. "All suffering is natural" ["*Jedes Leiden ist natürlich*"], they say, and of course, "good order is the foundation of all things" (p. 83). ["*Die Verhältnismässigkeit der Mittel ist dein Grundsatz*" (16-

17).] During this barrage, Kaspar's grammar begins to outpace his experience. He extrapolates, syllogistically, from a single experience to echo the truisms of the prompters, saying that "everything I can't pick up with my whole hand is a match" ["*Alles was ich nicht mit der ganzen Hand aufheben kann, ist ein Streichholz*"], "everything that cuts is only a table knife" ["*Alles, was schneidet, is nur ein Tafelmesser*"], and "everything that bites is only a closet door" (pp. 84-86) ["*Alles, was mich in die Hand beisst, ist nur eine Schranktür*" (16-17)]. At the same time Handke uses the spotlight to designate the places where Kaspar is moving the props. The spotlight begins to do more than simply follow Kaspar, however, it anticipates him and seems to represent his unspoken conceptualizations and thus to determine his actions. With this whole scene, in complicated and subtle visual and linguistic ways, Handke creates a picture of Kaspar as a being who illustrates the Sapir-Whorf hypothesis. Language is shown to anticipate experience and to define it according to its own terms.

The focus next turns from the relationship between language and experience to that between language and thought. The shift is from the external to the internal. To mark the change Kaspar stops moving around the stage and settles into a rockingchair. He is then taught, according to the stage directions, "the model sentences with which an orderly person struggles through life" (p. 90). ["*Jetzt werden Kaspar die Satzmodelle beigebracht, mit denen sich ein ordentlicher Mensch durchs Leben schlägt*" (18)]. What the prompters tell him follows the same pattern as before. So, they say: "You finish speaking: you finish thinking: if you couldn't finish speaking, you couldn't say this sentence: I finish thinking" (p. 90). ["*Du sprichst zuende: du denkst zuende: könntest du nicht zuende sprechen, könntest du nicht den Satz sagen: ich denke zuende*" (18).] Sentences and thoughts are, thus, coextensive and inseparable. Only when he absorbs this point is Kaspar capable of using language creatively. In Wittgenstein's terms he can play the language-game. He can make his contribution to the community of sentences. Yet he can only establish a relationship to himself through verb conjugations. After a struggle he seems to succeed by repeating "I am the one I am" (p. 102). ["*Ich bin, der ich bin*" (22)]. But then Handke, with a masterful touch, introduces a disturbing image of the sort seen earlier in the shoelace noose. Just when Kaspar's identity seems secure, he stops rocking his chair and asks "Why are there so many black worms flying about?" (p. 102). ["*Warum fliegen da lauter so schwarze Würmer herum?*" (22).] No linguistic formulation can fully prepare him for the illogic of black worms flying about. They come from the realm of Chaos. Logos seems overcome by them. They cannot be ordered or explained. As in *The Chairs*, language seems inadequate at a crucial moment.

The prompters register awareness of Kaspar's disturbing vision and attempt to soothe him, though they are, in fact, rubbing salt in his wound by repeating the faith of the adequacy of language:

You have model sentences with which you can get through life: by applying these models to your sentences, you can impose order on everything that appears chaotic: you can declare it ordered: every object can be what you designate it to be: if you *see* the object differently from the way you *speak* it you must be mistaken: you must say to yourself that you are mistaken and you *will* see the object: if you don't *want* to say that to yourself, then it is obvious that you want to be *forced*, and thus do want to say it in the end.

(p. 102)

[*Du hast Modellsätze, mit denen du dich durchschlagen kannst: indem du diese Modelle auf deine Sätze anwendest, kannst du alles, was scheinbar in Unordnung ist, in Ordnung setzen: du kannst es für geordnet erklären: jeder Gegenstand kann der sein, als den du ihn bezeichnest: wenn du den Gegenstand anders siehst als du von ihm sprichst, musst du dich irren: du musst dir sagen, dass du dich irrst, und du wirst den Gegenstand richtig sehen: willst du es dir nicht gleich sagen, so ist es klar, dass du gezwungen werden willst, es also schliesslich doch sagen willst.*

(22)]

They are reinforcing the "tyrannical hold that linguistic form has upon his orientation on the world," but now they are inverting things to suggest that experience is making the demand, that experience is coercing Kaspar's mind toward order. This is insidious because it refuses to allow for the possibility of disorder when experience inevitably provides disorder.

As the prompters go on, they extend their logic to offer a peculiar admission of the possibility that order can be absent: "Even if there are no limits: you can draw them" (p. 102). ["*Auch wenn es keine Grenzen gibt: du kannst welche ziehen*" (22).][15] They seem to be giving up ground before Kaspar's continuing and disturbing silence. But if they are attempting to be reassuring, their retreat has the opposite effect, and their logic is made to seem more treacherous than ever. This becomes clear when they announce: "You've been cracked open" (p. 103). ["*Du bist aufgeknackt*" (22).] Kaspar responds to the intended metaphor for enlightenment by dividing. A series of other Kaspars come on stage to mime reactions to promptings which draw attention to externals, such as "you become sensitive to dirt" (p. 103). ["*Du wirst schmutzempfindlich*" (22).] These other Kaspars seem to be exteriorizations of Kaspar's thoughts, and are external reminders of the problem raised by the ability of grammar to posit both *other than self* and *other self* at the same time it distinguishes *self*. Like the spotlight which earlier seemed to represent Kaspar's thoughts by anticipating his actions, they are another dramatic device by which Handke assures that Kaspar is a play and not a tract. Still another such device is mentioned in the introduction, where Handke says that the play might also be called a *speech torture*, and that "to formalize this torture it is suggested that a kind of magic eye be constructed above the ramp. This eye, without however diverting the audience's attention from the events on stage, indicates, by blinking, the degree of vehemence with which the PROTAGONIST is addressed" (p. 59). ["*Zur Formalisierung dieser Folterung wird dem aufführenden Theater vorgeschlagen, für jeden Zuschauer sichtbar, zum Beispiel über die Rampe, eine Art von magischem Auge aufzubauen, das, ohne freilich die Zuschauer von dem Geschehen auf der Bühne abzulenken, durch sein Zusammenzucken jeweils die Sprechstärke anzeigt, mit der auf den HELDEN eingeredet wird*" (9).] This formalizing of emotional intensity is one of the first rules in Brecht's program for the theater. The aim is to confront the audience, to produce thought, but not at the expense of a dramatic presentation in which discoveries can be made simple when "the natural is made to look surprising."[16]

The other Kaspars represent an identity crisis made terrifying in its obviousness. The crisis is, however, for the time being, short-lived. While the prompters remain silent, Kaspar "tries to catch himself" ["*Kaspar versucht sich selbst einzufangen*"], running in ever smaller circles until he "seizes himself with his own arm" (p. 109) ["*nur noch mit den Händen um den Körper herum sich einfangen will*" (24)]. With his identity thus temporarily recovered, he delivers a long speech which summarizes his inculcation of the doctrine of linguistic order. Unlike Lucky's comparable, extraordinary speech in *Waiting for Godot*, which causes the other characters, his "masters," so much discomfort that they must violently silence him, Kaspar speaks in a way designed to reassure his teachers.[17] He ends with the slightly troublesome recognition that objects seem sinister, but hurries to assert that the power to name them is enough to counter the danger. Handke takes immediate steps, however, to remind the audience of the danger.

Intermission breaks the action on stage at this point, but it does not interrupt the theatrical event. With tapes of the prompters' speeches and disjunctive, mangled sentences spliced together and piped through the theater loudspeakers, and even into the street, the audience is subjected to a speech torture, just as Kaspar has been. The snippets of speech which Handke offers as a possible text have an overtly threatening character, and they are intended to be interspersed with such violent sounds as saw blades penetrating wood with a screech, or braking cars, or jets, or sirens. The final section of the text repeats images of a knife, stabbing, death, and then is drowned out by a series of harsh sounds. This termination foreshadows the sounds created by the other Kaspars at the end of the play, and the tone of violence heightens the sense of physical danger and psychic destruction. The overall effect is unavoidably galvanic.

The prompters quickly pick up the tone of the intermission text at the recommencement of the events on stage. Two Kaspars now sit on a couch looking contented, in contrast to Kaspar's original expression of astonishment. But any sense of real contentment is undercut by the disturbing hint of schizophrenia. And when the prompters speak, their theme is that "water dripping regularly down on one's head" ["*Ein regelmässiger Wassertropfen auf den*

Kopf"], or other forms of torture, "is no reason to complain about a lack of order" (p. 117) ["*ist kein Grund über Mangel an Ordnung zu klagen*" (28)]. They endorse a violent imposition of sentence over sense, a principle that before had only been implicit in the coercion of their lessons, but now is shown in its full exaction as a linguistic principle.

Three other Kaspars arrive, and finally the original Kaspar comes on stage. He moves directly to the microphone to obey a prompting:

> Those who have been brought to order—instead of withdrawing into themselves and fleeing society—should now realistically seek without force or beatings but out of their own strength to show new ways of looking at sentences valid for all: they cannot choose they must choose and tell others the truth about themselves without phrases or bubbles: the others too should finally be able to want to do what they themselves now want and should do.
>
> (p. 121)
>
> [*Die in Ordnung Gebrachten—statt sich in sich selber zurückzuziehen und die Gesellschaft zu fliehen—sollen jetzt reell danach trachten ohne Zwang und Schläge aus eigener Kraft neue Wege zu zeigen indem sie nach für alle gültigen Sätzen suchen: sie können nicht wählen sie müssen wählen und den andern ohne Phrasen und Sprechblasen die Wahrheit über sich selber erzählen: auch die andern sollen endlich wollen können was sie selber jetzt wollen sollen können.*
>
> (29)]

Everyone is compelled to follow the rules of the language-game, in this schema, and the result is socially deterministic as well as individually deterministic.

When Kaspar goes to the microphone he is able to project his voice through an electronic medium as the prompters have been doing all along.[18] This tends to make his relationship to the audience something like the relationship between the prompters and himself. The stage directions add that "his voice begins to resemble the voices of the prompters" (p. 121). ["*Seine Stimme wird der der Einsager ähnlich*" (29).] By having Kaspar thus try to fulfill his social contract with the linguistic community represented by the audience, while making him represent something like the restriction of language itself, Handke again attempts to make the audience uneasy and thoughtful. He confronts them without the satiric relief that Havel gives to Lear's address in *The Memorandum*.

To emphasize the social determinism of language, Handke has Kaspar launch into a long list of social rules. While he explains what "everyone must do" ["*Jeder muss*"], though, the other Kaspars begin to make disturbingly unsocial sounds. These noises are like the vision of black worms that interrupted Kaspar before. But they are even more unsettling, because they so clearly come from those selves which grammar has led him to distinguish and which work so irrevocably against him. When he can no longer withstand the chaotic noises he gropes desperately for words, his final resource but also his first problem: "What was it that I said just now? If only I knew what it is that I said just now" (p. 131). ["*Was habe ich doch gerade gesagt? Wenn ich nur wüsste, was es ist, was ich gerade gesagte habe!*" (31).] As he is overcome, he begins giggling madly with the other Kaspars, and the prompters try to finish his speech. Kaspar is able to recover after a silence, and attempts to go on himself, but ends up again with the threatening problem of identity, which must always precede social responsibility:

> After I had learned to say the word I, I had to be addressed as I for a time because I did not know I was meant by the word you, since I was called I; and also, when I already knew the word you I pretended for a time that I did not know what was meant, because I enjoyed not understanding anything; thus I also began to enjoy responding whenever the word you was uttered.
>
> (pp. 135-36)

> [*Nachdem ich das Wort ich sagen gelernt hatte, hat man mich eine Zeitlang mit dem Wort ich ansprechen müssen, weil ich nicht wusste, dass mit dem Wort du ich gemeint war, da ich doch ich hiess; und auch, als ich das Wort du schon verstand, tat ich eine Zeitlang, als wüsste ich nicht, wer gemeint sei, weil es mir Vergnügen machte, nichts zu verstehen, so machte es mir dann auch Vergnügen, mich jedesmal zu melden, wenn das Wort du fiel.*
>
> (34)]

Kaspar tries to continue, but the other Kaspars again produce excruciating noises. After a terrific struggle, Kapar manages to speak a few lucid sentences. He manages to show that somehow he realizes his fate, that "already with my first sentence I was trapped" (p. 137). ["*Schon mit meinem ersten Satz bin ich in die Falle gegangen*" (35).] But finally the chaos lurking within the boundaries imposed by language reasserts itself: "By saying: the chair is harmless, it is all over with the chair's harmlessness" (p. 138). ["*Dadurch, dass ich sage: der Stuhl ist harmlos, ist es mit der Harmlosigkeit des Stuhls auch schon vorbei*" (35).] And Kaspar submits to the forces which showed themselves first in his shoelace noose, next in the vision of the black worms, and most powerfully in the infernal noises produced by the other Kaspars. His final breakdown comes with a soft chorus of "if only" ["*Möge doch*"] from the prompters. Imposed over this feeble, ironic lament are the sounds of the other Kaspars, the sounds of terminal psychic disruption. The curtain closes while Kaspar, accompanied by "the shrillest possible sound" ["*Mit dem schrillsten aller möglichen Geräusche trifft der Vorhang*"], the formal sign of the force which destroys him, repeats "goats and monkeys" ["*Ziegen und Affen*"]. He is echoing a line from *Othello*, Act 4, Scene 1, where Othello recalls words Iago had used earlier, showing that he has accepted Iago's poisoned characterization of human behavior, and revealing how the words themselves have taken their toll in poisoning his mind.[19] Handke's use of this allusion gives tragic resonance to the scene.

Kaspar is not a tragic hero, since he is without power to divert or counteract the forces which impose themselves upon him. But Handke shows him as a victim whose basic plight may be universal. And by presenting this plight as a matter of linguistic determinism, Handke attempts to make his audience sensitive to problems of an order which seems to preclude freedom. Yet the dramatization of Kaspar's fate also seems to be an attempt to open rigidly order-bound minds, based on Handke's belief in our ability to create propositions for new models of thought. It shows how serious, and dramatic, the creative use of linguistic theory can be.

Notes

1. See Ranier Nägele and Renate Voris, *Peter Handke* (Munich: Beck, 1978), pp. 14-17.

2. Ludwig Wittgenstein *Philosophical Investigations,* trans. by G. E. M. Anscombe (New York: Macmillan, 1966), p. 27e.

3. Jean Genet, *The Balcony,* rev. ed., trans. by Bernard Frechtman (New York: Grove Press, 1966), p. 94.

4. Václav Havel, "The Memorandum," trans. by Vera Blackwell, in *Three East European Plays* (Harmondsworth: Penguin, 1970), p. 198.

5. See Martin Joos, "Toward a First Theorem of Semantics," *Language* 34 (1958): 286.

6. Eugène Ionesco, "The Chairs," trans. by Donald Watson, in *Plays* (London: Calder, 1958), 1: 45.

7. Ibid., p. 34.

8. Handke does not adhere to Brecht's ideas on epic theater. But see "Strassentheater und Theatertheater," in *Prosa Gedichte Theaterstückte Hörspiel Aufsätze* (Frankfurt: Suhrkamp, 1969), pp. 303-06, where he says "Brecht hat geholfen, mich zu erziehen," and goes on to explain how he began to see in Brechtian theater the possibility for presentations which could produce the propositions needed for new thought, rather than reproducing the propositions of existing sentences.

9. For discussions of Handke's use of Anselm Ritter von Feuerbach's book on Kaspar Hauser, and of his distancing from this creative seed, see Manfred Mixner, *Peter Handke* (Kronberg: Athenäum, 1977), pp. 56-57, and Nägele and Voris, pp. 82-83.

10. Peter Handke, *Kaspar and Other Plays,* trans. by Michael Roloff (New York: Farrar-Noonday, 1969), p. 60. German text from *Suhrkamp Literatur Zeitung* 3 (1976): 9. Hereafter page references in text parenthetically.

11. Noam Chomsky, *Language and Mind* (New York: Harcourt, 1968), p. 32.

12. Edward Sapir, "Conceptual Categories in Primitive Languages," in *Language in Culture and Society,* ed.

Dell Hymes (New York: Harper, 1964), p. 128. This is the Sapir-Whorf hypothesis in its strongest form. Cf. Benjamin Lee Whorf, "Science and Linguistics," in *Language, Thought, and Reality,* ed. John B. Carroll (Cambridge: Technology Press of Massachusetts Institute of Technology, 1956), p. 212: "The background linguistic system (in other words the grammar) of each language is not merely a reproducing instrument for voicing ideas but rather is itself the shaper of ideas, the program and guide for the individual's mental activity, for his analysis of impressions, for his synthesis of his mental stock in trade."

13. *Language and Mind,* p. 53.

14. Cf. Antonin Artaud's explanation of cruelty and consciousness, in *The Theater and Its Double,* trans. by Mary Caroline Richards (New York: Grove Press, 1958), p. 102: "Cruelty is above all lucid, a kind of rigid control and submission to necessity. There is no cruelty without consciousness and without the application of consciousness." By making *Kaspar* a "speech torture" for both his protagonist and his audience, Handke may be engaging in a "theater of cruelty" designed to disclose the rigid control of language in consciousness.

15. This sentence derives from Wittgenstein. Handke closes one of his essays with an indignant observation on this urge to draw limits: "Wittgenstein sagte: 'Es gibt keine Grenzen, aber man kann welche ziehen.' Die meisten Leute scheinen damit beschäftigt su sein, ihre einmal (gar nicht von sich selber) gezogenen Grenzen immer wieder nachzuziehen. Und sie sind noch stolz darauf." See "Ein Beispiel für Verwendungsweisen grammaischer Modelle," in *Prosa Gedichte Theaterstücke Hörspiel Aufsatze,* p. 302.

16. See Bertolt Brecht, "Vergneugungstheater oder Lehrtheater," in *Schriften zum Theater,* ed. Siegfried Unseld (Berlin: Suhrkamp, 1957), p. 63: "Das 'Natürliche' müsste das Moment des Auffälligen bekommen."

17. See Samuel Beckett, *Waiting for Godot* (New York: Grove Press, 1954), pp. 28-30.

18. Perhaps Marshall McLuhan's observations on the effects of electronic media are relevant here. He argues that they are supposed to reintroduce sensitivity to auditory suggestion, so that "in our new software information environment sound images are back as magical forces for channeling perception." See *Culture is Our Business* (New York: McGraw-Hill, 1970), p. 152.

19. The allusion is as clear in German as in English, since the words Handke uses are the same in all standard German translations of *Othello.*

Jeanette R. Malkin (essay date September 1990)

SOURCE: Malkin, Jeanette R. "'Think What You Are Saying': Verbal Politics in the Early Plays of Handke and Kroetz." *Modern Drama* 33, no. 3 (September 1990): 363-379.

[*In the following essay, Malkin compares the play* Kaspar *to Franz Xaver Kroetz's dramas* Stallerhof *and* Geisterbahn.]

Peter Handke and Franz Xaver Kroetz have, as both will readily admit, very little in common.[1] If anything, they occupy opposite ends in the spectrum of contemporary German dramaturgy and, with each successive play, seem to move further apart. Handke's abstract subjectivity has in recent plays (such as *Über die Dörfer,* 1981) deepened into near mysticism. Kroetz, on the other hand, has moved from sub-proletarian naturalism to, more recently, an almost cinematic depiction of middle-class moral styles (as in *Furcht und Hoffnung der BDR,* 1984). Handke is a private person, an individualist with an aversion to labels, systems, and political affiliations.[2] His critical acclaim has always been greater than his popularity and some of his best writing has been done in the novel, rather than the dramatic genre. Kroetz is a highly prolific and popular playwright (and actor). Much produced, often interviewed, he is outspoken, polemical, politically engaged, a one-time member and even spokesman of the German Communist Party (KPD).[3]

It is perhaps the very disparity between these two contemporaries (Handke was born in 1942; Kroetz, 1946), in their personal as well as their artistic styles, that has attracted interest—both academic and in the media.[4] Handke himself seems to comment on Kroetz's dramatic language, to compare his own theatrical loquaciousness with Kroetz's stunted stage speech, when he has the tycoon Quitt, the protagonist of his 1973 play *Die Unvernünftigen sterben aus* (*They Are Dying Out*) say to his servant Hans:

> You're making fun of my language. I would much prefer to express myself inarticulately like the simple people in that play recently, do you remember? Then you would finally pity me . . . They too wanted tenderness, a life together, et cetera—they just can't express it, and that is why they rape and murder each other. Those who live in inhuman conditions represent the last humans on stage. I like that paradox.[5]

Quitt has recognized the social protest sounded through the inarticulateness, even though he mocks the naive naturalism of its idiom. His own protest, and Handke's, will also adduce the link between language and power, the gap between language and self-knowledge.

In probing the function and political implications of language as used in their early plays, plays written at the start of each man's career and in which—in both cases—

their distinctive and very different styles, and their perhaps not so different thematic concerns, are most uncompromisingly and sharply portrayed, I will focus on Handke's first and best known full-length play: *Kaspar* (1968). As for Kroetz, I have chosen two plays written in his socalled "early" style, i.e. before his 1972 shift to an ideologically more explicit and dramatically less extreme style.[6] These plays are: *Stallerhof* (*Farmyard*), and its sequel *Geisterbahn* (*Ghost Train*) (1972).

At first sight the differences between these two successful playwrights are impressive. The Austrian Handke has been identified with a formally difficult, analytical, anti-realistic type of theatre which—especially in his early *Sprechstücke* and in **Kaspar**—revels in the abstract and philosophical. **Kaspar** is almost devoid of plot. Dominated by disembodied voices and vocal interactions, its obsessive dramatization of language often seems wilfully obscurantist and oriented towards linguistic and philosophical insights. The play contains only one character/clown who is created and destroyed on stage by those "voices" which force him to acquire and conform to normative social language: a sophisticated but difficult theatrical proposition. Handke's (no doubt ironically meant) admission that he "dwells in the ivory tower" (this is the title of his 1972 collection of essays: *Ich bin ein Bewohner des Elfenbeinturms*[7]) reflects and seemed to confirm the accusations that he is a formalist, an aesthetist, an introverted, solipsistic writer in the vein of Beckett, a writer who is socially "nicht engagiert" (uncommitted).[8]

The Bavarian Kroetz, on the other hand, is considered one of the initiators of the German "New Realism" of the '70s.[9] His plays are concretely situated in a recognizable social milieu and present a set of specific, problem-ridden characters who speak a sparse, dialect-tinged German. Like most of Kroetz's early plays, *Stallerhof* and *Geisterbahn* are "family" dramas which deal with a fringe rural lower class. The plot of these two plays shows the disintegration of orderly life at the Farmer's home resulting from the rape and aberrant pregnancy of his retarded 14 year-old daughter, Beppi. The two plays include graphically distasteful bits of realism: masturbation, defecation, fornication—all polite terms for very basic bodily acts which are bluntly performed upon the stage. Kroetz, as opposed to Handke, was always considered to be a socially conscious, "committed" playwright who, as Marieluise Fleisser once put it: writes for and about the "little people" and their own real problems.[10]

Despite their obvious differences, Handke and Kroetz share certain thematic obsessions. Both write about the hidden and overt power-structures which manipulate and determine our existence, and—especially in these early plays—both focus that manipulation foremost within the repressive power of language: a language which exerts a violent and violating control over man's autonomy. In their different ways, both Handke and Kroetz posit language at the center of their plays and enact a power-struggle between that unseen force and the characters who people their stage.

The "language" to which I refer is not a mere abstraction. Handke, no less than Kroetz, and despite his unrealistic methods, grounds his language in a social reality which is concrete and particular. It is the reality of a middleclass well-formedness; the smooth language of the TV newsreel, the radio commentary, the fully grammatical, persuasively structured verbal patterns of the ruling organisation, patterns which contain and perpetuate a system of beliefs. It is a familiar language using the right words to teach the right behavior, the behavior of "aller anständig denkenden Menschen" (all right-thinking people) as the Prompters put it.[11] And thus, despite its analytical presentation, it is a concrete language.

However, this "language" is not merely concrete and socially grounded. Even Kroetz's dialogue is not actually "realistic"—despite the greater verisimilitude of his settings and plots. Kroetz's characters all speak a single and undifferentiated language, producing repetitive patterns of meager, unnuanced speech. The same structures and clichés, the same semantic blanks, the same limited vocabulary recur in play after play, with little variation. This is because Kroetz has created an *abstraction* of lower class speech, a "model" of verbal inhibitedness and poverty which, in its function and self-reflectiveness, parallels Handke's abstraction of middle-class well-formedness.

Thus the concrete and abstract interact.

Within the concrete and very different settings of both authors' plays, the language acts upon the characters as a determinism, pre-conscious and unwilled. Yet for the audience, the abstractions work almost like a didactic model, analysing and exposing the nature of language. These models, the repeated patterns of speech which we find in both playwrights, and the control they exercise over the characters' ability to think and act freely, reveal the "hidden" power structure of language. Language is not presented as a neutral expressive medium. There is an intimate connection here between the powerlessness of the characters, and the coercive power of their language.

Moreover, it seems clear to me that both Handke and Kroetz have a social, educational goal in their plays.[12] Through their portrayal of language's oppressive potential they sound a protest, call for our resistance, our awareness. Paradoxically, if we compare their reputations, Handke's attempt to activate his audience towards change is even more clear and overt than Kroetz's in these early plays. It is especially pronounced in his **Publikumsbeschimpfung** (*Offending the Audience*), and, most interestingly, in the "intermission text" of **Kaspar**. Here Handke, through loudspeakers which insistently invade the neutral spaces of intermission time (cafeteria, lobby, patios, etc.), subjects the audience to the same verbal torture which Kaspar suffers on stage. Thus the dramatic model of language's manipulative power is taken out of the theatre into reality; demonstration replaces literary efficacy and urges us towards recognition of, and protest against the voices which control and afflict us.[13]

The "plot" of *Kaspar* is quite simple. We see a clown-like figure, an uncoordinated *Kasperl* figure[14] on a cluttered stage. He, like his namesake Kaspar Hauser, is incapable of speech except for one sentence.[15] Three unseen Prompters—*Einsager*—speaking through loudspeakers placed above the stage, teach Kaspar in orderly fashion to become as orderly and preordered as the model sentences they espouse. Kaspar will develop from clown to suit-and-tied *Bürger* through the acquisition of language; and he will finally rebel against his forced incorporation into Procrustian structures. In a sense, *Kaspar* can be viewed as the parable of an attempted, and failed, socialization process.

In the opening section of *Kaspar* Handke describes the voices of the *Einsager*—the Prompters—as follows: "their manner of speaking should be that of voices which in reality have a technical medium interposed between themselves and the listeners: telephone voices, radio or television announcers' voices, the voice that tells the time on the phone, the voices of automatic answering services . . . the speech mannerisms of sports commentators, of stadium announcers . . . of language course records, etc. etc. . . ."[16] Handke's description is very precise. The Prompters' voices are to speak "from all sides" of the stage, are to be automatic, conventionalized, without overtones or undertones, without warmth, humor or irony. They remain formal—never personal—teachers: i.e., they embody a *principle,* not a personality. The voices speaking over some technical medium also implicate those same instruments of mass language transportation: media instruments which surround us "from all sides" with endless voices, endless words. Handke comments in the stage directions of section 8 that the text which the Prompters speak is not theirs ("einen Text, der nicht der ihre ist"). That is: we are not going to read spontaneous dialogue, thoughts which emerge from the psyche and personality of some unseen individuals. Rather, we will read a text which is taken, borrowed, "quoted" from the stock of social language, language which—like the Prompters' voices and the instruments through which they speak—surround *us,* no longer belonging to anyone, but directed "from above" against everyone.

An alternative title for *Kaspar,* Handke writes, would be *Sprechfolterung*—speech torture (p. 59). It is both torture through aural excess and cruel imagery; and the torture of separation from self. The Prompters place their text between Kaspar and his one original sentence: "I want to be a person like somebody else was, once." That sentence was originally uniquely Kaspar's, his only possession. The Prompters forcefully drive it out of him through a din of words and replace his sentence with their own system of sentences. As he is assured in section 17:

> You hear sentences: something like your sentence: something comparable. You can play off your sentence against other sentences and already accomplish something . . . You can no longer imagine your sentence all alone by itself: it is no longer your sentence alone: you are already looking for other sentences. Something has become impossible: something else has become possible.

Thereupon he is immediately taught a set of simple "model" sentences which contain rules of comportment and end with an intimation of what Kaspar will eventually become:

> Where are you sitting? You are sitting quietly. What are you speaking? You are speaking slowly. What are you breathing? You are breathing regularly . . . You are breathing in and out . . . You are speaking. What are you speaking? You are sitting. Where are you sitting? You are speaking in and out:
>
> Order. Put. Lie. Sit.
>
> Put. Order. Lie. Sit.
>
> Lie. Put. Order. Sit . . .
>
> Stand. Sit. Lie. Order.
>
> Lies. Stands. Sits. Completely ordered:

Like the Prompters, Kaspar too will learn to speak a text which is not his.

In an interview, Handke said of this play: "My point was to use words to encircle the audience . . . my words are not descriptions, only quotations."[17] And indeed many of the lines in the play are direct quotes—from Wittgenstein, Horváth, Shakespeare, from von Feuerbach's account of the education of the real Kaspar Hauser, etc.[18] These direct quotations merge with the abstracted, "quoted" forms of (so-called) normative social speech. Handke analyses and deconstructs the patterns of speech, the order of speech; and Kaspar's education to language is shown as an indoctrination to the reductive values of speech-order. Correct grammatical forms become both examples and inducements to orderly perception which, as we will later see, assure obedient behavior. As Kaspar is told in section 28:

> You have model sentences with which you can get through life: by applying these models to your sentences, you can impose order on everything that appears chaotic: you can declare it ordered: every object can be what you designate it to be: if you *see* the object differently from the way you *speak* of it, you must be mistaken: you must say to yourself that you are mistaken and you *will* see the object. . . .

Kroetz presents this same theme, and critique, realistically. In *Stallerhof* and *Geisterbahn* we don't see the characters acquiring speech: we see the resultant distortions of a highly restrictive and minimal language on their restricted lives. With the one exception of Beppi, who develops in these plays from nearly dumb to cliché-spouting, all of the characters are given within a fixed, uncommented, unconscious verbal mold. Kroetz has claimed that the speech of his characters doesn't function properly. He blames the social power structure for his characters' "Dumpfheit" (hollowness) and their resultant "Sprachlosigkeit" (inarticulateness).[19] But the impression of a language expropriated, stolen by society, is not available in the plays themselves. The social situation of the plays is given by the author without comment. Poverty and social deprivation are the reality, they are the implicit governing factors, but they are rarely the issue. Kroetz doesn't analyse a social situation—he merely presents it and lets it speak for itself in the clichés, quotes, and meaningless grunts of his characters. Indeed, the lack of analysis, the lack of authorial intrusion in any form, is one of the main reasons for the hopelessness of these plays. Kroetz offers us no outside spokesman, no *raissonaire,* no alternative voice. The world of these plays is claustrophobic and introverted: totally self-reflective. And so is the language of the characters.

The Farmer, his Wife, their retarded 14-year-old daughter Beppi, and the middle-aged workman Sepp who rapes her, fathers her son, and finally dies—whereupon Beppi kills the child rather than lose it to Welfare—are all caught within transparent clichés of thought and behavior of which they are unaware, and which govern their lives. The almost unbelievable gap between the incidents which occur on stage—rape, attempted abortion, infanticide—and the platitudes in which they are discussed, forces us to look to the language of these plays if we are to grasp their point. Take, for example, the following dialogue in which the Farmer confronts Sepp with the evidence of Beppi's pregnancy:

STALLER:

This is going to cost you ten years and me my honor.

SEPP:

But not because it was on purpose.

STALLER:

As if that helps. *Long pause.*

STALLER:

It leaves you speechless. *Pause.*

STALLER:

And we put our trust in him.

SEPP:

Then that's how it is.

STALLER:

Three months.

SEPP:

No one counted the days. *Pause.*

STALLER:

Want to hear a secret? She's pregnant.

SEPP:

Why?

STALLER:

That's right.

SEPP:

Not true. It's all lies.

STALLER:

We have proof.

SEPP:

Can't be.

STALLER:

Exactly.

SEPP:

Not right.

STALLER:

A test is made. Costs ten Marks.

SEPP:

Why?

STALLER:

It's made from piss.

SEPP:

Whose?

STALLER:

Hers. [. . .]

SEPP:

Pause. But it wasn't on purpose.

STALLER:

Cause you're a pig. No two ways about it.

SEPP:

Exactly.

(*Stallerhof,* II, 7)[20]

Truncated idioms, non sequiturs, silences. This is not so much a conversation as a collection of stock responses. Indeed, the language of *Stallerhof* and *Geisterbahn* is composed almost entirely of pre-formed units of speech strung together. These units fall into three groups: clichés; proverbs and other quotations; and semantic blanks (such as Sepp's use of "why" and "exactly," quoted above). The cliché is the most extensively used form, spiced and reinforced by proverbs and axiomatic wisdoms. It is characterized by a total absence of originality, by a sense of automatism, of unthinking, preconditioned response. Whole sections of dialogue often consist of such clichés:

WIFE:

. . . Wie mans macht, is es falsch [Whatever you do is wrong].

STALLER:

Genau . . . [Exactly] . . .

WIFE:

Wer die Wahl hat, hat die Qual. [Where there's a will there's a way]. *Pause.* Besser spät wie nie. [Better late than never].

STALLER:

Warum? (Why?).

WIFE:

Besser spät wie nie. [Better late than never].

STALLER:

Ja. Es is nie zu spät. [It's never too late]. *Pause.*

WIFE:

Das is jetz keine Zeit zum Kopfhängenlassn! [This is no time to throw in the towel!].

(*Geisterbahn*, III, 4)[21]

These disconnected clichés and empty formulas could easily have been culled from the long list of cliché precepts which the Prompters, as we will see, force upon Kaspar. Karl Kraus once warned that we should "Learn to see an abyss where platitudes abound."[22] It is into that abyss that Kaspar is drawn by the Prompters; certainly it is equally apparent in the abyssmal unoriginality of Kroetz's characters' language.

Quotations in Kroetz's dialogue are used in counterpoint to the clichés. Quotes are always in *Hochdeutsch*, a "foreign" language to these characters, one of authority and wisdom. To quote is to participate in this wisdom, to gain a momentary sense of borrowed power. Quotes are of two sorts: the quotation proper, i.e. quoting proverbs or biblical verse; and quoting axiomatic wisdoms, *Volksweisheiten*, which are usually preceded by the explanation "es heisst" or "man sagt" (it is said). Whenever decision-making is attempted by Kroetz's characters, we invariably find them quoting.[23] These two types of language—the cliché which the character treats as his own creation, and the quote which he borrows to support his cliché—create the powerful impression of a "found" language, a language superimposed upon them, uncreated and unowned.

But what is "owned" language? Owned language is language which is created out of a personality to fit a situation. It partakes of the public word, but is recreated in the private personality.[24] It is precisely this private recreation of which Kroetz's characters are most incapable. And since they don't own their language, they also reject responsibility for what they say. "Redn wird man durfn" (no harm in talking) becomes a common and recurrent defense for even the most indefensible utterances. In Act III scene I of *Stallerhof*, Staller and his Wife are on their way to church

with the underage and already pregnant Beppi. Fear of what the "neighbors will say" and despair as to the options open to them, motivate the following "discussion":

WIFE:

It is said [*es wird gsagt*] that backward people don't feel death the way we do.

STALLER:

Sure, a fly doesn't feel anything either. *Pause.*

WIFE:

Fifth commandment: thou shalt not kill.

STALLER:

Sixth: thou shalt not be unchaste. *Pause.* [. . .]

WIFE:

It is said [*es wird gsagt*] that the child goes on living in the mother's belly for hours after.

STALLER:

No. [*Des net.*] *Long Pause.* [. . .]

STALLER:

God helps those who help themselves. [. . .] *Pause.*

WIFE:

Blessed are the meek, for theirs is the kingdom of heaven.

STALLER:

I don't believe that.

WIFE:

The thoughts people get. Unthinkable.

STALLER:

We're only talking. [*Man redt ja bloss.*]

In disconnected sentences, between long pauses, the Farmer and his Wife discuss the possibility of killing their own daughter as a way out of the shame which her pregnancy will bring them. "Es wird gsagt" the Wife twice says and repeats the most fantastic superstitions as though they were fact. The use of "it is said" frees her to speak of her daughter's death and removes from her the responsibility for such thoughts: the quoted form gives them the air of objectivity. This is followed by verses from the ten commandments. Without explanation or preamble, the Wife quotes the fifth, Staller counters with the sixth. The two commandments cancel each other out; yet they don't develop into a discussion. The quotations are not an introduction to discussion, they *are* the discussion. In them the characters express their contrasting moral views without ever owning their positions. Meanings are not elaborated, the intention behind the isolated phrases is never developed. Each unit stands on its own, depleted, inconclusive. When the Wife finally protests against the thoughts they are having, Staller answers: "Man redt ja bloss." This defense—we're only talking, no harm in talking—is a recurrent denial of any inherent power in words. To their minds words and actions are always two separate realms: since the words which they possess can't mediate between their desires and the occurrences in their lives. Axiomatic language, quotations—a borrowed code—only give the characters the impression of having thought and discussed, while in fact brutally putting an end to any individual reflection.[25] In an article on the plays of Marieluise Fleisser, Kroetz wrote: "Fleisser's characters hold on to a language which is of no use to them, because it is not theirs."[26] This unoriginality of language, this "Enteignung von Sprache," as Kroetz puts it—expropriation of an "eigene Sprache," an original, owned language—is equally true of Kroetz's early plays:[27] like Kaspar, all Kroetz's characters speak a language which is not *theirs*.

This unowned, "found" language is not only restrictive: it is also shown to be immoral. Lack of verbal originality is insidious: it engenders a deeper lack of morality and compassion. Compassion for the suffering of others, a trait so sadly lacking in Kroetz's early plays in which rape and child murder are almost routine, depends on the capacity to imagine another's pain. But an automatic, pre-formed, unowned language alienates the characters from their feelings and responsibilities. Kroetz's characters, like Kaspar, can only *think* what they say, must think what they are capable of saying. As the Prompters tell Kaspar: "When you begin to speak you will begin to think what you speak even when you want to think something different" (section 27).

In 1946 George Orwell wrote the essay "Politics and the English Language" in which he denounces the corruption of language which, he claims, must necessarily lead to the corruption of thought.[28] He especially attacks the mechanical acceptance of pre-formed verbalizations, speech idioms which consist of "gumming together long strips of words which have already been set in order by someone else." Such language is tacked together "like the sections of a prefabricated hen house" and leads to a verbal automatism which no longer translates thought or emotion: it merely perpetuates dogmatic formulas. The result of this automatism, this ritualized repetition of jargon phrases and cliché sentiments, writes Orwell, is that man is literally "overtaken" by language, hypnotized, as it were, and forced to accept frozen formulas which can no longer express conceptual thought. It is here, he claims, that personal autonomy is most threatened. Ready-made phrases "will construct your sentences for you—even think your thoughts for you, to a certain extent—and at need they will perform the important service of partially concealing your meaning even from yourself."

Kroetz's characters speak almost exclusively in such prefabricated language. Indeed, it is interesting that their language manages to sound natural; for it is actually highly stylized, essentially artificial. Certain recurrent idiosyncra-

sies of sentence structure and typical idioms color the language with a Bavarian diction, but the plays are by no means in dialect—compared for example with the dialect plays of Harold Sommer or Peter Turrini.[29] Kroetz is not interested in reproducing a local language or in creating authentic spontaneous speech. In fact, his dialogues studiously avoid those devices which would give the illusion of verbal spontaneity. Spontaneous speech is typified by false starts, hesitations, retractions, interjections, i.e.: the struggle to verbalize is part of the speech itself. Naturalist drama uses this device abundantly. Kroetz's language, however, lacks such false verbal planning completely.[30] His syntax is undifferentiated, the language is foreshortened, emphatic, and minimal. Characters don't interrupt each other, sentences don't overlap, there is no attempt to create atmosphere or authenticity through language: all of those elements which transfer dialogue into lived and felt speech are missing. The reason is perhaps that unlike Naturalist language—which tends to *characterize* its speaker—Kroetz's characters are not differentiated through a verbal style. They all seem to speak the same language. Their inner life, their personal idiosyncrasies, don't break through the verbal mold. Language is imposed upon them, not created out of them.

This imposed, restricted language is the determining factor of Kroetz's early plays. Kroetz has written that "The proletariat in the province can no longer express itself or make itself clear; it can no longer organize itself. That is its fate."[31] Harald Burger and Peter von Matt, pondering on the lives and socio-linguistic context of Kroetz's proletarian characters, suggest that "the language itself is the unknown (unbegriffene) determinant of Kroetz's characters, and in fact to such a high degree that we must recognize in it the dramatic function of a *fate*—similar to heredity in Naturalism, blind vitality in Sternheim, or socio-economic factors in Brecht."[32] This is not to say that the language here is outside of the characters' socio-economic reality. On the contrary: that reality is channeled most concretely through the language. The poverty and restrictedness of their social existence is both given in, and conditioned by, their language. But the connection between environment and language can only be made by the audience. The characters themselves accept their limitations almost without question—since to question would be to being a process of change. This is precisely what does happen in Kroetz's later plays in which greater verbal capacity leads to a questioning of the molds of thought and behavior. In, for example, Kroetz's 1974 play *Das Nest (The Nest)*, Kurt's wife accuses him of being no better than a "trained monkey" who blindly repeats what he is told to think and do. This critique leads to discussion, awareness, and the responsible (if didactic) final action which differentiates Kroetz's post-1972 plays from his early ones.

In the early plays no such awareness is evidenced. Moreover, and unlike Handke's plays, no metacommunication about their language exists— or when it does, it is both ironic and painful. Sepp, after the birth of his son

Georg, tries to educate the backward Beppi to speech—so that their child might turn out differently than they. He has a vision of the boy's future success and power, a vision which is, ironically, totally rooted in verbal freedom: "Der Bub wird es ihnen zeigen, was mir können! Der werd gar net fragn, ob er gfragt is, der wird es ihnen einfach sagn, ohne dass er aufgrufn is" (*Geisterbahn*, II, 3): (The boy will show them what we can do. He won't ask them if he's being asked, he'll just tell them, without being called on.) In this stilted, undeveloped sentence, Sepp tries to verbalize his innermost hope while actually demonstrating to us the limited, hopeless language which the son will inevitably learn from his father—and which will certainly determine *his* future, as it has Sepp's.

The fatalistic control which language exercises over man is even more clearly demonstrated in **Kaspar.** By forcing Kaspar to assimilate the structures of normative speech, the Prompters are also forcing him to conform to normative behavior. In section 25, which shows a peak in Kaspar's education, the Prompters speak at him a row of cliché aphorisms which are not unlike those spoken by Staller and his Wife:

> Everyone is responsible for his own progress . . .
>
> The golden rule in life is moderation in all things . . .
>
> Good order is the foundation of all things . . .
>
> The room informs you about its inhabitant . . .
>
> A place for everything and everything in its place . . .
>
> In an orderly room the soul also becomes orderly . . .
>
> Disorder outrages all right-thinking people . . .

While the Prompters recite their platitudes, Kaspar gradually adjusts his movements to the rhythm of their sentences and puts the littered stage into order. He creates a perfectly arranged bourgeois salon, almost a parody of middle-class order with the requisite vase of flowers and bowl of fruit, even a painting which matches the decor. Finally he exchanges his own motley clothes for a suit and tie. Kaspar is now taught that complete conformity to language means not only submission, but moreover experiencing language as inevitable, as the primal reality. He is taught that language precedes thought: "Say what you think," he is told in section 27; "You can't say except what you think. . . . When you begin to speak you will begin to think what you speak even when you want to think something different . . . When you have begun to speak you will think what you are saying. You think what you are saying . . . you must think what you are saying because you are not allowed to think anything *different* from what you are saying. Think what you are saying."

Thus Kaspar is taught that speech is prior to, and the limits of, thought, and that his individuality must bend to its preconditions.

Yet it is difficult, or at least problematic, to speak of Kaspar as of an "individual." Kaspar is conceived and presented not as a "character" but as a contrivance. While

not quite as seamlessly artificial as Ionesco's Smiths and Martins, he is equally unreal. The theatre for Handke is always an "artifact,"[33] a contrived and artificial space; and within this space Kaspar is placed as an invention, a postulate, a theatrical device. Kaspar is never allowed to appear quite human. He is from the start distanced from the audience through his mask-face and the mechanical movements of his puppet-like body. Kaspar unfolds less as a person than as a process, the process of man's construction and destruction through language. This process brings Kaspar closer to the audience when moments of personality and struggle break through the speech-object he is becoming; it however also distances Kaspar, for as speech systems displace him he becomes increasingly inhuman. Kaspar is in many ways like the Subject in Structuralist analysis who is rejected and dissolved by systems which operate through him. Kaspar too is subjected to systems, viewed through generative rules of speech and thought. He is "displaced from [his] function as center or source" and thus, "the self comes to appear more and more as a construct, the result of systems of convention." These systems—and foremost among them is the system of language—generate rules, constantly expand as autonomous entities, and make "even the creation of new sentences a process governed by rules which escape the subject."[34] This process of the "decentering" of the subject (to use Foucault's term) shows the individual as assimilating the rules of his culture, incorporating them, but not as originating or controlling them. Meaning thus resides in systems of convention which are prior to the individual and escape his conscious grasp. *Kaspar* fits well into this Structuralist perspective, but with an essential difference: Handke is not writing from the point of view of knowledge as interpersonal systems of convention (as are the Structuralists), but from the point of view of *man* who is subjugated through these systems and victimized through the repression (or disavowal) of his individual "self." The "conflict" in **Kaspar** is between language—perversely represented though it is by the Prompters—as the ultimate system of order, and Kaspar who, although a product of this order, rebels against his absolute displacement by it. When Kaspar finally rejects the ideas of his Prompters, he also rejects their grammar (and vice versa) and speaks deranged nonsense as a rebellion.

Thus the very artificiality of the play and of its central (and only physical) character, strengthens the notion of **Kaspar** as parable, as a demonstration and a warning. Martin Esslin wrote of Ionesco's *La Cantatrice Chauve* (1948) that "What he deplores is the levelling of individuality, the acceptance of slogans by the masses, of ready-made ideas which increasingly turn our mass societies into collections of centrally directed automata."[35] These words could apply just as well to **Kaspar.** Ionesco dramatises this theme through the creation of an ultra-typical product of such language stereotyping: the Smiths and Martins. Handke, on the other hand, abstracts the theme, creates a blank central "character" and achieves not satire and wit—as does Ionesco—but a formal, conceptual exposé of language structures. Kaspar learns language only through sentences, never through words; i.e. he is taught pre-formed structures, a system of structures from which he can no longer extricate himself. "[A] sentence is a monster" he says in his last speech of the play; "with each new sentence I become nauseous . . . I am under someone's control" (section 65). The "monstrosity" of sentences is that to speak one is to be already integrated, subsumed within the larger system of language.[36] Kaspar finally speaks in the same voice as the Prompters and realizes that: "Already with my first sentence I was trapped" (section 64). He learns that to accept any pre-given system is to be controlled by that system.

Kroetz's characters never achieve such conscious insight. The characters of his early plays learn nothing, never change, rarely develop. Indeed, they are almost interchangeable. They all use the same expressions, display the same attitudes, inflict the same brutalities; they are all isolated, uncomprehending, devoid of emotional imagination, and thus, of compassion. Compassion for the suffering of others depends on the capacity to *imagine* another's pain. But verbal and emotional imagination are inseparable. To compare the murder of one's child with the death of a fly, to call the deliberate drowning of an infant "a death like any other,"[37] requires a peculiar lack of imagination—which both reveals and engenders a deeper lack of morality and compassion. Kroetz, unlike Handke, does not intrude into his bleak world. He offers no authorial comments, allows for no dramatic spokesman, neither slants blame nor passes judgement on his characters. The audience, like the characters, is shut out from any privileged information. But unlike the characters, it can, and indeed *must,* mediate between the insistently recurrent patterns of stunted speech and the mindless brutalities. Thus the language becomes a provocation and an indictment. Like Handke's tycoon Quitt, the audience is forced to recognize and interpret the connection between language and morality, between personal autonomy and free verbal options. In the face of Kroetz's stubborn refusal to comment, the burden of interpretation and of judgement falls on the audience.

In an interview, Handke claimed that "The only thing that preoccupies me as a writer . . . is nausea at stupid speechification (stumpfsinnigen Versprachlichung) and the resulting brutalization of people. . . . One should learn to be nauseated by language, as the hero of Sartre's *Nausea* is by things. At least that would be a beginning of consciousness."[38] The equation of speechification and brutalization is at the thematic center of both Handke's and Kroetz's early plays. Speechification implies the mechanical regurgitation of pre-formed and unowned language which both brutalizes the speaker and renders him, or her, more capable of brutality and immorality. Both Handke and Kroetz question the humanist concept of language as the apex of culture, the mark of man's humanity. Both show language-systems as power-systems with the potential to control and inhibit personal autonomy. Their characters, so seemingly different from each other, are all "overtaken" by language. As Orwell warned: they speak a language which constructs

itself, which "thinks your thoughts for you." Ultimately, both authors present characters who can only think what they are *saying,* and both sound a warning and a protest against our unthinking complicity. Language is a "hidden" factor, less obvious than political coercion or social disenfranchisement; but once it is exposed, as it is in these plays, it can be seen to underlie, and perhaps facilitate, both.

Notes

1. This is made quite clear in, e.g., the Handke/Kroetz debate, broadcast on *LiteraTour III,* ZDF, Mainz, 5 December 1976, moderator: Richard Hoffmeister. The debate is reprinted in Richard W. Blevins, *Franz Xaver Kroetz: The Emergence of a Political Playwright* (New York, 1983), pp. 247-255.

2. See e.g. Ibid., pp. 249-50; also, see "Ich bin ein Bewohner des Elfenbeinturms," in: Peter Handke, *Ich bin ein Bewohner des Elfenbeinturms* (Frankfurt a.M., 1972), pp. 19-28.

3. For an incisive biographical sketch see Rolf-Peter Carl, *Franz Xaver Kroetz* (München, 1978), pp. 7-18; also, Gitta Honegger, "Thinking in Public: An Interview with Franz Xaver Kroetz," in *Yale Theatre* 15,3 (Summer/Fall 1984), 24-31.

4. E.g., Denis Calandra, in his *New German Dramatists* (New York, 1983), dedicates a chapter to the comparison of Kroetz and Handke, pp. 29-52.

5. Peter Handke, *They Are Dying Out,* trans. Michael Roloff (London, 1974), p. 38. Original quote can be found in *Die Unvernünftigen sterben aus* (Frankfurt a.M., 1973), pp. 61-2.

6. After joining the German Communist Party in 1972, Kroetz made a conscious decision to accord his characters greater verbal capacity in order to make his plays clearer and more accessible, and in order that his characters might function as "models" for emulation. See "Ich sässe lieber in Bonn im Bundestag," an interview in *Theater heute,* February 1973; and "Die Lust am Lebendigen," a discussion with the editors of *kürbiskern,* 2 (1975). These interviews are collected in Kroetz's anthology of plays, articles, and interviews: *Weitere Aussichten . . .* (Köln, 1976), with relevant passages on pp. 586-7, and 601, respectively.

7. Cited, note no. 2, above.

8. Peter Hamm's article, "Der neueste Fall von deutscher Innerlichkeit: Peter Handke," in Michael Scharang, ed.: *Über Peter Handke* (Frankfurt a.M, 1972), pp. 304-313, is the strongest example of this accusation. See also, Martin Walser, "Über die neueste Stimmung im Westen," *Kursbuch,* 20 (1970), 19-41.

9. Kroetz himself refers to this "group" as "Dieser neue Realismus" in an interview with Hannes Macher, "Was alles zur Gewalt führt," *Die Zeit,* 27 June 1972,

p. 11. Richard Gilman in his "Introduction" to a selection of translations of Kroetz's plays, *Farmyard and Four Plays* (New York, 1976), p. 19, suggests "the collective name of 'new realists'" for this group.

10. See Marieluise Fleisser, "Alle meine Söhne. Über Martin Sperr, Rainer Werner Fassbinder und Franz Xaver Kroetz," in *Materialien zum Leben und Schreiben der Marieluise Fleisser,* ed. Günther Rühle (Frankfurt a.M., 1973), pp. 409-10. Kroetz has repeatedly acknowledged his indebtedness to both Marieluise Fleisser (1901-73) and Ödön von Horváth (1901-38). He and other of the "New Realists" consciously emulated Fleisser and Horváth's exposure of the "common man" through a portrayal of his vernacular speech. Fleisser returned Kroetz's tribute by naming him her "favorite son."

11. Peter Handke, *Kaspar* (Frankfurt a.M., 1967), p. 37. The English translation used in most of this article is by Michael Roloff: *Kaspar,* in *Kaspar and Other Plays* (New York, 1969). Roloff translates this phrase as: "decent-thinking men," p. 84. I prefer my own translation here.

12. Both are fairly explicit about this. For Kroetz see note no. 6, above. Handke has said that his goal in writing is to make the audience more aware, more sensitive, more conscious. See Peter Handke, as quoted by Artur Joseph in "Nauseated by Language: from an Interview with Peter Handke," trans. E. B. Ashton, *The Drama Review,* 15,1 (Fall 1970), 58. This interview originally appeared in Artur Joseph, *Theater unter vier Augen: Gespräche mit Prominenten* (Cologne, 1969), pp. 27-39. The English trans. will be quoted here throughout. Also see "Ich bin ein Bewohner des Elfenbeinturms," p. 20.

13. ". . . because no story will take place, the audience will not be in a position to imagine that there is a sequel to the story, other than their own," writes Handke in *Kaspar,* p. 8; English trans. p. 60. (The translation of this line is incomplete and I have added the missing last clause: i.e., there is no continuation of Kaspar the "character," although there is a continuation of the theme of *Kaspar*—and this "Intermission Text" is the link between the play and its sequel [and pre-quel] in reality.)

14. *Kasperl* is a traditional German clown or puppet figure, parallel to the English "Punch."

15. This is how Kaspar Hauser's original sentence is transcribed by A. Ritter von Feuerbach, in *Kaspar Hauser, Beispiel eines Verbrechens am Seelenleben des Menschen* (Ansbach, 1832): "Ich möcht a sochener Reiter warn, wie mei Voter aner gween is" (i.e. "I want to be a Horseman [or Rider] like my father was"). Handke changes this sentence subtly to "I want to be a person like somebody else was, once" thus pointing to a more general need for conformity.

16. These instructions are included in the rather long opening stage directions which Handke stipulates should be read over a loudspeaker, over and over

again, as the audience enters the theatre and waits for the play to begin. Thus Handke's intentions are meant to be explicitly understood by the audience from the start. The text of *Kaspar* is divided into 65 numbered units or "scenes." Subsequent quotations will be followed parenthetically by the scene number to which they refer.

17. Joseph interview, Eng. trans. p. 57.

18. The text contains other direct, although unattributed, quotes from a large variety of sources. Mechthild Blanke in "Zu Handkes *Kaspar*" in Scharang, pp. 275-6, gives the sources of some of these quotes, also to be found in *Der Spiegel,* 21, 2 (1968), 139. For example: sentences are lifted from the writings of Lenin, Mao, and a DDR pamphlet. These sentences are quoted in section 25, and are thus parodied.

19. These remarks were originally printed in the "Vorbemerkung" to *Heimarbeit* when first published in *Drei Stücke* (Frankfurt a.M., 1971), p. 6. In the *Gesammelte Stücke* (Frankfurt a.M., 1972), this Preface has been removed.

20. All translations from *Stallerhof* and *Geisterbahn* are my own. The German original can be found in Kroetz's *Gesammelte Stücke* and subsequent references to this edition will appear parenthetically within the text.

21. This translation is not literal; I sought English cliché-idioms which are parallel to the German ones and equally common.

22. Karl Kraus, *Beim Wort genommen* (Munich, 1955); quoted by Marianne Kesting, "The Social World as Platitude," trans. George Schulz-Behrend, *Dimension,* 2 (1969), 177.

23. See Harald Burger and Peter von Matt, "Dramatischer Dialog und restringiertes Sprechen. F. X. Kroetz in linguistischer und literaturwissenschaftlicher Sicht," *Zeitschrift für Germanistische Linguistik,* 2 (1974). This excellent and detailed article provides a careful socio-linguistic analysis of Kroetz, applied mainly to his play *Oberösterreich* (1972); but is equally useful for Kroetz's earlier work.

24. See Wilhelm von Humboldt, who in *Linguistic Variability and Intellectual Development,* trans. G. C. Buck and F. A. Raven (Philadelphia, 1971), p. 39, writes *a propos* of the interrelatedness of public and private language: "By the same act through which man spins language out of himself, he also spins himself into it."

25. See Burger/Matt, p. 290.

26. Kroetz, "Liegt die Dummheit auf der Hand?," in *Weitere Aussichten . . . ,* p. 525.

27. Kroetz, *Weitere Aussichten . . . ,* p. 605.

28. George Orwell, "Politics and the English Language," in his *A Collection of Essays,* 1954), pp. 162-76. The following passages are quoted from this edition.

29. E.g. Peter Turrini's *rozznjogd (Rat Hunt)*; or Harold Sommer's *A unhamlich schtorka obgong (An Unbelievably Strong Exit)*: both written in different Austrian dialects.

30. See Burger/Matt, pp. 274-5.

31. Quoted by Michael Töteberg in "Franz Xaver Kroetz: The Realistic Folkplay," trans. Ardon Denlinger, *Performing Arts Journal,* 2.3 (1978), 18. This article originally appeared in German in *Akzente,* 23 (1976), 165-73.

32. Burger/Matt, p. 291.

33. Joseph interview, Eng. trans., p. 57.

34. Jonathan Culler, *Structuralist Poetics* (Ithaca, 1975), p. 29.

35. Martin Esslin, *The Theatre of the Absurd,* revised ed. (Harmondsworth, 1968), p. 140.

36. See Benjamin Lee Whorf, *Language, Thought, and Reality* (Massachusetts, 1956), pp. 156 & 258. There he claims that language "is a system, not just an assemblage of norms" of which "sentences, not words, are the essence. . . ."

37. *Heimarbeit* (1969): in which Martha tries to abort her extra-marital child with a knitting needle, thus giving birth to a deformed and disturbed child; her husband eventually drowns the infant and justifies its death with these words.

38. Joseph interview, Eng. trans., p. 61.

David Barnett (essay date October 2000)

SOURCE: Barnett, David. "Dramaturgies of *Sprachkritik*: Rainer Werner Fassbinder's *Blut Am Hals Der Katze* and Peter Handke's *Kaspar." Modern Language Review* 95, no. 4 (October 2000): 1053-63.

[*In the following essay, Barnett discusses how* Kaspar *has become a modern classic through its exploration of language and unique staging techniques.*]

Twentieth-century literature has been fascinated by language, more precisely, perhaps, by the disjunction of word and meaning. Few literary works, however, have attempted to approach these problems from the perspective of their linguistic foundations. The dramatic medium, with its possibilities of contrasting text with image, might suggest itself as particularly well suited for such an investigation. Peter Handke's *Kaspar* (première 11 May 1967, Theater am Turm, Frankfurt and Städtische Bühnen, Oberhausen) is probably the best-known example of a play about the mechanisms of language.[1] Ever since its first performance it has generated interest and stimulated much critical comment. This major play is not the only one to make linguistics its focal point. Rainer Werner Fassbind-er's *Blut am Hals der Katze* (première 20 March 1971, Städtische Bühnen, Nuremberg) also focuses on the figure of the linguistic *tabula rasa,* yet it engages the medium in a very different way. To my knowledge, only one scholarly article has been published on the play.[2] In this article I examine the dramaturgical structures that support a comprehensive *Sprachkritik* in both plays, with a particular emphasis on the tension between stage and auditorium.

Kaspar now has the status of a modern classic and is a staple of many modern drama courses. By virtue of this I have assumed that its plot and the figures of Kaspar and the Einsager are familiar to the reader. *Blut,* on the other hand, has drifted into obscurity, and I shall thus spend some time outlining and analysing its defining dramaturgical moments, with a view to contrasting them with those of the better-known *Kaspar.* A couple of reasons may account for this discrepancy in reception (I should not, however, like to link any of them with the plays' aesthetic qualities, as should become evident later). Handke's profile at the time was far higher than Fassbinder's; he had achieved prominence through both his association with *enfant terrible* director Claus Peymann and his own much publicized attack on the *Gruppe 47* in Princeton, in 1968. Fassbinder, by contrast, had yet to develop as a 'media phenomenon'. He was known in the South (*Blut* was commissioned by the city of Nuremberg for the *Dürerjahr*) but his work was not as widely propagated as Handke's (the *antitheater* had no publishing deal with a firm such as Suhrkamp either). In fact, in certain reviews he was considered an epigone of the young Austrian.[3] His theatre work also seems to have been eclipsed by his films. It is not untypical to find remarks such as 'Fassbinder learned to make films in the theatre',[4] which see the cinematic output as the culmination of his apprenticeship at the *antitheater.*

Blut is about an alien, Phoebe Zeitgeist, who has come to Earth to find out about democracy. The character is in fact taken from an American comic-book series written by Michael O'Donoghue and Frank Springer. Her name, as will become evident, is ironic. As Fassbinder puts it in his introductory remarks: 'Phoebe Zeitgeist hat aber Schwierigkeiten, sie versteht die Sprache der Menschen nicht, obwohl sie die Worte gelernt hat.'[5] From the outset, then, a tension is established between the situations Phoebe encounters and the way in which she processes them linguistically. The tension between Saussure's *langue* and *parole* are signalled early. The same can be said of *Kaspar,* yet the way in which the material is treated by Fassbinder reveals a complex dramaturgical method that changes over the three phases of the play.

The first phase presents the spectator with the typologized characters who recur throughout the play (for example, Der Polizist, Die Frau des toten Soldaten). They either deliver monologues by themselves or address monologues to Phoebe, who is present but mute. The two scene types alternate. There are eighteen short scenes in the first phase. A symmetry emerges in that the first character to have a scene with Phoebe, Der Polizist, is the last to have his *solus*. Correspondingly, Der Metzger, the first *solus* (and the second scene), appears in the seventeenth scene with Phoebe. The only exceptions to this mirrored scheme are Scenes 9 and 10, which would have featured Die Geliebte and Phoebe, and Die Geliebte on her own. Instead we see Der Liebhaber and Phoebe, and then Die Geliebte *solus*. One assumes that this was so that Die Geliebte was not seen in some way as the central character. All the same, Fassbinder is still interested in maintaining the symmetrical structure for the most part, something that constructs a sense of order and cohesion to the spectator. The importance of this device within the dramaturgy of play as a whole will be addressed later.

The second phase consists of a further thirty-six short scenes. All feature two of the nine typologized characters and Phoebe, who observes the vignettes before repeating lines that she has heard within them at the end of each scene. The lines she chooses follow no ostensible pattern; she does not favour beginnings, middles, or endings (which might tell us something about her mind-set with respect to those of both the characters and the audience). Each character has one (and only one) dialogue with each of the others in the cycle.

The third phase is a party attended by all the characters, including Phoebe. It is here that Phoebe deploys the language she has learned in phase two. Towards the end of the party Phoebe starts to bite the necks of the party-goers, one by one, until she is the only one left alive.[6] Having done this she recites a section of Hegel's *Wissenschaft der Logik* (1812-16).[7]

From this brief outline, one can see that the central figures in *Blut* and **Kaspar** differ greatly, although they play similar roles as language learners. One of the main interests in **Kaspar** focuses on whether the protagonist is figuratively tortured[8] by the three Einsager (that the process of acquiring language is made painful by their mendacity)[9] or that pain is a prerequisite when learning a language, regardless of who is teaching it.[10] Such fundamental issues do not arise in *Blut* in that Phoebe is never really exposed to the pain of language acquisition in the play. Kaspar has to have the sentence with which he enters the stage driven out of him to make him receptive to the Einsager. Phoebe is more an imitator and is never required to have language beaten into her (we assume that this process has already taken place on her own planet). Her problems with language are based far more in the assembly of words into sentences. In both plays, however, the playwrights employ the central character as a means of investigating the structures of language in society by dint of the characters' linguistic artlessness.

The three phases of *Blut* treat the social personae of the typologized characters very differently. In the monologic first phase identity seems fairly cohesive. The nine give their individualized pictures of violence, suffering, and/or oppression. Der Metzger in Scene 2, for example, tells of

a girlfriend he once had, who made his dreary working life and the regular blows received at the hands of his 'Meister' seem bearable. She left him, and now he buys sex every Friday and continues the cycle of violence, for he is now the 'Meister'. Glimpses of personal tragedy and repeated inhumanity pervade the first phase. The characterizations appear to represent standard psychological-realist fare. The speeches paint bleak pictures of everyday life and the characters never break frame with metatheatrical discourse. In the second phase the potted biographies that provided the audience with stable points of contact are radically called into question. If we follow the plotting for Der Metzger we find the following scenarios: he plays a dog to Das Modell's dominatrix; he tries to calm Die Frau des toten Soldaten after having hit her; he is a cellmate in prison with Das Mädchen; he boasts of his earnings to a former football team-mate, Der Soldat; he is the sceptical investor in a car-wash that Der Lehrer is trying to set up; he is the other man in a love-triangle featuring Die Geliebte; he is a hard-nosed creditor when Der Liebhaber discovers his wife has run up huge debts; he is a worker who will not strike because he has his own capital, by contrast with his more sympathetic workmate, Der Polizist. The variety of roles and personae is highly disparate. It would be difficult to identify a single character or personality within the diversity. Even if one were to impose such an interpretation, by viewing the short vignettes as scenes from a life, their sheer break-neck speed refuses the actor the depth of interiority to sustain a character. The spectator is denied the consistency required to promote the identification that was possible in the first phase. As a result, the spectator is prevented from developing the relationship established in phase one and is forced to re-evaluate basic 'realist' categories and to adjust to a more active form of spectatorship.

The range of texts each actor is made to speak undermines a coherence in characterization. The order in which they are spoken also frustrates the spectator's ability merely to digest the performance and encourages a reconsideration of the more conventional mapping of one actor onto one part (or of one actor onto doubled, yet psychologically consistent parts). The structure of phase two is also at odds with a unifying sense of character. The near-symmetrical distribution in the first phase is severely disrupted by the apparently random set of encounters between the figures in the second. The order in which the characters take the stage and interact with each other follows no pattern; there is no numerical series that determines when or with whom a particular character appears. This is a deliberate device (by virtue of the fact that each character meets the other once and only once) to attack the cohesion of the characters of phase one and thus openly to challenge a set of psychological and dramaturgical assumptions. 'Characters' are replaced by 'figures' that are too contradictory to be reduced to helpful shorthands for either the actor or the audience.

The apparently random distribution of the second-phase scenes and the larger structure that exposes an underlying organizing principle signal two important points. First, they fail to privilege any one actor, so that potential meanings may not emerge through overexposure. The process of de-centring the individual affects all equally; none of the human subjects can stave it off, regardless of the social roles he or she plays. Second, the presence of enforced equality points back to the constructed nature of the piece. The paradox of 'controlled haphazardness' confirms the play's artifice and acknowledges its limits. Individuality, carefully crafted by the (almost perfect) symmetry of the first eighteen scenes is exposed as a dramaturgical ruse. Thus, the organization of the second phase not only allows the spectator to assess a discrepancy between actor and role but also contextualizes this strategy within the play itself.

The scenes themselves are also of interest because they have no stage-directions: all is suggested by spoken (and body) language. It is also fair to assume that because of the speed of the thirty-six scene changes there would be little by way of stage set to indicate where the scenes were taking place. Even costume might be ruled out as an interpretative sign, for reasons of expense and time required to change. The spectator has to find his or her way into the brief situations without the help of the usual visual signs. There is also no continuity of a distinguishable character, as was noted above, and no 'epic banner' to set the scene, which also frustrates the process of easy comprehension. Thus, by virtue of *the audience*'s ability to decipher meanings from the short scenes, it becomes implicated in the short bursts of action. The spectator's recognition of the unpleasant situations betrays a familiarity that by extension becomes disturbing. This mechanism of tacit identification is then ironically checked by the character who does not understand; Phoebe digests the scenes only in so far as she repeats certain lines or phrases at the scenes' respective conclusions.

In a short period of stage time the scenes' contexts are imparted without any direct verbal reference to them. In this sort of whirl, the spectator has to work quickly to make sense of the vignettes. Actors whose characters were at the receiving end of an act of oppression might become the oppressors themselves, only to return to the role of the victim once more later. The spectator is forced to realize that meaning is being generated by his or her recognition of linguistic and kinetic signs. The status of sign as indicator and not substance (and not, therefore, as inevitable) is attested in the closing line of each short scene. Its language is wrenched out of the context that was so familiar to the audience by the silent observer. Phoebe takes her linguistic material from phrases spoken by any of the characters involved in the scene from any moment in the scene and then forms a new sentence. Language that already required active input from the spectator in order to create meaning is put into a new sequence. The *langue* is given a new *parole*. The process calls the scene into question by undermining the semantic and syntactic basis that gave the spectator access to it in the first place. Fassbinder's critique of the clichés that oppress his figures extends into the auditorium.

At the party, which forms the third phase of the play, Phoebe goes on to reuse the language she has distilled in phase two. The characters who were introduced in the first phase, and were shattered into various personae in the second, return in the third as a similarly fragmented mixture. The party displays a fluid set of human traits within the social contexts already presented. The major interest in this phase is the relationship between what Phoebe says and how it is interpreted by the others. Töteberg defines the third phase as 'Dialoge mit Phoebe, wobei sie die gelernten Sätze falsch anwendet'.[11] MacDonald contends that her speech is 'a series of nonsequiturs' and that she 'shatters the structures necessary to maintain the other characters' narratives' (Macdonald, pp. 144-45). Phoebe is not, however, quite as out of step as the two critics may believe, rather her function here is altogether more challenging.

Phoebe's lines at the party are peculiar in that they seem to follow a pattern but then occasionally diverge from it. The pattern is quite straightforward: Phoebe delivers her lines at different points during the party in the order in which she has learned them, which seems to indicate a lack of discrimination. However, there are points where a line that should follow does not, and there are a couple of other discrepancies as well. The lines 'Bist Du Wahnsinnig?' (*B*, p. 518), 'Du Bist Gemein' (*B*, p. 520), 'Sie Sind Gemein' (*B*, p. 521), 'Das Hab Ich Night Gewollt' (*B*, p. 527), and 'Ich War Krank' (*B*, p. 532) are all missing at the party. The lines do not differ greatly in content from other utterances made by Phoebe in the phase, yet the attempts to experiment with language learnt by omitting it betokens conscious agency. In addition, the original Phoebe lines 'Ein Kind, Das Hat Man Doch Sicher. Wenn Du Kein Vertrauen Hast, Dann Ist Alles Zuviel' (*B*, p. 528) are inverted at the party (the second sentence comes first in *B*, p. 546), and the lines 'Die Zeit Macht Dich Reif Und Dabei Vergeht Sie. Gegen Kranke Gedanken Gibt Es Gebete' (*B*, p. 530) appear in the party scene with an extra 'Die Zeit Macht Dich Reif Und Dabei Vergeht Die' after them (*B*, p. 546). Again, the decisions seem arbitrary, none the less they signal an impulse to experiment and a certain playfulness. These modifications demonstrate that Phoebe is being selective; there is no reason to doubt her memory. because she is able to deliver all the other lines both in the correct order and with accuracy. This consciousness signals an attack on the dominant *parole* of oppression and thus functions more dynamically and purposefully than Töteberg's and MacDonald's contentions. The linguistic structures that confronted the spectator in the second phase and were revealed as insidious are consciously attacked by the usage of an outsider. Of course, Phoebe is met with incredulity and bemusement (for example, Liebhaber: Du hast zu viel getrunken (*B*, p. 541), or Metzger: Seltsam, diese Person (*B*539)), which is the audience's initial reaction, too. Yet more often than one would expect, her 'random' contributions evince curiosity or agreement (Lehrer: Ja, das ist die Weisheit des Volkes. Ich würde nicht wagen, das zu verachten (*B*, p. 538), or Polizist: Die hat Phantasie. Ihr Arschlöcher. Der fällt was ein, der Frau, im Gegensatz zu euch lahmen Enten (*B,* p. 546)). Not surprisingly, both Der Lehrer and Der Polizist later grow weary of her linguistic challenges and join the others in dismissing her. What is important is that she injects a vitality into the proceedings with her peculiar gambits. Vitality is something conspicuous by its absence throughout the play. To a certain extent this is because of the unimaginative and tired use of language throughout the play (which finds an analogue in the familiarity of the scenes in the second phase and the familiarity of their violence).

Clichés crop up throughout as ready-made solutions to or ways out of the many problems that arise in phases two and three. Phoebe's sometimes sententious lines have such qualities, too, yet seem to engage the characters in phase three because of their freshness in the of the banal chit-chat. Phoebe can only quote: she holds a mirror to the mannerisms and behaviour of the nine figures and distortingly reflects them back in unfamiliar contexts. This is contrasted with the use of cliché and dead metaphor (as well as the repetitive cycles of language-encoded oppression) by the nine figures. The discrepancy between Phoebe's usage and that of the others opens up new discursive possibilities and offers a language-based response to the recurring language and motifs in the short scenes.

Here it might be well to turn to *Kaspar,* where there is also a figure who is taught language by repetition and who then combines words out of context at the end of the play. The main preoccupation of *Blut* is clearly the role of language as a social phenomenon. The various speech acts to which the spectator is witness are a central factor in the course and outcome of each oppressive situation. *Kaspar,* too, introduces and then goes on to develop the social implications of language, here through a clever parody of Ludwig Wittgenstein's linguistic theories. References to the philosopher's *Logische-philosophische Abhandlung* (*Tractatus Logico-Philosophicus*) are placed at judicious points of Kaspar's speech-training. Handke prefaces what will become evident as Wittgenstein's thought with a modified quotation that Wittgenstein used to preface the *Tractatus.* In Scene 20 we hear from the Einsager, 'für einen ordentlichen Gegenstand brauchst du nur einen Satz mit drei Worten' (*K,* p. 127).[12] By Scenes 23 and 24 one finds direct evidence of the famous 'picture theory' of language, when the Einsager say, for example, 'jeder Gegenstand muß ein Bild von einem Gegenstand sein', or 'ein Tisch ist ein wahrer Tisch, wenn ein Bild von Tisch mit dem Tisch übereinstimmt' (*K,* pp. 129, 130). Handke sets up a method, through which Kaspar is to be indoctrinated, that superficially seems 'natural' or 'common-sense': that is, that language is directly derived from an objective outside world. As Malkin puts it, 'Kaspar is taught that speech is prior to, and the limits of, thought' (Malkin, p. 374). We perceive objects or events and find a useful shorthand, a word, to refer to them. The simplicity of the process is vouchsafed by the transformed Kürnberger quotation. A world of order is created in which

each word represents an ideal, essential, or Platonic version of the object or event. Thus a table that has been knocked over is no longer 'a table'; it is 'a table that has been knocked over'. Even in the most un-ideological of objects, a covert, orderly meaning is predicating its overt semantic one. The word no longer describes its object (because, for example, a table is no longer a table when it is not standing on its legs), it imposes a desired state upon that object, too. Human influence modifies the word considered a shorthand and creates a 'non-natural' meaning. The social implications of Handke's critique of Wittgenstein are enormous. The dominant ideology creates its own standards and then seeks to hide such artifice under the naive defence that language is merely a reading-off of the external world. *Kaspar* then deploys the 'transparent' vocabulary in a series of loaded slogans in Scene 25, such as 'Jeder ist für seinen Fortschritt verantwortlich', or 'Jede Neuordnung erzeugt Unordnung' (*K,* p. 131, 132). The frequent use of 'jeder' and its other forms, as well as a sententious use of verbs, help to bolster the universalizing tone of the pronouncements and to hide the loaded nature of the slogans. As spectators, however, we can appreciate the dramatic irony of the scene: there are sixty-six such phrases, which become all the more self-parodistic as the scene progresses. Also, Kaspar's actions during the scene (he tidies up the untidy stage, he makes it orderly) ironize the texts through his blind obedience. It is telling, and indeed a final nod to the audience, that by the scene's conclusion, one object, the wardrobe, will not bend and remains defiantly open. The transition from household objects (Scenes 21, 23, and 24) to social prescription (Scene 25) illustrates the pernicious divisiveness that underlies the 'picture theory'.

The linguistic and social critique of the play is highly theatrical. A cursory reading of the text makes one aware that there are almost always two texts at work in the play. Down the left-hand column are Kaspar's lines and stage-directions, on the right those of the Einsager. What the spectator sees, therefore, is a constant interaction between the two sides, which is sometimes in tandem, but mostly apart. The contradiction between the two texts pushes the spectator away from the events on stage because he or she is continually being made to contrast two differing sets of signs. The interpretation of meaning is the product of the audience's critical judgements with respect to the dialectical tension of the material. In this sense, the dramaturgy is solidly Brechtian. However, the audience is brought back to the quotidian during the interval: the conscious artifice of the theatre is contrasted with a collage of extracts from 'the real world'. The 'Pausentexte', which comprise Scene 59 and are to be played in the foyer, are only a suggestion for a text. Handke writes that whatever words are used, they should be '*zusammengesetzt aus Bandaufnahmen der Einsager, Geräuscheinschüben, Originalaufnahmen von echten Parteiführern, Päpsten, öffentlichen Sprechern jeder Art, auch von Staats- und Ministerpräsidenten, vielleicht auch von echten Dichtern, die zu Anlässen sprechen. Die Sätze sind niemals vollständig*' (*K,* p. 166). This shift of frame allows the audience to play Kaspar's role to the tapes' Einsager. The spectator is exposed to the intertextual construction of views, opinions, and 'the natural', too. Yet words are not the only object of the critique. The '*Geräuscheinschübe*' (*K,* p. 166), mentioned in the introduction to the 'Pausentexte', make us aware of the commodified nature of noises and sounds too. The most profound example of this is at the end of the scene, where a cacophony of bells, buzzers, gongs, sirens, and rattles signifies that the second part of the theatrical event is about to begin. The use of the traditional sign, the bell, and its *Verfremdung* within the gamut of aural signs, points to the conventions taken for granted and to a possible escape from them. (This possibility, and its attendant problems, will be discussed in connection with the use of intertexts and quotations later.) Consequently, the actor-audience dynamic in *Blut* is almost the reverse of that of *Kaspar.* In the former, the audience is drawn into naturalistic vignettes before it is distanced by Phoebe; in the latter it is critical from the outset because of the foregrounded theatricality, only to be confronted with its own insinuation in the signifying chain at the interval. The pronounced and enforced transformation of the audience's role in these plays is both didactic (in their *Sprachkritik*) and dynamic (in their changes of dramaturgical cadence).

Both plays criticize language as a means of social control by pointing to the restrictive contexts of language deployment. The repetition of oppressive situations points to an intertextual cycle, where each power relationship quotes another. The sense of language as quotation is important in *Kaspar* as well as in *Blut*. In *Kaspar* one finds a range of quotations and intertexts. As well as the intertexts from the *Tractatus* and 'the real world', there are (sometimes modified) lines and echoes from Goethe, Feuerbach and Daumer (see below), Horváth, Shakespeare, the Bible, and Büchner. Such employment of foreign texts leads Read to assert that Kaspar is able to go beyond the 'world of rational discourse and the purely functional use of language' (Read, p. 133) of the Einsager to investigate and experience the other, which unconsciously replaces the father figure in Kaspar's first sentence. The historical Kaspar Hauser, as described by Anselm Ritter von Feuerbach and G. F. Daumer, was supposed to have appeared in Nuremberg with the sentence, 'ein Reiter möchte ich werden, wie mein Vater gewesen ist'. Handke changes this to 'ich möcht ein solcher werden wie einmal ein andrer gewesen ist'. This distinction, which desires a state of otherness, is an important modification. Not only does it situate Kaspar somewhere between a past ('einmal') and a future ('möchte [. . .] werden'), it also calls his individuality into question, and I shall show why this is crucial presently. The other, however, is a peculiar category in *Kaspar* because it is not original. It is taken from a source just like the rest of his language, yet it is the only means of liberating language from its present context.

A Shakespeare quotation used by Handke will explain the paradox. *Kaspar* concludes with a quotation from *Othello* ('Ziegen und Affen', *K,* pp. 197-98, compare *Othello,* IV.i.259). It comes at the end of a speech that seems to form disparate nouns into pairs. By this time there are several other Kaspars[13] on stage, 'challenging' the objects on stage, such as the table or the chairs, by laughing at them, costuming them, imitating them, and pulling them offstage. Action and language seem to mirror each other: both try to make their objects, their referends, 'UNMÖGLICH' (*K,* p. 196). By now the Kaspars are indistinguishable (a theatrical critique of 'the original'), so the text directs the Kaspar furthest downstage to speak the final speech. His free combination of random words gets stuck at the Shakespearean intertext, which is then repeated a further eight times. Critics have responded to the curtain line in a variety of ways. Jeffrey Herrick detects a tragic resonance by tracing the intertext back to its source. Othello recalls words earlier used by Iago and has thus accepted Iago's distorted ideas on human behaviour. Gay McAuley looks to the content of the line itself and says Kaspar 'reiterates the animal nature that language was supposed to free him from'.[14] Both ideas point to a negativity, that Kaspar is unable to escape from a suffocating world created by language. Read, as I have already noted, suggests a more positive reading: that the intertexts offer a way of frustrating the linguistic oppression of the play through a poetic use of language. By making language do what it has not previously done, the speaker can postpone a final denotation and continue to connote. The obvious problem is that Kaspar's escape-route employs words already coined by another. He has not formed his own solution, he has reactivated an older phrase.

Handke's intertextual tactic is also worthy of further comment. Almost all the quotations in the play are neither that well known nor instantly identifiable. It would seem that Handke uses his intertexts to allow the audience to believe that unexpected linguistic usages can question the dominant context, only to discover afterwards, maybe from a volume of criticism, from the press, or by word of mouth, that that is not the case. The play can be seen to have a time-delayed effect: an idea for an evasion of the oppressive forces in the play is set up, only to be disappointed at some unknown date in the future. The spectator then has to reconcile this discovery with his or her experience of the lines in performance. Context is the only temporary escape, yet its emphasis marks the shift from the strictures of the 'picture theory' to the relative freedoms of Wittgenstein's later concept, the 'language game'.

Phoebe's final quotation from Hegel plays a similar role in that it presents familiar words in an unlikely context, but in this case the quotation also sheds light on all that has gone before it. Phoebe, of course, has been presenting learned lines in odd places for the whole of the third phase. She is, by virtue of this, a perfect vehicle for the final speech. For those unfamiliar with the text, I reproduce it here in full, in Fassbinder's capitalized letters:

> Durch Den Verstand Pflegt Das Vermögen Der Begriffe
> Überhaupt Ausgedrückt Zu Werden; Er Wird Insofern
> Von Der Urteilskraft Und Dem Vermögen Der Schlüsse
> Als Der Formellen Vernunft Unterschieden. Vornehm-
> lich Aber Wird Er Der Vernunft Entgegengesetzt; In-

sofern Aber Bedeutet Er Night Das Vermögen Des Begriffs Überhaupt, Sondern Der Bestimmten Begriffe, Wobei Die Vorstellung Herrscht, Als Ob Der Begriff Nur Ein Bestimmtes Sei. Wenn Der Verstand In Dieser Bedeutung Von Der Formellen Urteilskraft Und Der Formellen Vernunft Unterschieden Wird, So Ist Er Als Vermögen Des Einzelnen Bestimmten Begriffs Zu Nehmen. Denn Das Urteil Und Der Schluss Oder Die Vernunft Sind Selbst Als Formales Nur Ein Verständiges, Indem Sie Unter Der Form Der Abstrakten Begriffsbestimmtheit Stehen. Der Begriff Gilt Aber Hier Überhaupt Nicht Als Bloss Abstrakt Bestimmtes; Der Verstand Ist Daher Von Der Vernunft Nur So Zu Unterscheiden, Dass Jener Nur Das Vermögen Des Begriffes Überhaupt Sei.

(*B*, p. 550-51)

Hegel's dense style and unqualified use of philosophical terms makes the text difficult to comprehend at first. Its stockpiling of ideas in such a short space also adds to its perceived difficulty. This, I believe, is part of its theatrical appeal to Fassbinder. The text requires work on the part of the audience if it is to make any sense. It re-presents the linguistic problematic that has run through the play. The process of decoding and making sense of the lines refers back the themes of the play as a whole. Language has been revealed as a powerful means through which one character can oppress, cheat, humiliate, coerce, or disown another. Its instrumental function has routed all others. By calling language into question both by Phoebe's odd juxtaposing of learned lines and by the final speech, Fassbinder is able to criticize both the language of the three phases and the situations they depict. The partial explanation of this is found in the Hegel text itself. Understanding, 'Verstand', is primarily set against Reason, 'Vernunft'. But Hegel goes on to qualify this distinction. The interpretation of the Notion, 'der Begriff', is sanctioned by Understanding. Yet the Notion does not come from the abstract realm (some eternal, mystical site of universals), it is more material than that. The Notion becomes more contingent on its contexts.[15] Understanding and Reason are thus more flexible and are, in fact, closer to each other than the original opposition presumed. We can conclude, with respect to *Blut,* that the Notions, with which we are confronted in the many scenes, are only manifestations of a particular, historically dependent configuration of Understanding and Reason.

Contingency is a central theme in *Blut*. The social vignettes with which the audience is bombarded are to be found very much within the its experience. The swiftness of recognition on the audience's part points squarely to the contemporary, through familiar situations and accessible colloquial forms. In this way Fassbinder takes up Handke's social critique and attempts to historicize it within the frame of situations the audience recognizes. Yet the spectator is able to recognize them only because of their language (and their translation into body language). Fassbinder, like Handke, acknowledges the difficulties of breaking out of ossified social structures that are reinforced by equally rigid linguistic and semantic ones. Because language helps

construct social relations (as noted in Handke's critique of the 'picture theory'), language must become a central consideration if one wants to change them. The playwright's employment and foregrounding of intertext points to the potential for liberation as coming from a playful and challenging use of language, which none the less does not conform to a spurious bourgeois notion of originality.

In conclusion, then, one may register the similarities between Fassbinder and Handke. Both exploit the dramatic medium to expose the artifice of language (and to oppose its status as 'natural') in order to suggest the possibility of social change. Through a conscious reuse of intertext both signal the primacy of context over content: the words themselves may be familiar, but it is their deployment that opens the possibility of *Sprachkritik*. The most marked difference in their strategies is their manipulation of the actor-audience relationship. Fassbinder introduces the audience to recognizable scenes of everyday oppression. The scenes never directly announce their subject-matter and require input from the spectator to generate meaning. This task is not too testing, yet its continual repetition points to the tacit collusion between stage and auditorium. Phoebe makes this collusion overt by throwing the trusted words back at the spectator and thus causes irritation in the audience, which may lead to raised awareness of the linguistic issues. Handke, on the other hand, uses a conscious theatricality from the outset. Meaning is generated out of a contradiction between Kaspar and the Einsager. The mechanisms of signification are laid bare before the audience's eyes. The interval thus comes as more of a shock, when the audience is made to confront its own acceptance of linguistic commonplaces. Only once the spectator has experienced the prison house is the potential for escape presented in the form of poetically protean intertexts. Handke's dramaturgy moves between distance (Scenes 1-58) and proximity (Scene 59) and then returns to distance (Scenes 60-65) in a journey that demarcates the elements of its dynamic quite clearly. For Fassbinder, the process is one of a gradual awakening of curiosity in the spectator. The first phase sets itself up for its fall in the second. The rapid succession of second-phase scenes highlights the part played by the audience in the generation of meaning, and the spectator oscillates between spectacle and involvement. By the third phase, the audience is primed for Phoebe's attempt at bucking the system and exposing its foundations. Both plays require strategies to activate the audience to effect their *Sprachkritik*. Handke creates the context for criticism from the outset before confronting his audience with the 'real' examples of the processes explored on stage. Fassbinder uses a more covert technique in that he shams a more conventional dramaturgy in order to turn it back on the spectator later. Fassbinder ambushes the audience Handke treated with more respect with a subtle dramaturgy that ends up accusing the spectator of collusion in the acts of oppression that seemed confined to the stage.

Notes

1. In Peter Handke, *Stücke 1* (Frankfurt a.M.: Suhrkamp, 1972), hereafter *K.*

2. Erik MacDonald, 'Rainer Werner Fassbinder and the Politics of Simulation: Two Plays', *Journal of Dramatic Theory and Criticism,* 5 (1990), 131-50.

3. See, for example, Ernst Wendt, 'Dramen über Zerstörung, Leiden, Sprachlosigkeit im Alltag—auf der Flucht vor den großen politischen Stoffen?', *Theater heute,* 5 (1971), 32-40 (p. 32).

4. Christian Braad Thomson, *Fassbinder: The Life and Work of a Provocative Genius,* trans. by Martin Chalmers (London: Faber, 1997), p. 45.

5. *Blut am Hals der Katze,* in Rainer Werner Fassbinder, *Sämtliche Stücke,* ed. by Michael Töteberg, (Frankfurt a.M.: Verlag der Autoren, 1991), p. 498, hereafter *B.*

6. The alternative title of the play, which appeared in the programme of the world première, was *Marilyn Monroe contre les vampires.* What seems to be happening, therefore, is that Phoebe has observed the mutually parasitic behaviour of the characters and has become a vampire herself, reproducing her surroundings once more.

7. She recites the first paragraph of the first chapter of the section entitled 'Die Subjektivität' from the second part of the work (*B,* p. 239). I shall return to an interpretation of this concluding speech later. Both Denis Calandra, who has translated a selection of Fassbinder's plays, and MacDonald, who, I assume, read Calandra's introductory remarks to the volume of translations, name Kant as the intertext's source (Rainer Werner Fassbinder, *Plays,* ed. and trans. by Denis Calandra (Baltimore, MD: Johns Hopkins University Press, 1985), p. 11). MacDonald is keen to point to Kant as a symbolic father-figure, in Lacanian terms (p. 145), whereas Hegel could be seen as one of the bastard sons, self-confident and iconoclastic. Calandra may have identified Kant as the source because of the language and categories employed in the speech. Hegel, however, is a more controversial choice of philosopher. The associations with Marx, a figure still looming large at the time in the wake of the upheavals of 1968, are hard to avoid. Hegel is thus more provocative as the provenance of the final text; Kant, in comparison, is authoritative and untouchable.

8. This concept is taken from Handke's much-quoted preface to the play, in which he says he could have called *Kaspar* 'Sprechfolterung' (*K,* p. 103).

9. See, for example, M. Read, 'Peter Handke's *Kaspar* and the Power of Negative Thinking', *Forum for Modern Language Studies,* 29 (1993), 126-48, or Jeanette R. Malkin, '"Think What You Are Saying": Verbal Politics in the Early Plays of Handke and Kroetz', *Modern Drama,* 33 (1990), 363-79.

10. See, for example, Christa Dixon, 'Peter Handkes Kaspar: Ein Modellfall', *German Quarterly,* 46 (1973), 31-34, or Bettina Soestwohner, 'Kaspar oder das Theater der Sprache', *Colloquia Germanica,* 22 (1989), 137-50.

11. Michael Töteberg, 'Rainer Werner Fassbinder', in *Kritisches Lexikon zur deutschsprachigen Gegenwartsliteratur,* 9 vols, ed. by Heinz Ludwig Arnold (Munich: text + kritik, 1986), III, p. 6 of the entry.

12. The quotation comes from a fellow Austrian, Ferdinand Kürnberger: 'Und alles, was man weiß, nicht bloß, was man rauschen und brausen gehört hat, läßt sich in drei Worten sagen', in Ludwig Wittgenstein, *Tractatus Logico-Philosophicus/Logische-Philosophische Abhandlung,* trans. by C. K. Ogden (London: Routledge, 1981), p. 25. This appears as the work's motto.

13. Originally they had served the Einsager in Scenes 33, 35, 37, 39, 41, and 43 by illustrating ideal ways of dealing with situations suggested by the Einsager. After the interval they become more rebellious and anarchic. They also represent an attack on individuality, similar to that in *Blut.* The Kaspar of the first part of the play can no longer be separated from the others. His idiosyncrasies are reproduced by the other Kaspars and we are shown a world of faceless uniformity.

14. Jeffrey Herrick, 'Peter Handke's *Kaspar.* A Study of Linguistic Theory in Modern Drama', *Philological Quarterly,* 63 (1984), 219, and Gay McAuley, 'The Problem of Identity. Theme, Form and Theatrical Method in *Les Nègres, Kaspar* and *Old Times*', *Southern Review,* 8 (1975), 63.

15. It is interesting to note that there is a confluence of ideas between Fassbinder and Handke here. In Handke's *Büchner-Preis-Rede* of 1973, he rails against the abstraction of ideas, preferring to oppose it with the complexity of experience and memory.

DER RITT ÜEBER DEN BODENSEE (THE RIDE ACROSS LAKE CONSTANCE)

PRODUCTION REVIEW

Sarah Kaufman (review date 9 October 1998)

SOURCE: Kaufman, Sarah. "The Truth about *Lake Constance.*" *Washington Post* (9 October 1998): N41.

[In the following review, Kaufman discusses theatrical stagings in the 1930s, as well as tie-ins to German movie stars whom director John Spitzer uses for his adaption of Handke's The Ride across Lake Constance, performed by the Fradulent Production.]

The tiny, 45-seat theater at D.C. Arts Center is currently home to some Very Big Ideas.

The Ride across Lake Constance is FraudProd's fourth production by Austrian experimentalist Peter Handke, whom director John Spitzer calls the most important playwright of the late 20th century—despite the fact that he is little known on this side of the Atlantic. What the rest of the country hasn't yet discovered, says Spitzer, is Handke's take on reality.

Handke deals with that fundamental postmodern concept of multiple truths—"many divergent realities that are valid at the same moment. And if you're going to seize on one possible interpretation, you're going to close out 50 others," the director says.

Which is exactly the issue in *Ride.* In a properly appointed, 1931 drawing room, a mix of characters (all named for German silent-film actors) talk about events that may or may not be real, may or may not be fantasy. Nobody seems to know for sure, which is exactly the point. Who can be certain what is real? If there's no agreement on the truth, does it exist at all?

"Reality is an idea that we arrive at by consensus," says Spitzer. "'Did you see that? I did, too. Therefore, it must exist.' But what happens when that consensus doesn't exist?"

Spitzer first encountered the playwright 25 years ago when he stumbled upon his writings in a bookstore. "I can actually say reading him changed my life," says Spitzer, who until then had been dabbling in Shakespeare and Beckett. But while grasping the writer's ideas from the written page is one thing, bringing them to life in the theater is another.

When he began working on the production, Spitzer said, he had to "empty and open" his mind. He begins by taking notes on the text, whatever the words cause to pop into his mind. In *Ride,* Spitzer says, the idea of a 1930s living room seemed right, given the era's importance to German filmmaking as talkies first came into being.

Continuing the film theme, Spitzer likens the two main characters to "Laurel and Hardy in an existential hell." (Pictured above are Dan Awkward, left, as Emil Jannings and Matt Grayson as Erich von Stroheim.)

"It's not as dense and daunting as it sounds," Spitzer says. "It's really a lot of fun. . . . I hope the audience sits back and enjoys the ride—then wakes up the next day and argues with their spouse about it."

CRITICAL COMMENTARY

Nicholas Hern (essay date 1971)

SOURCE: Hern, Nicholas. *"The Ride Across Lake Constance."* In *Peter Handke: Theatre and Anti-Theatre,* pp. 90-94. London: Oswald Wolff, 1971.

[*In the following essay, Hern discusses the question of sanity versus insanity in Handke's work* The Ride Across Lake Constance, *comparing it to previous Handke plays such as* Kaspar *and* My Foot My Tutor.]

Handke's second full-length play [*The Ride Across Lake Constance*] is a critic's dream in that, while clearly re-using certain elements from the author's earlier plays, it equally clearly represents an advance on these plays; but it is also a critic's nightmare in that this advance is into territory almost totally devoid of those landmarks such as logic, consistency, sequentiality, by which a critic would normally find his way. Indeed, nightmare, or dream, is an apt description of the play, by far the most surreal of Handke's creations and reminiscent no longer of the abstract austerity of Beckett but rather of the cruel luxuriance of recent Bunuel (*The Exterminating Angel, Belle de Jour*) or of the baroque inventions of the neglected Polish dramatist, Gombrowicz. Talking in interview about his play, *The Marriage* (produced in Berlin in 1968, the first of a series of Gombrowicz productions in German theatres), Gombrowicz called it 'obscure and dream-like and fantastical: because it is so full of shadows, I wouldn't know how to analyse it fully myself . . . Like all my works [it is] a revolt against form, a travesty of form, a parody of "great drama".' These words could well apply to *The Ride Across Lake Constance.*

But, considering the persistence with which Handke has hitherto pursued his preoccupations, he is unlikely to have forsaken them merely for the decorative externals of surrealism. For a start, the new play is full of reminders of previous works. Thus, the five main characters (facetiously identified for the reader with the names of famous German stage and screen personalities of the 'twenties) all look like refugees from the cast of *Quodlibet.* They do have a set this time, though, which looks like an amalgam of musical comedy and drawing-room drama—'Chekhov's *Cherry Orchard* transported to Hollywood', wrote the critic of *Die Zeit.* Their costumes are similarly non-specific, although definitely theatrical—'intimations' rather than recognisable costumes. Like the figures in *Quodlibet,* they also indulge in apparently aimless conversation, but every word, every gesture is carefully laid down. And as at the end of *Quodlibet,* these characters too seem often more asleep than awake and they too fall prey to an unmistakably insidious silence and inaction, somehow connected with a large, very life-like doll, which is carried on by the black-faced woman who opens the play by vacuuming the room and removing the dust-sheets from the furniture.

Again, two of the characters, called Emil Jannings and Heinrich George, are locked in the dominant/subservient relationship familiar from *My Foot My Tutor.* But the other three, Elisabeth Bergner, Erich von Stroheim, Henny Porten, seem caught up in a distorted eternal triangle: this, and their interaction with the first two, are new elements.

Again, there are a number of speeches in the play which are counterparts to 'poems' in *The Inner World of the Outer World of the Inner World.* Particularly striking is the similarity between No. 20, *Mistakes* (*Verwechselungen*), where perfectly ordinary phenomena are misinterpreted as horrifying (a plane with its loading-doors open is seen as a hungry shark on the runway), and Jannings' account of a 'bad day' full of similarly disturbing mistakes (a 'madwoman' trampling on egg-shells is in fact breaking them up for the birds). Both the play and the suite of 'poems' consistently reject the orthodox *outward* expression of *inner* thoughts and feelings, in favour of a more real and disturbing *inner world* normally kept repressed and submerged.

At this point, the play's relationship to *Kaspar* also begins to emerge. There are several devices in the new play which Handke first used in *Kaspar*; for instance when Elisabeth lapses into schizophrenia following an encounter with her reflection, and Henny restores her self-integration by reciting a number of syntactically identical sentences until Elisabeth is induced to imitate the model with an example of her own; or when Jannings kicks George at the precise moment that Stroheim kicks Henny, and Elisabeth delivers a paean in praise of order and co-ordination. But also in *Kaspar* there were hints of the terrifying abyss beneath the superficial semblance of order and linguistic competence. And it is this abyss, this innermost world beneath a thin veneer of normality, which opens up beneath our feet when we take *The Ride Across Lake Constance.*

The title refers to a short ballad, *Der Reiter und der Bodensee,* by the Swabian poet, Gustav Schwab (1792-1850), which tells of a horseman who, without knowing it, rides across the frozen Lake Constance but dies of fright when he learns of the danger he was in. The analogy with the thin ice of rationality on which we are all skating is exact; and it is essential we remain unaware of how thin the ice is if we are not to disintegrate with shock. In the words of Botho Strauss in *Theater Heute*:

> The ride parallels the functioning of our grammar, of our system of co-ordinating perception and meaning, and of our linguistic and sentient powers of reason; it is only a provisional, permeable order, which, particularly when, as in Handke's play, it becomes conscious of its own existence, is threatened by somnambulism, schizophrenia and madness.

The question remains, however, whether what is called madness might not be preferable to accepted normality, just as Kaspar's original unco-ordinated innocence seemed preferable to the social co-ordinate he became. The answer is given by the Kessler twins, who make a brief appearance towards the end of the play. Their identical appearance in ordinary (untheatrical) clothes, looking as if they had 'come into the production by mistake', their banal conversation ('How do you do?. . . . Good day . . . What time is it?'), their symmetrical movements, and their brisk tidying of the set, all mark them out as representatives of the orderliness of normality. But how dispiriting their normality is made to seem, and how easily it is seen to disintegrate as the twins leave the stage in confusion.

Botho Strauss sees in one of Henny's dream-like speeches 'about water and madness, and the Ships of Fools on the great rivers' a reference to Michel Foucault's treatise on *Madness and Civilization* (1961). Much more important

than this single point of contact is the relevance Foucault's thesis has for the play as a whole. In attempting to define historically the 'moment of conspiracy' when the thin ice dividing Reason and Madness first froze over, 'Foucault makes it quite clear,' says the Introduction to the English edition,

> that the invention of madness as a disease is in fact nothing less than a peculiar disease of our civilization. We choose to conjure up this disease in order to evade a certain moment of our own existence—the moment of disturbance, of penetrating vision into the depths of ourselves.

And Foucault himself writes:

> The constitution of madness as a mental illness, at the end of the eighteenth century, affords the evidence of a broken dialogue, posits the separation as already effected, and thrusts into oblivion all those stammered, imperfect words without fixed syntax in which the exchange between madness and reason was made.

In *The Ride Across Lake Constance* Handke is concerned to re-establish that broken dialogue, to question the assumptions 'by which men, in an act of sovereign reason, confine their neighbours, and communicate and recognise each other through the merciless language of non-madness' (Foucault), and to reinstate the ancient belief that madness is an expression of 'the secret powers of the world'. Handke has moved from a Wittgensteinian distrust of language to a Foucaultian distrust of what our society calls reason. His play is by no means surrealist in externals only: it parallels the surrealists' cardinal desire—the liberation of men's minds from the constraints of reason.

Thus Handke continues to demonstrate that the consistently *anti*-theatrical stance which he has maintained throughout his dramatic writing can none the less lend concrete theatrical expression to abstract philosophical ideas, thereby generating a new and valid form of theatre.

DIE UNVERNÜNFTIGEN STERBEN AUS (THEY ARE DYING OUT)

PRODUCTION REVIEW

Robert Koehler (review date 1 August 1985)

SOURCE: Koehler, Robert. "Wunderbar Staging of *Dying Out*." *Los Angeles Times* 104 (1 August 1985): 2 sec. 6.

[*In the following review, Koehler gives a positive assessment to Rolf Brauneis's staging of Handke's* Die Unvernünftigen sterben aus.]

Peter Handke's German theater doesn't transfer easily to our cultural landscape. The comedy tends to be more emphatic and dichotomous than we're used to, the drama often highly expressionistic and political. And the language defiantly resists translation.

Against those odds, Los Angeles has had two fine stagings in a row of two of Handke's major works: last year's *Kaspar* at the Night-house, and now translator/director Rolf Brauneis' compelling version of *The Unreasonable Are Dying Out* at the Wallenboyd.

Brauneis, a quiet man with a countenance seemingly chiseled from a block of stone, has a few surprises in store for those who would like to meet the director who's elicited some very electric ensemble performances—highlighted by Kedric Robin Wolfe's startling portrayal of the industrialist Hermann Quitt.

For starters, this is Brauneis' first directorial assignment. His circuitous career, as he recalled it in the Wallenboyd office, began with painting. He later gravitated to Frankfurt's legendary Theatre am Turm in the robust late '60s.

'A lot of my friends were working there. Handke was living in Kronberg just outside Frankfurt. He had recently done *Offending the Audience* (which caused a huge sensation). Then *The Ride across Lake Constance* and *Kaspar* were both first staged at Theatre am Turm. It was a collaborative and very democratic theater in which the actors and crew decided what they wanted to do. As assistant director, I became hooked on theater. We weren't under the thumb of a single artistic director."

But the publicly funded theater *was* under the thumb of Frankfurt's city government. "At this point, Frankfurt was governed by the Social Democrats. When the Christian Democrats won locally in 1970, they managed to get (late film and stage director Rainer) Fassbinder as artistic director, and got rid of our democratic model."

As many of his friends ventured to friendlier haunts in Berlin with Peter Stein's Schaubuhne Theatre (where, as well as at Frankfurt's Stadtische Buhn, *The Unreasonable Are Dying Out* co-premiered), Brauneis turned to the visual arts again—as a fashion photographer. "But," he said, "I had this terrible split within me, like Hermann Quitt—I had a bad conscience doing that work rather than pursuing my art."

(Quitt is split between his capitalist desires and his yearning to be free, instinctual, wild, unreasonable. In the end—after cheating his corporate partners on a buy-out scheme and confronting them in one of the most deliciously biting sequences of the stage year—he rams his head against a huge boulder.)

Unlike Quitt, Brauneis survived his dilemma, dissolved his business and exiled himself to Los Angeles, where, he said, "art and I have come together again."

But what about the poor fellow who has to play Quitt?

"Kedric got a lot of excitement out of playing him. But at first he fought against the character so much. Quitt's very far from what Kedric is as a person and what he believes in. After a rehearsal, we talked about it, and I told him it might be interesting when playing Quitt to just watch what Quitt does. In a week, it suddenly clicked."

Just as surprising as the fact that Brauneis is new at this sort of thing is that he wasn't worried about directing American actors with such an imagistic, complex text.

"Probably *because* I was a first-timer, it didn't bother me," he said. "And when the cast read the play, they realized it was a challenge they wanted to take on."

It helped that the text was his own translation—"done in my naive English"—with refining by playwright Jeffry Freundlich. Though unacquainted with Michael Roloff's version, Brauneis is critical of Eric Bentley's English edition: "Handke's language is full of images and very poetic. I found none of that richness in Bentley's translation."

But the world created on stage is easily recognizable: the cutthroat methods of advertisers, the tragicomic self-loathing that lurks underneath. "Handke's people build up facades of prestige and bury themselves under a wave of words. But soon, the facade cracks. The true self comes out, along with fears and paranoias. This is the political breakdown, too, but the beauty of Handke is that he's never ideological and never works on just one level."

In his rookie year, Brauneis might well be speaking of himself.

DAS SPIEL VOM FRAGEN ODER (VOYAGE TO THE SONOROUS LAND)

CRITICAL COMMENTARY

Eva-Maria Metcalf (essay date 1990)

SOURCE: Metcalf, Eva-Maria. "Challenging the Arrogance of Power." *Modern Fiction Studies* 36, no. 3 (autumn 1990): 369-79.

[*In the following essay, Metcalf discusses Handke's usage of mythology and language to establish a quasi-fairy tale-like structure in* Das Spiel vom Fragen.]

I

In 1967 Peter Handke built himself an ivory tower, and he has resided in it ever since. The theories about language and writing that he exposed in his essay "Ich bin ein Bewohner des Elfenbeinturms" have continued to serve as his guiding principles throughout his more than twenty years of authorship. During the last decade, Handke has drifted further and further in the direction of mysticism, which has become the ultimate consequence of his rejection of current nonliterary discourse.

Based on Herbert Gamper's long interview with Handke, *Aber ich lebe nur von den Zwischenräumen*, and Handke's two most recent works, **Das Spiel vom Fragen: oder die Reise zum sonoren Land** and *Versuch über die Müdigkeit*, I will trace Handke's Nietzschean efforts to revalorize words and concepts and along with them the value scale of modern society. His attempts to reach out beyond the thoughtless superficiality of everyday language and the stale realism of the stories dominating modern fiction to a deeper or greater reality by means of a priestly, ecstatic, and often hermetic language have led to rather harsh criticism by those unwilling or unable to duplicate his efforts to rid himself of the shackles of rationalistic discourses. He has been reproached for conservatism and epigonism, and, indeed, the German literary tradition since classicism makes up much of the intertextuality in his works and guides his fundamental approach to writing. This orientation anchors him in modernism rather than in postmodernism.

Nevertheless, Handke's relationship with tradition is anything but imitative. Rather, it consists of a critical and creative adaptation of this tradition that is not altogether unambiguous. As I will show, Handke's desired manner of writing is an "*Erzählen im Erzählstrom, der stets offen und ohne geschichtliche Determiniertheit ist,*" for which he has created the imagery of somnambulism (*Zwischenräumen* 139). His aim is to approach writing in a postreflexive, spontaneous state of mind. Like the "*Mauerschauer*" in **Das Spiel vom Fragen,** Handke searches for the third path ("*der dritte Weg*") beyond the either-or confinement of logocentricity. It seems a hopeless, impossible task, but therein lies the challenge, and Handke meets it head on. This paper will investigate what is at stake in Handke's attempt to counteract the arrogance of power displayed in the pervasive and ever-growing dominance of instrumentalized reason and functionalized logic by means of a self-empowering discourse of the powerless.

Like much of modern fiction, Handke's writing centers on the epistemological and ethical question of how the speaking subject can and ought to confront the world. As he turns to his own lived experience for the illustration and inspiration of the philosophical and theoretical discussions of language, writing, and communication, his insights are at once profound and accessible, self-centered and freehanded. Handke's thematic focus mirrors the essential crisis of the modern writer whose role in society has become marginalized. The disappearance of a universally valid, prescriptive formative paradigm uniting society and cultures has pushed the modern writer into an offensively defensive position from which he explores the theme of the alienated and fragmented subject. In the essay "Ich bin ein Bewohner des Elfenbeinturms," Handke states clearly:

Ich habe keine Themen über die ich schreiben möchte, ich habe nur ein Thema: über mich selbst klar, klarer zu werden, mich kennenzulernen oder nicht kennenzulernen, zu lernen, was ich falsch mache, was ich falsch denke, was ich unbedacht denke, was ich unbedacht spreche, was ich automatisch spreche, was auch andere unbedacht tun, denken sprechen: aufmerksam zu werden und aufmerksam zu machen: sensibler, empfindlicher, genauer zu machen und zu werden, damit ich und andere auch genauer und sensibler existieren können, damit ich mich mit anderen besser verständigen und mit ihnen besser umgehen kann.

(26)

In order to achieve greater sensitivity and self-knowledge, Handke suggests a self-vivisection with the help of language and its signs. With their slippage of meaning, their contingency, and their connotations, however, signs are not sufficiently clean tools for this purpose, and Handke starts the cleaning and clarifying process by removing the words and concepts he uses from their "natural" context and by relocating them in an ahistorical setting. Handke calls this process "das bereinigende Mythologisieren," which seems a paradoxical notion by modern commonsensical standards (*Zwischenräumen* 140). Similar to the act of purification in a religious ceremony achieved by burning incense, which enveils and hides and thereby dissolves and transforms the profane object, Handke purifies colloquial language, newsspeak, or scientific jargon reflecting an increasingly profane and demythified world by enveloping everyday concepts in a veil of myth. Once formed, this ethereal veil severs established ties and dislocates and decontextualizes words and concepts, which, transformed, arouse a mild alienation that will create the sense of newness Handke called for in his essay from the ivory tower. It is Handke's hope that this measure will prevent his literary language from being coopted by market forces and that his writing will become a counter-discourse of meaningful quietness within a sea of hollow noisiness of newsmedia language. The question remains, however, whether Handke's beautifully crafted, descriptive language—which cannot avoid being situated and read in a specific historical context despite Handke's efforts to cleanse the words of any infectious connotations—has the cleansing power he claims.

The myth Handke evokes is based on the materiality of language. He relies on the power of single words and the images they invoke. By "recycling" words and concepts, Handke attempts a new, fresh beginning, disregarding their connotative roots in a free play of words. Words such as "Segen," "Fluch," "Frieden," "Krieg," "Volk," which have traditionally been endowed with an aura but have now been demythified and worn with usage, are reinstated to their old power but in a new framework. With "cleansed" words the world opens up to new insights, as it does for the protagonists in **Das Spiel vom Fragen.**

Kindergeschichte is just one example of the remythification of a demythified world by means of the remythification of words and concepts. In Handke's new yet very traditional terminology childhood, along with old age and insanity, represents a blessed state of closeness between the subjective and objective world. Childhood becomes the expression of his longing for rejuvenation, for imaginative power, spontaneity, wholesomeness, and wholeness. No concrete childhood is intended, least of all Handke's own, about which he relates much suffering. His concept of childhood is very similar in content and function to Hofmannsthal's concept of Präexistenz. As do emptiness in *Das Spiel vom Fragen* and tiredness in *Versuch über die Müdigkeit,* childhood serves as a screen onto which hope, change, and possibility are projected. The child becomes "der Palast des Fragens" (*Spiel* 129), and Parzival, like Saint Exupéry's little prince, finds fault with the poor, inhibited, and unimaginative way adults ask questions.

An ascetic purity of language also lies behind Handke's rejection of the story as a narrative device. Story, he argues, is compensatory; it disguises the sentences, merely entertains, and thus diverts attention from real life problems ("macht weltvergessen" [*Elfenbeinturms* 23]). Handke's dislike of stories has its roots in his desire to make visible that which exists behind the layers of cultural codes, poses, and conventions. It is at one and the same time demythifying and remythifying. But does myth not need the shroud of story or rituals to survive? Rejecting the story, Handke relies heavily on ritual. Ritual enters into the process of writing, for example, which Handke approaches with awe, as becomes apparent in the highly autobiographical *Nachmittag eines Schriftstellers,* and which resembles the codification of a visionary's divine inspiration because Handke barely ever revises or alters what he has written.

With the one possible exception of *Wunschloses Unglück,* none of Handke's writings have a storyline or any plot development imposed from the "outside." As a rule, Handke's language imposes—he would prefer to say generates—its own structure. What this structure reveals over and over again is the fundamental conflict of the post-Romantic writer, the conflict between mimetic and nonmimetic communication. It is Handke's language that sustains the tension and inner logic of his plays and narratives. Handke still clings to his dictum from the sixties: language should reveal, not cover up the methods used. "*Die naturalistischen Formen zerdenken, bis sich die didaktischen, zeigenden ergeben*" (*Gewicht* 321) is a demand that Handke applies both to a single word or phrase he uses and to the whole structure of a work. Thus far, Handke joins with the structuralists and poststructuralists in the analysis and resulting demythification of language, the medium through which we perceive the world within and without us. But with his demand, "*die didaktischen Formen zerdenken, bis sich die mythischen ergeben*" (*Gewicht* 321), Handke does not uncover the mythical content of signs and second order signs as did Roland Barthes. Instead, he remythifies language and the act of writing, which to him has become a quasi-religious experience.

Handke disdains being swept along in the constant flow of things, and he persists in writing, "*damit in dem formlosen Strudel der Welt irgendeine kleine Form entsteht*" (*Zwischenräumen* 27). He is very ambiguous about the essence of this form, however. In his interview with Herbert Gamper, he confirms both his belief in the existence of a law behind appearances and in the fictionality of this law by conceding that his search for truth beyond historical contingencies, conventional language, and structural patterns may be self-deception. In his search for stability within eternal flow and relativity he admits to resorting to a lie or a fiction, just as Nietzsche had to do. Identifying with a man who desperately continued to search for meaning against all odds, Handke lets Nietzsche express the dilemma he himself feels: "*Es gibt nur eine Welt, und die ist falsch, grausam, widersprüchlich, verführerisch, ohne Sinn. Das ist die wahre Welt.—Wir haben Lüge nötig, um über diese Realität, diese 'Wahrheit' zum Sieg zu kommen, das heißt, um zu leben . . .*" (*Zwischenräumen* 199). Handke fights the meaninglessness he perceives around him by means of illusion, that is, by means of language. Demanding of his language not only that it represent an object but also that it express its very essence, Handke the mystic reveals the patterns which Handke the writer generates. Or, as he states, "*ich muß mein Wesen durch die Form gelenkt und gereinigt wiedergeben*" (*Zwischenräumen* 51). Truth and lie are intermingled as the illusion of truth in reality is confronted with the truthful illusion in Handke's writing.

What is the motive for this intermingling of reality and illusion? If not seen "with the simplifying eye of habit," as Hofmannsthal has Lord Chandos observe, everything disintegrates into parts and does not let itself be encompassed by one idea (Hofmannsthal 134). Stemming the tide of total disintegration for Lord Chandos, as for Handke, is what Christa Bürger has called "intermittent mimesis" (Bürger 205). For short durations of time, relief is sought through a return to the Dionysiac spell of an archaic, ahistorical world of images induced and mediated by analytic thought and writing. But does this project really represent a counter-image to popular culture, as Handke would have it? It does in the slowness and awe-inspiring care devoted to the process of writing. Music videos, however, display the same spellbinding decontextualization of imagery that Handke evokes in print.

For Handke, conflation of truth and illusion, as well as total identification with the object, is brought on by approaching the object slowly and reverently, by means, for instance, of a special gaze ("Blick") or a general openness and receptiveness to the world as it appears, devoid of signs and names. Coincidence and happenstance in the form of the right space or setting, as well as the right state of mind, play an important role for this moment of intense inspiration. Coincidence, now reinterpreted as fateful setting, becomes an accomplice in the subject's striving for sense and aesthetic sensitivity. During certain moments, insignficant objects can form an image or a constellation which becomes the source of a mysterious revelation, as do the shining path of a snail and the markings like those of dice on the feather of a bird in *Das Spiel vom Fragen.* The objects seem carefully chosen despite an apparent randomness considering the symbolic value invested in them by our culture. Precious slowness and closeness to the earth, the sublime freedom of flight, and coincidence are brought together in this image. The revelation inevitably draws upon the writer's and the reader's cultural memory, that is, despite decontextualization and mythification, cultural knowledge is an inevitable source of the writing process, which Handke describes as a swinging back and forth between the objects of the world and their slow transition into text (*Zwischenräumen* 230).

II

The two fundamental experiences of the modern artist, that is, alienation and isolation, the feeling of not being able to span the gulf between one's immediate presence to oneself and one's indirect representational knowledge of everything else, are topicalized in *Das Spiel vom Fragen* and *Versuch über die Müdigkeit.* These two works can be seen as complementing each other. Each work comes to the problem from a different angle using a new set of images, although a basic core of reappearing images slowly unfolds with each new work by Handke. The figure of the outsider who simultaneously cherishes and loathes his or her challenging and painful state is one of the core images. Whereas these outsiders were presented as protesters and sufferers in Handke's earlier works, they are presented as preachers and prophets in the image of Zarathustra in his more recent work, thus reflecting Handke's own changing attitude.

Das Spiel vom Fragen gives us an introspection into the dilemma of the modern writer by way of a painstakingly detailed dramatization of Handke's literary creativity. The play is delivered with commentary, criticism, and self-analysis to give it openness and transparency and to preclude any emotional engagement that might cloud the issues. The self-critical (re)search culminates in a play within the play that unravels and replays its fundamental problematic in an argumentative fashion. The problem discussed among the performers is nothing less than how do we do the impossible? How can one perform and represent the nonperformable and the nonrepresentable? This paradox of the mimetic project has haunted Handke for a long time, and in this play it "dramatized itself" the way Handke described it to Gamper in 1987:

> Mir kommt es eher darauf an, die richtige Frage endlich zu finden. . . . Also daß aus einem Problem, das einem—was vielleicht auch zum Schreiben gehört— seit unvordenklicher Zeit beschäftigt, auf einmal die richtige Frage entsteht. Diese Frage kann ja sehr langwierig sein, auch sehr gewunden, das ist ja auch ein Merkmal einer dramatischen und sich selber dramatisierenden Frage.

> (*Zwischenräumen* 107)

Das Spiel vom Fragen comprises a quest in the form of a journey in search of a new kind of question. The ideal kind of question Handke envisions should neither display the quality of the "previously-known" (*das Vorausgewußte*") of a "*Lehrstück,*" nor should it be a trap, as in the "*Hereinlegefragerei*" of a Socratic dialogue. Instead, the right kind of question presupposes a state of disinterested purity. Seven nameless people, one for each star in the constellation of the Pleiades, set out on a journey into the unknown. Their aim is to come upon the right questions, questions that do not already presuppose the answers, questions that are not caught within the confines of their own discourse, questions that can reach beyond the sphere of the cultural artifact of language. They do not purposefully and systematically pursue one road or direction that may lead them to their goal; their Holy Grail can only be reached by means of a slow, meandering, discursive journey.

Handke refers to the basic tenet of the play as that of a research trip and to the basic tone as that of a psalm ("Psalmenton"). He intentionally combines the modern and the medieval frame of mind or what Lyotard has termed scientific and narrative knowledge (31-37). The play opens with a suggestive image of isolation. Initially, the actors do not communicate with each other. Their meandering through space on the stage, sometimes together, sometimes walking in different directions, ends in a mutual understanding that reaches beyond language. The two main protagonists, "*der Mauerschauer*" (the mystic) and "*der Spielverderber*" (the sceptic) represent the two conflicting poles in Handke, whose love of mysticism is as strong as his love of form. In the search undertaken by these two protagonists as well as by the others, Handke retraces his initial reluctance and anxiety before the different conflicting tendencies become a harmonious whole.

At the point when the main protagonists call each other by their first names and when Parzival, who is the body of inquiry, is freed from his chains, the play assumes concrete shape both literally and symbolically. The stage is set for the expression of the ineffable in words. The sounds produced by the "*Mauerschauer*" find resonance in the sonorous country of the play's title. As this final image vibrates and slowly fades away, a feeling of communion and of oneness with nature is conjured up yet remains caught in the fictionality of the play.

Handke uses both emotional and didactic theatrical tools to prepare the viewer or reader for the final moment of bliss. Mood shifts are induced by lighting and stage props. In his stage directions, Handke asks for a special "question light" distinct from the harsh light of inquisition, a glimmering shine to suggest that it emanates from the protagonists. Sound assumes a central function through the confrontation of "*unmusikalische Fraglosigkeit*" (*Spiel* 150) and "*musikalische Fraglosigkeit*" (*Spiel* 156) that dissolves completely into sound at the end.

In *Aber ich lebe nur von den Zwischenräumen,* it becomes clear that spatial relations are of utmost importance for Handke's aesthetic sensibility. His idiosyncratic experience of bare, open spaces as threatening and limiting, but small openings as liberating for the imagination and the soul translates into the sequence of stage settings. The action—paralleling plumbing the depths of the soul—proceeds in jolts from a next-to-bare stage, through territories with some vegetation and cultural artifacts, and down to a clearing in a lush virgin forest in the region's deepest interior (hinterland). There, a collage of plants from different vegetative regions surrounds ahistoricized and decontextualized cultural props from different ages and strata and permits a partial view of the wall of questions, the end of the journey.

Parzival, who as the "body of questions" fulfills a didactic function, resembles Kaspar in his speechlessness ("*Sprachlosigkeit*") and mute anger, but his fate is a reversal or continuation of Kaspar's. Turned mute on account of his socialization, he learns to speak again as the searchers approach their goal. On the way, Parzival jerks off layers of acculturation while producing disjointed, incoherent phrases. Later, as the group approaches a more profound state of questioning, he recognizes correlations between words and objects, and his speech becomes meaningful. Whereas Parzival is freed from the leash that has chained him to muteness and cultural clichés, the group, now freed from the ballast of civilization, is ready to "think in question form," and the play within the play commences in unbridled playfulness as the actors dance off in somber, Zarathustran joy. The play ends in a state of relieved questionlessness, a state of inner calmness, harmony, and fulfillment which comes very close to the state of tiredness in *Versuch über die Müdigkeit.*

III

"*Nur mit der Energie eines Schlafwandlers kann ich mich auf andere übertragen,*" wrote Handke in *Die Geschichte des Bleistifts* (132). Sleepwalking, a state of unconscious awareness and intuitively sure-footed competence, becomes the optimal state for artistic creativity and direct human interaction. Whereas Handke had dramatized his somnambulistic approach to writing in **Das Spiel vom Fragen,** he addresses the social and intersubjective aspect of communication in *Versuch über die Müdigkeit.* The story resembles a clinical self-analysis, patterned as a soliloquy and written in suggestively poetic prose in which Handke tries to come to terms with "*das Versagen in der Gemeinschaft*" (*Versuch* 9). Handke undertakes a classification of four states of tiredness, or "*die vier Verhältnisweisen meines Sprach-Ichs zur Welt*" (*Versuch* 56), which are closely interrelated to the individual's ability to communicate and function in a social setting. In ascending order, these four stages are: 1) autistic muteness; 2) the ability to perceive voices from the outside, rudimentary emotion breaking through muteness as screams and fits of anger; 3) the ability to communicate with a child or a close friend; and 4) the final and optimal stage of alert and receptive tiredness.

These are the same stages Parzival and his fellow-travellers traverse. The predominant feeling at the three lower stages of abandonment, solitude, and senselessness vanishes on the fourth, as the world becomes epic and inscribes itself into the receptive and perceptive consciousness. The parallel to the self-dramatization of questions is apparent. The semantic field of the word "tiredness" at the fourth stage touches on and even overlaps with other antidotes to the fast-paced, logocentric, and technocratic societies present in Handke's fiction and that of many contemporary writers. It incorporates slowness, passivity, playfulness, and the search for closeness. Handke presents the reader with an array of situations dating back to his boyhood, his early work experiences, and his experiences on the road in which tiredness could be a destructive state of exhaustion, blank emptiness, insensitivity, and alienation. At times, however, it could be a constructive state of relaxed openness and satisfaction derived from a job well-done or occasionally from sexual intercourse.

The "good" tiredness associated with the smell of camomile is contrasted to the "bad" tiredness associated with the smell of carrion, and, as in **Das Spiel vom Fragen,** qualities of light and sound carry part of the message. One could be tempted to call Handke's method of creation a *Gesamtkunstwerk* of the senses. Handke experiences community—"*Wir Müdigkeit*"—after a hard day's work of threshing in a barn in a light which is engulfing and soothing rather than blinding and glaring. This "stage-four" tiredness unifies and cleanses, as does the revelatory, mythical experience to which it is closely related. "*Wir Müdigkeit*" results in a feeling of relaxed, unquestioned belonging and of being able to take in the whole world. At this point communication turns into communion. Just as any profane object can be endowed with revelatory energy, any profane place or setting—a boulevard, a garbage dump, a jukebox, a Spanish field, or midtown Manhattan—can promote this specific feeling of tiredness. The theme of tiredness can be traced in Handke's earlier writings. *Versuch über die Müdigkeit* picks up a thread from *Langsame Heimkehr,* and even in *Wunschloses Unglück,* Handke experiences a pleasant, impersonal tiredness, in which the super ego is finally quiet, leaving a space of receptive, creative emptiness.

The process of mimetic experiences inspired by an inner stillness and preparedness and resulting in somnambulistic energy is eloquently described by Elisabeth Lenk in *Die unbewußte Gesellschaft,* in which she equates dream states with the state of artistic creativity to which Handke also subscribes.

> *Etwas, was substanziell schien, wird in einen Schwebezustand versetzt. Alles, auch die normalerweise durch Arbeit zugängliche Normalwelt, wird für die ästhetische Subjektivität zum Gegenstand der Unmittelbarkeit und des Spiels. Sie entwickelt so etwas wie ein sakrales Verhältnis zum Nichtsakralen. Sie entwirklicht die Dinge, um sich selber an ihre Stelle zu setzen. Sie stellt nicht die Ereignisse selber dar, sondern ihre Auswirkungen, die Schatten, die sie ins Innere werfen*

und die auf einmal anfangen, sich wie von selbst zu bewegen. Im Ausdrucksakt wird eine Energie freigesetzt, die in der Welt der geronnenen Sozialfunktionen gebunden war.

(24)

IV

In *Die Abwesenheit*, a fairy tale with neither fairies nor a tale, written in 1987, Handke portrays an age-old bard, a singer who has lost his voice and whose songs remain only in his seeing and hearing. This bard embodies Handke's view of literature and of his own role in it. Just like the bard, Handke can no longer communicate his thoughts and feelings in the traditional and familiar way. What remains is a faint hope that his fiction may stimulate and entice the sensibilities of his readers, because those with the heightened sensitivity to see emptiness and listen to silence can understand the bard. It is a select group, to be sure, especially as Handke explicitly excludes the bourgeoisie and the rich and powerful from the roster of people who are able to experience revelation (*Versuch* 43). They belong to civil society (*Gesellschaft*) and cannot participate in the aesthetic communion (*Gemeinschaft*) of the initiated elite. Just as the symbolists had reacted to the deconstructive and demythifying tendencies in art at the turn of the century by forcefully reinstating its aura, Handke reacts to the modern-day devalorization of literature by turning it into a sanctuary.

In spite of this elitism, or maybe because of it, Handke's basic dilemma remains—bridging the gap, that is, finding the means and methods to transpose his very personal, ephemeral revelations into a language that can be shared by his readers. How can the immediacy and fullness of experience be mediated in a language that lacks plenitude? One solution is the "recycling" of words and concepts, another is the rejection of words altogether and their dissolution into sights, sounds, gestures, and light in order to make the work of art into an awe-inspiring counter-world to, and refuge from, the "newsmedia word." This is the problem of Handke the "Mauerschauer," but the "Spielverderber" side of Handke makes formal demands which counteract such hopes and visions. Guided by these conflicting impulses, Handke seeks his "third path" between the Scylla of compensatory writing, in which a mythifying and entrancing text compensates for a demythified and disenchanted world, and the Charybdis of formalism and intentionalism. The ephemeral nature of the suspension bridge supported by the author's inner tensions strung across the abyss connecting author and reader makes this path a hazardous one. Handke's tendency to intersperse revelations with polemical outbursts makes it uneven.

The "third path" Handke pursues is that of ambiguity, which he creates by using such literary tools and methods of Romanticism as paradox, the merging of reality and illusion, and the merging of narrative and scientific knowledge. His impotent power is that of an alert dreamer,

who reifies through illusion, who reveals by obscuring and enveiling words and concepts, and who gains in presence by withdrawing. It is the difficulty of tracing the "third path" and of uniting his conflicting selves that makes the image of the surefooted sleepwalker balancing at the brink of an abyss so appealing to Handke.

By granting himself this subconscious and unquestionable competence, Handke succeeds in harmonizing his self through the process of writing. But can he reach out to others? In the play ***Das Spiel vom Fragen*** Handke provides an answer. Whereas the seven travelers—Handke's alter egos and members of the *Gemeinschaft*—reach the sonorous country, there are those who cannot be reached (presumably the uninitiated). In the first scene of the play the "Mauerschauer" reaches out to someone who is in danger of falling into the abyss of nothingness and meaninglessness. This gesture is unsuccessful.

Works Cited

Bürger, Christa. "Hofmannsthal und das mimetische Erbe." *Prosa der Moderne.* Peter Bürger unter Mitarbeit von Christa Bürger. Frankfurt: Suhrkamp, 1988.

Handke, Peter. *Aber ich lebe nur von den Zwischenräumen: Ein Gespräch geführt von Herbert Gamper.* Zürich: Ammann, 1987.

———. *Die Abwesenheit: Ein Märchen.* Frankfurt: Suhrkamp, 1987.

———. "Ich bin ein Bewohner des Elfenbeinturms." *Ich bin ein Bewohner des Elfenbeinturms.* Frankfurt: Suhrkamp, 1972.

———. *Die Geschichte des Bleistifts.* Salzburg: Residenz, 1982.

———. *Das Gewicht der Welt.* Salzburg: Residenz, 1977.

———. *Kindergeschichte.* Frankfurt: Suhrkamp, 1981.

———. *Langsame Heimkehr.* Frankfurt: Suhrkamp, 1979.

———. *Nachmittag eines Schriftstellers.* Salzburg: Residenz, 1987.

———. *Das Spiel vom Fragen: oder die Reise zum sonoren Land.* Frankfurt: Suhrkamp, 1989.

———. *Versuch über die Müdigkeit.* Frankfurt: Suhrkamp, 1989.

Hofmannsthal, Hugo von. "The Letter of Lord Chandos." *Selected Prose.* Trans. Mary Hottinger and Tania and James Stern. New York: Pantheon, 1952. 129-141.

Lenk, Elisabeth. *Die unbewußte Gesellschaft: Über die mimetische Grundstruktur in der Literatur und im Traum.* München: Matthes, 1983.

Lyotard, Jean-François. *The Postmodern Condition: A Report on Knowledge.* Trans. Geoff Bennington and Brian Massumi. Minneapolis: U of Minnesota P, 1984.

DIE STUNDE DA WIR NICHTS VONEINANDER DER WUBTEN: (THE HOUR WE KNEW NOTHING OF EACH OTHER)

PRODUCTION REVIEW

Alan Riding (review date 26 December 1994)

SOURCE: Riding, Alan. "The Drama before Language Intervenes." *New York Times* 144 (26 December 1994): 33.

[*In the following review, Riding discusses the production of Handke's* The Hour We Knew Nothing of Each Other *and how a play without words, only sound and actions, achieves a greater level of drama.*]

A play without words? Mime, of course. Well, no. In mime, gestures replace words and, in the end, little is left unsaid. Peter Handke's idea is different. He looks around and sees myriad brief encounters that never reach the stage of words. So he has written a play *before* words.

It is not hard to imagine. In the hurried solitude of urban life, individuals send out "here-I-am" messages through their appearance and body language. Without a word being uttered, they set off responses of fear, respect, curiosity, arousal, indifference, disapproval. Then the moment passes and the crowd moves on.

In *The Hour We Knew Nothing of Each Other,* Mr. Handke, an Austrian-born playwright and novelist, has taken this to its theatrical conclusion, turning the stage into a piazza where, over a 24-hour period, 400 characters played by 33 actors and actresses appear, observe, are observed and then disappear.

They include a gum-chewing airline captain and his crew, an old fisherman, grinning roller skaters, a sexual deviate, tourists, a transvestite, a man in a tuxedo who has a heart attack, a leggy actress making a movie, and more. In a touch of surrealism, there are even cameo appearances by the likes of Moses, Jacques Tati, Papageno and Tarzan.

The 100-minute play, which was first produced in February by Berlin's Schaubuhne am Lehniner Platz and was acclaimed by British critics at this year's Edinburgh Festival, completed a run of 10 performances at the *Théâtre du Châtelet* in Paris this month. It was also generally well received by French critics.

"Handke has composed a hymn to a life filled with humor and poetry and agitated by mongrel hordes distracted by love and crazed with loneliness," Odile Quirot wrote in Le

Nouvel Observateur. "Masterly and euphoric!" More critically, Le Figaro's Frédéric Ferney concluded that Mr. Handke had held up a mirror to "nothingness."

The production stirred special interest because it combined the recognized talents of Mr. Handke, who now lives in Germany, and those of the 46-year-old Swiss-born theater director Luc Bondy, who began his career in Germany in 1971. Over the last decade, Mr. Bondy has been busy throughout Europe directing theater, opera and movies.

This month, the Châtelet also put on Mr. Bondy's much-praised operatic version of Arthur Schnitzler's 1901 play, *Reigen,* with music by the Belgian composer Philippe Boesmans. Mr. Bondy wrote the libretto and directed the production, first seen last year at the *Théâtre Royal de la Monnaie* in Brussels. Next year, he will direct Verdi's *Don Carlo* at the Châtelet.

If Mr. Bondy is still making his name, though, Mr. Handke's experimentation with literary forms and his public squabbles with Günter Grass have already made him one of the best-known writers in the German language today. He is a poet and essayist as well as playwright and novelist, and he also wrote the screenplay for Wim Wenders's film *Wings of Desire.*

Mr. Handke, 52, has recounted that the inspiration for *The Hour We Knew Nothing of Each Other* came simply from sitting in a cafe in an Italian piazza and watching the world go by. From his reflections came 46 pages of stage directions for a play that, while wordless, echoed the sounds of his piazza: church bells, a distant radio, plates breaking, a passing motorcycle.

It was then up to Mr. Bondy to orchestrate the flow of people and scenes across Gilles Aillaud's mintmalist set, which has the white-washed facade of a Spanish-style hacienda on one side, an abandoned car hidden under canvas on the other and, in the center, a pole with a basketball net and a statue of an Egyptian dog deity. Holes in the floor provide additional points of entry and exit.

What the audience does not see is the extraordinary scramble back stage as the cast of French and German actors and actresses disappear and then reappear, sometimes barely a minute later, in different costumes and roles. Most of the players act out 10 to 15 characters in the course of each performance.

As it happens, Mr. Bondy did not want much acting from them. Even though there are many moments of humor, some of slapstick and a few of sentimentality, the director was eager for the cast to appear as normal as possible—as normal, that is, as the weird characters who might cross a piazza thinking of themselves as normal.

Early in his career, Mr. Bondy spent two years at Jacques Lecoq's mime school in Paris. Today, he thinks of mime as "too talkative." In this case, he wanted his cast to remain silent, but also to signal nothing too obviously. "Theater can extract the hidden relationship between people," he told one interviewer. "Whenever I see people, I imagine something more; I fabricate stories."

Here, he invites the audience to do likewise: to spot the exhibitionists, the self-important, the defeated, the cruisers, the handicapped and those so self-absorbed as to notice nothing around them. And as spectators watch them cross the stage or pause or look around, their hidden lives should be easy to imagine.

Not everyone is alone. There are young women going off on a date, circus performers with a well-trained little dog in two, army commandos settling some mysterious score. Then there are brief moments that grab everyone's attention: a mugging, a police chase, a streaker. At one point, with the piazza bustling with life, a woman starts crying loudly. Everybody looks, but no one moves.

Do Mr. Handke and Mr. Bondy make words redundant? Not really. The words are there, felt or thought or about to be spoken or spoken and unheard. It is simply up to the audience to pick them.

After seeing the play at the Edinburgh Festival, The Guardian's critic, Michael Billington, described it as "a spectacle of mesmerizing beauty." And he went on, "It is a dazzlingly original show that overcomes one's conventional qualms about physical theater."

Richard Mowe, the critic for the newspaper The Scotsman, said the play showed "action does indeed speak louder than dialogue." By tacking universal themes that cross national divides, he wrote, Mr. Handke "succeeds in speaking volumes about the human condition, the feebleness of words and the fragility of mankind."

More simply, perhaps, the play makes the ordinary seem less ordinary. Indeed, one recent evening, as the audience headed home from the show, the scene at the Châtelet subway station looked strangely familiar. An elderly immigrant swept the platform, a young couple embraced, a homeless man slept on a bench. And no words were being spoken.

CRITICAL COMMENTARY

Gitta Honegger (essay date summer 1993)

SOURCE: Honegger, Gitta. "Seeing through the Eyes of the Word." *Theater* 24, no. 1 (summer 1993): 87-92.

[*In the following essay, Honegger, an English translator of Handke's work, discusses the usage of speech pattern and sound in Handke's* The Hour We Knew Nothing of Each Other.]

. . . As though everyone everywhere in the world, day in, day out, always had his pictorial mission: the mission to be a picture to others: the woman walks "past the train station, along a puddle collecting the falling rain, as 'the housewife on her way to the market,' and further in the distance someone walks by as 'the man with the umbrella;'" thus, offering their pictures of themselves, they help one another (me, at least) . . .

—Peter Handke: *Fantasies of Repetition, 1983*

Peter Handke's most recent work for the theater, ***The Hour We Knew Nothing of Each Other,*** is a play without words. It takes place in a square, inspired by the piazza of a small town near Trieste. Handke had spent an afternoon there watching the goings-on, each passer-by suggesting the fragment of a story which takes its shape only in the context of all the preceding and succeeding moments witnessed by the spectator, who in turn entered his own associations. At one point a coffin was carried from one of the buildings. Then life went on as if nothing had happened. But those who came after would watch the ongoing movement in the square with different eyes from those who had seen the coffin.

In an interview, Handke talked about the play as a "sort of dream play,"

> about what one might experience in the square beyond the natural phenomena which are there anyway, and what enters in terms of fantasy, myth, memory. One sits and watches and the longer one watches, the more pictures emerge from (one's own) background, supplementing the pictures that are moving by. Personal experiences also enter the square. Imagined people move right along. The seasons change. Childhood returns. People one hasn't seen in maybe 40 years are remembered and hallucinated. And then one wakes up, the dream is over. . . .

It is Handke's genius—and the greatest challenge to the director of the play—that he keeps the figures on stage open enough for spectators to enter their own associations, allowing them to respond to the "pictures" according to their experiences. The stories suggested on stage can be endlessly varied and expanded through each spectator's imagination. A play without words turns out to be all about language—its possibilities contained in and released by images.

Always present in the square, though neither named nor suggested, is the challenging spirit of a figure who was crucial to Handke's innovative dramaturgy from the beginning: Ludwig Wittgenstein. Handke's early plays, notably ***Offending the Audience*** (first staged in 1966), ***Kaspar*** (1968) and ***The Ride across Lake Constance*** (1970), can be seen as dramatic models of Wittgenstein's investigations of grammar and speech's traps and errors. Handke's later development also seems to parallel Wittgenstein's: from the construction of a rather didactic model that exposes the abuse of language to a humble sense of wonder about its nature, possibilities, and even existence; from the famous dictum in *Tractatus Logicus Philosophicus*—

"Whereof one cannot speak, thereof one must be silent"—to the moving remark in the lecture on ethics, nearly two decades later: "I am tempted to say . . . that the true expression, in language, for the wonder of the world's existence is the existence of language itself."

A silence that uncompromisingly delineated the limitations of language becomes the resonant silence of the square, which generates language in those who look and see.

Handke's shift from the skepticism of his early plays to the sense of wonder that permeates his later work coincides with his return to Austria after many years of living and traveling abroad. He moved from Paris to Salzburg with his daughter Amina, so that she could attend school in the environment of her own language. They stayed there from 1979 to 1988. His return is reflected in the tetralogy *Slow Homecoming*, consisting of the dramatic poem *The Long Way 'Round* (1982) and three prose texts: *Slow Homecoming* (1979), which follows an Austrian geologist working in Alaska on his gradual homeward drift, a process of inner separation from the vast expanse of the Northern landscape that finally takes him on a night flight back to Austria; *The Lesson of St. Victoire* (1980), an intensely personal meditation in and on the landscape of Cezanne's paintings that leads the writer directly into the landscape near Salzburg; and finally *Child* (1981),which tells how the lessons he learned as a father expedited Handke's decision to return to Austria. In *The Long Way 'Round*, a successful man returns to his native village in southern Austria (also Handke's birthplace) after many years abroad.

The work is not only "about" a return home, it's Handke's homecoming into the language of theater. Handke hadn't written a play since **They Are Dying Out,** first staged in 1974 (American premiere, Yale Repertory Theater, 1980). After almost a decade, Handke now attempted to locate *origin* by reaching for his literary ancestors: the Greeks, and, closer to home, Hölderlin's poetic reimagining of the power and magnitude of the Greek model. His native characters, "simple" working people, balance with dignity the demands of modern survival and of maintaining a connection to their ancestors' wisdom. In their long ceremonious speeches, Handke seeks to restore to them the theatrical grandeur of Aeschylus and the visual power of Homer. (The loveliness of things in Homer: "The tripod on the fire," the "well washed cloak," "the sheath of freshly sawed ivory," he writes in *The Story of the Pencil—Die Geschichte des Bleistifts,* a collection of notes, written 1976-1980.)

Handke's next theater work, **Play of Questions,** was first staged in 1990 by Claus Peymann, the Vienna Burgtheater's controversial director, who also directed the 1992 premiere of **The Hour We Knew Nothing of Each Other.** Both productions are still running in the Burgtheater's repertory. (Peymann started his career with the first productions of **Offending the Audience, Kaspar,** and **They Are Dying Out**). In **Play of Questions,** Handke further explores

the game-like dramaturgy he had experimented with in his early plays: in German, *Spiel* means both *play* and *game*. A randomly gathered group of people sets out on a "Journey Into the Sonorous Land" (the play's subtitle)—a fairy-tale childhood hinterland where they arrive, through liberating games, at the child's capacity to ask "the right questions." Wittgenstein, with his later explorations of language games in *Philosophical Investigations,* again seems to be the invisible guiding spirit. The participants are theatrical stock characters: an old rural couple; young lovers, both actors; and Parzival, a **Kaspar** figure, naked and in chains, speaking in disturbed slogans and commonplaces, afraid of the other speaking characters as carriers of the kind of language of commerce and control that has imprisoned him.

Few and far between as these theatrical texts are, they stand out as signposts pointing to the major departures in Handke's other works of this period, which take him further and further away from story and character in his efforts to restore language's original sacred power of naming. "The most beautiful poetic imagination would be one that no longer creates images, rhythms, wordgames or stories, but where language itself comes to life and makes things nameable," Handke writes in *The Story of the Pencil*.

Andreas Loser, the narrator of the novel *Across* (1983), is a high school teacher of classical languages and, like Handke himself, a confirmed walker, taking long hikes from the modern suburbs of Salzburg to its historic, castle-crowned *Moenchsberg*. The landscape envelopes the narrator in quietly perceived pictures that shimmer with its long history, from the present to geological times. During one of his walks he comes across a man in the act of spraying swastikas on beech trees and kills him with a rock. Although ostensibly the story of a murder, the work is a text about *seeing*. It introduces in the most concentrated way the *raison d'être* of all Handke's subsequent writing; and it leads directly to the theater as theatron, *a place to look/see,* of **The Hour We Knew Nothing of Each Other,** which challenges the audience to participate in the imaginative act of seeing. From the Greek verb for seeing, Loser learns about a gift perhaps lost to all but the ancient Greeks:

> How can I give a more accurate picture of the sense that I lacked? Perhaps only Greek has a verb expressing that fusion of perception and imagination (which is essential). On the surface, this verb means only "to notice;" but it carries overtones of "white," "bright," "radiance," "glitter," "shimmer." Within me there was an outright longing for this radiance which is more than any sort of viewing. I shall always long for that kind of seeing, which in Greek is called *leuketin.*

If Handke's works exposed the dangerous and misleading speech patterns induced by educational drill and the media, the German language continues to be shaken by its perversion through Nazi rhetoric, which still leaves its mutilating signs everywhere. Loser's path, his sudden, inescapable confrontation with the instinct to kill, leads into the realm of Greek tragedy. As stand-in for the author—and the reader—he leads his witnesses towards earning language again through the gift of seeing: the pictures in the world around us, which have always contained the words, and, vice versa, the pictures contained in each word.

In this period, Handke was also preoccupied with translations as a way of expanding one's capacity to experience and name the world. An ardent reader of Greek texts since his high-school studies of classic Greek, Handke has translated Aeschylus' *Prometheus Bound*. He has also translated Walker Percy's *The Moviegoer*; a novel by his French translator Georges-Arthur Goldschmidt, *Le miror quotidien*; and works from Slovenian, his mother's native language. Resonances from his encounters with these writers come into play in **The Hour We Knew Nothing of Each Other**.

In his novel *Repetition* (1986), the Austrian narrator travels to Slovenia to trace his brother, who, like Handke's Slovenian uncle, had been missing in action in World War II. He brings along a Slovenian dictionary his brother left him. Through it he discovers the ways of the people who were his ancestors: peasants and farmers in the arid Karst mountains. Their vocabulary and idioms, passed on through centuries, reveal their intimate relationship to their native environment, their history and origin. Language becomes a celebration of survival. In the process of these discoveries the narrator becomes a writer.

It may no longer be possible to affirm continuity through writing new heroic epics; perhaps it can be accomplished by paying careful attention to the rich resonances in individual words and their idiomatic usage: they tell the story of a community, its perception of itself through generations deeply rooted in their native landscape.

The Slovenian word for village idiot is "he who stirs up wind while walking." The same term applies to an arrogant person; in more practical terms, stirring the wind while walking is a necessary skill in the dry heat of the Slovenian Karst mountains. The expression found its way into **The Hour We Knew Nothing of Each Other.**

His most recent prose text, *Essay About a Day That Worked* (*Versuch über den geglückten Tag*) is ostensibly an attempt to describe the kind of day where one lives fully in the present, in touch with the smallest, most trivial phenomena. For the writer this also means being completely open to words, that is, being able to receive them from the pictures through which the world (according to Wittgenstein) offers itself; yet what he receives are ultimately his own words, which made him *see* to begin with. The borders between his inner world and the outer world merge in what Handke, in the title of a much earlier work, called *The Inner World of the Outer World of the Inner World.* When this happens, the individual becomes one with the world, which constitutes a *day that works.* The challenge is "To look and to continue to look further with the eyes of the fitting word," and to pass on to the reader

not just the picture but the dynamics of *seeing.* Reading then becomes another way of looking, seeing. Seeing the picture contained in the words, the reader will then be able to transform the picture back into his own words and the story he tells will be his. "The best thing, story teller: get the others, gently, to tell stories—make it your goal; and do it in a way that afterwards they feel as if they had a story told to them (a wonderful one)."

Often foreign words cause the *jolt* (a favorite term that reappears in almost all later works) that opens one's eyes. In *The Afternoon of a Writer* the narrator remembers that in French, his partner's language, "now" literally means "holding hands." And from the letters of St. Paul he learns that the Greek word for "moment" (*augenblick* in German, as in "the twinkling of an eye") is literally "the throwing of the eye." Also through St. Paul he discovers that "to read" literally says "perceiving upward," a "recognition upward." The narrator mentions in passing that he is working on a sketch about translating. In a sense the entire book is about translation, as all his writing is an act of translation, of finding the *Urtext* as Handke calls it on another occasion, the original text that is already and has always been *there.* In translations, according to Walter Benjamin, this *Urtext* is contained between the lines. In those spaces between, all translations of a given text merge and the *Urtext* reveals itself in their silence.

Emerging in the silence of **The Hour We Knew Nothing of Each Other** are figures who have emerged time and again from the unspoken *Urtext* of many times and cultures, as the square itself in the Vienna production seemed to have emerged from an ocean. This *Urtext* can be sensed in the periodic surge of a mysterious roar encircling the stage, merging with the rustle above, like trees in the wind, which once carried the voices of the oracles. In this silence that can actually be *heard* like the silence in the desert, the spectator suddenly finds herself listening to her own words in response to what she sees. She is amazed at how clearly these words resound in herself, weaving her stories from and into the many fragments of possible stories suggested on stage. Thus the stage event becomes a continuation of the initial experience that inspired it, rather than its duplication. Handke's theater, in a reversal of the dramatist's gift of appropriating other people's speech, is *returning the gift,* so to speak, to his spectators: the gift of words, not as something drilled in from the outside, but as everyone's own power of naming, which arises from learning how to look and *see, schauen* in German.

And the spectator suddenly remembers that in her native language the term for actor is *Schauspieler,* someone who *plays to be looked at.* The term for spectator is *Zuschauer*; a much more active word than spectator or onlooker; *zu* implies a movement towards, suggesting participation in what is being seen. The English *place of action* shifts in German to a *place of seeing,* a *Schauplatz* (the dramaturgical—and cultural—differences between German—and English-language theater surface in this subtle shift).

Furthermore, the German word for square is *Platz,* place. For the patron of an outdoor cafe looking out on the *piazza,* it has already become a *Schauplatz,* a place to see. Transfered to the theater, there is no break in realities; they are contained in the same word. Handke doesn't cheat when it comes to words. All the possibilities and limitations of any imaginative act, in this case a work for the theater, are already given in language. The "inner (imaginative) world" of the *theatron*—the theatrical space and its original function of presentation—merge with the "outer world" of the *place* of action and its function represented by the work. When Handke calls this work a *Schauspiel,* he means it, literally. It is a play of looking and seeing: what *takes place.*

Most figures entering this place are introduced as *Einer als,* literally "one as. . . ." The emphasis on the theatricality of the endeavor (there is always the actor entering *as* someone other than himself) is obvious. But Handke is far more consistent and rigorous in his honesty than that. The phrase also contains the original experience of seeing a stranger passing by in a square, and perceiving, imagining him *as* a certain person. At the same time it puts into question the possibilities of authenticating perception and—throwing the issue back to the theater—any attempt at authoritative "characterization." The only figures who are directly introduced—e.g. *a skateboarder, a jogger*—are those who are identified simply by their activities. No further assumption is made about who they might be. The construction *someone as* is awkward in English, so in the translation the *as* often is replaced by a comma or a dash to indicate the moment of recognition.

A phrase often used in the text is *im Ansatz* (which has no English equivalent), meaning "only as a beginning," not definite, not completely followed through. It points to the most difficult task for the director, who must introduce the figures as the personae described in the text and also leave them open enough to allow the spectator the imaginative process of *seeing as.* Handke's French translator once pointed out that his most recent prose works concern perception. No wonder he should return to theater, a medium in which the process of perception can be physically examined. His genius as a writer for theater has always manifested itself in his understanding and use of the stage as a model that makes *visible.* His plays, like all his texts, are not "about" something above and beyond themselves, they *are;* in the Wittgensteinian sense they are "pictures;" whatever is inside the picture shows, reveals itself through it; it cannot talk about itself in the language that constitutes it. "Do not betray what you have seen. Stay inside the picture," says the "oracle" that introduces *The Hour We Knew Nothing of Each Other*—which Handke has invented, a modern oracle speaking of the limits and the power of language for those who have learned how to perceive it, be it as writer, reader or spectator.

Thus Handke's text isn't merely a sequence of stage directions. Each passage contains a complete picture, an episode. The structure, rhythm, and tense chosen for each sentence, the pitch and tonality of each word also contain the movement of each scene fragment—that is, the movement not only as it happened, might have happened, or should happen on the stage but as it was perceived by the person watching. The sequence of details, the connections between two separate episodes, follow with painstaking precision the movement of an observing eye, which might first catch that someone's hands are shackled and then that the person walks barefoot. In German, which allows the construction of many subclauses, each sequence is contained in a single sentence that moves on one breath, up and down a person, following around curves and corners, along circles, straight and zig zag lines, in leaps and bounds, at breathtaking speed, at a leisurely strolling pace, a jogger's bounce, or a business-like gait. Magicians build their technique on playing games with the human eye. Those games are also a part of Handke's *play* with and of perceptions; they constitute an important—ancient—aspect of the language of the theater. Sometimes Handke seems to ask for impossible images, and, more practically speaking, impossible transitions and costume changes. But he isn't telling us what to do, he is telling us what he sees. And what he is asking from a production, rather than literally to realize the impossible on stage, is to make us *see* the impossible. The English language reminds us that *to realize* also refers to seeing, to make real through the imaginative act of seeing.

Alfred Nordmann (essay date winter 1996)

SOURCE: Nordmann, Alfred. "Blotting and the Line of Beauty: On Performances by Botho Strauss and Peter Handke." *Modern Drama* 39, no. 4 (winter 1996): 680-97.

[*In the following essay, Nordmann compares the works of Botho Strauss with Peter Handke, focusing on Handke's play* The Hour We Knew Nothing of Each Other.]

The performance of a text or the staging of a play is often and easily imagined as the representation, in another medium, of its content or meaning. On stage can be shown what the script merely says; the rehearsal process and the production itself thus appear as means towards the end of communicating to the audience what an author has set down on paper. When this picture of what goes on in performance is extended to dance or the realization of musical scores, the notion of "representation" proves too narrow, and performances are, therefore, often said to "express" a feeling, content, or intention.

While the two notions of "representation" and "expression" are theoretically rich and lend themselves to sophisticated explorations of just what it means to represent or express something, Nelson Goodman proposed that performance might be conceived also in different terms entirely. He suggests that performance can be likened to the exemplification of a pattern or form and that the transition from a dramatic text to its theatrical production involves no ontological leap into a different realm of being: the recorded piano sonata exemplifies the musical score (and vice versa) just as a swatch exemplifies a fabric (and vice versa).[2] On this account, the term "performance" no longer designates a set of attributes which come into play only once the text ceases merely to be read but is enacted on stage. Instead, the dramatic text is on a par with the staging in that both involve performance, both establish a form, set a pattern, or inscribe a motion: performance is the execution of a work, whether this execution takes the form of writing or reading, (en)acting or staging.[3]

Rather than discuss the theoretical merits of Goodman's proposal, the following investigation playfully takes it up by treating "mere" texts as performances of sorts. It does not discuss theatrical performances of the plays by Peter Handke and Botho Strauss, but seeks to appreciate how their writing performs very different motions. I wish to clarify these differences between Handke and Strauss by comparing them to two British painters of the eighteenth century, William Hogarth and Alexander Cozens. In doing so, I am following the lead of Handke and Strauss, who themselves suggested that the antagonism of their scientific ways of literary world-making can be mapped on to the antagonism between Hogarth's and Cozens's techniques of artistic invention. This will allow me to return in a brief conclusion to further remarks on the relation between performance and script.

They are reclusive, rarely appear in public, cultivating a proper distance to the culture industry and the quick circulation of ideas and trends. Peter Handke and Botho Strauss serve as high-priests of literature and guardians of the German language, and unabashedly see themselves in the long line of descent from Homer to Hölderlin to Heidegger, from Gottfried Keller to Ernst Jünger to Handke and Strauss. They are prolific and successful playwrights and self-consciously reinvented the novel in its long and short forms; both experimented with the literary essay. Charges of mannerism, arrogance, or elitism are deflected by their earnest persistence. After all, they represent the dying breed of the truly sensitive person who is finely attuned and reacts viscerally to the nuances of speech, who hears the murderous in a wrong turn of phrase. Their plays create artificial and poetic worlds which take up and transcend the cultural sensibilities of a very literate middle class. Even when their plays experiment and expand the language of the theater, they arrive on stage with the assuredness of the modern classic, written for posterity.[4] In the early 1980s, Handke and Strauss were considered representatives of a New Inwardness (*Neue Innerlichkeit*), epitomizing a kind of subjectivism which seemingly surrendered political aspirations of the sixties and seventies. For the 1996/97 season, however, the premieres of their new plays are greatly anticipated, since both have recently politicized their own work, creating considerable scandal in the literary world—Strauss claiming his poetic home on a vaguely defined political right, Handke defending Serbia against world opinion and the jargon which produces it.[5] There is no open rivalry between them, but two recent essays serve as veiled polemics, drawing attention to their radically different *Bewegungsarten des Geistes* [habits of mental movement].[6] That exchange began quite innocuously with Peter Handke's reflections on a self-portrait by William Hogarth.

When Hogarth painted himself with his pug in 1745, he included in the lower left-hand corner of the painting a palette. Across the palette arches a curved line, and engraved next to it are the words "The LINE of Beauty."[7] As Hogarth confessed later, the enigmatic palette was intended to puzzle his contemporaries, to inaugurate fruitful speculation about its meaning. Peter Handke joined this play of questioning in 1991 with his *"Essay on the Successful Day"* [*Versuch über den geglückten Tag*].[8] In this essay, Handke's earlier enthusiasm for experiencing the world always anew[9] takes a more modest, more resigned turn. It is devoted to the possibly futile quest for a single accomplished day that is carried forward along the trajectory of Hogarth's serpentine line of beauty and grace.

Less than a year after Handke's essay there appeared Botho Strauss's *Beginnlosigkeit: Reflexionen über Fleck und Linie* [*Beginninglessness: Reflections on Blot and Line*]. It seeks to distance Strauss's poetics from "the unreflected art of the present," and appears to include an implicit critique of Peter Handke: "Many beautiful novels, much that is accomplished . . . many reveries, in short; but that beauty which is the bounty of botanizing senses pales pretty quickly for the most part."[10] Handke's botanizing search for beauty "shapes the blot into the figure with the idealized line." In opposition to this, Strauss defends the blot as "the blossom of explosion [*Blüte der Sprengung*]."[11] With barely a hint of irony he praises its masculinity, which lacks contour and represents all soulful intent, contrasting it with the feminine line whose mystery lies in the unpredictability of its progression:[12]

> Pure and strong sensations always lack contour, they are not bounded by countervailing thoughts or experiences. They dissolve into the neutral "color" of time.[13]

Strauss cites the drawings and etchings of Joseph Beuys and John Martin to argue for the blot as a vague center of energy from which thought and feeling emanates. He might have found an ally also in the painter Alexander Cozens, a contemporary of Hogarth's.

Cozens was a mediocre artist enjoying mediocre success when he worried, in 1785, that painters like himself might lack in experience and thus in an "original stock of picturesque ideas."[14] A sublime spectacle of nature hardly occurs to those who have seen such spectacles only in paintings and who otherwise move only along the well-trod paths of convention. He, therefore, discovered for himself and his less-endowed students the adventure of blotting: "To blot, is to make varied spots and shapes with ink on paper, producing accidental forms without lines, from which ideas are presented to the mind."[15] Cozens then places a transparent sheet on the blot, beholding it as an unarticulated nature-scene, establishing a foreground, drawing out the contours of a tree here, a glacier there. Without leaving his studio, he is thus able to derive several spectacles of nature from a single blot, thereby venturing boldly beyond the narrow confines of his imagination.

With ingenuous ardor Hogarth and Cozens elaborated in scientific tracts how their principles of artistic creation correspond to the principles of nature. Hogarth delivered, in 1753, his *Analysis of Beauty, Written with a View of Fixing the Fluctuating Ideas of Taste.* According to Hogarth, there are no straight lines in nature. Muscles and drifting clouds, graceful people and racehorses have intricately bent forms; nature draws them in waving serpentines, twists and turns:

> Intricacy in form, therefore, I shall define to be that peculiarity in the lines, which compose it, that *leads the eye a wanton kind of chace,* and from the pleasure that gives the mind, intitles it to the name of beautiful.[16]

Hogarth thus echoes the mechanistic theories of perception of John Locke and David Hartley: lightwaves take up impulses from objects and impart them as vibrations to the optic nerves, which imprint an undoubtedly wave-shaped impression in the mind.[17] Nature, perception, and mind are fundamentally related, and thus resonate, communicating wave to wave. Whoever is inspired by the serpentine line will take up the impulse of nature and pass it on, and so is a mediator and communicator.

Like Hogarth, Alexander Cozens speaks of experiments and principles of nature when he elaborates, in 1785/86, his *New Method of Assisting the Invention in Drawing Original Compositions of Landscape.* Like Hogarth, he does not conduct a philosophical investigation of aesthetic judgment, and like Hogarth he is not interested in the perception, evaluation, or effect of paintings. As opposed to Hogarth, however, Cozens considers the forms of nature distinguished not by lines, but by shade and color. "To sketch, is to delineate ideas; blotting suggests them."[18] The eyes should not follow nature nor nature follow ideas. Rather, the blot's suggestion prompts a meeting of mind and nature.

> Previous ideas, however acquired (of which every person is possessed more or less) will assist the imagination in the use of blotting; and on the other hand, the exercise of blotting will strengthen and improve the ideas which are impaired for want of application.[19]

Two English draftsmen and painters develop, in the eighteenth century, methods of pictorial invention, and by that they mean composition of form. Color, the true domain of the painter, is subordinated to principles of form. The inventive motions of Botho Strauss and Peter Handke are also bound to form and leave their worlds uncolored.[20]

The blackness of sorrow brightens in Strauss's *Beginninglessness* to pike- or cave-grey at best: "[a] grey glance cast towards the grey image, from within the dusk of the entire person." Or, elliptically: "In the black basket we grasp for that spot where that paler darkness, the words. . . ."[21] Only once in *Beginninglessness* does color rise from the dusk, like the sun, but right away it sets again in a horizontal rainy greyness. And, a visionary sunset awakens hope for a colorful night at the very end of the essay: the blushing night-sky is ashamed of that eternal grey in grey and awakens the blot, in all its vagueness, to colorful life.[22]

Handke, too, struggles for color, most significantly in his *Doctrine of Sainte-Victoire,* an essay about Cézanne, the most painterly of painters. "In the colors of daylight, this is when *I am*," he notes there, but cannot articulate this being in the colors.[23] Standing in Cézanne's landscape and Cézanne's colors, he confesses: "The distinction and more so the naming of colors has always been difficult for me."[24] As opposed to Strauss, however, Handke seeks an impulse or a beginning that will carry him beyond his debilitating limitation:

> I feel my ignorance always as distress; and from this results an aimless urge for knowledge which does not yield an idea because it does not have an "object" with which it could "agree." But then a particular object might suggest something and thus posit a "spirit of commencement"; now the pursuit can begin in earnest, which otherwise, for all its studiousness, would have remained mere desire.[25]

At the beginning stands an impulse which puts Handke in a state of grace and carries him forward on its serpentine trajectory. His cursory glance thus rises and sinks, climbs and falls, revolves and circumscribes, winds and curves along the elevations and hollows, heights and depths, lines and arcs of Cézanne's mountain chain Sainte-Victoire. Handke's inwardness proves merely apparent and quite transparent: it serves to impart his motion to the reader immediately, just as the ripples of an impulse are communicated from wave to wave. For decades Handke has already been a prime suspect on the charge of mannerism, and yet he unfailingly succeeds to enchant his readers anew by casting his serpentine line like a magic spell. Even those who follow the cursives of his strokes only reluctantly are set in motion by them.

Peter Handke's plays establish a continuity of motion. While they peak and ebb, accelerate and decelerate, shade from brightness into darkness and vice versa, they provide for no sudden breaks or blackouts between scenes. A "pause" in *The Hour We Knew Nothing of Each Other* is a moment of rest in a continuous and serene journey. And indeed, this play, as well as *The Play of Questions,* suggests (like many of his novels) that pilgrimage may bring about a transformation of sorts which lies outside the narrative bounds of the journey itself.[26]

The many characters embarked on these journeys (close to three hundred in *The Hour We Knew Nothing of Each Other*) are not conceived in terms of inner natures or personalities which are revealed in the course of the play. Instead, they are theatrical icons, emphatically conceived in terms of their visual likeness to what we may have seen or heard or read or remembered. More often than not they lack names, but by their visible likeness they are placed on a trajectory which resonates with our experience:

> And again a man and a woman approach each other from afar, he immediately lowering his head while hers is held up high; just before they cross, he suddenly looks up into the other's face, which she, alas, had turned away a moment before.
>
> Two beauties, as speedwalkers, in fitting gear, skitter by in a jiffy.[27]

Handke remarks in an interview that the theater should *almost* touch upon real life in order to create resonance in the audience: the director should "barely miss life." In the same interview, Handke elaborates that in these bare, but unconsummated encounters he sees people as he sees them when he is not unjust towards them, when he has no opinion of them, when he likes them.[28] As we pass each other by and do not confront, hold on to, or cling to one another, we remain free to take up an impulse, to find a beginning for a motion of our own. Handke's plays provide the pure pleasure of watching a motion which we can take up, in which we can join.[29] This free-flowing motion, barely touching, but not intruding upon characters as it weaves a tapestry of a city, is most familiar to viewers of his 1987 film, co-authored with director Wim Wenders, *Wings of Desire*. It is also intimated at the conclusion of his play without words *The Hour We Knew Nothing of Each Other*:

> And now, down below, the First Spectator tears himself from his seat. . . . Coming and going, coming and going. Then darkness fell on the square.[30]

Botho Strauss lacks entirely the external impulse sought out by Handke, the spirit of commencement. "It is futile to look for the roots of the fog. Every beginning is an echo."[31] He finds that the blot which lacks a beginning is recommended to him by the natural sciences which "impact on the habit of mental movement in all its conceptions."[32] He cites Marvin Minsky and Douglas Hofstadter, steady state and chaos theories, dissipation and autopoeisis, Ilya Prigogine and Stephen Hawking. According to that scientifically suggested cosmic disorder, human relations can no longer be represented in the linear format of the story with its beginning, middle, and end. In Strauss's words they belong much rather in

> an illegible order of thresholds, leaps, interdependencies, transitions, dissolutions, riches resulting from the exuberant deterioration of all boundaries, unbounded hues freely spilling into one another, so that nothing can be said anymore about human beings except that they are blots of heat [*Wärmefleck*]. A fusion. A swarm of doctrinaire desires. A cloud of uncertain resolve . . .[33]

The events are standing still while a glance rises from the dusk of the entire person and longingly sinks into the dusk of the blot, gradually bringing its ambiguities to light. "A

permanent readiness for dread [*Entsetzen*]" accompanies this mode of becoming aware [*Gewärtigen*].[34] Strauss's addiction to experience does not seek knowledge, but hopes for the "real presence" of dread. "The accidental [*das Versehen*] fights for its preservation with all the means that blind passion has available," he declares in *Beginningless-ness*. "It fights against the tendencies of enlightenment which inevitably unfold in the love-story."[35] As opposed to Handke, Strauss's inwardness is not merely apparent. He knows of no path which would lead beyond himself, he knows no stories and no History, and casts himself blindly and willingly into the accidents and catastrophes of dread or happenstance, of ambiguous entanglements and dissociations.

One of Strauss's earliest stories and one of his most recent plays exemplify how intensely felt states have to be defended against their dissolution into a linear story or biography. *Devotion* details the pathetic struggles of a man who has been left by a woman: "I must try with all my strength to touch Hannah's heart. Yet I know that ultimately only he whose all-out effort has failed can move her."[36] His attempts to foster and preserve the despair of the abandoned lover render him a comic figure: "Right, but the comedy is only a protective ether that keeps the pain fresh. If I hadn't grown eccentric, then I'd have become either industrious or apathetic."[37] His abandonment to precious moments of loss render his experience unlike anyone else's, profound and authentic. But, he fails to make permanent the suddenness of such moments and curses himself for his failings: "A nasty night. Sleep has cut me down to size. . . . I can see how my heroic and festive despair is shriveling into a miserable petty-bourgeois sadness. Perhaps I should admit that I overestimated my capacity for suffering."[38]

Most of the protagonists in Strauss's plays lose their balance. A seemingly incidental encounter overwhelms them, a momentary flash illuminates, redefines their lives. *Beginninglessness* describes a moment very much like the one at the heart of *Schlusschor*:

> Every woman can become a sanctuary of desire once the fleeting glance which has encountered her creates a sharply defined, highly resolved after-image. If only she becomes present to us beyond that one moment, in a sense becomes absolutely present, so that every adventure, every story, every word vanishes in this one instant of time, like matter beyond the horizon of events. This is incidentally the very same force which is active and confuses our senses also in the most banal occurrence, as when the maid in a hotel suddenly, i.e., by ACCIDENT [*aus VERSEHEN*], tears open the door and sees us in our stillness and inwardness (which in any case is a form of nakedness), apologizes, and turns around. Every desire can be traced back to a quick and violent accident like this.[39]

The main protagonist of *Schlusschor* attempts to recover from the moment in which he accidentally encountered a naked woman;[40] the play also revolves around the quick, violent, and unsettling accident of someone shouting

"*Deutschland*" during the taking of a group photograph.[41] The shutter [*Blende*] of a camera was used by Strauss also to structure the succession of scenes in *Three Acts of Recognition,* as indeed most of his plays use suddenness to plunge the audience from one encounter to the next. This is accompanied by an ironic distrust of the rambling speech by which his protagonists attempt to regain control, following their "base inclination" to create more order than there is. These attempts are gently exposed in their frailty and futility.[42] The drama of Strauss's plays derives from incidental shocks, trivial catastrophes, ruptures, and juxtapositions. None of these blossom into full-fledged stories or characters. Instead, the plays observe how the sense of possibility that is attendant to catastrophe shrivels up. Strauss's male protagonists, especially, generally falter in their efforts to make sense of what is happening and to turn it into a story. What remains is a diffuse and agitated swarm of people and desires, drawn like mosquitoes to the bright lights of the stage. One can upset and disturb that flittering swarm of energy, only to see it reconstituted under the next lamp-post.[43] It is in this sense that Strauss's plays provide illuminating snapshots of contemporary society, targeting a self-indulgent middle class, letting the audience glimpse its own startling reflection, hitting the nail pointedly on the head.

Peter Handke and Botho Strauss follow the entanglements of their senses, but Handke keeps finding a trajectory which leads him out into the world, while Strauss remains deeply skeptical, caught up in reflections of the self. Neither one considers language a means to achieve understanding or to communicate semantic content. Handke views communication on the model of resonance: as he sets out to write he provides an impulse, not quite an awakening, inviting his readers to harmonize with the subsequent sojourn of his words and images.[44] Botho Strauss insists that language should not "serve communication," but as "a communion," poetically affirming its origin while it probes the depth and scope of individual sensibility: speaking is a form of listening to the echo of one's own voice. He likens the language of humans to that of whales and dolphins, where each utterance bounces off the walls of an inscrutable space of meaning, a thousand-fold refracted.[45]

For different reasons, therefore, neither Handke nor Strauss is interested in the narrative communication of a particular content, metaphor, effect, topic, or story. In this, too, they agree with Hogarth and Cozens. While they invoke the scientific idiom and wish to mobilize the powers of reason, they do not, therefore, aim for knowledge and do not recommend the arts as a form of knowledge. While Strauss refers and defers to the authority of science in order to justify priority of the blot over the line, he nevertheless insists that art should never be concerned with cognition "but always with the development of mental acuity," and thus with a method for the cultivation of experience as envisioned also by Handke, Hogarth, and Cozens.[46] None of them claims the intellectual authority of science for himself. However, their methods of experiencing, their ways of world-making, their habits of mental movement participate in scientific epistemologies: they desire the world in the manner in which science desires it.

Handke and Hogarth savor the "love of pursuit." "The active mind is ever bent to be employ'd," declares Hogarth, "this love of pursuit, merely as pursuit, is implanted in our natures."[47] This natural inclination corresponds to the scientific virtue of being responsive even to the seemingly inconspicuous. The development of knowledge begins with a first impulse which prompts a felicitous motion leading from one thing to another and perhaps into a successful day.

> Otto's protocol at 17 minutes after 3: Otto's thinking-aloud at 16 minutes after 3 was: in the room was at 15 minutes after 3 a table perceived by Otto.[48]

According to philosopher of science Otto Neurath, protocol-sentences like these might mark the beginning of any quest for knowledge. Peter Handke celebrates the element of pleasure in an observational posture as disciplined and artful as Neurath's. The attempt to achieve a successful day, therefore, begins with "the clicking of the buttons, when I stripped my shirt off the chair this morning" with "globules of dew on a raven feather" or with a few lance-shaped pencils lying "on the windowsill along with a handful of oval hazelnuts."[49] Handke shares in the joys of science when he finds how careful attention can enlarge what appears incidental, and that a minute triviality can take on a life of its own as its leads the mind to other precious observations of telling detail. He commits himself to this scientific course of progression, trusting that, once excited, the serpentine line may transport him infinitely far afield. Like Neurath, Wittgenstein, and other positivists, Handke thereby rejects the metaphysical notion that the world is somehow deep or profound. He gladly remains on the surface of the appearances, he reads the world and does not attempt to penetrate it or guess its riddle.

In contrast, Alexander Cozens and Botho Strauss ready themselves for profound revelations. They cultivate a sense of anticipation which allows them to suddenly apprehend something where there seems to be nothing. Cozens and Strauss seek the encounter of mind and nature and develop an art of discovery and invention designed to bring forth what is hidden. The imaginative child might see fairy tale creatures in the clouds, and the interplay of hypothesis and observation can lead a theoretically sensitized scientist to anticipate strange particles in a cloud of electrons. Similarly, Cozens and Strauss explore the experience that is only darkly intimated in the vague texture of an ink blot. All these instances lack a beginning. Ideas give contour to the blot, and the blot gives contour to the ideas, without beginning or end: the knowers always encounter themselves. "A universe which didn't evolve the human being couldn't even exist," Botho Strauss assures himself.[50]

In our sudden confrontation with the vagueness of the accidental blot, we experience a disorienting rupture or shock: having lost our bearing, we find ourselves cast into nature and simultaneously thrown back onto ourselves. In contrast, the willfulness of the line recovers the world and cheerfully runs into eternity. The line weaves people together and carries them forward for the duration of the possibly short-lived harmony of world and perception.

Botho Strauss has claimed the profound poetic blot for the political right, denouncing the line as the signature of an obsolete utopianism. It is not clear, however, whether Cozens's method or Strauss's poetics are affiliated so firmly with a political ideology. Strauss might point to Ernst Jünger's celebration of the sudden, unsettling, illuminating encounter between the artist's or the soldier's mind and the world; and Jünger is certifiably an author on or of the right. And yet, this core experience of shock or "chok" does not reduce Strauss's habit of mental movement to political ideology. The "chok" is also at the heart of Walter Benjamin's aesthetics. Benjamin read and admired Ernst Jünger, but his endeavor to activate in moments of "chok" a history which our conscious intelligence has rendered vague and indistinct, serves the explicitly communist goals of justice and human emancipation. Similarly, Peter Handke's cheerful line cannot be equated with a liberal belief in the perfectibility of the world. Aware of its anachronistic character, Handke defends the serpentine line for its ability to resonate, to touch upon and possibly to amplify values which have become precarious in the age of postmodern science and politics.

> Nowadays, the Line of Beauty and Grace might be unlikely to take the same gentle curve as in Hogarth's eighteenth century, which, at least in prosperous, self-sufficient England, conceived of itself as a very earthly epoch. Isn't it typical of people like us that this sort of song keeps breaking off, lapsing into stuttering, babbling, and silence, starting up again, going off on a sidetrack—yet in the end, as throughout, aiming at unity and wholeness?[51]

The preceding observations may well be relevant for stagings of Handke's and Strauss's plays.[52] However, they do not warrant an empirical generalization of the sort that would declare that all stagings of Handke's plays exemplify the line of beauty or that any production of a play by Strauss enacts a moment of slippage and shock. For example, it is easy to imagine a theatrical performance in which Handke's flowing motions are brutally stunted and thwarted; indeed, such a performance would powerfully dramatize the fragility of his utopian conceit.

Since "exemplification" establishes a reciprocal relationship, one might argue to the contrary that every actual staging exemplifies some aspects or properties of the dramatic text. The script has no ontological status of its own to which a performance conforms more or less. Instead, the performance establishes the play to which the author has merely provided the script. The performance reads, interprets, or enacts the script. The form it establishes, the pattern it sets, the motion it follows are inevitably the form, pattern, and motion of the play.

This view opens the door for a multitude of possible readings, interpretations, and stagings, but it does not imply

that "anything goes" or that all interpretation is arbitrary. Instead, it proposes enactability as a non-trivial objective criterion which is safeguarded and monitored by the actors during the rehearsal process: whatever "concept" a director or dramaturg comes up with, the actors have to test it for its viability, have to demonstrate its enactability. An actual performance always achieves some agreement between what is happening on stage and what is set down in the text. What this agreement looks like on stage cannot be predicted by considering the text by itself.[53] Just like enactability, interpretability is a non-trivial objective criterion, safeguarded and monitored by readers who have to judge an interpretation plausible.[54]

I may hope that my remarks on blotting and the line of beauty are true to Handke's and Strauss's texts: do they really prescribe a flowing motion or the shocking encounter with blots? At the same time, I may worry that my interpretations are merely consistent with the texts: have I reduced the writings of Handke and Strauss to records or notations of my interpretive motion, and can one say only now that, whatever else their texts do, they orchestrate and exemplify flowing motions and sudden ruptures? As old as that dilemma may be, it is resolved by the notion of exemplification which renders my oscillation between hope and worry obsolete. Performance and interpretation exemplify properties which are shared with what they symbolize: the performance on stage and the interpretation on page perform the performance of or by the dramatic text.[55]

Notes

1. I would like to thank Robin Detje and Amittai Aviram for encouragement and criticism.

2. Nelson Goodman, *Ways of Worldmaking* (Indianapolis, 1978), 65. Goodman speaks more generally of symbolization: in contrast to representation and expression, exemplification symbolizes in such a way that *what* is symbolized is not outside the symbol. The swatch does not possess certain properties which enable it to symbolize something other than itself: the swatch *is* a swatch of the fabric and the fabric *is* the fabric of the swatch. Likewise, a theatrical performance *is* a performance of the text (exemplifies some of its properties) and the text *is* a notation of the performance (exemplifying some of its properties). However, there remains a difference between the symbol and what it symbolizes: in its execution and implementation a performance is very different from a dramatic text (and *vice versa*). Compare also Nelson Goodman, "Implementation of the Arts," *Journal of Aesthetics,* 40 (Spring 1982), 281-83.

3. The terms of this equation may seem unusual, but compare the relation of performance to ritual and consider that any performance is (also) the repetition of a previous performance (or rehearsal). Amittai Aviram asks whether the shift from "representation" to "exemplification" corresponds to a shift from

metaphor to metonymy. Also, how does the tripartition of exemplification, expression, and representation relate to Peirce's distinction of icon, index, and symbol? I hope to discuss these questions some day.

4. There is nothing vulgar, raw, or compulsive about their plays, which sets them apart from the majority of contemporary German plays (by, for example, Herbert Achternbusch, Rainald Goetz, Elfriede Jelinek, Franz Xaver Kroetz, or the recently deceased Werner Schwab and Heiner Müller). Peter Handke's plays include *Publikumsbeschimpfung* (*Offending the Audience,* 1966), *Kaspar* (1968), *Das Mündel will Vormund sein* (*My Foot My Tutor,* 1969), *Der Ritt über den Bodensee* (*The Ride across Lake Constance,* 1971), *Das Spiel vom Fragen oder die Reise zum Sonoren Land* (*Play of Questions,* 1990), *Die Stunde da wir nichts voneinander wussten* (*The Hour We Knew Nothing of Each Other,* 1992), and *Zurüstungen für die Unsterblichkeit* (opening in the 1996/97 season). Some of Botho Strauss's plays are *Hypochonder* (1972), *Bekannte Gesichter, gemischte Gefühle* (1975), *Trilogie des Wiedersehens* (*Three Acts of Recognition,* 1977), *Gross und klein* (*Big and Little,* 1978), *Kalldewey Farce* (1982), *Der Park* (1984), *Sieben Türen* (1988), *Die Zeit und das Zimmer* (1989), *Schlusschor* (1991), *Das Gleichgewicht* (1993), and *Ithaka* (1996).

5. For first reactions to Strauss's *Ithaka: Schauspiel nach den Heimkehr-Gesängen der Odyssee* see *Theater heute,* 37 (August 1996). Strauss's trouble began with his essay "Anschwellender Bocksgesang" in *Spiegel* 6 (February 1993), 202-07. It was further aggravated by his refusal to distance himself from rightwing appropriations of this text (cf. *Theater heute,* 35 [December 1994] and 36 [February 1995]). Handke published a series of articles in the *Süddeutsche Zeitung* which subsequently appeared as *Eine winterliche Reise zu den Flüssen Donau, Save, Morawa und Drina oder Gerechtigkeit für Serbien* (Frankfurt, 1996).

6. For this turn of phrase compare Botho Strauss, *Beginnlosigkeit: Reflexionen über Fleck und Linie* (Munich, 1992), 75.

7. "Hogarth's Line of Beauty is not actually engraved in the palette; it is stretched over it like a curved rope or a whiplash." (Peter Handke, *The Jukebox and Other Essays on Storytelling* trans. Ralph Manheim and Krishna Winston [New York, 1994], 163). See William Hogarth, *Analysis of Beauty, Written with a view of Fixing the Fluctuating Ideas of Taste,* ed. Joseph Burke (Oxford, 1955), 10: "I drew a serpentine line lying on a painter's pallet, with these words under it, THE LINE OF BEAUTY. The bait soon took; and no Egyptian hieroglyphic ever amused more than it did for a time, painters and sculptors came to me to know the meaning of it."

8. "Successful Day," in Handke, *Jukebox,* 119-67 (the essay originally appeared as a separate volume in

German). The title might also be translated as "Essay on a Felicitous Day" or "On a Day that Worked Out."

9. Compare, for example, Handke's 1967 poem on novel experiences in *The Innerworld of the Outerworld of the Innerworld* (New York, 1974).

10. Strauss, *Beginnlosigkeit,* 14. While descriptive of Handke's method, the allusion to "botanizing senses [*botanisierende Sinne*]" might also be taken as a reference to Ernst Jünger. However, it can be traced back much further to a remark from the year 1768 by Georg Christoph Lichtenberg, who was ready by Jünger, Handke, and Strauss: "There are two ways of prolonging life, the first is to move the two points birth and death further apart and thus to make the road longer. . . . The other method is to walk more slowly and leave the two points where God put them, and this is the method for philosophers, for they have found that it is best to always go botanizing, zic-zac, try and jump a ditch here and back again, and where it is safe and no one sees it, dare a somersault, etc." Lichtenberg expressed admiration of Hogarth (most famous are his "Explanations" of Hogarth's plates). Indeed, the quoted remark is almost immediately followed by a declaration of allegiance to Hogarth's serpentine line of beauty and Lawrence Sterne's "Manier *en Ziczac,*" compare Lichtenberg, *Sudelbücher* (Munich, 1973), 81f (remarks L 129 and 131).

11. Strauss, *Beginnlosigkeit,* 101, 14.

12. Ibid., 70: "Der Fleck und die Linie. *Er* ist alles seelisch Gemeinte, nicht konturierbar, in mehrdeutiger Gestalt sich verlaufend. *Sie* ist die gebündelte Helle, und ihr Mysterium ist ihr offenes Ende, ihre Unabsehbarkeit."

13. Ibid., 56.

14. Alexander Cozens, *A New Method of Landscape* (Wisbech, 1977), 13.

15. Ibid., 8.

16. Hogarth, *Analysis of Beauty,* 42, compare 34f., 45, 87f., 95ff., and 70 where Hogarth analyzes a goat's horn, observing "first, that the whole horn acquires a beauty by its being thus genteely bent two different ways; secondly, that whatever lines are drawn on its external surface become graceful, as they must all of them, from the twist that is given the horn, partake in some degree or other, of the shape of the serpentine-line: and, lastly, when the horn is split, and the inner, as well as the outward surface of its shell-form is exposed, the eye is peculiarly entertained and relieved in the pursuit of these serpentine-lines, as in their twistings their concavities and convexities are alternately offer'd to its view."

17. Ibid., 108 on "rays of light which are said to fall upon the eye from every object it sees, and to cause more or less-pleasing vibrations of the optic nerves, which serve to inform the mind concerning every different shape or figure that presents itself." Compare also 44 and 172.

18. Cozens, *A New Method,* 9.

19. Ibid., 16.

20. This exploration of two habits of mental movement matches Hogarth to Handke, and Cozens to Strauss by likening for dramatic effect the antagonism between Handke and Strauss to the antagonism between Hogarth and Cozens. All four engage in a similar project by elaborating a scientific way of literary (or painterly) worldmaking; that is, they are concerned with form and method in a colorless world. Reference to this shared empiricist background allows me to highlight further the performative difference between a pursuit of the line and the method of blotting.

21. Strauss, *Beginnlosigkeit,* 56, 60.

22. Ibid., 113, 133f.

23. Peter Handke, *Die Lehre der Sainte-Victoire* (Frankfurt, 1980), 26.

24. Ibid., 10.

25. Ibid., 34.

26. This is characteristic also of his early experimental plays like *Offending the Audience* or *Kaspar,* which present a journey of words that precedes the arrival at a here and now.

27. Peter Handke, "The Hour We Knew Nothing of Each Other," *Theater* 24 (1993), 98. For more detail compare Alfred Nordmann and Hartmut Wickert, "The Impossible Representation of Wonder: Space Summons Memory," forthcoming in *Theatre Research International.*

28. *Theater heute,* 35 (January 1994), 14-18, compare 15 and 18.

29. Handke already formulated this aesthetic ideal in his *Ich bin ein Bewohner des Elfenbeinturms* (Frankfurt, 1970), 88-125.

30. "The Hour," 105. While Handke made some films of his own (*Chronik der laufenden Ereignisse* [1971], *Die linkshändige Frau* [*The Left-Handed Woman,* 1978], and recently *Die Abwesenheit* [*The Absence*]), his collaboration with Wenders dates back to *Die Angst des Tormanns beim Elfmeter* (*The Goalie's Fear of the Penalty Kick,* 1972) and *Falsche Bewegung* (*Wrong Movement,* 1975). If Wenders's films best correspond to Handke's itinerant aesthetics, it is Robert Van Ackeren who is most attuned to Strauss's celebration of trivial catastrophes, compare especially his *Reinheit des Herzens* [*Pure of Heart,* 1979], but also *Die flambierte Frau* [*A Woman in Flames,* 1982].

31. Strauss, *Beginnlosigkeit,* 36.

32. Ibid., 75.

33. Ibid., 100.

34. Ibid., 128f. Strauss articulated some of these aesthetic ideas in an earlier essay on George Steiner's *Real Presences* (Chicago, 1989): "Der Aufstand gegen die sekundäre Welt: Anmerkungen zu einer Ästhetik der Anwesenheit," *Die Zeit* 26 (29 June 1990), 15.

35. Ibid., 104.

36. Botho Strauss, *Devotion* (New York, 1979), 30.

37. Ibid., 62.

38. Ibid., 96f.

39. Strauss, *Beginnlosigkeit,* 103f.

40. Another variation of that theme occurs in *Wohnen Dämmern Lügen* (Munich, 1994), 9-11. Here, a man suddenly sees the unfaithfulness of his wife in the incidental nakedness of another woman.

41. "Schlusschor" in *Spectaculum 55: Sechs moderne Theaterstücke* (Frankfurt, 1993), 187-230, especially 191, 199, 202-216.

42. Strauss, *Beginnlosigkeit,* 129; compare the scene in which a printer complains of an annoying sound at his workplace while struggling to consume hors d'oeuvres in *Three Acts of Recognition,* or Lotte-Kotte's monologue with an intercom in the doorway of an apartment house in *Big and Little,* or the artifully cruel and senseless jargon of *Kalldewey Farce.*

43. With this metaphor Strauss concludes his essay on the aesthetics of presence. Each of Strauss's plays serves as a lamp-post under which a buzzing, blot-shaped swarm of contemporaries gathers fashionably in vain.

44. Handke himself delights in this quite openly, as evidenced by an interview with André Müller in *Die Zeit,* 3 March, 1989: "I am intent on a world that is cleansed by language. *But that's why you should describe evil, in order to banish it, rather than all the time those hymns to goodness and beauty.* You're an idiot. *Possibly.* It quite pleases me to hear that I write hymns to beauty, because they are concrete and philosophical and the formulations are super-cool [*supergeil formuliert*]. . . . I don't know any living author who writes pure literature as I do. Everyone else disseminates opinions. The only accomplishment that I am really proud of is that I avoided an ideology [*Weltbild*]. My books give me pure reading pleasure. My chest expands when I read them, and I think, how beautifully this is written, he really knows how to write, well-done."

45. Strauss, *Beginnlosigkeit,* 32, 108f.

46. Ibid., 15. Compare Hogarth, *Analysis of Beauty,* 22: a "kind of doctrine that may teach us to *see with our own eyes.*"

47. Hogarth, *Analysis of Beauty,* 41, 42, 45.

48. Otto Neurath, "Protokollsätze," *Erkenntnis* 3 (1932/33), 204-214. Neurath was one of the founders of so-called Logical Positivism.

49. Peter Handke, "Successful Day," 135, 156, 139. "As I listen for a tone, the tonality of the whole day's journey reveals itself to me. The tone does not have to be a full sound, it can be indifferent, as often as not a mere noise; the essential is that I make myself all ears for it" (135).

50. Strauss, *Beginnlosigkeit,* 10, compare 11: "It is not an object which triggers the pleasant sensation of wishing to contemplate it, but a nameless errant sensation, devoid of images or appearances, seeks a self-satisfaction in which an object appears worthy of contemplation." Strauss refers to this as a *"circulus creativus."*

51. Handke, "Successful Day," 127. For his precarious optimism compare his postscript to the controversial *Winterliche Reise,* 130ff., which also alludes to the serpentine line as embodied by the Serbian rivers, the diversions of art, and art as diversion.

52. A performance of one of Handke's plays is analyzed along these lines in Nordmann and Wickert, "The Impossible Representation of Wonder." For quite another example, namely the performance of the falling motion which characterizes the work of Heinrich von Kleist, see Alfred Nordmann "Political Theater as Experimental Anthropology: On a Production of Heinrich von Kleist's *Prinz Friedrich von Homburg,*" *New German Critique,* 66 (1995), 17-34.

53. On the criterion of enactability as a way of testing interpretive claims about texts as well as more general claims about human agency and sociability, compare Alfred Nordmann and Hartmut Wickert, "Ende der Kritik, Beginn der Aufklärung: Aufführungsästhetische Reflektionen am Beispiel des Dokumentartheaters" (typescript).

54. The problem of performing a text or executing a work is thus akin to Wittgenstein's problem of rule-following. On the one hand, it is absurd to assume that the meaning of a rule somehow determines all its applications (or that the meaning of a text dictates our interpretive responses): the rule has to be re-asserted, perhaps re-invented in each application. And yet, there are objective criteria for correct rule-following, namely whether or not our application of the rule agrees with an established practice. In the theater, the rehearsal process seeks out and establishes an objective practice.

55. This reveals what is right and what is wrong with the somewhat casual notion of a performance *by* a text. That turn of phrase reflects the heuristic and hermeneutically inescapable assumption that one can get nothing out of a text which isn't somehow in it already; and yet, strictly speaking a text does not do or perform anything at all; its performance is attendant on its execution, that is, by way of writing and reading, interpreting or (en)acting.

DIE FAHRT IM EINBAUM ODER DAS STUCK ZUM FILM VOM KRIEG (THE CANOE TRIP OR THE PLAY OF THE FILM OF THE WAR)

PRODUCTION REVIEW

Reinhold Grimm (review date autumn 1999)

SOURCE: Grimm, Reinhold. "Die Fahrt im Einbaum oder Das Stuck zum Film vom Krieg." World Literature Today 73, no. 4 (autumn 1999): 728-29.

[*In the following review, Grimm dissects Handke's* Die Fahrt im Einbaum Oder Das Stuck zum Film vom Krieg *plot line and character development, giving the play a negative review.*]

Peter Handke's *faible* for the Balkans, and for Serbia in particular, is well known. In his new book, *Die Fahrt im Einbaum oder Das Stück zum Film vom Krieg's* (*The Voyage in the Dugout or The Piece about the Film on the War*), this penchant comes to the fore again, in however veiled or masqueraded a manner.

Handke's "piece" (i.e., play, or alleged play) is equipped with no fewer than three mottoes—from Ivo Andrić, Goethe, and the fourteenth-century laws of King Dušan—all of which are meant to justify his apologetic endeavors. The dramatic action, if indeed that is the proper term, takes place in the lobby of a hotel named "Acapulco," a legendary building situated in a small provincial town right in the midst of the innermost gorges and mountains of the Balkan peninsula. It is there that two moviemakers, the American John O'Hara and the Spaniard Luis Machado, have met in order to hold tryouts for a film they plan jointly to shoot on the (civil) war that raged in this area—probably Bosnia—a decade ago. One after another, or sometimes together, the prospective actors and (noticeably fewer) actresses for this international film project appear, describing and explaining their respective views of the bloody, murderous, atrocious events they then experienced.

These would-be characters comprise, among others, a guide, a chronicler, a historian, a threesome of "mountain-bikers" who are journalists from abroad, but likewise truly indigenous witnesses such as the *"Waldläufer,"* an exconvict and kind of wild man roaming the woods, or the fabulous beauty queen called *"Fellfrau"* or *"Fellmantelfrau"* (since she wears a fur coat). As might be expected, their various testimonies turn out to be highly subjective and conflicting, even plainly contradictory, whether regarding the descriptions they give of those events or the mutual verdicts of guilt they pronounce. In the end, the filmmakers realize that their ambitious project is doomed to founder. Machado states as curtly as explicitly, "*Wir wer-*

den den Film zum Krieg nicht machen." Then he adds: "*Hier, jetzt aber ist die Zeit aller Schuldigen. Es ist das Land, oder Europa, oder die Welt der Allerschuldigen [!]—nur daß die einen Schuldigen zu Gericht sitzen über die andern.*" Hence, not just the Serbs are guilty, according to Handke, but all other nations too, and the latter perhaps even more so, especially through their abuse of the media and because they have the effrontery to sit in judgment upon the former. The author thus arrives at Hobbes's bleak insight, *Homo homini lupus,* "*Der Mensch ist dem Menschen Wolf.*" However, he continues: "*Das Volk ist dem Volke Wolf.*" Which is to say, in Handke's opinion, that either no one or everyone is to be exculpated.

Structurally speaking, Handke doubtless claims that his text forms a drama, or at least a play. It does neither. ***Die Fahrt im Einbaum*** lacks both a dramatic plot and convincing character portrayals and could at best be labeled, to vary a definition of Émile Zola's, as a series of *monologues raisonnés,* albeit by far not so lucid. And as for said "dugout" in the title, it only serves to produce a turbulent and rather ridiculous spectacle toward the end of the "piece," though having been present and visible onstage from the outset. Supposedly, it is endowed with a mythical, indeed magical quality, for this "Einbaum," the author assures us, "*kann überall fahren, gleitet durchs Geröll, übers Gebirge, schafft im Fahren selber die Tunnels, Paßhöhen, Furten.*"

Handke's text, to repeat, is but a series or, more correctly, a conglomerate of statements, pronouncements, and vague proclamations. Furthermore, it is not even wholly original either; it unmistakably betrays certain borrowings from Bertolt Brecht as well as from Thornton Wilder. For instance, the Handkean "reitender Bote" (messenger on horseback) clearly stems from the *Three-Penny Opera.* More important yet, his *Ansager* (announcer), who occupies a central position throughout the text, bears a striking resemblance to the stage manager in *Our Town.* And what of Handke's liberal admixture of foreign words and phrases that sometimes amount to veritable macaronic sentences? Here, for example, is what he has to say about the defenders of a village and their ruthless aggressors: "*Die Dorfverteidigung . . . vastly outnumbered, bald out-*

counted. Nur noch Tote und Verwundete . . . , und die Angreifer: hineingefired in die bodies, die Messer hineingeplunged, die Schädel smashed," and so on.

In short, ***Die Fahrt im Einbaum*** constitutes—barely—a lightweight effort within Handke's rich and variegated oeuvre. I seriously wonder if, for his own sake, it should have been published.

FURTHER READING

Criticism

Marcus, J. S. "Apocalypse Now." *New York Review of Books* 47 (21 September 2000): 80-85.
    Detailed account of Handke's pro-Serbian politics and the scope of some of Handke's post-21st century works.

Marranca, Bonnie. "Peter Handke's *My Foot My Tutor*: Aspects of Modernism." *Michigan Quarterly Review* 16, no. 3 (summer 1977): 272-79.
    A study on *My Foot My Tutor,* with a discussion on the play's use of a natural environment and non-usage of dialogue.

Nägele, Rainer. "Peter Handke: The Staging of Language." *Modern Drama* 23, no. 4 (January 1981): 327-38.
    Discussion of how Handke's plays, without language, have changed contemporary theatre.

Schlueter, June. *The Plays and Novels of Peter Handke.* Pittsburgh: University of Pittsburgh Press, 1981, 213 p.
    Collection of essays dealing with Handke's English-translated work prior to 1981.

Falk, Thomas H. "Die Theaterstucke." *World Literature Today* 67, no. 3 (summer 1993): 604.
    Discusses Handke's works throughout the years, starting with his first play *Publikumsbeschimpfung,* and concluding with the play *Die Stunde da wir nichts voneirander der wubten.*

George S. Kaufman
1889-1961

American playwright, scriptwriter, journalist, and critic.

INTRODUCTION

A member of the Algonquin Round Table, Kaufman collaborated on more than forty plays during his long career. He is best known for the sharp, scathing wit that informs most of his works. He satirized such diverse subjects as politics, the entertainment industry, and pretentious middle class values by using put-downs and comic one-liners.

BIOGRAPHICAL INFORMATION

Kaufman was born in Pittsburgh, Pennsylvania, on November 16, 1889, and graduated from Pittsburgh Central High in 1907. While there he was encouraged to act by his rabbi. Kaufman joined a student group and later collaborated with a friend, Irving Pichel, to write a play. Kaufman briefly studied law at Western University of Pennsylvania (now the University of Pittsburgh), but still held an interest in working in the theatre. From 1909 to 1912 Kaufman worked as a ribbon salesman for the Columbia Ribbon Company in Paterson, New Jersey, where his father was a plant manager. In 1910 Kaufman enrolled in the Alveine School of Dramatic Art in New York, and from 1914 to 1915 he took courses on playwrighting and modern drama at Columbia. Kaufman began sending contributions to a popular newspaper column called "Always in Good Humour," featured in the *New York Evening Mail.* Franklin P. Adams, who wrote the column, later suggested to Frank Munsey, the publisher of *The Washington Times,* that Kaufman could write a daily humor column for the newspaper. Kaufman was hired in 1912 and continued to write for *The Washington Times* until 1913 when Munsey fired him for being Jewish. Kaufman's first broadway credit came during the 1917-1918 season, when producer George C. Tyler asked him to revise the comedy *Someone in the House.*

MAJOR WORKS

While working as a drama reporter and critic for *The New York Herald Tribune* and *The New York Times* during the 1920s, Kaufman began to collaborate on plays with Marc Connelly. Kaufman and Connelly's first play, *Dulcy* (1921), was a commercial and critical success. The play revolves around a scatterbrained heroine whose unorthodox

attempts to entertain her house guests result in ludicrous situations. *Merton of the Movies* (1922) clearly displays Kaufman's disdain for Hollywood in its story of an incompetent yet successful young filmmaker. Kaufman wrote one of his most ambitious plays, *Beggar on Horseback,* with Connelly in 1924. Based on the experimental drama *Hans Sonnenstossers Hollenfahrt* by Paul Apel, *Beggar on Horseback* centers on a young composer torn between artistic integrity and the financial security he could obtain by marrying into his girlfriend's wealthy family. During a dream sequence the protagonist becomes enraged at his fiancee's family and murders them. They come back to life to testify against him, and he is ultimately sentenced to work at an "Art Factory" where he is forced to produce only trite, commercial work. Kaufman's most enduring and accomplished plays were written with Moss Hart. *Once in a Lifetime* (1930), their first collaboration, introduces the multiplicity of characters and outrageous incidents that became a hallmark of their work. *You Can't Take It with You* (1936) concerns the eccentric Sycamore family and their friends, whose assorted activities include ballet, candymaking, manufacturing fireworks, playwriting, and painting. The contrast between the mad confusion of the Sycamore household and the staid behavior of a visiting family provides much of the play's humor; the determined individualism of the Sycamores is portrayed as the more fulfilling lifestyle. Kaufman and Hart also cowrote *The Man Who Came to Dinner* (1939). The play's protagonist, based on Alexander Woollcott, is an unpleasant, sophisticated man whose barbed wit is aimed at the conservatism of his middle-class hosts. Among Kaufman's most successful plays of the 1940s and 1950s are *The Late George Apley* (1944), written with John P. Marquand, and *The Solid Gold Cadillac* (1953), with Howard Teichman. One of Kaufman's last original productions, *Silk Stockings* (1955), coauthored with Leueen MacGrath and Abe Burrows, was a musical adaption of the film *Ninotchka*.

CRITICAL RECEPTION

The musical comedy *Of Thee I Sing* (1931), written in collaboration with Morrie Ryskind, was the first musical to be awarded the Pulitzer Prize for drama. Kaufman's direction of Abe Burrows's *Guys and Dolls* earned him the Antoinette Perry (Tony) Award in 1951. Some critics, including Joseph Wood Krutch, conceded that Kaufman was a formidable comic craftsman, but objected to what they saw as coldness in his writing. Eleanor Flexner and William Sheed criticized Kaufman's plays as superficial, but funny. Kaufman's plays during the 1940s and 1950s, though well received, were generally criticized as not matching the quality or achievement of his earlier works.

PRINCIPAL WORKS

Plays

Dulcy [with Marc Connelly] 1921
Merton of the Movies [with Marc Connelly] 1922
To the Ladies [with Marc Connelly] 1922
The Deep Tangled Wildwood [with Marc Connelly] 1923
Helen of Troy, New York [with Marc Connelly; music and lyrics by Harry Ruby and Bert Kalmar] 1923
Be Yourself [with Marc Connelly] 1924
Beggar on Horseback [with Marc Connelly] 1924
Minick [with Edna Ferber] 1924
The Butter and Egg Man 1925
The Cocoanuts [music and lyrics by Irving Berlin] 1925
The Good Fellow [with Herman J. Mankiewicz] 1926
The Royal Family [with Edna Ferber] 1926
Animal Crackers [with Morrie Ryskind; music and lyrics by Harry Ruby and Bert Kalmar] 1928
The Channel Road [with Alexander Woollcott] 1929
June Moon [with Ring Lardner] 1929

Once in a Lifetime [with Moss Hart] 1930
Strike Up the Band [with Morrie Ryskind; music and lyrics by George and Ira Gershwin] 1930
The Band Wagon [with Howard Dietz; music and lyrics by Arthur Schwartz and Howard Dietz] 1931
Of Thee I Sing [with Morrie Ryskind; music and lyrics by George and Ira Gershwin] 1931
Dinner at Eight [with Edna Ferber] 1932
The Dark Tower [with Alexander Woollcott] 1933
Let 'Em Eat Cake! [with Morrie Ryskind; music and lyrics by George and Ira Gershwin] 1933
Bring on the Girls [with Morrie Ryskind] 1934
Merrily We Roll Along [with Moss Hart] 1934
First Lady [with Katherine Dayton] 1935
Stage Door [with Edna Ferber] 1936
You Can't Take It with You [with Moss Hart] 1936
I'd Rather Be Right [with Moss Hart; music and lyrics by Richard Rogers and Lorenz Hart] 1937
The Fabulous Invalid [with Moss Hart] 1938
The American Way [with Moss Hart] 1939
The Man Who Came to Dinner [with Moss Hart] 1939
George Washington Slept Here [with Moss Hart] 1940
The Land Is Bright [with Edna Ferber] 1941
The Late George Apley [with John P. Marquand] 1944
Fancy Meeting You Again [with Leueen McGrath] 1952
The Solid Gold Cadillac [with Howard Teichman] 1953
Silk Stockings [with Leueen MacGrath and Abe Burrows; music and lyrics by Cole Porter] 1955

Other Major Works

Roman Scandals [with Robert E. Sherwood] (screenplay) 1933
A Night at the Opera [with Morrie Ryskind] (screenplay) 1935
Star Spangled Rhythm [with Arthur Ross, Fred Saidy, Melvin Frank, and Norman Panama] (screenplay) 1943
The Senator Was Indiscreet (screenplay) 1947

GENERAL COMMENTARY

Arthur Hobson Quinn (essay dates 1927)

SOURCE: Quinn, Arthur Hobson. "The New Decade." In *A History of the American Drama from the Civil War to the Present Day*, pp. 220-25, 284-86. New York: Harper & brothers, 1927.

[*In the following essay, Quinn examines the Kaufman/ Connelly collaborations and argues that neither wrote as well on an individual basis. Quinn also praises Kaufman's work with Edna Ferber in* Dinner at Eight *and with Hart in* Merrily We Roll Along.]

George S. Kaufman (1889-) and Marcus Cook Connelly (1890-), both born in Western Pennsylvania and both newspaper men, first attracted attention by their clever comedy *Dulcy* (1921). It was natural that they should dramatize the material of the newspaper and they selected a character created by Franklin P. Adams, then a columnist for the New York *Tribune*. *Dulcy* celebrated the stupid, well-meaning married woman, who almost wrecks her husband's prospects by her plans and revelations during the week-end party which has been given to secure them. The two playwrights recognized that dullness can be made entertaining, if it is constantly contrasted with cleverness, so they provided one of the best character parts in her young brother, and they aroused, in an inimitable scene, a responsive chord in all who have suffered from the recital of the plot of a moving picture.

To the Ladies (1922) is an improvement upon *Dulcy* because the types are less eccentric and the characters of Leonard and Elsie Beebe achieve reality. Elsie is the opposite of Dulcy; she is the guiding spirit of the household, saving her husband from the consequences of his stupidity or conceit and not only preserving his own self-respect, but also fighting hard for her own belief in him. Kaufman and Connelly recognized the truth that the most precious asset in our lives consists in our illusions, and Elsie Beebe won the hearts of her audiences and kept them. Her brave little speech at the end of the first Act when she talks to Mr. Kincaid, Leonard's employer, through Mrs. Kincaid, because she sees that Leonard has lost his chance to be invited to the great annual banquet of the Kincaid Piano Company, is her first high moment. Kincaid, who is a delightful picture of the self-important business man, has been deeply hurt by discovering that Leonard had borrowed money on his Kincaid Piano. He is about to leave, remarking that there is no reason why Elsie should explain the matter to him when she cries:

> Oh, but there is! If I—if I could only make you understand! But, of course, you've never been poor—either of you—I mean—really poor—so that a few dollars actually mattered, and you had to be awful careful what you did with them. So that you had to plan weeks ahead . . . so much for each little thing, and if something came up that you hadn't counted on, and that just *had* to be paid, why, it meant doing without something that you—almost had to have to live. But you see—we've—done that—ever since we're married. And then, when it looks as though you've almost helped each other out of it—and the chance comes—oh, if I could only make you understand . . .

The play was praised highly for its satiric portrayal of the "public banquet," and it was amusing, but the climax was one in which character is wrought out of situation. Leonard has copied his speech out of a manual of speech making and is horrified to hear his rival, who is called just ahead of him, make the very same speech. He is paralyzed with stage fright and then Elsie rises—tells the table that he has suddenly been taken with laryngitis but that he has given her his notes and she will try to make his speech. He plays up to her and she gives them a human talk, skilfully touching Kincaid's weakness for approval, and makes the success of the evening. But what swept the audience was not only Helen Hayes' remarkable performance as

Elsie; it was the quick response to the appeal of the young wife whose love had given her the inspiration that was to save them both. The light touch in *To the Ladies* concealed from many the really profound observation of life which gave birth to her, and the imagination that made her live. She has discovered that the wife who never lets her husband be discounted by the world achieves a glory for herself that is one of the actualities, and this study of young married life, treated with understanding, with sympathy and with reticence is worth many a bitter analysis of exceptional unhappiness. The authors placed in Elsie's mouth as many bright sayings as they had put stupid ones in *Dulcy*. Her words to Kincaid in the last Act—"Nearly every man that ever got any place, Mr. Kincaid, has been married, and that couldn't be just a coincidence"—are a contribution to philosophy.

Merton of the Movies (1922) is a dramatization of the story by Harry Leon Wilson and it would be difficult to assign the relative shares to the credit of the novelist, the playwrights and the actor, Glenn Hunter, in the delightful presentation on the stage. The figure of the movie-struck clerk whose sole value turns out to be his unconscious burlesque of the part he is trying to play sincerely, was certainly made to live. It was a popular success, but *The Deep Tangled Wildwood* (1923), a clever satire "upon the Winchell-Smith type of play" was a failure.

The capacity of the co-authors for satire was revealed, however, in a delightful dream play, *Beggar on Horseback* (1924). The idea of a play in which satire upon existing conditions is expressed in terms of dreams is not new, of course, but the immediate suggestion was made by Winthrop Ames, who derived the idea from reading *Hans Sonnenstössers Höllenfahrt* by Paul Apel. In order that the flavor of the satire should be native, the playwrights did not read the original German play[1] so any discussion of its effect is unnecessary. Indeed, one familiar with the work of Kaufman and Connelly hardly needs to be assured of their originality, for through all the vision of the musician, Neil McRae, who sees his future if he marries into the rich family of the Cadys, their unmistakable blend of humor steadily shines. In this dream, Mr. Cady, who manufactures "widgets," takes Neil into the business and Neil is tossed from one stenographer to another in the vain search for a pencil, in the clutches of the modern efficiency system that makes more impediments to progress by separating the individual from his job than the old decentralized business ever conceived. Even better is the scene of the four prison cells in which are working the greatest living novelist, poet, painter, and composer, the last being Neil himself. When the novelist stops a moment in his dictation the stenographer goes right on for he is dictating from his own last book! Neil is condemned to composing music for lines like

> You've broken my heart like you broke my heart
> So why should you break it again?

Then comes the most memorable line in the play. Neil in desperation tugs at his cell door and finds that it opens easily.

"Why," he exclaims, "it was never locked!"

The dream is remarkably like a real dream; it has the peculiar assertion of varity, combined with the uncanny revelation of self-scrutiny and of the observation of others that is the experience of competent dreamers. The play is a fine expression of the resentment of the artist, the man who can do things that no one else can do, for the attitude of the Cadys and their like, whose ambition is to do everything just like other people and who are contemptuous of those who show originality. The title is a clever use of the phrase recorded by Robert Greene in his *Card of Fancie* in 1588: "Set a beggar on horseback, they say, and he will never alight."

Beggar on Horseback is the last collaboration, so far, of Kaufman and Connelly. There was no difference, but it was felt by both that it would be well for them to write separately for a time. The result has hardly been fortunate for the drama. Kaufman has written since then one original play, *The Butter and Egg Man* (1925). This is a clever farce, dealing with theatrical life, but while it was a financial success, it is hardly significant. It is in fact, a backward step, for it is a farce made up of hard caricature types, and depends entirely upon its situations. *Minick* (1924), which he wrote in collaboration with Edna Ferber, is a dramatization of the latter's short story, *Old Man Minick*. The collaborators have published in one volume the short story and the play, together with an amusing account of the way in which the dramatization was made. *Minick,* however, is not important. It is the product of careful observation of life, which runs, however, to caricature, and there is little charm in it, however much amusement it provided on the stage. *The Good Fellow* (1926) was also a collaboration and was a failure.

Connelly has written one original play alone, *The Wisdom Tooth* (1926). It is a charming comedy, with a note of fantasy. Bemis is just the average senior clerk. He has had ambitions when he was a boy, but they have been submerged by the hard knocks of the city and an inferiority complex. In his boarding house, Sally Field sees the spark in him and tries to bring it out. He sees also in a dream the boy he used to be and he is visited by his grandparents, a delightfully conceived pair. Under their influence he braves his employer, to protest against injustice, and the way in which the boy of his visions goes with him concretely is very appealing. Of course even this interview turns out to be a dream and when he does call up his employer, he is promptly discharged. But he has Sally's appreciation and the consciousness of his own self-respect.

The Wisdom Tooth is of great interest, for it seems to settle the question as to which member of the original partnership contributed the imaginative quality that lifted *To the Ladies* and *Beggar on Horseback* into permanent value. There is hardly a spark of it in Kaufman's work done alone or in collaboration with others. And yet of the three other elements which made the success of the plays written together, he certainly contributed his share to the

compact structure, the brilliant dialogue and the keen satire. Neither has written alone as fine a play as *To the Ladies* and it is to be hoped that they will once more bring together the nimble wit and the vivid fancy that made the union an unusual one in American play writing. . . .

George Kaufman has continued to shape the material, usually in collaboration, of satiric comedy. His own contribution is not easy to evaluate, for in addition to a wit which has individual quality, he possesses a remarkable sense of the dramatic as well as of the theatrical. This knowledge of the stage shone in *The Royal Family* (1927) written with Edna Ferber. It is a glowing reproduction of the lure which the theater has for the members of the Cavendish family, which results in a temperamental life, furious at times in its inconsequence. It was a delightful evening in the theater, especially noteworthy through the performance of Haidee Wright as Fanny Cavendish, the trouper of the old days. *June Moon* (1929) was amusing but not important, and *Once in a Lifetime* (1930), a blistering satire upon the absurdities of Hollywood, written with Moss Hart before either of the authors had been there, did not reach quite to the level of the succeeding plays. In *Of Thee I Sing* (1932) Kaufman approached the standard of W. S. Gilbert in the use of political material for satire, without offence, but with penetration and a shrewd estimate of the stupidity, banality and falsity of much of our party manipulation. There is much more plot than is usual in a musical comedy, and it is coherent. Writers of this vein of satire will have to go far before they can equal the spectacle of the Vice-President presiding over the Senate during the impeachment of the President. The widely different fortunes of *Of Thee I Sing* and its sequel *Let 'Em Eat Cake* (1933) illustrate a dramatic law. The satire of the first of these bit deeply into the Toryism and lack of a constructive policy of the years preceding 1932, and came just at the right time. The sequel satirized an imaginary political revolution which bore no relation to the actual situation. Dramatic satire must have reality as a basis and above all it must be concrete.

Between these musical plays, Kaufman collaborated with Edna Ferber in a powerful social satire, *Dinner at Eight* (1932). It deals with the fortunes of various people who have been invited to dine with a social climber to meet two members of the British nobility, culminating in the death of one guest, the fatal disease of her husband and her daughter's danger, all of which seem to her of no moment compared to the calm breaking of the engagement by Lady Ferncliff. *The Dark Tower* (1933) with Alexander Woollcott was too reminiscent of *Trilby* to seem important. But in *Merrily We Roll Along* (1934) George Kaufman and Moss Hart progressed from the amusing burlesque of Hollywood to the searching drama of a playwright's spiritual disintegration. The trouble with most satires of modern life is that they are too abstract and general, but here we are never allowed to forget the three central characters. Niles, the playwright, is caught by the lure of success and by the clutch of a woman unworthy of him and writes plays that bring him merely money but no satisfaction. Crale, the painter, keeps his own standards. Julia, the novelist, cannot fight it out, because of her love for Niles, and drinks herself to disgrace. This friendship between two men and one woman is as real as life itself. The retrogressive method of the play, by which the scenes begin in 1934 and go back to 1916, was eminently successful. It is, of course, not new, the closest parallel being Zoë Akins' *Varying Shore,* but it is carried out in a much more telling way, without sentimentality. Every young playwright should see or read the scene between Niles and Crale in which the latter begs his friend to go back to his earlier high standard. The last scene, laid in the college chapel where Niles is giving his valedictory, full of ideals, is terrific in its irony, for the audience has seen the crash of these lofty aspirations. This play illustrates a principle which is often forgotten, that theatrical rules may easily be broken, while dramatic laws remain constant. It has been a theatrical rule that plays must proceed chronologically, but *Merrily We Roll Along* disproves this assertion. At the same time the dramatic law of which it is an evidence still holds good. An audience loves to know something that the characters do not know. The audiences of *Merrily We Roll Along* are in possession of the future, and it adds tremendously to their appreciation of the past. If the play proceeded chronologically, they would know only as much as the characters know. It is the same dramatic law as that which O'Neill made use of in *Strange Interlude,* though the theatrical device is quite different.

In *First Lady* (1935), written with Katharine Dayton, Kaufman returned to political satire. Around the leading character, supposed to be drawn from Mrs. Longworth, revolve the interrelations of social and political life in Washington. The ambitions of Lucy Wayne who wants her husband, the Secretary of State, to become President, were drawn skilfully and while most of the characters were types, as a group they presented a fine illusion of veracity.

Note

1. Statement to the writer by Mr. Connelly.

Joseph Mersand (essay date 1939)

SOURCE: Mersand, Joseph. "George S. Kaufman: Master of the Technique of Good Theatre." In *Traditions in American Literature: A Study of Jewish Character and Authors,* pp. 14-24. New York: Kennikat Press, 1968.

[*In the following essay, originally published in 1939, Mersand discusses Kaufman's ability to satirize American character and culture.*]

George S. Kaufman's *The American Way* (1939) is his thirty-second play written in collaboration. Though critics may argue as to the ultimate value of his plays in the history of American drama, they almost unanimously agree that he is the most successful collaborator working in our theater. His associates have included Irving Pichel, Larry

Evans, Marc Connelly, Edna Ferber, Katherine Dayton, Alexander Woollcott, Moss Hart, Ring Lardner and Morrie Ryskind. The only play he wrote alone was *The Butter and Egg Man* (1925). Superlatives of various kinds have been used with Kaufman. He is generally recognized as the most successful master of stage technique in our contemporary theater. He is acknowledged as our outstanding satirist, one of our best directors, one of the best writers of dramatic dialogue, and as our most capable "play-doctor."

The surprising thing about his wizardry on the stage is that he had already been credited with it in 1927 when he wrote *The Royal Family* with Edna Ferber. Since that time, when critics thought that he reached his peak, he has developed in the versatility of his technique, in the depth of his social consciousness, in the sparkle and wit of his satire, and in his understanding of human nature. Basing his plays on the occurrences in his immediate environment, he has been compelled to change his technique, his subject-matter, and his point of view with each new production. Consequently he has become unpredictable. His many admirers have come to expect a good and even exceptional evening in the theater, but their expectations are never as delightful as their experiences with the realities. Kaufman's play, *I'd Rather Be Right,* marked his twentieth anniversary as a dramatist, and his two decades of labor merit a new evaluation.

Kaufman's personal development has run parallel to that of the American drama in general. Twenty years ago, we had plays which were either diluted imitations of Continental and British successes or feeble attempts at portraying the American scene. Louis Anspacher's *The Unchastened Woman* (1915) was considered a significant study of the modern woman and Eugene Walter's *The Easiest Way* (1909) was a bold venture in the study of morals. It is doubtful whether either play could endure a successful revival.

Today our drama is watched by alert playgoers everywhere. Eugene O'Neill, Maxwell Anderson, S. N. Behrman, George S. Kaufman, Elmer Rice, John Wexley, Clifford Odets and dozens of other American playwrights have seen their plays produced on the stages from Stockholm to Vienna. Maxwell Anderson's *Elizabeth the Queen* won over the critical audience of Vienna, Eugene O'Neill's *Strange Interlude* was acclaimed in Stockholm, John Wexley's *Steel* was successful in Moscow, and Elmer Rice's *Judgment Day* was a hit in several countries.

Even though Kaufman's *You Can't Take It with You* was a failure in London, the circumstance was the occasion of lengthy comment by critics here and abroad. Kaufman's success has been so remarkable in New York that his failure in London seemed inexplicable. All sorts of explanations were made. Charles Morgan, the critic and novelist, writing from London, the novelist J. B. Priestley, writing in New York, and Brooks Atkinson, drama critic of the *New York Times,* covered almost the entire front page of the Sunday drama section of one issue of the *New York Times* in discussing the London debacle.

The career of Kaufman is similar to that of many dramatists of today: journalist, columnist, dramatic critic, dramatist. Such has been the experience of George Ade, Ring Lardner, and S. N. Behrman, all of whom came to the stage after a career in journalism.

Kaufman was born in Pittsburgh in 1889. After graduating from the public high school, he studied law for a few months and finally gave it up because he found it too difficult. His occupations were numerous and various and brought him into contact with all sorts of human beings who undoubtedly enriched his understanding of human nature. He worked as a chainman and a transit man on a surveying corps, a window clerk in the Allegheny County tax office, a stenographer, and a traveling salesman.

In 1908 he came to New York and began his literary career as a volunteer contributor to Franklin P. Adams' column in the *Evening Mail*. Through Adams' help he secured the position as columnist on Frank Munsey's *Washington Times* (1912-1913). Although Kaufman thought the column humorous, his employer seems to have disagreed with him. A year later Kaufman succeeded to Adams' column when his mentor joined the staff of the *Herald*.

From writing for a humorous column to reporting on the new plays was an easy step. Kaufman eventually became dramatic editor of the *New York Times*. Every dramatic critic, as some disappointed playwright has said, is either an unsuccessful or an expectant dramatist. Kaufman's interest in the practical side of the theater was not long in developing.

About this time, Henry R. Stern of the Joseph W. Stern Music Company formed an organization for the encouragement of young playwrights. Kaufman, who was recommended for his promising talent, submitted a check-raising farce called *Going Up.* The play was never produced, but among those who read it and admired its snappy dialogue and comic situations was John Peter Toohey, at that time an associate of George C. Tyler, the producer. Toohey suggested Kaufman's possibilities to Tyler, and Kaufman was soon working on *Dulcy.* It seems inevitable that John Peter Toohey is the press representative of Kaufman's new plays, for he is the dramaturgic godfather to Kaufman.

Before writing *Dulcy* (1921) Kaufman had collaborated with Irving Pichel on *The Failure,* which never reached production. With the late Larry Evans he wrote *Someone in the House* (1918), which was unsuccessful. The writing of *Dulcy* deserves detailed treatment, because it is one of those plays whose genesis is well known and is an illuminating insight to dramatic creation.

George C. Tyler needed a comedy for Lynn Fontanne, Ellen Terry's brilliant protégée. Kaufman and Marc Connelly were invited to write a play using material which had appeared in Franklin P. Adams' column in the *Herald* in 1914. Kaufman has described its composition thus: "We had a great break of luck with it—the various parts fell

into place all in one Sunday afternoon." It was fairly successful in New York, which was in a receptive frame of mind in the early twenties to plays deriding low I.Q.'s. Only a year later Sinclair Lewis' *Babbitt* appeared. Outside of New York the audiences were colder. Sophistication had barely reached the peripheries of the large cities. Not until another decade could satire and social criticism in plays succeed in such preliminary testing-grounds as Boston and Baltimore. Now Kaufman prefers to have his latest plays open out of town. *I'd Rather Be Right* put the Bostonians in quite a turmoil and then Kaufman knew he had nothing to fear. When *Bring on the Girls* appeared to be sending them homewards in Baltimore and in Washington, the play folded up and never reached Broadway.

Babbitt is perhaps the most enduring of the literary works of the early twenties which ridiculed rotarianism, hypocritical woman-worship, and frequent banqueting. For students of human nature who wish to compare the characters in a play written during the depression of 1921 with those of the Great Depression of 1929—the following two bits of dialogue are illuminating. They reveal that Kaufman often says the same clever things in different plays.

Gordon (in *Dulcy*) is a pompous business man, greeting Bill, who is more flippant and serves as the mouthpiece of the author:

GORDON:

I say, how's business?

BILL:

Haven't you heard?

GORDON:

(*a bit cheery*) Oh, I don't know. I have an idea it may pick up presently.

BILL:

You've been reading Mr. Schwab. "Steel Man Sees Era of Profits."

GORDON:

Well—I think he's right at that.

BILL:

Yes . . . Rockefeller expects to break even this year, too.

GORDON:

Just the same I look for improvement. (*Earnestly*) Bill, if it could just be arranged that all the outstanding accounts could be absorbed by the banks, and then these accounts into payable—

BILL:

I know. You mean—things would be better if we weren't all broke.[1]

In 1933 in what was known as the depth of the depression Kaufman again discussed business, this time with Morrie Ryskind, collaborator in *Of Thee I Sing.* For those students of contemporary drama who are curious to distinguish the contributions of Kaufman from those of his associates, the following Socratic dialogue is helpful:

Socratic Dialogue

By George S. Kaufman and Morrie Ryskind

(The scene is Mr. Ryskind's favorite speakeasy—the one where Mr. Kaufman signs the checks.)

MR. K.:

Another glass of beer, Mr. Ryskind?

MR. R.:

Don't care if I do. And thank you very much.

MR. K.:

Don't thank *me.* Thank Mr. Roosevelt.

MR. R.:

Say, that's right. If it wasn't for the President we'd still be drinking that 6 per cent stuff, instead of this 3.2.

MR. K.:

What's the matter with 3.2? That's not a bad percentage. Those Harriman depositors would settle for that in a minute.

MR. R.:

Yes, but will Harriman?

MR. K.:

Well, he hasn't decided yet. As I understand it, Harriman is going to get together with France, and they'll make us a combined offer.

MR. R.:

That means Harriman won't pay unless Germany disarms?

MR. K.:

No, it just means Harriman won't pay.

MR. R.:

There's just one sure way to keep the banks open. Pass a law against them, the way they did with the speakeasies.

MR. K.:

That wouldn't do. You'd have too many banks in one block.

MR. R.:

I guess you're right. With as many banks as that, the prisons would get too overcrowded.

MR. K.:

Tell me—with all the bankers going to jail, what do you think will happen?

MR. R.:

Well, the first thing they'll do is float a series of Mutual Welfare Gold Debentures, guaranteed by Singer and Marcus and S. W. Straus and Company, and payable in 1962, with time off for good behavior.

MR. K.:

That's all right for 1962. But what happens in 1934, when the bonds drop to three and a sixteenth asked, and one-sixteenth offered?

MR. R.:

What do you think'll happen? They'll close the jails.

MR. K.:

Then what? You mean we have prison reform?

MR. R.:

Sure. A bill is rushed through Congress giving the President dictatorial powers over the jails. So he opens the good jails and the rest of them stay closed. Maybe some of the Detroit jails will never open.

MR. K.:

But what about the Reconstruction Finance Corporation? Aren't they supposed to help out?

MR. R.:

Oh, sure. They keep right on lending money—good jails and bad. No matter what happens.

MR. K.:

Let me get this straight. The Reconstruction Finance Corporation just keeps on lending money?

MR. R.:

That's right. On condition that there's no security.

MR. K.:

Well, whose money is it? Whose money are they lending?

MR. R.:

It's very simple. You see, they take the money that the depositors put into the good banks.

MR. K.:

And lend it to the bad banks.

MR. R.:

Now you've got it!

Mr. K.:

But if they're going to do that, why don't they let Harriman keep it in the first place?

Mr. R.:

Don't worry—he's going to. Waiter! Two beers!

Mr. K.:

Make mine the same!

Mr. R.:

Two times 3.2—that's 6.4, isn't it? That's not bad beer, Mr. K.

Mr. K.:

That's what it isn't. But tell me—have you tried any of this 3.2 wine?

Mr. R.:

No, I haven't. Tell me about that.

Mr. K.:

I've been making some at home. You take two parts of hydrogen and one part oxygen, and mix them together. That gives you H_2O, or 3.2 wine.

Mr. R.:

H_2O? That's water isn't it?

Mr. K.:

Well, what do you think 3.2 wine is? Wine?

Mr. R.:

That depends on the Supreme Court. If they say it's wine, it's wine—with Brandeis dissenting.

Mr. K:

Just the same, Mr. Roosevelt is doing a pretty good job. He's got the whole country behind him, and we Democrats have got a right to be proud.

Mr. R.:

We Democrats? I thought you voted for Thomas?

Mr. K.:

I did. But that was in New York City, and it wasn't counted.

Mr. R.:

Then I'm a Democrat, too?

Mr. K.:

Sure you are. If you voted for Thomas.

Mr. R.:

Well, I'll be darned! We've got to celebrate that! Waiter! Four beers!

Mr. K.:

Make mine the same!

Mr. R.:

Yes, sir, he's doing a great job—Roosevelt. A great job. Tell me—is Roosevelt married?

Mr. K.:

Sure he's married. Been married for years.

Mr. R.:

Funny. You never read anything about his wife.

Mr. K.:

Waiter! One rotogravure section![2]

Comparing the two dialogues written twelve years apart, one notices certain elements which might well characterize the dramatist. There is a contemporaneity, first of all, which ties the play closely to its environment and which may work to its disadvantage in the final reckoning of the playwright's contributions. Ibsen's *A Doll's House* could be revived in 1937 as a moving, provoking drama, because of its timelessness. There is no need to summon the platitudes concerning Shakespeare's revivability. The season of 1937 saw the Mercury's *Julius Caesar,* Talullah Bankhead's *Antony and Cleopatra,* the Surrey Players' *As You Like It,* and Charles Hopkins' *Coriolanus.* In 1938-1939 Maurice Evans produced *Hamlet* and *Henry IV.*

Since Kaufman's wit is essentially the kind which takes one by surprise because of its appropriateness and its felicity of phrase, will the same wit amuse an audience the second time? Nothing is so boring as a wise-crack endlessly repeated. Kaufman is perfectly aware of the immediacy of appeal of his plays as his well-known remark about his opinion of satire indicates. When questioned why he did not write satire more consistently instead of his popular plays with a touch of satire, he is said to have answered: "Satire is what closes Saturday night."

There is no doubt of his popular success. After his happy experience with Marc Connelly in 1921, he lost no time in writing **To the Ladies** and **Merton of the Movies** in 1922. The following year they wrote in collaboration **The Deep Tangled Wildwood,** an exposé of New York's sophistication, which was a failure. Ten years later, with Edna Ferber, Kaufman tried again with the same theme in **Dinner at Eight,** a mordant criticism of Park Avenue society folk. In 1923 Kaufman wrote his first book for a musical comedy, **Helen of Troy, New York.** (1923) **Be Yourself** (1924), **The Cocoanuts** (1925), **Strike Up the Band** (1927), **Animal Crackers** (1928), **The Band Wagon** (1931), **Of Thee I Sing** (1931), **Let 'em Eat Cake** (1933), and **I'd Rather Be Right** (1937) are other musical comedies for which he has fashioned the plots.

A dramatist deserves more than passing mention when his works achieve not merely a success of the moment but also enrich the art-form, remove its limitations, and open new fields in which it may flourish. Has Kaufman been more than a wizard of stage-technique? Are his many popular successes readable and revivable? The two Pulitzer prizes for *Of Thee I Sing* (1932) and *You Can't Take It with You* (1937) indicate at least a certain committee's testimony to his merit. To the historian of the drama, perhaps his two outstanding achievements have been *Of Thee I Sing* and *I'd Rather Be Right*.

Of the first it might truly be said that it was a pioneer effort. Critics thought that they had touched the zenith of adulation when they spoke of it as the nearest American counterpart to the Gilbert and Sullivan operettas. Yet *Of Thee I Sing* was even superior to the immortal Savoy operettas in certain respects. There is about such productions as *Pinafore, Iolanthe* and *Ruddigore* a feeling of gayety, yes, but also a childish kind of gayety. To make sophisticates laugh, to have tickled the mind, not the ribs, that was Kaufman's feat. To wring a laugh out of the war debt tangle, to have made a Presidential campaign exciting before the 1932 and 1936 battles; to have dared to present the Nine Old Men on the stage in an attitude more prejudicial than judicial; to have taken the dullness out of politics and to have substituted laughter—that was something new in American drama.

Although John Corbin in an article in the May, 1933, *Scribner's* was displeased with the influence which dramatists like Kaufman exercised in American drama, he admitted that Kaufman's spirit of satire was not wholly worthless. Kaufman found so much in American life to ridicule, because there are so many foibles and follies that deserve only ridicule. Tin Pan Alley was the subject for his satire in *June Moon* (1929); the stupidities of the moguls of Hollywood were ridiculed in *Once in a Lifetime* (1930); joiners were told some unpleasant things in *The Good Fellow*; and the Republicans surely were satisfied with the criticism of the New Deal in *I'd Rather Be Right*.

As a satirist of the more obvious inanities and crudities of American life, Kaufman is easily the master. His training as a columnist twenty-five years ago has made him a kind of dramatic column-writer, writing ironically about things that have amused him. No one expects a unique philosophy of life from such a writer, any more than one expects gossip columnists to be included in a revision of Will Durant's *Story of Philosophy*. Yet no man of intelligence, living in such times as these, can have failed to adopt certain definite ideas about artistic, economic and social problems.

Kaufman's artistic philosophy is perhaps most clearly stated in *Merrily We Roll Along,* written with Moss Hart in 1934. The dramatic device of beginning a play with the present and then retreating into the past was effective, to be sure, but after all, only a dramaturgic trick. To many observers this story of the commercialization of the ideals of a young playwright seemed something in the nature of a confession on Kaufman's part. Certainly no American dramatist would understand better the emotions of a successful dramatist whose millions do not satisfy his artistic

cravings. The conquest of dollars over idealism has often been treated by our dramatists, but seldom with the poignancy and irony which Kaufman gave to his play. The times may have influenced the dramatist, for a few years later he was back to character comedy. His excursion into the field of literary art and its difficulties is one of the truly revealing contributions to this difficult subject.

What is Kaufman's general philosophy of life? Will he eventually join the immortals or is he just another successful dramatist, another Kotzebue, a Scribe, a Boucicault? Mere technical proficiency never produced an enduring playwright. Is Kaufman satisfied with his financial returns and content to leave dramatic art to his younger contemporaries?

In the opinion of Joseph Wood Krutch, drama critic of the *Nation,* Kaufman has not a consistent point of view. "He has said a hundred witty things; he is certainly on the side of good sense; yet it would be very difficult after reading his twenty-odd plays to say that they tend in any direction."[3] Since this statement was made in 1933, certain plays have appeared in which ideas play an important part. These are *Merrily We Roll Along* (1934), *First Lady* (1935), *Stage Door* (1936), *You Can't Take It with You* (1936), *I'd Rather Be Right* (1937), *The Fabulous Invalid* (1938), and *The American Way* (1939). Sometimes Kaufman's point of view is one of good common sense, such as expressed by Grandpa Vanderhof in *You Can't Take It with You.* Briefly, his philosophy of life is one of enjoying it while one can. Perhaps Kaufman, who knows what audiences want, gave them their own land of heart's desire. In our nerve-wracking civilization we all crave a Shangri-La, a haven of refuge.

Kaufman's philosophy of life may not be consistent, not even positive, but it is quite evident and animates his plays. In all his satires and comedies with satirical flavors he shows his refusal to be fooled by the things which befuddle most people. His superiority to other writers like Sinclair Lewis and H. L. Mencken, who likewise have capitalized on their clarity of vision, lies in his ability to preserve that attitude when the others have succumbed to illusions.

Kaufman has shown Americans how ridiculous some of their most cherished institutions are: their Rotary clubs, their hypocritical adoration of women, their thirst for the dollar, their worship of material success. To have become successful by condemning the pet notions of one's audiences is an unusual accomplishment. It was said of a certain performance of *You Can't Take It with You* that one of the spectators laughed so heartily that he fell off a balcony and yet was unharmed. There is something symbolic in that. Kaufman has turned some of America's most sacred prejudices upside down, but their possessors have survived the experience. Perhaps it does us much good to see the world sometimes standing on our head. Kaufman may be able to stand on his feet and see what a crazy, silly, yet happy world this is. Our age demands more people with eyes that cannot be fooled by superficialities, with minds which can sum up the absurdities of a situation in an epigram, with courage to laugh at the weaknesses of men, be they movie moguls or Presidents.

Notes

1. Reprinted by permission of Mr. George S. Kaufman.

2. Reprinted by permission of Mr. George S. Kaufman and *The Nation.*

3. "The Random Satire of George S. Kaufman," *The Nation,* August 9, 1933, pp. 156-8.

Russell W. Lembke (essay date October 1947)

SOURCE: Lembke, Russell W. "The George S. Kaufman Plays as Social History." *The Quarterly Journal of Speech,* 33, no. 3 (October 1947): 341-47.

[*In the following essay, Lembke argues that Kaufman's plays offer an important survey of the American social history of his time.*]

It is time that we took another look at the thirty-four plays written in the years between 1920 and 1946 which bear the name of George S. Kaufman as author or collaborator. They have been smugly passed over by drama critics; but as social history alone, as vivid pictures of the life, particularly the city life, of the times, they do not deserve such treatment. There is an economy, a consciously painstaking selectivity, in the technique of writing which is not only good but which can be identified as Mr. Kaufman's own. These plays form an important and an independent body of drama even though twenty or more collaborators have been involved in their production; they deserve re-examination as in large measure the work of one of our most successful theater men.

A survey of the Kaufman plays will reveal that they present American social history with vividness, economy, and thematic significance—qualities which are present to such a degree that the lack of critical appreciation is difficult to understand. At least the critics who seem to stress the importance of social consciousness might have been expected to recognize values as important as these.

I

It is remarkable, in view of the fact that he is known as a "topical" playwright of the "popular" and transient sort, that not one of Kaufman's plays in the 1920-1930 period caters to the craving for minor excitements of the time beyond his representation of fast tempo. What are alleged to be Kaufman's "thousand random comments" include few of those minor American fads and excesses of the decade set forth in Frederick Lewis Allen's *Only Yesterday* or the Lynd's *Middletown,* such as: Mah Jong, Coué, drinking, marathon dancing, flag-pole sitting, bootlegging, and

racketeering. The fabulous crossword puzzle craze, the Florida land boom, and Lindbergh are only mentioned by Kaufman characters as very incidental to the main dialogue. Kaufman concentrates rather upon satirizing the business-success creed, including the advertising business, speculation, and big deals; the hero racket; and the influence of the business and social scheme upon art. This is not mere topicality; it goes far deeper than that.

Note how vividly Kaufman presents his picture, how expertly he pierces certain core problems of the 1920-1930 decade. Examine the thousand things that Americans were doing as illustrated by their fads and notice how these derive or gain impetus from the fundamental scheme of living at the time. There was a wider participation in business and public life, a development of organized entertainment for more people; and an increased dissemination of information through the newspapers, the movies, and then the radio; and, as a consequence, an emphasis upon the celebrity—the famous "personality." These are the things with which Kaufman dealt; they are the basis for hero and celebrity worship, fads, marathons, fast living, and the like.

Dulcy (with Connelly, 1921), the first Kaufman play, is remarkable, considering the hectic age in which it was written, for including so few purely topical references of a minor sort. The craving for excitement and for the sensational which marked the 1920's is not used by Kaufman and Connelly to bolster dramatic action; rather, the authors have managed to catch the mood of the times with respect to the particular by transient bits strategically and economically chosen to emphasize the general application.

The fashions and manners satirized in *Dulcy* are significant manifestations of the use of the bromide in business and society; each incident in the play is a concrete expression of superficial attitudes. *Dulcy* contains comments on idiosyncrasies of personalities and the vogue for personality improvement. It deflates popular American heroes. The great movie "scenarist" is ridiculed, and the suave and important Schuyler Van Dyck is revealed as a harmless lunatic with hallucinations about owning big business interests. Tom Sterret, the "advertising engineer," is another of the many vividly drawn Kaufman fools. *Dulcy* satirizes moving-pictures, writing, and other "cultural" activities; the plot of a scenario, told seriously and with extreme histrionics by the "scenarist," is a part of Dulcy's parlor entertainment (also a point of attack here and in *You Can't Take It with You.*) This scenario is a grotesque patchwork of plots, a melodramatic burlesque of serious drama. Most telling comment upon big business and the gospel of success is the refusal of the tycoon, Forbes, to recognize Van Dyck, his "business opponent," as a mad man. The whole is expertly and economically organized by a dominant emotional quality, by the general attack on platitudes, and by the contrast between Dulcy and her brother, Bill Parker, the first of Kaufman's many sardonic characters. The bromides in Dulcy's last speech, because they are a part of her method, make it very clear that she has not reformed her interfering ways; and her trite phrases recall again the dominant satirical high points of the play, not the mere fact that Gordon, her husband, has succeeded in getting a 25 per cent share in his business merger with Forbes instead of the proffered $16_{2/3}$ per cent. As for Gordon, like many an American spouse, he finds his own values behind Dulcy's grotesqueries and makes his own choice—to condone her idiosyncrasies—in the genial, democratic way. The material is vividly and keenly presented; and no such basic attack on platitudes can be called merely topical and random. *Dulcy,* it may be said, reveals the patterns that were consistently followed by later Kaufman plays.

Other plays of the period between 1920 and 1930 reflect, as does *Dulcy,* core attitudes and essential problems of the time; but it is *The Beggar on Horseback* (with Connelly) of 1924 which gives us the clearest focus upon middle-class family life in America, the ways of the socially elite whose mode of life is aped by others, and the effects upon these groups of our industrial system. The protagonist, Neil McRae, is an artist who escapes from materialistic domination, the only Kaufman hero to dominate his surroundings. Neil McRae lives in a democracy where he and his fellow protagonists have at least a freedom of choice—to conform or to temporize with actuality, to dominate or to outdo disorder, or to improve their state. The whole of a Kaufman play, whatever the choice of the characters, reflects a geniality which looks toward the ideal logical order of things. This is true of his plays in the fretful twenties even more than in the later plays which look back upon our history.

The Butter and Egg Man (1925) makes good fun of the economics of the theater and indirectly comments upon American business at the time when flourished the gospel according to Bruce Barton and Red Grange, Henry Ford and Graham McNamee, the Kiwanis Clubs and Coolidge prosperity. There followed further comments along the same line illustrated by the Marx Brothers' antics in *Cocoanuts* (with Berlin, 1926) and *Animal Crackers* (with Ryskind, 1928,) and by *The Good Fellow* (with Menkiewicz, 1926,) a gibe at fraternal-order high jinx.

June Moon (with Lardner, 1929) is the last Kaufman play of the decade. There was political cynicism in 1929, but the country still sang the songs that Rudy Vallee crooned and prayed for a Big Bull Market. Even with love debunked Americans wistfully revived "Sweet Adeline"; and Kaufman and Lardner pointed maliciously at our June and moon rhymes while at the same time they allowed their moronic hero (just one of us) to have his fool's success.

II

The years of the next decade, the 1930's, were much more seriously lived in America. Prosperity was gone; there were fewer fads and more fears. Miniature golf, bathtub gin, and gambling seem to be overshadowed by slightly different interests in, for example, sports, G-men, the Lindbergh kidnapping, the Dionne Quintuplets, and technocracy and other religious and economic salvation schemes. In general, there was a unifying interest in politics. Kaufman carried over to the thirties his interest in the arts and in business and social life, but turned more to comment on politics and patriotism. Again he chose what constituted the core interest of the time.

I'd Rather Be Right (with Hart, 1937,) one of these later plays, has more transient references than any other of the Kaufman works. Predominantly they are references to particular people in the news of the day. The topical bits of most Kaufman plays, however, simply serve to set the scene and are few and easily understood. *Of Thee I Sing* (with Ryskind, 1931) becomes no more specific even in its satire on the handling of unfinished business in the U.S. Senate than to have a Senator recall a bill first brought up in 1804 and again in 1852 to provide a pension for Paul Revere's horse, Jenny. The Senator suggests a moment of silent tribute when he learns that Jenny is dead. Here is a good comic reference which serves all the purposes of specific critical satire and retains a wealth of generalized significance.

There were other Kaufman plays or musicals of the 1930-1940 decade concerned at least in part with politics. This was the era of depression, followed by Roosevelt and the New Deal. In this decade, too, came *Once in a Lifetime* (with Hart, 1930,) the superb attack on Hollywood "art" and super-promotion told with unrivaled expertness in terms of the wisecrack and all the gaudy grotesqueries of the American faddist; true the hey-day of Coué, Mah Jong, Bananas, and the crossword puzzle was past, but miniature golf, Huey Long, and talking pictures had come along by 1930, when Kaufman and Hart made this powerful comment upon our fads as they introduced into art and all aspects of the social scheme. Similarly, *You Can't Take It with You* (with Hart, 1936,) *The Man Who Came to Dinner* (with Hart, 1939,) and *George Washington Slept Here* (with Hart, 1940) are fine comic treatments of our cultural idiosyncrasies.

Most of the plays mentioned thus far dealt with core interests of a period; later Kaufman began to view the present in terms of the past. Even *Dinner at Eight* (with Ferber, 1932) revealed the passing depression years with all their frustration and spiritual poverty. The ugly and primitive, the conventional and the grotesque are there; the force of social conventions and the gospel of success characterize a moneyed aristocracy and point, in fact, to the very basis of capital-labor oppositions. We know the force of conventions and we pity those who are driven by them, even as we laugh at the absurdities and, perhaps, say that we are not so bound. (*You Can't Take It with You* and *The Man Who Came to Dinner* represent a freer, more abandoned side of the Dionysian in which we laugh at social conventions themselves, exult in our own freedom, and derive pleasure in having dull habits broken by novelty, conventions violated at will.)

III

But Kaufman's vivid and economical method of handling historical materials is demonstrated most clearly in the later, more definitely historical, plays. In these plays Kaufman was concerned chiefly with the time since 1900 during which each of four decades was marked, respectively, by ruthlessness but by an increasing social consciousness; by an interest in business and sentiment; by cynicism; and, finally, by patriotism and a growing concern over public issues.

With *Merrily We Roll Along* (1934) Kaufman and Hart turned toward the type of production which was to be carried further in *The Fabulous Invalid* (with Hart, 1938,) *The American Way* (with Hart, 1939,) and *The Land Is Bright* (with Ferber, 1941.) These plays depend for their effect upon a certain display of scenic richness and upon a theatrical treatment of the substance of American history. *The Fabulous Invalid* is not only the story of a theater but of American city life. It reveals Kaufman's general feeling that the artistic temperament has an unequal struggle in a materialistic world; but he is more of a democrat, has more faith in the ordinary person than, say, Joseph Wood Krutch. At the same time Kaufman has always been sensitive to too strong an underlining of a "moral" and to the opposite extreme of a too severely flagellating satire. *The American Way,* for example, avoids fatuousness; it is never weak intellectually, vain or silly, complacently dull or inane.

The theatrical display in these historical plays is in no sense extraneous to the expressive purpose of the playwrights; it results in a striking fulfillment of that purpose in each case. *The Land Is Bright* presents the raw materials of life, the evils of corruption, violent climaxes, and overdrawn details of setting and vocal attributes; it projects our confused, coarse, often vulgar, generally physical approach to national and world problems. We are shown a distinctive picture of the rough and coarse nineties; the slickness and slyness, the jazz and the imitation of Europe in the twenties; and the stock-taking attempt at a return to essential democracy, the more human yet foreboding quality of the forties.

Kaufman has always been primarily interested in the man who is ostensibly a success, showing at the same time how others ape the ways of the financially successful. In *Merrily We Roll Along,* playwright Richard Niles' two wives, Althea and Helen, are products of materialism at two levels of society, and thus are symbols of the sort of environment under attack. We are concerned with their effect upon him in the same way that we are concerned with the effect of other discordant elements in the environment.

The climax of this play comes in Act III when the purposive will of the playwright is completely beaten by the opposition of Helen, the first wife, and her father and mother—the Murneys. Richare stands motionless, alone and defeated at the end of Scene 1; the power of the

contrast with the noisy intensity of previous high points is typical of the way in which many Kaufman plays achieve a climactic moment, typical of Kaufman's contrast of the noise and disorder of the times with the need for spiritual sensitivity. Compare the scene in *The Land Is Bright* in which a member of the Kincaid clan, just freed from a concentration camp, totters slowly and silently across the stage. All of the significance of the play is gathered together vividly and economically in such moments of silent pain in the midst of bedlam. Both of these plays reveal a greater cynicism than before. The years of both, 1934 and 1940, were serious times; in 1934 economic recovery was lagging badly, and in 1940 England was fighting for her life. Perhaps, too, Kaufman felt more justification for cynicism with respect to the past and its relation to the present.

Here are vivid presentations not only of history but of social forces. Kaufman and his collaborators have again found core interests of their time; moreover, they have revealed, in addition to pertinent social criticism, the expert use of social structures as organizing means. *Of Thee I Sing* is not only an orchestration of social interests but is also an attack upon the whole social scheme. Satirizing a political campaign, it presents fashions and fugitive interests through distorted parade banners and movie slides farcically reporting election returns. Our manners are satirized in the parading, the exaggerated political speeches, and the beauty contest run in conjunction with the presidential campaign to select a wife for the future president. Government, laws, law-making, and justice are criticized through a fantastic picture of the Supreme Court, of pompous Senators making speeches on any provocation and passing bills to music in the Senate Chamber. *Of Thee I Sing* is based on a lampoon of romantic love, parenthood, and sexual interests. A great part of the entire American social scheme has been taken into the play. Through the method of exaggeration the core problems of American political and social life are presented and the significance of history is projected in terms of a vivid generalized experience which lacks nothing in individuality.

We would need to search the works of many authors to find a clearer socio-historical picture of the tragic, the satiric, and the Dionysian, with its variations of melodrama, ugliness, primitive freedom, exuberance, surprise, and theatrical richness, than Kaufman presents. The characters of his plays are revealed in terms of the language and actions of ordinary people in a democracy but at different social levels. The wisecracks and gags which predominate grow from the people of Kaufman's time and reveal a knowingness, a freedom of expression, which contributes to our understanding of them.

IV

Important themes accent Kaufman's pertinent comment upon living interests—themes which by implication reveal the ideal world. There is no grandiloquent presentation, but through the pictures of dissonance come thematic variations upon matters of great interest which may serve to clarify focus: the spiritual vs. the physical, the destruction of platitudes, the value of even the smallest esthetic phase in experience and art, the value of free expression.

In *Dulcy* the bromide is ribbed, and "success" is revealed as often a thing of mad men. In *The Beggar on Horseback* the artist discovers that his cell door was unlocked all the time; he was always really free to do as he pleased, and in this case he does escape the restrictions of materialism. *The Butter and Egg Man* symbolizes in the one word "sweetheart" all the sham of the promotion business. Maxie of *June Moon* asks, "And still grinding them out?", when told that the latest song writer is only sixteen; therein he makes the ultimate comment upon the popular song and the people who sing them. Certainly superior are the ego-puncturing scenes which picture a Supreme Court Justice's home life in *First Lady* (with Dayton, 1935,) and the Cream of Mush broadcast by Sheridan Whiteside in *The Man Who Came to Dinner*. *Dinner at Eight* presents a remarkable picture of fear dominating the lives of those who live behind a social front.

Perhaps Kaufman's strongest theme is the conflict of the spiritual vs. the physical. What better dramatic juxtaposition could be devised than the fist fight between the campaigning followers of Bryan and McKinley and the final killing by a fascist-minded gang in *The American Way*? The rough-and-tumble, even vicious, methods of business and politics seem natural, but the people are stunned when Martin Gunther is beaten to death by a mob. The physical approach of the American to his problems when taken to the ridiculous extreme of fascism is exposed again in *The Land Is Bright*.

V

Here in the Kaufman plays is social history presented with vividness, economy, and significance. The most obvious of all the errant nonsense contained in the defamation of the Kaufman plays is the contention that his social criticism is vitiated by a conventional story. That satire is only strengthened when Dulcy's husband successfully achieves his business merger. The success creed continues its insane hold and Dulcy continues her bromidic ways—certainly this satire is the strongest kind of comment; moreover, we in a democracy have the right to make fools of ourselves if we wish. George in *Once in a Lifetime* is no conventionally successful "little man" or "Cinderella man." He does not achieve his success through persistence, ambition, or simple virtues; he is an out and out fool, and the theme of that play is simply that only a fool can be a success in Hollywood. Merton is a hero-worshiping fool and he becomes a star in spite of himself—ergo, any fool may be a hero. *June Moon* says that it takes a fool to write the kind of songs we love and the more fools are we for singing them.

The contention that the *You Can't Take It with You* characters could not so indulge themselves without a steady income is completely beside the point. We know too well that we cannot live without money, but we enjoy the spectacle of people getting along very nicely without apparently having to worry about it. We enjoy the carnival spirit, the release from compulsion.

Every conventional story which Kaufman offers is set within a satirical pattern which reveals the conventional in its true light. The method is that of direct but genial ridicule; it is exaggeration. Penny writes plays because eight years ago a typewriter was delivered to the Vanderhof home by mistake. When a Saroyan character writes a book and each book consists of one word, such as "tree" or "brother"—the word whose meaning he has learned in an ecstatic moment, that method consists of understatement. The critic may prefer one method over another; but Kaufman has also made his choice and has done excellently by it.

Kaufman has reiterated the fact that our history reveals revolutionary effects resulting from scientific and economic changes, that our thinking and our artistic sensibility and freedom have not kept pace with these changes, and that we must, nonetheless, for the sake of our own sanity, maintain a genial attitude toward the present which seeks values wherever we may find them. Mr. Kaufman, himself, might scoff at this as too grandiloquent a conclusion, but I find that there is more than a passing pleasure to be gained from his work, that there is demonstrated more than a financially profitable energy and ingenuity.

Ben Hecht (essay date 24 June 1961)

SOURCE: Hecht, Ben. *Saturday Review* 44, no. 25 (24 June 1961): 5.

[*In the following tribute, Hecht laments that by the time of Kaufman's death, the kind of irony and satire he wrote had become passé.*]

In the last ten years of his life George S. Kaufman found himself as obsolete as a Smithsonian exhibit. He was a practitioner of irony and satire, with a side line of bon mots. The USA, hell-bent on making the whole world as noble as itself, had no welcome mat out for tricky-minded fellows poking fun at it.

Such a one was Kaufman. He was almost the last of the Broadway breed of iconoclasts, a breed that indulged in derision rather than breakage. It also preferred to lampoon American flaws under its nose, rather than clobber the cockeyed behavior of far-off Russians and Chinese.

Kaufman's writings for the stage and magazines varied in excellence but seldom in purpose. They investigated human clownishness and offered Americans a look at themselves in a sort of fun-house mirror.

After World War II, when the pontificators took over, when Social Consciousness drove sociability from the dinner board, and sex became a new kind of toothache for psychologists' probing—in the time of our emergence as the Leader of the World, Kaufman and his kind went into mothballs.

In the early Thirties I never understood what George was so glum about, and why so bright and famous a wag wore so funereal an air. Most of us who knew him settled for the notion that George was neurotic, and therefore unable to enjoy his stock in trade, laughter. Perhaps he was. Girls told of his shyness as a lover, and males revealed his aloofness as a companero.

But Kaufman's neurosis, if he had one, had small effect on his life. It was not his own but the pottiness of the world that begloomed him, that gave the Kaufman pompadour the look of the first plume on a hearse.

What can a witty man do but hang his head in a land that has resolutely turned its back on wit, that is ready to cry sabotage to satire, that has traded in its once famous slapstick for a global scepter?

There was an even worse enemy of wit than the world-saving binge on which the U.S. went whooping in the Forties. This was the demolishing flood of bush-wah released by television. How could any humorist take on an enemy of such proportions—such an apocalypse of tripe?

Looking back on Kaufman, I see him now as a man extinct before his time. His wit, his adroit hotfoot for pious fatheads and cliché-crowned patriots, his drollery, his sly irreverence—these Kaufmanish qualities were considered passé and trivial while George S. was still in the midst of his career.

George himself knew it. He once said to me, "Comedy has become like castor oil. People fight it."

How good a playwright was George S. Kaufman? At his best he was the best of playwrights, and more. He was part of a good time Americans were once able to enjoy—when they dared to laugh at themselves rather than yield that privilege to others.

George S. Kaufman, Ring Lardner, George Ade, Robert Benchley, Gene Field, H. L. Mencken, Gene Fowler, Finley Peter Dunne, George M. Cohan, Sinclair Lewis, all sitting in a room with the white-maned Mark Twain, make the American wing in heaven a more outstanding attraction than our current display on earth. Ask any visitor.

Charles Kaplan (essay date winter 1963)

SOURCE: Kaplan, Charles. "Two Depression Plays and Broadway's Popular Idealism." *American Quarterly* 15, no. 4 (winter 1963): 579-85.

[In the following essay, Kaplan explores the similarities between You Can't Take It with You *and Clifford Odets's* Awake and Sing.*]*

It is a truism that, as the most public of the arts and the one therefore most immediately responsive to the pressures of its times, the drama may be considered a reliable indicator of current popular thought and sentiment. For the social and cultural historian, the ideas, subjects and themes presented onstage in any era provide useful clues to the states of mind prevailing in that era. This topicality of the theater, which is at once one of its most appealing qualities and a major source of its weakness, holds true whether we are dealing with Aristophanes or Albee. In the hands of a second-rate playwright, where topicality is all, the play sinks rapidly into its earned oblivion, to be exhumed only by scholars prowling dusty stacks; in the hands of more gifted writers, the topical issue is merely the point of departure for an examination of more lasting and general concerns. No one today remembers a 1934 play by Philip Barber entitled *The Klein-Orbach Strike*; but somehow *The Cherry Orchard* manages to remain alive.

Prior to World War I, however, the American theater seemed to be an exception to the general rule; it was only about 1916 that the late-flowering drama began to have any relevance to the American scene, coming to a full and explicit relationship in the 1930s. During that rapidly receding period of social dislocation and economic depression, the theater played an unusually active part in the ferment of national self-examination and criticism. This was the period of the so-called "proletarian literature," a significant portion of which emerged in writing for the stage. The products of the WPA Federal Theatre constituted, for the most part, the high-water mark of that achievement; but, in addition, amateur groups, labor groups and left-wing "agit-prop" groups took to the empty lofts and stores and labor halls in order to present their ideas through the theatrical medium. This was the period of the Workers' Laboratory Theatre, the League of Workers' Theatres, Theatre Union, the New Theatre League, the Theatre of Action and the journal, *New Theatre,* which was the unofficial organ of these shifting and short-lived organizations. The common denominator for most of these groups—namely, their concept of theater—was defined by Joseph Freeman as "a school, a forum, a communal institution, a weapon in the hands of the masses for fashioning a sound society."[1]

Perhaps the best-remembered organization is the Group Theatre, an offshoot of the Theatre Guild, created by disgruntled younger artists who found the parent organization lacking in vision, forcefulness and relevance for the times. Certainly the single most important factor influencing the success of the Group Theatre was the discovery, within its own ranks, of a young actor-playwright named Clifford Odets. For a brief four-year period during its total existence of ten years, the Group flourished on Broadway (and even sent out a road company), and Odets became the candidate of the 1930s for the title of white hope of the American theater. After being variously hailed as the American Chekhov and the American O'Casey, Odets (like other members of the Group Theatre) went to Hollywood, and the Group eventually disbanded. But the impact of their achievement was powerful and memorable; and it was Odets' first full-length play, *Awake and Sing!,* presented at the Belasco Theatre on February 19, 1935, that established the Group as an important new element in the development of the American theater.[2]

Few plays and playwrights could avoid reflecting, in some measure, the malaise of the thirties, even when, superficially, the plays seemed to be setting out directly only to entertain, to provide for the spectators an evening's welcome escape from the disheartening Depression just outside the doors of the theater. In one sense, the choice of the play to receive the Pulitzer Prize for 1936 seems eminently appropriate today. Although the members of the Critics' Circle disagreed (they chose Maxwell Anderson's *High Tor*), the determinedly middlebrow Pulitzer Prize Committee gave the laurel to *You Can't Take It with You*, the comedy by George S. Kaufman and Moss Hart that has since become the archetypal American farce. Certainly, *You Can't Take It with You* was not the best play of 1936 by any conceivable criterion of artistic merit; but it has survived the immediate moment both by the sheer inventiveness of its lunatic action and by the fact that, like *Awake and Sing!*, it represents a recurring, if simplified, strand in American thought. *You Can't Take It with You* is, in fact, *Awake and Sing!* turned inside out or upside down or seen through a mirror—but taken together they offer a revealing glimpse into the ways of the theater in the Depression era.

Awake and Sing!, dealing with the fortunes and misfortunes of the Berger (burgher?) family of the Bronx, was regarded by most critics in terms similar to those used by Burns Mantle when he included it in his list of the ten best plays of 1934-35. He called it "an embittered protest against the injustices put upon the poor by the workings of the capitalist system."[3] But this evaluation, it seems clear today, is grossly over-simplified.

Odets' first words about his characters are that they "share a fundamental activity: a struggle for life amidst petty conditions." The family consists of Myron and Bessie Berger, their children Hennie and Ralph, and Grandpa Jacob. Myron has long since been defeated by life, but the domineering Bessie persists in trying to arrange her children's lives for them. Hennie, left pregnant and abandoned by a fickle suitor, consents reluctantly to Bessie's scheme to marry her off to a man she does not love, for the sake of respectability. Ralph, a stock clerk in his Uncle Morty's factory, is a naive and frustrated boy whose first love affair is broken up by Bessie, also in the interests of what she considers proper. The spokesman for rebellion against this spiritually as well as economically impoverished life is the grandfather, a retired barber (but, it is emphasized, an "artist"). Jacob is an old-fashioned idealistic revolutionary merely tolerated by his daughter; when he observes the bickering among the Bergers, he comments: "Marx said it—abolish such families." But it is his plunge off the tenement roof in an apparent accident that enables Ralph to begin a new life. He rejects the insurance money Jacob has left him, but the old man's sacrifice opens his eyes, and the revolutionary spirit presumably passes on to Ralph in a new and more vigor-

ous form. Ralph cries: "The night he died, I saw it like a thunderbolt! I saw he was dead and I was born!" At the same time, Hennie flees the Berger household with her old flame, the mordant racketeer Moe Axelrod, to "the place where it's moonlight and roses." Moe, who has lost one leg in the war, values nothing but the immediate moment. The complete hardboiled cynic, he finally persuades Hennie to break her family ties: "Christ, baby," he says, "there's one life to live! Live it!"

The two choices of the Berger children—one to flee, the other to stay and fight for a better life—however disparate they seem, have as their common source their discontent with life as they live it. Seen in this sense, *Awake and Sing!* is less a play dealing with the class struggle than one embodying the vague dissatisfactions of the lower middle class at the thwarting of normal human desires. "I never had a pair of black and white shoes!" cries Ralph, but it is not the shoes alone that he is crying for. That the play is not really a "revolutionary" play at all was recognized by the Left press; according to Harold Clurman, who directed the production, the *New Masses* "spoke gingerly" of it and the *Daily Worker* called it "an unimportant play whichever way you look at it."[4] Odets' original title, *I Got the Blues*, would seem also to indicate that he was less concerned with the uprising of "ye that dwell in the dust" than with the expression of a mood of widespread disquiet. But the final title, together with Ralph's outcry, as the play ends, that he is "twenty-two and kickin'" and ready to fight for a new life, seemed sufficiently ominous and specific to convince others besides Burns Mantle that Odets was calling for an immediate revolution.

With the popular success of *Awake and Sing!*, the Group Theatre, after years of promise, discouragement and continual near-failure, had finally arrived. Clurman's comment at the time was: "Now the Group has put on long pants."[5] During that winter of the Group's great success, Moss Hart, one of Broadway's most popular as well as professional playwrights, conceived of the idea for his next collaboration with George S. Kaufman. It was to be a play about another New York family—but quite unlike the Bergers of the Bronx. This comedy was to deal with an "utterly mad but lovable" family, each member of which did exactly as he pleased "and the hell with what other folks thought." Kaufman and Hart had gotten as far as suggesting the title of *Grandpa's Other Snake*—fortunately vetoed by Mrs. Kaufman—before they dropped the project in favor of another idea. This new plan involved dramatizing an unpublished novel by Dalton Trumbo entitled *Washington Jitters*, a political satire which they intended to do in the broad strokes of Kaufman's 1932 Pulitzer Prize winner, *Of Thee I Sing*. In the summer of 1936, Kaufman left New York to join Hart in Hollywood and work on this project; when he arrived, however, Hart persuaded him to revert to the original idea of the mad family, and they wrote *You Can't Take It with You* in thirty days.[6] But between the conception and the execution fell the political satire; and some buried element of that satire, with its reflections on contemporary American life, is present amidst the lunacies of the Vanderhof family.

It was the lunacies, of course, that made the play the immediate success it became. The Booth Theatre was sold out on the second night, and the play settled in for a long and prosperous run. Brooks Atkinson, with an unmistakable sigh of relief, applauded the fact that the play was not (for a change, evidently) "a moral harangue," and praised the authors for being merely "fantastic humorists with a knack for extravagances of word and episode and an eye for hilarious incongruities."[7] George Jean Nathan, although learnedly pointing out that the "loony household idea" was far from being original, called it "superior fooling," "thoroughly amusing" and "something winningly tender."[8] Another critic wrote that "it offers no serious contribution to social or political philosophy, and yet it is by all odds the most delightful American play to be seen so far this year."[9] The reviewer for *Theatre Arts Monthly* called it "all absurdity" and said of the characters: "There is not a single ounce of rational thinking or acting in the lot of them."[10] And Euphemia Van Rensselaer Wyatt, writing for the *Catholic World,* said that New York always had room "for such pleasant comedies" without any "cross or disagreeable" characters.[11]

There is no evidence that Kaufman and Hart deliberately conceived of **You Can't Take It with You** as a reply to *Awake and Sing!,* that they set out to convert Odets' basic situation, that of the middle-class New York family trapped by the Depression, into a farce comedy. But, whether by design or by accident, there are a number of echoes in the second play, and at one major point the lines of force emanating from these plays intersect. (To raise one minor detail, consider the names that Kaufman and Hart give mother and daughter. Whereas for Odets their names had been Bessie and Hennie, Kaufman and Hart call them Penny and Essie.)

It is a curious circumstance, however, that the titles of the two plays may be considered to be almost interchangeable. **You Can't Take It with You,** which is a jazzy restatement of the *carpe diem* theme, is what Jacob preaches and Ralph learns—that the making of money is not the end of man. Jacob's ironical comment on Uncle Morty's materialistic views is: "Don't live—just make success." Ralph leaves the insurance money to his mother, and vows: "Let me die like a dog, if I can't get more from life." Hennie and Moe, fleeing the Bronx for their tropical paradise, may be judged to be socially irresponsible, but they have made the decision to live life on their own terms. Conversely, also, the injunction to awake and sing is exactly what the uninhibited members of the Vanderhof household have obeyed—they not only sing, but they dance, perform on the xylophone, make candy, paint, write plays, throw darts, feed snakes and visit zoos and commencements, make firecrackers in the basement, and in general practice the twin gospels of total relaxation and total individualism. What is significant about both plays, seen in this light, is that, in their own ways—one melodramatic, the other farci-

cal—each examines the quality of American life, its values, its ideals, its actual practice and its apparent breakdown in the thirties.

The Berger family is full of tensions, frustrations and rivalries. "Everybody hates, nobody loves," is the way Jacob characterizes the situation. The home is the place to escape from. But the Martin Vanderhof home is a haven—not only for the immediate members of the family but for Rheba, the cook; her boy friend Donald; Mr. De Pinna, the iceman who has just happened to stay for eight years; Mr. Kolenkhov, the Russian ballet teacher; and all others who fall under its spell. Everyone seems to have adopted Grandpa Vanderhof's laissez-faire philosophy; and the rampant individualism, not to say anarchy, of the household where each does as he will produces happiness and peace with the world.

To be sure, this peace is attained only by resolutely ignoring the outside world. As Grandpa says at grace: ". . . all we ask is just to go along and be happy in our own sort of way." When that world occasionally intrudes, in the form of an Internal Revenue agent or Mr. and Mrs. Kirby, prospective members by marriage of the happy clan, the outside values are shown up as illogical and pointless; and at the end of the play, Mr. Kirby is revealed to be a frustrated saxophone player who has never really enjoyed making money on Wall Street, but who, unlike Grandpa, has lacked the good sense to "sign off" and start living. The Vanderhof values triumph over or convert the outside world.

The philosophic grandfathers who dominate the actions of both plays express apparently contrasting principles of conduct. Jacob's first statement is: "If this life leads to a revolution it's a good life. Otherwise it's nothing." Grandpa Vanderhof says: "Life's pretty simple if you just relax." But Odets undercuts his characterization of Jacob by calling him "a sentimental idealist with no power to turn ideal into action"; and the truth about Grandpa Vanderhof is that his strength and calm assurance derive precisely from the fact that he long ago made the crucial decision to turn his ideal into action—to leave the business world in favor of living and, in a strong Thoreauvian echo, having "time to notice when spring comes around." Fundamentally, their diagnoses of what is wrong with the world are identical: it is the old "late and soon, getting and spending" syndrome. Jacob rejects a life that is "printed on dollar bills" because it lacks dignity; Grandpa rejects it because it's no fun. "Do what is in your heart and you carry in yourself a revolution," cries Jacob—but this exhortation is closer to Emerson than to Marx.

It is at this point that the lines of force intersect. The ostensibly realistic "socially-conscious" drama and the extravagantly nonsensical farce are both expressions of the irrepressible American idealism that constantly lurks just below the surface of our brazen materialism. Idealism—and sentimental optimism as well. Ralph's final speech concludes vigorously: "I want the whole city to hear it—

fresh blood, arms. We got 'em. We're glad we're living." Grandpa Vanderhof's final grace is more restrained, but along the same lines: "We want to say thanks once more for everything You've done for us. Things seem to be going along fine. . . . We've all got our health and as far as anything else is concerned, we'll leave it to You."

It is not surprising that these plays were popular and successful in 1935 and 1936. Both are basically consolatory and sentimental comedies, restating a familiar and acceptable American principle: namely, the integrity of the individual and his right to rear back and assert himself. The terms of assertion are different in these two plays, but the underlying theme, evoked by the times, is identical. At a time when the individual seemed to be helpless and at the mercy of impersonal and powerful economic forces, the theme of individual dignity and freedom must be reckoned as a criticism of existing conditions and as an American ideal too important to be lost sight of.

Notes

1. Joseph Freeman (ed.), *Proletarian Literature in the United States* (New York, 1935), p. 264.

2. The indispensable history of the Group Theatre is Harold Clurman's *The Fervent Years* (New York, 1957).

3. Burns Mantle (ed.), *The Best Plays of 1934-35* New York, 1935), p. 236.

4. Clurman, p. 140.

5. *Ibid.,* p. 160.

6. New York *Times,* December 20, 1936.

7. New York *Times,* December 15, 1936.

8. George Jean Nathan, "Art of the Night," *Saturday Review,* May 8, 1937, p. 19.

9. Grenville Vernon, in *Commonweal,* December 25, 1936, p. 249.

10. Edith J. R. Isaacs, "Broadway in Review," *Theatre Arts Monthly,* Fall 1937, pp. 96-97.

11. Euphemia Van Rensselaer Wyatt, in *Catholic World,* Fall 1937, pp. 597-98. Her review of *Awake and Sing!* had begun: "The Bergers are such a very unattractive family!" In succeeding capsule summaries of the current Broadway plays, she continued to use "disagreeable" as the characterizing adjective.

George Freedley (essay date December 1964)

SOURCE: Freedley, George. "George S. Kaufman, 1889-1962." *Modern Drama* 6, no. 3 (December 1963): 241-44.

[*In the following obituary, Freedley reviews Kaufman's career from his early days as a newspaperman through his collaborations with Moss Hart.*]

This little essay will only be concerned with the earlier section of George Kaufman's long career as a playwright and director in one of the most exciting periods of our theater when American drama came of age in the period between the World Wars, roughly 1918-1939. All of Kaufman's serio-comic genius came to flower in that period. There is nothing of real significance after that if you disregard the dramatic recrudescence of John P. Marquand's brilliant novel of Boston society, *The Late George Apley* (1944) and the delightful spoof of big business provided by *The Solid Gold Cadillac,* written in collaboration with Howard Teichmann (1953).

Kaufman was the born collaborator. He wrote only one play alone and one adaptation from the French early in his career before he found success. He was a shrewd and demanding collaborator as has been evidenced by such distinguished writers as Edna Ferber and Moss Hart, in their memoirs, and by lesser commentators in newspaper columns. He had tremendous inventiveness and many original ideas, but he worked best in tandem. He soared in proportion to the abilities of his co-writers, but this does not mean that he could not and did not rise above them—as in moments of honesty they were willing to admit.

The fact that he liked to work on his feet, acting out and demonstrating ideas, scenes, and lines suggests the possibility that he may have been a frustrated actor unconsciously. Although he occasionally appeared in skits intended for his professional confreres, not the public, he did act for the public at the Buchs County Playhouse at New Hope, Pennsylvania, in a summer stock presentation of *The Man Who Came to Dinner,* which he wrote with Moss Hart. Possibly because of his memories of his own days on the Borscht Circuit prior to his success as a writer, he undertook the same role for an overseas tour for G.I.'s in Alaska and the Pacific. As the dramatic critic of the *Morning Telegraph* I was invited along with other drama reviewers in New York City to journey out to what used to be called Camp Yaphank in Irving Berlin's day as a soldier in World War I. With no intended disrespect to the late Moss Hart, he was wise to become a writer and leave acting to others. Aside from exceptions such as David Garrick, Colley Cibber, Noel Coward, and Sacha Guitry, few playwrights have been gifted actors.

Kaufman's playwriting began with the worthless *Someone in the House* (1918) written with Larry Evans and Walter Percival just about the time he was leaving the New York *Tribune* for the *Times.* He was a brilliant drama reporter and his Sunday news piece was widely read even when his newspaper did not have the preeminent position it now enjoys. He is credited with creating a character named Tecumseh, who scouted for theatrical news, as well as naming the Times Square area the Rialto, a term which still sticks. Lewis Funke is now the Sunday Tecumseh, but he doesn't use the title.

Kaufman really came into his own when he teamed up with another Algonquin wit (for which see Margaret Case Harriman's *The Vicious Circle* and her father Frank Case's books about the famous hostelry he created) Marc Connelly. Connelly was a former newspaper man, and they spoke the same language. From his own work we can surmise that Connelly supplied the whimsy and the light touch while Kaufman provided the structure and the more barbed lines which are now termed "wisecracks." The collaborators began with *Dulcy* (1921), a play about a beautiful dimwit which brought Lynn Fontanne to stardom under Howard Lindsay's crisp direction. Kaufman had not yet become a stage director. Then came *To the Ladies* (1922) in which Helen Hayes shone, and this play was followed by an entertaining spoof of the silent days of the films, *Merton of the Movies,* which brought stardom to Glenn Hunter. The playwrights' collaboration continued with *Helen of Troy, New York* (1923) and *The Deep Tangled Wildwood* (1923). It reached its high point in *Beggar on Horseback* (1924), which was the only commercially successful Expressionist play of American authorship. This drama satirized American worship of success and probably was based on a German original although it was denied at the time.

Kaufman and Morrie Ryskind amused themselves and the rest of us by writing the book for a musical romp for the Marx Brothers, *Animal Crackers* (1928). In 1929 in combination with Ring Lardner he wrote a spoof of Tin Pan Alley in *June Moon.* He had assisted Edna Ferber in dramatizing one of her short stories, a character comedy entitled *Minick* in 1924. In 1927 this duo returned with a satire on the Barrymores in a nostalgic but genuinely funny comedy, *The Royal Family.* This title could not be used in England where it was called *Theatre Royal* (1934) because the Angry Young Men had not yet demolished the reigning house and the title was considered an offense to them. Dame Marie Tempest under Noel Coward's direction played Sarah, matriach of the acting tribe, and a very young Lawrence Olivier acted the role of Tony, the madcap youngest son patterned on John Barrymore. This warm, rich play appealed greatly to English audiences just as it did to Americans although we were more conscious of the characters' likeness to the Drew-Barrymores than our British cousins. This writing team had fun with the Park Avenue social set and its theatrical confines in *Dinner at Eight* (1932) in which Constance Collier played a recognizable portrait of Maxine Elliott, famous American actress and financier soon to be the subject of a biography by her youngest niece, Diana Forbes-Robertson (Mrs. Vincent Sheean). Miss Ferber and Kaufman paid their last joint tribute to the legitimate theater in *Stage Door* in 1936. They chose the famous Rehearsal Club, a non-profit theatrical boarding house for young actresses.

Kaufman had a bout with Washington social politics in *First Lady* with Katherine Dayton which starred Jane Cowl during the Dolly Gann-Alice Longworth feud. Kaufman was the sole author of *The Butter and Egg Man* (1924) a comedy about American business men. Not altogether brilliant it had its measure of success although hardly a play to revive. He collaborated twice with Alexander Woollcott, the bristling, rotund drama critic who became a bellwether

for the Lambs on radio. Kaufman knew him from his days on the New York *Times* and as frequent jouster at the Algonquin round table. Woollcott had a depressant effect on Kaufman's wit and inventiveness. The first play was *The Channel Road* (1929) and the final was *The Dark Tower* (1933), a macabre drama which was hardly Kaufman's dish of tea. It was poor enough on Broadway, but I shall never forget a production I saw in Prague the following year. The Park Avenue apartment boasted a circular table, peasant shawl draped over it, with oil lamp and shade. The dowager wore a babuschka. *Mitteleuropa* had definitely moved in on Kaufman and Woollcott. Probably that was when he thought he might get even with Alec some time, but it was six years later that the idea flowered in *The Man Who Came to Dinner.*

After Connelly, Kaufman's happiest collaboration was with Moss Hart who came into prominence with him in *Once in a Lifetime* (1930) which is still the best comedy about Hollywood madness that exists. The play stands up in reading and even in summer or community theater production, a real test. Hart has recorded the agonies of collaboration in his autobiography, *Act One,* a brilliant autobiography, the continuation of which was prevented by his death in 1961. They renewed their writing combination which resulted in the superbly fantastic Pulitzer Prize comedy, *You Can't Take It with You* (1935). This play is as funny today as it was when first staged and curiously enough brings a certain nostalgia for those Depression days now happily behind us. The K. and H. combination decided to have some fun with the Franklin Delano Roosevelt administration in *I'd Rather Be Right* (1937) which boasted the services of George M. Cohan as President. Kaufman's deep love for the theater of yesteryear reappeared in 1938 with *The Fabulous Invalid* which unfortunately had a short life despite its lavish production. During Hitler's persecution of German Jewry, the collaborators came up with a flag waving demonstration in *The American Way* (1939) which out-starred and out-striped Mr. Cohan who perhaps inspired this overflowing stage presentation which burst the seams of the gigantic Center Theatre in Radio City with an enormous cast headed by the Fredric Marches.

The culmination of the Kaufman and Hart collaboration came really to an end with *The Man Who Came to Dinner* (1939) although they continued through the slight but amusing comedy, *George Washington Slept Here* (1940), an account of restoring an old house in the country in which both writers had actually participated. The brilliant comedy about a lecturer who slipped and suffered a broken bone while staying in the house of his hostess, the local chairman of a women's club in a Middle Western city, surely stemmed from Alexander Woollcott's triumphant lecture tours across America. Perhaps remembering his encounters with that intellectual porcupine, Kaufman conceived his revenge. Not only did Woollcott not sue or combat the play, he actually headed a touring company of this minor classic. Merely playing himself, he never rose to the acting heights which elevated the late well bearded

Monty Woolley to stardom. In this comedy Kaufman had fun with the theater, and American social customs as well as avenging himself at the expense of the porcupine. The irony lies in the fact that he shrugged it off without his usual shower of barbed quills.

George S. Kaufman is one of the best representatives of the highly competent craftsman in playwriting in America.

Jean Gould (essay date 1966)

SOURCE: Gould, Jean. "Some Clever Collaboratos." In *Modern American Playwrights* pp. 135-167. Dodd, Mead & Company, 1966.

[*In the following excerpted essay, Gould describes how Kaufman and Hart worked when they collaborated.*]

For exactly a decade, from 1930, with *Once in a Lifetime,* to 1940, with *George Washington Slept Here,* two masters of comedic playwriting, George S. Kaufman and Moss Hart, contributed their combined wit and humor to the American theater in the form of six plays and two musicals. Three of the plays were outstanding works, one of which captured the Pulitzer prize. Their initial effort was an achievement in high comedy that ran for two years and won the Rio Cooper McGrue prize.

George S. Kaufman, the older of the two by some fifteen years, was born in 1889, the son of Joseph and Nettie Kaufman, in Pittsburgh. There seems to have been little out of the ordinary in his background or upbringing. He went through high school and studied law for two years, but decided the intricacy of legal lore was "too hard" for his particular mind. He drifted from one job to another for a couple of years, discovering that he was an indifferent traveling salesman, but a rather good stenographer. Wherever he worked, he had a knack for entertaining his colleagues with an unexpected wisecrack, a dry wit, delivered in a laconic tone, which completely surprised them. He was tall, taciturn in appearance, even gloomy. He rarely smiled, and then but briefly. His black hair stood up in a broad bushy pompadour; his tortoise-shell glasses were apt to slip down on his large nose, allowing his piercing black eyes to peer out over the rims with startling penetration. His full lips were twisted in a wry expression which was at best a sardonic grin that occasionally emerged when his listeners burst out laughing at some off-hand, side-splitting remark.

His hum-drum jobs, however, had little to offer young Kaufman in return, either spiritually or financially. He found that he had a flair for comedy in the written as well as spoken word, and at about twenty, he left Pittsburgh for New York, where the lights of the theater blazed, and the newspapers offered an outlet for his native wit. He had admired F.P.A.'s (Franklin P. Adams) column in the *Evening Mail* for some time, and now became one of its regular contributors. Before long, George S. Kaufman

began to acquire a following—readers who looked for his tidbits, and requested more. By this route, he came into a column of his own on Munsey's *Washington Times.* While many readers thought it was riotously funny, Mr. Munsey did not appreciate its quality of broad exaggeration, of brash unadulterated attack on stupidity and narrowmindedness. After a "slight disagreement" with the publisher over one of his satiric verbal assaults, the future playwright walked out of the Washington office never to return.

He came back to New York, and for a while took FPA's place on the *Evening Mail* when that gentleman took his column elsewhere. From there, Kaufman went on to become theater news reporter on *The New York Times.* Because his interest in the theater was immense, he was soon promoted to the post of drama editor on the paper—a job he continued to handle with great efficiency long after he had succeeded as a playwright. Brooks Atkinson, who came to work for the *Times* in 1926, has described him as "even-tempered, amusingly sardonic, pleasant and obliging, though never exactly cordial; . . . he came in and out of the office several times by day and night to keep his work moving. His habits were his own; his work was authoritative and final. . . . Everything went like lightning when Mr. Kaufman stood on the south side of the makeup table. Although he was one of the most envied men on Broadway, you would never have suspected it from his informal and preoccupied appearance and his quiet concentration upon what he was doing." The playwright himself said that having a job "kept him out of such mischief as idle hours might suggest, especially with bridge and poker pals." It also prevented his wife, the former Beatrice Bakrow, whom he married shortly after joining the *Times* staff, from scheduling too many social engagements for him.

Kaufman's collaborations began as early as 1917. In spite of his extraordinary talent for the quick, devastating jest, the acid quip, the incisive criticism, he preferred to work with other writers from the start. *Someone in the House,* which he wrote with Larry Evans and Walter Percival, was produced in 1918; and, while it was not an outstanding success, the lines contributed by the young theater news reporter showed promise of a brilliant future to follow. The first big hit came in 1921, when he wrote *Dulcy* with Marc Connelly. It preceded a long and dazzling array of successes: two hits, *Merton of the Movies* and *Beggar on Horseback,* with Mr. Connelly and half a dozen others with a variety of authors, including such notables as Edna Ferber (*The Royal Family,* 1927), Ring Lardner (*June Moon,* 1929), and Alexander Woollcott (*The Channel Road,* 1929). Moreover, in 1925, he wrote two of Broadway's most hilarious offerings as the sole author of *The Butter and Egg Man* and the book of *The Cocoanuts* for the Marx Brothers in 1925. All of this was accomplished before Mr. Kaufman teamed up with Moss Hart in 1930.

That dynamic young aspirant to Broadway (later called "forked lightning" by his playwriting partner) was then emerging from the thorny path of a long, arduous period of training. He gazed upon Mr. Kaufman (already known as "the great collaborator of his time") with worshipful eyes, "very much as a boy of ten would come upon Dick Merriwell, or the captain of the winning eleven." George S. Kaufman had been Moss Hart's hero for almost ten years by the time the younger man met his idol face to face. It was, in fact, while sitting entranced in "the gallery of the Broadhurst Theatre, drinking in a performance of *June Moon,* that the idea" for their first collaboration came to him like a bolt out of the blue, demanding to be set down on paper that very night. It was typical of the way he had streaked through most of his life up to that point: not without reason did Kaufman compare him to "forked lightning."

Moss Hart was born under the heel of poverty in a crowded section of the Bronx toward the end of 1904, to the harsh strains of family discord, mainly over finances. Theirs was not abject, but "unrelieved," mean, niggling poverty, unmitigated by any harmony there might have been in the home if his parents, Barnett and Lillian Hart, had not been at silent swords' point most of the time. His father's unspoken complaint was against the in-laws who lived with the Harts but did not contribute to the family budget, particularly his wife's old-maid sister, who lived with them most of her adult life. But if she was a thorn in his father's side, Moss Hart's "Aunt Kate" provided the ointment in the otherwise prickly existence of his poverty-stricken boyhood. For Aunt Kate was in love with the theater, and she imbued her nephew with the same passion from the time he was a small boy. The tiny legacy left to her by relatives went for a Broadway show every week, and when she came home, she would regale Moss and his mother with an account of the performance she had seen. And every Thursday afternoon she took her nephew to the plays at the Alhambra Theater in the Bronx, so that by the time he was twelve years old, Moss Hart was stagestruck. His feet might be in the upper Bronx, but his eye was on Broadway, though he had never seen it. In his words, he had "the goad and the goal. The goad was poverty, the goal—Broadway and the theatre."

He took his first step in the desired direction at the age of twelve, when he went to work at a music store near his home, an afterschool job paying four dollars a week. Here he pored over the pages of *Theatre Magazine* every chance he got, dreaming of Broadway, the street he had never seen. His first glimpse of it came one day when the manager of the store sent him down to Schrimer's for some sheets of music. As he came up from the subway at Times Square, bands were playing, flags were flying and the carnival spirit of a parade pervaded the scene. He shortly learned it was an election parade, but he could never disassociate Broadway from the blare of trumpets and the beat of drums; the heady excitement of it never left him.

During his high school years, Moss Hart wrote festival sketches and one-acts, always bearing in mind his objective, to become a playwright; or perhaps, an actor, or a

director, something connected with the theater. He managed to work his way through high school, and a year or so at Columbia, but at that point his formal education ceased for lack of funds. He took a job in the garment district, which lasted just long enough for him to write the annual employees' show. Determined to work in the theater, he discovered that Augustus Pitou needed a secretary and typist—not exactly creative work, but an office-door entrance to the theater was better than none. Pitou was Manager for Fiske O'Hara, the Irish tenor and hero of melodramas produced by Mr. Pitou. He set his new secretary to play-reading, a dangerous assignment, for Moss Hart immediately got the notion to turn out a script himself, confident that he could match any he had read by the prolific Anne Nichols, playwright for O'Hara. Some imp of fancy made him give a fictitious name instead of his own when he handed the first act of his play, *The Beloved Bandit,* to Mr. Pitou. Surprisingly, the producer was taken with the work of such a promising new playwright as "Robert Arnold Conrad" seemed to be; before Moss Hart could complete the plot, his boss wanted to meet the author—and the cat was out of the bag! Nevertheless, Pitou produced the play, which unfortunately failed in its initial tryout in Rochester, and did no better under a change of title in Chicago. As Hart wrote long afterward, "*The Holdup Man* or *The Beloved Bandit* was a composite of all the plays Anne Nichols had written for Fiske O'Hara. The Rochester audience recognized it as a fake and a dishonest facsimile . . ." After the second fiasco in Chicago, the show folded, never to see the light of Broadway. Moss Hart was fired from his job, but by no means defeated. The year was 1923; he was only nineteen; he had time.

He turned to directing little theater groups in New York and New Jersey during "the season." In the summer, he became social director at adult resort camps in the Catskills; one year he staged the plays in the Labor Temple at Camp Utopia. His was a rough apprenticeship in the theater, one that required "constant invention and sheer physical endurance to provide vacationers with entertainment." He was lucky if he worked as little as sixteen hours a day, and he rarely found time to enjoy resort pleasures himself, as the supervisor who hired him had promised. Once or twice a summer, following a late rehearsal, he and his assistants took a dip at three o'clock in the morning, but otherwise they scarcely saw the out-of-doors. However, Moss Hart was well-suited to the demands of such a job, both physically and emotionally.

He was tall, and almost theatrically attractive, with black hair and snapping black eyes, full of fun and mischievous curiosity. Above them, the twin peaks of his eyebrows pointed toward his early, "humorously receding" hairline, which, as Atkinson noted, broadened in twin bays over the years, leaving "a satyric peninsula of hair in the middle of his scalp." More than one writer of the time remarked on his resemblance to a satyr, and he seems to have had much of the mercurial spirit, the love of riotous fun and merriment that marked the attendants of Bacchus in Greek mythology. The improvisations, the inventive stage business so necessary to Chatauqua and camp shows seemed to come naturally to him; his tremendous drive and firecracker enthusiasm sparked those who worked with him into meeting the stringent deadlines of resort entertainment. He soon gained a well-earned reputation in the field, and by 1929, on that fateful night when he sat in the gallery watching *June Moon,* he was known as "King of the Borsht Circuit," a title of dubious honor artistically, but of great significance as practical training in the theater.

As he related, he began writing his play the same night— the only occasion on which the title came to him first: he wrote on a big yellow paper pad, *Once in a Lifetime,* and proceeded from there. Three weeks later, he completed the script, and submitted it to six managers all of whom were interested; he chose to sell it to Sam Harris, principally because the producer promised to get George S. Kaufman to read it with an eye for possible collaboration. Shortly afterward, he received the magic message that the Great Collaborator had not only read his play but wanted to start working with him at once. They met in Harris' office—an historic meeting in theater annals, marked by Mr. Kaufman's extreme lassitude (wearily lifting one finger in greeting and uttering a barely audible, "Hi") and Mr. Hart's dewy-eyed hero worship.

Earlier in the same year, Moss Hart had written a musical with Dorothy Heyward, *Jonica,* which had been produced in the spring to fairly good notices. They had worked hard, but he was used to that. However, neither that experience, nor all his rigorous training in the borsht circuit had prepared him for the gruelling sessions that began the next day on the top floor of Mr. Kaufman's brownstone in the East Sixties. Here the two playwrights, congenial intellectually, but entirely opposite emotionally, temperamentally, slaved for several months, rewriting the script. They started at ten in the morning and worked straight through until two or three the next morning—or until they were about to drop from exhaustion. Moreover, Mr. Kaufman seemed oblivious to bodily needs for food, while young Mr. Hart had a lusty appetite, and found the fifteen-minute break for tiny tea sandwiches (and perhaps a piece of chocolate cake) in the middle of the afternoon so insufficient that he would leave for home weak from hunger as well as work.

Kaufman was methodical, even in his eccentricities. He would always scrub his hands in the little washroom off the study before starting the day's stint. (He liked to do four pages a session, but would sometimes spend a whole morning on a single line or a proper exit.) When concentrating, he stared hard at the floor, as if searching for the right words, and if he bent to pick up small pieces of lint, he would usually come up with a good line for the play as well. If he stretched out on the floor or paced the room, it meant trouble—or, as Hart later learned, he was trying to avoid the smoke from the younger man's cigar (which he could hardly bear, but never complained about). He liked to proceed according to plan, and usually did so; but if

there were delays, writing "humps" that took time, he was patient, good-natured, reassuring.

Moss Hart, on the other hand, was buoyant, enthusiastic, bursting out with rapid-fire ideas as he puffed away on the long black cigars he had taken to smoking during his directorship days. While *Once in a Lifetime* was in process of revision, the cigar-smoking was his sole outlet, for he was too terrified of the Great Collaborator to move from the overstuffed chair that Mr. Kaufman indicated the first day. Hart fondly recalled the whole period as "The Days of the Terror." Later on, when he felt at ease with Kaufman, and they had a roomy work place in the country, he would roam around while thinking out a situation, and seemed to click more rapidly if he had a few distractions. He was fond of hot dogs and other indigestibles that set Mr. Kaufman's pompadour even further on end (possibly the taste for Indian nuts that George indulges all during *Once in a Lifetime* could be traced to Mr. Hart); and he would wax wildly enthusiastic over a gourmet dinner, while Kaufman regarded meals as an interruption.

Eventually the first draft was finished, followed by a slight respite until rehearsals began, and then the treadmill pace resumed. The lines did not "play" as intended when they were typed; most of the scenes required some rewriting, and as rehearsals progressed, it became routine for the two playwrights to sit up half the night revising, and "to appear at rehearsals fresh and bright at ten o'clock the next morning." Kaufman himself took on the role of Lawrence Vail, the forlorn, forgotten playwright of the comedy—the only time he attempted to act in one of his plays. The initial performance of the tryout in Atlantic City elicited a terse message from the producer: "It needs work, boys"—as if they had been idling before!

But by the end of the second tryout at Brighton Beach, both of them knew Sam Harris was right. Drastic cutting and revision was necessary if their brainchild was to survive the final tryout in Philadelphia. Their working sessions (which had always been rugged) now seemed to Moss Hart like the confines of a concentration camp, "and an eraser took on all the semblance of a rubber truncheon." In contrast, Mr. Kaufman came to life as never before, and now seemed able to exist entirely without food. In spite of all their efforts, however, the script still ran way too long on opening night in Philadelphia. The collaborators went into hiding in their hotel room (except for the hours that Kaufman had to be onstage) and for six solid days worked around the clock to perform the herculean task of final revision before the New York opening. During one of their sessions toward the end, Moss Hart insisted on a break for fresh air. As they strolled by a little public park, they spotted a children's carrousel, and, to Hart's surprise, Kaufman made for it as eagerly as he. For half an hour they 'swung madly around' like a pair of truant schoolboys. Then they returned calmly to work, with an added feeling of comradeship. From the moment of that pre-dawn spree they were friends as well as collaborators.

Once in a Lifetime proved to be a hilarious satire on the movie industry, shown in the throes of adjustment to the "talkies." On opening night, September 24, 1930, at the Music Box Theater, the play and its authors received a standing ovation, which George S. Kaufman acknowledged with the briefest, most generous of curtain speeches. "I just want to say," he confided to the audience, "that this play is eighty per cent Moss Hart." The night before, as the final dress rehearsal was about to begin, he had smiled reassuringly at Hart, who for three days had a nervous stomach (and in fact usually spent opening night in the men's room). "Don't worry too much," he had comforted the younger playwright. "It's been swell anyway. And let's do another one."

Although they "married and had several beautiful children," as Mr. Hart put it, an interval of four years elapsed before the second one came along. During those years, the no longer impoverished Mr. Hart spent money as fast as it poured into his pockets. He transferred his whole family from their house in Sheepshead Bay (where they had moved some years before) to a hotel suite in Manhattan, leaving all their household possessions behind them, like unhappy memories. He bought a farm in Bucks County (on which he planted thirty-five hundred trees) as a retreat for both work and relaxation. Kaufman purchased an adjoining farm; and, when not writing, the two became "Broadway agriculturalists." The plot of their next play, **Merrily We Roll Along,** concerned a young playwright who leaps into fame with his first offering, and, while it is principally a character study in relation to moral values, there are certain surface resemblances to Hart's life: the sudden, stunning success after years of struggle; the thrill and glamor of moving in celebrity circles, hobnobbing with people in the theater who had been mere names before; the new sensation of having plenty of money, and plush surroundings in place of pinched pennies and patchy apartments. The title is ironic, for there is nothing "merrily" done except some of the bright chatter in the play, which is more of a melodrama than anything the two collaborators ever wrote together. Its experimental structure, with the scenes moving backward chronologically, in rapid succession (not to be confused with the backflash narrative) is diffusive and highly unsatisfying, because it never makes the connection between past and present. Nevertheless, the subject matter lent itself to clever Kaufman commentary on the theater, and there were enough admirers to give the play a fair-sized run.

Getting back into character, Kaufman and Hart followed the venture into serious drama with their most successful, laugh-evoking, and most human comedy, **You Can't Take It with You.** Produced in December of 1936, this delicious, captivating piece of playwriting depicted a family whose delightful idiosyncrasies and wise sense of values quickly won the hearts of American audiences. Awarded the Pulitzer prize for 1936-1937, the play, after a long Broadway engagement, became a classic of its kind, produced over and over again in theaters throughout the country; and its timeless quality was irrevocably proven when it was revived nearly thirty years later, in December of 1965, to the equal delight and unrestrained laughter of

jaded audiences. The family of Grandpa Martin Vanderhof, who, with him have been doing just what they like to do ever since he decided not to go to his office one morning, plus an odd assortment of people who came to the household and stayed, mark a high point in character creation for the Kaufman-Hart combine. Grandpa's married daughter, Penny Sycamore, for example, at rise of curtain, "is doing what she likes more than anything else in the world. She is writing a play—her eleventh." In Penny (whose flightiness is reminiscent of Kaufman's earlier Dulcy, minus the latter's irritating qualities, and with a charm all her own) the authors evidently enjoyed themselves immensely. She is a gentle spoof at playwriting, and a joyous one. The primary fact that she began writing plays—and left off painting—because a typewriter was delivered to the house by mistake, is hilarious enough; but when the audience is witness to her professional dilemma, as she switches her heroine from El Morocco to a monastery, asks everyone's advice on how to get her out after six years, and gets the following reaction from Rheba, the family factotum, "Six years? My, I bet she busts that monastery wide open.", the effect is side-splitting.

Penny's husband, Paul, makes firecrackers with Mr. De-Pinna, a former milkman, who came one delivery day and just stayed on. Her older daughter, Essie, loves to take ballet and make candy; her husband loves to play the xylophone, and operate a hand-press. Grandpa himself enjoys going to commencement exercises and the zoo—with equal pleasure. All, like Grandpa, do not believe in taxes, or in making more money than needed to live on (hence, the title). Even the younger daughter, Alice, although she does not share the philosophy of the others,—she has a job and seems to prefer a greater degree of social conformity—can appreciate their attitude, and regards them tenderly. It is undoubtedly Penny, however, who represents the authors' objective point of view and perhaps wishful thinking in regard to their profession. As she goes through her stack of manuscripts, murmuring the subject matter—"labor play . . . religious play . . . sex play . . ." (a riotous pun)—one has the feeling that both Kaufman and Hart might have longed to write plays for the sheer pleasure of it.

In reality, however, the outlook was more like Kaufman than Hart, who made the most of the monetary rewards of the theater; he took great delight in spending money—buying presents for friends, traveling, and entertaining. Kaufman was reserved, retiring, almost provincial in his preference for Manhattan; he rarely took trips. Yet both men hated the harassment of opening nights, and the petty quarrels of their world. Both were active in the Dramatists' Guild, which Kaufman had helped to build into an effective organization to combat contract abuses beginning in 1925, when a handful of playwrights had bound themselves to make the Guild more than a mere name.

It is interesting to note that, with the possible exception of **The American Way** (1939), all of the Kaufman-Hart plays brought in some aspect of the theater, in varying degrees.

Yet they never resorted to the "backstage story" so popular in the thirties; and fondness for the theater outweighs their criticism of it. As a matter of fact, the hero of **The Fabulous Invalid,** their next offering, was the theater itself—always dying, always being revived.

By this time the two had evolved a comfortable course of collaboration. If one or the other conceived an idea for a possible play, they would toss it around at random, sometimes for months, until it had enough substance to warrant a daily work schedule, free from interruption. With the exception of **Once in a Lifetime,** most of their playwriting was done in the country, where there was room enough for both to stretch out—or pace—as they chose. They continued to talk over an idea for several weeks before the typewriting stage began. (When it came to the actual typing, Moss Hart, now on an easy, first-name basis with his collaborator, was willing to "let George do it," while he roamed around, giving vent to pent-up energy, and making sure his cigar smoke did not offend his writing partner. They usually tried to produce four pages a day and often did; but just as often they fell short of the mark, trying to perfect a single speech or line. As much attention was given to stage directions and character descriptions as to dialogue. One of the things that makes **You Can't Take It with You** delightful reading is the ironic commenatry running through it. For example, following the description of Penny as, "A round little woman in her early fifties, comfortable, gentle, homey," comes the authors' aside: "One would not suspect that under that placid exterior there surges the Divine Urge—but it does, it does."

The first draft of a script was usually overwritten, on the theory that it was easier to cut than to pad, a premise on which most writers agree. The time it took to complete a script varied from as brief a period as five weeks, for **You Can't Take It with You,** all the way up to six months for **The Man Who Came to Dinner,** their third big hit. (In between two of their plays, these prolific collaborators turned out the book for the musical **I'd Rather Be Right,** and they worked separately on other projects—George S. Kaufman with Edna Ferber, in writing **Dinner at Eight,** and **Stage Door**; and Moss Hart in furnishing the book for musicals with Irving Berlin, *Face the Music,* and *As Thousands Cheer*; and with Cole Porter on *Jubilee,* after they had journeyed around the world together.) George worked better under a deadline, a hangover from his journalism days, and liked to set his own by having the theater rented, and the opening date set for the première before he started to write. Moss preferred more leeway, so they usually compromised by setting the dates when the primary "blocking out" of the acts was completed. **The Man Who Came to Dinner** written with the whirlwind personality of Alexander Woollcott, their colleague and crony, in mind, mushroomed as they went along, inventing scenes and surprises that were only a mild exaggeration of some they had witnessed in real life in which the fabulous Mr. Woollcott figured as the rascally, obstreperous protagonist. The dedication of the published work read,

"To Alexander Woollcott, *For reasons that are nobody's business.* The Authors."

In this spirit, the portrait of Sheridan ("Sherry") Whiteside was drawn, and superbly enacted by Monty Woolly. It was shown before thousands of appreciative playgoers (and, later, movie fans) from its opening night, October 16, 1939, for an extended run. Like **You Can't Take It with You,** this play has also been popular with little theater groups and repertory companies, although it is not as much of a perennial, does not withstand the changes of the times as well.

A year later, in 1940, Kaufman and Hart wrote their final comedy in collaboration, **George Washington Slept Here,** a rather obvious and contrived satire on city dwellers becoming country squires, set, naturally, in Bucks County. The redeeming feature of the play is the glimpse one gets of the inevitable summer theater, including the classic line from the actress, who, when asked what she expects of a summer theater, replies: "Not a great deal . . . I would just like them to take the pigs out before they put the hams *in,* that's all."

After 1940, the team of Kaufman and Hart separated professionally, though it remained steadfast in friendship, and through various business ventures in the theater and out. For one thing, Kaufman found a new collaborator in life as well as playwriting: he was divorced from Beatrice around this time, and married the actress, Leueen McGrath, with whom he subsequently wrote a number of plays, mostly comedy. Moss Hart, reaching out for more profound expression, underwent psychotherapy, and wrote *Lady in the Dark,* a play with co-ordinated music by Cole Porter, dealing with the effects of psychoanalytic treatment. As played by Gertrude Lawrence, the subject was distinctively, artistically handled, and made Moss Hart a name in his own right. In 1946, he was married to Kitty Carlisle, a happy combination; the ceremony was performed August tenth, in New Hope, Pennsylvania, close to the Kaufman-Hart farms. Two children—a son, Chris, and a daughter, Cathy Carlisle—were born in the next few years. Mr. Hart was notably happy in his matrimonial venture, yet his next play, *Christopher Blake,* dealt with the effect of divorce on a small boy. He seems to have had the desire to develop the serious side of his effervescent nature, but his reach exceeded his grasp. He was more successful in the lively and diverting first volume of his autobiography, *Act One,* of which he said that George S. Kaufman was the hero. (Kaufman, for his part, when asked how the collaboration started, replied, "I very quickly knew, when I met Moss, on which side my bread was buttered.")

Both men were interested in directing and producing in later years, although Kaufman wrote plays well into the fifties, with his wife, and others. Both died of heart attacks in the same year, 1961, six months apart. (The second and third "Acts" of Moss Hart's memoirs were never written.) But the Kaufman-Hart canon of comedy lives on, a laughing, sunny presentation of the American scene.

A. Cleveland Harrison (essay date August 1972)

SOURCE: Harrison, A. Cleveland. "Of Thee I Sing, Baby!" *Players: Magazine of American Theatre* 47, no. 6 (August 1972): 275-79.

[*In the following essay, Harrison argues that there are many similarities between* Of Thee I Sing *and the comedies of Aristophanes.*]

Presidents come and Presidents go, but *Of Thee I Sing* goes on forever, baby! A musical satire about the making of the President, the product of two playmakers collaborating with two music-making brothers, *Of Thee I Sing* remains forty years after its opening the touchstone for musical satire on federal government and the national election process. The approaching Presidential election once again calls it to mind and once again questions arise about the sources of its resurgent power. I want to suggest that George S. Kaufman and his collaborators were artistic descendants of Aristophanes, that *Of Thee I Sing* was a re-emergence of Old Comedy in the New World, and that the play's vitality issues from its Aristophanic parallels in function, form, and substance.

Although serious American drama of social criticism in the 1930's was usually somber in tone, with playwrights like Elmer Rice and John Howard Lawson convinced that social criticism was the primary function of the theater, there were many efforts in the period toward satire of a kind seldom attempted before or since. During the Great Depression, satire, whether or not consciously modeled after Aristophanes, came closer to realizing the purposes and exploiting the methods and structure of Greek Old Comedy than in previous periods. George S. Kaufman was in the forefront of the satirists.

In fact, the new point of departure in comedy had begun to reveal itself in American drama as early as 1921, when Kaufman collaborated with Marc Connelly on *Dulcy.* As collaborators they continued to attack typical American institutions in *To the Ladies* and *Merton of the Movies,* both in 1922, and climaxed their joint work by adding fantasy to satire in *Beggar on Horseback* in 1924. By the time Kaufman collaborated with Morrie Ryskind on the book of *Of Thee I Sing* in 1931, he had complete control of the techniques of dramatic satire while Ryskind shaped the book's political tone and mood. Reinforced by George and Ira Gershwin's equally effective words and music, *Of Thee I Sing* opened at the Music Box Theatre on December 26, 1931, and in the midst of the country's deepening financial depression ran 473 performances on Broadway, following that with a successful national tour.[1]

Most critics of the time were quick to note the production's several outstanding attributes, particularly those which appeared to advance the musical comedy genre. Many agreed with Richard Dana Skinner, who said it had a "sense of Rabelaisian fun which far outstrips anything of the kind previously attempted on a musical comedy stage."[2]

Although the playwrights started with musical comedy, Francis Fergusson detected an effort to "create effects that the musical comedy in this country has never achieved."[3] In their accomplishment, Gilbert Gabriel surmised that Kaufman, Ryskind, and the Gershwins were in danger of "having perpetrated a classic."[4]

Critical allusions to the Gilbert and Sullivan values in the play abound. Other comments stress that although the whole performance was the broadest, most merciless satire imaginable upon American politics, the play was remarkable for the curious way that "the ridicule is friendly." But the *New Republic* reviews found the play weakened by these contradictory qualities, suggesting that the Gilbert and Sullivan humor was out of character with the burleycue traditions of American musicals and that the satire was "padded with 32-ounce gloves."[5] However, two months later, both Stark Young and Richard Dana Skinner, approving the Pulitzer Prize Committee's award to *Of Thee I Sing,* noted an increasing Aristophanic blend in musical comedy and acknowledged that "the mere fact of having a musical accompaniment does not prevent a musical review from being a first-class satirical play."[6] Moreover, two years after its premiere, Montrose Moses could pronounce with clearer perspective and greater assurance that *Of Thee I Sing* was "certainly the best satiric extravaganza of its kind ever written."[7] Neither newspaper reviewers nor magazine critics went beyond a simple acknowledgement of the play's Aristophanic antecedents. Nor, of course, were all critics convinced of the high quality of Kaufman and Ryskind's work, and it may well be in the context of their severest critic, Joseph Wood Krutch, that some essential background to understanding the satirist's aims and methods may be established before taking a detailed look at the play itself.

In *The American Drama since 1918,* Joseph Wood Krutch insists that the wisecrack illustrates Kaufman's "most conspicuous, most persistent, and apparently most cherished weakness, his willingness to subdue himself to the stuff he works in, to write plays of Broadway as well as about Broadway, to let the least worthy of the drama's patrons establish its laws."[8] Such an appraisal is too severe on Kaufman, but it provides a forceful reminder of the occupational hazards of the satirist and of the critic's special difficulty in judging the worth of satirical works:

> In democratic countries [the satirist] attacks individuals only at the risk of grave financial loss to himself . . . in totalitarian countries the satirist risks death.[9]

The very ephemeral contemporary context of the social-political scene, which the effective satirist makes his own province and the mastery of which determines his success, is the strength of the artist and weakness of the critic. The artist cannot succeed with satire unless it points to a territory familiar to his audience; the critic cannot judge with an assurance the writer's position as a literary figure because the meaning of much he says is lost as conditions change and the circumstances and men who produce them are lost to memory.

So Kaufman's enduring accomplishment in *Of Thee I Sing* is even more remarkable in light of the rapid shifting of economic and political patterns in our society during the 1920's and 30's. Furthermore, in the theater the effect of satire is far more tenuous than it is in literature because everything in the theater depends upon the immediacy of response from a heterogeneous and volatile audience. Satire, to work in the theater, must make instantaneous sense to those whom Krutch condescendingly speaks of as "the least worthy of the drama's patrons."

The wisecrack is Kaufman's surpassing satirical technique, yet it is the focal point of Krutch's criticism of Kaufman as a playwright, revealing that the critic had a limited understanding of the objectives and materials of satire. The wisecrack, with its momentary currency, is so suspect to Krutch that he doubts it can have a serious function: "It may imply, perhaps, a philosophy in solution but it does not necessarily imply a consistently formulated attitude and it is quite compatible with a complete inability to expand any further the criticism which it suggests."[10] There are a number of vital truths about theatrical satire missed in such a critical attitude. First, the basic strategy of the wisecrack is to keep the audience with you, a fundamental condition if people are not to get up and walk out of the theater. Second, there is no necessity for the satirist to formulate a complete philosophy in a single play. From Aristophanes on, it has been increasingly difficult to know exactly what satirists are *for*. But on the other hand, the burden of proof has never really rested with the critic of society so much as with society itself. Third, the wisecrack functions as a synechdoche (a part is used for the whole) so that the rapidfire potshot is capable of indefinite extension in the auditor's mind and so may expand into an attack on the whole structure—people, events, and issues that produce the satirist's comments—of which the subject of the wisecrack is only a part.

Another of Krutch's major criticisms refers to the structure of *Of Thee I Sing*. Mr. Krutch says that shrewd flights of wit and touches of character are not enough to make a play. "It has to be held together by a plot and the plot must tend somewhere."[11] L. P. Potts speaks of such a demand placed upon comedies as *un*critical, since it is "based on an unscientific application to comedy of Aristotle's theory of tragic drama," demanding a logical sequence of cause and effect in the events from beginning to end. This is not the effect at which comedy is aiming. "For in comedy we must feel that man is free, not fated; if anything goes wrong with him, the remedy is in his own hands . . . A comedy may even fail in its effect simply because the author has taken pains to make the plot conform strictly to the law of cause and effect. The pattern we want in comedy is of a different kind; a grouping of characters rather than a march of events."[12]

It is this very pattern which Mr. Krutch has failed to detect in the similarity between Kauffman's plot design and those of Aristophanes. There is very little plot in the ordinary sense of the word in Aristophanes' plays; the episodes have a structure evolving out of episodes that furnish occasions for witty and satiric thrusts. The same structure characterizes the work of Kaufman. In fact, any clear understanding of the artistic accomplishments of Kaufman in *Of Thee I Sing* can best be realized through an examination of all those general characteristics it shares with Greek Old Comedy.

The play's structure is reminiscent of the Aristophanic in several distinct ways. Like Old Comedy, which fused the functions of poetry, dance and drama into one artistic whole, Kaufman and Ryskind, from the beginning, planned *Of Thee I Sing* to make all parts—music, humor, lyrics, chorus routines, production numbers—basic to the plot.[13] Their plot, on the surface, appears to link situations in a loose revue-like sequence, but closer analysis reveals the scenes are carefully related like matched beads on a string, each a logical accompaniment of the one preceding it without necessarily relying upon a cause-effect linkage. The Aristophanic single plot joins the episodes of the Presidential campaign story, not by a cause-effect sequence leading to an inevitable conclusion, but by related events which, while not necessarily producing one another, at least develop and conclude one aspect of the central topic appropriately.

The various locales utilized illustrate the plot design's simplicity. The scenes may be logically expected in a Presidential campaign: a convention hall in a large city, a room in a shabby hotel, the boardwalk at Atlantic City, a rally at Madison Square Garden, the Capitol steps at Washington, D.C., several White House rooms, and the carridors and chamber of the U.S. Senate.

In a similar fashion, given the party's choice of "love" as the central campaign issue, commonplace episodes of the musical comedy fall into place, developing the logical extremes to which the Aristophanic "happy idea" (love in politics) will lead. The domestication of the political candidate through love and marriage operates like a stichomythic strand upon which all the scenes are strung. A bachelor candidate will win votes from marrieds and singles alike if he has a prospective bride. He also needs publicity to succeed. These necessities are joined in a beauty contest that simultaneously furnishes the candidate an attractive fiancee along with free campaign advertising. Any red-blooded American political candidate, however, would want to choose his own bride. He refuses therefore to marry the winner of the beauty contest and selects for himself a practical rather than romantic type. The scorned beauty contest winner, her womanly fury aroused, vows revenge. Thus, the design of the play by relevant, though not inevitable connections, evolves through the most domestic of denouements, the birth of Presidential twins.

Such a single plot is ideally adapted to the expression of satiric ideas because it is allegorically significant, inherently dramatic, and potentially comic.[14] Like Aristophanes 2500 years before, Kaufman and Ryskind translate the clash of ideas into a conflict of allegorical and stereotyped characters. *Of Thee I Sing* in effect dramatizes the "ideal of democracy," as represented by the consent of the people, *versus* the "reality of democracy," as practiced through political parties. Consistent with satiristic practice beginning with Aristophanes, the writers leave the audience to deduce their ideal from the way in which the clash and contrast of political abnormalities are depicted.

The allegorical action (the visible presentation of invisible ideas), a distinctive part of Old Comedy,[15] ranges from the family-home-true-love metaphor of Mary Turner's corn muffins to the pure Aristophanic wrestlers at Madison Square Garden. Two grunting behemoths perform a choreography of wrestling holds as an accompaniment to Senator Jones' convention speech: "Gaze into the future, my friends, and what do you see?" The "rear elevation" of Vidovtich and Yussevitch. "Not for us the entangling alliances of Europe, not for us the allying entanglances of Asia."[16] At this point, the wrestlers have a complicated doubled scissors hold on each other. Throttlebottom's physical retreat and ineffective body behavior throughout the play similarly epitomize what was then the almost-forgotten office of the Vice-President.

Episodes dramatizing the political and social conflict of the country also have the basic ingredients of Old Comedy—the strife, decision, and consequences of the *agon* or debate. When President Wintergreen refuses orders to divorce his wife in order to marry beauty-contest winner Diana Devereaux, strife with France is threatened. The Senators angrily decide to impeach the President. The subsequent trial is interrupted by the fortuitous appearance of the President's wife who announces she is expecting a baby. The domestic announcement stops the impeachment but leads to international repercussions when France demands the baby as reparations. The other episodes of the plot follow a similar straight-line development, evoking complications without presenting much circumstantial meshing of events or of character entanglements.

Finally, as far as plot structure is concerned, the crisis, like that of an Aristophanic comedy, does not produce a traditional reversal of fortune or a recognition.[17] At the President's impeachment trial, Mary's pregnancy, which she refers to as her "husband's delicate condition," interrupts the proceedings and inspires the tumultuous song, "Prosperity is Just Around the Corner!" Her announcement momentarily revives but does not reverse the fortune of the expectant father. Throttlebottom's subsequent discovery of his obligation to perform the unfulfilled duties of the President (by marrying Miss Devereaux) cannot be called a recognition scene without stretching technical meanings to the utmost.

The Aristophanic single plot of *Of Thee I Sing* proves singularly useful in combining the motley crew of characters who express and satirize ideas.[18] Frances V. Gilhooley and Louis Lippman, the party committeemen, are allegorical representatives of Irish and Jewish power. The types are allegorical because they represent a class of people rather than a single person. Fulton, a thinlydisguised William Raldolph Hearst, owner of a newspaper empire, stands for the power of the press. In each instance, the family name indicates not only social class but certain qualities within each class as well. Mr. Lippman, to use the slang, gives everyone a lot of "lip"; a bit of "hooligan" is Gilhooley; and Benedict Arnold Fulton unmistakably alludes to both William Randolph Hearst and the U.S.'s earliest infamous Anglophile. The characters' motives exemplify their natures: boozing, babes, bribery, and bunkum, all in the cause of party power. In addition, although the party types are all closely allied in ideas, their personalities are carefully differentiated. Senators Lyons and Jones, for example, who are from the South and West respectively, each has his regional dialect to represent prejudices and pork-barrel motives.

The central characters, (Wintergreen, Mary Turner, and Throttlebottom), on the other hand, are presented as lively and full-blooded, though not fully rounded, human beings with some traits of individuality. Wintergreen is an exuberant common-man American "on the make"—boastful, paradoxically sanguine and cynical, but a sucker for wholesome girls and home cooking. Healthy Mary Turner is the girl next door with clear complexion, clear conscience, and clear wit who sees her way "clear" to the heart of first Wintergreen and then the country. While John and Mary do not command the degree of identification common to lovers in romantic comedy, they do generate enough warm reality to contrast markedly with most of the other characters.

But Alexander Throttlebottom seems to be the character who would gain the strongest audience sympathy. Perhaps the source of empathy in 1931 was that every one in the audience "felt himself something of a Throttlebottom—confused, lost and uncertain."[19] Even today Throttlebottom appears as an average citizen, trying to do his best, though it may be inadequate, in a country that wants to hear from him only when he can be of use. The other recurrent figure of the musical, Diana Devereaux, in contrast to Mary, is the proverbial conniving female masquerading under the soft, magnolia exterior of the southern *femme fatal*. The minx wants her way; and her behavior and speech leave little doubt she will get it, whomever she must lie to or with.

The minor characters are little more than types.[20] The chambermaid (Act I, Scene 2) only furnishes the love-and-marriage idea which generates the happy idea of the plot and then she disappears. While she is in the hotel room, though, her question—"Can I turn the bed down now?"—becomes a brief refrain, perhaps symbolically underscoring the old saw that "politics make strange bedfellows." The character is more mechanical than memorable. Unforgetable Diana Devereaux, in contrast, functions throughout to keep the action complicated long after the election is won and Mary and John are married. The Wintergreens' private secretaries, Miss Benson and Sam Jenkins, and the Senate Clerk are realistic and serve no other symbolic purpose. The White House guide and sightseers merely keep the plot moving by informing Throttlebottom of his Vice Presidential duties at the opportune moment in the plot's resolution. Furthermore, the abundance of public officials is purely Aristophanic—party delegates, senators, congressmen, diplomats, Army and Navy attaches, cabinet members, Supreme Court Justices, and ambassadors.[21] These and characters such as photographers, drink and hot-dog vendors, policemen, French soldiers and dozens of secretaries only lend an air of verisimilitude and contribute to a "more the merrier" atmosphere.

Unlike Aristophanes' plays, there is little historicity to prominent characters in *Of Thee I Sing*.[22] Faint resemblances to real persons just whet speculation without serving a parodic feast. Lippman's comment that John P. Wintergreen "even *sounds* like a President," may have reminded a few of the 1931 audience of a similar remark about Warren G. Harding, "Gee, but he'd make a good-looking President."[23] William Gaxton, who originally portrayed Wintergreen, reportedly made the role a takeoff on New York's Mayor James J. Walker.[24] In the main, however, characters in the drama bore only allusive resemblances to known personalities. What Kaufman and Ryskind do exploit for satirical purposes is the entire spectrum of Aristophanic character types and their functions.

Plot and character in *Of Thee I Sing,* then, are the visible personification of national attitudes about the U.S. body politic. Obviously, Kaufman and Ryskind want to amuse with a purpose. To do so, they make character and incident serve the principle of judicious comment on many sacred American traditions. In *Of Thee I Sing* they explore the U.S. political maze: the ludicrous, vacuous campaign slogans that politicians create and that people expect and/or accept; the cynical politicos behind the scenes who select the candidates by caprice, the impertinent and irrelevant kinds of reorientation that men undergo to prepare for the Presidency; the dangerous and demeaning practice of voters and politicians ignoring the Vice Presidency; the conniving to win at any cost that obscures significant issues in campaigns; the pie-in-the-sky promises and other appeals to emotion by standard shibboleths of God, mother, and country; and the tenuous nature of American foreign relations which sometimes evolve into absurd connections between them and our own domestic affairs.

Glancing but telling blows are delivered to the social midsection as well. The beauty contest scene pictures the backstage maneuvering that precedes it and the odd amalgam of irrelevant circumstances that determines the winner, the least of these being beauty. Jabs at newspapers are made repeatedly, emphasizing how they slight news to build circulation by an emphasis on cheesecake instead. But on the backstroke of the same punch, Kaufman and Ryskind hit the willingness of politicians (condoned by public apathy) to corrupt marriage and children for cheap publicity and meaningless glory. In Act Two, Scene One, the roll call of issues reviewed is long and varied: disarma-

ment, Latin America, the Southern race issue, dispossessed royalty, international debts, horseracing, farm problems, air flight, and political patronage.

Besides the allegorical actions and characters with which they attack American politics, the authors frequently scatter wisecracks about any reasonably relevant topic. Furthermore, in the tradition of Greek Old Comedy, the language texture of the play throughout delights with words which are poetic, dramatic, and comic. A dozen songs for individual characters and choruses are intrinsic parts of the plot. With dramatic relevance the bathing suit contestants sing of their aspiration: "The prize is consequential— / Presidential!" "Of Thee I Sing," the campaign love song, with the flip addition of "baby" to the phrase, joins the sacred and profane, exemplifying the very focus of the play's satirical attack. The marvelous pun of "Posterity is just around the corner," in one line snapped at the whole Hoover "boom."

Long before it was a customary convention in musicals, the Gershwins, within multi-versed choral songs, varied tone and topic with the character of the singer. In the song of thanks giving on the approaching birth of a presidential baby, Lippman, as Secretary of Agriculture, sings to the tune of "The Farmer's in the Dell"; Gilhooley, as Secretary of the Navy, sings of water, anchors, and sails; Senator Jones, from the West, refers to the cowboys on the prairie. Wintergreen too sings his inaugural address in his own idiom. The French soldiers who accompany their ambassador sing a parody of their language composed of names ("Lafayette" and "Maurice Chevalier") and phrases ("Chevrolet coupe" and "crepes suzette") familiar to Americans.

The range of verbal ingenuity of *Of Thee I Sing* extends from puns to parody. In between, Kaufman and Ryskind thrust at unpopular topics like France's debt to the United States: "What's the worst she can do? Sue us for what she owes us?" Wintergreen offers ribaldly to halt France's declining birthrate by making his own contribution through a personal tour of France. Fulton says it will be wonderful to have a baby in the White House, for "there's something about the patter of baby feet, trickling down the stairs . . ." Colloquialisms and slang are part of the total language fabric throughout the play.

The music which George Gershwin provided was just as varied and appropriate as his brother Ira's lyrics. The melodies and recitatives poke fun at grand opera in the stuffy Senate proceedings and at Viennese-waltz sentimentality in the song of Mary's imminent motherhood. "Wintergreen for President" is filled with quotations from Irish and Jewish tunes, from familiars like "Hail, Hail, the Gang's All Here," and "A Hot Time in the Old Town Tonight." "Gershwin never faltered in trying to find the exact musical equivalent for every shade and nuance of wit, humor, and malice of his text and lyrics."[25]

Judging from explicit and implicit stage directions (the former unmistakably by the wisecracking Kaufman), the spectacle integrates, punctuates, and illustrates the play's every satirical thrust. Opening the play, the noisy marchers with torchlights and campaign banners, "Vote for Prosperity and See What You Get," set the key for the irreverent tone to follow. Scenes skillfully alternate between large crowds and small groups, noise and quiet, rooms and auditoriums. Tense moments lead to an explanatory song climaxed by a jouous dance. From the fleshy costumes of the bathing beauties and wrestlers to the splendor of braided uniforms; from the ceremonial black of the Supreme Court justices to the morning suits of senators with Dundrearies, all are extravagantly clothed.

Election results (Act I, Scene 5), are scenery, a screen, on which photographs of the candidates, America's past heroes, and national monuments punctuate the returns, baseball and bridge scores, and sale prices at Macy's Basement. Portraits of George and Martha Washington look down benignly upon the Wintergreens in their "his and her" Presidential office. Mrs. Wintergreen's final appearance (wheeled into the yellow room in "a great canopied bed, hung with gold and silver, and baldheaded eagles," in the midst of assembled guests and white-wigged flunkies), provides a gigantic exclamation mark to the whole play. The pomp of the inaugural ceremonies at the Capitol when the Justices count off like soldiers is a fitting match to the swing-and-sway roll call of the Senators. Nowhere does the drama suceed more completely than in the harmony of its specatcle with its other dramatic values.

A given work is not a replica of the type it represents. *Of Thee I Sing* is no exception; but its characteristics, in significant respects, are clearly Aristophanic. It set a pattern and precedent for a recurrent line of musicals which unfortunately did not follow. Such astringent satire, brought up to date, would be a healthy sign in our theater today. *MacBird* and *Red, White, and Maddox* notwithstanding, *Of Thee I Sing* still awaits a fully worthy successor.

Notes

1. Morgan Y. Himelstein, *Drama Was a Weapon* (New Brunswick, 1963) p. 185.

2. Richard Dana Skinner, "Of Thee I Sing," *Commonweal,* January 13, 1932, p. 302.

3. Francis Fergusson, "Comedies, Satirical and Sweet," *The Bookman,* January-February, pp. 561-562.

4. Gilbert Gabriel, New York *American,* December, 1931; quoted in Bernard Hewitt, *Theatre USA* (New York, 1959), pp. 385-386.

5. M. C., "Burleycue and Whimsey," *New Republic,* January 13, 1932, p. 243.

6. Stark Young, "Town Notes," *New Republic,* March 9, 1932, p. 97.

    Richard Dana Skinner, "The Pulitzer Prize," *Commonweal,* May 18, 1932, p. 77.

7. Montrose Moses, "George S. Kaufman: A Satirist in the American Theatre," *North American Review,* CCXXXVII (January, 1934), p. 76.

8. Joseph Wood Krutch, *The American Drama since 1918* New York, rev. 1957), p. 148.

9. R. C. Elliott, "The Satirist and Society," quoted in Robert W. Corrigan (ed.), *Comedy: Meaning and Form* (San Francisco, 1965, p. 332.

10. Krutch, p. 149.

11. Krutch, pp. 148-149.

12. Potts, p. 209.

13. David Ewen, *The Story of America's Musical Theatre* (New York, 1961), p. 143.

14. Katherine Lever, *The Art of Greek Comedy* (London, 1956), p. 120.

15. Lever, p. 123.

16. All lines are from the version of *Of Thee I Sing* in William H. Hildreth and Wilson R. Dumble, *Five Contemporary American Plays* (New York, 1939), pp. 310-394.

17. Lever, p. 120.

18. *Ibid.*

19. Caspar H. Nannes, *Politics in the American Drama As Revealed by Plays Produced on the New York Stage, 1890-1945* (Philadelphia, 1950), p. 83.

20. Lever, p. 114.

21. Lever, p. 115.

22. Lever, pp. 115-117.

23. Nannes, p. 84n.

24. Nannes, p. 85.

25. Ewen, p. 144.

Wilfrid Sheed (essay date 1978)

SOURCE: Sheed, Wilfrid. "The Wit of George S. Kaufman and Dorothy Parker." In *The Good Word and Other Words,* pp. 159-63. New York: Dutton, 1978.

[*In the following discussion, Sheed argues that the wit of Kaufman and Parker should not be thought of as a compensation for or expression of a psychoneurosis, but that as writers they deliberately created recognizable and marketable brands of wit.*]

The lives of the wits make grim reading these days. To judge from John Keats's *You Might as Well Live,* Dorothy Parker had a wretched loveless childhood, got her own back at the world with some fine wisecracks, and came to a miserable end. According to Howard Teichmann's *George S. Kaufman,* little George was coddled and frightened into helplessness, learned to fight back with some splendid wisecracks, and came to a pitiable end.

Both stories may be true for all I know. The odds on any intelligent person having an unhappy childhood are better than fair, and the odds on a sad ending are practically off the board. However, there are a couple of things that bother.

First of all, there is the sheer ease and speed with which these conclusions are reached. Teichmann needs only a few pages to wrap up the Kaufman case. George's guilt over an older brother's death, his lifelong fear of sickness, his inability to play baseball—no wonder he had to be witty. It's all a bit like one of those magic insights in a 1940s' Hollywood psychodrama which show mother drinking, father killing himself, and baby screaming, all in one flashback. That this brand of glib psychologizing passes for biography nowadays is ominous. This sort of thing may be good enough for analyzing Richard Nixon, but surely minor playwrights deserve better.

Keats is not much profounder about baby Parker. His account of her early childhood is largely based on her own recollections given in interviews during her last bitter years. Mrs. Parker was notoriously hard on people who had left the room; and since parents and teachers came comfortably into this category, they got their lumps. But of the kind of adversary proceeding from which biographic truth emerges, Keats offers practically none.

In each case, the author uses only such material as points to a childhood wound. The possibility that Dorothy was a holy terror from the womb who drove her wicked stepmother crazy with her feline cleverness is not explored. Or that anyone who played the great American game of poker as well as George had no need to worry about baseball. (More boys are lousy at baseball than good anyway.) Or that both of them were artists with highly developed persons, and hence unreliable witnesses to their own pasts.

Take Kaufman's helplessness for instance. It seems he couldn't drive, swim, or tie his own shoelaces. But what Teichmann overlooks is that humorous authors have been coming on helpless since at least the days of Addison and Lamb (see Cyril Connolly, *Enemies of Promise*) and were still doing it under Leacock and Benchley. Kaufman was outrageously competitive and you can be sure no one was going to come on more helpless than he, even if it meant being carried from room to room. No doubt he had natural gifts in this direction, but like most successful people he could always be as tough as he needed to be, even to the point of imposing his helplessness on others. Likewise Dorothy's cynicism was at least partly a conscious literary manner—following after Edna St. Vincent Millay "in my own horrible sneakers"—which hardened into a characteristic as life belted her around.

The individualist-psychologizing of the 1940s left out all these questions of fashion and cultural artifice and what other people were doing at the time, and so was particularly at sea with entertainers, who live by those things. Thus we

had those films about Al Jolson's tragic flaw, etc., and now we have these books with the same period flavor, as if wit needs a tragic wound to explain it.

All available evidence suggests that *everyone* was trying to be witty in the twenties, just as everyone was trying to be authentic in the sixties. Each era is bullied by one temperament which seems like the only one to have. So, was the whole nation wounded that year? Probably about as much as England was wounded in the Restoration. Anyway, what created Kaufman and Parker was not primarily their warped temperaments, but the vast public demand for wit; and what distinguished them from a thousand aspiring wise guys was simply their success at providing it. If there was a neurotic component, it was in the success, not the wit—particularly in those wit marathons at the Algonquin with everyone whoring after laughs and press mentions, as much part of the period as six-day bike races and flagpole sitting.

Looking at Kaufman's wisecracks now, one is puzzled by the ones that have survived. By what evolutionary law does such a feeble off-Wilde as "a bad play saved by a bad performance" still find itself in print? Or such a mechanical switcheroo as "forgotten but not gone"? There is more wit in a single essay of Benchley's—or a single essay of Kaufman's. But the fact that it was purred or shot back or murmured by a living person gives a joke more value, even in print. (Thus the Algonquin may have spawned our current talk shows.)

The wit *apparat* of the twenties is more interesting than the individual toilers. The Algonquin wits were like comic-strip characters. Many of their lesser gags were almost interchangeable, but their well-publicized "characters" made them seem different—just as Durante and Hope would make the same material seem different. For a Parker line, you add a "she said gently." For Kaufman, one stresses the pause, the deadpan, the devastated victim.

The entrepreneurs, Franklin P. Adams and Alexander Woolcott and assorted press agents, circulated these images and fixed them forever. It was simply up to the originals to stay in type—a stultifying requirement that may have kept them all from growing as they might have. Mrs. Parker, at least, came to hate her comic-strip self. "But dammit it was the twenties and we had to be smarty." She tried to live another life and to stop being a waxwork in a brightly lit window. She spat venomously on the old Algonquin legend. Having to be Dorothy Parker had damn near ruined her.

Kaufman, on the other hand, seems to have been at some pains not to grow or change at all. Hand after hand of bridge, a contracepted mental activity if ever there was one; joke after joke put together like Erector sets—"a lot of bridge has passed over the water," he murmured gently (or was that the other one?); play after play, worked at compulsively, but showing no deepening of mind or leap of imagination.

For anyone who takes the American theater seriously, it is disheartening to find one of its most influential figures with as little inner life as Teichmann's book reveals in Kaufman. It is true that some excellent writers have barely seemed alive when they weren't working. But somehow the very forms they worked in urged them beyond Kaufman's sophisticated Norman Rockwell view of people and life. Kaufman either could not or would not see beyond the limits of the Broadway hit. The only escape for his obviously superior intelligence was in those wisecracks of his, some of which were indeed wonderful, and in playing cards, which was a much more neurotic evasion than his wit ever was. But these activities seem less a defense against some childhood trauma than against the adult thinking and feeling which could have threatened his Broadway career. In modern American style, his job, not his past, defined him.

He may have known best at that. Mrs. Parker's attempts to be more than a wit ended sadly: a few pretty good short stories, following Hemingway in those self-same sneakers, and some smart, formula verses, at the cost of enough derangement of the senses via booze and wanton melancholy to buckle a Rimbaud. The sick room of a minor artist is a glum place. And Keats's attempt to raise her stature only makes it worse, like the twitter of a near relative. Yet she knew the score about herself ("my verses are no damn good") and where she stood in relation to real artists ("the big boys") and that's more than something. The pity of it is that the Algonquin waxwork lives while the real Dorothy Parker has begun to fade. It isn't even a tale of great tragic waste. Maybe with a purer vocation she could have done a little better: but she tried much harder than she let on, and my guess is she squeezed out all she could.

Kaufman at least was perfect of his kind. "He gave me the walk and the talk," says Groucho, and that should be achievement enough for any man. In fact he was the real Groucho, of which Groucho is the imitation or platonic representation. The sequences Kaufman wrote created Groucho, and the latter has been trying to live up to them ever since. "Ah Emily, I can just see us tonight, you and the moon." Pause. "You wear a necktie." Quoted from loving memory. And much more in this vein, finest American dada, heartless, nonrepresentational, humor for humor's sake.

Unfortunately most Broadway comedies had to be adulterated with this and that—sentiment, human interest, etc., so Kaufman took on a raft of collaborators to help out with these, and with the jokes as well, so we'll never know just how true his comic gift was. We do know that he refused altogether to write love scenes, which suggests, not that he was scared of them but that he took his comic vocation seriously and was not going to adulterate himself so long as he could get Edna Ferber or somebody. The best comedy is always heartless, an alternative to rational emotion, and Kaufman dedicated himself to matching this product personally: again, not as a frightened child, but as a ruthless professional.

Teichmann has, about half the time, written the right kind of book about him, i.e., an old-fashioned collection of theater anecdotes. Those people lived in anecdotes, one couldn't imagine a life in between. The anecdotes still entertain, which is all Kaufman ever contracted to do. The life in between, now that we have it, is the usual mess and hardly worth telling. The mysterious psychic springs of humor are not here, and the rest is soap opera.

Laurence Shyer (essay date spring 1978)

SOURCE: Shyer, Laurence. "American Absurd: Two Nonsense Plays by George S. Kaufman and Morrie Ryskind, and Ring Lardner." *Theater* 9, no. 2 (spring 1978): 118-21.

[*In the following preface, Shyer discusses "nonsense plays" and Kaufman's contribution to the genre.*]

The next few pages . . . are devoted neither to the presentation nor discussion of contemporary plays; rather they look back at another era in the American theater, specifically, at two of its practitioners: George S. Kaufman, who spent a long and phenomenal career on Broadway as playwright, director, producer and drama critic, and Ring Lardner, whose stories and satires recorded the oddities of American life and language during the first few decades of this century. Although both the works presented here were written in the 1920's, we might, with some justification, call them new plays for both are coming before a contemporary audience for the first time—Lardner's *The Gelska Cup* has never been reprinted or collected (in fact it has even escaped detection by the satirist's bibliographers) and Kaufman and Ryskind's *Something New* is being published here for the first time.

We might even extend this aspect of contemporaneity a bit further; these two nonsense or "Dada" plays—the spirit of which, if not the exact form, is with us today in the creations of Kenneth Koch and Charles Ludlam—have at their core a rebellious nature that reflects a modern sensibility. Not only do these parodies repudiate the notion of a rational universe and its corresponding mimetic portrayal in literature; they also dispose of most conventional literary elements from metaphor to linear continuity to coherence itself. Lardner, the recognized master of the nonsense play, creates a novel imaginative world in which the non sequitur is made the elemental unit of a new syntax and incongruity determines every occurrence.

Many of the nonsense plays and absurdist parodies that came out of the twenties were infused not only with this appreciation of the ridiculous but with a critical attitude as well. They assaulted the conventions, contrivances and pretensions of a prospering commercial theater. The authors of such plays included Robert Benchley, Donald Ogden Stewart, Marc Connelly, Robert Sherwood, Kaufman and Lardner; all of whom came out of the newspapers and magazines, unencumbered by the theater's cherished traditions and inherited practices. These plays were often performed by the writers and their literary friends at such largely amateur entertainments as the Dutch Treat Club shows, the Lamb's Annual Gambols or at one of the annual Authors League benefits. The best known of these amusements was probably *No, Sirree!,* "an anonymous entertainment by the Vicious Circle of the Hotel Algonquin" in which critics and other writers mocked the plays of such contemporary dramatists as Samuel Shipman, Zoe Akins and A. A. Milne, reducing the style and substance of the imitated objects to absurdity. Later a number of these writers assembled a professional revue called *The 49ers* in an unsuccessful attempt to take Broadway; Lardner's first biographer, Donald Elder, described the satiric entertainment as a "gesture of defiance at the commercial theater."

Like European Dada, the native nonsense play also assaulted the seriousness of art and the holiness of the artist. Lardner, for one, cheerfully violated the sanctity of literary names throughout his career; one of his late parodies, *Abend Di Anni Nouveau* featured a character list made up of distinguished contemporary creators, among them Theodore Dreiser—a former Follies girl, Heywood Broun—an usher at Roxys, H. L. Mencken—a kleagle in the Moose, and Ben Hecht—a taxi starter. But if there was one supreme target at which the darts of parodists were aimed, it was Eugene O'Neill, the man who was to his era the very image of the artist. The awe and reverence he and his new kind of psychological drama inspired made him an inevitable candidate for comic deflation. It was Lardner who wrote the best known of the O'Neill parodies: a humorous alternative to *Mourning Becomes Electra,* the massive tragedy which stretched across three nights, thirteen acts and several dinner intervals. It was entitled *Quadroon*—"A Play in Four Pelts Which May All Be Attended in One Day or Missed in a Group," and consisted mainly of luncheon and dinner menus for the lengthy intermissions plus slightly altered cast lists (Lavinia, Christine, Fred Astire) and useful bits of information: "Leave your ticket check with an usher and your car will come right to your seat." The Great God O'Neill also came under the wary scrutiny of George S. Kaufman. In *No, Sirree!* he appeared as the "1st Agitated Seaman" (there were two others played by Marc Connelly and Alexander Woollcott) in "The Greasy Hag," a comic reduction of *Anna Christie* which democratically offered the audience an O'Neill setting of their own choosing: "Vote for One. Backroom of Billy the Bishop's saloon or Fireman's forecastle on a freighter bound east from Rio." And several years later in the Marx Brothers musical *Animal Crackers* (1928), which Kaufman wrote with Morrie Ryskind, the character of Captain Spaulding (Groucho Marx) periodically excused himself from the play—"Pardon me while I have a Strange Interlude"—and bared his sub-conscious to the audience in an O'Neill-inspired interior monologue:

> Strange how the wind blows tonight. It has a thin eerie voice . . . drab, dead yesterdays shutting out beautiful tomorrows. Hideous, stumbling footsteps creaking

along the misty corridors of time. And in those corridors I see figures, strange figures, weird figures, Steel 186, Anaconda 74, American Can 138 . . .

Such humorous replies to the "genius" of O'Neill (others were written by Frank Sullivan and Donald Ogden Stewart) express more than the comic penchant of a particular era. Like the nonsense play itself, these diversions somehow communicate the spirit of American comedy; they were independent, scornful of authority (be it literary or any other kind), irreverent and in full possession of a cheerful skepticism.

The first of the plays included here, *Something New* was copyrighted in 1929 by George S. Kaufman and Morrie Ryskind (who would later collaborate with Kaufman on the Pulitzer Prize-winner musical, *Of Thee I Sing*) and was probably written a few months after the opening of *Animal Crackers*; the two works were actually submitted for copyright on the same day. *Something New* is actually an amalgam of scenes that must have been modeled on similar moments in conventional Broadway dramas of the 1920's (and no doubt Kaufman witnessed many such episodes during his years as the theater critic of *The New York Times*), only here by means of some comic tampering and an arrangement that is to a sequence of individual scenes what the non sequitur is to dialogue, their potential absurdity is fully realized. After this short parody, Kaufman's next project was a collaboration with Ring Lardner, the author of our other selection. The play was *June Moon,* a satire on Tin Pan Alley that was to give Lardner what he had always wanted but had not yet achieved: a Broadway hit. This, incidentally, was not their first association; Kaufman had known Lardner for some years, he had appeared as an actor in two of his parodies for the Dutch Treat Club shows and he directed the first of Lardner's nonsense plays, *The Tridget of Greva.*

The second play in this section, Ring Lardner's *The Gelska Cup* was originally published in 1925 (the same year Lardner wrote his most famous short story, "Haircut") and appeared in the old *Life,* a humor magazine that featured the early writings of Benchley, Sherwood, Connelly, Kaufman and Dorothy Parker. Although the piece lacks the economy and some of the verbal agility of its better known counterparts, and a few of the jokes may elicit grimaces, it has all the features of the other nonsense plays: characters who fail to appear, deleted scenes, improbable settings, non sequitur, and also a few new elements that expand the possibilities of theatrical representation—stage directions and cues for the audience, running commentary on the low quality of the work and motivation for actors who want out of the play.

Lardner is perhaps the more radical of the two parodists discussed here. Whereas Kaufman exposes the current deficiencies and excesses of theater practices, Lardner obliterates not only traditions and conventions of the stage but also the absurdity of the form itself. His targets are not nearly so often the failings as they are the imperatives of the stage: program credits to identify actors and characters, the necessary division of action into acts, the limitations of realistic scenery, the methods of imparting information to an audience and easing a play forward—his is a comic indictment of the entire theatrical engine. But both Kaufman and Lardner move beyond the limits of criticism. In the end, they do not attack the absurdity of the theater, they celebrate it.

Note

An incidental note on the authorship of *Something New*:

Dec. 7, 1977

I can't give you the slightest bit of information about "Something New," since I have no memory of having written it. Are you sure you've got the right guy?

It is true George and I talked over a lot of ideas, and he would occasionally make notes and type them up afterward. But this one rings no bell at all . . .

Yours mystifiedly,

Morrie Ryskind

Jeffrey D. Mason (essay date 1988)

SOURCE: Mason, Jeffrey D. "The Fool and the Clown: The Ironic Vision of George S. Kaufman." In *Farce*, pp. 205-217. New York: Cambridge University Press, 1988.

[*In the following essay, Mason examines Kaufman's use of fools and clowns, with particular focus on his use of the Marx Brothers in his comedies.*]

Theater suggests two coextensive worlds. An actor is both himself and the character he plays; a stage is both a platform and an illusion. While all art engages in the creative interpretation of the human condition, theater actually re-enacts life, introducing the constant, tantalizing risk that the distance and the distinction between art and life will diminish to the vanishing point.

The farceur revels in reducing that distance to an excruciating minimum, forcing the audience to accept a double vision that will never quite come into focus. All theater employs artifice, contrivance and convention, but while comedy and tragedy might ask their audiences to suspend disbelief, farce embraces the separation between object and representation. Farce challenges the spectator, vacillating between an apparent depiction and a travesty—between what *seems* to be and what lurks, leering gleefully, just beneath the surface. The farceur acts on the knowledge that probability necessarily implies an improbability which carries a license for wild nonsense.

Both the form and the content of George S. Kaufman's farces derive from his recognition of the incongruous distance between actuality and imagination, his narratives incarnating the unlikely as he embraces farce's liberation from the merely apparent reality of the ordinary world. He

deals in opposites—he mingles the frank theatricality of farce with the realistic production style that prevailed on the commercial Broadway stage during his career, and his attitude towards humanity alternates between sentiment and cynicism. The form and content of his work are interdependent, for while Kaufman's farce expresses his ironic vision of life, the vision itself is farcical because it makes light of the limitations of the ordinary world.

Kaufman conveyed his double vision most clearly in two kinds of farce that he wrote from 1921 to 1930, depicting his American Everyman alternately as a fool and as a clown. The most characteristic examples of the fool farce are **Merton of the Movies** (1922, with Marc Connelly), the tale of a dreamer who travels to Hollywood to become a silent-screen star; **The Butter and Egg Man** (1925), the story of a gullible young man who believes that investing in a Broadway show is a sure thing; and **Once in a Lifetime** (1930, with Moss Hart), the history of a charmingly inept vaudevillean's rise to the top of a film studio. The clown farces include the scripts that Kaufman, with Morrie Ryskind, wrote to display the caricatures that Groucho, Chico and Harpo Marx had developed during fifteen years in vaudeville—the original Broadway versions of **The Cocoanuts** (1925) and **Animal Crackers** (1928), and the screenplay for **A Night at the Opera** (1935). Since **The Butter and Egg Man** is the only play Kaufman wrote without a collaborator and **The Cocoanuts** was his first vehicle for the Marx Brothers, each play may serve as the model for its kind.

OF FOOLS AND DREAMS

The story of **The Butter and Egg Man** is a variation of the archetypal tale of a young man who travels to the big city to win fame and fortune. Peter Jones arrives in New York with an inheritance that is not quite large enough to help him fulfill his dream of buying and managing a hotel back home in Chillicothe, Ohio. He has heard that investing in Broadway theater will make him rich in record time, so he introduces himself to Mac and Lehman, a pair of ex-vaudevilleans who seek backing for a script they control. He tries to treat the partners' extravagant promises with what he considers to be shrewd skepticism, but his resistance crumbles when he meets Jane, their sweet young secretary, and he gives the sharpers nearly all of his money in exchange for a forty-nine per cent share of the production. The plays opens out of town and it is clear to everyone but Peter that the script is a disaster. During the post-mortem conference, Lehman insults Jane, and Peter's sense of gallantry moves him to take an option on the entire production. He opens the play on Broadway, where it is, astoundingly, a smash hit, but he discovers that he is the object of an airtight plagiarism suit—the script turns out to be a shameless theft from a published short story. With the help of Fanny Lehman, the producer's wife, he sells the entire production back to his former partners, reaps a gigantic profit, and returns to Chillicothe with Jane to buy his hotel and live happily ever after.

Peter is an exemplary Kaufmanic fool, a natural hick whose ingenuousness first leaves him vulnerable to the city slickers and then enables him to defeat them. He is truly innocent, as pure and untouched as on the day he was born. Neither education nor experience have marred him, so he remains naïve and artless, eternally childlike, and forever honest and trusting.

Virtue is Peter's keystone. He believes that morality and ethics are simple and absolute, applying with equal strength and validity to all men in all situations; it never occurs to him that values might be complex, relative or situational. He believes that all men achieve success—as he hopes to do—through righteousness, dedication and hard work. He assumes that everyone else shares his faith in the power of good, and he takes for granted that others' motives towards him are benevolent and unselfish. His innocence makes him highly gullible, and it is difficult for him to imagine skulduggery or malice. He trusts Mac and Lehman because he *wants* to trust them, because skepticism and suspicion are completely alien to him. That his partners might find him ridiculous, that they might not respect him, that they would lie and cheat without qualm, that they befriend him only as a last resort to raise money—none of this occurs to him.

The catalytic episode in any Kaufmanic fool's life occurs when he stumbles upon a dream, finds that he cannot realize it at home, and decides to undertake a journey to a strange land, an Oz, a world that seems all fantasy and delight. Peter finishes act I alone in the producers' office, taking in the exotically unfamiliar atmosphere, admiring the photographs on the wall, and finally settling into the swivel chair and propping his feet up on the desk. He looks at a business that is marked by its anxiety and uncertainty, and he sees only the romance and the glamour, believing that to produce a show is to have a hit, for a flop is inconceivable to him.

Every fool learns that in order to realize his dream he must become part of the institution that dominates the new world, but the established members of the institution treat his overtures with suspicion or contempt. Peter discovers that the theater demands certain rites of passage before it is willing to accept him; the director and the leading lady consider Peter to be a rank outsider, beneath their notice, until he becomes the only owner of the property. After his fool's lucks turns a disaster into a smash, only a combination of farcical coincidence and foolish inspiration allows Peter to escape from the plagiarism suit with his prize intact. He wins *because* he is ignorant and innocent; those he befuddles are accustomed to the onslaughts of their own kind and they are vulnerable to the fool's ingenuousness. His triumph is the defeat of craft and sophistication by intuition, innocence, and faith.

There are two important women in the fool's life. The first is the ingenue, Kaufman's wholesome girl next door. Jane matches Peter in virtue, but she has learned a little from experience and she unobtrusively guides him when his intuition goes awry. When her talents aren't equal to the demands of the situation, in walks a character we might call the 'sophisticated lady'. Clever, experience and perceptive, Fanny Lehman is a survivor who expects the worst of everyone, so the fool's well-meaning helplessness startles her protective instincts into action. She passes out of Peter's life when the quest is finished, but Jane marries him and becomes the typical life of Kaufman's cynical version of the American dream.

The fool's quest and his beliefs combine to lead him into adopting certain endearing attitudes towards himself. First, he cannot imagine his own failure; he believes that to attempt is to succeed. Second, he never questions the source or the validity of his dream, even if he finds it in rumor, the contrived fiction of the movie screen, or the seductive advertisements in the back pages of a cheap magazine. Third, he is absolutely unable to perceive his own comic potential, making him a susceptible target for the laughter of others.

Even without the contrasting presence of the clown, the fool displays Kaufman's irony. The fool succeeds not because he is exceptionally brilliant or talented, nor because he is skilled or trained in any special way. He succeeds because he is himself; sheer existence is sufficient cause for reward. His career celebrates the common man and affirms the American dream of the simple backwoods boy who makes good, a myth which includes a contradiction, because while it applauds individual effort it also denies the uniqueness of the hero. It supports the belief that all men *are* created equal, that no one is better than anyone else, and that the best sort of citizen is the 'regular guy' who does not stand out from the crowd. The myth demands a hero without remarkable qualities— something for nothing. The fool's career resolves the contradiction because his very commonness makes him uncommon. His achievement also vindicates the American belief that a man can be free without violating the system, and that any little boy from humble origins can become President if he perseveres and doesn't upset the status quo.

Yet even while Kaufman neatly resolves these contradictions, the structure of the farce awakens the uneasy suspicion that the playwright mocks the American dream. The disciple and paragon of the dream is a fool—it may be that *only* a fool can place his faith in the dream and succeed according to its principles. While the tragic hero faces destruction because he is exceptional, the farcical fool enjoys success because he is ordinary; instead of tragic catharsis, Kaufman gives us a farcical slap in the face. The fool is an unsettling mirror held up to the complacently smiling gaze of Kaufman's audience—each spectator suddenly wonders whether or not he is seeing a reflection of himself. Kaufman may be offering a disquieting choice: to remain un-foolish and settle for less than a dream, or to become a fool and win.

OF CLOWNS AND NIGHTMARES

The clown is the fool's opposite: experienced where he is innocent, crafty where he is artless, cynical where he is trusting, committed to shattering the rules rather than living by them, a sly devil who would rather cheat than work. While the fool works within the system and ingenuously charms his way to the top, the clown takes control, creating the world anew at every moment, shattering the status quo and completely confusing the other characters. While the fool inspires our affection with his endearing smile, the clown is a frightening juggernaut. The fool makes us feel superior, for he is a man who lacks even average gifts, a rustic without even minimal polish and worldly wisdom, delightful because he is so clumsy and so inept; but the clown moves too fast, startling and bewildering us with his unexpected and inexplicable choices. Either fool or clown may be mad, but the fool's madness has more to do with happy, innocent idiocy than with manic terror. The fool is a collage of quite natural flaws, while the clown is artificial because he is too perfect a machine.

The clown is an emblem of disorder, or at least of an order that is separate and estranged from our own familiar order. He is free from restraint, a spirit of revelry and license. He scoffs at absolute values and questions everything, showing no willingness to adhere to any set principle or law. He is a vice figure in an amoral time, not a spirit of evil but a nihilist who espouses nothing but the mischief and chaos he so joyfully creates. Kaufman's clown is a grotesque travesty of mankind, a character who, like the farce itself, presents the appearance of reality without becoming that reality.

Each of the clown farces employs a tight structure, building from a simple situation that provides a foundation for character and story. *The Cocoanuts* is set in an hotel in the midst of a land boom in Florida, offering a location public enough and a situation open enough to allow the authors to move characters in and out with a maximum of flexibility and a minimum of justification. The phenomenon of the hotel leads the characters into certain associated formal behavior patterns, products of etiquette and custom that are almost rituals, offering a predictability that the clowns can shatter.

The cast includes a set of conventional characters—a gullible dowager, a couple of villains, a clumsy detective, and a pair of lovers—whose simplicity and artificiality leave them vulnerable to the clowns' tricks and susceptible to the playwrights' manipulation. The dowager is Mrs Potter, who seeks to maintain her status in society by arranging an acceptable match for Polly, her daughter. She chooses Harvey Yates, not knowing that he and Penelope, his secret paramour, are fortune hunters—the villains of the play—who covet the Potter millions. Groucho is on the scene as the manager of the hotel (named 'The Cocoanuts'), and he hopes to persuade Mrs Potter to invest in some chancy real estate. Chico and Harpo arrive to try to make a killing in land speculation, with a detective named Hennessey hot on their trail, an unwitting symbol of authority who offers an easy target for farcical assault on order. Finally, there are the lovers, Polly and a charmingly ambitious young architect named Bob Adams, whom Mrs Potter scorns because he is temporarily employed as a clerk. They are

an innocent, attractive, sentimental pair who recall the fool and his ingenue in their search for domestic tranquility.

Kaufman begins each of his clown farces by using the dowager as the catalyst as she attracts attention from the lovers, who need her approval or recognition; the villains, who covet her money or resent her social prominence; and from Groucho, who pretends to aid her social aspirations while actually making a fool of her. The action of *The Cocoanuts* follows a pattern of countervailing intrigues between the villains, the lovers, and the clowns. Harvey and Penelope steal Mrs Potter's necklace and hide it in a stump at Cocoanut Manor, Groucho's land development. Harpo finds the jewels during the land auction, and Hennessy arrests Bob for the theft because the young man has just bought the lot containing the stump. The clowns trick Mrs Potter in order to get the money for Bob's bail, and Harpo gives him a scrawled map of Cocoanut Manor that shows the location of the stump and the jewels. Polly tricks Harvey into drawing a similar map, and the lovers discover that the handwriting is the same on both. At the dinner celebrating Polly's engagement to Harvey, Bob produces the matching maps to prove that Harvey was the thief. The play ends happily as the villains quit the scene, the lovers plan to marry, and Groucho learns that a millionaire intends to make him a handsome offer for Cocoanut Manor.

Situation, character, and story are all subordinate to the buffoonery or *lazzi* of the clowns. Through verbal and physical mayhem, the clowns offer zany, alternative behavior patterns that assault the polite formality of the conventional characters. The *lazzi* range from Groucho's witticisms to Chico's *non sequiturs* to Harpo's taxi horn. Some offer slight development of character or story, while others digress wildly from the action, as when the Brothers turn Hennessey's investigation into a minstrel show, complete with music and 'Mr Bones', when the hapless detective gives them the traditional opening line, 'Ladies and gentlemen, be seated!' Still others have no relationship at all to the plot, as when Groucho interrupts the show to perform a brief vaudeville sketch. The ultimate form of *lazzi* shatters not only the conventional characters' expectations but also the audience's belief in the stage illusion, as in *Animal Crackers,* when Groucho protests, 'Why, you can't arrest them. That's the hero and the heroine.'[1]

BEYOND LANGUAGE

Through the Marx Brothers, Kaufman turns language into a madly comic weapon against the conventional characters, who are trapped in cliché, formula and banality. Kaufman creates a parody of a love scene so Groucho can make fun of Mrs Potter's desirability and femininity, of himself as a lover, of Bob and Polly as the genuine lovers, of the audience's expectations concerning love interests on stage, and of love scenes in general.

GROUCHO:

Well say that you'll be truly mine, or truly yours, or yours truly, and that tonight when the moon is sneaking around the clouds, I'll be sneaking around you. I'll meet you tonight by the bungalow, under the moon. You and the moon. I hope I can tell you apart. You wear a red necktie so I'll know you. I'll meet you tonight by the bungalow under the moon.

MRS. POTTER:

But suppose the moon is not out.

GROUCHO:

Then I'll meet you under the bungalow.[2]

The clowns also use pun mercilessly, pushing it to the limit when Groucho goes beyond mere words to reassemble sounds according to his whim.

Guatemala every night or you can't Mala at all. Of course, that takes a lot of Honduras. (**Animal Crackers,** 1, 2, 41)

The clowns raise the stakes by moving beneath language, working on the meaning it is intended to convey, and fracturing the logic of thought. Early in **The Cocoanuts,** Groucho addresses a crowd of underpaid bellboys:

I want you to be free. Strike off your chains. Strike up the band. Strike three, you're out. Remember, there's nothing like liberty. That is there's nothing like it in this country. Be free. Now and forever, one and indivisible, one for all, and all for me and me for you, and tea for two. Remember, I have only my best interests at heart, and I promise you, that it's only a question of a few years before some woman will swing [sic] the English Channel. I thank you.

(p. 209)

Kaufman uses word associations and the rhythms of phrases to turn Groucho's oration into a parody of political rhetoric, destroying the relationship of word to idea and permitting him to gull the bellboys into cheering the man who refuses to raise their wages.

Once meaning and language are divorced, Kaufman can twist them in different directions, forming a convolution or perversion of their original relationship. In this next passage, Chico and Harpo arrive at the front desk:

CHICO:

Hello. We sent you a telegram. We make reservache.

GROUCHO:

Oh. Welcome to Cocoanut Manor. What do you boys want? Garage and bath?

CHICO:

We go together him.

GROUCHO:

You go together him?

CHICO:

Sure me.

GROUCHO:

Would you mind coming in again and starting all over?

(*The Cocoanuts,* p. 213)

The clowns use their lingo to maintain their control over the situation, and the conventional characters are completely unable to follow them. The key quality is indirection—while most people value language that communicates simply, clearly and directly, the clowns prefer to say one thing while meaning another.

While the clowns impose their meta-language on the world they invade, the fool discovers that the world of his dreams demands that he learn a jargon, or target language, in order to succeed. At the beginning of **The Butter and Egg Man,** Mac and Lehman demonstrate their control of the situation by displaying their linguistic facility.

LEHMAN:

Anybody comes in on this trick'll clean up! I can do it for fifteen thousand. I'd take twelve.

MAC:

You'd take one.

LEHMAN:

You don't say? Let me tell you this, sweetheart, there ain't going to be no bargains, not if I have to throw it in the ash-can! This show's a pipe, and any bird that comes in is going to make plenty.[3]

This jargon depends heavily on slang, and it is boldly colloquial, idiosyncratic and crudely expressive. Peter discovers that his accustomed speech patterns brand him as a greenhorn, so he must master at least the style of the jargon, if not its content, in order to remove it as a barrier to his success. At first the new slang bewilders him—when Lehman informs him that 'I'm doing a wow,' Peter has to ask for a translation. Later in the play, he has retained enough fragments from several overheard conversations to be able to assemble a speech that will fool the uninitiated, even though he's not quite sure of what he's saying.

Everything happens to this girl—she marries a fellow, only she's going to have more sympathy. . . . It's going to make millions of dollars—thousands. It's going to be the biggest thing that ever was in the theatre . . . and it's going to have Hongkong [sic] in it! A great big scene instead of where it's a trial! It's wonderful—it's a hop joint and he turns out to be her father and she comes back at him with the strong talk and so-and-so and so-and-so and so-and-so.

(p. 166)

Peter captures just enough vocabulary and rhythm to produce the effect he seeks. Meaning is absent or fractured, so the jargon becomes a hastily-constructed mask that changes who he *seems* to be, not who he *is*.

CRAFTSMAN AT WORK

Although Kaufman's expertise shines most clearly through his re-creation of various lower forms of spoken American English, he is equally adept at creating farcical situation. He uses realism as the basis, creating a world that mimics—but does not become—the ordinary world. He begins with an apparently solid foundation of familiar materiality—walls, doors, everyday paraphernalia and recognizable people—in order to encourage his audience's conventional expectations and to lull them into a false sense of security. Then he distorts his creation, veering towards the improbable and introducing a logic that only resembles that of the ordinary world. If Kaufman departs from reality completely, he robs the audience of their point of reference and forfeits his ability to seduce their belief, while if he sustains a perfect or even apparent identity with the ordinary world, he must follow ordinary rules and sacrifice his control. To maintain that control is to be free from the predictable and the plausible, so the impossible is rife—rascally clowns escape the clutches of the law, and a fool finds the money he needs in the nick of time.

To its inhabitants, the farce-world appears to be as capricious and as unreliable as Alice's Looking-Glass World; not only does it refuse to follow the laws of the ordinary world, it declines to be consistent within its own context. It is inimical one moment and friendly the next, becoming an ineffable or hostile mechanism to the characters who are trapped within its closed system. It is the product of the tension between its realistic basis and the farcical artifice that dominates the action.

Kaufman mocks traditional farcical devices even while he uses them, again conveying two points of view. Harpo finds Mrs Potter's missing jewels with none of the suspense and anxiety that characterize Sardou's use of the trick in *A Scrap of Paper*. When the clown leads the matron to the tree stump, he points out not only the necklace but also the ease of the discovery and the folly of playwrights who build entire plots around such gimmicks. If one of Feydeau's dupes is caught in the hall without his trousers, reaching for the door just as it swings shut and locks, then he is simply an unwilling victim of the farceur's machinery. But in Kaufman's door-slamming scene, when the three clowns rotate positions between the hallway and the two adjoining rooms, befuddling the hotel guests and joyfully slamming doors as they dive in and out of their hiding-places under the beds, they are the farceur's accomplices, and they act with full awareness of their theatrical mischief. Lady Teazle may hide behind the screen merely to escape detection, but Kaufman's clown hides under the bed both to annoy the conventional characters and to create a parody of concealment, coincidence, and the rapid, mechanical pace that is farce's hallmark.

With relation to character, the classic farcical device is mask. For many of his creations, Kaufman offers two masks—the one the individual sees and the one that others see—making each role an exercise in dissonance and incongruity. The inept character has little self-awareness and he insists on the self-image he cherishes even when circumstances deny its validity. A mask acts as a disguise only when the wearer recognizes the distance between appearance and actuality; when the wearer's incomprehension turns that distance into a chasm, it becomes a trap. *Pour le Bain,* a sketch that Kaufman wrote with Howard Dietz in 1931, describes a society woman's discomfort when shopping for bathroom fixtures. Her mask of gentility so confines her that she cannot even bring herself to ask for a toilet by name; the mask stands between her and her needs. In the case of the clowns, character *is* mask. Groucho's character has little or no personality beneath the garish mustache, eyebrows and glasses; he is as fixed in his zaniness as the mask is in its features. The fool, on the other hand, creates and dons a mask in order to deceive others into believing he is someone he is not. His conscious masquerade raises him above simplicity and artlessness towards the realm of roguery. As long as Peter Jones *knows* he wears a mask, he is safe from its inherent trap, but when he loses sight of the distinction between his true self and his appearance, he begins to lose both Jane and the fortune he seeks. Kaufman uses the mask to explore the folly of those who wear them in the ordinary world.

THE VEILED COMMENTARY

With the mask, the playwright holds folly up to inspection but not to punishment. Does Kaufman embrace the cynical view of man as essentially foolish and given to error, or does he accept the sentimental vision of man as essentially weak but progressing inevitably towards goodness and perfection? He vacillates between the two, sometimes using one to undercut the other. In this moment, he attacks man's folly, using his acid wisecracks to ridicule and deride certain characters. In the next, he presents a warm picture of man striving for self-improvement and placing his trust in the generosity and benevolence of others. In a single play, he may offer an unashamedly sentimental couple whose romance holds the play together, while providing a contrast with a decidedly unsentimental couple whose unsurprised, experienced attitude dilutes the sweetness of the hero and heroine. The clown is the sharp instrument of cynicism, but the fool is the apotheosis of the sentimental dream.

Kaufman may present man as a weak, inept, and sentimental fool, but he approaches his folly with humorous tolerance. Kaufman never loses sight of man's absurdity—that is his cynicism. He prefers to use the fool as a focal point of laughter, and although the audience may laugh at the fool's mistakes, they also laugh with his victories. Kaufman tempers his cynicism with sentiment in that his fools survive their missteps and win the prizes they seek. The fool may be a boob, but he's improving just the same.

Kaufman's combination of cynicism with sentiment leaves little room for the spirit of saturnalia and revelry that farce often offers. Cynicism declines to believe in celebration, while sentiment crushes it with prudery. Another play-wright might find in sexuality a chance to explore the themes of birth and the renewal of the world, or an opportunity to present a wild, joyous, physical release at the end of the play. In Kaufman's work, sexuality loses the capacity for abandon. Beautiful women become untouchable, comfortless sex symbols, while others turn away from sensuality and formalize it into their social roles as wives and helpmates, defining themselves in terms of their men's success and taking a firm but discreet hand in the course of events. Sentimental, middle-class values insist on the wife helping the husband along the road of self-improvement, so there is little time for the wild affirmation of life that is Bacchanalia.

In the end, Kaufman is a pessimist. His farces end happily, but they neither affirm life nor offer genuine answers to real-world problems. There is no sense that the fool's victory carries any implication or message for those of us in the ordinary world. His fools solve or avoid the dilemmas confronting them, but their solutions work only within the controlled environment of the farce. He sees too clearly the absurdity in the world, and if one accepts absurdity, then one relinquishes the right to expect the consistency of cause-and-effect that social cures require. Kaufman does not believe in solutions, and his work seldom seriously questions the system or its values.

Joseph Wood Krutch criticized Kaufman for failing to adopt a single, coherent point of view, but Kaufman's ironic vision—the very vision that makes his work possible—prevents him from doing so.[4] Kaufman sees man as fool *and* hero, clown *and* dupe, so he cannot for more than a passing moment commit himself to one or another model of human nature. At one point Kaufman sees the world as a rationalist mechanism that submits to man's tinkering, a device that rewards craft and sophistication. At another point he sees the world as an organism that remains ineffable to the scientist but which encourages the trusting wanderings of that strange Romantic hero, the Kaufmanic fool. He cannot commit himself to a single interpretation because he looks at the world and sees its farcical reflection beside it, an image that reproduces the original with startling accuracy but without achieving or desiring genuine identity.

Notes

1. George S. Kaufman and Morrie Ryskind, *Animal Crackers*, TS, Sam H. Harris Collection, William Seymour Theatre Collection, Princeton University Library, 11, 1, 36.

2. George S. Kaufman, *The Cocoanuts* in Donald Oliver, ed., *By George* (New York: St Martin's Press, 1979), p. 219.

3. George S. Kaufman, *The Butter and Egg Man* (New York: Boni and Liveright, 264)

4. Joseph Wood Krutch, 'The Random Satire of George S. Kaufman', *The Nation*, 137 (1933), 157; and review of *First Lady*, *The Nation*, 141 (1935), 694.

David K. Sauer (essay date spring 1995)

SOURCE: Sauer, David K. "George S. Kaufman's Exploitation of Women (Characters): Dramaturgy and Feminism." *American Drama* 4, no. 2 (spring 1995): 55-80.

[*In the following essay, Sauer gauges Kaufman's development as a dramatist by the development of his skill in drawing characters.*]

George S. Kaufman's successes in the theater mark him as a theatrical genius: he wrote more than forty plays which appeared on Broadway (all but one with a collaborator), and he directed most of those plays, as well as 20 others, working simultaneously as director and "play doctor." But because his work is collaborative, it is difficult to say what exactly was his contribution to a given play. As a result, lacking a single auteur to give credit or blame, until recently scholars have not paid much attention to his contributions to American drama.[1] The purpose of this paper is to take a further step towards defining part of that contribution by examining Kaufman's earliest successes in sequence, to see what he learned, and how his dramaturgy changed through his first five plays: *Dulcy* (1921), *To the Ladies* (1922), *Merton of the Movies* (1922), *Beggar on Horseback* (1924), and *Butter and Egg Man* (1925). The first four were written with Marc Connelly; the fifth is Kaufman's only play written alone.

In order to give shape and meaning to the pattern discovered in this sequence of plays, I have used an approach focusing on women's roles. Underlying this perspective is that after forty years of campaigning, the nineteenth amendment finally passed on August 18, 1920. So women's suffrage forms a substantial background to Kaufman's emergence as a dramatist. Reflecting this political shift, the role of the female lead in Kaufman's plays changes radically from one play to the other, and some explanation of these shifts is necessary to understand his growth as a dramatist (and dramaturg). Those changes, in brief, begin with *Dulcy* (originated by Lynn Fontanne in her first starring role) who is a Gracie Allen kind of wife, continually trying to help yet creating disasters for her husband. The second play reverses these roles. In *To the Ladies* it is the husband whose follies propel the plot, and the wife (originated by Helen Hayes in her first adult role) who is the intelligent rescuer from each disaster. The fifth play in the sequence, finally, breaks free from both these clichés, and offers two naïve characters, male and female, who work their way through a series of disasters with wit and cleverness that feed off each other.

In one sense, this pattern seems simply to reflect a sexist view of woman as inferior to man, to a reverse view of woman as superior, to conclude with a humanist equality of the sexes. In fact the pattern is more complex and more interesting. Gayle Austin, following Sue-Ellen Case and Jill Dolan, traces three divisions of feminist discourse in *Feminist Theories for Dramatic Criticism* (5). Austin begins with liberal feminism which stresses women's equality with men based on "universal values." The second type, cultural feminism, views women as "both different from and superior to men," advocating this perspective through female forms of culture. Finally, materialist feminism "deconstructs the mythic subject Woman to look at women as a class oppressed by material conditions and social relations" (5). To some extent, Kaufman's dramaturgy loosely reflects these stages. In each of his plays, with growing emphasis, big business is seen as an increasingly villainous condition which constrains both men and women. How to achieve freedom from this oppression is what animates the plots of these early plays. As men and women begin to work together in this struggle, more complex characters, especially women, emerge. Consequently, Kaufman's dramaturgy develops from exploiting characters for plot purposes to letting them work together to create a plot. It is the growth of this view of characterization that is the focus of this article; female characters are used as a measure of Kaufman's development.

Of parallel significance to the political standpoints of his plays, Kaufman's growth as a dramatist shows a similar liberation from the exploitation of women characters; he first uses them to animate his plots and create their complications, then with an increasing sense of the material conditions which create the obstacle which characters must overcome. In this struggle, men and women are both seen as oppressed and needing to work together to achieve any measure of success against the oppressor. Dramaturgically, Kaufman moves from a simple structure which either blames or credits wife/woman and sees business itself as the environment that distorts, to a de-centered view in which business itself is not intrinsically evil and in which all characters work in a much more fluid environment without simple villians and heroes. The result is to spread the power of animating the plot among the cast, rather than concentrating it in one or two clever characters. The consequence of this is perhaps best seen in the plays Kaufman wrote with Moss Hart in the 1930s, in which a variety of characters work in diverse directions, giving much greater breadth and richness to the plays, and, therefore, a more complete view of a variety of characters, male and female, rather than the simplistic dramaturgy of the single plot with one protagonist and one (female) side-kick. But Kaufman learned to do this in his first plays written in the early 1920s.

Kaufman's first full length play, **Dulcy** (Aug. 13, 1921; 246 performances), written with Connelly, is set in a country house with nine characters who rather than acting as pairs in succession are fully involved in most of the action. The dramaturgical problem with this kind of play is how to get the plot to work.

The solution is Dulcy, the air-headed wife. She tries to help her husband, Gordon, who invented a process for making costume jewelry, but he and other small jewelry makers are being forced into selling out to a larger company for a small share of the profits. So from the start

the problems of business and unfair exploitation are raised; all the power is in the one businessman. To remedy this, Dulcy invites the take-over mogul, Mr. Forbes, and his wife and daughter to the country. Dulcy's brother is also present, as are, by accident, Mr. Starrett (originated by Elliott Nugent), and an admirer of the daughter, Vincent Leach, movie scenarist and object of the daughter's affection, and Schuyler Van Dyck, millionaire pianist whom Dulcy just met at a brunch and brought home. This is a large cast of characters to entertain on stage at once, and it takes great control to make them work. Dulcy is the main controller, scheming to match Mrs. Forbes with Van Dyck, and Angela Forbes with Vincent Leach. By matchmaking Mr. Forbes' daughter, Dulcy's purpose is to win over both his affection and Mrs. Forbes' good will.

Naturally, her plots result in catastrophe. Forbes hates Leach, the screenwriter, from the outset, so when Angela elopes with him, her father is furious. He's also resentful at his wife's interest in Van Dyke. Having a bad back, he hates the country and despises golf and polo. His only recreation, billiards, is ruined because Dulcy had the table moved, unbalancing it.

The culmination of the play is Dulcy's recognition that she has failed:

GORDON:

> I don't know what the future is going to do to us. You mean well, but you just don't stop to think.

DULCY:

> I guess I don't think—I just think I think. (*Rising and speaking bravely*) I'll let you go, darling—if you want me to. (*Smith is silent.*) I'm just—all wrong. I'm—a false note. I always wondered how I'd be able to make a man like you care for me—it seems too absurd for a man like you ever to love—a false note. And now we're finding out—he can't.

GORDON:

> (*Carried away for a second, crossing to her L.*) Dulcy, we can't end everything like this! You're not a false note—you're a melody—a whole tune. (*A pause. He reverts to his previous mood.*) But I don't know what to do. (*He turns away to c.*)

DULCY:

> (*Sadly*). I don't think I can reform . . . (*Realizing that it's old stuff but hopefully trying it anyhow*) I could make another promise. (*SMITH shakes his head. Dulcy pleads tearfully*) One that would take in everything.

GORDON:

> Oh, I know you'd try to keep it, but . . .

DULCY:

> (*Crosses to him with tears in her voice*) Oh, but I would keep this one. Dearest, if you'll let me, I'll promise that I'll never interfere with your business affairs again.

(111-112)

According to his autobiography *Voices Offstage,* Connelly wrote this kind of scene because the "only areas in our plays which he [Kaufman] shied away from were love scenes" (60). The excessive sentimentality places the woman, Dulcy, in a most degrading position of pleading with her husband to stay with her. This is clearly a sexist play, but it seems to have been redeemed by Lynn Fontanne for whom the play was written. In her first starring role, as Dulcy, she charmed the reviewers with her "warmth and good humor," according to Malcolm Goldstein in *George S. Kaufman: His Life, His Theater* (61).

Kaufman and Connelly had been commissioned by George Tyler to write the play for Fontanne, who had appeared as a similar character in a supporting role in a play for which Kaufman was Tyler's play doctor (Goldstein 61). So the essential outline of the foolish Westchester wife was not theirs; in the earlier play, however, both husband and wife were foolish. Here only the wife would be. Their concept was to merge that situation with a character from Franklin P. Adams' humor column, Dulcinea, who mouthed continual clichés, and place her in Westchester (Connelly 59). It is not clear whether the whole concept was Tyler's or Kaufman's, so it is difficult to assess credit or blame for the depiction of women in the play.[2]

In their next play, however, they were again asked by Tyler to write a play for another of his young actresses, Helen Hayes, in her first adult role (Goldstein 75). *To the Ladies* (Feb. 1922, 128 performances), according to Goldstein, was begun in 1921, but still lacked a third act and needed a serious re-writing a week before rehearsals opened. This time, however, the role of the wife and husband are reversed from what they were in *Dulcy.* The husband is now the foolish one who gets carried away by success and loses himself totally. He is saved by his wife who comes to his rescue and corrects his false vision of himself. This play is not based on a previous work source as are their other collaborations, and no one has offered any explanation of why the characters' roles reverse so completely.

The play's outline reveals its programatic structure; it has none of the integration of multiple plots interwoven in *Dulcy.* Instead, the plotting is sequential, as if the team started with an outline so that each could write the scenes he most preferred. In act one, Leonard and Elsie Beebe await a visit to their home from the boss of Leonard's piano factory—prelude to a promotion. But the visit is destroyed when their piano is repossessed because of their failure to make payments. Just when it seems all is lost, as the boss assumes Leonard is financially irresponsible, Elsie makes a valiant appeal which saves the day. From the start, however, we can see that she is the brains behind Leonard:

LEONARD:

> But when he sent for me, and—said all those nice things—why, that's where I got the work in. I mean, my telling him we had a Kincaid piano, and that you

sang little songs, and persuading him to drop in. (*He hastily picks up a magazine and begins to turn pages.*) The power of will!

ELSIE:

> (*Going into his arms. They are together R.C.*) Oh, yes, Leonard. I can't get over how—how smart you were.

LEONARD:

> It wasn't anything that anybody wouldn't have thought of.

ELSIE:

> Yes it was—and it was wonderful of you to think of it. Are you sure you did it just the way I—suggested.

LEONARD:

> Well, you hardly gave me more than just the—germ of it. You only said, if I ever did get a chance—

ELSIE:

> Oh, Leonard, I know it was you! You've got to take care of me, Leonard.

LEONARD:

> I will all right.

(10)

A passage like this shows how totally the male-female concept has changed in this play from the first. Here Leonard never knows—until the recognition scene at the end—that his wife is making his career for him, and without her he would be nothing. But it is apparent to the audience when Elsie hesitates over "as I—suggested." The playwrights do not make this any more obvious since it is not referred to again. But the audience knows from the start that Leonard is self-satisfied, self-deceived, and ignores his wife's contributions to his career. Elsie makes this clear to us and disguises it from Leonard when she quickly switches to the helpless female role, "You've got to take care of me, Leonard."

Elsie's superiority is demonstrated most clearly at the end of each act when she rescues Leonard from an impossible predicament. Her best effort is at the company awards banquet, where Leonard's rival gives the same speech he was about to give. Elsie steps in, as her husband collapses, to apologize for her husband's laryngitis, and speaks for him—a much better (and more praising to the boss) presentation which wins Leonard the promotion.

The issue of sexism is most prominently raised, however, in the third act when Leonard, now personal assistant to Mr. Kincaid, acts obnoxiously with new pride in his position toward everyone, even Elsie. The act opens with Leonard dictating a letter:

> . . . so I cannot say just what our attitude in the future will be in regard to the department. Mr. Toohey now has twelve girls in the mailing department, but believes with me that men not only could do the work better, but much more quickly, than women.

Paragraph. As you know, we believe that as a general rule women are not so capable as men in business.

(74)

No comment is ever made about this letter. It is simply there to show what Leonard has become, with the obvious inference that his sexism ("girls") is a result of his fatuous pride ("men . . . could do the work better"). But it is also apparent that the sexism is a product of "men in business," an environment that allows, if not encourages, this view of women. The play as a whole, in contrast, is designed to expose the blindness of businessmen.

Later in the act he is unmasked when it is revealed that he let his wife save him at the banquet, and so is demoted. Elsie comes to his rescue with Mr. Kincaid again:

ELSIE:

He's told me you've demoted him—on account of the speech.

LEONARD:

Elsie! Mr. Kincaid, she—she doesn't mean to—she doesn't understand—she's just a woman—

ELSIE:

Leonard, would you mind waiting out there—(*she points off R.*)—while Mr. Kincaid and I have a talk.

(92)

Leonard's casual disparagement, "she's just a woman," and Elsie's ignoring of it, make the point that digs against sexism are continual in this play, but not really underlined.

Indeed, the culminating speech of the play seems to try to address the sexism of Leonard, but does so by taking refuge in the cliché that behind every successful man there is a good woman.[3] Elsie gives the speech as a final appeal to Mr. Kincaid to reverse his view of her husband:

Why, nearly all the men you meet are just like you and Leonard. They don't let you know it—and I suppose sometimes they don't really know it themselves—always—but somewhere in back there's somebody—a wife or someone—who's helping them all the time—either giving them encouragement—or—perhaps doing real things, like Mrs. Kincaid [who makes all of Mr. Kincaid's business decisions]. Nearly every man that ever got any place has been married, and that couldn't just be coincidence!

(96-97)

The key thematic point is that "all the men don't really know it," but the full sexism of this blindness is not openly attacked. The only concession to a decent position for women is the glancing idea that the woman behind the man might be "doing real things," but that possibility is not really envisioned in this play.

Instead, the sentimental conclusion is Leonard's recognition, and admission, finally, of his need for his wife's help.

LEONARD:

This was—all your doing, and I want Mr. Kincaid to—know it.

ELSIE:

Why, no it wasn't, Leonard.

LEONARD:

Yes it was, but things are going to be different from now on. I'm going to make them different—(He hesitates; weakens a little)—if you'll help.

ELSIE:

But you may not—need me.

LEONARD:

Oh, yes I will—always.

(99)

Such a conclusion does not really address the underlying issues of male/female roles, nor does it address the source of the sexism in the business world which sanctions such views. Nor does the ending reveal any sophistication in dramaturgy. Still the foolish character creates the complications, and the smart one performs the rescue. The only shift from *Dulcy* is at least that the woman doesn't get the blame as the stupid one. But she still must play the background role, and Leonard's underlying business-based sexism is never fully addressed. His enlightenment is simply personal, not cultural: he recognizes Elsie's role, and humbles himself by making a public admission. But Leonard doesn't recognize, as the playgoers must, that his view of women is seriously skewed.[4]

In their next play, however, *Merton of the Movies* (November, 1922, 398 performances), the role of the woman is given a different treatment. Here she is able to be "doing real things" and is not only the brains hidden behind the man. And from this play forward, the business world is no longer seen as the cause of one individual's problems, as in the first two plays, but as a pervasive system which exploits anyone it can. The solution the playwrights offer is not to change the system, it is to outwit it; and women are key to doing this. Their third play, adapted from a serial in *The Saturday Evening Post,* has a foolish male character as in *To the Ladies,* but this time he is viewed more sympathetically. Merton Gill wants to be a movie star, and despises comedies, wanting only to do high art. He is rescued from his delusions of grandeur by "the Montague Girl" (significantly, her father's name is given, not hers). But she is a new kind of hero. She and her father look for work as extras or bit players, but she also pitches ideas for stories to directors, and is a stunt double for Merton's heroine of the movies, Beulah Baxter. So she is an independent woman, and one who is successful at that.

Merton's follies, which animate the plot, have nothing to do with her until the third act. He's seen in the first act as a dreamer who acts out movie stunts with store mannequins where he works in Simsbury, Illinois. In the second act, he lands his first role as an extra, but fails to do what the director wants and is fired. He is totally disillusioned at the end of the next act when he finds that Baxter doesn't do her own stunts. When he reaches total despair, the Montague Girl figures out a way to make him a success as she sells a new idea to Jeff Baird, the director of comedies which Merton despises:

GIRL:

> Don't you see? He looks like Parmalee [a movie star Merton idolizes] and he wants to do Parmalee stuff! All right, put him in a Buckeye comedy, and let him kid the life out of Parmalee! Only don't tell him he's supposed to be funny . . .

BAIRD:

> But suppose he finds out?

GIRL:

> That's the only thing I'm afraid of. We've got to keep it from him for a while, that's all. He's got a trusting way of looking at you that's sort of got me, Jeff, and if he ever finds out I did it, I couldn't stand it. He's a nice kid.

(72-73)

Although both Dulcy and Elsie manipulate people and use them for their own ends, this is the first Kaufman scene in which there is some consciousness of the consequences on the person manipulated. Nevertheless, the ethical questions implied are barely raised; perhaps this is because the movie system itself uses people all the time, so that considering such consequences is hardly encouraged.[5] The Girl's obvious concern for Merton, however, masks that she is using him. The tone of the quotation is very much like one from *Mr. Smith goes to Washington,* in which Jean Arthur does much the same thing, manipulating the James Stewart character and taking advantage of his innocence. The situation itself became a convention of works in the thirties. So did the idea of the comic genius who wants to be a success at high art, serious drama, as in S. N. Behrman's *No Time for Comedy* and Preston Sturges' screwball comedy *Sullivan's Travels.*

Like Mr. Smith, Merton's success is thus completely created by the woman behind the scenes. This technique resembles **To the Ladies,** but there is no marriage to require that she help him; and she is doing it to take advantage of him. He is not the talented actor he thinks he is, but a parody of one. What is intriguing about this situation is that Miss Montague is not working for Merton's best interest, per se, but rather for a successful movie, using him to achieve it. The main criterion for both the director and Miss Montague is simply making successful movies; using Merton to accomplish this is never questioned. The fact that he is destitute is not her main consideration at all.

The conclusion of the play is the recognition scene again, when Merton discovers that the Girl has made him a comic star. But the love that they share is presented in strangely maternal terms:

GIRL:

> (*Merton crosses to her and falls into her arms, sobbing.*) There, don't you worry! Mother's got you and she's never going to let you go.

MERTON:

> (*Sobbing*) It's like that night on the lot when I found out about you and Beulah Baxter and you were so—

GIRL:

> There, there. Don't you worry. Did he have his poor old mother going for a minute? Yes, he did. He had her going for a minute, all right. But he didn't fool her very long, not very long, because he can't ever fool her very long. And he can bet a lot of money on that.

MERTON:

> I feel a little better.

(93)

Perhaps the mother imagery of this final reconciliation reflects Kaufman's uneasiness with love scenes; it certainly shows him searching for a model for presenting a non-marital male/female relationship. The fact that this play was the most popular hit of Kaufman and Connelly, 398 performances,[6] indicates that as peculiar as the scene seems today, it made sense to the audience of its time.

The view of woman as mother, might also be appropriate to an America in the 1920s which whole-heartedly embraced psychoanalysis and Freud (as Kaufman's wife Beatrice did).[7] But for the dramatists, the image of woman as care-giving mother turns to nightmare in the last play Kaufman and Connelly wrote together, **Beggar on Horseback** (February, 1924; 144 performances). Here the twenties' grappling with the image and function of woman in relation to man is treated as a psychodrama. For the play is essentially a dream vision of the psychological struggle within Neil's mind of two stereotypes of woman. Rather than the virgin/whore dichotomy, here the conflict is two sides of wife/mother: supporter vs. suffocator. The duality is illustrated in two fantasies from the second act, as the would-be composer Neil moves from one woman to the other.

(The Supportive Cynthia:)

CYNTHIA AND NEIL:

> [*Reading in unison.*] "Your symphony will be played by our orchestra on December the tenth."

NEIL:

> Darling!

CYNTHIA:

Darling! They'll applaud and applaud! You'll have to come out and bow! (150-51)

(The Suffocating Gladys:)

NEIL:

Done for me? You've ruined me, that's all! You've given me a lot of money that I didn't want, and you won't let me do the one thing I want to do! Well, now I'm going to write my music! I'm going to finish my symphony!

GLADYS:

Oh, no, you're not! [*Crosses quickly to the piano and tears up the manuscript*] There's your old symphony! Now what have you got to say?

NEIL:

You tore it up! It was the only reason I married you, and you tore it up! All right—there's only one thing to do! [*He takes up the paper knife from the piano. . . .*]

(161-62)

The juxtaposition of the two views of woman, one helping and encouraging Neil as composer, the other hindering him and destroying his work, reveals the two views of women that seem to have alternated in the early work of Kaufman and Connelly. Dulcy destroyed her husband's efforts (though he still loved her). Elsie rectified her husband's blunders over and over again. So too did "the Montague Girl." But in the culmination of Kaufman and Connelly's partnership, the two visions seem to be at war over Neil's soul.

Interestingly, there is never any consideration by any character over whether it is moral or ethical to simply use Gladys for her money—all the characters accept that as a given.

CYNTHIA:

Oh, I've been thinking about it ever since she began coming here! You really *do* think it's the right thing for him? The wisest?

ALBERT:

I'm sure of it.

CYNTHIA:

But could he be happy?

ALBERT:

That's the only way he *can* be happy, permanently—if he's free to write his music. That's the most important thing in the end.

CYNTHIA:

It seems—and yet I'm afraid you're right.

ALBERT:

We only hurt people by being sentimental about them. That's one of the first things a doctor learns. Let's put this through, Will you? . . . You'll be here, and I've got to go away. And anyway, a woman can always do more than a man about this sort of thing.

(84)

This is an intriguing passage because of the way it ignores Gladys totally and only questions whether Neil will be happy: "that's the most important thing in the end."

The issues are so centered in the psychological realm that normal considerations of human relationships do not apply. Thus, here, even more than in the other plays, the women are simply used to make the plot, to create the conflict. They have no reality or purpose outside their simple dramatic (or perhaps psychologica) function.

Again, however, that is a factor of the kind of system in which the characters exist: the all-powerful business world. Neil is mercilessly exploited at the beginning of the play, writing endless arrangements of others' music for bare subsistence—that is why he has no time to write his own music. And in his dream vision of working for Gladys' father, business exploits him (as he seeks to exploit Gladys). Music is turned out on an assembly line, as Neil explains: "The ideas are brought from the inspiration department every hour on the hour. After I turn them into music they are taken to the purifying department, and then to the testing and finishing rooms. They are then packed for shipment" (220).

The conclusion allows Neil exactly what he wants without working for it: Gladys finds another man, and decides to break off the engagement to Neil. And self-sacrificing Cynthia, who left Neil so that he would marry Gladys for her money, simply returns: "Cynthia. (*Hesitatingly*). Want me, Neil? Neil. Do I want you? (*He continues playing as he hears her approaching.*)" (237). Kaufman's difficulty in writing a romantic scene could not be more evident than in this underplayed reconciliation, as Neil continus to play the piano. His acceptance of Cynthia, without making the least effort, other than to endure the dream vision psycho-machia, reveals how far the play is from dealing with characters as if they had reality outside the play. The solution posed is simply to reject the money of business, both as employee and as spouse.

Suggesting the pattern within the psyche of the playwright, Kaufman's first four major plays depict women as either helpers or hinderers. The last play in the sequence provides a test case, since it is the only play that Kaufman wrote alone. Lacking Connelly's assistance, though after working with Edna Ferber to adapt her story **Minick** for the stage (September 1924, 141 performances), Kaufman's **The Butter and Egg Man** (September 23, 1925, 243 performances) offers a fit ending for the psychic pattern, but in this play, again there is a less than astute hero—Peter Jones, hick from Ohio. But the new ingredient is Joe

Lehman, exploitative producer. It is he who initially sets the action running, duping Peter and keeping a production afloat. Lehman's secretary, Jane Weston, at first is used as simple sexual bait by Lehman. He has her enter with a fake letter just so Peter will see her—and join the business. When she discovers that Peter and his mother's whole savings is taken by Lehman, Jane looks to be the guiding and helping little woman, but instead she does not warn Peter of Lehman's plans to deceive him. She works for Lehman, and though she hasn't been paid for three months, continues to support him. She makes it clear to the audience that Peter is being duped, but he does not realize it.[8]

As the play progresses, however, both Jane and Peter become more independent. Peter increasingly speaks up with his suggestions for the production, and Jane finally objects to Lehman's treatment of him: "I simply say you're being unfair to him! I think—it's an outrageous way to treat him! You take his money—all you can get—for a play you must have known was worthless—" (142-43). Her objections, however, just get her fired, and Peter comes to her rescue: "I'll show you whether you can talk to people like that. Do you want to sell the rest of it to me—the show?" (145). Once his offer is accepted, and Lehman leaves, Peter realizes what he's done:

JANE:

Oh, Peter, it was foolish!

PETER:

But I had to show him, didn't I? I couldn't help it, when he started talking to you like that.

JANE:

I got you into it again.

(151)

PETER:

I—I'm just beginning to realize what's happened. I've given him—everything I had left and—that's all there is to it. It's gone. I guess I'm done for.

JANE:

Peter, you're not! Now, we're going to think of a way out.

(153)

In these passages, Jane accepts her partial responsibility for getting Peter into the dilemma, and signals the shift of the play's direction with "*we're* going to think of a way out." The *we* indicates the cooperation that will govern the rest of the play between woman and man, rather than having one manipulate the other.

They work together when Oscar Fritchie enters as a potential investor. Peter is given the first stage direction to indicate his recognition of Fritchie's possibility: "[*Slowly digesting this.*] Would you mind saying that over again?

OSCAR. The show business. I say—someday I'm going to get into it" (160). It is Jane, however, who first broaches the subject, working together with Peter to make the sale:

OSCAR:

Say—what's up?

JANE:

[*Leaping into the breach.*] Mr. Jones has a proposition to make to you! He's going to give you a chance to invest in this play that opened tonight! It's going to make an awful lot of money—

(164)

In this case both Peter and Jane are working together, but it is she who takes the initiative. Peter leads Fritchie on, explaining the glories of being a producer, and Jane assists, but it is she who must raise the issue.

As the scene progresses, however, they begin to work as a team to get Oscar to sign on as co-producer:

OSCAR:

Now wait! I—I don't know what to say. I know I'd like the theatrical business, and I been getting kind of tired of the hotel lately—

PETER:

Sure! I did too! Why—you're not the kind of man to stay cooped up in a hotel all his life.

JANE:

Mr. Jones got out, and look at him!

PETER:

Yah. [OSCAR *looks.*]

OSCAR:

I'd love to quit and tell Mr. Hemingway what I thought of him.

PETER:

That's the stuff!

JANE:

Then, why don't you?

OSCAR:

I'm scared.

PETER:

Well, this is your chance!

JANE:

A chance to leave this old hotel behind you!

(169-70)

Working together, Peter and Jane build up the fantasy for Oscar of escaping from his hotel life to be a New York producer. Once they realize that his fantasy is to tell off his boss, they work on that in tandem.

Jane's importance becomes more evident when the lawyer, Patterson, confronts Peter with the charge of plagiarism. She saves Peter by stalling for time:

PETER:

What do you think we ought to do, Jane?

JANE:

[*To the lawyer*] Must you—must Mr. Jones give an answer immediately?

PATTERSON:

I regret that he must.

PETER:

But it's—I haven't had time—

JANE:

Can't we—even talk it over? That is, Mr. Jones and I?

PATTERSON:

This young lady is your adviser?

PETER:

Yes, indeed.

(197)

Peter's deference to Jane, and her taking the lead in dealing with the lawyer, implies her status. But the final line confirms her elevation beyond secretary to full equality, as Peter agrees that she is his adviser.

It is Jane again who takes the lead as Peter again defers to her in the fifteen minute grace period. She comes up with the idea of getting both Lehman and McClure to pool their money to buy the show back:

PETER:

Well then, I guess we're-[*Almost as a matter of course, he turns to* JANE.]

JANE:

I know a way to fix things. Mr. Lehman has fifty thousand dollars and so has Mr. McClure.

LEHMAN:

Well?

JANE:

Why shouldn't they—buy it together?

PETER:

[*As it dawns on him.*] Oh, say! That's an idea. [*He gives Jane an approving pat on the shoulder.*]

(210)

By this time, Peter has come to recognize that if an idea is needed, Jane will come up with it, and so *"Almost as a matter of course, he turns to JANE."* And immediately, she replies without hesitation, "I know a way to fix things." Up until this point, Jane's function is essentially that of the witty servant in Plautine comedy—but finally the love interest is articulated.

The expression of love, typical of Kaufman, is limited to an *"approving pat on the shoulder."* Naturally, it is Jane who must say the words—which Peter is never quite able to return. As in the other plays, whenever the man gets an inflated sense of self-worth, the woman comes to the rescue, and it is in the interval when Peter seems doomed by the lawyer that Jane broaches the subject of love:

JANE:

Peter—may I tell you something? [*He is silent.*] I love you, Peter.

PETER:

Oh Jane, do you? [*He reaches for her hand.*]

JANE:

Wait, I wanted to tell it to you now, when things are looking black. It—it may be wrong, but—I'm glad this happened. . . . I did want you to be successful, but somehow you lost something that was you. It's just as you said, Peter—you're not that kind of person—you never could be. You belong back in Chillicothe, in the hotel. You're—simple, and—sweet, and—you don't really like all this, do you?

PETER:

I don't know. I thought I did, but I don't know.

JANE:

Don't you realize—how little it amounts to, really? You're too fine for it, Peter.

PETER:

Did you mean what you said, about—loving me?

JANE:

More than anything that ever was. I thought for a while you'd gone away from me, but now I know you never can. It made me so unhappy to think that—but now it's all over.

PETER:

It's over, all right. Being a success is over.

(199-200)

This is a nice, though not very moving, scene. At least it avoids the horrors of turning the woman into a mother. Yet the closest intimacy allowed is for Peter to reach for her hand (does he ever get it?). Perhaps no more is necessary, however, or allowed. More intriguing is the way that the business, ethical, and love considerations are all mixed together. In this play, as in the previous *Beggar on Horseback,* the idea of business and financial success is clearly revealed to be the destruction of a person's soul. Peter has become an imitation Lehman, exploiting the naive Fritchie without hesitation, and getting an inflated ego as a result. The only solution possible, as in *Beggar,* is to flee the world of commerce: "You belong back in Chillicothe, in the hotel. You're—simple, and—sweet, and—you don't really like all this, do you?" The world of money and business is seen as so corrupting and manipulative, that there is no way to survive by accommodating oneself. Only through escape is it possible for men and women to exist on equal grounds, and for love to be possible.

This play, of his earliest efforts, shows the most balanced view of men and women. Peter is still a complete fool at times, but he catches on fast, and begins to use Lehman's own language by the end, calling him "Sweetheart" (but not calling Jane that). The point is that in this last play of his first period, the only one he wrote alone, Kaufman was finally free from using women as mere plot devices. Unlike Dulcy, who animates the plot with her stupidity, or the helping women like Elsie, the Montague Girl, and Cynthia, Jane is a little less and so a little more. She is not simply the witty servant who helps out her stupid master. She and Peter seem to work together in three scenes, collaborating as they extemporize. And that is not only a more healthy relationship for them, but also a more liberated one for the playwright.

Coincident with this changing attitude towards women is the view of business which seems to create it. At first, business is simply embodied in one person: in *Dulcy* it is the take-over mogul, Mr. Forbes, and in *To the Ladies,* Leonard's employer, Mr. Kincaid. But in *Merton of the Movies,* it is clearly a whole system which takes advantage of would-be actors, pays them little or nothing, and uses them to create great profits. In this case, men and women are used in the same way, and the only way to deal with such a system is to try to outwit it, as the Montague girl and Merton finally do. The same vision is shown in Neil's dream in *Beggar on Horseback*—but the system there is so all encompassing, that the only way to deal with it is to escape, as Neil and Cynthia decide to do. In *Butter and Egg Man* the same is true; to save himself from becoming as ego-inflated as other producers in the business of Broadway, Peter must return to Ohio to run a hotel.

The later, greater successes of George S. Kaufman reveal the fruits of this early liberation from the exploitation of women (characters). In the plays of the 1930s, especially those he wrote with Moss Hart, the contrivance of reliance upon women characters to animate the plot by themselves is finally gone. And those plays distribute the work of making the events occur more equally across a wide variety of characters, especially in *You Can't Take It with You* (1936; 827 performances) and *The Man Who Came To Dinner* (1939; 739 performances). Such works not only reveal the maturity of the dramatist in age, but also his developed sense of the role of women which is much more complex than the early more exploitative plays written with Connelly.

Another development which stems from Kaufman's early plays can be seen in the movies of the 1930s.[9] This is no surprise since all five of these plays were made into (silent) movies in the 1920s. *Butter and Egg Man* (filmed in 1928 by First National) can be seen as a clear precursor of the screwball comedies of the next decade. And the less developed male/female relationships of *Merton of the Movies* and *Beggar on Horseback* lead to Frank Capra's use of the convention in Jean Arthur's intelligent helper to the naïve Mr. Smith, or Barbara Stanwyk to Gary Cooper's equally naïve John Doe. In Capra's work, the woman takes care of her man; but George S. Kaufman had advanced beyond that use of women (characters) which he had shed by 1925.[10]

Notes

1. Two scholars recently dealing with Kaufman have ignored the authorship problem and dealt with his work as a complete entity, defining his playwriting in conventional dramatic categories, one as a satirist, the other as a farceur. Rhoda-Gale Pollack sees Kaufman as a satirist "who molded American satirical comedy in to the form that we know today" (Preface). Rejecting the label of satirist, Jeffrey Mason places him entirely in the tradition of farce. The change in category results in each concentrating on different plays in this sequence of earliest successes. The categories also result in peculiar views of women. Pollack, for example, thinks that *To the Ladies* "would appeal to contemporary feminists" because of its theme that behind every successful man is a wife/woman. Mason has a more sophisticated vision of feminism, but his concept of farce requires that characters be seen as types, and results in a rather negative view of the characters discussed in this paper: "Gladys Cady is Kaufman's 'nice girl' gone berserk, and in compromising the female characters, Kaufman threatens the sentimental concept of domesticity. With her savvy sense of humor and firm dedication, the Montague Girl seems to offer a viable post-Twenties option as a wife until she reaches the grotesque and disturbing moment when Merton weeps and she holds him in her arms. . . . The most sympathetic option is Jane Weston, who succeeds simply because she does not offend" (26-27).

2. Scott Meredith quotes Kaufman claiming the combination of Dulcy and Helen Glendenning was his idea completely, but there is no attribution (78). Connelly implies that they both came up with the idea of using Adams's Dulcinea, and ignores the

earlier play in which Fontanne played Helen Glendenning (59). Goldstein gives the most complete account, but claims that Tyler gave them "by way of suggestion or instruction" that they turn "Adams's Dulcinea into some kind of comic heroine" (57) but he does not explain who suggested merging her with the earlier Fontanne character.

3. Pollack sees this instead as a feminist position: "Certainly the wisdom of Elsie and Mrs. Kincaid would appeal to contemporary feminists" (20). But this is "first stage" feminism at best. Mason seems closer to the truth in his description of Elsie: "Elsie dons folly as a mask in order to hide her intelligence as she manipulates her bumbling husband's career while convincing him that she is helpless without him" (24).

4. Alexander Woollcott's review in *The New York Times* implies a complete acceptance of this play as a kind of feminist statement, without questioning either the implied anti-feminism of Leonard nor of the view of wives as anything other than positive:

> It is not until after their marriage that she finds out he is the kind of young man who . . . if he is ever to amount to anything, she will have to manage it for him somehow. The play follows her campaign in this matter, and it is attended by many skirmishes and many agonies, the kind of everyday agonies that keep life agitating in your own home. It is a piece written on the observation that all men who have, as a matter of fact, amounted to anything have been married men, and on that theory that can hardly have been a coincidence.
>
> (26)

5. Mason describes the worlds of the three later plays, *Merton, Beggar,* and *Butter and Egg Man* in similar terms, as the business world out of control. For example "Merton's Hollywood is a farcical machine that has run amuck but has no 'off' switch. The industry makes the same films again and again, as writers and directors find 'new' material not in real life but in movies they've already made" (17). And in *Butter and Egg Man,* "We see Broadway through Peter's wide eyes as a closed system that forces all comers to live by its own unique logic, a set of crazy rules that seem to change whenever anyone nearly masters it" (14)

6. 398 is Goldstein's number (92); Pollack uses the same number (25). Mason gives the number as 381 (112). But without explanation Meredith lists it as 248 (656).

7. Goldstein notes Beatrice Kaufman's dependence on psychoanalysts through the 1920s and 1930s (49).

8. Mason sees Jane in much more passive terms: "Jane is a 'nice girl,' matching Peter in virtue, but she has learned a little from experience. And she knows that the sharpers have swindled him, so she unobtrusively guides him when his intuition goes awry" (14). This view completely ignores the increasingly active role she plays as she becomes freed from the "crazy rules" of the institution that Mason describes, and does much more than "unobtrusively guide," but actively leads the way. Pollack virtually ignores Jane, not even mentioning her by name: "Also Peter receives assistance in his efforts—as does Merton—from a knowledgeable ingenue who protects and promotes him" (36).

9. *Dulcy* presents a stereotype later made famous by Gracie Allen (and later by Lucille Ball on television), the wife whose attempts to help her husband creates disasters. But the later plays reverse this image of women entirely, giving prototypes of the Jean Arthur/ Barbara Stanwyk roles used in the movies of the 1930s. Another aspect of *Dulcy* also used by the screwball comedies of the 1930s is the madman who thinks he's a millionaire, making business deals only to be exposed so that the seeming solution falls through. The character of Harold Patterson, who thinks he's Schuyler Van Dyke, shows up on *The Twentieth Century* as well to deceive Carole Lombard and John Barrymore.

10. Another Capra-esque touch is the view of business as destructive. Grandpa Vanderhof in *You Can't Take It with You* is the archetypal Kaufman hero in this respect—having totally rejected the world of business in 1912, he and his family of eccentrics all live a kind of ideal life, free from the contamination of business or success. Capra made the film of *You Can't Take It with You* in 1938; it won the Academy Award for best picture in that year.

Works Cited

Austin, Gayle. *Feminist Theories for Dramatic Criticism.* Ann Arbor: University of Michigan Press, 1990.

Case, Sue-Ellen. *Feminism and Theatre.* New York: Methuen, 1988.

Connelly, Marc. *Voices Offstage.* Chicago: Holt, Rinehart, 1968.

Dolan, Jill. *The Feminist Spectator as Critic.* Ann Arbor, MI: UMI, 1988.

Goldstein, Malcolm. *George S. Kaufman: His Life, His Theater.* New York: Oxford, 1979.

Kaufman, George S. *Butter and Egg Man.* New York: Boni and Liveright, 1926.

Kaufman, George S. and Marc Connelly. *Dulcy.* New York: G.P. Putnam's Sons, 1921. Rpt. New York: Samuel French, 1948.

Kaufman, George S. and Marc Connelly. *To The Ladies.* New York: Samuel French, 1923.

Kaufman, George S. and Marc Connelly. *Merton of the Movies.* 1922. Rpt. New York: Sameul French, 1953.

Kaufman, George S. and Marc Connelly. *Beggar on Horseback.* New York: Boni and Liveright, 1924.

Mason, Jeffrey. *Wisecracks: The Farces of George S. Kaufman.* Ann Arbor and London: UMI Research Press, 1988.

Meredith, Scott. *George S. Kaufman and His Friends.* New York: Doubleday, 1974.

Pollack, Rhoda-Gale. *George S. Kaufman.* Boston: Twayne, 1988.

Teichmann, Howard. *George. S. Kaufman: An Intimate Portrait.* New York: Atheneum, 1972.

Woollcott, Alexander. "By the Authors of 'Dulcy.'" Review of *To The Ladies.New York Times,* 21 February, 1922. Rpt. in *On Stage: Selected Theater Reviews from The New York Times 1920-70,* eds. Bernard Beckerman and Howard Seigman, New York: Arno P, 1973: 26.

THE MAN WHO CAME TO DINNER

PRODUCTION REVIEWS

Joseph Wood Krutch (essay date 28 October 1939)

SOURCE: Krutch, Joseph Wood. "What Nothing Succeeds Like." *The Nation* 149, no. 18 (October 28, 1939): 474-75.

[*In the following review, Krutch objects to what he sees as a lack of warmth and merriment in* The Man Who Came to Dinner *although he recognizes that it is funny and skillfully crafted.*]

Not even the obvious virtues of farce as the Messrs. Kaufman and Hart have learned to write it seem quite adequate to explain the boundless enthusiasm with which their successive works are received. A very large and very mixed audience has taken them to its heart in some special way and greets them with a warmth seldom exhibited upon any other occasion, grave or gay. The glow begins at the first hint that a new piece is to be expected, and as the great night approaches, the elect assemble in the best of their good clothes ready to greet one another with happy smiles which say, "This is going to be good." When the curtain goes down upon the first act, the applause which breaks forth is as unanimous and as inevitable as the plaudits of the Reichstag, and yet it is not from the members of any single party. One touch of something—it probably isn't nature—has made the giddiest of debutantes and the tiredest of tired business men one with the critic. This, they all say, is what we really like. And thereby they confound the gloomiest critics of our civilization. Who says that the modern world acknowledges no "principle of unity"?

There is no doubt about the fact that *The Man Who Came to Dinner* (Music Box Theater) is one of the best and funniest of the farces which Mr. Kaufman has written with either Mr. Hart or any of the other numerous collaborators with whom he has worked. In a very general way it belongs in the category of *The Royal Family* and *You Can't Take It with You,* though it is technically smoother than either, and doubtless owes part of its effectiveness to the steadily accelerating tempo and the mounting complications which ensue as one character after another is introduced to keep the pot a-boiling. And yet, sound as the workmanship is, it is still, I think, not entirely clear just why the enthusiasm of an audience is quite so unreserved, unanimous, and unqualified as it actually is, just why the plays of Mr. Kaufman and Mr. Hart should be treated as absolutely *sui generis* and find audiences whose applause is not so much a judgment as the confirmation of a foregone conclusion. Perhaps the fact that they are so treated helps to give the authors an air of confidence, helps them to be what it is already taken for granted that they are. Perhaps Mr. Kaufman and Mr. Hart are made funnier by being thought funny, just as a beautiful woman is said to be made more beautiful by the knowledge that she is loved. But that probably does not prevent other comic writers from asking themselves what the unloved are said to ask: "What's he got that I haven't?"

The answer is as difficult in the second case as it is in the first, but part of it probably is that Mr. Kaufman and Mr. Hart have a certain power of suggesting that they are very much in the know, that to laugh with them is to laugh in the most up-to-date company, and that, contrariwise, to fail to see the point in this satiric thrust or that is simply to confess that one does not know one's way about the metropolis. *The Man Who Came to Dinner* has, that is to say, something of the warm, cosy malice of a gossip column. Of course the man in question, a man who came unwilling and stayed for weeks because he broke a hip on the doorstep, is not really Alexander Woollcott; Alexander Woollcott does not wear a beard as this man does. But were it not for this essential incongruity, that intimate inner circle—strictly limited to forty or fifty million persons—which shares the carefully guarded secret of the Town Crier's habits, tastes, and mannerisms might suspect that this sentimental egotist with a serpent's tongue was intended as a far from flattering portrait. Even as it is, one may speculate wickedly upon the question whether or not the British jack-of-all-theatrical-trades was intended to bear some resemblance to Noel Coward, and when a much-discussed character—a practical joker from Hollywood most mysteriously known as "Banjo"—finally appears, one may nudge one's companion and say, "That's probably Harpo Marx. 'Harpo' and 'Banjo.' Get it?" The play does, to be sure, poke fun at just the sort of celebrity worship to which it appeals, and on Christmas morning the gifts received by the man who came to dinner include, among others, little remembrances from Shirley Temple, William Lyon Phelps, and Admiral Byrd. But though you may laugh as you will, neither you nor I really know so many people whom any autograph hunter would prize.

Perhaps I am merely being perverse, for my laughter was as loud and as long as that of the audience about me. Perhaps Mr. Kaufman is only an Aristides who has been called "the funny" once too often. But I do not think that it is merely that. *The Man Who Came to Dinner* is too bright, too hard, and too competent. It is funny without being gay, and it leaves no pleasant chuckles behind. I do not mean merely that it is cynical, though, except for a few inevitable and incongruous passages of sentiment, it is as loveless as tinkling cymbals. I do mean that there is no ebullience even of cynicism, no real joyousness, in it. Laughable it certainly is; merry it certainly is not. And the best of comedies are somehow merry. All the parts are played with suave expertness, only one, I think, with more than that. Carol Goodner, an American whose successes have been mostly in London, brings to the part of the professional siren a human warmth lacking in the well-disciplined performances of the rest of the cast.

Morton Eustis (essay date November 1939)

SOURCE: Eustis, Morton. "*The Man Who Came to Dinner.*" *Theatre Arts* 23 (November 1939): 789-98.

[*In the following essay, Eustis describes Kaufman at work directing* The Man Who Came to Dinner.]

'All Right, Mr. Kaufman?' the stage manager asks . . . 'Yes, any time you're ready.' . . . George S. Kaufman has a whispered colloquy with Monty Woolley. He stands centre stage surveying the green living-room-hall in Mesalia, Ohio, which Donald Oenslager has designed for *The Man Who Came to Dinner.* He marks the spot where he wants Woolley's wheel-chair to rest, opens and closes the big doors leading to the library on the left to see that they slide smoothly, and rubs the edge of the stair bannisters in the centre to see that they are smooth enough for someone to slide down. Then he walks down the ramp which connects stage and auditorium during rehearsals and flops in an orchestra seat with his legs dangling over two of the chairs.

The scene is the Music Box Theatre. The time, 2 P.M., one Tuesday afternoon eight days after the Kaufman-Hart comedy has been in rehearsal. The first four days were passed sitting around a table, reading. Today a run-through of the entire play is to be attempted. Although the actors are still fumbling for their lines, none of them carry their 'sides', except Monty Woolley, who, in the Woollcottian role of Sheridan Whiteside—litterateur, lecturer, radio commentator, 'intimate friend of the great and near-great'—has a part which is almost as long as Hamlet's.

It is a little unusual in theater practice to have the set in place so early. But Kaufman is such a stickler for assurance in detail that, when the play is not an elaborate, many-scened affair, he likes his actors to get the feel of the set as soon as they walk on in their parts. The stage manager

sits at a prompt table on the right. A brilliant work-light hangs centre stage illuminating the set and the dark and empty theater in a garish manner.

'On stage for the end of the third act,' the stage manager calls out. Kaufman, a script in his hand, walks up the aisle to talk with his collaborator, Moss Hart. 'You may be right,' he says, 'but let's run through it this way and see how it plays.'

To see a play backwards—the final curtain first, then the last act, then the second and the first—is a curious and somewhat frightening experience to anyone who has ever tried to write a play. It shows—at any rate, this farce-comedy shows—that a play can be put together so that each scene is not only self-explanatory but a revelation of what has gone before. The last act of *The Man Who Came to Dinner* is just as funny, and just as clear, even if you have not seen the acts which preceded it and have but the haziest advance notion of what the play is about. Kaufman, in all the rehearsals of the show except the complete run-throughs, starts with the last act and works backward. Whether he does this deliberately because he thinks that it is one way to catch the dead spots—that each act, in other words, should be able to stand on its own feet as an entity—this writer cannot tell. But to see a backward run of a play that is as expertly constructed as the present Kaufman-Hart script is an object lesson in what William Archer calls 'playmaking'.

* * *

'All right, ready.' They start to run through the scene in which Sheridan Whiteside takes his sarcastic leave of the Middle Western family on whom he has imposed himself for over a month. Kaufman slumps in a seat next to Hart as the action commences.

Whiteside, the bewhiskered 'Big Lord Fauntleroy', as his secretary calls him in a moment of anger, bids farewell, in his graciously ungracious style, to his long suffering host and starts to make his exit.

'Merry Christmas, everybody,' he says as his parting thrust, puts his hat on with a flourish and walks out of the house.

'Wait a minute,' Kaufman says. 'The gesture with the hat is fine, Monty, but make it after the line. You'll hold the line that way and sustain it.' The exit is repeated and Kaufman proves to be right. The 'Merry Christmas' is funny in itself—after all that has occurred—and the gesture holds and builds the laugh.

'Now let's get this sound right,' says Kaufman, as he ambles up on stage and walks over to the stage manager's desk. Whiteside, in leaving the house, is supposed to slip on the icy stoop, emitting a loud groan. 'I want to try dropping a sand bag for the first sound. Then your groan, Monty, must be a long, agonized wail.' . . . 'How's this?' says Woolley, moaning eloquently. 'A little too sharp, I think,' Kaufman tells him. 'But try it once.'

'Merry Christmas, everybody,' Woolley flourishes his hat and goes out. A thud is heard, then Woolley's anguished groan. 'No, Monty,' Kaufman calls out, 'I get the feeling that you're standing right outside. Remember, the door is shut! All right, now key it down a little—*there,* that's just right.'

They run through this exit several times as Kaufman stands watching it, his long arms dangling loosely by his side, his shock of black hair standing up in disarray.

Kaufman, the director, is the complete antithesis of Kaufman, the playwright. The pungent, volatile drive, the sheer exuberance and vitality that illuminates almost every Kaufman script, is completely lacking in Kaufman, the man. He is not, like Noel Coward, a whole show in himself at rehearsals. He is quiet, unobtrusive; he never raises his voice, even at the most exasperating moments; he is kindly, sympathetic, quizzical. There is nothing of the human dynamo hammering the beat of a speedy, perfectly timed charade. On the other hand, he gives almost immediately the impression that the jobs of playwriting and directing are two parts of the same thing; that gesture, and the movement of the actors, singly and together, are as much a part of the play as the words. This accounts for the way he rewrites as he goes along, shifting a phrase, a line, sometimes a whole speech to suit the tempo and the rhythm of movement he wants to secure. He is nothing if not thorough. And as you see him standing, his head tilted a little to one side, his forefinger cocked or in the corner of his mouth, listening to the sound of a play that will be as quickly paced as any in New York, you realize that his genius for direction lies as much in the infinite capacity for taking pains as in a natural theater flair.

The new Kaufman-Hart opus is a kind of *You Can't Take It with You,* Algonquin style. Kaufman and Hart strand their Woollcottian prototype in Mesalia, Ohio, while on a lecture tour. The portly, quixotic 'road company Nero', as he describes himself in one bashful moment, breaks his hip (or is supposed to) when he slips on the ice on the doorstep of Mr. and Mrs. Ernest Stanley's home and he is obliged to spend a month in a wheel-chair in their house. He disrupts completely the life of every one in the establishment. He takes charge, arrogantly, of the living quarters; relegates the Stanleys to the service entrance; sends their children away from home and generally makes an alluring beast of himself. The thread of the play is hung on his thoroughly outrageous attempt to thwart his secretary's desire to marry a young reporter from the local gazette—an attempt which involves the kidnapping of an English actress he lures to Mesalia to entrap the young reporter. Like a good opus, it ends on the key in which it started—an exit and a fall on the ice.

* * *

'Hold it, Monty,' Kaufman calls out, 'I want to fill in here with a few little lines before you come in.' Whiteside's groan, on his final curtain fall, brings all the family and servants rushing into the room, down the stairs and from the doors to the left. After a moment's thought, as he scratches the edge of his steel-rimmed glasses, Kaufman gets the line he wants Whiteside's secretary to say: '"Bert, something's happened to Mr. Whiteside"—No, I beg your pardon. Bert's got to run out. I forgot. Turn to the doctor and say "Doctor—doctor". On that, you people run downstairs (the son and daughter and Mrs. Stanley). Not too highly keyed, please, you people on the stairs—*You* say (to the son) "What's the matter? What's wrong!"—You (to the girl) "Has something happened? What is it?"—You (to the mother) "What's the matter? What's the matter, Barbara!" . . . All right, try it.'

They run through it. 'Now a little faster,' Kaufman requests. 'You needn't wait for dead cues on this. You can overlap them . . . "What's the matter? What's the matter?" sounds wrong. Let's see. Change that to "Oh dear! Oh dear!"'

Kaufman watches with Hart as they work out this scene. 'The group on the stairs a little stronger vocally, please, he calls out. 'And Doctor, your entrance is too casual. You've got to come in with a good deal of eagerness.'

Back on stage he spends five minutes working out the cues with the stage manager so that each sound and movement is timed to create the right effect. The scene is played again and again. Whiteside is carried in for the final curtain, shouting for his nurse—whom he detested—and promising that he will sue the Stanley family for $350,000.

'We'll have to wait until we get this before an audience, Monty,' Kaufman says to Woolley, 'to see whether your line "I want Miss Preen, Miss Preen!" (the nurse) gets such a laugh that it will drown out the next one, or whether we can get the laugh and then build it again on "$350,000".'

'All right, let's try the third act from the beginning of the kidnap.' This is (or was) the scene in which a Harpo Marx character, named Banjo, and a crazy surrealist painter, named Miguel Santos, save the day for Whiteside by kidnapping the actress (played by Carol Goodner, the English actress). This is worked out very slowly, to get the mechanics of it exact. Binding the girl's legs and arms, and gagging her, require considerable routine work. Woolley also has a fast and continuous speech at this point and it is essential to have the kidnapping take no longer than Woolley's lines.

'All right, let's do this routine again,' Kaufman says, 'and time it.' It takes exactly twenty-seven seconds. 'We'll allow thirty seconds,' Kaufman says, 'in case of a slip.' They play it through again, first with the business alone, then with the lines. Kaufman calls: 'Put it together a few times, business and lines.' And he adds: 'Maybe in about two days, after this is better set, I'll fill it in a little more, but let's let it go as it is, now.'

Kaufman comes down into the house and has a long talk with Hart. Then he asks the stage manager to run through the third act.

* * *

Whiteside, looking intently at the picture of Mr. Stanley's sister, suddenly discovers that she is none other than Lizzie Borden, or as the dramatists choose to call her, Harriet Sedley. He looks at the picture, registers recognition, but that is all. Hart stands up. 'I think we've got to build this, George,' he tells Kaufman. 'I'd like to have him snap his fingers as he looks at the picture—and I'd even go so far as to have him say: "I knew I'd seen that face before." . . . You've got to let the audience realize the significance of what he's discovered and I don't think the facial expression is enough.'

Kaufman is a little uncertain. 'It may be too obvious,' he says, 'but O.K., let's try it.' Woolley does try it and it is much better. The slight confusion that was evident before is gone.

'I'd like you to run through the second act, Bernie,' Kaufman tells the stage manager. 'Then we'll try one little change.' And he and Hart retire to Sam Harris' office in the mezzanine to do some rewriting.

The second act runs fairly smoothly and without interruption, as its mentors are not present. There is a definite dead spot, however, in the middle where the Stanley son and daughter ask Whiteside to help them in their troubles. The son wants to become a professional photographer, 'but Dad won't hear of it'. The daughter has fallen in love with a young labor organizer and 'Dad won't hear of that' either. Each asks Whiteside's help, and of course he gives it, advising them to do exactly what their parents think they should not do. The two short scenes are nicely written. The son gives quite an eloquent speech, but somehow the interest lags the moment they start their pleas.

The run-through completed—to the tune of a typewriter pounding busily upstairs—Kaufman and Hart make their appearance with the new material. The sheets of paper are passed out to the company, Kaufman sits down on the sofa and asks them to read through the new scene, which is, needless to say, the dead spot of the second act. What Kaufman and Hart have done is quite simple. They have transposed, rearranged and cut the scene severely, giving to Whiteside the burden of the lines which the son and daughter formerly spoke. The net result is to keep Whiteside in the dominant position. He is now the one who suggests that the son should leave his family and follow his own bent; he is the one to tell the daughter that she must run away with her boyfriend. Even in a reading, the scene picks up. The sympathy of the audience is enlisted just as strongly on behalf of the children, but the fact that Whiteside, the supreme meddler, is the *deus ex machina* of the occasion, gives it a point and a breadth of humor lacking before.

'That's better, don't you think?' Kaufman says to the writer, as he strolls up the aisle. 'An audience always listens more to a lead than to a juvenile, and I think the shift has pulled up the scene. It's amazing, you know,' he says as he sits down. 'You think you have a script just as tight as possible. Then you get it on the stage and dead chunks appear all through it. When you get it in front of an audience, a whole new set of dead spots turn up. And three weeks after the New York opening you still find places you can cut.'

This, from a man of Kaufman's experience both as a playwright and a director, should be more than illuminating to young and earnest playwrights who feel that a script is an inviolable thing which cannot be desecrated by the change of even a word or a semi-colon. If anyone in our theater should be able to write a 'tight' script, it is George Kaufman and Moss Hart. And yet you see these two glittering dramatic jitterbugs rewriting whole scenes, filling in others, and cutting, cutting, cutting all along the line.

You see them also writing almost as they go along, taking a well-rounded script, not a skeleton by any means, and giving it a three-dimensional quality in terms of the complex medium in which it is expressed. Kaufman's method as a director is utterly different from that of Noel Coward or the Lunts, all three of whom are more dynamic in their approach than he is. Yet Kaufman, in his own way, produces a dynamic effect as well as anyone in our theater. And he can mold a rollicking script like ***The Man Who Came to Dinner*** just as well as a sombre play like *Of Mice and Men,* and with equal variety.

'All right! Stand by for a complete run-through this time.'

* * *

'Four props came today, and one was right,' Kaufman tells Hart with a wry smile two days later, but he does not let this disturb his equanimity. He paces up and down, in front of the orchestra pit, as the company runs through the play—backwards again. Now he is concentrating upon cueing the action to the word, upon the thousand and one details that an audience is never aware of. Fully ten minutes is spent gauging the exact moment at which the slam of a door should be heard at a certain exit. All the spots where the props may hold up the action are studiously worked over. The opening of a package, for instance, is timed so that the actual work of undoing the string is at a minimum. One realizes as never before how important little details are; how the opening of a letter, say, can slow up the whole action of a play unless someone is given a line to fill in the pause.

'Keep perfectly serious,' Kaufman adjures the doctor, who enters disguised as Santa Claus. 'The moment you smile, the moment *you* think you're funny, it's gone!' . . . 'In the line "four telephones crying", don't lose the word "crying",' he tells the actor impersonating Banjo. 'You've got to heighten "crying", or you get the laugh on "telephones".'

He and Woolley work out little details of the characterization. Woolley will tell him, for example: 'I think I would be delighted, George, when she says that.' Kaufman agrees and suggests a way to register that delight. He rarely plays out a part for the actor, though sometimes he will illustrate a bit of business. He works mostly by a kind of suggestion; an encouragement of the actor's own feeling.

'That line is killed by having the radio men come in,' John Hoysradt (the Beverly Carlton—Noel Coward of the play) tells Kaufman, which is quite true. So Kaufman has the men come in a beat later after the laugh is registered. But if an actor sees a line or a situation in a way that is out of key with the idea, Kaufman will tell him at once that that is not the way he wants the speech read, or the gesture made, and will explain his reasons.

One of the radio men has to enter a little later, to plug a cord into a light socket. 'Wait a minute,' Kaufman calls, after the actor has made his exit, 'I think we can get a laugh on that if you come in in a perfectly matter-of-fact manner, plug in, and then suddenly notice Miss Goodner standing there and retire in astonishment and confusion.' The actor tries it, looks up with a 'My-God-what's-this!' expression at the actress, turns quickly to run out and just before he exits casts another amazed glance over his shoulders at the siren. 'That's fine,' Kaufman says, 'particularly that last look.' And the point is proved emphatically at the first showing before an audience when the business gets a loud, spontaneous laugh—a perfect illustration of how a dull but essential bit of business can be transformed into a living part of the play by astute direction.

* * *

'Monty, I can't quite tell whether you're unsure of the lines or it's part of the characterization,' Kaufman says to Woolley after a run through of the first scene. 'That's bad.' Woolley *is* unsure of the lines, as is evidenced by his performance a few days later. His part is extremely difficult; he is on stage, seated in a wheel-chair, almost all the time, and he must dominate the scene even when he is not talking. Any actor knows how hard it is to get variety into a performance when he cannot move about the stage. And it is not until the lines and business are completely set that Woolley is able to incorporate the expressions and subtle gestures which enable him to dominate the show in eloquent fashion.

'If that's a laugh, take the door slam after the laugh,' Kaufman says to the stage manager, as he paces up and down, his right forefinger in the corner of his mouth.

He has an uncanny sense of rhythm—this playwright-director—even when he appears to be paying no attention to the goings-on. And he can tell instantly if, by accident, an actor inserts a word into his lines. His sense of timing is so acute that it may lead him, occasionally, to overlook details of characterization, providing only the time clock is clicking as he wants it to. People who have worked with him claim that sometimes he lets his ear control his mind. But there is only one scene in this play where there is

evidence of that—a scene which, to these eyes, is badly overplayed by one of the actors, but which does not appear to bother Kaufman—perhaps because he knows that it is bad and that it can easily be remedied before the opening.

'Monty, when you say: "Two years ago I was in a diving suit with William Beebe, but she got me"' (*she* referring to Gertrude Stein who always calls up Whiteside on Christmas Eve to let him hear the bells of Notre Dame), 'Don't break the line on "Beebe". The laugh will come then, and kill it. The really funny part is not that you were in the diving suit, but that she got you by telephone there.'

Woolley has a line that he cannot remember. Every time he tries it, he loses it. It is simple enough, something to the effect: 'What kind of skullduggery have you been up to?' The line follows one in which he promises to give an iron toothpick as a wedding present to an English Lord whose teeth, he says, always remind him of Roquefort cheese. 'Think from the teeth to the skull and you'll get it,' Kaufman suggests—and Woolley does.

* * *

So it goes, day in, day out, for three weeks; heigh tening here, keying it down there, building it up, tearing it down, and cutting, cutting, cutting. Once the play opens before an audience it will have to be retimed, reset, because as Kaufman says, 'you can never be sure where the laugh will come,' and a long laugh requires re-spacing and lengthening of all the business that surrounds the words. For although the action of a comedy must never seem to stop to give the audience a chance to catch up, it must, in practice, take account of laughter or applause. The first dress rehearsal before an invited audience was almost wrecked by the prolonged laughter that greeted Monty Woolley's first speech and by the unexpected (though not unwarranted) applause that followed his 'Merry Christmas' exit. But Kaufman's imagination went to work at once to fill, with new business, the gaps which seemed to hold the play suspended.

'Dress parade at 8 P.M., please,' the stage manager calls out. 'Yes. Everyone except the choir boys,' Kaufman says, strolling up on stage. 'Oh, and Bernie, ask the three men who carry in the totem pole to come half an hour earlier; I want them to get the movements exactly; when they're set, we'll see whether we need to fill in there with any extra dialogue.'

* * *

Note from Hartford, after the out-of-town opening. 'You may want to make some slight changes in the article to fit changes that we are making in the play. We are re-writing Act Three, eliminating the character of the surrealist, who turned out not to be funny. The kidnapping remains but will be managed differently. The lady will not be tied up.

Instead of a totem pole, the final gift will be a mummy case, and Miss Goodner will be carried out in it. . . . That's all—to date.'

FANCY MEETING YOU AGAIN

CRITICAL COMMENTARY

George Jean Nathan (essay date 1953)

SOURCE: Nathan, George Jean. "George S. Kaufman." In *The Theatre in the Fifties,* pp. 67-69. Alfred A. Knopf, 1953.

[*In the following review, Nathan dismisses* Fancy Meeting You Again, *a play about reincarnation which Kaufman co-wrote with his wife, Leueen MacGrath.*]

George S. Kaufman's *Fancy Meeting You Again,* in which his wife, Leueen MacGrath had a hand, deals with reincarnation, a subject that in one form or another was very appetizing to audiences in the early years of the present century. It was in that period that plays like *The Road to Yesterday,* written by a pair of elderly New England ladies who apparently believed quite seriously in it, and like *When Knights Were Bold,* written by a Britisher who believed it was just a lot of gumbo that would cash in at the box-office, attracted the impartial favor of our theatergoers. For the next two decades, however, the topic was forgotten until a believer who owned several million dollars' worth of oil wells in Texas thought it high time that it again be treated devoutly and confected something called *The Ladder,* which remains in history as the damnedest rubbish of its or any other era.

The exhibits of the genre, whether tolerable or awful, committed themselves in a general way to two plots. In one, advocated by the believers, it was argued that what you are in the present life is a reflection of what you were in previous incarnations and that if, for example, you have a long aquiline nose and are of a somewhat bellicose disposition you were once a Roman warrior under Caesar and before that in all likelihood an elephant. In the other, manufactured by those concerned only with an easy dollar, a comedian who jumped with fright every time the cuckoo-clock went off was involved in a sudden shift of scenery which disclosed him in a far past embodiment as a ludicrous knight in armor who, just as he was about to rescue the maiden fair from a murderous band of Turks, was scared into a dead faint by the screech of a hoot-owl.

Beginning with the late Thirties, reincarnation was discarded by playwrights as being altogether too rococo and idiotic and, preening themselves on their superior wisdom, they went in for what they were pleased to regard as scientific or psychiatric explanations of the delusion. Thus, instead of showing that their characters were something other than their contemporary selves in remote years, they attributed everything to Ouspensky's theory of spiral time, which proved, they assured us, that you lived through the centuries in an endless single pattern and that you are exactly the same jerk today that you were when you were playing house with Julia Agrippina in 42 A.D. and swindling the Earl of Shrewsbury's tailor out of a couple of suits in 1688. The playwrights who preferred psychiatry to any such complex hypothesis took an easier way out. If a character imagined, because he happened to break his wife's ribs while embracing her in joyous celebration of their seventieth wedding anniversary, that he was a reincarnated boa constrictor, they argued very simply that his mind was unhinged from having in his youth watched bartenders squeezing limes into gin rickeys and that the cure for his psychosis was milking cows. The circle was now at length spun 'round again, and it is reincarnation that once more tries to court the box-office.

As in the case of the *When Knights Were Bold* kind of thing, Mr. Kaufman and his collaborator have shrewdly elected to spoof the business and have written of a sculptress who cancels her marriage to a stuffy bore in the hope that a more likely candidate in the shape of the lover who pursued her in previous incarnations will appear in this to clasp her to his hungry bosom. The lover shows up in the person of an art critic, just to make things a little more complicated and a deal more fantastic, but after the usual misunderstandings everything is straightened out as usual and the couple as usual swoon in each other's arms.

The play which, as you have probably guessed, aims at nothing more exalted than selling tickets, consists mainly in a succession of gags, one or two of them comical and the rest of them not. The stage business is similarly at one or two times fresh and amusing and at all other times a reincarnation of what we knew in a much earlier period of our theatergoing. The scenery performs trickily as in other days, and so do the lights. And a number of the characters are veterans, including the female wisecracker, the starchy suitor, the sharp female committee member, and the inevitable figure from the other world dubbed, as always, A Visitor.

The box-office promptly spurned Mr. Kaufman's suit.

FURTHER READING

Biographies

Goldstein, Malcolm. *George S. Kaufman: His Life, His Theatre.* New York, Oxford University Press, 1979, 503 p.

Interweaves a biography of the man and study of his work.

Meredith, Scott. *George S. Kaufman and His Friends.* Garden City, NY: Doubleday & Company, Inc., 1974, 723 p.

An anecdotal biography based on the recollections of friends and collaborators

Pollack, Rhoda-Gale. *George S. Kaufman* Boston: Twayne Publishers, 1988, 144 p.

A comprehensive, chronological study of Kaufman's life and career.

Teichman, Howard. *George S. Kaufman: An Intimate Portrait.* New York: Atheneum, 1972, 372 p.

Charts the course of Kaufman's life and career by his collaborator on *The Solid Gold Cadillac.*

Criticism

Gassner, John. "The Kaufman Cycle." in *Masters of the Drama,* pp. 666-8. New York: Dover Publications, 1940, 804 p.

Provides a very brief overview of Kaufman's works and influence.

Mason, Jeffrey D. *Wisecracks: The Farces of George S. Kaufman.* Ann Arbor: UMI Research Press, 1988, 134 p.

A study of Kaufman's farces arguing they rank among the classics of the American theater.

Additional coverage of Kaufman's life and career is contained in the following sources published by the Gale Group: *Contemporary Authors,* **Vols. 93-96, 108;** *Contemporary Literary Criticism,* **Vol. 38;** *Dictionary of Literary Biography,* **Vol. 7;** *DISCovering Authors Modules: Dramatists;* *Drama for Students,* **Vols. 1, 10;** *Literature Resource Center;* *Major 20th-Century Writers,* **Ed. 2; and** *Reference Guide to American Literature.*

Arthur Schnitzler
1862-1931

Austrian short story writer, playwright and novelist.

INTRODUCTION

Known for his stylistic experiments in both drama and prose, Schnitzler's works analyzed pre-World War I Vienna society. His work was influenced by some of the theories of psychoanalyst Sigmund Freud.

BIOGRAPHICAL INFORMATION

Schnitzler was born in Vienna in 1862 in an upper-middle-class Jewish family. At the Akademisches Gymnasium in Vienna from 1871 to 1879, he was considered a model student, graduating with honors. Influenced by his father and maternal grandfather, Schnitzler went to the University of Vienna in 1879 to study medicine. He received his Doctor of General Medicine degree in 1885 and became editor of the medical journal *Internationale klinische Rundschau* in 1887. The following year he became an assistant at his father's practice. Despite his success as a physician Schnitzler began writing *Anatol,* (1893) one of his most important plays. After his father's death in 1893, Schnitzler spent more time writing than practicing medicine, and in 1895 one of his most popular plays, *Liebelei,* (1895) was performed for the first time at the Burgtheater. Schnitzler was also a member of the Jung-Wein group, a literary movement of impressionist writers that met at the Vienna Café Griensteidl. The Jung-Wein were strongly opposed to naturalism, popular in Berlin society of the time. It was with the Jung-Wein that Schnitzler met fellow Austrian playwright Hugo von Hofmannsthal. Schnitzler died of a cerebral hemorrhage in Vienna in 1931.

MAJOR WORKS

Schnitzler's plays generally focus on sex, death, and the turmoil of the human psyche. His first published play, *Anatol,* remains one of the most important works of his career. The play is comprised of seven one-act plays composed between 1888 and 1891; it is intended to be performed as a complete cycle, but each of the one-acts can stand alone and has been performed separately. The title character, Anatol, is a melancholy playboy given to self-analysis and narcissism. His sexual double standard—expecting purity of women while partaking in numerous dalliances of his own—is considered a conscious mirror

and criticism of Schnitzler's and all of *fin de siècle* (a term used to describe end-of-the-century culture) Vienna's views on sexuality. Perhaps not surprisingly, the play did not escape controversy. Censors in Austria and Germany objected in particular to the episode entitled *Abschiedssouper (Farewell Supper)*—the first of the one-acts to be performed separately in 1893—because of its frank handling of female infidelity. Schnitzler again addressed sexuality in *Liebelei* (performed 1895), using the paradigm of the *süßes Mädel* ("sweet girl") to examine relationships that cross class lines and, symbolically, abuses of the bourgeoisie by the upper classes. Schnitzler's most notorious play, *Reigen,* (1920) is also his most widely adapted. It was performed in various versions throughout the twentieth century despite the author's own ban. These versions include a film entitled *La Ronde* (1950). Based in form on the traditional dance in the round, *Reigen* consists of ten dialogues—nine of them dealing directly with various sex acts—between men and women who are involved sexually. Illustrating the dance motif of the title, one partner from each dialogue appears in the dialogue immediately following it, so that each is involved with two partners in the play. In this way Schnitzler emphasizes the pervasiveness of sexual desire across class and gender lines. *Paracelsus* (performed 1899) is set in sixteenth-century Basel and written in verse.

CRITICAL RECEPTION

Schnitzler's plays experienced widely divergent attention in his lifetime. *Zwischenspiel* (1905), *Der junge Medardus* (1910), and *Professor Bernhardi* (1912) received awards. On the other hand, many of his plays, including *Professor Bernhardi,* were censored, excoriated, and outright banned at one time or another, especially *Reigen* which Schnitzler banned himself, and remained banned until his son Heinrich lifted the ban in 1981. In their published form his plays were considered more accessible than those of his contemporaries, so he maintained a wide reading audience. But the increasingly hostile anti-Semitic atmosphere of early-twentieth-century Austria and Germany often led to public protests over the staging of works by Jewish writers such as Schnitzler. Additionally, his frequent exploration in his plays on the mores of the upper-middle-class Viennese resulted in an unfortunate stereotype of Schnitzler as a writer of frivolous, one-dimensional drawing-room comedies despite his concurrent focus on issues of ethics and mortality. Towards the late twentieth century, critical opinion of Schnitzler's plays shifted to recognize his subtle social criticism and psychological depth. He is now considered a serious, sophisticated examiner of the human condition.

PRINCIPAL WORKS

Plays

Das Abenteuer seines Lebens 1891
*Anatol 1893
Das Märchen 1893
†Liebelei 1895
Freiwild 1896
Das Vermächtnis 1898
Der grüne Kakadu 1899
Paracelsus 1899
Der Schleier der Beatrice 1900
Lebendige Stunden 1902
Der Puppenspieler 1903
Der einsame Weg 1904
Zwischenspiel 1905
Der Ruf des lebens 1906

Komtesse Mizzi oder der Familientag 1909
Der junge Medardus 1910
Der Schleier der Pierrette [*The Bridal Veil*] 1910
Das weite Land
Professor Bernhardi 1912
Komödie der Worte 1915
Fink und Fliederbusch 1917
Die Schwestern oder Casanova in Spa 1920
‡Reigen 1920
Komödie der Verführung 1924
Im Spiel der Sommerlüfte 1929
Der Gang zum Weiher 1931
Anatols Grössenwahn 1932
Die überspannte Person 1932
Halbzwei 1932

Other Major Works

Sterben: Novelle (novel) 1895
Die Frau des Weisen: Novelletten (novella) 1898
Leutnant Gustl: Novelle [*None But the Brave*] (novel) 1901
Frau Bertha Garlan: Novelle (novel) 1901
Die griechische Tänzerin: Novelle (novel) 1905
Dämmerseelen: Novelle (novel) 1907
Masken und Wunder: Novelle (novel) 1912
Frau Beate und ihr Sohn: Novelle [*Beatrice: A Novel*] (novel) 1913
Gesammelte Werke in zwei Abteilungen 9 vols. (collected works) 1913-23
Casanovas Heimfahrt: Novelle [*Casanova's Homecoming*] (novel) 1918
Fräulein Else: Novelle (novel) 1924
Die Frau des Richters: Novelle (novel) 1925
Traumnovelle [*Rhapsody: A Dream Novel*] (novel) 1926
Spiel im Morgengrauen: Novelle [*Day-Break*] (novel) 1927
Buch der Sprüche und Bedenken: Aphorismen und Betrachtungen (aphorisms) 1927
Die Erwachenden: Novelle (novel) 1928
Flucht in die Finsternis: Novelle [*Flight into Darkness: A Novel*] (novel) 1931
Abenteurernovelle (novel) 1937
Über Krieg und Frieden [*Some Day Peace Will Return: Notes on War and Peace*] (nonfiction) 1939
Jugend in Wien: Eine Autobiographie [*My Youth in Vienna*] (autobiography) 1968
Briefwechsel mit Otto Brahm [edited by Otto Seidlin] (letters) 1953
Georg Brandes und Arthur Schnitzler: Ein Briefwechsel [edited by Kurt Bergel] (letters) 1956
Der Briefwechsel Arthur Schnitzlers mit Max Reinhardt und dessen Mitarbeitern [edited by Renate Wagner] (letters) 1971
The Correspondence of Arthur Schnitzler and Raoul Auernheimer, with Raoul Auernheimer's Aphorisms [edited by Donald G. Daviau and Jorun B. Johns] (letters and aphorisms) 1972
The Letters of Arthur Schnitzler to Hermann Bahr [edited by Donald G. Daviau] (letters) 1978

*This work is comprised of the following seven one-act plays: *Die Frage an das Schicksal, Weihnachtseinkaüfe, Episode, Denksteine, Abschieds-*

souper, Agonie, and *Anatols Hochzeitmorgen. Anatol* was performed in English translation on numerous occasions; it was also performed in English as *The Loves of Anatol* in 1985.

†This work was performed in English translation as *Flirtation,* 1905; *The Reckoning,* 1907; *Light-o'-Love,* 1912; *Playing with Love,* 1914, and *Flirtations,* 1981.

‡This work was performed in English translation as *La Ronde* in 1960 and as *Rondelay* in 1969; it was also published in English as *Hands Around* in 1920. It was adapted to film as *La Ronde* in 1950.

GENERAL COMMENTARY

Joseph W. Bailey (essay date 1920)

SOURCE: Bailey, Joseph W. "Arthur Schnitzler's Dramatic Work." *Texas Review* 5, no. 4 (1920): 294-307.

[*In the following essay, Bailey addresses the supposed amorality that other critics found in Schnitzler's works, arguing that Schnitzler rightly puts his art above the "interests of a prudish morality."*]

In that classic of literary criticism which Mr. Joseph Conrad has appended as a preface to his inimitable novel, *The Nigger of the Narcissus,* we are given a statement of the author's artistic creed:

> To arrest, for the space of a breath, the hands busy about the work of the earth, and compel men entranced by the sight of distant goals to glance for a moment at the surrounding vision of form and color, of sunshine and shadows; to make them pause for a look, for a sigh, for a smile—such is the aim, difficult and evanescent, and reserved only for a very few to achieve. But sometimes, by the deserving and the fortunate, even that task is accomplished. And when it is accomplished—behold!—all the truth of life is there: a moment of vision, a sigh, a smile—and the return to an eternal rest.

Whether or not Arthur Schnitzler, dramatist, novelist, and physician of Vienna, will have been assigned a place in the pantheon of those "deserving and fortunate" ones, when the sickle of the critically iconoclastic years shall have thinned out the teeming numbers of our striving contemporaries, we cannot be certain. But, judging him as best we can without that breadth of vision which only the perspective of the years can bring to us, we can delegate to Schnitzler no subsidiary position in the ranks of those artists who have utilized their art to hold the mirror up to life itself and to cast what gleam of truth they may upon the dark riddle of our existence.

It is probable that, to the conscious moralist and the mawkish purist, the name of Schnitzler may be anathema, and it is true that he makes no concession to the popular desire for the triumph of a "supposed immediate ethical good

over a supposed immediate ethical evil". Schnitzler does not use his drama for the preaching of a moral; there is no sermonizing in it, and he does not distort and destroy the verisimilitude of his picture of life in the fatuous belief that he may show to a struggling humanity the path that leads to happiness and warn them from the path that leads to misery and woe. To Schnitzler, Art is something the glory and beauty of which is so transcending that it rises far above the domain of morals, and there is no doubt that the spontaneity and sincerity of any art must be destroyed if it be subjected to a moral or ethical purpose. Any such cheap conception of Art must bring as dismal a failure as that more mercenary conception which endeavors only to "split the ears of the groundlings" and to flatter the smugness of a self-sufficient generation. It has been strongly maintained that all Art has its foundation in the sexual instinct, and we cannot afford to condemn a work because it deals with this important aspect of our nature. Let it be understood at the first, then, that Schnitzler's work is not immoral, any more than the brilliance of a spring sunset or the voluptuous beauty of a summer night's high moon. The relation of lover to beloved is too natural, too beautiful, and too spontaneous for Schnitzler to see aught in it that is immoral. Even, however, if the relation itself were indefensible, the worth of Schnitzler's art would not suffer in the least, and his drama would no more deserve condemnation on account of it than does *Oliver Twist* on account of the brutal murder of Nancy Sykes. Schnitzler neither accuses nor condemns. He attempts merely "to snatch in a moment of courage, from the remorseless rush of time, a passing phase of life" and to leave the world to form its own judgement. There can be no impeachment of the honesty of his Art, and this very honesty makes it impossible for him to make his Art subservient to the supposed interests of a prudish morality.

The shortcomings of Schnitzler as a literary artist are more in the nature of limitations than of actual faults. That is to say, the greatest weakness of his work is the narrowness of his scope. What he does he does with a grace and deftness which approaches perfection, but as we shall see, the range of his activity is not very wide. He has been called "the perfect Viennese", and those who are qualified to speak with authority have said that he has interpreted faithfully the Viennese life and atmosphere. Ashley Dukes has said that "his dramatic method is the intellectualization, the refinement of the Viennese waltz". This, then, will constitute an important limitation to the scope of Schnitzler's work—it is restricted to city life and to the city life of Vienna in particular. Whether his scenes are laid in a suburb of Vienna or in some foreign city, his characters are distinctively urban and Viennese. In point of character types, he contents himself with dealing with those classes which he knew best—the cultured and idle representatives of the upper classes—and he deals with these only in their extra-official hours of recreation and love-making. Schnitzler does not concern himself with the *bürgerlich*; he is confined altogether to the aristocratic and artistic circles. His drama is always intensely personal; we find no suggestion of the social or economic problem in its broader aspects. The relation of sex to sex is his domain, and he reigns supreme within this province; but he seldom ventures beyond the limits which he has set for himself. The German dramatic critic, Rudolph Lothar, in the course of a not altogether sympathetic appreciation of Schnitzler, remarks:

> "His Weltanschauung! It would be better to say his Frauenanschauung. For at bottom Schnitzler is only a lover, and his world is woman."

The criticism may be justified, and is certainly true; but, even so, the imputation of a disproportional evaluation of life and a niggardliness of material is not warranted. The controversy between the Freudian and anti-Freudian schools of psychology over the influence exerted by the sexual function still rages; but we do know that there is no one of man's primal instincts, excepting the instinct for self-preservation, which is so powerful in determining our manner of living. There is no note in the whole gamut of human emotions which cannot be sounded by an appeal to this aspect of man's nature. And so it is that Schnitzler's work has also its scientific side. His dramas are, in the last analysis, little more than free studies in the psychology of sex, but let us remember that this field may ultimately be broadened to take in the whole of man's endeavor. We know not how much of maternal love, and paternal pride,—how much of our Art and Religion,—how much of our appreciation of a summer sunset or the joy in spring—may be possible only through the existence of this element in our make-up. Let us not then, minify the field of Schnitzler's endeavor until we are sure Lilliput will not become Brobdingnag when the microscope of our own ignorance is removed.

Arthur Schnitzler was born in Vienna on May 15, 1862, the son of a renowned Jewish physician. He studied medicine at the University of Vienna and obtained the degree of Doctor of Medicine in 1885. After graduation, he was engaged for two years in one of the large city hospitals. He began early to contribute poems and prose sketches to the literary journals of the day. It was as this early period of his life, also, that he became interested in psychic phenomena, especially hypnotism and suggestion, to which we find references in his *Anatol* and *Paracelsus*. After a short trip to England, he settled down in Vienna as a practicing physician. It is probable that Schnitzler's application to his literary labors was not altogether pleasing to his father, and we find many instances in his works of that "conflict of the generations"—that incompatibility of youth and age—which usually takes the form of a protest against interference on the part of a parent in the son's choice of a profession.

The case of a creative genius in the realm of letters who, at the same time, is an active and successful medical practitioner and to whom literature is only a side-line at best, is so extraordinary that we are justified in expecting to find a casual relation between the peculiar nature of his vocation and his manner of living, on the one hand, and the turn which his artistic labors has taken, on the other. This relation can be plainly established, I think, in the case of Schnitzler. It is, indeed, very probable that Schnitzler first became interested in the relation of the two sexes and in the psychology of sex, which topics are predominant in his literary work, as scientific subjects related to his profession. There is no doubt, of course, that Schnitzler knew and loved the Bohemian life of his native city. But, at the same time, there are innumerable indications in his works that his interest in this subject of the sex relation was partly a result of his scientific training. Even in his most convincing creations, we cannot rid ourselves of the impression that the author is playing the rôle of diagnostician, and is only desirous of investigating with the physician's eye the aberrations and reactions of the human organism. *Reigen,* for instance, is a frank, open, and very naturalistic study in the psychology of sex, and as such Edwin Bjorkman has said "it has not many equals". I do not think that we are justified in stressing this scientific aspect of Schnitzler's work to the exclusion of all others,—I do not think that the tendency on the part of some critics to regard him as a sort of Freud afflicted with the artistic impulse is indicative of sound literary judgment; but, at the same time, the student of Schnitzler cannot afford to ignore this scientific interest in the sexual nature which was undoubtedly very strong in Schnitzler's mind.

Another aspect of his work which may be traced to his experiences as a physician is his preoccupation with the theme of death. There is an underlying note of melancholy, a sort of brooding sadness, running through all of Schnitzler's works which must be due, in a measure, to his ever-present consciousness of the transiency of this life and of the threatening death that hovers over every human being. How the native melancholy of his sensitive soul must have been depressed by the endless, weary night in the sick-room, the babe breathing out its last feeble gasp on his breast, and the pitiableness of withered age closing its feverish eyes in the last sleep! Like Andreyev and Dostoievsky, Schnitzler finds himself again and again in contemplation of the mystery of dissolution, staring fixedly at the black hood of Death, attracted by the thing he fears more than anything else in the world. For Schnitzler belongs both racially and by environment to the languid and life-loving South rather than to the cold and fearless North; and we may expect to find his kindred spirit in the mysticism of the Slav and the impressionism of the Latin. Schnitzler, as I have said before, has been hailed as "the perfect Viennese just as Anatole France is the perfect Parisian", and Edwin Bjorkman has said of Vienna that "it is the meeting place not only of South and North, but also of Past and Present". He continues:

> "Like all cities sharply divided within itself and living above a volcano of half-suppressed emotions, Vienna tends to seek in abandoned gaiety, in a frank surrender to the senses, that forgetfulness without which suicide would seem the only remaining alternative."

And so it is that, in studying Schnitzler, we cannot hope to arrive at an understanding and appreciation of his genius unless we consider these salient facts of his life which have left their impress on his work—in the first place, that he is a Hebrew and is possessed of all the passionate fire and melancholy mysticism of his race; in the second place, that his experience as a practicing physician has led him into the half-world of poverty and suffering and brought him into contact with death in a thousand shapes; and, in the third place, that all his life has been spent in the free and sensuous atmosphere of the city of Vienna. These three factors, I think, may be made to account for everything in Schnitzler that seems to us morbid, revolutionary, and immoral, while the artist in him will account for everything that is fine, delicate, and attractive.

I have said that the scope of Schnitzler's art is limited, and, from the standpoint of the materialist, this is true; but in so far as the passions of desire and pity may touch the heart of mankind, there is no limit to Schnitzler's appeal. The mystery of love and death is everywhere his theme. The tragedy of love—for love, as life, by reason of its very transiency, must have something of the tragic in it—and the tragedy of death—which brings an end to the "Living Hours" of love—find expression, as it were, in ever-recurrent minor chords, and it is only in the lighter moments between that he allows himself, with a half playful air of cynical aloofness, to strike a major note. I do not wish to convey the impression that the dominant tone of his style is oppressively melancholy—quite to the contrary, it is replete with the tripping melody of wit and sarcasm—but, behind all his levity, we can sense the tell-tale note of pessimistic fatalism that his philosophy of "Living Hours" has left him.

The cycle of one-act plays, **Anatol,** was the creation for which Schnitzler first received recognition as a playwright, and, in spite of the fact that he has since produced plays of much greater merit, it is probably by this cycle of plays that he is best known even today. **Anatol** consists of seven scenes, the same man figuring in each one of them with a different woman. Anatol, the hero, is a wealthy and loose young man of the upper class of Viennese aristocracy, one of those idle and harried creatures who exhaust themselves in an effort to find amusement, seeking refuge in a multiplicity of mistresses from the ennui which pursues the wealthy idler. In each scene, the amour is at a certain well-defined stage in its short-lived existence, either the infatuation of both parties is just being born and the hero is enjoying the novelty of a new mistress, or the passion of love is at its height and the two are wrapped up in each other, oblivious of the world, or the old love is waning, and the separation that has been inevitable from the first is taking place. The third character is Max, the cynical, worldly, and incredulous friend of the hero, who is ever present to laugh at his friend's foibles—although he himself is guilty of the same folly—and to say the things that Schnitzler himself would probably have said. In the first scene, we find Anatol enjoying his infatuation for Cora, but, at the same time, knowing that she is unfaithful to him. When placed in a position where he can learn the real truth, however, Anatol refuses to read the answer of the oracle, and Max leaves them "clasped in a passionate

embrace". Anatol is unwilling to destroy his paradise, even though he knows it can last for only a short while. Schnitzler's interest in the psychic world and in hypnotism, which marks him as a strange combination of the scientist and the romanticist, and which reminds us strangely of the poetic interest which Wordsworth is said to have experienced for the study of higher mathematics, is brought to our attention in this scene, as Anatol's power of hypnotism is the means whereby he is enabled to question Cora.

The second scene satirizes the smug and self-conscious virtue of the respectable married woman. Anatol has met Gabrielle, an old acquaintance who has married, and she, having questioned him about his present innamorata, sends her the following message:

> "these flowers, my sweet little girl, were sent to you by a woman who, perhaps—might know how to love as well as you—but who hasn't the courage."

She leaves him standing in the street. And so the experiences follow one another in succession, the glance of interest at first meeting, the lowered eyelid and slight suggestion of a smile which usher in the new affair, the thrill of pleasure at a new conquest growing into a crescendo of passion, the first murmur of dissatisfaction signaling the coming rupture, the final meeting when the words of farewell are said with relief, with resignation, with a slight touch of sadness and regret or are growled between the hysterical sobbings of a furious woman; and the tireless one is ready for a new adventure and a new thrill. There is no end to the eternal procession of women; they come from the hero cares not where, and they go to where he neither knows nor cares. He lives in a world of mistresses, past, present, and future, dreaming in his twilight memories of those who have gone before, when, at the beck of his retrospective mood, the shades of past lovers come before him, "one from a simple tenement home, another from her husband's gorgeous drawing room, one from her stage dressing room, one from a milliner's shop, one from the arms of a new lover, one from the grave—one from here, another from there—until they all come—"; but in the present there is always *the* one, and in the future he sees only an endless succession of those who are to be. His "Weltanschauung" is truly only a "Frauenanschauung", but his world is an andro-centric one, and we cannot suppress a feeling of pity for the forlorn lot of the countless women who are drawn to him like moths to a light, and are left to perish in the dark when his pleasure dims.

Schnitzler's manner of treatment in these scenes is intensely naturalistic. All the shades and subtleties of feeling are recorded, and no external detail is slighted. The action is given a life-like accuracy, and there is no prudish shying away from the unconventional intimacy between Anatol and his mistresses, but, at the same time, we do not find in the play anything that savors of the exploitations of the "dirty" for its own sake. There is nothing that consciously panders to the baser instincts and no attempt to justify sexual irregularities. According to the creed of the naturalist, Schnitzler has attempted to represent faithfully a particularly chosen aspect of life as it is lived, and leaves the reader to justify or to condemn. There is no lesson of moral or ethical conduct to be drawn from the play; the story stands for its own sake without point or purpose. The significant thing about *Anatol* is the proof it gives of the singular powers of Schnitzler as an artist: his delicate touch in the creation of an atmosphere, his supreme ability in the interpretation of emotion, and in the manufacture of dialogue.

In *Reigen,* Schnitzler has dealt even more candidly with the same theme: the amenability of all classes of mankind to the common passions. *Reigen* consists of ten scenes, with as many characters, two of them figuring in each scene. Like *Anatol, Reigen* is expressive of the physician in Schnitzler, and is scientific in spirit as a study of the psychology of sex. In the broader significance it stresses the common nature of mankind and the fact that class distinctions are powerless before the onslaught of the basic passions of all men. On account of its unprecedented freedom in the treatment of the delicate question of sex, *Reigen* was not printed for some years after its production, and then only privately; and in Germany, is still *verboten.* There is, however, nothing intrinsically immoral in the book, and we feel that its proscription is only another manifestation of that crowd psychology which demands the removal of its paupers, its insane, and every suggestion of its social cess-pools to that "Half-Rome" which is to be shunned by the more fortunate of us.

In *Liebelei,* one of Schnitzler's most powerful and far-reaching creations, although the theme is still the eternal passion of the love which is frowned upon by society, we see the other side of the shield—the tragic, sombre side—, and the curtain to the final act is rung down before a new-made grave. Fritz, the young aristocrat, is this time in love with the wife of another man. His friend contrives a meeting for him with Christine, an innocent and credulous girl of the middle classes, who conceives a genuine passion for her destroyer. Fritz is challenged and killed in a duel by the husband of his former mistress, and Christine takes her own life. For the time being, Schnitzler transcends himself, and it seems that for once love, in the breast of Christine, is no longer a toy to be played with for the amusement of an idle hour, no longer a lovely flower which bursts quickly into bloom only to wither with the passage of a few short days, but, in the heart of the simple maiden, it has swelled into a passion which dominates fate. The undercurrent of brooding sadness is felt everywhere in the play. Schnitzler's ever-present consciousness of the transiency of life and love is emphasized through every line. There are two striking passages which express this feeling, and which, in the mouth of Fritz, make Christine's position pathetic from the start:

"We must not speak of forever. . . .

"Of course it's possible that we might not be able to live without each other, but we can't know about that, can we? We are only human."

And so, with his "Wir sind ja nur Menschen", Schnitzler gives his estimate of humanity, and leaves his characters to struggle against the odds which are pitted against them. The same spirit of resignation and melancholy hovers over the Schnitzler in all his creations. There is *Freiwild,* with the pathos of woman's sad lot and the folly of mankind destroying itself in obedience to a barbaric code of duelling; *Das Vermachtnis,* with its tragedy of prejudice and death; *Komtesse Mizzi,* with its demonstration of the eventual equality of mankind, the leveling of the barriers between cab-men and count, between countess and soubrette. There are times when the convictions of the artist assume the form of a delicate cynicism, but, in his more serious moments, Schnitzler has no heart for the smirk of the cynic; the heart overflowing with sympathy and the spirit hearkening to the "turbid ebb and flow of human misery" banish the leer of the scoffer.

Der Einsame Weg is, perhaps, Schnitzler's most powerful work. In this play, he rises to the height of his power in the depicting of human emotion. The inter-play of psychological reaction is so delicately subtle, the situations so realistic and lifelike in spite of the compression which is essential to the dramatic form, the appeal to the emotions of pity and regret so universal, that the play may be said to have ensured Schnitzler's reputation as a dramatist of the first order. The theme is still the same— the eternal tragedies of love and death, with the addition, as the title indicates, of the tragedy of loneliness, that twin shade and prelude to the final conqueror, Death—the unutterable pathos of continuing to breathe and to see when the passage of years has despoiled one's heart of all that life held dear. The plot is very simple, and there is very little action in it. Julian Fichtner, artistically inclined bachelor, is the father of Felix, who believes himself to be the son of Professor Wegrat. The latter has been a dutiful, kind parent to his daughter, Johanna, and to his supposed son, Felix. The play recounts the pitiful efforts of Fichtner, now growing old and lonesome after a lurid youth, to inspire for himself a spark of love in the heart of his son. He fails utterly. Von Sala, worldly cynic who has lived as Fichtner, is dying of an incurable disease. Johanna loves Sala, and discovers that he is a doomed man. Irene Herms is an old flame of Fichtner's who has lived out the golden hours of her youth in idle pleasure-hunting, and is now growing old, with no attachments or ties to mellow her declining years. Wegrat is bound up in his scientific work, and is oblivious of the finer sympathies and the love which Johanna's heart is hungering for. So each of them walks his "lonely way" to the end that is inevitable. "The process of aging must needs be a lonely one to our kind," says Sala and gives the secret of the tragedy of his life and of Fichtner's. The latter has sacrificed love and a family for his art and his freedom, and now he finds that, in his age, the iron of lonesomeness has been pressed into his heart by the procession of the years and that he is without consolation for his sadness. He has grown fond of Felix, and has a pathetic longing for the boy to recognize his fatherhood and to return his affection, but Felix feels only resentment toward him for his treatment of the injured mother. Schnitzler again takes occasion to satirize the cruelty and folly of one's sacrifice of love and honor for the sake of art.

In the treatment of the character of Sala, we see again the Hebraic and Eastern temperament in this haunting fear of impending death which is pursuing the doomed man There is something of the horror of Andreyev's pictures of the death-cell in the spectacle of the lonely man waiting for the death that he knows must come; and, I think, there is a note distinctly Russian in the cry that bursts from his despairing heart:

> "Is there ever a blissful moment in any man's life when he can think of anything else (than dying) in his innermost soul?"

Irene Herms, the lonely woman growing old, reminds us very much of the sisters in Arnold Bennett's *Old Wives' Tale*. She is profoundly pathetic in her seclusion and loneliness—fleeing from the memories of her youth which the old familiar scenes in Vienna have brought crowding to her mind—with her pitifully vain regrets and her visions and dreams of what might have been—with the agonizing cry of her mothering heart making itself heard when her halcyon days are gone and it is too late to begin life again.

Johanna is the most pathetically lonely of them all, and her seclusion and sadness is the more pitiable because she is in the golden hours of her youth when the blighting tragedy of time and sorrow should not be felt and when the spirit of youth should be upheld by the conviction of its own immortality.

And the great fact behind all the minor sadnesses of life is the eternal tragedy of the passing of time—crushing and rending in its inexorable march all that it has made beautiful and strong-creating, nurturing, and then destroying, only to begin again its cycle of interminable labor. In his last conversation with Christine, Sala sums up the life of every man in his reference to the enigma of time:

> "The present—what does it mean anyhow? Are we then locked breast to breast with the moment as with a friend whom we embrace or an enemy who is pressing us? Has not the word that just rings out turned to memory already? Is not the note that starts a melody reduced to memory before the song is ended? Is your coming to this garden anything but a memory, Johanna? Are not your steps across that meadow as much a matter of the past as are the steps of creatures dead these many years?"

The play ends with a tragic irony which is, I think, characteristic of Schnitzler's philosophy of life. Christine is dead, and Felix, the real son of Fichtner, has spoken to Professor Wegrat and called him "Father". Wegrat answers in a burst of penitence for his neglect of Johanna:

> "Must things of this kind happen to make that word sound as if I had heard it for the first time?"

Schnitzler's future is uncertain. We are not acquainted with his activities since the spectre of war invaded the shady retreats of his pleasure-loving Vienna. We do not even know whether he has survived the four years of strife and the succeeding months of starvation. If he is now alive, it would be difficult to prophesy the turn which his work will take as a result of his experiences in the war. But, whatever he may do in the future, we may be fairly certain that the author of *Liebelei* and *Der Einsame Weg* is not merely the favorite of a generation, destined to be forgotten like the shadowy loves of his Anatol.

Martin Swales (essay date 1971)

SOURCE: Swales, Martin. "Tragedy and Comedy." In *Arthur Schnitzler: A Critical Study*, pp. 181-214. Oxford: Oxford University Press, 1971.

[*In the following essay, Swales explores elements of tragedy and comedy in* Liebelei *and* Zwischenspiel.]

Liebelei is the nearest Schnitzler comes to writing tragedy. Here, he explicitly measures the sexual behaviour of the young man-about-town, of the Anatol figure, against the possibility of total and passionate surrender to love, and judges the young man accordingly. In this play Schnitzler takes issue with many of the moral conventions of his time. In this sense *Liebelei* recalls Ibsen, although it lacks the resolute social purpose of Ibsen at his most passionately critical. It must, however, not be forgotten that Schnitzler's concerns are somewhat different from those of his great Norwegian predecessor. In a play such as *Pillars of the Community*, Ibsen attacks the way society is run, the powers of social administration and, with them, specific concrete forms of social abuse. Schnitzler attacks above all prevailing social attitudes; he is concerned with the way people confront and formulate personal, *private* experience, rather than with social activities as such. He documents the extent to which personal experience is embedded in the social reality and class-structure of his time. Schnitzler's characters inhabit a different world from Ibsen's. Where Ibsen is concerned with the stifling, self-righteous world of the small provincial town, Schnitzler is concerned with a capital city which in its sophistication would repudiate self-righteousness as being in bad taste. One feels the difference of Ibsen's world even in those plays where he is concerned with the private sphere of experience, with marriage, family life. There is, for example, in Schnitzler no equivalent to the relentless certainty of Torwald Helmer (*A Doll's House*), and hence there is no equivalent to the final head-on confrontation between him and his wife. The all-pervasive Viennese irony, which concedes its own inadequacy and thrives on its disarming self-awareness, is a much more elusive organism for the would-be giant-slayer to confront than Ibsen's self-explanatory and often self-satisfied world. Where Ibsen is concerned with the juxtaposition of truth and falsehood, Schnitzler is concerned with their intermingling.[1] For the most part, Schnitzler is content to enter the minds of his characters and to imply that standard by which they are to be judged. Just occasionally, however, he does make his characters confront a world which lives by totally different and more genuine standards. Once Schnitzler admits such a confrontation, the comedy of the undisturbed baseness of the individual mind gives place to the new and rare possibility of tragic confrontation.

The figure of the 'süßes Mädel' appears frequently in Schnitzler's work. Very often she is seen in terms of the response she elicits from the man (one things of Anatol's famous description of her in *Weihnachtseinkäufe*). This means that she tends to play a passive role. She, like the actress, is 'Freiwild'; she is sexually accessible, grateful for any taste of romance and glamour, however brief, that is brought into her limited, practical existence by the young 'Lebemann'. Furthermore, she is socially undemanding. She has to accept the few hours allotted to her, to accept that she is accorded only a peripheral role in the life of her lover. In many of his works, Schnitzler focuses on the 'Lebemann' himself. In *Liebelei,* however, the 'süßes Mädel' is a figure equal in importance to the young man. Schnitzler here confronts two social worlds and their attendant attitudes towards human relationships. Although the confrontation itself, the relationship between Fritz and Christine is seen essentially in personal and psychological terms, the difference in social background is nevertheless an important factor. In this sense one could describe *Liebelei* as an example of Schnitzler's psychological Naturalism, in which even the most private and intimate sphere of personal experience is seen to partake of and reflect the social situation that surrounds it.

The confrontation between the two worlds, the central theme of the play, is articulated at the simplest level in the scene setting. Act I plays in Fritz's rooms. Schnitzler gives us no specific stage directions, as he does in most of his early dramas (*Das Märchen, Freiwild, Das Vermächtnis*). All we know is that the room must reflect Fritz's way of life, the kind of social existence which his independent means allow him, it must be 'elegant und behaglich' (D, i. 216). The last two acts are to play in a totally different environment, in a room that is, quite simply, 'bescheiden und nett' (240).

Act I opens with a dialogue between Fritz and Theodor. The latter reproaches his friend for his continued—and dangerous—relationship with a married woman, a relationship which in its insecurity and furtiveness brings both parties nothing but unhappiness, but which Fritz seems quite incapable of breaking. Theodor suggests that his friend should get away from Vienna for a few days. He points out how much good their brief stroll in the country has done him. He goes on to refer to another context in which Fritz has recovered all his former gaiety and good humour: 'Du weißt nämlich gar nicht, wie fidel du da draußen gewesen bist—du warst geradezu bei Verstand—es war wie in den guten alten Tagen . . .—Auch neulich, wie wir mit den zwei herzigen Mädeln zusammen

waren, bist du ja sehr nett gewesen . . .' (217). For Theodor, these two experiences function on the same level. In relation to the social world which both he and Fritz inhabit, both experiences take place 'da draußen': in this sense, both experiences represent a pleasant change. Theodor goes on to develop a whole theory of erotic relationships. Women are there as relaxation for man, and one only needs to look to a specific kind of world for happiness and distraction, 'wo es keine großen Szenen, keine Gefahren, keine tragischen Verwicklungen gibt' (219). The world to which Theodor refers is that of the 'Vorstadt', and Fritz is won over. He joins Theodor in the unanimous slogan of 'Erholung'. Theodor, delighted to have convinced his friend, issues an ultimatum: 'Ich hab' deine Liebestragödien satt. Du langweilst mich damit. Und wenn du Lust hast, mir mit dem berühmten Gewissen zu kommen, so will ich dir mein einfaches Prinzip für solche Fälle verraten: Besser *ich* als ein anderer. Denn der Andere ist unausbleiblich wie das Schicksal' (220). This opening dialogue of the play summarizes the spirit in which the two men receive Christine and Mizi, and crystallizes the framework of personal and social attitudes which encompasses the relationship between Christine and Fritz. Theodor argues that the relationship with Christine will finally put an end to Fritz's 'Liebestragödien'; in actual fact, however, the relationship with Christine is the nearest Schnitzler's world gets to yielding a love tragedy. Furthermore, Theodor sounds a theme that runs through the play, when he urges Fritz not to be troubled in his conscience about any relationship he may experience: the lover might just as well be he as anyone else, for fate decrees that lover will succeed lover in an almost unbroken chain. This notion of 'fate' is at the heart of the moral attitudes of the socially dictated code of behaviour: no one relationship must be allowed to acquire the aura of something uniquely valuable. No relationship is unique; love is the general name for a series of experiences. It is not an absolute, it is, like all experiences, repeatable. Ultimately, this sense of being one of a series, this 'Ahnung der Wiederholbarkeit des Unwiederholbaren'[2] produces the total heart-break in Christine. Thus psychologically and thematically the scene is set and ready for the appearance of that other world 'da draußen'—the world of the 'Vorstadt'. Mizi is the first to arrive. She is attractive to Theodor in her spontaneity, in her full-blooded enjoyment of life 'ohne Liebestragödien'. Mizi does indeed correspond to Theodor's depiction of the 'Mädel aus der Vorstadt', to borrow the title of the Nestroy play in which, arguably, the figure of the 'süßes Mädel' has her origins. Mizi has no illusions about her relationship with Theodor; she knows it cannot last, but she accepts it with both hands for the pleasure it can give:

THEODOR:

Ja, richtig—so lange währt die ewige Liebe nicht.

MIZI:

Wer wird denn im Mai an den August denken. Ist's nicht wahr, Herr Fritz?

(222)

Mizi guarantees the kind of unproblematical relationship such as Theodor has praised.

It is against this background that Christine enters. In contrast to Mizi, she identifies the whole purpose and beauty of her life with her love for a man—and specifically, of course, with her love for Fritz. She expresses the simple truth of her feelings to Fritz: 'du bist aber mein Alles, Fritz, für dich könnt' ich . . .' (225). Fritz cannot respond to the unadorned intensity of her emotion. His reaction is typical of him:

FRITZ (UNTERBRICHT):

Kind, ich bitt' dich . . . so was sag' lieber nicht . . . die großen Worte, die hab' ich nicht gern. Von der Ewigkeit reden wir nicht . . .

CHRISTINE (TRAURIG LÄCHELND):

Hab' keine Angst, Fritz . . . ich weiß ja, daß es nicht für immer ist . . .

(225)

Fritz mistakes uncomplicated intensity of feeling for 'große Worte', for a false dramatizing of feelings which are of necessity transitory. Fritz applies the moral—and linguistic—standard of his own social class to a girl who comes from a different social class, who has different presuppositions about love relationships. Fritz and his whole world are so distanced from the immediate realities of feeling that he mistakes genuine passion for a kind of childishness. It is significant how often he addresses her as 'Kind' in the course of the play. In so doing he relentlessly asserts a discrepancy between their emotional beings, a distance which always makes itself felt in the actual relationship. It is an implicit assertion of distance which does not escape Christine. She knows that they belong to different worlds, and hence she demands almost nothing in terms of the actuality of the relationship. But she gives—and demands—everything in terms of the emotional commitment from which it springs. This combination of passion and reticence, of being emotionally demanding yet socially undemanding, makes Christine's position such a paradoxical one. As J. P. Stern has said of the 'süßes Mädel': '[she is] only too ready to value herself no more highly than she is valued by the society to which she does not belong'.[3] Over and over again Christine is confronted by, and has to accept, the fact that the world in which Fritz moves is closed to her. The process begins, in this, their first scene together. She has seen him the previous evening in a theatre box together with a man and a woman. She asks who these people were—just as she will ask who 'der Herr' is later in the first act. And the only reply she receives is that she does not know these people: they are 'Bekannte—es ist ganz gleich, wie sie heißen' (224).

The scene between the two pairs of lovers is interrupted by the arrival of 'der Herr'. Critics, most recently Heinz Politzer,[4] have pointed out that the arrival of the husband in the middle of the convivial evening is the modern

equivalent of a supremely baroque moment, where Death summons Man to leave the good things of life. Only a few years after the appearance of *Liebelei* Hofmannsthal was to re-create explicitly the spirit of the baroque in his mystery play *Jedermann*. One cannot help agreeing with Heinz Politzer that Schnitzler's reinterpretation of this baroque *topos* within a modern context is more powerful and persuasive than Hofmannsthal's conscious attempt at cultural reinstatement. It should be stressed that Schnitzler has very carefully rethought the whole atmosphere of the scene. The booming church bells have become the doorbell, the allegorical Death figure has become the jealous husband with the authority of the duelling code behind him, the opulence of Jedermann's banquet has become the hastily organized evening meal during which the coffee boils over and Mizi drinks so much wine that she falls asleep. And yet dramatically the whole scene is as powerful and rich in its implications as is Hofmannsthal's overtly allegorical confrontation. The short scene between Fritz and 'der Herr' is one of the most terse and powerful that Schnitzler ever wrote. It is a significant tribute to the laconic power of this one page of dialogue that the great Viennese actor Mitterwurzer chose to play the small part of 'der Herr' at the play's first performance—and with stunning effect. Behind the icily polite exchange of formal courtesies, the automatic implementation of the time-honoured convention of the duel, there throbs an anger and despair that threatens to break through to the surface. The tension between the polite formulas and the rage and disgust behind them gives the scene a horrific power.

Acts II and III are set in Christine's room, the world of the 'Vorstadt'. Once again, Schnitzler's stage direction could hardly be simpler: 'Zimmer Christinens. Bescheiden und nett' (240). The stage directions evoke a mood rather than a specific room with furniture, properties, precisely indicated exits and entrances, and so on. The first few scenes of the act, however, serve to underpin the atmosphere of life in the 'Vorstadt', and above all to suggest commonly held attitudes towards human experience. The physical barrier between 'Innenstadt' and 'Vorstadt' can be bridged, as when, in Act II, Fritz arrives in Christine's room. But the psychological barriers are much more resilient: they make themselves felt almost every time Fritz and Christine speak to each other.

Act II opens with a dialogue between Christine and Frau Binder, a neighbour. The latter's husband has a cousin who is very much attracted towards Christine. Frau Binder describes him in glowing terms, terms by which the 'Vorstadt' measures the suitability of relationships between the sexes: 'Wissen Sie, Fräulein Christin', daß er jetzt fix angestellt ist? . . . Und mit einem ganz schönen Gehalt. Und so ein honetter junger Mensch' (240). Christine tries to terminate the conversation at this point, but Frau Binder persists. She recounts at length a three-cornered conversation that took place. Her husband reported seeing Christine in the neighbourhood escorted by an elegant young man. Frau Binder relates her own, highly revealing, reply to this comment by her husband: 'Das Fräulein Christin', die ist keine Person die mit eleganten jungen Herren am Abend spazieren geht, und wenn schon, so wird's doch so gescheit sein, und nicht grad in unserer Gassen!' (241). Here she becomes very much a mouthpiece for 'Vorstadt' attitudes. She is prepared to concede the possibility that a young woman could associate with men of higher social station, but then at least, it must be done discreetly. But to show oneself openly in the 'Vorstadt' with an elegant young man amounts to breaking the rules. One of the reasons, of course, why Frau Binder launches into this lengthy narrative is that she wishes to show Franz, her husband's cousin, in a good light: Franz was angry with Herr Binder and leapt to Christine's defence. He refused to hear a word against her good name and went on to defend her spiritedly in terms that constitute a 'Vorstadt' ideal of domesticity: 'Und wie Sie so für's Häusliche sind und wie lieb Sie alleweil mit der alten Fräul'n Tant' gewesen sind' (241). At this point Christine's father enters, and she slips away in order to meet Fritz. A conversation ensues between Weiring and Frau Binder and once again the topic is love and marriage. She mentions the cousin again, and all his good points, but Weiring surprisingly does not agree with the attitudes expressed: 'Ist denn so ein blühendes Geschöpf wirklich zu nichts anderem da, als für so einen anständigen Menschen, der zufällig eine fixe Anstellung hat?' (243). Frau Binder is not, however, to be put off, and she praises the certainty of such relationships over against the 'other kind' of relationships, which she describes as follows: 'Auf einen Grafen kann man ja doch nicht warten, und wenn einmal einer kommt, so empfiehlt er sich dann gewöhnlich, ohne daß er einen geheiratet hat' (243). Weiring does not, however, give way. He even goes so far as to defend the kind of relationship that Frau Binder has described. It may be impermanent, but at least the girl experiencing it is richer in her memories: 'Na, und was bleibt denn übrig—wenn sie—nicht einmal was zum Erinnern hat—? Wenn das ganze Leben nur so vorbeigegangen ist (*sehr einfach, nicht pathetisch*) ein Tag wie der andere, ohne Glück und ohne Liebe—dann ist's vielleicht besser?' (244). The scene goes on to reveal why Weiring should hold such views which, on the face of it, are completely out of keeping with the social class to which he belongs. The decisive experience has been his looking after his sister. On the death of her parents he took her to live with him, and he kept an anxious watch over her behaviour in the early years when she was a young, attractive girl: 'Aber dann später, wie so langsam die grauen Haar' gekommen sind und die Runzeln, und es ist ein Tag um den andern hingegangen—und die ganze Jugend—und das Mädchen ist so allmählich—man merkt ja so was kaum—das alte Fräulein geworden,—da hab' ich erst zu spüren angefangen, was ich eigentlich getan hab'!' (245). Either way, it would appear, there is only regret at the end of the road. Regret at having never experienced happiness and love or, as is implicit in one or two of Frau Binder's remarks, regret at having once experienced it, only to be subsequently deprived of it.

The scene constitutes an absolutely overt discussion of the central theme of the play. Indeed, one could argue, particularly as regards Weiring's statements, that the scene becomes rather too overt and thematically 'loaded'. This is indeed a fault in many of Schnitzler's plays. He cannot resist forcing a moral issue in that all the characters in a particular play or story are made to take part in an explicit discussion of that issue. It is, of course, largely a stylistic question. The first act of *Liebelei* with its casual opening discussion between the two men illuminates the central theme and establishes at the same time a powerful sense of the social normality of such views, of the way they are expressed, and of the whole context in which they are expressed. The overtness of the scene between Frau Binder and Weiring loses this kind of contact with social normality which in *Liebelei* is inextricably bound up with the articulation of moral attitudes.

Despite its faults, the scene between Weiring and Frau Binder does add a further layer to the thematic centre of the play. If Act I has evoked the attitudes of the 'Innenstadt' towards love relationships, the exposition of Act II reveals the attitudes of the 'Vorstadt' towards such relationships.

It should be added here—with reference to the whole question of socially typical attitudes—that *Liebelei* operates not simply with the contrast between Fritz and Theodor on the one hand, and Mizi and Christine on the other, i.e. between 'Innenstadt' and 'Vorstadt'. There is also the contrast between Theodor and Mizi on the one hand, and Fritz and Christine on the other. Both axes of contrast do, of course, relate to the basic tension of social attitudes with which Schnitzler is concerned. Theodor and Mizi function as uncomplicated representatives of the relationship between 'Innenstadt' and 'Vorstadt'. They are aware of the rules of the game, and they are careful to confine both their actual behaviour and the attitudes which motivate that behaviour to the pre-established code of behaviour. Fritz and Christine are, however, different in that they bring an individuality, a specific personal involvement to the question of human relationships, and both, in a sense, are destroyed by the code of which they partake, but which has not taken full possession of their being. Fritz is, of course, much more conditioned by the code to the point that his individual capacity for feeling all too often degenerates into a kind of sentimentalizing process. Even so his capacity for personal involvement is much greater than Theodor's. Fritz has become far too involved with the married woman for Theodor's taste. Furthermore, Fritz has forgotten one of the crucial rules of the game, despite Theodor's constant reminders—he has written letters to her. Fritz gets caught in the machinery of the game and acquiesces helplessly in the duel as being the only way out. However imperfectly and sentimentally, Fritz, as we see in Act II, does respond in some measure to Christine's being. Theodor may be able to talk him round, to persuade him to uphold the rules of the game, but this does not alter the fact that Fritz potentially is capable of a response that just does not exist in Theodor. Similarly, Christine does attempt to adhere to the rules of the game; she reminds herself over and over again that her relationship to Fritz cannot last. But this reminder simply does not correspond to the fact of her being; she can only love on her own terms, and these terms are those of a passionate, complete surrender that demands everything in return.

The contrast between Christine and Mizi—and the common denominator of social experience that unites them—is revealed in the short scene which precedes Fritz's entry in Act II. The discrepancy between the two girls' attitudes is straightforward. Mizi counsels caution where men are concerned. They are not to be trusted, and one must never allow oneself to become completely involved with one. Her advice falls on deaf ears: Christine is completely and irrevocably in love with Fritz. The conflict of attitudes is succinctly summarized in the following lines:

MIZI:

> . . . Ich sag's aber immer! Den Männern soll man überhaupt kein Wort glauben.

CHRISTINE:

> Was redst du denn—die Männer—was gehn mich denn die Männer an!—ich frag' ja nicht nach den anderen.—In meinem ganzen Leben werd' ich nach keinem andern fragen!

(248)

Mizi's experience focuses on men in general—on a series of relationships which represent, as it were, safety in numbers. Christine asserts the uniqueness of love experience with one man, and this intensity excludes any notion of repetition, of seeing the specific relationship as one of a series.

Fritz then arrives, and the scene that ensues between him and Christine is one of the most revealing in the whole play. Part of the scene is devoted to a discussion of Christine's room. Here, the general aura of 'Vorstadt', which has hitherto been implicitly revealed in terms of psychological attitudes, is evoked by means of the actual décor of Christine's room. The stage direction at the beginning of the act refers to Christine's room simply as 'bescheiden und nett'. It is this aura which surrounds Christine, and Fritz on seeing the room exclaims: 'Bin ich wirklich zum erstenmal da—? Es kommt mir alles so bekannt vor! . . . Genau so hab' ich mir's eigentlich vorgestellt' (250). What then follows is a page of dialogue in which specific details of the room are discussed. Schnitzler thereby evokes not only the actual physical details of the room, but also the way in which two people respond to and evaluate these details. Three specific features are picked out. Fritz looks first at the pictures—'Abschied—und Heimkehr'—and Christine describes another picture which hangs in her father's room: 'Das ist ein Mädel, die schaut zum Fenster hinaus, und draußen, weißt, ist der Winter—und das heißt "Verlassen"' (250). All the pictures show domestic scenes—or, in the final case, domestic betrayal. They all embody situations involving home and, by implication, there is in each picture a considerable emotional loading of the situation. Farewell, return,

betrayal are the conceptual patterns which generate an emotional response. Fritz can say nothing about such pictures—beyond a laconic 'so'. To him they speak volumes, and implicit in the pictures is a sentimental attachment to the home. He then looks at Christine's books. She has copies of some of the classics—Schiller, Hauff—the 'Konversationslexikon' which 'geht nur bis zum G . . .' (250), and a kind of compendium of articles of general interest, 'Das Buch für Alle'. The final detail of the room is a small bust of Schubert. This detail, too, generates an aura of simple domesticity. Christine goes on to explain that her father is a great lover of Schubert, that he used to compose songs himself. We know from earlier references in the play that Christine herself plays the piano and also sings to her father's accompaniment. The bust of Schubert comes, then, by a process of subtle association to suggest home music-making, the kind of music that links father and daughter, the kind of music that has both a domestic register and yet also expresses pathos and tragedy, longing and despair.

As the conversation develops, Christine reproaches Fritz for the fact that he tells her so little about himself, that he is always keeping things from her. She asks Fritz how he spends his day, to which he replies: 'Aber Schatz, das ist ja sehr einfach. Ich geh' in Vorlesungen—zuweilen—dann geh' ich ins Kaffeehaus . . . dann les' ich . . . manchmal spiel' ich auch Klavier—dann plauder' ich mit dem oder jenem—dann mach' ich Besuche . . . das ist doch alles ganz belanglos. Es ist ja langweilig, davon zu reden.— Jetzt muß ich übrigens gehn, Kind . . .' (251). Fritz's answer is evasive—largely because he does not know *what* he does with his days. He does very little with them, and such things as he does are 'ganz belanglos'. But Christine wants to know more. She articulates what she feels about their entire relationship—that she only knows a tiny segment of Fritz's experience, that she is relentlessly excluded from whole areas of his life: 'Schau', mich interessiert ja alles, was dich angeht, ach ja . . . alles,—ich möcht' mehr von dir haben als die eine Stunde am Abend, die wir manchmal beisammen sind. Dann bist du wieder fort, und ich weiß gar nichts . . . Da geht dann die ganze Nacht vorüber und ein ganzer Tag mit den vielen Stunden—und nichts weiß ich' (252). Fritz argues that partial possession of the self is all that is possible. He rejects her demands as being too exclusive, too total—not only on himself, but also on her own being. He answers that no one can know himself sufficiently well to be able to make the kind of total statement that Christine makes: 'Du weißt ja doch nur eins, wie ich—daß du mich in diesem Augenblick liebst . . . (*Wie sie reden will*) Sprich nicht von Ewigkeit. (*Mehr für sich*) Es gibt ja vielleicht Augenblicke, die einen Duft von Ewigkeit um sich sprühen.—. . . Das ist die einzige, die wir verstehen können, die einzige, die uns gehört . . .' (252). Christine answers him instinctively. She misses completely the kind of philosophical argument he has used—i.e. that man cannot perceive himself or other people in such a way as to make statements of total and lasting certainty. She simply reassures him that she is not trying to possess him entirely—that she is not asking him to abandon his freedom:

> Du bist ja frei, du bist ja frei—du kannst mich ja sitzen lassen, wann du willst . . . Du hast mir nichts versprochen—und ich hab' nichts von dir verlangt . . . Was dann aus mir wird—es ist ja ganz einerlei—ich bin doch einmal glücklich gewesen, mehr will ich ja vom Leben nicht. Ich möchte nur, daß du das weißt und mir glaubst: Daß ich keinen lieb gehabt vor dir, und daß ich keinen lieb haben werde—wenn du mich einmal nimmer willst

(253)

Here explicitly are the terms which Christine offers Fritz. She asks for no undertaking of permanency; she recognizes such factors as social unsuitability for marriage. But what she does insist on is the intensity and permanence of her own feelings—and that at this level Fritz can meet her, can reciprocate genuineness and commitment of actual emotion.

This scene between Fritz and Christine is important, particularly as regards the issue of sentimentality. Clearly, both Fritz and Christine are capable of sentimentality, and in this scene Schnitzler shows two kinds of sentimentality interacting. The scene itself is as a result balanced on a knife edge between being an illumination and exploration of sentimentality on the one hand, and succumbing to sentimentality on the other. Christine's notion of beauty (as in her description of the pictures) is unmistakably sentimental—viewed in any kind of objective terms. The pictures are, presumably, worthless in themselves, and yet they strike a chord of genuine response in Christine. Her existence is narrow and restricted, and yet within it there is an intense capacity for feeling. Inevitably, therefore, this intensity of feeling is poured out within a highly domesticized context. The discrepancy between experiential content on the one hand and intensity of emotional response to it on the other produces the kind of sentimentality that Christine displays here. But there is a certain genuineness about it. It is not simply a kind of cerebrally contrived substitute for feeling. And in the final act Christine shows that she is prepared to take the consequences of her emotional situation.

Fritz, however, is different. He is attached to Christine, and yet beside her he is an emotionally impoverished being. His capacity for feeling has, presumably, been largely dissipated by a series of affairs. His desperate infatuation with the married woman, which is referred to in the first scene of Act I, is perhaps very largely a sentimental forcing of the squalid, illicit affair to the proportions of a fatal fascination for the unattainable. In the crucial scene with Christine in Act II, Fritz becomes aware of a quality in her being and environment that he vaguely apprehends as precious. And yet it is only a vague apprehension. Fritz's inability to respond to this on its own terms is reflected in the quality of his language. I have already drawn attention to the frequency with which he addresses Christine, and

by implication conceives of her, as a child. Fritz is often patronizing towards Christine. When he confronts her, he is obliged to sentimentalize, to force his feelings to sound more than they are. He describes his sudden decision to come and see her as follows: 'plötzlich hat mich eine solche Sehnsucht gepackt, eine solche Sehnsucht nach diesem lieben süßen Gesichtel . . .' (249). He then goes on to praise the beauty of her room and the view from the window. Fritz does respond to the whole atmosphere of Christine's existence, but his response is limited because he sees himself as a complex, tormented figure entering a simple, secure, homely world. Ultimately, such moments are sentimentalization of a given situation. Potentially, however, there is in Fritz a capacity for feeling which is utterly foreign to the world of which he is part. It is this— albeit residual and ultimately questionable—response to the intensity of Christine's love that makes Fritz more of an individual than the terms of the code allow.

The interaction of kinds of sentimentality in this scene and in the play as a whole is one of Schnitzler's most impressive achievements. He shows how sentimentality can be very much part of real feeling, and also how sentimentality can obscure real feeling. It is this complexity of illumination which prevents the play from succumbing to the sentimentality which it depicts.

Theodor appears and confirms that Fritz has to 'go away' for a few days. He teases Christine when she asks Fritz to write, describing her request as 'sentimental' (254). Theodor's intervention convinces Fritz again of all the presuppositions of the social class from which he comes. He is persuaded to distrust his feelings: 'o Gott, wie *lügen* solche Stunden!' (254). Passion is by definition a suspect commodity because it cannot last: there are intense moments and no more. Whether the moments with Christine lie or not, Fritz *makes* them lie. Hence his way out is unreal as well: the sentimental leave-taking after the moment of anguished heart-searching.

Act III confronts Christine with the truth of her relationship to Fritz. As the curtain rises, we see her fearful of the imminent end of this relationship. She is forced to conceive the present actuality of what she said she knew would inevitably happen—and is unable to: 'nicht für immer, ich weiß ja—aber auf einmal hört ja das nicht auf!' (257). The 'auf einmal' gives the key to the point at which her attempt at being sensible breaks down. For her the relationship must continue to exist because of her continued emotional commitment to it. The end therefore will be incomprehensible and sudden. Weiring enters, obviously knowing what has happened: 'sie weiß noch nichts, sie weiß noch nichts . . .' (258). Such a statement seems very much out of place in the play, and savours, if anything, of melodrama. Schnitzler is here forcing the emotional charge by making it abundantly clear early on that everybody knows what has happened—apart from Christine. This is a crude device to heighten the emotional tension, and a moment such as Weiring's muttered aside is so obviously contrived that it disturbs the kind of laconic impact that

Schnitzler intended with his brief third act. Weiring tries to console Christine, to suggest that the relationship with Fritz was not a happy one. The point of the scene is perhaps reached when Weiring says: 'ich weiß, daß ich dich lieb hab', daß du mein einziges Kind bist, daß du bei mir bleiben sollst—daß du immer bei mir hättest bleiben sollen' (260). Here Weiring in his despair retracts his earlier remark about love, that the young girl must taste the joys of passionate love, even if it does not last. This pattern of argumentation about human experience is a familiar one: it is, once again, the sequence of Hofmannsthal's *Gestern*: 'im Anfang stellt der Held eine These auf, dann geschieht eine Kleinigkeit, und zwingt ihn, diese These umzukehren.'[5] Here, however, the process is peripheral to the main action. Weiring is not the centre of interest in the play, and this scene has a retarding function which may heighten the tension, but in some ways does so to the detriment of the central confrontation which is the only necessary concern of the third act.

When Mizi and Theodor enter, Christine guesses the awful truth that Fritz is dead. And yet—and this is the greatness of the final scene—Christine is made to face not simply a past event—Fritz has been killed in a duel—but also the emotional truth about their whole relationship. She asks if Fritz left some message for her, but there is none. Theodor tries to comfort her: 'am letzten Morgen, wie wir hinausgefahren sind . . . hat er auch von Ihnen gesprochen' (262). Christine picks up the one word that hurts her beyond endurance: '*Auch* von mir hat er gesprochen! Auch von mir! Und von was denn noch? Von wie viel anderen Leuten, die ihm grad so viel gewesen sind wie ich?' (262). What tears at her heart is not just the fact of Fritz's death, but the realization of the hideous deception that was their relationship. What to her was a unique, all-embracing experience was to him merely one of many. Christine is forced to confront the fact that Fritz never quite believed in the intensity of her love: 'Ich bin ihm nichts gewesen als ein Zeitvertreib—und für eine andere ist er gestorben—! Und ich—ich hab' ihn angebetet!—Hat er denn das nicht gewußt? (262).

Time and time again Christine turns to Theodor in order to find out the precise truth about Fritz, and time and time again he gives only evasive answers. She asks, for example, with whom he had his duel. Theodor replies: 'Niemand, den Sie kennen . . .' (261). She asks Theodor why he waited so long before coming to her. He can only offer the lame excuse that he had much to do organizing the funeral:

THEODOR:

> Auch hat das . . . es hat in aller Stille stattgefunden . . . Nur die allernächsten Verwandten und Freunde . . .

CHRISTINE:

> Nur die Nächsten—! Und ich—? . . . Was bin denn ich? . . .

MIZI:

> Das hätten die dort auch gefragt.

CHRISTINE:

> Was bin denn ich—? Weniger als alle andern—? Weniger als seine Verwandten, weniger als . . . Sie?

> (263)

The process of exclusion, whereby Christine is denied any admittance to Fritz's world, reaches its climax here. Theodor in effect refuses to recognize that she has any right to know about Fritz. The horrifying fact of this exclusion is not simply a past truth which Christine discovers in the final scene, it is also a present situation which is clearly expressed by Theodor and, in a sense, by everyone around her. Theodor is embarrassed by Christine's misery—but no more; he murmurs to Mizi: 'Schau' Kind, das hättest du mir ersparen können . . .' (262).

Finally, however, Theodor capitulates before the intensity of Christine's love, and he blurts out the real reason for his behaviour: 'Ich bin sehr . . . (*mit Tränen in der Stimme*) Ich hab' das nicht geahnt . . .' (263). Theodor had seen Christine and Fritz together; he had heard her speak of love, and yet he simply had not *believed* her. This disbelief is an existential degradation of Christine. And the present world partakes of the same uncomprehending disbelief. Neither of the two worlds evoked in the play, neither the 'Innenstadt' (Theodor) nor the 'Vorstadt' (Mizi, Weiring) can conceive of the full tragic intensity of Christine's situation. Words of comfort inevitably imply a return to social normality. And such a return is anathema to her: 'Und in einem halben Jahr kann ich wieder lachen, was—? (*Auflachend*) Und wann kommt der nächste Liebhaber? . . .' (263). Existentially the world has no place for Christine's being, for the kind of experience she craves. At the end of the play she stands in absolute isolation, an isolation that is totally unbearable because her being can only exist in relationship to another fellow being. Christine has loved in a void; she cannot and will not continue to live in that void.

With Christine's exit the play reaches its appointed end. One can only regret that the curtain falls just a few lines too late. Weiring's last words—'Sie kommt nicht wieder' (264)—are superfluous, one of those moments which in their thematic underpinning amount to melodramatic explicitness.

The specific tragic quality of **Liebelei** and, above all, the kind of fascinated clarity with which Christine in the last act perceives her own isolation in many ways remind one of Austria's greatest tragedian, Franz Grillparzer. Several of Grillparzer's plays are concerned with one central experiential pattern: the protagonist is drawn out of the world in which he belongs, most often by the force of love, into a new world. All too often, however, the pressure exerted on the relationship is too great, and the relationship—and with it that new world which the protagonist has sought to enter—disintegrates. At this point, however, there is no return, no simple way back to that framework of existential certainty which has been abandoned. Grillparzer's heroes and heroines perceive with relentless clarity that they are utterly alone, and this moment of existential homelessness is frequently the mainspring of Grillparzer's tragic experience. It is perhaps significant that when Schnitzler turns to tragedy he should produce something which so recalls Grillparzer. For both authors a concern for the existential being of man implies a vision of man in the context of human relationships, of some kind of 'home' where he belongs. Human relationships involve a surrender of the self, a preparedness to be changed, and with this process, as Hofmannsthal saw, comes the danger of losing one's self, of losing the 'home' within which definition of the self was once possible. Medea's anguished cry 'Allein wer gibt Medeen mir'[6] finds its parallel in Christine's helpless 'Und was bin denn ich?' (263) of the final act.

The comparison of Grillparzer and Schnitzler should not, of course, be allowed to obscure the differences between the two writers. One should stress immediately that Schnitzler very rarely attempts to write tragedy. More typical of his art is the comedy *Zwischenspiel*. It is perhaps worth noting at the outset that the theme of both *Liebelei* and *Zwischenspiel* is the destruction of love. And yet in the latter play neither of the principal characters is the unequivocal embodiment of love, as is Christine. The very completeness of Christine's surrender to her love is what makes her a tragic figure. In total, exceptional form she lives out the full implications of her social situation. In the radical—and untypical—intensity of her being she becomes the paradigm of, and catalyst for, all that is typical in the situation of the 'süßes Mädel'. She is a type in Roy Pascal's sense of the term: she 'combines in an extraordinary degree, exceptionally, the various qualities which are usually present only partially'[7] in the type of the 'süßes Mädel'.

Zwischenspiel lacks the tragic explicitness of *Liebelei*. It is concerned with the difficulty of apprehending a relationship for what it is, with the unclarity of human affairs. Both Amadeus and Cäcilie suffer because of this unclarity. And the misunderstandings and betrayals which result are supremely the subject for comedy.

Both Amadeus and Cäcilie are practising musicians, and the demands of their careers mean that they inevitably spend much of their time apart. Act I opens with Amadeus rehearsing a role from the opera *Mignon* with Gräfin Friederike Moosheim. She is clearly in love with him, and is very determined that they should have an affair. Amadeus reacts with a mixture of urbane scorn and occasional moments of anger. Friederike insinuates that Cäcilie is deceiving him, to which he replies with an assertion of the frankness and understanding that prevails between him and his wife: 'Zwischen Menschen unserer Art gibt es keine Geheimnisse' (D, i. 900).

The implications of this scene are important for the subsequent development of the play. Both Amadeus and Cäcilie are surrounded by an indolent, cultured world which accepts marital infidelities as the norm for famous performing musicians. Friederike expects to have an affair with Amadeus, just as she expects Cäcilie to be having an affair with Sigismund. And the strenuousness with which Amadeus insists on the frankness and truthfulness that prevail between him and his wife is the measure of their desperate attempt to retain some kind of fundamental moral integrity within their relationship. Both know of the temptations to which their everyday lives expose them. It is Amadeus's firm conviction that if they admit to these dangers they can arrive at a kind of personal moral code, which may not correspond to any traditional notions of physical fidelity, but which can serve to hold their marriage together.

This kind of attitude towards human relationships is the subject of the scene between Amadeus and Albertus Rhon in Act I. Albertus recognizes the seriousness and integrity behind this new approach to human relationships—but he raises certain objections: first, that complete frankness and 'understanding' is not a foolproof basis for a lasting relationship, and secondly, that the individual is capable of all kinds of psychological and physical infidelities, that it is false to assume that the more freedom for sexual adventure the individual has, the 'truer' will be his life.

It is in the context of this kind of moral argumentation that one has to view the three main confrontations between Amadeus and Cäcilie which are the high point of each act. In Act I, scene v, they begin by discussing Cäcilie's work schedule, and she asks Amadeus to come to her rehearsal the following morning:

CÄCILIE:

Ich fühle mich sicherer, wenn ich dich in der Nähe weiß; das ist dir ja bekannt.

AMADEUS:

Ich werde kommen—ja. Ich werde dem Neumann und der Gräfin absagen.

CÄCILIE:

Wenn du damit kein zu großes Opfer bringst——

AMADEUS (ABSICHTLICH TROCKEN):

Ich kann sie ja auch für Nachmittag zu mir bitten.

CÄCILIE:

Dann kämst du aber gar nicht dazu, für dich zu arbeiten. Lassen wir's doch lieber.

AMADEUS:

Was sollen wir lassen?

CÄCILIE:

Komm morgen nicht zur Probe.

AMADEUS:

Wie du meinst, Cäcilie. Ich dränge mich natürlich nicht auf.

(906f.)

This interchange is deeply revealing. It indicates the degree of personal awkwardness that results from Amadeus's and Cäcilie's working arrangement. They see very little of each other and attempt to exorcize the threat of their frequent separations by being completely frank with each other. What results is a curious diffidence, an embarrassment at the emotional and physical demands they place on themselves by being together. Much of their conversation functions as a kind of shadow-boxing. Neither wishes to be seen to make demands on the other, because this would be out of keeping with the sensible—i.e. unemotional—arrangement they have reached. Behind the verbal implementation of this arrangement, however, one hears the voice of feeling, the simple dictates of emotional attachment which drive them to ask for each other's help, interest, attention. Amadeus tries to retain the professional note in the conversation by discussing what Cäcilie should sing at a forthcoming charity performance:

CÄCILIE:

Nun, etwas von dir jedenfalls——

AMADEUS:

O nein, nein.

CÄCILIE:

Warum denn nicht?

AMADEUS:

Aus einem inneren Bedürfnis heraus singst du's ja doch nicht.

CÄCILIE:

Wie du meinst, Amadeus.—Ich dränge mich auch nicht auf.

(908)

Once again, the conversation touches on a point where their work commitments impinge on their personal relationship. Implicit in Amadeus's reaction is a kind of reproach to Cäcilie, a hint of simple jealousy. Cäcilie turns the tables on Amadeus by quoting his own phrase back at him—'ich dränge mich auch nicht auf'. In so doing she reminds him of the terms of their working arrangement, terms that he has already invoked in the course of their conversation.

Once again the conversation is deflected on to practical matters, until Amadeus asks Cäcilie about her relationship with Sigismund. Cäcilie is disinclined to say more than she has already told him:

CÄCILIE:

Glaubst du nicht, Amadeus, daß manche Dinge geradezu anders werden dadurch, daß man versucht sie auszusprechen?

AMADEUS:

Unter Menschen wie wir—nein!

(909)

Cäcilie's words crystallize what will be one of the central moral preoccupations of the play, namely the relationship between human emotions and their articulation in language. Amadeus is not to be put off, and insists on the simple fact: 'du fühlst dich zu ihm hingezogen' (909). Cäcilie answers with another kind of truth: 'Aber vielleicht gibt es heute etwas, das zurückhält, . . . das zurückhalten könnte, wenn es nur wollte' (910). Her words are commented upon by the stage direction—'sehr innig, beinahe zärtlich' (910). It therefore becomes clear that what she is referring to here is their love, a love which the working relationship has hitherto threatened, but not destroyed.

At one point later in the scene the conversation lapses and Amadeus plays a few notes on the piano, the theme of the 'Zwischenspiel' from the symphony on which he is working. Amadeus is considering changing its title: it will be called 'Capriccio', perhaps even 'Capriccio doloroso'. Cäcilie has taught him to realize the sadness of this little transitional movement:

AMADEUS:

Es ist seltsam, wie man manchmal seine eigenen Einfälle anfangs mißversteht. Die verborgene Traurigkeit des Themas hast du mir entdeckt.

CÄCILIE:

Du wärst schon selbst darauf gekommen, Amadeus.

AMADEUS:

Vielleicht.

(912)

Here briefly, the meaning of the play's title becomes apparent. It is an intermezzo, a seemingly gay and witty transition in a human relationship whose infinite sadness will yet become apparent to the participants.

Amadeus dominates the dialogue for the rest of the scene. Beginning with a discussion of Cäcilie's practical plans for her future concert career, he proposes that they should put their relationship on a totally different footing. They should simply concede that they have long ceased to love each other, but should maintain their professional and practical contacts as before. Over and over again Amadeus stresses that he is offering the obvious rational solution to the problem: 'es liegt doch eigentlich kein vernünftiger Grund vor, daß sich unsere musikalischen Beziehungen umgestalten müßten' (913), or again: 'Je ruhiger ich die

Sachlage überschaue, um so unsinniger erscheint es mir, daß wir wie die ersten besten geschiedenen Eheleute voneinandergehn . . .' (914). In vain does Cäcilie protest that frequent contact between them, as envisaged by Amadeus, would inevitably bring emotional troubles. Amadeus brushes aside her objections and continues to elaborate his notion of the ideally free relationship that will prevail between them, whatever conventional moral scruples may say: 'Wir haben wohl das Recht, einen etwas höheren Standpunkt einzunehmen. Wir gehören doch schließlich noch immer zusammen, auch wenn von hundert Fäden, die uns verknüpfen, einer zerrissen ist' (914). Here one begins to feel already the falsity of Amadeus's argument, or rather, of his response to human relationships. In terms of abstract argumentation Amadeus may well have a case, but love, passion, is not just *one* of the many threads that has held him and Cäcilie together: it is the essential one. To push this on one side as no longer relevant is to misunderstand human behaviour, and, above all, the attraction between man and woman. But Amadeus is not to be deterred. His image of the ideal relationship between himself and Cäcilie is founded first on complete emotional freedom, and secondly on complete truthfulness: 'Das wäre natürlich die Voraussetzung unserer weiteren Beziehungen: Wahrheit—rückhaltlose Wahrheit' (915). Here again Amadeus falsifies the substance of human relationships by conceiving of truth and truthfulness in purely cerebral terms, by conceiving of a whole relationship in terms of a kind of professional interchange. Amadeus's conviction carries the day. In a moment of curious rhetoric Amadeus sets the seal on their new relationship by embracing Cäcilie for the last time as his beloved and taking her hand as a pledge of the friendship which in the future is to be the link between them. What makes this grand gesture of Amadeus's slightly pathetic is Cäcilie's instinctive reaction to it. As he moves to embrace her she says: 'Was tust du? (*Neue Hoffnung im Blick*)' (915). This is a deeply eloquent hint which undercuts all Amadeus's grand words and intellectual enthusiasms by revealing the simple, unspoken basis of their relationship, namely the fact that they still love each other. But Cäcilie is forced to accept Amadeus's interpretation of their situation—and his future solution to it.

The first act closes with a brief example of how their new relationship will work. Amadeus rehearses a Brahms song with Cäcilie. Yet the collaboration on their art cannot simply remain a question of rehearsing technicalities. The relationship is involved; the attraction between husband and wife is latent. Twice Cäcilie breaks off, the second time remarking: 'Amadeus, du sollst nicht allen deinen Schülerinnen den Hof machen' (916). After a further interruption Cäcilie manages to devote herself to the song. One of the reasons for her difficulties is perhaps the song itself, on whose first line the curtain falls: 'Nicht mehr zu dir zu gehen, beschloß ich und beschwor ich, und geh' doch jeden Abend . . .' (916). Implicitly, the ending of the act relativizes the decision which Amadeus and Cäcilie have taken. They are united not simply by the practicalities of the same profession, but also by a love of music. And their relationship to music is of necessity more than purely cerebral. Amadeus, when he writes the solo part for the final movement of his new symphony, will think of Cäcilie's voice as he writes—and will want her to sing the part. The emotional involvement is there, just as it is hinted at in their rehearsing a song which is explicitly concerned with the discrepancy between intellectual decisions about relationships, and the sheer emotional force which these relations generate.

Acts II and III take place some months later. What has happened in the intervening period is both revealed and discussed in the scene between Amadeus and Marie Rhon. We learn that Cäcilie is returning from a brilliantly successful guest season at the Opera in Berlin, that during the summer Marie and Cäcilie were together in the Tirol, while Amadeus spent much of the time at the villa of Gräfin Friederike Moosheim, with whom he was having an affair. Marie is clearly perturbed about the relationship between Amadeus and Cäcilie, but he is at pains to assure her that all is well, that they have behaved completely within the terms of their agreement: 'Wir beraten uns über alles, liebe Marie; geradeso wie früher. Und mit noch mehr Objektivität vielleicht als früher' (918). Amadeus even goes so far as to be completely frank with Marie about the various infidelities, or supposed infidelities, that occurred during the holidays. Indeed, he talks quite happily about Sigismund having been in Berlin with his wife.

The discussion of the relationship is continued in the scene between Amadeus and Albertus Rhon. A further piece of information is given—Friederike's husband has fought a duel with a young painter who had had an affair with his wife. The irony—and this appeals to Albertus's acute sense of the tragicomic—was that at the time of the duel the affair between Friederike and the painter was over, in fact she was already involved with Amadeus. For Albertus, life is shabby and confused. It just needs to be heightened and concentrated by art to produce the perfect tragicomedy.

Albertus has read rumours in the paper that Cäcilie and Sigismund intend to marry, and he offers to stay with Amadeus until the worst is over. Amadeus is horrified by the amount of rumour that he and Cäcilie are exciting, and Albertus warns him: 'Neuerer wie du müssen das Urteil der Welt verachten, sonst geraten sie in Gefahr, Großsprecher gewesen zu sein' (924). Here Albertus raises one aspect of Amadeus and Cäcilie's behaviour which is not fully worked out in the play, but which is implicit in the social reactions which they cause. Their working arrangement amounts to a new kind of sexual morality which contradicts all traditional notions of propriety and fidelity. As such it questions many deeply ingrained social attitudes, and society draws the automatic conclusion that their marriage is simply breaking up. What it refuses to recognize or believe is the possibility that this relationship represents moral integrity just as much as the traditional 'happy marriage'. In one sense, what Amadeus and Cäcilie have done, is to recognize the pressure which is exerted on the social institution of marriage by prevailing trends of behaviour, and to attempt to formulate a new and appropriate morality. Amadeus answers Albertus very much in this spirit. Like so many of Schnitzler's characters, he asserts that he is concerned with a *private* issue: 'Ich bin ja kein Neuerer. Das Ganze ist eine Privatabmachung zwischen mir und Cäcilie, bei der wir uns beide so wohl fühlen als möglich' (924). Yet at the same time, Amadeus desperately wants to convince the outside world of the rightness with which he has solved this private issue: 'Sag' doch den Leuten, bitte, die dich fragen, daß wir uns nicht scheiden lassen . . . Mach' ihnen doch klar, daß von einem Betrug keine Rede sein kann, wo es keine Lüge gibt. Sag' ihnen, daß die Treue, die wir, Cäcilie und ich, einander halten, wahrscheinlich eine bessere ist als die in manchen andern Ehen . . .' (924). Their new relationship is the result of a process of general moral argumentation, and it is the generality of principle behind it that the world could be made to recognize. Albertus agrees that he could put this in a play, that he could allow the figure representing Amadeus to declaim his views, but Albertus warns that the play would end 'nicht sehr heiter, mein Freund'. He goes on to explain why: 'Das ist ja das Charakteristische aller Übergangsepochen, daß Verwicklungen, die für die nächste Generation vielleicht gar nicht mehr existieren werden, tragisch enden müssen, wenn ein leidlich anständiger Mensch hineingerät' (925). At the most obvious level, Albertus is making a social point here, that Amadeus and Cäcilie are trying for a notion of marriage which is so far in advance of their times that it will be threatened by prevailing social attitudes. And yet, as the play as a whole shows, there is a further implication in Albertus's words. Amadeus is concerned with a 'Privatsache'. However unpleasant the anonymous letters may be which he receives, he could, presumably, continue to live happily with his wife in spite of the furore which their relationship creates. The ultimate test of their relationship is not whether they can persuade society to recognize it, but quite simply, whether they can make it work. The play itself ends, 'nicht sehr heiter', and the relationship disintegrates from within. Amadeus and Cäcilie may indeed be right—on their own terms—when they reject traditional notions of sexual morality as excessively inflexible; and yet their answer to such notions is, in its turn, equally inflexible. Their 'new' ideal of a relationship does not correspond to their emotional being. Implicitly, however, the question is raised whether these emotional needs, which they falsify in their working relationship, are the eternal and immutable emotional needs of man, or whether they are themselves the result of a whole tradition of moral thinking which has falsified them in the first place. To this Schnitzler can give no answer. He can only offer that pragmatic response which is so typical of him: that the basic moral needs of the human being are ultimately indeterminable; that, in practical terms, some kind of moral restriction does help man to find lasting relationships and, with them a sense of personal security and wholeness. *Zwischenspiel* is about the destruction of love. And this destruction is directly caused by an attempt to formulate a code of moral behaviour that is right for this specific relationship. It is this

paradox at the heart of the play's vision which, as Amadeus senses towards the end of his scene with Albertus, makes not so much for heroes, but rather, for clowns and fools.

The scene between Amadeus and Cäcilie which concludes the second act is one of the most richly ambiguous that Schnitzler ever wrote. Dramatically, its most obvious function consists in the reversal of the position in the comparable scene in the first act. In the first act, Amadeus had dominated as the theorist of the new relationship, and Cäcilie had been hesitant. Now Amadeus feels himself again in love with Cäcilie, and she answers him with his own arguments.

Amadeus, as becomes clear in this act and subsequent developments, is jealous of Cäcilie's intimacy with Sigismund and Wedius. She assures him that nothing has happened:

AMADEUS:

  So ist eine Gefahr in der Nähe.

CÄCILIE:

  Gefahr? . . . Was ist für uns Gefahr? Wer keine Verpflichtungen hat, für den gibt es auch nichts mehr zu fürchten.

AMADEUS (SIE LEICHT AM ARM FASSEND):

  Spiel' nicht mit Worten!

                                                             (938)

Amadeus here angrily dismisses as playing with words the kind of argument that he himself has used. Similarly, later in the scene when Cäcilie says: 'wir werden uns immer die Hände reichen, selbst über die tiefsten Abgründe hinweg, Amadeus' (935), she directly echoes what her husband had said to her in Act I: '[wir] würden uns die Hände reichen, auch über Abgründe' (915). Ironically, Amadeus's only reaction to Cäcilie's quotation of his own words is a helpless 'Du sprichst wie gewöhnlich äußerst klug' (935). Similarly, he goes on to reproach Cäcilie with being so 'ruhig' in the present confused emotional situation, and yet it was precisely this quality which he so proudly displayed in this confrontation in Act I. Amadeus is alarmed at the kind of freedom Cäcilie displays, at the degree of moral independence which she claims for herself. He argues that Cäcilie will only cause herself pain, but she rejects this: 'Ich bin schon heute nicht mehr, die ich war, Amadeus . . .' (936). Here we are confronted by one of the central notions of Schnitzler's moral thinking: man is compounded of a whole mass of contradictory emotions and urges, and can only find a coherent sense of his own manageable identity if he is prepared to restrict himself, to circumscribe an area within the mass of possibilities which he chooses to convert into reality. When this principle is ignored, when, for example, as in Act I, Amadeus urges Cäcilie to fulfil many of the possibilities of her being, he is inviting her to change the definition of her self. Hence, in Act II, when Amadeus looks for the Cäcilie he has known, he finds she has vanished irrevocably. As he looks at her, this truth begins to dawn: 'du bist auch nicht die Cäcilie, die ich geliebt habe—nein! . . . Die, die heute kam, hat eine Stimme, die ich nie gehört, Blicke, die mir fremd sind, eine Schönheit, die ich nicht kenne . . .' (937).

At the end of Act II, Amadeus looks at the changed Cäcilie and falls in love with her again. She feels the erotic tension behind his words to her, and she attempts to resist. She reminds her husband of his principle that they should be simply friends and colleagues. He counters by reminding her of their promise to be truthful—and the truth is that they are not now friends, but lovers. She continues to resist, but Amadeus's passion mounts to a final outcry: 'Nicht dein Geliebter also . . . nein, etwas Besseres und was Schlimmeres: der Mann, der dich einem andern nimmt! . . . der, für den du einen verrätst . . . einer, der dir Seligkeit und Sünde zugleich bedeutet! . . .' (938). Not only the sentiments here, but also the language itself is different from anything we have heard from either Amadeus or Cäcilie up to now. It is a tone that first makes its appearance towards the end of this scene when Cäcilie speaks of her new identity, of her powerful sense of potential sexual adventures. This passionate, intense tone in its over-rhetorical fury is the linguistic and stylistic underpinning of the experiential truth about which both of them have spoken. Not only the voice is different: the whole language has changed. In grandiose emotional terms Amadeus coaxes Cäcilie into this most dangerous of adventures. The clock is turned back; this is, as it were, the voice of adolescence: the individual personality is an unrestricted tangle of possibilities, and it responds to that possibility which represents the greatest emotional intensity.

Act III takes place the following morning. Amadeus is violently jealous of Sigismund. He is in love with Cäcilie and therefore determines to challenge Sigismund to a duel. He tells this to Albertus, and asks him to convey his challenge to Sigismund. Albertus finds the whole thing absurd—if it were a play, no one would believe it. He coolly points out that Amadeus cannot possibly challenge Sigismund to a duel for behaving in a way that he (Amadeus) has explicitly invited.

Albertus's mission, is, however, forestalled by the arrival of Sigismund, and the ensuing scene is a fine example of Schnitzler's high comedy at its best. Sigismund finds the position in which he is placed intolerable and he asks Amadeus to offer Cäcilie a divorce in order that she may choose freely whether she wishes to marry him or not. Amadeus reveals that two of his friends are at present entrusted with conveying his challenge to Sigismund. Sigismund realizes that Amadeus has changed position so that Cäcilie will no longer be left in such a compromised situation, and immediately withdraws his suit. The neatly comic pattern of reversed roles which operates throughout the play is employed here with delightful precision.

Amadeus is convinced that he can assert possession of Cäcilie. But Cäcilie refuses. She argues that they cannot

simply forget what they were—what they meant to each other—nor can they trust the fleeting happiness of a night's love. Amadeus tries to answer her objections with his certainty—both about himself and about the rightness of their relationship. In a crucial exchange he offers her the protection of his love:

AMADEUS:

> . . . Jetzt bist du auch nicht mehr schutzlos, wie du es warst—meine Zärtlichkeit behütet dich.

CÄCILIE:

> Aber ich will nicht behütet sein.—Ich gebe dir das Recht nicht mehr dazu! . . .

> (956)

Cäcilie condemns the two of them for lacking the courage of their convictions, for being neither friends nor lovers: 'Wir waren weder geschaffen, uns ewig in Treue zu lieben, noch stark genug, um unsere Freundschaft rein zu erhalten' (957). With relentless intellectual clarity which recalls Amadeus's argumentation in the first act, she insists that what is now holding them together is nothing more than a shabby fear of the final leave-taking. To stay together would be as much a moral degradation as the kind of empty, convention-bound marriages of which they were so scornful. Their discussion is interrupted briefly by Albertus, who then leaves to play with Peterl's toy theatre. As he does so, he says: 'Na, Bub', komm, du sollst mir dein Stück vorspielen. Aber ich bestehe darauf, daß der Held zum Schluß entweder Hochzeit macht oder vom Teufel geholt wird; da kann man doch beruhigt nach Hause gehen, wenn der Vorhang gefallen ist' (959). In the play we are witnessing, however, the ending is neither happy nor tragic; it is an arid realization of the destruction of a relationship—and of the fact that both principal characters not only acquiesced in this process, but helped to bring it about. In a speech of infinite sadness, Cäcilie recalls the cardinal error they committed; a schematization of their emotional needs in the name of a cerebral partial 'truth':

> Wenn alles andere wahr gewesen ist,—daß wir beide uns so schnell darein gefunden in jener Stunde, da du mir deine Leidenschaft für die Gräfin und ich dir meine Neigung für Sigismund gestand—das ist nicht Wahrheit gewesen. Hätten wir einander damals unsern Zorn, unsere Erbitterung, unsere Verzweiflung ins Gesicht geschrien, statt die Gefaßten und Überlegenen zu spielen, dann wären wir wahr gewesen, Amadeus,—und wir waren es nicht.

> (960)

The insight comes too late, however.

And yet one should stress here that *Zwischenspiel* is a comedy—for all its serious undertones. It is comic in the sense of Bergson's definition: 'du mécanique plaqué sur du vivant'.[8] Throughout the play, Amadeus and Cäcilie become so involved in arguing out the implications of their relationship, in formulating a kind of new morality, that they always ignore the basic fact of present emotional attraction. In this sense, they are comic figures, uttering grand words, impressive intellectual arguments, and yet quite simply missing one of the essential points. And it is this essential point which continues to assert itself every time they are together—and which necessitates every time a fresh piece of argumentation to explain the situation yet again. And this is true even of the final act. Cäcilie speaks with considerable insight when she sees through their ideal of 'truthfulness'—and yet in a supreme stroke of comedy, she cannot see that she is now guilty of the same kind of misunderstanding as that perpetrated by Amadeus in the first act. Why should they not trust the previous night of love as much as their own ability to discuss and analyse it? Fundamentally, Amadeus and Cäcilie learn very little in the course of the play. They gyrate in perpetual confusion occasioned by their relentless desire for complete intellectual clarity. They are comic in the sense that the hapless Faulkland is comic in *The Rivals*. Their only insight is to be able to see each time where they have gone wrong—but they are never able to see where they are *going* wrong. At the end of the play they separate. Amadeus leaves—and then and only then does Cäcilie confront her sorrow at losing him. Their separation will put an end to their relentless self-tormenting. And yet even in the final act Cäcilie refers to the possibility of their perhaps coming together again: 'Aus allen möglichen Schicksalen können wir eher einmal zueinander zurück als aus dem Abenteuer dieser Nacht und aus dieser trügerischen Stunde' (957). This remains a possibility. If they do come together again, then presumably the whole process will repeat itself. The song which closes Act I perhaps stands as a kind of motto for the play—'Nicht mehr zu dir zu gehen, beschloß ich und beschwor ich, und geh' doch jeden Abend . . .' (916).

One should in conclusion stress the basically comic structure of *Zwischenspiel*. There is a sharp parallelism in all three acts. Each act opens with a scene—or several scenes—of exposition, then follows a discussion between Amadeus and Albertus, and then a discussion between Amadeus and Cäcilie. The parallelism is deliberate, and as I have tried to suggest on several occasions, it yields a neatly contrasting pattern as statements are repeated, transformed by context, and often reversed by characters who have completely changed position. The artificiality is further stressed by Albertus's frequent references to the similarities between what Amadeus and Cäcilie are doing and the performance of a play. And yet the neatness and wit of this comic illumination is never allowed to lose its serious undertone. Amadeus's and Cäcilie's shifting attitudes with regard to their relationship may be comic; but we know that all the time they are playing with something deeply serious, ultimately indeed, with their own reality as people. With the mechanical relentlessness of so many great comedies, they change and undermine themselves.

Notes

1. On the contrast between Ibsen and Schnitzler see Melchinger, *Illusion und Wirklichkeit im dramatischen Werk Arthur Schnitzlers*, pp. 17, 87, 94.

2. Richard Alewyn in the 'Nachwort' to *Liebelei, Reigen* (Fischer Bücherei, 1960), pp. 157f.

3. *Liebelei, Leutnant Gustl, Die letzten Masken*, ed. Stern, ed. cit., p. 13.

4. Heinz Politzer, *Das Schweigen der Sirenen*, p. 137.

5. Cf. p. 134 n. 1.

6. *Medea*, Act III, scene ii.

7. Roy Pascal, *The German Novel* (Manchester, at the University Press, 1957), p. 127.

8. Henri Bergson, *Le Rire* (Alcan, Paris, 1938), p. 50.

Reinhard Urbach (interview date 1973)

SOURCE: Urbach, Reinhard. "Early Full-Length Plays." In *Arthur Schnitzler*, pp. 35-71. New York: Frederick Ungar Publishing Co., 1973.

[*In the following excerpt, Urbach provides critical overviews of* Anatol, The Fairy Tale, *and* Light-O'Love.]

ANATOL: A SEQUENCE OF DIALOGUES

A superficial man soon finds something profound.

—Johann Nestroy

The cycle of seven loosely connected scenes entitled *Anatol* concerns a young bachelor, Anatol, who in each act experiences a new love affair and discusses it with his friend Max.

Scene 1: *Ask No Questions and You'll Hear No Stories (Die Frage an das Schicksal)*. Anatol possesses the power of hypnosis. He could ask his beloved Cora, who permitted him to hypnotize her, whether she is faithful to him. Yet, he does not ask the question, partly because he persuades himself that he does not want to know the truth, and partly because he is convinced that one cannot know the truth. He considers the question "What is fidelity?" to be just as unanswerable as the question "Are you faithful?" He has hypnotized Cora in vain, for she could have told him "just as well without hypnosis" that she loved him.

Scene 2: *A Christmas Present (Weihnachtseinkäufe)*. Fruitlessly Anatol adores Gabriele, a married woman, an elegant lady of high society. She helps him to select a Christmas present for his *süßes Mädel*, who is waiting for him in the outskirts and whom he describes as a girl who knows how to love deeply and naively. Gabriele is moved, and she has Anatol bring flowers to the girl from a woman "who perhaps can love just as deeply . . . and who did not have the courage to do so. . . ." (See the account of *Light-O'-Love* for a discussion of the *süßes Mädel*.)

Scene 3: *An Episode (Episode)*. Anatol asks his friend Max to keep the mementos of his love affairs so that he will not forget. Even at the time, he had regarded his brief relationship with Bianca as a casual interlude. It was his feeling, however, that this episode must have been an unforgettable experience for her. Bianca, the equestrienne, returns to Vienna and visits—Max. She has forgotten Anatol.

Scene 4: *Keepsakes* (*Denksteine*). While Bianca forgot her previous experiences, Anatol forces Emilie to revive her past. He requires her to spread out her past before him in order to cast it away along with the pieces of jewelry that reminded her of the individual episodes. Now he wants to marry her, for, as he will assure us later in *Megalomania*, he creates his own virgins. Yet his transformation of the "fallen woman" into a marriageable one proves to be illusory. Emilie retained two precious stones: the least valuable and the most valuable. The one reminds her of the day on which she became the kind of woman Anatol fell in love with as well as the kind of woman he would not want to marry. The other reminds her of her most profitable adventure. His jealousy and her greed are stronger than all of their protestations of love.

Scene 5: *A Farewell Supper* (*Abschiedssouper*). Anatol does not know how to inform Annie that he no longer loves her but someone else and that they must therefore separate. They had arranged things between them in this way: ". . . right from the beginning . . . as we swore eternal love to each other—Remember, dear Annie, whichever partner one fine day senses that our love is ending will tell the other straight out . . ."

Annie embarrasses Anatol. She beats him to the punch by being the first to confess that she wants to end the relationship. She, too, loves another.

But Anatol is not about to let her get away with this ploy. He claims that he has already deceived her with the other woman! At this news Annie is insulted. She would never have gone that far—that is, she would never have *told* him.

Scene 6: *Dying Pangs* (*Agonie*). Anatol loves Else, a married woman. But the constant circumspection, which they have to maintain because of Else's marriage, destroys his love. He realizes he is not the sole man in her life but only a convenient lover. In spite of the danger involved in the present situation, Else prefers that to fleeing with Anatol and losing the comfort of her marriage. For Anatol, it is unbearable never to be able to embrace his beloved but always the wife of another man.

Scene 7: *The Wedding Morning* (*Anatols Hochzeitsmorgen*). On the evening before his wedding, Anatol had attended a bachelor party, where he bade farewell to his "sweet, riotous bachelor life." After the party he had gone to a masquerade ball and met Ilona, an actress and former mistress of his. On the morning of Anatol's wedding Max finds the two together in Anatol's apartment. Ilona knows nothing yet of Anatol's impending marriage. When she learns of it from Max, she makes a

big, dramatic scene and threatens to go to the wedding herself and expose Anatol. Max is the one who discourages Ilona from carrying out her threat, assuring her that Anatol will return to her sooner or later anyway.

Anatol's Megalomania (*Anatols Größenwahn*). Schnitzler had written this scene as an alternative for *The Wedding Morning*. It was not performed or published, however, until after his death.

Years have passed, and Anatol has aged. But he has retained his illusions as well as the awareness that he has illusions. Both aspects of his character are tested when young Annette flirts with him, even though she is having an affair with Flieder, who is very jealous and just as sentimentally inclined as Anatol. Yet Annette cannot take Anatol's emotionalism. Even Berta, who was once Anatol's mistress, had made fun of him during their affair and never took his high-sounding declarations at face value.

ANATOL:

> And when we swore eternal love to each other . . . you knew all the time that that actually . . .

BERTA:

> Certainly—and you? Were you really intending to marry me?

ANATOL:

> But we worshipped each other!

BERTA:

> Certainly . . . but that is no cause to lose one's reason!
> . . .

Anatol drags his illusions and memories of past fantasies along with him—he has nothing else.

Anatol convinces himself that he believes in genuine love, which, however, is only genuine as a game. He does not believe it is a game, although he stages it and actually came to an agreement with Annie, for example, under its terms. He lives in constant self-deception. This is his megalomania.

Anatol accepts as genuine life, what in reality is only genuine as a game.

ANATOL:

> . . . Such is life!

MAX:

> Oh, . . . I beg your pardon . . . life is not that way!

Anatol deceives himself about the character of the game. Again and again he believes that what he is involved in is a binding relationship—one, however, that would exempt him from any responsibility. His attitude is shown by the way he turns even his wedding into a game for which one must be in the mood. He himself determines the rules, and he prevents the intrusion of reality into the game. Thus he does not question the hypnotized Cora beyond the boundaries of the game as played in the conscious state. Reality would invalidate the rules, for it is part of the game to swear eternal love to each other, a vow that is actually meant only for the moment, without thinking of the future (*Anatol's Megalomania*), of the husband (*Dying Pangs*), or of the past (*Keepsakes*).

Annie observes the rules literally and honorably without deceiving either Anatol or herself. Else transgresses against the sentimentality of Anatol's rules because she views eternal love as a relative matter. Emilie did not take literally Anatol's command to destroy the past. She wanted to preserve in their marriage both her jewelry and the memories that it represents. Berta has seen through Anatol. She is a worthy partner for him, since she knows and observes the rules, but she is superior to Anatol because she never takes the rules seriously (Annie had taken them seriously as long as they concerned her). Anatol acted according to the spirit of the rules and at the same time tried to circumvent them. Nevertheless, he always remains threatened by the destruction of his illusions and he never really lives—that is, except for the moment. His life is superficial and never reaches into the depths, it changes but never develops. Instead of being faithful, Anatol seeks new love affairs. Constant variation of the same theme with ever different partners is intended to suppress inner emptiness, but it cannot eliminate it.

First Anatol exploits his possibilities as a type and then repeats them in the endless emptiness of exhaustion. He undergoes no transformation through his wealth of experiences but remains chained to a round dance of ever the same occurrences. He asserts: "I mastered the art of deriving the most experience from the least number of external events. . . ." But that is not true. In spite of his very great effort (expended on collecting as many mistresses as possible) he gains little because he always experiences only the same thing. What he called multiplicity is only the sameness of superficial repetition. Multiplicity as a profound experience is possible in marriage, as Schnitzler later showed, or in realizing all of the potentialities of a relationship, in the struggle between guilt and responsibility, as expressed by Georg von Wergenthin in Schnitzler's novel *The Road to the Open*. Anatol's life could have taken a decisive turn and his character could have been deepened if he had been confronted by the problem of fatherhood. As it is, however, he remains only clever and superficial. He loves variation because he is indolent, comfort-loving, and incapable of fidelity and permanence.

Anatol does not acknowledge people as individuals but simplifies everyone to a type. He describes his girl in *A Christmas Present* as a *süßes Mädel,* but by contrast he makes Gabriele the self-absorbed elegant lady of society. He typifies and thus practices the very superficiality that he appears to resist.

Schnitzler's structural patterns utilize the parallel concepts of variation and association that represent the way his characters live and think. The theme determines the formal structure. The cycle is a circular form that signifies emptiness. By means of this form Schnitzler not only characterizes his figures but also permits them to unmask themselves.

The favorite mood of superficiality is melancholy, which derives from boredom. Melancholy is the mood of the surface, which conceals the underlying mood of depression that drives one into megalomania. Anatol's characterization of himself as a "frivolous, melancholy person" is not a contradiction, for "frivolous" is the logically consistent complement of "melancholy."

By contrast Max could be described as a reflective skeptic. It has been a technique of drama from the beginning to provide the seducer with a companion who keeps the record, consoles the deceived woman, and creates opportunities. Max, however, is not a servant to Anatol like Leporello, for instance, is to Don Juan, but Anatol's friend and counterpart. He is neither the voice of conscience nor a spokesman for Schnitzler but a corrective for Anatol's errors and foolish behavior. He is never Anatol's rival with women, but neither is he a moralist. Instead, he acts as the instigator for some of Anatol's adventures and remains on his side. His masterpiece, the soothing of Ilona, is a solution in terms of the prevailing rules of the game, one of which is that marriage is no barrier to casual affairs.

Even Ernst L. Offermanns begins the postscript to his 1964 *Anatol* edition with the statement that this cycle consists of a series of loosely connected scenes. It is only the new form that is confusing. But this form is closed and complete in itself. None of the scenes is interchangeable without destroying the logical sequence—which is not determined by the plot. The theme of the variations is Anatol's fate in his relationship to women. Anatol's downward course is shown, from the idyll of the first scene to the dilemma, the barely averted scandal of the last scene, along with the intermediate stages of flirtation, rapture, jealousy, farewell, and agony. The first scene shows that Anatol is still subject to his hypnotic powers. He could penetrate into the depths of a soul, learn the truth, and establish a genuine love. Cora's answer could remove all doubts, and thus there would be no cycle. Because of his fear of the depths, however, Anatol robs himself of the possibility of gaining certainty and consequently initiates the sequence of variations. Cora does not allow him to hypnotize her again. The moment of the height of Anatol's power to free himself from his illusions passes.

Anatol's doubt about Cora's fidelity is confirmed by his own actions in *A Christmas Present*. While he rhapsodizes about his love for his *süßes Mädel,* he woos Gabriele unashamedly and is rejected. Out of the moment of opportunity for fulfillment in *Ask No Questions and You'll Hear No Stories* develops the yearning in the second scene and the remembrance in the third. Anatol's decline begins. In the third scene he has no mistress and begins to survey his past. Then it happens that his former mistress Bianca, who loves too often to be able to experience the uniqueness of true love, confuses him with another lover. The time of love, hope, and belief is past. Anatol's star is sinking. He even wants to marry the "fallen woman" Emilie. She loves him and tells him the truth, but he does not mean everything to her and cannot eradicate her memories. In return for his raising her to his level, she is supposed to make every sacrifice. But he cannot forgive her—Anatol makes no sacrifices. In *An Episode* he is not forsaken, only forgotten. In *Keepsakes* he is still the one who breaks off the affair. Not until *A Farewell Supper* is he forsaken. Annie plays his own game and leaves him. *Dying Pangs* shows the death of the love Anatol had yearned for in *A Christmas Present.* Else takes him only for a lover. *The Wedding Morning* leads close to catastrophe. Ilona finally intends to punish him for what he has done to women. Anatol has made himself vulnerable, and Ilona cleverly knows how to utilize this advantage against him.

Of necessity the games that Anatol plays culminate in an affair with an actress. For Ilona life unexpectedly turns into a stage, the realm in which she is accustomed to dominate. Exaggerations are part of the game: "I have been crying over him for six weeks. . . ." Yet this did not prevent her from going to the masquerade ball where she meets and renews her affair with Anatol. In his apartment Ilona tries to overshadow the others by acting like the mistress of the house. When she is unsuccessful in this role—Anatol and Max cannot enter into the spirit of her performance because they are already committed to another play, Anatol's wedding—she stops acting and makes a real scene. In contrast to Anatol, who lives according to and is dependent upon moods (though he does not act them out, for he cannot render artificial feelings in a genuine manner), Ilona commands the nuances that enable her to make trivialities seem original. She can convey her feelings and emphasize them with gestures. Unlike Anatol, who with all his illusions still preserves his sense of shame, she does not feel embarrassed in front of the public because she is used to performing before an audience.

Ilona is sure of her feelings and her techniques, for she has tested their effectiveness on the stage. One can doubt her love but not her power of expression. Her outburst is to be taken seriously as a performance, although its effectiveness suffers from lack of truthfulness. And Max explains to her that if she declared her love for Anatol in public and made a scandal of his wedding, she would not only hurt Anatol, but she would also make herself appear "ridiculous" because no one would believe in her love.

At the same time Ilona does not lack grandeur, and during this scene there is truth in what she says. It is not she but Anatol who is lying. It is not she but Anatol who is attempting (unsuccessfully) to dissemble. Her recognition of his behavior causes her outburst. What other possibility does she have except to adopt a pose when the others justify themselves by indulging in windy rhetoric? She takes up the cue for revenge that Max had given to rescue

Anatol for the moment, and this provides her with a grand exit. Her actual despair and urge for revenge are not so great, however, that she can resist the temptation to appear grandiose and demonic to herself. Immediately she is attuned to the dramatic possibilities inherent in acting out the emotion of revenge.

Thus the cycle is concluded, but the possibilities for further variations are not yet exhausted. Therefore, Schnitzler offered an alternative to *The Wedding Morning,* which is really a preview of the future showing that the game will continue. His alternative is *Anatol's Megalomania,* which is a retrospective view demonstrating that the game did indeed continue.

Two additional variations to Anatol were found in Schnitzler's literary estate. *The Adventure of His Life (Das Abenteuer seines Lebens*; printed in Ernst L. Offermann's edition, 1964), the earliest scene on the Anatol theme, places Anatol between two women, like Fritz in *Light-O'-Love.* Cora in this early version, however, is not a *süßes Mädel* like Fritz's Christine, but a temperamental, carefree girl, who used to love lieutenants and now loves poets. Gabriele represents for Anatol only a temporary infatuation, not a real affair. Anatol lives in the illusion that both women love him. He loses both when they encounter each other at his home. Now he must find two new girls. But this causes this early Anatol no inner conflict. He is just too happy-go-lucky a person.

More significant is the fragment "Süßes Mädel," which Schnitzler wrote on 15 March 1892, after the cycle had already been completed. Before Anatol leaves to attend a ball, he and his *süßes Mädel,* Fritzi, act out the event that lies before him. He knows what the atmosphere at a ball is like, while she can only imagine. He plays the part of himself, and she plays the part of a socialite who belongs in the world of high society. Even in this rehearsal (which is not even a real rehearsal, since the *süßes mädel* is only filling in for the socialite), ostensible playacting turns into seeming reality. The scene that they are rehearsing threatens to become living reality because the *süßes Mädel* in her role as socialite hears the truth about herself, which makes her forget her role. Anatol, who actually wants to leave her, is distracted, and therefore his performance is genuine: he is supposed to act in a distracted manner, since while at the ball he is ostensibly yearning for his *süßes Mädel.* The fragment breaks off with Fritzi's lament that their relationship is only a game of pretending, that Anatol will never be in earnest.

In *Anatol* Schnitzler adumbrated many themes that were to recur in later works. *Ask No Questions and You'll Hear No Stories* contains in essence the theme of *The Puppeteer,* of assuming the role of destiny, symbolized by the power of hypnosis, which Paracelsus, in the one-act play by that name, also knows how to use. The love triangle that occurs in *Light-O'-Love* is foreshadowed in *A Christmas Present.* The motifs of recollection and egotism are brilliantly varied in *New Year's Eve. Keepsakes* treats the problem of the insurmountable past, as does also *The Fairy Tale,* with the difference that in the former play the burden of guilt is accorded to the "fallen woman," whose greed overcomes her pretended love. The thesis of *A Farewell Supper*—that lovers should always be completely truthful to one another—initiates the conflicts found in *Intermezzo.* The egotistically comfortable behavior of the mistress in *Dying Pangs* is treated again in *The Eccentric.* In the latter play, however, it is not the woman but the man who violates his partner's claims to unqualified devotion. The comic situation in *The Wedding Morning* finds its correspondence in *Literature,* the one-act play from the cycle *Living Hours,* in which a woman about to be married finds herself caught between two men. Finally, Ilona, Schnitzler's first characterization of an actress, was to have many successors.

. . . . .

The individual scenes constituting *Anatol* each had its premiere singly.

Josef Jarno, director of the Vienna Deutsches Volkstheater, was the first to concern himself with these scenes. In 1922 he recalled this early period. (In his discussion two errors of memory occurred: *A Farewell Supper* was premiered in 1893, and *Ask No Questions and You'll Hear No Stories* in 1896.)

> In the year 1890 at the Ischl Summer Theater I staged the premiere of Schnitzler's one-act play *A Farewell Supper,* and in the year 1895 in Berlin, on the occasion of a large soirée at the home of the Berlin attorney, Dr. Greling, at which the whole of literary Berlin was present, a performance of his one-act play *Ask No Questions and You'll Hear No Stories.* In both countries these occasions represented the first time that Arthur Schnitzler's works had been performed anywhere. In the year 1898 I met my wife, Hansi Niese, in Berlin and persuaded her to play [Christine in] *Light-O'-Love* and [Annie in] *A Farewell Supper* in a matinee at the Residenz Theater in Berlin. This represented a memorable moment in my wife's career, for actually through the performance of these two female characters she thanks Arthur Schnitzler for her rise to great fame.

A Christmas Present was premiered in 1898 in the Sofiensälen in Vienna. *A Farewell Supper* was also given at the same performance. Arthur Schnitzler wrote to Otto Brahm about this performance on 22 January 1898: "It was as if one had locked a canary in a bear cage."

In 1898 *An Episode* had its premiere in Leipzig. *The Wedding Morning* was premiered in 1901. The premier date of *Keepsakes* may be given as 10 January 1916, although Schnitzler had written to Otto Brahm about this work on 4 August 1909: "*Keepsakes,* which I naturally do not like either, has already proved itself on small stages."

At the end of the 1890s the well-known actor Friedrich Mitterwurzer was to have played Anatol under the direction of Oskar Blumenthal at the Lessingtheater in Berlin.

The project was not carried out, however, because of Mitterwurzer's death. In addition, on 9 March 1899, *The Wedding Morning* was banned in Berlin by the censor for moral reasons. Finally, five of the scenes of *Anatol* were performed together as a cycle on 3 December 1910 in Otto Brahm's Lessingtheater in Berlin and at the same time at the Vienna Deutsches Volkstheater. In connection with this performance Brahm wrote to Schnitzler on 24 July 1909:

> I have now read *Anatol* again and would like to perform it. I agree with your opinion, that not all of the scenes should be included, but I would not like to omit *The Wedding Morning.* We need it as a conclusion because of its humor. Why do you want to eliminate it? Certainly it becomes a little too boisterous toward the end where Anatol throws on his tuxedo, but otherwise I find it of a pleasant insolence. By contrast, *Keepsakes* and *Dying Pangs* seem to me to be less effective, and I would like to sacrifice them, partly also in order not to burden humanity with seven different things. I am not worried that this will make the evening too short. But I know that it will gain in impact.

Schnitzler was often critical of *Anatol.* He found *The Wedding Morning,* in particular, "objectionable." Not the least important reason for his antipathy was that the success of these plays was responsible for the cliché that labeled Schnitzler a frivolous poet and a *bon vivant.*

In a letter to Brahm of 14 August 1909, Schnitzler expressed this idea about *Anatol:* "A different kind of theatrical effect could be achieved if one had all five women [in *Anatol*] played by the same actress. The pleasure in the art of transformation of this one actress would in this case replace the pleasure in the change of performers or, if this actress were a genius, would be able to surpass it." This was once done for a performance in the United States.

In 1932 at the Vienna Deutsches Volkstheater Heinrich Schnitzler directed the alternate scene, *Anatol's Megalomania,* for the first time. The same year the Burgtheater added *Anatol* to its repertory, under the direction of Franz Herterich. The Viennese drama critic Raoul Auernheimer wrote in the *Neue Freie Presse:*

> Before the curtain opens for the first time, [Raoul] Aslan as Anatol is already seated on stage facing partly away from the audience. With a mocking side glance at the public of today, he speaks the prologue in a reverie, as if he were just thinking up his speech. Then the curtain parts, Anatol turns his face to the right, and without getting up or changing his position, he begins to speak to Max, who is sitting diagonally opposite him. This is an attractive idea and one that derives from the material. . . .

After World War II Karl Eidlitz staged *Ask No Questions and You'll Hear No Stories* at the Burgtheater on 7 October 1946. On 13 June 1952 Curd Jürgens, in a presentation of the cycle in the same theater, tried to eliminate all references to the time in which the play was written. Rudolf Holzer, writing about this "experimental production" in the *Presse,* stated that Jürgens had tried "to have these events, which after all are completely real, take place on a transparent, illusionist stage. It is, of course, contrary to Schnitzler's intention but . . . not without a strong illustrative effect."

Ernst Lothar's production in 1960 in the Akademietheater in Vienna had a successful run. Lothar's solution was to put *Anatol's Megalomania* at the beginning and thus to transpose the action into the irrevocable past. This transposition and subjective textural changes, however, met with vigorous objection.

Anatol has enjoyed more popularity in the United States than any other of Schnitzler's plays. It has been offered as drama and musical comedy, in small workshops and summer stock as well as on Broadway. Often American directors have produced one *Anatol* episode in combination with one-acters of other playwrights. *A Christmas Present* and *A Farewell Supper,* in particular, have been presented in this way.

Anatol was first brought to the American stage in 1912, when Winthrop Ames staged five of the episodes at the Little Theater in New York. In this production, John Barrymore played Anatol. The comedy was received enthusiastically by critics and public alike. Charles Darnton, of the *New York Evening World,* voiced the pleasure of the *Anatol* audience:

> If you have read Schnitzler's "Anatol" dialogues you know how good they are, but until you go to the Little Theater you cannot know how much better they act than read. . . . While this form of entertainment—five separate episodes—must be regarded as an experiment, there is no reason to fear it will not prove popular, for these "Affairs" are decidedly lively and witty. To theatergoers who have reached the age of discretion they are sure to prove delightful.

The *New York Dramatic Mirror* claimed that Anatol was John Barrymore's best role to date—"a lovable scamp who may be unmoral but never immoral."

In 1921 Cecil de Mille produced a film version, "Affairs of Anatol." It owed little more to Schnitzler's cycle than title and core plot.

It was almost twenty years before *Anatol* returned to the New York stage. On 16 January 1931 an adaptation of the Harley Granville-Barker translation opened at the Lyceum Theater. In this version, in which six episodes were presented, the female principal in the episode *Ask No Questions and You'll Hear No Stories* was renamed Hilda. The production was subjected to frequent comparison with its predecessor of 1912—a comparison that was seldom favorable. John Mason Brown, unhappy with the entire production, criticized the unsuccessful attempt to revise Granville-Barker's translation with Broadway lingo. Nor did he have good words for the principal actor, Joseph Schildkraut, whose Anatol was "insensitive to the illusions he seeks to preserve in each new experience. . . ."

In 1946 Mady Christians, star of *I Remember Mama,* directed a production by the Equity Library Theater, which showed, according to one critic, "just how good the theater off Broadway can be." The Directors' Theater presented six of the scenes for an off-Broadway showcase in 1956, in which each scene was developed by a different director. In 1958 Karl Mann and Alex Horn presented the entire seven-scene cycle at the Little Theater in New York, using Karl Zimmerman's translation. Critic Francis Herridge believed this production to have firmly carried out Schnitzler's intentions: "For although the central figure might easily be exaggerated to a ludicrous cartoon, they brought out the man's sensitivity and his anguish. They have given depth to what could be a two-dimensional farce."

In 1961 "The Gay Life," a musical inspired by *Anatol,* was produced by Kermit Bloomgarden at the Shubert Theater in New York. In this production Barbara Cook played Liesl, who finally trapped Anatol into marriage. Except for accusations that the musical "almost smothered the original 1893 work with a fresh story line," the production itself had some success.

THE FAIRY TALE (DAS MÄRCHEN)

The Fairy Tale is a drama in three acts concerning the transition to a new outlook on life, specifically to new attitudes of naturalness and emancipation that were developing at the time the play was written. This work retains its importance today not because of its theme of the "fallen woman" but because it demonstrates the enduring power of the past.

The past affects the present, and we cannot escape it. Fedor Denner, a young poet, loves the actress Fanny Theren, but he cannot forget that he is not her first lover. "What was, is! That is the profound meaning of the past." He cannot be deceived by his love and does not pretend even to himself that Fanny's past does not disturb him. To be sure, he is above the prejudice that girls who have a "past" are bad, but he cannot escape the knowledge that Fanny has had previous lovers. He has ventilated the musty rooms of his world with a bold spirit, but he has not abandoned it.

He is incapable of experiencing love in a timeless sense. While Fanny lives in the consciousness of the eternity of love, Fedor interprets this eternity as the moment that passes and is overshadowed by what has been.

Yet Fedor's fate is not the main concern of the drama. Fanny, not Fedor, plays the main role. She is thankful to him for not castigating her, as others have done, because she followed her "natural impulses." He helps her to live freely, that is, to follow her feelings without being bound by the chains of convention that prevail around her. Her career as an actress corresponds to her outlook on life. She must be able to enter fully into her roles. She cannot bring prejudices into her acting if she wants to accomplish an artistic achievement. Because she is an actress and a "fallen woman," she is doubly depraved in the eyes of the petty bourgeoisie and intellectuals, who, moreover, equate the one with the other. Fanny's artistic profession enables her to get over Fedor's failure (which stems from his genuine, though fanatic, devotion to truth). By finally accepting a promising engagement in Saint Petersburg, she resolves the suspense of the third act, which resulted from her repeated refusal of this offer while waiting for Fedor to reach a decision. "She has been restored to goodness through suffering and in the process has become an artist. A noble future is beginning, and we are shown a grandiose perspective. Purified and consoled, we are dismissed" (Hermann Bahr).

The characters of the play are all interconnected and all have a function in the drama. At the same time, unlike the figures in Schnitzler's earlier dramas, here they represent more than themselves. The relationship of two minor figures to Fanny may serve as an example: there is Agathe Müller, the aging actress, and Emmi Werner, the novice who wants to enter the theater.

Emmi is a young bourgeois girl who wants to follow the example of the successful Fanny. She badgers her parents into allowing her to take "elocution lessons," which she considers the first step to success—success with men who hold the title of baron or above. "In any event, I want first to become a great actress . . . I will make my way, and when playing comedy becomes ridiculous for me and I have gathered enough applause and fame—then I will marry a titled gentleman."

To be sure there are those who declare that Emmi's "enthusiasm for art" is "not completely genuine." Emmi is not concerned with art. She is concerned with using this detour through the theater to guarantee the fulfillment of her desire to climb socially. The theater is to serve as a means to an end; she views her future career not only as effortless but enjoyable as well. For this reason she cannot understand Fanny's extreme grief, except as a particularly emotional recitation.

At the other end of the path stands Fanny's older colleague, Agathe, who is experienced but hardly successful. She knows that in the world of the theater one must not be affected by personal matters. For her the world of the theater is a world of independence, of freedom; for Emmi it is a world of erotic wishes and dreams; for Fanny it is a world that causes rejection, a world by which one is condemned to unhappiness. Agathe and Emmi fail to see the tormented person in Fanny. Nevertheless, they are both related to her. For Agathe, Fanny represents her lost youth, for Emmi her future success. She is praised in retrospect by Agathe, while Emmi regards her as a model.

While Agathe acknowledges Fanny's accomplishment, Emmi flatters her. Emmi stands enthusiastically on the threshold of the theater world, but Agathe has become indifferent, beyond all feelings of rivalry or competitive envy. As part of this world Fanny is torn between her art

and her love for Fedor. The desire for adventure attracts Emmi to the theater. The desire for variety motivated Agathe's theatrical career. Fanny is prepared to leave the stage, although through love she has now become more mature in her art. She must, like Agathe, first experience rejection in order to find her direction. By this process she finally comes to acknowledge the theater as her world. Here she can find her way to self-acceptance, freed from the obligation of despising herself as prescribed by the bourgeois world.

The dialogue in ***The Fairy Tale*** is cleverly constructed, but it is not always successful because, although it was not Schnitzler's intention, the characters are actually discussing and interpreting themselves.

The drama was modeled on illustrious forerunners: theoretically on Friedrich Hebbel (the inescapable consequences of an act), abstractly on Ibsen (Fedor's hatred of the hypocrisy of life), and practically on the French writer Henry Murger (the life of the petty bourgeois artist).

. . . . .

The Fairy Tale was given its first performance at the Deutsches Volkstheater in Vienna on 1 December 1893. Concerning this production of the play, which he later described in 1912 as "a very respectable play," Schnitzler wrote on 12 June 1894 to George Brandes:

> It has been performed in Vienna, in the Deutsches Volkstheater. The first two acts found favor, but the third act failed so completely that it ruined the effect of the entire play. In particular, the audience seems to have found little edification concerning the moral qualities of the play. One critic called to me: "Decency, please." Another spoke pointedly about the "truly frightening moral depravity," to which the play bore witness. A Berlin theater that had already accepted ***The Fairy Tale*** withdrew from its contract because of this failure in Vienna, and thus I can probably consider the stage career of this play as finished.

Subsequently, however, the play was performed often and successfully in Russia. It appeared on 15 June 1912 in the framework of a Schnitzler cycle at the Deutsches Theater in Prague under the direction of Heinrich Teweles. Noteworthy also is a television presentation that was given in Hamburg in 1966.

LIGHT-O'-LOVE (*LIEBELEI*)

Schnitzler's next play, ***Light-O'-Love,*** a drama in three acts, also reminds one of Murger's sketches "Scènes de la vie de bohème." Although the young people in ***Light-O'-Love*** are not artists and the action is concentrated in two couples, Christine and Mizi bring to mind Murger's Mimi and Musette. Christine and Mizi represent two different variations of the *süßes Mädel* type. Judged in external terms, the circumstances of each girl's life are similar, but they experience them differently.

The *süßes Mädel* type may be described as a loving and frivolous young thing from the outskirts who, during the flower of her youth, seeks pleasurable experience with the young men of better social class and then, in maturity, marries a workman—a good man. The *süßes Mädel* brought unappreciated fame to Schnitzler: ". . . if one had the choice between being 'unrecognized' or 'falsely recognized'? Of course the latter happens to one after the seventeenth or twenty-eighth play rather than after the first, and it is more difficult to recover from," he wrote in a recently published letter, which he had written on 24 January 1908 to Marie Herzfeld. This type is not as uniform in Schnitzler as is commonly believed. There are naive (Cora in *Anatol*), wise, fickle, and corrupt variations—the latter appears in *Hands Around,* the only play in which Schnitzler actually names the character "Süßes Mädel," rather than having another of the characters simply refer to her as such. Schnitzler's reaction to the fact that all his young girls were labeled as *süßes Mädel* is reflected in the words of the puppet Liesl in the burlesque *The Big Wurstel Puppet Theater*:

> Just because I am a single girl,
> And Vienna's the scene of the plot,
> They call me "süßes Mädel,"
> Whether I am or not.

The *süßes Mädel* type can be found as early as Nestroy, in his *Mädl aus der Vorstadt* (*Girl from the Outskirts*). The carefree young people and the sweet young thing, who is pursued by dandies, appear in this farce of 1845. Nestroy modeled his seamstresses (Schnitzler's Mizi Schlager in *Light-O'-Love* is a milliner) on the pattern of French grisettes, and it is not far from French *vaudeville* via Murger to Schnitzler. Moreover, there are the variations of the type of *süßes Mädel* found in Berlin in the works of Theodor Fontane and Georg Hermann—not to mention Ernst Wolzogen, in whose works the actual term *süßes Mädel* appears for the first time. One should not, then, give Schnitzler sole credit for creating as a literary type the kind of girl that is spawned by urban life, and furthermore a type that he varied and portrayed ironically, without anyone noticing it.

Once the term was in vogue, all of Schnitzler's female characters were called *süße Mädeln* if they were unmarried. Schnitzler drafted an "Anticritique" but did not publish it. In it he speaks about *Liebelei* being used as a catchword and about *Anatol,* to whom all subsequent lovers in his works, including Sala, Medardus, Hofreiter, and later even Bernhardi, were compared as "aging Anatols."

> In a completely similar manner the same thing happened with another figure, or let me first say, with the words *süßes Mädel,* that appeared for the first time in a little scene entitled **The Christmas Present,** which was published in the *Frankfurter Zeitung* on Christmas Day 1891. The type to which these words refer surely did not signify anything new, not even in strictly literary terms. It is possible that by giving certain individualizing nuances to particular characters, to whom this designation is rightly or wrongly applied, I created the impression of greater naturalness and liveliness. What would remain completely baffling, however, if one didn't have to reckon continually with the intellectual laziness and maliciousness of a certain type of critic, is the circumstance that ever since (I mean ever since the designation *süßes Mädel* gained a place in the German language), scarcely a work of mine has appeared in which the *süßes Mädel* is not immediately recognized with shouts of joy among the characters. For this recognition it is only necessary that the character be unmarried. Their other qualities and destinies are not taken into consideration in the slightest, and not only Mizi, who, after all, may claim a well accredited right to this pet name or nickname, but also Johanna Wegrat in **The Lonely Way,** Anna Rosner in **The Road to the Open** and indeed (one might not consider it possible) even Princess Helene in **The Young Medardus** have all been greeted as *süßes Mädeln.* Thus, just as the masculine world is divided into Anatols and homosexuals, the feminine world consists of *süße Mädeln* and married women—it goes without saying, only when my works are being considered. If some of my works had appeared under a pseudonym, even the most perceptive reviewers would have failed to detect what now seems to be so clearly evident, namely, the relationship of my masculine and feminine characters to those prototypes, who were introduced to the public for the first time two decades ago. Moreover, if one remembers now that all of the relationships that exist between my characters of different sexes are designated once and for all as **Liebeleien** [flirtations], one can gain an idea of just how weak-minded, shallow critics have made it easy for themselves, by describing, with the help of words that I must take partial blame for making popular, the truly not inconsiderable variety of characters and destinies that I have portrayed, as merely a constant repetition of the same theme.

At the beginning of this "Anticritique," which must have been written about the year 1911, stands the passage about *Liebelei* being a catchword:

> Fairly near the beginning of my literary career I wrote a play in which I portrayed the love of an ordinary young girl for a student from a well-to-do home, showing the happiness, suffering, and death of this young girl. Since the young man is still entangled in a previous love affair, and thus at first takes his relationship with this young girl all too lightly, I named this play **Liebelei,** giving it an overtone of painful irony that can scarcely be missed. More seriously and with equal justification, although of course with somewhat less taste, I could have called the play "Christine's Great Love." The possibility of misunderstanding the exceedingly simple plot is completely out of the question, even for the most limited reader or spectator. This has not prevented a majority of the critics, however, from pretending to construe the word *Liebelei* strictly in its original meaning and acting as if they believed that my play did not concern any profound and strong feelings but merely involved a casual, frivolous escapade.

These comments of Schnitzler should suffice to indicate how he wanted his play understood. As was the case with almost every one of his dramas, Schnitzler worked on

Light-O'-Love for several years and wrote several versions. Lengthy segments of a folk play in eight scenes exist in his literary estate. The first scene was published in 1903 in a volume honoring Ferdinand von Saar's seventieth birthday. Schnitzler distanced himself from this work, as it were, by noting: "Only to comply with a friendly wish of Mr. Richard Specht do I make this manuscript available to him for publication in this volume." And yet, it is a scene that is complete in itself and that perhaps could even be performed. In a dancing school with its oppressively restrictive and formal environment, two couples meet for the first time. Against this unpromising background evolves a tender, fervent relationship. In this version Fritz and Theodor are not only characterized by opposing qualities—seriousness versus the carefree, melancholy versus frivolity—but also the basic distinction between the two, which lies in the depth of character of the one and the superficiality of the other, is clearly evident. In contrast to the completed version, in this early version Christine also has a past affair to forget. Thus, the uniqueness of Christine's and Fritz's love as the central idea of the play was not yet present in the folk play.

The plot of the final version: By means of an affair with Christine, a girl from the outskirts, Theodor wants to distract his friend Fritz from his passion for a married woman, a relationship that inhibits Fritz's freedom and that is threatening to become dangerous. But the husband challenges and shoots Fritz just as Fritz was becoming conscious of his love for Christine, to whom he had come to mean everything and who knew nothing about his affair, duel, and death. What she had taken seriously all along, he had only valued as a noncommittal game.

Fritz Lobheimer feels guilty toward Christine. He has deceived her and, without suffering a bad conscience at the time, has told her nothing about his life and problems. Nevertheless, within its fixed boundaries, his relationship to her was genuine. He simply left out his real life and did not bring it along into the game. His conscience and feelings of regret awaken in him when he senses that more than a game could have developed from this relationship. At their last meeting before the duel, Fritz realizes that he has deceived Christine by not telling her the whole truth. Deception occurs at the point where one begins to feel bound or wishes to be bound, where he begins to feel a sense of responsibility. While Fritz has unconsciously played a game with Christine, Theodor and Mizi act by mutual agreement, for they are fully aware of how their relationship will end. Fritz and Christine are more sentimental and romantic. They do not speak as candidly about the past and the future as the other two, who can do so because they only want to enjoy the moment. Both Theodor and Mizi know the rules of the game, but Fritz never lets Christine know that he is acting according to these rules. The affair is tragic, therefore, because Christine regards as deception what he intended as a game. She does not believe in the "repeatability of the unrepeatable." The game, on the other hand, is repeatable—it is based on the principle of repeatability. This discrepancy must of

necessity drive Christine to despair. Fritz has experienced the two types of the social game of love: an affair with a married woman and an affair with one of those "girls whom one does not marry" (the title of a collection of tales by Raoul Auernheimer). As long as the rules of the game are observed, and people do not deceive each other but tell the truth, the game is genuine. Fritz, however, is not capable of honest, casual, temporary relationships such as Theodor engages in; thus, even his passion for the married woman has become a lie. Hermann Bahr summarized the importance of this for Christine: "Because he dies of a lie, she realizes that she has lived on a lie."

While nothing could distract Christine from her devotedness, she was only a diversion for Fritz, not the meaning of his life. When she learns of his death, her life loses its meaning and she rushes off. Where does she go? To her death, the critics maintain in a rare display of unanimity. Even Schnitzler in the above cited "Anticritique" speaks of the "end" of Christine. Yet, he did not venture to express this conclusion explicitly in the drama. Her death is one, but not the only, possibility. Her father, old Weiring, believes with certainty that she will not return, but Schnitzler was honest enough to doubt her death. It would have been easy to show her death unambiguously, as Schnitzler did in *Free Game,* and as he avoided doing in *The Legacy* (in striking parallel to *Light-O'-Love*). With Christine's departure, however, the play is at an end; what will follow is left to the imagination of the spectator.

In 1897 Otto Stoessl, in his "Wiener Brief" (published in the *Neue Deutsche Rundschau,* Vol. 8, p. 205), described *Light-O'-Love* as a play about Vienna: "What gives this first work its emotional content other than the strong play of opposites? This naive, guileless, affectionate Christine with her completely unbroken, simple soul clings to an artful, sophisticated young man. The result is, perhaps more than one would like to believe, a 'Viennese' play; it contains very clearly, beautifully, and distinctly the nature of this city and its barbarity, which to be sure also has a certain charm."

. . . . .

Light-O'-Love is one of Schnitzler's most performed plays. The premiere took place on 9 October 1895 at the Burgtheater in Vienna, and the play remained in the repertory until 15 September 1910. In Berlin, Otto Brahm directed the play on 4 February 1896.

On 1 March 1918 *Light-O'-Love* was revived by the Burgtheater under the direction of Max Devrient. This production was performed in different theaters until 10 October 1930.

Then in 1946 the Vienna Burgtheater again produced *Light-O'-Love* together with *A Christmas Present* from the *Anatol* cycle. With reference to this performance Rudolf Holzer wrote in the *Wiener Zeitung* on 13 March 1946 that beginning the program with *A Christmas Present* "produced the truly curious effect of a humorous prologue to the following tragic **Light-O'-Love.**" In his opinion, however, the public remained indifferent: "The generation of today has experienced too much that is difficult, frightful, and shattering, to be able to empathize with the resentment toward life of a Fritz Lobheimer or the love tragedy of a Christine." Nevertheless, the play had a successful run from 9 March 1946 until 21 September 1946.

On the occasion of a new production on 12 June 1954 O. M. Fontana wrote: "Conditions change but not hearts." Under the direction of Ernst Lothar the main roles were performed by two well-known actors, Hans Moser and Inge Conradi. The spoken version of their unforgettable portrayals was made into a recording under the direction of Heinrich Schnitzler. **Light-O'-Love** found its place in the repertory of large theaters even in the 1960s. In 1968 it was performed, with staging by Heinrich Schnitzler, at the Theater in der Josefstadt.

Light-O'-Love enjoyed a brief period of popularity among Americans in the early 1900s. Under the title **Flirtation,** it was produced by the Progressive Stage Society in 1905 at the Berkeley Lyceum Theater in New York. In 1907, as **The Reckoning,** it was presented again at the Berkeley Lyceum. This second version was revived the following year.

Stephanie Hammer (essay date 1986)

SOURCE: Hammer, Stephanie. "Fear and Attraction: *Anatol* and *Liebelei* Productions in the United States." *Modern Austrian Literature* 19, no. 3-4 (1986): 63-74.

[*In the following essay, Hammer examines the American production histories of* Anatol *and* Liebelei *to unearth American perceptions of Schnitzler in particular and of European art in general.*]

The American production histories of **Anatol** (complete cycle 1910) and **Liebelei** (1902) are both intriguing and revealing. The divergent fortunes of Schnitzler's two seminal theatrical works in this country provide a useful comparative basis for measuring the image and impact of his plays in the United States. More importantly, however, a comparison of **Anatol**'s and **Liebelei**'s fortunes here not only sheds light on the considerable polarity in American perceptions of Schnitzler, but also points to the paradoxical nature of our own self-perceptions and obsessions as they emerge in our reception of European art.

In March of 1985 Schnitzler's **Anatol** returned to Broadway.[1] This Circle in the Square production, entitled **The Loves of Anatol,** was developed, adapted, and directed by Ellis Rabb and promised from its very inception to be highly controversial. Rabb had commissioned an in-house literal translation of the play, and from that he and Nicholas Martin created what they probably believed to be a truly American production. This act was in itself a radical departure from the past.[2] With his insistence on his own personal translation Rabb indirectly questioned the validity of the British influence which had always pervaded American productions of the play in this country. Most "important" American renditions of **Anatol** had employed British translations ranging from the Granville-Barker "paraphrase" of the 1912 New York première starring John Barrymore to Frank Marcus' version used in the critically acclaimed 1984 Hartford Stage production starring the play's director Mark Lamos.[3] In an even more drastic move Rabb decided first to reshuffle the order of the Anatol playlets, making **Episode** the frame story in which the other scenes would represent flash-backs, and second, to alter the ending to include **Anatol's Megalomania** (*Anatols Grössenwahn*).

The result of these innovations was utter disaster according to most critics. A brief summary suffices to indicate the degree to which the play was panned.[4] The *New York Times'* Frank Rich called the present production a "vulgar and unfunny boulevard farce" in which most of Anatol's lovers appeared to be "shrieking burlesque tarts" ("Schnitzler Reshuffled," 7 March 1985). Assessment of the lead performances was no more charitable. Mel Gussow, also of the *Times,* deplored the play's shift in emphasis which made of Max an "ubiquitous presence" (17 March 1985), and Brenda Gill of the *New Yorker* found that Stephen Collins played Anatol "as a strenuous distraught boyscout" (18 March 1985). Finally, Michael Feingold's *Village Voice* article "Boo Danube" concluded simply that Rabb had reduced Schnitzler to a Neil Simonesque "Sacher Suite" (19 March 1985). Only *TIME* magazine stubbornly withstood the tidal wave of censure, praising both the play's rearrangement of the playlets and the "smirky latently homosexual flavor of the exchange of titillating reminiscences between Anatol and Max" (William A. Henry III, 18 March 1985).

In any event, as dreadful—and perhaps as undeserved—as these notices were, they are not surprising when placed within the context of **Anatol**'s production history. At first glance the play seems to have been tremendously successful in this country simply because it has been chosen time and time again for all manner of productions:[5] John Barrymore, a matinee idol, used it as his vehicle in 1912;[6] in 1921 Jesse Lasky and Cecil B. DeMille chose the play's story-line as the basis for a lush and lavish adaptation starring Wallace Reid and Gloria Swanson;[7] countless amateur and regional companies performed some or all of the acts; in New York **Anatol** was revived in the 1930s with Joseph Schildkraut as the lead,[8] and again in 1958 with Owen Cunliff (Little Theater, dir. Alex Horn), in 1940 at the Bucks County Playhouse (with Louis Coltern, dir. Heinrich Schnitzler), in 1970 at Purdue University (with George McDaniel, dir. Raffael Nedomansky), at the Hartford Stage (dir. and star, Mark Lamos, 1984), and in New York in the 1980s (Circle in the Square, 1985). In addition to this already impressive list **Anatol** boasts two musical adaptations during the 1960s—the opulent cast of fifty Broadway production *The Gay Life*[9] and Tom Jones' smaller musical which played at Bucks County, Princeton, and at the

American Festival in Cambridge, Massachusetts.[10] Last but not least, Orson Wells adapted and starred in a radio version for his Mercury Theater in 1938 (Clipping—*Affairs of Anatol* [Radio], Lincoln Center) and channel KNXT Hollywood broadcast a ninety-minute teleplay in 1961 (Clipping—*Affairs of Anatol* [T.V.], Lincoln Center). Yet in spite of all these renditions the overwhelming majority of *Anatol* productions have experienced little if any critical success.

Why should this be the case? The lack of acclaim may have its source in the reverence of theater critics who still refer with wistful admiration to the original New York production starring the famed John Barrymore. When seen against this mythical backdrop any subsequent attempt understandably appears amateurish, unsubtle, and uncouth. However, it is important to note that the reviews of the 1912 *Affairs of Anatol* at New York's Little Theater reveal little if any of this critical exuberance. The *New York Times* in particular expressed admiration for the show's leading-man but not much enthusiasm for the production itself, which was "smart," "charming," but also "all very much in one key" (15 October 1912). Similar reactions are echoed later in other production notices. The response to the Schildkraut *Anatol,* for example, was tepid at best. The *New York Tribune* found the actor wooden and "lacking in suave persuasiveness" (Arthur Ruhl, "Schnitzler's *Anatol,*" 16 February 1931), while the *Times* maintained that he lacked spontaneity (J. Brooks Atkinson, "Schnitzler's Anatomy of Love," 16 January 1931). More interesting is the fact that these reviews did not speak very highly of the play itself. The *Tribune* referred to *Anatol* as "that slightly shopworn matinee idol's delight" (Ruhl). Similarly the *Times* concluded, "there is a murmur in the heart of Schnitzler's play" (Atkinson).

Given these assessments it is no surprise that the play came increasingly to be dealt with as either a curio or a farce. The latter attitude is clearly (and amusingly) articulated by the Seattle Repertory's flyer describing its 1936 production of *Anatol*:

> From the city of the aristocrats—Vienna—comes . . . *The Affairs of Anatol.* Gaiety and sophistication, as well as airy humor abound in the three subtly charming—but aimless—episodes which comprise the play. Each episode deals with one of Anatol's "affairs" which although Anatol would be the last to admit it, nearly always turn to his disadvantage. He fancies himself an irresistible Don Juan and is in and out of love with singular regularity. Yet none of his setbacks affect his unimpressionable ego. You'll thoroughly enjoy his laugh-provoking difficulties. The Granville-Barker translation is full of fun and laughter.
>
> (Seattle Repertory, *Playhouse News,* vol. IX, November 1936, No. 2).

Only with the off-Broadway production in 1958 did *Anatol* begin to win some serious respect as what the *New York Post* called a "comic satire," but the same review nonetheless dismissed the play merely as "little theater entertainment" (Frances Herridge, "Affairs of Don Juan off-Broadway," 4 September 1958).

After this point productions began to take a quite different direction. The *Lafayette Journal and Courier* found the 1970 Purdue production serious enough, but also tedious and wordy (Larry Schumpert, 4 December 1970), and by 1984 the play had become serious indeed. In his program essay for the Hartford Stage John Simon emphasized the importance of the *fin-de-siècle* world for the meaning of the play; he describes that milieu thus:

> . . . such a dying culture is characterized by world-weariness and a concomitant desperate hunger for living, philosophy scattering itself in bitter-sweet epigrams, wit suffused with a cynicism no less melancholy than biting, sensuality propelled into perversity. There is a frenzied concern with sex as the last possible panacea along with the excruciating awareness of the instability indeed impossibility of loving.
>
> ("Schnitzler: Poet of the Unfulfilled," Hartford Stage Program for *Anatol,* Lincoln Center).

We are clearly a long way from Seattle's gay Vienna and the zany fun-loving Anatol of that staging. Hartford's lugubrious-sounding production met with unfavorable reviews in Norwalk (Robert Vigas, *Norwalk Fairpress,* 24 October 1984) but had glowing notices in the *Times.* Mel Gussow saw this production as a modern psychodrama of "a hedonist who may in fact be suffering from anhedonia, and is perhaps incapable of love" ("Stage: Hartford Troupe in Schnitzler's *Anatol,*" 28 October 1984). In that same psychoanalytical vein Gussow concluded, "in his production and in his performance Mr. Lamos captures the self-deluding and self-melodramatizing aspects of Anatol, a man who in the name of romance entraps himself as victim."

With this interpretation it seems that American *Anatol*s have all but exhausted the gamut of theatrical possibilities: Barrymore's suave, sophisticated *homme fatal,* stock interpretations of Anatol as a light-hearted, egotistical, and somewhat stupid playboy, Lamos' existential neurotic, and most recently Collins' sexually ambiguous innocent. Surprisingly, then, scrutiny of *Anatol*'s production history in the U.S.A. reveals that a truly definitive theatrical interpretation has never been established. Instead (especially in the case of the major revivals) problematic production follows problematic production, each one differing radically from the last, each one in its own way disturbing and unsatisfying to some of the critics, regardless of whether the director and actors handle the play as comedy of manners, farce, or existential or psychological drama.

An opposite but equally peculiar fate awaited the arrival of *Liebelei* in the United States. Performed in English for the first time in 1905 at the Berkeley Lyceum in New York under the title of *Flirtation,* the play received respectful if not especially positive notices from a local newspaper.[11] Two years later this production (with translation by Grace Isabel Colbron) was revived at the same theater under the title of *The Reckoning* to very favorable reviews.[12] The play appeared sporadically in the following eighty years under varying titles, *The Love Game, Light O'-Love, Light of Love, Playing with Love,* and most recently *Flirtations.* Curiously, although it has yet to have a major American revival (a state of affairs which will probably not be remedied by Tom Stoppard's forthcoming adaptation *Dalliance*), small companies, theater societies, and university theater departments stubbornly persisted in staging *Liebelei* with surprising regularity. The Players' Cooperative staged the play in 1929 at the Cherry Lane Theatre (dir. Ruth Collins Allen). In 1939 Johann Reich, former producer from the Josefstadt Theater, directed *Liebelei* at Ithaca College. German performances of the play persisted from 1897 through the 1940s in such theaters as New York's Irving Place, the Young Men's Hebrew Association, and the Philadelphia German Theater.[13] In 1956 a small company performed the play in a New York studio.[14]

In 1962 the theater department at the University of California, Los Angeles staged what appears to have been an innovative production with a translation by Carl Mueller (dir. William Melnitz). The program notes to the production reveal a significant pairing of seemingly opposed artistic aims. The notes to the play are translated from Albert Schulze's *Theaterkritik 1952-60,* thereby revealing the director's desire to remain faithful to the work's Germanic origins. However, in his own notes to the translation Mueller anticipates Ellis Rabb's philosophy that American productions of Schnitzler must employ American rather than British translations (UCLA Program for *Liebelei,* Lincoln Center, 3-5). In this manner the program put forth the very exciting idea that an American performance of Schnitzler using American vernacular and accent would not in any way negate or invalidate the "Austrianness" of the theatrical settings; moreover, only an American translation could make the plays truly accessible to an American audience.

However, the production and the innovative attitude which it proposed seem to have had little success in enhancing *Liebelei*'s visibility. Five years later California State College at Los Angeles staged a theatrical potpourri called *The Lovers and The Losers,* which included scenes from all three acts of *Liebelei* (dir. Roger Altenberg). But from that point on the play went underground until 1981, when the Nassau Repertory Theatre (now the Long Island Stage) undertook another strictly American adaptation under the form of *Flirtations.* This production boasted an excellent new translation by A. S. Wensinger and artistic director Clinton J. Atkinson (in *Arthur Schnitzler: Plays and Stories,* New York: Continuum, 1982). But, while Mr. Atkinson's balancing of the play's opposing moods— romance with cynicism, gaiety with tragedy—received admiring notices from both the *New York Times* (Alvin Klein, "A Bit of Daring in *Flirtations,*" 14 February 1982) and *Newsday* (Aileen Jacobson, "Golden Old Vienna," 9 February 1982), this revival was for all intents and purposes ignored by the larger theater world.[15]

Liebelei's lack of impact on the American theater contrasts dramatically with its constant and continued success in Europe (for example, the major revival at Vienna's Akademietheater in 1972). This discrepancy seems especially bizarre when we consider the praise which the play received from literary critics in reviews of its early appearances in English. In his 1912 article for *The Drama* Baynard Quincy Morgan regarded the play as Schnitzler's "high-water mark" (No. 7 [August 1912], 13). In his foreword to his translation of the play P. Morton Shand admired its tragic quality and emotional intensity (*Playing with Love,* Chicago: A. C. McClury, 1914). In 1929 George March devoted an article to Arthur Schnitzler in *Poet Lore* and concluded that *Liebelei* was simply the best of Schnitzler's works (39 [1929]: 573-581).[16]

The peculiarity of this state of affairs becomes even more striking when we compare early translations of *Liebelei* with those of *Anatol.* Granville-Barker's highly successful version of the latter victorianizes the play's more off-color moments, as Harro Kühnelt has already noted in his 1981 article "Harley Granville-Barker und Arthur Schnitzlers *Anatol*" (in *Studien zur Literatur des 19. und 20. Jahrhunderts in Österreich,* Innsbruck: Kowatch, 69-77), while early translations of *Liebelei* are surprisingly true to the language and spirit of the piece.[17] Moreover, the immense popularity of Max Ophul's 1932 film version in this country[18] and its rediscovery at the New York Film Festival in 1974 with unconditional raves by such critics as Andrew Sarris (*Village Voice,* 10 October 1974) and Nora Sayre (*New York Times,* 30 September 1974) provide yet further evidence of the play's contradictory fortunes here.

This brief survey of *Anatol*'s and *Liebelei*'s production history raises an important if seemingly obvious question: Why on one hand stage repeatedly a dated, problematic, non-narrative piece which the American theater world sees as either totally frivolous or deeply depressing, and why on the other hand ignore a play by the same author which is agreed to be an excellent and significant piece of modern theater?

The answer, I suspect, lies in the nature of our expectations of European and especially Austrian theater and in the kinds of characteristics which we as Americans inscribe upon it. Just as we seek our own reflection—that is to say, the reflection of our concerns and problems—in our own art and theater, so do we usually seek the opposite in European art. It is common knowledge that Europe and its culture have traditionally represented the autocratic, amoral, sensual Other to our democratic essentially puritanical Self; not surprisingly, Americans have always been especially fascinated by those periods and those urban centers which have best represented the easy sensuality and decadence of European society.[19] This is the essence of the mystique which periods ranging from the late Roman Empire to the 1930s in such cities as Rome, Paris, Vienna and Berlin continue to exercise on the American imagination. Vienna in particular currently enjoys a privileged position within this pantheon as the incarnation of both decadence and fascism.[20]

It is this Otherness which probably first attracted American producers to the erotic gamesmanship and arch wit of

Anatol rather than to the more overtly moral and more evidently tragic *Liebelei.* But while the European Other is attractive, it is also frightening—frightening because it is not like us and is therefore evil and frightening because our overwhelming attraction to it suggests that it is like us after all. Taken to the limit, attraction to the Other dissolves the lines of demarcation between the Self and the Other, as Jean-Paul Sartre has argued in his discussions of the struggle between these apparent opposites,[21] either we become the Other or the Other becomes our Selves.

This ambivalence towards the European—and by European I mean amoral, hedonistic, sexual, and aristocratic—nature of Schnitzler's play surfaces continually in *Anatol* productions and in the critics' reactions to them but is most blatant—and therefore most useful for our discussion here—in the film and musical adaptations. In an interview with the *New York Times* Jesse Lasky explained that he was searching for exotic and new stories, specifically from Europe (Charles P. Cushing, "New and Old Faces on the Screen," 25 December 1921). He apparently found such a story in *Anatol,* which he decided to film upon the recommendation of Somerset Maugham (Charles Higham, *Cecil B. DeMille,* New York: Scribners, 1973: 84-5). Schnitzler's play then underwent a remarkable transformation. The story was completely revamped in such a way as to make it morally palatable to an American audience: Anatol became a wealthy and married New Yorker embarking on a series of philanthropic misadventures with various women. The *New York Times* review tells us, "On the screen Anatol is an exceedingly nice man whose affairs are all entirely innocent. If the girls are not so innocent, they are still not so very, very bad, and promise to be good before they are dismissed from the story" (12 September 1921). Then DeMille added his own—now notorious—directorial vision to the film, turning it, in spite of its new subject matter, into a highly suggestive work.[22] In this manner DeMille's *Affairs of Anatol* ceased to be either Schnitzler's original play or even an adaptation thereof; instead it represents a telling exercise in American fear and fantasy, fulfilling what Aldo Scaglioni once called the mission of all good pornography, which is "to *tell* you how bad sex is, and to *show* you how good it feels."[23]

A similarly mixed message is emitted from the Broadway musical's sanitized version of the story, in which Anatol is snared by Max's little sister in a combination of *Gigi* and *My Fair Lady* plot developments. But visually the production told a rather different tale; the costumes were decolleté, the dancing wild, the language cynical, and the musical ended in quintessential 1960s fashion with the premarital coupling of the bride and groom.[24]

This state of affairs leads me to suspect that Americans play *Anatol* obsessively and repeatedly because its eroticism simultaneously seduces and terrifies. The resulting ambivalence expresses itself in a stream of schizophrenic productions and bizarre adaptations. In this context the Hartford Stage's reduction of *Anatol* to a pathological category emerges as the latest in a tradition of attempts to make Schnitzler's ambiguous hero less threatening to an American public.

Following this line of reasoning, I would like to suggest that *Liebelei* suffers from a misconception stemming from the same ambivalence. Because the tragic and socio-critical aspects of the play were emphasized by English-speaking critics initially, *Liebelei* is generally considered to be a terribly serious theatrical undertaking. It is therefore not hedonistic, erotic, and amoral, that is to say, not European, not Austrian, and especially not Viennese enough to satisfy an American audience, which both craves and fears the artistic presentation of continental degenerateness. Sadly it seems that *Liebelei* must await the magic of Stoppardization in order to win the attention which it deserves on the U.S. stage.

A final observation: is it not ironic that these two Schnitzler plays should have production histories which prove so similar to the plays themselves? *Anatol* remains an obsession for directors, actors, and translators; it becomes more elusive the more they try to grasp it, just as the play itself deals with obsession, as the worldly but desperate protagonist moves from one woman to the next in a never ending and futile quest for the one true love. Likewise the American fortunes of *Liebelei* weirdly mirror the dynamics of that play. An artistic creation of recognized aesthetic merit is held to be of little account by a theater establishment, which like Fritz himself pursues another more dangerous love-object.

Notes

1. See Clippings—*The Loves of Anatol* at the Performing Arts Research Center at Lincoln Center. The primary sources used in this article (newspaper reviews, photographs, programs, flyers, etc.) can be located at Lincoln Center. *Anatol* materials are cross-listed. For *Liebelei,* however, separate catalogue entries for each of its various English titles must be consulted.

2. See Helen Dudar's interview with Ellis Rabb in the *New York Times,* 26 March 1985.

3. See Harley Granville-Barker, *Anatol* (New York: n.p., 1911) and Frank Marcus, *Anatol* (London: Methuen, 1982).

4. In addition to the articles discussed here see Douglas Watt, *Daily News,* 7 March 1985 and Clive Barnes, *New York Post,* same date. Also worthy of note is Stephen Collins' article for the *Daily News* in which he affirms his belief in the Rabb production despite its poor reviews, 26 March 1985.

5. For a survey of productions from the play's première in the U.S.A. through the 1960s see Luverne Walton, "Anatol on the New York Stage," *Modern Austrian Literature* 2, ii (1969), 30-44. For a general overview of Austrian plays on the New York stage see Leroy Shaw, "Modern Austrian Dramatists on the New York Stage," *Österreich und die angelsächsische Welt,* ed. Otto Hietsch, vol. 2 (Wien: n.p., 1961), 547-563.

6. *The Affairs of Anatol,* directed by John Foster Platt, The Little Theater.

7. *The Affairs of Anatol,* Famous Players—Lasky Corporation, September 1921. Prints of this film are difficult to find, and special arrangements must be made well in advance to view the film at UCLA, the Library of Congress, or the Eastman Film Collection in Rochester.

8. *Anatol, a play in 4 acts and 6 scenes,* directed by Marc Connelly and Gabriel Beer-Hofmann, Brooks Atkinson and Lyceum Theaters, 1931.

9. Book by Fay and Michael Kanin, lyrics and music by Howard Dietz and Arthur Schwartz, starring Walter Chiari and Barbara Cook. The show premièred 18 November 1961.

10. This rendition traveled to a variety of places. It was first performed by the Bermuda Theater Guild in May of 1960, then moved to Bucks County and to Princeton in August and September of the same year. This production was directed by Ellis Rabb. In July-August 1961 the musical came to Cambridge with a different cast and under the new direction of Warren Enters and then to the Boston Arts Center in the fall for a pre-Broadway try-out.

11. This production was staged by the Progressive Stage Society under the direction of Robert Whittier. See Program—*Flirtation* and unidentified Clipping—*Flirtation* at Lincoln Center.

12. See Clippings—*The Reckoning* (especially New York Herald and New York Commercial Herald) at Lincoln Center.

13. For discussions of all these performances see Clippings—*Liebelei,* Lincoln Center.

14. See Promptbook—*The Love Game* (anonymous) and catalogue entry—*The Love Game,* Lincoln Center.

15. During my recent conversation with Mr. Atkinson (25 April 1986) he indicated that, although he was generally pleased with the production (which captured the romanticism inherent in the play), he noticed that the audience had a mixed reaction to it.

16. The first part of this article is a (plagiarized?) translation of an earlier German essay by Richard Specht. See "Arthur Schnitzler," *Die Neue Rundschau* (May 1922), 488-498.

17. See, for example, Shand's and Morgan's translations.

18. *Liebelei,* starring Magda Schneider and Wolfgang Liebeneiner came to the U.S.A. in 1936. The film can be viewed at the Museum of Modern Art Film Archive in New York. For 1936 reviews of the film see Clippings—*Liebelei* (Cinema), Lincoln Center.

19. Taking her cue from Jean-Paul Sartre's discussion of the encounter between Self and Other, Simone de Beauvoir astutely links the straight-forward, virtuous

male Self to America and the mysterious, morally disruptive, chaotic female Other to America's perception of Europe. See *The Second Sex,* trans. H. M. Parshley (New York: Modern Library, 1968), 80, 259. The prevalence of this construct in current American popular culture can be seen, for example, in Jed Perl's recent article for *Vogue* magazine on contemporary art. Significantly, he notes: "Ever since the Puritans came here to escape the wicked ways of Europe, Americans have looked to Europe as the land of sexual secrets." See "Sex, Love and Art in the 80's," May 1986: 120.

20. A good example of this continuing interest is the *Vienna 1900* exhibition at the Museum of Modern Art in New York, 16 June-21 October (1986). *New York Times* art critic John Russell aptly expresses the American perception of this morally ambiguous time and place: "Paradox was everywhere in Vienna, from the first move towards the higher education of women in 1870 to the frenzy of abasement with which, almost 70 years later, the population ran to welcome Hitler's armies . . . it is worth saying that this was a killer among cities—one in which for every rose there was a poisoned thorn." See "The Brilliant Sunset of Vienna in its Final Glory," 29 June 1986.

21. Jean-Paul Sartre describes the terrifying and contradictory process by which man denies a part of himself, calls it Other and Evil and then feels increasingly attracted to it, gradually recognizes its presence in himself, and finally actually comes to desire to be all that he has heretofore denied: "It is his anxiety, his fundamental disbelief or his individuality that comes to him from without, like Another himself, to tempt him. It is what he wants but does not want to want. It is the object of a constant and constantly rejected will which he regards as other than his "true" will. . . . And it is himself insofar as he is for himself Other than Self. It is the will to be other and that all be Other." *The Philosophy of Jean-Paul Sartre,* ed. Robert Denoon Cumming (New York: Vintage, 1965), 387.

22. A representative example of the film's considerable ambiguity occurs in an early café scene in which Anatol watches Emilie. Although the titles tell us that he is "shocked at her decadence," the camera focuses on the actress' (Wanda Hawley) mouth as she slowly and suggestively applies her lipstick. See David Cook's discussion of this phase in DeMille's career in *A History of Narrative Film* (New York: Norton, 1981), 215.

23. Professor Scaglioni made this unforgettable observation in conjunction with Tasso during a lecture on the Renaissance at the University of North Carolina Chapel Hill, fall of 1979.

24. Lincoln Center possesses a fine collection of materials on this musical including photographs, caricatures clippings, script, and original cast LP recording.

ANATOL

CRITICAL COMMENTARY

Luverne Walton (essay date summer 1969)

SOURCE: Walton, Luverne. "*Anatol* on the New York Stage." *Modern Austrian Literature* 2, no. 2 (summer 1969): 30-44.

[*In the following essay, Walton discusses the production history of* Anatol *on the New York stage.*]

The dramas of Arthur Schnitzler were introduced to New York theater audiences in 1897, when *Liebelei* made its debut at the Irving Place Theater. The next two years witnessed the American premieres of *Freiwild* and *Das Vermächtnis,* plays equally somber in mood as *Liebelei,* and identified Schnitzler as a writer of tragedy. It was not until after the turn of the century that the world of this "leichtsinniger Melancholiker" was revealed to New York audiences, but since its appearance *Anatol* has surpassed all other plays of Schnitzler in popularity, longevity, and in the variety of media and languages in which it has been presented to American audiences. Though performed only once in its entirety, there have been seven full productions of the work,[1] and on six other occasions individual scenes have been extracted from the whole and performed separately. Adaptations of it have been made for the silent films, radio, television, vaudeville, and musical comedy. As a drama composed of a series of independent one-acts, it introduced a new dramatic form to Broadway. Scenes from it have been produced in English, French and Russian. The only thing lacking to complete its production history is a performance in German, the language in which it had its birth.

Anatol has become the symbol for Schnitzler. The work of the youth has justifiably become the token of the man, for within *Anatol* are the seeds of many of the concepts and characters which Schnitzler treats in his later dramatic works. Here is the philanderer, the *raisonneur,* the artist, the "süsses Mädel," and the woman who exists outside the bounds of respectable society. Here are the themes of illusion and reality—the *Lebenslüge*—infidelity, the longing to experience life to the utmost, and the self-deceptive centering of that search in the realm of the erotic. In its construction *Anatol* represents that form in which Schnitzler excelled: the one-act. Each scene is complete in itself. Each highlights a basically similar situation from a different angle and in a different mood. Together the scenes form a whole, but it is not the wholeness traditionally expected of a large dramatic work. Julius Kapp described its unity thus:

> So rundet sich der Anatolzyklus trotz seiner bunt schillernden Vielheit unvermerkt zu einem dramatischen Ganzen. Es ist das Drama des Junggesellentums mit all

seinen Freuden und Leiden. Der Einzelfall weitet sich dabei unter den zart zufassenden Händen des überall scharf beobachtenden und charakterisierenden Dichters zum allgemeinen Problem. Jeder Hörer fühlt sich ohne weiteres als beteiligt, vor seinem Inneren taucht die Erinnerung an Episoden seiner eigenen Jugendzeit auf.—Die einzelnen Bilder bestehen durchweg aus Dialogen. Die Personen sind Anatol, Max und in jedem eine andere Frau. Die Liebe bleibt immer die gleiche, nur der Gegenstand wechselt![2]

Schnitzler did not exhibit great ability to sustain dramatic conflict nor to develop plot complication, but he was a master of the succinct statement about a facet of human personality, he knew how to throw light upon human motivation in a variety of ways, to epitomize a relationship between two people, and he used the one-act with consummate skill as an ideal vehicle for these purposes. In the same way that *Anatol* is a kind of panorama of Schnitzler's dramas, so the production history of *Anatol* on the New York stage is a panorama of the history of all Schnitzler's works there. It first appeared only six years after the 1897 premiere of *Liebelei,* and the most recent production was in 1959, followed by a musical based on the work in 1961. The only other Schnitzler play to be produced in any form in the decade of the 1960's is *Reigen.* In an English translation titled *La Ronde, Reigen* was performed at the Theatre Marquee in 1960, and a French film with the same title, distributed in this country as *Circle of Love,* was shown in 1965. The adverse criticism of *Anatol* in the course of its fifty-eight-year production history contains all the major objections applied to his other plays: decadence, immorality, datedness, absence of character development and lack of traditional form. The media in which it has been produced encompass and exceed the number of media in which his other works have appeared and, with the exception of sound movies, include all major media of mass theatrical entertainment, even the twentieth century innovations of radio and television. But there is one way in which a view of the stage history of *Anatol* does not comprise a view of all Schnitzler's works on the New York stage. Generally speaking, the fate of his dramas has paralleled that of actor Oswald Yorke who, in the 1912 production of *Anatol,* played Max; in the 1931 production, the waiter. In like manner, Schnitzler's works have not completely disappeared from the stage, but the importance of their role in the theatrical repertory has greatly decreased in the course of the century. The general production history is a decrescendo, a decrease of popularity and, in most instances, final disappearance from the stage. In some cases the life of a play was brief and death swift; in others the demise was prolonged but nonetheless sure. Not so with *Anatol.* Though the first full production in 1912 was on most counts the high point of its history, almost every decade has seen its revival, and each revival has demonstrated the play's capacity to appeal to theater audiences and to elicit enthusiastic comment from the critics.

By 1912, the year of the first full production of *Anatol,* Schnitzler was already known to New York theater audiences through German or English performances of *Lie-*

belei, Freiwild, Das Vermächtnis, Literatur, Die letzten Masken and *Der grüne Kakadu.* The most popular of the productions had been an English translation of *Liebelei,* titled *The Reckoning,* staged in 1907. By 1912 *Anatol* had also appeared in New York twice in very abbreviated form: the first time in 1903, when *Abschiedssouper* was produced in French and again in 1906 when the same scene was performed in Russian. The 1903 production of *Abschiedssouper* marks the beginning of the history of individual scenes from *Anatol,* extracted from the whole and performed separately. Such productions have included three stagings of *Abschiedssouper*: 1903 in French, 1906 in Russian, and 1938 in English; two productions of *Anatols Hochzeitsmorgen* in English: 1926 and 1959; one production of *Episode* in English in 1959; and another unidentified scene in English in 1953. The introduction of *Anatol* to the New York stage in 1903 occurred when Madame Charlotte Wiehe and her French company made a guest appearance in New York and, under the title of *Souper D'Adieu,* included *Abschiedssouper* on a vaudeville bill which opened at the Berkeley Lyceum on October 21. Schnitzler's Annie, renamed Louise, was played by Madame Wiehe, and English program notes and plot summary aided the audience in understanding the French dialogue. Though Danish by birth, Charlotte Wiehe had reportedly experienced her greatest theatrical success in Paris, and her acting style was characterized with the vague phrase, "distinctly French." Her appearance on the New York stage drew very fashionable audiences, and the dramatic entertainment which she and her ensemble of actors provided was described as "bright and piquant, [appealing] pleasantly to those who enjoy the light humor of Paris."[3] Again in 1906, *Abschiedssouper* owed its appearance on the New York stage to a group of foreign actors, a troupe from Russia known in this country as the Russian Players and headed by Madame Alla Nazimova. With Madame Nazimova in the role of Annie, the Russian Players performed *Abschiedssouper* on the occasion of their last appearance in America, May 2, 1906.[4] Three days later most of the troupe sailed for Russia, but Madame Nazimova remained in America under contract to appear on the American stage on the condition that she learn English, and in less than five months she had developed sufficient fluency to perform Ibsen's *Hedda Gabler* in translation. In 1938, *Abschiedssouper* was performed in English, when the MacDowell Club Players staged it in conjunction with Thornton Wilder's *The Happy Journey* in the Guild Hall of the Little Church Around the Corner on March 11. With productions in French, Russian and English *Abschiedssouper* has the distinction of receiving the most international attention of any of Schnitzler's works in New York.[5]

On at least two occasions *Anatols Hochzeitsmorgen* has also been extracted from the larger work for separate performance in English, and *Episode* once. In 1926 Ye Curtain Players produced the wedding morning scene at the Princess Theatre[6] and from May 11-15, 1959, Neighborhood Playhouse School of the Theatre performed both one-acts.[7] Twice—in 1952 and again in 1953—the Equity-Library Theatre[8] chose scenes from Schnitzler to include in its "Scrapbook" programs, a series of productions described as "the project that brings Shakespeare and the classics without tears to student bodies in the metropolitan area."[9] According to the *New York Times* these programs were very popular. Both the 1952 and 1953 "Scrapbook" productions were presented, among other places, at the Lenox Hill Playhouse. The 1952 "Scrapbook" included scenes from Schnitzler, Rostand, Shakespeare and Wilde, but the advance publicity material about the program did not identify which of Schnitzler's works was to be performed. Because *Anatol* had been a part of the Equity-Library Theatre repertory for at least six years,[10] it is probable that the scene was an excerpt from this work, but this is only conjecture. The selection in 1953 was from *Anatol,* though which portion of it was performed was not reported in the newspaper review. The 1953 "Scrapbook" opened at the Lenox Hill Playhouse on November 5, and ran for the rest of that week.[11] The *Times* described the production as an exhibit of the show which would soon tour the public schools and reported that James Lanphier played the role of Anatol, but no other information about Schnitzler's work was given. From the standpoint of their critical reception in New York, little comment can be made on the production of the one-acts as almost no reviews are available, but the fact that they continued to be produced is in itself a critical comment. It is worth noting that two of the three which have been selected for individual production, *Abschiedssouper* and *Anatols Hochzeitsmorgen,* have also, along with *Weihnachtseinkäufe,* been most often singled out from the other one-acts in full productions of *Anatol* for their ability to entertain and for their dramatic value; and the actresses in these three scenes have most often been applauded for performance of their roles. It is possible that these actresses have always been the most accomplished actresses of the entire cast, but there is no question that these roles offer the greatest opportunities to display acting talent.

The premiere of the first full production of *Anatol* on the New York stage occurred on October 14, 1912.[12] The years of 1916,[13] 1931, 1946, 1956 and 1958 also witnessed full performances of the play, and there has been one production at the off-Broadway Cherry Lane Theatre for which no date has been established. John Barrymore was the first American Anatol, and the English text used for the 1912 production in which he starred was the Harley Granville-Barker paraphrase. This premiere was an occasion for critical attention not only after the opening, but in anticipation of the event:

> When Mr. Ames presents at the Little Theatre next month Arthur Schnitzler's *Anatol,* he will introduce to American theatergoers a novel form of dramatic composition—a sequence of dialogues. . . . We shall have a glimpse at five episodes in the life of a very episodical young gentleman from Vienna. Each episode is complete in itself, like a perfect bead, but it is only when they are strung together that they become the finished piece of jewelry. The string that holds them is the unfolding of Anatol's personality. Each bead has a

different color, given to it by the individuality of the *vis-a-vis* in the episode—always a woman, of course. Anatol is an arch-connoisseur of love.[14]

The question of the play's morality, its fitness for the stage, was discussed in the reviews of 1912. Some reviewers seemed to think that theatergoers would feel that a moral issue was involved, and these reviewers commented on the question in some way. But Anatol's promiscuity was obviously not the overriding issue in the judgment of the audience, as the play found immediate favor with theatergoers. The critics rejoiced and attributed its ready reception to three factors: the growing liberality of the American attitude toward the stage, the paraphrase of the work prepared by Granville-Barker in which he made certain changes in the text in deference to the strict British stage on which Anatol had appeared the previous year, and Schnitzler's finesse and taste in the characterization of Anatol and his composition of dialogue and situation that meticulously and gracefully avoid the coarse and common and concentrate instead on the amusing and charming figure of the incurable lover and the moods through which he passes as he falls in and out of love enroute from his first affair to his wedding day. Two summations of the moral question characterize the views of most of the critics. The first judges *Anatol* as theater entertainment:

> Of course, Anatol is a very reprehensible young man . . . and yet, as theatrical entertainment, he is such a clever and amusing figure that one almost loses sight of his moral enormities.[15]

The other is a judgment on Schnitzler's artistry:

> To the question whether these episodes are moral, one is tempted to equivocate by saying that they are artistic. Schnitzler's writing is always refined; there is nothing ugly or coarse or vulgar, nothing repellent here. One must be grateful to him for what he does not say. He has the gift of silence and says the unsayable without asterisks and without offending.[16]

It was a play to appeal to the sophisticates of the day, and the depth of condemnation voiced seldom sank below the level of "naughty." Perhaps one reason why objections to it in New York did not assume greater proportions was because as theatrical literature *Anatol* was not taken too seriously. It was considered a charming dramatic trifle,

> light but agreeable entertainment, fitted for an audience which has dined pleasantly, drifted in leisurely fashion to the theatre, and brought thither a readiness to accept for the moment the continental habit of treating "love" as an activity apart and sufficient unto itself, and not—as our literature assumes—necessarily associated with marriage.[17]

One may wonder whether Schnitzler's reaction to this lighthearted, uncritical approach to his work might not have been similar to the reaction of Hermann Bahr who responded indignantly to the "compliment and excuse" which those outside Austria often used when speaking of the works of Austrian writers: "Wir würden jedoch wün-

schen, strenger benandelt aber dafür ernster genommen zu werden!"[18] A search for meaning in the work usually ended in such banalities as "variety is the spice of life,"[19] or "no matter how comprehensive a man's experience with the gentler sex may have been; how much he may regard himself triumphant in the duel—in the end he remains their laughing stock,"[20] or in the feeling that "a search for either [a philosophy or a moral] is not worthwhile."[21] It was regarded as a novelty, particularly in form, and serious consideration of the play was largely confined to Schnitzler's gift for characterization and dialogue. As always, *The Farewell Supper, Christmas Present* and *Anatol's Wedding Morning* were considered to have the greatest theatrical value, with *Christmas Present* most appealing in its mood of nostalgic melancholy.

The play ran at the Little Theatre until the middle of December, then moved to Chicago for a limited engagement at the Fine Arts Theater. There the criticism of its morality was sharper, one critic even referring to the production as "an unsavory thing for the Chicago Theater Society . . . to bring before the town."[22] Its appearance there was occasion for a novelty in production. There were two theaters in the Chicago Fine Arts Building: the Fine Arts Theater and the Little Theater. While the professional company from New York performed *Anatol* in the larger Fine Arts Theater, a group of Chicago amateurs performed it in the Little Theater, a tiny auditorium on the fourth floor which seated ninety-nine persons. The amateurs offered an additional ingenious touch to their production: instead of preparing only five scenes and staging those five at every performance as John Barrymore and the New York cast did, they prepared all seven scenes, but omitted two different ones at each performance. After an engagement of approximately two weeks, the New York cast returned home and opened at Maxine Elliott's Theatre on January 6, where performances continued for several weeks. Their return to New York brought the comment from the writer for the *Telegram*:

> After facing the cultured atmosphere of the Theatre of Fine Arts in Chicago, John Barrymore and five leading women in Schnitzler's "The Affairs of Anatol" were no doubt glad to return to New York again.[23]

Soon after the play re-opened the role of Max was taken over from Oswald Yorke by Frank Reicher, and it was reportedly on this occasion that Barrymore added to his knowledge the meaning of the German expression "Hals- und Beinbruch!" *The New York Sun* reported the story:

> Half an hour before curtain time Monday night Mr. Barrymore overheard George Foster Platt, producer for Mr. Ames, tell Mr. Reicher that he hoped he would break his neck. As Mr. Reicher received the wish with marks of the highest appreciation, Mr. Barrymore asked for an explanation. He was informed that in Germany it is a sign of bad luck to wish an actor good luck when making his first appearance in a production and that to wish him some bodily harm or bad luck is considered an omen of good fortune.[24]

Whereupon Barrymore is said to have gone to the nearest telegraph office, from which he sent Reicher the following telegram: "Max Reicher, Maxine Elliott's Theatre: 'May you break every bone in your body.' Anatol."

No reviewer has ever admitted complete satisfaction with the portrayal of Anatol. No American actor has ever been able to capture completely the spirit of the "leichtsinniger Melancholiker" from Vienna, and John Barrymore was no exception. Though praised for his interpretation of the role, he was not able to convey the delicate nuances of mood demanded in the more subtle scenes, but found his greatest strength in the situations which called for farcical and comedy characterization. The 1912-1913 production of *The Affairs of Anatol* was a new experience for New York, and the novelty of it and its probable future effect on the theatergoer were summed up by *Collier's*:

> It will be seen that "The 'Affairs' of Anatol" is in a gallery a trifle remote from Broadway—so different, indeed, that the spectator, having got the "hang" of it, will probably enjoy it more the second time than the first.[25]

Having got the "hang" of it, New Yorkers did enjoy *Anatol* again several times, but when it closed at Maxine Elliott's Theatre in 1913, it was eighteen years before another major production of it occurred in New York. In the meantime Schnitzler's name was kept alive through productions of a number of his other dramatic works, and familiarity with *Anatol* was preserved through a small production at the Astor Hotel in 1916, the Ye Curtain Players performance of *Anatol's Wedding Morning* in 1926, and a silent movie based on the work in 1921. Titled *The Affairs of Anatol,* the silent film script, written by Jeanie Macpherson, had little similarity to Schnitzler's work and producer Cecil B. DeMille rightly billed it as "suggested by Arthur Schnitzler's play and the paraphrase thereof by Granville-Barker."[26] The *Times* called it "only a distant and thoroughly acclimated cousin of the continental work" featuring a married Anatol De Witt Spencer,

> an exceedingly nice young man whose affairs are all innocent. If the girls who, one after another, arouse his purely philanthropic interest are not so innocent, they are still not so very, very bad, and promise to be good before they are dismissed from the story.[27]

Hollywood was Hollywood even in 1921, and not only was Schnitzler's work altered almost beyond recognition though his title retained, his cast of eleven was increased to twenty-three. Although other films based on Schnitzler's dramas have circulated in the United States, *The Affairs of Anatol* is the only one that has been an American film. Among the cast were some of the famous names of silent movies: Wallace Reid, who played Anatol, Gloria Swanson, Bebe Daniels, Monte Blue, and Polly Moran.

In 1931 Bela Blau revived the Granville-Barker adaptation of *Anatol* and the point of departure for much of the criticism was the comparison of the new production with the production of 1912. The two most frequent comparisons made were the difference in moral attitudes with which the

1931 reviewers thought that the two generations viewed the play, and the comparison of John Barrymore and Joseph Schildkraut as Anatol. In the realm of moral judgment it is obvious that the reviewers of 1931 felt a superiority of sophistication over the reviewers of 1912. It is obvious too that in their sophistication they exaggerated the indignation with which the New Yorkers of 1912 had greeted the play. Little evidence was found in the 1912 New York reviews to substantiate the comment on that production which John Mason Brown made in 1931: "There were those who not only failed to surrender to its urbane charm but who felt outraged by the conscienceless way in which it chronicled the progress of a Viennese rake."[28] Continuing in this vein, Gilbert W. Gabriel sought for similarity between bathtub-gin America of 1931 and Schnitzler's old world Vienna: "We have caught up with Alt Wien. We can sip our 'Anatol' straight, unaffaired, unaffeared."[29] There were two kinds of superficial language changes between the 1912 and 1931 productions, one of which reflected this sophistication which the New Yorker of 1931 felt that he had achieved: into the Granville-Barker adaptation "a few damns [were] sprinkled here and there for purposes of modernization."[30] The other change made the dialogue less obviously British: "the 'Oh, I says' and 'Really, old chaps' and 'Frightfully sorrehs' and other specimens of Londonese" were omitted.[31] In the role of Anatol Joseph Schildkraut was even less in his element than John Barrymore had been. He was stiff and strident and lacked the suavity necessary to an Anatol. In the description of his acting, the new importance of the movies and the advent of the "talkies" is obvious. Schildkraut, who had come to Broadway from Hollywood, was reproached for such stage taboos as "looking into the camera"[32] and "talking like a talkie."[33] Most often commended for their acting were Patricia Collinge for her portrayal of Gabrielle, "the Lady who Didn't Dare,"[34] and Miriam Hopkins in the role of ballet dancer Annie; and, as usual, the corresponding scenes of *A Christmas Present* and *The Farewell Supper* received highest critical acclaim of all the one-acts. Even with sets designed by Jo Mielziner and under the direction of Gabriel Beer-Hofmann, the production did not convey a completely Viennese atmosphere, but in spite of this and in spite of the charge that the work was a bit dated and its delights thought to be fewer than in 1912, it was still considered to be one of the better offerings of Broadway 1931, and it ran for forty-five performances.[35] Almost all of the criticism in 1931 was confined to aspects of the production. There were few comments on Schnitzler and almost absolute absence of references to his other works. Brooks Atkinson came closest to a literary judgment when he combined his comparison of the 1912 and 1931 productions with a comment on the character of Anatol and his author:

> When "Anatol" was first mounted here nearly twenty years ago with John Barrymore it was reputed to be audacious. Anatol is a sinner. But not to Schnitzler, and hardly to the pernicious playgoer of today, for Anatol is a sybarite of love. He is punctilious about the deportment of conquest. He loves love. The six scenes in his affairs reveal his susceptibilities—his anxiety over the

fidelity of Hilda, his wounded vanity when Bianca no longer remembers him, his anger when he discovers one of his trollops coveting the booty of previous amours or another planning to supplant him with a chorus boy. For to Schnitzler love is full of savor and deception, honeyed tenderness and sweet languor. None of the hotblooded passion of the modern theatre bursts into his amorous hothouse. There is hardly a kiss visible to the naked eye. Silken in the writing, it is overlong in the acting. If it were half as long it would be twice as good in the theatre. Certainly this production would be brisker amusement if a half hour were taken out of it.[36]

A vaudeville act suggested by *Anatol* followed in that same year,[37] but except for it and the MacDowell Players production of *The Farewell Supper* at the Little Church Around the Corner on March 11, 1938, *Anatol* disappeared from the stage for fifteen years. During this long absence from the stage Orson Welles adapted it for the relatively young medium of radio, and in 1938 it was broadcast nationally on the Mercury Theater of the Air. The episodes were strung together by a narrative in first-person-singular style, related by Welles in the role of Anatol, with incidents enacted by him and other members of the Mercury Theater ensemble woven into the narrative. Anatol seems a strange choice of character for Orson Welles to undertake. He is best known for his characterizations in heavy, suspenseful dramas, and it is not surprising that his portrayal of the urbane, sophisticated Anatol drew the comment from a Massachusetts listener that

> The play began and, strange as it may seem, Mr. Welles became Charles Laughton and remained Charles Laughton to the end. Again he was good in the more serious parts, but inclined to be ponderous and monotonous in the lighter ones. I think Anatol was a tenor and Welles is Basso troppo Profundo, unable to portray the unscrupulous frivolity, the disarming wit and charm of the role.[38]

Eight years later, in 1946, reviewers thought for the first time that a true touch of Vienna was given to a production of *Anatol* when Mady Christians directed the play for the Equity-Library Theatre. In addition to Miss Christians' own continental heritage and directorial skill, two factors may have benefited her in the creation of the mood of *Anatol*: the prefacing of the performance with the *Prologue by Loris* and her own experience as Ilona in *Anatols Hochzeitsmorgen* in the 1924 Max Reinhardt *Kammerspiele* production of *Anatol* in Berlin. Though currently starring in the 1946 Broadway hit of *I Remember Mama*, Miss Christians worked into her schedule the rehearsals for *Anatol,* and for a while these rehearsals were held in her apartment but were later moved into the basement smoking lounge of the Music Box Theatre, reportedly because she thought her apartment was "too sunny for the romantic, by-candle-light mood of *Anatol*."[39] *Anatol* was an exception to the regular Equity-Library productions because its cast included a greater than usual number of experienced actors in types of roles in which they were not ordinarily cast. Tonio Selwart, chosen for Anatol, had

played "bright boys under 25" on Broadway, and villains—including Nazis—in Hollywood. Carmen Matthews, usually cast as a "regal, suffering woman," played Mimi[40] in *The Farewell Supper,* and Henry Jones, who "was always cast as older men, caricatures," was Max.[41] Opening June 5, 1946, *Anatol* was performed four times at the George Bruce Branch Library—all performances free to the public—and closed the Equity-Library Theatre local season on June 7.[42] George Freedley, who had helped to found the acting group, called *Anatol* "the most expert production which [Equity-Library Theatre] has had in its three seasons' existence," and claimed that with *Anatol* the Theatre's season had ended "in a blaze of glory and a roar of laughter."[43] Since Freedley was one of the founders of Equity-Library and might naturally be expected to be enthusiastic about the productions, it is gratifying to have a report from another source which corroborated his commendation. Writing for the *Post,* Vernon Rice said:

> To our way of thinking, [Miss Christians] couldn't have made a better choice, for the bill had variety, contrast and consuming interest. If she used wisdom in selecting her plays she also used a touch of genius in selecting her players. So important are just the right actors for these kinds of playlets, that one bit of miscasting would almost prove to be fatal. Schnitzler is a writer of atmosphere and mood. There is a touch of grace mixed in with portions of gentle passion, melancholy, charm, wit and delicacy in his writing and even a slight stroke of heavyhandedness on the part of the director or an actor and the playwright's whole fragile structure is ruined. Through the expert work of Miss Christians, however, and her assembled cast, the spirit of Vienna of 1900, the whirl of the Viennese waltz were retained.[44]

The only discordant note came from the *New Yorker Staats-Zeitung und Herold*: Miss Christians had indeed succeeded in her direction of the actors and her creation of mood: "Sie hat ein sehr gutes, echtes, Wiener Leben aus den Darstellem herausgeholt;" but she had committed one "Todsünde:" the inadequacies of the English translation used for the production had not been corrected. In *Weihnachtseinkäufe* two phrases occur which, more than any others, have become tokens of Anatol and his world: "Das süsse Mädel" has become the cliché which captures the essence of Schnitzler's "Mädel aus der Vorstadt;" "leichtsinniger Melancholiker," a phrase which Anatol uses to describe himself, has come to embody not only Anatol but the entire generation of Viennese young men of whom Anatol was representative. The English translation used by Miss Christians rendered the latter phrase as "amateur philosopher," a translation which utterly fails to capture the essence of the German. The *Staats-Zeitung* was indignant over the discrepancy in meaning and the resulting erroneous comprehension of Anatol's character:

> Es ist kaum noch eine Ähnlichkeit da zwischen den beiden Begriffen!! Ein Amateurphilosoph—ein Raisonneur, der neben der Handlung steht und gescheite Bemerkungen macht, den kennen wir ja aus hundertunddrei *französischen* Stücken. Aber Anatol steht ja zutiefst

in der Handlung . . . und was er sagt, ist gar nicht philosophisch überlegen—in den meisten Fällen blamiert er sich gründlich! Aber das ist wahr, dass seine Genusssucht gepaart ist mit einer nachdenklichen Melancholie, die ihn immerfort das Vergängliche, Vergebliche in aller Glucksüche ahnen lässt und damit all seinen Handlungen die Frische und Energie nimmt. Dieser Lebemann, der so viel seinen Pariser Vorbildern verdankt, ist doch *kein* Pariser—er ist Wiener von 1890— "fin de siècle"! Es ist ein Stückchen Hamlet in ihm—zu viel "Bewusstsein" macht ihn "feige"! Das Bewusstsein hat er freilich mit dem Philosophen gemein, aber in nichts die Lebenshaltung.[45]

The greatest number of Schnitzler productions in New York occurred in the first thirty years of the century, and by mid-century most of them had disappeared from the stage completely. Only in the case of *Anatol* and *Reigen* do the later decades represent a real continuation or upsurge of interest in Schnitzler's plays. In the fifties *Anatol* was played in New York on four occasions. Twice it appeared in cuttings on bills with other plays when Equity-Library Theatre and the Neighborhood Playhouse School of the Theatre chose scenes for production in 1953 and 1959 respectively. Twice—in 1956 and again in 1958— full productions were given. Both of the latter were smaller and less elaborate than those in which John Barrymore and Joseph Schildkraut starred, but each had its own small point of distinction. In 1956 six of the seven scenes were staged in Directors Theatre, a second-floor studio half a block off Broadway on West 46th Street. The producers were Laura Malin and Vivian Schectman, and their theater was described as an "off-Broadway showcase for directors."[46] Originally scheduled to open on August 8, the opening was postponed until August 15, and performances were advertised for Wednesday through Saturday nights until September 1.[47] The distinction of this production lay in the fact that each scene was staged by a different director, but this very point of distinction was undoubtedly responsible for lessening the impact of the whole, for there was a consequent lack of unity in interpretation of the work: "As some of the directors seem not too sure whether the audience should laugh or shudder at certain crucial moments, it is small wonder that the results are uneven."[48] In spite of this unevenness in interpretation and some amateurish acting, the production was recommended by its reviewer:

> As Schnitzler, with his translator, Grace Colbron, makes the rounds of 1900 Vienna's world of cafe lights and boudoir shadows with Anatol, his friend, Max, and assorted past-and-present mistresses, there lurks beneath the ceaseless flow of keen-edged wit, the disturbing comparisons between happiness-and-pleasure and truth-and-illusion which come up more harrowingly and not so well balanced in the same author's *Reigen*.[49]

The mention of *Reigen* suggests the possibility that it may have contributed to the impetus for the two new revivals of *Anatol* in the second half of the fifties. In 1954 a French film based on *Reigen*, titled *La Ronde*, received wide publicity in New York when attempts were first made to distribute it there. Censors objected to its appearance on New York screens and only a ruling by the United States Supreme Court made possible the film's distribution there. The following year the Eric Bentley English stage adaptation of *Reigen*, also titled *La Ronde*, had a long and successful run off Broadway.

The significant feature about the 1958 production of *Anatol*, a translation by Karl Zimmermann, is the fact that it is the only production which has included all seven of the scenes. Once again it was a "Little Theatre" in which the production occurred, but in 1958 it was not the Little Theatre in which the John Barrymore production of 1912 took place, but a newly named theater at 4 St. Mark's Square. Formerly known as the Tempo Theatre, it had produced Schnitzler's one-act, *The Gallant Cassian*, in 1956. *Anatol* opened the off-Broadway season there on September 3, 1958. Though one reviewer expressed the opinion that the play "today . . . belongs in a curiosity shop,"[50] another considered it a happy choice for little theater entertainment. The production was executed with artistry and with concern for correct interpretation of the author's intent, and in skillful hands the mood of Schnitzler's Vienna and the fortunes of his hero were not without appeal for another time and place. Reacting to the opening night performance a reviewer wrote:

> Although it was written at the turn of the century in a decadent Vienna where gentlemen had little to amuse themselves with but love, its barbs and its wistful mockery will do very well today . . . [Anatol] is the toy philosopher in a toy world of emotion, seeking a faithful mistress in a society where no one remains faithful, least of all himself. And in each episode, his disillusion is complete. You don't feel sorry for him, only slightly sad at what people accept as love.[51]

Since the performance by the Neighborhood Playhouse School of the Theatre of *Anatol's Wedding Morning* and *Episode* in May 1959, the year following the last full production, no appearances of *Anatol* have been actual presentations of the work itself on the stage,[52] but have included adaptations for television and musical comedy. Though there is no indication that the television version of *Anatol* was shown in New York, the adaptation is recorded here to illustrate the wide variety of media for which the work has been considered appropriate. In 1961 Hollywood TV station KNXT offered a ninety-minute telecast of three of the scenes. It was part of a series of programs made, reportedly, "in the interests of better television," but the result was disappointing:

> [It] was, indeed, better than most of what is seen on tv but, alas, fell somewhat shy of the special excitement one hopes for in what is classified as prestige entertainment. . . . Its native spirit of witty sophistication, delicate irony and subtlety of style as well as the intended endearing nature of its central characters [have been] tarnished by the passage of time, victimized by the modern viewer's acquired immunity to astonishment when confronted with the "naughty" manners of its rakish, but outmoded "lady's man" hero, and [it is] faintly incompatible with the supercharged requirements of the living room medium itself.[53]

Though the reviewer was not enthusiastic about the final result, it is worth noting in relating the production history of *Anatol* that it was chosen to be included as a part of a series intended to upgrade a theatrical medium.[54]

The years since 1959 have seen two musicals based on *Anatol.* Neither can properly be called an adaptation, except in the broadest sense, but through them the character of Anatol and the name of Arthur Schnitzler have been preserved for this decade of theater audiences. One of the musicals, *Anatol,* did not have the opportunity to make an impression on the New York theater world. Based on Schnitzler's work, the book and lyrics for the musical were written by Tom Jones;[55] the music was borrowed from Offenbach. It was performed twenty-four times at the Boston Arts Center in 1961,[56] and *Show Business Illustrated* called the Boston production a "pre-Broadway tryout."[57] If it was, as such it was a failure, as it was not performed professionally in New York although one amateur performance there is recorded for it: in 1959 Jones was associated with the theater program at St. Bartholomew's Community House in New York and there in the fall of that year he produced his *Anatol.*[58] The other musical based on *Anatol, The Gay Life,* was more successful. After pre-Broadway tryouts in Detroit and Toronto, it opened in New York at the Shubert Theatre on November 18, 1961, and was performed 113 times before it closed in February of the following year.[59] In keeping with the idea of the need for a special temperament to capture the character of Anatol, in both musicals "latin lovers" were chosen for the role. In the Boston production of *Anatol,* it was Frenchman Pierre Aumont; in *The Gay Life* Walter Chiari was imported from Italy for the occasion. *The Gay Life* was a Broadway "extravaganza" and Schnitzler's cast of eleven—Anatol, Max, seven women, a waiter, and a servant—was inflated to twenty-two, plus singing and dancing ensembles. Though *The Gay Life* is not an adaptation of Schnitzler's *Anatol,* the musical's debt to Schnitzler is greater than the acknowledgement which appears on the program might lead the audience unacquainted with *Anatol* to believe. Neither Schnitzler's name nor the title of *Anatol* appears on the page which contains all the other composition and production credits; but tucked away underneath the cast of characters is the note: "'The Gay Life' was suggested by Arthur Schnitzler's 'Anatol,'" almost like an oversight remembered just in time. Among the obvious debts to Schnitzler—in addition to theme, characters, and setting—is the incorporation of incidents taken from the various scenes, the reproduction of snatches of dialogue, as well as the episodic nature of a great part of the musical's structure which portrays through flashbacks some of Anatol's affairs. It is a tribute to Schnitzler and his drama that most of the reviewers welcomed a revival of the story of Anatol and the mood of the era which Schnitzler helped to romanticize: "It is still durable and, as it has been treated by its current creators, modernly old-fashioned or, if you prefer, old-fashionedly modern."[60] It is an opulent extravaganza cast in the operetta mood of gay Vienna at the dawning of this century. It is the era of Strauss waltzes, of hansom cabs clobbering on the cobbled pavements, of maidens in billowing full-length skirts, of high living and elite dining. This ebullient period is romantically distilled by every facet of the current production. Here is the charm of a period that may never recur. Here is a fiesta for nostalgic sentimentalists."[61] Its revival and its adaptation for a new medium attest to the continued appeal of the play and its 113 performances witness to theatergoers' approval of the new garb in which Fay and Michael Kanin, Howard Dietz, and Arthur Schwartz clothed it. To the "nostalgic sentimentalists" *Anatol* still has charm and the ability to delight, and the world that is revealed with the opening of the curtain is the same enchanted world which Alfred Kerr described in 1896, only three years after the work was published:

> Mit leisem Zauberschlag erscheint eine schmerzlichsüsse Welt, voll traurigschalkhafter Grazie, voll ironischer Melancholie, voll leiser, lachender Innigkeit. Sie ist von zartem Leichtsinn durchweht, von schwermütigem Zweifel umwittert, von holdem Betrug umspielt . . . Alles flutet durcheinander: Innigkeit und Eleganz, Weichheit und Ironie, Weltstädtisches und Abseitiges, Lyrik und Feuilletonismus, Lebensraffinement und volksmässige Schlichtheit, Oesterreichertum und Halbfranzösisches, Schmerz und Spiel, Lächeln und Sterben . . . Das ist die unvergleichliche Welt Arthur Schnitzlers.[62]

Notes

1. A full production is defined here as one which includes five or more of the seven one-acts in *Anatol.*

2. Julius Kapp, *Arthur Schnitzler,* (Leipzig, 1912), p. 40. A more recent comment on the nature of the unity of *Anatol* is that of Ernst L. Offermanns: "Trotz lockerer Fügung bildet die Einaktersammlung *Anatol* . . . ein Ganzes . . . : Anatols diskontinuierliche Persönlichkeit, die ihm das Leben zu einer Abfolge isolierter Episoden werden lässt, deren ängstigende Vergänglichkeit durch die turbulente Permanenz ständigen neuen Abenteuers verdeckt werden soll; sein Versuch, Einsamkeit und Langeweile mittels der Fülle immer neuer Beziehungen zu überwinden; wie er sich aber dabei in seinem Verhalten zu Welt und Du gerade nicht von deren Wesentlichem bestimmen lässt, sondern durch die impressionistische Nuance der jeweiligen Situation oder Stimmung, woraus sich die Austauschbarkeit aller Relationen des Ichs ergibt; wie Anatol schliesslich, die mittlere Linie der Klarsicht immer nur kurze Zeit behauptend, Depressionen oder schöner Täuschung erliegt. Diese Problematik erscheint in den einzelnen Akten des Zyklus' mannigfach entfaltet." *Arthur Schnitzler, Anatol, Komedia,* no. 6, Helmut Arntzen und Karl Pestalozzi, eds., (Berlin, 1964), pp. 174-175. Through a brief analysis of the one-acts, Offermanns then shows how each of them illustrates this main theme. Other aspects of *Anatol* dealt with in this present essay which Offermanns also touches upon are: the novelty of the dramatic form, the production history of the play and its reception by the critics.

3. *New York Dramatic Mirror,* October 31, 1903, p. 16.

4. It is possible that *Abschiedssouper* was performed by the Russian Players in New York before May 2, 1906, but no substantiation of an earlier performance can be made here from programs, reviews or other sources.

5. In the files of the Theatre Collection of the Lincoln Center for the Performing Arts in New York City there is a note about another English performance of *Abschiedssouper* at the Lyric Theatre in New York on April 11, 1916, but because no program, review or reference to it in newspapers or periodicals was found to substantiate the performance, it has not been included here.

6. The exact date of the performance is not available. A brief report of the production was found in *Billboard,* March 6, 1926, p. 40, and for that reason it is probable that it was performed in February of that year.

7. Program.

8. The Equity-Library Theatre was, as its name suggests, a combined effort by members of Actors Equity and the New York Public Library to accomplish three purposes: (1) to create a receptive attitude toward theater in New York neighborhood audiences; (2) to give acting opportunities to new actors; (3) to give established actors opportunities to appear in roles which they ordinarily did not play. *New York Morning Telegraph,* June 8, 1946.

9. *New York Times,* November 6, 1953. The *Times* added to the above description: "The presentations, usually about an hour long, are designed to demonstrate the vitality of the living theatre. They also are brought to life by experienced professional actors and are shown during the one-hour assembly periods in the city's public schools."

10. As early as 1946 the Equity-Library Theatre produced five scenes from *Anatol* at the George Bruce Branch Library. This production is discussed later in this essay.

11. Cuttings from other dramas included scenes from *Taming of the Shrew* and *Twelfth Night,* Maxwell Anderson's *Elizabeth the Queen,* and Oscar Wilde's *The Importance of Being Earnest.*

12. In her unpublished thesis, "The Reception of Arthur Schnitzler in the United States," (Columbia University, 1931) Beatrice Schrumpf dates the premiere performance and first run of this production as March 12, 1911, indicating that the October, 1912 show was a revival of the preceding year's production. Nothing in her thesis substantiates the 1911 date except the remark years later by Ward Morehouse, who recalled that "it was at the Little Theatre 'that John Barrymore held forth as Anatol back in 1911.'" (p. 5) All of Schrumpf's bibliographical references to the stage production refer to the October 1912 production.

Every reference examined for this present essay substantiates the New York premiere performance date of October 14, 1912. There was a production in London in March, 1911, which used the same Granville-Barker paraphrase, and both the London and New York productions took place in theaters named the Little Theatre. Because of these similarities it is possible that Schrumpf confused the two productions.

13. This production occurred at the Astor Hotel, May 24, 1916, but no information about the details of the performance is available.

14. This is the anticipatory comment of E. E. vom Baur, who wrote a lengthy review of *Anatol* prior to its stage premiere and quoted passages of dialogue from the scenes. *Theatre Magazine,* XVI (October 1912), 106.

15. *Munsey's Magazine,* XLVIII (December 1912), 527.

16. *Theatre Magazine,* XVI (October 1912), 110.

17. *Collier's Weekly,* November 2, 1912.

18. Quoted by Julius Kapp, *Arthur Schnitzler,* p. 11.

19. *New York World,* October 15, 1912.

20. *New York Telegram,* October 15, 1912.

21. *New York Evening Post,* October 15, 1912.

22. *Chicago Record,* December 20, 1912.

23. January 7, 1912.

24. Undated clipping of January 1913, in the Theatre Collection, Lincoln Center for the Performing Arts, New York City.

25. November 2, 1912.

26. Program from the Rivoli Theatre, New York, week of September 11, 1921.

27. September 12, 1921.

28. *Evening Post,* January 17, 1931.

29. *New York American,* January 17, 1931.

30. *Brooklyn Eagle,* January 17, 1931.

31. *Times,* January 11, 1931.

32. *World,* January 17, 1931.

33. *Brooklyn Eagle,* January 17, 1931.

34. *New York Evening World,* January 19, 1931.

35. Burns Mantle, *The Best Plays of 1930-31* (New York, 1955), p. 480.

36. *Times,* January 17, 1931.

37. Photographs in the Theatre Collection at Lincoln Center for the Performing Arts in New York City are evidence of a vaudeville production of *Anatol* in 1931, but research in 1931 periodicals and newspapers has produced no further details about the act.

38. *New York Post,* August 26, 1938.

39. *P.M.,* June 4, 1946.

40. Schnitzler's "Annie."

41. *P.M.,* June 4, 1946.

42. The performance was repeated at the U.S.O. Theatre on June 14, 1946.

43. *New York Morning Telegraph,* June 8, 1946.

44. June 8, 1946.

45. June 10, 1946.

46. Unidentified newspaper clipping of August 24, 1956, in the Theatre Collection, Lincoln Center for the Performing Arts, New York City.

47. *Times,* July 26, 1956.

48. Unidentified newspaper clipping of August 24, 1956, in the Theatre Collection, Lincoln Center for the Performing Arts, New York City.

49. Unidentified newspaper clipping of August 24, 1956, in the Theatre Collection, Lincoln Center for the Performing Arts, New York City.

50. *New York World-Telegram and Sun,* September 4, 1958.

51. *Post,* September 4, 1958.

52. This excludes the possibility that the Cherry Lane Theatre production, for which no date has been established, occurred after 1959.

53. *Variety,* April 12, 1961.

54. The adaptation for the ninety-minute program for television, *The Affairs of Anatol,* was written by Robert Boon, produced by Alexander Ramati, and directed by Ezra Stone. Members of the cast included John van Dreelen, Oscar Beregi, Kathleen Crowley, Susan Silo, Didi Ramati, Jack Tesler, and Ralph Smiley. *Variety,* April 12, 1961.

55. Jones is the author of the book and lyrics for the musical *The Fantasticks.*

56. Henry Hewes, *The Best Plays of 1961-62* (New York, 1962), p. 41.

57. September 19, 1961.

58. Confirmed in a telephone conversation with a staff member of St. Bartholomew's, March 18, 1966.

59. *The Best Plays of 1961-1962,* p. 270.

60. *Newsday,* November 22, 1961.

61. *Women's Wear Daily,* November 20, 1961.

62. "Arthur Schnitzler," *Neue deutsche Rundschau,* Jahrgang VII, 1 (1896), p. 287.

DER SCHLEIER DER PIERRETTE

CRITICAL COMMENTARY

Lawrence Sullivan (essay date spring 1993)

SOURCE: Sullivan, Lawrence. "Arthur Schnitzler's *The Bridal Veil* at the American Laboratory Theatre." *Dance Research Journal* 25, no. 1 (spring 1993): 13-20.

[*In the following essay, Sullivan explains the ways in which Schnitzler's* Der Schleier der Pierrette *allowed stage directors to break away from realist conventions and explore abstract and symbolist theatrical effects.*]

Whatever the particular intentions of the playwright, Arthur Schnitzler's **Der Schleier der Pierrette** (**The Veil of Pierrette**), a ballet-pantomime first performed in Dresden, January 22, 1910, with music by Ernst von Dohnányi, became, in the first year of its composition, a vehicle of avant-garde experimentalists on the Russian theatrical scene. In October 1910, Vsevolod Meyerhold used Schnitzler's ballet-pantomime for his own avant-garde interests in commedia dell'arte motifs, producing **Columbine's Scarf** (a variant title) at the House of Interludes in St. Petersburg. Three years later, in 1913, Alexander Tairov, as anti-Meyerholdean as he was anti-Stanislavskian, also staged a version of **Der Schleier** under the title **The Veil of Pierrette,** at the Mardzhanov's Free Theatre in Moscow. Both directors, relying on different aesthetic principles, used the commedia dell'arte ballet-pantomime as a statement against Stanislavskian psychological realism[1].

The historical significance of Schnitzler's ballet-pantomime was its appeal not only to experimental directors, such as Max Reinhardt, Vsevolod Meyerhold, and Alexander Tairov, but also to talented stage designers such as Nicholas Sapunov, Sergei Soudeikine, Antatoly Arapov, Alexandra Exeter, and Natalia Gontcharova. For example, Nicholas Sapunov's setting for Meyerhold's first version of **Columbine's Scarf** was based on his earlier design for Alexander Blok's anti-realist play *The Fairground Booth* (*Balagantchik*). Directed by Meyerhold in 1906, the scenery for *The Fairground Booth* consisted of a cardboard backdrop with cutouts through which the actors projected their heads, arms, and legs and from which they performed their roles. Such anti-realistic scenic devices, the use of commedia dell'arte stock characters, puppets, and Punch-and-Judy episodes, all aimed to reject the psychological and literal realism found in Stanislavsky's Moscow Art Theatre[2].

Something of a novelty in theatrical genre, the ballet pantomime provided these directors with a fresh artistic freedom where action of the drama could be expressed by theatrical devices without the aid of the written or spoken word. Konstantin Rudnitsky, Russian critic and historian, describes the new prevailing attitude aptly:

> But from 1910 onwards, an antipathy among Russian theatrical innovators to all "literature," including the classics—in fact against the written word in general, began to make itself felt. Theories were devised to justify the compulsion to rescue the actor from delivery of text of any kind. Wordless action was attractive because it created the possibility of proving the autonomy and intrinsic value of theatrical art, its complete independence from literature. Practice kept up with theory. Both the experienced Meyerhold and the still very young Tairov experimented with mime. They each staged the same mime by Artur [sic] Schnitzler set to music by Ernst Dohnany—Meyerhold under the title of *Columbine's Scarf,* and Tairov under the title *The Veil of Pierrette.* Although the productions were in no way alike, they both aroused lively interest in theatrical circles.[3]

Not only was there freedom from a literary text, but as one Viennese dramatic critic put it, the ballet-pantomime was "to liberate the dance from the ballet." The periodical *Tanzblätter* interprets this comment to mean that there was a need "to eliminate passages from a ballet that were dramaturgically unnecessary, to concentrate on the action, and to interpret it not only through pantomime but through dancing" (p. 11). Thus, Schnitzler's **Der Schleier der Pierrette** offered directors opportunities to explore new and compelling symbolistic theatrical effects as an alternative to the well-worn devices of realism found in traditional naturalistic presentations.

Given this historical Russian context of Schnitzler's ballet-pantomime, it is surprising that on January 21, 1928 the first American production of **Der Schleier der Pierrette,** under the title **The Bridal Veil,** opened in New York at the American Laboratory Theatre. This school and theatre, staffed by Russian emigrés from Stanislavsky's Moscow Art Theatre and dedicated to Stanislavskian theatrical principles, seems to be an unlikely place to stage a work that had earned its reputation in Russian productions as a non-realist vehicle. Yet, **The Bridal Veil** under the choreography and direction of Elizabeth Anderson-Ivantzova proved, as its critical reception revealed, to be one of the more successful ventures of the Lab Theatre.

Co-founded in 1923 by Richard Boleslavsky, formerly of the Moscow Art Theatre, and Mrs. Herbert Stockton, the American Laboratory Theatre started out as a school and eventually evolved into a "laboratory" theatre in the manner of Stanislavsky's Moscow Art Theatre. After deciding not to return to Russia with the Moscow Art Theatre then on tour in the U.S., Maria Ouspenskaya joined Boleslavsky in 1924 as dramatic coach and acting teacher[4]. Mme Anderson-Ivantzova, unlike Boleslavsky and Ouspenskaya, did not come out of Stanislavsky's Moscow Art Theatre. The young Anderson's theatrical training began in 1898 or 1899 at the Imperial Ballet School in Moscow, from which she graduated in 1906. She received her primary instruc-

tion from celebrated teachers and principal dancers Mikhail Mordkin and Vassily Tikhomirov. In addition, her dramatic coaching for principal ballet roles was from Alexander Gorsky, under whom she made her début in 1916 as Aurora in Tchaikovsky's *Sleeping Beauty*[5]. As an emerging, young ballerina, Elizabeth Anderson was specially cited by Oliver M. Sayler during his visit to Moscow in 1917 for her strength as a dramatic interpreter of the roles she assumed in *Sleeping Beauty* and *Swan Lake*[6]. Little is known of her connection, if any, with Stanislavsky in Moscow, save that Sayler notes her attendance among the "pillars of the Moscow stage" at a First Studio dress rehearsal of *Twelfth Night,* describing her as "the bewitching blonde inheritor of Pavlova's laurels in the ballet . . ."[7]. Mme Anderson-Ivantzova emigrated to the West during the 1918-1919 season to find a career in exile not only in dancing but also in choreography.

When she arrived in Paris in 1920, she performed with Nikita Balieff's Théâtre de la Chauve-Souris during its opening season and choreographed various dances for the first three programs. Nikita Balieff, an illustrious theatrical entrepreneur and performer from Moscow, was originally an actor with the Moscow Art Theatre before he founded his own Letuchaya Muish or Bat Theatre in 1908. His success in Moscow was legendary, and in Paris the critics declared the Chauve-Souris a sensation and a model avant-garde theatre[8]. After Mme Anderson-Ivantzova left the Chauve-Souris, we hear of her at Max Reinhardt's Kammerspiele des Deutschen Theaters in Berlin where, in September 1922, she first choreographed Schnitzler's **Der Schleier der Pierrette** for a production by the Kikimora Theatre Company of Moscow, for which Natalia Gontcharova designed the sets and costumes[9]. Having completed a season at the San Carlo Opera House in Lisbon in 1922-23, Anderson-Ivantzova returned to Paris to perform with Le Théâtre Balagantchik in a production of *Foire de Moscou,* directed by M. Korniloff with scene designs by Sergei Soudeikine[10]. While it is difficult from the sources to associate Mme Anderson-Ivantzova directly with Stanislavsky, we see that she had worked under Gorsky, who was directly influenced by Stanislavsky[11], under Balieff, who was a member of the Moscow Art Theatre, and with Boleslavsky, who in New York was an acknowledged spokesman for Stanislavsky's theories of acting and an illustrious product of the Moscow Art Theatre. Nevertheless, it was probably her own natural bent in dramatic performing and her professional experience with protégés of Stanislavsky that led to an invitation to teach ballet and body movement at the American Laboratory Theatre and to her direction of two dance-pantomimes, Arthur Schnitzler's **The Bridal Veil** (1928) and Jean Cocteau's *Le Boeuf sur le toit* (1930).

Of the first production, **The Bridal Veil,** some details are known concerning the lighting, costumes, and set design. Documents on the technical costs, letters to a costume maker and to an agent on royalty matters, a crayon sketch of the set for Scene I and of the costumes for the Bride (Pierrette) and the Groom (Harlequin), and a statement of what seems to be a declaration of aesthetic principles intended for the program notes by James Reynolds, the designer, are the only original sources presently available to the researcher[12]. From these documents, we learn that the set design required platforms, that Mrs. Walter Fleischer was offered a contract to make the costumes, and that the business manager, Richard Aldrich, expressed what apparently he saw as a unique optimism within the company about the production itself. In his letter to Mrs. Herbert Stockton, a founding member of the Board of Directors of the Lab Theatre, Aldrich reports that "for the first time in the history of the [American Laboratory] theatre, all the departments seem to be uniformly enthusiastic about the production. . . . They all feel that it is to be the most spectacular and interesting of any of our productions. Due to the costumes and the sets which Mr. James Reynolds has designed, *The Veil* will literally be a feast for the eyes and something quite unusual and new to New York City"[13].

Despite the optimism of Richard Aldrich's letter, according to J. W. Roberts, sometime prior to January 6, 1928 a significant disagreement arose between the choreographer and the designer[14]. Apparently Anderson-Ivantzova rejected Reynolds's designs for the pantomime because in her judgment they were "static and did not 'move'." A dramatic argument ensued between Boleslavsky and Anderson-Ivantzova, but in the end Boleslavsky forced the issue and called for a vote to determine whether to use Reynolds's proposal. Anderson-Ivantzova lost, and the production went forward with Reynolds's designs.

The altercation between choreographer and scene designer notwithstanding, Aldrich's letter contains a number of telling items. The participants, Aldrich writes to Mrs. Stockton, felt optimistic about the successful outcome of the production, and they believed that the aesthetic result would be "spectacular" and "interesting." It would be interesting because as a ballet-pantomime, a relatively novel genre to New York, *The Veil* would impose on audiences, as the reviewer in *Theatre Arts Monthly* later would note, the need to listen with their eyes. It would be spectacular because Reynolds's sets and costumes would be aesthetically effective in the merging of design, color, and lighting with the choreographic movement of the pantomime and with Schnitzler's verbal text and Dohnányi's music. Aldrich's letter concludes with the happy expectation of moving the production to Broadway through the influence of Jed Harris. Aldrich's ardent hope for a Broadway run was not fulfilled, but his judgment about the artistic success of the production seems to be confirmed by some of the details provided by reviewers.

James Reynolds (1891-1954), the designer, coming from such commercial Broadway successes as *The Vagabond King* (1925) and *The Royal Family* (1927), has left us with a credo that explains his interest in the American Laboratory Theatre's production of *The Bridal Veil.* His initial attraction to the theatre, he explains, began with an interest in the ballet, "its twin[,] pantomime," and seventeenth-century forms of the commedia dell'arte. His interest in

these forms, he tells us, embraced "the whole ballet tradition—the classic *Les Sylphides* as well as the modern work of the Diaghileff group and pantomime." He goes on to say that "pantomime depends like ballet upon stylized emotion, and like ballet aims above all for a visual effect. It thus provides the surest inspiration for the designer"[15].

This credo is significant in its context, I think, because it identifies pantomime with a particular kind of ballet, i.e., a scenario ballet either with character or narrative for its content (as in many of the Diaghilev ballets), and because the choreography or movement communicates its visual effect through "stylized emotion." From this statement it may be presumed that the design for *The Bridal Veil* evolved from Schnitzler's written text and from the rendering by the choreographer of the written word into dance movement or gesture. Because of its unknown date of composition, Reynolds's statement may have been written before or after the quarrel between the choreographer and the designer. In any event, the declaration of a unified aesthetic purpose between choreographer and scene designer may have become the basis for Aldrich's claim to Mrs. Stockton that a unique optimism prevailed in the company and that "all the departments seem to be uniformly enthusiastic about the production . . . ."[16].

Design created from movement and gesture was something that Reynolds could experiment with at the Lab Theatre since the kind of audience it attracted was receptive to innovation. The freedom offered at the Lab Theatre stood in direct contrast to what he met with in the Broadway theatre, for, as he says, "the designer who seeks expression in the commercial theatre in this country encounters an intolerably unintelligent point of view"[17]. An experimental theatre, with its low cost budget, its artistic priorities, and its relatively small but generally receptive audiences, afforded theatre artists an opportunity to discard well-worn formulas for innovative enterprises and new discoveries. Even as theatre artists, their commitment to financial success aimed at self-sufficiency rather than at investment returns to stolid stockholders. The judgment of the New York critics partially confirms the optimism of Aldrich, and their criticism, though aiming to reflect what they thought they saw on stage, actually revealed as much about their own tastes and assumptions as it did about the production itself. Thus, in acquiring as many critical opinions as possible, one hopes for a more balanced view of the undertaking of *The Bridal Veil* than what can be gained from a single assessment. With that aim in view, it is helpful to review the writings of as many critics as are available from press clippings and other sources.

Generally speaking, the critical reception of *The Bridal Veil* was mixed[18]. Of the ten reviews consulted, four were clearly favorable, though with some qualification three were plainly unfavorable, with occasional compliments; and two, those of the *New York Times* and the *New York Herald Tribune,* stood on neutral ground by being anonymous, essentially reportorial, and brief. *Theatre Arts Monthly,* on the other hand, without ostensibly reviewing the production itself, reviewed the reviewers, leaving little doubt in the reader's mind that the Laboratory Theatre had created something important[19]. Critical openness, it was urged, shapes a reviewer's attitudes and evaluative judgment. As a case in point, the commentator for *Theatre Arts Monthly* observed that:

> pantomime as a dramatic form has always been particularly popular in theatres where actors have style and where audiences have the listening eyes that belong to people of imagination—a limitation which has made it increasingly unpopular in the modern theatre. . . . Watching a pantomime takes almost as much grace and flexibility as acting in it. The interesting thing about the response to *The Bridal Veil* is its diversity—the audience (and incidentally the critics) liked it or disliked it according to their openmindedness and their ability to see without words.

(p. 232)

The writer then goes on to quote Richard Lockridge, assigned by the *New York Sun,* as an example of a critic with limited vision:

> Pantomime is a very definite art. It must have as its background a measurable sophistication and can only, before that background, posture at naïveté. The present cast provides the naïveté in full measure, but its sophistication is on the whole that of so many circus acrobats.

(p. 232)

Ironically enough, this judgment of *The Bridal Veil* has prevailed down to our own times when one sees in *The Encyclopedia of the New York Stage, 1920-1930,* published in 1985, the very same quote cited verbatim as representative of the *collective critical assessment* of the ballet-pantomime[20]. *The Theatre Arts Monthly* commentator clearly disagreed with Lockridge's judgment, preferring the review of "the new critic [Robert Littell] at the *New York Evening Post*" (p. 235), who obviously was able "to see without words"[21].

Another approach to assessing the ballet-pantomime was taken by Thomas Barrett, reviewing for *The Billboard*. In response to what he heard several members of the audience ask—"What's it all about?"—Barrett provided his readers with a note from the performance program that summarized Schnitzler's pantomime. The version of the plot implied the theme that artists and lovers are not survivors in this world. The quote here renders Schnitzler's plot somewhat poetically, omitting, however, some essential elements of the action:

> The sculptor is in no mood for merry making. His friends, in holiday attire, come to take him to a ball, but he refuses to be persuaded. He prefers to wait for his love, whom he has not seen for weeks. And then she comes. She comes not as his love but as a bride, for her parents have betrothed her to a rich man. She comes in her bridal veil, for this is the night of her wedding. She comes bringing a wine which will end

their sorrows, and the sculptor, draining the glass at a draft, leaves merry making and sorrow forever. Leaves also the bride, to drain as best she may the bitterer cup of dance and song and a love grown hateful. But this cup also proves too much for her strength. From the ball and its sinister gaiety she flees to her dead lover, only to be captured and derided by the bridegroom, balked of his prey, but swift in his revenge. When he has left her with her dead lover, her heart breaks, her mind becomes distraught and she joins him [the Sculptor] at last.[22]

This synopsis of the plot only cryptically alludes to some important details that make this ballet-pantomime a grotesque. For example, in Scene I the "wine" the Bride brings is a vial of poison to end their lives; the Sculptor alone drinks it and dies before her eyes; in Scene II the ghost of the Sculptor bearing her bridal veil in his hand appears to the Bride (something she alone sees) and pursues her during the dancing; her strange behavior enrages the Bridegroom, whom she then flees to return to the Sculptor's quarters, but the Bridegroom follows her to find the Sculptor lying on the floor. Thinking the Sculptor to be asleep, the Bridgroom picks up the body and props it up on the couch. Then he learns that the Sculptor is dead, and in revenge he locks the Bride in the apartment with the corpse of her dead lover. Frantically trying to escape from the room, she rushes about in every direction to be free, but goes mad in the attempt and dies, dropping along side the body of the Sculptor. The absence of some of these details certainly may have caused some consternation among those in the audience who may not have been able to discover why the characters behaved the way they did.

In the original text Schnitzler identified his main characters as Pierrot the Lover who was a painter (and not a sculptor), Pierrette the Bride, and Harlequin the Bridegroom. The Lab production did not use those traditional commedia dell'arte names, perhaps because they were less familiar to American audiences, but used general character types—a Sculptor, a Bride, and a Bridegroom. Following Schnitzler's text, the pantomime was divided into three tableaux or scenes: the Sculptor's quarters, the Bride's home, and again the Sculptor's quarters. The performance lasted about an hour, with the first and last scenes each taking about ten minutes to play, whereas the second scene, the wedding party at the Bride's house, took about forty minutes. As the reviews suggest, most of the dancing occurred during Scenes II and III, the Ballroom scene and the final scene of the Bride's demise into madness and death. A single piano provided the music for this production, which was something of a liability because the dramatic content of the action was so intense that, as some critics noted, the dance movement required a more substantial musical accompaniment to sustain the dramatic emotion than that afforded by the piano alone.

. . . As stated earlier, there is a technical design of the platforms to be built for Scene II, and two critics noted that the action took place on several levels. Stark Young, critic for *The New Republic,* offering us a sense of the visual effectiveness of the overall design, considered the "décor in both scenery and costumes . . . beautiful and fresh"[23], and Oliver Sayler, writing for *The Saturday Review of Literature,* found Reynolds's work and Anderson-Ivantzova's choreography well coordinated. Sayler says:

> Schnitzler's simple retelling of the legend of Pierrot, Pierrette, and the Bridegroom, and von Dohnanyi's score are fused by the choreography. The wedding of the two arts to make a third is blessed and perfected by James Reynolds's boldly original and exotic but strangely blending costumes which flash against his happily conceived settings.[24]

These observations, unfortunately, do not offer us much specific detail of the actual setting itself for Scene II or of the costumes worn by the dancing ensemble. The remaining critics merely acknowledge visual effectiveness with such remarks as "attractive and colorful costumes," "stage settings well done," or "gayly dressed couples." None expressed any fault with the settings or costumes.

The principals who played the Sculptor, Bride, and Bridegroom generally received good notices for their work. There was no agreement, however, in the selection of the best performer. Anne Schmidt, we are told, by Benjamin DeCasseres of *Arts & Decoration,* surpassed herself in the role of the Bride, whereas Stark Young, in his review for the *New Republic,* found her only "fair." Young felt that Harold Hecht as the Sculptor was "highly successful," and that "talent appears constantly in what he does, and most of all in that strange, indefinable absorption and awe in the stage movement that he feels—the quality that in this instance most singles him out from all the others of the company"[25]. Donald Hartman's Bridegroom was well received by all who mentioned the character in their review, except Thomas Barrett, who gave a qualified notice, saying Hartman overacted a bit because of the voice restraints required by pantomime, but otherwise offered "a forceful performance"[26]. The company players as a group were cited for their "youthful and conscientious performance" in the four-sentence notice by the *New York Times,* whereas Stark Young and Oliver Saylor noted the dancers' success in ensemble playing, a hallmark of the Stanislavskian legacy.

The reception of **The Bridal Veil** generally produced some extraordinary comments by the reviewers who did not have a personal aversion to pantomime or to Schnitzler's play. One reviewer found that the production, appearing as it did at the wane of the theatrical season, was a "most delightful surprise." The American Laboratory Theatre, says DeCasseres, revealed "the highest point of its career and, besides, it has produced one of the most artistic, best directed and best acted plays of the season." Robert Littell, writing for the *New York Evening Post,* said **The Bridal Veil** "is not only the best pantomime I have yet seen but also one of the most competent and imaginative items in a very remarkable New York theatrical season"[27].

Stark Young remarks that even with its shortcomings in the coordination of the musical accompaniment and movement and with its budget limitations, the American Laboratory Theatre production was "twenty times better than was the production of 'Pierrot the Prodigal,' for instance, in which Miss Laurette Taylor was starred; just as it is much more exact, competent and complete with regard to the movement, style and technical pains than the pantomime of the chorus at the Metropolitan Opera House"[28]. Such observations would have seemed to fulfill Richard Aldrich's prediction that the Laboratory's production would find its way to a Broadway run. While falling short of that happy event, these notices justified Aldrich's expectations and optimism expressed in his letter to Mrs. Stockton about the success of the production.

Even reviewers who liked neither pantomime nor Schnitzler's play tried to distinguish between their predilections and the efforts of the company. Barrett, to qualify his rather severe review, hastened to add that "the performance in reality is no reflection on the workmanship of the cast. On the contrary the players struggle bravely with a most awful theme—a pantomime that cries to the skies for words—and do their best with what from dancing, tugging and mugging might properly be classified as a muscle concert"[29]. Yet, even critics who were more sympathetic to the efforts of the cast had some reservations about the success of the production as well. Stark Young tempered his comments on the coordination between music and movement, saying that he did so on the "most demanding grounds." He felt that at times the dramatic texture of the macabre action was too "thin," and that the production would have had greater dramatic power if the movement had been joined more firmly to the "musical foundation" provided for it (p. 19). Oliver Sayler, like Young, also saw a discrepancy between the movement and the music, but he did not attribute the problem to the choreographic direction as much as to the thinness of the musical accompaniment. He wished that "a string quartet had replaced the single piano to give rhythmic and tonal variety and the strangely vibrant and dramatic quality of that musical medium" (p. 611).

It was, however, Robert Littell, who perceived the purpose of balletic movement of which James Reynolds spoke, namely, "stylized movement" for a "visual effect." Littell observes that this pantomime, unlike some other Schnitzler stories, does not contain actions and events from life by people we almost feel we know personally. These characters are somehow extraordinary. Thus, he says:

> **The Bridal Veil,** as framed by Miss Anderson-Ivantzova into a whole as delicate and as distinct as a painting on glass, is remote, fantastic, unreal. It isn't the dilution of fantasy or the sort of prettified unreality we are used to in pantomime. It is made of the same stuff throughout, it keeps the same key, and its remoteness comes to us with great strength and beauty.[30]

Scenes I and III were brief episodes, presented almost as miniatures or "tender little pictures" as Littell calls them, in contrast with Scene II, which was the longest tableau in the pantomime. For this scene, there was a significant change of pace and mood to offset the effects found earlier, lest the whole impression—"that of a strange and richly colored dream," as Littell expressed it—evaporated before the end of the pantomime. Littell explains later in his review:

> But the second act, an ever-changing pattern of gayly dressed couples dancing on several levels of the stage, dancing towards us, dancing away from us, dancing, running, in exquisitely arranged confusion, holds the other two [scenes] together and gives solidity and variety to the whole pantomime without ever breaking its mood. The gathering pace, the changes, the flowing movement and graceful vigor of this scene . . . in which a sad uneasiness, a reckless gayety and a new despair were expressed subtly by the coming and going of dancing figures, was for me something quite new in the art of the theatre.

Needless to say, Robert Littell gave the production its strongest review, and one likes to think the strength of that review was based on the resolved disagreement on the aesthetic intention between the choreographer/director and the scene designer. Whatever be the case, almost all the critics acknowledged that pantomime, to achieve its dramatic effect, required some sophistication on the part of the audience. That the American Laboratory Theatre took the risk of attracting a sophisticated audience nightly speaks only of their sense of artistic adventure and their commitment as an experimental theatre to introduce unfamiliar forms to their audiences. Aside from a reasonably successful run of forty-eight performances and although the company did not perform on Broadway, they must have taken additional satisfaction in Littell's judgment that "the whole thing [production] was staged by Elizabeth Anderson-Ivantzoff with a skill, a strength and a sense of design which would make a dozen Broadway directors I could think of look like amateurs"[31].

As a final word, Robert Littell's assessment of Mme Anderson-Ivantzova's choreographic ability was a foreshadowing of things to come. *The Bridal Veil* provided her with a showcase for those who would need to consider a choreographer with a special success in dance-pantomime. A year later, in 1929, she was engaged to choreograph the American premiere of Igor Stravinsky's *Les Noces* for the League of Composers' production at the Metropolitan Opera House. Anderson-Ivantzova proved to be a wise choice. The critical reception of her choreography for the complex Stravinsky ballet was enthusiastic and uniform among the major reviewers, such as Mary I. Watkins (*New York Herald Tribune*), Olin Downes (*New York Times*), and John Martin (*New York Times*), who were in no way reluctant to praise her choreographic talents[32].

Notes

1. For an overview of Schnitzler's ballet-pantomime in the hands of Meyerhold and Tairov in Russia, see Elisabeth Heresch, *Schnitzler und Russland: Aufnahme, Wirkung, Kritik* (Wien: Wilhelm Braumüller, Universitäts-Verlagsbuch handlung, 1982), pp. 103-111. An extended discussion of Alexander Tairov's productions of *The Veil of Pierrette* is found in Thomas Joseph Torda, "Alexander Tairov and the Scenic Artists of the Moscow Kamerny Theater 1914-1935," PhD Dissertation, University of Denver, 1977, pp. 162-178.

2. For an analysis of Meyerhold's *Columbine's Scarf,* see Edward Braun, *The Theatre of Meyerhold: Revolution on the Modern Stage* (New York: Drama Book Specialists Publishers, 1979), pp. 102-109. It is interesting to note here also that in 1909 Meyerhold performed the role of Pierrot in Mikhail Fokine's *Carnaval* and that in 1911 Alexander Benois's set design for Mikhail Fokine's *Petrushka* was modeled on Sapunov's set design for Meyerhold's *Columbine's Scarf.* See *"Der Schleier der Pierrette, 1898-1981," Tanzblätter,* 31 (June 1981): 11-12. For a discussion and the text of Alexander Blok's *The Puppet Show (Balagantchik),* see *The Russian Symbolist Theatre: An Anthology of Plays and Critical Texts,* edited and translated by Michael Green (Ann Arbor: Ardis Publishers, 1986), pp. 31-57. On Max Reinhardt's experiments with wordless drama and dance-pantomime, see Margaret Dietrich, "Music and Dance in the Productions of Max Reinhardt," *Total Theatre: A Critical Anthology,* ed. E. T. Kirby (New York: E. P. Dutton, 1969), pp. 162-174. Schnitzler's German text consulted for this paper was from *Der Schleier der Pierrette,* Pantomime in drei Bildern, von Arthur Schnitzler, Musik von Ernst von Dohnányi (Leipzig: Ludwig Doblinger [Bernhard Herzmansky]), 1910.

3. Konstantin Rudnitsky, *Russian and Soviet Theater: 1905-1932,* trans. Roxane Permar and ed. Dr. Lesley Milne (New York: Harry N. Abrams, 1988), pp. 10-11. On the use of the commedia dell'arte characters in Russia, see Kenneth Richards and Laura Richards, *The Commedia dell'Arte: A Documentary History,* (Cambridge, MA: Basil Blackwell for the Shakespeare Head Press, 1990), p. 303. The subject of wordless-drama-dance has not received sufficient attention in the critical and historical literature. It is helpful here, however, to know that two major productions of Max Reinhardt parallel Schnitzler's piece: *Sumurûn* (Berlin 1910), a wordless play in nine scenes by Frederich Freska with music by Victor Hollender that Reinhardt took to London (1911), New York (1912), and Paris (1912). *Tanzblätter* asserts that Grete Wiesenthal, a popular dancer from Vienna and a well-known performer for Max Reinhardt in Berlin, co-authored *Sumurûn.* "Die Tänzerin selbst [Grete Wiesenthal] was Mitautorin der Pantomime 'Sumurûn', die in der Inszenierung von Max Reinhardt weltberühmt werden sollte." ("The dancer herself was co-author of the pantomime 'Sumurûn', which was to become world-famous in the production by Max Reinhardt" p. 12.) Her name, however, usually does not appear among the credits. The second Reinhardt "big production" (which the

Germans refer to as *Grossrauminszenierungen*) of a wordless play adapted from a book by Karl Voll-möller, with music by Englebert Humperdink, was *The Miracle* (1912 in Berlin and 1924 in New York). Max Reinhardt's production of *The Miracle* was thought a huge success by New York critics because it demonstrated that theatre did not need words to accomplish its effects, that "theatricality" had its own ends and could create emotional responses in audiences by virtue of its own instruments. See Peter Bauland, *The Hooded Eagle: Modern German Drama on the New York Stage* (Syracuse: Syracuse University Press, 1968), pp. 34-36 and pp. 57-60, and Dietrich, pp. 165-166. Interestingly enough, Richard Boleslavsky of the American Laboratory Theatre directed the crowd scenes for Reinhardt's New York production, according to Ronald A. Willis, "The American Lab Theatre, 1923-1930," PhD Dissertation, University of Iowa, 1968, p. 206.

4. In addition to his dissertation, the only full-length study of the American Laboratory Theatre I know of, Professor Willis has an abbreviated discussion of the school and theatre in "The American Lab Theatre," *Tulane Drama Review,* 9, 1 (Fall 1964):112-116. In the same issue, a brief account of Boleslavsky's and Ouspenskaya's approach to teaching of Stanislavskian theory is given by their former student Francis Ferguson, in "The Notion of 'Action'," pp. 85-87. A later study is that of J. W. Roberts, *Richard Boleslavsky: His Life and Work in the Theatre* (Ann Arbor, Michigan: UMI Research Press, 1981), which covers the theatrical career of the founder and director of the American Laboratory Theatre. Maria Ouspenskaya (1876-1949) began her theatrical training as a coloratura soprano, but lacking sufficient financial support abandoned it for a career on the dramatic stage. She learned her art and seasoned her talent by touring with provincial companies. Out of 250 applicants, she was one of two accepted in 1911 by Stanislavsky into the Moscow Art Theatre. Between 1911 and 1923 she played about 150 roles with the Company. In 1923, she was a member of the visiting Moscow Art Theatre Company on tour in New York, but did not return to the USSR, remaining in the U.S. and joining Richard Boleslavsky at the American Laboratory Theatre the following year. In the 1920s and 1930s she appeared in many Broadway productions before she went to Hollywood, performing in a number of films as a character actress while under contract to Metro-Golden-Mayer. She maintained an acting school in Hollywood during the late 1930s and the 1940s. "Veteran of Character Role in Plays and Films Succumbs to Burn Injuries on Coast," Obituary, *New York Times,* 4 December 1949, p. 108.

5. On Mme Anderson's career, see the interview conducted by Marion Horosko, "In the Shadow of the Russian Tradition," *Dance Magazine,* January 1971, p. 37; on Mikhail Mordkin, Vasilly Tikhomirov,

and Alexander Gorsky, see Elizabeth Sourtiz, *Soviet Choreographers in the 1920s,* trans. Lynn Visson, edited with additional translation, Sally Banes, (Durham, North Carolina: Duke University Press, 1990), pp. 85-153.

6. Oliver M. Sayler, *The Russian Theatre* (New York: Brentanos, 1922), pp. 108-109.

7. Sayler, p. 17.

8. Lawrence Sullivan, "Nikita Baliev's Le Théâtre de la Chauve-Souris: An Avant-Garde Theater," *Dance Research Journal,* 18, 2 (Winter 1986-87): 17-29.

9. *Tanzblätter*: 16-17. This essay contains a photograph of Gontcharova's set. The chronology omits Alexander Tairov's first production of *Der Schleier* at Mardzhanov's Free Theatre in 1913 and a later production at the Kamerny Theatre in 1915 in Moscow, and Vsevolod Meyerhold's second production of *Columbine's Scarf* in St. Petersburg in 1916, to mention only three. The article, however, documents over twenty different performances of the ballet-pantomime, most in central Europe and one in the United States.

10. Souvenir Programme for "*Le Foire de Moscou,* spectacle présente en juillet 1923 par Théâtre Balagantchik," Dir. M. Korniloff, Théâtre Femina. Rondel Collection, Bibliothèque de l'Arsenal, Ro 9595. Many of the members of this company also appeared in a production called *Maria Kousnezoff et sa companie,* directed by Richard Boleslavsky. See *Comedia Illustré,* avril-mai 1922, Rondel Collection, Bibliothèque de l'Arsenal, Ro 12674.

11. Natalia Roslavleva, *The Era of the Russian Ballet* (London: Victor Gollancz, 1966), p. 159. Souritz, p. 118.

12. Copies of these documents were provided through the kindness of Professor Ronald A. Willis, who has in his possession the surviving documents from the American Laboratory Theatre. Unfortunately, the prompt book for this production, to which Oliver Sayler refers in his review for "The Play of the Week," *The Saturday Review of Literature,* 18 February 1928, p. 611, appears to have been lost. Prompt books at the American Laboratory Theatre usually had the literary text pasted on loose-leaf pages in a loose-leaf binder. The margins contained handwritten comments on the interpretation of the text, key phrases on character analysis, sketches of directions in movement, and other technical details. One such prompt book is still extant for a production of Eugéne Labiche's *The Straw Hat* (1926), directed by Maria Ouspenskaya, in which one finds her technical notes on the play. For example, she used the metaphor the "spine of the play" as a means to convey the basic theme of the play and the "spine of the characters" to identify the characters as types, through brief descriptions often with specific details.

Memorabilia of Maria Ouspenskaya, Box Number 7, Rare Book Collection, University Research Library, University of California Los Angeles, Los Angeles, California.

13. Richard S. Aldrich, "Letter to Mrs. Herbert K. Stockton," 6 January 1928. Richard Aldrich (1902-1986) had a long career in the theatre, was prominent in the development of summer theatre in America, and produced over thirty Broadway shows during his career. In 1940, he married Gertrude Lawrence and produced a successful revival of Shaw's *Pygmalion* for her. Tim Page, "Richard Aldrich, a Producer; Influenced Summer Theater," Obituary, *New York Times,* 16 April 1986.

14. Roberts, pp. 203-04.

15. From an untitled, signed statement by James Reynolds among the papers of the American Laboratory Theatre. For a brief résumé of his scene and costume designs, see Bobbi Owen, *Scenic Design on Broadway: Designers and Their Credits, 1915-1990* (Westport, Connecticut: Greenwood Press, 1991), pp. 151-152.

16. Aldrich, "Letter to Mrs. Herbert K. Stockton."

17. Reynolds' "Statement."

18. The following reviews were consulted: Anonymous, "American Laboratory Theatre Introduces Pantomime in America," *New York Times,* 27 January 1928, p. 15; Anonymous, *New York Herald Tribune,* 19 February 1928; Anonymous, *New York Telegram,* 27 January 1928, p. 8; Thomas Barrett, "American Laboratory," *The Billboard,* 4 February 1928, p. 10; Benjamin DeCasseres, "Broadway to Date," *Arts & Decoration,* February 1928, pp. 72, 115; Robert Littell, "Two on the Aisle," *New York Evening Post,* 13 February 1928 [Reprint]; Richard Lockridge, "Pantomime," *New York Sun,* 27 January 1928, p. 18; R. S. "The Theatre: A Directoire Tragedy," *Wall Street Journal,* 28 January 1928, p. 3; Oliver M. Sayler, "Play of the Week," *Saturday Review of Literature,* 18 February 1928, p. 611; Stark Young, "As the Weeks Pass," *The New Republic,* 22 February, 1928, pp. 18-19.

19. "The Great World Theatre," *Theatre Arts Monthly,* 12 (April 1928): 232-35.

20. Richard Lockridge's statement appears in *The Encyclopedia of the New York Stage, 1920-1930,* editor-in-chief Samuel L. Leiter, Volume I (Westport, Connecticut: Greenwood Press, 1985), p. 91.

21. The ability of audiences "to see without words," as *Theatre Arts* puts it, is something expected of dance or ballet audiences. For example, the glittering pyrotechnics of the Black Swan variations and grand pas in Act Three of *Swan Lake* can create emotional reaction in the viewers. Aristotle's affective reactions of the audience may obtain: fear that Prince Siegfried will indeed abandon Odette for Odile because of her dazzling pirouettes and thirty-two fouettés, and pity that Odette will not be delivered from Rothbart's curse. And all the audience has to do is "to see without words" or "to listen with their eyes."

22. Barrett, p. 10.

23. Young, p. 19.

24. Sayler, p. 611.

25. Young, p. 19. At the age of sixteen, Harold Hecht (1908-1985) began his theatrical career in 1924 as an assistant to Richard Boleslavsky at the American Laboratory Theatre. He later appeared as one of the Drushki (Bridesmen) in the American premiere of Igor Stravinsky's *Les Noces,* April 26, 1929, Metropolitan Opera House, under the choreography of Anderson-Ivantzova, spent several years as a dancer with the Martha Graham Company, and became a dance director with Busby Berkeley in New York and in Hollywood. In the 1940s and 1950s, he collaborated with Burt Lancaster to found the Hecht-Lancaster Productions, later augmented by James Hill, forming the Hecht-Hill-Lancaster Productions. Esther Fein, "Harold Hecht, Film Producer and a Burt Lancaster Partner," Obituary, *New York Times,* 28 May 1985, p. D 16.

26. Barrett, p. 10.

27. Littell, *New York Evening Post.*

28. Young, p. 19.

29. Barrett, p. 10.

30. Littell, *New York Evening Post.*

31. It was perhaps this comment by Robert Littell that Herbert Stockton, Chairman of the Board of Directors for the Lab Theatre, had in mind when in a letter to Maria Ouspenskaya he briefly alluded to *The Bridal Veil* as one of the models of the school's success. In a gentle admonishment, Stockton noticed that Mme Ouspenskaya had allowed certain actors (Blanche Tancock and George McCready), active individuals with an "avid reach for leading parts" and "political activities within the Theatre," to be cast in leading roles to the detriment of the professional reputation of the Lab Theatre. He went on to say that "I do not mean to argue in personalities but you will understand impersonally what I mean when I say that to my mind there is a greater promise for the Lab indicated in the human qualities plus the technique of such performances as [Donald] Hartman's and [Anne] Schmidt's in 'The Veil'. . . ." Letter from Herbert K. Stockton to Madame Maria Ouspenskaya, 8 April 1928, page 2. *Memorabilia of Maria Ouspenskaya,* Box Number 6, Rare Book Collection, University Research Library, University of California Los Angeles, Los Angeles, California.

32. On the critical reception of the Anderson-Ivantzova choreography for Stravinsky's *Les Noces,* see Lawrence Sullivan, "Les Noces: the American Premiere," *Dance Research Journal,* 14, 1 & 2 (1981-1982): 3-14.

DIE SCHWESTERN ODER CASANOVA IN SPA

CRITICAL COMMENTARY

Brigitte L. Schneider-Halvorson (essay date 1983)

SOURCE: Schneider-Halvorson, Brigitte L. "*Die Schwestern oder Casanova in Spa.*" In *The Late Dramatic Works of Arthur Schnitzler,* pp. 15-43. New York: Peter Lang, 1983.

[In the following excerpt, Schneider-Halvorson provides a plot overview and a critical analysis of Die Schwestern oder Casanova in Spa.]

BACKGROUND OF THE PLAY AND STATEMENT OF PURPOSE

The drama ***Die Schwestern oder Casanova in Spa***[1] was published in 1919 by S. Fischer Verlag and produced a year later with some success at the Burgtheater on March 26, 1920. It is one of the rare productions which the author designated as "Lustspiel." He seems to have reached here the ability to create such "wundervolle Heiterkeit" which was a necessary condition, "um das wahre Lustspiel hervorzubringen."[2] Schnitzler himself confesses his fondness for the work in a letter to Hofmannsthal: "[. . .] mir selbst ist selten was von mir so lieb gewesen."[3]

Whenever a date of completion is mentioned for a work by Schnitzler, it must be remembered that it is really only a "date." Most of his works took years to grow into their final form, and since he was usually engaged in several pieces of writing at the same time, it is generally possible to find specific links between the emotional content of a given piece and the course of his life at the time of its composition. *Casanovas Heimfahrt*[4] and ***Die Schwestern,*** for instance, date from roughly the same years. According to Reinhard Urbach, Schnitzler had his first inspiration on March 28, 1908, at which time the working title reads *Eifersucht.* It was conceived as a one-act play.[5] After Schnitzler's perusal of the Casanova Memoirs in 1914 he changed the title to *Spion,* and by summer of 1916 he had decided to mold the text into a three-act play which he now called *Die Wiederkehr.* Only after that year did the

play receive its present title. His prose writing ***Casanovas Heimfahrt*** progressed parallel with the play, and both works were finished by 1917.

A letter to Georg Brandes explains how he became interested in Casanova: "Meine beiden Casanova-Sachen, das Lustspiel 'Die Schwestern' und die Novelle 'Casanovas Heimfahrt' sind so entstanden, dass mir zwei Stoffe, die schon geraume Zeit unter meinen Papieren lagen durch die Lectüre [sic] der Casanova Memoiren plötzlich lebendig geworden sind."[6] Here is proof that Schnitzler chose to reconstitute faithfully a fragment of history because of his desire to illustrate a theme, and to study a psychological problem interesting to him.[7] These two productions stand outside Schnitzler's "popular" works and therefore are customarily neglected. Josef Körner, who in his study of Schnitzler's "Spätwerk", for example, does not hesitate to lay the comedy aside because it seems to him of "little importance,"[8] shows the Novelle not much more respect in his monograph of 1921.[9]

The purpose of this analysis is to demonstrate that this play has been underestimated until now and to prove that Schnitzler is better as a dramatist than critics have given him credit for. All major characters in the drama are interpreted in their relationships, problems and challenges. Recurring "Leitmotive" and "Leitgestalten" are discussed to show how they gain in complexity and depth, thus demonstrating a process of maturation and thereby a distinct positive development in Schnitzler's late dramatic works. "Ich empfand es als meinen Beruf," says the author in a letter to the Austrian historian Richard Charmatz, "Menschen zu gestalten und habe nichts zu beweisen, als die Vielfältigkeit der Welt. Eine Handlung so zu führen, dass jede an ihr beteiligte oder nur an sie anstreifende Figur ihr innerstes Wesen preisgeben genötigt wird, darin liegt am Ende das Geheimnis aller dramatischen Energie."[10] Indeed, the "Vielfältigkeit der Welt" is a key idea for a better appreciation of the author's late dramatic work. In it he depicts many life styles and also shows the consequences as a result of selecting one over the other; however, he neither condones nor condemns any of his characters for whatever choice they made, because each one represents an aspect of his soul.[11] "Every play is produced in the soul of the dramatist before it is staged in a theater," he tells George Sylvester Viereck in an interview, and continues: "A play is a conversation of the dramatist with himself. In portraying dramatic conflicts the dramatist wrestles with his soul."[12]

OUTLINE OF THE PLAY

All conditions are provided in the play to create a staging favorable to the unfolding of frivolous and joyous incidents. The scene is set in an elegant inn in the health resort town of Spa, on a lovely summer day. The characters are nearly all young, beautiful and charming. As age begins to touch them (a case in point is Herr von Gudar, who is over sixty) they make up for their lack of physical attraction by their polished manners and complacent philosophy of life. The less important characters are all "types" and include a nobleman, a rich widow from Amsterdam, eager to find a new husband, and a mother and daughter from Lyon, who are rivals in false prudery. They are all attracted by the preparations for an excursion into the countryside, preceded by a sumptuous outdoor banquet which is given by the false baron named Santis. He is eager to retrieve the cost of the dinner by inviting his guests to a gambling party afterwards. His wife Flaminia is young and sexy and just as scheming as her jealous husband, whom she deceives in order to further her own style of business. Then there is the famous dancer Teresa, who travels through Europe from one theater and lover to the next; and finally Tito, the hotel page, bold and hardworking in the duties of lover as well as servant. All, dominated by the legendary figure of Casanova, surround Andrea and Anina, the central couple, a wealthy young man of Ferrara and a young woman from the same city, with whom he has eloped and whom he counts on marrying very soon.

The play in its time sequence is limited to a few hours; it starts about mid-morning and ends before the feast has taken place. Act I of the comedy serves to disclose Anina's changed attitude toward the question of faithfulness. On the preceding night she received a visit from Casanova and yielded to his advances. Her confession provokes Andrea to outrage and, subsequently, a change of marriage plans at the moment when he discovers by chance conversation with his rival that Casanova, deceived by darkness and the location of their rooms. believed he was visiting Flaminia. Andrea, thus comforted, would be willing to pardon Anina, but she resents the motives which led to his change of mind. When Flaminia learns of Casanova's confusion of the previous night, she reasserts her rights over the man she considers as her conquest.

In Act II Andrea casts the existing quarrel into a fable. Santis and later Casanova himself are invited to bring a solution to the enigma that is posed. The question which justifies the entire play is this: "What does true fidelity consist of?" or, as Schnitzler formulated it: "Welcher Mann hat mehr Berechtigung, eifersüchtig zu sein: der, dem seine Frau gesteht, sie möchte gern einem anderen angehören, oder der, dessen Frau bewusstlos von einem anderen besessen ward?"[13]

In Act III all of the main characters—the two women, Santis, Andrea, Casanova—discern that what they took for a theoretical debate, the invention of a strict moralist, represents in fact a hurt which each one feels in his or her own vanity. The men conclude by drawing their swords to defend their injured honor at the cost of their lives. At this point, outside intervention is necessary to keep the tenor of the comedy. The dancer Teresa, introduced by Gudar, arrives on the scene just in time to restore peace among the rivals. She returns to Casanova with new plans for their future, thus reclaiming him for herself alone. This scene then brings reconciliation for all concerned, but only on the basis of an anti-social understanding of the term

"fidelity." All except Andrea go off to enjoy the pleasures of the outdoor dinner and thus drown their disappointments and heartaches in the excitement of the evening. Andrea is lost in thought; he learns from Casanova the moral from the standpoint of an adventurer, who considers Teresa the most faithful of all, for "sie kehrte mir zurück. Nur das ist Treue" (733).[14]

REVIEW OF CRITICISM

Ernst L. Offermanns is the only recent critic who analyzes the drama *Die Schwestern oder Casanova in Spa* in any detail.[15] Part of his title for the chapter reads: "Die erborgte Idylle des 'Lustspiels'" (110), referring to the designation which Schnitzler himself gave to the play. Offermanns recognizes the special position which this drama occupies within the context of the author's entire dramatic work. The carefully chosen term "erborgte Idylle" acknowleges the fact that Schnitzler's experience in writing a "Lustspiel" remained an isolated attempt to work with this genre, "dessen 'Spielheiterkeit' und Anmut nicht darüber hinwegtäuschen können, dass jenseits des Festes das Chaos und hinter der Göttermaske das Nicht-mehr-Menschliche lauern. Die nächste Komödie," Offermanns points out, "impliziert denn auch den Widerruf oder die Zurücknahme des 'Lustspiels'."[16] He refers to *Komödie der Verführung,* where the three women characters—Aurelie, Judith, and Seraphine—are not inclined to embrace each other. Max in his rather passive role as "Casanova" reports in the end for military service. "Die für eine Weile erborgte Idylle," concludes Offermanns, "musste zerbrechen."[17]

In theme as well as in terms of motives Offermanns considers this play a continuation of previous comedies, because the phenomenon of "impressionistischen Weltverhaltens" is associated with the Casanova-figure. To see this drama as a continuation of previous comedies is debatable, especially in light of the women characters who have gained in complexity, as this analysis will demonstrate. "Es wird auch, wie zuvor, eine Reihe von Konflikten vorgeführt," adds Offermanns, "die sich aus dem Gegensatz einer kontinuierlichen und einer auf den Augenblick gestellten Lebensform ergeben."[18] This polarity principle, however, received more attention in this play, as well as in subsequent dramatic works, than in earlier writings. The polar constellation of characters—Offermanns discusses in this respect Anina-Andrea, Anina-Flaminia, Casanova-Andrea—can be amplified by similar arrangements of incidents as well.

Klaus Kilian, on the other hand, does not examine any details of the play. His book, published in 1972 under the title *Die Komödien Arthur Schnitzlers. Sozialer Rollenzwang und kritische Ethik,* includes only a brief chapter devoted to "Schnitzlers 'erstes' Lustspiel."[19] His discussion focuses primarily on the adventurous role Casanova chooses to play which in his later years leads to complete isolation, rejection, and death. Kilian formulates the result of his considerations of the "role"-concept in modern sociology as well as of the range of meaning of the word "comedy"—as Schnitzler used it—in his central thesis as follows:

> "Komödien als Bauform"—und zwar im Drama wie in der Erzählung—entsteht bei Schnitzler immer dann, wenn "Komödie als Verhaltensweise des Menschen" thematisch und in entlarvender oder vermittelnder Tendenz problematisch und programmatisch für das soziale Verhalten des Menschen wird.[20]

Earlier than Offermanns, Kilian considers *Die Schwestern oder Casanova in Spa* "am Endpunkt einer geistigen Entwicklung," and states: "Im Rahmen der Komödienproblematik bietet dieses Werk nichts eigentlich Neues, das nicht latent schon in der Thematik früherer Dramen und Erzählungen angelegt gewesen wäre."[21] Kilian does not find an unequivocal and final answer to the question,

> ob Schnitzler hier tatsächlich zu einer echten Vermittlung der Ebenen von Realität und Rolle gelangte, oder ob diese Vermittlung nicht vielmehr erst durch die Aufgabe der Aktualität, eine resignierte Flucht in die Distanz der Historie, erkauft wurde [. . .].[22]

In line with the explanations Schnitzler provides for his diagram "Der Geist im Wort und der Geist in der Tat,"[23] Kilian points out the negative realm of the adventurer who is not bound by "social roles and comedies of society."[24]

Similarly, Friedbert Aspetsberger in his article "Drei Akte in einem" addresses himself to the "Formtyp von Schnitzlers Drama"[25] and concentrates on the character of Casanova. Because of the double title of the drama, he considers *Die Schwestern oder Casanova in Spa*

> eine Exempeldichtung; Träger des Geschehens ist hier die Casanova zugedachte Geisteshaltung, der Sinnzusammenhang ihr sich stets wiederholendes Handelnsschema, das 'Funktionieren,' mit dem er immer wieder die eigene Wahrheit ins Licht rückt.[26]

He points out correctly: "Die bedeutendste der Bedingungen für den reibungslosen Ablauf der 'Drei Akte in einem' ist der Verzicht auf die Zeit als Bestimmung des Lebens."[27] However, I disagree with his conviction that Anina and Andrea serve merely as background for the unfoldment of Casanova. As the analysis will show, the lack of development within Casanova is caused by his self-imposed isolation from society, whereas Anina and Andrea emerge as more mature human beings by the end of the drama.

Mme Derré by virtue of her all-inclusive study of Schnitzler's works provides excellent explanations for the 18th-century atmosphere chosen for the play.[28] Her outline of the play contains some commentary on nearly all characters, with most of her attention directed toward Casanova.[29]

Richard Alewyn in his article "Casanova"[30] provides the most detailed background information with regard to the historical figure of Casanova. He portrays him not only as adventurer and eroticist, but also as "Renaissancemensch" because of the diversity of his talents and interests.[31] Alewyn concludes with a valuable discussion of the Baroque and Rococo heritage which is evidenced in *Die Schwestern oder Casanova in Spa.*

Several scholarly studies recently published include a discussion of this drama with an emphasis on the women characters. They are important for the present study, because in his late dramatic works Schnitzler provides for more complexity of his women portrayals, no longer presenting them as mere types. Among these doctoral dissertations which deal specifically with women in Schnitzler's works, is the most recent thesis, submitted to the University of Wisconsin in 1973 by Willa Elizabeth Schmidt. It carries the title "The Changing Role of Women in the Works of Arthur Schnitzler," correcting some areas of neglect by scholars in their research and criticism. She points out that

> the most significant deficiency [. . .] is a unanimous failure to take into account the development which occurred in Schnitzler's attitude as he matured as a human being and as an artist. He has generally been judged, especially where his female figures are concerned, on the basis of his early writings, although even these are often seen in too superficial a light.[32]

She goes on to criticize "observers such as Boner, Derré, Rey and Körner, who are aware that the later works are different" and yet "do not offer detailed evidence of the effects of the change [. . .] but rather tend to persist in their original assessment of the women as all belonging to one or several static types."[33]

Schmidt's last chapter, entitled "Woman in Her Own Right," is still concerned with earlier types such as wives, fiancées and mistresses, but in the late dramatic works these characters have for better or for worse changed their roles, becoming more comprehensive, differentiated individual expressions of being. This chapter includes a brief discussion of the female characters analyzed in my study.[34] Schmidt "detects in the author an increasing tendency toward reflection and character analysis" in his late dramatic works which she finds "apparently better served by the prose medium, where he had time to study and dwell on psychological detail."[35] This leads her to agree with William H. Rey "that in the final period of his writing Schnitzler's narrative works are superior in quality to the dramas."[36] I disagree with this notion on the grounds that Schmidt herself overlooks some of the complexities encountered in Schnitzler's late dramatic production.

Another dissertation, submitted in 1949 at the University of Vienna by Susanne M. Polsterer, is entitled "Die Darstellung der Frau in Arthur Schnitzlers Dramen." Although the title indicates only a study of the dramatic works, the prose writings seem to receive as much attention as the dramas. She depicts Schnitzler as a threat to Austria and Austrian womanhood, accusing him of fabricating women characters in his mind in order to work off his own psychological problems: "Keinesfalls können diese Frauen als typische Wienerinnen aufgefasst werden."[37] She recommends Schnitzler's type of writing only for mature and stable people, and sees the work less fit for youth and for foreigners, because "die Jugendlichen müssen zu unrichtigen Vorstellungen über die Geschlechtsbeziehungen gelangen und die Ausländer zu unrichtigen Vorstellungen über die Österreicher."[38] Her work, therefore, appears to be an attempt to protect the national image of Austria in general and its charming Viennese women in particular rather than to recognize the reasons behind Schnitzler's concerns. As I see Schnitzler, his concern was a search for truth which he pursued with total honesty not only toward himself but also toward facing the prevailing conditions in his country. Such an endeavor most certainly attracts enemies, and Schnitzler, indeed, had plenty of experiences during his lifetime in this respect. Numerous articles have been written on behalf of Schnitzler to correct deliberate and inadvertently damaging criticism. Among those authors are Heinrich Schnitzler, Robert A. Kann, and Rena R. Schlein, to name a few.[39] One finds the slightness of such a study as Polsterer's even more striking when one looks at her interpretation of statistics compiled in an effort to justify her own moral and ethical prejudices. I concur with Schmidt's conclusion which states: "[. . .] her [Polsterer's] study cannot be taken seriously. It is a prime example of poor scholarship [. . .]."[40]

A third dissertation, submitted in 1930 by Georgette Boner at the University of Basel, entitled *Arthur Schnitzlers Frauengestalten* is mentioned here mainly for its significance in reflecting a welcome change in critical attitudes toward Schnitzler's women characters.[41] Her goal is, "das Besondere von Schnitzlers Frauengestalten im Gegensatz zu seinen Männerfiguren hervorzuheben."[42] A priori, she assumes, "dass Schnitzler durch die Frauen seiner gedichteten Welt ein positives Element beizufügen trachtet."[43] Although the author states at the beginning of her work that she will address herself mainly to the dramatic works, "[. . .] weil in diesen die Konflikte meistens akuter, die Entscheide dringender sind als in den epischen Werken [. . .],"[44] she seems to cite for her discussion almost as many examples from the narrative works as from the plays. A chapter entitled "Schwestern" discusses the polarity of negative and positive members within the male and female categories, which is based on Schnitzler's theoretical essay "Der Geist im Wort und der Geist in der Tat" (1927).[45] It also includes a discussion of the play *Die Schwestern*. Although Boner develops some excellent insights into Schnitzler's treatment of women in his works, she fails to see in his later dramatic production any changes in the nature of these women who, in their quest for emancipation, exert personal freedom and choice in such matters as love and marriage. Furthermore, she overlooks the complexity which the author realizes for his female characters in the later works.[46]

ANALYSIS OF THE DRAMA

The title: The first part of the title *Die Schwestern* [. . .] places the emphasis upon the three female characters in the play: Anina, Flaminia, and Teresa. They are, however, not related to each other by family ties, nor do they share other common interests on the basis of education, life style, personality traits, or family background. What allows them, nevertheless, to move into such a close relationship is revealed in the second part of the title [. . .] *oder Casanova in Spa.*[47] Casanova is the character who combines all three acts into one because through him the three women become "sisters of fate." He is the sophisticated adventurer, placed in the setting of the Rococo period around the middle of the 18th century, whose travels on a lovely summer day lead him to Spa, a plush health resort city in Belgium, at precisely the right time for another round of passionate relationships.[48] He encounters these three women who are united solely by their common ability to give themselves completely to a moment of pure sensuality. They are light-hearted, carefree people, as are most other characters in the play, without too much thought spent on the consequences of their moments of passion.

The Rococo theme: These characters help in bringing alive the Rococo period of the 18th century—Johannes Jahn calls it the end phase of the Baroque tradition—[49] which is characterized by fanciful, frivolous and light-hearted modes. Even though the psychological problem in this play was perhaps most interesting to the author, he carried the Rococo theme through the entire play. Because the style of literature in the first half of the 18th century was typified by light-hearted, playful lyric pieces, often with erotic hints, this comedy is written in verse. The tone of the play, as Mme Derré points out, "is livelier, the rhythm often breathless, the phrasing broken up by exclamation points and marks of hesitation; the vocabulary and syntax are adapted to the violent and perverse 18th century."[50]

The setting, with its alcove to the right of the stage, further emphasizes this period. Preparations for the evening dinner are made in the garden and not in the banquet hall of a Baroque palace. Most important, however, are the characters in the play, each of whom contributes to the Rococo atmosphere already prevailing. As Richard Alewyn points out:

> Das Rokoko ist der Erbe des Barock [. . .]. Man lebt hastiger und gieriger [. . .] man misst auch das eigene Leben nicht mehr nach den Massen der Stände oder der Geschlechter, die man repräsentiert, sondern man lebt sein persönliches Leben, das mit dem Tod unweigerlich ein Ende hat, ja schon vor dem Tod mit dem Alter. Man hat keine Zeit zu verlieren und will sich des Augenblicks bemächtigen, ehe er zerrinnt.[51]

In Act I, Herr von Gudar, a retired Dutch officer in his sixties, leads this kind of life. In his conversation with Anina he points out that aging people do not sleep: "Uns Greisen frommt kein Schlaf. Zu töricht wär' es, / Dem Wucherer Tod, der bald des Daseins Schuld / Im ganzen holt, allnächtlich Vorschuss zahlen" (652). He does not find Anina very receptive to his "Lebensweisheit"; as a result of her youth, she is only seventeen, she connects the key words "Schuld" and "Vorschuss zahlen" with gambling. This leads her to believe that Gudar might have lost the game last night to Andrea, her fiancé, who returned with many gold pieces. But Gudar does not care whether he wins or loses, for to him gambling is fate, which he battles every time anew (653). To satisfy Anina's curiosity, he tells her that not he but Herr Casanova lost, thus introducing Casanova to the audience early in the play.

Twice more, to nourish his inspiration, Schnitzler had recourse to an actual personage of petty history, Casanova, attributing invented circumstances to the exploits of the celebrated seducer whom he used in this drama as well as in his Novelle. Thus, Schnitzler continues his treatment of the adventurer, a "Leitgestalt" appearing throughout his work from Anatol to Casanova. In his late work, however, he has reworked the adventurer figure to a greater complexity.[52]

Polarity: With the introduction of Casanova through Gudar, a polarity between age and youth is provided. Although polarity and inner tension are basic forms of all Baroque thought, of Baroque world experience and art expression,[53] Schnitzler carries them over into this play with its Rococo setting as well. This polarity principle appears to be the key to an overall understanding of the message which the poet conveys to us through his entire work. It relates such seeming opposites as youth and age, truth and falsity, dream and reality, gaiety and solitude, love and hate, reason and emotion, skepticism and belief, tragedy and comedy, life and death, fate and chance as equally justified components. Schnitzler says about fate and chance: "In logischem Sinne sind also Schicksal und Zufall niemals Gegensätze, sondern durchaus das Gleiche und um so unwidersprechlicher identisch, von je höherem Standpunkt aus wir ein Ereignis betrachten."[54]

This explains in part why Gudar looks upon his gambling activity not in terms of chance but of fate. The world around him may see in gambling nothing but chance; for Gudar, however, it is an important part of his life style. It provides him with pleasant memories of younger years, whether he thinks of his courage in combat or of his amorous adventures in Casanova-style. Gudar has been acquainted with Casanova for more than ten years, long before he "unter dem berühmten Bleidach / Freigeisterei und leicht're Sünden büsste [. . .]" (654). He knows him as part of himself and therefore does not seem to be worried about Casanova's credibility as an honest debtor, but Anina certainly doubts that Casanova can be considered a man of honor (654). Nevertheless, later she calls him a "nobleman." Now it is Gudar's opportunity to correct the picture in her mind, by saying that Casanova is a nobleman "wie Santis ein Baron, wie ich ein Fürst, / Und wie Flaminia etwa Nonne wäre—" (655).

Another aspect of polarity, that of "Schein" and "Wirklichkeit,"—comes into play at this point, and involves each character. Gudar, as was seen, speaks not only for himself but also for Casanova, Santis, and Flaminia, when he describes the false roles each one of them is playing. Even Anina is not free of falsity. She pretends that she has only

heard of Casanova's name; yet the audience sees her write a letter which she has the page boy Tito deliver to Casanova (657). Later on, in the scene with Andrea, she confesses to him her intimate relationship with Casanova the night before, which has changed her concept of faithfulness.

Although Gudar appears only twice on stage, at the beginning of the first and toward the end of the third act, the author has given him the major task of casting the proper light upon nearly all of the main characters, not only in negative, but also in positive ways as in the case of Andrea. When Gudar finds out from Anina that Andrea is not her husband—though twice before she did not correct him regarding her relationship—(653) Gudar pictures him as a respectable "Bürger" who will no doubt settle down to marriage. Later in the play, Casanova has the same opinion about Andrea. He sees himself bring "Ehrbiet'gen Gruss dem edlen Paare" for Andrea's goal "heisst Frieden, Ordnung und Gesetz / Wie Heimkehr Ihrer Wand'rung letzter Sinn" (681). As Gudar describes Casanova to Anina in his various roles as "Exzellenz," "Dieb," "Handelsmann," "Dichter," "Polizeiagent," "Millionär," "Bettler," "Bürger," "Falschspieler," "Lügner," "Gauner," "Ehrenmann," "Frauenheld" (656), he speaks actually of himself just as Casanova later discusses Gudar's life only to reveal the various stations in his own life (681). Thus, Schnitzler expands his polarity concept of age and youth to include a relationship between the two characters on the social as well as the intellectual level.

> Ein Gewinn ohne Risiko erscheint ihm schlechterdings als unmoralisch. Er ist eine Spielnatur, jederzeit bereit, alles auf eine Karte zu setzen, und jederzeit gefasst, seinen ganzen Einsatz zu verlieren. Das Risiko ist es überhaupt erst, was dem Gewinn seinen Wert verleiht.[55]

Even though Casanova had spent his money, he continued his game on borrowed gold from Gudar. But he does not want to stay long indebted to Gudar. In order to return the money to his friend who is not a rich man, according to Casanova (679), we see him appear before Andrea to whom he had lost the night before, offering him an unsecured thirty-day promissory note. Among "men of honor," he considers his signature enough of a guarantee for return of the money. He reasons that Andrea is rich and, in addition, had won so much the night before. Besides, Casanova might return the money sooner, for he plans to travel with Gudar when he leaves town and hopes to win the money back at that time: "Ein Spielchen—auf der Fahrt, im ersten Posthaus;— / Und lächelt mir das Glück wie gestern ihm— / Und die Wahrscheinlichkeit spricht sehr dafür—, / So hab' vor Abend ich mein Gold zurück" (680). So we see Casanova scheming and manipulating, always taking advantage of the opportune moment, thus living up to the description Gudar gave of him earlier.

However, the real specialty for which Casanova is noted in European history is of course his adventurous love life: "Er sucht weder den Kauf noch den Raub, sondern das Geschenk," observes Alewyn and explains:

Zu diesem Zweck gab es nur einen Weg: die Verführung, eine Kunst und ein Spiel, dem das Rokoko
verfallen war und dem es in Bildern und Büchern ge-
huldigt hat wie kein zweites Zeitalter, von dem wir
wissen. Ohne die Herstellung des seligen Einverneh-
mens, ohne die völlige Verschmelzung der Wünsche
mit denen der Geliebten gibt es für Casanova keine
Liebe.[56]

Andrea's suspicion that Casanova may have gained
entrance to their bedroom and to Anina by force (672-673)
is not confirmed, because Anina was at the open window
expecting Andrea after a long night of waiting, and instead
attracted Casanova, as she tells him:

> Er war's. Und eh' die Lippen mir
> Zu einem Schrei sich auftun, hat er über
> Die Brüstung ins Gemach sich frech geschwungen,
> Ist mir so nah, dass über meine Lider
> Sein Atem weht, dass seiner Pulse Beben
> Den meinen sich gesellt;—in seinem Hauch—
> Der kühl und heiss zugleich—kein Kuss, viel eher
> Ein Flüstern ohne Wort, ein Fleh'n, ein Bann—
> Doch endlich, ach, von meinem Mund ersehnt,
> Zum Kusse wird—löst all mein Sein sich auf,
> Und auf den Traumeswellen dieser Stunde,
> Vergangner nicht, zukünft'ger nicht bewusst,
> Treibt es, wie von sich selbst befreit, dahin.
>
> (673)

This moment in time, "der Augenblick," turns to an
interval outside of time without effect or fear of consequences. Life was for the moment discontinued for Anina
in favor of a dreamlike state of being, from which she
awakens

> So reulos wie aus Kinderschlaf erwacht?!
> Unfassbar gestern noch—und heut erlebt?!
> Und fühle mich die gleiche, die ich war,
> So unverwandelt und so unverwirrt
> Und deiner Zärtlichkeit so wert. . . .
>
> (674)

Casanova, after shocking Anina mildly at first, thus
achieves total harmony with her. He surrenders to her, and
his devotion for the moment in time is reciprocated by
Anina and remains lovingly in her memory: "In der Tat
übertrifft Casanova alle seine Vorgänger in Schnitzler's
Werk durch den Reichtum seiner Natur," comments William Rey.

> Er trägt, wie sie, impressionistische Züge, da ja sein
> Leben aus einer scheinbar endlosen Folge erotischer
> Episoden besteht. Aber es wäre doch falsch, ihn deswe-
> gen als einen flachen Genüssling zu bezeichnen. Im
> Grunde sucht er nicht so sehr das eigene Glück, als
> vielmehr die Beglückung seiner Liebespartnerinnen.[57]

The adventurer, then, is a frequent character in Schnitzler's work and is present not only in *Die Schwestern,* but
also in other parts of the late dramatic works, where he
belongs to nobody and nobody belongs to him. In his diagramm accompanying the essay, "Der Geist im Wort und

der Geist in der Tat" (1927), Schnitzler himself relegates
the figure of the adventurer to the lower triangle, thus
indicating that the adventurer as a state of mind
("Geistesverfassung") belongs to the negative type. Schnitzler comments: "Das Verhältnis der negativen zu den posi-
tiven Typen im Diagramm 'Der Geist in der Tat' entspricht
völlig den Verhältnissen im Diagramm 'Der Geist im
Wort'."[58] In Casanova, the author created one of those
significant personalities which, according to him, can also
exist in the negative realm of the lower triangle; really
great human beings, however, only occur in the positive
area (*AuB,* 141). The author admits: "Erregend, belebend,
öfter freilich noch beunruhigend, nicht nur durch seine
Leistungen, sondern schon durch sein Dasein, wirkt
manchmal der Repräsentant des negativen Typus in
höherem Masse als der positive; wahrhaft fördernd nur
dieser" (*AuB,* 141).

This description fits Casanova, for he evokes excitement
wherever he is present, but his philosophy is based on
anti-social premises. In his desire for unlimited freedom,
he shies away from any responsibility or commitment.
Schnitzler remarks in his *Buch der Sprüche und Bedenken:*
"Das muss schon ein Mensch von hoher Art sein, dem die
Sehnsucht nach Freiheit etwas Anderes [sic] bedeutete als
die Begier nach Verantwortungslosigkeit."[59] By the author's
own definition Casanova does not rank with a "hoher
Mann." He lives only one day at a time:

> Der negative Typus lebt ohne das Gefühl von Zusam-
> menhängen; das Gestern ist tot für ihn, das Morgen un-
> vorstellbar, nur im Raum vermag er sich auszubreiten,
> er hat im wahren Sinn des Wortes 'keine Zeit'; daher
> seine Ungeduld, seine Unruhe und seine Unbedenklich-
> keit in der Wahl seiner Mittel.
>
> (*AuB,* 142)

The adventurer, therefore, follows an impressionistic life
style.[60] He knows only the present, which consists for him
of a sequence of isolated moments. Schnitzler deplores
this kind of life, for "Wer aber nur die Gegenwart hat, der
hat nur den Augenblick, somit eigentlich nichts" (*AuB,*
149).[61]

This restlessness which Casanova demonstrates by his
quick change of travel plans, for instance, is a hopeless
flight from his nothingness. To be sure, he is the "life of
the party" wherever he goes; everybody remembers him
and yet one may never penetrate the wall that is built
around him, may never know anything beyond that which
Casanova is willing to share. He is sociable but isolated,
as the author defines the negative type (*AuB,* 142).
Casanova only seems to stand in the stream of life; in
reality he is rather distant from it. Gudar, Casanova's polarity, has even less to look forward to. The cardgame appears to be the only pleasure at his age, a means to fight,
even though fate seems the only battle left for him, an old
retired officer.

In his conversation with Anina, Gudar does not reveal
much personal detail about Casanova beyond his amorous
proclivity, which was already common knowledge in

European resorts. Anina is eager to find out more; her encounter with Flaminia adds much to complete her picture of Casanova. Flaminia does not believe his story of escape from Venice, and therefore calls him a "liar"; his gambling habits are those of a "fraud"; his "age" makes him less desirable to women—just three days ago the famous dancer Teresa "walzed away from him"; and finally, with her last breath of disappointment and jealousy perhaps, Flaminia labels him "Trauerweide," "Schatten," "Narr," "Geck" (661, 666).

Anina, the polar opposite to Flaminia, does not seem to believe much of her talk; in fact, Anina realizes that Flaminia was driven to Anina's room by curiosity. Flaminia sees in Anina her younger sister in "trade" as well as personality, even the innkeeper considered them to be sisters (662). She is eager to share with Anina her own experiences and "tricks of the trade." We find Flaminia identifying so much with Anina that she ignores completely the latter's feelings and her efforts to set the record straight regarding her own reputation as well as the integrity of Andrea.

FLAMINIA:

Wie lange schon reisen Sie mit ihm umher?

ANINA:

Drei Wochen,—*rasch* und wir werden uns vermählen.

(662)

Much to Anina's dismay, she hears Flaminia speak of "providence" that the four had to share a carriage before they reached the town of Spa, and Santis, we hear from Flaminia, was already calculating:

Wenn zwei Paare sich
Wie ich und du, und Bassi mit der Seinen
Zu Arbeit und Vergnügen klug gesellten—
Zum grössten Vorteil schlüg's uns allen aus.
Denn dieser Bassi—Santis' Worte sind's—
Als meinen Meister muss ich ihn erkennen.

(662)

Anina has not been able to stop Flaminia's double-mindedness, for neither did Andrea ever gamble before, nor is he a "Meister"—"in anderen Dingen" (663). She takes every possible opportunity to let Flaminia know that they have nothing in common, that their lives and affairs are miles apart. Her explanation as to why they eloped is cut short by Flaminia's answer:

So fängt es eben an. Aus Flucht wird Reise,
Aus notgedrungener Reise heitere Fahrt,
Leicht wird der Sinn, und in der Fremde lernt sich,
Was uns der Heimat Enge vorenthielt,
Meist nur allmählich,—manchmal über Nacht.

(663)

Flaminia even tells Anina how funny it is when she and Santis share their adventurous love affairs, "Denn, ach, die Welt ist dumm. / Zumal die Männer—" (663).

Flaminia seems to consider herself rather superior, and yet her "intelligence" is nothing more than natural calculation and cunning. She has attached herself to Santis who is nearly twice her age, mainly for reasons of social advantage, security, and protection—as a matter of convenience. When Santis had won heavily in his gambling activities, she seized upon the opportunity of acquiring a precious string of pearls. Now she assumes that Anina likewise is receiving pearls this morning from Andrea which, as she conjectures, must be the reason for his absence. Since this is not the case, she immediately judges him to be stingy (661). However, it is Anina who emerges as the intelligent woman from this dialog with Flaminia. With wit and humor she is able to counteract every one of Flaminia's exaggerated stories, whether they depict Casanova, Teresa, and Santis, or attempt to fasten upon Andrea's reputation. She easily sees through all façades and has already proven herself in this respect during her conversation with Gudar. She shows it again with Santis, who at this point enters the scene, boasting about the supper he will give in honor of twelve important wealthy people, while at the same time discrediting Andrea in the eyes of Anina as he blames him for wearing the mask of a philosopher (665-66). It is interesting to note that Flaminia used the same term earlier in the play (661). Thus, she and Santis display the same mentality in their thinking and reactions. They establish a polarity to Andrea and Anina.

In Act II, Anina continues to control her relationship with Flaminia by means of humor, but now it is used as a weapon of defense in her own behalf. She no longer protects Andrea and his reputation by the kind of love, concern and respect we saw her employ before. Her argument with Andrea over the night she spent with Casanova and the ensuing changes in Andrea after his conference with Casanova have left her with heartache and disappointment. She is ready to break her relationship and leave him without delay. This provides a humorous incident when Andrea opens the door to part with Anina just at the moment that Flaminia has come to the door inviting them to the table for the festive evening meal (695-96). She seems to be familiar with marital quarreling, which she calls "Liebeszank." Probably her own experience of having been beaten by the husband is recalled, as she projects it into this situation. Her advice to Anina is simple: "Man hat gezankt— / Man söhnt sich wieder aus. So ist's der Brauch" (696). Two more reasons for reconciliation are of a practical nature to her: a thunderstorm may break out at any moment and, furthermore, as no carriages are available in Spa this afternoon, walking in such weather is not the thing to do (696).

As soon as the spotlight falls on Flaminia and her disappointing "night in waiting for Casanova," and Andrea creates suspense in releasing the real reason for Anina's sudden departure, the "older sister" is no longer interested in repairing discrepancies and disharmonies between Andrea and Anina. She turns instead in self-pity to her own misery, throwing insults at them at every opportunity. Her dramatization develops along the lines of polarity:

Ins Leere durstig breitet sich mein Arm—
Indessen schlingt der ihre sich um ihn?!—
Die Nachtluft trink' ich, seine Küsse die—

(697)

Flaminia's eyes are red from crying, staring sleepless into the gray dawn; Anina's are slumbering blissfully, dreaming happily into the sweet morning. Another polarity with a double twist refers to their bedrooms. Flaminia is waiting passionately in her "chaste" bedside, whereas Anina knows how to lure Casanova into her "voluptuous" bed (697-98). Apparently, Flaminia regards herself as virginal before each new sexual encounter but considers a rival as innately wanton if the same man is the object of desire.

The insults increase in intensity as she questions Anina's origin and relegates her to a "Mädchenkammer, Freudenhaus" (698), where Andrea must have bought her from a procuress. Flaminia considers herself a good-natured fool to have given them a ride in her husband's carriage to Spa, treating Anina as a "girl friend and sister" in the face of this deception. Her earlier arrogance about "die Welt ist dumm—zumal die Männer" is taking its toll on Flaminia because now "die Welt is dumm—zumal die Frauen" fits Flaminia's situation much better in more than one way. When one compares the two women in their distress, Anina behaves in a more dignified manner, whereas Flaminia shows a rather vulgar personality. Another polarity occurs with regard to the women's intentions. At the beginning of the encounter it was Anina who was rushing after Casanova, according to Andrea; now, it is Flaminia who discloses her desire to forgo the dinner gladly and "fly after Casanova" (699).

Clearly, it is Flaminia who has lost her temper in this mutual rivalry, which has the opposite effect upon Anina. She perceives keenly in Flaminia a reflection of her own fate, and this helps her to gain distance. She is able to adopt an attitude of humorous observation which turns Flaminia to greater outrage, hatred, and bitterness. The stage directions read: "Anina hat zuerst starr, dann immer gelöster und heiterer den Worten der Flaminia gelauscht. Der Ausdruck ihres Antlitzes zeigt, dass sie den Humor der Sachlage zu erfassen beginnt und immer bereiter wird, sich ihm selbst anzupassen" (699). In Anina's reply to Flaminia she repeats the same words of advice given to her earlier about the stormy weather and the shortage of carriages. Flaminia finally resorts to cunning in hopes of winning out over Anina, who insists just as stubbornly now on her right to Casanova as does Flaminia. The dispute in its polar situation becomes a serious psychological problem for both:

FLAMINIA:

Was kommt dich Böse an,
Dass du mir nehmen willst, mir vorenthalten,
Was Rechtens mein?! Du Unersättliche!—
Dass du, sei's nun durch Zufall oder Lust,
Doch unverdient gewiss, die Seine warst,
Ist das nicht Glücks genug? Willst du noch mehr?

ANINA:

Ich war die Seine nicht.

FLAMINIA:

Wer denn als du?

ANINA:

Viel eher du.

FLAMINIA:

Für ihn, doch nicht für mich.

ANINA:

Er weiss nicht, dass ich's war, so war ich's nicht.

FLAMINIA:

Ich war's nicht, denn ich weiss, dass ich's nicht war.

ANINA:

So hätten beide wir ein Recht an ihn.

(701)

Both women suffer in their vanity because only a portion of their love has been fulfilled. Anina is longing for Casanova's individual affection, since he only desired her because he thought she was Flaminia; and the latter is longing for the physical consummation of love with Casanova which he gave to Anina. The inner disturbance and disappointment present in both women finds opposite relief. Rage and anger in Flaminia intensify to an open attack against Anina: "Und da die finst're Nacht dir hold gesinnt, / Sei ewig sie um dich. Mit dieser Nadel—" (703). The attempt of blinding Anina with the hairpin fails, but it shows clearly the pinnacle of Flaminia's jealousy, grudging her any daytime encounter with Casanova, just as Anina is too jealous to allow Flaminia a night with Casanova. This day and night polarity finds also a parallel in the behavior of both women. Anina, although she is just as insistent and stubborn as Flaminia, handles the entire encounter from beginning to end with humor, even though the humor is aimed at Flaminia as a challenge. Flaminia, on the other hand, is unable to recognize this maneuver which places her out of control entirely; her only responses are insults.

However, at the moment of greatest danger, Andrea comes to the rescue of Anina by stepping between the women and taking each by the hand. Forgetting his own trouble for the time being, he assumes the role of mediator and tries to handle with reason and objectivity a situation which cannot be resolved in the presence of flaring emotions. He objectifies the happenings by lifting them out of the highly charged personal realm and dressing them in a parable about two sisters, one of whom is to be married soon but finds herself in the arms of her sister's lover before her own wedding has yet taken place. With the consent of Flaminia and Anina, the controversial question from the parable is to be answered by Santis who, "etwas betrunken, noch in der Tür" (703), is urging Flaminia to get ready for the celebration. It is ironic that Santis is considered qualified for the job of arbiter on the supposition that he is facing this question "unverwirrten Sinns" (709). But Santis, by reason of his intelligence and, mainly his physical condition, is unable to tell the end of the story. He suggests instead that Casanova fulfill the task because

> . . . was Erfahrung anbetrifft, so findet
> Zu so verzwickter Rätsel Lösung sich
> Wohl mancher, der in Liebeslanden weiter
> Als ich gereist und mehr sich umgetan.
>
> (709)

Nevertheless, Andrea handled this situation with more elegance than he had managed his own quarrel with Anina. This time he succeeded in lifting the circumstances from the sphere of mere passion into the proposition of a mathematical problem (718), and even succeeded in having both women agree with his story in their identification as "sisters" (705), a phrase which translates more accurately into "sisters of fate." Thus, Andrea in his role as mediator finds his polar counterpart in Casanova.

The name "Casanova," and Santis' assurance that he is safely back in town as an invited guest to the evening dinner, has an electrifying effect upon Anina and Flaminia. At the end of Act II, they seem to have forgotten their quarrel and are now impatiently waiting for him.

FLAMINIA:

> Wo bleibt er denn?

ANINA:

> Warum lässt er uns warten?
>
> [. . .]

FLAMINIA:

> Er ist es!
>
> [. . .]

ANINA:

> Er! *Anina und Flaminia öffnen das Fenster.*
>
> (712-13)

But why had Casanova left town in the first place? Returning to the first Act, we find Andrea and Anina in an argument over a letter to Casanova. Andrea knows that Anina wrote this letter, but he is even more humiliated that she employed Tito, the lad of the inn, to deliver it. Andrea's reproach grows stronger with every new idea he expresses. He suspects that Anina in her vanity has inquired more in detail about the lace from Brussels which Casanova had promised to buy from a friend at more favorable prices. Andrea had overheard the conversation between them the night before. Anina could have left Andrea in his belief,

but faithful to her promise "Du weisst, dass ich nicht lügen will, noch kann" (668), she tells him the truth: her letter contained a request "Dass er noch in dieser Stunde / Die Stadt verlasse" (669). This knowledge creates even more anxiety within Andrea, because his pride and vanity are hurt. "[. . .] ihm verfallen—? Und ich bin nichts [. . .]?" (669). He continues with ideas very close to Schnitzler's own heart.

> [. . .] Als wäre Sehnsucht nicht
> Um Tausendfaches schlimmer als Erfüllung,
> Weil sie fortwühlend in der Seele Gründen
> Den reinen Lauf ihr bis zur Quelle trübt—!
>
> (670).

Andrea gives here the answer to a problem which Schnitzler pondered in his aphorisms:

> Ist der berechtigter zur Eifersucht, dessen Frau früher einen Geliebten hatte, mit dem sie nun völlig fertig ist, oder einer, dessen Frau als Mädchen geliebt hat, ohne den Geliebten zu besitzen, so dass sie noch immer voll Begehrens ist?[62]

Since Andrea senses in Anina a longing for Casanova, not realizing as yet that she has been fulfilled, he has an impulse to leave the place immediately, thus breaking his relationship with Anina. He considers her confession a joke, and is disappointed that she would become so friendly with those adventurous people as to follow through with a type of trick that must have been suggested to her. The fact that she really had spent the night with Casanova and has demanded his departure in return does not register with Andrea at this point. However, he at least recognizes that neither Anina nor he himself fits into this kind of company. He also regrets the gambling activity he engaged in the night before, because he realizes the risk in leaving Anina alone for so many hours. This town, as he sees it, is a potential danger and a source of confusion for them; so he is ready to leave together with Anina at the same hour. This presents a comic situation for the audience, because all negatives have already befallen the couple and they will, in fact, sharpen in focus as the scene goes on into the next act.

Anina's statement "Ob wir uns trennen müssen, steht bei dir" (672) places the proof of true love and continued trust upon Andrea. The thought of searching her own conscience does not enter her mind at all. She explains that all came about because she felt neglected by Andrea, longing and waiting all night for him. She considers her experience with Casanova an involuntary dream state which has passed as quickly as it came upon her, never to return again and not having any consequences "weil nichts geschah" (674). But Andrea needs to go full circle before he is able to gain a similar conviction.

The thought "Weil nichts geschah" would never mean anything to the opposite couple, Santis and Flaminia. They are set up in the play as polarities to Andrea and Anina. We have already heard Flaminia's motives for marrying

Santis, who himself is not necessarily a faithful husband. His main purpose in life is to attract money by whatever means available. He speaks about this freely with Flaminia; indeed, she helps him in her own way to reach this goal. Whenever they spend time together, they seem to speak freely about their individual activities, looking upon the world and mankind as an open field to play their cunning game. Andrea and Anina, on the other hand, come from an honest and sincere background; they find themselves temporarily out of place in this company and this resort town.

Andrea regrets his weak moment in accepting a place at the gambling table. However, he does not make any allowance, nor shoulder part of the blame, for what happened to Anina during his absence. He is unable to grasp that moment in time which Anina spent with Casanova as a discovery of her own identity. Neither does he comprehend that in her confession she is releasing the secret of that moment and thereby relegating it to her past.[63] No real communication has taken place between the two of them because they cannot see beyond the circle of their personal involvement; thus no understanding is reached.

At present Andrea sees only a prostitute in Anina and considers the money he won from Casanova as ransom which Casanova paid to gain her favors; therefore, he wants to dispose of this "Teufelsgold," as he calls it, by giving it to Anina as whore money:

> Hier ist das Teufelsgold, du wirst es brauchen—
> Fürs erste jedenfalls, bis von Flaminia
> Das weit're du gelernt.
>
> (675)

As Martin Swales points out:

> The prostitute is often seen as the female counterpart of the adventurer in that she surrenders over and over again to erotic experience, but without ever being totally committed to the actuality of each relationship.[64]

Therefore, Flaminia and Teresa fall into this category, for they really are attached to their "counterpart of the adventurer" in this non-committed way. Andrea, however, is never portrayed as an adventurer at any point in the play. By placing Anina in this category, Andrea indeed degrades himself to the role of whoremaster. In addition, he demonstrates a considerable lack of sensitivity in listening to Anina's story as she reveals her thoughts, her feelings, and the circumstances which led her into this experience. But she emerged from it still totally committed to Andrea. His uncontrolled reaction now leads to new difficulties.

Not only has Anina's individuality been damaged, but also his own, for he sadly recognizes that his relationship with her was not so unique after all: he could be replaced, exchanged. We see here that Andrea struggles with the egotism and vanity of which he had accused Anina earlier in their dispute. His motivation to leave her has its founda-

tion in this inner conflict. After this dark hour of personal insult, Anina too, sees no basis for any future companionship. "Das Band ist zerrissen" (677), she exclaims, just as Andrea had said earlier. When Casanova's visit is announced by Tito, she seems to seal their separation with these words: "[. . .] merke: Kein Bräutigam, nicht meiner Ehre Anwalt— / Du bist ein fremder Mann für mich—wie er" (677). This second Act ends in the disagreement between them. Apparently, Anina felt no obligation to her honor and Andrea's to resist Casanova, who she knew was not Andrea, although he was deceived as to her identity. She is not an inexperienced woman and therefore would be expected to have sufficient loyalty to her prospective husband to handle the advances of a deluded visitor such as Casanova. On the contrary, she thoroughly enjoys the experience and on awakening the next morning feels herself in a state of innocent bliss, for her excessive vanity tells her that no guilt attaches to one who has not sought out a sexual experience outside the stable relationship which she already enjoys with Andrea.

As the discussion shows, it is possible in this argument to take sides for and against Andrea and Anina at the same time. What Schnitzler is demonstrating here is the complexity of the issue which involves the polarity of honor and vanity. Honor in men requires dignity, integrity and especially excellence of character which Andrea did not demonstrate entirely, as shown by the weakness for gambling, thus leaving Anina alone and unprotected. Honor in women involves chastity in light of a marriage commitment, to which she felt not obligated in the loneliness of the night. Both, therefore, were carried off on the wings of vanity.

This polarity of honor and vanity is shown in other characters as well. At this point, Casanova is just as uninformed about events as Andrea was earlier, and as Santis will be later. The purpose of Casanova's visit is to borrow money from Andrea in order to repay Gudar. This desire to honor his debt, however, is not really motivated by genuine principles of honesty and integrity. Instead, Casanova intends to gamble with Gudar during their forthcoming mutual journey and win the money again from him, so that he can repay Andrea, hopefully sooner than within thirty days. This activity of losing and winning is set up here by the author in a polar sequence, and he works with this polarity principle, as has already been shown, throughout the play. Not only are the characters in polar position to each other, but incidents as well.

It can be seen at this point in the "open window." The night before, Casanova was attracted by it; presently, during his visit with Andrea and before he has started any conversation, he is repelled by it and asks that it be closed. Another polarity occurs within Andrea himself. At first, he is very reserved toward Casanova because he feels uncomfortable in his role as cuckold. Later on, as he regains his bearings when Casanova tells his story, thus revealing that he really does not know whom he seduced the night before, Andrea is more outgoing. He no longer is interested in securing Casanova's promissory note by asking questions about his sources of income; he gathers the gold rather quickly to hand it to him. He is also able to recover from Casanova the letter Anina sent him. Thus, Andrea wipes away all traces of any proof to the contrary, for Casanova assumes that Flaminia sent him this note to warn him of her jealous husband, who already looked for him in the morning. Andrea is now changing his mind about Anina considerably. To make certain that Anina would not fall into another temptation, Andrea suggests to Casanova that he might seek a safer refuge in Holland or England instead of Belgium; at any rate, further away from them.—What is one man's loss is another's gain!

The polarities between Andrea and Anina change in the ensuing scene. Whereas Andrea is ready for reconciliation, Anina wants to be left alone so that she can pack her suitcase. "Neu fängt mein Leben an" (693), she proclaims. The letter which started the original dispute between them is now again the cause of disagreement—this time in the opposite direction. Anina believes it was bought back with gambling money which Andrea had in the drawer and which has now disappeared. "Dafür das Gold—ein Handel?—Schmach und Torheit!" (692). Anina sees in this bargain nothing more than a reduction of human relations and problems, whereas for Andrea it is a reinstatement of his integrity as well as Anina's. When she asks him how he came into possession of this letter he replies by repeating her own words: "Neu fängt dein Leben an" (694); therefore, it should not matter. As she insists on hearing about it, Andrea tells her that Casanova assumes this letter has come from Flaminia to warn him of her jealous husband and his revenge. Andrea admits that he gladly left Casanova in this belief, for he considers this circumstance a special act of fate, thus providing a new level of consciousness upon which to rebuild their relationship. In the measure of forgiveness he sees a first step on their new path. As Anina questions this "big" word of forgiving, he reduces it to mean understanding and forgetting, but Anina at this point is not ready to forget all the insults, mental abuse, and hatred that have been heaped upon her. She repeats the same words Andrea originally said to her:

> Nimmt er nicht die Erinn'rung jener Stunde,
> Den Duft von meinem Leib, von meinen Küssen
> Den Nachgeschmack, der Seufzer Wonnehauch
> Für ewig mit—?
>
> (694)

thus setting again herself and Andrea in opposition to one another. He thinks he is ready for reconciliation, while she is still trying to cope with the mental damage suffered as a result of these strong accusations and is at the same time questioning the motives behind his sudden change of mood. As she grabs her coat and gets ready to leave, she rightfully poses this question to Andrea:

> Genest, weil Eitelkeit des Stachels ledig,
> Ein Herz so rasch, das todverwundet schien?
> Nun erst verlor ich dich!—Fahr hin!
>
> (694-95)

Schnitzler himself has a dim view of this subject, for he maintains that understanding and forgiving rarely stem from goodness, but from indifference and lack of love. In a series of aphorisms, he explains his standpoint on this matter quite distinctly: "Alles verstehen heisst alles verzeihen;—das wäre sehr edel gedacht und gesagt. Nur schade, dass das Verzeihen neunundneunzig Mal unter hundert aus Bequemlichkeit und höchstens einmal aus Güte geschieht [. . .]."[65] In another instance, he observes that these mental processes of "Verstehen," "Verzeihen," and "Vergessen" are almost too great for human nature to handle: "Du hast verstanden? Du hast verziehen? Du hast vergessen? Welch ein Missverständnis! Du hast nur aufgehört zu lieben."[66]

Andrea's "Eitelkeit" (694), as Anina calls his vanity, is suddenly no longer in distress, only because the fear of being ridiculed as a cuckold has been dissolved, so that his honor has been rescued. On a psychological level Andrea's willingness to forget may translate into suppression, but the more human aspect of Andrea's change of mind can be seen in his explanation to Anina that Casanova did not carry away her "Bild" (694), because her countenance was not recognized by him as Anina, nor was it the face he had expected that night. Since she was taken for somebody else "[. . .] so ist es nie gescheh'n" (694).

Although different ways of thinking were involved, Andrea arrives at the same evaluation of the situation as did Anina earlier, when she said "Weil nichts geschah" (674). But she no longer has this conviction. Because Casanova has loved her as Flaminia and not as Anina, she has a strong urge from wounded vanity to repair her individuality and integrity. By this revelation of her personality, Schnitzler neatly convicts her of excessive vanity and of delinquency in the most vital area of a woman's honor. "Jetzt lieb' ich ihn . . . und nun erst wird es Glück" (695) represents a renewed commitment to Casanova, and she held firm on that position during her encounter with Flaminia, as has been seen. The only concession both women have made is to put this dilemma into a fable and present it as a problem to Casanova, who is asked to find the solution.

In Act III, Casanova joins the two couples on stage; his stage directions read: "Er springt über die Brüstung ins Zimmer" (714), which is the same way he entered the night before. Thus Casanova arouses negative emotions and memories immediately in all players with the exception of Santis, whose remark "Er ist's gewohnt" (714) comes ironically close to the truth of which he is not aware at this point. Santis' eyes are geared only to material things; immediately he discovers the emerald on Casanova's snuff box. Casanova generously parts with this jewel box and gives it to Santis, thus paying the husband for the pleasures he thought he had had with his wife. This is another subtle polarity to the scene before, when Andrea considered his gambling money in a similar way. On the surface, of course, Casanova finds another reason for this generosity. He considers Santis his "savior" who through interference in his flight plans "saved" him from running after another "unfaithful woman" and probably into "death" (712).

Because Santis had the original idea of involving Casanova in this affair, he is supposed to tell the story about the two sisters and let Casanova find the proper ending. Throughout the drama Santis has been playing with the terms "Philosoph" and "Dichter" because he saw these qualities in Andrea. Now he has the opportunity to imitate Andrea by telling the story. He enjoys this new role so much that he pays no attention to proper sequence; in fact, Andrea impatiently labels it "Unsinn" (717) and helps out with a short summary. Casanova's answer, which seems to catch everyone by surprise, singles out the young man as being the one who is most deceived of all because he is the victim of a two-fold cheat in that he actually possessed neither one of the women (719).

Before Casanova can justify his decision, they are interrupted by considerable noise from the garden, where the guests are complaining about the fact that they have received neither drinks nor food. Tito appears to collect advance payment from Santis before anything can be served. Santis is outraged: "Ein Arzt herbei, der Wirt ist krank! Ich zahle, / Wenn ich vom Mahle aufsteh', nicht vorher!" (720). But Tito stands firm: "Und meine Bestellung lautet: Kein Bissen auf / die Teller, kein Tropfen in die Becher, ehe die Rechnung / beglichen ist" (720). Santis calls the bill "Betrug," "Erpressung," "Gaunerei," but is willing to pay half of it in advance and give him securities for the other half in the form of jewelry. Finally, Casanova saves Santis from any further embarrassment by paying the entire bill: "Wo Casanova man zu Gaste lud, dort muss der Wirt nicht für die Zeche zittern" (721). In addition, he is still in a position to repay Andrea the gold which he had borrowed from him earlier.

Although Casanova and Santis are both adventurer types, Schnitzler has set them up as polar opposites. In Casanova we see the carefree, self-centered but generous person who does not pretend to be anything other than an adventurer. Santis, on the other hand, has an elevated social consciousness; hence, his title "Baron" as well as his conformity to social customs such as marriage, however open such marriage may be. His self-centeredness is carried to a further extreme by the combination of cunning and of deliberate deception of other people for his own benefit. In contrast to Casanova, he is not a generous person; part of his personality is his suffering from unsatisfied greed. Instead of paying the bill, he first tries to reduce the amount; then to pay half now and the rest at an indefinite later time; then to secure the remaining amount as if at a pawn shop. He even wanted to take away the pearls from Flaminia, but probably had not reckoned with her own crafty skill, for she had had the clasp soldered in wise anticipation. Nor does he measure up to Casanova in terms of intelligence and education. In Schnitzler's diagram Santis would certainly occupy a lower position than Casanova in this triangular arrangement of types and states of mind.

Casanova, through his generosity in paying the dinner bill, has now switched places with Santis in becoming the host of the evening. In that capacity he invites everyone to the garden banquet: "Und nun, es blinkt der Wein, die Schüsseln dampfen. / Ich denk' es wäre Zeit, zu Tisch zu geh'n" (722). But he must first find an end to the unfinished story; so he has the following solution:

> Betrogen alle drei: Der Jüngling zweifach,
> Einfach die Frau'n auf ihre Weise jede.
> So glich sich alles aus, und ich erkläre:
> Ungültig war das ganze Abenteuer.
>
> (722)

Andrea sees the problem as solved, but not yet the "Novelle," because the women still have the daggers in their hands and have only agreed to a temporary armistice. What has happened cannot be erased from memory—especially since neither of the women wants to relinquish her claim nor share with the other (722). Santis, with his new suggestion in that matter, is setting himself up as a cuckold, for this time it will be Flaminia who will realize the pleasure with Casanova, while he is dreaming of Anina. Although Santis is still ignorant with regard to the women involved, Casanova is catching on; stage instructions for him read: "[. . .] hat bei diesen Worten in sinngemässer Weise bald auf Flaminia, bald auf Anina geblickt" (723). He may also remember that he did not feel the string of pearls the night before. Besides, Andrea's drawing his sword gives him the final perception. But Casanova, who has watched the delicious food being served at the table is asking for "zwei Bissen und ein Schluck, nachher der Tod!" (723). This request complies with his impressionistic life style of enjoying always the present moment. Andrea insists that only one of the two will be physically able to go to the table. Santis now surmises that it must have been more than simply "ein Problem" and immediately suspects Flaminia, so that the audience now sees two swords pointing against one.

At this point some outside intervention is necessary because the play is no longer moving along the lines of a comedy. In connection with several earlier experiences during theater visits, Schnitzler speaks in his autobiography "vom Ineinanderfliessen von Ernst und Spiel, Leben und Komödie, Wahrheit und Lüge," which stirred and occupied him "immer wieder, auch jenseits alles Theaters und aller Theaterei, ja über alle Kunst hinaus" and considers it a "Grundmotiv" in his thinking and in his entire works.[67] Indeed, the realms of seriousness and playfulness have moved dangerously close together; not just two but three swords are involved.

Gudar interrupts the duel by bringing in Teresa, who has just arrived to claim her lover and take him along to Vienna, where her next engagement as a dancer is scheduled. With her appearance Schnitzler creates a polar opposite to Casanova, because both characters experience each aspect of their life just for the moment. Teresa had broken her relationship with Casanova only three days ago, as we heard earlier from Flaminia (660); yet, her new sexual adventure has cooled off already. She answers Casanova's curious question: "Liegt er im Grab?" with these words: "Viel tiefer! In Vergessenheit. [. . .]" (726). Death, contrasted here with oblivion instead of life, creates an unusual polarity. However, when this is seen in the context of time and space, oblivion does appear at the opposite end of the scale. A person who has sunk into oblivion in the mind of another has truly ceased to exist for that individual. If, on the other hand, a person had departed through death, he may still be kept alive in the memories of those he left behind.

Teresa, who exists only in and for the moment, and so uses life's opportunities always to her greatest benefit and enjoyment regardless of responsibility and commitment to another person, drops each of her experiences into the sea of oblivion, as soon as it is over. She handles another situation in a similar way later in the play. Tito reports the arrival of two guests at almost the same time, each asking for Teresa. He locked each of them into a room because they acted rather irritated, and is awaiting instructions now. But Teresa is brief: "Ich kenn' sie nicht, man jage sie zum Teufel," later adding: "Ich kenne sie nicht mehr" (730).

Given the standards which she sets for herself, it can be argued that she lives in harmony with her nature: she exists only in the present moment. According to Schnitzler's diagram she would rank as a negative type: "Der negative Typ lebt ohne das Gefühl von Zusammenhängen; das Gestern ist tot für ihn, das Morgen unvorstellbar [. . .]."[68] Quite noticeably, Schnitzler here mentions this loss of the sense of time so characteristic of the negative types, a deficiency which is also the cause of their irresponsibility in the choice of their means. As soon as Teresa finds Casanova again, she becomes very possessive, almost aggressive, past happenings notwithstanding. When she sensed his involvement with the two women, Flaminia and Anina, she could have become jealous, but quickly changed her attitude: "Doch tu' ich's nicht. / Ich hab' dich wieder, so ist alles gut" (727). However, she urges him to pack immediately because they must soon be on their way. Casanova pretends to have other plans, and of course, at present, he still has the duel on his mind. But Santis is swift in extending his hand for peace; whereupon Andrea follows grudgingly: "Wer kann wem was wehren?" (728).

The three women form a polar opposite to the men. Earlier Teresa had embraced Flaminia and called her "teu're Freundin" (725). Now, she turns to Anina with these words, in a sense emphasizing the double meaning: "Auch Sie, mein schönes Kind? Nun ja, wer kann / Ihm widerstehn" (728). These episodes are over; she alone lays claim to Casanova now: "Ewig bin ich dein" (730). Not one of his plans has been acknowledged by Teresa, who in this way shows her insensitivity to any other person outside her own frame of reference. She is certain that they will travel together and has even made arrangements to take along Tito as their servant, since he has proven himself to be

rather clever. Casanova's insistence on having dinner first is finally granted under one condition, that she will eat with him with the two other women on her side. Teresa thus becomes the peacemaker in this inevitable encounter between Casanova and the two couples. In this activity she functions like Casanova, who earlier had a similar task as mediator between Flaminia and Anina. Now they have gone hand in hand into the garden in sisterly harmony; it appears so, at least on the surface.

All but Andrea seem to have overcome their injured vanity so as to join the other guests at the evening meal, and nobody but Casanova appears to have noticed Andrea's difficulty in overcoming his inner conflict. "Ich bin Ihr Freund" (731), are the opening remarks which eventually lead to a deeper understanding between the two men on the subject of faithfulness. Andrea at first rejects this offer of friendship, but the gesture is seen correctly as "Knabentrotz" (732) in Casanova's estimation. If Andrea's heart is closed to Casanova, at least it should not remain so toward Anina, the woman he loves. Passionately, Andrea explains that he cannot marry an unfaithful woman, nor is he able to understand Casanova, who seems to have selected the most unfaithful woman of them all as his companion. But Casanova looks at fidelity from a completely different angle:

> Ich frage Sie, mein Freund, gibt's bess're Treue,
> Gibt's, frag' ich klarer noch, gibt's eine and're
> Auf Erden zwischen Mann und Weib, Andrea,
> Als die Teresa eben mir bewies?
> Sie kehrte mir zurück. Nur das ist Treue,
> Die einz'ge, die mit Fug so heissen darf.
> Denn was uns sonst Gewähr der Treue gilt,
> Das hält nicht stand vor philosoph'scher Prüfung.
>
> (733)

The point of return represents for Casanova the highest level of fidelity, for it demonstrates to him a renewed desire for a certain companionship as a result of inner growth toward maturity. What other proof can there be, he asks: "Sexual closeness after a long struggle? A holy oath? To shoulder some danger? To kill herself and hopefully conquer all doubts in the partner?" (733).[69] For each of these questions Casanova has his own defeating answer such as the one for the first question: "Wer weiss, von wem sie träumt in Ihrem Arm!" (733).

Recurrently in his work, Schnitzler has pondered over the degree of commitment between two people; in his *Buch der Sprüche und Bedenken* he gives the following advice:

> Nicht früher darfst du dich von einer Frau geliebt glauben, ehe du nicht sicher bist ihre ganze erotische Sehnsucht auf dich allein vereinigt und alle andren Möglichkeiten ihres Wesens, auch die ungeahntesten, zur Wirklichkeit erlöst zu haben.[70]

Andrea is not convinced by Casanova's argument and creates a polarity to the concept of "Wiederkehr": "Ja, wenn sie Heimkehr wäre, dann vielleicht" (733). If the woman were coming home, then he might be better able to accept her. The degree of frequency with which one steps outside a relationship becomes the focal point here. "Heimkehr" relates to a close relationship such as a marriage. After previous longings for variety in sexual experiences are satisfied, the partner comes home because of a desire for order and stability, and for a deeper sense of sharing and caring. "Wiederkehr, von wo es immer sei" (733), on the other hand, carries a degree of uncertainty to the point of chaos in the relationship, because it would include maximum freedom for the individual to come and go and as such create a disruptive element. It certainly describes Casanova's life style, for he lives in and for the moment and does not belong anywhere. It might also leave him free of jealousy and anxiety, because he does not feel possessive about any partner.

Jealousy, responsibility, freedom, fidelity are key issues, not only for Andrea and Casanova, but throughout the entire play. These are the points of polarity between "vanity" and "honor," that is, honor in its basic connotation as "personal integrity." Schnitzler himself has formulated the difficulty in his *Buch der Sprüche und Bedenken*:

> Dass wir uns gebunden fühlen mit der steten Sehnsucht nach Freiheit—und dass wir zu binden versuchen, ohne die Überzeugung unseres Rechts dazu, das ist es, was jede Liebesbeziehung so problematisch macht.[71]

Andrea feels obligated to a serious relationship; yet, at the beginning of the play he also struggled with the freedom to gamble and drink and take exception to his commitment to Anina for one night—at least his suggestions to Santis regarding the excursion for that evening seems to indicate his secret desire:

> Wenn sich die Nacht senkt, werden schleierlos
> Von Busch zu Busch des Waldes Nymphen schweben
> Und ihre Gunst an Sterbliche verschwenden—
> Weh dem, der sie am Morgen wieder kennt—
> Und—rat' ich recht?—anstatt des grünen Tuchs
> Wird uns ein leuchtend weisser Frauenleib—
> Das Los entscheidet welcher—Spieltisch sein,
> Darauf das Glück in gold'nen Wellen rollt—
> Und wer verliert—der sei der Hauptgewinner.
>
> (667)[72]

Still, Andrea acts extremely jealous and hurt in his vanity that Anina did just that: take leave for one night from her otherwise solid commitment to him.

There are discrepancies in Anina's behavior as well. If she was serious in turning the page on her experience with Casanova by sending him the letter, she should have followed through with this decision. The love relationship between Santis and Flaminia, on the other hand, does not seem problematic at all in the sense Schnitzler formulated it, because they do not take their commitment to each other seriously, nor do they restrict each other in their freedom. Casanova and Teresa are so independent that their companionship does not reach any problematic state,

either. Thus, Schnitzler shows here a variety of possible relationships and allows the audience to see their merits and deficiencies.

"Aus einem bestimmten Anlass betrügen, heisst beinahe schon treu sein"[73] is another statement Schnitzler gave us in his *Buch der Sprüche und Bedenken,* which is rather all-inclusive in its application. The key words are "distinct occasion" for being unfaithful. This stipulation would fit the situation of each of the main characters. Their independence would be without restrictions; thus, true fidelity could not exist.

This independence is perhaps the reason for Casanova's total rejection of Andrea's concept of "Heimkehr," as he expresses himself in this way:

> Heimkehr?—O Wahn! Als wenn ein Mensch dem andern
> Heimat zu sein sich jemals schmeicheln dürfte.
> Ist Wand'rung nicht der Seele ew'ger Ruf?
> Was gestern noch als fremd uns angefröstelt,
> Umfängt's uns heute nicht vertraut und warm?
> Und was uns Heimat hiess, war's jemals mehr
> Als Rast am Weg, so kurz, so lang sie währte?
> Heimat und Fremde—Worte tauben Klangs
> Von Vorurteil, verschüchtert vom Gesetz
> Und feig verstrickt im Wirrsal des Gewissens,
> Sich Ordnung lügt ins Chaos seiner Brust,
> Der aufgetanen Sinns und freier Seele—
> Gleich unsereinem aus dem Stegreif lebt.
>
> (733-34)

This last one of Casanova's long dialogs (which seem like monologs) touches upon another polarity which was expressed at the beginning of their first encounter; it is the opposition "Bürger" and "Abenteurer." The life style which a "Bürger" like Andrea leads, according to Casanova, is hampered by prejudice, adherence to law, fears from one's conscience, and determination to see order where disorder truly reigns (733). Yet, it must be remembered that Casanova used the term "Heimkehr" earlier in the play in a rather positive way. He observed during his conversation with Andrea: "Ihr Ziel heisst Frieden, Ordnung und Gesetz / Wie Heimkehr Ihrer Wand'rung letzter Sinn"—and almost enviously he added: "Ein frühgeschloss'nes ist das stärkste Band, / Weh dem, der ewig sucht; wohl dem, der fand" (691). Andrea, who did not believe his ears, asks: "Ein solcher Spruch aus Casanovas Mund?" He is reassured by Casanova: "Bewahren Sie ihn sorglich im Gemüte, / Noch keinem gab ich höh're Weisheit kund" (691).

A further seeming paradox regarding the adventurer who travels "aufgetanen Sinns und freier Seele" and lives "aus dem Stegreif" (734) appears in contrast to what Casanova had said earlier. To sleep in strange beds, eat in all kinds of inns, and travel in the company of all sorts of people (691) is void of excitement and color; as if Casanova—had he the choice to start his life all over—would this time settle down early with a young woman, "schön wie

Anina, klug und tugendhaft" (691). Thus, Casanova has gained certain insights, and he seems to give Andrea the key as to what their conduct in marriage should be. Andrea will have to be Anina's conscience. Casanova seems to feel that women do not have a conscience, and this is one of his reasons for ranking Teresa superior because she has come back to him who is her substitute for conscience. Regret, envy, and a certain weariness seem to emanate from Casanova's words to Andrea, an indication that "Wahrheit" and "Lüge" are polarities equally present within Casanova. For a split second he is able to glance into the future and foresee his later years, which Schnitzler describes to his readers brilliantly in his Novelle *Casanovas Heimfahrt* (EW II, 231-323).[74]

Andrea whose objections to Casanova become progressively shorter in this last scene, calls him a "Sophist" and does not recognize him as a "Philosoph." Casanova seems to accept when he replies: "Mag sein. Daher ist's mir bestimmt, zu irren" (734). The word "irren" in its twofold meaning of making a mistake and of roaming applies ironically in each respect to Casanova, thus pointing to his fate in later years as a result of earlier mistakes. Davis interprets this passage quite differently, when he observes: "Casanova, the ebullient egoist, is proud of his deviation from the bourgeois norm. He can find no connection between himself and another person except for the fortuitous crossing of their paths or meeting of their desires."[75] However, when seen in context with the thoughts Casanova expressed earlier, he does not appear so "proud of his deviation."

Significantly enough, the play ends with the focus on the three "sisters" who are seen in the garden arm-in-arm, chatting, smiling and laughing, completely reconciled. They have forgotten and forgiven each other, a task which Andrea was not able to accomplish with Anina. "Wie schwesterlich vereint," remarks Casanova, "[. . .]—Und könnten Männer je / So Brüder sein wie alle Frauen Schwestern" (735). This expressed desire may not work for all men, but Casanova at least puts it into action for himself and Andrea as he walks arm-in-arm with him into the garden, seeing in him the "Bruder meiner Wahl!" (737).

Boner in her dissertation offers the following interpretation of the term "sisters": "Es ist die Fähigkeit des Selbstvergessens in Momenten höchster Daseinsintensität, die ein Band schwesterlicher Ähnlichkeit um Schnitzlers Frauen schlingt."[76] This ability is possible for them, because "Sie alle kennen uneingeschränkte Ergriffenheit und Hingabe. Sie alle vermögen das Reflektieren auszulöschen. Sie alle stehen jenseits des Postulates der Rechtfertigung durch Wort oder Tat."[77] Men, on the other hand, function differently. Boner concludes: "Diejenigen Männer dagegen, die in ihrem Geiste das Leben begreifen und durch eine Leistung rechtfertigen wollen, errichten um sich einen Wall."[78] Casanova seems to be aware of this rampart around him which prompts him to imitate the women by holding on to Andrea's arm. Besides, the invitation to join is there. The women have already called the men's names; Anina has called Andrea twice.

It is a happy note upon which the drama ends, demonstrating the perplexity and complexity of human nature. Man is uncertain of himself and uncertain of his relationship with others, a problem which Schnitzler handled throughout his works, and especially with greater detail and seriousness in his late dramatic works. The question of fidelity which the author posed time and time again must also be understood in this context. "Human acts and human emotions are the result of many shifting and interlocked causes that may reach back even beyond the birth of consciousness," ponders Liptzin. "Hence, none are guilty. All live as they must."[79] He continues to remind us: "Let us, therefore, not judge, Schnitzler would emphasize; and, above all, let us hesitate to condemn."[80]

Körner seems to be "guilty" of both judging and condemning. He finds, "[. . .] dass in jeden Weibes Seele ein Dämon schlummert, den nicht zu wecken höchste Weisheit ist."[81] He sees this "demon" lurking in all of Schnitzler's women characters and upon closer scrutiny considers them "allesamt als Dionysias Schwestern."[82] It is obvious that Körner's assessment represents a gross generalization and does not take into consideration the complexity of the female characters in later works, such as *Die Schwestern*. Certainly, Boner in her evaluation of the three women characters shows more sensitivity in this respect.

Definite evidence toward a change can already be seen in Schnitzler's selection of the title. The focus is on the women as they present themselves in their various predicaments. They are no longer reflected through the eyes of their male counterparts, as they were in the Anatol-cycle, for example. These women display much more personality and individuality as compared to the women of earlier works. Most dominant is their emancipation in matters of companionship, courtship, and marriage.[83]

Although only one of the four dramas considered here carries the title *Komödie der Verführung,* it became apparent that *Die Schwestern* is also a comedy of seduction. The emphasis, however, is placed upon human relationships rather than a mere act of seduction. In this play, as well as in the other three late dramatic works, "[. . .] die Bedeutung der Schnitzlerschen Gestalten liegt nicht in 'ihrem Schicksal,' sondern in 'ihrem Wesen'." Solutions to the various problems in the play are achieved on psychological rather than moral grounds. As we know from his *Buch der Sprüche und Bedenken,* Schnitzler distrusted any dogmatic system, be it religious, philosophical, political or social laws of morality. Yet Schnitzler was by no means immoral. "Our chief moral fault lies in our not listening to the infallible measuring instrument in our souls," which Liptzin calls "a moral seismograph that registers every minute deviation from the right path."[85] Because we do not understand ourselves, Liptzin points out:

> All moral confusion results from the fact that but few people know their own true nature, and that only a very small minority of these have the courage to act in accordance with it. Yet these alone are on the road to freedom.[86]

In challenging conventional thought, Schnitzler himself traveled the road to inner freedom, as his diversified writings demonstrate. He realized that there is no absolute knowledge with regard to human nature and the world as a whole. What is true for one person may not be so for another, for each one is unique in his own expression and sees the world according to his level of consciousness and understanding. Schnitzler's literary production shows how he as a humanist has collected these observations from the realm of everyday experience, in protest against old established systems of thought and ancient prejudices. This seems to be the reason for his satisfaction with "Weltbetrachtung" instead of "Weltanschauung". "'Dies ist's, woran's vor allem dir gebricht: / Die tief're Weltanschauung hast du nicht.' / Nun, lächelnd Eurer zünftigen Verachtung, / Bescheid ich mich in Weltbetrachtung."[87] "Weltanschauung" would indicate to him an authoritative evaluation of the world in its entirety, without leaving room for the ever-expanding, ever-questioning mind.[88] It would also mark for him a narrower point of view instead of openness and receptiveness.

This suggests distinctly a shift in emphasis from the outer world to the complexity of the inner world of man, which is part of the maturing process in Schnitzler's late dramatic work. In an interview with Viereck, he discusses the relationship between his early works and his later production as follows:

> I think the critics are sometimes disposed to overestimate some of my earlier works at the expense of my more mature production. Every talent has a countenance of its own. It took me some time to find myself—to discover my own face so to speak.[89]

Schnitzler's lifelong struggle for truth is related to these words of the interview, for as he realized the many facets of truth, he also discovered that human action and interaction relates to truth in complex ways. Körner points out that "Arthur Schnitzler vom sittlichen Relativismus, ja Amoralismus seiner Frühwerke sachte aber stetig zu immer strengerer sittlicher Bewertung vorgeschritten [sei]."[90] In *Die Schwestern,* and with each new work, he either revises earlier conceptions or adds another dimension to his literary and philosophical development. This change in adopting a stricter ethical and moral standpoint is the key to a better understanding of his late dramatic works. "Wer diesen Wandel des Standpunktes nicht beachtet," admonishes Körner, "mag leicht den irrigen Eindruck empfangen, der Dichter wiederhole sich, habe sich ausgeschrieben, wisse nichts Neues mehr zu sagen. In Wahrheit sind diese Wiederholungen Widerlegungen und sinnvolle Absicht."[91]

The acceptance of free will and individual responsibility represents a relatively late stage in his work. Asked about free will by Viereck, Schnitzler remarks:

> I believe in Free Will. Man is responsible for his actions. He could not live in a world without responsibility [. . .]. In the moral sphere as well as in the sphere of space, conduct is self-determined. Man is the master of his soul, even if his freedom of choice be limited by circumstances and hampered by heredity.[92]

How did Schnitzler know that the will is free? He gives an answer to Viereck in these words:

> If you ask me to prove that the will is free, I must confess my inability. Certain things cannot be argued. One must rely on intuition. One knows that they are so [. . .]. Intuition is an invaluable guide in art, in politics, in business, in love. Even our friendships are largely determined by 'hunches'.[93]

The conditions under which any will is able to function are, according to Schnitzler, "Selbstüberwindung, Erkenntnisdrang und Opfermut."[94]

In overcoming his ego as the center of attention, man is free to direct his interest toward the world around him and to be of service to his fellow men. As we have seen in *Die Schwestern,* this noble concept could not easily be carried out; it required great struggle both within and without, for most egos were still self-centered. Some characters such as Santis, Flaminia, and Teresa only exerted free will, but assumed no responsibility. Gudar, Casanova, Andrea, and Anina had usually more desire to express free will than to show responsibility, but exercised occasional responsibility. Gudar interfered in the duel which was about to start; Casanova paid the bill for the banquet when Santis had reached the pinnacle of irresponsibility; Andrea saved Anina from losing her eyesight when Flaminia attacked her with a hairpin; and Anina wrote the letter to Casanova to prevent more serious consequences from happening in her relationship with Andrea.

Working with the concept of individual responsibility in this drama, Schnitzler again placed it on the scale of polarity. Some characters can handle responsibility to a certain degree; others are not as yet aware of it. The principle of polarity, therefore, becomes an important key in understanding the play *Die Schwestern* and Schnitzler's work as a whole. This idea is based on Urbach's suggestion regarding the method of interpretation: "Die Gestalten müssen zueinander in Beziehung gesetzt werden, aus ihnen und nicht aus Hypothesen oder Ideen entwickelt sich das dramatische Geschehen. Einzig durch Konfigurationen lassen sich Schnitzlers Stücke begreifen."[95] Not only are Schnitzler's "Leitgestalten" used in polar arrangement such as "Bürger" and "Abenteurer," respectable woman and "Dirne," but each part of a polarity can give rise to a new polarity within the sphere of "Leitmotive." Casanova, the youthful adventurer, for example, has his counterpart in Gudar, the aging adventurer. "Letzten Endes also umfasst das Dasein für Schnitzler [. . .] alle Gegensätze," Rey observes, "[. . .] und verbindet sie zu einer Ganzheit, deren Wesen zwar geahnt, aber nicht mehr definiert werden kann."[96]

Within a single character Schnitzler also develops polarities such as truth and falsity (Casanova), dream and reality (Anina), gaiety and solitude (Casanova), love and hate (Flaminia), reason and emotion (Andrea). Although all characters have these qualities, some seem to become more aware of the polar opposites within them and their synthesis on a different plane; Andrea, for example, remarks that "Irrtum und Wahrheit sich wunderbar verschlingen" (722). On the other hand, we see Santis who recognizes: "Die Rollen sind vertauscht [. . .]" (723), but he is not aware that his statement rings true on different levels, for he only considers the change in hosts for the banquet. His idea of "zweifach glücklich [. . .] zweifach betrogen" (723) does not grasp the whole truth, either.

Boner in her chapter entitled "Vom gelebten Leben" observes this polarity in terms of "Sehnsucht" and "Wollen" which creates suffering in Schnitzler's characters:

> Schnitzlers Gestalten bewegt zweifache Sehnsucht, diejenige nach dem Fernen und Unbekannten, diejenige nach Rückkehr und Geborgenheit. Da sind Gestalten, die nur eine, da sind Gestalten, die nur die andere Sehnsucht kennen; aber die meisten haben zwei Seelen in ihrer Brust, und wenn sie der einen leben, sehnt sich die andere nach Verwirklichung.[97]

This polarity principle, of course, represents an important part of Baroque thought. Austria has a strong Baroque heritage, which significantly influences modern Austrian thought to this day, and which had an impact upon the author's production. Swales summarizes best the Baroque aspect of Austria, when he says:

> Many of the themes from Baroque literature are restated in a way that gives them a peculiarly modern resonance. The notion of the 'theatrum mundi,' of man as a player on the stage of life, the juxtaposition of 'Schein' and 'Sein,' of 'dream' and 'reality,' these and many other legacies from the Baroque assert themselves in one form or another in much of the literature of the 'Jahrhundertwende'.[98]

This modern resonance of earlier Baroque themes which Swales mentions is demonstrated in *Die Schwestern* not only by the lightness of tone in the drama but also by the carefree attitudes of its characters. The Rococo flavor already discussed earlier in this analysis is prevailing on every level: setting, plot, characters. Alewyn's assessment of Rococo serves to highlight the play again:

> Das Rokoko ist eine durch und durch ephemere und vordergründige Welt, ohne die barocken Spannungen zwischen Vernunft und Leidenschaft, aber auch ohne die unheilbare Diskrepanz zwischen Wunsch und Wirklichkeit [. . .] eine Welt ohne Tiefe, ohne Dunkel, ohne Geheimnis, ohne Vergangenheit und ohne Zukunft—die Entdeckungen der Romantik. Seine Menschen sind jeden Augenblick durchaus identisch mit sich selbst, freilich um den Preis, dass ihr Selbst von heute selten dem Selbst von gestern gleicht. Man will lieber zu leichtfertig erscheinen als zu schwerfällig.[99]

Indeed, the concept of "Augenblick" was very important in *Die Schwestern*; all significant turns in the play were prompted by a momentary action, beginning with Casanova's jump through the wrong window. The "Augenblick" is an important leitmotif in Schnitzler's entire work, one which increases in significance with each new drama in

his late period. In *Die Schwestern* it was used to create this carefree attitude among nearly all characters in the play; it served also to highlight opposite situations, those rare moments in time when a certain understanding or realization was reached within a particular character.

To see in the Rococo aspects of the play merely an escape of Schnitzler's from the political and social realities of the time, constitutes a rather one-sided view.[100] Schnitzler indeed was interested in the events of his time in so far as they did not involve revolutionary movements of post-war Europe. Such activities met with his utter disapproval and disdain. The following aphorism most closely expresses his thinking:

> Der Pedantismus missverstand die Menschenliebe;—das Resultat ist als Marxismus bekannt. Das Ressentiment missverstand den Marxismus, da wurde der Bolschewismus daraus. Das Literatentum missverstand den Bolschewismus, da galt er wieder als Menschenliebe;—aber nun sah sie auch danach aus.[101]

Schnitzler was not a politician by profession who would step on the platform and proclaim the necessity of certain measures for social change. As a writer he certainly gave an accurate "portrait of the intellectual climate of his times" in describing "the kind of psychological situation which individual participation in that society produces."[102] Even though the play takes place in the Belgian resort town of Spa and portrays the summer guests of various European countries, it easily parallels the Viennese society of Schnitzler's time. When once questioned about his country of post-World War I, Schnitzler answered with these words: "Das wird unsere Generation nicht mehr übersehen und schon gar nicht mehr gestalten können."[103]

This may be one reason why *Die Schwestern* remained the only play which Schnitzler designated as "Lustspiel." He could justify ending it on a happy note in the Rococo atmosphere of light-heartedness and frivolity among the characters. Brandes' admiration is cast into the following words: "Ich finde das Stück sehr fein, sehr unterhaltend und echt, bin leise erstaunt, dass Sie in so trauriger Zeit sich den Muth und die Spannkraft bewahrt haben, ein Lustspiel zu schreiben."[104] Jakob Wassermann in his remembrance of Arthur Schnitzler goes one step further with enthusiasm:

> Einer, der das Diktum prägt: mehr Haltung und weniger Geist! muss viel Geist besitzen, um es zu rechtfertigen. Nach meiner Meinung, die ich ihm nie verhehlte, war er der geborene Lustspieldichter. Er hat es bewiesen, er hatte die Leichtigkeit, er hatte Welt, sein Witz war sublim und traf stets in den Mittelpunkt einer Schwäche oder Lächerlichkeit, aber in späteren Jahren hat er diesen Bezirk seines Talents brachgelegt, kaum begreiflich, warum.[105]

The answer, however, can be found in the psychological depth and complexity which Schnitzler creates for his main characters and in the principle of polarity which involves dynamic action within each character, either to evolve and grow or at least to recognize the limitations imposed upon himself by the nature of his own thinking.

In *Die Schwestern,* to be sure, we have only witnessed the meager beginnings of greater complexity in characters and psychological insight, which develops even further in the subsequent dramas, as will be seen. Rey in his study *Die späte Prosa* denies any such development, at least in so far as the person of Casanova in *Die Schwestern* is concerned. He only observes, "[. . .] dass Schnitzlers Darstellung des alternden Casanova höheres Gewicht und höheren Rang besitzt. Denn das Lustspiel kennt weder die Schwere des Lebens, noch den Ernst der ethischen Problematik."[106]

It is true that the nature of a "Lustspiel" does not detail the difficulties of life; "ethische Problematik," however, was handled in such characters as Andrea and Anina, and even Casanova saw glimpses in the discrepancies of his own life style. The audience of *Die Schwestern* certainly had emotions similar to those which Rey experienced when reading the Novelle: "Wir fühlen Bewunderung, Abscheu, Mitleid zur gleichen Zeit—ein Anzeichen dafür, dass es Schnitzler gelungen ist, aus dem Abenteurertyp eine Gestalt von überraschender Komplexität zu entwickeln."[107]

Casanova's diminishing attraction to women in the Novelle has very natural physical and physiological reasons and does not constitute greater complexity, only a different range of clientele to be expected. "Erst in seinen späteren Jahren lichtet sich der Reigen der weiblichen Gestalten," Alewyn points out, "der durch sein Leben zieht: Herzoginnen und Näherinnen, betagte Matronen und halbwüchsige Mädchen, Nonnen und Kurtisanen."[108] To identify the aging Casanova with Schnitzler's own predicament of aging is not true to the facts, either. Even at age sixty-three, Schnitzler considers himself by no means old; instead, he only speaks about "Grenzjahre," those borderline years which follow the prime of man's life. This is revealed in a letter to Brandes in which Schnitzler also states that he has no reason to complain, "[. . .] weil ich mich in meiner Schaffenslust eher noch wachsen als abnehmen fühle. Auch an äusseren Erfolgen fehlt es nicht [. . .]."[109]

Rey's study concentrates on five of the later Novellen; he bases his study on the following assumption:

> Da die dramatische Produktion im letzten Lebensjahrzehnt des Dichters an Bedeutung verliert, darf in der späten Prosa die Krönung seines Schaffens gesehen werden. Dass auch hier Qualitäts-unterschiede festzustellen sind, versteht sich von selbst.[110]

Schmidt concurs with Rey, "that in the final period of his writing Schnitzler's narrative works are superior in quality to the dramas."[111] One of her reasons mentioned is the author's tendency to reflect on psychological detail. Yet, the trend in modern drama seems to move in this direction.[112]

It is not the purpose of this study to argue that Schnitzler is a better dramatist than prose writer; instead, I want to show that his late dramatic work is more significant than has been recognized heretofore. Nevertheless, in order to place Schnitzler in proper context as a dramatist, one needs to be reminded that the author's talent for both genres was exceptionally strong, and many dramas started out as prose works. In this respect, it is perhaps useful to draw upon the characterization Hofmannsthal gave Schnitzler in his Wiener Brief of April 1922, written with the authority of a close friend and contemporary:

> Arzt und Sohn eines Arztes, also Beobachter und Skeptiker von Beruf, ein Kind der obern Bourgeoisie und des endenden 19. Jahrhunderts, einer skeptischen, beobachtenden und 'historischen' Epoche, nicht ohne innere Affinitäten mit französischem Wesen und der Kultur des 18. Jahrhunderts, wäre es fast ein Wunder, wenn dieser grosse erfolgreiche Theaterautor nicht auch ein bedeutender Novellist wäre; denn in der Tat sind sich nie zwei Kunstformen näher gestanden als das psychologische Theater und die psychologische Novelle der letzten Generation.[113]

In Hofmannsthal's view, therefore, Schnitzler is a "great and successful playwright." He is also a "significant prose writer" because of the literary proximity of the two art forms, the psychological theater and the psychological Novelle. Even Schnitzler's narrative works show certain characteristics of the drama which Rey in his interpretation of *Casanovas Heimfahrt* recognized keenly. "Das Geheimnis der Form," according to Rey, "besteht in dem meisterhaft bewahrten Gleichgewicht von epischen und dramatischen Elementen."[114] Further on we read: "Seine Gestaltungskraft zeigt sich darin, dass er die formsprengenden Kontraste des Seelendramas einzuordnen vermag in die geschlossene Form des pseudohistorischen Berichts."[115] Earlier Rey wrote about "dramatische Spannung," "die dramatischen Höhepunkte," "die Erzählung zerfällt in fünf Akte," "die Dramatik der inneren Bewegung," "nach den dramatischen Erschütterungen," "Akt der Selbstverleugnung," "die Bühne ist vorbereitet," "in ihrem dramatischen Kontrast," "in der ganzen Szene."[116] These details are merely mentioned to show that Schnitzler's preoccupation appears to be that of a dramatist, even when he was writing prose.

In his concluding remarks Rey admitted "die Typenhaftigkeit der Darstellung [. . .] bei den weiblichen Hauptgestalten [. . .]" and contrasts "die Differenzierung der männlichen Charaktere ist viel stärker entwickelt. Hier stehen Abenteurer und Wahnsinniger als Gegensätze gegenüber."[117] "Typenhaftigkeit," however, points to Schnitzler's earlier works. If this aspect is still present in his late prose works, then they do not seem to qualify as the high point of Schnitzler's artistic achievement.[118]

His late dramatic works, on the other hand, show distinctly a process of maturation, especially with regard to the women characters. The author's characters in the late dramatic works begin to assume command of their own lives. They no longer are victims of moral and conventional customs which earlier would have hindered their individual expression and freedom of choice. They gain control over their lives and affairs and try to take advantage of social and economic situations to fulfill their inner desires, good or bad. In most cases, Schnitzler's characters show a sense of self-acceptance and self-authority. They authorize their own decisions and deeds, and take responsibility for the consequences, whatever the result may be. Because the emphasis in this drama is placed on the unfoldment of the women characters, I consider this drama—contrary to Offermanns' view, a departure from previous comedies in spite of Casanova's "impressionistischen Weltverhaltens."[119] *Die Schwestern oder Casanova in Spa* represents the beginning not the "Endpunkt einer geistigen Entwicklung"[120] for indeed Schnitzler's women characters take the lead in his late dramatic productions. This point will be developed more convincingly through the analyses of the subsequent dramas.

The key issues raised in the drama *Die Schwestern oder Casanova in Spa,* namely the principle of polarity exhibited in both the characters and the incidents in their lives, the complexity of human nature especially with regard to women characters, the question of fidelity in terms of "Heimkehr" or "Wiederkehr," the acceptance of free will and individual responsibility, also occur in the drama *Komödie der Verführung* (1924). However, new aspects added to each issue create even more complexity, as the large number of characters in the play demonstrates. The principle of triangularity receives more attention in *Komödie der Verführung.* In *Die Schwestern oder Casanova in Spa* triangular constellations occurred only among characters as for example the triangle of Flaminia-Anina-Teresa, Flaminia-Santis-Casanova, Anina-Andrea-Casanova. The triangularity in *Komödie der Verführung* not only includes the relationship of characters, but also important political and social themes in addition to psychological issues.

Notes

1. Arthur Schnitzler, *Gesammelte Werke. Die dramatischen Werke.* Zweiter Band (Frankfurt am Main: S. Fischer Verlag, 1962), pp. 651-737. All quotes from this second volume pertaining to the text will hereafter be referred to by page number only.

2. Oskar Seidlin, ed., *Der Briefwechsel Arthur Schnitzler-Otto Brahm. Schriften der Gesellschaft für Theatergeschichte,* Band 57 (Berlin: Selbstverlag der Gesellschaft für Theatergeschichte, 1953), p. 61. (Hereafter referred to as *Schnitzler-Brahm-Briefwechsel.*)

3. Therese Nickl/Heinrich Schnitzler, eds., *Hugo von Hofmannsthal-Arthur Schnitzler. Briefwechsel* (Frankfurt am Main: S. Fischer Verlag, 1964), p. 286. (Hereafter referred to as *Hofmannsthal-Schnitzler-Briefwechsel.*) The letter to Hofmannsthal is dated October 1, 1919.

4. Arthur Schnitzler, *Gesammelte Werke. Die erzählenden Schriften.* Zweiter Band (Frankfurt am Main: S. Fischer Verlag, 1961), pp. 231-323. Reference to the prose works are indicated hereafter by ES I or ES II.

5. Urbach, *Kommentar,* pp. 128-29.

6. Kurt Bergel, ed., *Georg Brandes und Arthur Schnitzler. Ein Briefwechsel* (Bern: Francke Verlag, 1956), p. 134. (Hereafter referred to as *Brandes-Schnitzler-Briefwechsel.*) Letter S 49, dated January 30, 1922. Cf. Richard Alewyn's comments regarding the Memoiren: "In ihnen wird — wie immer es um die Zuverlässigkeit des einzelnen bestellt sei — eine Form der Existenz zu Ende gelebt, ohne die unser Bild von den Möglichkeiten des Menschseins ärmer wäre: das Abenteurertum." ("Casanova," *Neue Rundschau,* 1959, 102).

7. Cf. William H. Rey, "Schnitzler in neuer Sicht. Ein bedeutender Forschungsbericht aus Frankreich," *Modern Austrian Literature,* 1, No. 1 (1968), 34: "Erst wird man Schnitzlers Casanova (sei es der junge in *Die Schwestern* oder der alte in *Casanovas Heimfahrt*) nicht als historische Figur, sondern als höchst aktuelle und zugleich mythische Verkörperung des Abenteurertums in all seinem Glanz und seinem Elend sehen müssen."

Cf. Heinz Otto Burger, "Dasein heisst eine Rolle spielen," *Germanisch-Romanische Monatsschrift,* N. F. 11 (Oct., 1961), 373: "Vom Dichter erwartet man nicht, dass er historisch getreu schildere oder frei erfinde, sondern dass er die 'Muster der Lebensweisen' finde und wiedergebe."

Cf. Susanne M. Polsterer, "Die Darstellung der Frauen in Arthur Schnitzlers Dramen," Diss. Wien, 1949, Paragraph 2.27. (There are no page numbers used in the main body of the text. Therefore, one has to depend solely on the numbered paragraph divisions.

Cf. Urbach, *Kommentar,* pp. 129-30.

8. Körner, "Spätwerk," p. 57.

Cf. Bernhard Blume, *Das Weltbild Arthur Schnitzlers* (Stuttgart: Buchdruckerei Knöller GmbH, 1936), p. 29: "Der glückliche Casanova erscheint in einem von Schnitzlers Nebenwerken, in dem Verslustspiel 'Die Schwestern oder Casanova in Spa'."

9. Körner, *Gestalten und Probleme,* pp. 26, 81, 97, 111, 115.

10. Letter dated January 4, 1913, quoted by Klaus Kilian, *Die Komödien Arthur Schnitzlers. Sozialer Rollenzwang und kritische Ethik* (Düsseldorf: Bertelsmann Universitätsverlag, 1972), p. 89.

11. Cf. p. 134 of this monograph where Schnitzler places his concept of the soul on a cosmic scale as well.

12. Viereck, p. 399.

Cf. Robert Roseeu, *Arthur Schnitzler,* p. 43: "Die Grösse des Schauspiels beruht eben nicht in der Führung der Handlung, vielmehr in der Schilderung der modernen Seele, in den weiten und grossen Lebensanschauungen, die daraus hervorleuchten." (Berlin: Wilhelm Borngräber Verlag Neues Leben, 1913.)

Cf. Theodor Reik, *Arthur Schnitzler als Psycholog,* p. 301: "Das eigentliche Produktive des dichterischen Schaffens bleibt eben im unbewussten Seelenleben." (Minden/Westf.: J. C. C. Bruns, n.d., Foreword 1913.) This spiritual concept of the soul conceiving the ideas for the mind appears to be the latest conclusion which Schnitzler reached in his search as to the nature of creativity. Some years earlier in his aphorisms (1927) we hear the scientist speak: "Ebenso, wie nun eine solche Zelle alles in sich aufnimmt, was ihr zur Nahrung, zur Vollendung dienlich ist, so nimmt auch jener Stoff alles in sich auf, was aus des Dichters Erlebnissen, Erfahrungen, Gefühlen ihm nutzbar sein mag, verschmäht das Unverwertbare, stösst es aus und dehnt sich allmählich immer weiter, so dass er endlich den ganzen Inhalt der Dichterseele zu bilden, ja dass die Dichterseele selbst in den Stoff umgewandelt scheint." (Arthur Schnitzler, *Buch der Sprüche und Bedenken. Aphorismen und Fragmente,* Wien: Phaidon-Verlag, 1927), p. 191. (Hereafter referred to as *BdSp.*)

Schnitzler has frequently allowed us "glimpses" into the active mind of a dramatist: "Dramatiker sein, heisst an den freien Willen glauben, wie, nein als einen Gott. Denn was ist das Drama? Der Widerstand, der Kampf des Einen, des Willens des Einen mit dem Schicksal? Die Summe, das Quadrat, kurz irgendeine Zusammenfassung aller andren freien Willen plus den unabänderlichen Naturgesetzen." (Schnitzler, "Gedanken über die Kunst," *Neue Rundschau,* 43, 1932, 38). An unavoidable prerequisite for the drama is the presence of a distinct "Weltanschauung" and the acceptance of certain paramount ethical values (Schnitzler, *BdSp,* 181).

13. Arthur Schnitzler, *Gesammelte Werke. Aphorismen und Betrachtungen.* Ed. Robert O. Weiss (Frankfurt am Main: S. Fischer Verlag, 1967), p. 287. (Hereafter referred to as *AuB.*)

14. For further detail of plot see also Sol Liptzin, *Arthur Schnitzler* (New York: Prentice Hall, Inc., 1932), pp. 256-58; and Françoise Derré, *L'œuvre d'Arthur Schnitzler. Imagerie viennoise et problèmes humains* (Paris: Librairie Marcel Didier, 1966), pp. 294-95.

15. Ernst L. Offermanns, *Arthur Schnitzler. Das Komödienwerk als Kritik des Impressionismus* (München: Wilhelm Fink Verlag, 1973), pp. 110-127.

16. *Ibid.,* p. 127.

17. *Ibid.*

18. *Ibid.,* p. 110.

19. Kilian, pp. 110-116. It was originally a 1969 dissertation at the Ruhr University of Bochum.

20. *Ibid.,* pp. 132-33.

21. *Ibid.,* p. 114.

22. *Ibid.,* p. 111.

23. Schnitzler, *AuB,* p. 142.

24. Kilian, p. 113.

25. Friedbert Aspetsberger, "'Drei Akte in einem.' Zum Formtyp von Schnitzlers Dramen," *Zeitschrift für deutsche Philologie,* 85 (1966), 285-308.

26. *Ibid.,* 291.

27. *Ibid.,* 296.

28. Derré, pp. 284-85.

29. *Ibid.,* pp. 293-96.

30. Richard Alewyn, "Casanova," 110-116.

31. *Ibid.,* 103.

32. Schmidt, p. 14.

33. *Ibid.*

34. Cf. Schmidt, pp. 248-57; pp. 308-328.

35. *Ibid.,* p. 243.

36. *Ibid.,* p. 242.

37. Polsterer, Paragraph 1.3.

38. *Ibid.,* Paragraph 1.3.

Cf. Rena R. Schlein in her more balanced view of Schnitzler: "Schnitzler's writings that have remained unparalleled represent a fusion of scientific insight, intuitive knowledge and perception, and artistic genius. This is the explanation of the renaissance his works are enjoying today. They will be read with joy by future generations, for, as all masterpieces, they are timeless." ("Arthur Schnitzler: Author-Scientist," *Modern Austrian Literature,* 1, No. 2, Summer 1968, 37.)

39. Heinrich (Henry) Schnitzler, "'Gay Vienna' — Myth and Reality," *Journal of the History of Ideas,* 15, N. 1 (Jan., 1954), 94-118. Robert A. Kann, "The Image of the Austrian in Arthur Schnitzler's Writings," *Studies in Arthur Schnitzler. University of North Carolina Studies in the Germanic Languages and Literatures.* Eds. Herbert W. Reichert and Hermann Salinger (Chapel Hill: The University of North Carolina Press, 1963), 45-70. Schlein, 28-38.

40. Schmidt, p. 6.

41. Reik dissects female as well as male characters according to psychoanalytic theories. Körner stresses the sensual as well as the emotionally overbalanced nature of women in Schnitzler's works who generally are shown in a state of dependency upon men. (*Gestalten und Probleme,* p. 34.)

42. Georgette Boner, *Arthur Schnitzlers Frauengestalten* (Zürich: Wintherthur Buchdruck, 1930), p. 15. Boner's dissertation was originally submitted at the University of Basel under the same title.

43. *Ibid.*, p. 16.

44. *Ibid.*, p. 15.

45. Schnitzler, *AuB*, pp. 135-166.

46. Most other aspects of Boner's study have been mentioned in Schmidt's analysis and need not be repeated here. Cf. Schmidt, pp. 2-5. The drama *Die Schwestern oder Casanova in Spa* is mentioned in some other dissertations; however, only certain aspects were treated as they fitted the overall purpose of these writings. These dissertations include: Evan B. Davis, "Moral Problems in the Works of Arthur Schnitzler," Diss. University of Pennsylvania, 1950; Reinhart Müller-Freienfels, "Das Lebensgefühl in Arthur Schnitzlers Dramen," Diss. Frankfurt, 1954; John Nelson Whiton, "The Problem of Marriage in the Works of Arthur Schnitzler," Diss. University of Minnesota, 1967. These dissertations will be recognized in the course of this study.

47. Aspetsberger, 291.

48. Whiton points out that "Throughout Schnitzler's works, resorts serve as the locals for the concentration of erotic temptation, and as a symbol of the erotic. This is especially true in [. . .] *Die Schwestern*, [. . .] *Komödie der Verführung*," p. 246.

49. Johannes Jahn, *Wörterbuch der Kunst* (Stuttgart: Alfred Kröner Verlag, 1966), p. 591.

50. Derré, p. 285.

51. Alewyn, "Casanova," 115.

52. Cf. William H. Rey, *Arthur Schnitzler. Die späte Prosa als Gipfel seines Schaffens*, p. 30: "In Schnitzlers Spätzeit wird die Auseinandersetzung mit dem Abenteurertum auf einer höheren Ebene fortgeführt [. . .]. Auf der Schwelle des Alters beschwört Schnitzler also noch einmal den Glanz und das Elend des Abenteurers und zeigt damit, wie bedeutungsvoll die schöpferische Auseinandersetzung mit dieser Gestalt für seine eigene Entwicklung gewesen ist." (Hereafter this work is referred to as *Späte Prosa*.)

53. Gero v. Wilpert, *Sachwörterbuch der Literatur* (Stuttgart: Alfred Kröner Verlag, 1964), p. 55.

54. Schnitzler, *BdSp.*, p. 70.

Cf. William M. Johnston, *The Austrian Mind. An Intellectual and Social History 1848-1938* (Los Angeles: University of California Press, 1972), p. 165. Cf. Jon D. Green, "The Impact of Musical Theme and Structure on the Meaning and Dramatic Unity of Selected Works by Arthur Schnitzler," Diss. Syracuse University, 1972, p. 42: "Schnitzler's mind actually seems to have functioned through a keen awareness of polarities. The fact that his works, almost without exception, contain a central conflict created by competing polar forces (Schein-Sein, freedom-determination etc.) creates a dramatic setting not unlike musical conflict and resolution."

55. Alewyn, "Casanova," 105.

56. *Ibid.*, 108.

57. Rey, *Späte Prosa*, p. 31.

Cf. Swales, *Arthur Schnitzler. A Critical Study* (Oxford: University Press, 1971), pp. 16-17: "The adventurer seeks erotic experience on the one hand, because it is the most intense form of physical experience, and yet, on the other, he refuses to be bound by it, because ultimately his spirit continues to reassert the insufficiency of each specific erotic experience. Each experience must be known in its intensity and yet transcend each time." (Hereafter this work is referred to as *Critical Study*.)

58. Schnitzler, *AuB*, p. 164.

59. Schnitzler, *BdSp.*, p. 165.

60. Bernhard Blume in his study certainly goes too far, when he equates the characteristics present in Casanova with the nature of the author himself: "Der utopische und in sich unmögliche Versuch, den Ablauf der Zeit aufzuhalten und sich in den Genuss des Augenblicks zu retten, wie ihn die Schnitzlersche Lieblingsfigur des 'Casanova' symbolisiert, gleichsam die materialistische Verfallsform des Don Juan, ist freilich ein notwendiger Versuch für den Menschen des Verfalls, und deshalb ein Grundzug von Schnitzlers Wesen." (p. 13)

See also Rey, *Späte Prosa*, p. 192. Cf. Heinz Politzer, "Diagnose und Dichtung," *Forum*, 9 (1962), 270. He shows a more sensitive view of the author: "Der Dichter Arthur Schnitzler war ein guter Arzt. Stück um Stück, Buch um Buch stellte er die tragikomische Verwirrung fest, die über die Menschheit hereingebrochen war. Er analysierte die Psyche einer dem Untergang bestimmten Gesellschaft, weil er den epidemischen Charakter der Neurosen fürchtete, die hier gebrütet wurden. Aber er war zu sehr eins mit den Gestalten, die er schuf, um sie, wie seine Nachfolger auf dem Gebiet der Tragikomödie — Jean Cocteau etwa, Tennessee Williams, Samuel Beckett — von oben her blosszustellen und einem über sich selbst erschrockenen Gelächter preiszugeben. An ihren Betten, welche Betten der Liebe und des Todes waren, verweilte er lange und litt. Er wusste um ihr Geheimnis, und da er es wusste, bewahrte er es."

61. What Uwe Rosenbaum in this context says about the "Graf" can be related to the "Abenteurer" as well. He is also "einer jener im Gesamtwerk Schnitzlers immer wiederkehrenden 'Augenblicksmenschen,' un-

terliegt einer illusionistischen Vorstellung. Denn auch der Augenblick ist in den Zeitlauf mit einbezogen, er ist Zeit, partielle Zeit." ("Die Gestalt des Schauspielers auf dem deutschen Theater des 19. Jahrhunderts [. . .]," Diss. Köln, 1971, p. 190).

62. Schnitzler, *AuB*, p. 290.

63. Cf. Schnitzler, *BdSp.*, p. 64: "Ein Schicksal mag äusserlich abgetan sein, es bleibt immer noch Gegenwart, solange wir es nicht völlig verstanden haben. Erst wenn es geheimnislos für uns wurde, haben wir das Recht, es Vergangenheit zu nennen."

64. Swales, *Critical Study*, p. 17.

65. Schnitzler, *BdSp.*, p. 114.

66. *Ibid.*, p. 118. Cf. also pp. 80, 97, 106 with regard to understanding and forgiving.

67. Schnitzler, *Jugend in Wien. Eine Autobiographie* (Wien-München-Zürich: Verlag Fritz Molden, 2nd. ed., 1968), p. 28.

Cf. Gudar at the beginning of the play speaking about Casanova: "So wie er oft mit wahren Worten lügt" (656).

68. Schnitzler, "Der Geist im Wort und der Geist in der Tat," *AuB*, p. 142.

69. This last idea is a problem which Schnitzler examines again in more depth in his next drama, *Komödie der Verführung*. Falkenir's first wife committed suicide to prove her fidelity. Similarly, the idea of "Wiederkehr" receives Schnitzler's most detailed attention in the present drama. Prior to this play, it occurred briefly in *Der grüne Kakadu* (1899), where the actress Léocadie for seven years returned periodically to Henri who finally marries her. From that point on, however, Henri no longer tolerated the escapades of his wife and, in fact, killed her lover Von Cadignan in the dressing room of the theater. Nevertheless, this episode only fills a minor detail within the political context of this one-act play on the evening of the French Revolution. The play *Die Schwestern oder Casanova in Spa*, on the other hand, deals with the idea of "Wiederkehr" at greater length and also provides entirely different circumstances. *Der grüne Kakadu* shows life as a crossroad between reality and illusion, wakefulness and dream, as the various entertainers within the play perform their act.

70. Schnitzler, *BdSp.*, p. 118.

71. *Ibid.*, p. 117.

72. This is a Dionysian idea which the one-act play *Bacchusfest* handles in detail; it occurs again in *Komödie der Verführung* and *Im Spiel der Sommerlüfte*.

73. Schnitzler, *BdSp.*, p. 116.

74. Cf. Alewyn, p. 110: "Es bestünde auch für ihn kein Grund, dieses Spiel nicht endlos zu wiederholen, gäbe es nicht eines: das Altern. Casanova hat ein für

seine Zeit hohes Lebensalter erreicht; aber schon auf der Mitte seines Lebensweges, mit fünfunddreissig Jahren, erklärt er, dass er sich alt werden fühle, und mit vierzig beginnt seine Spannkraft nachzulassen, und damit erlischt seine Magie. Er wird von Frauen betrogen und versetzt, er muss betteln, wo er sich zu bedienen gewohnt war." Cf. Kilian, pp. 111-12. He worked out comparisons between the two stories.

75. Davis, p. 127.

76. Boner, p. 30.

77. *Ibid.*

78. *Ibid.*

79. Liptzin, *Arthur Schnitzler*, p. 174.

80. *Ibid.*

81. Körner, *Gestalten und Probleme*, p. 94.

82. *Ibid.*

83. The dissertation by Georgette Boner represents the first positive contribution in sharpening the focus upon Schnitzler's women figures.

84. Modified from the original quote which reads: "[. . .] die Bedeutung der Schnitzlerschen Gestalten liegt nicht in 'ihrem Wesen,' sondern in 'ihrem Schicksal'" (Bergel, *Brandes-Schnitzler-Briefwechsel*, p. 68).

85. Liptzin, *Arthur Schnitzler*, p. 224.

86. *Ibid.*

87. Schnitzler, *BdSp.*, p. 26.

88. Cf. Christa Melchinger, *Illusion und Wirklichkeit im dramatischen Werk von Arthur Schnitzler* (Heidelberg: Carl Winter Universitätsverlag, 1968), p. 131. See also Rey, *Späte Prosa*, pp. 10-11. Richard Plant, on the other hand, gives a superficial evaluation of "Schnitzler as a juggler of psychological situations which he wheels around and around [. . .]" ("Notes on Schnitzler's Literary Technique," *Germanic Review*, 25 (February, 1950), 18.

89. Schnitzler, quoted by Viereck, p. 407.

90. Körner, "Spätwerk," 54-55.

91. *Ibid.*, 56-57.

92. Viereck, p. 400. See also Schnitzler in *BdSp.*, p. 56: "Ohne unseren Glauben an den freien Willen wäre die Erde nicht nur der Schauplatz der grauenhaftesten Unsinnigkeit, sondern auch der unerträglichsten Langweile. Verantwortungslosigkeit hebt jede ethische Forderung, kaum dass sie ins Bewusstsein trat, als wesenlos wieder auf: das Ich ohne das Gefühl der Verantwortung wäre überhaupt kein Ich mehr [. . .]." Cf. Herbert Lederer, "The Problem of Ethics in the Works of Arthur Schnitzler," Diss. Chicago, 1953, p. 159. Selma Köhler, "The Question of Moral Responsibility in the Dramatic Works of Arthur Schnitzler,"

Journal of English and Germanic Philology, 22 (1923), 410, denies that freedom of will and choice are possible. She calls it a "[. . .] delusion, however, contrasted with the more potent influences of environment, epoch, and heredity, and particularly is the power of choice a delusion when social conventions are brought to bear upon the individual." Cf. also her concluding remarks (411): "The question of individual responsibility," she says, "is replaced, in his estimation, by the vaster conception of man as a being subject to laws over which he has little or no control, those of physiological, biological, and social science." Her statement may have had more application in Schnitzler's early works, certainly not in his late dramatic works.

93. Viereck, p. 400.

94. Schnitzler, *BdSp.,* p. 65: "Selbstüberwindung, Erkenntnisdrang und Opfermut sind die einzigen wirklichen Tugenden unter allen, die man so zu nennen pflegt, denn nur in ihnen ist der Wille betätigt."

95. Urbach, *Arthur Schnitzler,* p. 27.

96. "Arthur Schnitzler" in: *Deutsche Dichter der Moderne. Ihr Leben und Werk,* ed. Benno v. Wiese, 3rd ed. (Berlin: Erich Schmidt Verlag, 1975), p. 243.

97. Boner, pp. 83, 89.

98. Swales, *Critical Study,* p. 23. For a discussion regarding "time," see p. 21.

99. Alewyn, "Casanova," 116.

100. Cf. Kilian, p. 110, who feels that Schnitzler needed to gain perspective of the political situation.

    Cf. Offermanns, p. 110: "Der impressionistische Abenteurer des Fin de Siècle wird in die kulturgeschichtlich verwandte Epoche des Rokoko projiziert und so der ungleich bedrängenderen aktuellen Wirklichkeit entrückt." Also see p. 125: "Das Lustspiel 'Die Schwestern' mag als der Versuch eines Gegenbildes zum 'grauenhaften Weltzustand' genommen werden."

101. Schnitzler, *BdSp.,* p. 168. In an interview with Viereck, the author expands his position this way: "I oppose Bolshevism, not for political reasons but because Bolshevism denies differentiation. Differentiation is a fundamental law of nature. If man were not differentiated, he would be a monstrosity standing outside the pale of nature. To negate personality is to repudiate culture. I am disgusted by men of letters who coquette with Bolshevism."

102. Swales, pp. 28-29. Cf. Offermanns, p. 179.

103. Max Krell recorded this conversation with Schnitzler. He is quoted by Urbach, *Schnitzler,* p. 17.

    Cf. Swales, *Critical Study,* p. 26. He states: "Yet there is more to Schnitzler than this stereotyped image. In a very real way he partakes of the total

upheaval that his world is undergoing and he embodies not only the traditional and backward-looking but also the modern and forward-looking aspects of the 'Jahrhundertwende.' He does, therefore, claim our attention as a representative figure of an important age, and not just as a patron saint of one limited segment of that age [. . .]."

104. Bergel, *Brandes-Schnitzler-Briefwechsel,* p. 126. B 44, dated June 13, 1920.

105. Jakob Wassermann, "Erinnerungen an Arthur Schnitzler," *Neue Rundschau,* 1 (Januar, 1932), 13.

    Cf. Politzer, "Diagnose und Dichtung" (II) who has an answer to Wassermann's 'warum': "Aber die Grundspannungen, die Schnitzlers reifes Werk tragen, haben weit eher mit der konkreten Wucht des Barock zu tun als mit der sublimen Eleganz des Rokoko." (*Forum,* 102, Juni 1962, 269.)

106. Rey, *Späte Prosa,* p. 30.

    Cf. also Blume, *Weltbild,* p. 29: "Hier wird er fast mehr genannt als gestaltet, dient als Umriss, der vom Wissen des Zuschauers gefüllt werden muss, als die Zitierung eines berühmten Namens, die die Entwicklung eines Charakters erspart [. . .]." It is true that much has been learned about Casanova before he enters the stage in Act II, but this is the kind of information that comes to mind in any audience, whenever the name Casanova resounds. However, he most definitely is involved in the central conflict raging about fidelity and imposes his antisocial convictions rather strongly upon all characters involved.

107. Rey, *Späte Prosa,* p. 30.

108. Alewyn, "Casanova," 107-108.

109. Bergel, *Brandes-Schnitzler-Briefwechsel,* p. 148, S 58.

110. Rey, *Späte Prosa,* p. 14.

111. Schmidt, p. 242.

112. Cf. Chekhov, Pirandello, Maupassant, Beckett, Dürrenmatt, Frisch — to name a few writers.

113. Hofmannsthal, *Gesammelte Werke in Einzelausgaben. Aufzeichnungen,* ed. Herbert Steiner (Frankfurt am Main: S. Fischer Verlag, 1959), p. 272.

114. Rey, *Späte Prosa,* p. 48.

115. *Ibid.*

116. *Ibid.,* pp. 40-45.

117. *Ibid.,* p. 191.

118. See Swales, who seems to have similar objections in his "Kritik an 'Arthur Schnitzler. Die späte Prosa als Gipfel seines Schaffens' — Rey," *Modern Language Review,* 65, No. 1 (January, 1970), 224: "And yet, for

all the virtues of this study, one has reservations about many of its conclusions. One wonders firstly if the late prose works are in fact the high-point of Schnitzler's artistic achievements. It could, for example, be argued that none of the stories analyzed approaches the mastery and subtlety of 'Leutnant Gustl' [. . .]. Indeed, one feels at times that Professor Rey tries too hard to demonstrate the maturity and richness of the late work; he seems, for instance, excessively determined to prove the moral worth of the various characters involved."

119. Offermanns, p. 110.

120. Kilian, p. 114.

REIGEN (LA RONDE)

CRITICAL COMMENTARY

Hunter G. Hannum (essay date January 1962)

SOURCE: Hannum, Hunter G. "'Killing Time': Aspects of Schnitzler's *Reigen*." *Germanic Review* 37, no. 1 (January 1962): 190-206.

[*In the following essay, Hannum locates* Reigen *within the Austro-Germanic* fin de siècle *literary trend, focusing on the play's preoccupation with time.*]

> Betrachte die Herde, die an dir vorüberweidet: sie weiß nicht, was Gestern, was Heute ist, springt umher, frißt, ruht, verdaut, springt wieder, und so vom Morgen bis zur Nacht und von Tage zu Tage, kurz angebunden mit ihrer Lust und Unlust, nämlich an den Pflock des Augenblicks, und deshalb weder schwermütig noch überdrüssig. Dies zu sehen geht dem Menschen hart ein, weil er seines Menschentums sich vor dem Tiere brüstet und doch nach seinem Glücke eifersüchtig hinblickt— denn das will er allein, gleich dem Tiere weder überdrüssig noch unter Schmerzen leben, und will es doch vergebens, weil er es nicht will wie das Tier. Der Mensch fragt wohl einmal das Tier: warum redest du mir nicht von deinem Glücke und siehst mich nur an? Das Tier will auch antworten und sagen: das kommt daher, daß ich immer gleich vergesse, was ich sagen wollte—da vergaß es aber auch schon diese Antwort und schwieg: so daß der Mensch sich darob verwunderte.[1]

This passage from Nietzsche's *Vom Nutzen und Nachteil der Historie für das Leben* can be taken not only as one of the most striking specimens of German prose in the last hundred years but also as a thematic epigraph, as Walter Sokel has said, for much of modern German literature.[2]

With advancing time, writers have moved farther and farther backwards to locate their images of a paradisiacal innocence for which the burden of time does not exist. The traditional images for this state, Arcadian Greece and Eden before the Fall, began to yield around Nietzsche's time to yearning depictions of innocent animals, such as the cows described above, who are blessed with immersion in the present moment and as a result have no crippling consciousness of a before and after. Here too a curve of regression may be traced from Rilke's lions, for example,[3] to the coral in Kaiser's play of that name and to Benn's protozoic slime:

> O daß wir unsere Ururahnen wären.
> Ein Klümpchen Schleim in einem warmen Moor.
> Leben und Tod, Befruchten und Gebären
> glitte aus unseren stummen Säften vor.[4]

Before this extreme retrograde position was reached, a group of writers at the turn of the century had already demonstrated in their works a consciousness of the problematic nature of human time. Generally described by the French formulation "décadent" or "fin de siècle," they located themselves with nostalgia at the end of an epoch of human culture and, since the idea of inevitable progress held no force for them, looked forward with little hope to the future. When they turned their attention to the present, they saw an instant of time, made melancholy by echoes of a rich past, sinking into nothingness before their eyes. Two Austrian authors of that era, Arthur Schnitzler and Hugo von Hofmannsthal, were particularly obsessed with this theme. The latter's first play, *Gestern* (1891), describes the difficulties of a hero who aspires to live, like the members of Nietzsche's herd, "kurz angebunden . . . an den Pflock des Augenblicks." Andrea, the princeling of a late Renaissance court, finds that a life consistent with his varying moods, the only "true" life for him ("Laß dich von jedem Augenblicke treiben, / Das ist der Weg, dir selber treu zu bleiben"),[5] demands inconsistency, inconstancy, in his tastes and affections. The pale dress which his mistress Arlette had worn the day before no longer pleases him, for today is a "Correggio" day requiring rich and glowing colors; the pictures in his gallery also must be changed to fit his present mood, be it ascetic, sensuous, demonic, or whatever. Following the same aesthetic principle of selection, Andrea chooses and rejects his companions on the basis of their congruence with his feeling of the moment: in an ascetic frame of mind he prefers Marsilio; in a war-like mood, Lorenzo; in a mood for the pleasures of the table, he prefers the Cardinal of Ostio, whose very appearance awakens appetite ("Durch deine Augen seh ich Trüffel winken"[6]). Andrea is dutifully practising here what Kierkegaard, writing in *Either/Or* some fifty years earlier, had described as "the rotation method." The aesthete, the purely sensuous, ethically uncommitted man who wishes to enjoy the world as an aesthetic phenomenon must, according to the Danish writer, beware of cultivating too long and too exclusively any one area of experience; otherwise he will be left with nothing but a feeling of dull satiety, and thus fail to attain his goal of greatest possible enjoyment. He must carefully avoid consistency, "willing one thing," and choose arbitrariness in his approach to the world, or else his experiences will lose that freshness which he so strongly desires in them. It is of paramount importance for the devotee of the aesthetic life as described by Kierkegaard and as exemplified by Andrea to be in command of "the general categories of *remembering* and *forgetting*. Life in its entirety moves in these two currents, and hence it is essential to have them under control."[7] Andrea will not be shackled in his surrender to the moment by acts and choices of the past. When Arlette reproaches him for his changing taste in her clothes, he retorts angrily:

> Mußt du mit gestern stets das Heute stören?
> Muß ich die Fessel immer klirren hören,
> Die ewig dir am Fuß beengend hängt,
> Wenn ich für mich sie tausendmal gesprengt![8]

It would appear from these lines that Andrea has a firm control over his memory, that in thousands of present moments he has been able to demolish just as many past ones successfully; but the *dénouement* of the playlet shows him to be the victim of a crucial miscalculation. Arlette has been unfaithful to him the night before with his best friend Lorenzo, and the force of this past betrayal, contrary of course to Andrea's expressed philosophy, is sufficient to poison the present to such an extent that he must send his mistress away with these words:

> Dies Gestern ist so eins mit deinem Sein,
> Du kannst es nicht verwischen, nicht vergessen:
> Es *ist,* so lang wir wissen, daß es *war.*
> In meine Arme müßt ichs täglich pressen,
> Im Dufte saug ichs ein aus deinem Haar!
> Und heute-gestern ist ein leeres Wort.
> Was einmal war, das lebt auch ewig fort.[9]

The characters in this play are like figures in a charade who act and dress in a certain way to illustrate a point—in this case the point that the hero's lyric-philosophic meditations are belied by human experience. The multi-dimensional quality of that experience finds no place within the framework of this little fable, in which the characters other than the hero are present merely to act out the implications of his thesis. This is in keeping with Andrea's schematic way of apprehending his fellow beings, who are for him mere representations of abstract qualities, such as "Behagen" in the case of the Cardinal; for Andrea, as for Kierkegaard's aesthete, "experience is reduced to a sounding-board for the soul's own music."[10] The simplistic nature of *Gestern* is also of course in keeping with the youth and comparative inexperience of the play's author, the seventeen-year-old Hofmannsthal. In any case the play gives scant signs of the dramatic mastery with which the author will depict the confrontation of aesthete-adventurer and everyday human world in such a comedy as the later *Christinas Heimreise.*

Despite the limitations of *Gestern* as a dramatic work of art, it is understandable that Arthur Schnitzler, hearing the play read aloud by its young author to a select company, was deeply impressed, for the preoccupation of his own characters with time was always of Schnitzler's literary essence. The remainder of this paper will trace the varying relations between human beings and time in several of Schnitzler's works, concentrating finally on one of his chief theatrical successes, ***Reigen.***

In a novella entitled *Sterben,* which appeared the year after *Gestern,* Schnitzler depicts the predicament of a time-haunted hero ironically named Felix who discovers that the disease from which he is suffering allows him at the most another year of life. The plot of this novella gives its author the opportunity for a satiric psychological examination of a projected *Liebestod.* (A striking thematic parallel is offered here by the abortive love-death of the hero of Heinrich Mann's novella *Pippo Spano,* which appeared approximately a decade later.) When Felix' mistress, Marie, learns of his impending fate, she cries out instinctively that she will not be able to live for a day—not even for an hour—without him: "Sie flüsterte: 'Ich will mit dir sterben.' Er lächelte. 'Das sind Kindereien. Ich bin nicht so kleinlich, wie du glaubst. Ich hab' auch gar nicht das Recht, dich mit mir zu ziehen.'"[11] As the year passes, both partners of this dialogue gradually change their resolutions under the attrition of time. Marie, as the cheerless exhausting months drag by, finds her love for the querulous and selfish invalid dying, can only think of escaping from him and living again; Felix, on the other hand, finds more and more comfort in the thought that he need not die alone, that the young and vital Marie, whom healthy men glance at so admiringly in the street, will join him in the grave. The final *Liebestod* is not a romantic one: Marie outlives Felix; it is her love for him which dies, turning into horrified revulsion when at the last moment before his death he tries to kill her.

Felix clearly represents an extreme case of a sufferer from time by consciously experiencing his life, in a now famous phrase, as a "Sein zum Tode" (Heidegger). Near the beginning of the narrative, he has an insight both modern and ancient: "Es gehen eigentlich lauter zum Tode Verurteilte auf der Erde herum."[12] This knowledge, however, does not bring the stoic composure which he hopefully envisages for himself ("ich bin der Mann, der lächelnd von dieser Welt scheidet"[13]) but rather ever-increasing anxiety and despair. Like the majority of Schnitzler's male characters, Felix enjoys an elevated social station with corresponding income that allows him to surrender himself carelessly to the so-called "good things" which the passing moment offers. Yet his inability to live merely in the present moment progresses with the story. Sometimes he succeeds, by an effort of the will, in forgetting past and future:

> Der Wein war gut, schmeichelnd klang die Musik herüber, der Sommerabend war berauschend mild, und wie Felix zu Marie hinüberschaute, sah er aus ihren Augen einen Schein unendlicher Güte und Liebe strahlen. Und er wollte sich mit seinem ganzen Wesen in den gegenwärtigen Moment versenken. Er stellte eine letzte Anforderung an seinen Willen, von allem befreit zu sein, was Vergangenheit und Zukunft war. Er wollte glücklich sein oder wenigstens trunken.[14]

But more often Felix experiences a phenomenon, so common in Schnitzler's works, that Bernhard Blume has aptly characterized as an "immerwährende Vernichtung der Gegenwart durch die Zeit. . . ."[15] This can occur in various ways: either an experience from the past can poison the present (as was the case too with Hofmannsthal's Andrea) or a future event, such as Felix' approaching death, can have the same effect; or (and this has often been overlooked) the lack of those relative points of reference, past and future, can rob all substance from the present. In terms of Nietzsche's parable: the man who admires the happiness of the herd finally attains their state without however finding the imagined "happiness," since he has reached their oblivious condition at the price of all consciousness of it. (As Nietzsche had indeed foreseen: "er . . . will es doch vergebens, weil er es nicht will wie das Tier.") Alfred, Felix' friend and physician, finds the invalid in this state towards the end of his sickness and recognizes it as a fatal symptom; he sees Felix entering into a "Zeitabschnitt, in dem es keine Hoffnung und keine Furcht gibt, wo die Empfindung der Gegenwart selbst, dadurch, daß ihr der Ausblick auf die Zukunft und die Rückschau ins Vergangene fehlt, dumpf und unklar wird."[16]

The next work of Schnitzler to be considered here, **Anatol** (with its famous prologue by the author's friend "Loris"), appeared the year after *Sterben*. The chronology alone points to the probability of common concerns in the novella and the play. With Anatol, Schnitzler turns to the figure of the erotic adventurer, which in the following decades was to reappear so often in his own works as well as in those of Hofmannsthal. To return here briefly to *Either/Or*: Kierkegaard too has portrayed in that book the erotic adventurer as the exemplary aesthete; Don Juan, as embodied in Mozart's music and reincarnated in the Seducer, was the traditional figure the Danish philosopher chose in order to present the aesthetic way of life, just as Schnitzler and Hofmannsthal later chose Don Juan's Rococo successor, Casanova, for a similar purpose. Again Kierkegaard has defined some fifty years before the fact the predicament of the aesthete-heroes of the Austrian writers when, in discussing in his notebooks that section of *Either/Or* devoted to the erotic adventurer, he states: "The first part [of the book] always comes to grief upon time. . . ."[17] With this insight and the related one that the aesthete typically suffers from "tungsind," a brooding melancholy, "a dreaming, almost crazy wallowing in imagination,"[18] Kierkegaard comes close to prophesying the character of Anatol. The play is such a loose sequence of scenes that it scarcely matters where one begins to try to arrive at the essence of its titular hero. Its "plot" is of such a nature that Aristotle, for example, who found that "of all plots and actions the episodic are the worst," would never have approved of it. This lack of causal and consequential progression, however, is again in keeping with a statement of Kierkegaard's that the aesthetic life is incapable of "becoming history, of acquiring history . . . ," a direction which for him, as no doubt for Aristotle too, "is the significance of the temporal and finiteness."[19]

In an early episode of the play, Anatol calls himself a "leichtsinniger Melancholiker,"[20] and in a later scene sharply entitled "Agonie," we approach the heart of his sadness. He is unable to give the passing moment, which is for him typically the moment of love, that fullness and self-sufficiency which he feels he and his partners deserve to find in it. He is not one of the happy members of the herd: ". . . ich beneide ja doch die andern . . . die Glücklichen, für die jedes Stück Leben ein neuer Sieg ist!—Ich muß mir immer vornehmen, mit etwas fertig zu werden; ich mache Haltestellen—ich überlege, ich raste, ich schleppe mit—! Jene andern überwinden spielend, im Erleben selbst . . ." (p. 62). Anatol feels melancholy for himself and guilt towards his partners: "Hatten wir nicht die Verpflichtung, die Ewigkeit, die wir ihnen versprachen, in die paar Jahre oder Stunden hineinzulegen, in denen wir sie liebten? Und wir konnten es nie! nie!—Mit diesem Schuldbewußtsein scheiden wir von jeder—und unsere Melancholie bedeutet nichts als ein stilles Eingeständnis" (p. 62). Max, the *raisonneur,* must analyze the situation for his friend and us: "Deine Gegenwart schleppt immer eine ganze schwere Last von unverarbeiteter Vergangenheit mit sich . . . Und nun fangen die ersten Jahre deiner Liebe wieder einmal zu vermodern an, ohne daß deine Seele die wunderbare Kraft hätte, sie völlig auszustoßen.—Was ist nun die natürliche Folge—?—Daß auch um die gesundesten und blühendsten Stunden deines Jetzt ein Duft dieses Moders fließt—und die Atmosphäre deiner Gegenwart unrettbar vergiftet ist . . . Und darum ist ja ewig dieser Wirrwarr von Einst und Jetzt und Später in dir" (pp. 62-63).

The chaos of past, present, and future which, according to Max' analysis, defines the character of Anatol comes to light in the swiftly shifting scenes of the play. In the very first, the force of the past is already present, inhibiting Anatol's surrender to the moment: the thought that Cora, his mistress, might at some time have been unfaithful to him robs his love for her of any naïve assurance and happiness. The theme of infidelity, one of the only constants in the impressionistic worlds of Schnitzler and Hofmannsthal, illustrates dramatically the power the past has to vitiate enjoyment of the present moment. Logically, both Andrea and Anatol should be flattered that their partners share their own hedonistic philosophies, but in practice the suspicion that such might be the case is a source of endless torment. Having successfully hypnotized Cora, Anatol balks at asking her the crucial question which would establish the facts of her past behavior. For the moment he chooses to forget the past. We recall that the aesthete must have the two faculties of remembering and forgetting under his control; but Anatol, that dramatic performer of the "rotation method," again and again comes to grief because he cannot constantly exercise this control. Again and again he is haunted by the pasts of his partners, by the fact that he cannot forget—likewise, however, he is beset at times by his inability to remember, to recapture the past. In the third scene, entitled "Episode," Anatol comes to his friend Max seeking a refuge for his past, in this case represented by mementos of the women he has loved. The friends find an envelope containing a flower which has now turned to dust, and this discovery gives Anatol occasion for rueful reflections on transience: "Es war nur eine Episode, ein Roman von zwei Stunden . . . nichts! . . . Ja, Staub!—Daß von so viel Süßigkeit nichts anderes zurückbleibt, ist eigentlich traurig.—Nicht?" (p. 35).

Regret at passing time, chagrin "daß alles gleitet und vorüberrinnt," is of course a widespread literary theme, often accompanied by the "carpe diem" reaction. In this same "Episode," however, Schnitzler introduces his peculiar treatment of this motif, which will reappear with radical force in *Reigen*: the aesthete's "day," often diminished to a few hours or less, may even sink away completely under the conscious weight of past and future. Nothing is so difficult for Anatol as to capture the present moment. While he is making love to Bianca, the experience is already past for him: "Während ich den warmen Hauch ihres Mundes auf meiner Hand fühlte, erlebte ich das Ganze schon in der Erinnerung. Es war eigentlich schon vorüber" (p. 36). Anatol and the other characters of the play also suffer more conventionally from time. The titular hero, in the scene in which he calls himself a "leichtsinniger Melancholiker," questions wistfully: "Weiß man denn überhaupt im Herbst, wem man zu Weihnachten etwas schenken wird?" (p. 23), and in answer to the question whether he means everything to the girl he presently loves he replies: ". . . Möglich! . . . Heute . . . *Schweigen*" (p. 29). In Schnitzler's world, clocks or watches are always ticking inexorably in the background, just as in Baroque literature the sand is always slipping through the hourglass. Such a scene as the following is typical:

ANATOL:

> *die Hände faltend*: Ich bitte dich!—Kannst du dich denn nicht wenigstens sekundenlang unverheiratet denken?—Schlürfe doch den Reiz dieser Minute—denke doch, wir zwei sind allein auf der Welt . . .
>
> *Glockenschläge.*

ELSE:

> Wie spät—?
>
> (p. 65)

Seize the moment between the pulsebeats of time—but here again that moment has been vitiated by thoughts of before and after. In "Abschiedssouper," Anatol has decided to inform his beloved, Annie, that his erotic interests have for some time found another object; Annie, who has also experienced such a shift of interests, anticipates him by announcing the necessity of their parting. Infuriated by her "infidelity," Anatol exclaims: "Man kann sich bei euresgleichen nicht genug eilen—sonst kommt ihr einem zuvor!" (p. 59). Again Schnitzler introduces a personal note in the theme of hastening to capture the moment of erotic bliss: one must be aware, at this very moment, of the past and future infidelities which take from it its aesthetic value. Comparison with an earlier treatment of the theme points up this divergence. In a seventeenth-century poem such as "Ach Liebste, laß uns eilen, / Wir haben Zeit . . ." the poet is at least sure that he and his beloved have "time," even if it be, as Leonard Forster has commented, "occasio" rather than "tempus" in this particular case.[21] The Baroque poet is able to tear his pleasures "through the iron gates of life" and, for the moment at least, to enjoy them wholly. For Anatol and his coevals, however, these moments are all to a greater or lesser degree "sonderbar täuschende . . . Augenblicke . . ." (p. 61).

Reigen, written in 1896/97, is a masterful dramatic statement of Schnitzler's attitudes toward time. No longer does the author find it necessary to have a *raisonneur* such as Max comment after an especially glaring example of Anatol's inconstancy: "es ist eben das Leben!" (p. 83)—now all such comments are firmly embedded in the structure of the play itself. The scenes, their Janus-faced composition pointing to both past and future, inexorably locate the characters in that context of time which they more or less consciously are always trying to escape. The aesthete's "day" has, as already anticipated in *Anatol,* been reduced to the most evanescent of moments, the moment of sexual satisfaction as experienced by two persons who are seeking only that from one another. It is surely psychological naiveté on Soergel's part to find "paltry" Schnitzler's use of the sex act as a metaphor for "die Fülle des Lebens,"[22] for Schnitzler's characters, heirs of those eighteenth-century sensationalists who had converted the famous Cartesian dictum into "I feel, therefore I am," seek certainty of their existence in the experience of pleasurable sensations—and the stronger the sensations, the surer their existence seems to them.[23] They show curiosity about one another's capacity to perceive "happiness": the poet is questioning "das süße Mädel":

> . . . Sag mir, mein Kind, bist du glücklich?

DAS SÜSSE MÄDEL:

> Wie meinst das?

DER DICHTER:

> Ich mein im allgemeinen, ob du glücklich bist? . . . Ich mein . . . wenn du dich einfach leben spürst. Spürst du dich überhaupt leben?

DAS SÜSSE MÄDEL:

> Geh, hast kein Kamm?
>
> (p. 561)

The count does not have any greater success with the prostitute:

> Sag mir einmal, bist du eigentlich glücklich?

DIRNE:

> Was?

GRAF:

> Also ich mein, gehts dir gut?

DIRNE:

Oh, mir gehts alleweil gut.

. . . . .

GRAF

bleibt wieder stehen: Du, sag einmal, dir ist schon alles
egal—was?

DIRNE:

Was?

GRAF:

Ich mein, dir machts gar keine Freud mehr.

DIRNE GÄHNT:

Ein Schlaf hab ich.

(pp. 580-81)

Like Nietzsche's human being, Schnitzler's characters
here receive singularly unilluminating answers from the
"happy" herd.

Regardless of their degree of sophistication in the pursuit
of pleasure, the figures in *Reigen* all encounter one
obstacle between them and their goal—the obstacle of
time. The first and most concrete form that time takes for
them is the clock; it is the enemy of the soldier in the first
scene who must return to the barracks, of the young wife
in the fourth scene who has only five minutes for her illicit rendezvous, of the count in the ninth who finds the
early hour inauspicious for courtship. In all these cases,
however, the act of love does take place, in spite of clock
and time. Consciousness of the clock seems to work like
an aphrodisiac upon the characters of the play. The
prostitute in the first scene states the motive behind this
response: "Geh, bleib jetzt bei mir. Wer weiß, ob wir morgen nochs Leben haben" (p. 518), and the young gentleman in the fourth scene restates it as a part of his perora-
tion for the young wife: "Das Leben ist so leer, so
nichtig—und dann—so kurz—so entsetzlich kurz!" (p.
533). Like Felix in *Sterben* but without his reason for
urgency, the people in *Reigen* realize that their living is a
"Sein zum Tode" and act similarly to the earlier hero by
seizing upon the moment of pleasurable sensation as their
only guarantee of existence. The temporal aspect of this
behavior has been described by Bernhard Blume as "aus
der 'Zeit' in die 'Fülle' flüchten,"[24] and it is now necessary
to examine this "Fülle."

"Fülle" can of course be only a matter of minutes for
Schnitzler's characters—a fleeting, momentary thing. The
action of *Reigen* emphasizes this without the aid of any
overt philosophizing on the part of the characters by building its brief scenes around a sexual act with no "before"
or "after" (the "before" was with another partner as the
"after" will be). The act refuses thus to "acquire history,"
to become a part of time; it is discontinuous, its very
nature precluding duration. In an episode unique in *Reigen,*
Schnitzler presents a love scene between man and wife.

Married love, committed to duration, would seem to be
out of place in a play such as this, until we learn through
the dialogue of the peculiar history of this marriage. The
husband is explaining to his young wife that their five-
year-old marriage has been successful only because in the
course of it they have had "ten or twelve" love affairs with
each other:

Hätten wir gleich die erste [Liebschaft] bis zum Ende
durchgekostet . . . es wäre uns gegangen wie den Mil-
lionen von anderen Liebespaaren. Wir wären fertig mit
einander . . . Darum ist es gut, immer wieder für einige
Zeit nur in guter Freundschaft hinzuleben.

DIE JUNGE FRAU:

Ach so.

DER GATTE:

Und so kommt es, daß wir immer wieder neue Flitterwochen miteinander durchleben können, da ich es nie
drauf ankommen lasse, die Flitterwochen . . .

DIE JUNGE FRAU:

Zu Monaten auszudehnen.

DER GATTE:

Richtig.

(pp. 539-40)

For the moment at least, the husband's expressed philosophy seems to be valid and the warning of the aesthete-
author of "The Rotation Method" that "one must never
enter into the relation of *marriage*"[25] appears unnecessary.
Readers or viewers of *Reigen,* however, may well question the validity of this particular marriage—even on
purely aesthetic grounds—after witnessing the scenes
before and after the one directly depicting it. Positive
views on the wedded state are of course not generally to
be expected from the characters of this play; conventional
proposals are neither proffered nor desired here. Schnitzler's figures on the whole would agree with the following
passage from "The Rotation Method" which appears
directly after that on marriage, although they would no
doubt smile condescendingly at the quaint decorum of the
first sentence:

But because a man does not marry, it does not follow
that his life need be wholly deprived of the erotic element. And the erotic ought also to have infinitude; but
poetic infinitude, which can just as well be limited to
an hour as to a month. When two beings fall in love
with one another and begin to suspect that they were
made for each other, it is time to have the courage to
break it off; for by going on they have everything to
lose and nothing to gain.[26]

This "poetic infinitude, which can just as well be limited
to an hour as to a month," is what Schnitzler's characters
are seeking under the name of "Fülle": *Reigen* chronicles
this search with its increasing and inevitable frustrations.
It is usually felt that this particular play, with its title and

analogous structure, precludes any form of dramatic development. Insofar as "dramatic development" suggests a progressive action with a beginning, middle, and end, and a cast of characters who to greater or lesser extents come to realizations of their human condition through this action, this usual skepticism about **Reigen** is well founded. (It will be seen later why conventional development of character is impossible in this play.) But to deny any kind of development in **Reigen** is to overlook the author's careful evolution and increasingly sharper statement of theme in the frenetic rondo of his ten scenes.

Among the more conventional deterrents to the full enjoyment of the present moment in **Reigen** is the characters' consciousness of the pasts of their partners. Anatol too had been tormented by the infidelity of others, but in the later play this sentiment is both more widespread (both male and female characters share it) and even more ironic; for Anatol is a model of constancy compared to these figures whose brief unions are so clearly framed for us by those of the preceding and following scenes. Anatol had found a sort of solution to the shock caused by his partners' infidelities: hasten to anticipate them in this sphere. But he probably would not have been capable of formulating the perverse coda of this motif as played by the Poet and the Actress near the end of **Reigen**:

SCHAUSPIELERIN:

Nun, wem bist du in diesem Moment untreu?

DICHTER:

Ich bin es ja leider noch nicht.

SCHAUSPIELERIN:

Nun tröste dich, ich betrüge auch jemanden.

(p. 565)

Just before the embrace obligatory in these scenes, the Actress returns to the subject:

SCHAUSPIELERIN:

Nun, wen betrüg ich?

DICHTER:

Wen? . . . Vielleicht mich . . .

SCHAUSPIELERIN:

Mein Kind, du bist schwer gehirnleidend.

(p. 566)

The Poet, however, is not so insane as his companion suggests, for he and all the other characters are inevitably and uniformly betrayed by their very presence in a play whose structure permits no illusions about the uniqueness of the affairs depicted in it. Nor is he likely to find comfort, as the Actress advises, in the fact of the universality of this betrayal, since this very fact, as we know, poisons the presents of all Schnitzler's devotees of the moment.

The present was the most precarious among the chaos of tenses which defined Anatol's character. We recall that during the course of an erotic experience he already imagined it to himself as past, as a tender memory among many others. Another and even more effective way to undermine the present moment is to forget rather than remember it as it occurs. Anatol at least has his memories to shore up against his ruins; by browsing among the mementos of past love affairs which he deposited with Max, he can be sure that he has existed, although saddened by the consciousness of the tense. But if such a character has a bad memory, how can he be certain of his existence at all? "Forgetting," then, becomes a motif which is stated with ever-increasing strength in **Reigen** until it represents the final and fatal triumph of time over the characters; for by robbing the aesthete of his consciousness of sensation, he is thereby robbed of his very existence. The motif is first stated in the scene between the Little Miss and the Poet; the latter speaks in the darkened room:

Es ist seltsam, ich kann mich nicht mehr erinnern, wie du aussiehst.

DAS SÜßE MÄDEL:

Dank schön!

DER DICHTER ernst:

Du, das ist beinah unheimlich, ich kann mir dich nicht vorstellen—In einem gewissen Sinne hab ich dich schon vergessen—Wenn ich mich auch nicht mehr an den Klang deiner Stimme erinnern könnte . . . was wärst du da eigentlich?—Nah und fern zugleich . . . unheimlich.

(pp. 557-58)

By losing their grasp on the present moment, as here, the characters in **Reigen** also lose the clear contours of personality, also lose their identities. If the aesthete exists ony for and in the present moment, he necessarily loses all reality when that moment loses reality. The first step in this process is the growing indistinctness of the partner in an erotic experience, as in the scene cited above; the next and inevitable step for Schnitzler is the blurring of the experience itself for the subject.

Although, as we have already remarked, **Reigen** has no *raisonneur* like Max, who stands somewhat outside the action and comments upon it in neatly-turned epigrams, Schnitzler has given his later play a "philosopher" of sorts, and, by making him an integral part of the action, the author is able to give his play both increased dramatic objectivity and irony. The Count in the last two scenes is a near relation of those other aesthetes, Felix and Anatol, with the possible difference that his station in life permits him an even more exclusive and spectacular dedication to the pursuit of pleasure. As we would expect, then, his "tungsind" is even deeper than theirs. Through his practice of the "rotation method," he has come to feel that all fields are equally unexciting and essentially interchangeable.

When stationed in Hungary he looked forward to the diversions of Vienna; once arrived in Vienna he found that the only difference was that the crowds in that city were larger. He envies the Actress whom he is visiting because he assumes that she must know why she is living: she has the lofty goal of her art to pursue. When she denies any knowledge of purpose in her life, he points out that after all she is famous, celebrated. Then a highly significant conversation takes place about the central problem of "happiness" and its relation to time:

GRAF:

Ich bitt Sie, Fräulein—berühmt—gefeiert—

SCHAUSPIELERIN:

Ist das vielleicht ein Glück?

GRAF:

Glück? Bitt Sie, Fräulein, Glück gibts nicht. Überhaupt gerade die Sachen, von denen am meisten g'redt wird, gibts nicht . . . zum Beispiel die Liebe. Das ist auch so was.

SCHAUSPIELERIN:

Da haben Sie wohl recht.

GRAF:

Genuß . . . Rausch . . . also gut, da läßt sich nichts sagen . . . das ist was sicheres. Jetzt genieße ich . . . gut, weiß ich, ich genieß. Oder ich bin berauscht, schön. Das ist auch sicher. Und ists vorbei, so ist es halt vorbei.

SCHAUSPIELERIN GROß:

Es ist vorbei!

GRAF:

Aber sobald man sich nicht, wie soll ich mich denn ausdrücken, sobald man sich nicht dem Moment hingibt, also an später denkt oder an früher . . . na, ist es doch gleich aus. Später . . . ist traurig . . . früher ist ungewiß . . . mit einem Wort . . . man wird nur konfus. Hab ich nicht recht?

SCHAUSPIELERIN *NICKT MIT GROßEN AUGEN:*

Sie haben wohl den Sinn erfaßt.

(p. 572)

Here is the time philosophy of the characters in **Reigen** made explicit, but, as we shall see, this is not Schnitzler's own final statement on the theme in the play. The isolated moment with no before or after is the only element in which these characters can exist; and insofar as the moment is discontinuous, the character too must be discontinuous. For this reason, as was hinted earlier, there can be no conventional development of character in a play such as **Reigen.** In the scenes toward the end involving the Actress and the Count, this discontinuity of character becomes so pronounced that we are confronted with a constant stream of non sequiturs. The figure of the actor or actress is supremely suited for the dramatic presentation of this inconstancy. The actor, as Nietzsche pointed out (and Schnitzler must have agreed with him), with his capacity for lightning-swift "changes," typifies "falseness with a good conscience," shows "the joy in dissimulation breaking out" to such an extent that it "pushes the so-called 'character' to the side, drowns it, at times even extinguishes it."[27] In her scene with the Poet, the Actress voices changing opinions in practically every speech, referring for example to her present lover as a "whim," then as a man for whom she is "dying" with love. When, in the next scene, she discovers the Count just as clearly contradicting himself (most conspicuously by making love to her at the early hour contrary to his "program"), she cries out: "Und du hättest Schauspieler werden sollen!" (p. 575).

Indeed, we cannot expect any consistency on the part of the aesthete, for whom the "actors" here are heightened representatives. The aesthete, in his turn, stands for man himself—for, as Hofmannsthal defined him, he is a dovecote: impulses fly out like doves and others return, making it a metaphor to speak of the "self" at all. The "I," as Hermann Bahr repeated after Ernst Mach, is "irretrievable." Schnitzler illustrates this dissolution of the psychologically consistent traditional character most strikingly in the figures of the Actress and the Count; and with the latter he goes one step farther and shows the existential consequences of the discontinuous "I" with a psychological sharpness equalling that demonstrated by Nietzsche in his fable of the herd. The aesthete-Count is sure of only one thing: the pleasure of the moment. "Jetzt genieße ich . . . gut, weiß ich, ich genieß"—that is something so certain that he can say with the sensationalist: "I feel, therefore I am." In the dim dawn scene which follows the interview with the Actress and is the final episode of **Reigen,** the intoxicated Count has accompanied the prostitute of the first episode home to her sordid room. He awakens and tries to orient himself in his at first unfamiliar surroundings. Schnitzler here shows us a character close to psychological annihilation and at the same time illuminates with mordant irony the paradoxical aestheticism of his characters. The Count, in the previous scene, had stated that the time before and the time after that of the most pleasurable sensations was essentially sad but that the time of that pleasure was something certain: "I know I enjoy . . . that is something certain," and he might have added: that is all that is certain. Now, throughout the scene with the Prostitute, he tries to establish with only halting success whether he has actually enjoyed her favors, whether the pleasure he is so sure of actually took place. The motif of forgetfulness takes on nihilistic proportions, for here, in the most real sense, is a man fighting for his existence and meeting only blank nothingness. As he regards the sleeping girl, the Count, "philosopher" still, speculates upon the similarity of sleep and death; he fails to realize, however, the similarity of his own state with death, for he too in this shadowy scene has lost contact with the real space and time surrounding him. He has reached the state of that "happy" member of Nietzsche's herd who always "forgets" his happiness of the moment before, and this state, as Nietzsche recognized, is psychological death for the human being. By seeking to isolate the "moment," which alone has meaning for him, he has succeeded in "killing" time in the real sense of that often thoughtlessly used phrase. Human existence at any given instant is contiguous with and dependent upon the coordinate points of past and future. Increasingly for the modern mind, there is no such thing as "absolute" time: a moment cannot be isolated from its surroundings, to which it is supremely relative, and then be spoken of as "real." Schnitzler here shows us characters seeking "fullness" of time outside the domain of measuring clocks and finding inevitably (and most dramatically in the case of the Count)—nothing. Baroque poets sensed with a similar urgency that the moment is our only possession, but had at their disposal, as one last contrast will show, a formula of transformation which set them in a different world from Schnitzler's characters:

> Mein sind die Jahre nicht, die mir die Zeit genommen;
> Mein sind die Jahre nicht, die etwa möchten kommen;
> Der Augenblick ist mein, und nehm ich den in Acht,
> So ist der mein, der Zeit und Ewigkeit gemacht.[28]

Readers of *Reigen* never fail to mark Schnitzler's social comment in the last scene—that the highest and lowest levels of society are equal before the power of Eros, as in the Middle Ages they were seen to be equal in the universal Dance of Death. A further comment, however, needs to be underscored: that these two creatures of pleasure, sophisticated and unsophisticated, are equally cheated. In answer to the Count's anxious questions about her happiness, the Prostitute answered "Was?" and (yawning) "Ein Schlaf hab ich." The Count's assurance concerning his own enjoyment, although eagerly sought ("Und was ist denn passiert . . . Also nichts . . . Oder ist was . . . ?" [p. 578]), is equally inadequate. Schnitzler, like Kierkegaard, emphasizes the essential paradox of the aesthetic life by showing how such a life, so basically committed to time, inevitably comes to grief upon it. Like Kierkegaard and Nietzsche, Schnitzler realizes the inanity of the idolization of the moment, whatever form it may take: "Das Vergangene abgetan sein lassen, die Zukunft der Vorsehung anheimstellen—beides heißt den eigentlichen Sinn der Gegenwart nicht verstehen, die überhaupt nur so weit als Realität gelten kann, als sie durch Treue des Gedächtnisses das Vergangene zu bewahren, durch Bewußtsein der Verantwortung die Zukunft in sich einzubeziehen versteht."[29] These lines were not written by a philosopher or Christian apologist; the fact, however, that their moral insight might suggest such authorship discloses an aspect of Schnitzler's genius which is often overlooked in conventional treatments of the Austrian dramatist, and particularly of this play.

The characters in *Reigen* "forget" themselves so completely near the end of the play that we can refer to them only metaphorically as having conventional "selves." The circular structure suggests that the play might begin again at the ending with the same cast of characters (the Prostitute meeting the Soldier the evening after her episode

with the Count, and so forth), for they have not developed or won any insights into themselves in the course of the action. These features must strike a modern theater-goer as amazingly like those of an "anti-play" such as *The Bald Soprano*. The seeds of absurdity present in Schnitzler have come to blossom in Ionesco's "Theater of the Absurd." Here the characters have become so unreal to themselves and one another that they must constantly state their names and the most obvious facts about themselves in order to gain some assurance of their existence (husband and wife rediscover that they are married by finding they have the same daughter). They are so discontinuous that they constantly contradict themselves, usually in an even shorter space of time than *Reigen*'s figures:

MR. SMITH:

> She has regular features and yet one cannot say that she is pretty. She is too big and stout. Her features are not regular but still one can say that she is very pretty. She is a little too small and too thin. She's a voice teacher.[30]

The characters are interchangeable in *The Bald Soprano,* as—for certain purposes—they are in *Reigen* also. The French play ends with Mr. and Mrs. Martin seated in the same places occupied by Mr. and Mrs. Smith at the beginning and speaking the same lines which the latter couple had at the opening of the scene. The circular structure both here and in *Reigen* suggests absurdity. The self, the psychologically consistent entity capable of duration, so threatened at the end of the century and already declared then to be "irretrievable," collapses for the French playwright with farcical results. This juxtaposition of Ionesco and Schnitzler is not meant as a value judgment of either author or of the virtue of modernity as such; it is merely intended to suggest that Schnitzler, like the scenes in his *Reigen,* is Janus-faced. He may indeed look back wistfully, as all the textbooks tell us, to the charms of a declining society, but he also assuredly looks forward to the peculiar confusions and torments of our own times. By devoting himself with such perspicacity to his own "moment," he succeeded at that feat which his characters were so signally unable to perform: he transcended his time.

Notes

1. Friedrich Nietzsche, *Werke in drei Bänden,* ed. Karl Schlechta (Munich, 1954), I, 211.

2. Walter H. Sokel, *The Writer in Extremis: Expressionism in Twentieth-Century German Literature* (Stanford, 1959), p. 102.

3. "Blühn und verdorrn ist uns zugleich bewußt. / Und irgendwo gehn Löwen noch und wissen, / solang sie herrlich sind, von keiner Ohnmacht." Rainer Maria Rilke, *Sämtliche Werke,* hrsg. vom Rilke-Archiv (Wiesbaden, 1955), I, 697.

4. Gottfried Benn, *Gesammelte Werke in vier Bänden,* ed. Dieter Wellershoff (Wiesbaden, 1960), III, 25.

5. Hugo von Hofmannsthal, *Gedichte und lyrische Dramen,* ed. Herbert Steiner (Vienna, 1952), p. 149.

6. Hofmannsthal, p. 168.

7. *A Kierkegaard Anthology,* ed. Robert Bretall (Princeton, 1946), p. 26.

8. Hofmannsthal, p. 148.

9. Hofmannsthal, p. 179.

10. *A Kierkegaard Anthology,* p. 27.

11. Arthur Schnitzler, *Ausgewählte Erzählungen* (Frankfurt am Main, 1950), p. 13.

12. Schnitzler, *Erzählungen,* p. 21. Pascal clothed the same insight in the same image in his *Pensées:* "Qu'on s'imagine un nombre d'hommes dans les chaînes, et tous condamnés à la mort, dont les uns étant chaque jour égorgés à la vue des autres, ceux qui restent voient leur propre condition dans celle de leurs semblables, et, se regardant les uns et les autres avec douleur et sans espérance, attendent à leur tour. C'est l'image de la condition des hommes." *Oeuvres de Blaise Pascal,* publiées par Léon Brunschvicg (Paris, 1921), XIII, 124.

13. Schnitzler, *Erzählungen,* p. 17.

14. *Erzählungen,* p. 39.

15. Bernhard Blume, *Das nihilistische Weltbild Arthur Schnitzlers,* Diss. (Stuttgart, 1936), p. 33.

16. *Erzählungen,* p. 60.

17. *The Journals of Søren Kierkegaard,* a selection ed. and trans. Alexander Dru (Oxford University Press, 1938), p. 128.

18. *Journals,* p. 128.

19. *Journals,* p. 128.

20. Arthur Schnitzler, *Meisterdramen* (Frankfurt am Main, 1955), p. 27. Page references to this edition will appear hereafter in the text.

21. Leonard Forster, *The Temper of Seventeenth-Century German Literature,* An Inaugural Lecture Delivered at University College, London, 7 February, 1951 (London, 1952), p. 12f.

22. He speaks of the "Armseligkeit dieses Gleichnisses": cf. Albert Soergel, *Dichtung und Dichter der Zeit: Eine Schilderung der deutschen Literatur der letzten Jahrzehnte,* 20. Auflage (Leipzig, 1928), p. 506.

23. Typical is a statement of Casanova (who, if he had not existed, would certainly have had to be invented by Schnitzler): "Je sais que j'ai existé, car j'ai senti; et le sentiment me donnant cette connaissance, je sais aussi que je n'existerai plus quand j'aurai cessé de sentir." Casanova, *Mémoires,* Texte présenté et annoté par Robert Abirached et Elio Zorzi, Préface de Gérard Bauer (Paris, 1958), I, 4.

24. Blume, *Das nihilistische Weltbild,* p. 20.

25. *A Kierkegaard Anthology,* p. 29.

26. *A Kierkegaard Anthology,* p. 30. Cf. *Reigen:*

> Der Dichter:
>
> Ich hatte es mir schön vorgestellt, mit dir zusammen, allein mit dir, irgendwo in der Einsamkeit draußen, im Wald, in der Natur ein paar Wochen zu leben. Natur . . . in der Natur . . . Und dann, eines Tages Adieu—voneinander gehen, ohne zu wissen, wohin.
>
> Das süße Madel:
>
> Jetzt redst schon vom Adieusagen! Und ich hab gemeint, daß du mich so gern hast.
>
> Der Dichter:
>
> Gerade darum—
>
> (p. 561)

27. These quotations from Nietzsche are my translation of fragments of Section 361 of *Die Fröhliche Wissenschaft.* Schnitzler speaks of a "Kernlosigkeit . . . die übrigens vorzugsweise bei reproduzierenden Talenten, vor allem bei genialen Schauspielern, insbesondere Schauspielerinnen, zu beobachten ist." *Buch der Sprüche und Bedenken: Aphorismen und Fragmente* (Vienna, 1927), p. 96.

28. Andreas Gryphius, "Betrachtung der Zeit," *Deutsche Barocklyrik,* hrsg. und mit einem Nachwort versehen von Max Wehrli (Basel, 1945), p. 22.

29. Schnitzler, *Buch der Sprüche,* pp. 83-84.

30. Eugène Ionesco, *Four Plays,* trans. Donald M. Allen (New York, 1958), p. 12.

Gerd K. Schneider (essay date 1986)

SOURCE: Schneider, Gerd K. "The Reception of Arthur Schnitzler's *Reigen* in the Old Country and the New World: A Study in Cultural Differences." *Modern Austrian Literature* 19, nos. 3-4 (1986): 75-89.

[*In the following essay, Schneider addresses differences in reactions to the stage, book, and film versions of* Reigen *in various countries.*]

Since the reception of Schnitzler's **Reigen** up to 1925 is generally known, only a few points need to be emphasized. The play was written in the winter of 1896-97 and was published in 1900 in a private printing that was not for sale. The work was well received by his friends, but as early as 1903, the year scenes four to six were first staged in Munich, sharp criticism was voiced by Törnsee:

> **Reigen** ist nichts als eine Schweinerei oder, ist das zu deutsch, eine Cochonnerie, die bloß der Esprit eines Parisers oder die Satire eines Künstlers, der moralisch hoch genug steht, um das Lüsterne des Themas sa-

chlich verurteilend zu behandeln, aus dem Reiche des Pornographischen in das Gebiet der Kunst hätte emporheben können.[1]

The use of the subjunctive indicates that Törnsee did not consider Schnitzler to be the artist to raise this work to the elevated level of art. One of the reasons for this apparent inability was supplied by Ottokar Stauf von der March:

Der Verfasser [Arthur Schnitzler] stellt sich in die Reihen der gewissenlosen Sudler, deren mephitische Erzeugnisse die Spalten der sogenannten 'Witz'-Blätter *ad majorem Veneris vulgvagae gloriam* füllen. . . . allenthalben [ist] der bekannte *foetor judaicus* zu spüren . . . [*Reigen*] *ist mit hündischer Geschlechtsgier geschrieben, daß es einem ekelt.*[2]

One year later the book edition of **Reigen** and the performance of the play were banned throughout Germany. However, Schnitzler was aware that **Reigen** was staged in Russia and in America, because he noted in his diary: "Wenn man hätte, um was man in Rußland, Amerika bestohlen würde."[3] Another diary entry shows that Schnitzler knew of unauthorized **Reigen**-performances in Hungary: "**Reigen,** ungarisch in Budapest gespielt, ordinär wie es scheint, polizeilich verboten."[4] Because unauthorized performances of **Reigen** increased after 1918, Schnitzler considered a stage performance, first in Berlin and then in Vienna.

Initially the press gave the Berlin performance of 23 December 1920 an excellent review. Herbert Ihering saw in the **Reigen** "graziöse Liebesspiele, ohne geistige Verfälschung,"[5] and Alfred Kerr called Schnitzler in the *Berliner Tageblatt* "mehr launig als faunisch," as someone who showed "mit nachdenklichem Lächeln den irdischen Humor der unterirdischen Welt. Nicht Schmutzereien: sondern Lebensaspekte. Auch das Vergängliche des Taumels: das komisch-trübe Schwinden des Trugs. Alles umhaucht von leisem, witzigem Reiz."[6] Interesting to note is that, according to some reviews, **Reigen** is a Viennese, not a German, product: "**Reigen** ist Wien, ist der betäubende, lockende verführerische Schimmer dieser herrlichen, fauligen, sinkenden, versunkenen Stadt."[7] It was not long before Regierungsrat Karl Brunner, who called himself the "Bannerträger der neuen deutschen Kultur," denounced this "Viennese decadent work" in strong terms. Working for the Government as an expert adviser attached to the "Zentralstelle zur Bekämpfung unzüchtiger Schriften," he succeeded in his attempt to activate nationalistic and anti-Semitic groups; this attack led to the famous, or rather infamous, theater scandal on 22 February 1921. The subsequent *Reigen-Prozeß* lasted from 5 November to 18 November; the trial transcripts published by Wolfgang Heine constitute a valuable historical document for the strong anti-Semitic feelings that existed during the so-called "Golden Twenties," twelve years before the Nazis officially assumed power. Anti-Semitism is reflected in the statement of one witness who shifted from the specific *ich* to the generalizing *unser,* finally culminating in *das ganze deutsche Volk*:

[Während der Aufführung] konzentrierte ich [hauptsächlich] mein ganzes Empfinden und meine Gedanken darauf, zu beobachten, in welcher Weise das Familienleben, das Eheleben, unser religiöses Leben, unsere christliche Religion, der Stand der Offiziere, schließlich auch der Stand der Schauspieler so restlos durch diese Akte der Unzucht in den Schmutz gezogen sind. Da sagte ich mir: ja, was ist denn das eigentlich hier? Soll das als Kunstwerk angesprochen werden? Wenn ja, so kann ich nicht glauben, daß man das als deutsche Kunst ansprechen wird, es muß etwas anderes sein, und zwar das, womit man das ganze deutsche Volk nach der Revolution und namentlich unsere Jugend mit aller Macht demoralisiert.[8]

This "something other" which demoralized German youth was stated directly by another witness: "Das verdanken wir dem Judenpack! Das wäre noch schöner, wenn wir uns das gefallen ließen, wenn wir auf diese Weise das deutsche Volk vergiften ließen."[9] These invectives came not only from organized Nazi groups such as the *Hakenkreuzler* but also from other right-wing associations which saw an opportunity during the trial to publicize their anti-Semitic bias. Again and again the following statements could be heard: "Mit diesen Juden muß Schluß gemacht werden! Wir sind doch schließlich Deutsche! . . . diese Saujuden . . . diese Bande . . . dieser jüdische Direktor . . . die Juden muß man alle ausräuchern . . . dieses Gesindel . . . die Juden sollen nach Palästina gehen. . . ."[10] Sentiments like these probably led the defense to the following conclusion: "Für die Verteidigung kommt es darauf an, festzustellen, daß es sich gar nicht um einen Kampf gegen den **Reigen** handelt, sondern um einen Kampf gegen die Juden, daß man den **Reigen** nur benutzt hat, um in dieser Form eine antisemitische Aktion ins Werk zu setzen. . . ."[11]

Schnitzler was skeptical about having **Reigen** performed in Vienna, as one of his diary entries shows:

Über "Reigen" aufführung. Bedenken und Gegengründe. Im Volksth[eater]. Wies Bernau [Direktor des Deutschen Volkstheaters] auf die Schwierigkeiten hin; u[nd] besonders auf die voraussichtliche Haltung der Presse. Schimpfereien der Antisemiten—und Lauheit der andern. Skandäle, die schädigen können, ja ev[entuell] selbst Censurverbot nach der Aufführung.[12]

The Viennese performance of **Reigen** took place on 21 February 1921 without any disturbances. The reviews, however, were quite biased; thus one could anticipate a scandal similar to the one in Berlin. The official organ of the Christian-Socialist Party, the *Reichspost,* issued the following attack:

Mit dem Reigen hat Schnitzler das Theater, das uns ein Haus edler Freuden sein sollte, zu einem Freudenhause, zum Schauplatze von Vorgängen und Gesprächen gemacht, wie sie sich schamloser in keiner Dirnenhöhle abwickeln können. . . . Schnaufende Dickwänste mit ihrem weiblichen Anhange, der den Namen der deutschen Frau schändet, sollen sich jetzt dort allabendlich ihre im wüsten Sinnentaumel erschlafften Nerven aufkitzeln lassen. Allein wir gedenken den Herrschäften das Vergnügen bald zu verleiden.[13]

A more vicious attack was published in the *Neue Montagsblatt* of 7 February 1921:

> Bordellprologe des Juden Schnitzler . . . typischer jüdischer Schiebereinfall, um mit der Wohltätigkeit unsaubere Geschäfte zu versuchen und hungernden Kindern Brotsamen vom Tische der Geilheit zu offerieren . . . das Schmierigste, das auf dem Theater je dagewesen ist . . . geilste Pornographie . . . Es ist die Pflicht all jener Katholiken, die in ihrem Kampf gegen Schmutz und Schund wieder diesmal allein zu stehen scheinen, sich zu mächtigen Protestaktionen zusammenzutun, die von den Behörden nicht überhört werden können.[14]

The Catholics soon followed the call to action; on 13 February the "Katholische Volksbund für Österreich" gathered for a demonstration which drew 800 people who listened to the anti-Semitic statements made by the state councillor Seipel. On the evening of the same day Schnitzler attended the ***Reigen*** performance; his experience is recorded in his diary as follows: "Sie waren schon dabei, als ich hinkam. Über 300, von einer Katholikenversammlung kommend, wo ich beschimpft wurde, insultiren die Theaterbesucher, die eben kommen, johlen: 'Man schändet unsere Weiber! Nieder Reigen! Nieder mit den Sozialdemokraten' usw. Polizei vertreibt sie. Viel Polizei an den Eingängen."[15]

Public opinion became more prejudiced the following day after the "Deutsch-Arischen Vereinigungen" had met to protest against the "Schande Wiens." The attack came on the 18th of February during a performance which Schnitzler was attending:

> Lärm . . . Garderobiere stürzt herein, weinend . . . [Schauspielerin] Carlsen von der Bühne fluchtartig, Geschrei, Toben, Brüllen;—Leute aus dem Zuschauerraum—ein paar hundert sind eingedrungen,—attakiren die Besucher, Publikum flieht, wird insultirt;—ich auf die Bühne, ungeheure Erregung, eiserner Vorhang vor, Spritzen in Thätigkeit, Publikum flieht auf die Bühne, Requisitenkammer,—das Gesindel tobt, schmeißt Sachen an den Vorhang, will die Thüren einbrechen;— Wasser fließt in die Garderoben . . . wir [A. S. und Heinrich Schnitzler] gehen in den Zuschauerraum;— Bänke und Sessel aus den Logen heruntergeworfen . . . Polizei verbietet die 10 Uhr Vorstellung . . . Der ganze Abend ein Unicum in der Theatergeschichte.[16]

After the ***Reigen*** trial in Berlin in November 1921 this controversial play was staged again in Vienna on 7 March 1922. Police were present to maintain public order, but in order to avoid a recurrence of another scandal Schnitzler withdrew his permission to have the play performed. The last showing in Vienna took place on 30 June 1922, and not until 1982 could Schnitzler's ***Reigen*** be seen again.

Some of the prejudices called forth by the ***Reigen*** in the Old Country were also imported into the New World. A case in point is the German emigrant Fritz Endell who had come to the United States to start a new life. Comparing the American concept of freedom with the lack of freedom in the Old Country, he noted in his article on "Der ***Reigen*** in Amerika" the following, without being aware of the contradiction:

> Es dürfte den meisten Deutschen unbekannt sein, daß in dem Lande der Freiheit . . . an eine Aufführung des ***Reigen*** niemals gedacht werden könnte, da bereits die Verschickung des Buches durch die Post in den Vereinigten Staaten eine strafbare Handlung ist, während uns [in Deutschland] die öffentliche Aufführung durch berittene Schutzmannschaft und Strafprozesse aufgezwungen ist.[17]

Embarrassed by the "Junggesellenkunst" of a leading German dramatist, he advised Schnitzler that it was now, especially after the war, "mehr denn je vaterländische Pflicht, *unseren literarischen Ehrenschild rein zu halten.*"[18] Schnitzler wrote a conciliatory letter to Endell in which he stressed the importance of ***Reigen*** for himself, that he would regret "wenn ich in meinem Leben nichts anderes geschrieben hätte als dieses Buch, daß ich es aber unter den ungefähr zwei Dutzend, die erschienen sind, keineswegs missen möchte, sowohl um meinet- als um der deutschen Literatur willen."[19] Because Endell had done Schnitzler a favor by sending him some antique prints, Schnitzler felt obliged to mail him a copy of this disputed work. Endell's reaction was:

> Nachdem ich die zehn Akte mit ihrer ermüdenden und herausfordernden Schlußpointe gelesen, war mir zunächst klar, daß man ein solches Buch unmöglich in einem deutschen Haus aufbewahren könne, ich riß daher den Text fein säuberlich heraus und verbrannte ihn, nur den Deckel und das Widmungsblatt des Dichters zurückbehaltend. Ich bin zwar kein Literaturkritiker, aber soviel glaube ich sagen zu können, daß die künstlerische Form dieser Bühnenbilder kaum so bedeutend ist, daß um ihretwillen der Inhalt der deutschen Literatur, dem deutschen Theater hätte gerettet werden müssen.[20]

Some of Endell's reservations were shared by his American compatriots. ***Reigen,*** which was translated into English by F. L. Glaser and L. D. Edwards and published under the title ***Hands Around*** in 1920, appeared with the following inscription: "Of this edition, intended for private circulation only, 1475 copies have been printed after which the type has been distributed."[21] A performance of ***Reigen*** in the Green Room Club in New York City, planned for March 1922, had to be changed to a reading because of the intervention of some interest groups aimed at guarding public morality, especially the Society for the Suppression of Vice. The first American performance of ***Reigen*** took place in October 1926 at the Triangle Theater in New York City. The reason that there were no disturbances probably had to do with the exclusive showing of this play before a male audience which had subscribed to the seasonal offerings. No other theater dared to perform ***Reigen,*** however, because the book had been banned in New York State by John S. Sumner, Secretary of the New York Society for the Suppression of Vice. The court test came in the fall of 1929 when a raid on a bookstore produced a copy of the 'decadent' work. Charged with violation of Section 1141 of the Penal Law, the bookstore owner had to stand trial, but the charges against him were dismissed by the Magistrate Louis Brodsky in the City's Magistrate's Court in the Borough of Manhattan with the following ruling:

> Although the theme of the book is admittedly the quite universal literary theme of men and women, the author deals with it in cold and analytical, one might even say scientific, manner that precludes any salacious interpretation. A careful scrutiny of the text reveals not a single line, not a single word, that might be regarded as obscene, lewd, lascivious, filthy, indecent, or disgusting within the meaning of the statute.[22]

Other justices, on the other hand, found the book indecent and obscene; they fought so furiously against the lifting of the ban that the *Publishers' Weekly,* the American Book Trade Journal, issued the following warning:

> In the Court of Special Sessions "Hands Around" was held to be an obscene book, and the long arm of Mr. Summer is free to interrupt its sale in New York. Justices Frederick Kernochan [and others] differed with Magistrate Brodsky, holding that the book is "obscene and indecent, being a lurid story of ten illicit love relations." It is becoming necessary for the bookseller in New York to watch his courts very closely in these hectic times.[23]

The lifting of the ban was affirmed in 1930 with the decisions by the Appellate Division of the Supreme Court of New York and the Court of Appeals of the State of New York.

The censorship of **Reigen,** however, was not ended yet. This time the target was not the book nor the play but the French movie version which was directed by Max Ophuls in 1950 and released in America under the title **La Ronde.** While the British Film Academy had voted **La Ronde** as the best film in 1951, it was banned in New York State by the Division of Motion Pictures of the State Education Bureau and the National Legion of Decency, which placed it in its 'C' category, 'C' standing for condemned. The film distributor for the United States had anticipated this reaction as the *Souvenir Programme,* which carried the warning "Strictly for Adults Only," clearly shows: "We take pleasure in presenting this exciting French film, **La Ronde.** No doubt it will create a good deal of controversy and perhaps even bitter criticism, but we feel that film-goers should at least be given the opportunity to see it. . . . We must add, however, that **La Ronde** is a film for adults and that it is most unsuitable for children."[24]

The chief reason for refusing **La Ronde** a license in New York was, according to Otis Guernsey, "on the grounds of immorality and tendency to corrupt morals," and because "it openly refutes the legitimacy of family life."[25] The ban imposed by Dr. Flick, the Director of the State Board of Regents' Division of Motion Pictures, was upheld by the

State of New York. This ruling was overturned on 18 January 1954 by the Supreme Court on the grounds that the state's order had infringed upon the constitutional right of freedom of expression. **La Ronde** could now be seen in the State of New York without violating state law. The more conservative forces did not admit defeat, however, because, as Andrew Sarris pointed out, the showing of **La Ronde** "in New York State remained restricted to a mutilated print . . . while the rest of these United States enjoyed the original version."[26]

In the same article Sarris attacked Eric Bentley for his review of **La Ronde** which "is very knowingly malicious as it demolishes the film for the sake of the play."[27] The review in question had appeared in the *New Republic* in 1954 where Bentley had rated the film "not utterly banal" because "it is better than that. There are real actors in it. There is a real sophistication in the showmanship. Late Saturday night, if you feel like seeing a little French bedroom comedy, and don't mind its not being of the best, you can see **La Ronde** and like it. Go really late, so you'll be nearly as tired as Mr. Ophuls must have been when he made the scenario."[28]

Bentley, objecting strongly to the film version, published a new translation of **La Ronde** which was used in the 1955 production in New York's Circle in the Square in Greenwich Village. It opened on 27 June 1955 and ran for 132 performances.[29] Directed by José Quintero, the play was hailed by Lewis Funke in the *New York Times* as a first-rate performance, because "as a clinical study of the game of sex, it is a devastating part of the truth. . . . *La Ronde* is hardly the sort of comedy to make you laugh. It is sardonic, pitiless and penetrating in elemental forces. . . . [The play] does not present an especially pretty picture. But it does present a fascinating one."[30]

The next performance of **La Ronde** took place in the Studio-Theater in Washington, D.C., an intimate theater with a seating capacity of 247. Directed by June Havoc and Donald Cook, it sold out for the entire three-week engagement. The opening on 28 November 1955 was a much-touted social event attended by dignitaries like Vice President Richard Nixon heading the political delegation and Mrs. Gwen Caffritz the socialites. The reception of this production was not favorable. Richard Coe remarked that "the local theater world is set back a few light years with the opening of the Studio . . . for [La Ronde] is a cynical mess."[31] Criticism was directed mainly against the reduction of the ten different players to four who had to double in the ten roles, but the Eric Bentley translation was also faulted: "As for Eric Bentley's adaptation of the Viennese doctor's worldly treatise on venereal disease, it closely follows the Frank and Jacqueline Marcus translation. . . . [In addition], the project's sleazy worthlessness was underscored by [the malfunctioning of] technical matters. The Studio is more to be censored than pitied. Roundly. As in zero. Or, more accurately, minus zero."[32]

Another possible explanation for the play's failure is that the public's level of expectation was set too high because the Max Ophuls film version was generally known, or as

Tom Donelly remarked in the *Washington D.C. Daily News* on 29 November 1955, not without local pride: "You must know about *La Ronde,* since the elegant film version of this classic set of dialogs ran for years in Washington, without the least bit of trouble from the censors. (In provincial New York it was a different matter.)"

Donelly was not far off with his reference to "provincial New York," not only because the Ophuls version had been censored, but also because of another incident at Bard College, a coeducational college of about 275 students. The Episcopal clergyman, the Reverend John Quincy Martin, charged the college administration with having abandoned its moral role and demanded that it should resign. The reason for this moral outrage was that two male students, who subsequently were expelled, had visited the women's dormitory during the night the drama department had staged a "French" play—*La Ronde.*[33] These two events were probably linked in the clergyman's mind because he referred to the students' behavior and the play as "immoral." Bard's president, Dr. James H. Case Jr., replied to this charge as follows:

> *La Ronde* is written as a serious attack on human weakness with a serious moral story to tell. In converting it to American movie standards, it emerged as a frothy comedy. We went back to the serious play ***. We used the original version, not the movie version. While there may have been a question of taste and judgment in staging the play, I do not see how it could be construed as immoral.[34]

The moral outrage evoked in the 50s as a result of the Bard College production had disappeared by the time the play was revived on 9 May 1960 at New York's Marquee Theater. The *Playgram* carried the following message:

> It is our belief that Schnitzler's writing has not been fully appreciated in this country, perhaps partly because of a lack of understanding due to our more robust national characteristics. In any case, now, with the passing of time . . . we believe Mr. Schnitzler's delicate dissertation can be leisurely and appropriately explored on all its levels.[35]

The "our" and "we" in the above quotation refer to Patricia Newhall and Hans Weigert, who had translated Schnitzler's work anew in order to replace the "somber" Bentley version. The main difference between the two versions was the substitution of humor for cynicism or, as Patricia Newhall remarked in an interview: "Schnitzler wrote a brilliant satire on human nature and I feel its comment is made through humor."[36] This new translation, however, could not save the play. It was superior to the Bentley version but, as Peter Bauland pointed out, it "misses the lightness and humor of Schnitzler. According to most reviewers, the performance was dull and heavy-handed. *Reigen* had lost its charm and its usefulness, particularly for a young audience that shares none of the nostalgia for the old days in *mittel-europa*."[37] In addition to these shortcomings the shock-value was gone; sex was more acceptable to a modern audience, or as Brooks Atkinson observed in

his review: ". . . the Freudian revolution in attitudes toward sex has tempered the audacity of the material. Now we can hardly avoid regarding the ten episodes as repetitious, each being less interesting than its predecessor, although the writing of the English text by Hans Weigert and Patricia Newhall retains the humor and taste of Schnitzler's view."[38]

Walter Kerr, on the other hand, whose final verdict in the *New York Herald Tribune* of 10 May 1960 was that "*La Ronde* makes it about a third round the carousel," attributed partial blame for the failure to the new translation, "which is not really prepared to give us the delectable verbal relief that will refresh interest, bout by bout." To other reviewers "verbal relief" was present, but in the wrong situations, because "people say some quite profound and often humorous things, but they are always getting undressed or dressed while they talk, and this is disconcerting."[39] All in all, this production "to be found in an off-Broadway action on a small but broad-minded stage,"[40] was not a success and one could assume that the interest in Schnitzler's play had dissipated.

This was, however, not the case. Eight years later, a brief notice in the *New York Times* announced that *La Ronde* would appear as a musical on Broadway: "*La Ronde,* Arthur Schnitzler's 1902 [sic] treatise in 10 episodes on illicit [sic] love, will be presented as a musical in May."[41] This announcement was premature; not until the 1969-1970 season was *La Ronde* staged under the suggestive title *Rondelay* which ran for only eleven performances. A revival of the play was attempted in 1972 when the "Moving Company" decided to try its luck. The result was almost predictable; the play was turned into a "tired formula, not Schnitzler's cynical depiction of the sexual mores and hypocrisy of his time."[42] At fault were the youth of the actors and the failure to differentiate among the assorted middle-European types: "So they have brought the play down to a rather pedestrian level of 1972-American-apple-pie, not Viennese sacher torte, circa 1900. The mores of that time not being sufficiently re-created in the characterization, the essential elements in the play are missing."[43]

Rondelay was back again in 1975, publicized as a play by Peter Swet based on Schnitzler's original and performed by actors from the "Impossible Ragtime Theater." New were the time and locality of the action since the play was transplanted to New York City in the 1970s. The main requisite was, according to one critic, "a bed . . . swinging like a turntable from Central Park to a suite at the Pierre."[44] Arthur Schnitzler lost out in this production while Peter Swet should have created his "own love play instead of adapting Schnitzler's."[45]

Another major production of *La Ronde* was attempted at the Tyrone Guthrie Theater in Minneapolis in July 1977. Ken Ruta, the director, intended to stress the play's social criticism and the characters' existential despair. This message is clearly stated in the *Guthrie Theater Program*:

"The laughter [the play] liberated is the laughter of loneliness and despair. . . . If the characters were able to uncouple long enough to really look at each other, they might see that they share more urgent needs: social, moral and human ones. But they cannot. Instead they waltz on and on, ever closer to the brink of disaster."[46]

Joan Bunke, in her review "Good Play, Bad Guthrie," which was published in the *Des Moines Sunday Register* on 26 June 1977, disagreed with this interpretation. She felt that this approach contradicted Schnitzler's intention since "Vienna's glossy, phony veneer and the rot spreading under it were Schnitzler's targets. Ruta's production is too much corruption and too little veneer." Equally devastating was the review in the *New York Times*: "*La Ronde,* Schnitzler's circular chain of seductions and solitudes in turn-of-the-century Vienna, lacks shape in the Guthrie production. The 11 [sic] episodes do not share the ghost of style and tone they need if they are to become truly a circle."[47]

Reigen was back in New York when the Impossible Ragtime Theater decided to give this play another chance, this time without the changes made by Peter Swet. The play opened on 7 September 1978—and closed on the 24th of the same month. Directed by Rob Pherson, the cast's excellent acting and the adding of two mimes were commended,[48] but Terry Curtis Fox from the *Village Voice* found that the true message of the play did not come through. What Schnitzler had wanted to show was the combination of

> an amoral sexual radicalism with severe social criticism. Two strands flow through the work: sexual pursuit is its own erotic end . . . and that men and women act differently when their partners are of a different social class. Schnitzler defined sexual attraction as something that happens between people of different social standings. He also understood that women were viewed by his society as socially distinct, thus enhancing their otherness; the minute they were known, they lost their erotic interest.[49]

The Rob Pherson production lacked "the delicate balance of speech and gesture," and because of this "Schnitzler's pomp becomes mere posturing; his wit becomes strained. Soon there is no longer any of the elegance left, just sexual moaning and groaning in the dark. The champagne zest is gone. What is as sweet and well-carved as a Viennese cake ends up like a dry doughnut."[50] Equally disappointing was the 1979 production of the Equity Library Theater in New York. Directed by Warren Kliever, this play premiered on 1 February and closed on 18 February. A New York critic attributed the closing to the fact that "the playwright's cynical rendering of amorally amorous deception, once thought daring, has been rendered innocuous by changing standards of behavior."[51] The same conclusion can be found in the *New York Theater Review*: "Without the fin-de-siècle Viennese atmosphere, Arthur Schnitzler's once-daring and still bittersweet effective portraits of casual sex seem silly and charmless."[52]

One year later another musical version of *La Ronde* appeared, this time produced by Center Stage, a resident repertory theater of Bergen County in New Jersey. This musical, consisting of sixteen musical numbers, a Prologue, and a Finale, opened on 26 June 1980, at the Playhouse on the Mall in Paramus, directed by Charlz A. Herfurth. The one-sidedness of this production can be seen in the titles of some musical numbers: "Oh, Herr Alfred;" "It's Most Difficult;" "A Perfect Lady;" "Whipped Cream;" "Time for Bed;" and "We'll Join the Night." The success, according to one critic, was moderate:

> The characterizations lack charm and wit and offer little contrast. Love may appear in many guises, but is marked by poor performances, and while a few singers display voices of modest merit, others are notably untrained. The music is, at best, ambitious and as orchestrated for piano and harp, becomes gratingly repetitive. The lyrics are awkward, and lack a suitable balance of pre-Freudian Viennese humor and cynicism.[53]

The fall of 1984 saw yet another production of *La Ronde,* this time at the new Ohio Theater in New York. Sammy Cucher's direction turned Schnitzler's original into a travesty because now the action took place in New York during the 1920s. This added a not-appreciated estrangement effect:

> There is a strange and meaningless bit when a character crosses the stage gesticulating silently while a broadcast voice talks about Calvin Coolidge. Another time, the cast comes out waving little American flags. Why? Well, Cucher is a graduate of NYU's experimental theater wing and he has to show off what presumably he learned there.[54]

Another drawback was the Bentley translation written in "textbook English," and the old-fashioned European setting: "[The] text is filled with references to private dining rooms, poets writing for the theater, a count who pays a visit to a leading lady, etc. All of that is highly continental. Here we do not refer to dramatists as 'poets,' and a restaurant's private dining room used for a seduction is a phenomenon of other times and other places."[55]

Despite this negative comment it seems that *La Ronde* will not vanish from the American stage. More successful performances of this challenging play include the Arthur Storch production at Syracuse Stage in November of 1974, the Eric Conger production with the Barter Intern Company in Abingdon, Virginia, in August of 1975, and the 1985 summer-staging at the Williamstown Theater Festival with David Trainer directing. There have also been numerous productions at American universities, including the ones by the Experimental Theater of Vassar College in May 1969, by the Theater of the University of North Carolina at Asheville in May 1972, and at the Juilliard School in May 1976. In all reviews not one derogatory remark was made referring to Schnitzler's Jewish background. The bulk of the American reviews stress Schnitzler's cynicism and to a certain extent, the 'immoral' sexual content of *La Ronde.*

Nietzsche once said that every writer projects himself into what he writes. This is also true of literary critics and others who have commented on **Reigen** or **La Ronde,** the book, the stage performance, or the film and will probably remain true of future critics in the Old Country as well as in the New World.

Notes

1. Fr. Törnsee, in *Neue Bahnen,* 3 (1903), p. 245. Quoted by Otto P. Schinnerer, "The History of Schnitzler's *Reigen,*" *Publications of the Modern Language Association,* 46 (1931), p. 841.

2. Ottokar Stauf von der March, *Ostdeutsche Rundschau,* 17 May 1903, quoted by Schinnerer, ibid.

3. Unpublished diary entry of 27 November 1906.

4. Arthur Schnitzler, *Tagebuch* 1902-1912, ed. Werner Welzig et al. (Wien: Verlag der Österreichischen Akademie der Wissenschaften, 1981), p. 361.

5. Herbert Ihering, "Reigen," *Börsen-Kurier,* 24 December 1920; reprinted in H. I., *Von Reinhardt bis Brecht. Eine Auswahl der Theaterkritiken* 1909-1932, ed. Rolf Badenhausen (Reinbek bei Hamburg: Rowohlt-Verlag, 1967), pp. 77-78; also in *Theaterkritiken für die Republik 1917-1933 im Spiegel der Kritik,* ed. Günther Rühle (Frankfurt am Main: S. Fischer Verlag, 1967), pp. 280-281.

6. Günther Rühle, *Theaterkritiken,* pp. 279-280.

7. Herbert Ihering, "Reigen," p. 78.

8. Wolfgang Heine, ed., *Der Kampf um den Reigen. Vollständiger Bericht über die sechstägige Verhandlung gegen Direktion und Darsteller des Kleinen Schauspielhauses Berlin* (Berlin: Rowohlt, 1922), p. 93.

9. Ibid., p. 95.

10. Ibid., pp. 161-165.

11. Ibid., p. 164.

12. Unpublished diary entry of 19 April 1919.

13. Quoted in Otto P. Schinnerer, "The History of Schnitzler's *Reigen,*" p. 851.

14. Ibid.

15. Unpublished diary entry of 13 February 1921.

16. Unpublished diary entry of 16 February 1921.

17. Fritz Endell, "Der *Reigen* in Amerika," *Deutsches Volkstum,* 5, vii (1923), p. 284.

18. Ibid., p. 285.

19. Ibid.

20. Ibid.

21. See Richard H. Allen, *An Annotated Arthur Schnitzler Bibliography* (Chapel Hill: The University of North Carolina Press, 1966); C 13, e 1, p. 55. The same edition of 1475 copies was published for members of the Schnitzler Society in 1929.

22. "When Judges Disagree," *The Publishers' Weekly,* xxiv, no. 116, 14 December 1929, p. 2758.

23. Ibid., p. 2759.

24. *Souvenir Programme,* dated 29 July, part of the Schnitzler collection in the Beaumont Library, a branch of the New York Public Library at Lincoln Center.

25. Otis L. Guernsey Jr., *The New York Tribune,* 28 March 1954, p. 1.

26. Andrew Sarris, "films in focus," *The Village Voice,* 16 October 1969, p. 55.

27. Ibid.

28. Eric Bentley, *New Republic,* 5 April 1954, p. 21; reprinted as "Reigen Comes Full Circle" in E. B., *The Dramatic Event: An American Chronicle* (New York: Horizon, 1954), p. 210.

29. See Peter Bauland, *The Hooded Eagle. Modern German Drama on the New York Stage* (New York: Syracuse University Press, 1968), p. 174.

30. Lewis Funke, "Theatre: A Clinical Study of Sex," *New York Times,* 28 June 1955, L+:24.

31. Richard L. Coe, "One on the Aisle: Square Peg—Round Stage, "*The Washington Post and Times Herald,* 30 November 1955, final ed., p. 26.

32. Ibid.

33. In April 1986 I inquired whether this "French" play was indeed Schnitzler's *Reigen.* William Driver, Flint Professor of Drama at Bard College replied: "Indeed, yes, the play was Schnitzler's *Reigen*; it was produced in the College's new theater, director Ted Hoffmann, date 1955. No one survives on campus who played in or saw the play, and Dr. Case and Father Martin are both dead."

34. "Pastor Critical of Bard College," *New York Times,* 29 March 1955, L++, p. 20.

35. *Playgram—Theatre Marquee,* May 1960, part of the Schnitzler collection in the Beaumont Library.

36. Arthur Gelb, "New *La Ronde* Stresses Humor," *New York Times,* 14 March 1960, L+, p. 25.

37. Peter Bauland, *The Hooded Eagle,* p. 175.

38. Brooks Atkinson, "'*La Ronde*' Arrives at the Marquee," *New York Times,* 10 May 1960, L, p. 44.

39. John McClain, "*La Ronde*—Heady Stuff," *New York Journal American,* 10 May 1960, p. 15.

40. Rowland Field, "Around Again. *La Ronde* Revival Parades Untired Lovemakers," *Newark Evening News,* 10 May 1960, p. 54.

41. Sam Zolotow, "*La Ronde* Turns Into Musical," *New York Times,* 19 December 1967, L, p. 58.

42. Martin Oltarsh, *Show Business,* 30 November 1972, p. 13.

43. Ibid.

44. Mel Gussow, "La 'Rondelay'," *New York Times,* 26 November 1975, L, p. 14.

45. Ibid.

46. *The Guthrie Theater Program* 1977, issue 1:13.

47. Richard Eder, "In This Theater the Stage Becomes an Actor," *New York Times,* 21 July 1977, L C, p. 19.

48. See *Show Business,* 14 September 1978, p. 12.

49. *The Village Voice,* 25 September 1978, p. 127.

50. Donald R. Wilson, *Soho Weekly News,* 14 September 1978, p. 58.

51. Tom Buckley, "*La Ronde,* Seduction in Vienna," *New York Times,* 3 February 1979, L, p. 14.

52. "*La Ronde* at Equity Library Theatre," *New York Theater Review,* March 1979, p. 50.

53. Dani, "Love Games," *Variety,* 9 July 1980, p. 94.

54. "Ohio Theater Makes Travesty of *La Ronde*," *New York City Tribune,* 15 November 1984, p. 5 B.

55. Ibid.

Gail Finney (essay date 1989)

SOURCE: Finney, Gail. "Female Sexuality and Schnitzler's *La Ronde.*" In *Women in Modern Drama: Freud, Feminism, and European Theater at the Turn of the Century,* pp. 25-50. Ithaca and London: Cornell University Press, 1989.

[*In the following excerpt, Finney uses Schnitzler's ambivalence toward Freudian psychoanalysis as a starting point in addressing the playwright's focus on women and sexuality in* La Ronde.]

FEMALE SEXUALITY AND SCHNITZLER'S *LA RONDE*

I will make a confession which for my sake I must ask you to keep to yourself and share with neither friends nor strangers. I have tormented myself with the question why in all these years I have never attempted to make your acquaintance and to have a talk with you. . . . The answer contains the confession which strikes me as too intimate. I think I have avoided you from a kind of reluctance to meet my double [aus einer Art von Doppelgängerscheu].

This often cited confession forms the center of Freud's third letter to Arthur Schnitzler, written in 1922 to congratulate the author on the occasion of his sixtieth birthday.[1] By this time Schnitzler's dramas and prose works had won him international renown as the sharp-eyed critic of fin-de-siècle Viennese society; indeed, until the late 1930s he was more famous than Freud. Freud's "reluctance" to meet Schnitzler stemmed from his conception of the double, which he had adopted from Otto Rank and described in his paper "The Uncanny" in 1919. During the stage of primary narcissism which dominates the minds of children and primitive adults, Freud writes, the idea of the double operates as an insurance against the destruction of the ego; once this stage has passed, however, the double reverses its character and becomes the uncanny harbinger of death, and confrontation with one's double causes identity confusion.[2]

But Freud overcame his reservations about Schnitzler. The birthday letter of May 1922 prompted Schnitzler to suggest that they meet at last, and Freud responded with a dinner invitation. The following August, Schnitzler visited Freud in Berchtesgaden, where he was vacationing. Yet although they continued to exchange their publications, between 1922 and Schnitzler's death in 1931 they saw each other only five more times: three times by accident and on two occasions when Schnitzler visited Freud in a sanatorium located down the street from Schnitzler's house.

Freud had good reason to see himself mirrored in Schnitzler. The parallels between the two men begin on the biographical level: Freud was only six years older than Schnitzler; both were products of the same milieu, Vienna at the height of the Hapsburg monarchy; both were educated, upper-middle-class, nonpracticing Jews; they traveled in the same circles and Freud was well acquainted with Schnitzler's brother Julius, a surgeon. Perhaps most important, both Freud and Schnitzler were doctors with an interest in psychiatry, although Schnitzler eventually chose to specialize in laryngology, the same field in which his father had distinguished himself.

Schnitzler's first exposure to Freud dates from 1886, when he attended and reported on a meeting at which Freud spoke on male hysteria. That same year Schnitzler worked under the neurologist Theodor Meynert, just as Freud had done a few years before. In Meynert's psychiatric clinic Schnitzler learned hypnosis, with which he carried out sensational experiments in his father's polyclinic. Schnitzler's most extensive medical treatise was a discussion of the treatment of hysterical voicelessness through hypnosis and suggestion, and in the late 1880s and early 1890s he reviewed several of Freud's translations of psychiatric works by Charcot and Bernheim. Hypnosis appears in two of his dramas, where it is used to express characteristically Schnitzlerian ideas. In one of the one-act plays included in **Anatol** (1893; dates following plays refer to year of publication), which launched Schnitzler's career as a playwright, the title character hypnotizes his lover in order to learn whether she is truly faithful to him but is then afraid to ask her the question, preferring his illusions to certainty. **Paracelsus** (1898), in which the noted Renaissance doctor discovers a married woman's secret sexual fantasies through hypnosis, astonished Freud with its knowledge about "these things"[3]—the conscious and unconscious desires that complicate married life.

Schnitzler's writing increasingly took precedence over his activities as a physician, especially after the death of his father, who had from the beginning been the motivating force behind his medical career. Throughout, Schnitzler's works reflect his fascination with the dynamics of the human psyche; it is no accident that he was the first writer in the German language to use the technique of the autonomous interior monologue (in the novella *Leutnant Gustl*, 1901). He makes frequent use of dreams in his prose writings, notably in *Traumnovelle* (1928) (*Rhapsody: A Dream Novel*). And many of his works, such as the novella *Fräulein Else* (1924), are akin to case studies in their minute exploration of psychologically troubled characters.

In light of Schnitzler's preoccupations, it is little wonder that the renaissance in Schnitzler scholarship in recent decades has in large measure consisted of efforts to detail the affinities between the Viennese writer and the founder of psychoanalysis. Thus we find attempts to demonstrate that Schnitzler anticipated Freud's most important ideas and categorizations of the psychoses in Schnitzler's oeuvre.[4] But critics of such attempts hold that there is little point in arguing about whether Freud or Schnitzler was the first to make this or that discovery,[5] particularly since Freud himself repeatedly observed that many of the insights he gained through analysis and experimentation were not original with him but were known to creative writers. Moreover, "Freudian" interpretations of Schnitzler's works, of which there have been a considerable number, overlook or underestimate Schnitzler's expressed reservations about psychoanalysis. Although Schnitzler claimed in an interview, "In some respects I am the double of Professor Freud,"[6] he could never overcome his sense that there was something monomaniacal about Freud's way of thinking and that psychoanalysis, dominated by "fixed ideas,"[7] tended to overinterpret. It seems plausible to conclude that the differences between the two men were as responsible as the similarities for the infrequency of their personal contact. Schnitzler's ambivalence is perfectly captured in a diary entry made on the day he arrived in Berchtesgaden to visit Freud in 1922: "His entire being attracted me again, and I feel a certain desire to talk with him about the various chasms in my works (and in my life)—but I think I'd prefer not to."[8]

Schnitzler's ambivalent attitude toward Freud's thinking is probably nowhere clearer than in the writer's views on female sexuality. Both sex and women play such a prominent role in his oeuvre that the importance of this issue for Schnitzler can scarcely be overestimated.[9] One of the works most useful in exploring his conception of female sexuality is ***Reigen*** (1903) (***The Round Dance***), probably best known outside Austria and Germany through Max Ophüls's romanticized film version of 1950, ***La Ronde***.[10] (Since the appearance of Ophüls's film, the French title has taken precedence, even in English translations, and I will use that title here.) Schnitzler's drama quite literally revolves around sex: nine of its ten dialogues frame an act of sexual intercourse, conveyed by a row of dashes in the text and, in early productions, by a lowering and raising of the curtain on stage; in each case one of the partners has appeared in the previous scene and the other appears in the following scene—A-B, B-C, C-D, and so on. Character A's reappearance in the last scene completes the "round" and creates the impression that the cycle will be repeated endlessly. The play's innovative structure, unique not only in Schnitzler's oeuvre but in the drama of the time, is the perfect vehicle for its message—so daring in its day—about the universality of sexual desire. In its relentless portrayal of sexuality *La Ronde* stands as a summation of many of the themes that preoccupied Schnitzler: marriage and adultery, the roles and linguistic games men and women play with each other, the tension between reality and illusion and, concomitantly, between honesty and deception, both self-deception and deception of others.

The production history of ***La Ronde*** reveals just how shocking its subject matter was. "Dear Pornographer": thus the salutation of a tongue-in-cheek letter from Hofmannsthal and Richard Beer-Hofmann to Schnitzler advising him, in the face of Fischer's refusal to publish the play, to take care in his selection of a publisher for his "piece of dirt" (*Schmutzwerk*) and to demand a lot of money in advance, since the book would surely be confiscated by the censors.[11] Their prediction was realized in 1904, the year after the play's publication. Although unauthorized versions of ***La Ronde*** were occasionally performed outside Austria and Germany during the first decades of the century, the first full production in German did not take place until 1920, in Berlin. Within a year its cast and director were tried for obscenity, but acquitted. In every German city in which the play was performed, riots and demonstrations erupted, many of them anti-Semitic; theater patrons came armed with rotten eggs and stink bombs. But nowhere was the scandal greater than in Vienna, the setting of the drama and thus the "scene of the crime." Here the controversy even led to fights in parliament, suggesting that a statement made about Vienna in 1981, fifty years after Schnitzler's death, was true at the turn of the century as well: "Hardly any other city is as unhesitatingly tolerant of sexual freedom as Vienna—as long as one condition is met: that it is never talked about."[12] In 1922 Schnitzler, thoroughly fed up with the whole affair, forbade any further productions of his much-maligned drama. Fifty years after his death, however, his son Heinrich lifted the ban, and since then directors have attempted to make up for the play's long period of dormancy.

The scandalous quality of ***La Ronde*** lay at least in part in the fact that it spares no social class. The play's use of nameless, paradigmatic types, spanning all levels of society from prostitute to count, has often been noted. Yet these characters represent not only social types but also gender types—"the parlourmaid," "the young gentleman," "the actress," and so forth. A close look at the play in terms of Freudian categories reveals the degree to which its characters strain against the confines of these gender stereotypes.[13] As we shall see, Schnitzler often sets up conventional masculine-feminine dichotomies only in order to problematize and undermine them. I should emphasize that I am not interested in determining Freud's influence on Schnitzler or, since Freud's writings on femininity postdate *La Ronde,* in demonstrating the degree to which Schnitzler anticipated Freud. Rather, my intention is to use Freud's thinking as a lens through which to examine the play's treatment of the kinds of roles and stereotypes assigned to women in turn-of-the-century Vienna. Because of the range of types encompassed by *La Ronde,* close study of this work should also prove illuminating for the dramas discussed in subsequent parts of this book.

As I mentioned in the Introduction, the issue of female sexuality has been crucial to the history of psychoanalysis, though its fate has been a turbulent one. Steven Marcus calls the discussion of female sexuality since Freud a "tragicomedy"; in Kate Millett's words, the question has been a "scientific football or a swamp of superstitious misinformation."[14] No one was more perplexed about the subject than Freud. One finds expressions of his uncertainty from his first writings on the topic to his last—from his statement in *Three Essays on the Theory of Sexuality* (1905) that the erotic life of women "is still veiled in an impenetrable obscurity" to his characterization of the nature of femininity as a "riddle" in "Femininity" (1933).[15] Surely one of his most frequently quoted utterances is that in which he described to Marie Bonaparte "the great question that has never been answered and which I have not yet been able to answer, despite my thirty years of research into the feminine soul": "What does a woman want?" ("Was will das Weib?").[16] And yet he did construct a theory of female sexuality, and one whose ramifications were far-reaching. An understanding of this theory necessitates a brief rehearsal of his conception of the early development of sexuality.

In his essays on infantile sexuality (notably the *Three Essays* and "The Infantile Genital Organization," 1923) Freud postulates the concept of sexual monism: child sexuality for both sexes is masculine, since both girls and boys recognize only the male genital organ. (He was to persist throughout in viewing libido as masculine, as he indicates in, for example, "Femininity," 131.) From the child's point of view the clitoris is simply a substitute for the penis; "the little girl is a little man" ("Femininity," 118). Thus Freud labels the phase following the oral and anal phases the phallic phase in both sexes. In both sexes the girl's lack of a penis leads to a castration complex, since children believe that the girl had a penis and lost it. But the castration complex manifests itself differently in the two sexes, and these distinctions are closely bound up with differences in the Oedipus complex in boys and girls, outlined in "The Dissolution of the Oedipus Complex" (1924) and elsewhere. For Freud the Oedipus complex, which has been described as "a shibboleth on which psychoanalysis stood or fell,"[17] was the central phenomenon of the sexual period in early childhood. After the boy discovers that the girl lacks what he has, Freud hypothesizes, he comes to

dread the possibility of castration, perhaps as a punishment for masturbation brought on by his oedipal desires for his mother. His castration complex leads him to repress these desires and to begin internalizing his father's authority, thus forming the kernel of his superego, which will maintain the prohibition against incest.

The situation is different with girls. Whereas in boys the Oedipus complex is terminated by the castration complex, the girl's Oedipus complex is produced by the castration complex. Accepting her castration as having already occurred, she comes to envy the boy his penis: "She has seen it and knows that she is without it and wants to have it."[18] Yet she gradually replaces her wish for a penis by her wish for a child, and with this purpose in mind she rejects her mother, the primary object of her preoedipal affection, and takes her father as a love object. At this culminating stage of her Oedipus complex, the girl's relationship with her mother is colored by jealousy: "The girl has turned into a little woman" ("Some Psychical Consequences of the Anatomical Distinction between the Sexes," 256). Freud emphasizes that these two desires—to possess a penis and to bear a child—are crucial in helping to prepare the woman's nature for its subsequent sex role. Significantly, because her castration has already taken place, the girl has less reason to move beyond the Oedipus complex than the boy. The two results are that women may remain until a late age strongly dependent on a paternal object or on their actual father, and that their superego does not become as well developed, as "inexorable," as it does in men; thus women show less sense of justice than men and are more influenced in their judgments by feelings of affection, envy, or hostility. In "Female Sexuality" Freud sums up the significance of this difference in the development of child sexuality as follows: "We should probably not be wrong in saying that it is this difference in the reciprocal relation between the Oedipus and the castration complex which gives its special stamp to the character of females as social beings."[19] Perhaps most important, according to this theory that takes the male as the norm and defines the female in terms of a lack, the castration complex leads both sexes to disparage woman, the castrated being.

To repeat, this summary of Freud's conception of the early development of sexuality is not intended as an indictment but rather, interpreted metaphorically, as representative of the attitudes of his social order. What about Schnitzler, who belonged to precisely the same social order? Did he take a different stance? We may best answer this question by interweaving more specific considerations of Freud's writings on women into a close analysis of the text of *La Ronde.*

Inherent in Freud's definition of libido as masculine is his attribution of a less pronounced sex drive to women. He never gave up his belief, expressed as early as *Three Essays,* that "the tendency to sexual repression seems in general to be greater [in girls than in boys]" (219), and in "The Taboo of Virginity" (1918) he writes of the "general female tendency to take a defensive line [toward sex]."[20] He simply does not regard female sexuality as an active, independent drive. What seems to Freud to be more important to women than sex is love; as he states in "Anxiety and Instinctual Life" (1933), the fear of castration found in men is replaced in the female sex by a fear of loss of love.[21] Concomitant with these views is his often repeated association of masculine sexuality with activity and feminine sexuality with passivity. Indeed, he notes that the contrast between masculinity and femininity must frequently be replaced in psychoanalysis by that between activity and passivity (*Three Essays,* 160). Although he occasionally qualifies this equation,[22] he clearly believes in its essential validity, since many of his most important claims are based on this dichotomy (such as his definition of libido as masculine), and in one of the last works to be published during his lifetime he refers to the male's "struggle against his passive or feminine attitude."[23]

Turning now to Schnitzler, we find that such dichotomies do not hold up under scrutiny, although at first glance they may seem to. In two scenes—those between the young gentleman and the young wife and between the "sweet girl" (*süßes Mädel*) or grisette and the poet—men rip women's clothes in their haste to get on with things. Similarly, the male characters are often in a hurry to get away from their partners once the sexual act is over—thus the soldier with both the prostitute and the parlour-maid, the young gentleman with the parlourmaid, and the husband with the sweet girl, whose observation that he is "different" after their intimacies[24] sums up this phenomenon. By contrast, the reaction of the parlourmaid with the soldier and of the sweet girl with the husband following intercourse is to ask their partners whether they care for them. These conventional gender roles are not maintained, however; in the scenes between the young gentleman and the young wife and between the sweet girl and the poet it is the men who express concern about the women's love for them afterward and the women who are in a hurry to get home, and in the play's final scene even the count seems to wish he meant something more to the prostitute than the other men she has been with. And several of the female characters are anything but passive in their sexual relations. The prostitute approaches the soldier even though she claims not to want any money from him, hence falling out of her social role; the parlourmaid's interest in the young gentleman is evident in the way she primps before taking him the glass of water he requests; the young wife goes to her rendezvous with the young gentleman in full awareness of what awaits her; and, most obviously, the actress initiates sex with both the poet and the count.

A similar pattern emerges in *La Ronde* in connection with a characteristic Freud often associates with women, shame. In *Three Essays* he observes that the development of the inhibitions of sexuality, such as shame, takes place in little girls "earlier and in the face of less resistance than in boys" (219), and in a frequently cited passage in "Femininity" he writes: "Shame, which is considered to be a feminine characteristic *par excellence* but is far more a

matter of convention than might be supposed, has as its purpose, we believe, concealment of genital deficiency" (132). He then goes on to describe women's invention of plaiting and weaving—one of their few contributions to civilization, he notes—as an unconscious imitation of the interwoven hair that conceals their genitals. In commenting on this passage Sarah Kofman points out the ambiguous nature of Freud's conception of feminine shame as "both a *conventional* virtue (more or less linked to cultural repression) and a *natural* one, since, in her invention of weaving, woman was only 'imitating' nature."[25] Moreover, Kofman adds, this "natural/conventional artifice" serves to excite and charm men: "Feminine modesty is thus a trick of nature that allows the human species to perpetuate itself" (49).

Kofman's observations are illuminating apropos of *La Ronde,* which unmasks the contradictions of traditional conceptions of shame such as those expounded by Freud and shows it to be a supposedly natural but in fact artificial convention that serves to enhance seduction. The parlourmaid's embarrassment as the young gentleman opens her blouse and kisses her breasts in broad daylight, heightened when she learns that he has seen her undressed in her room at night, does not deter him but rather intensifies the desire of both. Similarly, the fact that the young wife comes to the young gentleman's flat "heavily veiled" (iv, 12) and her insistence that if she becomes conscious of what she is doing she will "sink into the earth with shame" (iv, 16) are simply part of her game of seduction, just as her feeble protestations in the drawing room that "it is so light here" (iv, 17) only move the young gentleman to lead her into the bedroom. Indeed, the implicit comparison of the young wife to a popular contemporary actress suggests that she is merely playing a role expected of her: when the young gentleman is taken aback to discover that she is not wearing a corset, she responds that the actress never wears one either. Neither she nor the sweet girl (with the poet) can bear to have their partners look on while they get dressed, although they have just had sex with them. Schnitzler takes his unmasking of shame one step further, however; he does not limit it to women: in the scene between the actress and the count it is the count who is reluctant to engage in love in the daytime. The actress has a simple solution: "Close your eyes if it's too light for you" (ix, 59).

The blurring of conventional sex-typed distinctions in *La Ronde* complements a pattern in the play which might be labeled "one-upwomanship," a pattern in which female characters repeatedly get the better of male characters whose views on women are very similar to Freud's. One of the best illustrations of this pattern is the bedroom scene between the young wife and her husband, who is a perfect embodiment of patriarchal values. His attitude toward his wife, whom he addresses as "my child," is intimated right from the beginning of the scene, when he urges her not to read anymore that evening since it will "ruin her eyes" (all quotations from the play in this paragraph are from scene v). For him, male and female spheres of activity are clearly separate, as his adaptation of lines from Schiller's "Das Lied von der Glocke" ("The Song of the Bell") at the end of the scene demonstrates: "One can't always be a good lover. One has to keep going out into a hostile world. One must fight and one must strive." Nowhere are the differences between men and women clearer to him than in the area of premarital and extramarital sexual experience, as we learn from his explanations to his wife. Whereas women like herself come to their husbands pure and relatively ignorant about love, he tells her, men are forced before marriage to rely on those "poor creatures" who sell themselves. (This distinction is of course class-bound; both the husband and the poet question the sweet girl about her previous lovers.) Similarly, whereas the husband forbids his wife to associate with adulterous women—women whose lives are full of "lies, trickery, deceit and danger"—he admits that he was once involved with a married woman.

In his belief in a double standard Schnitzler's husband typifies the "civilized sexual morality" described by Freud in "'Civilized' Sexual Morality and Modern Nervous Illness" (1908). The main intention of this essay, whose claim that civilization is founded on the suppression of instincts anticipates *Civilization and Its Discontents* (1930), is to lament the debilitating effects of a social code that prohibits sexual intercourse outside of monogamous marriage. As a corollary Freud calls attention to the "double code of morality" that tolerates lapses in the male but condemns them in the female. He points out that this double code is buttressed by women's education, which employs drastic measures to keep them ignorant of sex until marriage. Freud goes on to link women's ignorance in sexual matters and their intellectual inferiority in general:

> [Women's] upbringing forbids their concerning themselves intellectually with sexual problems though they nevertheless feel extremely curious about them, and frightens them by condemning such curiosity as unwomanly and a sign of a sinful disposition. In this way they are scared away from *any* form of thinking, and knowledge loses its value for them. . . . I think that the undoubted intellectual inferiority of so many women can . . . be traced back to the inhibition of thought necessitated by sexual suppression.[26]

Despite his criticism of the conditions that foster the "double code," Freud offers no alternatives or proposals for reform, and he obviously does not believe that civilization can or should be done away with.[27] Later statements on the issue show him to be even closer to the position represented by the husband in *La Ronde.* In *Civilization and Its Discontents,* for example, he writes, "Women represent the interests of the family and of sexual life. The work of civilization has become increasingly the business of men, it confronts them with ever more difficult tasks and compels them to carry out instinctual sublimations of which women are little capable";[28] similarly, in "Femininity" he regards women as "weaker in their social interests and as having less capacity for sublimating their instincts than men" (134).

Taking a close look at the fifth scene of *La Ronde* against this background, we find that the traditional moral code embodied by the husband does not have the last word but that his wife acts as a kind of satiric "corrective" at every juncture. Her fascination with his premarital sex life and with the life of prostitutes already shows her transcending the double standard that did not allow middle-class women to express such interests. Similarly, when her husband feigns pity for the lot of prostitutes, she responds that she does not find such pity appropriate, since she thinks they must lead quite a pleasant life. When he reminds her that these women are destined to fall lower and lower, she observes, "It sounds rather pleasant." And when he struggles to describe the existence of adulterous women, she supplies the word "pleasure." As we might expect, her husband is shocked by these formulations. His attitude is encapsulated by his reaction to her veiled threat to withhold sex if he does not answer a pressing question she has: "You do have a way of talking . . . please remember, you're a mother . . . that our little girl is asleep in there . . ." (Schnitzler's ellipses). This response anticipates his anger in the next scene at the sweet girl's suggestion that his wife is as unfaithful as he is. He simply cannot accept the thought that a respectable woman possesses the same kind of sexual desire as a man.

The most graphic manifestation of this attitude is the husband's practice of alternating periods of platonic "friendship" with "honeymoons" in his marriage, thereby rendering his wife newly pure in his mind before each honeymoon. One such instance is depicted in this scene, in which the couple's sexual encounter follows closely on the husband's statement that "one can only love what is true and pure" and his exclaimed wish that he had known his wife as a child. His reliance on the fantasy of renewed virginal purity in his wife is illuminated by Freud's diagnosis in "The Taboo of Virginity," which describes the demand in civilized societies for virginity in women at marriage as a "logical continuation of the right to exclusive possession of a woman, which forms the essence of monogamy" (193). Freud adds that a woman's experience of losing her virginity "creates a state of bondage in the woman which guarantees that possession of her shall continue undisturbed and makes her able to resist new impressions and enticements from outside" (193). In light of the young wife's adultery, it is hardly necessary to point out the extent to which such attitudes are ironized in Schnitzler's play.

The husband's inability to reconcile sexuality with motherhood and his overall idealization of his wife reflect a further tendency that Freud considered characteristically male, the need to overvalue the love object. In "On the Universal Tendency to Debasement in the Sphere of Love" (1912) he theorizes that this need grows out of incestuous fixations that cause men to make unconscious associations between the women they love and their mothers and/or sisters. But because the incest taboo prohibits sexual relations with such women, the tendency to overvalue the *love* object produces a counterpart need in men to debase the *sexual* object in their estimation in order to maintain potency. That the union between love and sexual fulfillment realized in the bedroom scene between the husband and his wife in Schnitzler's play is a rarity for them is evident in her wistful remarks about the encounter.

This dissociation of love and sensuality seems perfectly exemplified in **La Ronde** in the scene between the young wife and the young gentleman, whose explanation for his impotence with her is "I must love you too much" (iv, 18). As support for this position he brings in Stendhal's *De l'amour,* which, he tells her, relates tales of cavalry officers who suffered a similar misfortune during their first encounters with the women they most loved. Yet a closer look at both this scene and Stendhal's book suggests that the reason for the young gentleman's failure may not be an excess of love. Just a few lines before the couple's unsatisfactory encounter, the following exchange occurs:

(*He undoes her shoes and kisses her feet. She has slipped into bed.*)

WIFE:

Oh, it's cold.

GENTLEMAN:

Soon, it'll get warm.

WIFE (LAUGHING QUIETLY):

You think so?

GENTLEMAN (UNPLEASANTLY DISTURBED, TO HIMSELF):

She shouldn't have said that.

[iv, 17]

What "disturbs" the gentleman here is the sexuality manifested by the wife's question and accompanying laughter.[29] In her open acknowledgment of her sexuality she strains against the confines of the conventional role that her society assigns to middle-class women and continues the process of subordination prefigured on the gestural level when the gentleman removed her shoes and kissed her feet. Hence we see that his sexual performance in fact suffers not because of an overvaluation of her, as the Freudian diagnosis would have it, but for precisely the opposite reason.

A further explanation for the gentleman's difficulties is supplied by the chapter in *De l'amour* which he refers to but does not name, "Des Fiasco" ("Concerning Fiascos"), a kind of miniature treatise on impotence. Here Stendhal writes that if a first rendezvous is expected and eagerly awaited, a man often suffers a "fiasco through imagination." The gentleman's eager anticipation of his tryst in **La Ronde** is evident in his careful preparations before the wife's arrival at the flat he has rented: spraying the rooms and bedpillows with violet perfume; making sure the blinds are closed; removing a tortoiseshell comb—a remnant of a former rendezvous—from a drawer in the bedside table;

laying out cognac, candies, and dishes; combing his hair and moustache. The factor of surprise accounts for the gentleman's success in his second attempt with the wife, which occurs unexpectedly, just after she has announced her intention to leave in five minutes.[30]

Because *De l'amour* is so clearly relevant to this scene, it is not inappropriate to compare Stendhal's text to the gentleman's retelling of it. The comparison reveals that the gentleman alters Stendhal's story of the lieutenant who could do nothing but kiss his beloved and weep for joy during his first three nights with her: whereas Stendhal makes no mention of the woman's tears, in the gentleman's narration both she and the lieutenant weep—a version much more in keeping with his traditional notions of what is fitting behavior for women. That this alteration is more than a picayune detail is evident in the wife's reaction; she not only finds it hard to believe that the woman cried along with the man, she goes on to object, "But there are surely a lot who don't weep at all" (iv, 19). She brings these sentiments to a head a few lines later with her sarcastic response to the gentleman's exclamation that he is happy: "But you don't need to cry as well"—a remark that enrages the gentleman in its veiled reference to his impotence and her resulting dissatisfaction. The young wife's skeptical reaction to the gentleman's romanticized tale, indicating her pragmatic approach to sex, once again calls into question the conventional gender roles sanctioned by her society and epitomized in Freudian doctrine.

The Freudian theory that men dissociate love and sexuality and tend as a consequence to choose sexual objects who are ethically or socially inferior to them would seem to be borne out by the entire framework of **La Ronde**: in every case where there is a class difference between partners, it is the man who belongs to the higher class. Yet the female figures in these scenes also problematize the hierarchical thinking at the foundation of Freud's views on sexuality. The degree to which the prostitute transcends stereotyped conceptions of her role, announced as we have seen in her offer of free services to the soldier, is heightened in the scene in which she reveals to the count that she is on the job at the same early hour every day, like any conscientious employee. The parlourmaid's position makes her appear to be the quintessential incorporation of the association between femininity and servitude implicit in Freud's writings.[31] But when her sexual encounter with the young gentleman is interrupted by the doorbell and he irritably says that it probably rang earlier and they didn't notice it, she responds, "Oh, I've been listening all the time" (iii, 11), thus considerably undermining any impression of devoted subservience we may have formed. Her final gesture in the scene—stealing a cigar from the young gentleman's smoking table after he has left the room—caps off the commentary.

A similar pattern emerges in the scenes focusing on the sweet girl, an example of the famous character type that became inextricably bound up with Schnitzler's name early in his career. Based on an actual type—the girl from the petty bourgeois suburbs of Vienna—the *süßes Mädel* was first "defined" by the playboy Anatol in one of the one-act plays in the *Anatol* cycle, *Weihnachtseinkäufe* (*Christmas Shopping*): "She's not fascinatingly beautiful . . . she's not particularly elegant—and she's not at all clever. . . . But she has the soft appeal of a spring evening . . . and the grace of a bewitched princess . . . and the spirit of a girl who knows how to love!"[32] Both the husband and the poet seem to have a similar image of this type of girl, to judge from their condescending treatment of the sweet girl in *La Ronde*. Again and again, however, she thwarts their expectations. The husband is repeatedly taken aback by her worldliness, for instance, especially by the fact that she guesses from his behavior that he is married. And when he tells her that he would like to see her on a regular basis but that he has to be able to trust her since he cannot be around to watch out for her, she retorts, "Oh, I can look after myself" (vi, 39), a remark that emphasizes the independence he finds so difficult to reconcile with his idea of what a girl like her should be.

The poet takes an even more patronizing tone with the sweet girl. A caricature of the fin-de-siècle aesthete, he is not interested in hearing about her domestic responsibilities—which as Schnitzler was aware were only too real for girls of this class[33]—but prefers to beautify everything, including what he perceives as her stupidity: "Of course you're stupid. But that's why I love you. Oh, it's so beautiful when women are stupid" (vii, 41). Following their sexual encounter he stands over her with a candle, declaiming: "You are beautiful, you are beauty, you are perhaps even nature itself. You are 'sacred simplicity'" (vii, 44). His raptures are ended, however, when she cries out that he is dripping wax on her. Thus his condescending aestheticism is satirically—and symbolically—deflated on the gestural level, the level on which so much happens in this play, dealing as it does with matters that are "not to be spoken of."

The poet is put in his place much more directly by the actress, who is his intellectual superior. When he tries his patronizing, beautifying phrases on her, often repeating exactly the same expressions he used with the sweet girl in the previous scene, she simply dismisses them as "rubbish" and tells him he is talking "like a complete idiot" (viii, 49). Her pragmatism in sexual matters contrasts sharply with his feigned romanticism; when he leaves her room in the inn briefly, she sarcastically warns him not to start something with the waitress, and she shows her greater sexual awareness in her revelation that a mutual friend of theirs is homosexual, something the poet has had no inkling of.

The actress merits a closer look for a number of reasons. As we have seen, all the characters in *La Ronde* are role-players. In contrast to Freud's association of secretiveness and insincerity with women (*Three Essays,* 151), Schnitzler presents men and women alike as partners in a round of deception. (This notion is by no means limited in Schnitzler's oeuvre to *La Ronde,* as is evident in the last

line spoken by the title character in Schnitzler's *Paracelsus*: "We are always playing; he who knows this is wise.") Hence the actress in *La Ronde,* a role-player by profession, is in a sense the most "authentic" character in the play. She is also the most narcissistic, bragging about her acting abilities to both the poet and the count and reminding them that many other men would like to be in their place. She emerges, in fact, as a virtual parody of Freud's conception of the narcissistic woman, in his opinion "the type of female most frequently met with, which is probably the purest and truest one."[34] Such a type results, he writes, when at the onset of puberty a girl's primary narcissism is intensified, so that her ability to form outward attachments is impaired. Especially common in attractive women, secondary narcissism manifests itself in a self-contented coolness toward men, who tend to be fascinated by such women precisely because of their inaccessibility and self-sufficiency. Freud compares this fascination with the charm exerted by children, cats and larger beasts of prey, great criminals, and humorists, all of whom "compel our interest by the narcissistic consistency with which they manage to keep away from their ego anything that would diminish it" ("On Narcissism," 89). Exemplifying such a personality type in the extreme, the actress mocks both the poet and the count at every turn, tells the poet at one point that he is nothing but a "whim" for her (viii, 52), and insists to both the poet and the count that she hates people and has nothing to do with them—all of which serves to heighten the fascination she seems to possess for both lovers. Similarly, she elicits in both men complaints about her enigmatic nature, a trait Freud singles out as the reverse side of the narcissistic woman's charm.

Such a conception of femininity is unusual in Freud, whose entire theory of sexual development, as we have seen, rests on the definition of women as lacking that which men have, a lack that leads to their denigration by both sexes. Kofman argues that "On Narcissism" opened up a new and frightening path in Freud's thinking in its attribution of self-sufficiency to women and that he overcame this difficulty by defining excessive narcissism as pathological: "It is as if Freud . . . 'knew,' dream-fashion, that women were 'great criminals' but nevertheless strove, by bringing about such a reversal as occurs in dreams, to pass them off as hysterics" (*Enigma,* 66). Not so Schnitzler: one might say that in his depiction of the actress he travels down the path that Freud does not take. She not only strains against conventional female roles, as do the other women characters in *La Ronde,* she adopts male roles, in effect switching places with various male figures in the play. She addresses the poet as "my child," the designation that he and the husband have used with other female figures, and she calls the poet patronizing names, as he has done with the sweet girl; her assurance to the count that her bedroom door will not open from the outside echoes the husband's assurances to the sweet girl in their *chambre séparée*. Most notably, it is the actress who is on the offensive sexually. It is her idea to go to the country inn with the poet, and she sends him away from her room only in order to call him back again when she is undressed and in bed. After the count kisses her hand, she astonishes him by kissing his in return. Having appropriated the power associated with the male role—a transferal symbolized by her request that he remove his saber—she succeeds by gradations in getting him into her bed despite his protestations against making love in the daytime. The description of his final submission—"The Count resists no longer" (ix, 59)—is reminiscent of similar phrases used earlier in the play in connection with female figures. And in a final reversal of traditional role conceptions, Schnitzler suggests that the actress's sexual capacity is greater than the count's: whereas she wants to see him again that evening, he would prefer to wait until two days later.

The count's manifest fear of the actress is elucidated by a passage from "The Taboo of Virginity" in which Freud attempts to explain the primitive custom demanding that defloration of the bride be carried out before marriage and by someone other than the husband-to-be:

> Wherever primitive man has set up a taboo he fears some danger and it cannot be disputed that a generalized dread of women is expressed in all these rules of avoidance. Perhaps this dread is based on the fact that woman is different from man, for ever incomprehensible and mysterious, strange and therefore apparently hostile. The man is afraid of being weakened by the woman, infected with her femininity and of then showing himself incapable. The effect which coitus has of discharging tensions and causing flaccidity may be the prototype of what the man fears; and realization of the influence which the woman gains over him through sexual intercourse, the consideration she thereby forces from him, may justify the extension of this fear. In all this there is nothing obsolete, nothing which is not still alive among ourselves.

[198-199]

Perhaps this suspicion of the primitive, untamed nature of female sexuality is at the bottom of Freud's famous statement that "the sexual life of adult women is a 'dark continent' for psychology."[35] As we have seen, however, it is not in Freud but in his contemporary Schnitzler that we find an exploration of the powerful and liberating potential that lay within this "dark continent."

Not surprisingly, although Schnitzler did not take a stand on the women's movement per se, he was enthusiastically received by a number of feminist groups.[36] And yet any claim about the emancipatory quality of *La Ronde* must be qualified in at least two respects. First, on an existential plane, it is with good reason that this play has often been seen as a modern variation on the medieval dance of death, which represented Death as leveling class distinctions by dancing with all social types from poorest to richest. Schnitzler's play, in which sex is the great leveler, is a kind of round dance of dead souls in which men and women alike objectify each other in their easy progression from one partner to the next. The impersonal, even anonymous quality of their intimacies is emphasized by the repetition of the same or similar lines in different

scenes, by the observation made by several characters that their partners remind them of someone else, and by the fact that they are frequently unable to see each other's faces. And numerous references to transience and death reveal the deepest motivating force behind these frenzied sexual encounters. Second, on a social plane, it must be kept in mind that *La Ronde* is above all a portrayal of its time. Indeed, Schnitzler himself described the work as a "series of scenes which . . . if dug up again in a few hundred years would provide a unique illumination of an aspect of our culture."[37] As a portrait of Viennese society under the Hapsburg monarchy, the play can only go so far in presenting emancipatory possibilities for women. Although it clearly problematizes conventional masculine-feminine distinctions in its depiction of female characters transcending traditional conceptions of their role in the bedroom, these characters nevertheless remain limited to marginal positions in society: the status of the prostitute and the parlour-maid requires little comment; the actress, though a professional, practices an occupation that her society does not respect; and the sweet girl can expect little more than a modest version of the domestic confinement experienced by the young wife.

In its wide-ranging portrayal of sexual desire *La Ronde* covers the spectrum of all the female character types we will examine in the rest of this book: we will encounter the prostitute again in Wedekind's Lulu; the working-class girl in Synge's Pegeen Mike, Hauptmann's Rose Bernd, and Hofmannsthal's Dyer's Wife; the performer in Lulu and in Wilde's Salomé; the middle-class wife and mother or would-be mother in Ibsen's Hedda Gabler, Shaw's Candida, and Strindberg's Laura. But insofar as Schnitzler's female figures belong to a patriarchal society, they are, metaphorically speaking, all daughters. . . .

Notes

1. *Letters of Sigmund Freud,* ed. Ernst L. Freud, trans. Tania and James Stern (New York: Basic Books, 1960), p. 339. Schnitzler had begun their correspondence on the occasion of Freud's fiftieth birthday in 1906. For the original versions of Freud's letters to Schnitzler, see Sigmund Freud, "Briefe an Arthur Schnitzler," ed. Heinrich Schnitzler, *Neue Rundschau,* 66 (1955), 95-106. Schnitzler's letters to Freud have been lost.

2. Freud, "The Uncanny" ("Das Unheimliche"), *SE,* XVII, 234-235.

3. Quoted in Ernest Jones, *The Life and Work of Sigmund Freud,* ed. and abr. Lionel Trilling and Steven Marcus (New York: Basic Books, 1961), p. 225. Freud also refers to *Paracelsus,* with reference to resistance, in a footnote to his case study of Dora; see "Fragment of an Analysis of a Case of Hysteria" ("Bruchstück einer Hysterie-Analyse," 1905), *SE,* VII, 44n.

4. E.g., Frederick J. Beharriell, "Schnitzler's Anticipation of Freud's Dream Theory," *Monatshefte,* 45 (1953), 81-89, and "Freud's 'Double': Arthur Schnit-

zler," *Journal of the American Psychological Association,* 10 (1962), 722-730 (these essays are revised and combined in Beharriell, "Schnitzler: Freud's Doppelgänger," *Literatur und Kritik,* 19 [1967], 546-555); Robert O. Weiss, "The Psychoses in the Works of Arthur Schnitzler," *German Quarterly,* 41 (1968), 377-400.

5. See, e.g., Hartmut Scheible, *Arthur Schnitzler und die Aufklärung* (Munich: Fink, 1977), pp. 47-48. In "Arthur Schnitzler und Sigmund Freud: Aus den Anfängen des Doppelgängers," *Germanisch-Romanische Monatsschrift,* 24 (1974), 193-223, Bernd Urban, in describing Schnitzler's medical knowledge and experience in the early days of research on hysteria in order to demystify what Freud saw as Schnitzler's "intuition" of his ideas, also invokes Freud's disavowal of his originality.

6. George S. Viereck, "The World of Arthur Schnitzler," in Viereck, *Glimpses of the Great* (London: Duckworth, 1930), p. 333.

7. Commenting on a study of his works up to *Anatol* by Freud's student Theodor Reik, one of the first to draw parallels between Schnitzler and Freud, Schnitzler writes that it is "not uninteresting" but that it "lapses into the fixed psychoanalytic ideas toward the end"; Arthur Schnitzler, diary entry of 27 June 1912, *Tagebuch, 1909-1912,* ed. Werner Welzig et al. (Vienna: Österreichische Akademie der Wissenschaften, 1981), p. 339. (Unless I have noted otherwise, all translations are my own.) Ernest Jones, with whom Schnitzler also argued about these matters, mentions that he had particular difficulty accepting Freud's ideas of incest and infantile sexuality (Jones, *Life and Work of Sigmund Freud,* p. 435). Michael Worbs follows a survey of Freudian configurations in Schnitzler's works with a discussion of Schnitzler's criticisms of psychoanalysis; see Worbs, *Nervenkunst: Literatur und Psychoanalyse im Wien der Jahrhundertwende* (Frankfurt: Europäische Verlagsanstalt, 1983), pp. 225-258.

8. This quotation of 16 August 1922 from the unpublished diaries is cited in Urban, "Arthur Schnitzler und Sigmund Freud," p. 223. In addition to Urban and Scheible, scholars who have warned against a facile identification of Freud and Schnitzler include Henri F. Ellenberger, who in *The Discovery of the Unconscious: The History and Evolution of Dynamic Psychiatry* (New York: Basic Books, 1970) writes that Schnitzler, in contrast to Freud, emphasized the importance of role-playing in hypnosis and hysteria, the unreliability of memory, the thematic rather than the symbolic element in dreams, and the self-deceptive rather than the aggressive component in the origin of war (pp. 471-474); and Wolfgang Nehring, "Schnitzler, Freud's Alter Ego?" *Modern Austrian Literature,* 10, nos. 3 and 4 (1977), 179-194, who observes that Schnitzler focuses on individuals in a particular society, whereas Freud's

findings are universal; that unlike Freudian analysis, Schnitzler's diagnoses do not lead to self-awareness; and that whereas Freud strives to detect the genesis of neuroses, Schnitzler analyzes psychological phenomena only as they appear in the present.

9. In "Schnitzler's Frauen und Mädchen," *Diskussion Deutsch,* 13 (1982), 507-517, Renate Möhrmann points out the abundance and variety of female figures in Schnitzler's works, a feature particularly striking in his dramas, since the unusually high proportion of female characters has caused difficulties in producing his plays (507).

10. On the film's transformations of the play see, e.g., Anna Kuhn, "The Romantization of Arthur Schnitzler: Max Ophuls' Adaptations of *Liebelei* and *Reigen,*" in *Probleme der Moderne: Studien zur deutschen Literatur von Nietzsche bis Brecht. Festschrift für Walter Sokel,* ed. Benjamin Bennett et al. (Tübingen: Niemeyer, 1983), pp. 83-99.

11. Hofmannsthal and Beer-Hofmann to Schnitzler, 15 February 1903, in Hugo von Hofmannsthal/Arthur Schnitzler, *Briefwechsel,* ed. Therese Nickl and Heinrich Schnitzler (Frankfurt: Fischer, 1964), pp. 167-168.

12. Ernest Bornemann, Profil no. 18, 1981, quoted in Renate Wagner, *Arthur Schnitzler: Eine Biographie* (Vienna: Molden, 1981), p. 338. For a full account of the play's scandal-ridden production history see Wagner, pp. 325-338, and Ludwig Marcuse, *Obscene: The History of an Indignation,* trans. Karen Gershon (London: MacGibbon & Kee, 1965), pp. 165-214.

13. See Barbara Gutt, *Emanzipation bei Arthur Schnitzler* (Berlin: Spiess, 1978), for a survey of female types in Schnitzler's works in general. For the most part Gutt focuses on describing and illustrating these types rather than on the attempts of the women characters to break out of them. On character types in Schnitzler's dramas see also Jürg Scheuzger, *Das Spiel mit Typen und Typenkonstellationen in den Dramen Arthur Schnitzlers* (Zurich: Juris, 1975).

14. Steven Marcus, introduction to Freud, *Three Essays on the Theory of Sexuality,* trans. and ed. James Strachey (New York: Basic Books, 1975), p. xxxviii; Kate Millett, *Sexual Politics* (New York: Ballantine, 1969), p. 164. For psychoanalytic views of female sexuality since Freud see, e.g., *Female Sexuality: New Psychoanalytic Views,* ed. Janine Chasseguet-Smirgel (London: Virago, 1981); *Women and Analysis: Dialogues on Psychoanalytic Views of Femininity,* ed. Jean Strouse (New York: Grossman, 1974); Harold P. Blum, *Female Psychology: Contemporary Psychoanalytic Views* (New York: International Universities Press, 1977); and Zenia O. Fliegel, "Half a Century Later: Current Status of Freud's Controversial Views on Women," *Psychoanalytic Review,* 69 (1982), 7-28.

15. Freud, *Three Essays on the Theory of Sexuality (Drei Abhandlungen zur Sexualtheorie), SE,* VII, 151, and

"Femininity" ("Die Weiblichkeit"), in *New Introductory Lectures on Psycho-Analysis, SE,* XXII, 113.

16. Quoted by Jones, *Life and Work of Sigmund Freud,* p. 377.

17. Juliet Mitchell, "On Freud and the Distinction between the Sexes," in *Women and Analysis,* p. 33.

18. Freud, "Some Psychical Consequences of the Anatomical Distinction between the Sexes" ("Einige psychische Folgen des anatomischen Geschlechtsunterschieds," 1925), *SE,* XIX, 252.

19. Freud, "Female Sexuality" ("Über die weibliche Sexualität," 1931), *SE,* XXI, 230.

20. Freud, "The Taboo of Virginity" ("Das Tabu der Virginität"), *SE,* XI, 201.

21. Freud, "Anxiety and Instinctual Life" ("Angst und Triebleben"), in *New Introductory Lectures on Psycho-Analysis, SE,* XXII, 87.

22. E.g., in "Instincts and their Vicissitudes" ("Triebe und Triebschicksale," 1915), *SE,* XIV, 134, and "Femininity," 115-116.

23. Freud, "Analysis Terminable and Interminable" ("Die endliche und die unendliche Analyse," 1937), *SE,* XXIII, 250.

24. Schnitzler, *La Ronde,* trans. Sue Davies and John Barton (Harmondsworth: Penguin, 1982), scene vi, p. 37. Subsequent quotations are from this edition and are identified in the text by scene and page number.

25. Sarah Kofman, *The Enigma of Woman: Woman in Freud's Writings,* trans. Catherine Porter (Ithaca: Cornell Univ. Press, 1985), p. 49. Subsequent page references appear in the text.

26. Freud, "'Civilized' Sexual Morality and Modern Nervous Illness" ("Die 'kulturelle' Sexualmoral und die moderne Nervosität"), *SE,* IX, 198-199.

27. Cf. Peter Heller, "Freud as a Phenomenon of the *Fin de Siècle,*" in *Arthur Schnitzler and His Age: Intellectual and Artistic Currents,* ed. Petrus W. Tax and Richard H. Lawson (Bonn: Bouvier, 1984), pp. 4, 7. See pp. 4-7 of Heller's essay for a detailed reading of "'Civilized' Sexual Morality and Modern Nervous Illness."

28. Freud, *Civilization and Its Discontents (Das Unbehagen in der Kultur), SE,* XXI, 103.

29. Martin Swales's association of laughter with sexual excitement in the scene between the soldier and the parlourmaid is applicable to this scene as well; see Swales, *Arthur Schnitzler: A Critical Study* (Oxford: Clarendon, 1971), p. 237.

30. Lotte S. Couch's claim, paralleling Freudian doctrine, that the young gentleman fails with the young wife because they belong to the same class does not explain his successful second attempt; see Couch,

"Der Reigen: Schnitzler und Sigmund Freud," *Österreich in Geschichte und Literatur,* 16 (1972), 221-222. Her article points out a number of similarities between Freud and Schnitzler manifested in *La Ronde* but does not take note of the ways in which the play problematizes such parallels.

31. Cf. Maria Ramas, who in "Freud's Dora, Dora's Hysteria," in *In Dora's Case: Freud—Hysteria—Feminism,* ed. Charles Bernheimer and Claire Kahane (New York: Columbia Univ. Press, 1985), argues that for Freud, "femininity was linked with service specifically with regard to sexuality" (174), that indeed for him "servitude was a metaphor for femininity" (176).

32. Schnitzler, *Anatol,* trans. Frank Marcus (London: Methuen, 1982), p. 19 (Schnitzler's ellipses). On a more pragmatic note, W. G. Sebald adds another dimension to the "sweetness" of the sweet girl by pointing out that she was more likely to be sexually hygienic and thus free of venereal disease than prostitutes; Sebald, "Die Mädchen aus der Feenwelt: Bemerkungen zu Liebe und Prostitution mit Bezügen zu Raimund, Schnitzler und Horvath," *Neophilologus,* 67 (1983), 112-114. The prevalence of venereal disease in Schnitzler's milieu is evident in the remarks of Theodor Reik, who relates that one of his physician friends speculated about the "tragicomedy" that would have resulted if even one of the characters in *La Ronde* had had gonorrhea; see Reik, *Arthur Schnitzler als Psycholog* (Minden, Westphalia: Bruns, 1913), pp. 79-80.

33. See e.g., the descriptions in his autobiography of the harsh living and working conditions suffered by Jeanette Heger, a girl from this background with whom he had a brief relationship; Schnitzler, *Jugend in Wien* (Vienna: Molden, 1968), pp. 307-308.

34. Freud, "On Narcissism: An Introduction" ("Zur Einführung des Narzißmus," 1914), *SE,* XIV, 88. To repeat, I am obviously not suggesting that Schnitzler parodied Freud, since "On Narcissism" appeared after *La Ronde* was written, but rather that Schnitzler's depiction of the actress can be seen as a parody of female narcissism as Freud was later to describe it.

35. Freud, *The Question of Lay Analysis (Die Frage der Laienanalyse,* 1926), *SE,* XX, 212. Freud uses the English "dark continent" in the original. Sander L. Gilman describes it as a "phrase with which [Freud] tied female sexuality to the image of contemporary colonialism and thus to the exoticism and pathology of the Other"; Gilman, *Difference and Pathology: Stereotypes of Sexuality, Race, and Madness* (Ithaca: Cornell Univ. Press, 1985), p. 107.

36. See Gutt, *Emanzipation bei Arthur Schnitzler,* pp. 157-168.

37. Schnitzler to Olga Waissnix, 26 February 1897, in Schnitzler/Waissnix, *Liebe, die starb vor der Zeit: Ein Briefwechsel,* ed. Therese Nickl and Heinrich Schnitzler (Vienna: Molden, 1970), p. 317.

Ian F. Roe (essay date July 1994)

SOURCE: Roe, Ian F. "The Comedy of Schnitzler's *Reigen*." *Modern Language Review* 89, no. 3 (July 1994): 674-88.

[*In the following essay, Roe examines comic elements in* Reigen, *noting that critical analysis of and audience reaction to the play have historically neglected these elements.*]

It is now a decade since the ban on the performance of Schnitzler's *Reigen* came to an end, and the productions that have been mounted during that time have only added to the controversies surrounding what is arguably the most famous and certainly the most infamous of Schnitzler's works. Surprisingly, however, there has been no marked shift of emphasis in the critical appreciation of the play in recent years. On the whole, two major themes still dominate critical analysis: the extent to which the play is a mirror of the Viennese society of Schnitzler's day, and the play's depiction of human sexuality as a repetitive and seemingly empty and meaningless activity.[1] What has received almost no attention, even during the years in which it has been possible to see the play performed, is the question of *Reigen* as a comedy. Such neglect becomes all the more surprising when one considers the traditions of comedy for which the Viennese theatre is rightly famous. Even the one book that sets out to explore the comedies of Schnitzler scarcely mentions the play and confines the few comments that are made to aspects of the characters' behaviour and social roles,[2] whilst most studies of German comedy make little reference to Schnitzler, let alone to *Reigen*.[3] It may be that such critical attitudes reflect or have even shaped the reception of the play in the theatre: a performance that I attended at the Akademietheater in Vienna in 1984 was watched in a mood of reverence tinged with apprehension, with even a transparently comic line such as the actress's post-coital sigh of satisfaction, 'das ist doch schöner als in blödsinnigen Stücken spielen', failing to raise a single laugh (my own having been swiftly stifled).

Sex is of course a very serious topic, and probably not suitable as a spectator sport, as one reviewer of the 1982 production at the London Aldwych reminded us.[4] Whether it is quite as 'unbarmherzig und todernst' as the by-now obligatory critical references to the medieval dances of death would have us believe is open to question, however.[5] Schnitzler's admission, after the Viennese premiere in 1921, that he was surprised that the play's 'Lustigkeit' had been outweighed by its 'Melancholie' indicates that he had intended the former to predominate.[6] The comedy is most certainly not one of cheap laughs such as characterized the 1982 Munich production (a flesh-coloured corset for the Count, a floor-length nightshirt for the husband, or a pose modelled on Tischbein's celebrated painting of Goethe for the writer) but Schnitzler's handling of his potentially risqué subject is full of comic touches, whilst some scenes, in particular those involving the young wife, the writer, and the actress, are excellent comic vignettes in their own right.

Nevertheless the play accords uneasily with many of the generalizations that have been put forward concerning the nature of comedy. There is no 'Antagonismus von dramatischer Anspannung und komischer Entspannung',[7] no comic plot that tightens almost to breaking-point before unravelling in the comic dénouement; no 'Zuschauer- oder Kommentarfigur';[8] no 'Spielverderber' who refuses to play the game or who plays but breaks the rules,[9] unless one sees the actress in that role, but the plot is not then designed to integrate or unmask her. One may certainly detect elements of the *Konversationsstück* beloved of dramatists such as Bauernfield (the conversation in the early scenes is admittedly of a somewhat rudimentary kind!),[10] whilst a British reader may see a more risqué variation on the Wildean comedy of manners, although lacking the verbal fireworks and *bon mots,* or even a precursor of an Ayckbourn comedy such as *Bedroom Farce.* On the other hand, there is none of the grotesque comedy of Dürrenmatt, nor the audience-involvement or 'play within a play' motif that are features of much modern comedy, and it is surely an exaggeration to see *Reigen* as a pointer to the absurd theatre of Ionesco.[11]

If the atypicality of *Reigen* therefore requires one to resist the straitjacket of a 'typology of comedy' of the kind that can reduce even the wittiest play to a dry philosophical tract,[12] it is nevertheless apparent that one particular source of the comedy is provided by the very structure of the play, in that the audience gradually becomes aware that in each scene the two characters' words, behaviour, and above all their sexual strategies are not to be viewed in isolation, but may either be compared with the preceding scene or judged in anticipation of the one that is to follow.[13] Whether such a structural feature needs to be underlined by the introduction of a character who links or supervises the various encounters, as in the 1989 production at the Theater in der Josefstadt, must remain debatable. Indeed, if such a change also adds a voyeuristic touch, then it may detract from an appreciation of the play's comedy to an even greater extent than the impression created in Max Ophuls's film version of *La Ronde* that the characters are figures on a fairground merry-go-round that have been brought to life under the benign and ironic gaze of the showmaster. Given the motif that links all ten scenes, it may seem strange that one feels the need to stress that all the characters are to a greater or lesser extent individual creatures of flesh and blood,[14] but the degree to which they are individualized as such and differentiated from one another is in no small part a result of the comedy that dominates or underscores much of the characterization. It is that comedy that is the main subject of my present investigations; bearing in mind the general agreement, recently reiterated by Bruce Thompson, that the female characters are treated rather more favourably than their male counterparts,[15] it will also be important to consider whether such a distinction is borne out in the use of comedy: in what ways does the comedy contribute to our view of the respective roles and characters of male and female; to what extent are the women the source of the comedy of which the men are the object?

In the early scenes the comedy is almost entirely that of situation; indeed, a number of elements acquire an added poignancy and also a certain comic connotation only by virtue of their recurrence in later scenes. Even in the first encounter it is the woman who is interested in a more lasting relationship, as the prostitute thinks of the soldier in terms of a potential lover rather than a client (p. 328), whilst the man's main concern is to expedite the act of sexual intercourse (in this case with a degree of haste that takes even a prostitute by surprise) and afterwards to make his excuses and escape as quickly as possible. The soldier's concern for the right ambience ('da ist nicht das Rechte' (p. 328)) is also a brief adumbration of the male concern with creating the right mood and atmosphere that is later explored more fully.[16] In the first scene, however, the prostitute takes the initiative to an extent matched only by the actress amongst the female characters, and the second scene is rather more typical of the play as a whole, with its comic contrast of the assertive male and the more cautious but far from reluctant female, a contrast that is underscored by the (from an English point of view) untranslatable interplay of different modes of address. Although she is initially reluctant to use the informal 'Du', the maid's final word before the first of two lines of dashes is 'komm!', her wish between the two copulations is to see his face,[17] and afterwards it is she who uses the informal mode of address as the soldier's total lack of commitment is indicated by his return to the formal 'Sie' (p. 331), to which the maid does not revert until she has realized his lack of interest in her and even his desire to go back to the dance in order to find another woman.

As already implied by the emphasis on comedy of situation, the characters encountered in the first two scenes are not particularly witty or humorous in themselves. The soldier's two attempts at jokes are either decidedly feeble ('Morgen früh ist schon wieder licht') or predictable ('Das wär z'viel!'), and the comedy arises chiefly from the repetition of lines already used in the first scene: the references to darkness, the fear that someone may be coming, or the soldier's concern with when he should be back in barracks. Similar remarks could apply equally well to the third scene, although the comedy is slightly more subtle, as the young gentleman desperately thinks of more excuses to call for the maid until he is finally emboldened to take a more direct approach, not least by her coquettish behaviour and her smile that is partly one of amusement and partly one of encouragement (p. 334). Once more the woman's line is that someone may see or disturb them ('wenns draußen läut—'), but the maid's repeated protestations ('Aber, Herr Alfred . . .') carry much less conviction than in the previous scene, and the sighs that are her response to the kiss that he places on her breast merely add to the impression conveyed throughout the scene that the desire for at least some form of intimate encounter is entirely mutual.[18]

Indeed, the maid's behaviour in the third scene might even be thought inconsistent with her earlier caution in the encounter with the soldier, who in the meantime has after all provided her with the security of a more lasting relationship, even if, as may be surmised, a not entirely stimulating or socially rewarding one. If she does hope for higher things from the young gentleman, then her hopes are dashed in the by now familiar way, as he fends off her attempts to continue the relationship (p. 336) and rushes away to the secure male domain of the coffee-house, thereby returning to the social normality that he may have neglected and of which the sound of the doorbell rather rudely reminds him.[19] The maid is left to gain at least some material reward for her indiscretion by stealing a cigar, presumably for her boyfriend, and in the process inviting us once again to recall the prostitute of the opening scene.

The young man's nervous uncertainty both before and after the 'climax' of the scene is potentially a source of comedy, more particularly when contrasted with the woman's behaviour, which indicates a much greater degree of self-assurance despite her lower social status as both maid and female. If at this stage only in embryonic form, the comedy of the scene derives from the contrast between the gender roles demanded by social codes and conditioning, and on the other hand the behaviour that results from the protagonists' actual character and psychology. Such a contrast is clearly evident in the fourth scene, the first in which the female character is more fully prepared to depart from her socially determined role, not only by asserting her intellectual superiority but also by admitting to her sexuality. Whilst the young man's initial behaviour, as he paces up and down inspecting the contents of the flat or jumps nervously at the sound of the doorbell, is simply a more elaborate version of his antics in the earlier scene, the behaviour of the young woman is considerably more complex. Although arriving heavily veiled, although insisting that she can only stay for five minutes and that even remaining for that length of time is a great risk that has drained her emotionally, she nevertheless uses the warmth of the room as a pretext for raising no objection to the young man's removal of her veils and other outdoor garments. Her repeated adieus and references to his promise to be 'brav' (pp. 339-42), her apparently painful memories of earlier meetings, are contrasted first with the long-drawn-out kisses to which she readily responds (p. 340), and later with the overtly erotic gesture of offering him half of the glazed pear that she holds in her mouth (p. 342).

Her talk of guilt and vengeance, of the torture, shame, and disgrace she must endure (pp. 339, 341), may at first seem merely a comic parallel to the young man's more exaggerated talk of bliss, of the uniqueness of their encounter in the midst of life's transience: 'Das Leben ist so leer, so nichtig—und dann—so kurz—so entsetzlich kurz! Es gibt nur ein Glück . . . einen Menschen finden, von dem man geliebt wird—' (p. 342). Yet whilst the man's philosophizing appears pompous and shallow, the young woman's melodramatic references to dishonour and social disgrace gradually appear to be part of an elaborate charade designed to frustrate the young man's desire for intimacy until she herself is ready to take the initiative:

DIE JUNGE FRAU:

(*ist ins Bett geschlüpft*) Oh, mir ist kalt.

DER JUNGE HERR:

Gleich wirds warm werden.

DIE JUNGE FRAU:

(*leise lachend*) Glaubst du?

DER JUNGE HERR:

(*unangenehm berührt, für sich*) Das hätte sie nicht sagen sollen. [. . .]

DIE JUNGE FRAU:

(*zärtlich*) Komm, komm, komm!

(pp. 342-43)

Having earlier evoked conventional codes of social behaviour and the consequences of offending such codes as a means of keeping him at a distance, she now draws on and deliberately misunderstands conventional role-models to tease or even to mock him as he desperately seeks literary parallels in Stendhal for his own sexual failure. Such teasing involves an increasing use of irony as she applauds the fact that he has indeed been 'brav' and that they can just be good friends (pp. 344-45), as she implies that normally only older men are afflicted by impotence, or pretends that she thought all cavalry officers wept instead of making love (p. 344), a motif to which she continually returns, to his increasing annoyance. It is then no surprise when the comic reuse or reversal of motifs from earlier in the play finds the young man, like the maid earlier with the soldier, asking for proof of the other's love and she in turn suggesting she has just proved it:

DER JUNGE HERR:

[. . .] Wenn ich nur überzeugt wäre, daß du mich liebst.

DIE JUNGE FRAU:

Verlangst du noch mehr Beweise?

(p. 344)

It is now the young woman who claims to be in a hurry, a rendezvous with a sister being the latest variation on the excuses that earlier took the form of coffee-house or barracks. But the young man, echoing the young woman's words, begs for five minutes more, and by the end of the scene and after the young man's more successful performance second time round, it is already eight o'clock and more than an hour and three-quarters have elapsed, rather than the five minutes that she had originally been prepared to stay.

Whilst obviously not lasting as long on stage, the fourth scene is the first in which the action is more fully developed around a series of comic parallels and contrasts, but whereas in earlier scenes the comedy had arisen merely

from such parallels or through the juxtaposition of words and actions, the ironic comments of the young woman suggest a character with a sense of humour, whose words and behaviour are an explicit as well as an implicit source of comedy. The fourth scene is also the first in which the sexual act seems mutually and lastingly enjoyable rather than being followed by an abrupt change of mood on the part of one or both participants. The young woman's haste to leave is not the lack of involvement exhibited by the male characters of the earlier scenes, and she still finds time to continue with her earlier games, insisting that he will never see her again, allowing only for the possibility of chance encounters, apparently determined to stay away from any gatherings where he may be (p. 346), yet then proposing to discuss any future rendezvous the very next day (p. 347).

The young woman's fears are not to be taken too lightly, even though the emphasis is on the comic aspect of such exaggeration and repetition, and although it is clear that she is turning such worries to her advantage as a weapon in her dealings with the young man. Nevertheless her concern with how to explain her absence to her husband, her contemplation of the disgrace that would result from the discovery of her liaison, and the fear that it could have fatal consequences for both of them, these are real fears, as the young man's reaction (*höchst unangenehm berührt*) and also a glance at the fate of Fritz in *Liebelei* make only too apparent. For the woman of Schnitzler's day, the concern was not so much the man's fear of death in a duel as the need to preserve her reputation as an 'anständige Frau', unsullied by any sexual experience other than with her husband. The total hypocrisy of the situation and the gulf between appearance and reality is indicated in the young man's delight at finally embarking on an affair with such a woman, who at this point if not long before has ceased to be 'anständig' except in respect of the veneer of social respectability that she can still maintain as long as her extra-marital affairs remain undetected. This is not a criticism of the young woman; on the contrary, when the 'rules' of socially acceptable sexual behaviour are enumerated by the husband in the fifth scene, the author's and also the audience's sympathy is very much on the side of the young woman forced by social convention to conceal her naturalness, wit, and vivacity behind a façade of subservient innocence or even stupidity.[20] The argument that the one entirely legal act of sexual intercourse is the most sordid precisely because of the hypocrisy that underlies the supposed 'Heiligkeit' of the marital contract, or that the depiction of sex within marriage goes a long way to explain the need for the relationship in the other scenes, does not need to be demonstrated again here;[21] in the present context it is more important to stress that the woman's moral and intellectual superiority is indicated through her sense of humour and irony, which she can never fully suppress despite her attempt to play the role of the naive and dutiful wife, whilst the comedy of the scene is at the expense of the husband, whose pomposity and arrogance not only are comic by virtue of the exaggerated and self-pitying terms in which they are stated but are also cast in an ironic light thanks to the audience's awareness of his wife's earlier behaviour and their expectations of similar indiscretions on his part.

From the very start, the young woman's surprise at her husband's renewed interest in her is revealed in her ironic comments ('wirklich?', 'was hast du denn?'), and the same irony underpins her laconic responses to his excuse that it is the sanctity of marriage which necessitates his frequent suppression of or, as she sees it, lack of erotic interest:

DER GATTE:

> [. . .] hätte ich mich von Anfang an meiner Leidenschaft für dich willenlos hingegeben, es wäre uns gegangen wie den Millionen von anderen Liebespaaren. Wir wären fertig miteinander.

DIE JUNGE FRAU:

> Ah . . . so meinst du das?

DER GATTE:

> Glaube mir—Emma—in den ersten Tagen unserer Ehe hatte ich Angst, daß es so kommen würde.

DIE JUNGE FRAU:

> Ich auch.

DER GATTE:

> Siehst du? Hab ich nicht recht gehabt? Darum ist es gut, immer wieder für einige Zeit nur in guter Freundschaft miteinander hinzuleben.

DIE JUNGE FRAU:

> Ach so.

DER GATTE:

> Und so kommt es, daß wir immer wieder neue Flitterwochen miteinander durchleben können, da ich es nie drauf ankommen lasse, die Flitterwochen . . .

DIE JUNGE FRAU:

> Zu Monaten auszudehnen.

DER GATTE:

> Richtig.

(p. 348)

Her suggestion 'wenn es aber . . . bei mir anders wäre', that in other words she may not at that moment be interested in a renewal of intimacy,[22] is ignored or genuinely misunderstood by the husband, as he develops his elaborate image of young men compelled to seek sexual experience from fallen women, whilst the daughters of good families are able to preserve a more ideal vision of love as they wait in cloistered innocence for the 'men of honour' to complete their unsavoury and demeaning course of sexual initiation (p. 49). As the wife imagines with a certain envy the delights that such 'fallen women'

experience and begins to snuggle up to her husband (p. 350), she might be in danger of revealing the truth about herself, were it not for the fact that the husband is quite incapable of conceptualizing her except through the socially defined categories of 'anständige Frau' and mother of their daughter. The husband's division of women into the categories 'Frau' and 'Weib' (he will later refer to the 'süßes Mädel' as the latter) is an indication of the cliché-ridden artificiality of his thinking but more particularly a convenient way of justifying his own behaviour and of keeping his wife in what he imagines to be a state of docile innocence.

Not for the first time in the play it is the woman who presses for more details of the man's life and experiences; this is not the desire for a more lasting attachment, which after all she already has, but it does reflect the hope for a more fulfilling one, in which she will be seen as both wife and mistress. The comic irony of the scene lies above all in the fact that it is the husband who knows so little about his own wife; indeed, as he continues to talk in ridiculously pompous terms of fallen women having a 'Heimweh nach der Tugend' and dying young, as he sees his wife as an equally unrealistic ideal of 'Reinheit und Wahrheit' and asks her not to have anything to do with any woman involved in an extra-marital affair, whilst she however contemplates the pleasure and intoxication of her own such affair (pp. 351-52), one has the impression that they both finally make love to someone else or at least to a figment of their imagination. After they have slept together, they remain in the marital bed, but in other respects the pattern of other scenes is preserved, with the wife keen to maintain the level of intimacy and emotional commitment she has briefly regained, whilst the husband is quick to return, at least emotionally and metaphorically, to ordinary reality outside ('man muß [. . .] hinaus ins feindliche Leben' (p. 353)) and to re-establish the distance that he had earlier seen as a prerequisite for married life (pp. 348, 353). Once more he refers to her condescendingly as 'mein Kind'.

Whilst the audience may find the husband's self-righteousness amusing, he himself is scarcely blessed with a sense of humour, whilst his wife's natural wit is also considerably more muted than in the previous scene. The husband's presence means that the same is true in reverse order of the two scenes involving the 'süßes Madel'. In the first of these she reveals glimpses of self-assurance and independence beneath the required façade of innocence and malleability, and cleverly evades his probing for details of her past, questions that unlike those of the female characters in other scenes are not designed to find out more about the partner as a person but to elicit confessions of sexual experience that may pave the way for his own enjoyment of similar favours. On the whole, however, the comedy of the sixth scene is more muted than in the previous two, and derives principally from the recurrence of by now familiar motifs,[23] not least the contrast between the woman's apparent attempt to keep her distance and an obvious enjoyment of intimacy (*langer heißer Kuß* (p.

357)), that is particularly clear from the stage-direction immediately after they have made love (*lehnt mit geschlossenen Augen in der Diwanecke*), even though she once more seeks to blame her lack of resistance on the wine (p. 360).

Also as in earlier scenes, after intercourse the woman loses her desire to leave and instead seeks assurances of genuine affection, but the equally familiar motif of the man's post-coital desire for distance is even more extreme than usual, as his immediate fear is that he has been less than careful and may have contracted some disease, a fear that also informs his increased interest in her previous lovers (pp. 360-61). As the girl emphasizes, the man's mood has totally changed: 'Du bist aber wie ausgewechselt' (p. 361), a line that sums up the male characters in a number of scenes, whilst the audience's awareness of the true state of affairs injects a large touch of comic irony into the final section of the scene, as the husband returns to his irreconcilable categories of 'Frau' and 'Weib' and is enraged by the girl's suggestion that his wife may herself be having an affair (p. 362).

The sixth scene ends with the husband claiming to live in Graz, but apparently prepared to set up the young girl in a place where he may visit her as long as she promises not to entertain any other lovers. If any such promise is made it has inevitably been forgotten in time for her encounter with the writer, the opening section of which is a virtual reprise of the fourth scene, as the girl is persuaded without too much difficulty to take off her hat and cape despite her protestations that she can only stay for a minute (p. 364). The comedy of the scene results largely from the portrayal of the writer as a self-centred poseur who sees every situation, every sentence, as a potential literary gem to be used in a subsequent work (pp. 365-66). His vocabulary is littered with words such as 'göttlich' (pp. 365-68), 'Herrgott' (p. 370); he calls the girl 'Engel' (pp. 367, 369) and idealizes her apparent stupidity as divine (p. 365), her simplicity as holy (p. 369). He is more particularly obsessed with his own importance and fame as a writer, torn between the fleeting delight at realizing that he may have attracted the girl as an ordinary human being (p. 369), yet on the other hand distraught to discover that there may be those who do not know or may be indifferent to his identity as a writer (pp. 367, 369); indeed, he is so insecure without his literary persona that he feels he will know the girl only when he discovers what she thinks of his plays (p. 371).

Considerable comic effect is achieved as she ignores or seems to misunderstand his poeticizing, not least when he apostrophizes her as the ultimate ideal:

DER DICHTER:

Du bist schön, du bist die Schönheit, du bist vielleicht sogar die Natur, du bist du heilige Einfalt.

DAS SÜSSE MÄDEL:

O weh, du tropfst mich ja an! Schau, was gibst denn nicht acht!

(p. 369)

or when his attempts to elicit an answer to the question of whether she is happy or aware of being alive are met only with a request for a comb (p. 370). On occasions, the comedy is even gentle irony at her expense, as she appears genuinely bewildered by his literary devices and role-playing:

Ja, jetzt kenn ich mich aber nicht mehr aus

(p. 369)

Jetzt, die G'schicht mit dem Biebitz—da bin ich schon ganz blöd

(p. 371)

Yet such responses are not simply the result of naive innocence; in the face of the writer's egoism and artificiality, the young girl appears considerably more self-assured and assertive than in the earlier scene, and at times seems to be deliberately misunderstanding him in the manner of the young woman in the fourth scene, or openly mocking his pretentious language:

DER DICHTER:

Deine Augen müssen sich an das Halbdunkel gewöhnen.—Diese süßen Augen—*küßt sie auf die Augen.*

DAS SÜSSE MÄDEL:

Dazu werden die süßen Augen aber nicht Zeit genug haben.

(p. 364)[24]

Indeed, when she repeats virtually word for word her earlier explanation for having been in a *chambre separée* (p. 366), again assuring the partner that the only other man she thinks of is her former fiancé and that she is ashamed of her current indiscretion (p. 369), she conveys the strong impression that she has used such lines on other occasions and that she is acting out her role as the 'süßes Mädel' to the same extent as the writer adopts his literary poses.

With the exception of the prostitute, the behaviour of all the characters can be seen in that light, and indeed is a feature of so many of Schnitzler's creations, whether it be the eponymous central figure of *Leutnant Gustl* or *Casanovas Heimfahrt,* or Anatol, whose playing of an elaborate role inspired Hofmannsthal to capture what he saw as the quintessence of Schnitzler's work but also of his own precocious aestheticism in the famous lines from the prologue. As in **Reigen,** the roles played in **Liebelei** are not so much aesthetic posing as socially determined gender roles, accepted by Theodor and Mizi and abandoned with disastrous consequences by both Fritz and Christine. In **Liebelei,** however, the breaking of rules is often accidental and partly subconscious: Fritz pays for the acknowledged folly of exchanging letters by accepting the need for a fatal duel, whilst even Christine's refusal to allow things to return to normal ('und in einem Monat ganz getröstet, wie?') is born of total despair rather than of any conscious challenge to socially conditioned patterns of behaviour. In **Reigen,** however, a number of the characters are very aware that they are both playing and also subverting an accepted role, and the comedy is often a direct result of that awareness and of the concomitant refusal to take the role entirely seriously. The culmination of such play acting, and arguably the most comic scene of the whole cycle, is the confrontation, one might say thespian duel, between the writer and the actress. The former wheels out the big guns of poetic hyperbole that he has already used in the earlier scene: 'Du bist das Göttliche, du bist das Genie . . . Du bist . . . Du bist eigentlich die heilige Einfalt' (p. 372). Just as earlier he had contemplated a romantic idyll in the isolation of nature (p. 370), so now he imagines spending time amongst pious, simple country folk (p. 373), and he continues to philosophize right up to the climax of the scene, as he imagines the actress being unfaithful to an imaginary painter of her own invention (p. 375); on this occasion, however, he is met not with incomprehension or unintentional put-downs but with straightforward sarcasm: 'Rede keinen Stiefel', 'Du redest wie ein Idiot' (p. 373), 'Ich bitte dich, rede nicht so märchenhaft blöd' (p. 375). The actress mocks his arrogance by implying that he thinks of himself as God, or by asserting that he has no talent (p. 372). In particular she teases him mercilessly, and the game of seduction is played very much on her terms, as she makes him wait under the window whilst she undresses and tells him not to start an affair with the waitress in the meantime (p. 373), as she suggests he get into bed with her but then tells him not to move a muscle (p. 375). Erna Neuse has suggested that the characters never have any moral scruples about intercourse, only social or aesthetic ones (Neuse, p. 361), and while that is not true of all the characters, the actress openly acknowledges the immorality of the situation by inviting him to imagine whom she is being unfaithful to (p. 375). If this also serves to negate any attempt at a romantic heightening of the episode, then the same is true of her later insistence that he is a mere whim (p. 376).

The comedy of the scene continues as she repeatedly calls him arrogant, again taunts him with names such as 'Grille' or even 'Frosch'. Here there is a further instance of comic reversal of motifs from an earlier scene, as he no longer wishes to be called by his literary pseudonym Biebitz, and certainly not by one of her less flattering nicknames, but by his real name Robert, which she however rejects as far too stupid (p. 377). Her own self-centred arrogance is revealed as she confesses to having nothing to do with her fellow actors (p. 376), or boasts of her sensational performance on stage the previous night ('Die Menschen sind blaß geworden' (p. 377)). The link between theatrical and sexual performance is one that the actress specifically makes in the line already quoted at the start of this article, and the parallel is in fact continued in an exchange in which it is not clear what sort of 'Stück' is being discussed (p. 375). Certainly the actress and writer reveal a consummate ability to act a part, thereby demonstrating in extreme form what the play suggests is a feature of all human sexual behaviour; in this particular instance, however, both characters appear to be in full agreement as far as the play's direction is concerned (even though the writer may

have doubts about some of the lines that the actress has given him!) and neither has anything to hide or be embarrassed about. Significantly this scene is, with the partial exception of the fourth, the only one in which the sexual act is not followed by an obvious change of mood in at least one of the partners, and the uneasy and self-conscious transition from pre-coital assertiveness to post-coital anxiety and introversion that frequently characterizes the male partner is in this case displayed neither by the male writer nor by the female actress who is adopting the conventional male role. Any changes of mood in the actress are quite independent of her desire to sleep with the writer and are in any case entirely artificial and able to be manufactured as and when required. Hence by the end of the scene she has reversed her earlier distinction between her adored Fritz and the writer who is a mere whim: now she is dying of longing and love for the writer, whilst Fritz is dismissed as a galley slave (p. 377).

Much has been made of the suggestion that the actress adopts a male role in the play,[25] and she does indeed share a number of lines with the male characters in other scenes, asking for a kiss (pp. 372, 374), tempting the writer into bed (p. 374), or refusing to use his real name and referring to him as 'mein Kind' (p. 376).[26] However, the actress has an obvious sense of humour that distinguishes her from the all too serious self-importance of her male counterparts and links her especially with a female character such as the young wife. As in the fourth scene, the comedy derives from the reversal of conventional gender roles, but whilst the young woman still pays lip service to those roles and to the social codes that underpin and dictate them, in this eighth scene those codes are quite consciously overturned. Yet precisely because the actress is aware of what she is doing, the part she chooses for herself is so exaggerated and transparent that she cannot take it seriously, unlike the writer, who at times appears genuinely enmeshed in his literary conceits and his own self-importance as Biebitz. Nevertheless, under her influence even the writer is moved to essay the odd witty or ironic comment of which he seemed incapable in the earlier scene with the 'süßes Mädel' (joking that he currently has the best chances of starting an affair with her (p. 375)), although his witticisms are more a means of self-defence than a sign that he has fully come to terms with the role assigned to him by his female director.

The extent to which the writer is indeed a match for the actress is revealed only in the following scene with the Count. He, unlike the writer, readily accepts as the truth the actress's protestations of illness (p. 378) and also her claim that she is a misanthropist, or that she was performing only for him (pp. 380-81). Fortunately for his sake, the mockery she had hurled at the writer is here used more sparingly and indirectly, no doubt out of respect for his military rank and concomitant social standing, but she quietly pokes fun at his philosophizing (pp. 382, 384-85), his insistence on a schedule or on the importance of the right ambience for seduction, which she finds 'süß' (p. 383), or which drives her to call him an old man (pp. 379,

384). She refrains, however, from any open criticism of his desire to paint a Hungarian sunset (p. 380), where previously she had poured scorn on the writer's similar apostrophizing of nature, and her earlier delight in calling people names is here restricted to her giving him the name of what he describes as a Godforsaken garrison town in western Hungary: 'Adieu, Steinamanger!' Although she is also more cautious than before in taking the initiative, it is once more the woman who does so, kissing his hand or asking for a kiss (pp. 378, 382), repeatedly telling him to come nearer or to remove his sword (pp. 381-83), lying to him that they cannot be disturbed because the door (through which he has only just entered!) cannot be opened from outside (p. 382), or being the first to switch to 'Du' in yet another instance of the elaborate to and fro between formal and informal modes of address. It is she who then appears to want to impose distance afterwards, although this is very much in the nature of a grand dramatic gesture ('ich [will] dich nie wiedersehen' (p. 384)),[27] as is her final staging of the formal farewell which she then herself disrupts with her ironic reference to Steinamanger. As in the previous scene, the actress does nothing to hide her enjoyment of sex, and once more performance in that sphere is equated with acting ability: the Count, she suggests, should have been an actor (p. 384)!

The Count has been considered as the most sympathetic of the male characters,[28] yet in his way he is just as wrapped up in his own affairs and his philosophizing as the writer, and arguably has rather less intelligence. His cliché-ridden philosophy (people are the same everywhere, there is no such thing as happiness, one must abandon oneself to the moment (p. 380)) can hardly be taken seriously and leads to the actress's ironic comment: 'Sie haben wohl den Sinn erfaßt' (p. 381),[29] or she reminds him of one of his own clichés:

GRAF:

Ich bin sehr glücklich.

SCHAUSPIELERIN:

Nun, ich dachte, es gibt kein Glück.

(p. 382)

The actress accuses him of being a 'Poseur' (pp. 382-83), which was true of the writer but not of the Count, for the simple reason that he is unaware of the artificiality of his stance. Schnitzler's most scathing criticism of the military is, of course, to be found in *Leutnant Gustl,* but the Count is just as empty-headed as (if perhaps more idealistic in his acceptance of the military way of life than) the young lieutenant, whose existence is threatened by the very code that gives his otherwise empty life some semblance of meaning. Certainly the Count's language is as artificial and exaggerated as that of the writer ('gespielt wie eine Göttin', 'kolossal' (p. 378)) and with his insistence on routine and order and his determination to see the actress as a problem or as somehow mysterious (pp. 379, 382), not least because she does not fit in with his male order of

things, he is as much a comic character as the young man and the writer, whilst his penchant for philosophizing and his concern for atmosphere, ambience, and routine link him with all other male characters except perhaps the soldier.

If, as the actress suggests, he does revert to his formal exterior, 'als wär nichts geschehen' (p. 384), then he is once more conforming to the archetypal male pattern, although his reaction to such an implied criticism may indicate that this is another example of the actress's role-playing. Indeed, if the Count *is* one of the more sympathetic male characters, then it is in part because he finds himself cast in the female role, seeking excuses for leaving and worried about being disturbed (pp. 382-83), and very much at the mercy of the actress who, as in the previous scene, takes over the behaviour patterns that elsewhere characterize the play's male protagonists. Perhaps it is inevitable that as a result, and also in view of his rather exaggerated chivalry and sense of decorum, there appears to be something of the artist *manqué,* even of the fop or dandy about him, although the continual references to his male colleagues that may lead a late twentieth-century reader to pursue such a line of enquiry further are almost certainly not to be understood in that way.[30] In any case, the actress's implicit praise of his performance also negates any attempt to read significance into his removing his sabre before sex, despite the tempting link with similar imagery in *Leutnant Gustl.*

The cycle of erotic encounters is completed by the character who makes a living out of man's sexual urges and who has by now progressed from furtive coupling on river banks to a room of her own, admittedly a decidedly dilapidated one, and is even dreaming of a move to the more salubrious Spiegelgasse. In other respects, however, the final scene is somewhat different from the rest. The sexual aspect is already some hours past, and the Count has no recollection of having slept with the prostitute and is quite convinced that he did not. He is otherwise determined to see the prostitute as 'tugendhaft' and 'unschuldig', as a princess (pp. 386-87), a motif that strikes one as a grotesque variation on the young man's desire for a relationship with 'eine anständige Frau'. In a way that once more links him with the female characters in the play, he convinces himself that she reminds him of a former love. When forced to acknowledge that his meeting has had the inevitable outcome, he regrets the fact that he has missed out on what would have been a somewhat different experience: 'Es wär doch schön gewesen, wenn ich sie nur auf die Augen geküßt hätt. Das wär mir beinah ein Abenteuer gewesen' (p. 390). The Count may wish he could have momentarily escaped the never-ending cycle, but it is known that at midday the prostitute will be seeking her next client, and the play's cycle resists final closure in a way guaranteed to satisfy even the most ardent disciples of Lacan and Kristeva.

The concluding scene is also unusual in that there is no explicit comedy to speak of, certainly not by comparison with the preceding scenes, but merely a certain gentle irony at the Count's expense which arises out of the contrast between his philosophizing and the prostitute's very down-to-earth approach, a contrast reminiscent of the scene with the writer and the 'süßes Mädel'. What little comedy there is does conform to the established pattern: at the expense of the male character even if not specifically generated by the woman's humour. This contrast applies even where, as in the case of the actress, it is the woman who reveals the usually male characteristics of an unscrupulous pursuit of the sensual goal and a lack of emotional commitment. That a major source of the play's comedy derives from the contrast between the behaviour of male and female characters might be seen as a conventional ingredient of many comedies, but there is the further contrast between the characters' actual behaviour and that which the social codes of Schnitzler's day might lead one to expect. The men in Schnitzler's play range from the slightly pathetic (the Count and the young man) to the unsavoury or simply vulgar (the husband and the soldier), with the pomposity of the writer somewhere in the middle. He at least has some flashes of the humour and irony that is otherwise reserved for female figures such as the 'süßes Mädel' and more especially the young woman and the actress.

On the whole, however, the women are more witty and amusing, but also as a result more warm and sympathetic, whilst the men appear shallow and lacking in warmth and humanity. For all the male characters, empty philosophizing and a concern with order and ritual replace or even indicate a lack of genuine emotional involvement. The men may be keen to stress the depth of their love and the uniqueness of the present relationship, but their partial dislike and fear of sexuality, witnessed most clearly in the characters of husband and Count, mean that they are quick to break any romantic spell and to return to the security of male-oriented social normality once they have had their brief moment of pleasure. According to Klaus Kilian, for all characters, including the women, 'geht es ausschließlich um die Befriedigung ihrer Begierde, um reine Sexualität' (Kilian, p. 60), yet the women, unlike their male counterparts, retain an awareness of past loves, with which they are happy to compare present experience. They appear to derive a more lasting pleasure from sexual experience, showing less furtiveness and fewer signs of post-coital guilt. Even the prostitute regrets that she could not sleep with the soldier in more comfortable surroundings, whilst the final scene finds her sleeping contentedly after her night with the drunken Count. For the women, sexuality is a weapon that gives them a certain power over men, or at the very least an awareness of equality with them, and the humour displayed by the female characters derives in no small part from that awareness; in this respect, if not in the others so often asserted (see note 13 above), it may be correct to agree with the Count that 'der Schlaf macht alle gleich'. For the same reasons, however, the men find sexuality a threat, a potential source of inferiority and, not merely in a sexual sense, impotence.

Paradoxically, it is the men's own codes of social behaviour, stated in their most extreme and ludicrous form by

the husband in the play's pivotal scene, which demand that they go in search of sex as a proof of their superiority and virility, and which lead inevitably to the more sordid aspects of sexuality depicted in the first and last scenes of the cycle, from which there is no escape except the Count's naively romantic ideal of merely kissing the prostitute's eyes.[31] It is scarcely surprising, therefore, that in the final scene 'Lustigkeit' is indeed outweighed by 'Melancholie', as the cycle returns to the character who owes her *raison d'être* to the suppression of more natural and mutual sexuality that is codified in social convention. If only by implication, however, **Reigen** invites us to rethink such socially determined patterns of behaviour and the conventional gender roles they produce. Certainly the actress has manipulated or openly flouted the rules set by male society and turned them to her own advantage, whilst the young woman is prepared to play her own game and assert her superiority although apparently following rules that dictate the opposite, and it is they who communicate the greatest sense of humour and of *joie de vivre*. To borrow the terminology of the often unsatisfactory distinction between *Komödie* and *Lustspiel*,[32] **Reigen** not merely is concerned with unmasking the inadequacies and false values of human life and society but also reveals a good-natured understanding of human foibles and limitations that is expressed in the wit and humour of certain characters. As such comedy is surely meant to indicate, sexuality is not to be seen in exclusively negative terms as 'rein animalisch', 'sinnlos und seelenlos', as a source of disappointment, 'Ausweglosigkeit', or 'experiential impoverishment',[33] and Schnitzler's portrayal of human behaviour is perhaps rather less a metaphor of death and despair than the massed ranks of (predominantly male!) literary critics have so frequently claimed.

Notes

1. Typically Ursula Keller, *'Böser Dinge hübsche Formel'. Das Wien Arthur Schnitzlers* (Berlin: Guttandin & Hoppe, 1984), pp. 177-94; Bruce Thompson, *Schnitzler's Vienna* (London: Routledge, 1990), pp. 63-68; Johanna Bossinade, '"Wenn es aber . . . bei mir anders wäre". Die Frage der Geschlechterbeziehungen in Arthur Schnitzlers Reigen', in *Aufsätze zu Literatur und Kunst der Jahrhundertwende,* ed. by Gerhard Kluge (Amsterdam: Rodopi, 1984), pp. 273-328 (pp. 276-77). For earlier critics, see Rolf-Peter Janz and Klaus Laermann, *Arthur Schnitzler. Zur Diagnose des Wiener Bürgertums im Fin de Siècle* (Stuttgart: Metzler, 1977); Martin Swales, *Arthur Schnitzler: A Critical Study* (Oxford: Clarendon Press, 1971).

2. Klaus Kilian, *Die Komödien Arthur Schnitzlers. Sozialer Rollenzwang und kritische Ethik* (Düsseldorf: Bertelsmann, 1972). Ernst L. Offermanns devotes one short paragraph to what he considers one of the 'Vorformen von Schnitzlers Komödie' (*Arthur Schnitzler. Das Komödienwerk als Kritik des Impressionismus* (Munich: Fink, 1973), pp. 12-13). More recently, Peter Skrine has described the play as 'a *tour de*

force of comic invention' but is unable to develop the matter further within the constraints of a general introduction to three dramatists (*Hauptmann, Wedekind and Schnitzler* (Basingstoke: Macmillan, 1991), p. 131); see also W. E. Yates's reference to the play's intention 'to function as a sexual *comedy*' (*Schnitzler, Hofmannsthal and the Austrian Theatre* (New Haven, CT, and London: Yale University Press, 1992), p. 133).

3. The second volume of *Das deutsche Lustspiel,* ed. by Hans Steffen (Göttingen: Vandenhoeck & Ruprecht, 1969), includes an essay on *Der grüne Kakadu* by Herbert Singer (pp. 61-78) but otherwise studies of comedy and compilations of essays on individual comedies seldom refer to Schnitzler, let alone to *Reigen;* see, for example, *Wesen und Form des Komischen im Drama,* ed. by Reinhold Grimm and Klaus L. Berghahn (Darmstadt: Wissenschaftliche Buchgesellschaft, 1975), *Die deutsche Komödie vom Mittelalter bis zur Gegenwart,* ed. by Walter Hinck (Düsseldorf: Bagel, 1977). One exception is Morton Gurewitch, *Comedy: The Irrational Vision* (Ithaca, NY, and London: Cornell University Press, 1975), but his one brief comment that 'Schnitzler's *Reigen* [. . .] splendidly illustrates the imagination of irony' (p. 18) is difficult to interpret.

4. Robert Cushman, *The Observer,* 17 January 1982.

5. Richard Alewyn, postscript to the edition of the play published by Fischer Verlag (Frankfurt a.M., 1981, pp. 175-76). See especially Helga Schiffer, 'Arthur Schnitzlers *Reigen*', *Text und Kontext,* 11 (1983), 7-34; also Swales, p. 234; Claudio Magris, 'Arthur Schnitzler und das Karussell der Triebe', in *Arthur Schnitzler in neuer Sicht,* ed. by Hartmut Scheible (Munich: Fink, 1981), p. 73; Gerhart Baumann, *Arthur Schnitzler. Die Welt von Gestern eines Dichters von Morgen* (Frankfurt a.M.: Athenäum, 1965), p. 15. The only critics who have rejected the link are Hartmut Scheible, *Arthur Schnitzler* (Reinbek bei Hamburg: Rowohlt, 1976), p. 65; Jon Barry Sanders, 'Arthur Schnitzler's *Reigen*: Lost Romanticism', *Modern Austrian Literature,* 1 (1965), 56-66 (p. 57); also Bossinade, pp. 276-77, Janz and Laermann, pp. 56-57, and Skrine, who concludes that 'there is scant evidence in the text to suggest that the spectre of mortality is waiting in the wings' (p. 132).

6. Letter to Dora Michaelis, 5 February 1921, in Arthur Schnitzler, *Briefe 1913-31,* ed. by Peter Michael Braunwirth and others (Frankfurt a.M.: Fischer, 1984), p. 231. Quotations from *Reigen* are from *Gesammelte Werke. Die dramatischen Werke,* 2 vols (Frankfurt a.M.: Fischer, 1972), 1, 327-90.

7. Bernd Schoeller, *Gelächter und Spannung. Studien zur Struktur des heiteren Dramas* (Zurich: Atlantis, 1971), p. 9.

8. Fritz Martini, *Lustspiele—und das Lustspiel* (Stuttgart: Klett-Cotta, 1974), p. 32.

9. Introduction to *Deutsche Komödien. Vom Barock bis zur Gegenwart,* ed. by Winfried Freund (Munich: Fink, 1988), p. 12.

10. The links between Schnitzler and Bauernfeld are stressed by Helmut Prang (*Geschichte des Lustspiels* (Stuttgart: Kröner, 1968), p. 280), and more recently by W. E. Yates, who refers specifically to Schnitzler's debt to the *Konversationsstück* (pp. 68-70). The social uncertainties that undermined the fashion for the *Konversationsstück* are examined by Hans-Peter Bayerdörfer ('Vom Konversationsstück zur Wurstelkomödie. Zu Arthur Schnitzlers Einaktern', *Jahrbuch der Deutschen Schillergesellschaft,* 16 (1972), 516-75 (pp. 519-20)).

11. Hunter G. Hannum, 'Killing Time: Aspects of Schnitzler's *Reigen*', *Germanic Review,* 37 (1962), 190-206 (pp. 205-06); also Swales, p. 251. The modern aspects are more justifiably stressed by Bayerdörfer in the context of the slightly later *Zum großen Wurstel*; see also Swales, p. 273.

12. One need look no further than the theories summarized in the *Metzler Literatur-Lexikon,* ed. by Günther and Irmgard Schweikle (Stuttgart: Metzler, 1990), pp. 243-48. See the comment of Winfried Freund: 'Fast drängt sich dem Leser all der schwergewichtigen Definitionen und tiefernsten Erörterungen der Eindruck auf, als habe man die Komödie mit der tragischen Elle gemessen, sie gewogen, aber zu leicht befunden' (p. 7).

13. The linking motifs have been examined in some detail, if not always entirely accurately, by Erna Neuse, in 'Die Funktion von Motiven und stereotypen Wendungen in Schnitzlers *Reigen*', *Monatshefte,* 64 (1972), 356-70, but with only the briefest mention of what she recognizes as their comic impact. See also Keller, pp. 182-83.

14. There is a tendency amongst critics to paraphrase the Count's words in the final scene and stress that 'die Liebe macht alle gleich': Kilian, p. 61; Neuse, p. 367; Michaela L. Perlmann, *Arthur Schnitzler* (Stuttgart: Metzler, 1987), pp. 41-42. Swales (p. 233) writes of 'faceless, nameless marionettes', similarly Alewyn, p. 174. Not surprisingly, critics who question such an interpretation are often those who distance themselves from the parallel with the *Totentanz* (for example, Janz and Laermann, p. 57; see above, note 1). Others seek an uneasy compromise: for Schiffer the characters are 'sowohl Individuen als auch Marionetten' (p. 28), whilst Keller's insistence 'sie sind beileibe keine papierenen Abstraktionen' (p. 190) is outweighed by her constant references to 'das Immergleiche'.

15. Most recently Thompson, pp. 67-68. It is surprising that this view has managed to coexist with the insistence that all are equal: perhaps women are more equal than others! W. E. Yates, however, argues that 'the sexes are given equal weight and presented with equal irony' (p. 133).

16. One is also reminded of Anatol's insistence on 'Stimmung' (*Die dramatischen Werke*, 1, 57).

17. In this scene especially one can only concur with Robert Cushman (see note 4) that the Viennese had 'enviably rapid powers of recovery!'.

18. Swales underlines the contrast between stage directions and verbal protestations (p. 236).

19. That women lack the possibility of escape to a social normality that is male-dominated and male-orientated is undoubtedly true, but Bossinade's repeated suggestions of 'eine latent homoerotische Dimension' (pp. 297, 300, and elsewhere) seem questionable.

20. To accuse the young woman of being frivolous and coquettish (Thompson, p. 65) is surely to overlook the extent to which she is playing a game according to the rules dictated by her husband. Even more questionable is the categorization of her as 'die dämonische Frau' (Barbara Gutt, *Emanzipation bei Arthur Schnitzler* (Berlin: Spiess, 1978), p. 54).

21. See Thompson, p. 65; Janz and Laermann, p. 59; Swales, p. 245. Lotte S. Couch writes of 'die Verbannung der Sexualität aus dem bürgerlichen Familienleben' ('Der *Reigen*: Schnitzler und Sigmund Freud', *Österreich in Geschichte und Literatur*, 16 (1972), 217-27 (p. 223)).

22. For Bossinade (pp. 313-15) this indicates the young woman's desire for the kind of contact with other women rendered impossible by a male-dominated society in which women have no independent identity but can exist only as a function of male desire.

23. The to and fro between the forms of address as the husband encourages her to use the more informal 'Du'; the girl's desire for a more permanent relationship, which in this case leads her to go with someone who reminds her of her boyfriend who abandoned her; her increasingly feeble attempts to resist the husband's advances (*sie wehrt kaum ab* (p. 360)) and to find excuses to go home to her mother (pp. 357, 360); the usual fear that someone may come in and disturb them (p. 360).

24. Similarly, as he fantasizes about forgetting her or about overcoming the barriers between near and far ('Geh, was redst denn—?' (p. 367)), or as he contemplates the natural idyll of their relationship or their future parting (p. 370).

25. For example, Janz and Laermann, p. 67. Gutt rightly denies that such an exchange of roles means that the actress is presented as a masculine type: 'In seinem Werk finden sich die Rollen häufig vertauscht, ohne daß die Geschlechtszugehörigkeit ihrer jeweiligen Träger in Frage gestellt wird' (p. 117). Less convincingly, Bossinade sees the actress as a plaything of writer and audience (Count) respectively, because she is a product of the male world of the theatre.

26. It is noteworthy that, with the exception of the actress (and almost inevitably the prostitute), the women more often refer to the men by name, whereas the men are more likely to refer to the partner as 'Fräulein' or 'Kind'. This detail of characterization is inevitably overlooked in any insistence that the characters remain nameless, which is only true of the list of characters (Heinz Rieder, *Arthur Schnitzler* (Vienna: Bergland, 1973), p. 53; see also Alewyn, p. 174, Swales, p. 233).

27. The juxtaposition of a farewell for ever and arrangements for a rendezvous again links the actress with the young woman in the fourth scene.

28. Neuse, p. 364, Keller, p. 181; also Ernst L. Offermanns, in *Handbuch des deutschen Dramas*, ed. by Walter Hinck (Düsseldorf: Bagel, 1980), p. 332.

29. Hannum manages to see the actress's words as the summation of a highly significant conversation on the 'time philosophy of the characters' (pp. 202-03).

30. Rather surprisingly, Bossinade appears to find the Count a less productive source of 'homoerotische Dimensionen' than other male protagonists.

31. To see this as the play's message (Sanders, p. 65) is surely to misunderstand the play almost entirely.

32. Otto Rommel, 'Komick und Lustspieltheorie', in *Wesen und Form des Komischen im Drama* (see note 3 above), p. 49 (first published in *Deutsche Vierteljahrsschrift*, 21 (1943), 252-86); Gero von Wilpert, *Sachwörterbuch der Literatur* (Stuttgart: Kröner, 1964), p. 397.

33. Respectively Neuse, p. 367; Rieder, p. 53; Janz and Laermann, p. 72; Schiffer, p. 27; Swales, p. 51.

IM SPIEL DER SOMMERLÜFTE

CRITICAL COMMENTARY

Brigitte L. Schneider-Halvorson (essay date 1983)

SOURCE: Schneider-Halvorson, Brigitte L. "Im Spiel Der Sommerlüfte." In *The Late Dramatic Works of Arthur Schnitzler*, pp. 113-135. New York: Peter Lang, 1983.

[*In the following essay, Schneider-Halvorson discusses various critical commentary, as well as Schnitzler's use of themes and symbols in the play* Im Spiel Der Sommerlüfte.]

BACKGROUND OF THE PLAY AND STATEMENT OF PURPOSE

The first performance of Schnitzler's play *Im Spiel der Sommerlüfte* took place on December 21, 1929, at the Deutsches Volkstheater in Vienna.[1] First publication was in

1930 by S. Fischer Verlag, Berlin.[2] According to Schnitzler's diary notes, he completed this three-act drama between February and April of 1928.[3] His first ideas, however, date back to 1898, when he recorded: "Ein Stück 'Sommernacht' wird lebendig [. . .]. Im Kaffeehaus entwarf ich den Plan eines dreiaktigen Stückes 'Sommernachtstraum'."[4] More sketches and notes were added between 1911-1913; five years later a new sketch was written under the present title, *Im Spiel der Sommerlüfte.* The term "Spiel" points to the fluctuating atmospheric conditions of summer, which, as analysis will demonstrate, affect significantly not only the various moods of the characters in the play, but also turn some of these characters further inward where life is truly lived.

Hartmut Scheible measures the success of this drama merely in terms of respect paid to the author and calls it an "Achtungserfolg."[5] It is a play, he states without further elaboration, "[. . .] das alte Motive aufgreift, sie aber in einer Schwebe lässt, die sonst nur von Chekhov erreicht wurde [. . .]."[6] The present study reveals some of the reasons Schnitzler may have had for leaving these motifs in limbo. The conflicts between generations in the play remain without consequences and catastrophes, it is true. The fact that everything ends well in it, even secondary plot lines, can only be attributed to the protagonists' regaining reason and recovering their internal balance, which had been disturbed by a troublesome confusion of the senses or of the imagination, just as after a brief violent thunderstorm the sun begins to shine again. In this respect, Scheible's comparison of Schnitzler to Chekhov discloses a number of similarities. A detailed comparison with Chekhov's plays, however, exceeds the scope of this work.[7]

The analysis discusses essential problems of modern individuals who find themselves living in a complex society. It shows how this society threatens their feelings of human worth and self-respect and why they are pushed, at times, into passive patterns of living. The symbolism of the weather is examined, along with its relationship to emotional patterns such as jealousy, doubt, guilt, despair. The antinomies of life as expressed in the thoughts, emotions, and concerns of the characters are discussed as they are exposed in youth and age, in art and love, in love and hate, "Pflicht und Neigung." The chapter closes with a study of comparative points as they can be found in the other late dramatic works (*Die Schwestern oder Casanova in Spa, Komödie der Verführung, Der Gang zum Weiher*), thus providing for detailed analysis of most aspects of the play. Each character is analyzed and also viewed in polar relationship to other persons in the play as well as comparative characters in works previously discussed.

OUTLINE OF THE PLAY

Vincenz Friedlein, a prominent sculptor in Vienna, his wife and former model Josefa, and their seventeen-year-old son Eduard occupy a summer house in Kirchau, a village in southern Austria, not far from Vienna, where the action takes place around 1900. In the morning, Vincenz generally leaves for the city to conduct his business. He returns late in the evenings and sometimes not until the next day. Thus, he gives the audience the impression of being liberal in his morals and unconventional in his manners. His appearance is that of a successful artist; he is cheerful and positive about his talent. The marriage is merely an arrangement of convenience. He enjoys all the pleasant features without giving of himself in return. He takes Josefa's loving devotion to husband and child for granted without realizing that she might feel neglected in her desires as a woman of only thirty-six years of age. They have invited their niece, Gusti Pflegner, to their country home to help her regain health and strength before taking up her first engagement as an actress in Innsbruck. Only eighteen years of age, Gusti is aware of her attractiveness and uses this gift flirtatiously. Vincenz looks at her with the eyes of a sculptor, always in search of new models; young Eduard becomes her ardent admirer while assisting her in the study of *Romeo and Juliet.* Dr. Faber, a Viennese physician, considers himself virtually engaged to her. Lieutenant Robert Holl, the twin brother of the village chaplain, Ferdinand Holl, is attracted to her acting and hopes to resume acquaintance in Innsbruck, where he is to be stationed. He has left a deep impression upon her and with that confession to herself, "Der hat mir aber besonders gut gefallen" (994), the first act closes.

Act II unfolds the life of each of these characters as it is lived on deeper levels, where hidden desires and longings are exposed and waiting for expression. Vincenz uses the arrival of the "Exzellenz" from the Kassel theater as an excuse to spend the night in Vienna. Josefa hears about it by telegram, when she is on her way to the railway station to pick up her husband and walk home with him. Eduard is disappointed about the afternoon because the botanic excursion with the Kaplan has been cancelled on account of the sudden visit of the latter's twin brother. He now seeks to interest Gusti to follow him on a hike to Fallenböckhütte, a place in the mountains, where he will be waiting for her. Gusti will hike with Eduard, but first she has to finish a letter to her friend, Dr. Felix Faber. This letter contains a sensitive message: she decided not to bind herself to him at this point. Her career and the prospect of meeting other men are more attractive and important to her. After mailing the letter, she follows Eduard into the mountains to avoid disappointing him. Throughout the play Eduard has been forcing himself upon Gusti on every occasion, and her presence under the same roof keeps him inflamed. The unstable weather which is mentioned throughout the drama affects the balance of nearly all the characters. Finally, the rain begins to fall, trapping these young people in a mountain cabin. The closeness intensifies their emotions "and, without making any serious effort at resistance, they yield to the temptation of the moment. Gusti is delighted by the freshness and naturalness of the boy in contrast to the premature seriousness of [. . .] the physician. For Eduard she signifies the first experience of manhood."[8]

The relation between the Kaplan and Josefa develops within the last part of Act II. It is characterized by restraint on physical levels. Of course, they are more mature than their younger counterparts, but on the other hand, they have allowed greater frustration and even resignation to build up within themselves. The sultriness of the evening moves them to be more at ease in disclosing their innermost feelings.

The Kaplan, who is linked by friendship to Eduard in their common interest in botany, but also in the young man's need for tutorial help, has always performed his priestly duties with exactness and devotion. However, various references in the play indicate that he had been promised a different destiny, for he is a man cultivated in all subjects and full of the most varied intellectual curiosities. He might have become, for instance, an officer like his twin brother, if his mother had not decided to send Ferdinand to the seminary from his fourteenth year. His officer brother is now bound to him by profound affection mixed with gratitude. The priest soon confides to Josefa that his brother, who has just paid him a visit, left behind a letter in which he announces his intention of fighting a duel. The text ends in these words: "Und Deiner Liebe werde ich es zu danken haben, Deiner Fürbitte, wenn ich frei von Sünden vor den höchsten Richter trete. Und so wage ich in unerschütterlichem Gottvertrauen, diesen Brief mit dem Wort zu enden: Auf Wiedersehen! Dein Robert" (1010).

This event and Josefa's words of comfort give rise between them to a free conversation that soon takes on the aspect of a confession in which each person admits doubt. Their discussion of faith brings both of them to the brink of a great temptation. A juxtaposition develops in which Josefa helps him to recognize challenges of everyday life, and the Kaplan leads her into higher, previously unsuspected regions where she can see in new perspective her role of wife and mother. This enables them to resist the temptation, and their reward is not long delayed.

In Act III, Robert Hall, the lieutenant, retires unharmed from the duel, only lightly wounding his adversary; the Kaplan finds his balance again and continues reading of the mass. Josefa regains the love of her husband; Eduard tries to forget in botany his first disappointment in love. Gusti decides to leave the next morning in preparation for her acting career. Felix, whom she left in uncertainty about her contract in Innsbruck and who heard about it through the newspaper, does not want to accept the end of their relationship. But Gusti reminds him: "Wir gehen ja beide nicht aus der Welt. Wir werden uns ja wiedersehen. Wir wollen ja Freunde sein, Freunde bleiben—Freunde werden" (1024-25). Disappointed, Felix resumes his hospital practice. Josefa continues her devotion to her husband who in turn may give more of himself than before. The action closes in the light of a beautiful summer morning, just as the characters emerge untroubled by last night's storm.

Review of Criticism

In general one can observe that *Im Spiel der Sommerlüfte* has not received such extensive reviews and criticism as the other three late dramatic works. In February 1930,

Robert Arnold reviewed the play with his usual negative attitude toward Schnitzler and his dramas. In the end, however, he concedes that the play in its Christian and worldly resignation is an appreciated complement to the erotic "Reigen."[9] A year later the play was performed in Giessen. It received the attention of Hans Thyriot, who finds it impossible to give a plot summary of the play, "das weniger ein Drama als eine dialogisierte Novelle ist und völlig von Umrissen, Andeutungen und verschwebenden Stimmungen lebt."[10] As a possible motto, he suggests the *Paracelsus* verses: "Es fliessen ineinander Traum und Wachen [. . .]," the favorite stand-by quote of many critics.[11]

In Scheible's view the respect paid to the author saved the play from being rejected. It has nothing new to offer so far as motifs are concerned; they have already surfaced in previous dramas. The only difference, according to Scheible, can be seen in the happy ending.[12] Nevertheless, this difference constitutes a significant change which must be recognized. It prompted Schnitzler in a similar situation to write the following lines in a letter to Rilke: "Aber Sie wissen ja; ich bin in das Kastl mit der Aufschrift 'Liebelei' hineingethan (sic); die Kritiker haben das nicht gern, wenn die Taferln gewechselt werden."[13]

In the view of Mme Derré, the author in this play "semble avoir voulu pour une fois encourager la maîtrise de soi et donner une leçon d'optimisme."[14] But she admits: "Si tout y finit bien, et même les intrigues secondaires, c'est moins [. . .] grâce a l'intervention de données suprarationelles que parce que les protagonistes redeviennent raisonnables, retrouvent leur équilibre interne un temps rompu, par un trouble emballement des sens ou de l'imagination [. . .]."[15] "Still," she maintains, "Schnitzler has made a pretense of this somewhat slender plot, for at the end of it nothing has happened to compound the serious debate" (between the priest and Josefa) [. . .].[16] She considers it false to see in the play anything other than a psychological study or to seek in it a profession of faith.[17] Although Schnitzler parted early with his profession as a physician, he maintained nevertheless throughout his life a certain interest in the progress achieved in the field of depth psychology and dream interpretation. Schnitzler's diaries reveal numerous entries in this regard.[18] It is this depth psychology which in Schnitzler's late dramatic works receives ever-increasing attention, thus reducing its content to a "slender plot," as Mme Derré has chosen to call it.

Körner, who is concerned with Schnitzler's "Spätwerk" in a lenghty article, does not even mention this play.[19] A. E. Zucker in his review of the drama states that it "deserves full recognition" and places it above *Die Schwestern* and *Komödie der Verführung*,[20] but he does not substantiate his argument. To Martin Swales, on the other hand, the drama is "a deeply flawed work," because "moral thinking is not intrinsically conducive to great literature."[21] Referring to the "threatening storm" which "passes and leaves the secure, simple order cleansed and refreshed," he considers the play "reminiscent of Stifter" in its thematic and structural progression.[22]

In Offermanns' view, *Komödie der Verführung* represents "das letzte bedeutende Stück, das Schnitzler vollendete—und das sicherlich beziehungsreichste."[23] He completely ignores even the existence of *Der Gang zum Weiher,* a significant play, which likewise combines Eros and war, a major point of discussion in Offermanns' study. The play *Im Spiel der Sommerlüfte* turns his audience to the inner realms of the soul, where life is really experienced. With this new focus on the total human being, it is a logical consequence that exterior events are less well illuminated.

In his study entitled "Das Lebensgefühl in Arthur Schnitzlers Dramen," Müller-Freienfels admits, "Schnitzler will nicht in einem völligen Nihilismus enden und den Menschen jede Hoffnung und Zuversicht nehmen."[24] He seems to lean too much on Blume's evaluation of Schnitzler's *Weltbild,* which the latter placed on the level of pessimism and nihilism. Körner's viewpoint serves as another guideline closely followed by Müller-Freienfels. An example is the following conclusion about the play: "Man darf jedoch nicht übersehen, dass dieses letzte Stück des Dichters Märchencharakter besitzt und dass der gute Ausgang nicht dem eigentlichen Lebensgefühl seines Schöpfers entspricht. Im Grunde bleibt Schnitzler bis zu seinem Lebensende der Skeptiker und Zweifler, der er immer war."[25] Without referring to textual evidence, it is difficult for the reader to follow Müller-Freienfels' argument in pinpointing the "Märchencharakter," particularly in this rather realistic life situation. Furthermore, who is to say with certainty that this last play was written in an effort to represent the actual "Lebensgefühl seines Schöpfers?"

Sol Liptzin separates the author from his characters. He deals with this drama in his chapter entitled "Dream and Reality" and observes that Schnitzler has two ways to return his characters from dangerous experiences: "[. . .] they may either awaken, as from a dream, and return to their accustomed ways, or they may be transformed in body and soul. After employing the latter ending in many serious works, Schnitzler chooses the former alternative for his drama 'Im Spiel der Sommerlüfte'."[26] During his summary of the play, Liptzin also analyzes each character in his particular predicament. However, not all characters appear to be in a dream. Josefa, for example, truly is engaged in soul searching which lifted her to a higher level of consciousness.

"Das Abenteuer," writes Reinhard Urbach, "[. . .] gewinnt im Spätwerk eine therapeutische Funktion [. . .] oder löst sich in eine fast schon selbstverständliche Form augenblicklichen Lebens und momentaner Gemeinsamkeit auf, jenseits von Vorurteilen und Problemen der stickigen Luft der Jahrhundertwende."[27] The relationship between Felix and Gusti would be an example of such "momentaner Gemeinsamkeit." While no details are given in the play as to the nature of Vincenz's overnight stays in Vienna, Josefa seems to feel intuitively when an extramarital adventure is involved. The therapeutic effect Urbach speaks about can be seen in the end of the play. Vincenz renews his interest in the marriage. He shows again greater affection toward his wife. Long-promised travels are discussed more seriously. He also wants to take her along to participate in the festivities on the occasion of his latest work of art which he completed recently. Urbach further points out: "Das unbedenkliche—und früher als leichtsinnig oder zerstörerisch und schuldhaft Empfundene—gewinnt die Dimension des Harmlosen und Verantwortungsfreien."[28] With regard to Schnitzler's last work, Urbach concludes: "Diese Einstellung stiftet noch Verwirrung, aber nicht mehr Zerstörung [. . .]."[29]

Mme Derré seems to think that Schnitzler gave one of the principal roles to the priest, not as a "profession of faith" but rather to demonstrate the ease with which the author is able to manage the religious values in a central dialog.[30] Her interpretation is certainly valid, provided that one recognizes this aspect as part of Schnitzler's larger frame of reference: his never ending quest for truth. In his aphorisms he wrote down many statements pertaining to religion, all of which seem to underline his conviction against any kind of dogmatism.[31]

Willa Schmidt, on the other hand, finds that Josefa and Gusti have the most important roles. "It is in the portrayal of these characters that is found one of the most noteworthy elements of the play, since the difference between the past and the new era in the making, so typical of Schnitzler's later works, is emphasized in *Im Spiel der Sommerlüfte* mainly by means of the two women."[32]

This brief review of criticism demonstrates the variety and discrepancy of views, a situation which usually occurs when only certain aspects of the play are discussed to the exclusion of other important parts. Let us now turn to an attempt at a comprehensive analysis, viewing the play as a totality.

ANALYSIS OF THE DRAMA

The title in view of Goethe's Faust: "Sind wir ein Spiel von jedem Druck der Luft?"—This verse from Goethe's *Faust*[33] was used by Schnitzler as motto for his last drama. It was a popular question to ask at that time of world-wide disarray, for it had application to all aspects of human existence.[34]

The scene in *Faust* in which this verse occurs is entitled "Abend" and shows Margarete's small but immaculately neat room which Faust soon enters. The function of this scene is to make vivid the basic antagonism between Margarete's simple purity of heart and the baseness of the threat to her peace. Neither Faust's heedless passion nor Mephistopheles' lewd sensuality is compatible with the cleanliness of this room and its occupant. The atmosphere of the room, therefore, translates into simplicity, serenity, and contentment which has its effect upon Faust. He recognizes the despicable nature of the intention which brought him there. His passion is, for the moment, sublimated in a romantic analysis of the objects around him, until he realizes the incongruity of his present endeavor with his former standard of conduct. Although his biological urge is strong, some change has come over him. The forthright impulse to animal indulgence has changed, with the disillusion of his emotions, into a dream of love.[35] Thus, his unrestrained nature that might have erupted like a storm and destroyed everything with its intensity is momentarily arrested, and a new, deeper aspect of Faust emerges in his quest for truth. But under the influence of Mephistopheles, events take their turn, and when Faust in the end returns to his nobler self, it is too late to alleviate the suffering which he has caused to Gretchen. Although Faust is dazed in the last scene of the drama, Gretchen's voice still reaches him; it is the voice of love which will not pass away from his memory.

The detail recalled from Goethe's *Faust* serves as an important point of reference to understand Schnitzler's interpretation of the verse "Sind wir ein Spiel von jedem Druck der Luft?" in his play. The atmospheric pressure Faust experienced in Gretchen's room influences his moods and emotions. In Schnitzler's play the self appears not dependent on moods but on weather conditions; thus, the rain after a sultry evening clears the air and returns every character to reason. The evening scene in *Faust,* on the other hand, is characterized by more "Streben," however inconsistent as this striving may be in Faust's yet confused understanding of his services to God.[36] It is not on the strength of "good deeds" but of his human striving that Faust is granted ultimate salvation. The real world of Faust's actions and meditations, of his physical experiences and spiritual endeavors, is surrounded by another and "higher" reality.[37] In Schnitzler's *Im Spiel der Sommerlüfte,* on the other hand, earthly lives are not interrupted from the realm of the transcendental. Urbach observes correctly that Schnitzler's style of the late period places emphasis upon "little causes and large effects which remain, however, without great consequences. And the causes disappear and are charged to the account of summertime."[38]

The games initiated in *Faust,* therefore, represent man's "journey" through life, as he is torn by two forces: the dictates of his nature and the demands of his reason, a duality which can be observed in Schnitzler's characters as well without the experience of their entire earth journey. In contrast to the game played by Faust, which had disastrous consequences for Margarete, her mother and brother, the games in Schnitzler's *Im Spiel der Sommerlüfte* have a happy ending. Some characters are more or less drawn into the game and, because of their passivity, they have no control over it. They wait and, because they do not use their will power, they are "ready to follow every lure which presents itself until a thunderstorm ends everything."[39]

Faust, on the other hand, exerts tremendous will power in his strivings. He needed to stay active and use his will power, for the negative force tried every moment to keep Faust at rest and in one place, in an effort to deliver him from life to destruction, thereby gaining control over his soul and winning the wager with Heaven. By comparison the games played in *Im Spiel der Sommerlüfte* are of less serious nature by far, but they likewise constitute matters of the soul.

Character analysis in light of triangularity: Different from Goethe's drama, Schnitzler's places his women characters in the foreground. The two women in their contrasting representations of "the past and the new era in the making," in Willa Schmidt's words, are also at opposite ends in their activity of playing the game in their relation with others. Gusti, who represents "the new era in the making"—relating to political and social change, is instrumental in setting the game in motion in her relationship with Eduard and Felix, whereas Josefa, who signifies "the past," is for the most part "Mitspieler" in her position as part of a triangle with Vincenz and the Kaplan.

a) *Gusti-Felix-Eduard.* Gusti's attractiveness has drawn both men for different reasons into her orbit. Felix is seriously interested in Gusti, but in his capacity as "Sekundararzt im Krankenhaus [. . .] mit einem Monatsgehalt von sechzig Gulden" he finds it impossible to start a family (988). His visits to Kirchau on weekends are "im Grunde nur eine Quälerei" (987), for it is no pleasure for him to spend the night away from Gusti in a guestroom at the nearby inn. Still, he is happy that he can see her early in the morning for a hike in the forest. In his possessive nature he suffers from feelings of jealousy. With "gerunzelter Stirne" (984) he shows displeasure toward Gusti as she lets Eduard drink the rest of her milk. What bothers him even more is the fact that Gusti practices her roles with Eduard. Felix considers this activity utterly unnecessary (986). When he finds out that Gusti might stay two or three weeks longer in the countryside, he wants to persuade her to return to Vienna earlier (986), since her health has already improved enough for the journey.

Quite concerned over the possibility of Gusti's engagement at the theater away from Vienna, he inquires whether she had received any more letters in that respect. "Liegen keine neuen Engagementsanträge vor? Deutschland, Amerika, Australien—?" (987). He would like to see her study another winter in Vienna, he says, so that she can ask for a larger honorarium the following year. This is a thin veiling of his own selfish interest in such a proposal, for it would keep her away from other possible suitors until his own promotion. Already we have seen him "verstimmt" (985) when Gusti asks the Kaplan whether his brother Lieutenant might visit him a longer time. Her decision to return to Vienna the next day, and from there in a few days to Innsbruck, may have something to do with the officer's transfer to Innsbruck and the possibility of meeting him there soon. In fact, Felix is suspicious of the Kaplan as well. He would bet that Josefa "mit dem Kaplan was hat" (988), admonishing Gusti at the same time by saying, "Du bist übrigens auch verliebt in ihn" (988). Gusti leaves that possibility open just to underline again her point made earlier: "keine Lust" (988) of getting married so soon.

The relation between Eduard and Gusti develops along different lines. In contrast to Felix, Eduard admires Gusti's talents as an actress. He is happy to provide Romeo's lines as prompter, especially since he has a chance in that role as Romeo to give Juliet a kiss, a moment for which he waited long, always trying to be near Gusti. She denies him that privilege because "auf den Proben wird nur markiert" (991). Eduard, too, is jealous at the thought that any strange man in Innsbruck might kiss her just because he is cast in the role of Romeo on stage. The name Innsbruck creates other associations in Eduard's mind as well. Jealously he asks Gusti: "Was sagt denn dein Doktor dazu, dass du nach Innsbruck gehst?" (990), thus revealing that he knows about Gusti's secret. In fact, Innsbruck arouses the desire in him of becoming an actor likewise. "Möchtest mich nicht mitnehmen nach Innsbruck?" (1004) is his candid question to Gusti. It would serve two purposes: First, he would be close to Gusti, as he really begins to like her very well; and second, he would not have to finish his school, especially since he does not like to learn Greek in the first place, and would have no need for it as an actor, anyway. "Der Vater hat auch keine Matura gemacht und ist ein berühmter Mann geworden und Professor dazu" (996), he reasons more confidently from the time his mother mentions at the beginning of Act II that Felix, the physician, is not betrothed to Gusti but is only an acquaintance (995). Many ideas and questions apparently fill his mind and distract him from his studies. Finally he closes his notebook and with the question, "Möchtest du vielleicht später mit mir spazierengehen?" (996), he addresses himself to Gusti, obviously in the hope of firming up his future plans with Gusti's help.

It is easy to open his heart to Gusti for still another reason. She looks upon him as an equal, thus placing him in the adult world. This is first indicated by her manner of address to him: "junger Herr," "junger Mann" (984, 1033). Although in Eduard's absence or in conversation with his parents, she picks up on "Bube," a term his parents like to use—not just out of habit. At one point in the drama, however, Gusti and Eduard have a quarrel over the word "Bube." In Gusti's eyes Eduard behaves like an adolescent when in a moment of jealousy he speaks his mind regarding Felix, whom he would prefer to kill because of the favored position with Gusti (1002). When he realizes his negative behavior, he begs forgiveness from Gusti and in a theatrical gesture throws himself on the floor crying — later laughing, truly playing a role (1002-1003). The serious point underlying this encounter is made by Eduard. He wants to erase the image of a child and be counted among the adults, especially since he is only one year younger than Gusti. So he tells her: "Ich versteh' überhaupt mehr, als gewisse Leute meinen," and further, "Ich bin kein Bub, Gusti" (1002-1003).

He has a more difficult time establishing himself as an adult among the members of his family than elsewhere. Both the Rainer-Mädeln, for example, address him without hesitation as "Herr Eduard," and Kathy, the servant at Friedleins, has breakfast "für den jungen Herrn" (979);

later on she praises "Herrn Eduard" for his diligence in his study habits (995). The real initiation into manhood, however, results from his mountain experience with Gusti during the night of the rainstorm. The next morning, his heart is overflowing; he wants to share with everybody, but Felix, above all, needs to know about the tables that have turned—no more visits in Kirchau to see Gusti! Some more guidance is necessary on Gusti's part, for discretion is a man's first duty (1018); Eduard must learn this right from the beginning. When she sends him affectionately to sleep (1018), he does not know yet that she has decided to leave the next morning for Vienna.

Liptzin describes Gusti as being "delighted by the freshness and naturalness of the boy in contrast to the premature seriousness of her betrothed, the physician."[40] But the text does not reveal any such statement, nor is she betrothed to Felix, as has already been pointed out in the discussion. Stage directions only tell "nimmt plötzlich seinen Kopf zwischen beide Hände, sieht ihn zärtlich an [. . .]" (1018). She shows some emotions but is silent about the experience. Her conduct suggests a logical reason with regard to the advice she gave the young man: "Diskretion ist die erste Pflicht," a rule pertaining to both partners.

Indeed, she seems to have her emotions very well under control, especially with respect to farewells. The night spent with Eduard appeared to both of them a joyful experience, unhampered by feelings of parting. She uses a similar pattern in her relation with Felix. Knowing that he is already troubled by jealousy and the prospect of her engagement in Innsbruck, she withholds any further information in order to make their time spent together as harmonious and pleasant as possible. Finally, she reminds him: "Wir haben's doch immer gewusst, vom ersten Monat an, Felix. Du genau so gut wie ich, dass es so kommen wird [. . .]. Deswegen haben wir uns um nichts weniger gern gehabt und sind um nichts weniger glücklich gewesen. Vielleicht sogar mehr—als wenn wir an die Ewigkeit geglaubt hätten" (1024).

Müller-Freienfels, who is concerned in his study with the "Lebensgefühl" of Schnitzler's characters, summarizes relations of short duration as follows: "Gerade das Wissen um die Kurzfristigkeit der Verbindung kann manchmal auch noch den Genuss vertiefen und ihm den Charakter der Einmaligkeit verleihen."[41] These sudden farewells have, according to him, still another advantage: "Man vermeidet durch die zeitliche Begrenzung auch das allmähliche, qualvolle Absterben und Verfallen einer Liebesbeziehung, das Schnitzler's Personen noch mehr fürchten als das Ende selbst."[42]

It is, therefore, best to avoid the word "Abschied," as Gusti suggests to Felix: "Sag nicht Abschied. Durch so ein Wort macht man sich das Schwere, das man ja doch durchmachen muss, nur noch schwerer, als es sowieso schon ist" (1024). Bernhard Blume, who discusses this subject also, adds: "Sich schmerzlos zu verabschieden, wird also ihr Bemühen. Natürlich sind es die eigenen Schmerzen, die sie vermeiden möchten, nicht die des anderen, auch wenn sie das Gegenteil behaupten."[43] Schnitzler, of course, knew best the problems involved in love relationships. The following aphorism from *Buch der Sprüche und Bedenken* laments the discrepancy of commitment involved in any more or less long-term relationship: "Dass wir uns gebunden fühlen mit der steten Sehnsucht nach Freiheit— und dass wir zu binden versuchen, ohne die Überzeugung unseres Rechts dazu, das ist es, was jede Liebesbeziehung so problematisch macht."[44] The concept of freedom, however, cannot be viewed in isolation—other areas of human conduct enter into it, such as a sense of responsibility and commitment to oneself as well as others. Liptzin reads Schnitzler this way: "Freedom is, to Schnitzler, that ideal state in which a person understands himself and the world around him. No person can enter on the road to freedom so long as he lies to himself, nor so long as he feels conscience-stricken when others condemn those actions of his which he deems justified."[45] The key words are "to understand oneself," which is such a difficult task because one has to master honesty with oneself first. Schnitzler's characters are always shown in various stages of their own understanding, which therefore influences their concept of freedom accordingly. Gusti also values freedom most of all, and so she tells her aunt Josefa: "Und—was den Doktor anbelangt—du hast gestern schon recht gehabt [. . .] ich werde Schluss machen, noch ehe ich ins Engagement fahre. Wird g'scheiter sein" (1019). The real motive, however, is her desire to make the acquaintance of the Lieutenant in Innsbruck.

b) *Josefa-Vincenz-Kaplan.* Josefa's decisions, on the other hand, are not as easily made, for she is married and has responsibilities. For various reasons I call her "Mitspieler" in her triangular constellation with Vincenz and the Kaplan. To begin with, her husband's extensive absences from the family disrupt the flow of communication between the two partners considerably, and this in turn affects their affinity and reality. On the surface she appears to be a complacent wife and mother, devoted to her husband whenever he is home. In her devotion she is motivated by admiration of the artistic talent that brings him recognition and success. Her expression of love has lost spontaneity because her husband does not reciprocate; in fact, he pays her almost no attention. That has changed her, and when the play begins, Schnitzler gives the following description of her: "[. . .] etwa 36, sehr jugendlich [. . .] spricht und bewegt sich etwas müde, doch häufig und immer häufiger bricht durch ihr Wesen die Lebhaftigkeit ihres Temperaments" (976). Her sense of unfulfillment creates a great deal of frustration hidden behind a rather transparent facade. Her role as mother provides a partial outlet for pent-up emotions; she is interested in her son's activities, especially those which he undertakes with the Kaplan of the village. On occasion she participates in their excursions, the highlights of which are stimulating discussions with the Kaplan. This contrasts with the small talk that takes place with her husband about weather, Gusti's fling with the Doctor, and her theatrical engagement in Innsbruck. In the eyes of Gusti and probably of Vincenz as

well, Josefa appears as a harmless, simple person; Felix is the only one who senses a deeper involvement between Josefa and the Kaplan:

FELIX:

Harmlos? Die? Ich—wette—

GUSTI:

Was denn?

FELIX:

Dass sie mit dem Kaplan was hat.

GUSTI:

Aber du bist ja verrückt.

FELIX:

Pass nur einmal auf, wie sie ihn anschaut [. . .].

(988)

The underlying reason, of course, goes back to Vincenz, who is so occupied with himself and his work that he has neither time nor courtesy to give her approval, encouragement and appreciation. Naturally, Josefa becomes insecure and turns against herself in judgment and self-condemnation, thus losing self-confidence. Twice stage directions describe her as tired: "[. . .] bewegt sich etwas müde" (976); "kommt langsam, etwas gedrückt durch die Gartentür" (1006).

At only thirty-six years of age, she feels herself old and unattractive. She probably interprets her husband's frequent solitary travels as rejection. "Berufsreisen—Geschäftsreisen sozusagen" (982), he explains to the Kaplan; however, he still hopes to go to Italy on a vacation trip with Josefa, but she shrugs her shoulder in a gesture of doubt and disbelief (982). Earlier, when Vincenz had spoken about his trip to Kassel for the unveiling of his newest piece of art and had turned to Josefa with these words: "Und du fährst mit—diesmal!—Wenn's dir Spass macht" (982), she only looked at him "befremdet" (982). Later in the play, this gesture translates into a question to her husband: "Liegt dir denn was dran, dass ich bei so was dabei bin?" (1027), which is another expression of her deeper feeling of inadequacy.

In a reminiscent mood she looks back to her youth, when she was engaged as a model for Vincenz. Now she is jealous of the girls which he may have used in his "Dionysoszug," his latest work, for they may be more beautiful than she was. Even her husband's protest does not erase her deep-seated suspicions to the contrary. "Also das kann ich beschwören, Josefa, ein schöneres Modell hab' ich nie wieder gefunden als—," and Josefa continues: "—als ich einmal gewesen bin" (980), indicating again how far into the past she places everything. Vincenz tells her: "Also, Josefa, auf die ältere Dame brauchst du dich wirklich noch nicht hinauszuspielen" (980), but his words lack the warmth which only comes from a loving heart and therefore draw a somewhat stubborn response from her. Previously, she has already reminded him not to call her "Madame," a term she probably associates with older age.

The reason for this irritation goes in part to Gusti, the cause of Josefa's jealousy. When Gusti tells Josefa how her mother was able to rent out the large room but kept "das gelbe Kabinett," jokingly adding that this was done in case she might be sent home from Innsbruck, Josefa replies spontaneously: "Sie werden dich schon nicht nach Hause schicken. Mit dem G'sichtl und mit der Figur! [. . .] Das ist immer die Hauptsache beim Theater" (997). Of course, she speaks from experience, because attractiveness and a good figure were important factors in her own short profession as a model. Once she married Vincenz, he did not use her as a model anymore, especially since their son was born a year later. One might surmise that her early marriage was necessitated by the pregnancy and that she has not reconciled within herself the changes in her life style.

When Gusti mentions that Felix will visit her regularly in Innsbruck, at least once a month, Josefa advises: "Es tut kein gut. In solchen Fällen gibt's nur ein Entweder—Oder. Sei froh, dass du hinaus in die Welt kommst mit deinen neunzehn Jahren, in die Freiheit und ins Leben . . ." (998). In retrospect, Josefa actually regrets the development her career took, for Vincenz, too, might have visited her too often, thus ending her life as a single person and with it the prospect of freedom, as she sees it. Gusti, in a moment of ill humor, exclaims in reply to Josefa's advice: "Ich wollt', ich wär' lieber neunzig, und alles wär' vorbei" (998). In a passion, Josefa admonishes her, for Gusti does not know what it means "all over." Gusti deems Josefa ungrateful, especially since she has an attractive husband and a boy of eighteen. Josefa finds it necessary to register a correction about the boy's age; he is only seventeen. If this situation was not such a sore spot in Josefa's heart, she might have reacted differently by not placing so much importance upon it. Josefa's somewhat subdued and disillusioned "happiness" in her marriage is another indication that she faces difficulties within herself. Her devotion to Vincenz and the child might be motivated by a sense of duty instead of her heart's desire. Therefore, she is more of a "Mitspieler" rather than wholeheartedly in it, letting circumstances rule her life instead of accepting the turn of events in the knowledge that she has primary responsibility in her life and affairs.

"Jeder muss seinen eigenen Weg gehen," points out William Rey, "Er muss aber auch die Verantwortung für seine Entscheidung auf sich nehmen. Das Wagnis der Freiheit bleibt keinem erspart. Nur wenige erkennen, dass der höchste Sinn der Freiheit die Bindung ist."[46] Both partners, therefore, have the same responsibility to work toward a happy marriage. Schnitzler, however, seems to demand more of his women characters because of their finer insight, of which his male characters without exception seem to be incapable. John Nelson Whiton, who studied the problem of marriage in Schnitzler's works, places Vin-

cenz in the category of "the dull, complacent husband who provides his wife with status and material security, but not with love."[47] The kind of double standard which Vincenz has created in his marriage, as indicated by his frequent late returns home, is not conducive to a happy marriage, especially since it is clear that he reserves these evenings or overnight stays for extra-marital pleasures. Of course, these extra freedoms on the part of Vincenz are thinly veiled under the pretense of work that has to be accomplished, but Josefa intuitively knows the truth: "Nur ihr Kunstwerk interessiert diese Menschen," writes Müller-Freienfels, "und das lebendige Modell ist ihnen gleichgültig geworden, sobald es seine Aufgabe erfüllt hat."[48]

Vincenz is not vicious, however, as was his artistic counterpart Gysar in *Komödie der Verführung*; a certain amount of ignorance in understanding himself and others prevents him from recognizing Josefa's deeper desires as a woman. "Es kümmert sie auch nicht, ob dieses lebendige Modell dadurch, dass es von ihnen nur als Instrument und Mittel für ihre künstlerischen Zwecke gebraucht wurde, vielleicht selbst Schaden genommen hat," observes Müller-Freienfels.[49] "Der Weg zum Mitmenschen besteht nur für denjenigen, der keine Maske trägt, beständig und innerlich gefestigt ist," says Anna Stroka.[50] But Vincenz hides behind the image of a successful artist and Professor; he is not as steadfast and secure a person as he shows in outer ways. His frequent absence from home indicates that he needs constant reassurance as a man. His marriage is for him a matter of convenience more than anything else, and this places a twofold responsibility upon Josefa. Not only does she have the same responsibility in working toward a happy marriage as her husband does, but also an additional accountability toward the child.[51] Her sense of devotion and her unselfishness help her to shoulder these responsibilities remarkably well, even though occasional frustrations upset the balance. The paradox of "Selbsterfüllung in der Selbsthingabe," which Rey discovers in some of Schnitzler's women characters, applies in general to Josefa also, so that "die männliche Eroberungslust [. . .] ihren Gegenpol in der weiblichen Opferbereitschaft [findet]."[52]

Her moments of frustration on the one hand find a pleasant relief on the other hand in the challenging and inspiring dialog with the Kaplan, and the understanding and sensitivity he shows her toward the end of the discussion uplift her in consciousness. No physical enjoyment takes place between them, but they both had their weak moments, to be sure. Significantly enough, the long dialog between Josefa and the Kaplan is placed in the center of the drama, preceded by one of the more disappointing moments in Josefa's marital experience. She had intended to meet her husband at the railway station and looked forward to walking home with him. But she returns alone, having received a telegram on the way which informs her that Vincenz is staying in town, entertaining his guest from the Kassel theater. Seeing that she is somewhat depressed, Gusti tries to console her aunt: "Es ist ja nicht das erste Mal, dass der Onkel drin übernachtet." This prompts Josefa to say: "Nein. Es kommt sogar ziemlich oft vor. Aber manchmal muss man's im Gefühl haben . . . Ob man einen allein lassen darf oder nicht" (1007). It appears that her feelings this time are mixed, and suspicious as well. Her churning emotions find a corresponding expression in the embroiled state of nature: the wind has increased, there is summer lightning on the horizon with a rolling of distant thunder, and people hurry by to get home before the rain begins. Among them are the Rainer-Mädeln (1007-1008).

Just at that moment the Kaplan is passing by the fence and, looking into the garden, he unintentionally hesitates. He is not looking for Eduard this time; instead his goal is the railway station, but Josefa invites him to seek shelter there until the rain has passed. Thus their encounter not only takes place in the middle of the drama, but also at the height of a storm and in the absence of most occupants of the house. Vincenz, Eduard and Gusti—all have left to experience their own pleasures. Josefa has a keen perception of the situation which at one point in the dialog she communicates to the priest this way: "[. . .] keine Mutter hat ihren Sohn, und keine Frau hat ihren Mann—so, wie sie ihn haben möchte. Wenn es gerade ruft und lockt von irgendwoher, so laufen sie ins Wetter, in die Nacht und ins Leben hinaus—und man bleibt allein" (1013). Indeed, her son has gone off with Gusti into the storm, her husband into the night—all three for the purpose of experiencing life differently. The combination of weather, night, and life has symbolic meaning which will be discussed later on. The fact remains that Josefa finds herself alone at a moment when she most needs the presence of some company. In contrast to her previous role as "Mitspieler," she now initiates the game with the priest. In keeping with her generally unselfish nature, she allows him to speak his mind first, but during the course of their conversation she is able to reflect upon her own concerns as well, not always accepting as advice or reassurance the cleric's convictions which at times seem to her to be out of touch with the reality of life.

An alarming letter from Robert Holl, informing his brother, the Kaplan, indirectly of a serious duel, gives rise to a philosophical discussion about guilt, temptation, inner struggle, self-conquest, doubt; it also brings these two people to a better understanding of themselves and of each other. The Kaplan resigns himself to an attitude of waiting and praying, although he is painfully aware that prayer in its miracle-working power cannot undo what has been done—the sin remains, in his way of thinking. Josefa is an understanding woman, knowing that there are many temptations for a young person. But the Kaplan in his stoic attitude insists that it is one's duty to fight temptation, for weakness in this regard is a sin as well. "Not everyone is probably created for such a struggle," replies Josefa, reminding the priest of God's concept of mercy for those who miss the mark (1011). Unaware that Josefa's words might be based on experiences of herself and her family, the Kaplan considers her a "Good woman" and expresses his gratitude for her empathy which comes from "the peace of her pure heart and the shelter of this home" (1011). This invites opposition from Josefa: "Wer ist denn

überhaupt geborgen, wer in dieser Welt? Wem ist ein friedliches Herz geschenkt?" (1011). Again, the Kaplan's answer is remote from any real life situation: "Through inner struggle and self-conquest to peace and happiness" (1011). His words sound like a mindless slogan to Josefa, who had just raised the question as to whether or not everyone is equipped to handle such inner difficulties. In her mind, it takes more courage to accept happiness on the basis of life's polarities—joy and sorrow, good and bad, beauty and ugliness, but she is told that this kind of courage often looks more like sin because the happiness attained is followed by remorse (1012).

The argument is brought down to more concrete levels, when Josefa applies the priest's line of thought to the situation of his own brother. How can he be so sure about his brother's state of mind? Perhaps he cherishes the very same experiences that brought him into the present position so much that they are worth any remorse felt afterwards. Josefa's daring ideas are foreign to the Kaplan and perhaps a bit frightening, because he hides now behind the word "Absolution" (1012), mentioned in his brother's letter, giving it his own clerical interpretation. Actually, Robert expressed gratitude toward his priestly brother for everything he had done for him in the past, at the same time assuring him that every word, handshake and embrace will mean absolution to him, when they see each other tomorrow (1009-1010). In a sudden move, the Kaplan puts the spotlight back on Josefa, interpreting her behavior as adverse reactions to the letter that must have caused anxiety and perhaps even doubt. However, Josefa considers doubt as a part of her nature and emphasizes instead those rare moments in a person's life when the real truth from within is revealed, when a new perspective of life is gained (1012-1013).

In light of Josefa's profound realization about herself and her family, the priest's position on the various issues raised seems rather inflexible, merely touching the surface of Josefa's concerns. Even when she speaks about the lure which draws husband and son into the weather, the night, and life, his only consolation is that they will be back soon (1013). Josefa's reply: "Und werden beide nicht da sein" (1013) opens up a whole new vista of her psychological insight. She knows well that they will return, but for a while thereafter they are only physically present, while on mental and emotional levels they are still involved with the experiences gained from those nocturnal activities.

Finally, the priest changes his attitude and becomes "beinahe herzlich" (1013), only to miss the point again, as he interprets Josefa's words to be a kind of confession, consoling her that tomorrow her anxiety will have passed. He is perplexed by Josefa's quick response: "Ja, das wird sie gewiss. Und man wird sich wieder belügen, sich und die andern dazu" (1013). Josefa's ideal is a truthful life, and this kind of role-playing does not satisfy her any longer. Throughout the dialog she is searching for deeper answers beyond conventional religious views of guilt, temptation, inner struggle, and self-conquest, but every one of her concerns has been misinterpreted or superficially answered. Step by step she has drawn a tighter mental circle around the priest in the hope of hearing words of deeper sincerity. She is greatly puzzled, therefore, to hear the priest abruptly change the subject by pointing out that it is time for him to attend his duties elsewhere. She considers this latest move on his part nothing less than flight, and wonders whether he would leave if there had been a true confession on her part. She had wished to speak to him as a friend, for in her mind a priest is above all a human being, and as such a friend. Of course, he cannot deny his human nature, which does not give him any greater virtues or rights, but he does believe that his vocation exacts higher duties, and as a priest he sets himself apart. Certainly, one such "higher duty" might have called for a more distinct effort to understand Josefa's concerns, which were born out of a sudden realization of the discrepancies between ideal and real life situations, as well as states of consciousness.

There is still more disagreement in store for her which finally breaks the distance which the priest tries to maintain under all circumstances:

KAPLAN:

[. . .] Kommen Sie zur Besinnung, Frau Josefa. Versuchen Sie Ihre abirrenden Gedanken wieder auf den richtigen Weg zu leiten.

JOSEFA:

Wissen das Hochwürden ganz bestimmt, welches der richtige Weg ist? Mein rechter Weg?

KAPLAN:

Der ist vorgezeichnet, wie nur je einer war, es ist der Weg einer Gattin, einer Mutter.

JOSEFA:

einfach Ich bin auch eine Frau, Hochwürden, und ich bin nicht so sicher, ob ich meinen Weg als Frau so gehe und gegangen bin, wie Gott ihn mir vorgezeichnet hat

(1014).

When the Kaplan tries to tell her that such thoughts have nothing to do with God, Josefa closes in on him. How does he know where thoughts come from; which thoughts reach us from above and which from below and which are within us? And what about our prayers? Is Heaven or Hell responding to them?

Josefa in Schnitzler's character portrayal demonstrates deeper insight than the priest, for she knows that everything in life is of rather complex nature. Just as in the beginning of their discussion, she now draws again upon his brother to demonstrate her point. As he prays for Robert and wants him to be saved because he is his brother, does he not at the same time invite death for the other person, who most likely is less guilty than the brother? The discussion about

a "believing heart" (1015) finally helps the Kaplan realize that he himself has been a doubter all along, and that he had no right to judge Josefa for her doubts. Of course, the difference between these two characters lies in the degree of self-honesty. Josefa felt free to speak to the priest about her innermost concerns. This was perhaps easier for her to do than for the Kaplan, for she revered him, as was already apparent by her form of address. He, on the other hand, as one sworn to strict vows before the altar of the priesthood, wanted to uphold this priestly aura of strength and faith, thus forgetting that he still is a human being and as such troubled with certain weaknesses as well. He finally has the courage to reveal to Josefa that he is more than a doubter, because when he read the letter he felt rebellion, dissatisfaction with his calling as a priest, even jealousy toward his brother who experiences life in such diversity. He fears, therefore, that his prayers may have dissipated in space, for they were spoken without belief and conviction (1016).

There seems to be a lack of balance within the priest, for when he condemns himself for being worse than a doubter, he leaves out his feelings of love and concern for his brother. Josefa can see these connections very clearly, and when the Kaplan passes by the garden in Act III to meet the mailman, she knows intuitively that he will carry a good message to him. This time the priest is freer in his expression toward Josefa. He even tells her about last night's dream he had, which involved the two of them in reverse roles and how his earthly longing for her through confession changed at the end of the dream to clarity of thought, purpose, and action. Josefa does not consider it a sin "[. . .] dass wir einander—beinahe—verstanden hätten" (1021). The priest understands now that Josefa is stronger than he himself, but she corrects him "frommer, Hochwürden" (1021). It seems, however, that each has learned from the other and emerged as a stronger and more balanced personality in the end, ready "to return to their daily life with renewed appreciation for its values," points out Davis.[53] "Everything ends on a conciliatory note."[54]

Concerning the first part of the dialog, Müller-Freienfels' observations are correct: "Der Kaplan erscheint im Grunde unehrlich: er sucht sich in seine Kirchen und seine Dogmen zu flüchten, allen Fragen und Bedenken ängstlich auszuweichen und nach aussen hin einen festen Glauben vorzutäuschen, den er innerlich gar nicht besitzt."[55] A significant change, however, has occurred within the priest at the beginning of Act III as a result of the dream. Vicariously, he experienced with Josefa what Vincenz and Eduard that night looked for in the physical world. He also seems to be closer now to his God, strengthened in his faith, and more in tune with his inner nature.

Herbert Lederer's evaluation of the Kaplan is, that he does "not quite come up to the high ideals expected of [him]."[56] One must ask the question here: How valid are expectations? In general, the Kaplan is portrayed as a devoted "shepherd of the flock" at Kirchau. He sees people, comforts those near death like the Hofrat, and also has time for the interests of the younger generation, as seen in his relation to Eduard. Only in his encounter with Josefa does one find his human nature revealed in all its hidden aspects. He had repressed a broad scale of emotions, including the aspect of doubt, so that what might have appeared insincere within him was really a result of this long history of emotional repression.

Schnitzler addressed himself to this problem in connection with belief: "Auch Glaube und Zweifel sind nicht allzu häufig als Charakteranlage vorhanden. Gerade sie sind fliessende Seelenzustände [. . .] und häufig genug kommen sie sogar nur als Stimmungen vor. Wie könnte man sonst verstehen, dass auch gläubige Naturen nicht selten an ihrem Gott irre werden—und dass immer wieder Zweifler sich zu einem Glauben oder ganz allgemein zum Glauben bekehren."[57] Furthermore, since Schnitzler gives the Kaplan these words: "Ich bin Priester, Frau Josefa" (1014), it is clear that he wanted him to be a positive character on the left side of his triangular diagram as "Erfüller einer Sendung [. . .] einer göttlichen Aufgabe."[58]

Davis believes that the Kaplan's "doubts are dangerous to him, but he has the touch of mysticism essential to his calling."[59] This cannot be proven with certainty through textual evidence, unless the dream is considered as a "touch of mysticism." Indeed, priests should have a mystic inclination; "[. . .] doch fehlt es nicht an Priestern [. . .] die zweiflerisch oder skeptisch angelegt sind [. . .]," Schnitzler adds in his discussion.[60] This reflects more truly the role of the priest in his particular drama. Georgette Boner sees this polarity of doubt and belief, balanced by a new courageous attitude, in the context of Schnitzler's effort to eliminate impressionistic elements from his work.[61]

Polarities: Schnitzler uses this concept of courage to establish a synthesis for such polar opposites as doubt and belief. Referring to Boner's observation (footnote 61), the priest has the courage to express the "heroic belief" of the woman, and Josefa finds the courage to address herself to the "heroic doubt" of the man. This was only possible when both were willing to take off their masks, particularly in the case of the priest. Other polarities find a balance as well, which could be considered a synthesis along Boner's line of thinking. The Kaplan spoke of inner struggle and inner peace: "Niemandem bleiben innere Kämpfe ganz erspart. Aber ohne die wäre wohl auch der innere Friede nicht viel wert [. . .]. Erst Selbstüberwindung ist Friede, ist Glück" (1011). If this somewhat negative attitude of "self-conquest" could be seen in light of "self-mastery," it represents a much desired synthesis. Self-control through inner guidance creates a balanced person who can face the antinomies of life and still remain peaceful at heart. This would also include the polarities Josefa pointed out: "Freude und Leid—Gutes und Böses—Schönes und Hässliches auch" (1012). These, too, are "fliessende Seelenzustände," to use Schnitzler's expression, which can be controlled through knowing the self.

Related to this concept of self-mastery is the polarity of "Stadt und Land." The lure and complexity of the city, as opposed to the sheltered atmosphere and simplicity of the countryside, demand balance. Throughout the drama, there is movement between these two poles.[62] Every morning Vincenz leaves for the city to carry out his work, but instead of returning home in the evening, he often stays overnight to experience the night life of the city. Finally, when feelings are held in check, there is less urgency to be in the city. Vincenz at the end of the play tells Josefa to her surprise: "Dass du gerade jetzt auf die Idee kommst, in die Stadt zu ziehen, wo ich mir vorgenommen habe, einmal vierzehn Tage lang in Ruhe da heraussen auf dem Land zu verleben" (1030).

Regarding the urban motif, mention must be made not only of Vienna but of Innsbruck as well. Innsbruck is the city where Gusti found her first employment as a professional actress. In that respect, it corresponds to Vienna where Vincenz' art studio is located. What lures Gusti away from her countryside "spa" several weeks earlier than she had planned, is the expectation of excitement. She is motivated not only by her desire to stay away from Felix in Vienna, but by her need to gain distance from Eduard. Furthermore, the lieutenant's transfer to Innsbruck presents an opportunity for new adventure in her quest for freedom of expression.[63]

But in all fairness to Gusti, one must not forget her sincerity as an actress. Although she is on vacation, we observe her immersed in the role of Shakespeare's Juliet, which is her first assignment at the Innsbruck theater. She demonstrates energy and enthusiasm for her profession, and talent in addition, as indicated by the nature of her first role in Innsbruck. Even the mere practice of her lines earned heart-felt "bravos" from passersby such as the lieutenant (992). She also reveals a seriousness of purpose when she speaks of her work. In a discussion with Eduard, her ardent admirer, about her contract for the coming season in Innsbruck, she explains rather firmly: "Ich hab' was Gescheiteres und was Wichtigeres zu tun in Innsbruck, als Besuche von Herrn zu empfangen oder Schulbuben. Ich hab' zu arbeiten. Ich muss schau'n, dass ich vorwärts komm'. Ich muss Geld verdienen für mich und für die Mutter. Seine Pflicht hat man zu tun vor allem" (1006). Uwe Rosenbaum, who investigates "Die Gestalt des Schauspielers auf dem deutschen Theater," offers this comment: "Es ist das Verhältnis des bürgerlichen Mädchens, das den Beruf der Schauspielerin als einzig möglichen ergreift, um sich eine Lebensgrundlage zu sichern, weniger aus künstlerischen Gründen."[64] Whether or not Gusti had artistic reasons for her career as an actress is difficult to evaluate, because the information given in the drama is limited. But her family background seems to point to an artistic orientation. Gusti's aunt Josefa probably selected her brief career because she was attracted to artistic circles.[65]

The characteristics of the two women relating to polar opposites have already been discussed, but ultimately Josefa and Gusti achieve a synthesis through better understanding of each other's innermost nature. When Gusti returns with Eduard from the mountain, having spent the night together in the cabin, she is prepared to give Josefa all kinds of excuses: "[. . .] grad' noch im richtigen Moment bin ich in die Hütte gekommen. Sonst—ich glaub', es hätt' mich heruntergeschwemmt" (1019). But Josefa suggests smilingly: "Ich glaub', es ist besser, du redest nichts" (1019), which is a gesture of understanding. Later on, the embarrassment is Josefa's, because Gusti wants to know how she knew about the lieutenant's duel. Josefa is prepared for a lengthy reply, all in an effort to justify the priest's evening visit, when nobody else was in the house. But Gusti helps her out—even the tone of her voice and the words are the same as Josefa's: "Ich glaub' halt, es ist besser, du redest nichts" (1030). A further gesture seals the secret between them: "Dann nimmt Gusti Josefas Kopf in ihre Hände und küsst sie" (1030).

The harmony which exists now between the two women, in spite of age differences, is not apparent between Vincenz and his son Eduard. Unlike Josefa, Vincenz is never outwardly concerned about his own age, to judge by anything he says in the course of the play. His experiences in town seem to give him assurance that he is still attractive to women. At home, the fact of a seventeen-year-old son might remind him of his age, but he handles that on psychological levels. He does not recognize his son as an adult. First he laughs when the Rainer-Mädeln send a greeting to "Herrn Eduard," repeating this form of address to himself as if he were rather amused about it. Perhaps he has been away so much that he has not really had a chance to watch his son grow up. He is complaining to Josefa about it early in the drama: "Ich hab' überhaupt nichts von dem Buben da heraussen (978). Josefa and Gusti pick up on this term also, at one point adding "insult to injury," when they call Eduard "dummer Bub" (996). However, Josefa is keenly aware of Eduard's feeling in this respect and tries to convince her husband also: "Der ist kein Bub mehr. Das ist ein väterlicher Wahn. Ein junger Herr ist er, ein Jüngling. 'Ein schlanker Jüngeling' hat gestern der Doktor gesagt. Hast du denn noch gar nicht bemerkt, wie die Weiber ihn anschau'n?" (980).

As his mother, Josefa is deeply conscious of this stage in Eduard's life, for it signals to parents that the time has come to release their child to make his own life.[66] The Kaplan is the only one who never calls Eduard "Bube." But he uses the term, when he talks about his own childhood: "[. . .] wie wir noch Buben gewesen sind—Kinder—" (999), referring to his twin brother Robert also. The age of twelve, it seems, is the last year of childhood in the mind of the priest, for, as he entered his teens, serious considerations were given to his future career. His twin brother went to the Military Academy at the same time that the Kaplan entered the Seminary. With regard to Eduard, much emphasis is placed on his school work, for he seems to have failed his examinations or part of them once before. Now his parents are concerned that he pass "die Nachprüfung,"[67] and he is constantly reminded to take tutoring lessons from the priest rather than going on hiking tours with him (979). Whenever Eduard is interested in some aspect of the adult world, the magic word "Nachprüfung"

resounds and pushes him back to the childhood level: "Schau lieber, dass du bei der Nachprüfung [. . .] nicht durchfliegst."[68] Thus, there is a correlation between "Bube" and "Nachprüfung," neither of which Eduard cares to hear about. Thereafter, the word "Bube" occurs in the drama only in passing, among the various characters, but hardly in the presence of Eduard.[69]

An exception can be observed in the relation between Gusti and Eduard, who wanted to establish himself as an equal adult (1003, 1005). At the end of the play Eduard is uncontrolled in his disappointment over her sudden decision to depart. She copes with his outburst by reminding him that he must show that he is a man. But to Josefa and Vincenz she admits: "Er ist ja doch noch ein Bub" and, asking his permission, she kisses him with these words: "Also denk manchmal an mich, junger Mann!" (1033).

Symbolism (weather, Dionysos, the mountains): The one term which is mentioned consistently by almost every character in the play is the weather.[70] It is already anchored in the title ***Im Spiel der Sommerlüfte*** and indeed involves many components: wind, thunder, lightning, rain, sunshine. Weather usually is related to the sensation of the characters. In the beginning of the drama, Vincenz justifies taking his overcoat along in spite of the warm weather: "Ich trau' dem Wetter nicht. Und wenn ich abends drin in der Stadt bleib'—" (977). That he does so is indicated by the telegram he sends later.

Gusti during her vacation in the countryside "ist förmlich aufgeblüht" (984), and Vincenz attributes this improvement either to the milk she drinks or to the good air. In the late afternoon of that day, Josefa knows "Es kommt ein Wetter," but Kathi does not think much will happen before the night (995). It is interesting to observe Schnitzler's method: he lets a simple girl utter some simple words that prove to have far-reaching consequences. Gusti finds the weather sultry and, just in case of rain, takes an umbrella along as she goes to the mailbox (1007, paralleling Vincenz' earlier provision for the coat, for she will need that umbrella as she follows Eduard into the mountains.

A dramatic turn in the weather occurs when the Kaplan visits Josefa. "Stärkeres Wetterleuchten" is accompanied by a "Windstoss" as he greets her; "Windstoss" again as she invites him in (1008). "The wind," points out J. E. Cirlot, "is air in its active and violent aspects, and is held to be a primary element by virtue of its connexion with the creative breath or exhalation."[71] Although no overt act takes place during the ensuing dialog between the priest and Josefa, their heightened mental activity certainly stirs up inner turmoil. This sheds light not only on traditionally accepted concepts but also on spiritual horizons, as "Wetterleuchten" does in nature. Cirlot points out that "Jung recalls that in Arabic (and paralleled by the Hebrew) the word *ruh* signifies both 'breath' and 'spirit'."[72] Spirit, of course, is recognizable by its luminous intensity, just as lightning for a split second releases large amounts of energy. Through the long process of dialog, Josefa and the priest are able to understand themselves better, as they turn to the spirit of truth.

Josefa, in the course of their discussion, speaks about her husband and son who run into the weather, into the night, and into life, leaving her alone (1013). The common symbolic denominator of this triangularity of concepts is creativity and light. Weather in this drama is synonymous with rain which "has a primary and obvious symbolism as a fertilizing agent, and is related to the general symbolism of life and water," according to Cirlot.[73] As with the water symbol, rain "signifies purification,"[74] a creative power at work. Purification involves a clearing process which seems to be active within Vincenz, Eduard, and Gusti. Their nocturnal experiences clear up false ideas and thought patterns to achieve clarity in their future actions. "Night is related to the passive principle, the feminine and unconscious," writes Cirlot.[75] The feminine principle in man is also the creative aspect within him, and the Greeks thought that night and darkness preceded the creation of all things. Night "is an anticipatory state in that, though not yet day, it is the promise of daylight."[76] It is symbolic of the principle of understanding in the mind. Thunder is also an active force, "a symbol of the supreme, creative power [. . .] at the same time, the flash of lightning is related to dawn and illumination."[77] The night, therefore, with its outbursts of illumination in nature, brought light into the mind and heart of each character who was away from his usual habitation.

A related symbol, perhaps less complex than weather, is that of Dionysos. Vincenz has just finished a large sculpture for the Kassel theater which he calls "Dionysoszug" (980). It represents "einen Fries für das neue Schauspielhaus in Kassel. Zwölfeinhalb Meter lang" (981). When asked by the Kaplan whether he created it in antique style, Vincenz replies: "[. . .] in ziemlich freier Auffassung" (981). This reply includes not only the physical aspect of the artwork, but also Vincenz' moral and ethical convictions regarding the relations between an artist and his various models. Dionysos is described by Cirlot as "an infernal deity, and a symbol of the uninhibited unleashing of desire, or of the lifting of any inhibitions of repression."[78] Vincenz seems to answer all. In *Komödie der Worte* (1915), consisting of three one-act plays, Schnitzler devotes the third play to the Dionysian aspect. He calls this play *Das Bacchusfest*. What Felix the poet created in words, Vincenz the sculptor changed into visual form, allowing himself the freedom to experience every aspect of his creation. Felix explains to Guido the details of this custom in these words:

> Das Bacchusfest war [. . .] ein religiöser Brauch [. . .]. Er bestand darin, dass einmal in jedem Jahr, eine Nacht hindurch, zur Zeit der Weinlese [. . .] der Menschheit—in gewisser Hinsicht uneingeschränkte Freiheit gegönnt war [. . .]. Für diese eine Nacht waren alle Bande der Familie, alle Gebote der Sitte einfach aufgehoben. Männer, Frauen, junge Mädchen verliessen bei Sonnenuntergang das Haus, dessen Friede sie sonst umgab und behütete, und begaben sich in den heiligen Hain [. . .] um dort unter den schützenden Schleiern der Nacht das göttliche Fest zu feiern [. . .]. Bei Anbruch des Tags—war das Fest vorbei, und jeder Teilnehmer war verpflichtet zu vergessen, mit wem er

> für seinen Teil das göttliche Fest gefeiert hatte. Verpflichtet. Das gehörte mit zum religiösen Brauch—wie die Feier selbst [. . .]. Und wie die Sage berichtet, sollen die Festteilnehmer zuweilen etwas ermüdet, aber doch erfrischt, ja gewissermassen geläutert nach Hause wiedergekehrt sein"

> (DW II, 551).

Vincenz, too, returned home the next morning with no trace of fatigue, but rather refreshed in spite as well. He bought the atlas for Eduard; he now has travelling plans for the family, and meets Josefa in her somewhat embarrassed behavior with an embrace and these rather symbolic words: "Es muss doch ziemlich arg gewittert haben da heraussen" (1031). The promise of a new, different life becomes apparent—a life that will be spent in closer sharing of interests.

When Eduard receives the atlas, he feels that this wonderful illustrated edition is not his alone to enjoy; he thinks immediately of the priest as well: "Und der Herr Kaplan wird auch eine Freud' haben" (1031). Indeed, a deep friendship connects these two men, a friendship that has taken them on many excursions into the mountains. As the drama ends, the Kaplan appears "im Touristenanzug" (1031), ready to hike with Eduard just as he had hiked with his brother a year ago for a whole week in Kärnten and around the Grossglockner (999). This time their goal is the Gaisental, where they hope to find some rare orchids that grow usually only in the Dolomites (998). When Eduard first appears in the drama, he has just returned from the Katzenstein in record time (978). He meets Gusti at the Fallenböckhütte which later gives them shelter for the night (1006, 1019), and even Josefa has been up there to testify to the beauty of the surroundings.

The mountains represent an exalted state of mind: the priest finds new inspiration and enthusiasm for his calling; Eduard seems drawn to the mountains whenever his book learning overwhelms him; Josefa joins her son and the Kaplan on their hikes, whenever she is disturbed by marital frustration. The mountains, therefore, can symbolize a state of spiritual realization and uplift, but in the case of Gusti and Eduard that is also a state of physical enjoyment. Deriving from the idea of height "are interpretations such as that of Teilhard, who equates the mountain with inner 'loftiness' of spirit, that is, transposing the notion of ascent to the realm of the spirit."[79] One also gains a clear view from the mountain top. The characters in the play see their lives more clearly, and have a better perspective, whenever they return from the mountains.

Comparison with other late dramatic works: The symbolism of the mountain can be compared with that of the tower in *Der Gang zum Weiher*. Both are symbols of ascent and denote also spiritual elevation. Yet, the tower experience in *Der Gang zum Weiher* did not achieve anything comparable to the mountain experience in *Im Spiel der Sommerlüfte*. All characters, except Vincenz who had never time to be in the mountains, enjoyed them, because they felt uplifted; whereas the guestroom in the tower only involved Sylvester and Konrad. It had an adverse effect upon Sylvester, who did not even spend a single night there. After burning his diary notes page by page, he still had not been able to lift himself into a new state of awareness by accepting the truth about himself at his present station in life. He felt uncomfortable with himself and, rather than facing himself in self-honesty this time, he ran away—as so often before—to avoid this promising lifting experience.

Konrad enjoyed the tower guestroom as he would have any other bedroom after his experience of sex with Leonilda. The memory of his encounter lingered on. In that respect he can be compared with Eduard who experiences his sexual initiation in the mountains. Another comparison between Konrad and Eduard involves the question of adolescence. Both young men wanted to be counted as adults. In contrast to Eduard, Konrad was only once called "Bube" when he was challenged by Sylvester to a duel (834). That was an issue of biological difference in age. Eduard never had strong feelings toward age, because unlike Konrad (cf. 805), he did not perceive a threat to his self-esteem from this direction.

The idea of the duel is present in all four dramas. In *Die Schwestern oder Casanova in Spa* and *Im Spiel der Sommerlüfte* it is actually carried out, but no serious difficulty arises; in fact, Casanova and his two opponents are prevented from fighting through the intervention of Teresa, the dancer (726). In *Komödie der Verführung,* it was established that Prince Arduin was rather duel-happy but never entered a fight; in *Der Gang zum Weiher,* the outbreak of war prevented the duel between Konrad and Sylvester, but Konrad had already indicated that their ages were incompatible (834). With regard to Schnitzler's position in this matter, Davis concludes that "if Schnitzler [. . .] were really concerned about this point, we should expect to find the same process of constant clarification of his attitude that we have found on other subjects."[80] No death is caused by any duel in the late dramatic works, and this represents a significant difference from Schnitzler's earlier dramatic writings. According to Davis, "Schnitzler in his late works uses the duel frequently as a tool to point out something important about a character, and as poetic justice."[81]

On the other hand, one could suspect that the issue of the duel may be rooted in Schnitzler's inability to accept the changes from Old Vienna to postwar Vienna. The duel is a holdover from the past which he retains to keep evergreen the precious memories of his own youth. In his book *Jugend in Wien* Schnitzler recalls vividly his feelings of younger years about the duel:

> Es war vom Duell die Rede, und wir alle, ohne uns gerade als prinzipielle Anhänger dieser Sitte zu fühlen, betonten aus unserem Studententum heraus und mehr noch als Einjährige-Freiwillige und künftige Reserveoffiziere unsere Bereitschaft, erforderlichenfalls ritterliche Satisfaktion zu geben [. . .]. Wir waren zwar alle

> weder Raufbolde noch besonders tüchtige Fechter, und keiner von uns lechzte daher nach einem Waffenhandel, aber ebensowenig hätte es einer versucht, sich einer studentischen Mensur oder selbst einem Duell zu entziehen, wenn es den geltenden Regeln nach als unausweichlich gegolten hätte."[82]

One can glean from this discussion that Schnitzler never believed in any procedure justifying the duel, but that he would not have retreated, had there been a serious necessity of fighting one. Schnitzler, therefore, did not change his position throughout his life. His stand had always been against this convention, but in the last analysis dueling is a matter of inner conscience. If one does not heed inner guidance, one will find himself no longer balanced, no longer centered, a condition which some characters in the various plays call "Schuld."

To Leonilda in *Der Gang zum Weiher* guilt is present only when one knowingly turns the wrong way (789). In this she moves away from conventional thought patterns, by which a person is made to feel humiliated by imputations of guilt made by someone else. Gusti, in *Im Spiel der Sommerlüfte,* continues in Leonilda's footsteps. When Felix tries to blame her for his anxiety, fear, and painful thoughts during her absence from Vienna, she defends herself: "An denen bin ich nicht schuld. Das ist nur deine unglückselige Natur. Wenn du mehr Vertrauen hättest—" (1024). Schnitzler indicates here through Gusti that the responsibility for one's emotional wellbeing rests within each person. Strong negative emotions such as hate, anger, fear, jealousy, guilt hamper a person's ability to master life's challenges successfully.

The priest, on the other hand, represents traditional theological thinking in the matter of guilt: he blames himself for Josefa's stirred-up emotions on account of the letter he has read to her: "[. . .] morgen wird Ihre unruhvolle Stimmung—an der ich leider auch mir einige Schuld zumessen muss—, morgen wird sie wieder vorbei sein" (1013). He does not comprehend that his visit to Josefa that evening was "mehr freundschaftlicher als amtlicher Natur" (981), just as the Hofrat needed to confide in a friend, when he called for the Kaplan.

In *Komödie der Verführung,* the question of guilt rests with Falkenir. He blames himself for the suicide of his first wife, which shapes his decision to withdraw from his marriage proposal to Aurelie. "[. . .] du wagst es nicht, glücklich zu sein—als hättest du irgendetwas zu sühnen—, was du doch nicht verschuldet" (871), she tells him, in order to remind him that he has a choice in life. Falkenir does not grasp this idea at all, for he accepts guilt. "Ist Vorhersicht nicht Schuld?" (871) is the question to which he finds no answer, and when he meets Aurelie again at the Danish coast, he has accepted additional guilt for her present state of abandon. "Wenn es hier etwas wie eine Schuld gibt, so liegt sie bei mir allein" (950).

An interesting polarity is created with the term "Rechenschaft oder Treue schuldig sein": Judith wants to enjoy irresponsibly without being accountable to anybody (865);

Gysar lures Aurelie by reminding her of independence (894); Arduin asks Aurelie: "Bist du irgendeinem Menschen, wer es auch sei, Treue schuldig?" (947). In *Die Schwestern oder Casanova in Spa,* the term "Schuld" has likewise two connotations. On the one hand, Casanova is constantly concerned with his obligation of paying his debt[83]—on the other hand, the question arises as to whether the two women feel any guilt for their assignations with him (694, 699).

The theme of "Schuld," then, has been treated by Schnitzler in all four dramas, the lighter aspect of which is represented in *Die Schwestern oder Casanova in Spa.* The more conventional concept of feeling guilty for another person's actions is developed in *Komödie der Verführung.* The absence of "Schuld" is demonstrated in *Der Gang zum Weiher* through Leonilda, the emancipated woman, who determines for herself what course her life will take instead of feeling compelled to bow to a hypocritical social code. Her father likewise showed this conviction when the message reached him about Sylvester's drowning. He knows: "Sie trägt keine Schuld" (840), speaking of Leonilda. Each person rules his own moral actions and is responsible for them. The last drama, *Im Spiel der Sommerlüfte,* deals again with a juxtaposition between old and new ideas in this respect, thus connecting to the first drama and completing the circle. Schnitzler's contemporaneity rests on his assumption for his characters that no guilt attaches to any behavior so long as one accepts the responsibility for the consequences of one's decisions and actions.

There is another correspondence between the first and the last drama in terms of the women characters. Flaminia and Anina considered themselves sisters in that they both felt a strong attraction to Casanova, once they had physical contact with him. But the quarrel over Casanova brought out the worst within them and even their seeming harmony at the end of the play was not sincerely demonstrated. Josefa and Gusti, on the other hand, became sisters because of their states of mind. They understood each other's concerns on deeper levels, so that no significant disharmonies interrupted their life in the countryside. Gusti and Leonilda are mental sisters in their desire to remain unmarried for a while, and both offer friendship to their suitors. Neither Sylvester nor Felix, however, feels inclined to accept it (824, 1025).

Another combination justifies a brief comparison: Josefa and Aurelie. Both were models for artists, one for a sculptor and the other for a painter. Whereas Josefa was trained professionally for this work and enjoyed her brief career, Aurelie never had such ambitions for the profession and only yielded under pressure from Gysar. In consequence, her despair of soul confused her. Josefa married and has, apart from certain frustrations, lived a sheltered life in devotion to her husband and son. She is a mature woman who deepens her understanding of herself through a healthy quest for truth, even if it means doubting the validity of certain traditions and conventions. Aurelie, rejected

as a marriage partner, is left without balance or discernment, in a state of mental disarray. She never reaches a state of healthy introspection.

The polarity of "Stadt und Land" in *Im Spiel der Sommerlüfte* finds a correspondence in all four dramas. The complexity of city life—its business atmosphere as well as the lure and excitement after working hours—related to one's personal code of conduct in Schnitzler's last drama. The movement between the two poles of "Stadt und Land" in *Der Gang zum Weiher* has its cause in political maneuvers. The main reason for the entire drama's taking place in the countryside of castle Mayenau is the dismissal of the Freiherr as chancellor to the emperor six or seven years earlier. Whereas the main characters seem to have adjusted to this quiet, peaceful life, Dominik, the servant, is bored and nostalgically awaits the moment when he can be with his master in the stream of events again. Leonilda breaks the news of pending war by talking about the two messengers on horseback who stopped briefly in the village on their way to the emperor to deliver secret documents. Konrad, who carries a letter from his father to Mayenau, is moving on to the capital. Finally, Mayenau himself is on his way to the city—first, to catch his adversary and then, together with him to be on a peace mission to the emperor. After Mayenau is reinstated as chancellor, preparations begin for moving to Vienna to take up permanent residence at the court.

In *Komödie der Verführung* the movement is first between countries, as Arduin fulfills his diplomatic mission. Money speculations carried out by Westerhaus also take place between countries, as the various telephone calls are interpreted. Later, when most of the characters meet again away from Austrian city life in the simplicity of a Danish sea resort village, the declaration of war sends them into frantic preparations to meet the last train in Copenhagen to cross the border. The polarity of "Stadt und Land" in this drama involves its greatest complexity of the international political situation.

In *Die Schwestern oder Casanova in Spa,* it is the Belgian resort town of Spa which has become "unsafe" to some characters on account of Casanova's presence. Andrea, therefore, suggests at one point to Anina that they should leave this place so as to expose themselves no longer to the lure of the various pleasures which are there. The polarity of "Stadt und Land" shows a gradual increase of importance and urgency, as each drama unfolds from a personal realm to international politics, then local politics, to end up again on a note of personal conduct, thus completing a circle.

In summary: There is a coherence among the last four plays which in terms of their publication dates all appeared after the First World War. Of course, one must not forget that Schnitzler began collecting ideas for these dramas over a long period of time. Anna Stroka's observation about "Schnitzlers Tragikomödien" can also apply in part to these four weeks: "Mit diesen Werken hat Arthur

Schnitzler ein ernstes Problem des Menschen seiner Epoche behandelt und gleichzeitig kritisch zu diesem Stellung genommen. Er deckte die feinsten Seelenregungen dieser Menschen auf, enthüllte ihre innere Leere, wollte mithin nicht nur entlarven, wollte seiner Zeit nicht nur einen Spiegel vorhalten, sondern auch warnen."[84]

The soul had always been an area of interest and concern to Schnitzler because of his own training in psychology. Each drama is concerned with the souls of its characters, but the most complete study takes place in ***Der Gang zum Weiher.***[85] One of Schnitzler's aphorisms speaks of the immortality of the soul, a conviction seldom dwelled upon in his works: "Unsere Seele ist ewig, ja, aber nicht mehr in gleicher Weise die unsere. Das, was in uns Seele war, ist ewig, wie auch das, was in uns Körper war, ewig ist, wie überhaupt alles ewig ist, da innerhalb der Unendlichkeit nichts verloren gehen kann."[86] "That which in us was soul is eternal," says Schnitzler in a carefully worded way which places the soul on a cosmic scale, "das All" in Schnitzler's words. For Karl Joël the soul is the center of life,

> nicht weil sie zufällige Mitte [. . .] sondern weil sie Einheit des Lebens ist, und mehr, weil sie bildende Kraft des Lebens ist. Sie ist das eigentlich Lebende, der Leib das Gelebte, Durchlebte, ja das grosse Mittel des Lebens; denn die Seele lebt durch den Leib hindurch, in die Welt hinein. Der Leib ist die letzte Gliederung der Seele, ihre Instrumentierung auf die Welt hin, und die Seele waltet durch den Leib so unsichtbar wie der Dirigent unhörbar durch das Orchester."[87]

The soul, therefore, is the most important part of a human being. Within the soul antinomies are unified to a harmonious concert. As Joël says so eloquently:

> Die Seele ist Mann und Weib, Krieg und Frieden, Scheidung und Bindung, Spannung und Lösung, Lust und Leid. Sie ist wie das von ihr beherrschte Leben gerade der Ineinanderklang von Gegensätzen. Es ist das Wesen des Lebens, dass es nicht eindeutig ist, sondern Reibung und Ausgleich. Noch jeder hat gelogen, der das Leben auf einen Begriff zog. Optimismus und Pessimismus sind hier so parteiisch wie Monismus und Dualismus. Denn die Gegensätze bedingen sich."[88]

The soul, as the part of man that is forever searching, is a characteristic ingredient of Schnitzler's own career and his fascination with Goethe's *Faust.* He questioned himself in the same way Faust did: "Sind wir ein Spiel von jedem Druck der Luft?" Schnitzler's own answers would be based upon the antinomies of life, the polarities—as I called them throughout the study. The more man turns within for answers, the stronger mastery he gains over these opposites.

It is in light of this inner search that his last drama, ***Im Spiel der Sommerlüfte,*** gains in value and deserves more recognition than it has been accorded so far. Without violence, each character in the play emerged as a more complete person with deeper understanding of himself and the world around him, through the searching of his soul. Each character reaches a synthesis, so to speak. The answer to the question: "Sind wir ein Spiel von jedem Druck der Luft?" depends upon the strength of character to maintain its identity[89] and to govern the intensity of one's life experiences.

Notes

1. Arthur Schnitzler, *Gesammelte Werke. Die dramatischen Werke,* Zweiter Band (Frankfurt am Main: S. Fischer Verlag, 1962), pp. 975-1034, 1042. All quotes from this second volume pertaining to the text will hereafter be referred to by page number following the quote.

2. Urbach, *Kommentar,* p. 197.

3. Arthur Schnitzler, *Tagebücher,* Mappe 126-127. Cf. Gerhard Neumann und Jutta Müller, *Der Nachlass Arthur Schnitzlers* (München: Wilhelm Fink Verlag, 1969), p. 64.

4. Arthur Schnitzler, quoted by Urbach, *Kommentar,* pp. 196-97.

5. Hartmut Scheible, *Arthur Schnitzler in Selbstzeugnissen.* Rowohlts Monographien, Ed. Kurt Kusenberg (Reinbek bei Hamburg: Rowohlt Taschenbuch Verlag GmbH, 1976), p. 127.

6. *Ibid.* With regard to Chekhov, Scheible reminds his readers that Schnitzler himself entered a note in his diary on February 10, 1929: "Die Russen könnten es spielen."

7. Cf. Gerhart Baumann, "Arthur Schnitzler: Die Tagebücher. Vergangene Gegenwart — Gegenwärtige Vergangenheit," *Modern Austrian Literature,* 10, Nos. 3/4 (1977), 159.

8. Liptzin, *Schnitzler,* p. 253.

9. Robert F. Arnold, *Die Literatur* 32, V (1930), 290: "Mag die betreffende Erörterung sich auch etwas lang gestalten, sie liegt auf so hoher Ebene, dass wir ihrer nicht entraten möchten und den erotischen Reigen gerne durch christliche und durch weltliche Resignation ergänzt sehen. Überraschungen freilich hat das anmutige Spiel nicht zu bieten, es wäre denn die, dass die Hand seines Schöpfers noch immer mit alter Leichtigkeit und Sicherheit gestaltet und lenkt."

10. Hans Thyriot, *Die Literatur* 33, IX (1931), 514.

11. *Ibid.*

12. Scheible, p. 127.

13. Schnitzler's letter dated July 4, 901 [sic], published in *Wort und Wahrheit,* 13 (1958), 288.

14. Derré, p. 408.

    Cf. also A. E. Zucker, "Criticism to 'Im Spiel der Sommerlüfte'," *Germanic Review,* 6 (1931), 92. He underlines "the hidden depth of the souls of (Schnitzler's) characters" which allow for an optimistic conclusion of the play.

15. Derré, p. 408.

16. *Ibid.,* pp. 408-409.

17. *Ibid.,* p. 409.

18. Cf. also Baumann, "Tagebücher," 157.

19. Körner, "Spätwerk," 53-83; 153-163.

20. Zucker, 93.

21. Swales. *Critical Study,* p. 75.

22. *Ibid.*

23. Offermanns, p. 128.

24. Müller-Freienfels, p. 191.

25. *Ibid.,* p. 192.

26. Liptzin, *Schnitzler,* p. 251.

27. Urbach, *Kommentar,* p. 38.

28. *Ibid.*

29. *Ibid.*

30. Derré, p. 409.

31. Cf. Schnitzler, *AuB,* pp. 51, 84, 85, 254-266.

32. Schmidt, p. 255.

33. Johann Wolfgang von Goethe, *Goethes Werke. Hamburger Ausgabe in 14 Bänden, Dramatische Dichtungen,* Dramen I, Band 3, 8th ed., ed. Erich Trunz (Hamburg: Christian Wegner Verlag, 1967), Vers 2724, p. 88.

34. According to Urbach, Richard Beer-Hofmann also worked with this motto for his *Novellen* (*Kommentar,* p. 197).

35. *Faust I,* Vers 2723, p. 88.

36. *Ibid.,* Vers 308, p. 17.

37. At the end of Part I, when Gretchen is dismissed by Mephistopheles with a rude "Sie ist gerichtet!", this other reality appears in the "Stimme von oben: Ist gerettet!" (Part I, 4611), thereby indicating that the supernatural, "heavenly" world may at any time assert its judgment in the empirical world of human affairs.

38. Urbach, *Schnitzler,* p. 94.

39. *Ibid.*

40. Liptzin, *Schnitzler,* p. 253.

41. Müller-Freienfels, p. 81.

42. *Ibid.*

43. Blume, p. 32.

44. Schnitzler, *BdSp.,* p. 117.

45. Liptzin, *Schnitzler,* p. 211.

46. Rey, *Späte Prosa,* p. 17.

47. Whiton, p. 141.

48. Müller-Freienfels, p. 139.

49. *Ibid.*

50. Anna Stroka, "Arthur Schnitzlers Tragikomödien," *Acta Universitatis Wratislaviensis,* No. 128, *Germanica Wratislaviensia,* XIV (1971), 66.

51. Cf. also Davis, p. 185.

52. Rey, *Späte Prosa,* p. 17.

53. Davis, p. 153.

54. *Ibid.,* p. 152.

55. Müller-Freienfels, p. 190.

56. Lederer, "The Problem of Ethics," p. 195.

57. Schnitzler, "Ein Zwischenkapitel über Begebungen und Seelenzustände," in *AuB,* p. 158.

58. Schnitzler, "Der Geist im Wort," in *AuB,* p. 142; cf. also p. 146.

59. Davis, p. 153.

60. Schnitzler, "Der Geist im Wort," *AuB,* p. 142.

61. Boner, p. 25: "Die Müdigkeit des Impressionismus wird durch einen neuen stosskräftigen Mut überwunden. Schnitzler hat diesem Mut durch das unerbittliche Zu-Ende-Denken des 'Reigens' einen Grundstein gesetzt und ihm eine Spitze gemeisselt durch das Gespräch in 'Im Spiel der Sommerlüfte,' in dem die menschliche Maskierung es mit sich bringt, dass der Kaplan den heroischen Glauben der Frau und Josefa den heroischen Zweifel des Mannes ausspricht. Der Weg ist weit vom frühen Impressionismus bis zu diesem Dialog, in dem der Mut sich zum verzweifelten Wort steigert: 'Auch Schwäche ist Schuld, Schwäche ganz besonders'."

62. The train or necessity to reach it in time is mentioned many times: Cf. pp. 978, 983, 984, 985, 995, 997, 1000, 1001, 1007, 1008, 1011, 1027.

63. The name "Innsbruck" is mentioned most frequently by Gusti herself, but almost as often by Eduard and Felix and the rest of the family. Cf. pp. 978, 985, 990, 993, 994, 997, 1004, 1005, 1006, 1022, 1023, 1026, 1027, 1032.

64. Uwe Rosenbaum, "Die Gestalten des Schauspielers auf dem deutschen Theater des 19. Jahrhunderts mit der besonderen Berücksichtigung der dramatischen Werke von Hermann Bahr, Arthur Schnitzler und Heinrich Mann," Diss. Köln (1971), p. 84.

65. Rosenbaum concludes: "Die Flucht aus der Wirklichkeit in die Welt des Theaters ist die Flucht vor der Lüge, vor dem Schein in neue Lüge, neuen Schein" (p. 219) which does not apply to Schnitzler's last

drama, either. Gusti is serious about her career. Perhaps she is able to reverse the opinion commonly held about the theater. Rosenbaum summarizes one such opinion as follows: "Der schlechte Schauspieler, der Komödiant, der Gaukler ist zum 'Symbol' der Zeit geworden" (p. 219).

66. Schnitzler had dealt with this theme on previous occasions, last in *Das weite Land* (1910), where the center of dramatic interest gradually shifted to the new theme, namely, the conflict of generations: age giving way to youth. Cf. Liptzin, p. 172: "Mrs. Meinhold-Aigner has no [. . .] illusions. She has frankly capitulated to the younger generation, and she does not feel obliged to maintain even a semblance of authority over her Otto. She reminds Genia that sons, also, grow up to be men." Cf. Singer, p. 139.

67. Cf. pp. 979, 990, 995, 996, 1006, 1028, 1032.

68. Cf. pp. 990, 995, 1006, 1028.

69. Cf. pp. 998, 1000, 1007, 1008, 1028.

70. Cf. pp. 976, 977, 981, 982, 984, 995, 996, 1004, 1006, 1007, 1008, 1011, 1013, 1017, 1018, 1028, 1031, 1032, 1034.

71. Cirlot, p. 353.

72. *Ibid.*

73. *Ibid.,* p. 259.

74. *Ibid.*

75. *Ibid.,* p. 218.

76. *Ibid.*

77. *Ibid.,* p. 324.

78. *Ibid.,* p. 78. Cf. also *Wörterbuch der Antike* 7th ed. (Stuttgart: Alfred Kröner Verlag, 1966), p. 124: "Gott des Weines und des drängenden Lebens in der Natur, deren zeugende Kraft in ihm Gestalt gewinnt."

79. Cirlot, p. 208.

80. Davis, p. 174.

81. *Ibid.,* p. 175.

82. Schnitzler, *Jugend in Wien,* p. 155.

83. Cf. pp. 690, 721, 732.

84. Stroka, 73.

85. Cf. pp. 745, 746, 751, 759, 761, 773, 775, 777, 778, 788, 794, 803, 810, 817, 827, 828.

86. Schnitzler, *AuB,* p. 257.

87. Karl Joël, *Seele und Welt. Versuch einer organischen Auffassung* (Jena: Eugen Dieterichs, 1912), p. 123.

88. *Ibid.,* p. 121.

89. Cf. Richard Alewyn, with regard to Hofmannsthal: "Der junge Hofmannsthal schon ist tief bewegt von der Erfahrung, dass die Seele keinen Grund hat und keine Grenze. Wir sind 'nicht mehr als ein Taubenschlag,' ein 'Spiel von jedem Druck der Luft,' wie die jungen Wiener gerne aus dem 'Faust' zitieren. Es ist diese Beschaffenheit, die es ihnen schwer macht, gegenüber dem unendlichen Andrang der Dinge die Identität der Person zu behaupten, es ist aber gerade auch diese Beschaffenheit, die Hofmannsthal zum Dichter macht. Denn sie erlaubt ihm jenes mystische Kommunizieren mit dem Kern aller Dinge, das diesen ermöglicht, aus dem Dichter mit seiner Stimme zu sprechen." (*Über Hugo von Hofmannsthal,* 2nd ed. (Göttingen: Vandenhoeck & Ruprecht, 1958/1960, p. 8).

DER GANG ZUM WEIHER

CRITICAL COMMENTARY

Brigitte L. Schneider-Halvorson (essay date 1983)

SOURCE: Schneider-Halvorson, Brigitte L. "*Der Gang Zum Weiher.*" In *The Late Dramatic Works of Arthur Schnitzler,* pp.83-111. New York: Peter Lang, 1983.

[*In the following essay, Schneider-Halvorson discusses various critical commentary, as well as Schnitzler's use of themes and symbols in the play* Der Gang Zum Weiher.]

BACKGROUND OF THE PLAY AND STATEMENT OF PURPOSE

Although Schnitzler had reached a preliminary conclusion of this play by June 11, 1921[1] and had written in 1924 to his friend Georg Brandes "[. . .] und ein Versstück wird vielleicht auch bald fertig sein [. . .],"[2] this five-act verse play was not published until December of 1926 by S. Fischer Verlag, Berlin.[3] As a serious artist, Schnitzler rarely allowed publication of any work until he had convinced himself that it expressed truly his innermost convictions and that it had reached the most perfect form which he could create for it. As in other cases, this dramatic work was first conceived as a prose work entitled *Der weise Vater* in 1907. More sketches and notes were added between 1907 and 1914 and the new title *Der Weiher* given to it in 1915.[4] This new designation announces a shift in focus. In the final version of the drama water has even more significance than in the previous play ***Komödie der Verführung.*** This points to another aspect in Schnitzler's artistic career which heretofore has rarely attracted attention in the field of literary criticism. Eight months before his death (October 21, 1931), Schnitzler attended the premiere of the drama on February 14, 1931. During the first theater season the work had fourteen performances within two months.[5]

Upon first acquaintance with ***Der Gang zum Weiher,*** it is possible to become literally overwhelmed by the complexity of its thematic structure. For almost four decades Schnitzler had wrestled with essential problems of life, seeking to divest them of the conventional thought associations of his own time and place, in order to suggest their universal importance among mankind and to reveal all facets of their inner meaning. With some justice Josef Körner writes that even "der grösste Dichter" would find it difficult to force "so Mannigfaltiges zur Einheit."[6]

But was it unity which really captured Schnitzler's interest? Is it perhaps not more important to recognize that he concerned himself primarily with the diversity of human relationships as he observed them in the course of daily life, concluding that the ideal premises, such as unity and harmony, desirable for well-balanced personal interactions are rarely present. Schnitzler recognizes that these are worthwhile goals to strive for, but to attain them, one often experiences adverse states of mind first. Therefore, he emphasizes the dialectic pulse of the world, where polarities reign supreme. The analysis of this drama reveals that the antinomies of life are expressed in attraction and repulsion, intimacy and detachment, realism and surrealism, youth and age, art and life, life and death, peace and war, love and hate, selflessness and egotism, for gratification of physical desires and those of the psychic personality exist side by side, and often within the same personality.

It is the purpose of this analysis to show how Schnitzler's characters face the antinomies of life on physical, mental, and spiritual levels in an effort to achieve balance and restore inner peace. Beyond the desire for truth and well-being in their own lives they have an urge to better understand their relations to other people. The discussion indicates that Schnitzler's use of symbolism allows some insight into the mystical content of his Weltanschauung. More than fifty years have passed since Körner wrote his assessment of Schnitzler's play. I share the predictions of recent criticism which states that "Many will come to regard this poetically beautiful play as one of his supreme achievements, a pinnacle in his lifelong struggle to express his uniquely personal view of life."[7]

OUTLINE OF THE PLAY

The action takes place in the mid-eighteenth century, paralleling in this respect the period of ***Die Schwestern oder Casanova in Spa.*** However, the setting in ***Der Gang zum Weiher*** is presumably Austria. The first act introduces the ex-chancellor, Freiherrn Albrecht von Mayenau, in peaceful retirement at age fifty, dictating his memoirs. He lives at a distance from the city, in his castle, previously just a vacation place (741). In his company are his unmarried sister Anselma, over forty but still beautiful (741), and his lovely daughter Leonilda, a precocious young woman of nineteen, who has recently finished her education in a convent. They expect the arrival of Sylvester Thorn, an aging poet and friend of Mayenau, who is returning to his homeland after ten years of self-imposed exile. Among the preparations for his visit are instructions from Leonilda to decorate the guest room in the tower of the castle with fresh lilac. Many branches have already wilted because Sylvester is several days late. Meanwhile, Mayenau and his sister speak about Leonilda, thus preparing for her late appearance on stage. Anselma expresses her concern for her niece as she tells the brother of Leonilda's nocturnal walks to the pond, a secluded place in the forest, where she has been bathing in secret. This activity in the solitude of moon-flooded summer nights is always climaxed by a ritualistic dance around an ancient stone. The chancellor does not share Anselma's worries; he only sees innocence in his child and insists that they both keep silent about their knowledge of Leonilda's secret, her nightly "Gang zum Weiher."

With the appearance of Leonilda begins the historical theme of the drama. She brings news from the village that war is imminent. The youthful Konrad von Ursenbeck, officer and son of the military commander, enters the stage shortly. He informs the chancellor that war with the neighboring state is unavoidable and conveys the hopes of his father, an old friend of the house of Mayenau, that the ex-chancellor will persuade the indecisive emperor without delay. The arrival of Sylvester Thorn interrupts their conversation and leads into Act II.

Schnitzler portrays both Sylvester and the chancellor so affectionately and in such detail that one could easily suspect a superimposed self-portrait. Sylvester has returned to Mayenau primarily to retrieve his past, captured in diary notes which he left in safekeeping with Anselma. Prior to burning each page in the fireplace, he wants to read his old writings again. Today he is confident of being able to compare himself with his own youth, thus preserving the sense of progress in his life. He is growing old, and he will soon be forced to admit that he no longer possesses the talent and vitality of his youth. He can try to forestall this conclusion by burning the papers and turning to the present and future, for he is in the process of preparing a home for the mistress he plans to marry and the child they are expecting. Sylvester meets Leonilda briefly, and she recalls all the fairytales he once told her in her childhood, hoping that he would add new stories. Meanwhile, the chancellor resumes the dictation of his memoirs, but the political discussions of the morning have excited his mind so that he stops the dictation.

Act III takes place late that evening; Sylvester has burned his papers and wants to leave the castle that same night. He is delayed by Andreas Ungnad, the secretary of the chancellor. In his role as a psychopath he entrusts Sylvester with a secret. Because Sylvester is conscious of his own egocentricity, he tends to see in his interlocutor a caricature of himself. While still baffled, he meets Leonilda, who with youthful admiration expresses concern about his future. This he interprets as a declaration of love. Flattered by Leonilda's words, he misunderstands them entirely and suddenly is prepared to desert the woman he supposedly loves. Instead, he asks the ex-chancellor for Leonilda's hand in marriage. Mayenau is appalled and speaks to his friend harshly. Finally, he tells Sylvester that he may return after he has put his own house in order. This decision will also provide time and distance for Leonilda to think things over. Should Sylvester still love her and find her the same, Mayenau will not withhold his blessing. Neither man is aware as yet that Leonilda is a free spirit and does not intend to bind herself in marriage. Anselma enters and intuitively knows what has happened. She withdraws with her brother into the darkness of the trees, from which they see Leonilda on her walk to the pond. Anselma foresees also Mayenau's reinstatement as chancellor and envisions for Leonilda the fulfillment of "ein fürstliches Geschick" (796-97).

The sudden appearance of Konrad returns the scene to the level of reality, as the threat of war looms more seriously now than ever. The document from the emperor restores to Mayenau all rights as chancellor. Mayenau, however, appears a disappointment to Konrad and the war party, for he will intercede only for the sake of peace. As he leaves immediately on this peace mission to the capital, Konrad stays in the castle impatiently. He wants to cool off and remembers the pond from his childhood days. Mayenau denies at first the existence of such waters, but his cryptic remarks made later on are actually intended to direct Konrad to the pond. When the chancellor returns from his trip to the emperor in Act IV, the inevitable, of course, has happened: Leonilda and Konrad have found each other and are "married before God" (832). A sharp argument follows between Mayenau and Konrad about the political situation and its consequences. The latter becomes suspicious of the chancellor's motives for keeping him at the castle; he sees in him nothing but an adversary and refuses to appear before the emperor.

Act V begins with the official return of Sylvester, who has had a brief encounter with the foolish secretary Ungnad in the previous act. He reports that his mistress and child have died in the travail of birth. "Von kaum geschloss'nen Särgen" (822), he comes still with the desire to marry Leonilda. Mayenau informs him of the changed circumstances, but only a long conversation with Leonilda convinces him of his wrong assumption. Mayenau is in error also about Leonilda's relationship to Konrad. "[. . .] mir beliebt es nicht [. . .] so bald mich zu vermählen" (832) she replies to her father. The last phase of the drama returns to the political scene. Mayenau has failed to preserve the peace. Konrad becomes more hostile as he disagrees in matters of strategy. He is finally free to leave, but Sylvester steps in his way by challenging him to a duel. The first shots of war are fired, thus averting Sylvester's provocation. While Konrad takes leave, not without properly addressing Leonilda and her father, Sylvester

disappears unnoticed to start his walk to the pond. Schnitzler has no official exit for him. Ungnad, who followed Sylvester and observed his drowning in the pond, returns with this message to the house. His state of mind is very confused. Meanwhile, Mayenau prepares to move to the capital and Leonilda begs him to take her along because "dreifach gespenstisch schleicht Alter, Wahnsinn, Tod durch dieses Haus, / Nicht eine Nacht mehr will ich hier verweilen" (841). The work ends with the hope for early peace and a happy future for Leonilda.

REVIEW OF CRITICISM

In Körner's view the drama does not hold together because the various themes are not developed in order of their priority.[8] He criticizes Schnitzler for the fact that his characters, happenings, and thoughts appear "mehr ersonnen als erlebt, mehr durchgrübelt als durchlitten [. . .]" and attributes the unsatisfactory impression it leaves with the reader to the circumstance, "dass der Dichter in einer seelisch-sittlichen Wandlung begriffen ist, die uns von ihm in jedem Sinne neue Werke noch erwarten lässt, die aber vorläufig nur zu einer zwiespältigen, unausgeglichenen Dichtung geführt hat."[9]

Sol Liptzin sees this work as an epilogue which Schnitzler wrote in loneliness and concern for age "in the last decade of a contemplative career" where "he gives utterance to his deep disillusionment with art as a substitute for active life, and to his sad recognition of the fact that fame is not in itself an end worth striving for."[10]

Françoise Derré, who in her detailed presentation of Schnitzler combines creatively historical, biographical, and thematic aspects, finds that the drama concentrates upon two aging characters: Thorn, the poet thwarted in his effort to recover wasted younger years through marriage with young Leonilda, and Freiherr von Mayenau, the statesman unsuccessful in his attempt to prevent the outbreak of war with the neighboring country. Her interpretation stresses the issue of war and peace, which she feels constitutes the center of the drama, "le heurt entre la bonne volonté des hommes et leur méchanceté, le conflit de la liberté avec le destin."[11] Although he is less carefully drawn, the emperor in this play is reminiscent of Rudolf II, as he is represented in Grillparzer's *Ein Bruderzwist in Habsburg,* for his weaknesses are marked by indecisiveness.[12] In Sylvester she seems to recognize an extension of Schnitzler's own experience, who like his protagonist, was suffering from discrimination, deliberate misunderstanding, and false criticism.

Martin Swales in his chapter, "Schnitzler's World: Restriction and Resonance," focuses on the "dialectic of attraction and repulsion" which "is central to Schnitzler's vision of human relationships."[13] This attraction can be felt toward another person, as Konrad experiences it with a young man in the opposing army. At the end of the play Konrad's main interest in war is to kill his "Doppelgänger."[14] Another form of "Doppelgänger," Swales shows, can be observed appearing in characters like Leonilda, Sylvester, and the Sekretär, who "have a sense of other people's existing as another part of their own being."[15] These states are further explored in an excellent article by Harold D. Dickerson.[16] He points out the "significance of the pond" as "the one symbol in the drama that gives coherence to its disparate and seemingly unrelated parts" because it is "both a place and a state of mind."[17]

Although all of the above interpretations contribute to an understanding of the drama, the analysis given by Dickerson is to date the most comprehensive effort in focusing on aspects of water and vision.

The present analysis explores the idea of unity in diversity from the standpoint of the polarity principle. In his late dramatic works Schnitzler creates frequently polar opposites in order to find answers in his search for truth and the deeper meaning in life. Often he establishes a synthesis which is equivalent to his concept concerning "die Ganzheit des Lebens." It also includes those states of consciousness beyond the rational mind. The tower symbolism in addition to that of water and vision is discussed in an effort to show how various characters in the play leave the firm ground of reality to seek answers from the higher mind.

Analysis of the Drama

Symbolism: The symbolism begins with the carefully chosen title *Der Gang zum Weiher.* "Der Gang" refers to the means, the path which various characters seek to get to their goal. The path is symbolic of life itself. It represents the burning path of life's desires. In connection with the second part of the title, "zum Weiher," the path to the water is important to all major characters in the play, because they recognize the pond as a point of reference which connects earlier experiences with the present moment and gives them a sense of direction for the future. For example, Konrad recalls his childhood days, when he was playing with Leonilda by the pond and one day lost her ball in the water. After a long day's journey on horseback, he now wants to return to the place and refresh himself (802-03).

For Leonilda, the pool seems to provide more than physical comfort, now that she has returned from the convent as a mature young lady, who is sensitive to the difference between life in a sheltered, restricted, cloistered atmosphere and life in a worldly environment with its social, economic, and political issues. During her nocturnal walks and activities at the pond she is seeking insight from the higher mind, that part of the mind which transcends the waking conscious and subconscious mind—the superconscious mind, the voice of intuition. With regard to the water symbolism Juan Eduardo Cirlot points out that "a secondary meaning [. . .] is found in the identification of water with intuitive wisdom."[18] Thus, the water represents mental potentiality, that is, unexpressed possibilities in the mind.

Commonly it is said that a man is "at sea" when he is in doubt about a mental process; in other words, he has not established his thoughts in line with the principle involved;

he is not balanced. The sea is capable of production, but must come under the dominion of the formative power of the mind, the imagination. Leonilda is moved by the power of her imagination, whether she is dancing or immersing herself in the cool water. The waters, according to Cirlot, symbolize the universal convergence of potentialities which precedes form and creation.[19] Immersion intensifies the life force, and Leonilda certainly experiences in her nocturnal walks to the pond the awakening of her body as well, between mysticism and myth.

Sylvester, on the other hand, experiences the opposite: death and annihilation. In earlier years, the pond inspired his creative talent to tell Leonilda many fairytales, as they walked together along the water. When his endeavor of turning their friendship into a love relation fails, he loses the purpose in life and is ready to end it.

To Anselma who secretly observes Leonilda's nightly activity, the situation appears quite different. She is convinced that Leonilda engages in pagan worship which may lead her to other temptations as well. Indeed, she questions the wisdom of her brother and wonders, whether it was such a good idea "aus des Klosters Schirm und Frieden / Ein Kind— / [. . .] eh' sich ein Eidam fand, / In eine ringsum aufgetane Welt / Der Rätsel und Versuchungen zu stellen" (745). Hesitatingly, she tells him that she has been aware for a long time of Leonilda's nightly visits to the pond in the forest. She witnessed Leonilda's nocturnal swim and only "der Wellen Sang" (747) disclosed her proximity until she reached the other side, culminating in mystic dances around an ancient stone— "ein ungefüger Block" (748)—with arms outstretched, as if transfigured in the moonlight."[20]

Anselma's description, so vividly alive, seems to create a sensual atmosphere around the pond, Anselma herself being drawn momentarily into a magic spell as if she re-experienced her own years as a young woman and projected her feelings onto Leonilda. At this point Anselma's eyesight is transcending human limitation, when she recounts minute details from across the pond: "Es rinnen langsam / An ihrem Leib die blauen Tropfen nieder" (747). To her description on the physical level she adds mental and emotional aspects. In her mind's eye she observes the countenance of a god, embracing this beautiful naked child who gave herself "ahnungsheiss dem Blick des Gottes" (748). "Es war kein Menschenantlitz," she confides to her brother, but it was attuned to Leonilda's spirit—"es gab sich kund" (748) to the extent that Leonilda became aware of her own beauty in the presence of the onlooking god: "Wie sie berauscht von diesem Wissen war, / Und zwiefach trunken, weil ein Gott sie sah—" (749).

Anselma's vision is paralleled later in Act IV by an exceedingly charming and enchanting love scene between Leonilda and Konrad as they recall the moment, when they—as if by magic—found each other at the edge of the pond and under its spell entered together the domain of sexual love. The experience represents to Leonilda her initiation into womanhood, answer to and fulfillment of her spiritual dance around the "ungefüger Block" (748). This change within her is further evidenced by her firm attitude toward Sylvester to remain on the level of friendship with him. To Konrad these nights of love are the consummation of a strong attraction to Leonilda that began by the same pool in their childhood days. He is so overwhelmed by his powerful feelings for Leonilda that he prepares to leave the castle even before the Freiherr has returned. However, when Mayenau's arrival is announced and Leonilda unselfishly tries to help Konrad escape through a side door, the young man reveals to her his real reason for leaving: "Noch eine dritte Nacht an dich, / An diesen Mund, an dieses Herz gedrängt,— / Und all mein Wesen trankst du so in dich, / Dass ich mit Leib und Seele dir verfiel. / Und davor war mir bang. D'rum wollt' ich fliehn" (810).

The motif of flight as it relates to the pond is of antithetical significance to Sylvester Thorn. In contrast to Konrad, Sylvester flees because of unrequited love for Leonilda. Whereas Konrad, after the second night, draws away from the pond, the magic place of his spellbound relationship with Leonilda, Sylvester is attracted to the pool in his final moments of existence. ". . . als wenn / Der Waldpfad, den er ging, sich unsichtbar / Fortsetzte unterm Wasserspiegel," reports the Sekretär, "schritt er / Vom Ufer immer weiter in die Flut— / Und immer tiefer, bis sie ihn ihn verschlang" (838). Contrary to Leonilda's experience in the water, which imparted vital energy to her, Sylvester's immersion brings him death. Again, the path serves as a means to achieve a goal, which was not reached at the edge of the pool. Watching Sylvester on that path, Ungnad felt the path continued invisibly under the surface of the water. This may suggest a continuation of existence beyond physical limitations. Reinhard Urbach points out: "Selbstmord kann als Selbstbestimmung und nicht nur als Selbstverlust gedeutet werden [. . .] er kann [. . .] auch als bewusste Entscheidung und freiwillige Aktion begriffen werden, als Verfügung über die eigene Person [. . .]."[21] The Freiherr feels that his friend decided his departure "mit letzter Würde / Und eben noch zu rechter Zeit" (840). His thoughts this time are very tactfully expressed in contrast to the blunt words he used in the dispute which they had had previously.

Water in its different negative aspects represents weakness, lack of stability, negation—all of which can be linked to Sylvester. In his lifetime he has not found the spirit of the law which governs human existence in its actions and interactions. His selfish concept of freedom and detachment let him always stand alone in the world, free of commitment or obligation of any kind: "Und also schwebt' ich über fremder Erde, / Von Wurzelkräften nirgends festgehalten, / Ein Gast und frei" (769). His adventurous life, exciting as it might have been in younger years, has never taught him a sense of responsibility and concern for anyone else; now the aging poet stands alone. He has never known the simplest but profoundest of human emotions, a loving feeling for another human being.

Too late Sylvester recognizes the futility of such an egocentric life and even the changes he is prepared to make upon his return to the country are marked by weakness, lack of stability, and dishonesty. On the one hand, he wants to prepare a home for his mistress and the child they expect; on the other, he hopes for their demise so that he could be free for Leonilda: "In meiner Seele Gründen / Hab' ich's gewollt" (826). With these words he admits to Leonilda his feelings of guilt for having wished their death. He shows no remorse for having forgotten, or having been prepared to abandon them in favor of Leonilda. Every thought and word, of course, is recorded in his consciousness, and all the weak and characterless words and expressions gather in the subconscious mind as water collects in holes. Mayenau, who cannot hide his astonishment over Sylvester's return as suitor immediately after the funeral, receives this answer from him:

> Als Freier ging ich schon.
> Und gab ich an der Beiden Totenbett
> So heissem Schmerz mich hin, wie je ein Gatte,
> Ein Vater ihn gefühlt,—mich drein verlieren
> Wär' Schwäche;—zu verweilen, wo mich nichts
> Mehr hielt, wär' Heuchelei [. . .].
>
> (822)

Sylvester's selfish attitude demonstrates a polar opposite to the author's own ideas which Liptzin captured in these words: "Schnitzler himself specifies in the codicil to his will, dated April 29, 1912, that, after his death, absolutely no one is to wear mourning for him. He forbids funeral orations and elaborate funeral rituals [. . .] he feels that no amount of oratory or weeping can warm the dead, and that the living should not succumb to gloom because of those who have passed on."[22] Schnitzler wanted to relieve everyone of a burden in the event of his death. Sylvester, on the other hand, burdened himself by wishing for the death of Alberta. In time of need there is nobody to sustain him. One such moment arrives in Act V, when the poet reveals the complete emptiness in his heart and pleads for acceptance of his marriage proposal. At that time Leonilda reaffirms her position of friendship and admiration for him as an eternal artist, because youth does not understand nor respond to the suffering of age and loneliness. As contorted as Sylvester's reply appears, it closes with the essential word which takes away any positive outlook on life: solitude (828).

It is again this despair that wells up in protest against Konrad's youth, when he challenges him with these lines: "Nur mir verstattet, [. . .] / Ein Abschiedswort Euch nachzurufen. Bube!" (834). It is a complement to Sylvester's earlier remark: "[. . .] 's wär eine arme Welt, / Wenn Jugend alles wär'—" (822). Even though he tries to end his life in a duel, the message about the outbreak of war at the border interrupts everything and he cannot even have the satisfaction of a "heroic" death. Ironically enough, the death by duel of one man is prevented by the bloodshed of many in war. But Konrad would not have agreed to such a fight, because it would have been "ein ungleich' Spiel" (834). He recognizes that Sylvester is "[. . .] wen'ger / Zu töten als zu sterben aufgelegt" (834). Therefore, the real issue is not moral but biological. It is a struggle not between the two personalities but between youth and age. As the Freiherr pointed out to Sylvester earlier: "Du bist ein ausgelesen' Buch, ein Name / Auf einem Grabstein" (823). The ensuing exchange between the Freiherr and Konrad allows Sylvester to leave unnoticed and start his final walk to the pond. He seeks the water to find not atonement but escape from this present state of affairs.

Water, however, stands not only for mental potentialities, weakness, negativeness, vital energy, regeneration, and birth; according to Arnold Whittick it is also a symbol of purification."[23] In this play so abounding with symbolism, there is the possibility that Sylvester's suicide can be interpreted as an act of purification. He is escaping from his egoism, thereby releasing himself from the narrow confines of his selfishness. In this sense his death is "inseparably linked with the theme of man's purification."[24] In Whittick's view death, as we commonly understand it, affects only physical man, while the rebirth is that of spiritual man, a dimension of which Schnitzler's characters indeed rarely are aware during their lifetime. "They pass their lives with no hope of ever penetrating the essential mystery," points out Dickerson. "But Schnitzler relieves the intransigency of this situation by endowing his characters with an instinctive and mystic awareness of life's secrets which enables them ultimately to come to terms with the unknown forces that both create and destroy them."[25]

It is hard to determine, however, where the Sekretär, the mad solipsist, stands in his "awareness of life's secrets." He looks upon other characters in the play as figments of his imagination. Schnitzler arranges to have scarcely any importance attached to Ungnad's notions, which, rather than a reasoned conviction, translate into a fixed idea bordering on insanity.[26] He is the only witness to the suicide: "Er sprang / Aus meinem Schädel in die Welt hinaus, / Wir waren zwei mit einmal auf der Erde" (838). The influence of the pond to which the Sekretär was exposed while watching Sylvester drown seems to have helped him clarify the "Doppelgänger"-problem he struggled with throughout the play. As he tells the Freiherr, Sylvester gave the sign for the rest of the world to come to life: "Nun leuchtet, braust es, heult, es lebt ringsum— / Und wider eine Welt steh' ich allein" (841). Thus, the Sekretär experiences a sense of separation which he might have picked up from Sylvester, who not only felt separated from the outer world, but also from the innermost part of his being.[27] Kammeyer sees in this character only a technical means to an end, namely, to carry out stage effectiveness: "Schnitzler stellt diese Figur als schweren Psychopathen dar, um an die Irrealität des gesamten Bühnengeschehens erinnern zu können. Der Zuschauer soll durch diesen allerdings nicht leicht zu durchschauenden Kunstgriff, wie schon in der Überleitung zum zweiten Akt, Abstand gewinnen."[28]

The term "Irrealität" is perhaps ill-chosen to describe "das gesamte Bühnengeschehen" because the drama also deals with politics and the looming war issue which certainly have a realistic basis. The important concept which dominates all four of Schnitzler's dramas discussed here is the principle of polarity.[29] Life's expression would not be complete without the two poles. William Rey summarizes this principle of composition as follows: "Letzten Endes also umfasst das Dasein für Schnitzler [. . .] alle Gegensätze, Kosmos und Chaos, Sinn und Unsinn, Gut und Böse, und verbindet sie zu einer Ganzheit, deren Wesen zwar geahnt, aber nicht mehr definiert werden kann," and concludes: "angesichts dieser Ganzheit, deren Schrecken und Wunder ihn immer von Neuem faszinieren, wird Schnitzler zu dem, was Hofmannsthal einen Mystiker ohne Mystik nennt."[30]

On the one hand, Schnitzler's concern is the question of reality, but in order to understand reality, one must look at the opposite as well, which in *Der Gang zum Weiher* leads some characters to a search beyond the physical senses. Richard Specht calls Schnitzler a "Dichter der seltsamen Zusammenhänge."[31] Oskar Seidlin, who recognizes that the Schnitzler research has bypassed certain aspects of Schnitzler's work, summarizes these neglected sides of the author's artistic development by stating: "[. . .] es lässt sich kaum leugnen, dass hinter der eleganten Fassade, hinter der weltweisen und abgeklärten Skepsis, die gesamte Apparatur des Spuks und der Zauberei am Werke ist."[32]

Surrealism: Schnitzler has no ready answers to any of the problems posed, for he recognizes that it is not a condition he is dealing with but it ultimately narrows down to states of consciousness, states of mind. Quite often he has been misunderstood and harshly criticized for this.[33] "Was er immer wieder darstellt," observes Rey in defense of Schnitzler, "ist die Einsicht in die unerhellbare Hintergründigkeit des Daseins."[34] This impenetrable ambiguity is not only related to the symbolism of water and vision, it also finds application in the political realm discussed later. The focus again is on "Ganzheit." Herbert Cysarz in his excellent comparative study broadens the spectrum, when he admits: "Doch freilich ist Schnitzlers Erscheinungswelt immer auch ein Spiegelsystem, ein Medium unsichtbarunsagbarer Mächte. Oft bilden sie gleichwie einen Schleier vor transzendierenden Weiten, bisweilen gewinnt sie ihr Relief wie unter metaphysischer Matrize."[35]

The influence of the inexplicable upon man, Cysarz's "Spiegelsystem," is seen by Gerhart Baumann as a twofold activity which takes place "halb vor und halb hinter der Wirklichkeit [. . .]; die Gestalten erleiden dabei ein Doppelschicksal: ein unwichtiges, das sich an ihnen vollzieht, und ein wichtiges, das sie nicht erfahren. Die Mehrzahl verbringt ihr Dasein im Vorfeld des Noch-nicht-Eingetretenen oder im Schatten eines längst unwiderruflich Vollzogenen."[36] Sylvester belongs to this category. He lives either in the past or projects into the future, bypassing the only opportunity for constructive activity: the present. The first critic, however, who became aware of the conflicting element in Schnitzler's work is Körner, who wrote as early as 1921: "Wider Willen fast scheinen sich diese Okkultismen dem Dichter aufgedrängt zu haben, denn sein waches Bewusstsein liebt dergleichen durchaus nicht."[37] Perhaps Schnitzler's own ideas in this respect will help to clarify his position: "Das Wesen der sogenannten okkulten Erscheinungen liegt nicht darin, dass sie geheimnisvoller sind als tausend andere, die wir nur darum nicht als okkult bezeichnen, weil wir sie gewohnt sind, sondern dass sie sich den uns bekannten Naturgesetzen nicht einfügen, sondern ihnen gerade zu widersprechen scheinen."[38]

It seems that Schnitzler uses the natural laws known to science as parameters to place so-called "occult phenomena" in their proper perspective. There appears nothing mysterious about them to him; the mystery is only in man's mortal concept of them, because not all natural laws are known to man as yet. Thus Schnitzler, the natural scientist, the realist, allows space to grow, and this is reflected in *Der Gang zum Weiher*. Its complex symbolism includes that aspect of the work which Michael Imboden, in his examination of Schnitzler's prose works, calls "die surreale Komponente."[39]

Although the concept of "Surrealismus" originates in a movement in French literature, Imboden found a quote by Maurice Nadeau which redefines the term and allows its application to certain works of Schnitzler: "Die surrealistische Gesinnung, d.h. die surrealistische Verhaltensweise kommt [. . .] zu allen Zeiten vor, sofern man sie als die Bereitschaft auffasst, das Wirkliche tiefer zu ergründen, ohne es damit sogleich transzendieren zu wollen [. . .]."[40] Seen in this context, surrealism in the work of Schnitzler helps to complete "das Bild der Wirklichkeit und bringt es zu einer Ganzheitsdarstellung."[41] This total picture by necessity includes also phenomena which defy rational explanation, interpreted by Imboden this way: "Der Surrealismus stellt eine Welt dar, die dadurch mehrdeutig wird, dass sie nicht nur Oberflächen-Realität darbietet, sondern auch das Geheimnis jenseits des Verständlichen miteinbezieht. Die Gestalten der Dichtung leben in einer Alltagswirklichkeit, die durch das Hervortreten des Hintergründigen, der Dinge hinter den Dingen, brüchig geworden ist."[42]

Surrealism can be discovered not only in Schnitzler's prose works, but also in his dramatic production, and increasingly so in his late dramatic works. In *Der Gang zum Weiher* emphasis is placed upon "die surreale Komponente" as it occurs in the symbolism of water, vision, and the tower, discussed in the following pages.

Water and vision: The pond had immediate attraction for Leonilda, Konrad, and Sylvester. They were physically drawn into its seeming magic water for various reasons, whereas the Sekretär, Anselma, and the Freiherr kept a physical distance, but their mental activity displayed a vivid imagination about the pool. The Sekretär calls the pond "Zauberweiher" (838), because he witnesses an event peculiarly different from any of his previous experiences with water. The forest path in his state of mind magically

seemed to continue for Sylvester directly underneath the water. In reality Sylvester is drowning, but Ungnad is not aware of it in this context. The spell of the water attracts him. The word "Zauberweiher" invites the immediate response from the Freiherr: "Wer sagt, dass hier ein Zauberweiher sei?" (838); yet, in his earlier conversation with Konrad he refused to give him direction to the pond because "Es heisst, der Weiher sei / Verzaubert, / Seit Märchenzeiten" (804). Adding to the "Märchen"-atmosphere, the Freiherr tells about evil spirits present there at night and nixies who are not necessarily from the spirit world, hinting at Leonilda's nocturnal dances (804-05).

The pond clearly has a deceiving influence upon the chancellor: Not only does he misguide Konrad by being vague regarding the existence of the pond, and by creating curiosity in Konrad with his reference to the nixies, but he is also duped by his own failing eyesight. His memory tells him the water "ist eher / Ein Sumpf zu nennen" (804), while Konrad can "swear" that he remembers from his childhood "Quellklares Wasser, wiesengrün umrandet, / Durchsichtig bis zum kieselblauen Grund" (804). At this point the Freiherr readily admits: "Vielleicht, dass Kinderaugen tiefer schau'n" (804), a comment prompted by his morning's activity in dictating another chapter of his memoirs. Dickerson, who correctly recognizes "that the eye plays a role only second to that of the pond,"[43] concludes that "in youth the chancellor had also enjoyed the mystic vision of 'Kinderaugen' and was able to grasp intuitively the common bond of humanity that joins all men."[44]

Indeed, in his case it was a special bond, for when they were twelve years old, the Freiherr felt a great sense of loyalty toward his playmate who was to wear the crown of the emperor later (751). This loyalty turned into a deep friendship with the emperor which seemed "ewig unzerreissbar" (783). As everything in human nature is subject to change, he learns that this "Band von Mensch zu Menschen [. . .] zerriss, wie jedes Menschenband" (783). There is a parallel yet different experience in Konrad's military life which draws again upon the water symbolism in the meaning of separateness. A small brook divides two opposing armies, and each side is carefully patrolled because they await orders to go to war against each other. Instead of feeling hostile toward one another, Konrad has found a friend of his age and rank across the water: "Und unbedenklich spinnt sich das Gespräch / Vertraut und heiter über das Gerinnsel, / Das uns zu Füssen weiter Grenze lügt" (763). They talked about everything and even embraced as friends and brothers before Konrad received orders to go to the chancellor and then to the emperor (764). But suddenly Konrad experiences a change. The friend becomes an enemy: his "Kinderaugen," which could see clearly to the depth of the pond before, suffer blurred vision; no longer are they a source of light, inspiration, and understanding: "Und nicht eher / Will ich ihm wieder Aug' in Auge stehn, / Als—meiner Schmach in Blut mich zu entsühnen— / Ich's mit gezücktem Degen darf und muss" (764).

Distrust and suspicion interfere with his intuitive nature. He questions the chancellor's honesty in his dealings with him, and when he finds Leonilda by the pond one night, he is uncertain two days later whether she may not have waited for somebody else, and wonders who may have seen her and been with her on other nights. He reasons that the place is "nicht eben unzugänglich" (808) and hardly doubts "dass auch vom Dorf ein Weg zum Weiher führt" (808). The chancellor, however, is convinced that nobody else ever saw his daughter because nobody knows the gate and the path "Und zu dem Weiher führt kein zweiter Weg" (749). Anselma, too, considers the path unknown to anybody and only sees a "weglos abgeschied'nen Weiher" (747), which lifts this location from the physical into the mental realm: it becomes a state of consciousness in the lives of certain characters. In fact, she equates this pond with "einem schillernd grünen Riesenauge" (747). It is the single eye which suggests one-pointedness and a spiritual equivalent to the possession of two eyes, which in human beings conveys physical normalcy.[45] Imboden calls this spiritual intuitive vision "Blick nach innen."[46]

According to Cirlot, it is the center of clairvoyance and vibrational perception. However, it also relates to the "symbolism of the number three: for if three can be said to correspond to the active, the passive, and the neutral, it can also apply to creation, conservation, and destruction."[47] All three processes are likewise related to the symbolism of water in the drama, constituting an ongoing cycle in nature from start to completion. The water has creative as well as conserving and destructive powers, forming a cycle in nature which also relates to the life cycle in man. Because of man's diverse emotional nature, life is complex. Schnitzler demonstrates this complexity in his drama *Der Gang zum Weiher.* Each character has reached a certain station in life which becomes the motivating factor for his human actions and interactions. Together they convey the author's concept of "Ganzheit," a total experience.

The life-giving forces of the pond have their complement in the human experience of love as it came to Leonilda and Konrad; while the destructive forces of the water correspond to death, as seen in Sylvester's case and to an extent in the clouded mind of the Sekretär. Anselma and her brother are the characters who are neither positively nor negatively affected by the pond. They observe everything from a distance: Anselma watched her niece from afar during the latter's nocturnal activity at the pond. Mayenau draws his sister into the darkness of the trees, as Leonilda begins her walk to the water another time. In their own personal experiences brother and sister come more closely in contact with the forces of fate than others, because they believe in such powers. An example is Anselma's status as an unmarried woman. Whatever happiness prevails in her life, she never experienced the joy of sharing it in an intimate one-to-one relationship. It is easiest for her to dismiss any future possibilities of companionship in the name of fate. There is a hint that Sylvester may

return for her sake, but Anselma has released this affinity from her mind: "Ich und er . . . / Wie lang ist das vorbei—wenn's jemals war!" (744). Time has indeed weakened Sylvester's memory because he addresses Leonilda with "Anselma?" (776), thus giving away, through gesture and the question mark in his voice, the difficulty he faces in associating the correct name with the right person. A second intervention by fate occurs toward the end of Act IV.

The Freiherr speaks of his guilt feelings toward Anselma for having prevented a possible marriage between the emperor and his sister, who, though equal on emotional and intellectual levels, "doch nimmermehr / Den kühnen Blick so hoch erheben durfte" (817). Anselma does not want unwarranted sympathy: "Hätt' ich mich für mich selber nicht bewahrt,— / Mehr als nur einem müsst' ich dann gehören. / Und dass ich's wusste, —das bewahrte mich" (818). Her brother's answer suggests a different viewpoint: "Und wär's vielleicht ein Dirnenlos gewesen, / Du hättest doch dein Frauenlosgelebt" (818). However, the question arises as to which of the two possible relations could have been meaningful to Anselma. Sylvester's negative attitude toward responsibility and commitment may have been more suggestive of a type of open marriage, especially in light of his suggestions to Leonilda (827). The question of "Dirnenlos" versus "Frauenlos" arises after Anselma and her brother have discussed the emperor and his unhappy marriage, which has just concluded. The Freiherr feels guilty toward the emperor also, for, in an effort to protect his own sister, he also guided his friend in another direction. The whole country might have experienced happier times had he not given distorted advice (818). Although these guilt feelings are self-inflicted, they constitute a heavy burden. In addition, the Freiherr was dismissed as chancellor, an event which for years unpleasantly interrupted his friendship with the emperor. Fate, therefore, has left its mark on both their lives.

Although the neutral attitude which Anselma and the Freiherr have toward the pond is more pronounced on the physical level, it should be pointed out that on the intellectual level Anselma is very active. Her intuition produces a prophetic vision three times in Act III. Intuitively she knows that Sylvester is serious about Leonilda (796). She also predicts that her brother will be reinstated as chancellor (796) and, at that time, should consider taking Leonilda along so that "a princely fate" (797) may be fulfilled, especially since the year of mourning for the death of the emperor's first wife has just ended (797). Anselma speaks "seherisch," according to Schnitzler's own stage instructions (797).

The end of Act V emphasizes Leonilda's intuitional gift again. In her mind's eye, the process of Sylvester's disintegration and return to the "All" speeds up "Und wesenlos zu nichts sein Bild verzittert [. . .] Denn keine Welle bringt, / Was jemals in des Weihers Tiefe sank, /

Nicht Ding noch Mensch bringt je die Welle wieder" (841). The "Ding," of course, may relate to the event in Konrad's childhood, when he lost Leonilda's ball, which never surfaced.

Sylvester and the Sekretär, on the other hand, are blind to inner vision and the truths that are revealed. In fact, the opening lines of the drama emphasize the "meist offenen, wie ins Leere schauenden Augen" (740) of the Sekretär. The same emptiness is present in Sylvester's eyes, for he is not able to remember his experiences from younger years for the purpose of adjusting to his present station in life. Instead, he had to undertake a long journey in order to read his diary notes again. By physically releasing page after page of his past into the fire, he believes himself able now to direct his efforts and aspirations to the present and to the future. But in his limited, ego-bound expression of life, Sylvester is imperceptive, unable to effect a release of the past intellectually. He is blind to the necessity of facing himself with honesty. It is impossible for him to recognize the natural progression in life from youth to age; neither can he see the difference between art and life, past and present. This intellectual burden in the end contributes to his self-surrender to destructive forces.

Among the minor figures Dominik deserves to be mentioned in this context. Although his physical station in life is only that of a servant, on intuitive levels he is more advanced than other characters in the drama. He has taught himself to concentrate on each letter that arrives in the mail: "Man lernt allmählich / Auch hinter unerbrochne Siegel schau'n" (741), which the Sekretär does not comprehend in its significance.

Even the term "Aug' in Auge" (764, 812) is used antithetically. On the physical level, Konrad wants to meet his enemy-friend "Aug' in Auge" in order to kill him; the chancellor, however, meets with the ambassador of the opposing country, on occasion that enables them to dissolve prejudice, misconceptions, inharmonies, arrogance and to step before the emperor as peacemakers (812-13). The chancellor, therefore, can be viewed as the balancing force in the drama. Not only does he influence Sylvester during his sudden outburst of passion for Leonilda, he also "cools off" temporarily Konrad's fanatic ambitions to involve his country in useless war with the neighbor. Although the Freiherr is not able to remove the blindness from their eyes—this task is one that each must do for himself according to his level of awareness, Mayenau's hospitality provides an opportunity for reflection.

Tower symbolism: It is probably no coincidence that the guestroom is located "im Turmgemach" of the house (772, 803), which at first is prepared for Sylvester's visit and later serves to accommodate Konrad. The tower, as well as the house, carries ancient symbolic meaning. House means consciousness. The idea of ascent and spiritual elevation is implicit in the tower which connotes transformation and evaluation. Unfortunately, Sylvester does not experience any change; he intends to run away from it, as indicated by his desire to return home on the same night he arrived. According to Cirlot, the tower "is a determinant sign denoting height or the act of rising above the common level in life or society."[48]

At the beginning of Act II, Sylvester has just returned to the life and social customs of his native city, and he now prepares to settle down with his mistress Alberta into marriage and parenthood. But he is still filled with misconceptions and distorted views about himself and his earlier life. He mentions his house "in der Residenz" in which he lived "So lang, bis man den Fremdling d'raus verjagt" (767) because his mother's ancestors came "aus fremden Land hieher gewandert" (767). He equates "Fremdes" with such negative terms as "verhasst," "niedrig," "gemein" without realizing that his erroneous thinking may have been the cause of his own flight into "fremdes Land." In his desire to rise "above the common level of life," Sylvester had submitted to self-imposed exile rather than ask his friends for help. It is Mayenau who interrupts Sylvester's distorted presentation to Konrad in an attempt to balance the scales of truth: "Kein Mensch hat dich verjagt" (768), he tells him, and had somebody tried, not only the law of the land but also his friends would have been strong enough to protect Sylvester.

This exile, however, was more than just physical distance from his friends and everything dear to him. It was at the same time an escape from his own self: "Mir selbst entronnen, / Ein and'rer wandelt' ich durch kühle, klare, / Von keiner Ford'rung überhang'ne Welt" (769). Although he was "Wunschlos und keinem als [sich] selbst verpflichtet" (769), he recognizes slowly that nothing was gained during these ten years: as a "fool" he left, and he is returning in like manner (769), for to run away from challenges is to never meet them. As he communicates his feelings to the Freiherr and to Konrad, he appears to reach a certain perspective over his life which helps him to untangle its intricacies.

However, the most important task of coming to terms with life's progression from youth to age seems to fail him. He takes his diary notes to the tower guestroom, the place of spiritual elevation, but he is not able to free himself from self-deception, from his concept that the power of language is superior to the intuitive insights of the inner eye and the human heart. Mayenau tries in vain to call Sylvester's attention to the power of the word which continues to linger in memory long after it has vanished from the page, but Sylvester does not accept memories at all. In his view memory is "Ein Ungestaltes, Niezu-Fassendes" (775), but the written word is "ein Zaubergriff" which connects "Verfliessendes, Verflossenes [. . .] / Und schafft, wenn's aus erfüllter Seele kam, / In übermächt'ge Wirklichkeit es um" (775).

Sylvester does not fit into the group of characters who, in Schnitzler's words, experience life three-dimensionally: "Man erlebt alles Wesentliche in dreifacher Art: im Vorgefühl (auch wenn man es nicht geahnt hat), in der

Erinnerung (auch wenn man vergass) und endlich in der Wirklichkeit: diese aber bekommt erst ihren Sinn in Hinsicht auf Vorgefühl und Erinnerung."[49] Because Sylvester rejects memory, he is never able to come to terms with reality in the present moment. Instead, he is afraid that in later years he might discover that his past, the youth of his life, is better than the aging process of the present. By burning his diary, he believes he can destroy the domination of the past because: "Heute bin ich meines Sieges noch gewiss, / Ob über's Jahr, ob ich es morgen wäre? / Drum sei es heut gelesen—und verbrannt" (775).

But the past is closing in before he has a chance to reach the tower guestroom to destroy it. Leonilda leads him back in memory to the time when she was a child listening to the fairytales he told her. She proves to him: "Ich weiss sie alle noch— / In Worten nicht, doch besser als in Worten. / Sie träumen stumm in meiner Seele fort" (777). She is the second person who tries to awaken Sylvester from his lifelong deception, to assist him in removing the blindness from his eyes which are the windows of his soul. Just as the pond reflects in its "Riesenauge" the truth of his soul, his inner being. Yet he is afraid of the truth. Finally, Leonilda urges him to look into her eyes and see the reflection of his true nature: "Und siehst du mir nur lang genug ins Aug', / Erblickst du selber durch den Maskentrug / Dein mir vertrautes, wahres Angesicht;—" (778). His poetic talent shall create a new beautiful fairytale, and it shall belong to both of them as a child is shared by father and mother (778). Little is she aware yet of the dual role which Sylvester would have to play as father: However, she is keenly aware that Sylvester would follow her "trotz aller Geister— / [. . .] üb'rall hin, wo's [ihr] beliebt" (781).

Later on the drama reveals that Sylvester's experiences in the tower have not brought him any closer to present realities, for his reaction is the one usual to him, that of flight in order to reach less complicated territory. "Die Menschen hausen meistens nur im mittleren Stockwerk ihrer Lebensvilla," observes Schnitzler with his psychological insight, "dort, wo sie sich behaglich mit guten Öfen und sonstigen Bequemlichkeiten eingerichtet haben. Selten steigen sie in die unteren Räume hinab, wo sie Gespenster vermuten, vor denen ihnen schaudern könnte; selten klimmen sie zum Turme auf, wo der Blick ins Tiefe und Weite sie schwindeln macht."[50] Sylvester's abrupt change of plans would indicate his uneasiness at the prospect of spending the night high up in the tower. He is mentally unprepared for any uplifting experiences. Schnitzler is aware of two kinds of people when he says: "Manche Leute freilich gibt's, die sich just im Keller aufzuhalten lieben, weil ihnen im Dämmern und Gruseln wohler ist als in Licht und Verantwortung, und andere wieder klettern gerne auf den Turm, um den Blick in unergründliche Fernen zu verlieren, die ihnen ewig unerreichbar bleiben."[51]

If the basement can be compared to the past, then Sylvester tends to remain there for fear of facing his present and future desires. He wastes the precious moment, the only time for him to fill with meaningful activity. But in his tower symbolism Schnitzler considers a third group of characters and comes closer to describing Sylvester's state of mind: "Die unseligsten Subjekte aber sind diejenigen, die zwischen Keller und Turm ruhelos treppauf und treppab rennen und die zum eigentlichen Wohnen bestimmten Räume verstauben und verwahrlosen lassen."[52]

This restlessness within Sylvester is a result of his nonchalant nature. During his carefree life he had crossed paths with Alberta numerous times, only to drift apart again after a while. This time he wants to create a permanent relationship through marriage because they are "des Schicksals vorbestimmtes Paar" (773). This is a deception when compared to the statement he makes to Leonilda later (829). Furthermore, he tells Mayenau they stay together "um immer wieder, nach erfüllter Zeit, / Aufs neu' zu scheiden" (773). Mayenau in his balancing nature issues a warning, indirectly pointing to the responsibility and commitment involved in marriage: "Und dennoch denkst du ernstlich an Vermählung?" (773), but his words fall on deaf ears. This insincerity on the part of Sylvester, together with the fact that he is suffering from self-deception, apparently is the cause of his sudden change in marriage plans. In Leonilda's presence he misunderstands every word she speaks, especially when she touches upon the concept of sin in life: "Mit seh'ndem Aug' den falschen Weg zu geh'n" (789). This Sylvester interprets to mean that the right path leads along Leonilda's side. "Hielt Treue mir dies wunderbare Kind? / Und stürzt aus ihrem glaubensjungen Herzen / Sich Glaub' und Jugend endlich auch in meins—?" (789), he says, conjuring up his youth again, which he said he had come to leave behind by burning the pages of his diary.

Konrad, on the other hand, has little trouble with the tower guestroom. He has his first sexual experience during this stay. As soon as the chancellor leaves him at the end of Act III, he frees himself from the idea of adolescence (805). Suddenly, he knows "Ich bin ein Mann" (805). However, in Act V he is faced with a challenge with regard to his newly gained consciousness of being an adult, when the Freiherr for reasons of political differences demands his sword. The sword, as Whittick explains, is the symbol of power, authority, protection, justice, and knighthood.[53] When taken away, these attributes would reduce Konrad again to the status of adolescent. But Leonilda intervenes in the name of justice to let him be a free man (834). It is this new state of consciousness which leads him without difficulties to the pond, where he finds Leonilda likewise ready for her first sexual experience. The hours Konrad spends in the guestroom up in the tower are filled with his memories of that joyful experience. However, with the awareness of manhood often comes that of jealousy, and Konrad proves to be no exception. Two days later he begins to wonder why Leonilda was not frightened when he suddenly appeared and disturbed her nocturnal devotion. Something else puzzles him: "Mir war, als hätt'st du mich, nein Leonilda, / Nicht eben mich—nein, irgendwen erwartet" (808). Leonilda's simple but serious answer does not satisfy him, for there may be other paths that lead to the pool, and if so, who has seen her emerge from the pond on other nights? When she playfully leaves this possibility open, Konrad at the height of his jealousy wants to die, but not without taking her life also (809).

Whenever the chancellor is not present to balance one-sided views, it is Leonilda who takes his place. As she stepped into this role with Sylvester, she now does so with Konrad. With distinct self-authority she places the situation in perspective: "Hab' ich in dem Augenblick, / Da wir verzaubert ineinanderglitten, / Zum Herrn dich über mich gesetzt? Gab ich / Mit meinem Heut mein Gestern und mein Morgen,—" (809), thus maintaining again the freedom of her own choice.

Her words are a firm rejection of Konrad's assumption that he now has a voice in what she does. She requires that he first earn the right through responsible behavior: "Nein? Jetzt gilt es erst zu werben. / Dein war die Nixe. Willst du auch das Weib,— / Mit Jünglingsfrechheit wirst du's nicht gewinnen. / Und auch die Nixe, gib nur acht, steigt wieder, / Wie sie emporgetaucht, hinab zum Grund" (809). Although Leonilda dislikes being called "Nixe," she now uses the word twice herself as a means to distinguish Leonilda, the woman, from the water sprite, an incomplete state of being. Seen in connection with the term "Jüngling," it indicates a state of spiritual incompleteness on both their parts; sheer sensuality without responsibility lacks the foundation of truly deep love that is desired in marriage. With the words "hinab zum Grund," she establishes the need to know more about her potential as a woman in order to feel the same harmony as she does with the forces of nature signified by the pond, which are the same forces that underlie the secret of life and love. Leonilda, this "âme indépendante et fiere," as Mme Derré characterizes her,[54] represents the woman of the future, who moves beyond the conventions of a romantic idealization of love and marriage.

Leonilda's awakening: Her experience with Konrad also provides better understanding of her own feelings toward Sylvester. Davis points out that "she wakes from adolescence and dreamy fantasy into the reality of womanhood. Before the encounter with Konrad at the pool, she is vague, uncertain, and remote in her mind [. . .]."[55] Such generalizations contribute little to the interpretation of this important character. It is necessary to recognize that Leonilda actually becomes aware of deeper levels within her nature. This awareness helps her to realize that her attraction to Sylvester was not based on love but admiration. In the beginning of the drama she insists to her father: "Er lebt in mir" (754), because she was inspired by Sylvester's fairytales and his spirited artistic temperament, which impressed her so strongly as a child that Leonilda, the woman, could not forget him. As a woman, she has reached a new level of maturity; she refuses Sylvester's marriage proposal in lieu of friendship, which seems to her "das edlere Geschenk" (825), begging him to reciprocate forgivingly: "Lass mich nicht entgelten, / Dass ich nicht früh'r

erkannt, was mich zu dir— / Das Kind schon übermächtig zu dir zog, / Und jenseits meines Irrtums bleib mir nah" (825). But mere friendship does not comfort Sylvester, who is longing for a youthful wife to regain his own youth. He does not understand Leonilda's new state of awareness and in fact is led to believe that she is "unter allen Frau'n auf Erden / [ihm] bestimmt von Anbeginn der Welt" (829). With these words he alienates her even more.

Leonilda is similarly upset at her father, who attempts to arrange a marriage ceremony to give his daughter honorably to Konrad before the young man leaves to meet an uncertain fate at the front. She however rejects even the thought of a wedding: "Verzeih, mein Vater, mir beliebt es nicht, / Mit wem's auch sei, so bald mich zu vermählen" (832). Without hesitation she grants to Konrad the same freedom which she desires for herself: "Frei zieh' er hin. Ich bleibe frei zurück. / Wie und—ob wir einander wiederfinden, / Weiss nur der Gott, vor dem wir uns vermählt" (832). Konrad accepts her terms, although he declares himself "feierlich verlobt" (836). However, when Leonilda emphasizes for the second time that Konrad should be free from any past memory to experience joyfully whatever life has in store for him (836), Konrad senses a note of farewell rather than a blessing or an assuring message from her heart that would give him courage during the lonely hours of his war mission.

Unity: The two parts of the play. In his desire to contrast matters of the heart with political issues, Schnitzler has carefully proportioned the two parts of the drama. It is unfortunate that this intentionally created balance of the plot has been mostly overlooked by Schnitzler critics. Körner insists: "Im 'Weihergang' ist das politische Geschehen, trotzdem es mit der Liebeshandlung im Grunde nichts zu tun hat, zu sehr ausgedehnt, macht sich mit seiner eigenen Problematik breit, benimmt der Haupthandlung Lust und Raum."[56] He fails to recognize that the "Haupthandlung" really spreads over two-thirds of the drama. In addition to the war issue pushed by Konrad and his father, the remaining part of the play deals with peace efforts on the part of the chancellor, as well as with the problem of friendship between himself and the emperor. This complexity is Schnitzler's tool to sharpen the conflict which arises from human action and interaction.

Further criticism is raised in terms of the various arguments. Körner asks: "Handelt es sich um das Problem des zum Weib erwachenden Mädchens? Oder um das der freien Frau? Um den alternden Mann? Um das Heimatproblem? Um den Pazifismus? Oder verbirgt sich der eigentliche Sinn des Stücks in dem wahnsinnigen Sekretär Ungnad [. . .]."[57] Schnitzler defends himself in a letter to Körner, dated July 11, 1927, in which he can barely hide his anger and annoyance: "Niemals ist ein Einfall in mir mit solch zwingender Einheitlichkeit aufgetaucht, vom ersten Augenblick an [. . .] waren die erotischen Vorgänge in die politische Atmosphäre gestellt, das Verhältnis des Dichters zum Krieger, des Kriegers zum Politiker, der Leonilda einerseits zum Dichter, andererseits zum Soldaten war mir von Anbeginn an das Wesentliche, unter einem anderen Himmel als dem, den ich über sie gespannt habe, konnten die seelischen Vorgänge, auf die es mir ankam, sich überhaupt nicht entwickeln [. . .]."[58]

Consequently, the drama does not outline a single problem, but deals with the complexity of life which affects human conduct. Schnitzler's insight into human nature reveals that there are no ready answers. He reproves Körner for not recognizing "die Notwendigkeiten der Verknüpfungen und die Verknüpfung der Notwendigkeiten" which "'hätten Ihnen aufgehen müssen."[59] Furthermore, he clarifies Körner's question with regard to "Probleme": "Es handelt sich ja in der Kunst—verzeihen Sie die Selbstverständlichkeit—überhaupt a priori nicht um Probleme, sondern immer nur um Gestalten und um das Schicksal der Probleme, in den vom Dichter geschaffenen oder der Wirklichkeit nachgebildeten Gestalten."[60]

Liptzin's observation, on the other hand, is more applicable than Körner's, when he says: "[. . .] though Schnitzler fails to solve the important questions which he poses, he does remove a maze of prejudices with which these questions are normally surrounded, so that they stare at us in their sphinxlike majesty."[61] They remain questions, indeed, "[. . .] denn Lösungen gibt es nicht," according to Schnitzler.[62]

Polarities: Schnitzler's dialectic approach allows him to show various aspects within one character as well as the relationship to others in the play. Leonilda combines within her filial love such natural polar qualities as loyalty and rebellion. So too does Konrad project the same opposites in his war interest. Leonilda is devoted to her father but rebels when he tries to hasten her into marriage. She shows loyalty toward Sylvester, for she not only remembers him and his artistic talent, but feels that he lives within her and tells her father that the same poet will return, who left ten years ago (754). Yet, when Sylvester wants to bind her to his side, she withdraws in protest. Konrad, eager to prove himself as a warrior, is faithful to his father's interests which stand in sharp contrast to Mayenau's philosophy as a statesman. The reader and audience are already familiar with the chancellor's viewpoint from his conversation with Leonilda, who carries the war issue into the play as a distinct antithesis to the aspect of Eros, likewise initiated by Leonilda. Her visit to the village that morning did not result in play, as her father suspected, but in a political discussion because "ein schwarzer Reiter" came through the village with documents presumably containing a decision to go to war. Pensively the chancellor questions: "Entscheidung—für den Krieg?—[. . .] Befehl zum Angriff?" (753). He imagines it possible, especially since the proper moment—as so often in the past—had already been lost because of the emperor's indecisiveness. It has always been this way, always is, and always will be the same: "[. . .] inmitten des Zufrüh und des Zuspät / Ratlos einher, von jedem Hauch erschüttert" (753).

"Encore que moins nettement dessiné," Mme Derré has opportunity to show, "l'empereur de 'Der Gang zum Weiher' n'est pas sans rappeler un autre célèbre monarque de la littérature autrichienne, Rudolf II tel que le représente 'Ein Bruderzwist in Habsburg'."[63] In her excellent discussion she discovers relationships between Schnitzler and Grillparzer in that they both deal in their dramas with polarities such as loyalty and rebellion, hesitation and action. These associations between the two great Austrian dramatists have hardly been noticed in earlier criticism. Five years later Swales points out: "The shadow of Grillparzer falls unmistakable on Schnitzler's 'Der Gang zum Weiher.' Human action is seen as an inevitable caricature of the intention from which it sprang."[64]

Unfortunately, Swales does not support his idea beyond this general statement. It is important to recognize the close relationship between these two monarchs. The emperor in *Der Gang zum Weiher,* like Rudolf, is a wise man but incapable of acting. He does not like to make decisions and so creates within himself a conflict between "Pflicht und Neigung." He also tries to ignore the demands of a changing society, thereby resembling Rudolf closely.[65] In Schnitzler's play the emperor is drawn between war and peace, between introversion and the public life of a politician, between thought and action, leaning toward a contemplative rather than an active style of life. He, too, has to deal with the conflict between individual interests and the welfare of the entire empire. There exists an antithesis between earthly anarchy and cosmic order, between his role as a human being and that of an emperor. This latter conflict has been the reason for withdrawing his friendship from Mayenau. As emperor he developed a strong feeling of distrust, which the chancellor recalls not without sadness in a conversation with Konrad: "düst're Hast" was disguised "als Drang zur Tat, / Unschlüssigkeit als kluger Vorbedacht, / Schwachheit als Güte, müd' geword'ner Hass / [. . .] als Gerechtigkeit / [. . .] kaum bezwung'ner Ekel [. . .] als Menschenliebe" (759-60). In Rudolf's situation there exists also a conflict between Protestantism and Catholicism, but this religious aspect is not apparent in *Der Gang zum Weiher.*

Instead, more emphasis is placed on intuition, present in degrees within all major characters. Mayenau is the first one to emphasize "Ahnung" when he answers Anselma: "Muss Leonilda *wissen*? Ihrer *Ahnung* / Vertrau' ich mehr als and'rer Wissenschaft" (744). William Rey explains Schnitzler's dialectic approach in these words: "Als überzeugter Feind eines jeden Dogmatismus, ob nun religiöser oder wissenschaftlicher Natur, entwickelt er ein dialektisches Denken, das von der Einsicht in den gleichberechtigten Geltungsanspruch des Gegensätzlichen beruht und durch die Bejahung der im Dasein angelegten Widersprüche eine höhere Ebene der Erkenntnis zu gewinnen sucht."[66]

It follows that Schnitzler in his dialectic thinking recognizes a deeper meaning in that which is commonly considered negative. In his *Buch der Sprüche und Bedenken* he formulates this idea as follows: "Das Sinnvolle hat nur Bedeutung, ja Daseinsmöglichkeit durch die Annahme des Sinnlosen [. . .]. Gerade der Schmerz über das unvermeidliche Scheitern des Menschen kann zur Quelle innerer Bereicherung werden."[67]

Sylvester experiences this kind of pain in his sudden passion for Leonilda, but instead of gaining inner strength and enrichment, he is overcome by despair. His polar opposite, Konrad, the warrior, is not successful in his political mission and withdraws to a position of rebellion, but in the end he is able to reconcile the differences with Mayenau. For the third time within seven weeks, he carries the same message to the emperor and this time invites the ex-chancellor to accompany him in order to lend more force and urgency to the task at hand. But Mayenau, who was forced to leave his political appointment seven years ago (759), declines his help. Even after he is reinstated as chancellor in Act III, he does not share Konrad's philosophy of war, namely, that this hostile encounter is an inevitable destiny. Instead, Mayenau believes in the power of thought whose energies have influence upon the cosmos: "Ich fühle nicht geheimnisschwer vom Schicksal / Mich überhangen. Über mir die Wolke / Ist auch nur Nebeldunst aus Menschenland, / Und am Verhängnis über mir braut so / Mein Will' auch mit" (802). Unfortunately, his peace mission comes too late, war has already broken out. In loyalty to the emperor, Mayenau joins his regiment, thus restoring a better relationship with Konrad.

Significantly enough, the "dialectic," in Swales's terms, of intimacy and detachment, of attraction and repulsion, which is a central issue in Schnitzler's vision of human relationships,[68] also plays an important role in the chancellor's loyalty to his emperor. In his memoirs the Freiherr recalls a certain attraction to an intimacy with the young man who was to become emperor. His position as chancellor increased the closeness and friendship between them. Yet, when the emperor detached himself, Mayenau ceased to maintain an active interest in his country and its destiny. To him Schnitzler gives his own view of intellectual pacifism, that war is a waste of human values and the triumph of injustice (761). Much to Leonilda's surprise, her father draws a distinction between "Reich und Vaterland." When he fails to accomplish this task, then the political power struggle invites duality, as seen in the conflict between the emperor and the marshal. If the emperor decides against the marshal's recommendation to go to war, which was outlined in the letter Konrad delivered, then Konrad is convinced the army will decide in favor of the marshal (765). In this event the chancellor speaks of rebellion, but Konrad calls it "obedience to the proper master" (765). Similarly, he is of the opinion that the letter to the emperor provided choice and not a threat, as Mayenau sees it.

This polarity between the conservative judgment of the older statesman and the liberal ideas of Konrad creates differences between age and youth. At the end of Act II Mayenau proclaims: "Und nach Jugend riecht die Welt!" (783); whereas Act IV ends with Konrad's disgusted expression: "Vergiftet ist die Welt von Greisenateml!" (806), an inner rebellion of youth against age. It is a sensi-tive issue with Mayenau, who corrects Konrad in his reference to Sylvester as "der sonderbare alte Herr" by saying: "Nicht eben alt, doch sonderbar, mag sein" (804). He needs to take this position, for whatever is said about Sylvester would also ring true for himself as Sylvester's friend. Konrad does not change his mind at all and indeed insists, when alone on stage later: "Ich bin ein Mann—und er ist grau und alt" (805), referring to Mayenau. Leonilda, on the other hand, looks at Sylvester differently. Interestingly enough, she is correcting her father: "Der, den ich meine, Vater, altert nicht, / So wenig jemals Jugend von ihm strahlte" (754). Age in her frame of reference is not an issue of chronology; she sees him in his spirit nature, forever young. Yet, at the end of the play she no longer has this idealistic view. Because of the most recent incidents of suicide and Ungnad's psychopathic behavior, the castle has turned into a nightmare for her, and she begs her father to be taken along to the court: "Vater, nimm mich mit dir. Dreifach gespenstisch / Schleicht Alter, Wahnsinn, Tod durch dieses Haus, / Nicht eine Nacht mehr will ich hier verweilen" (841).

Sylvester, however, knows that the storms of youth have gone by; his only chance to bring them back to life is by reading the diary notes, but the spirit of his youth (778-79) will not be redeemed, not even by way of Leonilda as a marriage partner. Twice Sylvester addresses Mayenau as "Freund meiner Jugend" (791), until he stands corrected "entschwund'ner Jugend Freund" and furthermore is reminded: "Schlimmer als alt—wir beide—nicht mehr jung" (792). The Freiherr, conscious of the limitations that age may impose upon him, agrees in the presence of Sylvester to accommodate himself to this situation of being no longer young on a physical level. These limitations, however, by no means have influence upon his mental capacities. He would call any man a fool if not "ein Geck" (793), because he knows that at this age a man may be able to conquer the heart of a teenage girl but not to keep her happy in marriage.[69]

Sylvester refuses to accept his friend's viewpoint, defending himself with these words: "[. . .] 's wär eine arme Welt, / Wenn Jugend alles wär'—" (822). This philosophy parallels that of Fenz, the old "Kammersänger" in *Komödie der Verführung*. Interestingly enough, Schnitzler discloses the age of neither of these two characters. The only reference with regard to Sylvester is contained in a letter to Brandes where he says: "In meinem nächsten Stück soll der neunzigjährige [sic] als Sieger übrig bleiben."[70] Because the final version of the drama did not grant the victory to Sylvester, it is perhaps safe to assume that Sylvester was not ninety years of age either, possibly closer in age to Mayenau. Schnitzler, of course, addresses himself to the problem of age and aging numerous times in his late dramatic work. His own conviction is perhaps best expressed in the letter cited above to Brandes: "[. . .] das Alter ist nur eine Intrige, die die Jugend gegen uns einfädelt."[71] But another cycle of seven years expired in Schnitzler's life between 1924 and 1931, which left Jakob Wassermann with a different impression. He visited Schnitzler six months before the latter's death and recalls the following: "Was ihn von Mal zu Mal tiefer bedrückte, war die Tatsache des Alters und Alterns, die er sich nicht mehr verbarg. Ich [Wassermann] las neulich ein entzückendes Wort von Alice Berend: Das Schlimme im Altern ist nicht, dass man älter wird, sondern dass man jung bleibt. Damit ist der seelische Zustand des alternden Schnitzlers umfassend gekennzeichnet [. . .]."[72]

Wassermann's statement reverses Mayenau's earlier convictions: "[. . .] schlimmer als alt [. . .] nicht mehr jung" (792). This really amounts to a matter of attitude toward the complexity of this problem. Wassermann seems to come to the same conclusion about Schnitzler, when he writes: "[. . .] Mit jedem Atemzug wehrte er sich trotzig und angstvoll gegen das unerbittliche Gesetz, bis zum Zorn, bis zur Paradoxie oft, wobei zugleich der Arzt in ihm, der Denker, das aufsässige Kind zur Ordnung rief."[73]

Not only is Schnitzler the thinker at work in an attempt to come to terms with this problem, but especially Schnitzler the poet. Freud offers the following consolation in a letter to him: "Zum Schluss aber—ich weiss nicht ob Sie dieses Trosts bedürfen—lassen Sie sich sagen, dass der Dichter später altert als gewöhnliche Menschenkinder, und dass nach dem Dichter noch der Denker herauskommt."[74] Earlier, however, it was the poet whom Freud jealously admired in Schnitzler, because this poetic talent seems to have given Schnitzler access to knowledge which opened up for Freud only after laborious efforts of scientific research.[75]

This knowledge is based upon Schnitzler's dialectic approach to presenting a problem. The anger and indignation which Wassermann spoke of are not Schnitzler's last words about the deficiencies in human existence, such as age. "Auch Leid ist Gnade," we read in *Der Gang zum Weiher* (789). And his aphorism in *Buch der Sprüche und Bedenken* underlines this statement even further: "Dass wir geschaffen sind, das Unfassbare zu fassen und das Unerträgliche zu ertragen—das ist es, was unser Leben so schmerzvoll und was es zugleich so unerschöpflich reich macht."[76] It is truly an acceptance of human existence in all of its contradictions which Schnitzler stresses. In *Der Gang zum Weiher,* Mayenau is the character whose wisdom strikes a perfect balance between Konrad's unstructured vitality of youth and Sylvester's inability to see his age in proper perspective. His philosophy reveals a firm belief in the power of the spirit, which allows life's energies to expand within the context of responsibility and commitment. Friedrich Wilhelm Kaufmann observes this polarity of youth and age in a similar way: "In 'Der Gang zum Weiher' aber wird eine Synthese der ziellosen Vitalität der Jugend und der rückwärtsschauenden, begrifflichen Unlebendigkeit des Alters in der Forderung und Schaffung eines Jugend und Alter gemeinsamen höheren Zieles gewonnen."[77]

It is certainly exaggerated to say that the problem of aging forms the center of the drama, as Körner does.[78] Rey recognizes the situation more accurately when he stresses

Schnitzler's view of the adventurer: "Es ist aber bezeichnend, dass sich in dieser Periode die Kritik Schnitzlers am Abenteurertum noch verschärft [. . .]. Hier wird der Abenteurer, auch wenn er Künstler ist, entlarvt als der grosse Egoist, der nie ein Opfer gebracht hat, der nie wahrhaft geliebt hat."[79] Therefore, Mayenau and Sylvester are opposite yet complementary characters; opposite because the chancellor is a man of action and not an egoist, a combination rather rare in Schnitzler's work; complementary because he, too, is unable to comprehend women's souls. He misunderstands both Leonilda and his sister Anselma. Worried by the thought that he might have sheltered Anselma too well, he now is in a hurry to arrange for Leonilda's marriage to Konrad. But neither as father nor as brother could he fulfill their destinies. Schnitzler goes with his ideas beyond the customs of the day, because in his drama each woman is responsible for her own life and essentially accepts the freedom of her own choice. But Mayenau is motivated in all his actions by a sense of responsibility, whether it be the war issue or more sensitive emotional matters within his own household.

In this respect too he is the opposite of Sylvester who really wavers between frivolity and responsibility. Most of his frivolous life has been given to debonair selfish pleasures. He has never committed himself beyond the narrow limits of "I, me, and my," and even now he withdraws from his commitment to Alberta. Herbert Lederer, discussing the problem of ethics, finds other ethical concepts which Schnitzler arranges in contrasting pairs such as: "Altruismus und Egoismus, Erlebnis und Sensation, Sachlichkeit und Opportunismus, Stolz und Überheblichkeit."[80] Each one of these concepts can also be found in *Der Gang zum Weiher,* for they are motifs, all connected to the central conflict in human relationships.

Another form of polarity can be recognized in the "Doppelgänger" motif, discussed by Swales.[81] Schnitzler presents this motif in different variations. Konrad, for instance, was attracted to the young man in the opposing army because they shared many interests; but when war is declared, he is eager to find his "Doppelgänger" again and destroy him, thus cancelling human relations in favor of political differences. Leonilda, on the other hand, feels Sylvester's existence as another part of her own being. Early in the play, she tells her father "Er lebt in mir" (754); later she urges Sylvester to capture his true self in the reflection of her eyes in an effort to erase his false identity (778). Sylvester, who for the most part cannot look beyond the periphery of his personality, constantly compares earlier images of himself or escapes from them. He tells his friend: "Mir selbst entronnen, / Ein and'rer wandelt' ich [. . .]" (769). The purpose of reading his diary notes again is "Den, der ich bin, an dem zu messen, der / Ich einmal war" (775), a false competition within himself. His own fierce egocentricity, the only thing he is conscious of, culminates in the encounter with the Sekretär. In him Sylvester tends to see his own "Zerrbild" (787). Andreas Ungnad is Schnitzler's most extreme version of subjective ideals. The "confusion of dream and reality borders on the insane," one reads in Liptzin's account.[82] Ungnad has strange notions about himself and the world: "[. . .] wenn ich sterbe, stirbt / Die Welt mit mir.—Herr Sylvester Thorn / zerfliesst in nichts, wenn ich mich von ihm wende" (786). Just the opposite occurs, however, and Swales describes it in this way: "Significantly, the collapse into total insanity of the Sekretär is parallel to and in part caused by the collapse of Sylvester Thorn."[83]

At the expense of any social relationships, this solipsist cultivated such extreme indulgence of and concern with the self that at the death of his only contact he sank into total oblivion also. Schnitzler's aphorism in *Buch der Sprüche und Bedenken* sums it up best: "Manche flüchten sich in den Wahnsinn wie andere in den Tod:—und beides kann sowohl Mut als Feigheit gewesen sein."[84] Sylvester's death is linked with the water of the pond and can be interpreted as his desire for purification rather than as a lack of courage.[85]

Other polarities in the drama are Anselma and her niece Leonilda. They are opposites in age and in their relationship to Mayenau and to the established order he represents. Anselma's cautious nature conforms to the rules of society. Susanne Polsterer, discussing the symbology of names in her study of women, asks the question: "Sollte es ein blosser Zufall sein, dass die einzige Aristokratin, die virgo intacta bleibt, weil ihr Bruder liebevoll aber streng über ihre Mädchenehre wacht, den Namen Anselma trägt, das bedeutet: 'Gott als Helm,' von einem Gott beschirmt?"[86] She ignores Anselma's own assessment with regard to "brüderliche Strenge" (818). Of her own choice Anselma leads "a useful life," Willa Schmidt points out, "is fulfilled and happy in her own way, and is loving and perceptive where others are concerned."[87] It is her own choice to forgo any intimate relationship (818).

Leonilda, however, is searching to find different ways. She is "an excellent example of Schnitzler's increasingly positive feelings about emancipation of women."[88] Though Leonilda, "the nixie," has given herself to Konrad, the woman Leonilda does not want to enter a permanent relation with him, sanctioned by either Church or State. The intimacy experienced with Konrad does not leave her with feelings of remorse, either; she only answers to her own conscience, which Liptzin considers as "inner fulness" or "conforming to the laws of her personality."[89] Boner, who was the first among critics to see Schnitzler's attitude toward women in realistic perspective, explains the change within Leonilda this way: "[. . .] sie gewann Konrad [. . .] die Übertragung des Glaubens an einmalige Idealität in gläubige Bereitschaft jedem Lebendigsein gegenüber. Sie wirft die Fesseln der Konvention von sich, da sie die wertvollere Fessel ihrer eigenen Konzessionslosigkeit fühlt. Sie vermag die Tragik eines Einmaligen durch die Annahme des Vielmaligen aufzuheben."[90] Boner's sensitive observation with regard to Leonilda's sexual behavior represents a sharp contrast to Polsterer's semantic interpretation of Leonilda's name: "Ich würde ihn als Leon + Hilda deuten, die 'Löwenkämpferin.' Die Kaltblütigkeit, Rücksich-

tslosigkeit und Entschlossenheit mit der die erst 19-jährige Baronesse im 'Gang zum Weiher' um die von Schnitzler's Frauen so hoch gehaltene völlige sexuelle Freiheit kämpft, würde jedenfalls diese Namensdeutung rechtfertigen."[91]

Attributes such as "kaltblütig" and "rücksichtslos" can hardly be proven through textual evidence. Leonilda's role in the drama is that of an emancipated woman who desires the freedom to choose and to decide her own fate, just as Anselma exercised choice to experience her life in harmony with her inner nature. Their physical desires are, of course, on opposite ends of the scale, perhaps as a result of age difference. On mental levels, however, Anselma and Leonilda are complementary characters. They both have highly developed intuitional gifts, and lead strong inner lives which give them self-acceptance and stability. Leonilda's nocturnal dances by the pond may be considered as freedom to express one's inner feelings in line with Wolfdietrich Rasch's findings about the dance, which he considers: "[. . .] als Mittel der Befreiung und Ausdruck jener geistigen Freiheit, Freiheit der Frau [. . .] als Ausdruck der übermässigen und nicht aussprechbaren Spannung."[92] The movements of the individual body and soul find expression in the dance and "mit diesem individuellen Ausdruck ist der Tanz zugleich Verbundenheit mit den überpersönlichen, universalen Mächten, mit den—wie man damals sagte—cosmischen (sic) Kräften."[93] Anselma quite accurately sensed Leonilda's spiritual experience and felt it was "kein Menschenantlitz" but "Blick des Gottes" (748). Rasch calls it "die Verbundenheit alles Lebendigen, der grosse Zusammenhang"[94] which made itself known to Leonilda. Seen in this larger context, the dance symbolizes "Lebenstanz" which never ends, but Rasch points out "seine symbolische Darstellung durch den Tanz eines einzelnen Menschen endet, wie das Einzelleben, mit dem Tod."[95]

Comparison with other late dramatic works: Schnitzler used the motif of the dance in addition to other symbols in the previous drama *Komödie der Verführung* as well. Each situation, however, is unique, so that a comparative study is in order. Leonilda carries out the dance in the quiet of the night, as if spirit was dancing through her. The joy which she expresses during the dances, as observed by Anselma from afar, signifies a sense of harmony with herself and the world around her. This harmony is also with her during the day, when she frequently strolls through the meadows to pick flowers and explore nature.

The dance that ends in death for Aurelie, who is only six years older than Leonilda, was imposed upon her by Falkenir, who gained pleasure in watching her dance first with Max and later with Gysar. It was not a spiritual dance, although it likewise took place near the waters of a pond in the park. It became a fateful dance for Aurelie, for it changed the direction of her life. Her dance movements emphasized her youth and so prompted Falkenir to withdraw his marriage proposal. His action pushed Aurelie into a state of bewilderment. Gysar took advantage of her confused state of mind, from which she never recovered, and eventually she and Falkenir ended their lives by drowning. Leonilda, who is balanced on physical, mental, and spiritual levels, understands the concept of self-authority increasingly as the play unfolds. Aurelie, on the other hand, is motivated by a feeling of insecurity, hiding her true self behind masks. When a critic fails to recognize these subtle psychological differences which Schnitzler so carefully develops in the two dramas, it is easy to draw superficial conclusions such as the one in Körner's evaluation of Aurelie: "[. . .] sie nimmt sich bloss Freiheiten heraus, sie handelt nicht in einer selbstverständlichen Ungebundenheit, sondern aus Trotz und Widerspruch [. . .]."[96]

Willa Schmidt has corrected Körner's viewpoint with regard to Leonilda: "He thereby both distorts the character and misses the author's message, i.e. that women share with men not only the need to express their sexuality but also the desire to determine for themselves what course their lives will take regardless of their experience in this realm, rather than being compelled to bow to a hypocritical social code."[97]

The water symbol also pertains to both women. Whereas Leonilda is reticent about the refreshing bathing activity at night which leads her into the dance afterwards, Aurelie speaks freely about her boating on the ocean. To Falkenir, she relates her ability to hear "die ewigen Stürme rauschen" (964-65), just as he first confided the same phenomenon to her (872).

With regard to the contrasts between Mayenau and Sylvester, Schnitzler uses similar configurations in each of his late dramatic works, but his characters seem to grow older with each play he writes. Andrea and Casanova in *Die Schwestern oder Casanova in Spa* are young; the dominant male characters in *Komödie der Verführung* are about forty; in *Der Gang zum Weiher* and *Im Spiel der Sommerlüfte* they are in their fifties. The dialogs between these characters often express Schnitzler's deepest feelings and wisest thoughts. Liptzin compares them with Schnitzler, who is also growing older and observes that "they change form and clime, but they rarely leave him. They point to a dualism in his nature."[98] On the other hand, one must guard against identifying the author too closely with the characters he has created and the opinions they put forward. As Schinnerer points out: "Every creative artist will resolve the complexity of his nature by creating a variety of characters all of whom may be to some extent his spiritual and intellectual offspring."[99]

With regard to the major male characters in both dramas, *Komödie der Verführung* and *Der Gang zum Weiher*, Schnitzler contrasted youth and age. Arduin would like to marry Aurelie but is refused in favor of Falkenir, the older of the two. Konrad, on the other hand, who had no marriage plans at all upon his arrival at the castle of Mayenau, was "married before God" to Leonilda one night by the pond. Both men share a similar childhood experience in that they recall pleasant hours with their playmates at the pond (855, 803). Falkenir in turn did not believe in his

"Spätglück"[100] and allowed his doubts to destroy not only a potentially happy marriage but also both their lives through drowning. An antithetical situation exists in *Der Gang zum Weiher*. The aging poet Sylvester Thorn reaches confidently for a "Spätglück," but is not able to capture it and so ends his life by drowning likewise.

In both dramas, therefore, water and death by drowning play a significant role. For Aurelie and Falkenir it is a joyful moment as they swiftly sink beneath the surface of the sea, "as if they were kissing," and smiling "blissfully" (973). For Sylvester it is "ein Gang zum Weiher" in utter loneliness and disappointment just in time to save his dignity, as the Freiherr puts it (840). Sylvester's name is significant. Sylvester is the patron saint for the last day of the year—in the drama Sylvester lives the last day of his life. In both of these works water transcends its natural qualities in that "Nicht Ding noch Mensch bringt je die Welle wieder" (841), predicts Leonilda, whereas Gilda knows with certainty "noch in dieser Nacht wird die See beide an den Strand bringen" (973). However, the Direktor had commented earlier that only "die irdischen Ursprungs sind, die werden von den Wellen ans Ufer gespült" (934), and indeed, when Gilda's mother drowned, the sea did not return "ihre sterbliche Hülle" (934). Gilda like her mother spends much time in the water, earning the description "Nixe," an epithet she shares with Leonilda as well.

The significance of the pond has already been discussed in this chapter, but it is also a central motif in *Komödie der Verführung*. In both dramas, emphasis is placed on the fact that no other paths lead to the pond (749, 808, 853), which would indicate that only certain characters are attracted to the pool. Indeed, these waters effect changes of inner direction not only within the lives of Leonilda, Konrad, and Sylvester, but also within Falkenir and, most ominously, within Aurelie. She lost her mother's necklace near the pond, where Max found it and returned it. If she were superstitious, Falkenir suggests, she would not wear it again, or she would throw it into the pond (873). At this point in the play, Aurelie is still in control of herself and her life, and does not follow this joking advice, but at the end of Act I she "löst ihren Schmuck, wirft ihn in den Teich" (889), thereby symbolically giving away authority over her life, self-identity, personal freedom, and power of choice.

A certain magic surrounds the ponds in both dramas. Leonilda asks Konrad: "Weisst du nur, ob ich mich selbst dir gab" (809). A similar question arises within Max, but he feels that Aurelie gave him "unendlich viel—nur nicht (sich) selbst" (897). Judith reminds Max of her individuality in a way similar to Leonilda's with Konrad (865). In each situation the woman character seems to view her experience remotely, removed from reality into a world of dreams.

Related to the pond is the park, present in both dramas, and the significance of the tree symbol. "Alleen" are frequently mentioned in *Der Gang zum Weiher*.[101]

Sylvester was most creative when strolling with Leonilda down the "Alleen" to tell her fairytales. Leonilda's creativity inspired her dances under the trees by the pond. Mayenau and his sister Anselma seek shelter under the trees so as to remain unseen by Leonilda as she starts her "Gang zum Weiher" (796). In **Komödie der Verführung** all important aspects of the plot take place in the park under the trees (Act I).

The obvious symbolism about the tree is that it is capable of developing from a small seedling into a large, upright, calm, stable, sturdy plant with its roots firmly anchored in the ground. In that respect the symbolism relates to man and his ideal relationship to life. When man has strong roots, firm values, he is able to withstand the storms of life by drawing upon inner resources. Mayenau and his sister Anselma are examples. As father, he has been able to impart this secure feeling to his child Leonilda. Aurelie, on the other hand, experienced insecurity on account of an unstable household because of unfaithful parents. She conducts her own life without firm values. The adventurous characters such as Sylvester, Arduin, Gysar, Santis, and Casanova fall short of the qualities attributed to the tree as well. "The tree is one of the most essential of traditional symbols," points out Cirlot. "In its most general sense, the symbolism of the tree denotes the life of the cosmos: its consistence, growth, proliferation, generative and regenerative processes. It stands for inexhaustible life, and is therefore equivalent to a symbol of immortality."[102]

Schnitzler rarely elaborated on the question of immortality beyond his term "Aufhebung des Individuums ins All" for reasons he conveyed to Körner in his letter of July 11, 1927.[103] But as a psychologist he is interested in what Rey formulates as "Undurchdringlichkeit der Zusammenhänge" and "Ganzheit des Lebens."[104] It is the author's "Staunen vor dem einfachen Sein" which Rey considers a significant trait of Schnitzler's "religiosity."[105] "Wenn er es als Agnostiker auch ablehnt, den Schöpfer näher zu definieren," Rey continues, "der Ehrfurcht vor der Schöpfung kann er sich doch nicht entziehen."[106]

Along similar lines, the symbol of lilac branches is used in both plays in an intriguing way, which rules out any argument suggestive of coincidence. From the many spring flowers Schnitzler selects lilac, a flower which prevails in many love songs as a symbol of spring and love, just as its scent permeates a garden. In **Komödie der Verführung** it is Max who shares his branches with the women who invite him later for closer relationships.[107] Twice Aurelie mentions "den Duft des Flieders" (890, 964), which influences her senses and allows her to glide willingly into the arms of a lover. The lilac branches in **Der Gang zum Weiher** serve to decorate the guestroom for Sylvester. Although the maids handle this task, they are directed by Leonilda who also watches carefully to make sure they are fresh each day (741-44). Because Leonilda worships the ideal poet in Sylvester and later rejects any closer relationship with him beyond friendship, it would be farfetched to assume sexual overtones similar to those of **Komödie der**

Verführung.[108] The wilted lilac branches in **Der Gang zum Weiher** have symbolic importance in this respect. Sylvester's spring of life has long passed and his efforts to win Leonilda's love are likewise in vain, as predicted at the beginning of the drama symbolically through the wilted lilac in his room.

Not only symbols but also trends of thought provide a foundation for comparison in Schnitzler's late dramatic works. Just as the symbols imply deeper levels of meaning, trends of thought are re-examined for the purpose of deeper understanding and awareness. Ideas which in **Komödie der Verführung** were presented in triangular arrangement are considered as polarities in **Der Gang zum Weiher.** Foremost in Schnitzler's mind rank the ideas of war and peace because he wrote both dramas under the influence either of war or of its devastating consequences for Germany and Austria. In **Der Gang zum Weiher** this idea comprises one-third of the drama. The chancellor has played a great part in the history of his country and is shown now in his peacekeeping efforts, combining his capacity both as a diplomat and as a wise friend to the younger generation, represented by Konrad, who can see only the excitement of war. **Komödie der Verführung** emphasizes the powers at work in an effort of profitmaking by plunging the country into war; the drama also pointed out the irresponsibility in diplomatic and banking circles as represented by Arduin and Westerhaus. The ideas in **Der Gang zum Weiher,** however, move beyond the war issue to register also the abuse of the word "Vaterland," which Schnitzler had so often noticed in German and Austrian power politics. Alfred Apsler points out that the author "differentiates between Vaterland and Heimat" and explains that "'Heimat' is the noble conception of home, 'Vaterland' the catchword of the politicians."[109]

Schnitzler expresses this viewpoint through Mayenau, the wise statesman. Davis, on the other hand, emphasizes a moral adversity within Mayenau: "Once he has left his retirement, however, and moves in the field of power and action [. . .] the land becomes his fatherland, when he can use it to express his demand for power [. . .]. Albrecht sees only a field for action whether in war or peace."[110] All indications in the drama, nevertheless, point out that Schnitzler's idea of pacifism was not intended to be merely an intellectual exercise.

The idea of "Heimat" is also picked up again in the context of love relationships, as a temporary place of peace and immunity to which a loved one can return after physical and emotional detours. In **Die Schwestern oder Casanova in Spa** it was Casanova who introduced this idea and considers that place as "Rast am Weg" (733), since in his frame of reference a more permanent place would pose a threat to his concept of freedom. In **Komödie der Verführung,** Falkenir has the desire to provide a temporary "Heimstatt" for Aurelie, "deren Frieden niemand stören darf" (952). In **Der Gang zum Weiher** the term "Heimat" recurs most frequently.[111] The emotionally most intense expression comes from Sylvester, who would be so happy to watch over Leonilda's sleep even if it was only for one night (827).

Schnitzler judges progressively more severely the behavior of his "Abenteurer," for the deeper problem is the question of commitment and responsibility. These adventurers try to preserve a state of isolation because they shy away from either inner or outer relations with other human beings, in an effort to maintain unlimited freedom. They limit their emotional involvement to short periods of time and never attempt continuity and lasting relationships. Marriage looks to them like all other ties to family and country, that is, an encroachment on their personal freedom. In no way are they prepared to commit themselves to another being because they do not want to shoulder responsibility or any sharing-caring attitude. This desire for noncommitment is apparent not only in relationships with other human beings, but in other areas as well. It certainly is not by chance that these adventurers mostly belong to independent professions, for they would reject any activity that tied them down to regular working hours and a permanent seat of residence.

Müller-Freienfels concludes: "Gerade zu den Beziehungen zu ihren Mitmenschen zeigt sich immer wieder, dass sie nicht nur die äusseren, sondern ebenso sehr auch die inneren Bindungen fürchten. Sie scheuen im Grunde jedes echte, tiefgehende Gefühl für einen anderen Menschen, da sie auf diese Weise innerlich an ihn gebunden werden würden."[112] He poses the question whether or not these people really stand with both feet in the stream of life, and suggests: "Im Gegenteil, ein solcher Mensch, der niemals etwas von seiner inneren oder äusseren Freiheit einbüssen möchte, distanziert sich im Grunde vom Leben, will sich in einem Abstand halten. Dieser Gedanke der Distanz vom Leben und von den Menschen ist bei den meisten von Schnitzler's Personen auch der tiefste Sinn ihres gesamten Strebens nach Bindungslosigkeit."[113] Bernhard Blume, who discusses the problem of distance also, feels that these characters stay away from the "Strudel des Daseins [. . .] der ihnen unausweichlich mit Vernichtung droht."[114] He attributes this behavior to the life style "des Lebensschwachen, der in der Flucht sein Heil sucht."[115] Casanova is able to avoid serious consequences,[116] but Falkenir and Sylvester pay with their lives. As will be seen in the last drama, entitled *Im Spiel der Sommerlüfte,* a summer rain clears the air and returns everybody to their senses before it is too late.

The idea of "Gespenster" and "Geister" from the past invading the present moment form a close connection. The common denominator would be "die Macht der Erinnerung." In the last act of *Komödie der Verführung* Aurelie fearfully raises this question, but Falkenir believes they are both strong enough to avoid recalling the past for the sake of a harmonious marriage. But he himself is not able to do it, even moments after Aurelie has left him to change into a bridal dress (966-67). In *Der Gang zum Weiher*

Schnitzler deals with these problems more in detail. Mayenau does not believe in "Geister der Vergangenheit" (762), yet tells Konrad about "böse Geister" which reign at night near the pond (804). But he is firmly convinced that "Erinnerungen" continue to glow (774), a fact he demonstrates most vividly by dictating his memoirs. Sylvester, on the other hand, discredits "Erinnerungen" (774), but "die Geister der Jugend" are so vivid in him that he needs to destroy them by fire in the hope that they may never return. Even Leonilda, who triumphed over Sylvester's "Geister" (781), wants in the end to flee her surroundings because they are "dreifach gespenstisch" (841) and quite real to her.

The question might be asked: Why was Schnitzler the rational scientist interested in these ideas? Ideas can be reduced to thought forms meandering mostly uncontrolled through the mind. As such they would fall into the same category of intuition and vision for which Schnitzler himself has the following definition: "Gewiss handelt es sich auch hier um nichts anderes als um eine nicht mehr zu kontrollierende Geschwindigkeit des Gedankenablaufs. Scheinbare Gleichzeitigkeiten von Eindrücken, die durch grosse Geschwindigkeit vorgetäuscht wird."[117]

To have a vision means to form a mental picture, "ein Bild." This idea of "Bild" occurs first in *Die Schwestern oder Casanova in Spa,* but it seems to become more important with Schnitzler as time went on. In this play the idea of "Bild" is central to the dispute between Anina and Andrea over the night she spent with Casanova, who had intended to be with Flaminia. Anina maintains that Casanova still takes along eternally "die Erinnerung dieser Stunde" (694), but Andrea insists "doch nicht dein Bild" (694), thus providing a basis to forgive and forget, because the whole affair can remain a secret between the two of them. "Erinnerung," therefore, is not identical to "Bild," although both are mental processes, because even Anina's picture would have to be a mental vision. In *Komödie der Verführung* the idea of "Bild" relates to Aurelie. The picture which Gysar painted of her and which she rejected at first for not representing her true nature, becomes more real to her as the play unfolds. In her outer life she lives up to the sensuality which Gysar's picture portrayed, until she finally transforms her entire being into the picture, thereby losing her inner balance completely. She reduces herself to "Maske und Lüge" (962) and suffers the consequences of this total rejection. The "Bild" is symbolic of replacing her self-image with a mask to hide behind. In her "Erinnerung," the devastating garden party at Gysar's house has grown into a mental monster, dangerously impairing her sanity. In this drama "Erinnerung" and "Bild" have become one and the same in a negative way.

The concept of "Bild" in *Der Gang zum Weiher* is related to Leonilda's idealistic vision of Sylvester. She tells him that in her mind's eye "dein ewig Bild hab' ich in mir bewahrt" (788). Looking beyond the personality, she beholds Sylvester's poetic soul which is forever perfect and pure. When he later pleads with her to marry him, she speaks about "dein edles Bild" (827), which refers to the never-aging spirit self of Sylvester. On the physical level, she knows that more than thirty or forty years of age difference are not a realistic basis on which to build a lasting marriage. At the end of the drama she speaks about Sylvester and visualizes how "wesenlos zu nichts sein Bild verzittert" (841)—perhaps as indication of Leonilda's concept of death. At that point all earthly riddles are resolved.

Connected with Sylvester is the idea of "Märchen" in this drama. Leonilda remembers the fairytales he told her in her childhood days, but he denies "Nein—Märchen waren meine Sache nie" (777). In Act V Sylvester renounces the idea of immortality as a fairytale and equates "Märchen" with "Lüge." In *Komödie der Verführung* the concept of "Märchen" received much more extensive attention. Since it was used there within the context of triangularity, one might conclude that Schnitzler redefined the idea of "Märchen" and narrowed it down again to its original meaning of telling stories, as Sylvester did before his exile.

In contrast to *Komödie der Verführung,* where the triangularities connected certain ideas with various characters, *Der Gang zum Weiher* emphasizes the characters in their triangular position. Mayenau stands between the emperor and Konrad, who is motivated by his father, over the issue of war and peace. Leonilda forms a triangle with Konrad and Sylvester with regard to the expression of love and marriage. Sylvester stands between Anselma and Leonilda in his effort to create a deeper relationship: the one with Anselma failed years ago; the one with Leonilda never gets started. Mayenau has a triangular relationship with Anselma and Leonilda in an effort to correct his mistake of overprotection.

The contrasts, however, seem to have been more important to Schnitzler, since he mentions them especially in his letter to Körner: "[. . .] das Verhältnis des Dichters zum Krieger, des Kriegers zum Politiker, der Leonilda einerseits zum Dichter, andererseits zum Soldaten, war mir von Anbeginn an das Wesentliche."[118] Many polarities are sharply delineated in the lines of various characters (759, 762). Especially significant is the contrast relating to the political part of the drama, i.e., the friendship between Konrad and the enemy soldier, and Mayenau and the emperor (763, 783), as well as the concept of "Aufruhr und Gehorsam" (765), "Treue und Verrat" (827), "Geisel und Gast" (830). Through Mayenau, Schnitzler emphasizes again his concept that opposition can be links of the same chain as "Wild und Jäger," "Herz und Pfeil," "Mörder und Opfer" (801), just as on ethical grounds "Schuld" is related to "Sühne," and "Verdienst" to "Tat" (801).

In summary, the results of the preceding analysis of the drama, *Der Gang zum Weiher,* add another view to Schnitzler's already established reputation as a writer concerned with complex issues. Imboden's conclusion regarding the prose works can also be extended to Schnitzler's late dramatic works: "Das scheinbar Immer-Gleiche der von ihm beschriebenen Welt hat weit auseinanderliegende Pole. Nicht wenigen seiner Gestalten gleitet plötzlich der feste Boden der Realität unter den Füssen fort; viele werden in die pfadlosen Bezirke des Geheimnisvollen hineingestossen. Von wem? Weshalb? Fragen, die in Hinsicht einer heilen Welt berechtigt wären, doch, auf doppeldeutige und unkontrollierbare Weiten bezogen, vergeblich gestellt werden."[119]

Considerable skill is required to treat in literary prose the complexity of this world, which extends, in Imboden's words, to far-reaching poles, often reaching beyond the area of scientifically acknowledged information, "that area of reality and truth which is not accessible to the cerebral capacities of man," as LoCicero formulated it.[120] The task seems even more complicated when the information needs to be compressed into drama form. But Schnitzler achieved it convincingly, proving that he is a better dramatist than critics have been willing to acknowledge. Imboden sees two factors as being responsible for Schnitzler's newly increasing interest in surrealism: "Nach dem Kriege verliert Schnitzler den Kontakt mit der Umwelt; sie versteht ihn und er sie nicht mehr. Ferner entfremdet ihn auch der fortschreitende Verlust des Gehörs den Menschen und dem Alltagsgeschehen."[121] While these points cannot be disputed, one should not forget that Schnitzler to the end of his life was interested in the events of the world around him. In *Der Gang zum Weiher,* he presents the rebellious activities of the young generation as an opposite to the peace-loving loyalty of the old statesman which, according to Rey, "demonstrieren Schnitzlers Bemühungen, sich für die Auseinandersetzung zwischen politischen Ideen offen zu halten."[122]

The idea of freedom formed an important aspect, for without freedom there cannot be individuality. But Schnitzler conveyed clearly his message that freedom in itself is no absolute value. It is connected to the question of responsibility and commitment, and the willingness of human nature to accept these premises. If the concept of freedom is misunderstood, it leads to selfishness and thus in the end to utter loneliness.[123]

Schnitzler's main concern in the drama, *Der Gang zum Weiher,* centered on the area of the I-Thou relationship, the all-important basis for the concept of the total human being. It is true, as Foltin points out, that the total human being is "not just the well defined, rational 'ego,' but also the rebellious, not conscious, subconscious, unconscious, irrational 'id.'"[124] But this human being, as total in itself as it may be, only leads a balanced, fulfilled life in its relationship to others through sharing of love on different levels as the highest form of living; for living means giving in its various ways—to be of service to others. This purpose in life, this high call, is hard to achieve, but being on the road to this goal is better than not trying at all. Schnitzler's characters in *Der Gang zum Weiher* show the degrees of effort in this respect. Liptzin describes this struggle most appropriately in the following way:

During our all too few years on earth, however, we make frantic efforts to escape from our absolute solitude. In work we find a drug that helps us to forget, but it is only during the intoxication of love that we are enabled really to break through the bars that separate individual existence. Schnitzler's men—cool, rational, ironic—may, at best, resign themselves to work and forgetfulness. His women, on the other hand, do, at times bridge the gulf between soul and soul; and in ecstatic abandon they do attain perfect communion with the All. His women are, on the whole, more courageous than his men. The latter hesitate, deliberate, weigh all possible risks, and seek to postpone their decisions. If forced to act, they try to minimize their responsibility and to avoid every possible consequence of their act. The women, on the contrary, answer the call of life heroically, brave all dangers readily, and lose themselves successfully in others. They, thus more easily, experience true love [. . .]. Western civilization for a long time emphasized male superiority, and thereby made man ever more self-centered and egoistic. While woman has retained her capacity to respond naturally, naively, instinctively, man has been handicapped by an overabundance of rationalization. Schnitzler's women want love, Schnitzler's men offer understanding.[125]

Schnitzler's interest in this complex area of the I-Thou-relationship continues in his last drama *Im Spiel der Sommerlüfte.* It is relatively unknown and appears to be merely concerned with the moods of its characters and their feelings about themselves and those with whom they interact. In the end, no drastic changes take place, no deaths occur, but great gains have been made in human understanding which was, after all, Schnitzler's own search in life. In his last drama, he turns further inward where life is truly lived.

Notes

1. Urbach, *Kommentar*, p. 195.

2. Bergel, *Brandes-Schnitzler-Briefwechsel*, pp. 142-143. Letter dated December 14, 1924.

3. Arthur Schnitzler, *Gesammelte Werke. Die dramatischen Werke*, Zweiter Band (Frankfurt am Main: S. Fischer Verlag, 1962), pp. 739-843. All quotes from this second volume pertaining to the text will hereafter be referred to by page number following the quote.

4. Cf. DW II, 1038; also Urbach, *Kommentar*, p. 195.

5. Urbach, *Schnitzler*, p. 127.

6. Körner, "Spätwerk," 82.

7. Harold D. Dickerson, Jr., "Water and Vision as Mystical Elements in Schnitzler's 'Der Gang zum Weiher'," *Modern Austrian Literature*, 4, No. 3 (1971), 24.

8. Körner, "Spätwerk," 70.

9. *Ibid.*, 83.

10. Liptzin, *Schnitzler*, p. 260.

11. Derré, p. 452.

12. *Ibid.*

13. Swales, *Critical Study*, p. 45.

14. Davis, p. 142.

15. Swales, *Critical Study*, pp. 45-46.

16. Dickerson, 24-36.

17. *Ibid.*, 25. Cf. Davis, p. 138: "This pool is mysterious and symbolically treated."

18. Juan Eduardo Cirlot, *A Dictionary of Symbols*, transl. Jack Sage (New York: Philosophical Library, 1962), p. 345.

19. *Ibid.*

20. "Natürlich ein Phallussymbol," determines Körner, "Spätwerk," 69 (footnote). Anselma does not go that far. She relates "ungefüger Block" to "Opferstein," which places its existence back in ancient times, prior to Christianity. Mayenau does not share his sister's view. For him it is a stone like a thousand others, standing at that particular spot by mere chance (DW II, 748).

21. Urbach, *Kommentar*, p. 37.

22. Liptzin, *Schnitzler*, p. 10.

23. Arnold Whittick, *Symbols — Signs and Their Meaning and Uses in Design* (London: Leonard Hill, 1971), p. 348: "Cleansing by water appears to have been a purification rite with many religions before Christianity, as it was with the Jews. In Christianity the symbolism of water has survived chiefly in the rite of baptism. Its significance appears to cover purification, regeneration or rebirth."

24. Lore B. Foltin, "The Meaning of Death in Schnitzler's Work," *Studies in Arthur Schnitzler*, eds. Herbert W. Reichert and Hermann Salinger (Chapel Hill: The University of North Carolina Press, 1963), p. 39.

25. Dickerson, 30. "Mystic awareness" is neither apparent to the senses nor obvious to the intelligence; it is spiritual insight, intuition. Cf. LoCicero, 18.

26. It is important to pay attention to the name symbolism related to Ungnad, which means "without mercy." He is treated with compassion by Mayenau, Sylvester and everyone he comes in contact with, but Ungnad does not have compassion for himself nor for others. He is ill adjusted and therefore incapable of overcoming.

27. The idea of separation in connection with water symbolism has also been mentioned by Whittick (p. 348), who points out that "water has also been considered symbolically with the significance of separation, because rivers and seas are natural barriers."

28. Kammeyer, pp. 104-05.

29. Cf. pp. 99f. of this study for a more detailed discussion of this important concept in Schnitzler's late dramatic work.

30. Rey, "Schnitzler," p. 253.

31. Richard Specht, *Arthur Schnitzler. Der Dichter und sein Werk. Eine Studie* (Berlin: S. Fischer Verlag, 1922), p. 153.

32. Seidlin, *Schnitzler-Brahm-Briefwechsel*, p. 28.

33. Cf. Herta Singer, "Zeit und Gesellschaft im Werk Arthur Schnitzlers," Diss. Wien (1948), p. 22.

34. Rey, "Schnitzler," p. 256.

35. Herbert Cysarz, "Das Imaginäre in der Dichtung Arthur Schnitzlers," *Journal of the International Arthur Schnitzler Research Association,* NS. 1, III (1968), 8.

36. Baumann, *Schnitzler,* p. 30.

37. Körner, *Gestalten und Probleme,* p. 171. "Okkultismen" relates to surrealism in the terminology used by Imboden.

    Cf. Specht, *Schnitzler,* p. 152.

38. Schnitzler, *AuB,* p. 73.

39. Michael Imboden, *Die surreale Komponente im erzählenden Werk Arthur Schnitzlers* (Bern, Frankfurt am Main: Verlag Herbert Lang & Cie AG, 1971).

40. Maurice Nadeau, *Geschichte des Surrealismus,* deutsche Übersetzung von Karl Heinz Laier, rde. Bd. 240/41 (Reinbek b. Hamburg, 1965), 8. Quoted by Imboden, p. 9.

41. Imboden, p. 9.

42. *Ibid.,* p. 11.

43. Dickerson, 30.

44. *Ibid.*

45. Cirlot, p. 95.

46. Imboden, p. 19.

47. Cirlot, p. 95.

48. *Ibid.,* p. 326.

49. Arthur Schnitzler, "Bemerkungen aus dem Nachlass," *Neue Rundschau,* 3 (1962), 351.

50. Schnitzler, *AuB,* p. 278.

51. *Ibid.*

52. *Ibid.*

53. Whittick, p. 329.

54. Derré, p. 372.

55. Davis, p. 141.

56. Körner, "Spätwerk," 70.

57. *Ibid.*

58. Schnitzler, letter to Körner, dated July 11, 1927, quoted by Davis, p. 185.

59. *Ibid.*

60. *Ibid.,* p. 187.

61. Sol Liptzin, "The Genesis of Schnitzler's 'Der einsame Weg'," *The Journal of English-Germanic Philology,* 30 (1931), 392-93.

62. Schnitzler, letter to Körner, quoted by Davis, p. 187.

63. Derré, p. 452.

64. Swales, *Critical Study,* p. 53.

65. Franz Grillparzer, *Ein Bruderzwist in Habsburg* in *Sämtliche Werke.* Historisch-kritische Gesamtausgabe, Part 1, vol. 6, ed. August Sauer (Wien: Verlag von Anton Schroll & Co., 1927), 182-83.

66. Rey, "Schnitzler," p. 251.

67. Schnitzler, *BdSp,* p. 139.

68. Cf. Swales, *Critical Study,* p. 45.

69. We recall that Flaminia already used the term "Geck" to refer to Casanova (DW II, 666), and Andrea uses the same word for him (p. 670).

70. Bergel, *Brandes-Schnitzler-Briefwechsel,* p. 143.

71. *Ibid.*

72. Wassermann, "Erinnerungen," 12.

73. *Ibid.*

74. Freud to Schnitzler, letter dated May 14, 1912, *Neue Rundschau,* 1 (1955), 96.

75. *Ibid.,* 95.

76. Schnitzler, *BdSp.,* p. 66.

77. Friedrich Wilhelm Kaufmann, "Zur Frage der Wertung in Schnitzlers Werk," *PMLA,* 48 (March 1933), 215.

78. Körner, "Spätwerk," 56.

79. Rey, "Schnitzler," p. 254.

80. Lederer, p. 76.

81. Swales, *Critical Study,* pp. 45-46.

82. Liptzin, *Schnitzler,* p. 244.

83. Swales, *Critical Study,* p. 46.

84. Schnitzler, *BdSp.* p. 86.

85. Cf. also Foltin, 42.

86. Polsterer, Section 3.3. She continues that "[. . .] die diversen süssen Mädels aus verschiedener Herren Länder dagegen Namen tragen wie Annie, Anita, Annina, Annette, Ninette [. . .]. Auch wissen wir ja aus verschiedenen Aussprüchen seiner Figuren, dass der Dichter sich wohl über die Bedeutung der Namen und ihrer Verbreitung Gedanken machte."

87. Schmidt, p. 310.

88. *Ibid.,* p. 316.

89. Liptzin, *Schnitzler,* p. 269.

90. Boner, p. 38. Cf. also Schmidt, p. 314.

91. Polsterer, Section 3.31 entitled "Semasiologische Deutung."

92. Wolfdietrich Rasch, "Tanz als Lebenssymbol im Drama um 1900," in: *Zur deutschen Literatur seit der Jahrhundertwende* (Stuttgart: J. B. Metzlersche Verlagsbuchhandlung, 1967), p. 64.

93. *Ibid.*

94. *Ibid.,* p. 77.

95. *Ibid.*

96. Körner, "Spätwerk," 62.

97. Schmidt, p. 314.

98. Liptzin, *Schnitzler,* p. 32. Cf. also p. 4.

99. Otto P. Schinnerer, "The Literary Apprenticeship of Arthur Schnitzler," *Germanic Review,* 1 (1930), 67.

100. Körner, "Spätwerk," 71.

101. Cf. pp. 777, 778, 784, 785, 796.

102. Cirlot, p. 328.

103. Quoted by Davis, pp. 186, 189.

104. Rey, "Schnitzler," p. 253. In Judeo-Christian theology, this is called the "Brotherhood of Man."

105. *Ibid.,* p. 252.

106. *Ibid.,* pp. 252-53.

107. Cf. pp. 860, 864, 878, 971.

108. Lilac in Schnitzler's work dates back to *Liebelei* (1896).

109. Alfred Apsler, "A Sociological View of Arthur Schnitzler," *Germanic Review,* 18 (1943), 105.

110. Davis, pp. 145-46.

111. Cf. pp. 755, 766, 767, 769, 770, 771, 772, 773, 782, 788, 789, 791, 792, 825.

112. Müller-Freienfels, p. 97.

113. *Ibid.,* p. 101.

114. Blume, p. 34.

115. *Ibid.*

116. Schnitzler's later prose work entitled *Casanovas Heimfahrt* (1918) catches up with the old adventurer and pursues him into death.

117. Schnitzler, "Gedanken über Kunst. Aus dem Nachlass," *Neue Rundschau,* 43 (1932), 37.

118. Schnitzler, letter to Körner, quoted by Davis, dated July 11, 1927.

119. Imboden, p. 125.

120. LoCicero, 18.

121. Imboden, pp. 124-25.

122. Rey, Schnitzler, *Späte Prosa,* p. 18.

Cf. Kammeyer's statement (p. 127 footnote 93) regarding Schnitzler and the first World War which shows a rather hasty assessment: "Die geistige Auseinandersetzung mit dem ersten Weltkrieg hat Schnitzler aus seinem dramatischen Schaffen ausgeschlossen; es existieren jedoch essayistische Aufzeichnungen aus seinem Nachlass [. . .]."

123. Cf. Rey, "Schnitzler," p. 262.

124. Foltin, 36.

125. Liptzin, *Schnitzler,* pp. 47-48.

Cf. also Boner, p. 8: "Es sucht nach dem internen Gleichgewicht des Menschen, nach dem geistigen Jenseits der materiellen Aktionen und Gegenaktionen."

FURTHER READING

Criticism

Alter, Maria P. "From *Der Reigen* to *La Ronde*: Transposition of a Stageplay to the Cinema." *Literature Film Quarterly* 24, no. 1 (1996): 52-56.
    Comments on the differences in tone between *Reigen* and its film version, *La Ronde,* noting in particular the less banal, romanticized attitude towards sex depicted in the film.

Nehring, Wolfgang. "Schnitzler, Freud's Alter Ego?" *Modern Austrian Literature* 10, nos. 3-4 (1977): 179-94.
    Uses Freud's letters to Schnitzler to address the extent to which Schnitzler may have been influenced by Freudian psychoanalysis in his plays and novels.

Norden, Edward. "From Schnitzler to Kushner." *Commentary* 99, no. 1 (January 1995): 51-59.
    Examines similarities in themes of and critical reaction to the plays of Schnitzler and contemporary playwright Tony Kushner.

Yates, W. E. *Schnitzler, Hofmannsthal, and the Austrian Theatre*. New Haven and London: Yale University Press, 1992. 286 p.

Book-length treatment of Schnitzler and his friend and contemporary Hugo von Hofmannsthal, focusing on their roles in turn-of-the-century Viennese theater.

Additional coverage of Schnitzler's life and career is contained in the following sources published by the Gale Group: *Contemporary Authors,* **Vol. 104;** *Dictionary of Literary Biography,* **Vols. 81, 118;** *European Writers; Literature Resource Center; Reference Guide to Short Fiction; Reference Guide to World Literature; Short Story Criticism,* **Vol. 15; and** *Twentieth-Century Literary Criticism,* **Vol. 4.**

Oscar Wilde
1854-1900

(Born Oscar Fingal O'Flahertie Wills Wilde, also wrote under pseudonyms C. 3. 3. and Sebastian Melmoth) Irish playwright, novelist, essayist, critic, poet, and short story writer.

INTRODUCTION

Wilde is recognized as one of the foremost figures of the late nineteenth-century literature Aesthetic or "art for art's sake" movement, which defied convention, subordinating ethical instruction to aesthetic value. This credo of aestheticism, however, indicates only one facet of a man notorious for resisting any public institution—artistic, social, political, or moral—that attempted to subjugate individual will and imagination. Wilde is best known for his critical essays and popular plays, which are humorous comedies of manners that focus on upper-class English society.

BIOGRAPHICAL INFORMATION

Wilde was born and raised in Dublin, Ireland. He began his advanced education at Dublin's Trinity College and concluded it with an outstanding academic career at Oxford. In college Wilde was influenced by the writings of Walter Pater, who in his *Studies in the History of the Renaissance* (1873) urged indulgence of the senses, a search for sustained intensity of experience, and stylistic perfectionism in art. Wilde adopted such aestheticism as a way of life, cultivating an extravagant persona that was burlesqued in the popular press and music-hall entertainments, copied by other youthful iconoclasts, and indulged by the avant-garde literary and artistic circles of London wherein Wilde was renowned for intelligence, wit, and charm. Wilde published his first volume of poetry in 1881. A few years later he married, and embarked on successful lecture tours of the United States, Canada, and Great Britain. In the 1880s, Wilde and his family settled in London, where he continued to crusade for aestheticism as a book reviewer and as the editor of the periodical *Lady's World,* whose name he immediately changed to *Woman's World.*

During this period of creativity, Wilde met and became infatuated with Lord Alfred Douglas, son of the Marquess of Queensbury. His relationship with Douglas, the Marquess's violent disapproval of this relationship, and his own ill-advised legal action against the Marquess scandalized London. *The Importance of Being Earnest* was in production at the time of Wilde's 1895 trial on

charges of "gross indecency between male persons." His conviction and subsequent imprisonment led to ignominy for Wilde and obscurity for his works. He continued to write during his two years in prison. Upon his release, however, Wilde was generally either derided or ignored by literary and social circles. At the time of his death in 1900, the scandal associated with Wilde led most commentators to discuss him diffidently, if at all. While critical response no longer focuses so persistently on questions of morality, Wilde's life and personality still incite fascination. Biographical studies and biographically oriented criticism continue to dominate Wilde scholarship.

MAJOR WORKS

Wilde arrived at his greatest success through the production of four plays in the 1890s. The first three—Lady *Win-*

dermere's Fan (1892), *A Woman of No Importance* (1893) and *An Ideal Husband* (1895)—are well-made comedies of manners revolving around social codes of the English upper classes. They are distinctively Wildean for the epigrams and witticisms delivered at frequent intervals (a show of rhetoric which often brings the action of the drama to a standstill). A fourth play, *The Importance of Being Earnest* (1895), marked the height of Wilde's popularity and is considered his best and most characteristic drama. Bypassing the more realistic characters and situations of its predecessors, *The Importance of Being Earnest* forms the apogee of Victorian drawing-room farce. Its stylish characters, stylized dialogue, and elegant artificiality are for many readers and critics the ultimate revelation of Wilde's identity as both man and author.

CRITICAL RECEPTION

Wilde's plays have been popular with both audiences and critics, who praise his humorous and biting satire of English manners at the turn of the twentieth century. Analysis of sexuality in his work have been a rich area for critical discussion, as commentators investigate the role of androgyny and homosexuality in his comedies. Possible influences on and sources for his work has been another subject for critical study. Commentators on Wilde have also come to stress the intellectual and humanist basis of his plays. Traditionally, critical evaluation of Wilde's work has been complicated, primarily because his works have to compete for attention with his sensational life. Wilde himself regarded this complication as unnecessary, advising that "a critic should be taught to criticise a work of art without making reference to the personality of the author. This, in fact, is the beginning of criticism."

PRINCIPAL WORKS

Plays

Verna, or the Nihilists 1883
Guido Ferranti: A Tragedy of the XVI Century 1891
Lady Windermere's Fan 1892
A Woman of No Importance 1893
An Ideal Husband 1895
The Importance of Being Earnest 1895
Salomé 1896
A Florentine Tragedy [opening scene by T. Sturge Moore] 1906
The Picture of Dorian Gray 1913

Other Major Works

Poems (poetry) 1881
The Soul of Man under Socialism (nonfiction) 1890
The Happy Prince, and Other Tales (short stories) 1891

A House of Pomegranates (short stories) 1891
Intentions (essays) 1891
Lord Arthur Savile's Crime, and Other Stories (short stories) 1891
The Picture of Dorian Gray (novel) 1891
The Ballad of Reading Gaol, and Other Poems (poetry) 1898
De Profundis (letter) 1905
Collected Works. 14 vols. (poetry, essays, short stories, novel, plays, and criticism) 1908
The Letters of Oscar Wilde (letters) 1962

*This work was not published in its entirety until 1949.

GENERAL COMMENTARY

Joseph Bristow (essay date spring 1994)

SOURCE: Bristow, Joseph. "Dowdies and Dandies: Oscar Wilde's Refashioning of Society Comedy." *Modern Drama* 37, no. 1 (spring 1994): 53-70.

[*In the following essay, Bristow discusses the defining characteristics of Wilde's plays.*]

I

"London Society," according to Mrs Cheveley in **An Ideal Husband** (1895), is "entirely made up of dowdies and dandies."[1] Reported by Mrs Marchmont to Lord Goring, Mrs Cheveley's words have a far greater function than simply making her the centre of attention among this group of gossipy aristocrats and their various hangers-on. Her acute observations of London Society disclose that this particular milieu is dull and yet dazzling. Rather like the interest she manages to generate around her own persona, Mrs Cheveley's insights about this contrastive culture of "dowdies and dandies" have an element of sparkling wit about them while appearing not a little predictable to at least one of their company. For although Lord Goring tells Mrs Marchmont that Mrs Cheveley is in principle "quite right," his dandiacal instincts compel him to qualify how one might affirm this lively view of London Society. "The men are all dowdies," he says, "and the women are all dandies" (152). By this point, Mrs Marchmont is unsure whether or not she ought to agree. "Oh!" she exclaims, after a pause, "do you really think that is what Mrs Cheveley meant?" (152).

I begin with this exchange because it foregrounds at least two of the main issues at stake in Wilde's contentious handling of the late-Victorian Society comedy. The first is that these dramas constantly thrill the audience with their spectacular displays of the wealth enjoyed by these generally idle characters, only to reveal how grayly monotonous their everyday lives truly are. This play, after all, begins with Mrs Marchmont complaining that the Hartlocks give "Horribly tedious parties" (133), a view with which Lady Basildon wholly concurs. "Horribly tedious!" she exclaims. "Never know why I go. Never know why I go anywhere" (133). Yet the repetitious lifestyles of these people are framed by the grandeur of the stage setting which places them in a richly tapestried environment that cannot but impose its aesthetic qualities upon us. The dreary day-to-day rounds of the Season may well make Mrs Marchmont and Lady Basildon look rather bored with their world yet in spite of this—if not because of it—the stage directions insist that their "*affectation of manner has a delicate charm.*" For all their superficality, it is still the case that "*Watteau would have loved to paint them*" (133). Similar comparisons with the work of favoured artists extend to practically all of the men and women in the play. Lest we might think that these stage settings have a purely decorative function, Ian Small reminds us that Wilde's selection of these specific art-objects "implicate[s] the political values which are so central to the play's development." Thus Watteau immediately encodes a sense of "delicate eroticism."[2] If these luxurious descriptions were not enough to emphasize the visual allure and social glamour of this drama, then there is the whole question of the role of the London fashion houses that used the West End stage to advertise their creations. For, as Joel H. Kaplan has remarked, Wilde collaborated with up-and-coming designers of *haute couture* in order to "turn [those] icons of mid-century melodrama—the Magdalen, the Adventuress, the Puritan Wife—into fashion 'statements' that cut provocatively across moral and generic boundaries."[3] So even if the routines of Society make this world seem, as it were, dowdyish, these women none the less inhabit an environment that one might, at the risk of straining a metaphor, describe as dandiacal. Its attractiveness refashioned how an audience could and should look at Society.

The second, and equally important, point that emerges from Lord Goring's response to the lives of these "dowdies and dandies" is that the meaning of the original observation is far from cut and dried. By transforming the men into the usually feminine "dowdies" and representing Society women as the conventionally masculine "dandies," Lord Goring employs one of Wilde's most characteristic tropes. This is the figure of peripety—or the dramatic reversal in fortune—where a given structure is rapidly turned upside down and back to front. For everywhere we look in Wilde's works, we encounter an arresting changeover of familiar devices into things that often seem completely unanticipated—sometimes by hilariously testing the limits of dramatic plausibility. Jack Worthing, after all, having pretended for some time to be "Ernest," becomes genuinely Ernest in "e(a)rnest," as Wilde's farcical final comedy hurtles to its close. Whether we are examining the improbable coincidences shaping his comedic plots or looking at the axiomatic tricksiness of his phrases and philosophies, there is always a marked tendency for Wilde to outwit us just at the point where our expectations ought to be confirmed. Small wonder, then, that Mrs Marchmont is left to consider whether Mrs Chev-

eley really meant that the gentlemen were "dowdies" and the ladies the "dandies" of the day. What, indeed, might be the point of refashioning Mrs Marchmont's sense of how London Society looks and behaves? Why should there be this rapid *volte face* in how we are made to look at, as well as think about, the roles given to men and women on this visually and verbally irresistible stage?

These questions are worth raising because it has proved persistently difficult for critics to contend with the inconsistencies that would for some appear to mar Wilde's Society comedies. For example, when discussing **A Woman of No Importance,** Kerry Powell emphasizes his dissatisfaction with the conclusion to a play in which "all the major characters exhibit contradictory and unpredictable behaviour."[4] This is an aspect of Wilde's drama that frequently vexes Powell's painstaking investigation of Wilde's borrowings from his theatrical predecessors. Especially confounding in this respect is Lord Goring, who, for Powell, does not behave in a manner that would fulfil our expectations of the dandy as a man of independent spirit and incisive wit. Lord Goring, by all accounts, appears to be the least likely candidate to conform to Society's wishes by becoming engaged to Mabel Chiltern in Act IV. "Brilliant though [Lord Goring] is," writes Powell, "what can we make of a dandy who links love and politics so sentimentally, who preaches such a retrograde sexual ethic as the one he expounds to Lady Chiltern [263-65], and who ends the play by choosing a domestic life in preference to any other?"[5] Powell is hardly alone in questioning how one character comes to a thoroughly unpredicted end. Not only has it long been the case that Wilde's protagonists have struck his audiences as lacking the depth and sincerity that would lend men such as Lord Goring a satisfying unity of purpose, from the earliest days of these dramas, countless commentators have also expressed impatience with the way that they are scattered so liberally—if not repetitiously—with "Oscarisms" that it proves hard indeed to tell one character apart from another.[6] It is as if Wilde, rather than his dramatis personae, ruled the stage. Worse still has been Wilde's seeming contempt for the traditions in which he had chosen to work. One of his most hostile critics, writing on **The Importance of Being Earnest** in 1895, stated that the "story is clumsily handled, the treatment unequal, the construction indifferent, while the elements of farce, comedy, and burlesque are jumbled together with a fine disregard for consistency."[7]

One can, of course, turn Wilde's blatant defiance of conventions to his advantage. But the desire to do so has, on occasions, made him look just as capricious as he appeared to those who found his "Oscarisms" a source of irritation. In the study that has done more than any other to restyle our understanding of Wilde's *oeuvre*, Regenia Gagnier makes one point undeniably clear right at the start of her discussion. "Oscar Wilde," she observes, "wanted to have it all ways."[8] He becomes, for Gagnier, the figure of contradiction par excellence. On this view, his life and writings, together with the large corpus of biography that has swollen around the Wilde myth, present him as romantic and cynical, sentimental and satiric, and martyr and mannequin at one and the same time. Such manifestations are, according to Gagnier, the outcome of Wilde's relations with the main forces of cultural production that impose their competing demands on his work. Although Gagnier's emphasis on the need to position the figure of Wilde in the context of various social institutions is a welcome one, it may well suggest that the contradictoriness of his writing is the mystified and unresolved result of the machinations of capital. I should wish to argue instead that the inconsistent, contradictory, and unpredictable elements that characterize the authorial sign of "Wilde" are part and parcel of his wholesale critique of a culture that foolishly wants its meanings and its morals clearly laid out. Dowdies and dandies are, in this respect, hardly discrete. But, there again, they are not quite the same thing either.

Rather than labour the interchangeability of "dowdies and dandies" any further, this essay proceeds to discuss a handful of episodes from the Society comedies that accentuate how and why Wilde was consistently absorbed, as it were, by inconsistency. For if one thing becomes patently obvious in these dramas, it is that their moral system is difficult to gauge. Each plot fails to secure an ending that provides a magical resolution to the crises it has opened up—not least in the divided, undecidable, and factitious personalities that catch our attention with those "Oscarisms" which, by definition, could hardly be called their own. The greatest problem arising from the deliberate contradictoriness that typifies almost every aspect of these Society comedies is whether they are necessarily progressive or avant-garde. It remains to be seen whether Wilde's generic and moral transgressions are, so to speak, transgressive.[9]

II

Let me move, first of all, to one of the most vexed aspects of *Lady Windermere's Fan* (1892). For it was there that the meaning and motivation of Wilde's characters became the source of considerable friction between Wilde, George Alexander, and Clement Scott. Wilde's disagreement with them lay in the figure of Mrs Erlynne, who, he told Alexander, was an "adventuress, not a cocotte," and should be played as such.[10] But his insistence that this carefully designed character should not reveal her identity as Lady Windermere's mother until the close of Act IV kept much of the play beyond the audience's grasp. "For two-thirds of the evening," wrote Scott in the *Daily Telegraph*, "people were asking one another, who is she? . . . Is this adventuress a mistress, or can she be a mother?"[11] The audience, to be fair, was not entirely to blame for feeling so bewildered. Wilde had, as he informed Alexander, sought to create in Mrs Erlynne "a character as yet untouched by literature."[12] But she proved to be too innovative by far. To overcome the confusion she aroused among those who attended the opening night, Wilde reluctantly capitulated to Alexander's directorial demand that this woman's true identity as the mother of Lady Win-

dermere be made clear much earlier in the play. (In his public pronouncement on this marked alteration to his script, however, Wilde declared that Alexander had been right to urge him to make the change so that "the psychological interest of the second act would be greatly increased.")[13]

At first sight a stock-in-trade adventuress, Mrs Erlynne comes to Lord Windermere's home to bribe him so that her true identity shall not become public knowledge. Any family connection with such a disreputable person would, he knows for sure, ruin his marriage. It is, as Lord Windermere sees it, imperative that his Puritan Wife is not disabused of the belief that her own mother died when she was a small child. But no sooner has most of the first act been given over to preparing the audience for Mrs Erlynne's entrance onto the stage than she undergoes a transformation that could never have been imagined in any of her theatrical precursors. The intractable difficulty with Mrs Erlynne is that she is placed in a position where she begins to espouse precisely those puritanical values that, to all intents and purposes, she should and must despise. Perhaps more puzzling still is the rapid turnabout in Lady Windermere's behaviour. For this young wife impulsively disregards the moral strictures of her upbringing by abandoning her husband and child on the grounds that she believes him to be conducting an adulterous affair with the woman who is, in fact, her mother. Wilde's plot, therefore, swiftly places one apparently incongruous moral layer upon another.

At the start of Act III, it goes without saying that the diametrically opposed Puritan Wife and the Adventuress have, if only momentarily, changed places. Mrs Erlynne has followed Lady Windermere to Lord Darlington's room to dissuade her from deserting Lord Windermere and their baby. The Puritan Wife's actions come as a great surprise, since she has in the opening scene made her strict views on the rights and wrongs of marriage known to her flirtatious admirer, Lord Darlington. Underpinning her moral precepts at the start of Act I is the high-minded virtue of sacrifice. Spiritual values are for her sharply opposed to those of the stock exchange. "Nowadays," she declares, "people seem to look on life as a speculation. It is not a speculation. It is a sacrament. Its ideal is Love. Its purification is sacrifice."[14] Lord Darlington offers the first, and unsuccessful, challenge to this unbending orthodoxy, since he thinks that life is "too complex a thing to be settled by these hard and fast rules" (11). She, however, does her utmost to resist his charms. Under no circumstances whatsoever will Lady Windermere admit any compromise.

But Lady Windermere does so only in principle. For by the time she is waiting for Lord Darlington to return she has surely transgressed Society's moral code of honour. Scott, not surprisingly, found this aspect of the play most unpalatable. In his indignant review in the *Illustrated London News*, Scott turned his paragraphs over to an imaginary monologue spoken by Wilde. In this derogatory guise of Scott's invention, the playwright reels off each and every insult that he has managed to blow in the public's face, much in the manner of the cigarette that he chose to smoke while addressing the audience on the opening night of the play, and which caused considerable offence in some quarters of the press. Reminding his readership of Nora's abandonment of her child in Ibsen's *A Doll's House* (1879), Scott projects these words into Wilde's mouth. "You have seen how the good mother can desert her new-born infant without a pang." Scott then identifies how Wilde has sought to add insult to injury in his depiction of Lady Windermere. "I will show you," he writes, "a mother who leaves her daughter for ever, unkissed, and goes downstairs to accept the hand of a *roué* admirer on her deserted daughter's doorstep."[15] Scott clearly is sickened by the thought that such an action should be found "amusing" by a prurient public. No doubt Lady Winderemere is like Nora in doing "a thing that one of the lower animals would not do."[16]

Yet Scott misleads his readers by implying that Wilde's comedy extends and heightens the shocks induced by Nora's desertion of her husband and child. For Lady Windermere, of course, does not ultimately fall foul of Society. Mrs Erlynne unexpectedly comes to her rescue."Oh! to save you from the abyss into which you are falling," she exclaims in words that have a more than familiar melodramatic ring to them, "there is nothing in the world I would not dare" (55). Yet this morally righteous act of salvation is the direct result of Mrs Erlynne's brazenly corrupt behaviour. Mrs Erlynne has learned of Lady Windermere's intentions through the slyest of actions by intercepting the letter that the Puritan Wife has impulsively left for Lord Windermere. The Adventuress, therefore, has done something shameful in order to spare her daughter from "shame, yes, shame and disgrace" (56). The scene reaches an incredibly emotive pitch when Mrs Erlynne launches into a speech that berates Society's intolerance towards the woman with a past. "One pays for one's sin," she says, "and then one pays again, and all one's life one pays" (57). Such words force home the point that Mrs Erlynne—"a character as yet untouched by literature"—is not beyond redemption. But the comedy does not struggle either to reform or to punish her so that the moral system of the drama can be easily resolved. "I have," she tells Lord Windermere in Act IV, "no ambition to play the part of a mother . . . I want to live childless still" (80).

The crucial point about this lengthy speech in Act IV is that it reminds us that the lives led by members of Society are nothing more than already scripted roles. And such roles have to be enacted to secure one's own best interests. For social advantage, as Mrs Erlynne knows only too well, is maintained by the appearance one makes in Society, and little else. Sincerity, depth of feeling, authenticity—none of these things can be risked in her chosen way of life. "I lost one illusion last night," she remarks, "I thought I had no heart. I find I have, and a heart doesn't suit me, Windermere. Somehow it doesn't go with modern dress" (80). So even if Mrs Erlynne discovers that she has a fundamental humanity, she dare not risk becoming sentimental since

it "makes one look old" (80). Better by far to maintain the illusions enabled by "modern dress" where age can masquerade as youth. Mrs Erlynne, after all, has never admitted to being older than thirty. Her decision to keep up appearances in "modern dress" ensures that the truth of her identity continues to be withheld from Lady Windermere. Yet at the moment that Mrs Erlynne confesses to having lost one "illusion," she insists to Lord Windermere that his wife must not lose hers. Her daughter must, by all accounts, remain devoted to the "memory of this dead, stainless mother" (80). The unmotherly Mrs Erlynne is certainly at her most manipulative when she takes the moral high ground by reminding Lady Windermere of one's duties as a "mother" (85). These emollient words serve to salve Lady Windermere's conscience so that she can stay happily married at Selby. But they emerge from a most ironic source. Consequently, Lady Windermere's ignorance of Mrs Erlynne's strategic handling of "modern dress" shall guarantee her marital bliss. The play, however, does not return Lady Windermere to a state of innocence. This comedy resists, as always, such an easy equation between moral alternatives.

For, in living contentedly with her "illusions," Lady Windermere cannot retreat back to her earlier moralistic self. Even if she remains committed to the "memory of this dead, stainless mother," she has none the less had radically to shift her perspective on the double standards of the Society she inhabits. Whereas in Act I she declared that life would be more "simple" if everyone lived by "hard and fast rules" (11), by Act IV she is protesting to her husband in Mrs Erlynne's favour that she does not "think now that people can be divided into the good and the bad, as though they were two separate races or creations" (73-74). Her mature outlook leads her to insist in Act IV that Mrs Erlynne, whose engagement to Lord Augustus has just been announced, is without question "a very good woman" (89). But, there again, her judgement is based on only a partial knowledge of the Adventuress who has paraded across the stage in the endlessly deceitful guise of "modern dress." So even if Lady Windermere has discovered some wisdom in not dividing the world into virtuous and vicious types, her final declaration about the goodness of Mrs Erlynne must surely make the audience pause for thought. How does one genuinely know the moral value of another person? Are there any exact standards by which one may measure the truth or falsity of another's motives? Since it is "illusions" that lead Wilde's heroine to label the adventuress who saved her as a "very good woman," it remains unclear which of the two is supposed to be valued most highly. The play is far from explicit about who, indeed, is the "good woman" being honoured in its subtitle.

III

Purity, one of the conventional signs of virtue, is cast under equal suspicion in *A Woman of No Importance* where the two figures who embody the "higher ethical standard" (22) are challenged by a man who ostentatiously dons "modern dress." The Puritans, in this instance, are the self-satisfied philanthropist, Lord Kelvil MP, and a young woman hailing from the New England bourgeoisie, Hester Worsley. Their high-minded pronouncements on the social ills of modern life are contested by the dandiacal Lord Illingworth. Yet here, too, the system of moral oppositions between each party is far from as stark as these character types might initially encourage us to believe.

Hester, for example, spends most of the first three acts expressing her dismay at those Society people who take it upon themselves to "sneer at self-sacrifice" (52). Her assault on the English upper classes is harsh indeed, and her indictments at times invite us to see her as the strong voice of political conscience in the play. In Wilde's drafts, Hester's invective is especially pungent. "You cultivated people," she declares, "don't know *why* you are living. You never think of *that*" (n. 52). In the text used in performance, she rails against a class of persons who "throw bread to the poor . . . merely to keep them quiet for a season" (52). Such outpourings would seem to underline Wilde's dissatisfaction with a property-owning Society that he forcefully criticizes in *The Soul of Man under Socialism* (1890). But Hester, as the play proceeds, hardly fulfils any socialist ideal. She is only too clearly an insurgent member of the aspiring *nouveaux riches* who is treated to not a little irony when Lady Caroline informs her that "In my young days . . . one never met anyone in society who worked for their living" (15). Hester is, for all to see, in England to obtain a husband, and to gain access to upper-class life. And so, by the final act, she has secured her engagement to an Englishman.

What is more, Hester's punitive moral principles, which she sustains right up until Act III, eventually founder as her friendship with Mrs Arbuthnot develops. Having declared in her brash manner that "all women who have sinned be punished" (53), she later recognizes in Mrs Arbuthnot qualities that are apparently lacking in other members of Society. Hester, on the face of it, could not have drawn a more wrongheaded conclusion. For she does not know that Mrs Arbuthnot is a woman who has had to live the life of an outcast for bearing a child outside wedlock. Hester, as a consequence, fails to realize that her fiancé, Mrs Arbuthnot's son, is illegitimate. So when Hester later calls on Mrs Arbuthnot to agree with the view that a "woman who has sinned should be punished" (88), Wilde's dramatic irony is painfully obvious. In Mrs Arbuthnot—described elsewhere by Lord Illingworth as "excessively handsome" (64)—Hester perceives "a sense of what is good and pure in life" (83). Yet once the truth of Gerald's parentage has been disclosed in the final line of Act III, she will have to revise her opinion. For what happens to Hester is that she is abused by Lord Illingworth in a way that enables her to sympathize with Mrs Arbuthnot's long history of silent suffering. The dandy, playing up to his role as a philanderer, makes an unwelcome pass at the young woman. Having screamed out the words "He has insulted me!" (95), Hester later joins forces against him, extravagantly informing Gerald that in his mother "all womanhood is martyred." "Not she alone,"

she adds, "but all of us are stricken in her house" (108). Although her puritanical discourse is sustained throughout this comedy, the important point that arises from Act IV is that Hester's retributory position on the woman with a past has been turned on its head. In the closing tableau, she accepts Mrs Arbuthnot as her "mother" (120).

This would appear, on the surface, to be a reconciliatory scene, one that set the moral priorities of the play in order. Yet for all the changes in conscience that have beset the "Puritan in white muslin," as Lord Illingworth wryly names Hester (113), it is still the case that the compromise made by Mrs Arbuthnot and Gerald is morally incomplete. Rejecting the dandy's offer of marriage, Mrs Arbuthnot cannot so easily be rendered acceptable as a "martyr" when she is, by her own admission, like all women who "live by our emotions and for them" (117). "A kiss," as she tells her former lover, "may ruin a human life" (112), making us question the ferocity of Society's opprobrium against those who follow their desires. Mrs Arbuthnot, in any case, does not exactly pass muster as an icon of self-sacrificing motherhood. Her sexuality was, in Alexander's original production, strongly signalled by her style of dress. Playing Mrs Arbuthnot in 1893, Mrs Bernard Beere, according to a writer in the *Sketch*, "wore two severe-looking gowns, both black." Such costumes, we are told, were "appropriate to a betrayed woman, and had the advantage of standing out strongly in grim, sombre majesty against the brilliant dresses of the butterfly women of the play."[17] Accoutred in this manner, she stands out much in the same way as Illingworth does himself. And her style of clothing confounds, rather than clarifies, the resolution to her plight.

Mrs Arbuthnot, however, is not unique in sending out contradictory signals about how she is supposed to be understood by the audience. In Wilde's dramas, it remains mainly in the hands of the dandy to problematize the question of how appearances may reveal or conceal moral truths. This is certainly not to say that Lord Illingworth provides anything like a reliable index against which the relations between acts and consequences can be confidently measured. For in Illingworth, as with many of Wilde's dandies, it is not always easy to make hard and fast distinctions between levels of depth and superficiality. "People nowadays are so absolutely superficial," he tells Gerald Arbuthnot, "they don't understand the philosophy of the superficial" (75). It is, as he himself acknowledges, tempting to view his style as simply an inconsequential display of egotism and wit. To a degree, that is precisely what it is. But his dramatic purpose is also to raise the audience's awareness that there may be something to be learned from his well-oiled axioms, not least when it comes to mocking Society. The badinage in which he and Mrs Allonby indulge at great length in Act I provides perhaps the best examples of how his discourse refuses to settle on either side of an argument. The tone of their lively exchange is constantly shifting. Flippant remarks often carry the weight of considerable import. "I never intend to grow old," he informs Mrs Allonby. "The soul is born old but grows young. That is the comedy of life." She matches his wit by playfully turning these apothegmatic statements upside down. Thus she replies that "the body is born young and grows old. That is life's tragedy" (38). Large philosophical speculations roll off the tongue in such glib turns of phrase that one may well take them as frivolous in the extreme. And yet the rapid reversibility of comedy and tragedy, age and youth, and life and death in these feats of rhetorical one-upmanship assuredly has a larger point to make about the unstable nature of the oppositions featured here. Their dialogue suggests that comedy and tragedy are always implied in one another, and to extricate them is difficult indeed. This is surely the case when we consider the outcome of the play. For in refusing Lord Illingworth's belated offer of marriage, Mrs Arbuthnot leaves England to join a son and daughter-in-law whose strict moral code looks like a very bleak alternative to the life she might have led with him. This comedy, therefore, remains haunted by doubts. To be a "mother," in this context, could very possibly be viewed as another kind of tragic denial.

For it is, time and again, the evident intention of each of Wilde's Society comedies not to present the audience with ideal endings. Marriage, in particular is the institution that fails most visibly in this respect, and the ambivalence with which marriage is treated in the closing moments of comic resolution is surely symptomatic of the changing legal status of the ties that bound men and women together in wedded bliss. Many critics have noted that Wilde's comedies show a marked responsiveness to the broadening of the Married Women's Property Act in 1893. In Act II, Mrs Allonby wittily observes that "All men are married women's property." "That," she adds, "is the only true definition of what married women's property really is" (42). Such remarks give Lady Stutfield good reason to ask Mrs Allonby for her views on what might go into the makings of the "Ideal Husband" (47). For her such an "ideal," given that her own husband is pejoratively described in legalistic terms as a "promissory note" (43), simply cannot exist. But the suggestion that she might sketch an outline of the "Ideal Man" prompts Mrs Allonby to remark that he would "talk to us as if we were goddesses, and treat us as if we were children" (47). In one regard, this is exactly what middle-class upholders of the doctrine of "Woman's Mission" promulgated from the 1830s onwards. Mrs Allonby appears to be celebrating nothing other than the devoted angel-wife who is forever infantilized by her authoritarian husband. But no sooner has Mrs Allonby made these conservative sentiments clear than she promptly adds that the "Ideal Man" should "forbid us to have missions." "[C]aprices," she jokingly asserts, are what women should have instead (47). What, then, are we to believe?

There is obviously no unequivocal answer. And that is precisely the point of the play. Eager to collapse clear-cut distinctions, Wilde surely must have felt that his intentions had been fulfilled when reading A. B. Walkely's generous review of this comedy. For Walkely sees "verbal antithesis" as "not only the secret of Mr Wilde's dialogue, but of his

dramatic action as well." His attention focuses in particular on the links between the final line of the drama and its title. Mrs Arbuthnot closes Act IV by remarking that the glove with which she has lightly hit Lord Illingworth across the face belongs to a "man of no importance" (120). "What," asks Walkely, "is the opposite to 'a woman of no importance'? Why, 'a man of no importance.'" These phrases strike him as "the two contrasted *most de la pièce*."[18] These "*mots*," to be sure, mark out the points of convergence and disparity between Lord Illingworth and Mrs Arbuthnot. Their likeness and dissimilarity are held in an entirely purposeful tension—in so far as the play's strongly marked interest in structural contradictions is concerned.

IV

The debate about the makings of the "Ideal Husband" and the "Ideal Man" are, of course, carried over into *An Ideal Husband* itself. Here, too, the closing scene of the play strikes one or two "antithetical" notes against the perfect qualities supposedly enshrined in its title. Lord Goring, having announced his intention to marry Mabel Chiltern, is gently reproved by his father. "[I]f you," declares Lord Caversham, "don't make this young lady an ideal husband, I'll cut you off with a shilling" (270). This half-serious threat prompts Mabel to remark: "An ideal husband! Oh, I don't think I should like that. It sounds like something in the next world" (270). Her rather naïve response, however, also has a profound resonance, since it is juxtaposed to the plight of Sir Robert and Lady Chiltern, for whom, after many personal difficulties, "a new life is beginning" (270). The Chilterns have, throughout the course of the play, had to make compromises of the kind already established in the two previous comedies. But Wilde's unusual handling of Sir Robert exerts innovative pressures on the ways in which men of high standing are to be regarded in Society drama. For once Sir Robert's sordid history comes to light, he appears to us in rather feminized terms. Like the stock-in-trade "woman with a past," he has prostituted himself, if not sexually, then to the God of Mammon. His whole fortune, we discover, is based on the monies he gained from selling a Cabinet secret to a foreign aristocrat. Once this heinous act has been revealed to Lady Chiltern, she conforms to her role as the Puritan Wife by despising herself for ever having looked up to him as "something apart from common life, a thing pure, noble, honest, without stain" (210). The remainder of the drama undertakes to bring them together, if on wholly revised terms. In this respect, their "ideal" marriage suffers much the same fate as that of the Windermeres. Yet, in this play, Wilde's interest in unsettling the distinctions between "good" and "bad" types is focused on one theatrical device that is used to much more elaborate ends than in *Lady Windermere's Fan*. In *An Ideal Husband*, the intercepted letter literally serves to rewrite Society's rigid manual of conduct where no one—not even a traitor to the government—is unduly punished.

Lady Chiltern's letter of desperation to Lord Goring undergoes a series of startling rescriptings. It emerges, first of all, at the opening of Act III shortly after Sir Robert has confessed his painful history to her. The truth has had to come out because of the political inveiglings of Mrs Cheveley, who has attempted to bribe him in much the same manner as Baron Arnheim did before. Dispatched to Lord Goring, her missive simply reads: "I want you. I trust you. I am coming to you" (215). However, Lady Chiltern's words are consequently subjected to a wilful misreading. And for some time it looks as if this hastily written piece of paper may serve to incriminate her. Let us follow, then, the perilous passage of this letter through Acts III and IV so that Wilde's aesthetics of appropriation and politics of social change can be understood in all their structural intricacy.

The Adventuress, given her stealthy behaviour, fulfils her role by filching Lady Chiltern's letter while waiting for Lord Goring to return to his rooms. She sees how a highly sexual gloss may put upon this document, one that would suggest that Lord Goring is committing adultery with the Puritan Wife. The letter consequently becomes a significant bargaining tool in the war of words that ensues between Mrs Cheveley and Lord Goring. And the intensity of the situation is increased because, as Act III reveals, these two people were formerly lovers. She finally declares that she will hand over the letter if he agrees to marry her. It is hardly a decent proposal, and he dismisses her offer out of hand. Right at the centre of the cross-fire of insults that they subsequently aim at one another is a punishing critique of marriage. Discovering that Lord Goring will consent to her wishes so that Sir Robert shall be saved, Mrs Cheveley derides his inability to rise "to some great height of self-sacrifice" (235). Failing to meet with her expectations, he insists that "self-sacrifice is a thing that should be put down by law." "It is," he adds, "demoralizing to the people for whom one sacrifices oneself. They always go to the bad" (236). The enmity between them goes from bad to worse precisely because these rivals— the dandy and the adventuress—are only too aware of how masks and roles are constantly being manipulated to maintain specific appearances and exert certain forms of power in high Society. They attend, more than anyone else, to questions of fashion. Outward displays count far more for them than do inward forms of denial. When Lord Goring asks Mrs Cheveley for the letter, for example, she claims not to have it with her because a "well-made dress has no pockets" (232). Similarly, when commenting on the virtues of the Puritan Wife, Mrs Cheveley ridicules the ungainly size of Lady Chiltern's hands: "A woman whose size in gloves is seven and three-quarters never knows much about anything" (236). The surprising thing is that the play encourages us to see that Mrs Cheveley and Lord Goring, for all their corrupt wranglings, are in many respects correct. This point is made explicit in "The Truth of Masks: A Note on Illusion" (first published in 1885) where Wilde remarks that "Costume is a growth, an evolution, and a most important, perhaps the most important, sign of the manners, customs and mode of life of each century."[19] To understand fashion, as Lord Goring and Mrs Cheveley claim to do, is to comprehend the inner workings of a culture. Such fashion-conscious people, by and large, are in a better position than most to come to terms with some of Society's deepest contradictions.

That is why the "snake-brooch with a ruby" (238) features so centrally in Act III. Like the intercepted letter, it has the potential to be refashioned in a style that has not been previously anticipated. For the brooch that Mrs Cheveley has lost in Act I is clasped upon her arm by Lord Goring as a bracelet. Never before has she known that it could be worn like this, and her ignorance of this fact spells her doom. For she finds that she cannot remove it. She is, at this point, outsmarted by her adversary, who informs her that this piece of jewellery once belonged to his cousin, from whom Mrs Cheveley has stolen it. Although many critics have expressed dissatisfaction with the heavy-handed treatment of this device—since it obviously ensnares the Lamia-like adventuress in her own snakish coils—it none the less signals the larger interests of the comedy in unexpected reversals.

Mrs Cheveley is only momentarily manacled by the bracelet that she once believed to be a brooch. By Act IV the letter, her ultimate weapon, is still in her hands, and eventually it is sent to Sir Robert with the clear purpose of ruining the Chilterns' lives. But here, too, Mrs Cheveley is foiled. Particularly revealing is the conflict that rages between Lord Goring and Lady Chiltern when they learn of Mrs Cheveley's vengeful act. For here the moral consequences of telling the truth have immoral implications. When Lord Goring declares that it would be better if Lady Chiltern explained that it was she rather than Mrs Cheveley who was expected in his rooms, Lady Chiltern is seen *"Looking at him with amazement that is almost terror"* (255). Lady Chiltern recognizes only too clearly that this disclosure would incriminate her in exactly the way that Mrs Cheveley has desired since intercepting the letter in Act III. What saves them is the fact that the letter has not been addressed to anyone. All it contains is Lady Chiltern's message and her signature. It arrives in Sir Robert's mail just at the moment when he felt that there was no future for their marriage. And her words—"I want you. I trust you, I am coming to you. Gertrude" (257)—renew his confidence in their love. Lord Goring, aware that this is indeed a fortunate mistake, implores her to accept the situation and welcome Sir Robert's error. Potential tragedy is usurped by comedy. This ironic reversal—or peripety— could not be more sudden and complete.

This error serves, in some respects, to expand and strengthen Lady Chiltern's moral education. For she learns that the cost of disclosing the truth may be too high, and that tactful dissimulation may serve her interests altogether better. When persuading her husband that resigning from public office would be a "useless sacrifice" (265), she is repeating Lord Goring's advice to her that "men and woman are not made to accept such sacrifices from one another" (264). Yet the additional lines that she has learnt from Lord Goring on this matter sound somewhat hollow. "A man's life," she explains to her husband, "is of more value than a woman's. It has larger issues, wider scope, greater ambitions" (265). If such words provide the rationale for the enlightened belief that her husband should not sacrifice his career, they none the less suggest that Lady Chiltern can only assert this view on the grounds of her inferiority as a woman. Given the rather leaden nature of the speech she reiterates at Lord Goring's bidding on the ways in which women's "lives revolve in curves of emotions" while it "is upon lines of intellect that a man's life progresses" (265), surely a shadow of doubt hangs over the integrity of these sentiments. One suffrage writer observed how here the "fatuousness of such a summing-up of the lives of the two sexes is painfully obvious." This speech, she remarked, put before us a "picture of male-organized society" where woman is alloted nothing more than a "parasitic" role.[20] Yet the position of Lady Chiltern's remarks on the subordination of women look, given her earlier remonstrations, rather paradoxical. For these creakingly rehearsed lines, which are designed to tug at her husband's heart-strings, undoubtedly issue from exactly the kinds of "separate spheres" ideology that she, as a reeducated Puritan Wife, has learned to renounce. In making this observation, I am not wishing to identify a basic flaw in the dramatic design to this part of Act IV. The purpose instead is to show that Wilde's repeated concern with accomplishing certain ends through unexpected means may well be not as progressive as we might think. It is tempting to be overwhelmed with the sense, as was Bernard Shaw, that Wilde "plays with everything: with wit, with philosophy, with drama, with actors and audience, with the whole theatre." Shaw regarded this as a positive aspect to *An Ideal Husband.* "Such a feat," he adds, "scandalizes the Englishman."[21] This impulse to "scandalize," according to Shaw, can be readily attributed to the playwright's distinctive Irish heritage. But such a view may obscure the idea that Wilde's energetic rewriting of the Society comedy, perhaps of necessity, keeps his plays enmeshed in the systems of value that they strive to subvert. To refashion something does not always mean that it will adopt a politically more progressive style.

V

It is with this specific issue in mind that I wish to conclude by addressing several questions to assess the political dimensions of Wilde's strenuous rewriting of Society comedy. Can the inconsistency and contradiction that appear as the main structural features of these works be little more than formal devices? Is there something necessarily subversive about the provocative moral, generic, and characterological transformations that appear in each and every scene? Is it really the case, as Gagnier has claimed, that Wilde's dramas provide important antecedents for the modernist manifestos comprising Antonin Artaud's "Theatre of Cruelty"?[22] Even if the pattern of his works sets out to overturn our expectations of moral values, social types, and generic conventions, there is the danger that his contradictoriness sets in motion an all too predictable logic where each and every outcome remains ruptured and nothing more. The plays, after all, even when challenging orthodoxies, remain structurally repetitive. And on countless occasions their most polished apothegms migrate from

one play to another, making it seem as if they themselves were stereotyped. *Earnest,* it has to be said, at times reads like a compilation of the most memorable phrases that Wilde has implanted in his earlier works. Shaw's enthusiasm for *An Ideal Husband,* we should bear in mind, turned on its head within a matter of weeks when *Earnest* left him with the sense of having wasted his evening. He experienced a "miserable mechanical laughter . . . at every outburst," especially as the farcical structure to the play struck him as belonging to the 1870s. So if the general drift of the Society comedies is to subvert the limits imposed upon the conventions in which Wilde chose to operate, then it has to be recognized that his contestation of those conventions is necessarily defined against them, if not entrammelled by them. For all their innovations, his dramas could, as Shaw's comments indicate, ultimately seem outdated.

One needs to emphasize this point because there has recently been a tendency to see Wilde as an indisputably avant-garde figure whose artistic mission was to undermine the normative assumptions of a largely puritanical culture that would express its brutality most forcefully when it sentenced him to gaol for committing acts of "gross indecency" in 1895. Jonathan Dollimore, for example, insists that there is a "transgressive aesthetic" enshrined in the axioms that Wilde brought together in "Phrases and Philosophies for the Use of the Young" (1894). Dollimore claims that such well-known maxims as "Man's deeper nature is soon found out" display "a non-centred or vagrant desire" that "is both the impetus for a subversive inversion, and what is released by it." He stresses how these phrases and philosophies parody received proverbial wisdom while provocatively retaining its axiomatic form. Thus they "enact one of the most disturbing of all forms of transgression, namely that whereby the outlaw turns up as inlaw, and the other as proximate proves more disturbing than the other as absolute difference."[24] Although it is assuredly the case that these mocking turns of phrase caused sufficient offence for them to be cited as evidence against Wilde in the first trial of 1895, it is easy to be misled by the belief that the contradictory axiom—that which, as Dollimore says, makes what is most familiar most strange to itself—is integral to a radical sexual politics of "perversion" and "inversion." (Wilde, to be sure, never subscribed to the model of the "invert" that would be taken up by homosexual enthusiasts of sexology such as Edward Carpenter.) Surely these "disturbing" axioms are also the stuff and substance of a well-worked routine that runs the risk of making their defamiliarizing qualities become somewhat too familiar.

To grasp the repetitious familiarity—rather than the structurally defamiliarizing aspect—of the axiom, it is useful to take a final look at the figure who turns out each of these "Oscarisms" with such systematic regularity. This is the man of fashion himself, the dandy, who draws on Society's codes of dress to reveal how power is wielded through the use and abuse of appearances. Some of Lord Goring's pronouncements are typical of how the rhetorical force of Wilde's maxims can cut in both radical and reactionary directions. Anticipating Wilde's "Phrases and Philosophies," Lord Goring remarks to Sir Robert in Act II that "no man should have a secret from his own wife. She invariably finds it out" (175). Such a comment neatly lays bare the peculiar epistemology of the secret. For a secret can never be known for what it is until, paradoxically, it stops being one. But Lord Goring's brilliance leads him to make another quip that has an altogether more ambivalent resonance to it. "Women," he remarks, "have a wonderful instinct about things. They can discover everything except the obvious" (175). This sentiment can be taken in at least two ways. On the one hand, it would seem to be a virtue not to recognize the "obvious," since that could be a sign of intelligence. Yet, on the other, to miss even the "obvious" might be taken as an outright condemnation of women's inherent stupidity. Since Wilde's dandies, in any case, frequently air unflattering views of women, Lord Goring's discourse could be thought to be inflected with a rather misogynistic tone.

In her comparative study of the dandy in late-Victorian writing, Rita Felski claims that by "exalting appearance over essence, decoration over function," such a refined man of leisure "voices a protest against prevailing bourgeois values that associate masculinity with rationality, industry, utility, and thrift." But his opposition to the cherished pieties of the middle classes is "implicated in, rather than dissolved by, the espousal of a self-reflexive and parodistic consciousness."[25] For it is most obviously on the question of femininity that the dandy's conservatism comes into view. Felski's general point is that the dandy's misogyny derives from the fact that it is Society women who are his most visible rivals in this fashionable world. The narcissistic interest of fashionable women in being the centre of attention constantly threatens to undermine the social authority that the equally vain dandy seeks to command. But Felski's persuasive account of the dandy's damning comments on women's narrow intelligence does not fully explain how someone like Lord Goring resigns himself to marriage. It is only by seeing how the dandy must take on something of Sir Robert's social disposition as an "ideal husband" that the repeated structure of dramatic contradiction can be more completely understood. Like the Puritan Wife, the adventuress, and the self-sacrificing husband, the dandy keeps being repositioned in a drama that allows no one person at any one time an entirely fixed place from which to speak and act.

Thoughts such as these lead me back to Lord Goring's exchange in Act I with Mrs Marchmont, who remains unclear whether Mrs Cheveley really meant that the men were all "dowdies" and the ladies the "dandies" of the day. Like her, we cannot say for sure whether we might agree. There is, in this perpetual dialectic, no closure to be had. All that can be asserted is that these plays beg us to see how the distinctions that we make are often arbitrary ones. The "dowdies and dandies" can and must be looked at from unexpected angles. But it needs to be borne in mind that the reversible structures that shape and define

Wilde's writings may well negate their wilful impulse to overturn commonplace assumptions. For in learning from Lord Goring how to see that "dowdies" and "dandies" may not be complete opposites we are surely anticipating, and in some measure growing less responsive to, the subversive intent of those contradictory strategies that Wilde undertook to refashion Society comedy. We may grow as tired, languid, and idle as the dandy himself. It goes without saying that, for all his dissident behaviour which mocks men and women of his own class, his verbal pyrotecnics are hardly likely to ignite the fires of any coming revolution.

Notes

1. Oscar Wilde, *Two Society Comedies: "A Woman of No Importance" and "An Ideal Husband,"* ed. Ian Small and Russell Jackson (London, 1983), 152. Further page references are in parentheses.

2. Ian Small, *Conditions of Criticism: Authority, Knowledge, and Literature in the Late Nineteenth Century* (Oxford, 1991), 119 n.9.

3. Joel H. Kaplan, "Bad Dressmakers and Well-Arranged Worlds: Fashion and Society Comedy," *Modern Drama,* 34:3 (1991), 329.

4. Kerry Powell, *Oscar Wilde and the Theatre of the 1890s* (Cambridge, 1990), 70.

5. Powell 105.

6. See, for example, the unsigned review, *Truth,* 21 February 1895, 464-65, repr. in *Oscar Wilde: The Critical Heritage,* ed. Karl Beckson (London, 1970), 192.

7. Unsigned review, *Theatre,* 1 March 1895, 169-70, repr. in *Oscar Wilde: The Critical Heritage,* 200.

8. Regenia Gagnier, *Idylls of the Marketplace: Oscar Wilde and the Victorian Public* (Stanford, 1986), 3.

9. My thoughts on this issue are indebted to Elizabeth Wilson's provocative essay, "Is Transgression Transgressive?" in *Activating Theory: Lesbian, Gay, Bisexual Politics,* ed. Joseph Bristow and Angelia R. Wilson (London, 1993), 107-17.

10. Wilde, Letter to George Alexander, [mid-February 1892,] in *More Letters of Oscar Wilde,* ed. Rupert Hart-Davis (London, 1985), 113.

11. Quoted in Joel H. Kaplan, "A Puppet's Power: George Alexander, Clement Scott, and the Replotting of *Lady Windemere's Fan,*" *Theatre Notebook,* 46:2 (1992), 61.

12. Wilde, Letter to George Alexander, [mid-February 1892], in *The Letters of Oscar Wilde,* ed. Rupert Hart-Davis (London, 1962), 309.

13. Wilde, letter to the editor of the *St James's Gazette,* 26 February 1892, *The Letters of Oscar Wilde,* 313.

14. Wilde, *Lady Windermere's Fan,* ed. Ian Small (London, 1980), 9. Further page references are in parentheses.

15. Clement Scott, review of *Lady Windermere's Fan, Illustrated London News,* 27 February 1892, c, 278, repr. in *Oscar Wilde: The Critical Heritage,* 125.

16. Scott, "A Doll's House," *Theatre,* 14 (1889), 19-22, repr. in *Ibsen: The Critical Heritage,* ed. Michael Egan (London, 1972), 114.

17. Unsigned review, "Dress at the Haymarket Theatre," *Sketch,* 26 April 1893, repr. in *Two Society Comedies,* ed. Small and Jackson, 295.

18. A. B. Walkey, review of *A Woman of No Importance, Speaker,* 29 April 1893, 484-85, repr. in *Oscar Wilde: The Critical Heritage,* 151.

19. Wilde, *The Complete Works,* ed. J. B. Foreman (London, 1966), 1074.

20. C. S. B., review of *An Ideal Husband* at the St James's Theatre, *Votes for Women,* 3 January 1914, 549. I am grateful to Joel H. Kaplan and Sheila Stowell for drawing my attention to this review.

21. Bernard Shaw, review of *An Ideal Husband, Saturday Review,* 12 January 1895, repr. in *Oscar Wilde: The Critical Heritage,* 176.

22. Gagnier, 109ff.

23. Shaw, review of *The Importance of Being Earnest, Saturday Review,* 23 February 1895, 249-50, repr. in *Oscar Wilde: The Critical Heritage,* 195.

24. Jonathan Dollimore, *Sexual Dissidence: Augustine to Wilde, Freud to Foucault* (Oxford, 1991), 14-15.

25. Rita Felski, "The Counterdiscourse of the Feminine in Three Texts by Wilde, Huysmans, and Sacher-Masoch," *PMLA,* 106 (1991), 1096, 1099.

Alan Sinfield (essay date spring 1994)

SOURCE: Sinfield, Alan. "'Effeminacy' and 'Femininity': Sexual Politics in Wilde's Comedies." *Modern Drama* 37, no. 1 (spring 1994): 34-52.

[In the following essay, Sinfield explores Wilde's utilization of effeminacy and femininity in his plays.]

Lytton Strachey saw *A Woman of No Importance* revived by Beerbohm Tree in 1907:

> Mr Tree is a wicked Lord, staying in a country house, who has made up his mind to bugger one of the other guests—a handsome young man of twenty. The handsome young man is delighted; when his mother enters, sees his Lordship and recognises him as having copulated with her twenty years before, the result of which was—the handsome young man. She appeals to

Lord Tree not to bugger his own son. He replies that that's an additional reason for doing it (oh! he's a *very* wicked Lord!). . . . The audience was of course charmed.[1]

If the play had been read generally in this way, it could not have been performed on the West End stage, in 1907 or initially in 1893.

EFFEMINATE MEN

Silences, deconstruction has taught us, are significant; it might seem that this point has been well taken among commentators on Wilde, for any silence is likely to be read as a deafening roar about homosexuality. Now, Lytton Strachey's interpretation of *A Woman of No Importance* seems all too inviting. Ian Small and Russell Jackson link Lord Illingworth with Sir Henry Wotton in *The Picture of Dorian Gray:* both "instruct and educate a younger man, and become in the process sinister and attractive figures of authority. This in its turn suggests one of the stereotypes of homosexual relationships: the surrogate father."[2] Today the "earnest," which it is so important to be, must be "homosexual." To Patricia Behrendt, "earnest" sounds like *Urning,* the term for boy-lovers proposed by Karl Heinrich Ulrichs in the 1860s, and even more like the French variant, *uraniste;* this is mooted also in Alan Hollinghurst's novel *The Swimming-Pool Library.*[3] Timothy d'Arch Smith's idea seems better: there may be an allusion to John Gambril Nicholson's book of poems, *Love and Earnest* (1892).[4] But who would hear such an allusion? And for whom, in *The Importance of Being Earnest* (1895), is it important to be a uraniste? No one. To the contrary, as Chris White remarks, "'Ernest' is the name that the men must adopt in order to be acceptable to the women they wish to marry."[5]

Then there is Bunburying. Christopher Craft unearths seven respects in which *Earnest,* as a text, "'goes Bunburying'—in which, that is, Wilde lifts to liminality his subcultural knowledge of 'the terrible pleasures of double life.'"[6] One is engraved cigarette cases, in the play and in Wilde's liaisons; but, of course, Wilde himself did not know, when he wrote *Earnest,* that cigarette cases would prove embarrassing at his trials. Craft is concerned more with intertextual instabilities than with material allusions to a homosexual subculture. Others claim more. Bunburying "was not only British slang for a male brothel, but is also a collection of signifiers that straightforwardly express their desire to bury in the bun," Joel Fineman asserts. Behrendt declares that Bunburying "blatantly calls forth the image of a promiscuous sodomite and foreshadows the epithet 'somdomite' [*sic*] applied to Wilde" by Lord Queensberry (I don't understand the foreshadowing point). Linda Gertner Zatlin has another idea: that Bunbury was "the term for a homosexual pickup."[7] As far as I can discover, there is no historical ground for any of these assertions. *Bun* does not mean "buttock" in Eric Partridge's *Dictionary of Slang,* from the first edition (1937) to the eighth (1984). In John Farmer's dictionary of 1890 it means the *pudendum muliebre,* which is what Partridge says (it's to do with squirrels and rabbits). The meaning "buttock" occurs in the United States from around 1960, according to the *Oxford Dictionary of Modern Slang*.[8] So the implication in Algernon's Bunburying is heterosexual. Even now, "buns" has no necessary connection with brothels, promiscuity, or pick-ups; such inferences seem to derive from narrow stereotypes of modern gay behaviour. Above all, if these meanings were current in Wilde's time—how could Wilde have got away with it? Even today, the plays are sufficiently ambiguous to pass, perhaps with some uneasiness, before boulevard audiences.

We need to recover the initial perceptions of Wilde, and of his dandy characters—before the notoriety of the trials. It is a mistake to suppose that Wilde and his audiences "really" had a concept of gayness like our own, but kept it behind a mask; that it is lurking, therefore, beneath the text—as if it were a statue under a sheet, fully formed but waiting to be unveiled. The modern idea of the homosexual was in the process of getting constituted—largely, I argue elsewhere, through the figure of Wilde himself.[9] For us, it is hard to regard Wilde as other than the apogee of gay experience and expression, because that is the position we have accorded him in our cultures; the principal mid-twentieth-century stereotype was made in his image. For us, he is always already queer. But that is after the event—after the trials helped to produce a major shift in perceptions of same-sex passion. Even in 1907, we must suppose, Strachey's reading of *A Woman of No Importance* was not widely available. To presume a twentieth-century homosexual identity in the blind or hesitant approximations out of which it was (partly) fashioned is to miss, precisely, the points of most interest. The interpretive challenge is to recover the moment of indeterminacy—when Lord Illingworth, like Wilde, is on the brink of manifesting *the homosexual*.

Before he knows that Gerald Arbuthnot is his son, Illingworth asks him to become his secretary. "I took a great fancy to young Arbuthnot the moment I met him," he says; "It is because I like you so much that I want to have you with me," he tells him.[10] To be sure, such language sound amorous to us. However, other characters find no impropriety. "It means a very brilliant future in store for you. Your dear mother will be delighted" (*WNI* 16), Lady Hunstanton enthuses; in fact, she had thought of proposing it herself. "Lord Illingworth seems to have taken quite a fancy to him," Lady Caroline observes, without any evident sexual innuendo (*WNI* 15). For the audience, though not for the other characters, Illingworth acquires the alibi that Gerald is his son—the outcome of Illingworth's treacherous behaviour towards Mrs Arbuthnot (as she calls herself). This seems to afford a double distraction from any suspicion of homosexuality: Illingworth appears heterosexual enough to have conceived Gerald (we see him harassing another woman in the course of the play); and it seems only natural that he should be attached to his son.

Even so, the situation is strange and uneasy. Illingworth expostulates, to the outraged Mrs Arbuthnot: "if I were a perfect stranger, you would allow Gerald to go away with me, but as he is my own flesh and blood you won't. How utterly illogical you are!" (*WNI* 69). And yet, are her fears altogether illogical? For the more explicitly heterosexual Illingworth appears, the more he is a self-ish cad—having seduced and abandoned Mrs Arbuthnot; and hence the less likely, suddenly, to be drawn to his son by wholesome familial ties. Illingworth discovers "paternal feelings he never even suspected he had," says one recent reviewer; "[T]he basis of his change of heart is never dramatized," notes Kerry Powell.[11] The more Illingworth claims the devotion of a father, the more he may seem to manifest a strange excess of male-to-male attachment.

Of course, Wilde was aware of the dangerous possibilities here—already Lord Queensberry was harassing him. Illingworth's amorousness is stronger in drafts of the play, and in some cancelled dialogue the knowing Mrs Allonby seems to have twigged something. "How you delight in disciples!" she teases; "What is their charm?" Illingworth replies: "It is always pleasant to have a slave to whisper in one's ear that, after all, one is immortal. But young Arbuthnot is not a disciple . . . as yet. He is simply one of the most delightful young men I have ever met" (*WNI* 272). When Lady Hunstanton reiterates how Illingworth has "taken such a fancy" to Gerald, Mrs Allonby comments: "Lord Illingworth would talk about nothing else but Mr Arbuthnot, the whole of yesterday afternoon. He looks on him as his most promising disciple. I believe he intends him to be an exact replica of himself, for the use of schools" (*WNI* 281). Wilde deleted this more provocative dialogue.

Still, the point is not that Illingworth is "really" homosexual. There is no "truth" of the play or its characters, to be discovered by peering round behind it at cancelled drafts. Cecil Graham, a dandy in *Lady Windermere's Fan* (1892), is open to divergent readings. He becomes very appreciative of Mrs Erlynne: she "looked very handsome tonight", Graham says; he has become as Lord Darlington observes, "one of her admirers."[12] Graham, here, could certainly be the heterosexual philanderer. But he appears to have no personal attachments to women, and could equally (in the manner we might associate with some gay men today) be admiring the style with which the stigmatized Mrs Erlynne is managing her re-entry into Society (rather like Judy Garland making a come-back). Asked how long he could love a woman who didn't love him, Graham replies: "Oh, all my life!" (*LWF* 66). This might indicate either boundless passionate devotion to women, or a preference for relations that never get anywhere. Simply, the representation labelled "Graham" allows two readings. The critical task is not to give priority to one of them, but to recognise an indeterminacy; one that is not to do with Graham's personal ambivalence as a character, but with the scope of the idea of the dandy in that culture. Wilde contrived a scenario that would pass on the Haymarket stage, while perhaps figuring his own preoccupations and suggesting such possibilities to a few informed observers. Working out the complex codes that enabled this double vision will tell us a good deal about Wilde and the sex-gender system of his time, and about how those phenomena have been circulating subsequently in our cultures.

At the back of modern notions that Wilde and his dandy characters must, somehow, be homosexual is "effeminacy" (as with "the feminine," I use current constructs—recognising that they are misogynist, and hoping to gain a purchase upon the oppression that they encode). "The future belongs to the dandy. It is the exquisites who are going to rule," Illingworth declares, offering Gerald tips on buttonholes and how to knot a tie. "I have always been told that a man should not think too much about his clothes," Gerald replies—intrigued yet somewhat uneasy (**WNI** 75). The dandy is "exquisite"—not like "a man"—but this did not necessarily, before the Wilde trials, signal male homosexuality.

Generally, Ellen Moers shows, the dandy was a heterosexual philanderer. In Edward Bulwer's *Pelham* (1828), for instance, he is said repeatedly to be effeminate in respect of his philandering with women (after many flirtations and affairs, he settles to wedded bliss); he is not linked with same-sex practices.[13] For the most part, Wilde's dandies are heterosexually passionate, and/or philanderers. Lord Darlington in **Lady Windermere's Fan** tries to persuade Lady Windermere to run away with him. Lord Augustus, in the same play, is especially effeminate. He has been married and divorced several times, and is infatuated with Mrs Erlynne despite evidence of her unreliability. He falls too easily for female charms; he is flabby; men insult him. "Tuppy," they call him, mocking his ramish proclivities. Even in *Dorian Gray,* where the plot springs from the response of Wotton, the dandy, to the attractions of Dorian, Wotton's other involvements seem to be with women. He reflects with wonderment upon Basil Hallward's infatuation with Dorian—"He remembered something like it in history. Was it not Plato, that artist in thought, who had first analyzed it?"[14] Hallward is the homosexual, if anyone is, but he is not a dandy; he is earnest—moral and hard-working.

According to Gwendolen in **The Importance of Being Earnest,** the dandy is positively sexy. "[O]nce a man begins to neglect his domestic duties he becomes painfully effeminate, does he not? And I don't like that. It makes men so very attractive" (**IBE** 65). The obvious "modern" reading is proposed by Behrendt: "[t]he attraction that the effeminate man would hold for Gwendolyn [sic] would be his lack of sexual interest in her."[15] Such a reading not only unravels the plot of *Earnest,* it flies in the face of the "interest" shown in women by Darlington, Augustus, and Illingworth. Believing "Earnest" to mean "uraniste," Behrendt thinks Gwendolen is "attracted specifically to men of questionable sexual preferences" (176). Rather, "Earnest" means *earnest.* The effeminate dandy, despising responsible, middle-class domesticity and finding nothing better to do, spends his time flirting. He is dangerously attractive because he shows he is available.

Dandy effeminacy signalled class, far more than sexuality. The newly dominant middle class justified itself by claiming manly purity, purpose, and responsibility, and identified the leisure class, correspondingly, with effeminate idleness and immorality. In the face of this manoeuvre, there were two alternatives for the wealthy and those who sought to seem wealthy. One was to attempt to appear useful and good; the other was to repudiate middle-class authority by displaying conspicuous idleness, immorality, and effeminacy; in other words, by being a dandy. Wilde presents extreme versions of this strategy. Jack and Algy in **The Importance of Being Earnest** are thoroughly effeminate young men, and this includes their leisured idleness, their indifference to moral conventions, their exploitation of and romantic devotion to women, and suggestions of diverse further profligacies. "It is awfully hard work doing nothing", Algernon complains; "However, I don't mind hard work where there is no definite object of any kind" (**IBE** 46). The women's demand that their beaux be "earnest" is a characteristically frivolous reworking of prevailing middle-class mores; a further mark of the excessive leisure-class frivolity of all the principals.

Effeminacy came to function as a broad signal of aristocracy during the eighteenth century. Eve Sedgwick writes of "the feminisation of the aristocracy as a whole," whereby "the abstract image of the entire class, came to be seen as ethereal, decorative, and otiose in relation to the vigorous and productive values of the middle class."[16] The impact of this is evident in Michael Rey's study of police records of men accused of same-sex practices in Paris from around 1800:

> to people of the lower class, a noble—powdered, pomaded, refined—was both elegant and effeminate; but that bothered no one as long as the mode of attire remained faithful to the specific superior social condition which its wearer represented. If someone lower on the social scale assumed this costume . . . not only did he betray his social condition, but in addition, his effeminacy, by losing its accepted association with elegance and the upper class, became an indication of the wearer's real effeminacy.[17]

I don't agree that what was revealed was "real effeminacy": rather, it was another cultural mode. However, this does not spoil the relevance of Rey's observation. The aristocrat was expected to be effeminate, so same-sex passion was not foregrounded by his manner; with lower-class young men, it was otherwise.

The Wildean dandy, therefore—so far from looking like a homosexual—was distinctively exonerated from such suspicions. Because of his class identification, or aspiration, he above all need not be read as identified with same-sex practices. At the same time, however, the dissolute aristocrat might indulge in any kind of debauchery; so while same-sex passion was not ruled in, neither was it ruled out. Hence the texts afford some basis for knowing interpretations such as Strachey's, and for the readings of modern criticism. The subsequent, and partly consequent,

Wildean image of the male homosexual has made such readings inevitable—though still dependent upon intricate and insecure nuances, and still scarcely audible for conservative audiences.

Lord Goring, in *An Ideal Husband* (1895), has been regarded as a candidate for homosexuality; Behrendt credits him with a "passionate attachment" to Sir Robert Chiltern.[18] For most of the play Goring flirts honourably with Mabel Chiltern, but that does not affect the case either way. Indeed, she is generally the initiator, and Goring is preoccupied with the troubles of his friend, Sir Robert. However, Goring's apparent disinclination could, very likely, be the off-hand, dandy way of undertaking a romantic courtship; he was once in love with Mrs Cheveley. Reluctance to marry is not distinctively suspicious to Goring's father, Lord Caversham; in fact, it is quite understandable: "Damme, sir, it is your duty to get married," he says; "You can't be always living for pleasure. Every man of position is married nowadays. Bachelors are not fashionable any more. They are a damaged lot. Too much is known about them."[19] Once more, the text licenses the modern assumption that a bachelor is probably, or "really," gay; but it is able to do this because that inference was scarcely there for Wilde's initial audience.

Sexuality will not come properly into focus in *An Ideal Husband* because the play is not interested in it. Goring's dandyism makes fuller sense if we observe its embeddedness in the prevailing alignment of effeminacy and class. Mabel Chiltern is teasing when she denies that he leads an idle life; "How can you say such a thing? Why, he rides in the Row at ten o'clock in the morning, goes to the Opera three times a week, changes his clothes at least five times a day, and dines out every night of the season. You don't call that leading an idle life, do you?" (*IH* 136). Goring appears not just idle, but conspicuously so; he almost, as Miss Chiltern suggests, works at it. Caversham's wish for him to marry involves an entire repudiation of this dandy programme: "You must get a wife, sir. Look where your friend Robert Chiltern has got by probity, hard work, and a sensible marriage with a good woman" (*IH* 217). Goring, too, might become useful and good—Sir Robert is an idealistic and energetic government minister who, though not from an old family, has established himself by affirming, with his wife's specific support, middle-class earnestness. According to the *Times* critic, Chiltern was played by Lewis Waller "in his manliest and most robust style."[20]

Chiltern's vulnerability to blackmail (because of a fraud) derives from the contemporary alignment of class and earnestness, as Mrs Cheveley points out: "In old days nobody pretended to be a bit better than his neighbours. In fact, to be a bit better than one's neighbour was considered excessively vulgar and middle-class. Nowadays, with our modern mania for morality, everyone has to pose as a paragon of purity" (*IH* 161). Mrs Cheveley has a point. "Prior to the 1830s," Frank Mort observes, "personal morality had not been seen as necessary for political eminence." This pattern was challenged "both by organ-

ised evangelical pressure groups and by the structural shift in the overall balance of power in favour of the middle-classes."[21] Manliness remains at issue when Chiltern attempts to justify his dishonesty. "[T]here are terrible temptations that it requires strength, strength and courage, to yield to. To stake all one's life on a single moment, to risk everything on one throw, whether the stake be power or pleasure, I care not—there is no weakness in that. There is a horrible, a terrible courage" (*IH* 181). Thus Chiltern reworks manliness, niftily abandoning the earnest, middle-class version for a heroic, Nietzschean mode.

Nonetheless, there is authority in Goring's statement that Chiltern has merely become involved in a "loathsome commercial transaction of a loathsome commercial age" (*IH* 237). Indeed, Goring, though a dandy, proves both principled and effective—his interventions save the Chilterns from disgrace. The standard expectations of the dandy and the earnest gentleman are reversed.

In fact, the manly man figures more strongly in *An Ideal Husband* than elsewhere in Wilde's plays. Generally, dandy values are allowed to hold the stage. There are no military officers (Jack's father in *Earnest* was a general, but he is long absent; Lady Bracknell, his sister-in-law, cannot recall his first name). Other men are doormats. Sir John in *A Woman of No Importance* is cosseted and pursued by his wife; Lord Bracknell is so dispensable that he commonly dines upstairs to make the numbers right at dinner. Not that he is busy with manly affairs—he is entirely domesticated, Gwendolen says: "Outside the family circle, Papa, I am glad to say, is entirely unknown. I think that is quite as it should be. The home seems to me to be the proper sphere for the man" (*IBE* 36, 65). There is no equivalent of the pugnacious Lord Queensberry. Even Herod, in *Salomé*, is all too ready to give away half his kingdom for an infatuation.

The uncertain balance of moral authority between Chiltern and Goring shows manly earnestness under contest from effeminate idleness. This is not resolved in the play—to the perplexity of critics. William Archer supposed that Wilde meant to show that Chiltern's old peccadillo should not incapacitate him for public life, but inadvertently indicated the opposite. Small and Jackson find it "difficult to believe in the new life which awaits these characters," and particularly in the future of the Chilterns' marriage.[22] However, such indeterminacies are too persistent to be mere blunders. Consider *Lady Windermere's Fan,* where the happy-family ending depends on Lady Windermere remaining ignorant of the identity of her mother and Lord Windermere unaware that his wife meant to leave him. It is indeed disconcerting to suppose that our rulers are like Sir Robert, and his marriage certainly looks less promising than that of Goring and Mabel; Wilde allows dandy values to outweigh earnestness.

Powell argues that it is a mistake to expect these plays to conclude tidily, in the manner of a contemporary problem play. He sees, rather, "an unresolved struggle between the author's own fragmented personality—socialist and socialite, husband and homosexual, father and feminist, Paterian and puritan."[23] I would add that the stresses and indeterminacies in Wilde's life and writings were not his alone. They manifest the ideological faultlines, in class, gender, and sexuality, that fractured his culture.

Feminine Women

Mrs Cheveley is said to have complained that Society is made up of dowdies and dandies. Lord Goring quips: "She is quite right, too. The men are all dowdies and the women are all dandies, aren't they?" (*IH* 152). Goring accepts the idea of the dowdy woman, but chivalrously (he no doubt thinks) reapplies it to men: they are dull, plain, and domesticated, whereas Society women—such as Mrs Cheveley herself—display dandified leisure-class frivolity. In so far as he caps Mrs Cheveley's remark, Goring contrives to rise above his own analysis: he proves himself a dandy rather than a dowdy.

In fact neither is right. In Wilde's version of Society, male and female characters, equally, may be dowdily earnest (Lord Bracknell, Miss Worsley), and either may display dandy attributes. Mabel Chiltern keeps pace with Lord Goring's banter; when it comes to a marriage proposal it is he who asks her to "be serious" (*IH* 251). Illingworth and Mrs Allonby spar on even terms (one of her aphorisms is shared with Wotton in *Dorian Gray*: "The secret of life is never to have an emotion that is unbecoming").[24] Mrs Erlynne in *Lady Windermere's Fan* gets her way by playing along the male dandies. This is feminine power.

Many leisure-class men in fact worked hard, in civil affairs or running their estates. But Society women were expected to be conspicuously idle and frivolous. "The reason for the more extreme insistence on a futile life for this class of women than for the men of the same pecuniary and social grade," Veblen argues in *The Theory of the Leisure Class* (1899), is that such women constitute "a vicarious leisure class." The uselessness of the leisure-class female made her an ornament for the male upon whom she depended. "Riding, dancing, flirting and dressing up—in short, entertaining and being entertained—all occupations which imply the consumption and not the production of commodities and services, were the very substance of her life before marriage and a large and important part of it after marriage," Beatrice Webb recalls.[25] To live thus was regarded as feminine; and the dandy was effeminate because of his skills and pleasure in his women's arena. Young and unmarried men might leave cards and call, Leonore Davidoff observes, but "they were rather pitied for having to do so as it was considered very much a part of a wife's or daughter's duty."[26] The dandy is good at entertaining and being entertained by women; he enjoys activities that were coded "feminine"—trivia, chit-chat, flirting, gossip, scandal.

The social round was not without utility, however. As Davidoff shows, leisure-class women were "arbiters of social acceptance or rejection."[27] Lord Windermere can give Mrs Erlynne money, but only Lady Windermere can get her readmitted to Society. Windermere tells his wife: "She has been to several houses—not to houses where you would go, I admit, but still to houses where women who are in what is called Society nowadays do go. That does not content her. She wants you to receive her once" (*LWF* 24). Windermere can invite Mrs Erlynne to a dance at their house only at the cost of his first row with his wife, and it remains open to Lady Windermere to destroy the whole effect by cutting her unwanted guest.

The policing of Society was effected crucially through marriage—a distinct responsibility of the leisure-class woman. The management of class boundaries through marriage, C. Wright Mills says, served "to keep a propertied class intact and unscattered; by monopoly of sons and daughters, anchoring the class in the legalities of blood lines."[28] This was a delicate matter, because merely arranged marriages were no longer acceptable; the young people's opportunities, affections, and interests had to be carefully manipulated if an outcome satisfactory to the requirements of property was to be obtained. This was achieved through the feminine regime of calling, tea, dinners, and balls. Lady Berwick in *Lady Windermere's Fan,* like Lady Bracknell, accomplishes it without reference to her husband.

In Walter Bagehot's view, an "order of nobility" prevented "the rule of wealth"; it would be more precise to say that Society arranged an accommodation between birth and wealth, deciding when, and through what face-saving mechanisms, money made in business was to be allowed to count alongside family and breeding.[29] For although there were a few noble families at the core, the many commercial and industrial peerages from about 1886 and the arrival of monied South Africans, Europeans, Jewish, and U.S. people made Society's edges, as Geoffrey Best observes, "permanently blurred by the jostling of the thousands who were trying to get in with the hundreds who were trying not to be pushed out."[30] "There were no fixed caste barriers; there seemed to be, in fact, no recognised types of exclusiveness based on birth or breeding, on personal riches or on personal charm; there was no fastidiousness about manners or morals or intellectual gifts," Webb says; the implicit test of membership was "*the possession of some form of power over other people*."[31] Lady Windermere imagines that her moral preoccupations can influence Society, but the play discloses an intricate shuffle of money, status, and talent. Mrs Erlynne almost makes it back; she fails because she is moral, not because she is immoral. Society was organized not to maintain a fence around an established order, but to handle a chronic instability.

The ideology purveyed in the new popular press was that everyone in Society was, at once, noble, rich, and amusing—until found out. The actuality, as Wilde's comedies suggest, was continual improvisation and compromise. It was not a matter of deciding who was authentically upper-class, but of negotiating a partly permeable system. Miss

Worsley in *A Woman of No Importance* and Mr Hopper in *Lady Windermere's Fan* are desirable because they are rich; they are mocked as outsiders (American and Australian with trade connections), but the mockery is part of the process whereby they are being accommodated. Being amusing was not as effective as being rich, but might get one a long way. "Talent, brain and beauty could, with the right patronage, rise quite high"—to the point, Best says, where Society seemed accessible to "every kind of attractive or plausible 'outsider' (e.g. Disraeli, Millais, Taine and Bagehot)."[32]

If charm, sophistication, and fluency could help one into Society, Wilde makes it even more important in policing the boundaries—negotiating the categories, the hierarchies. That is what the witty cross-talk of the feminine woman is often doing—for instance over degrees of familiarity with a spade (*IBE* 67). Mrs Allonby is a bit too adventurous for some of her acquaintance. "Remarkable type, Mrs Allonby," Lady Caroline avers. "She lets her clever tongue run away with her sometimes," Lady Hunstanton responds, picking up the critical implication but damping it a little. "Is that the only thing," Lady Caroline wonders, "Mrs Allonby allows to run away with her?" (meaning a man). This goes a bit too far for Lady Hunstanton—who, after all, has invited Mrs Allonby to her house: "I hope so, Caroline, I am sure" (*WNI* 29). Lady Hunstanton does not altogether discount the exotic possibility, but Mrs Allonby is allowed to pass. "There seemed in fact to be a sort of invisible stock exchange in constant communication with the leading hostesses in London and in the country; the stock being social reputations and the reason for appreciation or depreciation being worldly success or failure however obtained," Webb reports.[33]

The frivolous and knowing stance of the dandified, feminine woman was nearly as much of an affront to middle-class ideas of womanliness as the effeminate dandy was to ideas of manliness. Good women were supposed to be innocent. "[T]he public world of work was dirty, brutal and often immoral," Philippa Levine says, "while the home, the domain of the woman, signified peace and purity. The sexual articulation of that polarity had an irresistible logic: man's sexuality was active, often violent and certainly dominant, a mirror of his public involvements, while that of woman was circumscribed by the demands of purity."[34]

Feminists and reformers often accepted the earnest model of woman. They used the idea of female purity as a way of campaigning against male exploitation, especially by upper-class men and in prostitution. They also insisted on work; many, Martha Vicinus says, "saw work as the key to the single woman's liberation."[35] This is the stance of Lady Chiltern in *An Ideal Husband.* She serves on committees where they consider "Factory Acts, Female Inspectors, the Eight Hours' Bill, the Parliamentary Franchise," and loves her husband because she believes he has "brought into the political life of our time a nobler atmosphere, a finer attitude towards life, a freer air of

purer aims and higher ideals" (*IH* 188, 174). However, Lady Chiltern's earnestness is questioned, and not just by the bad Mrs Cheveley. Lady Basildon and Mrs Marchmont are sardonic about her attempts to inculcate "some serious purpose in life," and Mabel Chiltern rejects the thought of marrying a man like Sir Robert (*IH* 134, 196). So Wilde's women construct a contest parallel to the effeminate/manly dichotomy displayed by the men: the feminine, leisure-class woman stands together with the male dandy against middle-class earnestness.

In *A Woman of No Importance* purity is asserted by Mrs Arbuthnot, the earnest American, Hester Worsley, and the MP, Mr Kelvil. The latter complains that Illingworth "regards woman simply as a toy," whereas she is "the intellectual helpmeet of man in public as in private life. Without her we should forget the true ideals" (*WNI* 30). However, Kelvil has packed his own wife and eight children off to the seaside while he pursues his career; and although Mrs Arbuthnot wins out against the unpleasant Illingworth, it is at the cost of appearing narrow and obsessive. Meanwhile, feminine, dandified values are maintained by the leisured women. Mrs Allonby leads them in an after-dinner assault on marriage, domesticity, and the manly man. "[H]appy marriages," Lady Caroline observes, are getting "remarkably rare." "Except among the middle classes, I have been told," Lady Stutfield reports (disavowing first-hand knowledge); "I have noticed a very, very sad expression in the eyes of so many married men." Mrs Allonby elaborates: "they are horribly tedious when they are good husbands, and abominably conceited when they are not." She dismisses the very notion of an ideal husband: "There couldn't be such a thing. The institution is wrong." Her husband—Ernest—is no dandy: he has "a very strong chin, a square chin," but is "absolutely uninteresting," with "no conversation at all"—though he talks all the time. Miss Worsley is appalled. On her definition of natural womanly purity, the entire conversation should have been impossible: "I couldn't believe that any women could really hold such views" (*WNI* 42-50).

Wilde's awareness of and readiness to respond to earnest feminist ideas and attitudes is displayed in his editing of *The Woman's World* (1887-89), where he supplemented trivia, fashion, and gossip with thoughtful and improving topics. There, he undermined the stereotypical idea that women cannot handle serious matters. The plays deploy an opposite strategy; as Laurel Brake puts it, "It is just these qualities rejected as unsuitable for women—a taste for triviality, dress, gossip, and pleasures such as music—which are valorised in Wilde's own writing." The alternatives derive from the polarity described by Jonathan Dollimore—between "the natural, the sincere, and the authentic" in the manner of André Gide, and the anti-essentialism that we more often associate with Wilde.[36] A key feminist victory was the Married Women's Property Act of 1882, which enabled women to continue to own property after marriage. Mrs Allonby claims not to need such reforms. Turning the phrase around, she declares: "All men are married women's property. That is the only true definition of what married women's property really is. But we don't belong to anyone" (*WNI* 42). In the plays, Wilde undermines the earnest woman, and empowers the correlate of the effeminate man—the boldly feminine woman.

THE IMPORTANCE OF IMPOTENCE

Effeminacy and femininity do not sound like progressive representations; they sound like exploitative patriarchal stereotypes. However, the reformers' endorsement of earnest middle-class purity, also, was not entirely progressive; as Levine observes, "Feminists took hold of the position to which they were limited by Victorian ideology and inverted its precepts." By definition, it is difficult to achieve progressive aims from such a compromised starting point. "In conforming to these precepts, however subversively, feminists were aligning themselves, in one sense, with values associated with the middle classes."[37] The earnest rhetoric of purity led campaigners into demands for state regulation; and, as tends to happen, whatever the initial intentions of the reformers, the new laws bore upon the victims rather than the powerful. Miss Worsley, in that vein, wants fallen women punished along with men, and the children as well (*WNI* 88-89). Like Lady Windermere, she learns to reconsider her values. The purity lobby scarcely touched the upper-class men with whom it had begun; it produced instead the Criminal Law Amendment Act of 1885, which increased penalties for brothel-keeping, raised the age of consent for girls to sixteen, and criminalised male homosexual acts in private.

We should not be surprised at this outcome. The reformers deployed the ideology of purity because it is hard to conceive dissidence without *some* grounding in the current framework of language and representation. They "drew on the only vocabulary able to bear the moral and intellectual weight of their challenge," Frank Mort argues; "religious language not only provided a link between different political constituencies, it offered a set of concepts, a rhetoric of resistance and a strength of moral certainty powerful enough to take on the weight of the medical and political establishment. Even more importantly, it supplied many mid-Victorian feminists with a critical perspective on existing social relations."[38] It was the same, I suggest, for Wilde with leisure-class effeminacy and femininity: though at an ideological price, they afforded some critical purchase upon dominant attitudes, and upon some of the less attractive stances of the reformers. The dandy and the feminine woman were figures around which issues of class, culture, and sexuality might be contested. They offered the opportunity, and the risk, that dissident strategies often admit: they disturb certain orthodoxies at the expense of admitting other regressive implications.

Deciding whether Wilde's games with gender are, in essence, progressive or reactionary is in my view not an appropriate project. His comedies have held the stage before basically conservative, boulevard audiences for a hundred years; they afford ample scope for indulgence in deference towards the upper classes. At the same time, successful plays are usually risky; they flirt, at least, with the danger that prevailing values might not be satisfactory, or might not prevail. In the face of such a production, some audience members will retreat into conformity, while others will entertain more radical possibilities. It is a mistake to posit a unitary "audience response."[39]

The resistance that Wilde's vision of feminine power has aroused is illuminating. It tends to replicate the ideology that it aspires to assess; the ideology that Wilde observed and redeployed. In the view of Patricia Behrendt, the representation of Mrs Allonby and the others is misogynist: these women are "tyrannizing, materialistic, and petty by nature."[40] I suppose that is broadly true; but, also, it is how women tend to get regarded in our cultures when they do not confine themselves to domestic duties. Behrendt complains that "Lady Bracknell has usurped the traditionally masculine role of dominating the household and of granting permission for Gwendolyn [sic] to marry"—no wonder there is a "tendency to cast a man in her role" (177). Wilde's dandified women embody a threat that women might exercise power far beyond the purity and innocence that was allowed in middle-class ideology. Further, by claiming femininity they unsettle the idea that the good woman is the truly womanly one. Take Mrs Arbuthnot's handwriting. "She is one of the sweetest of women. Writes a beautiful hand, too, so large, so firm" (Lady Hunstanton). "A little lacking in femininity, Jane. Femininity is the quality I admire most in women" (Lady Caroline). "Oh! she is very feminine, Caroline, and so good too" (Lady Hunstanton; *WNI* 32). If femininity is womanly and hence naturally good, Mrs Arbuthnot is "very feminine." But she asserts herself and her goodness in a middle-class way, and thereby becomes, like her writing, almost manly. "You should hear what the Archdeacon says of her. He regards her as his right hand in the parish," Lady Hunstanton adds (*WNI* 32). The common phrase, which we almost hear, is "right hand man." Mrs Cheveley says Lady Chiltern has large—manly—hands and sees in her handwriting "[t]he ten commandments in every stroke of the pen, and moral law all over the page" (*IH* 236-37, 222).

In fact, Society women might exercise political influence. "[I]f the secret political history of the past forty years could be written," one commentator remarked in 1885, it would be found to depend upon "a judicious course of Whig hospitality during the months of autumn." Davidoff comments: "[T]he filtering of personnel through the sieve of Society regulated access to political power, economic position and the accumulation of capital."[41] Women were confined to socialising, but feminine power could be effective through that mechanism. "No man has any real success in this world unless he has got women to back him, and women rule society," Illingworth says (*WNI* 76); Mrs Cheveley and Lady Chiltern determine Sir Robert's career.

To be sure, even the leisure-class woman was subordinated in late-nineteenth-century society. As we see in the plays, she may not go down to supper without getting a man to pay her attention (*IH* 154-55). This perhaps did set witty, flirtatious interchange at a premium; and hence, in Wilde's version, the empowerment of the fluent, dandified woman. Political scenarios such as Wilde depicts did occur, but the pertinence of his representations of effeminacy and femininity does not depend on that, or even on people such as his characters actually existing. The woman on top is a perpetual anxiety in cultures, such as those we call "western," that cannot manage with, or without, powerful women. Of course, it is a joke when Lady Hunstanton remarks: "Dear Mr Cardew [presumably the prime minister], is ruining the country. I wonder Mrs Cardew allows him" (*WNI* 26). But Wilde was evoking an anxious fantasy. This is plainer in the more exotic mode of *Salomé.* Iokanaan (like Hester Worsley) inveighs against and resists the immorality of the ruling elite, whereas Salomé (like Mrs Cheveley) depends upon feminine power. Herod offers Salomé half his kingdom if she will dance for him—the woman intrudes on male authority. But she doesn't want the kingdom, she wants destruction; and that is the male fantasy about feminine power. Initial reviewers, Jane Marcus points out, linked Salomé with Ibsen's strong female characters. The subsequent move with such women, as the concept became current, was to label them "lesbian." The 1918 production of *Salomé* was subjected to such allegations. As Marcus observes, there was no justification in the text or the performance for this. "Nothing overt in the play indicates that Salomé was a lover of her own sex. She kills a man, therefore she must be a lesbian, runs the reasoning of the trial."[42] The same logic informs the film *Basic Instinct.*

The feminine woman, as Wilde represents her, together with the effeminate man, effects a disturbance of categories that reaches beyond the oppressive terms in which both are framed. According to Alan Bird, "the men are impotent triflers, the women domineering, powerful, ruthless, self-possessed and absolutely determined in their obsessive desires and loves, whether of money, marriage, social standing, or a son."[43] That is right: conventionally good women are undermined and, apart from the stand-off between Goring and Chiltern, the conventionally active man is written out. This is Wilde's challenge.

Camille Paglia rehearses the Victorian debate about true womanly attributes. "Never for a moment are Gwendolen and Cecily persuasively 'female'. They are creatures of indeterminate sex who take up the mask of femininity to play a new and provocative role"; if the parts are played properly, "[l]anguage, personality, and behaviour should be so hard that the play becomes a spectacle of visionary coldness. The faces should be like glass, without gender or humanity."[44] Paglia imagines essential, transhistorical male and female principles, which she thinks ought to be aligned with masculine and feminine attributes as conventionally understood; anything else is a failure in humanity. Wilde's version of feminine power indeed effects an aggressive splitting apart of these violent hierarchies.

Initial audiences, I have argued, were unlikely to hear homosexuality in Wilde's dandy characters, but the subsequent impetus of these plays is inseparable from the popular knowledge that their author is the most notorious homosexual of modern times. This tends to influence hostile accounts of their deployment of gender categories. The "hieratic purity" of *The Importance of Being Earnest,* Paglia says, "could best be appreciated if all the women's roles were taken by female impersonators."[45] Wilde was unable to create authentic women characters, we are led to infer; after all, Paglia remarks, gay men are dedicated to thwarting "nature's procreative compulsions." This is not an irrelevant perspective: Wilde was indeed undermining constructs that Paglia deems natural. She resists this by turning back the challenge: "of course nature has won, as she always does, by making disease the price of promiscuous sex" (14-15). So not only are gay men unable to write plays with "humanity," they get AIDS as well.

Dandy effeminacy, I have argued, did not necessarily mean homosexuality in the nineteenth century, but sometimes it came close to it; the mid-twentieth-century stereotype was at the point of forming. There is Graham's evasiveness, Goring's attachment to Chiltern, Hallward's love for Dorian, the Page's love for the young Syrian in *Salomé.* And there is Illingworth's excessive liking for Arbuthnot. "You have missed not having a father, I suppose, Gerald?" he asks, placing his hand on his shoulder (*WNI* 74). Leisure-class men did have intimate secretaries, and they didn't turn out to be sons. In 1894, Lord Alfred Douglas's twenty-five-year-old brother, Francis, Viscount Drumlanrig, was found dead from a gunshot wound. Drumlanrig was assistant private secretary to Lord Rosebery, then Foreign Minister, and the Douglas family were convinced that his death was brought about by the pressures of a same-sex relationship with Rosebery.[46] "The world will know him merely as my private secretary," Illingworth tells the hostile Mrs Arbuthnot, "but to me he will be something very near, and very dear" (*WNI* 66).

Strachey's reading has a subversive plausibility—even, and perhaps especially, for those who detest such Wildean frivolity. According to the *Evening News,* the trials exposed Wilde as what he always had been: "a social pest, a centre of intellectual corruption . . . who attacked all wholesome, manly, simple ideals of English life."[47] Wilde's dandified characters may be artificial constructs—subversive puns upon conventional gender categories; but he makes them persuasive. Frivolity, it appears, overcomes earnestness. That Wilde was astute in his sense of what would engage an audience's interest is shown by his success in the theatre. That orthodoxies are not easily overthrown is shown by the fact that he was tried, convicted, and sentenced.

Notes

1. Quoted in Michael Holroyd, *Lytton Strachey: A Biography* (London, 1971), 357-58 n. 14.

2. Introduction to Oscar Wilde, *Two Society Comedies: "A Woman of No Importance" and "An Ideal Husband,"* ed. Ian Small and Russell Jackson (London, 1983), xxv.

3. Patricia Flanagan Behrendt, *Oscar Wilde: Eros and Aesthetics* (London, 1991), 172-73; Alan Hollinghurst, *The Swimming-Pool Library* (London, 1988), 177.

4. Timothy d'Arch Smith, *Love in Earnest* (London, 1970), xix. In 1894 Nicholson appeared alongside Wilde and Douglas in the *Chameleon*, so the connection is not illfounded.

5. Chris White, "The Organization of Pleasure: British Homosexual and Lesbian Discourse 1869-1914", unpub. diss. (University of Nottingham, 1992), 289.

6. Christopher Craft, "Alias Bunbury: Desire and Termination in *The Importance of Being Earnest*," *Representations*, 31 (Summer, 1990), 19-46.

7. Joel Fineman, "The Significance of Literature: *The Importance of Being Earnest*," October, 15 (1980), 89; Behrendt, 174; Linda Gertner Zatlin, *Aubrey Beardsley and Victorian Sexual Politics* (Oxford, 1990), 151.

8. Eric Partridge, *A Dictionary of Slang* (London, 1937); 8th edition, ed. Paul Beale (London, 1984); John S. Farmer, *Slang and Its Analogues* (London, 1890); John Ayto and John Simpson, *The Oxford Dictionary of Modern Slang* (Oxford, 1992). See also William Green, "Oscar Wilde and the Bunburys," *Modern Drama*, 21 (1978), 67-80; Neil Bartlett, *Who Was That Man?: A Present for Mr Oscar Wilde* (London, 1988); Joseph Bristow, in Oscar Wilde, '*The Importance of Being Earnest' and Related Writings*, ed. Joseph Bristow (London, 1992), 16-19; cited hereafter in the text as "*IBE.*"

9. See Alan Sinfield, *The Wilde Century: Effeminacy, Oscar Wilde and the Queer Moment* (London, 1994); Ed Cohen, *Talk on the Wilde Side: Toward a Genealogy of a Discourse on Male Sexualities* (New York, 1993); Michael Hurley, "Homosexualities: Fiction, Reading and Moral Training," in *Feminine, Masculine and Representation,* ed. Terry Threadgold and Anne Cranny-Francis (Sydney, 1990), 164; Eve Kosofsky Sedgwick, *Between Men: English Literature and Male Homosocial Desire* (New York, 1985), 94, 216-17; Martin Green, *Children of the Sun: A Narrative of "Decadence" in England after 1918* (London, 1977), 23-40; Ellen Moers, *The Dandy: Brummel to Beerbohm* (London, 1960), 304.

10. Oscar Wilde, *A Woman of No Importance*, in Wilde, *Two Society Comedies,* ed. Small and Jackson, 23, 35; cited hereafter in the text as "*WNI.*"

11. Pat Moorman, reviewing a Royal Shakespeare Company production, *Brighton and Hove Leader*, March 26, 1992, 26; Kerry Powell, *Oscar Wilde and the Theatre of the 1890s* (Cambridge, 1990), 71.

12. Oscar Wilde, *Lady Windermere's Fan,* ed. Ian Small (London, 1980), 60; cited hereafter in the text as "*LWF.*"

13. Moers, 81, 172 et passim.

14. Oscar Wilde, *The Picture of Dorian Gray,* ed. Isobel Murray (Oxford, 1981), 36; and see 101-2.

15. Behrendt, 176.

16. Sedgwick, 93; see also 174-76; and Frank Mort, *Dangerous Sexualities* (London, 1987), part 3; Regenia Gagnier, *Idylls of the Marketplace* (Stanford, 1986), 67-90; H. Montgomery Hyde, *The Other Love: A Historical and Contemporary Survey of Homosexuality in Britain* (London, 1970), 139; Jeffrey Weeks, *Sex, Politics and Society: The Regulation of Sexuality since 1800,* 2nd ed. (London, 1989), 110-11).

17. Michael Rey, "Parisian Homosexuals Create a Lifestyle, 1700-1850: The Police Archives," in *'Tis Nature's Fault,* ed. R.P. Maccubbin (Cambridge, 1988), 189.

18. Behrendt, 163.

19. Oscar Wilde, *An Ideal Husband,* in Wilde, *Two Society Comedies,* ed. Small and Jackson, 217; cited hereafter in the text as "*IH.*"

20. Quoted in *Two Society Comedies,* ed. Small and Jackson, 131.

21. Mort, 88.

22. Review of *An Ideal Husband* (1895), in *Oscar Wilde: The Critical Heritage,* ed. Karl Beckson (London, 1970), 174; *Two Society Comedies,* ed. Small and Jackson, xxxv.

23. Powell, 72; see 86-87.

24. *WNI* 84; Wilde, *Picture of Dorian Gray,* 84.

25. Thorstein Veblen, *The Theory of the Leisure Class,* with introduction by C. Wright Mills (New York, 1953), 229; Beatrice Webb, *My Apprenticeship* (New York, 1977), 47.

26. Leonore Davidoff, *The Best Circles: Women and Society in Victorian England* (Totawa, NJ, 1973), 44. A deleted line of *The Ideal Husband* said, by way of showing the sheepishness of a husband, "If I allowed him he would have tea with me at five every afternoon" (ed. Small and Jackson, 151).

27. Davidoff, 16.

28. C. Wright Mills, introduction to Veblen, xvi; see Webb, 48; Davidoff, 49.

29. Walter Bagehot, *The English Constitution, Collected Works,* ed. Norman St John-Stevas, vol. 5 (London, 1974), 263; see Geoffrey Best, *Mid-Victorian Britain 1851-75* (London, 1979), 251-68; Joseph Bristow, *Empire Boys: Adventures in a Man's World* (London, 1991), 55-58.

30. Best, 262.

31. Webb, 49.

32. Best, 274-75.

33. Webb, 51.

34. Philippa Levine, *Victorian Feminism 1850-1900* (Tallahassee, 1987), 130. See Mort, *Dangerous Sexualities,* 77-83; Nancy Armstrong, "The Rise of the Domestic Woman," in Nancy Armstrong and Leonard Tennenhouse, eds., *The Ideology of Conduct: Essays on Literature and the History of Sexuality* (New York, 1987), 96-141.

35. Martha Vicinus, *Independent Women: Work and Community for Single Women 1850-1920* (London, 1985), 24; see Elaine Showalter, *Sexual Anarchy: Gender and Culture at the Fin de Siècle* (London, 1990), chs.2, 3.

36. See Laurel Brake, "Gendered Space: *The Woman's World,*" *Women,* 2 (1991), 149-62; Jonathan Dollimore, *Sexual Dissidence: Augustine to Wilde, Freud to Foucault* (Oxford, 1991), 14 and ch.1.

37. Levine, 133.

38. Mort, 89; and 116-30. See Sheila Jeffreys, *The Spinster and Her Enemies: Feminism and Sexuality 1880-1930* (London, 1985); Judith R. Walkowitz, *Prostitution and Victorian Society: Women, Class, and the State* (Cambridge, 1980); Richard Dellamora, *Masculine Desire: The Sexual Politics of Victorian Aestheticism* (Chapel Hill, 1990), 199-205.

39. On such complications of interpretation, see Rita Felski, "The Counterdiscourse of the Feminine in Three Texts by Wilde, Huysmans, and Sacher-Masoch," *PMLA,* 106 (1991), 1094-1105; Alan Sinfield, "Private Lives/Public Theatre: Noel Coward and the Politics of Homosexual Representation," *Representations,* 36 (Fall 1991), 43-63; Alan Sinfield, *Cultural Politics—Queer Reading* (Philadelphia and London, 1994).

40. Behrendt, 152.

41. Davidoff, 17; T. H. Escott, *England: Its People, Polity and Pursuits,* rev. ed. (1885), quoted in *Two Society Comedies,* ed. Small and Jackson, xxxi.

42. Jane Marcus, *Art and Anger: Reading Like a Woman* (Columbus, 1988), 17.

43. Alan Bird, *The Plays of Oscar Wilde* (London, 1977), 128.

44. Camille Paglia, *Sexual Personae: Art and Decadence from Nefertiti to Emily Dickinson* (New Haven, 1990), 536, 535.

45. Paglia, 535.

46. Hyde, 166-67; Gagnier, 206.

47. Quoted in Mort, 113-14.

John Stokes (essay date spring 1994)

SOURCE: Stokes, John. "Wilde Interpretation." *Modern Drama* 37, no. 1 (spring 1994): 156-74.

[*In the following essay, Stokes surveys the critical reaction to three productions of Wilde's plays in the 1990s, finding insight into the theatrical scene of the 1890s.*]

We live in an age of interpretation, a fact that is constantly mentioned in the theatrical journals. Some think that it has always been this way, that there never has been representation without mediation; others, like the director Jonathan Miller, that the power of interpretation is a recent phenomenon with complex origins. "[H]istorical change has accelerated so much in the last fifty years that the differences between 'now' and even a quite recent 'then' are much more noticeable" says Miller, "the bequests of the past arouse our interpretative energies as never before." "Besides," he goes on, "the life of the mind has now taken a distinctively 'interpretative turn', and with the development of self-consciously hermeneutic interests the problem of meaning assumes a paramount importance."[1]

Hence, among many other things, the ascent of the theatre director, the individual who gives meaning to texts. Yet Miller also believes that acts of theatrical interpretation must, if they are to be valid, respond to elements already in the work, inherent in the initial choice of genre, and that all interpretations, if only to that extent, are still part of the author's "intention." On the basis of these theoretical principles it would follow that an account of recent productions of Wilde plays ought not only to identify trends currently in operation, but, in the course of analysis, reveal meanings that were already present, though sometimes hidden or unacknowledged, within the texts themselves.

It is certainly true that ever since Peter Hall's National Theatre *Importance of Being Earnest* in 1982, the full-scale professional productions in London have shared a number of characteristics. An extreme adventurousness in design and costume has tried to match Wilde's linguistic extravagance with visual images, with sets that expand far beyond the backcloths and box-sets he must normally have envisaged. There have also been consistent attempts to make theatrical capital out of biographical connections between the work and its author. And there has been consistent engagement with the mixed modes of the play-texts: attempts to make the best, if not the most, of the strong elements of melodrama they undoubtedly contain. This last probably represents the greatest investment of directorial energy. Whereas Wildean insights invite an impassive delivery that distances speakers from the world they are commenting upon, in the simplified moral universe of melodrama the important statements are expressed in a highly emotional and pictorial manner. These mixed modes now demand our undivided attention because, in today's theatre, the contrasts seem more than just stylistic: they seem to reflect issues of social and sexual ethics at the very heart of Wilde's plays.

What follows is an experiment in two parts, inspired by Miller's ideas. The first part takes as its primary material the reviews of three major London productions, sifted and sorted according to my own memories and impressions.[2] The second considers what this survey of productions from the 1990s might tell us about the theatre of a century ago. Backtracking from "now" we head for "then."

1990s

A WOMAN OF NO IMPORTANCE

Philip Prowse's production of *A Woman of No Importance,* first seen at the Glasgow Citizens in 1984, revived at the Royal Shakespeare Theatre's Barbican home in October 1991, offered a superbly high-handed solution to some basic problems.[3] Prowse collapsed the play's four acts into three, and then demanded two twenty-minute intervals to allow for elaborate changes of the sets he had, as is his custom, designed himself. His production was unashamedly operatic in its scale, full of colour, imported incident, and metatheatrical devices. By keeping his actors always on the move, even in quite crowded scenes, by relying on formalised blocking, close to choreography, and a rhetorical delivery that addressed lines directly at the audience, Prowse overcame all risk of dramatic stasis.

With typical boldness he opened his production with an addition to the text: the ominous appearance, before the lights were fully up, of a golden youth lazily, pointlessly, miming a game of croquet. (In appearance obviously reminiscent of Lord Alfred Douglas, this eventually turned out to be the excessively minor character, Lord Alfred Rufford.) Michael Coveney (*Observer* 6.10.91) described the subsequent picture: "a staggering haven of gilded urns and a circular pond of daffodils, narcissi and bamboo reeds." Irving Wardle (*Independent on Sunday* 6.10.91) found it "breathtakingly ornate: a park, backing onto a gigantic gilt-framed Claude landscape, where everything from the masonry to the vegetation has changed to gold. Nature is painted out."

The obvious question was whether Prowse's fascination with seductive artifice could coexist alongside what appeared, in general, to be a toughly critical attitude to characters that derived from the moral orthodoxy of melodrama. "Prowse invests the melodramatic revelations about Gerald's parentage and the caddishness of Lord Illingworth . . . with a reality and weight they may not have. But he thus releases the rhythms and vicious satire of the piece in a way no one else has ever imagined," was Coveney's verdict. Wardle shrugged his shoulders: "The main plot is irreclaimable; partly for the obvious reason of its sentimental contrivance (as Hugh Leonard said, it makes one 'long for the corruscating saltiness of *East Lynne*'); but also because everyone in it can get up and go. The moralising American, the 'fallen' woman and her bank-clerk son, all have a life elsewhere." "Melodrama all the way," judged John Gross (*Sunday Telegraph* 6.10.91), though he thought that Prowse's production got away with it, "partly because he takes it seriously, with no sugges-

tions of unease. As soon as it's over, you realise that it is the stilted period piece that you always thought it was; but it is oddly moving while it lasts."

Listen for Oscar Wilde in *A Woman of No Importance* and you are first of all likely to hear him in Lord Illingworth: "the vile seducer and Wildean philosopher," played here by John Carlisle with "the smirking poise of a replete crocodile" (Wardle). Animal images crept into several critical minds: "sleekly dangerous lounge-lizard" (Michael Billington, *Guardian* 5.10.91), "cold and hawklike, obnoxiously sophisticated and majestically corrupt" (John Peter, *Sunday Times* 6.10.91). Gross found himself "wanting to strangle him." For Lindsay Duguid (*TLS* 11.10.91) it became "unpleasant to hear him exercise his wit, rolling out his decadent paradoxes about life, or trying to win over a good woman with wry, elegant seductiveness." Benedict Nightingale (*The Times* 3.10.91) thought Carlisle's performance historically suggestive nonetheless:

> He does, after all, espouse Wilde's own aestheticism. His professed philosophy is all about the virtues of insincerity, inconstancy, and well-tied neckties. His author called him "a figure of art. Indeed, if you can bear the truth, he is MYSELF", and yet made him the villain.

Was Lord Illingworth Wilde's attempt to impose himself on his public or an instance of genuine self-criticism?

Michael Billington, for one, thought he knew the extent of Wilde's involvement with the character. Admitting that *A Woman* might look like a "proto-feminist play," Billington finally decided that "it doesn't play like that."

> Wilde clearly poured his talent, if not his genius, into the aphoristic aristo modelled on Dorian Gray's Lord Henry Wotton: the wronged woman on the other hand is a real pain in the Arbuthnot, ready to sacrifice her son's future to her stored-up revenge.

Lindsay Duguid spotted autobiographical connections as well:

> The scene in which a virtuous woman tries to prevent her only son from being led astray by the man who ruined her, may echo scenes with Speranza or Constance Wilde. It is also a strange precursor to the letter which Wilde wrote to Lady Queensberry in November 1893 (seven months after the first performance of *A Woman of No Importance*), begging her to keep Bosie away from the dangers of society.

And Charles Spencer (*Daily Telegraph* 4.10.91) would have agreed:

> There is no mistaking the cruelty of the society Wilde depicts, or its hypocrisy. The conversation is brilliant but heartless, and in the fate of Mrs Arbuthnot, whose whole life has been wrecked by a sexual indiscretion, it is impossible not to be reminded of Wilde's own tragic last years. One wonders if he caught a premonitory glimpse of them himself.

If Lord Illingworth isn't exactly the Wilde we hope for, then perhaps his voice sounds more convincing when it issues from a female body—from Mrs Arbuthnot, for example, or from one of the play's several strong and witty women. Like most of Wilde's plays, this has quite a range of female characters. Gross distinguished distinctive notes in a well-balanced chorus—"the acidulous Mrs Allonby (Nichola McAuliffe), the dragonish Lady Caroline (Cherry Morris), the empty-headed Lady Stutfield (Mary Chater)"—and enjoyed "the flutterings of the seemingly soft and scatterbrained but ultimately invulnerable Lady Hunstanton," a character Spencer found "charmingly forgetful, terrifying complacent and with a delivery that makes even commonplace lines irresistible."

Cataloguing the varieties of female in a Wilde play can easily develop into a critical sport—a sport admittedly played mainly by men. Billington had "the pearl-choked Lady Hunstanton" and "the eternally vigilant Lady Pontefract who views her husband as a piece of permanently lost property." For Coveney, the women ranged from "the wronged Mrs Arbuthnot (Carol Royle) as a pinched and vengefully pained salon outcast" and "Barbara Leigh-Hunt's blinkingly impervious Lady Hunstanton" to Nichola McAuliffe's "splendidly butch and world-weary Mrs Allonby" and "Cherry Morris's dragon-like Lady Caroline." But then there was Prowse's master-stroke: "the casting of a black actress, the admirable Julie Saunders, as the American woman of the future who witnesses the last exhalations of these social dinosaurs while assisting on the melodrama's poignant resolution."

Wardle began with Mrs Allonby: "the boldest of them (Nichola McAuliffe in quasi-hunting kit, one hand permanently on her hip) . . . a Mme de Montreuil to his [Lord Illingworth's] Valmont" and went on to "the hatchet-faced Lady Caroline (Cherry Morris) whose one aim is to keep her husband away from the youngest of the ladies; and whose distracted panic when he finally escapes her clutches would do justice to a Racine heroine." The list ended with Barbara Leigh-Hunt, "best of all . . . as the ineffably complaisant hostess, who excuses a beating husband—'it runs in the family'—as though he suffered from asthma, and underscores her most mindless comments with deliciously ironic ambiguity."

Finally Wardle judged this to be a woman's play not just because it pleaded equal sexual justice, but because the women's "chatter" was its most dramatic element. For Lindsay Duguid too it was the staging of the all-female set-pieces, the introductory scene in particular, which showed Prowse's directorial skills at their most incisive. These witty women are "practised": their riddles and paradoxes may be funny, but they are old-fashioned, concealing an inner panic. "They say the first thing that comes to their heads because they are very anxious to hold on to their position and their men."

AN IDEAL HUSBAND

Philip Prowse directed **An Ideal Husband** in Glasgow in 1986 and it has been revived fairly frequently in recent years, though never to the kind of critical attention accorded Peter Hall's production at the Globe in 1992.

Again the sets, though less strikingly so than those designed by Prowse, set up a strongly meaningful mood. But this time the emphasis was on solidly material matters. Carl Toms's gilded interiors were fronted by a huge Victorian golden sovereign displaying the profile of the monarch. Correspondingly, Hall tended to deploy costumes as evidence of conspicuous wealth rather than as symbols of moral worth. Careful to keep all his effects both stylised and serious, he modified the clumsy melodrama of the eavesdropping scene by substituting an opening door for the notorious falling chair, yet ended each act with a emotional tableau in an authentically Victorian way.

On the morning of the London opening, Hall set out his basic principles in an article for the *Guardian* (11.11.91):

> All Wilde's characters are extravagantly emotional and are quite naturally eccentric. But they do not show their feelings or release their emotions; that would be un-English. They utter witticisms instead. The more emotional they become, the more extravagant the wit. It is a type of English stiff upper lip; and it informs all Wilde's theatre. Beneath the wit there is always an intense emotional reality. The actor must investigate it, know it, and create it every night. Then he must mask it completely with the wit.

Hall went on to identify areas of interest that would soon be taken up by his critics: the play's contemporary relevance to politics and to scandal-mongering journalism, its concern with a feminism based on femininity, its ultimately compassionate vision and its autobiographical element. According to its director all this came from the play's personal origins, but resulted in a universal vision nevertheless, since Wilde was bisexual and "we are just beginning to come to accept that vast numbers of people are bisexual."

The critics seemed satisfied enough. Even Billington (*Guardian* 13.11.91) saw the play as a comprehensive attack on Victorian values: "the false idealisation of men by women, the worship of wealth, the gap between public morality and private behaviour." Few could resist extending the list in time to include the difficulties experienced by British cabinet ministers in 1992 (the Matrix Churchill affair, which involved the selling of arms to Iraq, was currently in the news). On the opening night the "audience tittered, clearly sensing parallels with you-know-what and guess-who" (Benedict Nightingale, *The Times* 13.11.91). By insisting throughout that the melodrama lay in the public rather than the personal sphere, Hall's production became, surprisingly, all the more realistic.

Paul Taylor (*Independent* 13.11.92) quoted Wilde himself on the personal dimension. The subject of the play, Hall had once said, was "'the difference in the way in which a man loves a woman from that in which a woman loves a man.'" Aware that this reversed the more familiar belief that it is men who idealise women ("you don't hear much of Beatrice's Dante"), Taylor allowed that there might at least be a historical truth here, that "it isn't fanciful to discern a link between the heroine's behaviour in the play and the mentality that sent men off to the front to prove that they were heroes in the Great War."

With Mrs Cheveley there were few problems, "a sleek carnivorous butterfly, poised and dangerous, with eyes that miss nothing and a voice of cream and prussic acid" (John Peter, *Sunday Times* 15.11.92). Lady Chiltern was more difficult. Billington, who saw the central pair as "a quasi-Ibsenite couple whose married life is founded on a lie," called her "fatuously adoring" and applauded the psychological realism that had Sir Robert almost strike his own wife. Peter nevertheless found in this "saintly female unicorn a touch of sensuality." Though the actress playing the role (Hannah Gordon) came in for some stiff criticism from the *Daily Telegraph* (13.11.91) for "entirely missing the character's icy calculation and smug moral complacency," Taylor thought her:

> the Lady Macbeth of virtuous career-guidance. With smiles that are forever curdling into snarls of righteousness and sudden passionate kisses that are tactically reserved as good conduct badges, there's a voracity about her that seems just as ruthless in its way as Anna Carteret's captivatingly unscrupulous Mrs Cheveley.

This disturbing comparison gave some evidence that for Wilde women would always be "second-class citizens." Nightingale too, had difficulty with the proposition (given in the play to Lady Chiltern) that women's "curves of emotion" don't compare with men's "wider scope and greater ambitions."

The more morally ambiguous the older women appear in this play, the more weight is likely to fall upon Mabel Chiltern. "Plain and feisty," Charles Spencer (*Daily Telegraph* 13.11.92) called Victoria Hasted's interpretation, but Alastair Macaulay (*Financial Times* 13.11.92) judged that "to play this role as a bespectacled, nasal, energetic hoyden is an amusing mistake. Wilde's stage directions compare her to both a flower and a Tanagra statuette." Billington thought that she could see "right through her future husband." Taylor decided that "to make the marriage go, Lord G, you feel, would have to develop an improbable passion for lacrosse."

Once again there was the sense that Wilde himself was up on stage, palpably so this time in the figure of Lord Goring as played by Martin Shaw.

> Boasting an Oscarish tummy, mournful eyes and an insolent langour, Mr Shaw makes the character far more than a walking jokesmith: he suggests that the mask of flippancy conceals infinite reserves of charity and shrewdness.

> (Billington, *Guardian* 13.11.92)

> Martin Shaw, long-haired and padded at the waist, plays most attractively as a philosophising dandy with a high tolerance of human fallibility.

> (Michael Coveney, *Observer* 15.11.92)

John Gross (*Sunday Telegraph* 15.11.92) came right out with it—"a closet gay if ever there was one"—though Nightingale found that the physical identification with Wilde "sorts oddly with the robust heterosexuality the plot demands of the character." Spencer said that Shaw "gets to the heart of the play, touchingly suggesting a man who uses affected dandyism to disguise both personal hurt and an innate decency." Peter also related Goring to the essential schizophrenia of his creator: careless wit and moral arbiter at one and the same time.

> Martin Shaw presents a saturnine dandy, both magisterially epicene and soberly masculine who once has been athletic in body and inquisitive in mind. What seems to have happened to Goring is that he began to find the answers that life was providing increasingly fatuous, and, as his waistline grew more ample, his manner grew more florid to screen his disappointment. The exquisite triviality of his conversation is only a cover for a fastidious distaste.

> (*Sunday Times* 15.11.92)

A few felt dissatisfied with Goring's distaste. Wardle (*Independent on Sunday* 15.11.92) concluded that "the transitions from cold-blooded epigrams to clammy declarations of feeling have become unplayable." Macaulay (*Financial Times*) applauded Martin Shaw because "he has the authority to convey the moral seriousness behind the dandy's facade. Yet he radiates not only self-satisfaction but also affectation." Taylor was reminded of "Noel Coward in his finger-wagging, mother-knows-best mood."

THE IMPORTANCE OF BEING EARNEST

Time and again reviewers of *A Woman of No Importance* and of *An Ideal Husband* refer to *The Importance of Being Earnest* as if it were the only logical direction for Wilde's theatrical career to take—a brilliantly self-concealing answer to the clash between overt melodrama and evasive wit. As Jane Edwardes was to put it in her review of Nicholas Hytner's production of the play which opened at the Aldwych in March 1993:

> If as I suspect, we are only just becoming acquainted with the true emotion, not the melodrama, behind Wilde's wit, then *The Importance of Being Earnest* may not be so pleasing. It was, after all, the play in which Wilde completely hid his feelings, concentrating instead, through the role playing of Jack and Algernon, on the deceptions that his sexuality forced him to play.

> (*Time Out* 17.3.93)

John Peter made much the same point:

> Style wins over sincerity because Wilde despaired of finding any of the latter. In one sense this play, like all great comedies, is about nothing in particular: it exists to justify its own existence. But behind the wit and the ostentatious elegance of the writing, you get a glimpse of a barren, glittering desert.

> (*Sunday Times* 14.3.93)

There was evidence nevertheless that Wilde's elegantly theatrical solution to his own problems now puts a director in something of a quandary. Perhaps Nick Hytner's expensive, star-laden production raised expectations it never could fulfil. For each of the play's three acts the designer, Bob Crowley, produced sets that were not merely stunning, they seemed suggestive as well—though precisely of what, no one was quite sure. The first act, Algy's flat in Half Moon Street, "a slant-roofed property with sinful crimson walls which melt into carnation green" (Paul Taylor, *Independent* 12.3.93), was overlooked by an enormous mock-up of Sargent's portrait of W. Graham Robertson. The second act was "dominated by an extraordinary hedge of salmon pink roses excessively topiarised into the shape of peacock with an enormous, expanding tail" (*Time Out* 17.3.93). The third act was a creamy curved interior "like a skew-whiff Heartbreak House" (*Observer* 14.3.93)

The extraordinary plethora of references in descriptions of these extraordinary sets testifies to the general bemusement: "surreal" (*Plays and Players* May 93), "expressionist" (*What's On* 17.3.93), "Odilon Redon" (John Peter, *Sunday Times* 14.3.93), "Lewis Carroll" (Sheridan Morley, *Spectator* 20.3.93), "post-modernist" (Jack Tinker, *Daily Mail* 17.3.93). Wardle felt obliged to construct a whole surrealist tradition: "This is Wilde as seen in the rear-view mirror of Orton and Stoppard . . . on nodding terms with Magritte: or, as Cecily might have put it, 'This is not a spade' (*Independent on Sunday* 14.3.93).

Who could inhabit such a world? Only fantasists and narcissists. Cecily (Claire Skinner) was "an almost terrifying study in fresh-cheeked single-mindedness, believing her own diary fantasies with a fundamentalist's unblinking literalism" (*Independent* 12.3.93). Algy (Richard E. Grant) was "an ostentatious velvet dandy," "a peacock on heat, but one who seeks most especially to love himself" (*Sunday Times*), reminiscent to some of the young Wilde. But this is also where the problems began, for much of the acting was judged rather too conventional for the louche surroundings. There were strong reservations about Gwendolen (Susan Harker) and about Richard E. Grant too when he had "to struggle, paradoxically, to be languid and debonair as the smugly smiling Algernon" (*Independent*). Of the four young leads, only Jack, played by Alex Jennings as "a petulant, opinionated cherub, pompous and mean" (*Sunday Times*), offered a really surprising and therefore successful interpretation.

Curiously, very few critics referred to the production's most provocative, and puzzling, moment: the kiss of greeting that Jack bestowed on Algy at his first entrance. Was it critical pudeur, or did the actors simply forego the gesture on some nights early in the run? Even so a colour picture of the two men on the back of the souvenir brochure made its own unmistakeably homoerotic point. Those who did refer to the kiss were cautious. Robert Tanitch (*Plays and Players* May 93) thought it might suggest "that the director . . . is about to explore a Victorian gay sub-text and

that the true meaning of being 'earnest' and 'bunburying' will be revealed." To Tanitch's personal relief that suggestion turned out to be false. Sheridan Morley found the idea of "gay young things" intriguing, "but one incapable of being sustained once the girls appear" (*Spectator* 20.3.93).

The main focus of attention, commercially and theatrically inevitable, was upon Maggie Smith's Lady Bracknell. For Taylor, Coveney, Morley (*Spectator*), and many others, Smith offered an exact study in the mores of the English class-system.

> When she first sweeps in, the head may be reared back but the chin is tucked down, in tight disapproving mode, against the chest. Replace that imperious feathered hat with a head-scarf and milady's pursed moues and her air of pinched, almost predatory respectability would start to look distinctly suburban. . . . The titled monster may be dead set against her daughter forming an alliance with a parcel, but you could deduce, from this production, that her own lofty social position has come about only thanks to Lord Bracknell's willingness to form an alliance with a parvenue. In which case, his wife's tireless penchant for making dogmatic discriminations emerges as the compulsive behaviour of the arriviste turned beady-eyed expert at border-control.
>
> (*Independent* 12.3.93)

> This is no haughty old dowager guarding a bank of magisterial put-downs, but a scheming whirlwind, body askance in dove-grey silks, flyaway hat and perfect coiffure, a figure of frightening elegance who is not to be tampered with. . . . She certainly inspects the young people like a beaky, agitated adjutant on parade . . . her body language is as tightly corseted as her physical frame.
>
> (*Observer* 14.3.93)

When it came to animal imagery, Nightingale (*The Times* 10.3.93) went the whole hog, first invoking the human vultures, ravens, and crows of *Volpone*, then describing Maggie Smith as "maybe a lady griffin." Jane Edwardes spotted an unexpected sexual alignment along with the ornithological:

> Smith is an exotic bird, looking with hawk-like disdain on her prey, while Edith Evans was an immovable tank. Smith's fixed stare is accompanied by a fluttering of her wings and a quick turn of the head. Dressed in shimmering grey with a hat dramatically angled, she gives a definitive, hilarious performance which threatens to soar into a stratosphere all of its own. Such high camp almost puts her on the side of her decadent nephew rather than the forces of bourgeois authority.
>
> (*Time Out*)

For Jack the final irony will come when he realises that Gwendolen, like all women, has grown up into her mother. Further bizarre comparisons cropped up in Wardle: "part suburban *parvenue,* part drag artist, part vigilantly suspicious rodent" (*Independent on Sunday*), while Nicholas de Jongh (*Standard* 10.3.93) simply found the whole performance "high-camp."

That Maggie Smith possesses rare theatrical power is a truth that usually goes unquestioned. Wardle admired "her mastery of the stage, which she rakes with laser eyes on every entrance." Peter noted the same thing, but thought it further evidence of the character's *parvenue* status:

> What gives her away is the impertinent look of appraisal with which she scrutinises new arrivals. This is not the practised glance of the true upper-class matriarch, who takes in everything with the blink of an eye, but the ruthless inquisitorial stare of the middle-class climber who has had to learn what to look for.

Respectful to the point of reverence, most London critics gave Maggie Smith the kind of reception that a Dame should expect. There was a single, important exception: Michael Billington. "Dame Maggie," he pronounced, "is a bundle of fussiness forever fidgeting."

> She also constantly seeks laughs instead of letting them come to her. . . . When assessing Cecily's profile Dame Maggie indulges in an orgy of wide-eyed moues and stares far removed from the character's patronising beneficence . . . in stealing the show, Dame Maggie's hyperactive performance subtly undermines it.
>
> (*Guardian* 11 March 1993)

And in a review for *Country Life* (18.3.93) Bilington took these strictures even further:

> Dame Maggie, employing a strangulated, nasal tone, presents us with a Lady Bracknell who is bustling, fidgety and forever signalling her emotions. She gets huge laughs, on her first entrance, by shooting withering, disdainful glances at Mr Worthing as if he is a piece of untidy refuse, which makes nonsense of her second entrance when she recognises him instantly. In the famous interview, she clutches her stomach in revulsion on learning that he was found in "the cloak-room at Victoria Station". Again, this gets a big laugh. But it runs clean counter to the aristocratic temperament which registers high-voltage shock with maximum economy. In short, there is a strenuousness about Dame Maggie's performance that violently contradicts Lady Bracknell's indomitable self-assurance.

Later Billington had some reason to feel vindicated when the London *Standard* in June ran a piece under the heading "The Importance of Being Maggie Smith" which reported disturbing developments down at the Aldwych:

> The audience erupts into applause at the mere sight of her; she pauses, discreetly acknowledging the adulation, before launching into a performance of comic grotesquerie that is not so much Wilde as *wild*. For a moment, one is whisked from the seats of the Aldwych to the studio audience of *I Love Lucy*. . . . Every classic line, every gesture, is stretched to infinity for laughs. If an eccentric gesture doesn't get a laugh, she repeats it until it does. If a movement gets a laugh straight away, she repeats it for another one.
>
> (*Standard* 15.6.93 with later correspondence on 21.6.93)

There were, then, two schools, though of very unequal size. There was the minority view, headed by Billington, for whom Smith had indulged her technical skills at the expense of the role, and there was the majority view which saw nothing but creative comedy of a high order.

1890s

The danger with Jonathan Miller's theory is that it all too easily assumes the historical relevance of the interpretations it choses to address. A form of hermeneutic circling may come into play through which desired meanings are merely ratified by production style, and the validating process of historical discovery is lost. To avoid false inferences we sometimes need to be sparing with our conclusions.

Or what if a production is so visually attractive, so persuasively acted, that the text dissolves in performance, transformed into something quite different, but of undoubted power? That is certainly possible, though none of the recent productions of Wilde go quite that far. Even the lavish sets, essential for the success of a modern West End show, serve a function. Design is a prime mediator between action and audience, and the best work—Crowley's sets for *The Importance,* for instance—register the ambiguities that now surround the plays, as the comments of critics testify.

Acting styles are produced by the cultural moment as well, not just individually, but in the relation between a single performer and the surrounding company. One of the lessons to be learnt from Maggie Smith's performance, and from the responses to it, is that we are still living in a time, which probably originated in the later nineteenth century, when star performances and ensemble styles coexist rather uneasily.

Not that in 1895, when *The Importance* played at the St James, the problem would have centered on Lady Bracknell. Few critics of the first production spent much time with Rose Leclercq's reading of the part: George Alexander's Jack inevitably got the most attention. One critic explained that his failure to say much about any of the acting was evidence of the way in which Wilde dominated his own play.[4]

It took time for Lady Bracknell to become everybody's favourite joke. When Alexander revived the play in 1909, Max Beerbohm didn't even bother to give the name of the actress playing her. Nigel Playfair's production at the Lyric, Hammersmith in 1930 had Mabel Terry-Lewis in the role, greatly overshadowed by her nephew John Gielgud as Jack. Only later did Lady Bracknell achieve centrality, probably because she could now be more clearly seen in class terms. In her famous book on comedy, first published in 1943, Athene Seyler, who had played Lady Bracknell at the Old Vic a decade before, stresses that *The Importance* "shows the absurdities of the well-bred, cynical, easy manner of the 'upper classes' with its levelling of all emotion and experience to apparent indifference."[5] When Edith Evans seized command of Gielgud's 1939 production, and the extremely popular 1953 film, making Lady Bracknell a part of great importance, she did so by mining the full possibilities of this "apparent indifference." Evans's performance style perfectly matched that concept of the role because it was part of her brilliance as an actress to seem to be unaware of the effect she was creating, almost daring you to laugh. Judi Dench's notable Lady Bracknell in 1982 carried on the tradition by appearing equally blind to social circumstance.

But Maggie Smith's 1993 performance went in quite another direction: she almost dared you *not* to laugh. This technique clearly has many admirers, but the pained protests from Billington and a few others indicate a more established idea of what Wilde's most typical roles ask from actors and actresses: a self-effacing opacity that obliges an audience to respond with a mixture of bemused recognition and baffled surprise. A performer who controls our response to the extent that we find ourselves laughing at the exaggerated role they are playing can severely reduce the satirical complexity of an imperturbable face. Maggie Smith's *parvenue* was fearsome, yet coercive. Nor was she quite human—"a hawk," "a vulture," "a griffin"—a fabulous female creature.

In Wilde's theatre, rather in the manner of Restoration comedy, there are conscious wits and there are unconscious wits, and there are some, the most interesting, who are hard to keep in either category—they keep jumping from one to the other. Lady Bracknell belongs with these: Edith Evans was the actress who brought the manner to perfection, and, ever since, we have looked on the part as a supreme opportunity for a comic actress.

It's intriguing, then, that one or two critics should have referred to Smith as a "drag-artist." Perhaps they meant that she was pretending to be one (an actress imitating a man imitating a woman) or perhaps that, in some sense, Lady Bracknell really is male (the actress playing a woman with male characteristics). Though the latter seems the more likely explanation, both possibilities are oddly plausible: there are undoubtedly some who would say that she is a woman as only a man could imagine a woman. Yet even in *The Importance* with its relatively small cast, there are a number of rather different women with whom to compare her. Is the point that Lady Bracknell's maleness lies in her autocratic behaviour rather than in any fluke of biology? Jack does after all rebuke her for "her masculine mind." Then again, what precisely does female behaviour amount to in a Wilde play? These are the questions that we are now likely to ask.

In their versions of the two society plays both Hall and Prowse defused the moral melodrama of sexual relationships by playing the passionate scenes according to convention. This left them free to bring out the more interesting complexities created by wits, in particular by female wit. All three productions tried to persuade us that

Wilde's interest in group female discourse eclipses those elements of melodramatic idealisation (and, just possibly, misogynistic fear) that may also be felt in his work. In their different ways they all suggested that Wilde's most long-lasting—or prophetic—contribution to feminism was to allow his women to be articulate, and then to subject them to moral evaluation according to the ways in which they put their verbal dexterity to amusing and constructive use. It is this, we are led to conclude, that shows him to be a contemporary of the New Woman.

The other lesson, appropriately paradoxical, is that the plays are, more than ever, inseparable from their author's own experience, and depend greatly upon our seeing that to be the case. One obvious reason why the new stagings have gone for the autobiographical element is the enormous popularity of Ellmann's best-selling biography. We have also experienced a new frankness and curiosity about gay history and gay relationships. Yet the Wildean presence only works on stage today because it makes manifest a quality endemic to the plays: an interplay between performance, audience, and outside world that was already active in the conditions of late Victorian theatre, though taken to new extremes by Wilde—from the very start of his career.

An inveterate theatre-goer, Wilde made a point in the 1880s of attending the first nights of personal favourites like Helena Modjeska and Lillie Langtry. He knew how important it was for his own professional progress that he should be seen to be there on grand theatrical occasions. Lyceum *premières* were particularly grand (in fact it was Irving's manager, H. L. Bateman, who had first realised the full publicity potential of the first night) and Wilde rarely missed one. When *Othello* opened on 2 May 1881 with Booth as Othello and Irving as Iago, the audience were apparently also "entertained by the ubiquity of Oscar Wilde who, combining elegance and agility, was seen now leaning languidly from a box, now chatting in the stalls, and a moment later figuring prominently in a box opposite to the first."[6] Already, when he reviewed Irving's Hamlet in 1885, his reference to the audience betrayed a characteristic self-awareness:

> It sometimes happens that at a *première* in London the least enjoyable part of the performance is the play. I have seen many audiences more interesting than the actors, and have often heard better dialogue in the *foyer* than I have on stage. At the Lyceum, however, this is rarely the case, and when the play is a play of Shakespeare's, and among its exponents are Mr. Irving and Miss Ellen Terry, we turn from the gods in the gallery and from the goddesses in the stalls, to enjoy the charm of the production, and to take delight in the art. The lions are before the foot-lights and not in front of them when we have a noble tragedy nobly enacted.[7]

Throughout the 1880s the papers regularly reported his presence in among the fashionable throng. Attendant at the first night of *Faust* were the Princess Louise, the Prince of Wales (officially in mourning but he got over the problem by watching the play from behind) and "the once famous apostle of high art in dress, with hair cut short, quite bland and harmless, who has evidently renounced the vegetarian cult and dines on diet more generous than lilies." With him was his wife, "Mrs Oscar," wearing "a wonderful ruffle like an oyster shell standing on end."[8]

When the author took to the stage and addressed the first-night audience for **Lady Windermere's Fan** with "I congratulate you on the *great* success of your performance,"[9] he was simply offering an elegant variation on what had become a very familiar theme. "With many writers," the *Court and Society Review* announced in 1886, "the audience is regarded as hardly second in importance to the play itself."[10]

Wilde could cross from audience to stage and back again with consummate assurance because in the Victorian theatre the gap between the two was already narrow, and he had himself closed it even further by making his own presence so theatrically conspicuous within the actual auditorium. This established mode of exchange between two spectacles did more than enable Wilde's own first-night wit ("Mr Oscar Wilde is not in the house," he announced at the opening of **A Woman of No Importance**),[11] it encouraged his audiences to see and hear him on stage, speaking through the characters of his plays.

Today, of course, that familiarity has been reduplicated many times over by films, documentaries, biographies, the whole myth-making machinery. In which case the surprise is less that directors should build Wilde into their shows than that anyone other than Wilde should ever appear in them at all. The explanation for this singular achievement must surely be that, in time, the "Wildean" has come to stand for so much more than just one man.

A related curiosity of recent reviews is their regular recourse to the notion of "bisexuality," as if that somehow helped to explain the plays. There may be an implicit acknowledgment of the all-embracing nature of Wildean sexuality here—the strongly homosexual tone brought to ostensibly heterosexual relationships, for instance—but there is paradox at work as well. Until the final confrontation with authority in 1895 Wilde had managed to be provocative, and to survive, by making paradox his weapon and his shield. The recent *TLS* reviewer (19.3.93) who complained that Nick Hytner's production of **The Importance** failed to follow through the gay signposting of its first act was surely being rather obtuse. That a play should set down a premise in its first act, but come to an apparently different conclusion in its third, is entirely in line with Wilde's dramaturgy. The structure of **The Importance** we should recognise to be paradoxical in just this way: it zig-zags from start to finish. Men who fraternize with men turn out to like some women, and luckily some women turn out to like some men too; some men behave like women and some women behave like men. This is a bisexual drama in which "bisexuality" is not just a state of sexual desire (though it is, of course, exactly that), but a model for the sympathetic, if contrary, dramatic imagination.

In the 1890s Wilde was a public figure, in the 1990s he is the public itself: we want him to be a liberated gay man and a witty feminist, a worried parent and a guilty husband. Being Irish he necessarily becomes multicultural. When the all-black Talawa Theatre Company put on a comparatively low-budget **Importance** in London in 1989 it announced:

> In producing **The Importance of Being Earnest,** Talawa set out to be as truthful to the text as it was humanly possible to be, bearing in mind that an all-black production of **The Importance of Being Earnest** was probably very far from Wilde's wildest imagination. We found great support in his attitude to English society: his commentary was all the clearer perhaps because he was Irish. We felt it was important to set the play in England in 1895, but not ever to disguise or trivialise the fact that we were black.[12]

There was to be nothing trivial about this performance of Wilde's "trivial comedy," which doesn't mean to say that it wasn't wonderfully funny. Some differences have to be emphasised if others are to dissolve.

At which point we should remember that Wilde's favourite formula for jokes always was based on difference. "Women are never disarmed by compliments. Men always are. That is the difference between the two sexes." Most of Wilde's jokes work through this kind of self-cancelling comparison, the point being not only to suggest absurd oppositions, but, in exemplary deconstructive fashion ("to be premature is to be perfect," remember), to defer resolution by requiring reconsideration of the premise. They foreshadow those ideal modes of collective living that always lie just beyond us, and even now can only be glimpsed on stage.

Notes

1. Jonathan Miller, *Subsequent Performances* (London, 1986), 70.
2. I am grateful to Professor Joel Kaplan for supplying me with copies of the major reviews. The picture of Wilde as member of the audience is by Maurice Greiffenhagen and first appeared as an illustration to George Moore's *Vain Fortune.* I am much indebted to Dr. Russell Jackson, who originally drew my attention to it.
3. For further information about Prowse's remarkable productions of Wilde see Michael Coveney, *The Citz.: 21 Years of the Glasgow Citizens Theatre* (London, 1990) and Joel H. Kaplan, "Wilde in the Gorbals: Society Drama and Citizens Theatre," in *Rediscovering Oscar Wilde,* ed. G. Sandulescu (London, 1994).
4. *Oscar Wilde: The Critical Heritage* ed. Karl Beckson (London, 1970), 193.
5. *The Craft of Comedy: An Exchange of Letters on Comedy Acting Techniques with Stephen Haggard* (London, 1990), 68.
6. Laurence Irving, *Henry Irving* (London, 1961), 375.
7. *The Dramatic Review,* 9 May 1885, repr. in Robert Ross, ed., *Reviews* (London, 1908), 16.

8. Report of the first night of *Faust, Pall Mall Gazette,* 21 December 1885.

9. Richard Ellmann, *Oscar Wilde* (London, 1987), 346.

10. "'First Nights' at the Play," 7 October 1886, 931.

11. Ellmann, 360.

12. From the programme notes to the Talawa Theatre Company production, directed by Yvonne Brewster, at the Bloomsbury Theatre, 15-27 May 1989.

GUIDO FERRANTI

PRODUCTION REVIEW

Critic (review date 7 February 1891)

SOURCE: Review of *Guido Ferranti. Critic* 15, no. 371 (7 February 1891): 73.

[*In the following review of* Guido Ferranti, *the unnamed critic finds inconsistencies in the dialogue and acting.*]

The degree of popular favor that has attended the performances of Oscar Wilde's five-act tragedy *Guido Ferranti* at the Broadway Theatre must be attributed to the effective theatrical quality of certain scenes, rather than to the poetic charm or power or dramatic interest of the work as a whole. Apart from the fact that it is written in smooth blank-verse, and contains isolated passages of indisputable imagination and vigor, it is nothing but an old-fashioned 'blood-and-thunder' melodrama, put together in a very unworkmanlike manner, and with a curious disregard for anything in the nature of probability. Guido Ferranti, the hero, is a youthful gallant who has been reared in luxury and instructed in all the accomplishments of his age (the sixteenth century), but knows nothing of his family or origin. One day he receives a mysterious summons to Padua, and there, in the market-place, he meets a dark and gloomy stranger, one Morozone, who reveals to him the startling fact that he is the son of the late Duke, and that his father was betrayed to death by a false friend, who thus secured the Dukedom for himself.

Hearing this Guido swears an oath of deadly vengeance, and, with Morozone's help, obtains a place in the inner circle of the Court. Here, unmindful of his mission, he permits himself to fall in love with Beatrice, the lovely young wife of his ducal foe, and soon discovers that she is only too ready to reciprocate his passion. Reminded of his oath by the vengeful Morozone, he tells Beatrice that their union is impossible and bids her consider his vows unspoken. The lady, however, has no intention of letting

him escape her so easily, and forms a resolution which brings about one of the most effective scenes in the play. At midnight, Guido, in spite of guards and bars, is in the Duke's bed-chamber, but, being there, begins to entertain doubts about the propriety of assassination. In spite of the expostulations of Morozone, who turns up everywhere in the most bewildering fashion, he resolves to do no more than lay his dagger upon the Duke's breast, and is advancing to the bed with that object in view, when the Duchess suddenly appears and announces that she has killed the tyrant herself and thus cleared the way to their union. Guido shrinks from her in horror, upbraids her bitterly, and is about to leave her forever, when she summons the guard and accuses him of being the assassin. This scene is absurdly improbable as it stands, but is, nevertheless, theatrically effective and was received on the first night with great applause from the galleries.

The Duchess then becomes a fury. She presides over the trial of her lover and insists that he shall be put to death without being permitted to speak in his own defence, but he refuses to be silenced, and describes the midnight scene in a striking speech, ending with a confession of his own guilt, instead of the expected accusation of his judge. This, again, is a very striking though wildly improbable and unnatural scene. In the last act the Duchess visits Guido in his cell, and after taking poison, offers him the means of escape. He refuses to avail himself of them, and after another passionate love-scene, just as the headman is approaching to claim him as a victim, he kills Beatrice first and then himself.

Very little comment is necessary upon a story of this kind, which is not only in defiance of experience but of human nature itself. The best scenes, undoubtedly, are those of the midnight murder and of the trial, but the value of these is only theatrical. The general dialogue is of very uneven merit, and many phrases, and not a few ideas, are borrowed unblushingly from Shakespeare and minor dramatists. The play, however, considered altogether, is something out of the common rut, and Mr. Barrett is entitled to praise for giving it a chance, and to congratulations on the reception accorded to it. His own acting is vigorous and impressive throughout, and especially in the third and fourth acts. Miss Gale is overweighted in the part of the Duchess, which requires an actress of tragic force.

LADY WINDERMERE'S FAN

PRODUCTION REVIEWS

Spectator (review date 26 November 1892)

SOURCE: "Oscar Wilde's Comedy." *Spectator* 69 (26 November 1892): 767.

[*In the following positive assessment of* Lady Windermere's Fan, *the reviewer asserts that "we are grateful to Mr.*

Wilde for a straightforward comedy which professes no purpose but comedy's best and truest—to entertain. "]

We shall not be suspected of any great sympathy with the methods and the feats of Mr. Oscar Wilde. In this journal we have always disclaimed respect for the forms of charlatanism in which it has pleased him to indulge, and which he would, we suspect, be about the first himself to admit. But a charlatan may be a man of conspicuous ability; and on the withdrawal from the stage for the present of his first-acted comedy, after a career of great success, it is but appropriate in us as it is fair to him to signalise the addition to our acted plays of a comedy of society-manners pure and simple which may fairly claim its place among the recognised names in that almost extinct class of drama. We have, indeed, too much amongst us of Ibsen and his parallels not to note it with satisfaction. We can ourselves find nothing in *A Doll's House* beyond a fairly interesting domestic drama, with a story and characters which are nothing if not old, a kind of Martin Chuzzlewit married to Dora Copperfield, and a type of such very old-fashioned heredity as belongs to a gentleman who has the gout because his father drank; and we are grateful to Mr. Wilde for a straightforward comedy which professes no purpose but comedy's best and truest,—to entertain. A reproduction of contemporary "polite conversation" after the manner which we noticed long since in reviewing a republication of Swift, and which Sheridan idealised in the *School for Scandal,* **Lady Windermere's Fan,** as a specimen of true comedy, is a head and shoulders above any of its contemporaries for some years syne. It has nothing in common with farcical comedy, with didactic comedy, or the "literary" comedy of which we have heard so much of late from disappointed authors, whose principal claim to literature appears to consist in being undramatic. It is a distinguishing note of Mr. Wilde that he has condescended to leave his business, and has written a workman-like play as well as a good comedy. Without that it would be worthless, and how much he may owe to his manager's skill and help, according to another endless controversy, lies between those two, and concerns us not. If Mr. Alexander is as helpful as he is modest, it may be much. For the character of Lord Windermere affords him little opportunity of personal distinction. Indeed, the peculiarity as well as the weakness of the play consists in the fact that the interest lies entirely with two women,—as well acted as they well could be.

The story, for those who have not seen it, lies in a nutshell. We regret the disappearance of the old method of publication, for **Lady Windermere** would be worth reading. Lord Windermere has married for love a young lady whose mother they suppose dead, but she turns up in the guise of a *divorcée* of some notoriety in society, and Lord Windermere submits to be blackmailed in order to conceal the fact from his wife, and pays her many sums of money. The object of this Mrs. Erlynne, as she calls herself, is, like the heroine of *Forget-me-not,* to regain a place in society, and she gets an invitation to a ball given by Lady Windermere, who, meanwhile, has been informed by some

good-natured friends of the gossip of society about her husband and Mrs. Erlynne, whose appearance at the ball causes a sensation. Outraged in her feelings, Lady Windermere leaves a note to wish her lord good-bye, and flies to the rooms of an admirer, a certain Lord Darlington. Thither Mrs. Erlynne, who intercepts the letter, follows to save her daughter, for whom her heart and better feelings are thus suddenly aroused. Determined to save her at any cost, she takes upon herself the ownership of an accusing fan, her husband's gift, which, on the rooms being invaded by a circle of men, he being one of them, she mislays in a room she hides in. In again losing herself, Mrs. Erlynne thus saves her daughter, who at the end is thoroughly reconciled with the husband who really loves her; while Mrs. Erlynne finds a husband in an adoring lordling, and leaves England, where she never knows "whether the fogs cause the depressed people, or the depressed people cause the fogs," the secret of her relationship to the heroine remaining a secret still.

It will be seen that there is nothing new in the old story which has more or less framed half the comedies of intrigue which fine-folk comedy has so freely inspired. But the novelty of drama lies in treatment; and while there is no suggestion of coarseness in Mr. Wilde's play, there is plenty both of good feeling and of complex character, while there is opportunity for good acting, which is plentifully used. Miss Winifred Emery plays Lady Windermere with a charm and skill which has placed her quite in the front rank amongst our emotional actresses, the more remarkable because she was not the first representative of the part. Her acting suggests both heart and brains, and most effective is the contrast which she supplies with Miss Marian Terry, who, if not a little overshadowed by the fame of her elder sister, would bear even a better stage-name than she does. To those who remember the eldest and earliest Kate, she brings many curious shades of association. These old stage-families, to which both the Terrys and the Emerys belong, have singular aristocracies of their own, which, with a Gray or Webster at their side, it is curious to contrast with the Vane Tempests and Nutcombe Goulds, who bring new blood of another kind into the theatrical ranks. Mr. Gould is a quite remarkable figure in the comedy for bearing and breeding, combined with quiet force and skill. Indeed, the whole cast is in its manner as noteworthy as the play. Mr. Wilde's dialogue, which is the chief feature of the comedy—as, given the essentials, of course it should be—is throughout conveyed with point and appreciation. The genial and *blasé* tone which modern society of the special class affects is as admirably caught and sustained as were the would-be smartnesses of Miss Neveroul and her friends in Swift's *Polite Conversation.* All the close observation and thought which the comedy-writer requires Mr. Wilde has brought to bear upon the "puppets" with whom, in his capacity of advertising author, he has waged newspaper-war, and his puppets have repaid him in kind. If his Duchess is rather trying, it is more because she indulges in certain odd circular sweeps with her arm which nobody could possibly perform in a drawing-room, than because duchesses are supposed to be unlike other people. In conversational respects, they are perhaps as "much of a muchness" as Mr. Wilde makes them. The way in which she secures a fresh young Australian for her meek daughter, who is sent out of the way to inspect photographs, or to look at the moon, whenever her mother proposes to talk scandal, and her delightful summaries of the male sex, who "grow old, but never grow good," and are brutes who only want to be cooked for, are very amusing stage-talk to listen to. Another refreshing element in the play is the entire absence of the stage-servant, who seems so terrible a necessity in comedy. We all know what use even Sheridan made of them, amusing as that was. And to find nothing but a man-servant and maid-servant, who do just what they are engaged for, their business and no more, is a piece of "realism" in the right direction. Indeed, the whole comedy, its plan and its writing, its people and its dresses, its co-louring and its tone, deserve, as we think, these lines of record from us on its withdrawal from the boards, as an unique specimen in our day—as far as we know, absolutely unique—apart from all questions of its merits and demerits, of the comedy of fine-life manners. Since the club scene in *Money,* there has been no simply "man's scene" so clearly marked as that in Lord Darlington's chambers. Otherwise. Lord Lytton's favourite sentimentalities in *Money* interfere with it woefully as a comedy-picture. Not the least pleasant reminiscene to playgoers, in connection with **Lady Windermere's Fan,** will be the very amusing skit which it evoked at another comedy theatre, under the title of *The Poet and the Puppets.* As a thoroughly good-humoured piece of burlesque, not so much on the play as on the eccentricities and methods of the well-known author, it has not often been beaten. Not the least amusing reminiscence, on the other hand, will be the ferocious wrath which, on its first appearance, the play provoked among the regular stage-critics, almost to a man. Except that Mr. Wilde smoked a cigarette when called on, it is difficult to see why,—unless it was because the comedy ran off the beaten track, which is just what they are always deprecating.

Critic (review date 11 February 1893)

SOURCE: Review of *Lady Windermere's Fan. Critic* 19, no. 573 (11 February 1893): 84.

[*In the following mixed review of* Lady Windermere's Fan, *the critic discusses Wilde's dialogue as well written, but chides the production values.*]

The faults and merits of Mr. Oscar Wilde's four-act comedy, **Lady Windermere's Fan,** just produced in Palmer's Theatre after successful careers in London and Boston, may be summed up briefly in the statement that the piece is smartly written and constantly amusing, but very badly made. Not only is the construction extraordinarily clumsy, when Mr. Wilde's long experience in theatrical matters is taken into account, but the whole plot is founded upon suppositions wholly at variance with human experience and commonsense. The story, as pretty nearly everybody knows by this time, deals with the adventure of a young wife and mother, of a devotional tendency and exquisite natural purity of character (these qualities being insisted on with great particularity), who flings herself into the arms of another man, because her husband has insisted upon inviting to her house a woman of whom she is jealous, and whom she believes to be of immoral character. That she might leave her home, in such circumstances, is conceivable, but that she should seek revenge in personal dishonor is absolutely inconsistent with the whole theory of her nature. Not less ridiculous is the supposition that an affectionate husband, only anxious to shield his wife from unmerited disgrace, should compel her to receive publicly a woman whose very presence she regards as a contamination, and thus put the cruellest of all slights upon her, with all her friends for witnesses. These are not by any means the only glaring flaws in construction to be found in the first two acts, but they are all that need be quoted for present purposes.

The simple fact is that Mr. Wilde evidently set out to write a play around a situation, that situation being found in the third act, where Lady Windermere, having deserted her own home and taken refuge in the bachelor apartments of Lord Darlington, is rescued by the intervention of the very adventuress whom she had scorned, and who is, as the audience has known all along, her own disreputable mother. This is a well-devised and well-written scene, in which the characters of the two women are contrasted with skill and effect, and no small knowledge of human nature. The distrust, scorn and jealousy of the daughter are particularly well depicted. The fortune of the play depends upon this scene, but the succeeding situations, including the discovery of the fan, the self-sacrifice of Mrs. Erlynne and the escape, under fearfully improbable conditions, of Lady Windermere, maintain the interest to the end of the act. The final ending is by no means convincing, although there is considerable cleverness in the triangular scene between the adventuress, her daughter and her son-in-law. What is peculiarly puzzling is the position of Lord Windermere, who fails to see anything strange in his wife's sudden esteem and affection for Mrs. Erlynne, whom, an hour or two before, she had denounced as the vilest of creatures. His previous conduct had proved him a dull man, but this unexplained metamorphosis would excite suspicion in an idiot. It must be remembered that Lady Windermere, to the end, remains in perfect ignorance of her mother's identity.

As has been said the piece is very brightly and smartly written. The epigrams and paradoxes, which are the author's chief stock in trade, savor rather strongly of the lamp, but they are set in happy phrases, and rarely fail to excite laughter. His cynicism is of a rather cheap quality, but contributes to the general amusement. There can be no doubt that the comedy made a favorable impression, which was due in no small degree to the good acting. Miss Brookyn revealed unexpected capacities as the adventuress, and Mr. Barrymore, Mr. Holland, Mr. Ramsey, Mr. Saville, Mrs. D. P. Bowers and Miss Julia Arthur all did very well, while the minor parts were in perfectly satisfactory hands.

CRITICAL COMMENTARY

Christopher S. Nassaar (essay date fall 1995)

SOURCE: Nassaar, Christopher S. "Wilde's *The Picture of Dorian Gray* and *Lady Windermere's Fan*." *Explicator* 54, no. 1 (fall 1995): 20-24.

[*In the following essay, Nassaar views the four male characters in* Lady Windermere's Fan *as versions of the protagonist of* The Picture of Dorian Gray.]

In *The Picture of Dorian Gray,* Dorian develops from childlike innocence to a state of serious depravity in four states. The first stage is when he is still twenty and posing for Basil Hallward. Here he is the innocent young man who has not yet come in contact with evil. The second is when he is in love with Sibyl Vane. At this state evil has entered his life, but he is still largely innocent. The third is what might be called the "limited corruption" stage. Basil and Wotton become the opposing forces within him. Although he clearly leans toward Wotton, he is still balanced between good and evil, for his conscience is still alive and there are certain crimes, such as deliberate murder, that he would shrink from committing. In the fourth stage, all control is lost. He murders Basil, then tries to kill his conscience, which he identifies with his picture. Instead, he himself dies: human nature is "gray" and no one can become completely evil.

In *Lady Windermere's Fan,* Dorian Gray is fragmented and reincarnated in the four main characters, each of whom embodies one of the aforementioned stages, but within the framework and atmosphere of social comedy. Wilde often based his works on earlier works of his. In *Dorian Gray,* Dorian's development mirrors the drift of Victorian life and art toward corruption. In *Lady Windermere's Fan,* this same drift is shown in the juxtapositon of the four main characters, but it is simultaneously obscured by being cast in the mold of social comedy.

Dorian's first stage, childlike innocence, is embodied in Lord Windermere. Although he exists in a corrupt late-Victorian environment, Windermere is wrapped in a cocoon of early-Victorian morality that is never penetrated by his immoral surroundings. He is the object of much slander in the play, and even his wife becomes convinced that he is having an affair with Mrs. Erlynne. But he remains moral from beginning to end. His interest is in "saving" Mrs. Erlynne and in protecting his wife.

The art he admires is also that of spiritual innocence and purity. In Act 4, he attacks Mrs. Erlynne for having drifted away from a miniature of herself that his wife "kisses every night before she prays.—It's the miniature of a young innocent-looking girl with beautiful *dark* hair." This miniature typifies the kind of art that D. G. Rossetti produced in the 1850s and that Basil Hallward created in the picture of Dorian before it began to change. The Victorians have drifted away from such art, however, toward Pater's *Mona Lisa,* decadence, and Dorian's picture after its corruption. But Windermere has not developed with the age. He remains frozen at the state of purity and innocence.

In Lady Windermere we see the second stage of Dorian's development, which began when he fell in love with Sibyl Vane and ended when he rejected her and she committed suicide. Dorian's picture registers the change in him by adding lines of cruelty around the mouth, but it remains otherwise unaltered.

When we meet Lady Windermere, she is still pure and innocent, but during the play she rejects her husband, decides to become Lord Darlington's lover, then draws back from this immoral decision and—with the help of Mrs. Erlynne—is able to return to her previous life and preserve her marriage. It is significant that as soon as she steps into the world of corruption she is overwhelmed by a sense of guilt and decides to withdraw: "No, no! I will go back, let Arthur do as he pleases. I can't wait here. It has been madness my coming. I must go at once" (Act 3). Mrs. Erlynne's role is to open the trap and allow her daughter to slip away.

This episode changes Lady Windermere irrevocably. She becomes aware of an immoral streak in herself and as a consequence becomes more forgiving and stops categorizing people as good or evil. At the end of the play, she is tainted but still basically pure, much like Dorian's picture after the suicide of Sibyl Vane. Her sense of guilt parallels Dorian's after Sibyl's death. And like Dorian, she hides her secret from the world.

In his recent biography of Oscar Wilde, Richard Ellman observed of Lord Darlington:

> Lord Darlington, who has been taken as a man about town, and who talks like Lord Henry Wotton, differs from Wotton in his possession of deep feelings. . . . When the play was given in New York with Maurice Barrymore . . . in the role, Wilde complained that Barrymore had failed to see that "Darlington is *not* a villain, but a man who really believes that Windermere is treating his wife badly, and wishes to save her. His appeal is not to the weakness, but to the strength of her character (Act II): in Act III his words show he really loves her." It is because of her that he is leaving England for many years; he is a better man than Windermere.

> (363-64)

Darlington may not be a better man than Windermere, but there is more goodness in him than people have generally recognized. He sums up the third stage in Dorian's development, and there is within him a very delicate balance between goodness and corruption. The two opposites struggle in Darlington throughout the play, and the battle is not resolved at its end.

As the play begins, Darlington is in love with Lady Windermere, a married woman, and wants her for his mistress. But his great paradox is that he loves Lady Windermere for her purity and innocence: through her, he wants to recapture his own lost innocence. He says of her: "She is a good woman. She is the only good woman I have ever met in my life" (Act 3). And: "This woman has purity and innocence. She has everything we men have lost" (Act 3). The moral situation of Darlington is captured in Act 3, when he says to Cecil Graham and Dumby, "We are all in the gutter, but some of us are looking at the stars."

But Darlington's problem is that he cannot recover his lost innocence through Lady Windermere. She is already married, and if he wins her, he will only be dragging her into the gutter and corrupting her. Definitely not a fool, he realizes the impossibility of his situation but corruptly continues to pursue her. And yet part of the reason he appeals to her to leave her husband in Act 2 and to go with him is quite moral: he is thoroughly convinced that Windermere is a monstrously corrupt man who does not deserve her for a wife. Darlington's motives are a very complex and fascinating fusion of goodness and corruption, for black and white are mixed inextricably in him.

His final decision to leave England is ambiguous: he leaves as much for Lady Windermere's sake as for his own. It is true he decides to leave after her apparent rejection of him, but it is also true that she is at her most vulnerable at the end of Act 2 and that his chances with her have never been better. Indeed, that same night she reverses her decision and goes to his rooms. His hasty departure is both selfish and self-sacrificial. At least in part, he leaves because his stormy conversation with her leads him to realize how painful social disgrace would be for her. On the other hand, he does not want her to come to him mournfully, in tears, but with a smile and courageously or not at all. Even Lord Darlington's name is ambiguous, marking him both as a dandy and a "darling."

Mrs. Erlynne represents the final stage in Dorian's development. Although she does not commit any action quite as drastic as murder, she is nonetheless an immoral woman, devoted to leading a life of pleasure. In the play she discovers the goodness in herself and makes a major sacrifice to save her daughter. But she discovers that motherly love is too exhausting and strange an emotion for her, and she returns to the life of pleasure. She declares to the shocked Windermere: "I have no ambition to play the part of a mother. Only once in my life have I known a mother's feelings. That was last night. They were terrible—they made me suffer—they made me suffer too much" (Act 4). And: "No—what consoles one nowadays is not repentance, but pleasure" (Act 4). Far from being the conventional fallen woman of Victorian melodrama,

Mrs. Erlynne deliberately rejects the goodness in herself and returns to a life of corruption (Nassaar 78-80). As Ellmann has observed, "*Lady Windermere's Fan* is a more radical play than it appears. . . . Wilde . . . shelves the stereotype of the fallen woman: Mrs. Erlynne is singularly impenitent" (363-64). Wilde regarded this point as so basic that he wrote, in one of his letters, that her character is "as yet untouched by literature" (*Letters* 287-88).

Mrs. Erlynne's rejection of motherly love parallels Dorian's attempt to destroy his conscience by stabbing his picture. Far from dying, however, she tricks the infatuated Lord Augustus into marrying her and travels with him to the Continent. She also retains an affection for her daughter, albeit from a distance: human nature being "gray," the goodness in Mrs. Erlynne cannot be eliminated.

In *The Critic as Artist,* Wilde wrote:

> To an artist as creative as the critic, what does subject-matter signify? No more and no less than it does to the novelist and the painter. Like them, he can find his motives elsewhere. Treatment is the test. . . . [Criticism] works with materials, and puts them into a form that is at once new and delightful. What more can one say of poetry?
>
> (1027)

Treatment, then, or form, is what is vital in all art, not subject matter. In *Lady Windermere's Fan,* Wilde applied this principle quite successfully. He took the raw subject matter of his novel and gave it a new form. The result was his first successful play.

Works Cited

Ellmann, Richard. *Oscar Wilde*. New York: Knopf, 1988.

Hart-Davis, Rupert, ed. *Letters of Oscar Wilde.* New York: Harcourt, Brace and World, 1962.

Nassaar, Christopher S. *Into the Demon Universe: A Literary Exploration of Oscar Wilde.* New Haven: Yale UP, 1974.

Powell, Kerry. *Oscar Wilde and the Theatre of the 1890s.* Cambridge: Cambridge UP, 1990.

Raby, Peter. *Oscar Wilde.* Cambridge: Cambridge UP, 1988.

Wilde, Oscar. *Complete Works.* London: Collins, 1966.

AN IDEAL HUSBAND

CRITICAL COMMENTARY

E. H. Mikhail (essay date 1968)

SOURCE: Mikhail, E. H. "Self-Revelation in *An Ideal Husband.*" *Modern Drama* 11 (1968): 180-86.

[*In the following essay, Mikhail perceives* An Ideal Husband *as a reflection of Wilde's personal torment and a foreshadowing of the scandal that would ruin his career.*]

Despite its apparent objectivity, *An Ideal Husband* is self-revelatory. In a letter to his friend Reginald Turner, written in 1899, Wilde said:

> I read a great deal, and correct the proofs of *An Ideal Husband,* shortly to appear. It reads rather well, and some of its passages seem prophetic of tragedy to come.[1]

A sense of damnation, a foreboding of tragic failure, is to be found in the writings of Oscar Wilde long before it is sounded in *An Ideal Husband.* It is the theme of the sonnet *Helas!* as it is of *The Picture of Dorian Gray.* The motive of the outcast is conspicuous in Wilde's two previous comedies, *Lady Windermere's Fan* and *A Woman of No Importance,* where both Mrs. Erlynne and Mrs. Arbuthnot describe in moving words the lot of an outcast; but it reaches an ominous significance in *An Ideal Husband,* written shortly before Wilde's own fall. One cannot avoid the impression that *An Ideal Husband* is an oblique expression of Wilde's inner torment, using Sir Robert Chiltern as a mask. Wilde has described in Chiltern's person his own fear of an imminent scandal. Charles Ricketts remembers Wilde saying of the play when he insisted on Ricketts being present at the first night: "It was written for ridiculous puppets to play, and the critics will say, 'Ah, here is Oscar unlike himself!'—though in reality I became engrossed in writing it, and it contains a great deal of the real Oscar."[2] Mrs. Cheveley, while threatening Sir Robert, actually presages with amazing accuracy one prominent feature of Wilde's downfall, when she says:

> Sir Robert, you know what your English newspapers are like. Suppose that when I leave this house I drive down to some newspaper office, and give them this scandal and the proofs of it. Think of their loathsome joy, of the delight they would have in dragging you down, of the mud and mire they would plunge you in. Think of the hypocrite with his greasy smile penning his leading article, and arranging the foulness of the public placard.[3]

In the sin of Sir Robert's youth the guilt feelings which Wilde had tried to suppress all his life break through again. "The sin of my youth," Sir Robert exclaims, "that I had thought was buried rose up in front of me, hideous, horrible, with its hand at my throat." There is no doubt that for some time a shadow, a threat, had hung over Wilde. At the time when *An Ideal Husband* was written, it was clear that he had the feeling of a great fate hanging over him—it was part of his personal myth; and months before it happened he believed in the reality of his own downfall, in his destiny to become one of the great failures and sufferers of the world, as, indeed, he did become. André Gide, who met him in Algiers when the scandal against him was moving to a climax, and when it already seemed clear to many of his friends that he was riding for a fall, describes him as being resigned to and even longing for the precipitation of his fate; he said, "My friends are extraordinary; they beg me to be careful. Careful? But can I be careful? That would be a backward step. I must go on as far as possible. I cannot go much further. Something is bound to happen."[4] This is echoed in Sir Robert Chiltern's words to Lord Goring:

> Arthur, I feel that public disgrace is in store for me. I feel certain of it. I never knew what terror was before. I know it now. It is as if a hand of ice were laid upon one's heart. It is as if one's heart were beating itself to death in some empty hollow.[5]

and in his fear that:

> if it is all taken away from me now? If I lose everything over a horrible scandal? If I am hounded from public life?[6]

Some of Wilde's intimate friends had observed in him something similar to Chiltern's inner agitation; Wilde, too, like Chiltern, had shameful things to conceal from his contemporaries, and subconsciously, perhaps, he must have been dreading the approach of a cruel and terrible disaster which would expose him to public contempt and "a long farewell to all his greatness," to a fatal mischief that would shatter his career and rob him of his laurels. "I knew," he said once to Gide, whom he met in Paris after his release from Reading Goal—"I knew a catastrophe would come. This one or that one. I expected it. It had to end like that."[7] This was a feeling that must have weighed heavily upon his mind. We have in *An Ideal Husband* continual references to secrecy, double lives, masks. It is, in fact, in this third comedy that Wilde's preoccupation with masks as symbols begins positively to shout. Lady Chiltern cries out to her husband—the "ideal" husband, now unmasked: "Oh! what a mask you have been wearing all these years! A horrible painted mask!" And Phipps, "the ideal butler," is called "a mask with a manner." When Lord Goring threatens to fetch the police for Mrs. Cheveley, she is described thus: "A mask has fallen from her." As in the two previous comedies, the central scene is that in which the sinner confesses his sin and makes an impassioned plea for forgiveness and acceptance. There are touches of self-defence in *An Ideal Husband,* which reveal a great deal of the real Oscar. When Wilde lets Sir Robert escape from punishment, it is here that the motive of pardon comes in. Already in the two earlier plays Wilde shows sympathetic understanding for the "sinners," but here he is outspoken against the conventional morality which would have insisted on the confession and expiation of the crime. This preoccupation with sin, conscience, and pardon renders *An Ideal Husband* the most serious of Wilde's comedies and gives it psychological bearing as one of the most open "confessions" of Wilde's soul.

The technique of self-identification manifests itself in *An Ideal Husband.* In his creation of Lord Goring Wilde produced a replica of himself. Like Wilde, Goring misrepresents his age—he is thirty-four, but admits only to thirty-two. Wilde always gave his age as two years less than it was. When he went on a lecture tour of America he was twenty-eight years old, but he told the reporters that he was twenty-six. Though not a convincing deception, it gave him the illusion of having youth still before him.[8]

Like Wilde, Goring professes an adoration for youth: "Youth is an art," he says. He dresses much like a dandy: as a stage direction says, "He is the first well-dressed philosopher in the history of thought." Wilde was innately kind, and Goring is also kind. Both preferred to disguise this quality by an amused superficiality; both enjoyed shocking their friends by this outward coldness. Even his father repeats over and over again that Goring is heartless, but Goring was more of a stranger to his father than to the Chilterns, to whom he proved an invaluable friend. Both Wilde and Goring are fond of buttonholes. "I am the only person of the smallest importance in London at present who wears a buttonhole," says Goring to his butler.[9] Goring admits that he never knows when he is serious and when he is not. "He is fond of being misunderstood. It gives him a post of vantage."[10] His tongue drips Wilde-isms: "Everybody one meets is a paradox nowadays. It is a great bore."[11] Richard Le Gallienne tells us that Wilde was "one of those natures who find an unfading fascination in not being able to understand themselves."[12] Nor is Lord Caversham able to understand his son Goring:

LORD CAVERSHAM:

(*Turning round, and looking at his son beneath his bushy eyebrows.*) Do you always really understand what you say, sir?

And in the last act we also have the following between father and son:

LORD CAVERSHAM:

Have you been thinking over what I spoke to you about last night?

LORD GORING:

I have been thinking about nothing else.

LORD CAVERSHAM:

Engaged to be married yet?

LORD GORING:

(*Genially.*) Not yet: but I hope to be before lunchtime.

LORD CAVERSHAM:

(*Caustically.*) You can have till dinner-time if it would be of any convenience to you.

LORD GORING:

Thanks awfully, but I think I'd sooner be engaged before lunch.

LORD CAVERSHAM:

H'm. Never know when you are serious or not.

LORD GORING:

Neither do I, father.

Furthermore, Wilde's habit of unpunctuality is reflected in Lord Goring's remark that "it is always nice to be expected, and not to arrive."[13] But Lord Goring is also a kind of providence who settles all troubles by quick brain-work and utter detachment. Outwardly a dandy and an idler, he is inwardly a philosopher, even a man of action and decision if need be. All Wilde's friends remarked that in spite of his frivolous attitude to life, his trifling air and lazy inconsequence, his advice in mundane affairs was singularly shrewd; and each of these characteristics is given to Goring. There is further an echo of Dublin home life, of the disreputable Sir William Wilde and Lady "Speranza," in Goring's generalisation: "Fathers should be neither seen nor heard. That is the only proper basis for family life. Mothers are different. Mothers are darlings."

There are also many remarks in ***An Ideal Husband*** which were no doubt meant to have a personal application. The basic theme of the play is the innate corruption of political life. In this connection it should be remarked that Wilde showed a consistently hostile attitude towards politics and politicians, not only in his writings, but also in his personal life. "He despised politics," says Ernest Bendz, "and took no part in the strifes of the day. Those great social movements which reached his ears . . . left him an indifferent or uneasy onlooker, or roused him to scornful antagonism."[14] There were those among his friends who regretted that, with his gift for talking, he did not go into parliamentary life; one of these was Yeats, who, with his odd idea that Wilde was by nature a man of action, said to O'Sullivan: "He might have had a career like that of Beaconsfield, whose early style resembles his, being meant for crowds, for excitement, for hurried decision, for immediate triumphs." Anything less calculated for crowd appeal than Wilde's conversational or literary style it is difficult to imagine, and when Oscar was told of the idea that he was a man of action, he remarked disparagingly, "It is interesting to hear Yeats's opinion about me." According to Lord Alfred Douglas, Wilde professed to be a Liberal, but he mocked the Liberals as much as the Tories, and Douglas thought that he never showed enough interest in either party to vote in an election. When his political friends, admiring his conversational gifts, tried to persuade him to accept a safe seat in Parliament, he turned down the offer without hesitation. This is echoed by Goring's remark to his father: "My dear father, only people who look dull ever get into the House of Commons, and only people who are dull ever succeed there."[15] In ***An Ideal Husband*** this strongly critical attitude towards political life occurs in many quite deliberate statements of opinion in various parts of the play. For instance, when Robert Chiltern is trying to prepare his wife for a revelation of his predicament, which he knows will shatter the pedestalled ideal she has always made of him, he says to her:

Gertrude, truth is a very complex thing, and politics is a very complex business. There are wheels within wheels. One may be under certain obligations to people that one must pay. Sooner or later in political life one has to compromise. Everyone does.[16]

Then there is the even more revealing conversation between Chiltern and Goring,[17] in which Chiltern tells Goring how he was corrupted by Arnheim with his philosophy of power. Goring, who acts as Wilde's personal voice, expresses his complete disagreement with this philosophy. This attitude towards politics and the political life is supported by a whole series of epigrams scattered throughout the play. An example is Lady Markby's remark that "now that the House of Commons is trying to become useful, it does a great deal of harm."[18] Auden says about Wilde's view of politics:

> To do Wilde justice he seldom indulges in the all-too-easy role of political satirist. When, for instance, in *An Ideal Husband,* Lord Chiltern, in a fit of emotional remorse, resolves to quit public life it is Wilde's *alter ego* Lord Goring who dissuades him, knowing that Chiltern is by nature a politician and would be miserable doing anything else. This is not satire but sound sense.[19]

Wilde's dislike of journalism can also be traced in this comedy. "Oh, spies are of no use nowadays," says Sir Robert Chiltern. "Their profession is over. The newspapers do their work instead."[20] When Vicomte de Nanjac says that he reads all English newspapers and finds them so amusing, Lord Goring retorts: "Then, my dear Nanjac, you must certainly read between the lines."[21] Mrs. Cheveley reminds Sir Robert: "Sir Robert, you know what your English newspapers are like."[22] Nor was Wilde enthusiastic about religion. "I can't understand this modern mania for curates," says Lady Markby, "In my time, we girls saw them, of course, running about the place like rabbits. But we never took any notice of them, I need hardly say. But I am told that nowadays country society is quite honey-combed with them. I think it most irreligious."[23] A little later we have the following conversation:

MRS. CHEVELEY:

(*Rising.*) I don't mind waiting in the carriage at all, provided there is somebody to look at one.

LADY MARKBY:

Well, I hear the curate is always prowling about the house.

MRS. CHEVELEY:

I am afraid I am not fond of girl friends.[24]

Wilde had no liking for professional philanthropy, and used to tell a story about a certain man who spent twenty years of his life trying to get some grievance redressed or some unjust law altered: "Finally he succeeded, and nothing could exceed his disappointment. He had absolutely nothing to do, almost died of *ennui,* and became a confirmed misanthrope."[25] Lord Goring says to Sir Robert Chiltern who has given a deal of money to public charities, "Dear me, what a lot of harm you must have done, Robert."[26] Mrs. Cheveley also remarks, "Philanthropy seems to me to have become simply the refuge of people

who wish to annoy their fellow-creatures."[27] We further have in this comedy the elaborate compliments Wilde was fond of in actual life:

LADY MARKBY:

. . . I really must go to Vienna next winter. I hope there is a good chef at the Embassy.

SIR ROBERT CHILTERN:

If there is not, the Ambassador will certainly have to be recalled.[28]

In the same act Sir Robert says to Mrs. Cheveley: "To attempt to classify you, Mrs. Cheveley, would be an impertinence."[29] Like Wilde's wife, Constance, to whom "sin was a thing impossible to her nature,"[30] Sir Robert's wife, Gertrude, "can never" be touched by sin.[31] It is a fair assumption that Wilde's experience of blackmail in actual life suggested blackmail as the theme for his third piece. Finally, when Mrs. Cheveley offers to pay Sir Robert so that he may support the Argentine Canal Scheme, Sir Robert answers:

SIR ROBERT CHILTERN:

(*Rising indignantly.*) If you will allow me, I will call your carriage for you. You have lived so long abroad, Mrs. Cheveley, that you seem to be unable to realise that you are talking to an Englishman.[32]

This reply anticipates Wilde's own reply to the Governor of his prison when on the eve of the expiration of his sentence an American reporter called upon the Governor, and gave Wilde to understand he would pay him £1,000 for a long talk on his prison experiences. "Sir," said Wilde, "I cannot understand how such a proposal can be made to a gentleman."[33]

Notes

1. Hart-Davis, Rupert, ed. *The Letters of Oscar Wilde* (London, 1962), p. 787.

2. Ojala, Oatos. *Aestheticism and Oscar Wilde, Part I: Life and Letters* (Helsinki, 1954), p. 189.

3. *An Ideal Husband,* Act I, p. 181. Page references for Wilde's plays are to *Oscar Wilde: Five Famous Plays,* ed. by A. Harris (London, 1952).

4. Woodcock, George. *The Paradox of Oscar Wilde* (London, 1950), p. 40.

5. *An Ideal Husband,* Act II, p. 196.

6. *Ibid.,* p. 192.

7. Brasol, Boris. *Oscar Wilde; The Man, the Artist* (London, 1938), p. 269.

8. In spite of the exposure of this little deception, the date 1856 instead of 1854 for Wilde's birth is still frequently seen in print.

9. *An Ideal Husband,* Act II, p. 215.

10. *Ibid.,* Act I, p. 171.

11. *Ibid.,* Act III, p. 219.

12. Le Gallienne, Richard. "Introduction" to *The Writings of Oscar Wilde* (New York, 1907), p. 12.

13. *An Ideal Husband,* Act III, p. 216.

14. Bendz, Ernest. *Some Stray Notes on the Personality and Writings of Oscar Wilde; In Memoriam 30th November 1910* (Göteberg, 1911), p. 306.

15. *An Ideal Husband,* Act IV, p. 236.

16. *Ibid.,* Act I, p. 187.

17. *Ibid.,* Act II, p. 193.

18. *Ibid.,* Act I, p. 167.

19. Auden, W. H. "A Playboy of the Western World: St. Oscar, the Homintern Martyr," *The New Partisan Reader 1945-1953,* ed. by William Phillips and Philip Rahv (New York, 1953), p. 607.

20. *An Ideal Husband,* Act III, p. 223.

21. *Ibid.,* Act I, p. 172.

22. *Ibid.,* Act. I, p. 181.

23. *Ibid.,* Act II, p. 208.

24. *Ibid.,* Act II, p. 209.

25. Pearson, Hesketh. *The Life of Oscar Wilde* (London, 1946), pp. 172-173.

26. *An Ideal Husband,* Act II, p. 195.

27. *Ibid.,* Act I, p. 169.

28. *Ibid.,* Act I, p. 168.

29. *Ibid.,* Act I, p. 168.

30. Winwar, Frances. *Oscar Wilde and the Yellow 'Nineties* (New York, 1958), p. 176.

31. *An Ideal Husband,* Act IV, p. 251.

32. *Ibid.,* Act I, p. 179.

33. Esdaile, Arundell. "The New Hellenism," *The Fortnightly Review,* LXXXVIII (October 1910), p. 708.

THE IMPORTANCE OF BEING EARNEST

PRODUCTION REVIEWS

Athenaeum (review date 12 January 1895)

SOURCE: Review of *An Ideal Husband. Athenaeum* 105 (12 January 1895): 57.

[*In the following excerpted review, the anonymous critic offers a favorable assessment of* An Ideal Husband.]

One of the constituent elements in wit is the perception of analogies in things apparently disparate and incongruous. Accepting this as a canon and testing by it the pretensions of Mr. Oscar Wilde in his latest play, that writer might be pronounced the greatest of wits, inasmuch as he perceives analogies in things absolutely antagonistic. His presumable end is gained, since a chorus of laughter attends his propositions or paradoxes. It requires, however, gifts of a kind not usually accorded to humanity to think out statements such as "High intellectual pleasures make girls' noses large," "Only dull people are brilliant at breakfast," "All reasons are absurd," and the like. Uttered as these things are by Mr. Charles Hawtrey, who for once is entrusted with *fadaises* instead of fibs, they pass muster and create amusement, and it is not until one turns to them again that one perceives how impertinent and extravagant they are. As parts of the trapping of a vigorously ridden hobby-horse of affectation, they beget amusement rather than offence. It is difficult to be angry with the author or displeased with his play. **An Ideal Husband** has a certain amount of story, the development of which proves not uninteresting. Accident is too potent a factor in the action to permit of its being genuinely dramatic. Without the aid of *ficelles* the required termination could never have been reached. When reached even it is wholly disproportionate to what the author holds to be the offence, and a man whom Mr. Wilde sets before the audience as a traitor and a scoundrel escapes with no worse penalty than a fright and with one of the most coveted of human rewards. Nothing, in fact, beyond a curious complication is brought about by human folly. Separate scenes and characters are amusing and interesting, and the whole, with the salt of Mr. Wilde's impertinence, wins acceptance. The scenes and costumes are exquisite, and much of the acting is praiseworthy. Mr. Hawtrey and Mr. Brookfield, the latter as a servant, are seen to most advantage in a cast that comprised Mr. Waller, Mr. Bishop, Miss Fanny Brough, Miss Florence West, Miss Vane Featherston, Miss Maude Millett, and Miss Helen Forsyth.

Critic (review date 27 April 1895)

SOURCE: Review of *The Importance of Being Earnest. Critic* 23, no. 688 (27 April 1895): 316.

[*In the following review of* The Importance of Being Earnest, *the critic praises the play as lighthearted.*]

This three-act farce, one of the latest productions of Oscar Wilde, which has been running successfully for a number of weeks in London, was presented at the Empire Theatre on Monday evening, and met with a most favorable and often very merry reception. The piece is of the lightest possible texture, and never was intended to be subjected to the test of serious consideration or analysis. Its story is a whim, and its personages are mere vehicles for the utterance of those epigrammatic conceits which constitute so large a share of its author's literary stock in trade. When the curtain rises, two young fashionable idlers are exchanging experiences. John Worthing, known in London as Earnest, confesses that in the country, where he lives in a fine house with a charming ward, he is called Uncle Jack and is regarded as the pink of all proprieties. When he wishes to enjoy an outing, he explains that he is obliged to go to town to lookafter the affairs of a troublesome and wholly imaginary brother called Earnest, who for many years has been the scapegoat for all his own derelictions. Algernon Moncrief, the younger man, conceives the idea of visiting Worthing's country retreat in the guise of Earnest and making love to the beautiful ward. He has already made great progress in his wooing, when Worthing returns home unexpectedly in deep mourning, to announce that his brother Earnest has died suddenly in Paris. Out of this situation a number of amusing, but wholly preposterous incidents arise, including some entertaining passages of jealousy between the two young women who are prominent figures in the dramatic tangle. In the end, of course, everything is straightened out, and the importance of being Earnest is supposed to be established.

The piece is undoubtedly clever in its way, full of bright or rather "smart" sayings, and with some well-directed thrusts at social foibles and hypocricies, but, as a rule, the satire is not very keen or very powerful and the fun is rather shallow and labored, with very little of the freshness and spirit observable in W. S. Gilbert's best work, which was, rather too plainly, the model set up for imitation. Of the performers the most successful was Viola Allen, whose mock earnestness was capital. Henry Miller's touch is rather heavy for such flimsy material, while Mr. Faversham's work is spoiled by an apparent self-consciousness which is exceedingly aggravating. Agnes Miller, May Robson and Ida Vernon had purely conventional characters, but played them very well. The general representation was brisk and pleasing, and the audience retired in great good humor.

CRITICAL COMMENTARY

David Parker (essay date June 1974)

SOURCE: Parker, David. "Oscar Wilde's Great Farce: *The Importance of Being Earnest*." *Modern Literature Quarterly* 35, no. 2 (June 1974): 173-86.

[*In the following essay, Parker offers a thematic and stylistic examination of* The Importance of Being Earnest *and places it within the context of nineteenth- and twentieth-century farces.*]

It is generally agreed that *The Importance of Being Earnest* is Oscar Wilde's masterpiece, but there is little agreement on why it should be thought so or on how it works as a play. Though we can sense a solid substance beneath the frothy surface, the nature of that substance

remains an enigma. Surprisingly little real criticism has been written about the play, and much of that which has is sketchy or tedious. One of the few critics whose mind seems to have been genuinely engaged by the play is Mary McCarthy, but she has written about it only briefly, and despite her admiration clearly finds it repugnant. "It has the character of a ferocious idyll," she says, and complains that "Selfishness and servility are the moral alternatives presented."[1] Most of what she says about the play cannot be denied, yet there is a wrong note somewhere. Though it is almost always feeble to complain about critics using the wrong standards, I think we have to do so here. *The Importance of Being Earnest* does not tackle problems of moral conduct in the way that most plays do. In it, Wilde expresses a comic vision of the human condition by deliberately distorting actuality and having most of the characters behave as if that vision were all but universal. It is fair enough to complain about the vision entire, but to complain simply about the selfishness, without asking what it suggests, is on a par with complaining about the immortality of *Tom Jones*.

Though McCarthy uses the wrong standards, and therefore sees the play through a distorting lens, what she sees is there and needs to be studied. Her notion about the play's advocacy of selfishness may be got into better focus if we compare it with what William Empson says about the heroes of Restoration comedy: "There is an obscure paradox that the selfish man *is* the generous one, because he is not repressed, has 'good nature', and so on."[2] This seems to represent more accurately what goes on in Wilde's play, if only because it resembles Wilde's own way of thinking. Moreover, the play clearly owes something to the Restoration comic tradition. "My duty as a gentleman," says Algy, "has never interfered with my pleasures in the smallest degree,"[3] thus neatly summing up the principles by which the young bloods of Restoration comedy lived. They were understood to be gentlemen because they were Natural Men, responsive to impulse, capable of falling in love, and so on, in contrast to the inhibited, conventional, rule-obeying, theory-loving tradesmen, Puritans, and pedants, whom they despised. The heroes of Restoration comedy have been criticized too, often with justice, but one thing should be clear by now: their roguishness, their carelessness about money and sexual behavior, was presented not simply to be admired as such. These things had symbolic value as well. The suggestion was that aristocratic young men needed to abandon conventional morality and get back to basic impulse, if the values they represented (moral independence, for example) were not to be annihilated by commercialism and Puritanism. Their roguishness was a proof of freedom, as well as an excuse for scourging the bourgeoisie. Algy's selfishness, and that of the other characters, demands a similar interpretation. It has a satirical force, of course: the manners of the upper classes are being laughed at; but there is more to it than that. In Wilde's vision, a sort of honorable selfishness becomes not merely a virtue, but a moral *sine qua non*.

Wilde's play, it seems to me, is more successful than most Restoration comedies because it is more pure—more purely absurd, if you like. The process of distorting actuality for expressive purposes is carried out more thoroughly, and the play's moral and aesthetic integrity is better maintained. In the dialogue alone, there is a more consistent heightening, amounting to a transfiguration of everyday conversation. The trouble with many Restoration comedies is that they express values only half-believed in by the audience for which they were intended. The characters praise aristocratic recklessness and sneer at commerce, yet the original courtly audience was committed to, and dependent on, commerce for at least a large part of its wealth.[4] As a result, because of a secret uncertainty in the playwrights, there is often a confusion between symbolic action and action seriously recommended to the audience for imitation. We are presented with hyperbolic actions and sentiments, which we find not entirely convincing and perhaps a shade hysterical. There is the standard paradox of Restoration comedy, for instance: all moralists are hypocrites; only libertines can see the truth and maintain a fundamental decency. The confusion carried over into real life. Many of the court wits and gallants tried to live out such paradoxes, not always with happy results. Wilde too tried to live out his own paradoxes, with decidedly unhappy results, but in his greatest play artifice and advice do not get mixed up. "I don't quite like women who are interested in philanthropic work," says Cecily. "I think it is so forward of them."[5] This is funnier, and more percipient, than jokes about hypocritical Puritan tradesmen. Wilde's symbol for sensual vitality and obedience to impulse is itself more wisely chosen than that of the Restoration playwrights: instead of using sexual behavior, he uses eating, something much more easily distanced. Contrary to what McCarthy says, *The Importance of Being Earnest* rarely slips over into recommending attitudes that are morally repellent—relative to Restoration comedy, at any rate. You have to stand a long way off from the play to be able to think so. It is difficult to get indignant with the characters.

The farcical structure helps distance what we see, and Wilde exploits it in other ways too. Farce is not necessarily trivial, and even when it is, through its very nature it usually makes assertions and raises questions about human identity; that is what makes the same situations enduringly popular. The hero of farce is usually a cunning rogue who, in order to gratify some impulse, spins an elaborate deception, which his victims seem constantly on the verge of exposing, so that he is constantly threatened with defeat, punishment, or humiliation. We admire the hero because he has the courage to obey his impulses and because his tricks render him protean—free from imposed identity. We despise his victims because they are prisoners of manners, which repress impulse and forbid deception. They seem narrow and timid. A more highly wrought and expressive sort of farce is that in which all (or most) of the protagonists are rogues, who compete to satisfy their

impulses. The moral independence of the most versatile, the most protean, is endorsed by success. *The Importance of Being Earnest* belongs to that sort.

Moreover, Wilde consciously exploits the concern of farce with human identity. The joke in the title is often thought of as a mock-pompous piece of frivolity, but it is more than that. The play might as justly be named "The Importance of Being." The whole thing is comically addressed to the problem of recognizing and defining human identity; we are made to see wide significance in Jack's polite request, "Lady Bracknell, I hate to seem inquisitive, but would you kindly inform me who I am?" (p. 107). The pun on *earnest* and *Ernest* merely makes the title more suitably comic. Neither being earnest nor being Ernest is of much help when confidence is lost in the substantiality of human identity. The concern with identity is repeatedly underlined in the text of the play, where statements that seem superficially only to poke fun at upper-class frivolity continually edge the mind toward a contemplation of the insubstantiality of identity. "It isn't easy to be anything nowadays," complains Algy in the first act. "There's such a lot of beastly competition about." And only a few lines later, Gwendolen feels obliged to deny that she is perfect: "It would leave no room for developments, and I intend to develop in many directions" (Maine, ed., p. 327).

More than most writers of farce, Wilde was conscious of this concern with identity, so natural to the form, and he uses it to express a preoccupation which the nineteenth century gave birth to, and the twentieth century cherishes. Lurking always in the depths of the play is a steady contemplation of Nothingness, of *le néant*, which is all the more effective for its being, in contrast to most of its manifestations, comic in mode. Instead of making Nothingness a pretext for despair, Wilde finds in it a challenge to the imagination. For him, Nothingness in human identity, in human claims to knowledge, in the organization of society, becomes a field to be tilled by the artist—by the artist in each of us.

In many ways a writer owing more to French than to English traditions, in this respect too Wilde shares a quality of vision with Flaubert, Villiers, Zola, Barbey d'Aurevilly, and Mallarmé. They differ from each other, of course, as Wilde differs from them, but in the vision of each, as Robert Martin Adams says, "The shell of personal identity collapses, the yolk of individuality is split. Even grossness is a form of transparency, even knowledge is a form of complicated and difficult ignorance (Flaubert)."[6] Yet for Wilde this brings liberation, not despair. Though he has Algy complain about what we might call the epistemological complacency of the English, he has him do it gaily: "That is the worst of the English. They are always degrading truths into facts, and when a truth becomes a fact, it loses all its intellectual value" (p. 12).

If *The Importance of Being Earnest* looks back to the French nineteenth century it also looks forward to the twentieth century and the drama of the absurd. The plot is absurd, in an obvious sense, and many critics have argued that it should be dismissed as a Gilbertian fantasy. It seems to me, however, that it is important, in the negative way that plots are, in the drama of the absurd. Everyone responds to preposterous situations in a way that is crazily systematic, defending his responses with absurdly sententious generalizations. Besides being used as a symbol for sensual vitality, eating becomes a subject for absurd imperatives. Algy, for instance, declares that "One should always eat muffins quite calmly. It is the only way to eat them" (p. 85). People's behavior and sentiments act as a parody of the real world; such, it is suggested, is the nature of all action, all moralizing. But Wilde carries off this parody better than most of the playwrights whom we now describe as dramatists of the absurd. He is never obvious. His parody always works at two levels, which enrich each other: it pokes fun at the manners of a particular class, and it satirizes the human condition. To my knowledge, only Pinter and Albee do anything at all like this, with comparative success.

Nothingness is repeatedly evoked in the verbal texture of the play in a way that prefigures techniques of the drama of the absurd. Characters are always using words like *serious* and *nonsense* in a manner that sends out little ripples of significance. "If you don't take care," Jack warns Algy,

JACK:

your friend Bunbury will get you into a serious scrape some day.

ALGERNON:

I love scrapes. They are the only things that are never serious.

JACK:

Oh, that's nonsense, Algy. You never talk anything but nonsense.

ALGERNON:

Nobody ever does.

(Maine, ed., p. 337)

Serious was recognized as a canting expression in the nineteenth century. "No one knows the power," wrote "F. Anstey" in 1885, "that a single serious hairdresser might effect with worldly customers" (*OED*). Algy's quasi pun works as a protest against the importance attached by the Victorians to the very business of attaching importance (parodied more broadly in Miss Prism); for them, it is often apparent, this was a means of imposing form and stability on a world whose evanescence they half-suspected, a procedure of course unacceptable to Wilde. The joke is parallel to the one about *earnest*.

The play on the word *nonsense* expresses a sensibility that is recognizably modern, though it lacks the anguish that is now usually part of it. The sense of futility that arises out of the contemplation of Nothingness is felt only by those whose belief in human dignity requires support from a religious mythology, or a quasi-religious mythology, such as that subscribed to by many humanists. When his mind was at its most creative, Wilde felt no such need, willingly abandoning intellectual comfort and security for intellectual adventurousness in the unknown and unknowable. Algy's perception of universal nonsense is cheerful; it has the gusto of quick intelligence; and because it also works as a gibe at Algy's class, it has a quality of immediate practical shrewdness that makes it the more acceptable.

In the middle of the play, *absurd* itself is used repeatedly to evoke a sense of immanent Nothingness. Jack cannot understand how he should have a brother in the dining-room: "I don't know what it all means. I think it is perfectly absurd" (p. 48). Algy will not deny that he is Jack's brother: "It would be absurd" (p. 53). Jack says the same about the notion that Algy should lunch twice (p. 57), and he thinks Algy's presence in the garden at Woolton "utterly absurd" (p. 58). Algy disagrees with the contention that he has no right to "Bunbury" at Woolton: "That is absurd. One has a right to Bunbury anywhere one chooses" (p. 83). Gwendolen and Cecily agree that it is "absurd to talk of the equality of the sexes" (p. 91).

These words are used in jokes and casual comments that do not stand out in the text and are likely to be delivered in a carelessly cynical manner, as bits of flimflam designed simply to gain the speaker a tactical advantage in the argument; but they crop up repeatedly and affect the whole flavor of the play.

The use of paradox performs the same function much more obviously. Each paradox is a sort of miniature stylistic enactment of the notion expressed in one of the boldest: "In matters of grave importance style, not sincerity, is the vital thing" (p. 90). This pokes fun at the beau monde, of course, but it also hints at an answer to the problems raised in the jokes about *earnest* and *serious*. Once belief in epistemological certainty is abandoned, style, liberally interpreted, is more important than sincerity. By imposing a consciously provisional order onto evanescent reality, it makes practical decisions possible. Paradox imposes this order in a particularly striking way. It confounds conventional notions about order, identity, and dissimilarity, synthesizing new orders out of the confusion it exposes. Far from concealing chaos and disharmony, it rejoices in them, embraces them courageously, and takes them as a challenge to human wit and ingenuity. Wilde's rapid sequences of paradox after paradox picture for us a world in which men make, undo, and remake reality with almost every sentence they utter.

Of course, not all the paradoxes in **The Importance of Being Earnest** are purely verbal or confined to one remark. There is a sustained effort in the play to dissolve conventional notions of order in fields where they tend to hypertrophy. Wilde depicts a world in which the socially endorsed certainties are continually evaporating; values respecting social class, education, the Church, money, love, and the family undergo constant metamorphosis. Attitudes toward the family, in particular, are grotesquely transformed. Algy cheerfully dismisses the sentiments associated with kinship: "Relations are simply a tedious pack of tedious people, who haven't got the remotest knowledge of how to live, nor the smallest instinct about when to die" (p. 25). Others invert the normal sentiments. Lady Bracknell speaks of an acquaintance whose husband has died: "I never saw a woman so altered, she looks quite twenty years younger" (p. 13). Gwendolen complains about her lack of influence over her mother: "Few parents nowadays pay any regard to what their children say to them! The old-fashioned respect for the young is rapidly dying out" (pp. 30-31). She approves of her father's domestication, however: "The home seems to me to be the proper sphere for the man. And certainly once a man begins to neglect his domestic duties he becomes painfully effeminate, does he not?" (p. 74).

In plot and action, too, conventional notions about family life are broken down. The handbag in Jack's family history excites Lady Bracknell's famous protest: "To be born, or at any rate bred in a handbag, whether it had handles or not, seems to me to display a contempt for the ordinary decencies of family life that reminds one of the worst excesses of the French Revolution" (p. 23). The comedy is enhanced, of course, by the oddity of Lady Bracknell's own notions (or at least her way of expressing them). She seems to conceive family as something subject to human volition, and can advise Jack "to make a definite effort to produce, at any rate, one parent, of either sex, before the season is quite over" (p. 24). Though we may see parody of upper-class snobbery here, others do will relations into—and out of—existence, without there being any feeling of parody. Jack invents a brother; the girls invent ideal husbands. (Algy's Bunbury is only a friend, but the effect is much the same.) At the other extreme, the characters accept the family relationships revealed at the end of the play, with an absurd eagerness that is just as effective in ridiculing conventional notions. This is particularly evident in Jack's outburst, when he mistakenly assumes Miss Prism to be his mother. She indignantly reminds him that she is unmarried. "Cannot repentance wipe out an act of folly?" he cries. "Why should there be one law for men and another for women? Mother! I forgive you" (p. 107). The family is a category of everyday understanding that is one of the first to crumble before the vision of Nothingness. That is what enables Wilde's characters to adopt such a variety of postures with respect to it.

Individual identity, too, dissolves before the vision of Nothingness. That is why farce, and its traditional concern with human identity, was so useful to Wilde. Each character in *The Importance of Being Earnest* is a sort of vacuum that attains to individual identity only through an effort of the creative imagination. They are like Sartre's famous waiter in *L'Être et le Néant,* except that they make their decisions consciously, and that we are pleased rather than nauseated by the process. Each attains to identity in the mode of *being what he is not.*[7]

It is a sense of the insubstantiality of human identity which causes Wilde to place such emphasis on impulse (on selfishness, if you like). Admit all the problems of epistemology, and impulse still remains. Obedience to impulse is a defiant way of asserting some sort of basic identity. Algy's obsession with food is an example. "I hate people who are not serious about meals," he complains. "It is so shallow of them" (p. 12). Beneath the parody of manners, we can detect in this a perception, truthful within the terms of reference the play allows. Algy is prepared to use the word *serious* here because there is something fundamental to relate it to. When appetites are all that is substantial in human identity, all else must seem shallow. The two girls place a similar reliance on impulse. Both have faith in first impressions, and both are surprisingly candid about their sexual appetites. Cecily tells Algy, "I don't think you should tell me that you love me wildly, passionately, devotedly, hopelessly. Hopelessly doesn't seem to make much sense, does it?" (Maine, ed., p. 348).

They are quick to change, though. When, after mutual declarations of devotion, Algy tells Cecily he will wait seventeen years for her hand, she replies, "Yes, I felt it instinctively. And I am so sorry for you, Algy. Because I couldn't wait all that time. I hate waiting even five minutes for anybody. It always makes me rather cross. I am not punctual myself, I know, but I do like punctuality in others, and waiting even to be married is quite out of the question" (pp. 100-101). Changeability, in fact, is a corollary of obedience to impulse. As impulses vary, so must the attitudes of the individual. The protagonists of Wilde's play recognize this, particularly the girls. "I never change, except in my affections," Gwendolen announces (p. 110). Their changeability is most amusingly demonstrated in the first meeting of Gwendolen and Cecily, when, in the course of a single scene, they proceed from mutual suspicion to mutual affection, thence to mutual detestation, and finally to mutual affection again, all the time firmly maintaining that they are consistent. The audience is likely to laugh at this sort of thing because it realizes that literary and social conventions are being ridiculed, but there is more to the comedy than that. There is a core of truth in what we are presented with: human beings do change. The joke lies in the way the characters are neither distressed nor surprised at their own changeability. In Wilde's world nothing else is expected.

Love might seem a surprising ingredient in such a world, but it is a play of courtship, and love does have importance in it. Love is based on impulse, after all, and for Wilde it is action, not object; a courageous creative effort of the will, not a substantial inner something; the free play of the imagination, not a faculty. The characters of the play constantly deny the substantiality of love, in speech and action. Their courtships consist in patterns of interlocking fantasy and wit; they woo through imposture and fancy; they pursue and fly; they test and torment each other. Never is there anything static or certain about their relationships. "The very essence of romance is uncertainty," says Algy. "If ever I get married, I'll certainly try to forget the fact" (p. 4). Wilde is following Restoration comedy again, here. "Uncertainty and Expectation are the Joys of Life," says Congreve's Angelica. "Security is an insipid thing, and the overtaking and possessing of a Wish, discovers the Folly of the Chase."[8] And as with Restoration comedy, we admire the lovers for their courage and their wit. We feel that they are absurd too (all action in the play is absurd; the secret is not minding), but at the same time we are made to feel that they are somehow right as well. The theme of sentimental education, normally found in romantic comedy, is parodied by inversion. Fantasies the lovers have about each other are confirmed rather than cured, almost as if wit, the creative imagination (call it what you will), were able magically to force the world into the shapes it suggests to itself. We feel, at any rate, that the lovers earn their partners by growing toward them, through wit.

Because the characters live in a world in which order is constantly vanishing, they scorn theory, consistency, and the appearance of simplicity. "The truth," as Algy says, "is rarely pure and never simple" (p. 9). Certainly, in matters of identity, seeming intelligibility is to be distrusted. "The simplicity of your nature," Gwendolen tells Jack, "makes you exquisitely incomprehensible to me" (p. 31). The characters are alert, not to a harmonious universal nature, but to a proliferation of separate, deceptive, and contradictory sense-impressions. Knowledge comes only through the imagination. Gwendolen laughs at Jack's misgivings over her delight in his being called (as she thinks) Ernest. He cautiously inquires how she might feel were his name not Ernest, but she will not listen. "Ah, that is clearly a metaphysical speculation," she says, "and like all metaphysical speculation, has very little reference at all to the actual facts of real life, as we know them" (p. 17). This is an ironic node. The observation by itself fits in with the general theme of the play, but in the immediate context the joke is against Gwendolen (and Jack, when we think how he must feel). He has only assumed the name of Ernest; her notions are just as "metaphysical"; and what seem to be the actual facts of real life thoroughly justify such a speculation. Yet at the end of the play, Gwendolen's faith in the name, her conviction that she will marry an Ernest, and her insistence that her lover conform to her ideal are all justified; we learn that Jack's true name is Ernest. One effect of all this is to satirize faith in ideals by having it vindicated absurdly, but there is more to it than that. We feel delighted at the outcome, not like the recipients of a warning. We are made to feel that confident fantasies justify themselves, that a bold imagination is more useful than plodding attention to apparent facts.

In Wilde's world truth itself dwindles into insignificance. The characters have a strictly practical attitude to the relationship between statements and actuality, the latter being so elusive. Charged with being named John, Jack declares, "I could deny it if I liked. I could deny anything if I liked" (p. 81). And he is embarrassed when required to utter things in strict correspondence with what seem to be facts: "it is very painful for me to be forced to speak the

truth. It is the first time in my life that I have ever been reduced to such a painful position, and I am really quite inexperienced in doing anything of the kind, so you must excuse me if I stammer in my tale" (pp. 81-82). He goes on to say that he has never had a brother, which turns out to be untrue; Algy is his brother. Once again the inference is that truth cannot be discovered through the senses and the intellect alone. Jack's witty lies are more percipient. The comic inversion of truth and untruth is maintained in Jack's dismay, when he learns that what he had thought to be lies are true. "Gwendolen," he says, "it is a terrible thing for a man to find out suddenly that all his life he has been speaking nothing but the truth. Can you forgive me?" She can. "There is always hope," she says, "even for those who are most accurate in their statements" (p. 114). Even when it is the art of living, we are tempted to gloss, "Lying, the telling of beautiful untrue things, is the proper aim of Art."[9]

Jack and Algy certainly attain their ends through lying. They are true rogues, impulsive, lovers of deception and imposture. They fulfill themselves in the way of all rogues: by discovering human freedom in protean identity. Doubtless what they do permits us to laugh at the mad antics young gentlemen get up to, even to disapprove mildly, but the candid spectator will admit that their tricks inspire above all else a feeling of moral liberation. Jack's double life may be exposed, Algy's Bunbury may be deprived of his existence, but these deceptions serve their purpose, and part of us at least is glad.

Gwendolen and Cecily rely on beautiful untrue things as much as their suitors do, but instead of deceiving the world through imposture, they demand that the world accept the pleasing fantasies they choose to project onto it. The heroes adopt identities to suit the occasion; the heroines imagine identities to suit the persons with whom they choose to associate. Gwendolen explains her principles in love: "We live, as I hope you know, Mr Worthing, in an age of ideals. The fact is constantly mentioned in the more expensive monthly magazines, and has reached the provincial pulpits, I am told. And my ideal has always been to love someone of the name of Ernest. There is something in that name that inspires absolute confidence" (p. 16). She is very firm about this, and Cecily, whose words on the subject are almost identical (p. 70), is nearly as firm. The comic parallel generates a certain irony against the girls; we are tempted to laugh at them for sharing a folly, yet we cannot help admiring the strength of their resolution, absurd though it is. Though idealism is burlesqued, we are made to admire the wit and courage required to impose a pattern on the world, even such a one as this.

The women in the play are generally stronger and more resourceful than the men. The latter are forced to prevaricate in a way that at times seems shuffling, even abject, whereas the former are always perfectly poised and move with imperturbable grace from one contradictory posture to another. I suspect that this has something to do with Wilde's own personality and personal history, but the pattern makes sense on its own terms. The play may be seen as a disquisition in favor of a set of attitudes more normally associated with women than with men. It commends the sort of character that accepts experience, with all its confusions, and accommodates itself through provisional opportunist adjustments—through style, in short. It pokes fun at hard and fast ideas about reality, at that aggressive kind of intelligence which seeks to control reality through theory. Rightly or wrongly, women are thought of as conforming more often to the subtle stereotype; men are thought of as conforming more often to the aggressive stereotype. Wilde was not simplistic about this. The embodiment of aggressive masculine intelligence in the play is Miss Prism, but that is part of the joke against her. The other women are naturally more at home in Wilde's world than the men.

Lady Bracknell, of course, is the character that most thoroughly exemplifies feminine strength. Delightful though she is, she is likely at first to baffle the audience's expectations because she is cast in the role of obstructionist to the lovers; in a conventional romantic comedy she would have to be defeated and humiliated. Yet that is not what happens to her, and it is difficult even to imagine it happening. The critics have recognized that she rises above this role; she has even been called a goddess. Satisfaction is what Lady Bracknell requires, not defeat, because, irrespective of her role, she is the character that embodies most forcibly Wilde's notions about the creative power of the imagination. Out of the nebulous material of society fashion, she wills into being a world of rock-hard solidity, obedient to her dispensation, before which all other worlds, real and imagined, fade into ghostly insubstantiality. The audience may laugh at the burlesque of a fashionable hostess, but there is reverence in the laughter. Her directives on the acceptable and the proper are not empirical observations on the state of fashion; they are the utterances of a lawgiver, endowed with all but divine afflatus. Her response to Jack's Belgrave Square address is typical:

LADY BRACKNELL:

> The unfashionable side. However, that could easily be altered.

JACK:

> Do you mean the fashion or the side, Lady Bracknell?

LADY BRACKNELL:

> Both if necessary, I presume.

> (p. 22)

In contrast to the characters of farce who are imprisoned by manners, Lady Bracknell makes manners, and all the trivia of fashion, the building material of a world in which her will is law. She obtains freedom through manners, and she is powerful because she can impose her world on others.

Miss Prism and Dr. Chasuble are funny because they fail to impose their worlds on others, and in failing weakly parody the central characters. Their trouble is that they do not realize what they are doing and think that their rules and theories represent a real, substantial, unchanging world. Dr. Chasuble calls Miss Prism Egeria (an appellation much better suited to Lady Bracknell), but though she enunciates laws and definitions, they are tamely borrowed, not her own. Her paradoxes are amusing, not because they represent an attempt through wit to impose order on confusion, contradiction, and human folly, but because they indicate an unawareness of these things. Indeed, she does not realize that they are paradoxes. The audience laughs at her, not with her, when she describes her novel thus: "The good ended happily, and the bad unhappily. That is what Fiction means" (p. 35). Clearly she is a fit partner for Dr. Chasuble, who is thoroughly insensitive to the present moment (he is always misinterpreting the situation) and given to forcing an all-purpose moral onto any situation. His famous sermon is an example: "My sermon on the meaning of the manna in the wilderness can be adapted to almost any occasion, joyful, or, as in the present case, distressing. I have preached it at harvest celebrations, christenings, confirmations, on days of humiliation and festal days" (pp. 44-45). Both Miss Prism's novel and Dr. Chasuble's sermon, it is clear, recommend an ordered picture of the world, which excludes the sense of absurdity behind order, central to Wilde's vision, a sense that *The Importance of Being Earnest,* in its entirety, practically demonstrates.

It is beyond the scope of this essay to fit the suggested interpretation of the play into the general scheme of Wilde's ideas, but it is not difficult to see how it may be reconciled with Wilde's views on art, individuality, morality, crime, politics, and so on. What I have tried to do is to provide an interpretation fitting in with notions concerning farce, the drama of the absurd, and existentialist theories of identity, all of which have been fashionable in recent years. This can certainly help us like and understand the play, but I do not wish it to be thought that I am suggesting it be admired because it is "relevant" (whatever that word might mean nowadays). It seems to me that it should be admired, not simply because it expresses a characteristically modern sensibility, nor even because it does so before its time, prophetically, but because it does so supremely well. It is possible to dislike the play, on grounds similar to those set out by Mary McCarthy, if only because it is possible to dislike the sort of sensibility it expresses. Its vehicle, the literary tradition to which I suggest the play belongs, is one that readily allows the writer to sink into self-indulgence. Some feel it permits little else nowadays. But I think that if we are prepared to accept the sensibility and the tradition as capable of producing excellence (if, in other words, we are prepared to adopt appropriate standards in judging the play), we are compelled to recognize the excellence of Wilde's play. To the contemplation of Nothingness, of the absurd, Wilde brings qualities of wit, intelligence, and (not least) appetite for life, rarely found so abundantly in such a context. *The Importance of*

Being Earnest is a great farce because it transcends the normal limitations of the form. Wilde used the form to make a play that is sparkling, but profound as well.

Notes

1. *Sights and Spectacles, 1937-1958* (London, 1959), pp. 105-106.

2. *The Structure of Complex Words* (London, 1951), p. 192.

3. *The Importance of Being Earnest,* in *The Works of Oscar Wilde,* ed. G. F. Maine (London, 1948), p. 346.

4. See H. R. Trevor-Roper, *The Gentry, 1540-1640,* Economic History Review Supplements, 1 (London, 1953), pp. 52-53.

5. *The Importance of Being Earnest,* ed. Vyvyan Holland (London, 1957), p. 73. Unless otherwise stated, all subsequent references are to this edition of the original four-act version of the play.

6. *Nil* (London, 1966), p. 244.

7. Jean-Paul Sartre, *Being and Nothingness,* trans. Hazel E. Barnes (London, 1957), pp. 59-60.

8. *Love for Love,* in *Comedies by William Congreve,* ed. Bonamy Dobrée (London, 1925), pp. 310-11.

9. "The Decay of Lying," in Maine, ed., p. 931.

Geoffrey Stone (essay date January 1976)

SOURCE: Stone, Geoffrey. "Serious Bunburyism: The Logic of *The Importance of Being Earnest.*" *Essays in Criticism* 26, no. 1 (January 1976): 28-41.

[*In the following essay, Stone examines the metalinguistic aspects of Wilde's* The Importance of Being Earnest.]

A meta-language is a language you use to deal with given statements and their relations with actual facts. 'In order to speak about the correspondence between a statement S and a fact F, we need a language (a metalanguage) in which we can *speak about* the statement S *and state* the fact F' (Popper, *Objective Knowledge,* p. 316). Analogically the concept of meta-language can be extended into literature by differentiating between an *actual* and an *implied* statement or word-set. Meta-activity is occurring when actual and implied word-sets and the reality they both claim to relate to are being dealt with *together.* The concept is not empty; some examples may make its usefulness clearer.

The old 'New Criticism', for example, tended not to be metalinguistic, because it concentrated on the word-set (typically a poem) alone and often excluded any facts the 'statement' related to. It was a reaction against earlier criticism, which had decayed into total attention to supposedly related facts and almost complete inattention to

the literary 'statement'. The most valuable modern criticism (e.g., in the 'New Criticism', that of I. A. Richards and Empson) must, it seems clear, always be concerned with both the literary work and the aspects of life it is related to—and so must be inherently metalinguistic. Works of literature overtly metalinguistic are not uncommon, frequently in the specialized metalinguistic form of self-reference.

Tristram Shandy is wholly metalinguistic. Fielding started as a novelist in the metalinguistic form of parody and continued it in the 'commentary' chapters of *Tom Jones.* Jane Austen's characters, notably in *Pride and Prejudice,* discuss the novelistic propriety and convincingness of their own conduct and characterization (and, by logical inversion, the propriety of the contemporary novel). In a wonderful phrase I borrow from an excellent work on ethics, all metalinguistic works are full of 'overt or covert inverted commas'.

Oscar Wilde, in his earlier 90s plays, which are not metalinguistic, is compelled to write in a spokesman, usually an Intelligent Bad Man, for the views and wit his chosen form must otherwise exclude. *A Woman of No Importance* shows the clash between his genre, Strong Society Drama as we may call it, and much of what he really wants to deal with and do. Indeed, Wilde's struggles with his awful plots are extremely like Dickens's in his early novels—and for the same reason. They even fall into the same stagy bombast at the points of greatest strain.

For commercial reasons *A Woman of No Importance* is (i) a 'well-made play' with a strong plot, strong situations and powerful curtain-lines and (ii) one possessing (subject to (i)) social verisimilitude. But (iii), as one would expect from a First in Greats writing for commercial success, there is also an agreeably large quantity of Aristotelian irony, peripeteia and both literal and moral anagnorisis—Gerald's reversals, Hester's reversals, Lord Illingworth's unmasking, to name but a few. They give pleasure at both levels of audience awareness. It has too (iv) wit, but almost disconnected from the plot and held down by the requirements of verisimilitude and the necessity of not frightening the audience, and (v) a very funny running joke of savagely black humour about the Archdeacon's offstage wife, who we learn is 'wonderfully cheerful' though a martyr to headaches (Act I), stone-deaf (Act II) and rapidly going blind (Act II), her hands immobilized for the last ten years by gout (Act III), her memory gone 'since her last attack' (Act III), and her food entirely limited to jellies (Act III); 'she has nothing to complain of' are the Archdeacon's last words. This almost Swiftian attack upon God's arrangements and man's complacency contradicts the genre's premises, but is accidentally made possible by the theatrical convention of the comic clergyman. However, the other aspects of reality which Wilde evidently wants to deal with have no accidental convention to help them and get into the play either in a distorted form or, when in, threaten to break it up completely and have to be suppressed again. Attacks on contemporary class and sexual exploitation have to be assigned to the outsider American girl Hester Worsley, and consequently overstated and (as a result, metalinguistically considered) understated simultaneously. The treatment of women is at least relevant to the plot, but that of the poor, though an obsessive recurrent theme ('The problem of slavery', says Lord Illingworth; 'And we are trying to solve it by amusing the slaves'), has no relevance at all. Besides unpleasant social realities, unpleasant psychological ones are buzzing in the play; what is and will be the relationship between a bastard son and a mother who deliberately keeps him to herself in mediocrity? The plot, and Wilde's intelligence, are compelled to raise the theme, but since it has no place in the genre it is bundled away again as soon as raised. (In this and several other ways one is reminded of Shaw's early plays; a comparison of Shaw's and Wilde's different methods of half-solving similar problems would be of interest.) As the play proceeds, it devolops an enormous and comic gap between the characters' situation and their language. This culminates in the uproarious but unintended comedy of the curtain-scene of Act III and all Act IV ('Gerald, no! He is your father!') in which the Fallen Mother is revealed, the Seducer is unmasked, the True Love (with a large fortune) is discovered, and the Son's determination to force the Seducer into Atonement and Justice (Gerald, Act IV) by marrying the Betrayed Mother is thwarted only by the Mother's spirited moral and personal objection to doing anything of the sort ('What son has ever asked his mother to make so hideous a sacrifice?'). We are here dealing with perfectly serious matters, but the characters Wilde has attempting it are quite incapable of it; they are trapped by their nature, their idiom, the very conditions of their existence—the Strong Society Drama. Now if this gap is accepted and exploited, these masks become (so to speak) not characters but meta-characters; they relate indirectly to life, and directly to a certain representation of life—that acceptable to the 90s theatre audience, or loose sentimentalists anywhere anytime. A play containing them then becomes a criticism of, or a set of variations upon, that particular mode of inadequacy to life and its highly complex relations to reality. Further, being a meta-play, a work of art whose subject is art (literally art for art's sake, in fact), many things cease to be a temptation and become an artistic necessity; for example, perfect phrasing and epigram, the greatest possible elegance of expression, of plot, of situation. The author can legitimately aim at a perfection of form usually found only in music or mathematics. At the same time, by having its roots deep in the rich manure of the 90s commercial drama and reality, the work is preserved from abstraction or triviality. Anyone can be elegant trivially (Wilde himself in his earlier works); it is, for example, the multiple reality it embraces that gives Old Bill's phlegmatic explanation of the shell-hole ('Mice') its intense punch. In fact, if Wilde is going to write a genuinely good play it must relate to at least some of the 90s otherwise unmanageable realities, it must allow his wit to work with not against his art, it must also be produceable in the 90s commercial theatre and consequently relate to the established form as well as the facts that form pretended to correspond

with. It must therefore be inherently and essentially metalinguistic, a special and powerful sort of verbal structure; must be, in fact, the meta-play *The Importance of Being Earnest*. Hence its anti-natural yet legitimate stylization, its otherwise baffling combination of perfect seriousness in its internal structure with (ostensibly) perfect frivolity in its apparent structure ('a trivial comedy for serious people' is Wilde's own definition), and its numerous outcrops of granite-hard sense. These assertions will perhaps become plausible, indeed comprehensible, by a close examination of the play itself.

The people of the play are Mr. Worthing (Ernest in town, Jack in the country), his ward Cecily Cardew, his fiancée Gwendolen Fairfax (daughter of Lady Bracknell), and his friend Algernon Montcrieff (nephew of Lady Bracknell); the plot is that Algernon, as her guardian's fictitious younger brother Ernest, becomes engaged to Cecily, so both girls are engaged to 'Ernest' but neither to Ernest; more detail is unneeded. The play opens with a passage exhibiting, and implicitly commenting upon, the simple theme of master-servant relations and, by implication, those of the upper and lower orders. The social reality of the 90s was peculiarly one of power, of dominators and dominated, and in every passage of *The Importance* there is continuous conflict. Just as Byron boxed with his valet to reach physical grace-with-power, so Algernon spars verbally with his manservant. This is sporting of Algernon, and helps set the tone of civil decency that characterizes the play, because he loses every exchange. The opening question and answer ('Did you hear what I was playing, Lane?' 'I didn't think it polite to listen, sir') carry a number of elements; (*a*) regulative social conventions, (i) the upper order's access to art, and the lower orders' lack of it (cf. Yeats), (ii) the lower orders' 'knowing their place'; and (*b*) Lane's implied comments on the conventions and related facts. (i) Since society exacts deference, this exempts Lane from the duty of listening; indeed, since (ii) Algernon has no access to genuine art, it is personally polite not to have listened. In 'polite' sense (i), as a servant, Lane is outside the 'polis' or civilized group (in Athens he would have been a slave); in sense (ii), he is, as an independent intelligence, exquisitely within it. If this and the following exchanges were cruder in feeling, they would exhibit the covert insolence generated when an upper order character is attempting fraternity but being denied it; if they were coarsened the other way, by making Algernon's wit superior to Lane's, we would have the familiar figure of the comic but fundamentally inferior servant. The next exchange—on the champagne—deals with the expropriation of the expropriators, or—in the language of the time— the servant problem. Lane assumes and establishes his right to steal as much as he pleases, counters Algernon's probe with successive flank attacks on the upper order's taste, competence, major regulating social conventions (marriage, and a respectful attitude to it), and finally defeats Algernon's desperate but unsporting attempt at a snub by (judo-like) completely agreeing with him and consequently exposing a total complicity on Algernon's part with Lane's social subversion. Algernon's direct speech to the audience then points out (i) that they live off the lower orders, (ii) cant about them in several different ways at once, and (iii) their listening to and laughing at his speech shows they have publicly agreed to all that is entailed. The audience, like Algernon with Lane, has been trapped by entering the dialogue. (In Aristotelian terms, the one page of dialogue so far has supplied five peripeteias and two anagnorises. In its speed and veracity it is a little like Shaw's message to Archer about their joint play; 'Have finished plot and first Act; send more plot'.) Finally, although it apparently abandons the exposition usually the business of a play's first moments, it is actually carrying out the very necessary business of training the audience in the kind of social and linguistic relations that will compose the play. We should not deny to Wilde, any more than to Marvell, that well-known 'tough reasonableness beneath the slight lyric grace'.

The Importance of Being Earnest then moves to conflict and pretence within one social class, a theme necessarily shading into raw-material human conduct. As the play and characters must be convincing to the audience at the object-level, providing them with a fixed base on which they can rely, this is convenient. Jack and Gwendolen are the most simply presented (in technical terms, Jack despite his duplicity is Algernon's straight man, as Gwendolen is Cecily's); Algernon plays a much larger part in the meta-activity; and Lady Bracknell, ruthlessly accurate about the real world in every way, with almost every word exists fully, indeed irresistibly, at both meta- and object-level. In Jack's beautifully exact terminology, she is a monster without being a myth, which is rather unfair. Psychic energy is obtained by abandoning lies, and identifying with such liberated persons; what the audience gets indirectly through the rest of the play it gets directly from Lady Bracknell—just as Lady Bracknell's standards of fact-facing would shatter any conventional 'strong drama' she was placed in. The Jack-Algernon relationship is clearly one of conflict, in which Algernon is the dominator. He makes most of the jokes and even forces Jack into telling the truth, despite Jack's powerful defences—simple mendacity, convincing detail, accusation of class impropriety in reading a *private* cigarette-case, the symmetry that complements Algernon's real argument with Jack's fictitious one, and the Carrollian logic of country presents carrying country names. When Gwendolen and Cecily meet the dramatic conflict is so rooted is reality that it emerges not only in dialogue but virtually at the animal level; in half a page of dialogue Cecily has not only withstood, sometimes snubbed, Gwendolen's verbal overtures four times, but Gwendolen has delayed sitting down, though asked, until her first friendship-assault (as we may call it) is completed and there is a tiny armistice. 'A pause. They both sit down together.' Gwendolen moves to open aggression by formally announcing her intention of looking fixedly at Cecily and demanding Cecily's acquiescence on meta-linguistic class grounds: 'Mamma, whose views on education are remarkably strict, has brought me up to be extremely short-sighted; it is part of her system; so do you mind my looking at you through my glasses'—an elegant combination of upper order and animal behaviour. This is equally elegantly countered by Cecily on equally good social grounds with, in the circumstances, a strongly aggressive social implication—'Oh, not at all, Gwendolen. I am very fond of being looked at.' The struggle shifts—temporarily—to the purely verbal level; a meta-reference to sentimental drama—'Dearest Gwendolen, there is no reason why I should make a secret of it to you'—introduces a passage of conflict in which, with neat structure and rising complexity, Cecily's 'little country newspaper' and 'next week' are countered by Gwendolen's *Morning Post* (class and sophistication superiority) and 'Saturday' (time), Cecily's 'ten minutes ago' by 'yesterday afternoon at five-thirty', Cecily's diary by Gwendolen's diary, and the struggle shifts implicitly to the metalinguistic question of the logical category of a proposal of marriage. Is it a letter of intent, when the most recent one is valid, or a contract, when the earliest is the only valid one? Gwendolen brings a new rhetorical form into play, but her soliloquy is overcome by Cecily's stronger one, which uses metaphor—'entanglement'—to beat mere literalism. Since both speeches are delicately sentimental and 'out of character', the play is here metalinguistic in relating to the forms and content of 'strong drama', where maidens make and exchange just such innocent confidences. The sequence closes in yet another class-reference—'I am happy to say I have never seen a spade'—used as attack and self-assertion. The society of *The Importance* is an intensely class-based one, but it is also extremely dynamic. Considering human capabilities, while we watch the meta-characters Gwendolen and Cecily we are seeing real tigers pretending to be cats in contrast to the 'strong drama' the play relates to, where we see cats roaring.

Since the characters are firmly established in the audience's minds as acceptable and consistent at the object- and meta-level, and the necessary exposition is unobtrusively inserted, the play can afford to carry a great deal of comment by the characters about reality, both direct and in the metalinguistic form of combined reference to reality and to what people say about it—pretence. Lady Bracknell is notoriously the most copious source of examples, as in her examination of Jack's eligibility. It opens metalinguistically with the minor themes of upper order parasitism—Jack's smoking as 'an occupation. . . . There are far too many idle men in London as it is'—and the double-standard sexuality central to the 90s self-concern: 'a man who desires to get married should know either everything or nothing. . . . Ignorance is like a delicate exotic fruit; touch it and the bloom is gone.' The technique of comparison by substitution—'ignorance' for 'innocence', application to Jack instead of Gwendolen—is a Wildean favourite, often exasperating elsewhere; here it can work with the play, not just as external decoration. Lady Bracknell's beautiful aria on education is a direct comment on social reality, rising to the (fulfilled) prophecy of 'acts of violence in Grosvenor Square', and is followed by an equally accurate and prophetic aria upon land ownership. (It is directly no part of an artist's business either to prophesy or literally describe actuality; but the better grasp he has of what is the case, however he chooses to work from it, the longer his product will last and the more strikingly the world will move to conform to it.) The point about changing the fashion and the side of Berkeley Square is a joke about fact and quasi-linguistic behaviour—a metalinguistic joke, in fact. Jack's income is naturally the major point and is the only one actually noted in Lady Bracknell's book. 'Now to minor matters. Are your parents living?' is direct in form and metalinguistic in its play of actual fact against conventional utterance. The audience is also naturally pleased to find Lady Bracknell is wrong, since it is this 'minor matter' which, she finds, forbids the engagement. Her description of Jack as 'born, or at any rate bred, in a handbag' derives from the phrase 'born and bred', and consequently Lady Bracknell is modifying a reality to suit a language-structure, a rather nice inversion of normal metalinguistic procedure. Her refusal to allow Gwendolen to 'marry into a cloakroom, and form an alliance with a parcel' is a perfect verbal formulation of the upper order's habit of treating people as things, in accordance with her and their highly material mode of existence. When informed of Cecily's fortune, she continues 'A hundred and thirty thousand pounds! And in the Funds! Miss Cardew seems to me a most attractive young lady, now that I look at her. Few girls of the present day have any really solid qualities, any of the qualities that last, and improve with time. We live, I regret to say, in an age of surfaces'. Elsewhere in the play, too, Lady Bracknell is a fountain of good, often brutal, sense: feeling well opposed to behaving well, the Lady Harbury sequence, illness in others not a thing to be encouraged, the upper order's reaction to French and German (the play has a high proportion of jokes *about* language), 'the Influence of a permanent income on Thought', arguments regrettable as always vulgar and often convincing, and 'the General was essentially a man of peace, except in his domestic life'. Lady Bracknell is not of course the only truth-speaker. Algernon warns us 'the truth is rarely pure and never simple', Jack that a high moral tone is bad for health and happiness, and Gwendolen produces that poignantly exact definition of tension ('this suspense is terrible, I hope it will last'), and even Miss Prism regards the death of a black sheep as 'a blessing of an extremely obvious kind'. The play continually illustrates the observation (through Gwendolen, truly her mother's daughter) that 'it becomes more than a moral duty to speak one's mind; it becomes a pleasure'.

Since *The Importance of Being Earnest* is itself so completely structured, there is an added elegance in the presence within it of smaller structures which by their formal quality or reversal of expectations or both operate as a kind of model of the play itself—that is, as yet another meta-level above the ostensible one. Very few works of literature are of such formal complexity. There are the traditional, the classic ironies of plot—foreshadowings and echoes; Lady Bracknell's 'the line is immaterial', 'try and acquire some relations as soon as possible' (she is addressing her nephew in his brother's flat); the prophecy 'Half

an hour after they've met, they will be calling each other sister'—'Women only do that when they have called each other a lot of other things first'; and Algernon's masquerade as the younger brother he actually but unknowingly is. There is the very simple structure of the offstage running joke—Lady Harbury, Lord Bracknell; the more complex one of the onstage wit-combat, itself full of language-devices (inversion, category and subject-shift, and even points of pure logic—'There is no good offering a large reward now that the thing is found')—the battle of the cigarette-case, of Algernon-as-Ernest rebuked by Jack, of who has the right to be christened; and most complex of all, the circular sequence early in the play about the 'clever people' and the fools, which is funny at the simplest level ('What fools'), funnier when one realizes Jack has been defined as one of the fools whose non-existence he has been lamenting, and funniest when one realizes that the fool's cap also fits the audience and oneself—any critic of the play, in fact—since its characters are eminently 'clever people', and the whole audience has come to the theatre solely to meet and talk about them. So—for a second—the level-above-level structure has reached out and pulled, not this listener and that, or this common pretender and that, but the—any—audience, purely *qua* audience, inside the play—a very metalinguistic effect indeed.

The characters of *The Importance* are often seriously, even passionately, concerned about food. They are equally serious about property (preferably in its most 'real' form, money or its equivalent the Funds); and they are all, as we have seen, incessantly engaged in struggles for power. We can in fact take these as equivalents, whether we follow the Freudian judgment which makes food the reality and property and power its masks, or our metalinguistic interpretation which would make property and power the realities, 'good taste', 'civilized values', etc., the normal language about them, and 'food' the metalanguage Wilde employs to deal with the facts and the normal language simultaneously. Certainly Algernon has an exactly Freudian passage on food—'When I am in really great trouble, as anyone who knows me intimately will tell you, I refuse everything except food and drink. At the present moment I am eating muffins because I am unhappy'—another example of very hard sense. (The play clearly is the most centrally Wildean thing its author ever wrote—his getting so fat, that curious phrase about 'feasting with panthers', all those suppers at Willis's, the sinister foreshadowing of Carson's cross-examination by the cigarette-case scene—but unless we regard Wilde as the inventor of the non-fiction play seventy years before the non-fiction novel we had better stick to the literature.) The characters are surprisingly often engaged in unashamed, overt, onstage eating—cucumber sandwiches and bread and butter in town, cake, bread and butter, tea, sugar, muffins and tea-cake in the country. When not conspicuously consuming they are arranging to dine at Willis's, emphazing the moral importance of being serious about meals, the necessity of 'regular and wholesome meals' when one is going to lead an entirely new life, or the social impropriety of ever going without one's dinner. The food is always used as a weapon of domination; as in Act I, when Algernon, whose food it is, directs Jack's choice, or Act II, where Gwendolen employs it for social domination ('No, thank you. Sugar is not fashionable any more') and Cecily in turn uses it for physical revenge ('Gwendolen drinks the tea and makes a grimace. Puts down cup at once, reaches out her hand to the bread and butter, looks at it, and finds it is cake. Rises in indignation'), or later in Act II, when Jack attempts to dominate Algernon morally ('I say it's perfectly heartless your eating muffins at all, under the circumstances'), then, abandoning his moral position, is completely defeated by Algernon, who denies Jack the slightest share of his own muffins. The quasi-omnipresence of food is meta-significant; the 'strong drama' of the 90s seldom shows its characters coarse (or real) enough to take food and yet the actual 90s, like the following Edwardian era are notorious for the gross appetites of its upper orders. The literal food on stage acts as a sharp contradiction to the audience's favourite lies-in-art. Further, it acts as literal though trivial property, which can be struggled for, and also as representative of more substantial power; Algernon is entitled to eat sandwiches specially ordered for Lady Bracknell since 'she is *my* aunt'; Jack eats the bread and butter intended for Gwendolen 'as if you were going to eat it all. You behave as if you were married to her already'. Algernon's attitude to his aunt's sandwiches and Jack's muffins exactly parallels his aunt's attitude to Cecily's £130,000—which Algernon will also get. It is interesting to note that Algernon and Lady Bracknell, the two dominant, even predatory, characters of the play, are or were acquisitive by necessity; Algernon has nothing but his debts, and Lady Bracknell before her marriage 'had no fortune of any kind'. Lady Bracknell's attitude to Cecily's money is, however, deeper and more poetic than mere greed. When she refers to 'qualities that last, and improve with time', and later, when it is found Cecily can't get it until she is thirty-five, asserts that 'Thirty-five is a very attractive age. London society is full of women of the very highest birth who have, of their own free choice, remained thirty-five for years. Lady Dumbleton . . . has been thirty-five ever she arrived at the age of forty, which was many years ago. . . . There will be a large accumulation of property', there is the distinct intimation of the themes of Eternity against Time, the Unchanging against human ageing and mortality, of Hamlet with Yorick and of Keats's Grecian Urn. To put it another way, Lady Bracknell's imagination, like a good poet's, reverses the poles of reality, makes the abstract concrete, and looks through the mere shows of being—eighteen-year-old Cecily—to the unchanging Gold.

Indeed, *The Importance of Being Earnest* is sufficiently related to the world as it is to touch the great standard themes of art—Love and Marriage, Death and Rebirth, and Appearance and Reality—though they indeed occur very obliquely. Love and Marriage is of course used structurally rather than emotionally, and the crucial insistence is not on the fact—lovers' earnestness—but the word—their Ernest-ness, so to speak. The theme arises in the play's first minute, and runs through to the traditional

Triumph of Hymen in the last one, with such occasional strokes of appalling human truth as Gwendolen's 'I never change, except in my affections', or metalinguistic improvements on sentimental drama as 'though I may marry someone else, *and marry often,* nothing . . . can alter my eternal devotion to you'. Death and spiritual or nominal Rebirth are nearly as omnipresent. Quite early in Act I Jack anounces 'I am going to kill my brother' (Jack is *totally* his 'brother's' keeper) . . . 'I am going to get rid of Ernest. And I strongly advise you to do the same with . . . your invalid friend', and accordingly in Act II he appears, a tall basalt column in 'the deepest mourning, with crepe hatband and black gloves' to announce that Ernest is 'Dead! . . . Quite dead'. Algernon carries out a parallel phantom homicide: 'Bunbury is dead . . . I killed Bunbury this afternoon . . . he was quite exploded'. The aggression usually underlying comedy, and peculiarly strongly in this play, is in these examples quite cheerfully open. And though it may be over-fussy, I cannot help feeling Lady Bracknell's phrase about persons whose origin is a Terminus, though directed against Jack's social misfortunes, both prefigures Beckett ('We give birth astride a grave') and plays on a reversal of the Christian view of death—that our end is our beginning. This is, spiritually speaking, what happens in the sacrament of baptism, in which the baptisant dies to the Old Man and regenerates as the New in his symbolic drowning and resurrection. It is again the underlying logical *structure* which makes Jack's diffident negotiations with Dr. Chasuble so funny ('if you have nothing better to do . . . I might trot round about five if that would suit you'), and with Algernon ('I have not been christened for years.' 'Yes, but you have been christened. That is the important thing'—as, theologically, it is. 'Quite so. So I know my constitution can stand it.'). Lady Bracknell brings society and sacrament—Mammon and God—together in an explosion of short-circuits—'grotesque and irreligious . . . I will not hear of such excesses. Lord Bracknell would be highly displeased if he learned that that was the way you wasted your time and money', while at a proper age she includes christening among 'every luxury that money could buy'. *The Importance* is closely if obliquely related to religion, or at least religion-in-society, even down to Gwendolen's determination to crush her doubts on Jack's sincerity—'this is not the moment for German scepticism'.

Lastly, the theme of that age-old and ultimate pair, Appearance and Reality, is overtly with us from the cigarette-case, through all the metalinguistic truths and object-level deceptions, rising to the highest points of concentration in such scenes as Algernon's masquerade as Jack's brother (yet he *is* Jack's brother), his logic ('it is perfectly childish to be in deep mourning for a man who is actually staying for a whole week with you in your house as your guest'), and the total disappearance of Ernest. The very basis of objective reality is subverted in the perfectly accurate account of Memory, which 'usually chronicles all the things that have never happened, and couldn't possibly have happened', and the proferred documentary alternative of the two diaries (respectively 'a very young girl's record of her own thoughts and impressions, and consequently meant for publication', and 'something sensational to read in the train'). The extreme difficulty of valid description is finally exampled explicit: 'Is this Miss Prism a female of repellent aspect, remotely connected with education?' 'She is the most cultivated of ladies, and the very picture of respectability.' 'It is obviously the same person.'

If the metalinguistic structure of the play and the characters is not grasped, then not only is the nature of the play unrealized, but the play and characters *look* too fragile to handle, and consequently its beautiful substructures— social and general human satire on food and power, religion, death and resurrection, appearance and reality— have to be overlooked and ignored and criticism creeps away in a flurry of embarrassed and misdirected compliments. What a Theatre of Black Comedy and the Absurd we might have had in England under Victoria if only some enlightened lover of literature had saved Wilde for thirty years more playwriting by firmly propelling Bosie under a bus.

Camille Paglia (essay date winter 1985)

SOURCE: Paglia, Camille. "Wilde and the English Epicene." *Raritan* (winter 1985): 85-109.

[*In the following essay, Paglia explores what she calls the* "Androgyne of Manners" *in Wilde's* The Importance of Being Earnest.]

Oscar Wilde is the premiere documenter of a sexual persona which I call the Androgyne of Manners, embodied in Lord Henry Wotton of *The Picture of Dorian Gray* and in the four young lovers of ***The Importance of Being Earnest***. The Androgyne of Manners inhabits the world of the drawing room and creates that world wherever it goes, through manner and mode of speech. The salon is an abstract circle in which male and female, like mathematical ciphers, are equal and interchangeable; personality becomes a sexually undifferentiated formal mask. Rousseau says severely of the eighteenth-century salon, "Every woman at Paris gathers in her apartment a harem of men more womanish than she." The salon is politics by coterie, a city-state or gated forum run on a barter economy of gender exchange.

Elegance, the ruling principle of the salon, dictates that all speech must be wit, in symmetrical pulses of repartee, a malicious stichomythia. Pope's complaint that Lady Mary Wortley Montagu and the epicene Lord Hervey had "too much wit" for him alludes to the icy cruelty of the beau monde, to which moral discourse is alien because it posits the superiority of the inner life to the outer. Sartre says of Genet, "Elegance: the quality of conduct which transforms the greatest quantity of being into appearing." The salon, like the object-realm venerated by the esthete, is a spectacle of dazzling surfaces—words, faces, and gestures exhibited in a blaze of hard glamour.

Occasionally, Pope was drawn to the idea of spiritual hermaphroditism. But he was deeply hostile to the Androgyne of Manners, whom he satirizes as the Amazonian belles and effeminate beaux of *The Rape of the Lock,* because this psychological type is ahistorical in its worship of the ephemeral. The salon is populated by sophisticates of a classical literacy, but its speed of dialogue inhibits deliberation and reflection, recklessly breaking with the past through fashionable irresponsibility. Pope might have said, had the word been available, that the salon was too chic. The Androgyne of Manners—the male feminine in his careless, lounging passivity, the female masculine in her brilliant, aggressive wit—has the profane sleekness of chic.

In the Decadent nineties, before his career abruptly ended in arrest and imprisonment, Wilde was moving towards an Art Nouveau esthetics. Art Nouveau, then at its height of decorative popularity, is a late phase in the history of style, in many ways analogous to Italian Mannerism. Kenneth Clark says of one of Giambologna's streamlined Mannerist bronzes:

> The goddess of mannerism is the eternal feminine of the fashion plate. A sociologist could no doubt give ready answers why embodiments of elegance should take this somewhat ridiculous shape—feet and hands too fine for honest work, bodies too thin for childbearing, and heads too small to contain a single thought. But elegant proportions may be found in many objects that are exempt from these materialist explanations—in architecture, pottery, or even handwriting. The human body is not the basis of these rhythms but their victim. Where the sense of chic originates, how it is controlled, by what inner pattern we unfailingly recognize it—all these are questions too large and too subtle for a parenthesis. One thing is certain. Chic is not natural. Congreve's Millamant or Baudelaire's dandy warn us how hateful, to serious votaries of chic, is everything that is implied by the word "nature."

Smoothness and elongation, the Mannerist figure is a series of polished ovoids hung on a mannequin's frame. Lord Henry Wotton, with his "long, nervous fingers," is an ectomorph, an undulating ribbon of Mannerist Art Nouveau. The ectomorphic line is a suave vertical, repudiating nature by its resistance to gravity, but the Mannerist figure, overcome by worldly fatigue, sinks back toward earth in languorous torsion. The Androgyne of Manners may be seen in complete effete collapse in Henry Lamb's painting of Lytton Strachey turning his back to a window, his long denatured limbs draped over an armchair like wet noodles. Because of its swift verbal genius, however, the Androgyne of Manners is best represented as sleekness and speed. Count Robert de Montesquiou, the decadent model for Huysmans's Des Esseintes and Proust's Charlus, was once described as a "greyhound in evening dress," a phrase we might readily apply to Lord Henry Wotton.

Sleekness in a male is usually a hermaphroditic motive. Cinema, the cardinal medium of modern sexual representation, evokes this theme in its topos of the well-bred English "gentleman," a word of such special connotations that it cannot be perfectly translated into any other language. From the thirties through the fifties, movies used actors of this type to illustrate a singular male beauty, witty and polished, uniting sensitivity of response to intense heterosexual glamour: Leslie Howard, Rex Harrison, Cary Grant, David Niven, Michael Wilding, Fred Astaire. The idiomatic representational qualities here are smoothness and elongation, smooth both in manner and appearance, long in ectomorphic height and cranial contour. I think, for instance, of the astounding narrowness of Cary Grant's shiny black evening pumps in *Indiscreet*. The smoothness and elongation of figure are best shown off by a gleaming tuxedo, which signifies a renunciation of masculine hirsutism. The cinematic "gentleman" is always prematurely balding, with swept-back hair at the temples. His receding hairline is sexually expressive, suggesting hermaphroditic gentility, a grace of intellect and emotion. His sleek head is a promise of candor and courtesy, of eroticism without ambivalence or suffering. Smoothness always has an exclusively social meaning: it is nature subdued by the civil made second nature.

In *The Importance of Being Earnest*, the English gentleman, in whom the crudely masculine has been moderated by courtesy, may be seen turning into the Androgyne of Manners, in whom smoothness has become the cold glossiness of a bronze surface, like the "armored look" (*Panzerhaft*) of Bronzino's Mannerist portraits. Meeting and finally mating with their counterparts, the Art Nouveau androgynes of the play speak Wilde's characteristic language, the epicene witticism, analogous to their formal personae in its hardness, smoothness, and elongation. The Wildean epigram, like a Giambologna bronze, is immediately identifiable by a slim spareness, an imperious separateness, and a perverse elegance. Speech in Wilde is made as hard and glittering as possible; it follows the Wildean personality into the visual realm. Normally, it is pictorialism that gives literature a visual character. But there are few metaphors in Wilde and no complex syntactical units. Vocabulary and sentence structure are amazingly simple, arising from the vernacular of the accomplished raconteur. Yet Wilde's bon mots are so condensed that they become *things*, artifacts. Without metaphor, the language leaps into concreteness.

Language in Wilde aspires to an Apollonian hierarchism. His epigrams turn language from the Dionysian Many into the Apollonian One, for as an aphoristic phrase form and conversation stopper, the epigram thwarts real dialogue, cutting itself off from a past and a future in its immediate social context and glorying in its aristocratic solitude. It is the language of the Apollonian law giver, arbitrarily assigning form, proportion, and measure. A character in Wilde's *An Ideal Husband* declares, "Women are never disarmed by compliments. Men always are. That is the difference between the sexes." The iron rod of classification is thrust before us—even if it does not fall where expected. In form and in content, the Wildean epigram is a triumph of rhetorical self-containment. No one in English,

or probably any other modern language, has produced a series of utterances more mysteriously delimited. The epigram, as practiced in the Renaissance, was a poem of sharply ironic or sententious concluding verses. But the *epigramma* of antiquity was literally an inscription, as on a tombstone. Wilde may therefore be said to have restored the epigram to its original representational character, for his language has a hieroglyphic exactitude and cold rhetorical stoniness, separating itself from its background by the Apollonian incised edge.

In *The Importance of Being Earnest* the courtship of youth and maiden, at the traditional heart of comedy, loses its emotional color in the Wildean transformation of content into form, of soul into surface. Jack Worthing and Algernon Moncrieff, idle gentlemen-about-town, and Gwendolen Fairfax and Cecily Cardew, the well-bred objects of their affections, are all Androgynes of Manners. They have no sex because they have no real sexual feelings. The interactions of the play are governed by the formalities of social life, which emerge with dancelike ritualism. The key phrase of the English fin de siècle was Lionel Johnson's axiom, "Life must be a ritual." In *The Picture of Dorian Gray* Wilde says: "The canons of good society are, or should be, the same as the canons of art. Form is absolutely essential to it. It should have the dignity of a ceremony, as well as its unreality." In *The Importance of Being Earnest* the ceremony of social form is stronger than gender, shaping the personae to its public purpose and turning the internal world into the external.

The play's supreme enforcer of form is Lady Bracknell, who remarks with satisfaction, "We live, I regret to say, in an age of surfaces." In a stage direction to another play, Wilde says of a lord's butler: "The distinction of Phipps is his impassivity. . . . He is a mask with a manner. Of his intellectual or emotional life, history knows nothing. He represents the dominance of form." An optimal performance of *The Importance of Being Earnest* would be a romance of surfaces, male and female alike wearing masks of superb impassivity. The Anthony Asquith film, made in 1952, though it shortens and questionably edits the text, comes close to achieving this. Joan Greenwood's entranced and nearly somnambulistic performance as Gwendolen— slow, stately, and ceremonious—is the brilliant realization of the Wildean esthetic. But the effort to make Dorothy Tutin's Cecily sympathetic at Gwendolen's expense is sentimentally intrusive, a misreading of the play disordering the symmetry between the two young ladies, twin androgynes who fight each other to a standoff.

Productions of *The Importance of Being Earnest* are often weakened by flights of Forest of Arden lyricism which turn what is sexually ambiguous in Wilde into the conventionally heterosexual. The hieratic purity of the play could best be appreciated if all the women's roles were taken by female impersonators. Language, personality, and behavior should be so hard that the play becomes a spectacle of visionary coldness. The faces should be like glass, without gender or humanity. *The Importance of Be-*

ing Earnest takes place in Spenser's Apollonian "world of glas," a realm of glittering, sharp-edged objects. Chapman says of the goddess Ceremony, "all her bodie was / Cleere and transparent as the purest glasse." Gwendolen and Cecily are the goddess Ceremony conversing with herself, her body transparent because she is without an inner life. That Wilde may well have thought of his characters in such terms is suggested in *The Picture of Dorian Gray,* where Lord Henry Wotton longs for "a mask of glass" to shield one from the "sulphurous fumes" of life.

Gwendolen is the first of the women to enact a drama of form. Soliciting Jack to propose to her, she announces in advance that she will accept him but still insists that her bewildered suitor perform the traditional ritual, on his knees. Gwendolen's thoughts never stray from the world of appearances. At the climax of their romantic interlude, she says to Jack, "I hope you will always look at me just like that, especially when there are other people present." This voyeuristic series of observers is a psychosexual topos of Decadent Late Romanticism, first occurring in 1835 in Gautier's *Mademoiselle de Maupin.* Gwendolen imagines Jack looking at her while she looks at others looking at *them.* As a worshipper of form, Gwendolen craves not emotion but display, the theater of social life.

Gwendolen's self-observing detachment is exhibited by Cecily in precisely the same situation. When Algernon ardently declares his love for her, Cecily replies, "If you will allow me, I will copy your remarks into my diary." Emotion is immediately dispatched into a self-reflexive Mannerist torsion. Going to her writing table, Cecily exhorts her suitor to continue his protestations: "I delight in taking down from dictation." Intimacy is swelled into oratory, and poor Algernon is like Alice grown suddenly too big for the White Rabbit's house. Despite their impending marriage, Cecily declares it quite out of the question for Algernon to see her diary. Nevertheless, it is "meant for publication": "When it appears in volume form I hope you will order a copy." The Sibylline archivist, with professional impartiality, grants no special privileges to her sources of data.

Never for a moment in the play are Gwendolen and Cecily persuasively "female." They are creatures of indeterminate sex who take up the mask of femininity to play a new and provocative role. The dandified Algernon and Jack are simply supporting actors whom the women boldly stage manage. Gwendolen and Cecily are adepts of a dramaturgical alchemy: they are Cerberuses on constant guard to defend the play against encroachment by the internal, which they magically transform into the external. *The Importance of Being Earnest* is one long process of crystallization of the immaterial into the material, of emotion into self-conscious personae. In Shakespeare's volatile Rosalind and Cleopatra, automanipulation of personae arises from a Renaissance abundance of emotion, which flows into a multiplicity of psychodramatic forms. But Wilde's Gwendolen and Cecily inhabit a far more stringently demarcated world, the salon of the Androgyne

of Manners, and their personae are radically despiritualized, efflorescences not of psyche but of couture.

Lady Bracknell, too, ruthlessly subordinates persons to form. If Algernon does not come to dinner, "It would put my table completely out," and Lord Bracknell will be exiled upstairs. In one of Wilde's most wonderful lines, Lady Bracknell rebukes Jack for being an orphan: "To lose one parent, Mr. Worthing, may be regarded as a misfortune; to lose both looks like carelessness." Matters of form are uppermost, in death as in life. The emotional intensities of Victorian bereavement are cancelled. Nothing is of interest but the public impression. Once again there is the Late Romantic stress upon visual cognition: "may be *regarded* as a misfortune;" "*looks* like carelessness." Every event occurs with naked visibility on a vast, flat expanse; life is a play scrutinized by a ring of appraising eyes. This illustrates one of Wilde's central principles, as cited by Dorian Gray: "To become the spectator of one's own life is to escape the suffering of life." Late Romantic spectatorship is an escape from suffering because all affect is transferred from the emotional and tangible into the visual: no wounds can pierce the glassy body of the Wildean androgyne. The self is without a biological or historical identity. Self-originating, it has no filial indebtedness. A parent is merely a detail of social heraldry. To lose both parents, therefore, is not tragedy but negligence, like tipping the tea service into the trashbin.

The liturgy of the religion of form of which Lady Bracknell is a communicant, and in which she has instructed her daughter Gwendolen, is determined by fashion, whose bible is any one of "the more expensive monthly magazines." Lady Bracknell declares, "Style largely depends on the way the chin is worn. They are worn very high, just at present." The chin is imperiously "worn" like an article of clothing because the human figure is merely decorative, like the mummy's foot which serves as a paperweight in a Gautier tale. There is a latent surrealism here, for once the chin, like the eyebrow of Gautier's hieratic Cleopatra, has been detached from the body by Decadent partition, there is no reason why it cannot be worn elsewhere—on the shoulder, perhaps, or hip. Gwendolen, requesting Cecily's permission to examine her through a lorgnette (Cecily graciously makes the expected Late Romantic reply, "I am very fond of being looked at"), boasts that her mother "has brought me up to be extremely short-sighted." The body is sculpted at the whim of fashion, responding to its commands with plastic ductility.

At the tea table, Gwendolen declines Cecily's offer of sugar: "No, thank you. Sugar is not fashionable any more." To the choice of cake or bread and butter, she replies ("in a bored manner"), "Bread and butter, please. Cake is rarely seen at the best houses nowadays." For Gwendolen, tastiness is irrelevant, since the body has no needs in the world of form. Sugar and cake are items of decor, marks of caste by which one group separates itself from a lower group. Personal preference is renounced for hierarchical conformity. And note that cake is "rarely *seen,*" not eaten—its status is visual and not gustatory. Gwendolen is an Androgyne of Manners rapidly approaching the android. She is so completely the product of fashion that she is a machine, seeing myopically by maternal edict, eating, drinking, hearing, thinking, and speaking by preprogrammed desire. Mallarmé says, "Fashion is the goddess of appearances." Fashion is the divinity of this world of form, which Lady Bracknell and Gwendolen uphold with apostolic fervor.

The literary term "high comedy" is often rather loosely applied to any comedy of manners that does not descend to broad verbal or physical humor. I would argue that the most advanced high comedy is a ceremoniously mannered "presentation of self," the style of *The Importance of Being Earnest,* as most splendidly exemplified by Gwendolen. Indeed, in Gwendolen Fairfax, Wilde has reached the generic limit of high comedy. Gwendolen's self-hierarchization is so extreme that other characters are virtually dispensable, for they impinge on her only feebly and peripherally. But without at least two characters, drama as a genre cannot exist. When Gwendolen speaks it is not to others as much as to herself or to some abstract choir of celestial observers. Like the picture of Dorian Gray, which is not content to remain in its assigned place and rejects its entelechy, she seems ready to abandon drama for some extrageneric destination. Here is Wilde's greatest departure from the Restoration dramatists, for he detaches the witticism from repartee, that is, from social relationship. The Wildean witticism is a Romantic phenomenon in its proud isolationism. In this mode of high comedy there is an elaborately formal or ritualistic display of the persona, indeed a brandishing of it, like an aegis. The practitioner is in a double relation to the self, acting and also observing. But more importantly, there is a distinct trace of Late Romantic "connoisseurship": the self is the subject of Decadent studiousness and scholarship.

Let us examine several of Gwendolen's incomparable utterances, with their unyielding uniformity of tone. Late in the play she says, "I never change, except in my affections." This could serve as a darkly ironic caption to Walter Pater's Decadent "Mona Lisa." But what Gwendolen means is that, just as one might expect, she is rigidly punctilious in formal and external matters, while emotional events are beneath notice, flotsam and jetsam aimlessly adrift. Observe how she "brandishes" her personality, flaunting her faults with triumphant self-love. Her speech always has a hard, even, relentless, and yet rhetorically circumscribed character, as in her first words in the play:

ALGERNON:

Dear me, you are smart!

GWENDOLEN:

I am always smart! Am I not, Mr. Worthing?

JACK:

You're quite perfect, Miss Fairfax.

GWENDOLEN:

Oh! I hope I am not that. It would leave no room for developments, and I intend to develop in many directions.

If we were to speak of a psychodramatic "music," then in this last clause we are hearing the monody of a Gautierian contralto, the husky self-pleasuring of hermaphrodite autonomy. Identical into nations are present in two other of Gwendolen's remarks. At one point she gratuitously informs her suitor, "In fact, I am never wrong." And in the last act, as Jack struggles to regain her alienated affections, she says to him, "I have the gravest doubts upon the subject. But I intend to crush them." Such lines must be properly read—with slow, resonant measure—in order to appreciate their intractable severity. "I intend to develop in many directions": there is an extraordinarily distinctive sound to this in British diction, flat, formal, and sonorous, forbidding with self-command. Note the way personality is *distributed* throughout the sentence, filling the narrow channel of its syntax with a dense silvery fluid, acrid and opaque. Gwendolen's willful, elegantly linear sentences fit her like a glove. Smooth with Mannerist spareness, they carry not an extra ounce of rhetorical avoirdupois. There is no Paterian mistiness in Gwendolen. She overtly relishes her personality, caressing its hard edges, which are echoed in the brazen contours of her sentences. In this doyenne of Art Nouveau worldliness, Wilde has created a definitively modern selfhood, exposed, limited, and unsentimental, cold as urban geometry.

Above all his characters, it is Gwendolen whom Wilde has charged with creating an Apollonian dramatic language. Her speech, like Wilde's epicene witticisms, has a metallic self-enclosed terseness. She spends her words with haughty frugality for the same reason that Spenser's Belphoebe dashes off in the middle of sentences: the Apollonian is a mode of self-sequestration. The bon mot in general is jealous of its means, prizing brevity above all. It is a kind of sacramental display, permitting the self to be seen only in epiphanic flashes, like the winking of a camera shutter. These spasms of delimitation are attempts to defy the temporal character of speech or narrative, turning sequences of words into discrete *objets*. Ideas are never developed in the Apollonian style because of its antipathy to internality. Instead, as we find in Gwendolen and in the classic maliciously witty Androgyne of Manners of the salon, language is used confrontationally, as a distancing weapon, like a flaming sword. Gwendolen's self-exhibiting utterances follow the principle of *frontality* in painting and sculpture, which, as Arnold Hauser observes, is intrinsic to "all courtly and courteous art." Abjuring the modesty of the unmarried maiden, the potent Gwendolen turns herself full-face to her suitor, bathing him with a rain of hierarchical emissions.

Admiration of *The Importance of Being Earnest* is widespread, but discussion of the play is scarce and slight. Critics seem to have accepted Wilde's own description of it—"exquisitely trivial, a delicate bubble of fancy."

Scholarship has never distinguished itself in studying this kind of high comedy, with its elusive "sophistication." Frye-style myth criticism, for example, can do little with *The Importance of Being Earnest.* From the point of view of Decadent Late Romanticism, however, there is scarcely a line in the play which fails to yield rich implications.

Here are two examples. In the midst of her dispute with Cecily, Gwendolen declares, "I never travel without my diary. One should always have something sensational to read in the train." The latter sentence comes as a surprise, for ordinarily one travels with a diary not to read but to write in it. Gwendolen, however, as an Apollonian androgyne, does not keep a journal for self-examination—inwardness always being distasteful—but for self-display. To read one's diary as if it were a novel is to regard one's life as spectacle, which Wilde of course advocates. Gwendolen contemplates her life with appreciative detachment, acting both as objet d'art and Late Romantic connoisseur. Reading is normally a medium of expansion of personal experience; one reads to learn what one does not know. Here, however, reading is an act of Romantic solipsism: Gwendolen reads not to enlarge but to condense herself. Far from Emily Dickinson's mobile frigate, a book has become a mirror in which one sees only one's own face. The diary is a self-portrait. Hence Gwendolen reading her diary in a train compartment is exactly like Dorian Gray standing before his picture in the locked room. Both are performing their devotions to the hierarchized self.

The life which this diary records is, according to Gwendolen, "sensational," a source of public scandal and eroticized fascination. But to find one's own life sensational is to be aroused by oneself. The eyes, as always in Late Romanticism, are sexual agents: Gwendolen reading her diary is lost in autoerotic skeptophila, a titillation of the eye. If books can corrupt, and we know from *The Picture of Dorian Gray* that they can, then it is possible to be corrupted by one's own diary. To be corrupted by oneself is a perfect pattern of sexual solipsism, like Goethe's twisting Venetian acrobat Bettina, self-delectating and self-devirginizing. Gwendolen is an uroboros of amorous self-study, an Art Nouveau serpent devouring herself. Train reading is casual reading, a way to pass time with minimal effort. The life recorded and contemplated in the diary is therefore reduced in significance, trivialized: it is simply a series of sensational incidents without moral meaning.

Reading one's diary like a novel implies that one has forgotten what is in it. It demonstrates a lack of moral memory characteristic of the Decadent in general. In Wilde's *A Woman of No Importance,* Lord Illingworth declares, "No woman should have a memory. Memory in a woman is the beginning of dowdiness." The internal erodes the perfection of surfaces. In *An Ideal Husband,* Sir Robert Chiltern says of an antagonist, "She looks like a woman with a past," to which Lord Goring replies, "Most pretty women do." But as we see from Gwendolen's relations with her diary, the person with a past has no past.

The self is a tabula rasa open only to sensationalized Paterian "impressions." There is no moral incrementation; experience corrupts, but it does not instruct. In *The Picture of Dorian Gray* Lord Henry Wotton reflects, "Experience was of no ethical value. It was merely the name men gave to their mistakes." Reading one's diary is a diversion of the "late" phase of culture. Memory is inhibited precisely because one has done *too much,* like Pater's "Mona Lisa," fatigued by history. Her information retrieval system blocked by sensory overload, the robotlike Gwendolen is a stranger to herself, a stranger-lover.

Gwendolen never travels without her diary because it is her familiar, the inseparable escort which enables her to keep herself in a state of externalization. This is one of many traits she shares with Cecily, who uses her diary to similar effect, as we saw in the proposal scene, where Cecily instantly petrifies Algernon's sentiments midair, as if engraving them upon stone tablets. Gwendolen's diary, again like the picture of Dorian Gray, is a repository of the soul which she is able to carry about with her like a hatbox, preserving her soulless Apollonian purity. The diary is also a chronicle, the testament of her cult of the self. For both the High and Late Romantic, a diary is a personal cosmogony, a book of first and last things.

Hence it can be seen that Wilde's witticisms contain a wealth of unsuspected meaning. Even his most apparently nonsensical *boutades* are Late Romantic gestures. For example, Lady Bracknell attempts to terminate the stormy scene at the Manor House by declaring to Gwendolen, "Come, dear, we have already missed five, if not six, trains. To miss any more might expose us to comment on the platform." These bizarre lines have that air of skewed lunatic certainty we know from Lewis Carroll, who I believe strongly influenced Wilde. What is Lady Bracknell saying? Missing a train, even "five, if not six" (a studied Decadent enumeration) normally has only private and not public consequences. In the Looking-Glass world of form, however, failure to adhere to plan is an affront to natural law, bringing murmurs of complaint from passersby. But how do others learn of one's deviation from a train schedule? Since everything is visible in this landscape of externals, and since the mental life of these androgynes, like their bodies, has a glassy transparency, their intention may be said to precede them, like a town crier, alerting the populace to their tardiness. In its visionary materialism, *The Importance of Being Earnest* reverts to the Homeric world of allegorized psychic phenomena, in which the enraged Achilles feels Athena tugging at his hair. If we characterized Lady Bracknell's remark in naturalistic terms, we would have to speak of a megalomaniacal paranoia: she imagines a general consciousness of their every move; everyone knows what they are doing and thinking. But this is a development of aristocratic worldliness. Fashionable life, as Proust attests, does indeed take place before the unblinking eyes of *le tout Paris.*

"To miss any more might expose us to comment on the platform": Lady Bracknell exists in a force field of visual sightlines. Like Gautier's chaste Queen Nyssia, tainted by the gaze of another, Lady Bracknell fears being "exposed" to infection, in this case an infection of words. Barthes says of the sadomasochistic relations in Sade's novels, "The master is he who speaks . . . ; the object is he who is silent." Lady Bracknell will lose caste if she is subject to public "comment." Her hierarchical dominance will drain from her, like divine ichor. The scene of shame which she envisions on the railway platform is one of ritual exposure, like Hawthorne's Hester Prynne braving public scorn on the town scaffold. In Wilde's world, of course, crime is not sin but bad form.

The Importance of Being Earnest was the last thing Wilde wrote before his fall. Its opening night coincided with the initiation of the Marquess of Queensberry's most virulent campaign against him, and the play continued to be performed, to great acclaim, during his two trials. Now it is a strange fact that Wilde's passage to prison was a terrible fulfillment of this remark by Lady Bracknell. In *De Profundis,* written in *Reading Gaol,* Wilde recalls:

> On November 13th, 1895, I was brought down here from London. From two o'clock till half-past two on that day I had to stand on the centre platform of Clapham Junction in convict dress, and handcuffed, for the world to look at. . . . When people saw me they laughed. Each train as it came up swelled the audience. Nothing could exceed their amusement. That was, of course, before they knew who I was. As soon as they had been informed they laughed still more. For half an hour I stood there in the grey November rain surrounded by a jeering mob.

> For a year after that was done to me I wept every day at the same hour and for the same space of time.

Lady Bracknell's railway platform was to be the site of Wilde's greatest humiliation. Who can doubt that the imagination can shape reality to its will? So close are these two scenes of ritual exposure that one wonders whether Wilde's memory of Clapham Junction was not a hallucination, a variation on a fictive theme in the solitude and squalor of prison. But granting its truth, it is another example of Wilde's shamanistic power to bring his own imaginative projections into being. Publication of *The Picture of Dorian Gray* produced Lord Alfred Douglas, the beautiful boy as destroyer, who brought Wilde to his ruin. Clapham Junction came as the agonizing materialization of Wilde's principle of life as "spectacle." The entire Late Romantic tradition of concentrated visual experience reaches a disastrous climax on that railway platform, and it ends there, with Wilde the dizzy center of the visible world, like the Ancient Mariner the focus of cosmic wrath, here taking the unbearable form of laughter. The comedian, losing control of his genre, is devoured by the audience.

. . . . .

The epicene witticism has received little attention partly because it is sexually heterodox and partly because it does not fit into received critical categories. Thus Wilde's plays are suitable for explication while his conversation is not. But the Androgyne of Manners, of which Wilde was his own best example, makes an art of the spoken word. With his radical formalism, Wilde created an original language which I will call the *monologue extérieur.*

The salon dialogue of the Androgyne of Manners is a duel of "cutting" remarks. Language is used aggressively as an instrument of masculine warfare designed to slash, stab, pierce, and penetrate. Dorian Gray says to Lord Henry Wotton, "You cut life to pieces with your epigrams." It is no coincidence that terms describing a witty exchange—thrust, parry, riposte, repartee—are drawn from swordplay. The close interrelations of language and martial contention in Western culture are demonstrated by fencing parlance which speaks of a "conversation" or "phrase" of action. In other words, a fencing match is imagined as a sequence of competitive speech. It is plain how a woman of the salon who commands this sharp, challenging rhetoric is masculinized into an Androgyne of Manners. The male Androgyne of Manners achieves his hermaphroditism by combining aggressive language with a feminine manner, graceful and languid, archly flirtatious and provocative. The persona which Wilde projects in his epicene witticisms is a conflation of masculine intimidation and attack with feminine seduction and allure.

To "cut" someone is to wound him, but it is also to sever social connections with him. This duality is the subject of a pun by Lewis Carroll, when Alice is introduced to the leg of mutton:

> "May I give you a slice?" she said, taking up the knife and fork, and looking from one Queen to the other.

> "Certainly not," the Red Queen said, very decidedly: "it isn't etiquette to cut any one you've been introduced to. Remove the joint!"

Wilde's witticisms operate by a systematic "cutting," separating the self from communality and withdrawing it into an aristocratic sequestration. In *The Importance of Being Earnest* Wilde makes language into a mode of hierarchical placement. It is a series of psychodramatic gestures, each remark asserting a caste location with regard to some other person or class of person. The speakers are constantly positioning themselves at fixed distances from others. This even occurs, as we have seen, in the marriage proposals, where the heroines of the play befuddle the heroes by ceremonial demarcations, exclamatory bulletins of incipient intimacy, which they narrate like play-by-play sportscasters. To paraphrase: "We will shortly be intimate"; "We are now being intimate"; "Pray continue to be intimate." The Wildean heroine is a hierarchical commentator, plotting the relations of personae upon a mental map.

The use of language as signs of placement is often overt, as in the tea table dispute between the young ladies.

CECILY:

When I see a spade I call it a spade.

GWENDOLEN:

> [*satirically*] I am glad to say that I have never seen a spade. It is obvious that our social spheres have been widely different.

In this literalization of metaphor, a characteristic Wildean materialization, a spade becomes, like sugar or cake, a calibrator of caste. Gwendolen glories in her self-expanded hierarchical distance from Cecily. Such language appears everywhere in *The Importance of Being Earnest.* For example, the play opens with Algernon playing the piano: "I don't play accurately—anyone can play accurately—but I play with wonderful expression." "Anyone can play accurately": this self-absolving and demonstrably untrue premise, like a ladder leaned against a wall, stretches a great chain of being before our eyes, with Algernon exulting over the mass of the many from a topmost rung of esthetical "sensibility." The technique is used throughout Wilde. His polemical spokesman in *The Critic as Artist* says, "When people agree with me I always feel that I must be wrong." And a character in *An Ideal Husband* says, "Only dull people are brilliant at breakfast." Rhetorical energy is entirely directed toward social differentiation and segregation. Wilde was committed to an Apollonian enterprise—to create hierarchy through wit, ennobling himself, like the self-naming Balzac, through a magisterial persona construction.

Hence the epicene witticism is a language of hierarchical command in sexually aberrant or rather sexually denatured form. Wilde's "pointed" hierarchical style ultimately descends from the eighteenth century and in particular from Pope, whose poetry Wilde vociferously disliked. Brigid Brophy asserts: "Wilde's vehicle, the epigram, is in fact an adaptation of the logical axiom and the scientific definition. The Irish—perhaps originally theological—habit of paradox . . . is (like the paradoxical mysteries of Christian theology itself) nothing else than an exposure of the ambivalence concealed in our morality." But more precisely, Wilde's epigrams, which so impede the quickness of Restoration repartee, have acquired their substantiveness from eighteenth-century generalization. It is his power of generalization which gives Wilde's writing its permanent distinction. A modern play in the Wildean manner, Noel Coward's *Private Lives,* has only one truly Wildean line: "Certain women should be struck regularly, like gongs." And even this generalizing axiom is a vulgarization of Wilde, in whom contemplativeness is never distorted by action.

It was Pope who first made poetic beauty out of philosophy, devising a discursive style of elegant containment and high finish. Pope's rhetorical and social assumptions were transmitted to Wilde, apparently against his will, by the conservative Jane Austen, in whom we first detect Wilde's distinctive voice, tart, bantering, and lucid. Consider, for example, the great opening sentence of *Emma*:

> Emma Woodhouse, handsome, clever, and rich, with a comfortable home and happy disposition, seemed to unite some of the best blessings of existence; and had lived nearly twenty-one years in the world with very little to distress or vex her.

There is a delicate play of modern irony around the psychological edges of this sentence which is almost impossible to arrest and define. It is a meteorological disturbance or atmospheric rippling, an undulating vocal convection. Philosophically, Jane Austen's novels, although contemporaneous with High Romanticism, affirm the eighteenth-century world view, with its neoclassic endorsement of the sexually normative. Only in *Emma* can we find anything sexually ambivalent—in Emma's infatuation with Harriet—and even there it is slight and discreet.

Wilde diverts Jane Austen's comedy into the epicene first through his own character as a Decadent Late Romantic. Eighteenth-century wit is aligned with nature, from which Wilde makes a Late Romantic swerve. But this antinaturism enables Wilde to eliminate the sexual specificities of Restoration comedy. Human lusts no longer exist in *The Importance of Being Earnest.* Even Algernon's perpetual hunger is an angelic appetite, for the characters of the play feed on things insubstantial as manna: bread and butter, cucumber sandwiches, muffins, crumpets, and tea cake. They are like the Bread-and-butter-fly of *Through the Looking-Glass,* whose head is a lump of sugar and who lives on weak tea with cream. Wilde uses Jane Austen to *clarify* high comedy, stripping away the broad and farcical elements which had been present in it since Shakespeare. There are no longer any low-comic or crudely dialectal interludes. Even the secondary characters of *The Importance of Being Earnest* are erudite verbalists. (*Miss Prism*: "I spoke horticulturally. My metaphor was drawn from fruits.") Wilde has pruned and simplified high comedy by eighteenth-century standards of taste, decorum, and correctness.

But there is a second influence in Wilde's epicene transformation of Jane Austen. He is aided in this project by the one wit who stands between himself and her—Lewis Carroll. It is Carroll who detaches English comedy from the ethical (which it displays even in the bawdy Restoration plays, with their virtuous finales) and prepares it for its definitive amoralization at the hands of Wilde. After Wilde, this genre of glittering high comedy is confined to the epicene and can be practiced only by sex-crossing imaginations—Ronald Firbank, Noel Coward, Cole Porter. The sexual ambiguity in Lewis Carroll is not textually overt; that development was to be implemented by Wilde. But it is perfectly evident in his life. His friends and biographers speak of his long hair and "curiously womanish face," his fascination with little girls, his detestation of boys, which was "an aversion, almost amounting to terror." Carroll's self-identification was thoroughly feminine.

The dramatic force of the *Alice* books rests upon the stability of the Victorian social structure which invisibly supports them. Alice is an imperialist of custom. Thrust into an irrational dream-world, she remains serene and self-assured, a model of well-bred composure. In her firm sense of the limits of appropriate behavior, she is twin to that menagerie of potentates, human and animal, who chide her for transgressions of mysterious local codes of conduct. There is even a surprising cultural kinship between Alice and her chief critic, the fierce Red Queen, whom Carroll elsewhere describes as "formal and strict, . . . the concentrated essence of all governesses." But the Red Queen is a governess only insofar as the governess is the first and most immediate representative of the hierarchical in the lives of English children, ruling as a regent in the name of society.

Carroll did not, I contend, hold the Romantic or modern view that social laws are artificial and false. On the contrary, he took an Apollonian pleasure in them, admiring and cherishing them as he did the equations and theorems he manipulated as an academic mathematician. One of the first pieces Carroll published as a young man at Oxford was a list of nonsensical principles, "Hints for Etiquette; or, Dining Out Made Easy."

I

In proceeding to the dining-room, the gentleman gives one arm to the lady he escorts—it is unusual to offer both.

III

To use a fork with your soup, intimating at the same time to your hostess that you are reserving the spoon for the beefsteaks, is a practice wholly exploded.

VI

The method of helping roast turkey with two carving-forks is practicable, but deficient in grace.

VII

We do not recommend the practice of eating cheese with a knife and fork in one hand, and a spoon and wine-glass in the other; there is a kind of awkwardness in the action which no amount of practice can entirely dispel.

VIII

As a general rule, do not kick the shins of the opposite gentleman under the table, if personally unacquainted with him; your pleasantry is liable to be misunderstood—a circumstance at all times unpleasant.

It would be a typically modern error to assume that this is an essay in "debunking," that Carroll is reducing manners to the absurd in order to demonstrate the fictiveness of social custom. But everything we know about Carroll's private and public deportment shows him to be an inflexible advocate of order. A contemporary speaks of the "rigid rule of his own life," his fixed daily routine. Another says that he was "austere, shy, precise, . . . watchfully tena-

cious of his dignity, stiffly conservative in political, theological, social theory, his life mapped out in squares like Alice's landscape."

The evidence suggests that the rules and manners of "Hints for Etiquette" and the *Alice* books draw much of their force from Carroll's belief in their tradition-consecrated and even a priori character. Nearly all the comedy of Carroll's work arises from a natively English love of formality and ceremony. There is a tonality of wit in Carroll which has no parallel in premodern literature but which appears throughout Virginia Woolf, particularly in her masterpiece, *To the Lighthouse*. Note the similarities of voice, for example, between Carroll's "Hints for Etiquette" and this passage from a letter to Victoria Sackville-West in which Woolf reviews the comments roused by her newly bobbed hair:

1. Virginia is completely spoilt by her shingle.
2. Virginia is completely made by her shingle.
3. Virginia's shingle is quite unnoticeable.

These are the three schools of thought on this important subject. I have bought a coil of hair, which I attach by a hook. It falls into the soup, and is fished out on a fork.

This sophisticated comic style, with its subtlety of ironic inflection, seems to be produced in England by some unexplored interaction between language and persona.

The deep structure of such passages is as follows. An excessive or unforeseen event occurs within the strict confines of convention. The dining table is the favored locus of display, as the arena of daily domestic ritual. However, the incident elicits no reaction, or only a muted one. All personae remain in a state of dignified flat affect, restoring and preserving the rule of normality. The highest English comedy is predicated on a Wildean impassivity of countenance. One can see in the Woolf letter, in fact, how three diverse reactions are allowed to cancel each other out, cleverly effecting a return to stasis. The energy deflected from reaction flows into the social structure of the occasion, which is felt with architectural solidity, vibrating with public power.

Lewis Carroll covertly introduced an epicene element into English humor which, consolidated by Wilde, has continued in force to the present. It took immediate cultural root because of certain abiding features of upper-class English personality, foremost of which is the hermaphroditic type of the "gentleman," upon which I have already remarked. English society has also been noted for a toleration of eccentricity, a proliferation of sadomasochistic erotica, and a high incidence of male homosexuality stimulated by the monasticism of public-school and university life.

Lewis Carroll, in his two strange and inexhaustible books, synthesized several of the most potent elements in English high culture: wit, hierarchy, and spiritual hermaphroditism. After Carroll, English comedy, in literature and in educated dialogue, often tends towards the absurd and incongruous, in which there is always a shadow of the epicene. What Carroll did was first to invent a nonchthonian animism, giving Romantic nature a social voice. The *Alice* books are a din of creatures, speaking as uncompromising social hierarchs. There is no "tenderness" in Carroll's characters, save in the bumbling and ineffectual, like the feeble White Knight. All are sharp, forceful personalities, nodes of aggressive selfhood. The *Alice* books, like *The Importance of Being Earnest,* are glutted with rules of behavior, which pop up at the most improbable moments. Formality is the preeminent principle in Carroll, governing not only the narrative design (a pack of cards structures the first book and a chessboard the second), but also the psychodramatic style of the characters, a punctilious ritualism not unlike Carroll's own. The Red Queen's draconian championship of manners is merely the most blatant of the ritual formulas of Carroll's animistic world, and manners are the language of the hierarchical. Veblen remarks: "Manners . . . are symbolical and conventionalised survivals representing former acts of dominance or of personal service or of personal contact. In large part they are an expression of status,—a symbolic pantomime of mastery on the one hand and of subservience on the other."

It is the ancient history of manners as articulations of power which energizes the climactic confrontation between Gwendolen and Cecily, the center not only of *The Importance of Being Earnest* but probably of Wilde's entire oeuvre. In a tableau of brilliant formal beauty, a tea table is made the scene of a ferocious wargame, with manners the medium of ritual advance and retreat. Gwendolen and Cecily manipulate their personae with chill virtuosity. Nowhere else in the play is it more evident that the gender of the Androgyne of Manners is purely artificial, that "femininity" in the salon is simply a principle of decorum shared equally by male and female. The escalating emotion of the conversation between Gwendolen and Cecily is entirely absorbed by the ceremonial framework and by the formality of their social masks.

CECILY:

> [*rather shy and confidingly*] Dearest Gwendolen, there is no reason why I should make a secret of it to you. Our little county newspaper is sure to chronicle the fact next week. Mr. Ernest Worthing and I are engaged to be married.

GWENDOLEN:

> [*quite politely, rising*] My darling Cecily, I think there must be some slight error. Mr. Ernest Worthing is engaged to me. The announcement will appear in the *Morning Post* on Saturday at the latest.

CECILY:

> [*very politely, rising*] I am afraid you must be under some misconception. Ernest proposed to me exactly ten minutes ago. [*Shows diary.*]

GWENDOLEN:

> [*examines diary through her lorgnette carefully*] It is very curious, for he asked me to be his wife yesterday afternoon at 5:30. If you would care to verify the incident, pray do so. [*Produces diary of her own.*]

Each gesture, each rhetorical movement is answered by a symmetrical countermovement of balletic grandeur. Language becomes increasingly elaborate, in baroque convolutions of ironic restraint: "It would distress me more than I can tell you, dear Gwendolen, if it caused you any mental or physical anguish, but I feel bound to point out that since Ernest proposed to you he clearly has changed his mind." There is no hysteria, or even excitement. The immovable wills of the two young women press so fiercely against the social limits of the moment that the hierarchical structure of manners leaps into visibility, another of Wilde's characteristic materializations. Stylization and ritualism approach the Oriental. The scene is a Japanese tea ceremony in which gracious self-removal has yielded to barely concealed Achillean strife.

It was Lewis Carroll who made this greatest of Wildean episodes possible. In Carroll, manners and social laws are disconnected from humane or "civilizing" values. They have a mathematical beauty but no moral meaning: they are absurd. But this absurdity is predicated not on some democratic notion of their relativism but on their arbitrary, divine incomprehensibility. In the *Alice* books, manners are meaningless, but they still retain their hierarchical force; they are Veblen's "pantomime" of mastery and subservience. Wilde, influenced by Carroll, appropriates his view of the mechanisms of social power and sets it into a much larger system of aristocratic presuppositions derived partly from his self-identification as a Baudelairean Late Romantic (always reactionary and antiliberal) and partly from his reading of English drama, in which aristocracy is one of the leading moral "ideas."

In the century of the middle class, Wilde reaffirms aristocratic *virtù*, fabricating it out of its accumulated meanings in English literature. *The Importance of Being Earnest* is a reactionary political poem which takes aristocratic style as the supreme embodiment of life as art. Through its masquelike use of manners as social spectacle, the play seeks out the crystallized idea or Platonic form of aristocracy, which resides in rank, in the ascending gradations of the great chain of being. Wilde's bon mots bring an Apollonian world into being: language and ceremony unite to take the hierarchical to its farthest dazzling point, until it appears as form without content, like the icy latticework of a snowflake. Thus it is that the characters of *The Importance of Being Earnest,* and especially the women, have abnormal attitudes, reactions, and customs and embark upon sequences of apparently irrational thought, for they are a strange hierarchical race, the *aristoi.*

Wilde's play is inspired by the glamour of aristocracy alone, divorced from social function. In this it is quite unlike Augustan literature, which celebrates Queen Anne for her wisdom and stability of rule. In Wilde no collective benefits flow from throne or court, where the upper class is preoccupied with fashionable diversions. No contemporary regime is eulogized, no past one nostalgically commemorated. Indeed, social order has no legal, economic, or military aspects whatever; it is entirely divorced from practical reality. Class structure in Wilde exists as *art,* as pure form. This markedly contrasts with Ulysses's sermon on "degree" in Shakespeare's *Troilus and Cressida*: in *The Importance of Being Earnest* order is admired not because it is right or just but because it is beautiful. In fact, order here makes no intellectual sense at all; in Carrollian terms, it is absurd. Hence it is an error, and a common one, to say that Wilde is "satirizing" Lady Bracknell, making her ridiculous in her haughty presumptions. Lady Bracknell is beautiful *because* she is absurd. Aristocracy in *The Importance of Being Earnest* satisfies esthetic and not moral demands. The world of the play is *kosmios,* well-ordered and comely. And that it is ruled by the chic makes perfect sense when one realizes that the etymological descent of this word resembles that of *cosmetic* from *cosmos,* for the French *chic* is apparently a version of the German *schick,* meaning taste, elegance, and order.

Outside his art, Wilde found himself in the same quandary as Coleridge and Swinburne, anxiously attempting apologia and moral revision of their daemonic poems. Thus Wilde declares in *The Soul of Man under Socialism*: "All authority is quite degrading. It degrades those who exercise it, and it degrades those over whom it is exercised." Wilde was torn between his instinctive hier-archism as an Apollonian idealist and the liberalism to which he was impelled by the miseries of being homo-sexual in a Christian society. This led him into glaring self-contradictions, as in the testimony at his two trials.

The Wildean epicene unites the great English dramatic theme of aristocracy with Late Romantic Estheticism and Decadence. The first step in this process is Wilde's sever-ance of the hierarchical social values of the eighteenth century and Jane Austen from the ideal of commonweal. The second step is his sexual volatilization of English wit. The bantering rhetoric of the celibate Jane Austen and Lewis Carroll becomes epicene in Wilde because of his sexual experience, with its shift into decadence. Works of epicene wit are typically dominated by image—a tyranny of the visual—and by scandal and gossip. There is little scandal or gossip in Lewis Carroll because the *Alice* books have no sexual "free energy": Carroll is an annalist of ag-gression but not of eroticism. In Wilde, however, gossip is a primary force, intensifying the aura of glamour by which prestige is measured in the salon. The erotic excitation of scandal and gossip produces the volatility of Wildean wit, aiding its transformation into the epicene. Words cast off their moral meanings and escape into the sexually transcendental, leaving only vapor trails of flirtation and frivolity.

Neil Sammells (essay date September 1986)

SOURCE: Sammells, Neil. "Earning Liberties: *Travesties* and *The Importance of Being Earnest*." *Modern Drama* 29, no. 3 (September 1986): 376-87.

[*In the following essay, Sammells links Tom Stoppard's play* Travesties *with Wilde's* The Importance of Being Earnest.]

David Rod has argued in *Modern Drama* that critics of Stoppard's *Travesties* have paid insufficient attention to the views on art and politics of Henry Carr, the minor consular official who regales us with his version of life as it most certainly was not in Zürich during the Great War.[1] Carr, Rod insists, rejects the various idealisms of Tristan Tzara, James Joyce and Lenin to present an independent position of his own, founded upon a practical consideration of what art has been and what it has accomplished; Carr contributes tellingly to the debate as Stoppard creates a balance "among the four opposing aesthetic viewpoints presented in the play, a balance that does not tip in Carr's favor even though his memory controls most of the events in the play."[2] Rod is right to suggest that Stoppard does not allow any one of his antagonists to win the debate, but his remarks do less than justice to the complexity of *Travesties*. As important as *what* is said is *how* it is said; Rod's notion of a "balance" among the opposing view-points does not locate the real centre of Stoppard's dramatic strategies, which is the *form* of the play itself. It is the paramount achievement of *Travesties* that it ad-dresses itself to the debate about the nature of art not by means of a spokesman (whether Carr or anyone else) but by its own method of procedure.

Many critics, however, have been keen to lobby for James Joyce, to identify his as the voice of Stoppard in the great debate on art and politics.[3] Significantly, though, the play first presented itself to Stoppard as a debate between Tzara and Lenin based on the fact that although they were in Zürich at the same time they never met: "This seemed a rather interesting fact of history to keep in one's mind. I never quite forgot it and never quite did anything with it, and then I started working on *Travesties*." As he did so he became "dimly aware of James Joyce's part in all this."[4] Lenin, of course, calls for a literature that conforms. "Today," he bellows at us, alone on the stage, "literature must become party literature! Down with non-partisan literature! Down with literary supermen!"[5] His art which must not question but simply obey is directly opposed to the self-conscious delinquency urged by Tzara. The artist, Tzara claims, was the priest-guardian of the magic which first conjured the intelligence from the appetites, putting humanity on the first rung of the ladder to consecutive thought. His own anti-art is a protest against the abject prostitution of this exalted heritage. "Art created patrons and was corrupted," he raves: "It began to celebrate the ambitions and acquisitions of the paymaster. The artist has negated himself: paint—*eat*—sculpt—grind—write—*shit*" (p. 47). Joyce's deferred entry into the scheme of things does not, of course, necessarily preclude Stoppard's turn-ing to him as a spokesman, as an alternative to the mutual antagonism of Tzara and Lenin. What does preclude it is not just Joyce's inescapably parodic treatment but the nature of the play itself. The opposition between Tzara and Lenin restates to some extent that between the conformist realism of Donner and the avant-garde, delinquent gestures of Beauchamp; Stoppard, indeed, adapts many of the speeches from *Artist Descending a Staircase* to construct the debate in *Travesties*. Conformism and delinquency are the twin poles between which Stoppard's best drama in general, and *Travesties* in particular, chooses to function; in investigating that polarity Stoppard needs no spokesman, the play stands up and speaks for itself.

Travesties is unabashed in declaring the intricacy of its own design, and its flamboyant cleverness has distressed some of its critics. Kenneth Hurren, for instance, felt there was something intoxicated about Stoppard's achievement on the first night of the original London production. "Everything was gathered together again consummately," he acknowledged of the play's climax, "after the fashion of an amiable drunken actor who trips over a chair and walks through the scenery but steadies himself with amusing insouciance and carries off his big moment as though nothing had happened."[6] Elsewhere in the auditorium Michael Coveney was afflicted by the suspicion that Stoppard was setting himself a challenge for the sake of it. While admitting the brilliance and audacity of the design, he could see little point to it: "I find that a lack of any dramatic accumulation in the play induces a response of indifference."[7] Kenneth Tynan experienced not indifference but downright hostility. Identifying something both sterile and arbitrary at the heart of the enterprise, Tynan described Stoppard's imposition of Wilde's baroque plot upon his own burlesque version of wartime Zürich as "crossbreeding the bizarre with the bogus."[8] To dismiss the design of the play in such a fashion as brilliant but arbitrary is, quite simply, wrong. Stoppard does not just re-use the plot of the *The Importance of Being Earnest: Travesties* is evidence of a *critical engagement* with Wilde's play. The manner of that engagement is its own statement about what art can and cannot do.

Stoppard's critical strategies are both interpretive and transformational. He exploits the host-play by pinpointing a recurrent element and elevating it to a position of ostentatious prominence. An explicit burden of literary comment runs through Wilde's original, from Jack's dismissal of modern culture as not "the sort of thing one should talk of in private,"[9] and his withering condemnation of the "corrupt French Drama," (pp. 353-4) to Algy's claim that if life were either pure or simple modern literature would be "a complete impossibility," (p. 352) and Gwendolen's utter certainty about the kind of play she is appearing in: "This suspense is terrible," she announces; "I hope it will last" (p. 400). In *Travesties* such matter becomes a full-blown debate about art and the artist. Fittingly, the first-class ticket to Worthing and the cigarette-case which set in motion Wilde's plot are replaced by Stoppard with a library ticket divulging Tzara's Bunburying between the Library and the Meierei Bar; if we are in any danger of accepting **The Importance of Being Earnest** as simply a social comedy of manners the hyper-literary self-consciousness of *Travesties* ensures that we take a second look. It is interesting to note that in the closing moments of his play Stoppard cannot resist a brilliant reversal of Miss Prism's confusion of art and life when she loses baby Jack, pushing around in a pram the manuscript of her three-volume

novel. Carr here parodies Lady Bracknell's half of the dialogue, thus usurping the role which up to this point had been taken by James Augusta Joyce. The remarks applied in Wilde's play to Miss Prism are here made with reference not to a person but to a manuscript of Joyce's "Oxen of the Sun":

CARR:

> And is it a chapter, inordinate in length and erratic in style, remotely connected with midwifery?

JOYCE:

> It is a chapter which by a miracle of compression, uses the gamut of English literature from Chaucer to Carlyle to describe events taking place in a lying-in hospital in Dublin.

CARR:

> It is obviously the same work.

> (p. 97)

The exchange has, in fact, a dual function. It prevents Joyce from claiming a victory in the battle of the books, from establishing the unquestioned pre-eminence of his way of using language. It also points to the deformation that Stoppard has enacted upon **The Importance of Being Earnest**: making his own substitution of art for life, he replaces the personal and social vicissitudes of Wilde's protagonists with the play's revelations about the nature of our fictions.

The Importance of Being Earnest is saturated by fictions. Each of the main characters is directly associated with a document (or documents) which counters the fictions of others and attempts to impose its own configurations upon the fictional world in which they live. In the opening scene of the play the relationship between Algy and his servant Lane is defined by Lane's book in which he keeps the household accounts. This, it transpires, is a fictional account of Algy's expenditure: a cover for Lane's plundering of the Moncrieff wine-cellar. The book, the first of the fictions to appear in the play, defines precisely the nature, extent and self-consciousness of the duplicity between master and servant. Cecily, on the other hand, has two sets of fictions: the love-letters and her diary, both of which give a completely fictional account of her relationship with the equally fictional Ernest. For Cecily, life, primarily, is of use according to the degree to which it can be turned into fiction. "You see," she tells Algy of her diary, "it is simply a very young girl's record of her own thoughts and impressions and consequently meant for publication. When it appears in volume form I hope you will order a copy" (p. 377). Indeed, the conflict between Cecily and Gwendolen is bolstered by their mutual appeal to documentary evidence for verification of their respective engagements to the fictional Ernest. The announcement of her engagement will, Cecily insists, be made in "Our little county newspaper," while Gwendolen notes, calmly, that the news of hers "will appear in the *Morning Post* on Saturday at the latest" (p. 383). Gwendolen fights fire with fire; she matches newspaper with newspaper and the fictions of Cecily's diary are countered with those of her own. "He asked me to be his wife yesterday afternoon at 5.30.," she insists, "If you would care to verify the incident, pray do so. (*Produces diary of her own.*) I never travel without my diary. One should always have something sensational to read in the train" (p. 383). In her case, no less than in Cecily's, all aspects of experience are subjected to the fictionalising mind and the contortions of fictional form. History itself can be contained within the contours of the "bodice-bursting" historical melodrama. Of Jack she remarks, "Disloyalty would be as impossible to him as deception. But even men of the noblest possible moral character are extremely susceptible to the influence of the physical charms of others. Modern, no less than Ancient History, supplies us with many most painful examples of what I refer to. If it were not so, indeed, History would be quite unreadable" (p. 382).

Gwendolen's mother, Lady Bracknell, is of course, quite inseparable from her list of eligible young men—a document which threatens to seal Jack's fate—and Jack himself has recourse to the Army Lists to prove his assumed identity. In the original four-act version of the play this obsession with documents reaches a more explicit climax in the final scene when all the characters are handed a volume each by Jack in order to track down his father's name in the army records. The Lists prove not to be what was expected of them: the meticulous researchers find themselves leafing through handsomely-bound catalogues and railway timetables. These can be added to the "certificates of Miss Cardew's birth, baptism, whooping-cough, registration, vaccination, confirmation, and the measles; both the German and the English variety," (p. 394) which Jack cites in order to prove Cecily's identity in the face of Lady Bracknell's assertion that she has known "strange errors" (p. 393) in the Court Guides. The documents of private fiction are complemented by those of officialdom and neither proves more reliable than the other, the official publications making the fallacious and confusing claim that Jack is indeed earnest.

It is, however, Dr. Chasuble's unpublished sermons which provide the most explicit comment in *The Importance of Being Earnest* on the duplicity of literary production. Chasuble calmly explains that he is prepared for any eventuality. "My sermon on the meaning of the manna in the wilderness can be adapted to almost any occasion," he assures Jack, who has just announced the sudden demise of young Ernest, "joyful, or, as in the present case, distressing. I have preached it at harvest celebrations, christenings, confirmations, on days of humiliation and festal days. The last time I delivered it was in the Cathedral, as a charity sermon on behalf of the Society for the Prevention of Discontent among the Upper Orders" (p. 372). Chasuble's sermons are all form, content is obliterated; far from revealing the truth, these fictions enact whatever distortions are deemed suitable. Yet it is Miss Prism who gives the most dramatic form to that substitution of art for life,

of form over content, which is so vital to her social superiors. By putting the three-volume novel in the bassinette and the baby in the handbag she confuses document with person, a confusion propounded by Cecily and Gwendolen as they sensationalise their lives by means of their diaries.[10] To write is to distort. Hidden away in the closing scenes of the play is the voice of Wilde as Formalist, asserting art as lie, revelling in the impossibility of direct description:

LADY BRACKNELL:

Is this Miss Prism a female of repellent aspect, remotely connected with education?

DR. CHASUBLE:

She is the most cultivated of ladies, and the very picture of respectability.

LADY BRACKNELL:

It is obviously the same person.

(p. 398)

Miss Prism is both and neither; she exists only in terms of the lying descriptions made of her, prismatically, by others. The exchange is as vital to our pinpointing of the central strategies of *The Importance of Being Earnest* as is the parallel passage in *Travesties* to our understanding of Stoppard's tactics. This is Wilde as artist-critic, playing with the strident anti-naturalism of his *Intentions*.

"Memory, my dear Cecily," opines Miss Prism, "is the diary that we all carry about with us." "Yes," comes the reply, "but it usually chronicles the things that have never happened, and couldn't possibly have happened" (p. 367). This exchange reiterates the play's concern with the untrustworthiness of all writing: the diary is assimilated to the sensationalising activities of the imagination. The remark would also seem to give Stoppard his cue in *Travesties*. The play is under the erratic control of Old Carr's memory, telling of things that did not happen, and couldn't possibly have happened, in pacific Switzerland during the Great War.[11] His memory lies in the way that all fiction lies, and his rewriting of history is, at a basic level, a dismissive parody of that most "truth-telling" of all fictional forms, the Lukácsian historical novel. Lucács identifies as a fundamental technique of the historical novelist the use of a hero from the middle rank whose adventures shed light on the fabric of society as he encounters both high and low, the representatives of the people and the world-historical personalities.[12] Carr is such a hero, his adventures bringing him into contact with the great champions of art and anti-art and the word-historical personality of Lenin. In *Travesties,* however, the hero places himself very much centre-stage: history, and the society in which he has lived, are displayed solely in order to show the part he has, or has not, played in them. Carr, in the act or reminiscence, is attempting to define his own relevance. Just as Rosencrantz and his partner attempt to grasp their significance in the story of Hamlet, so Carr attempts to define his in relation to Lenin's flight from Switzerland and the events which followed. In fact, Old Cecily reminds him of the fictional nature of the dilemma he has posed himself; he had never really been the Consul and, by the time he came to play Algy, Lenin had long gone. The play's view of history is, then, far from objective in the Lukácsian sense but is, according to Peter Wood (who directed the first production), "seen prismatically through the view of Henry Carr. At one point Tom was thinking of calling it 'Prism' . . ."[13] The echo of *The Importance of Being Earnest* is quite unmistakable. Memory is the diary that Carr carries with him; his chronicle imposes a whole gallery of stereotyped figures and images upon his fictional experience, and memory is seen to function in the same duplicitous way as the fictionalising imagination.

Travesties is replete with stereotypes. We have James Joyce as a comic stage-Irishman speaking in limericks and looking for a loan, Tristan Tzara as a Rumanian nonsense complete with monocle and fractured English. At one point in the second act the stage is dominated by a huge slide of Lenin, captured on celluloid in an attitude of iron-willed resolution: '*a justly famous image*' (p. 84). Parenthetically but significantly Stoppard adds "*This is the photo, incidentally, which Stalin had retouched so as to expunge Kamenev and Trotsky who feature prominently in the original*" (p. 85). History has frozen into familiar form, and that form is a lie. The public lie of the historical stereotype is complemented by Carr's private lies. He refashions himself and his rivals in the same way as the characters in *The Importance of Being Earnest* use the established literary types of the wicked brother, the officious guardian, the gorgon-aunt, etc., to give shape and significance to their lives. Types make the world manageable, distribute the dialogue for a specific end. To stereotype people is to control them, and this is precisely what Carr is attempting to do, to slot himself into a history which, apparently, has largely passed him by.

When recasting the events he purports to recall in the overall shape of *The Importance of Being Earnest* Carr takes the role of Algy, transmuting the egoism of the Dandy, living solely for pleasure, into that of the peripheral figure who will no longer be ignored. His sense that identity can only be truly appraised through action (defining who he *is* by what he has *done,* what significance he has attained) allows Carr to assign Lenin a supporting role in his own personal drama. "I might have stopped the whole Bolshevik thing in its tracks," he tells Old Cecily, "but, here's the point. *I was uncertain*" (p. 81). "And don't forget," he continues, plaintively, "*he wasn't Lenin then! I mean who was he*? as it were" (p. 81). The shifting of perspective which comes with historical hindsight makes direct description a plain impossibility: there is no "natural" way of describing the Lenin who knew the rented obscurity of 14 Spiegelgasse. Such a consciousness of the relativity of historical evaluation sanctions Carr's own History as Egoism and his exuberant espousal of an enormously variegated range of possible ways of describing and proving what did, and did not, happen.

The fundamental lesson of *The Importance of Being Earnest* is that all writing is a lie we cannot do without. In the debate with which *Travesties* plays, documents are used as offensive weapons: memoirs (Gorki's, Fitz Platten's), letters (Lenin's to Karpinsky, his memos to Lunacharsky and Gorki), diary extracts (Hugo Ball's), legal documents (court records of the Bezirksgericht Zuerich) and public speeches (Lenin's) are referred to, cited, or quoted by the various antagonists in order to make their version of history prevail. *Travesties,* however, demonstrates a complete breakdown in the hierarchy of evidence: no single document or form of written proof (particularly newspapers: *The Neue Zuricher Zeitung* and *The Zuricher Post* contradict each other in their partisan reports of the state of the war as completely as the *Morning Post* and its rival in their announcement of the fictional Ernest's engagements), no one argument is allowed to silence the others. Similarly, and crucially, the play refuses to admit that any single *style* of writing enjoys a uniquely privileged relationship with what it purports to transcribe: the play is an argument of styles to match its argument of documents. The opening scene shows Stoppard's basic tactic at work: in the library Lenin's Russian is set alongside Tzara's verbal hat-trick, a quotation from Lenin's papers, snippets of *Ulysses* and Cecily's 'Sssssssh' which is, ironically, the only utterance we fully understand. The scene prepares us for the sheer range of parody and interpolation that the play will have at its command. Joyce contributes limericks, a rendition of *Mr. Dooley* and an interrogation of Tzara in the constabular style of the 'Ithaca' section of *Ulysses.* Carr contributes massacred dialogue from *The Importance of Being Earnest* and his own idiosyncratic prose steeped in travel-brochure clichés. Cecily lectures us on the history of Leninism and joins Gwendolen in a parody of a Gallagher and Sheen routine. Tzara brings us English in a variety of fractured forms including comic pidgin and mangled Shakespearean verse. Carr summons the historical giants to the stage, lets them have their say, and then dismisses them. The play invokes style after style, exploits each to the point of exhaustion, and moves on.

Stoppard's sensitivity, then, to Wilde's metafictional preoccupations (the involution of his critical concerns with his dramatic practice) sanctions both his own use of extensive parody and stereotypes, and his focus on the role of duplicitous fictions in the making of our meanings, the encoding of our world. Interpretation and transformation of Wilde's play go hand in hand; at its most playful *Travesties* reduces *The Importance of Being Earnest* to a series of costume-changes. As summarised by Joyce for the sartorially fastidious Carr the play *is* nothing but looks everything. "The curtain rises," explains Joyce, "A flat in Mayfair. Teatime. You enter in a bottle-green velvet smoking jacket with black frogging—hose white, cravat perfect, boots elastic-sided, trousers," he adds, ominously, "of your own choice . . . Act Two. A rose garden. After lunch. Some by-play among the small parts. You enter in a debonair garden-party outfit—beribboned boater, gaily striped blazer, parti-coloured shoes, trousers of your own choice" (p. 52). This is, indeed, a triumph of form over content, and again it points to (burlesques almost) Stoppard's own way with *The Importance of Being Earnest*: he brings the form of the play into the very foreground, and makes it a subject of attention. The structure of Wilde's play is that of travesty: Jack's proposal to Gwendolen is played again, and travestied, by Algy and Cecily; Lady Bracknell's interrogation of Jack in Act One reappears in a different form in her haranguing of Miss Prism. Similarly, individual scenes are themselves structured by travesty with one voice restating and confounding the other. It is precisely according to this principle that *Travesties* assembles itself.

Travesties has an argument with itself, constantly doubling-back to contradict and deny those shapes it has itself given to the past. Tzara, for instance, first enters as a "*Rumanian nonsense*" (p. 32). This is both a parody of Jack Worthing's first entrance and itself the subject of later parody. Soon this Rumanian joke is joined by an Irish joke: Joyce spouting limericks and looking for a loan. Carr's memory hurtles spectacularly off the rails as the entire scene is played out in limericks (pp. 33-36). Tzara, however, re-enters when this frenetic dialogue has exhausted itself. This time he is straight out of *The Importance of Being Earnest*, exhibiting a "perfect English languor."[14] Carr swaps one stereotype for another; he criticises one patently ludicrous version of history and embarks upon another that is equally untenable. The central contention of Wilde's *Intentions* is that art which pretends to reproduce mimetically is a lie and that the only honest alternative is to turn this vice into a virtue. Carr's chronicle is almost a parody of the literature Wilde intends, criticising one set of lies by means of another.

Travesty and contradiction are evident even at the fundamental level of language. The text of *Travesties* is woven together by repetition: phrases, turns of expression recur in travestied, often contradictory form. In the replaying of the scene in which Carr and Tzara discuss politics and art the reversal of initiative is expressed through a repeated verbal pattern. First, Tzara's heated dismissal of the traditional sophistries for waging wars of expansion and self-interest brings forth Carr's pained protest that "You are insulting my comrades-in-arms, many of whom died on the field of honour" (p. 39). In the second version, Carr counters Tzara's belief in the importance of art by describing it as, in essence, simply a beautifier of existence and denying that it can lay claim to any serious political efficacy. Tzara's cold rebuff is a pointed travesty of what has gone before: "You are insulting me and my comrades in the Dada exhibition" (p. 46). Repetition is employed specifically for the purpose of contradiction. At times, however, repetition evolves towards a higher complexity. This is the case when Carr infiltrates the library and attempts to woo Cecily, Lenin's devotee. The scene parodies that in which Algy attempts to woo Cecily, while posing as Ernest. Yet this parody is itself reflected in another as it develops into a travesty of the earlier discussion between Carr and Tzara. Once more we are given successive versions of the same scene and verbal motifs

are repeated and travestied. In high dudgeon Cecily rejects Carr's critique of Marxist theory: "you are insulting me and my comrades—" (p. 76). Stoppard is characterising art as a hinged mirror, in which the leaves reflect nothing but each other.

The self-inspection and self-contradiction in the play's structure is reflected not just in repeated verbal motifs, but also in the very prose itself. It is in Carr's opening monologue that Stoppard's dramatic prose denies and cancels itself most effectively. There is indeed an irony here. "If there is any point in using language at all," he insists to Tzara, "it is that a word is taken to stand for a particular fact or idea and not for other facts or ideas" (p. 38). This is a precept Carr can hardly be said to put into practice: his own speeches pay no such attention to the conventional division of sense and nonsense. Each of his descriptions is immediately cancelled as the prose advances in a halting parody of the deferential friend of the famous who no sooner attributes a quality to a great man than he feels impelled to deny that it is in any way carried to excess. Joyce exhibits "a monkish unconcern for worldly and bodily comforts, without at the same time shutting himself off from the richness of human society, whose temptations, on the other hand, he met with an ascetic disregard tempered only by sudden and catastrophic aberrations" (p. 23). Carr's description of life in Zürich is couched in a prose which takes no account of the external state of affairs it is supposed to transcribe. Even watchful, it advances by denying and criticising itself. "'Twas in the bustling metropolis of swiftly gliding trams and greystone banking houses," he begins, establishing a closed field of linguistic possibilities within which he then proceeds to play, "of cosmopolitan restaurants on the great stone banks of the swiftly-gliding snot-green (mucus mutandis) Limmat River, of jewelled escapements and refugees of all kinds, e.g. Lenin" (p. 23). This is prose as self-evident sham: the trams are mentioned purely to pun on *bustling*, the great stone banks present a critical reworking of greystone banking houses, the river is snot-green by virtue of the excruciating Latin pun it facilitates. The "naturalness" of the description is also undercut by the river's murky literary parentage. Its progenitors are Joyce's "grey sweet mother," the "snotgreen sea"[15] and Kipling's "great grey-green greasy Limpopo River."[16] A little later Carr works a further variation on his material: "Meet by the sadly-sliding chagrinned Limmat River," he counsels, "strike west and immediately we find ourselves soaking wet, strike east and immediately we find ourselves in the Old Town, having left behind the banking bouncing metropolis of trampolines and chronometry of all kinds for here time has stopped" (p. 24).

Hersh Zeifman suggests, in attempting to locate Stoppard's allegiances, that the plethora of puns in the play is its most effective stratagem nudging us towards Joyce's point of view.[17] Yet the puns are less a veiled acknowledgement of literary influence than a function of the play's structure. The design of *Travesties* is the design of denial; self-inspection and self-contradiction are combined in self-criticism as the play continually examines its own conventions and terms of existence. The puns deny the claims of the prose to describe the world, proclaiming its processes as fictionalisation; they contradict both the primary, transitional sense attempted and the claims of Carr that, for language to work, a word must be taken to stand for a particular fact or idea and not for other facts or ideas. When seen in this way the puns do indeed help to locate Stoppard's allegiances. The presiding genius of *Travesties* is not Joyce, but Oscar Wilde: the Wilde who, in his criticism and his drama, championed a literature which, by contradicting its own claims to tell the truth, could tell a truth of sorts.

"All poetry" says Tzara, offering Gwendolen a scissored sonnet in his hat, "is a reshuffling of a pack of picture cards, and all poets are cheats" (p. 53). "Cleverness," he has told Carr earlier, "has been exploded, along with so much else, by the war" (p. 37). By offering Gwendolen Shakespeare's eighteenth sonnet drawn at random and piecemeal from a hat he hopes to deny that rational premeditation of the creative act which has led to its prostitution. His rewriting of the artist's signature in the hand of chance is also a protest against the indigence of traditional art, the tired tricks it works with an all too familiar routine. In a sense, Old Carr's memory works in precisely the same way: reshuffling the picture cards of the past, cheating history with the dog-eared trump-card of *The Importance of Being Earnest.* In an important sense, however, his approach differs from that of the anti-artist and the traditional artist; the form of the play is a contradiction, a denial, of the traditionalism of the views Carr expresses. Unlike Tzara he does not abandon design to chance, but unlike the traditionalist he makes no attempt to disguise the trick he is playing. Old Carr does not just pull history from a hat, nor does he rest easy with the form it has been allowed to assume. He tells it in his own lying, designing way.

In fact, the play refuses the stark choice presented by conformism and delinquency, by art and anti-art, by the twin extremities of the pendulum swing. This refusal is an act of criticism: by isolating and using techniques employed by both alternatives (creating design, for instance, which denies design) *Travesties* frees itself from each. Stoppard seizes the pendulum and speeds it to the beat of his will. *Travesties* is an acute refinement of Stoppard's Theatre of Criticism; at all levels (from its engagement with *The Importance of Being Earnest,* to its anthologising of divergent styles and its marshalling of mutually exclusive arguments) we can see that disciplined observation of and conformity to established ways of seeing, thinking, and saying, coupled with the sudden and pointed departure therefrom, which is the province of the critical work.

In *The Importance of Being Earnest* "playing" is the attainment of freedom. The two pairs of young lovers undergo a process of self-creation, becoming the fabrications of their own fictionalising imagination. "The only thing that one really knows about human nature," claims Wilde, "is that it changes. Change is the one quality we can predicate of it."[18] The lovers, in this quintessential comedy of disguise and mistaken identity, make a virtue of the changeability that Wilde proclaims; they learn both the truth of masks, and that personality can be constructed by a critical refusal to leave well alone. It is this conscious espousal of duplicity which fascinates Wilde. The actor and the Bunburyist are united in their "playing" and become types of the artist who asserts his dissatisfaction with a narrowly-conceived notion of truth-telling, by indulging in the brazen and palpable lie. Stoppard's Henry Carr attempts to reconstruct his history and personality in the same way as Wilde's young lovers; his is a gesture towards self-definition and freedom, but the manner of this gesture (his continual recourse to historical and literary stereotypes) is a recognition of restraint. In effect, Carr "plays with" the past in the same way as Stoppard "plays with" literary procedure, displaying it to deny it, criticising it in the act of freeing himself from it. "Playfulness" in both *Travesties* and *The Importance of Being Earnest* is not just a spirit of fun, it is the act of criticism itself.

In *The Soul of Man under Socialism* Wilde extends his anti-naturalism from the literary to the political sphere, announcing his contempt for all political systems which interfere with the fundamental human right, and need, to change; his literary concerns receive a consistent political articulation in his assertion of the need to reject and replace prevailing social, political, and institutional forms. Annoyed by Carr's description of Wilde as indifferent to politics, Kenneth Tynan rightly commends *The Soul of Man under Socialism* to anyone who believes this, and claims that the hard polemical purpose of *Travesties* is to argue that art must be independent of politics.[19] Yet, if we acknowledge the way in which the *form* of the play contradicts the traditionalism of Carr's views, we can see that Tynan is wrong and that *Travesties* makes a far more positive assertion, and one of which Wilde would have approved: that art can embody a freedom that is inseparable from criticism. The "play" of *Travesties,* the brilliance and the point of its design, is a refusal and a criticism of the available alternatives of conformism and delinquency; the play needs no spokesman to free itself from the claims of a Lenin or a Tzara alike. In the true spirit of Oscar Wilde, and by means of a critical engagement with his masterpiece, Stoppard has produced a play which has earned its liberty and taken none.

Notes

1. David Rod, "Carr's Views on Art and Politics in Tom Stoppard's *Travesties," Modern Drama,* 26 (1983), 536-542.

2. Ibid., 541.

3. Michael Billington, for instance, in reviewing the original London production, suggests that Joyce "emerges as a truly great man, shaping the way future generations view reality" (*The Guardian,* 11 June 1974, p. 12). For a full discussion of the various lob-

bies for a spokesman in the play, see Craig Werner, "Stoppard's Critical Travesty, or, Who Vindicates Whom, and Why," *Arizona Quarterly,* 35 (1979), 228-236.

4. Quoted by Werner, 230-231.

5. *Travesties* (London, 1975), p. 85. All subsequent references will be to this edition.

6. Kenneth Hurren, *The Spectator,* 22 June 1974, p. 776.

7. Michael Coveney, *The Financial Times,* 11 June 1974, p. 3.

8. Kenneth Tynan, *Show People* (London, 1980), p. 109.

9. *Oscar Wilde: Plays, Poems and Prose Writings* (London, 1975), p. 350. All subsequent references to *The Importance of Being Earnest* and Wilde's critical writings will be to this edition.

10. In the uncut original Wilde allows Algy the most explicit and stylish declaration of this confusion of document and person. Miss Prism expresses the "sincere hope that you will now turn over a new leaf in life." "I have already begun an entire volume, Miss Prism," comes Algy's reply. See the Four Act version of the play in *The Complete Works of Oscar Wilde* (London, New ed., 1966), p. 357.

11. For the most succinct discussion of how Stoppard, or Old Carr, cheats history by telescoping four years into one in order to create the events and meetings in *Travesties,* see Richard Ellmann, "The Zealots of Zürich," *Times Literary Supplement,* 12 July 1974, p. 744.

12. See Georg Lukács, *The Historical Novel,* trans. H. and S. Mitchell (London, 1969), especially pp. 36-39.

13. Peter Wood, interview with Ronald Hayman, *The Times,* 8 June 1974, p. 9.

14. Quoted in Ronald Hayman, *Tom Stoppard* (3rd ed., London, 1979), p. 4. Stoppard is here describing John Hurt's performance in the original production.

15. *Ulysses* (London, 1969), p. 11.

16. "The Elephant's Child," *Just So Stories* (London, 1962), p. 46.

17. Hersh Zeifman, "Tomfoolery: Stoppard's Theatrical Puns," *Yearbook of English Studies,* 9 (1977), especially 216-218.

18. *Oscar Wilde,* p. 283.

19. Tynan, pp. 112-113.

Peter Raby (essay date summer-winter 1995)

SOURCE: Raby, Peter. "'The Persons of the Play'": Some Reflections on Wilde's Choice of Names in *The Importance of Being Earnest." Nineteenth Century Theatre* 23, nos. 1-2 (summer-winter 1995): 67-75.

[*In the following essay, Raby explores the sources and context of some of the character names in* The Importance of Being Earnest.]

On 14 February 1995, part of *The Importance of Being Earnest* was performed in Westminster Abbey, during the service of dedication of a memorial window to Oscar Wilde in Poets' Corner. This constituted a significant moment in the reacceptance of Wilde by the English establishment, a kind of re-christening. The geographical distance from the Abbey to the site of the St James's Theatre cannot be more than a mile; the social and moral distance rather further. Certainly for the late Victorians, the idea of Wilde being publicly received into the tribal temple would have seemed grotesque and irreligious. Yet a century later, at the dedication service, Dame Judi Dench delivered Lady Bracknell's inquisition of Jack, and as she proceeded the extract became less of a reading than a performance, a performance of a text by now accepted as one of the few instantly recognized passages in English literature. Lady Bracknell's view that the whole theory of modern education is radically unsound produced the first collective, confident laugh: "Fortunately in England, at any rate, education produces no effect whatsoever. If it did, it would prove a serious danger to the upper classes, and probably lead to acts of violence in Grosvenor Square." Spoken to an audience which included many members of the great and the good, former cabinet ministers and privy councillors as well as actors, writers, academics, and enthusiasts, the lines held a special resonance. After a hundred years, some things had not changed. The joke could be appreciated both by the English and, from a different perspective perhaps, by the non-English members of the audience. (When Seamus Heaney began his address, following a Cathedral canon, Judi Dench, and John Gielgud, I heard my neighbor say—"At last, an Irish voice.") The lines, written by one of the best educated people in England, work, like so many of Wilde's lines, in several directions: quite precisely, in approval of Jack's natural ignorance; as an unexpected and vaguely alarming digression; as an insight into the extraordinary mind-set of Lady Bracknell; and as a self-standing observation which was and is disturbingly close to the truth. Wilde's voice spoke resoundingly through his created persona, Lady Bracknell.

Two weeks later, the London *Times* second leader, on the subject of the collapse of Baring's Bank, began: "Lady Bracknell was a firm believer in unexciting but safe investment portfolios. She might have accepted, however, that the first catastrophe in Barings' history—the great depression of the 1890s in the risky Latin American market—was a misfortune. Its second—as the result of recent rogue trading activities—looks more like carelessness. How, she might ask, could head office . . .". A platform in Westminster Abbey followed by a quotation in a *Times* leader inspires a certain confidence. The persona of Lady Bracknell has acquired an extra dimension which allows her to operate outside the confines of the play, and so achieve an independent existence. She is one example of Wilde's rare ability to create characters who are triumphantly fictional and yet who maintain unsettling relationships with the supposedly factual reality to which they are opposed.

This essay begins to explore two aspects of the fictional/factual tension, in the context of some of the names Wilde has given to his persons. The use of the description "The Persons of the Play" is not, of course, Wilde's prerogative, though it does seem particularly apt. I am not clear when it became common practice to translate "Dramatis Personae" as "The Persons of the Play" in published texts, or when there was a shift to a plain list, or to "Characters in order of appearance," following the style of a theatre program. "Persons," rather than characters, suggests more strongly the idea of mask and role, of the artificial, and provides an appropriate introductory framework to the tone of Wilde's dramatic writing.

Wilde chose names for his characters with great care, and there were often changes between early drafts or between even relatively polished typescripts and the versions selected for the first production. There is, in fact, only one name in the first scenario of *Earnest,* which Wilde sent to George Alexander in August, 1894, which remains the same in the final three-act version: Miss Prism. The other names in the scenario are, perhaps, in the nature of convenient working titles: Lord Alfred Rufford occupies the role later occupied by Algernon Moncrieff; his mother (not aunt) is the Duchess of Selby, and her daughter is Lady Maud Rufford (the aristocratic connections are pitched somewhat higher in the scenario). Some of these names Wilde had used already in previous works. Lord Alfred Rufford has a minor role in *A Woman of No Importance*; Selby, in Yorkshire, is the name of the country house in *Lady Windermere's Fan.* Wilde frequently used place names for the aristocrats in his social comedies, taking care to incorporate only those names and titles which were not currently held by living people, presumably to avoid the risk of libel. Windermere, Darlington, Berwick, Pontefract, Illingworth, Hunstanton, Goring, Bolton: some of these places held private significance for Wilde (for instance, by commemorating the place he was staying when he wrote a work) but, more crucially, they all *sound* authentic, for landed English families naturally take, or took, their name from the areas they lived in, and from the lands they owned. Illingworth is a place, and a house—"Illingworth is entailed, of course, but it is a tedious barrack of a place," as Lord Illingworth patronizingly explains to Mrs Arbuthnot in *A Woman of No Importance.* "He [Gerald] can have Ashby, which is much prettier, Harborough, which has the best shooting in the north of England, and the house in St James's Square. What more can a gentleman require in this world?" (Ashby, coincidentally, is the village in Lincolnshire where Wilde's uncle was rector.) Further, the surnames are used frequently within the spoken text: the formality of conversation ensures that they are repeated like a litany. The movements of the "real" aristocracy around England, and Europe, were recorded

during the 1890s in the columns of fashionable newspapers such as the *Morning Post,* and Wilde's fictional names could have been inserted effortlessly into a paragraph, like the inventions of Evelyn Waugh's Adam Simes for the Mr Chatterbox column in *Vile Bodies*: "The Duke and Duchess of Berwick are taking the waters at Homburg; Lord Illingworth has joined Lady Hunstanton's houseparty at Hunstanton Chase. On Saturday, eight hundred brace of partridge were shot."

In *The Importance of Being Earnest,* Wilde, by making the mother of Gwendolen Lady Bracknell, was incorporating a private reference to the house where the Marchioness of Queensberry lived, and so scoring a glancing blow against the Marquis himself. He was also locating his fictional Gorgon in a specific and conspicuous locality, likely to be recognized by the majority of his audience. The connotations are in this instance not primarily comic, as they are when Pinter, another playwright with an acute ear for the possibilities of place, makes use of a town such as Basingstoke. Bracknell is just the other side of the Great Park from Windsor Castle; and Lady Bracknell shares more than her imperious manner with Queen Victoria. She drives through the same landscape, and inhabits the same territory.

Of the other persons in the play, Prism and Chasuble belong to an established tradition of comic naming, as exploited by Sheridan and Congreve. Lane and Merriman seem to reflect subtle differences between cool, urbane manservant (cucumber sandwiches) and country butler (cake). Worthing has its own wonderfully literal explanation, in contrast to the more resonant Moncrieff. Fairfax and Cardew suggest Yorkshire and Cornwall respectively. Fairfax may recall Cromwell's general, to whose daughter Andrew Marvell was tutor. Gwendolen Fairfax and Cecily Cardew form a beautifully balanced and musical pairing, symmetrical in syllables but contrasted on the tongue. The Cardew family maintain a firm family tradition that Miss Cicely Cardew was born when Wilde was staying with the family in May 1893. Wilde promptly announced that he would name the heroine of his next play after her. In view of the way many of Wilde's friends distanced themselves from him after 1895, so emphatic a claim seems entirely credible. Indeed, among Wilde's fellow undergraduates at Magdalen College, Oxford, was Arthur Cardew, who appears with Wilde in a contemporary photograph.

The choice of name, apart from its assonance, its combination of sweetness and crispness, its suitability for an apparently innocent young ward in the country, was more than a charming tribute to the infant daughter of old friends. Cardew was the sort of name which sounded right, not just for someone in a play, but for someone whose father had three addresses. The Cardews, and families like them, formed the dominant class in Victorian, imperial England. Their sons were Oxonians. They possessed large accumulations of property; they served in the army; they invented things; one Cardew was the controversial governor of Sierra Leone; another was a Director of the

London and South Coast railway, responsible for the Brighton line, as would be Cicely's father. A consultation of those delightful records, the Army Lists, for 1894 reveals no less than eight Cardews on the Army's books. Their collective careers offer a microcosm of British imperial history: one took part in the battle of Alma—severely wounded, horse shot; another survived the Zulu campaign; a third served in the Burmese Expedition. There are, besides, seven Moncrieffs, and even, on the Indian Supernumerary list, a General Bunbury. George Hay Moncrieff, Major General, was actually in command of the Dublin District at the very moment that Wilde borrowed his name. The England which Wilde wrote about was one still engaged in ruling, or attempting to rule, a large proportion of the world. The Army List is some 1500 pages long. The sheer size of the establishment, active or on the reserve, of the British officers is astonishing. Every individual in the St James's audience must have had a relation or friend, perhaps many relations or friends, in those same Army Lists, which are used by Wilde to authenticate the outrageously improbable. Countless Indian army children were brought up, though usually not lost, by their aunts; the fact that Jack's parents died in India, or at least of India, is an implication so obvious that it did not need to be stated.

Wilde's ability to draw from and lightly suggest the social structures around him, even while he is mocking or undermining them, is remarkable. A glance through the columns of a newspaper such as the *Pall Mall Gazette* for August, 1894, when Wilde was working on *The Importance of Being Earnest* in Worthing, throws up casual echoes and parallels to the play: the revolutionary outrages of continental anarchists; the theft of a handbag at Euston Station (by a clergyman, who escaped imprisonment by entering a temperance home); a relentless correspondence about the London, Brighton and South Coast Railway, and the punctuality, or lack of punctuality, of its trains; and a long article, suitable for the silly season of high summer, "What's in a Name: Some Curiosities of Christening." The piece cites the example of Balzac searching the length and breadth of Paris for the precisely correct name for one of his characters. Wilde's choices, while they have been authenticated for us by a hundred years of performance, were selected with unerring judgment for the ears of their first audiences, so as to convey subtly and subversively the tribal connotations of the English upper-middle classes. The fictions he creates bear an uncanny relationship to the facts. Even the name of an off-stage character such as Markby, inflated to absurdity by its tripling, Markby, Markby, and Markby, commemorates the name of an old established London legal firm which is still active, and still incorporating the name Markby, in 1995, a firm which was known to Robert Ross and therefore, plausibly, also to Wilde. One of the Mr Markby's would certainly have been seen at dinner parties. Jack remarks about the list of generals: "What ghastly names they have!" But they were names which reflected and suggested the experience of Wilde's

audience, who were, by the recognition of their laughter, implicated by them and so, like the townspeople of Gogol's *The Government Inspector*, seduced into laughing at themselves.

Wilde, like Shaw and Joyce, positioned himself "offshore, at a tangent to Ireland's own history," in Professor Marilyn Butler's phrase. "A work of fiction," she comments, "may be at once minutely localized in what it represents and very large in its sense of an audience" (Edgeworth 36-37). A second way in which Wilde opens up his plays to audiences is his reflection of and quotation from other kinds of literature—for example, from the high tradition of comic writing, such as the plays of Congreve and Sheridan, and his glances at the motifs, if not the manner, of Victorian farce. Wilde's social comedies convey, in addition, echoes of the nineteenth-century novel: within the urbane rhythms and references of *An Ideal Husband* can be heard the polished satire of Disraeli's political novels. Behind the distilled essence of *The Importance of Being Earnest* may lie something of the distinctive and ironic style of Wilde's Anglo-Irish predecessor in the dissection of class, gender, and race, Maria Edgeworth, and principally the first of her Tales of Fashionable Life, *Ennui*. The grounds for suggesting this have partly to do with motif, partly with tone.

Edgeworth, like Wilde, operates through the precise and creative use of names:

> Lady Ormsby was just come to the country, with a large party of her fashionable friends—some Irish, some English. Lord and Lady Kilrush; my lady Kildangan, and her daughter the Lady Geraldine—; the knowing widow O'Connor; the English dasher Lady Hauton; the interesting Mrs Norton, separated but not parted from her husband; the pleasant Miss Bland; the three Miss Ormsbys, better known by the name of the Swanlinbar Graces; two English aides-de-camp from the Castle, and a brace of brigadiers; besides other men of inferior note.
>
> (201)

Nearly a century separates this catalogue from *A Woman of No Importance,* but there is a correspondence between Edgeworth's account of Ormsby Villa and Wilde's description of the house party at Hunstanton Chase. The central character of Edgeworth's "Fashionable Tale," Lord Glenthorn, the victim of ennui, lived in his youth a life of extravagance. His servants drank nothing but claret and champagne, and he was at the mercy of tradesmen. (This phase of his life was passed in England, in a manner that Algernon Moncrieff would have recognized.) Later in the story it is revealed, by his Irish wet-nurse Ellinor, that he is not Lord Glenthorn at all: he has been changed at nurse with Ellinor's own baby, Christy O'Donoghoe, now the local blacksmith. The substitution took place at a seaside resort. The proof lies in a scar on Christy's head, received when he was dropped on a fender by a drunken servant. The scar is carefully examined, rather like the injury which Miss Prism's handbag suffered. Later, when the erstwhile

Lord Glenthorn, by this time Christy O'Donoghoe once again, is attempting to marry, he follows his patron's advice, not precisely to be christened again, but at least to change his name.

The woman he wishes to marry is Cecilia—Cecilia Delamere. The author deals with this part of the narrative briskly. Cecilia, like Cecily Cardew, is direct and to the point. "She believed, she said, that a man capable of conquering habitual indolence could not be of a feeble character; and she therefore consented, without hesitation, to intrust her happiness to my care" (320).

In certain respects, the messages conveyed by *Ennui* are in sharp contrast to the polished evasiveness of *The Importance of Being Earnest*. Edgeworth's satire offers a more direct critique of the values of a society intent on achieving wealth and position by any means; and the two main male characters in the story, the protagonist and his friend Devereux, and up by actually earning their living, the one as a lawyer, the other as a civil servant in India. Edgeworth presents the history of a man who discovers the difference between pleasure and happiness. But the remarkably proactive role of the young women, Cecilia and Geraldine, seems to anticipate the assurance of Cecily Cardew and Gwendolen Fairfax. Cecilia is being questioned:

> "As to Lord Glenthorn," said Mrs Delamere, "he was no fool, I promise you. Has he not been living prudently enough these three years? . . ."
>
> "But I have been told," said Cecilia, "that he is quite uninformed, without any taste for literature, and absolutely incapable of exertion—a victim to ennui. How miserable a woman must be with such a husband!"
>
> "But," said Lady Y—, "what could be expected from a young nobleman bred up as Lord Glenthorn was?"
>
> "Nothing," said Cecilia; "and that is the very reason I never wished to see him."

The discussion concludes:

> "Lord bless you child! how little you know of the matter! After all, I dare say, if you had been acquainted with him, you might have been in love yourself with Lord Glenthorn."
>
> "Possibly," said Cecilia, "if I had found him the reverse of what he is reported to be."
>
> (300)

"If I had found him the reverse of what he is reported to be": the phrase might come from Wilde's Cecily. This exchange is overheard through the folding doors by "Mr O'Donoghoe," the erstwhile Lord Glenthorn, in a scene that seems intentionally organized like a play, while the reader is continuously reminded of the artificial nature of the plot by such comments as "Changed at nurse! One hears of such things in novels, but, in real life, I absolutely cannot believe it!" ("In families of high position, strange coincidences are not supposed to occur.")

At an earlier point in the story, Lady Geraldine, locked up in the temple of Minerva by some hoydenish members of the house party, finds herself proposed to by Lord Glenthorn. This is a situation that her formidable mother Lady Kildangan, who exhibits traces of both the Duchess of Berwick and Lady Bracknell, has been striving to engineer: a reversal of Gwendolen's stage-management of Jack. Lady Geraldine, like Gwendolen, is fully able to control the situation, and as they are released she whispers to her proposer, "For mercy's sake, my lord, don't break my poor mother's heart! Never let her know, that a coronet has been within my grasp, and that I have not clutched it." Lady Geraldine departs, in due course, with her husband Devereux, for India, which offers the potential of escape from the constrictions of a colonial Irish society—a shift that prefigures the "world elsewhere" philosophy of Hester Worsley in *A Woman of No Importance.*

Certain elements of plot and theme in *Ennui*—the motif of the exchanged baby, the young man who finds that after all he has a kind of brother, the preoccupation with master and servant—bring *Earnest* to mind, as does the sense of paradox and reversal which permeates the text. These alert one to the possible echo of Edgeworth's Cecilia and Geraldine in Wilde's Cecily and Gwendolen. Maria Edgeworth's assured handling of form, her sharp dissection of social manners, her acute ear for the incriminating rhythms of dialogue, and her depiction of young women who seize the initiative with aplomb and who create and shape their own stories offer a model for Wilde to assimilate and reflect. She, too, looked at life from an unusual angle, and with a sophisticated and penetrating sense of style that encompasses an adroit manipulation of names and titles. As W. J. McCormack has commented, "Maria Edgeworth, like Wilde, understood that style is a miniature politics."

The partnerships of Cecily Cardew and Gwendolen Fairfax, John Worthing and Algernon Moncrieff, Miss Prism and Canon Chasuble, under the presiding queen-empress of Lady Bracknell, form a significant part of Wilde's verbal music and patterned reference.[1] The names and their associations ride the frontier between fact and fiction, between the assured solidity of place and property and power, and the shifting distortions of the surreal and the absurd. The names in his plays demonstrate Wilde's extraordinary power of suggesting more than he states, as he does conclusively by authenticating the fictional triviality of *Earnest* by reference to the most serious book in the English language for the imperial Victorians: the Army List.

Note

1. *The Cardew connection makes one more minor appearance in Wilde's life. The Director of the London, Brighton and South Coast Railway had an engine named after him; it was the Cardew, which always pulled the boat train to Newhaven. If Wilde looked back at England after his release from prison as he left for Dieppe on the cross-channel ferry in May, 1897, he would have seen the Cardew steaming gently on the quay.*

Works Cited

Maria Edgeworth. *Castle Rackrent and Ennui.* Ed. Marilyn Butler. Harmondsworth: Penguin, 1992.

W. J. McCormack. *Ascendancy and Tradition in Anglo-Irish Literary History from 1793 to 1939.* Oxford: Clarendon, 1985.

W. Craven Mackie (essay date summer 1998)

SOURCE: Mackie, W. Craven. "Bunbury Pure and Simple." *Modern Drama* 41, no. 2 (summer 1998): 327-30.

[*In the following essay, Mackie proposes the obituaries as a source for the name Bunbury, a character in Wilde's* The Importance of Being Earnest.]

Sometime in late July 1894 Oscar Wilde wrote to George Alexander requesting an advance of £150 so that he might go away to write a comedy. In that letter he outlines a scenario of the play that within a month and a half would become a rough draft of *The Importance of Being Earnest.* In this early untitled version the names of Jack Worthing, Algernon, Cecily, Gwendolen and Lady Bracknell have yet to be invented. There is yet no play upon the word *earnest* and no Bunbury.[1]

By early August, only a few days after writing to Alexander, Wilde had traveled with his family from London to the seaside resort of Worthing in Sussex, where he continued to work on the new play. In notes that quickly followed and expanded upon the first scenario, Wilde had come up with a working title, *The Guardian.* Further, he had settled on the names Worthing and Gwendolen, had introduced dialogue expressing Gwendolen's passion for the name Ernest and had noted "Mr Bunbury—always ill—."[2]

Since 1960 there has been much speculation about the source for Bunbury. The earliest inquiry and assumption on the subject appeared that year in the London *Sunday Times.* It came from an antiquarian in Cheshire, Reverend Ridgway: "As vicar of Bunbury I have always been puzzled as to why Oscar Wilde decided to pick on this remote village (if he did) to coin his phrase 'bunburying' in *The Importance of Being Earnest.* Can any reader throw light on the link?" William Green includes the letter among the endnotes to his article "Oscar Wilde and the Bunburys" and explains, "Although [Ridgway] did receive some interesting replies to his letter, his investigation came to naught."[3] Thirty years later Kerry Powell would echo Reverend Ridgway's disappointment: "Bunbury's name, like so many in Wilde's plays, is difficult to pin down in terms of its source."[4] Green himself rejects the possibility of place names as a source, arguing instead for names of actual people. He concludes that Bunbury was "a composite" of two contemporary figures, classical scholar Edward

Herbert Bunbury and an acquaintance of the Wilde family in Dublin during Wilde's youth, Henry Shirley Bunbury. Among the replies to Ridgway's inquiry, Green discovered a letter from Henry's son Walter recalling, "My father gave me to understand that it was he whom Wilde had in mind" at the time the play was written. Walter further recalls that his father "was in rather poor health," convincing Green that Henry Shirley Bunbury was indeed "the primary model."[5]

Without crediting Green, Richard Ellmann adopts the family friend thesis: "Many of [Wilde's] relations lived in England, and so did friends like Henry S. Bunbury . . . who would give his name to the errant behaviour of Algernon in *The Importance of Being Earnest.*"[6] Kerry Powell argues that "the concept of Bunburying—and its name—could have been suggested to Wilde by the recent success of *Godpapa*,"[7] an unpublished farce that had enjoyed a modest run in 1891 and in which an aspiring drunk named Bunbury unwittingly facilitates a kind of Bunburying by the hero. Joseph Donohue and Ruth Berggren reason that "Wilde appears to be following his habit of deriving surnames from place names,"[8] citing the village in Cheshire, and Peter Raby dutifully reports that the name can be found in the Army Lists of 1894.[9]

Do any of these speculations, however, provide a logical explanation for what prompted the hastily scribbled note "Mr. Bunbury—always ill"? Wilde had not seen or heard from the family acquaintance for sixteen years. He never met or acknowledged the classical scholar. That he would have had any desire to recall a nearly forgotten play by a rival playwright seems doubtful. And there is no proof that he had any knowledge of the village in Cheshire or of the Bunbury tucked away in the 1500 pages of the Army Lists. "All the evidence," Peter Raby explains, "points to Wilde constructing *The Importance of Being Earnest* with great rapidity and zest, incorporating material which lay conveniently at hand,"[10] bringing into question why any of the usual suggestions concerning Bunbury's origin would have occurred to Wilde at the seaside resort of Worthing in August 1894—particularly since another eminently more "convenient" source was available.

Daily newspapers like the *Times* and the *Pall Mall Gazette* supplied a wealth of topical material for Wilde's comedy: the gold rush in barren southwest Australia, lost luggage in railway stations, a running debate on the virtues of the three-volume novel, and numerous fashionable English names. The newspaper that Wilde most associated with news of fashionable society is identified in Gwendolen's assertion that the announcement of her engagement to Mr. Ernest Worthing "will appear in the *Morning Post* on Saturday at the latest." Announcements of births, marriages and deaths appeared prominently on the front page of the *Morning Post.* Engagements were relegated to page five.

On Monday 23 July 1894 in the *Post,* Wilde could have scanned the following names in the obituary list: Andrew, Beresford, Blofeld, Brooke, Bunbury—Lady Frances

Joanne Bunbury, "aged eighty . . . wife of the late Sir Charles Bunbury . . . at the Manor House, Mildenhall . . . after a sudden and severe attack." Mildenhall is located about sixty miles northeast of London. Notices of Lady Bunbury's funeral appeared in both the *Post* and the *Times* on 24 July.

Then on Wednesday 25 July on the front page of the *Post* under deaths, after Baylis, a second Bunbury: Thomas Charles, "aged eighty-two . . . late 60th Rifles, eldest son of the late General Bunbury . . . at Pembroke House, Freemantle, Southampton," about sixty miles southwest of London. Amazing. Two Bunburys in three days. Typically, the Bunbury name surfaced once or twice a year in the *Post* obituaries, with only one prior instance (7 May) in 1894.

Incidentally, on 30 July, on page five of the *Post,* Wilde could have read that a marriage had been arranged for Ernest Douglas Money.

And then on Tuesday 31 July, again on page one under deaths: Barrett, Bickham, Bonser, Bunbury! Phenomenal odds. Captain Philip Mill Bunbury, "aged seventy . . . late 7th Dragoon Guards, eldest son of the late Hugh Mill Bunbury . . . at Slindon, near Arundel, Sussex," fifty miles south of London and only twelve miles from Worthing. All three Bunburys were, like Algy's fictional invalid, located well "into the country."

Surely Wilde must have been amused and delighted by this sudden and convenient Bunbury epidemic. One can imagine him with his family, passing through Victoria Station to the Brighton line, joking that "to lose three Bunburys looks like carelessness." Or perhaps in answer to the question "Is Bunbury dead?" Wilde replied, "No. But he's always ill."

As fortuitous as this timely series of obituaries may have been, it is doubtful that Wilde would have noticed had not the particular recurring name possessed such resonance and potential meaning. Three Beresfords or Blofelds would have been of little use. Of course, Wilde was perfectly capable of creating Bunbury without assistance from external sources, but it appears there was no need to do so.[11]

For Wilde, at that time and place, the inspiration for Bunbury was hardly more subtle than that which prompted the name Jack Worthing. As an experienced comic and social commentator, Wilde knew the importance of building upon material that was familiar to his audience, which, like Wilde, relied constantly upon the newspapers. Also, the specific chronology for the progress of this inspiration confirms that the last week of July 1894 was a fairly productive period in the making of **The Importance of Being Earnest.**

Notes

1. Peter Raby, "The Making of *The Importance of Being Earnest*: An unpublished letter from Oscar Wilde," *Times Literary Supplement* (20 December 1991), 13.

2. Peter Raby, "The Origins of *The Importance of Being Earnest*," *Modern Drama* 37 (1994), 143.

3. William Green, "Oscar Wilde and the Bunburys," *Modern Drama* 21 (1978), 76.

4. Kerry Powell, *Oscar Wilde and the Theatre of the 1890s* (Cambridge, 1990), 183.

5. Green, 72. See note 3.

6. Richard Ellmann, *Oscar Wilde* (New York, 1988), 37.

7. Powell, 127. See note 4.

8. Joseph Donohue & Ruth Berggren, ed., *Oscar Wilde's "The Importance of Being Earnest": A Reconstructive Critical Edition of the Text of the First Production* (Gerrards Cross, 1995), 123.

9. Peter Raby, "'The Persons of the Play': Some Reflections on Wilde's Choice of Names in *The Importance of Being Earnest*," *Nineteenth Century Theatre* 23 (1995), 71.

10. Raby, "Origins," 143. See note 2.

11. To his credit, William Green was on track in pursuing a source among actual people.

SALOMÉ

PRODUCTION REVIEWS

***Critic* (review date 12 May 1894)**

SOURCE: Review of *Salomé. Critic* 21, no. 638 (12 May 1894): 331.

[*In the following negative review of* Salomé, *the critic discusses Wilde's usage of dialogue and theme from various other literary sources.*]

The downward course of a certain current in English literature and art has probably not reached an end in Oscar Wilde's ***Salomé.*** Some one will, doubtless, arise who shall be as incoherent as Blake, as hysterical as Rossetti, as incapable of decent reserve as Swinburne, and as great a humbug as Wilde. But it is doubtful whether the latter's cleverness in patching up sham monsters can go much farther. A large part of his material he gets from the Bible, a little has once belonged to Flaubert. He borrows from Maeterlinck his trick of repeating stupid phrases until a glimpse of meaning seems almost a flash of genius. But it must be admitted that he adds something of his own, and that what he has taken bears but the same relation to what he has made of it as does the farmer's pumpkin to the small boy's bogy lantern. A single example will perhaps suffice to show the nature of his improvements. There is a vulgar simile that likens a pair of black eyes to "burnt holes in a blanket." This Mr. Wilde expands into:—"It is his eyes above all that are terrible. They are like *black holes burnt by torches in a tapestry of Tyre.*" The play was originally written in French, and Mr. Wilde has been so happy as to secure a noble lord as his translator into English.

His illustrator, Mr. Aubrey Beardsley, searches in as many fields for the elements of his fantastic drawings. He takes from modern fashion plates, ancient designs for jewelry, the inevitable Japanese print and the caricatures of Caran d'Ache. He has the boldness to steal Whistler's butterfly and Willette's Pierrot. He answers the conundrum about the morality of Burne-Jones's type of beauty by employing it to convey decidedly immoral suggestions. Several of his pictures appear to have nothing to do with the text, but he satirizes Oscar as a showman whose "grand attraction" is his grotesque Herodias. He has the decorative instinct which tells him where to put a line or a spot of black, and he misuses it as wilfully as some Frenchmen do their more valuable artistic gifts. Five hundred copies of the book have been printed "for England"; how many for America does not appear.

Edward E. Hale Jr. (essay date 1 July 1894)

SOURCE: Hale, Edward E., Jr. "Signs of Life in Literature." *Dial* 17 (1 July 1894): 11-13.

[*In the following essay, Hale contrasts Hamlin Garland's* Crumbling Idols *and Wilde's* Salomé, *providing a mixed review of Wilde's play.*]

There are in Paris during the Spring of the year a good many exhibitions of pictures which trouble the soul of the conscientious lover of the arts. Not only at the two great Salons are there generally certain alarming manifestations, but there are also smaller collections gathered together by Independents, Rosicrucians, or other such persons, in which the wildest gymnastics in the name of art are not only allowed but encouraged. Dazed and antagonized by these indulgences, the feeling of many an ordinary and honest art-lover must be, "Almost thou persuadest me to be a Philistine." Fortunately, however, Paris herself furnishes an antidote to any such despair, in the annual exhibition of the pictures and sculptures entered in competition for the Prix de Rome. One goes to these shameless revelations of academic horror, and becomes in a great degree reconciled to the existence of new notions in art, however extravagant. They really do but little harm (except to their ingenious sponsors), and they are extremely useful in keeping up a healthy circulation of ideas.

Now I am not familiar with any evil things in literature analogous to these Prix de Rome exhibitions, unless perhaps we might count college oratorical contests and commencements. But the feeling that there might be something worse should make us look with benignity, if not pleasure, on such books as Mr. Hamlin Garland's *Crumbling Idols* and Mr. Oscar Wilde's *Salomé*. Different as they are in all other points, both books are of that foam and froth of literature which is indicative of true life and action somewhere, which is itself shortly blown away and lost to sight and remembrance.

Mr. Garland's book, we are informed by an unknown sponsor, is "a vigorous plea for the recognition of youth and a protest against the despotism of tradition." It might have been added that it is an assertion of the necessity of Americanism in American Literature. Surely these things are very good things, looked at in their ordinary light. But when we look at them in Mr. Garland's light, it must be confessed that the feeling is not one of approbation but of irritation. One is led to inquire, What earthly use can there be in Mr. Garland's saying all this? For the main points in Mr. Garland's discourse are by no means new. He takes Walt Whitman's thesis as to a native literature, looks at it in the light of the experience of the last twenty-five years, and puts forth the whole thing as his own prophecy for the future.

As one reads *Crumbling Idols* it comes more and more strongly to mind that the book is a sort of apology for existence on the part of its author. Now Mr. Garland of course need make no such apology. "Main Travelled Roads" and "Prairie Songs" are reasons enough for anyone's existing, temporarily. They are their own excuse for being; no one doubted the fact, until Mr. Garland set himself to force us into admitting it. For, unfortunately, Mr. Garland is not persuasive: he is bellicose, obstreperous, blatant. Nobody could possibly agree with him, whatever he said.

The real difficulty seems to be that Mr. Garland, being himself able to write excellent things of a certain sort, cannot conceive that there can be anything else excellent of a kind totally different. Feeling himself very virtuous, he becomes enraged that anyone else should venture to be still attached to cakes and ale. Now this is all wrong. Literature in America may never come to anything without plenty of local color and provincialism (to use Mr. Garland's expressions), but it will never be a great literature so long as it has nothing besides. Mr. Garland would do us but poor service if he could persuade people to write nothing but "local novels."

But of course one need not take the book very seriously. Mr. Garland's engrossing fear seems to be that Americans will turn their entire attention to writing "blank-verse tragedies on Columbus or Washington," or that they will "copy the last epics of feudalism." Such an apprehension seems to have very slight basis. It is probable that during the last year there have been thousands of what Mr. Garland would call "local" stories written by young America for every single blank-verse tragedy or epic of feudalism that has seen the light this side the Atlantic.

Everybody writes "local," stories nowadays; it is as natural as whooping-cough. There is no need of encouragement: to tell the truth, a little restraint would do no harm. For, even with the best of intentions, one may write a "local" story so badly that it will be worse than a blank-verse tragedy on Washington or anybody else,

But to turn from such serious foolishness to a more sprightly trifler. Mr. Oscar Wilde never troubles one with taking himself too seriously, and the history of *Salomé* is Oscar Wilde all over. It was written in French and produced in Paris. Desirous then of favoring his own countrymen, Mr. Wilde made preparation to present it in London. In this worthy attempt, however, he was hindered—so the papers told us—by some official folly which enraged him so much that he was even strongly tempted to stop being an Englishman, in favor of that less imbecile people across the Channel. But not wishing to keep his anger forever. Mr. Wilde finally allowed his noble friend Lord Alfred Bruce Douglas to do the play into English. It was then "pictured," as the phrase is, by Mr. Aubrey Beardsley, and is now ready for the delight of a somewhat indifferent world.

Such an extraordinary conjunction of affectations is ominous. But, strangely enough, there are some things in *Salomé* that are good. It is impossible to read it without feeling curiously moved and stirred. The careless talk of the loungers on the terrace, the soldiers and the Cappadocian, is good; the squabbling of the Jews, the Pharisee, the Sadducee, the Nazarene, is good. So, also, is Herod,—indeed the character of Herod is quite the best conceived thing in the play, as his description of his treasure is the best written. The play may well have been very effective on the stage, for there is a constant feeling of movement, of life, and it is certainly worth reading now that it is published.

With all this, however, the play is wholly ephemeral. Its action is trivial and its dialogue affected. Its ideas, and its language too, are extravagances, without much more foundation than the extravagances of Mr. Hamlin Garland. But while in Mr. Garland we have the prophet of Literature as Life, we have in Mr. Wilde the follower of Literature as Art. Mr. Garland is a "veritist," and prefers the fresh novelties of nature. But Mr. Wilde seeks beauty, in art and art's most latent subtleties. He contrives expressions and conceptions of the most curious and self-conscious refinement, of the strangest and most ultra-precious distinction. As ever, he scorns the ordinary, the every-day, the generally pleasing, and is unremitting to attain the romantic beauty, the strange, the wonderful, the remote, the reward of no art but the most devoted, the delight of no taste but the most distinguished.

As such, his work lends itself eminently to the illustration of Mr. Aubrey Beardsley. Mr. Aubrey Beardsley receives a good many hard words nowadays,—and certainly his pictures are strange things, more affected than Oscar Wilde himself, and more remote from obvious apprehension.

What one is first inclined to criticise in Mr. Beardsley is his lack of originality. His pictures remind us of almost every phase of art that has ever existed; or, at any rate, of every phase which had ever a tinge of the grotesque or the trivial in its character. From the bald priestly pictures mingled among Egyptian hieroglyphics, down to the graceful frivolities of Willette of the Red Windmill. Mr. Beardsley seems to have laid everything under contribution. His work seems by turns one thing and then another— Japanese, Gothic, Preraphaelite, what you will. So it seems at first. But the great excellence is that, however Protean. Mr. Aubrey Beardsley, like Satan in *Paradise Lost* is always himself, even in the midst of his disguises. Just what is his own quality, is hard to say; but there can be little doubt that it exists, and it would be worth somebody's while to determine it in the shifting dazzle of his influences,—to fix it for an instant for us, to get its true character and flavor unadulterated. But whatever be his quality, it is eminently in keeping with the work of Mr. Oscar Wilde.

Of our two literary eccentrics, some will prefer Mr. Wilde and some Mr. Garland. If they could be seized each with an admiration for the other, it would have an excellent effect on the work of both. But even as they are, they are good evidence of life in literature, and an assurance that it will not yet awhile harden down into utter conventionalism.

CRITICAL COMMENTARY

William Saunders (essay date September 1922)

SOURCE: Saunders, William. "Oscar Wilde's *Salomé*." *Drama Magazine* 12, no. 10 (September 1922): 335.

[*In the following essay, Saunders considers* Salomé *as "essentially Greek in character" and "one of the greatest tragedies of recent times."*]

About twenty years ago, after having completed the usual three years' course in French grammar and syntax, I devoted a year to reading practically nothing except modern novels and plays in the French language. The purpose I had in view in following out this self-imposed curriculum was the acquisition of as extensive a vocabulary as possible, and of such conversational fluency as an adequate study of contemporary dialogue in a foreign language alone can give. In making a choice of works for the purpose of this study, I adopted no system of purely scientific selection, beyond the fact that the periods of publication of the various works I made use of, had to be of comparatively recent date say, not later than ten years back. Within this category, all was fish that came to my net, and during that year I read several hundred plays. Yet although, as I have since had every reason to believe, I completely effected the aim I had set myself, I do not now remember more than a dozen of even the titles of the plays I devoured. But there was one of these plays which made so deep and vivid an impression upon my mind that it has to this day never been erased, and it is as clear now as it was on the occasion upon which it was first engraved.

The play in question was Oscar Wilde's **Salomé**. I remember all the inauspicious circumstances of that memorable encounter. It was a cold November evening and, rummaging through the scanty collection of French plays in the reference department of our local free library, I suddenly came upon a small volume dated 1893, and claiming to have been issued from the *Librairie de l'Art Indépendant,* Paris, and *Elkin Mathews et John Lane, Londres—Salomé, Drame en un acte.* Of what particularly attracted me to the volume, I have no clear recollection, but no doubt it was partly the fact that it was by Oscar Wilde, with two at least of whose plays I was already familiar, and partly the curious and bizarre device with its motto *"Non hic piscis omnium,"* on the title page. I read the play at a single sitting, under the impression all the time that it was a translation from an English work by the famous dramatist. Although later on I had added the volume to my own private library, I did not again read it until the evidence in a libel action gave it such an advertisement as nothing else in the world could have accomplished. Yet all the time the powerful and salient aspects of the play, and the rare imagery of the language in which it is couched, never faded from my memory. During the long interval of more than twenty years I thought about it often and on more than one occasion meant to read it again, but somehow I never found either the time or opportunity until the necessity of absolutely making a renewed acquaintance with the play, in view of my original and vivid impression of it was forced upon me by the evidence submitted at the trial in question.

On that occasion the chief indictment against the play seemed to lie in the frequency with which the various characters refer to the moon, and the evidence of several eminent alienists was given to prove that such references were understood only by moral perverts. That Oscar Wilde, when he wrote the play, intended his lunar allusions to be taken in that sense, I do not for one moment believe. If the witnesses who argued in the manner referred to are right, then the almanac is the most dangerous book in circulation, and the same reasons that were urged against **Salomé** are equally potent for the banning of that useful, if too frequently uninspired, publication. The whole of the evidence, so far as it tended to the condemnation of this play, was, I am convinced, entirely *ex post facto.* Had the career of the author ended otherwise than it ended, I doubt that we should ever have heard anything about the perverted morality of his work. **Salomé** is essentially a work of art, just as its creator was before everything, an artist.

Wilde lived at the time when the Wagnerian influence in music was beginning to make itself universally felt, but this influence was by no means confined to music and

musicians alone. The *leit-motif* principle, based as it was upon a foundation of pure artistry, exercised a fascination, not only upon the musicians, but to almost as great an extent upon the writers and poets of the eighties and nineties of the last century. Wilde early evinced a fondness for it. We find it both in **A Woman of No Importance** and in **Lady Windermere's Fan,** the end of Act 1, of the former play, for example. Mrs. Allenby and Lord Illingworth are *tête-à-tête,* discussing the ingenious young American, Hester Worsley, in the course of which, the following dialogue takes place:

MRS. ALLENBY:

You think there is no woman in the world who would object to being kissed?

LORD ILLINGWORTH:

Very few.

MRS. ALLENBY:

Miss Worsley would not let you kiss her.

LORD ILLINGWORTH:

Are you sure?

MRS. ALLENBY:

Quite.

LORD ILLINGWORTH:

What do you think she'd do if I kissed her?

MRS. ALLENBY:

Either marry you, or strike you across the face with her glove.

And at the very end of the act, Lord Illingworth sees Mrs. Arbuthnot's letter on a table, and taking it up, he looks at the envelope and thus rounds off the conversation:

LORD ILLINGWORTH:

What a curious handwriting! It reminds me of the handwriting of a woman I used to know year ago.

MRS. ALLENBY:

Who?

LORD ILLINGWORTH:

Oh! no one. No one in particular. A woman of no importance.

Now, these are clearly *leit-motifen,* especially designed as fore-shadowing the *dénouement* of the play. When, in the final scene, Mrs. Arbuthnot, the woman that Lord Illingworth had ruined, had been left alone, while her son and his *fiancée,* Miss Worsley, go for a turn in the garden together, in the little house in which she had endeavoured to hide herself, she is visited again by her lover of former days. He trys to reopen friendly relations but is repulsed.

LORD ILLINGWORTH:

[*Rises slowly and goes over to table where his hat and gloves are.* MRS. ARBUTHNOT *is standing close to the table. He picks up one of the gloves and begins putting it on.*] There is not much then for me to do here, Rachael?

MRS. ARBUTHNOT:

Nothing.

LORD ILLINGWORTH:

It is good-bye, is it?

MRS. ARBUTHNOT:

Forever, I hope, this time, Lord Illingworth.

LORD ILLINGWORTH:

How curious! At this moment you look exactly as you looked the night you left me twenty years ago. You have just the same expression in your mouth. Upon my word, Rachael, no woman ever loved me as you did. Why, you gave yourself to me like a flower, to do anything I liked with. You were the prettiest of playthings, the most fascinating of small romances. . . . (*Pulls out watch*) Quarter to two! Must be strolling back to Hunstanton. Don't suppose I shall see you there again. I'm sorry, I am, really. It's been an amusing experience to have met amongst people of one's own rank, and treated quite seriously too, one's mistress, and one's—"

[MRS. ARBUTHNOT *snatches up glove and strikes* LORD ILLINGWORTH *across the face with it.* LORD ILLINGWORTH *starts. He is dazed by the insult of his punishment.* GERALD *and* HESTER *return immediately after* LORD ILLINGWORTH *has gone.* GERALD *goes to table L. C. for his hat. On turning round he sees* LORD ILLINGWORTH'S *glove lying on the floor, and picks it up.*]

GERALD:

Hallo, Mother, whose glove is this? You have had a visitor. Who was it?

MRS. ARBUTHNOT :

[Turning round] Oh! no one. No one in particular. A man of no importance.

But to return to the so-called luner allusions, we have this in *Salomé*:

Une grande terrasse dans le palais d'Herode donnant sur la salle de festin. Des soldats sont accoudés sur le balcon. A droite il y a un énorme escalier. A gauche, au fond, une ancienne citerne entourèe d'un mur de bronèe vert. Clair de lune.

LE JEUNE SYRIEN:

Comme la princesse Salomé est belle ce soir!

LE PAGE D'HERODIAS:

Regardeê la lune. La lune a l'air très étrange. On dirait une femme qui soit d'un tombeau.

Elle ressemble à une femme morte. On dirait qu'elle cherche des morts.

LE JEUNE SYRIEN:

Elle a l'air très étrange. Elle ressemble à une petite princesse qui porte une voile jaune, eta des pieds d'argent. Elle ressemble à une princesse qui a des pieds comme des petites colombes blanches* . . . On dirait qu'elle danse.

LE PAGE:

Elle est comme une femme morte. Elle va très lentement.

When Salomé enters from the banqueting-hall, she also remarks upon the appearance of the moon, and it may perhaps be said that this is the one instance in the play where the reference might have been omitted without doing violence to the principle involved:

Que c'est bon de voir la lune! Elle ressemble à une petite pièce de monnaie. On dirait une toute petite fleur d'argent. Elle est froide et chaste, la lune. . . . Je suis sûre qu'elle est vierge. . . . Qui, elle est vierge. Elle ne s'est jamais souillés. Elle ne s'est jamais donnée aux hommes, comme les autres Déesses.

It is a tragic note that these lunar allusions are designed to strike, and never throughout the whole of the drama is this more apparent than when, on the occasion after the young Syrian has ordered the prophet to be brought out in response to Salomé's demand, the page again remarks:

Oh! comme la lune a l'air étrange![1] On dirait la main d'une morte qui cherche à se couvrir avec un linceul,

And the Syrian replies:

Elle a l'air très étrange. On dirait une petite princesse qui a des yeux d'ambre. A travers les nuages de mousseline elle sourit comme une petite princesse.

And after the prophet has appeared and cursed and prophesied as was his wont, Salomé, dwelling upon his emaciated condition, remarks:

Je suis sûre qu'il est chaste, autant que la lune. Il ressemble à un rayon de lune, à un rayon d'argent.

And again: *Les roses du jardin de la reine d'Arabie ne sont pas aussi blanches que ton corps. . . . ni le sien de la lune quand elle couche sur le sien de la mer.*

But when she has been repulsed once, she retracts and curses his body:

Ton corps est hideux. . . . Les longues nuits noires, les nuits ou la lune ne se montre pas, ou les étoiles ont peur, ne sont pas aussi noires.

The first real manifestation of the impending tragedy occurs however, when the young Syrian kills himself on realizing that the passion of Salomé for John the Baptist is indeed an undoubted fact, and in the torrent of grief which his friend the page immediately pours out, he claims to find a realization of what the moon had foretold:

Je savais bien que la lune cherchait un mort, mais je ne savais pas que c'était lui qu'elle cherchait, Ah! pourquoi ne l'ai-je pas cachè de la lune? Si je l'avais caché dans une caverne elle ne l'aurait pas vu."

The strange mystical appearance of the moon strikes Herod in much the same manner as it has done to the others, when he enters from the banqueting-hall, with Herodias and all his court. But to the latter, hard, practical, and utterly lacking in artistic taste, or appreciation of the beautiful, the moon is just the moon. This is one of the most brilliant strokes of genius that Wilde had ever made:

HEROD:

La lune a l'air très étrange ce soir. N'est-ce pas que la lune a l'air très étrange? On dirait une femme hystèrique, une femme hystérique qui va cherchant des amants partout. Elle est nue aussi. Elle est toute nue. Les nueges cherchant a la vétir, mais elle ne veut pas. Elle se montre toute nue dans le ciel. Elle chancelle à travers les nueges comme une femme ivre. . . . Je suis sûr qu'elle cherche des amants. . . . N'est ce pas qu'elle chancelle comme une femme ivre? Elle ressemble à une femme hystérique, n'est-ce pas?

HÉRODIAS:

Non. La lune ressemble à la lune, c'est tout. . . .

And evidently with this still simmering in her mind, Herodias, bored nearly to death by the wrangling of the Jews, some time afterwards flashes out:

Ces gens lá sont fous. Ils ont trop regardé la lune . . .

And still again we hear the voice of worldly wisdom when John having prophesied in these terms:

En ce jour la le soleil deviendra noir comme un sac de poü et la lune deviendra comme du sang, et les étoiles du ciel tomberont sur la terre comme des figues vertes tombent d'un figuier, et les rois de la terre auront peur.

The queen replies:

Ah! Ah! Je voudrais bien voir ce jour dont il parle, on la lune deviendra comme du sang et on des étoiles tomberont sur la terre comme des figues vertes. Ce prophète parle comme un homme ivre.

The words there attributed to John are strictly Scriptural, although there is no Biblical authority as to their having actually been uttered by the Baptist.[2]

The crux of the tragedy is Salomé's Dance of the Seven Veils, and it is to that and the all-pervading death theme that the *leit-motifen* apply. While Salomé's slaves are in the act of removing her sandals, and arraying her head and face in the famous seven veils, in preparation for the dance, Herod remarks:

Ah! vous alleè danser pieds nus! C'est bien! C'est bien! Vos petits pieds seront comme des colombes blanches. Ils resembleront à des petites fleurs blanches qui dansent sur un arbre.

Compare this with the passage in the first speech of the young Syrian, and the point of the argument will at once appear. Herod continues:

"Ah! regardez la lune! Elle est devenue rouge. Elle est devenue rouge comme du sang. Ah! le prophète l'a bien prédit. Il a prédit que la lune deviendrait rouge comme du sang. N'est-ce pas qu'il a prédit cela? Vous avec tous entendu. La lune est devenue rouge comme du sang. Ne le voyez-vous pas?

Herodias, still sceptical and sarcastic, assents:

Je le vois bien, et les étoiles tombent comme des figues vertes, n'est ce pas? Et le soleil devient noir comme un sac de poil, et les rois de la terre ont peur. Cela au moins on le voit. Pour une fois dans sa vie le prophéte a eu raison. Les rois de la terre ont peur. . . .

What follows in reference to the moon has little significance. The real crisis of the play is the dance, and all that then succeeds is the merely inevitable consequence of that tremendous episode. The king had promised to give the daughter of Herodias anything that she chose to ask, "even to the half of his kingdom," as a reward for her dancing, and when she demands the head of the Baptist on a silver charger, he immediately repents his promise, and offers her anything else she cares to ask for. In the most entrancing language, he reels off a catalogue of all his possessions from which she is free to take whatever she fancies, if only she will not ask for such a gruesome thing as the severed head of a half crazy prophet. In his garden he has a hundred wonderful white peacocks,—*"la pluie vient quand ils crient, et quand ils se pavanent la lune se montre au ciel,"*—fifty of these he offers to Salomé and promises that *"ils vous suivront partout, et au milieu d'eux vous serez comme la lune dans un grand nuage blanc."* And where should one derive a more beautiful figure of speech than Herod's description of his four-tier collar of pearls?—*"On dirait des lunes enchainées de rayons d'argent. On dirait cinquante lunes captives dans un filet d'or."* And from the catalogue of his possessions,—*"J'ai des sélénites qui changent quand la lune change et deviennent pâles quand elles voient le soleil. J'ai des saphirs grands comme des oeufs et bleus comme des fleurs bleus. La mer erre dedans, at la lune ne vient jamais troubler le bleu de ses flots."*

At last the crime is consummated, and, overcome with horror, the terrified king desires only to hide, and to be hidden:

Viens! Je ne veux pas rester ici. Viens, je te dis. Je suis sûr qu'il va arriver un malheur. Manassé, Issachar, Ozias, éteignez les flambeaux. Je ne veux pas regarder les choses. Je ne veux pas que les choses me regardent. Eteignez les flambeaux. Cachez la lune? Cachez les étoiles? Cachons-nous dans notre palais, Hérodias. Je commence à avoir peur.

And as the slaves obey his order to extinguish the torches, the stars likewise, as if in obedience to his will, disappear, and a great black cloud passes over the moon and obliterates it from the view. It is then, in the darkened court, that Salomé kisses the mouth of the dead head on the charager, and when once more the moon comes out, it reveals to Herod the woman who had thus brought him to shame, in a state of ecstacy and exaltation, and his crisp and rapid command, "*Tuez cette femme!*" brings the tragedy to its logical and inevitable conclusion.

Its logical and inevitable end! *Salomé* might as easily have been a tragedy of Euripides as an essay in histrionic creation by the greatest dramatic epigrammatist of the nineteenth century. The tragedy is essentially Greek in character, and after making the necessary allowances for the difference in periods, purely Euripidean in style. From the first word to the last, the inevitability of the tragedy is clearly demonstrable, and the *leit-motifen* merely accentuate the fact. The atmosphere of gloom and tragedy is never absent, but a gleam of light does occasionally fall across the scene,—a spark of wit suddenly flaring up, blazing forth with all the glamour of Wilde's genius for a moment, and then as quickly dying out again; or a flash of passionate love borne along in a chariot of momentary happiness that more than atones for the age of misery it leaves behind,—and there is surely no straining of metaphors in utilizing the moon as the symbol of such resplendent episodes. Like the plot of the Greek tragedy, that of *Salomé* evolves, and develops in a scene of shadow and depression, but if all is darkness, there are yet degrees and differences of its intensity, and there could be no apter exemplification in concrete form of this, than that which the author, with the true and unhesitating confidence of genius, has actually adopted. The point of my argument then centers in this, that the tragedy of *Salomé,* being Greek in conception and character, is dependent to a large extent for its power and terrifying qualities upon figures that are Greek in spirit and pagan in effect. Yet there is a vast difference between pure Hellenic paganism on the one hand, and moral obliquity on the other, and to suggest that the one term connotes the other, or *vice versa,* is indeed merely to attempt the reconciliation of opposites one with another, and the comparison of things that are absolutely unlike. Apart from its alleged moral degeneracy, a fault which, in spite of the *dicta* of some of the so-called greatest men of our time, *Salomé* is one of the greatest tragedies of recent times, and had its author never written another line, there is enough genius embodied in the ninety pages on which it lies,—not emblamed, but a virile and living force for good, and a source of never-ending intellectual joy and satisfaction to all who are capable of appreciating it, to ensure for him an immortality in the world of artistic humanity, and an everlasting niche in the Valhalla of literature, and of pure and unquestioned psychological delineation.

Notes

1. This was a favorite simile of the young Syrian. Later on, referring to Salomé, he remarks, "*La princesse a cache son visage derriere son eventail! Ses petites mains blanches s'agitent comme des colombes qui s'envelent vers leurs colombiers.*" And again, "*Elle est comme une colombe qui s'est egaree.*" The passages so treated are the really significant ones from the *leit-motif* point of view.

2. See Matthew, xxiv-29.

Richard Ellmann (essay date spring 1969)

SOURCE: Ellmann, Richard. "Overtures to Wilde's *Salomé*." *TriQuarterly* 15 (spring 1969): 45-64.

[*In the following essay, Ellmann traces the influence of Wilde's friendships with John Ruskin and Walter Pater on his* Salomé.]

Salomé, after having danced before the imaginations of European painters and sculptors for a thousand years, in the nineteenth century turned her beguilements to literature. Heine, Flaubert, Mallarmé, Huysmans, Laforgue and Wilde became her suitors. Jaded by exaltations of nature and of humanism, they inspected with something like relief a Biblical image of the *un*natural. Mario Praz, bluff, and skeptical of Salomé's allurements, seeks to limit them by arguing that she became the type of no more than the *femme fatale.* By type he means, he says, something "like a neuralgic area. Some chronic ailment has created a zone of weakened resistance, and whenever an analogous phenomenon makes itself felt, it immediately confines itself to this predisposed area, until the process becomes a matter of mechanical monotony."[1] But like most medical metaphors, this one doesn't apply easily to the arts, where repetition of subject is not a certain contra-indication to achievement. Most of these writers were conspicuous for their originality, and if they embraced so familiar a character from Biblical history, it was to accomplish effects they intended to make distinctive. As there are many Iseults, many Marys, so there were many Salomés, without monotony.

The fact that Wilde's *Salomé* is a play, and a completed one, distinguishes it from other versions and helps to make it more original than Mr. Praz would have us believe. Mallarmé was not merely flattering when he congratulated Wilde on the "definitive evocation" of Salomé,[2] or when he took care to avoid seeming to copy Wilde when he returned to work on his own *Hérodiade.*[3] Wilde's simple sentences and repeated words may indeed owe something to Maeterlinck or even (as a contemporary critic suggested) to Ollendorff—the Berlitz of that age—but they have become so habitual in modern drama as to seem anticipatory rather than derivative. The extreme concentration upon a single episode which is like an image, with a synchronized moon changing color from pale to blood-red in keeping with the action, and an atmosphere of frenzy framed in exotic chill, confirms Yeats's oblique acknowledgment that he had learned as much from Wilde as from the Noh drama for his dance plays.[4] A torpid tetrarch (three Herods telescoped into one), lusting yet inert, a prophet clamoring from a well below the floorboards, are more congenial figures now that Beckett has accustomed us to paralysis, senile drivelling, voices from ashcans, and general thwart.

Mr. Praz, quick to deny Wilde any novelty, insists that the play's culminating moment, when Salomé kisses the severed head of Iokanaan, is borrowed from Heine's *Atta Troll*.[5] But in Heine's version kissing the head is a punishment after Herodias's death, not a *divertissement* before it, and the tone of caricature is quite unlike that of perverted horror which Wilde evokes. If some source has to be found—and it always has—I offer tentatively a dramatic poem called *Salomé* published in Cambridge, Massachusetts, in 1862, by a young Harvard graduate named J. C. Heywood,[6] and subsequently republished during the 1880s in London in the form of a trilogy. I have to admit that in Heywood as in Heine, it is Herodias, not Salomé, who kisses the head, but at least she does so while still alive, and in a sufficiently grisly way. Wilde knew one part of Heywood's trilogy—he reviewed it in 1888, three years before writing his own play[7]—and he may well have glanced at the other parts. Still, he isn't really dependent on Heywood either, since he exchanges mother for daughter and, unlike Heywood, makes this monstrous kissing the play's climax. [*Author adds in a footnote*: According to E. Gomez Carrillo, a young Guatemalan writer who saw much of Wilde during the composition of the play, other details changed considerably in the planning, but the climax was always the same.[8]].

To read Heywood or other writers about Salomé is to come to a greater admiration for Wilde's ingenuity. The general problem that I want to inquire into is what the play probably meant to Wilde and how he came to write it. Villainous women were not his usual subject, and even if they had been, there were others besides Salomé he could have chosen. The reservoir of villainous women is always brimming. The choice of Salomé would seem to inhere in her special relationship to John the Baptist and Herod. Sources offer little help in understanding this, and we have to turn to what might be called praeter-sources, elements which so pervaded Wilde's imaginative life as to become presences. Such a presence Amadis was for Don Quixote, or Vergil for Dante. In pursuing these I will offer no *explication de texte,* but what may well appear a divagation; perhaps to give it critical standing I should pronounce it *divagation,* though I hope to persuade you of its clandestine relevance. It includes, at any rate, those fugitive associations, often subliminal, which swarm beneath the fixed surface of the work, and which are as pertinent as is that surface to any study of the author's mind.

It will be necessary, therefore, to retrace certain of Wilde's close relationships. If Rilke is right in finding a few moments in a writer's life to be initiatory, then such an initiatory experience took place when Wilde left Ireland for England. He later said that the two turning-points in his life occurred "when my father sent me to Oxford, and when society sent me to prison."[9] Wilde matriculated at Magdalen College, Oxford, on October 11, 1874, at the age of nineteen. The two men he had most wanted to know at that time, he said, were Ruskin and Pater,[10] both, conveniently enough, installed at the same place. He managed to meet Ruskin within a month, and though he didn't meet Pater so quickly, during his first three months at Oxford he made the acquaintance of Pater's *Studies in the History of the Renaissance,*[11] which he soon called his "golden book,"[12] and subsequently referred to in a portentous phrase as "that book which has had such a strange influence over my life."[13]

Three weeks after Wilde arrived, Ruskin gave a series of lectures on Florentine painting. During one of them he proposed to his students that, instead of developing their bodies in pointless games, in learning "to leap and to row, to hit a ball with a bat,"[14] they join him in improving the countryside. He proposed to turn a swampy lane near Ferry Hincksey into a flower-bordered country road. Such muscular effort would be ethical rather than narcissistic, medieval rather than classical. [*Author adds in a footnote*: Pater, on the other hand, much preferred the activities of what he called in italics the palaestra.]. Although Oscar Wilde found rising at dawn more difficult than most men, he overcame his languor for Ruskin's sake. He would later brag comically that he had had the distinction of being allowed to fill "Mr. Ruskin's especial wheelbarrow" and even of being instructed by the master himself in the mysteries of wheeling such an object from place to place. At the end of term Ruskin was off to Venice, and Wilde could again lie late abed, comfortable in the thought that, as he said, "there was a long mound of earth across that swamp which a lively imagination might fancy was a road."[15] The merely external signs of this noble enterprise soon sank from sight, but Wilde remembered it with affectionate respect, and his later insistence on functionalism in decoration and in women's dress, and on socialism based upon self-fulfillment in groups, were in the Ferry Hincksey tradition.

The road proved also to be the road to Ruskin. Wilde met his exalted foreman often during the ensuing years. In 1888, sending him a book, he summed up his feelings in this effusive tribute: "The dearest memories of my Oxford days are my walks and talks with you, and from you I learned nothing but what was good. How else could it be? There is in you something of prophet, of priest, and of poet, and to you the gods gave eloquence such as they have given to none other, so that your message might come to us with the fire of passion, and the marvel of music, making the deaf to hear, and the blind to see."[16] That (like this prose) the prophet had weaknesses, made him if anything more prophetlike. Wilde was aware of Ruskin's weaknesses as of his virtues. His letter of November 28, 1879, by which time he had taken his Oxford degree, mentions that he and Ruskin were going that night to see Henry Irving play Shylock, following which he himself was going on to the Millais ball. "How odd it is," Wilde remarks.[17] The oddity lay not only in attending this particular play with the author of *The Stones of Venice,* but in proceeding afterwards to a ball which celebrated the marriage of John Everett Millais's daughter. Mrs. Millais had for six years been Mrs. Ruskin, and for three of those years Millais had been Ruskin's friend and protégé. The details of Ruskin's marriage and annulment were no doubt as well known at that time at Oxford by word of mouth as they have since become to us by dint of a dozen books. It was the fact that Ruskin and the Millaises did not speak to each other that obliged Wilde to leave Ruskin with Irving and proceed to the ball alone.

To call the Ruskin ambiance merely odd was Oxonian politeness. As soon as Ruskin was married, he explained to his wife that children would interfere with his work and impede necessary scholarly travel. Consummation might therefore wisely be deferred until later on, perhaps in six years' time when Effie would be twenty-five. Few of us here could claim an equal dedication to learning. In the meantime Effie need have no fear about the possible sinfulness of their restraint, since many early Christians lived in married celibacy all their lives. Effie tried to accommodate herself to this pedantic view, and Ruskin in turn was glad to oblige her on a lesser matter: that they go to live in Venice, since he was already planning to write a book about that city.

In Venice, while Ruskin sketched buildings, Effie survived her boredom by going about with one or another of their friends. Ruskin encouraged her, perhaps (as she afterwards implied) too much. If he accompanied her to dances and masked balls, he often left early without her, having arranged that some gentleman friend escort her home. If she returned at 1:30 in the morning, he duly notified his parents in England, at the same time adding that he was completely at rest about her fidelity.[18] Yet her obvious pleasure in pleasure, her flirtatiousness, her impatience with his studies, her delight in frivolity and late hours, struck Ruskin sometimes—however much he repudiated the outward thought—as forms of misconduct and disloyalty. He said as much later. That Effie wasn't sexually unfaithful to him didn't of course prevent Ruskin, any more than it prevented Othello before him, from considering her so, or from transposing her mental dissonance into larger, vaguer forms of betrayal.

The Stones of Venice will always stand primarily as a work of art criticism. But criticism, as Wilde said, is the only civilized form of autobiography,[19] and it is as a fragment—a large fragment—of Ruskin's autobiography that the book claims an added interest. In novels and poems we take for granted that some personal elements will be reflected, but in works of non-fiction we are more reluctant, and prefer to postulate an upper air of abstraction in which the dispassionate mind contemplates and orders materials that already have form and substance. Yet even the most impersonal of writers, Thucydides, writing about the fortunes of another city, shaped his events, as Cornford suggests, by preconceptions absorbed from Greek tragedy. Ruskin made no pretense of Thucydidean impersonality, and the influence of his reading of the Bible is manifest rather than latent. But some problems of his own life also

were projected onto the Venetian scene. Rather than diminishing the book's value, they merge with its talent and add to its intensity.

It may be easier to be convinced that *The Stones of Venice* is in part autobiographical if we remember Ruskin's candid admission that *Sesame and Lilies,* a book he wrote a few years later, was a reflection of one particular experience. His preface expressly states that the section in it called "Lilies" was generated by his love for Rose La Touche. This love impelled him to idealize women, he says, even though "the chances of later life gave me opportunities of watching women in states of degradation and vindictiveness which opened to me the gloomiest secrets of Greek and Syrian tragedy. I have seen them betray their household charities to lust, their pledged love to devotion; I have seen mothers dutiful to their children, as Medea; and children dutiful to their parents, as the daughter of Herodias. . . ." His love for Rose La Touche also covertly leads him to quarrel in the book with pietism because Rose was that way inclined. *The Stones of Venice* deals less obviously, but with the same insistence, on the virtues and defects of the feminine character. As Ruskin remarks in *Sesame and Lilies,* "it has chanced to me, untowardly in some respects, fortunately in others (*because it enables me to read history more clearly*), [My italics], to see the utmost evil that is in women. . . ."[20] To Ruskin Venice is always *she* (to Mary McCarthy, invariably *it*), and the gender is not merely a form of speech but an image to be enforced in detail.

Accordingly Ruskin distinguishes two stages, with medieval Venice as virgin and Renaissance Venice as whore. The moment of transition is, apparently, the moment of copulation, and the moment of copulation is therefore (as in a familiar view of the Garden of Eden) the fall. When Ruskin describes the fallen state, he attributes to the city the very taste for masqued balls and merriment which he had ostentatiously tolerated in his wife. "She became in after times," he declares, "the revel of the earth, the masque of Italy: and *therefore* is she now desolate, but her glorious robe of gold and purple was given her when first she rose a vestal from the sea, not when she became drunk with the wine of her fornication."[21] At the end of the first volume he again asserts, "It was when she wore the ephod of the priest, not the motley of the masquer, that the fire fell upon her from heaven. . . ."[22] After that fire came another which changed the virgin city to its contrary: "Now Venice, as she was once the most religious, was in her fall the most corrupt, of European states; and as she was in her strength the centre of the pure currents of Christian architecture, so she is in her decline the source of the Renaissance. It was the originality and splendour of the Palaces of Vicenza and Venice which gave this school its eminence in the eyes of Europe; and the dying city, magnificent in her dissipation, and graceful in her follies, obtained wider worship in her decrepitude than in her youth, and sank from the midst of her admirers into her grave."[23] Ruskin cannot bring himself to sketch out "the steps of her final ruin. That ancient curse was upon her, the curse of the cities of the plain, 'pride, fulness of bread, and abundance of idleness.' By the inner burning of her own passions, as fatal as the fiery reign of Gomorrah, she was consumed from her place among the nations, and her ashes are choking the channels of the dead salt sea."[24] Just how passions should burn except inwardly may not be clear, especially since we can't suppose Ruskin favored the translation of sensual thought into sensual action, but pride, gluttony, and sloth secure a more sinister confederate in the unnamable sin of lust, whose self-generated fire is contrasted with that fire which had earlier fallen on the city from heaven.

Ruskin's stridency shows how much he had this problem at heart. In fact, consummation and defilement were irrevocably united for him, in his life as in his criticism. The Renaissance (a new term then but already favorable in its connotations)[25] was for him not a rebirth but a relapse. (In *De Profundis* Wilde accepted this view.) Ruskin's revulsion extended from coupling to begetting to having been begot. He had more trouble than most people in allowing that he was himself the product of his parents' intercourse. A small indication is to be found in an epitaph which he wrote for his mother (who already had an epitaph) long after her death, consecrating a memorial well, as he writes, "in memory of a maid's life as pure, and a mother's love as ceaseless. . . ."[26] In Ruskin's mind his mother had immaculately passed from maid to mother without ever becoming a wife.

This singular epitaph may illuminate a point never adequately explained, why Ruskin dated the fall of Venice not only to an exact year, but to a specific day, May 8, 1418.[27] His own explanation is that this was the deathday of the aged Venetian military leader Carlo Zeno, and he makes his usual citation of Pierre Daru's *Histoire de la République de Venise* as his authority. But Daru doesn't give Zeno's death such consequence.[28] Ruskin might more easily, and more consistently with his own views, have taken the year 1423, when the old Doge Tommaso Mocenigo died and the new Doge, Foscari, began his less glorious rule. He is alone among writers on Venice in attaching this significance to Zeno's deathday, and in view of his known penchant for numerology the date invites attention. If Ruskin had been born exactly four hundred years after this date, in 1818, rather than in 1819, the choice might seem related to his theatrical self-laceration, as if to regret he had even been born. But his terrors were for intercourse and conception rather than for birth. At the risk of impugning my own sanity as well as Ruskin's, I venture to propose that the date so carefully selected was, putatively, four hundred years to the day before his own conception—that act so impossible for him to meditate on with equanimity. That the moment of Venice's fall should be reiterated in the moment of his own begetting and be followed by his birth into an England only too ready (as he announces on the first page of his book) to fall—like a semi-detached Venice—anchored firmly the relationships Ruskin wished to dwell upon. In his parents' fall as in that of his first parents, he saw the determination of an age's character and of his own.

There was this difference, however, that Margaret Ruskin's marriage had made her a mother, while Effie Ruskin's "dissolute" behavior in Venice had made her—in fancy if not in fact—an adulteress. Moral blame, from which his mother was freed, was shunted to his wife. Ruskin's own later summary of *The Stones of Venice* confirms that he had this theme in mind. In *The Crown of Wild Olive* (1866) he wrote, "*The Stones of Venice* had, from beginning to end, no other aim than to show that the Renaissance architecture of Venice had arisen out of, and in all its features indicated, a state of concealed national infidelity, and of domestic corruption."[29] The trip to Scotland which Ruskin, his wife, and Millais took in 1853 strengthened the metaphors, and in later life he accused Millais of infidelity—artistic infidelity he called it[30]—to the Pre-Raphaelite principles as Ruskin had earlier enunciated them. Venice, his wife, and his friend were all guilty of the same crime.

Necessary as Ruskin found it to think of himself as wronged, there were moments when he recognized his own culpability. After the annulment of his marriage he came, by a series of mental leaps, to try a revision of his character. In 1858, while looking at Veronese's "Solomon and Sheba" in Turin, he suddenly felt a wave of sympathy for the "strong and frank animality" of the greatest artists.[31] He disavowed his earlier religious zeal, and became (though at the urging of his father and of Rose La Touche's mother he didn't publicly say so) quite skeptical. Then, as Wilenski points out, he began to acknowledge that his theory of history in *The Stones of Venice* was mistaken. Writing to Froude in 1864, he stated firmly, "There is no law of history any more than of a kaleidoscope. With certain bits of glass—shaken so, and so—you will get pretty figures, but what figures, Heaven only knows. . . . The wards of a Chubb's lock are infinite in their chances. Is the Key of Destiny made on a less complex principle?"[32] This renunciation of historical law was intellectually daring, and emotionally as well, for it meant that he was trying to alter those "pretty figures" which earlier had enabled him to lock his own conception and marriage into the history of Venice. As part of this change, he resolved to propose marriage to Rose La Touche, and in 1866 he at last did so. The day he selected for the proposal was probably an effort to change his temperament as well as his luck by another numerological flurry, for it was February 2, his parents' wedding day. By this symbolism he planned, perhaps, to overcome his revulsion at the thought of both consummation and procreation. Rose La Touche, no mean calendar-watcher herself, said she could not answer for two years, or perhaps for four. Ruskin abided her verdict with desperation; his diary records the passing of not only these anniversaries but, since she died soon after, of year after year following her death.[33] No one will mock Ruskin's pain, or his struggle to overcome his fears and become as animal as Veronese.

Rose La Touche had been dead less than a year when Ruskin and Wilde met and took walks together. Neither professor nor pupil was reticent, and Wilde probably divined the matters that Ruskin was unwilling to confide. At any rate, the moral law as imparted by Ruskin, even with the softenings he now wished to introduce, was for Wilde sublime—and berserk. In Ruskin, whom everyone called a prophet, the ethical life was noble and yet, in its weird chastity, perverse. Against its rigors life offered an antidote, and what life was had been articulated by Walter Pater, who saw it not in terms of stones but of waters, not of monuments but of rivery passions. Pater was like Wilde in that, at the same age of nineteen, he too had fallen under Ruskin's sway. He soon broke free, his conscience unclenched itself. He surprised a devout friend by nonetheless attempting, although he had lost his faith, to take orders in the Anglican Church. His friend complained to the bishop and scotched this diabolic ordination. The *Studies in the History of the Renaissance,* Pater's first book, doesn't mention Ruskin by name, but uses him throughout as an adversary. Pater's view of the Renaissance did not differ in being more detached; in its way it was just as personal, and it ended in a secular sermon which ran exactly counter to that of *The Stones of Venice.* It is Ruskin inverted. Pater is all blend where Ruskin is all severance. He calls superficial Ruskin's view that the Renaissance was "a fashion which set in at a definite period." For Pater it was rather "an uninterrupted effort of the middle age."[34] One age was older, one younger, they encountered each other like lovers.

An atmosphere of suppressed invitation runs through Pater's book as an atmosphere of suppressed refusal runs through Ruskin's. The first essay of *Studies in the . . . Renaissance* recounts at length how the friendship of Amis and Amile (in a thirteenth-century story) was so full and intense that they were buried together rather than with their respective wives. Later essays dwell with feeling upon such encounters as that of young Pico della Mirandola, looking like a Phidian statue, with the older Ficino, or as that—planned but prevented by murder—of Winckelmann and the still callow Goethe. For Ruskin the Renaissance is an aged Jezebel, while for Pater it is a young man, his hair wreathed in roses more than in thorns, such a youth as Leonardo painted as John the Baptist. In describing this painting, Pater lingers to point out that the saint's body doesn't look as if it had come from a wilderness, and he finds John's smile intriguingly treacherous [*Author adds in a footnote*: Wilde wrote from Algiers in 1895 to Robert Ross, "The most beautiful boy in Algiers is said by the guide to be 'deceitful'; isn't it sad? Bosie and I are terribly upset about it." (Unpublished text from Sir Rupert Hart-Davis)] and suggestive of a good deal[35]— which may be Victorian hinting at the heresy, a specially homosexual one, that Christ and John (not to mention Leonardo and his model) were lovers.[36]

Whatever Ruskin says about strength and weakness, Pater opposes. The decay against which *The Stones of Venice* fulminates is for Pater "the fascination of corruption,"[37] and images of baleful female power, such as Leonardo's Medusa and other "daughters of Herodias," are discovered to be "clairvoyant" and "electric,"[38] when Ruskin had

found the daughter of Herodias monstrously degraded. Instead of praising the principle of *Noli me tangere,* so ardently espoused by Ruskin, Pater objects to Christian asceticism that it "discredits the slightest sense of touch." Ruskin had denounced "ripe" ornamentation in terms which evoked elements of the adult female body: "I mean," he said, "that character of extravagance in the ornament itself which shows that it was addressed to jaded faculties; a violence and coarseness in curvature, a depth of shadow, a lusciousness in arrangement of line, evidently arising out of an incapability of feeling the true beauty of chaste forms and restrained power. I do not know any character of design which may be more easily recognized at a glance than this over-lusciousness. . . . We speak loosely and inaccurately of 'overcharged' ornament, with an obscure feeling that there is indeed something in visible Form which is correspondent to Intemperance in moral habits. . . ."[39] But for Pater overcharged ornament is rather an "overwrought delicacy, almost of wantonness," or "a languid Eastern deliciousness."[40]

Ruskin combated strenuously what he considered to be a false fusion of classicism and Christianity in the Renaissance. "It would have been better," he said, "to have worshipped Diana and Jupiter at once than have gone through life naming one God, imagining another, and dreading none."[41] Galleries had no business placing Aphrodite and the Madonna, a Bacchanal and a Nativity, side by side.[42] But this juxtaposition was exactly what Pater endorsed. For him European culture was what he called, following Hegel to some extent, a synthesis. To countervail Ruskin's diptych of Venice as virgin of the Adriatic and whore of Babylon, he offered as his Renaissance altarpiece the Mona Lisa of Leonardo. His famous description begins, "The presence that rose beside the waters," and it is clear that he is summoning up not only Lisa, but Venus rising like Ruskin's favorite city from the sea. Lisa has, according to this gospel of Saint Walter, mothered both Mary and Helen, exactly the indiscriminateness, as well as the fecundity, which Ruskin condemned. Pater's heroine, as Salvador Dali has implied by giving her a moustache more suited to Pater, is an androgyne: the activities attributed to her, dealing with foreign merchants and diving in deep seas, seem more male than female. She blends the sexes, she combines sacred and profane. Like Saint John, she has about her something of the Borgias.

Against Ruskin's insistence upon innocence, Pater proffers what he bathetically terms, in the suppressed and then altered and reinstated conclusion to the *Renaissance,* "great experiences." He urges his readers to seek out high passions, only being sure they are passions; later, only being sure they are high. The Renaissance is for him the playtime of sensation, even its spiritual aspects being studies in forms of sensation. W. H. Mallock parodied this aspect by having Pater, as the effete "Mr. Rose" in *The New Republic,* lust for a pornographic book. Something of the extraordinary effect of Pater's *Renaissance* comes from its being exercises in the seduction of young men by the wiles of culture. And yet Pater may not have seduced them in any way except stylistically. When Wilde presented Lord Alfred Douglas to him, the flagrancy of the homosexual relationship was probably, as Lawrence Evans conjectures, the cause of the rift between Pater and Wilde which then developed.

Pater and Ruskin were for Wilde at first imagined, and then actual figures; then they came to stand heraldically, burning unicorn and uninflamed satyr, in front of two portals of his mental theatre. He sometimes allowed them to battle, at other times tried to reconcile them. A good example is his first long published work. This was an ambitious review of the paintings in a new London gallery; he wrote it in 1877, his third year at Oxford, for the *Dublin University Magazine*. The article takes the form of a rove through the three rooms, which had been done, Wilde said admiringly, "in scarlet damask above a dado of dull green and gold." (Ruskin, who also attended, complained that this decor was "dull in itself" and altogether unsuited to the pictures.) Upon entering, Wilde immediately belauds Burne-Jones and Hunt as "the greatest masters of colour that we have ever had in England, with the single exception of Turner"—a compliment to Ruskin's advocacy of Turner and to the sponsorship of the Pre-Raphaelites by both Ruskin and Pater. Wilde then, to praise Burne-Jones further, quotes Pater's remark that for Botticelli natural things "have a spirit upon them by which they become expressive to the spirit," and as he swings through the gallery he finds occasion to savor the same sweet phrase again. He also manages to mention the portrait of Ruskin by Millais, though it was not on exhibition. Reaching the end, he salutes "that revival of culture and love of beauty which in great part owes its birth to Mr. Ruskin, and which Mr. Swinburne and Mr. Pater and Mr. Symons and Mr. Morris and many others are fostering and keeping alive, each in his peculiar fashion." He slipped another quotation from Pater into this final paragraph, but a watchful editor slipped it out again.

Wilde's review of the exhibition is not so interesting as Ruskin's, in *Fors Clavigera* 79, which roused Millais to fury and Whistler to litigation. But it did result in Wilde's finally meeting Pater who, having been sent a copy of the review, invited him to call. Their subsequent friendship afforded Wilde a chance to study the student of the Renaissance. He did not lose his admiration, as we can surmise from the poem "Hélas" which he wrote a little later. In it he invokes both of his mentors as if they were contrary forces tugging at him. After owning up to frivolity, Wilde says,

> Surely there was a time I might have trod
> The august heights, and from life's dissonance
> Struck one clear chord to reach the ears of God.

The chief reference is to Gothic architecture, celebrated by Ruskin because, though fraught with human imperfection—"life's dissonance"—it reached towards heaven. In the next lines Wilde confesses to having fallen away a little:

> Is that time dead? Lo, with a little rod,
> I did but touch the honey of romance.
> And must I lose a soul's inheritance?

Here he is quoting Jonathan's remark to Saul, "I did but taste a little honey with the end of the rod that was in mine hand, and lo! I must die," which Wilde remembered Pater's having conspicuously quoted and interpreted in the *Renaissance* in his essay on Winckelmann. For Pater Jonathan's remark epitomizes "the artistic life, with its inevitable sensuousness," and is contrasted with Christian asceticism and its antagonism to touch.[43] If the taste for honey is a little decadent, then so much the better. Wilde is less sanguine about this appetite here. But as Jonathan was saved, so Wilde, for all his alases, expected to be saved too, partly because he had never renounced the Ruskin conscience, only foregone it for a time.

The tutelary presences of Pater and Ruskin survived in Wilde's more mature writings. If he mentions one, he is almost certain to call up the other. In *The Picture of Dorian Gray*, for example, Pater is enclosed (like an unhappy dryad caught in a tree trunk) in Lord Henry Wotton. Lord Henry's chief sin is quoting without acknowledgment from the *Renaissance*. He tells Dorian, as Pater told Mona Lisa, "You have drunk deeply of everything . . . and it has been to you no more than the sound of music." He predicts, against the "curious revival of Puritanism" (a cut at Ruskin), a new hedonism, the aim of which will be "experience itself, and not the fruits of experience." It will "teach man to concentrate himself upon the moments of a life that is but a moment." These are obvious tags from the Conclusion to the *Renaissance*. Lord Henry's advice to Dorian, "Let nothing be lost upon you. Be always searching for new sensations," was so closely borrowed from the same essay that Pater, who wrote a review of the book, was at great pains to distinguish Lord Henry's philosophy from his own. Wilde seems to have intended not to distinguish them, however, and to offer (through the disastrous effects of Lord Henry's influence upon Dorian) a criticism of Pater.

As for Ruskin, his presence in the book is more tangential. The painter Hallward has little of Ruskin at the beginning, but gradually he moves closer to that pillar of esthetic taste and moral judgment upon which Wilde leaned, and after Hallward is safely murdered, Dorian with sudden fondness recollects a trip they had made to Venice together, when his friend was captivated by Tintoretto's art. Ruskin was of course the English discoverer and champion of Tintoretto, so that the allusion is not vague. The ending of *Dorian Gray* executes a Ruskinesque repudiation of a Pateresque career of self-gratifying sensations. Wilde defined the moral in so witty a way as to content neither of his mentors: in letters to newspapers he said *Dorian Gray* showed that "all excess, as well as all renunciation, brings its own punishment."[44] Not only are Hallward and Dorian punished by death, but, Wilde asserted, Lord Henry is punished too. Lord Henry's offense was in seeking "to be merely the spectator of life. He finds that those who reject the battle are more deeply wounded than those who take part in it."[45] The phrase "spectator of life" was one that Wilde used in objecting to Pater's *Marius the Epicurean.*[46] However incongruous his conception of himself as activist, with it he lorded it over his too donnish friend. For Pater, while he touted (sporadically at least) the life of pleasure, was careful not to be caught living it. He idealized touch until it became contemplation. He allowed only his eye to participate in the high passions about which he loved to expatiate. Dorian at lest had the courage to risk himself.

In *Dorian Gray* the Pater side of Wilde's thought is routed, through not deprived of fascination. Yet Hallward, when his ethical insistence brings him close to Ruskin, is killed too. In *The Soul of Man under Socialism,* also written in 1891, Wilde superimposes Ruskin's social ethic upon Pater's "full expression of personality," fusing instead of destroying them. In *Salomé,* to which I come at last, the formulation is close to *Dorian Gray,* with both opposites executed. Behind the figure of Iokanaan lurks the image of that perversely untouching, untouchable prophet John whom Wilde knew at Oxford. When Iokanaan, up from his cistern for a moment, cries to Salomé, "Arrière, fille de Sodome! Ne me touchez pas. Il ne faut pas profaner le temple du Seigneur Dieu," a thought of Ruskin, by now sunk down into madness, can scarcely have failed to cross Wilde's mind. By this time Wilde would also have recognized in the prophet's behavior (as in Ruskin's) something of his own, for after his first three years of marriage he had discontinued sexual relations with his wife. Iokanaan is not Ruskin, but he is Ruskinism as Wilde understood that pole of his character. Then when Salomé evinces her appetite for strange experiences, her eagerness to kiss a literally disembodied lover in a relation at once totally sensual and totally "mystical"[47] (Wilde's own term for her), she shows something of that diseased contemplation for which Wilde had reprehended Pater. Her adaptation, or perversion, of the Song of Songs to describe a man's rather than a woman's beauty also is reminiscent of Pater's *Renaissance* as well as of Wilde's predisposition. It is Salomé, and not Pater, who dances the dance of the seven veils, but her virginal yet perverse sensuality is at home in Paterism.

Admittedly the play takes place in Judea and not in Oxford. Wilde wanted the play to have meaning outside his own psychodrama. Yet his tutelary voices from the university, now fully identified as forces within himself, seem to be in attendance, clamoring for domination. Both Iokanaan and Salomé are executed, however, and at the command of the tetrarch. The execution of Salomé was not in the Bible, but Wilde insisted upon it [*Author adds in a footnote*: Gomez Carrillo says that the play was originally to be entitled "La Décapitation de Salomé," thus slighting St. John by precisely equating the two deaths.[48]]. So at the play's end the emphasis shifts suddenly to Herod, who is seen to have yielded to Salomé's sensuality, and then to the moral revulsion of Iokanaan from that sensuality, and to have survived them both. In Herod Wilde was

suggesting that *tertium quid* which he felt to be his own nature, susceptible to contrary impulses but not abandoned for long to either.

Aubrey Beardsley divined the autobiographical element in Herod, and in one of his illustrations gave the tetrach the author's face. Herod speaks like Wilde in purple passages about peacocks or in such an epigram as, "Il ne faut pas regarder que dans les miroirs. Car les miroirs ne nous montrent que les masques." Just what Wilde thought his own character to be, as distinct from the alternating forces of Pater and Ruskin, is implied in a remark he made in 1883 to George Woodberry, who promptly relayed it to Charles Eliot Norton. Wilde told Woodberry that Ruskin "like Christ bears the sins of the world, but that he himself was 'always like Pilate, washing his hands of all responsibility.'"[49] Pilate in the story of Christ occupies much the same role as Herod in the story of John the Baptist. In other letters Wilde continues to bewail his own weakness, yet with so much attention as to imply that it may have a certain fibre to it. In March 1877 he wrote, "I shift with every breath of thought and am weaker and more self-deceiving than ever,"[50] and in 1886 he remarked, "Sometimes I think that the artistic life is a long and lovely suicide, and am not sorry that it is so."[51] What he more and more held against both Ruskin and Pater was a vice they shared equally, that of narrowness. To keep to any one form of life is limiting, he said in *De Profundis,* and added without remorse, "I had to pass on."[52]

Herod too passes on, strong in his tremblings, a leaf but a sinuous one, swept but not destroyed by successive waves of spiritual and physical passion, in possession of what Wilde in a letter calls "a curious mixture of ardour and of indifference. I myself would sacrifice everything for a new experience, and I know there is no such thing as a new experience at all . . . I would go to the stake for a sensation and be a sceptic to the last!"[53] Here too there is martyrdom and abandonment, with a legal right to choose and yet stay aloof. Proust had something of the same idea when he said of Whistler's quarrel with Ruskin that both men were right.[54] In that same reconciling vein Wilde in *De Profundis* celebrates Christ as an artist, and the artist as a Christ. And in Wilde's last play, when Jack declares at the end, "I've now realized for the first time in my life the vital Importance of Being Earnest," he is demonstrating again that Ruskin's earnestness and Pater's paraded passionateness are for the artist not mutually exclusive but may, by wit, by weakness, by self-withholding, be artistically, as well as tetrarchically, compounded.

Notes

1. Mario Praz, *The Romantic Agony,* tr. Angus Davidson (Meridian Books, 1963), p. 191.

2. ". . . cette jeune princesse que définitivement vous évoquâtes." Unpublished letter, Mallarmé to Wilde, March 1893.

3. "J'ai laissé le nom d'Hérodiade pour bien la différencier de la Salomé je dirai moderne . . ." Draft of a preface to *Hérodiade,* in Stéphane Mallarmé, *Les Noces d'Hérodiade* (Paris, 1959), p. 51.

4. See Yeats's comments on *A Full Moon in March* and *The King of the Great Clock Tower.*

5. Praz, p. 299.

6. This edition was anonymous.

7. Heywood's *Salomé* was one of several books discussed in Wilde's review, "The Poets' Corner," *Pall Mall Gazette,* XLVII:7128 (January 20, 1888), 3.

8. E. Gomez Carrillo, *En Plena Bohemia,* in Collected Works (Madrid, n.d. [1919?]), XVI, 170 ff.

9. Oscar Wilde, *Letters,* ed. Rupert Hart-Davis (London, 1962), p. 469.

10. Vincent O'Sullivan, *Aspects of Wilde* (London, 1936), p. 139.

11. Wilde, *Letters,* p. 471.

12. Yeats, *Autobiography* (New York, 1965), p. 87.

13. Wilde, *Letters,* p. 471. At the Marquis of Queensberry trial Wilde spoke of Pater as "the only critic of the century whose opinion I set high. . . ."

14. John Ruskin, *Sesame and Lilies* (London, 1900), p. 203.

15. Based on newspaper clippings of Wilde's American tour, 1881-82.

16. Wilde, *Letters,* p. 218.

17. *Ibid.,* p. 61.

18. Derrick Leon, *Ruskin, The Great Victorian* (London, 1949), p. 152.

19. In *The Critic as Artist.*

20. *Sesame and Lilies,* p. xxxiii.

21. Ruskin, *The Stones of Venice* (New York, n.d.), I, 150.

22. *Ibid.,* p. 8.

23. *Ibid.,* pp. 38-39.

24. *Ibid.,* III, 165.

25. Wallace K. Ferguson, *The Renaissance in Historical Thought* (Cambridge, Massachusetts, 1948), pp. 142-44.

26. Entry for 30 November 1880, in *The Diaries of John Ruskin,* ed. Joan Evans and John Howard Whitehouse (Oxford, 1959), III, 995. Ruskin's earlier dedicatory tablet had been taken down because the well became polluted. It specified that the name "Margaret's Well" be given, but did not otherwise mention his mother, though the donor's name was given as "John Ruskin Esq., M.A., LL.D." The new inscription, never installed, was to read in full:

"This Spring

In memory of a maid's life as pure

And a mother's love as ceaseless,

Dedicate to a spirit in peace

Is called by Croydon people,

Margaret's Well.

Matris animae, Joannes Ruskin

1880."

27. *The Stones of Venice,* I, 18.

28. Pierre Daru, *Histoire de la République de Venise* (Paris, 1853), II, 198-99.

29. Ruskin, *The Crown of Wild Olive* (1866), in *The Works of John Ruskin,* ed. E. T. Cook and Alexander Wedderburn (London, 1903), XVIII, 443.

30. "But the spectator may still gather from them some conception of what this great painter might have done, had he remained faithful to the principles of his school when he first led its onset." *Fors Clavigera* 79 (July 1877), in *Works,* XXIX, 161.

31. Ruskin, *Diary,* II, 537, and Notes on the Turin Gallery. Quoted by R. H. Wilenski, *John Ruskin* (London, 1933), pp. 231-32.

32. Wilenski, p. 69.

33. *Diary,* II, 720, 737.

34. Walter Pater, *The Renaissance,* ed. Kenneth Clark (Meridian, 1961), p. 214.

35. "It is so with the so-called *Saint John the Baptist* of the Louvre—one of the few naked figures Leonardo painted—whose delicate brown flesh and woman's hair no one would go out into the wilderness to seek, and whose treacherous smile would have us understand something far beyond the outward gesture or circumstances." *Ibid.,* p. 118.

36. See Wilde, *Letters,* p. 756.

37. Pater, *Renaissance,* p. 108.

38. *Ibid.,* p. 116.

39. *The Stones of Venice,* III, 8.

40. Pater, *Renaissance,* p. 47.

41. *The Stones of Venice,* III, 109.

42. *Ibid.,* p. 110.

43. Pater, *Renaissance,* p. 211. Compare Ruskin, *Diary,* III, 972, for 1 January 1878: "And now, thinking of the mischief done to my own life and to how many hundred thousand, by dark desire, I open my first text at I Corinthians Vii.1. ['It is good for a man not to touch a woman. Nevertheless . . . let every man have his own wife, and let every woman have her own husband.'] And yet the second verse directly

reverses the nobleness of all youthful thought, expressed in a word by Dr. King: 'Not to marry that they may be pure; but to be pure that they may marry.'"

44. Wilde, letter to the Editor of the *St. James's Gazette,* June 26, 1890, in Wilde, *Letters,* p. 259.

45. *Ibid.*

46. Wilde, *Letters,* p. 476.

47. Jean Paul Raymond and Charles Ricketts, *Oscar Wilde: Recollections* (London, 1932), p. 51.

48. Gomez Carrillo, p. 214.

49. Unpublished letter in the Houghton Library, Harvard.

50. Wilde, *Letters,* p. 31.

51. *Ibid.,* p. 185.

52. *Ibid.,* p. 475.

53. *Ibid.,* p. 185.

54. "Whistler is right when he says in *Ten O'clock* that Art is distinct from morality; and yet Ruskin, too, utters a truth, though on a different level, when he says that all great art is a form of morality." Marcel Proust. *Correspondence avec sa mère,* ed. Philip Kolb (Paris, 1953), p. 279. Quoted in George Painter, *Marcel Proust* (London, 1965), II, 29-30.

Jason P. Mitchell (essay date spring 1996)

SOURCE: Mitchell, Jason P. "A Source Victorian or Biblical?: The Integration of Biblical Diction and Symbolism in Oscar Wilde's *Salomé*." *Victorian Newsletter* 89 (spring 1996): 14-18.

[*In the following essay, Mitchell asserts that Wilde's diction in* Salomé *was borrowed from the Old Testament as well as the Belgian author Maurice Maeterlinck.*]

The Salomé legend has its beginnings in the Gospels of Matthew and Mark (Matthew 14: 3-11, Mark 6: 17-28), which relate the beheading of John the Baptist at the instigation of Herodias, wife of Herod, who was angered by John's characterization of her marriage as incestuous. In both accounts, Herodias uses her daughter (unnamed in scripture but known to tradition, through Josephus, as Salomé) as the instrument of the prophet's destruction. According to the Gospel of Mark:

. . . when a convenient day was come, that Herod on his birthday made a supper to his lords, high captains and chief estates of Galilee. And when the daughter of the said Herodias came in, and danced, and pleased Herod and them that sat with him, the king said unto the damsel, "Ask of me whatsoever thou wilt, and I will give it thee." And he sware unto her, "Whatsoever thou shalt ask of me, I will give it thee, unto half of

my kingdom." And she went forth and said unto her mother, "What shall I ask?" And she said, "The head of John the Baptist." And she came in straightway with haste unto the king, and asked, saying, "I will that thou give me by and by in a charger the head of John the Baptist." And the king was exceeding sorry; yet for his oath's sake and for their sakes that sat with him, he would not reject her. And immediately the king sent an executioner, and commanded his head to be brought, and he went and beheaded him in prison. And brought his head in a charger, and gave it to the damsel; and the damsel gave it to her mother.

(6: 21-28, King James Version)

Clearly, if we are to follow this account, all guilt rests with Herodias, and such was the prevailing belief until the Baptist became a more widely venerated saint, with the result that the image of Salomé became increasingly negative (Zagona 20).

The Salomé theme was a prominent one in both literature and the visual arts until the end of the Renaissance, when its prominence began to lessen, until it was revived in the nineteenth century by Heinrich Heine, whose *Atta Troll* served to inspire an entire series of explorations by such divergent authors as Flaubert, Mallarmé, and Huysmans, ending with Oscar Wilde's *Salomé.*

Critical reaction to Wilde's effort has been mixed. Mallarmé, in a letter full of praise, commended Wilde for his portrayal "*de cette jeune princesse, que définitivement vous evoquâtes*"[1] (Ellmann, *Oscar Wilde* 375). Maurice Maeterlinck wrote his thanks for the presentation of the volume after reading it for the third time, describing it as a "*rêve dont je ne me peux pas expliquer la puissance,*"[2] and assuring Wilde of his "*admiration très grande*"[3] (Ellmann, *Oscar Wilde* 375). Pierre Loti said of *Salomé.* "*c'est beau et sombre comme une chaptre de l'Apocalypse—je l'admire profondement*"[4] (Ellmann, *Oscar Wilde* 375). Other critics were less favorably impressed. William Butler Yeats, though often an admirer of Wilde's works, considered *Salomé*'s dialogue "empty, sluggish, and pretentious" (259). (His dislike of the play was not, however, so strong as to prevent his rewriting it not once but twice [Worth 72].) Even one of Wilde's friends, Edgar Saltus, was not sure quite what to make of *Salomé,* describing it as a product "of genius wedded to insanity" (22).

Many have viewed Wilde's *Salomé* as a mere composite of earlier treatments of the theme overlaid with Belgian playwright Maurice Maeterlinck's characteristic diction. Typical of this appraisal is a anonymous review appearing in the (New York) *Critic* of 12 May 1894 accusing Wilde of literary theft, declaring that "a large part of his material he gets from the Bible; a little has once belonged to Flaubert. He borrows from Maeterlinck his trick of repeating stupid phrases until a glimpse of meaning seems almost a flash of genius" (Anonymous 285). Pearson notes that Wilde's *Salomé* "shows the influence of Maeterlinck . . . who wrote symbolical dramas . . . with a rigid simplicity of language and a haunting balladic effect" (201). Robert

Ross considered Maeterlinck "among the obvious sources on which [Wilde] has freely drawn" (Zagona 129). Ernst Bendz states his perception of Wilde's debt to the Belgian rather plainly: "*en ecrivant son drame de Salomé Oscar Wilde s'est fortement inspiré d'un . . . ouvrage d'un ecrivain contemporain, je veux parler des* Sept Princesses *de Maeterlinck*" (92).[5]

The matter of inspiration (or derivitiveness) does merit some examination. Wilde never made a secret of his literary borrowing; to Max Beerbohm he once said, "Of course, I plagiarize. It is the privilege of the appreciative" (Ellmann, *Oscar Wilde* 375-76). Wilde was certainly familiar with those who had gone before him; he revered Flaubert and Mallarmé, the latter of whom was a friend for many years, and his admiration for Huysmans is also well known (Ellmann, *Oscar Wilde* 213). Further, Wilde once remarked that he found only two modern playwrights interesting: Hugo and Maeterlinck (Worth 54). When asked why he had chosen to write *Salomé* in French, Wilde cited Maeterlinck as an example of the interesting effect resulting when an author writes in a language not his own (Worth 54). Once allowed reading material in prison, Wilde requested, among many other items, Maeterlinck's complete works (Harte-Davis 521-22).

However, while Wilde's debts are undeniable, the question of whether he created something new from the materials which inspired him remains. Wilde surely did. While the kissing of the head was an element not only of Heinrich Heine's *Atta Troll* but also of an American work on the Salomé theme by J. C. Heywood, there are some important distinctions. The horrible kiss does take place in the former work, but as Ellmann notes, "it is a punishment after Herodias' death, not a *divertissement* before it, and the tone of caricature is quite unlike that of perverted horror which Wilde evokes" (*Golden Codgers* 41). In the works of Heine and Heywood, the character who kisses the head is Herodias, not Salomé, and neither author makes "this monstrous kissing the play's climax" (Ellmann, *Golden Codgers* 41). Even Zagona, who holds that Wilde based the structure of his work on that of Flaubert's *Hérodiade,* praises Wilde's great improvement in dramatic unity (124).

Further, Mallarmé's *Hérodiade* seeks to "triumph over all her longings" (Fowlie 139) which is quite different from the flaw (compulsion?) of Wilde's *Salomé*, who is distinguished by her inability to restrain a human nature "entirely evil because entirely uninhibited and unmodified by any restriction" (Nassaar 92). Both heroines are obsessed with chastity, but the similarity ends there. As one examines the earlier works, Wilde's original approach becomes clear; Ellmann observes that "to read Heywood or other writers about Salomé is to come to a greater admiration for Wilde's ingenuity" (*Golden Codgers* 41).

Given Wilde's penchant for borrowing and his admiration for his contemporaries, it is certainly not unreasonable to assume that his choice of diction was inspired by his Belgian contemporary. However, a reasonable assumption

is not proof. While Wilde would certainly not have hesitated to borrow Maeterlinck's technique, *Salomé*'s unusual diction is too closely integrated with the play's symbolism to be a mere overlay. Consequently, it is more plausible that Wilde's inspiration was something far older than "a work of a contemporary author," namely the poetic works of the Old Testament. Wilde, raised in the Church of Ireland, was very familiar with the Old Testament, and his debt to it, particularly to the Song of Solomon, is often acknowledged but never discussed at length. Pearson, in the context of citing a possible Maeterlinckian influence does note the "obvious influence of the Song of Solomon on some of the longer passages" (226). Ellmann likewise observes that Salomé's description of Jokanaan is "an adaptation, or perversion, of the Song of Songs" (*Golden Codgers* 57). The influence of Old Testament verse on *Salomé* is clear from an examination of the text alone, but not, it seems, widely discussed.

Wilde, in his *Salomé,* not only employs a number of the images favored by Israel's kingly poets, but also makes masterful use of their chosen modes of poetic expression. The main technique of Old Testament versification is parallelism, the use of paired phrases containing some common element, with that in the second phrase answering, echoing or otherwise corresponding to that in the first. The types of correspondence tend to be fairly regular, often dealing with subordination, sequence of actions, and even repeated words (Kugel 4-7). The latter element is closely akin to another poetic device, repetition, in which "phrases, verses or short passages [known as repetends] recur, sometimes in different forms, at varying intervals" (Fox 210).

The play opens with what is to become a repetend, the statement of the Young Syrian: "How beautiful is the Princess Salomé tonight!" (392). This is repeated twice. After the second repetition, the same character remarks on the paleness of the Princess, in an example of parallelism: "How pale the Princess is. Never have I seen her so pale" (39).

The Page of Herodias also enters with a repetend. "Look at the moon," which is repeated (with variations) by Salomé, the Young Syrian, and Herod, each of whom sees very different significance in the moon. To the Page, "She is like a woman rising from the tomb. She is like a dead woman. . . . she is like a woman who is dead" (393). To the Young Syrian, enamored of Salomé, the moon "has a strange look. She is like a princess who wears a yellow veil, and whose feet are silver. She is like a princess who has little white doves for feet" (393). To Salomé, the moon is pure and virginal. "She is cold and chaste. I am sure she is a virgin. Yes, she is a virgin. She has never defiled herself. She has never abandoned herself to men, like the other goddesses" (397). However, Herod, as does the page, sees a sinister aspect in the moon:

> The moon has a strange look tonight. Has she not a strange look? She is like a mad woman who is seeking everywhere for lovers. She is naked, too. She is quite naked. She shows herself naked in the sky. She reels

through the clouds like a drunken woman. . . . I am sure she is looking for lovers. Does she not reel like a drunken woman? She is like a mad woman.

(407)

Only Herodias, of all the main characters of the play, sees nothing in the moon: "No; the moon is like the moon, that is all" (407). Thus do these characters share variations on the repetend "Look at the moon," expressing it in language filled with parallelisms.

As noted, some have proposed that Wilde simply copied the frequent repetition employed by Maeterlinck. Phillip Cohen suggests that this proposal, as well as San Juan's theory that the repetition in Salomé's and Jokanaan's speeches "opposes their fixated state to the wavering indecisiveness of Herod" (164), simply does not apply. Instead, Cohen maintains, "verbal repetition functions as a complement to repetition of plot. In a significantly structured manner, characters echo the words and re-enact the deeds of others" (164).

True as this observation is, however, it does not go far enough, ignoring as it does the important role which repetition and parallelism play in the exposition of the work's symbolism and failing to take into account *Salomé*'s near complete integration of Biblical poetic devices with symbolic expression. Because of this integration, one must approach the play's use of Biblical diction in the context of its symbolism.

Such language as we find in *Salomé* is certainly well-suited to an effective use of symbols, allowing the author to give them much greater stress than would otherwise be possible while minimizing the risk of monotony. For example, the repeated references to the moon cited earlier serve to accentuate its importance as a symbol, yet are saved from tediousness by the judicious use of variation. This same method of repetition also makes it possible to reveal through different characters the various aspects of this most crucial symbol.

The link between the moon and Salomé's paleness is our first clue to the former's importance. From the very beginning, it is clear that the moon is to be identified with Salomé; the juxtaposition of the Young Syrian's opening remark on the beauty of the Princess with the subsequent exhortation of the Page of Herodias to look at the strange and deathlike moon is but one clue. The Young Syrian himself identifies the "dancing" moon with Salomé in his description of it as a princess. To reinforce the point, Salomé, herself protective of her virginity, remarks on the moon's chastity (which quality is later the source of her attraction to Jokanaan). In short, repetitions and parallel statements serve to intensify the reader's awareness of these correspondences, just as they were once used for purposes of intensification in Hebrew poetry (Alter 11).

What is to be made of the Salomé-moon relationship, once established? Nassaar proposes that "the moon is meant to suggest the terrible pagan goddess Cybele," who, like Salomé, was obsessed with preserving her virginity and thus took perverse pleasure in destroying male sexuality (84). The priests who served Cybele had castrated themselves and sacrificed their own blood to her. Their self-mutilation parallels the suicide of the Young Syrian, and, Nassaar asserts, serves to reinforce the connections between Cybele, the moon, and Salomé (86).

Repetition may also serve to grant an incantatory quality, as in Salomé's beseeching of Narraboth (the Young Syrian) to bring her the Prophet, in which the statement "Thou wilt do this thing" is repeated, with variations eight times. Almost as though Salomé has cast a spell over him does Narraboth consent to do what inevitably leads to his death. If we grant Nassaar's parallel to Cybele, then Salomé's power over the unfortunate young man is clearly an analogy to that of the goddess over her devotees; thus the presentation of her demand in the form of a litany is very apt.

With the entrance of the prophet comes an important series of parallelisms and repetitions involving crucial color symbols. Salomé, first looking on Jokanaan as he emerges from his cistern, remarks on the blackness of his eyes, saying,

> They are like black holes burned by torches in a tapestry of Tyre. They are like the black caverns of Egypt in which the dragons make their lairs. They are like black lakes troubled by fantastic moons.

(402)

Immediately after, she marvels at his paleness, just as others had remarked on hers:

> How wasted he is! He is like a thin ivory statue. He is like an image of silver. He is like a moonbeam, like a shaft of silver. I would look closer at him, I must look at him closer.

(402)

Quite a bit in these two passages demands closer examination. In the first, the idea of blackness is repeated, with images of holes, caverns, and lakes. As Nassaar notes, all of these things suggest depth, and thus, coupled with the color of death, the tomb. Salomé's fascination with the blackness of Jokanaan's eyes clearly implies an attraction based upon his deathly quality. Again, repeating images of extreme blackness and depth aids in stressing an important aspect of the play's symbolism.

The second of the passages is even richer. Salomé extols the Prophet's paleness, a quality which she and the moon share, yet does so in images which suggest lifelessness: statues and moonbeams. This is an important point; white may symbolize chastity or death, and which of these is at issue in the passage is crucial. The repetition of whites and silvers serves to reinforce their status as important symbols, and the parallelism: "He is like a moonbeam, like a shaft of silver," in its identification of Jokanaan with the moon, may answer which aspect of white so fascinates Salomé.

Having seen how the Biblical diction in this passage reinforces the image of a lifeless (as opposed to pure) chastity, one must concur with Nassaar that "it is the death-like coldness of [Jokanaan's] flesh that attracts" Salomé (84). The Princess, in her Cybelic obsession with virginity, is drawn to the corpse-like Jokanaan because he poses no threat to her (Nassaar 83). As San Juan suggests, the final pair of phrases, "I would look closer at him. I must look at him closer," does powerfully suggest Salomé's fixation.

Acting upon her sterile attraction to Jokanaan, Salomé tempts him three times, resuming and extending the theme of color symbolism. Once again, she praises the Prophet's whiteness:

> I am amorous of thy body, Jokanaan! Thy body is white like the lilies of a field that the mower hath never mowed. Thy body is white like the snows that lie on the mountains of Judea, and come down into the valleys. The roses in the garden of the Queen of Arabia are not so white as thy body. Neither the roses of the garden of the Queen of Arabia, the garden of spices of the Queen of Arabia, nor the feet of the dawn when they light on the leaves, nor the breast of the moon when she lies on the breast of the sea. . . . There is nothing so white as thy body. Suffer me to touch thy body.
>
>   (403)

Not only is the word *white* used four times, it is employed in parallelisms that not only allow great stress to *white* without the risk of monotony, but also extend yet further the identification of Jokanaan with the moon—he is whiter still.

After the Prophet rejects her advances ("Back! Daughter of Babylon . . ."), Salomé begins the second phase of her temptation of him, by claiming that his body is "hideous . . . like the body of a leper" and that in reality she is attracted to his hair.

> It is thy hair I am enamoured of, Jokanaan. Thy hair is like clusters of grapes, like the clusters of black grapes that hang from the vinetrees of Edom in the land of the Edomites. Thy hair is like the cedars of Lebanon, the great cedars of Lebanon that give shade to the lions and to the robbers who would hide in them by day. The long black nights, when the moon hides her face, and when the stars are afraid, are not so black as thy hair. The silence that dwells in the forest is not so black. There is nothing in the world that is so black as thy hair. . . . Suffer me to touch thy hair.
>
>   (403-04)

So Salomé turns once again to blackness, with imagery nearly as sinister as before. Though the grapes seem innocent enough, one cannot say the same for the cedars of Lebanon: beautiful as they are, they give shelter to lions and robbers. Black as is the moonless night, "when the stars are afraid" is a particularly foreboding comparison, given the supreme importance that Salomé attaches to the moon. Repeatedly, Salomé stresses black in contexts that serve to reinforce its negative associations.

Rebuffed once more, Salomé enters the third phase of her temptation, this time asserting that it is not the blackness of the Prophet's hair which attracts her but the redness of his mouth:

> Thy mouth is like a band of scarlet on a tower of ivory. It is like a pomegranate cut in twain with a knife of ivory. The pomegranate flowers that blossom in the garden of Tyre, and are redder than roses, are not so red. The red blasts of trumpets that herald the approach of kings and make afraid the enemy, are not so red. Thy mouth is redder than the feet of doves who inhabit the temple and are fed by the priests. It is redder than the feet of him who cometh from a forest where he hath slain a lion, and seen gilded tigers. Thy mouth is like a branch of coral that fishers have found in the twilight of the sea, the coral they keep for kings! . . . It is like the vermillion that the Moabites find in the mines of Moab, the vermillion that the kings take from them. . . .
>
>   (404)

These images are the most sinister of all, recalling as red does blood, and thus sacrifice, suggesting Salomé's realization, given the Prophet's immunity to her charms, that she may only possess him by killing him (Nassaar 91). The reference to the pomegranate, like that to grapes, seems innocent, until Salomé's declaration, after Jokanaan's death, that she "will bite [his mouth] with [her] teeth as one bites a ripe fruit" (427). As Nassaar notes, it is only in this passage that imagery of sacrifice appears: the knife described as ivory-handled (suggesting a ceremonial blade) and "the slaying of lions" (91). The temple doves also suggest sacrifice rather strongly, forcing one to recall how those too poor to afford a lamb or kid could offer turtledoves as a sacrifice in the temple. Blood, we must remember, was a key element in the worship of Cybele. Again and again in this passage red is emphasized, its value as a symbol of blood, sacrifice and martyrdom enhanced by its repetition in contexts involving such elements of religious worship.

Not only are colors important symbols whose effectiveness is increased by the use of repetition combined with parallelism and other variations; this is also true of the word *look*. Throughout the work, characters exhort one another to look or not look. As though in warning, the Page of Herodias urges the Young Syrian to look at the moon (393), where perhaps there is some sign of Salomé's true nature, and not to look at Salomé herself, because "something terrible may happen" (393, 396-97). Salomé, too, is aware of the significance of looking: she knows only too well why Herod looks at her as he does. Likewise, she appreciates the significance of looking at the moon (397), and is eager to see Jokanaan after hearing his voice from the cistern, saying, "Bring out the prophet. I would look upon him" (399).

Clearly we are not dealing with an ordinary meaning of the word *look*, but rather with action as symbol. To look, in this context, is obviously to accept or to make oneself vulnerable to something. The Page fears that disaster will result if the Young Syrian looks upon Salomé. Salomé is well aware of the significance of the Tetrarch's looking at her "with mole's eyes under shaking lids" (397). Jokanaan says of Salomé, "I will not have her look at me" (402), and averts his eyes from her. Each of these characters knows that to look upon Salomé is to accept her evil nature, or at least to confront it, and none is willing to do so. The continued repetition of *look* by such dissimilar characters makes clear the word's status as an important symbol.

Herodias's frequent berating of Herod for looking at Salomé reinforces the point: "You must not look at her. You are always looking at her" (406). Herod, while quite willing to look upon Salomé, at least her body, refuses to confront what frightens or displeases him. He locks the prophet in the cistern, hiding him from view, yet John's shouted denunciations continue to reach all within earshot. When the Tetrarch comes onto the terrace and sees the body of the young man who has slain himself, he considers it "an ill omen" and says, "I will not look on it" (407).

After Salomé has danced and made her terrible demand, Herod declares,

> Thy beauty has grievously troubled me, and I have looked at thee overmuch. Nay, but I will look at thee no more. One should not look at anything. Neither at things nor at people should one look. Only in mirrors is it well to look, for mirrors do but show us masks.

(423)

Herod now knows Salomé's true nature and cannot bear to confront it. As Nassaar notes, "a mirror will show Herod a mask, but Salomé reveals his soul to him" (94).

Both the color symbols and the word *look* are stressed by continued repetition combined with images and parallelisms in whose contexts their meanings are made yet clearer. This is the weakness of the argument that the parallelisms and repetitions in *Salomé* are simply a superficial stylistic overlay adapted from Maeterlinck or the Bible. Though most certainly inspired by the latter and quite possibly influenced by the former, Wilde created, in *Salomé,* a work in which diction and symbolism are inextricably linked. Far from being a pastiche of all that had gone before it, Wilde's **Salomé** is admirably unified; the language which struck Yeats as "empty, sluggish and pretentious" serves a clear purpose: the greater emphasis of important symbols. Through modes of expression favored not by his beloved Greeks but rather by the poets of Israel, with their songs and prophecies, Wilde achieves a masterpiece of drama in which language and symbol are one.

Notes

1. "of this young princess, whom you have definitively evoked," (my translation).

2. "dream whose power I cannot explain to myself" (my translation).

3. "very great admiration" (my translation).

4. "it is beautiful and solemn like a chapter from the Apocalypse—I admire it profoundly" (my translation).

5. "in writing his drama of Salomé Oscar Wilde was strongly inpired by a work of a contemporary writer; I speak of Materlinck's *Seven Princesses* (my translation).

Works Cited

Alter, Robert. *The Art of Biblical Poetry.* New York: Basic Books, 1985.

Bendz, Ernst. "A Propos de la Salomé d'Oscar Wilde." *Oscar Wilde.* Folcroft, PA: Folcroft P, 1969.

Cohen, Phillip K. *The Moral Vision of Oscar Wilde.* Camden, NJ: Associated UPs, 1976.

Ellmann, Richard. *Golden Codgers: Biographical Speculations* New York: Oxford UP, 1973.

———. *Oscar Wilde.* New York: Alfred A. Knopf, 1988.

Fowlie, Wallace. *Mallarmé.* Chicago: U of Chicago P, 1962.

Fox, Michael V. *The Song of Solomon and the Ancient Egyptian Love Songs.* Madison: U of Wisconsin P, 1985.

Harte-Davis, Rupert, ed. *The Letters of Oscar Wilde.* New York: Harcourt, Brace and World, 1962.

Kugel, James L. *The Idea of Biblical Poetry: Parallelism and Its History.* New Haven: Yale UP, 1985.

Nassaar, Christopher S. *Into the Demon Universe: A Literary Exploration of Oscar Wilde.* New Haven: Yale UP, 1974.

Pearson, Hesketh. *Oscar Wilde: His Life and Wit.* New York: Harper, 1946.

Saltus, Edgar. *Oscar Wilde: An Idler's Impression.* New York: AMS P, 1968.

Wilde, Oscar. *Salomé: The Portable Oscar Wilde.* New York: Penguin, 1982. 392-429.

Worth, Katherine. *Oscar Wilde.* London: Macmillan, 1983.

Yeats, W. B. Letter to T. Sturge Moore, 6 May 1906. *Oscar Wilde: The Critical Heritage.* Karl Beckson, ed. New York: Barnes & Noble, 1970.

Zagona, Helen Grace. *The Legend of Salomé and the Principle of Art for Art's Sake.* Paris: Librarie Minard, 1960.

Christopher S. Nassaar (essay date winter 1999)

SOURCE: Nassaar, Christopher S. "Wilde's *Salomé.*" *Explicator* 57, no. 2 (winter 1999): 89-90.

[*In the following essay, Nassaar considers the symbolic significance of the fan in Wilde's* Salomé.]

Lady Windermere's Fan was Oscar Wilde's first mature play, and it established him overnight as a successful playwright. It also created in the minds of playgoers an association between Wilde and the fan. Soon afterward, Wilde wrote a second play, *Salomé,* and he included in it eight references to a fan. The references constitute Wilde's signature—his constant reminder to reader and audience that he is the author of this new play. But the fan in *Salomé* also serves a functional and symbolic purpose, much like the one in *Lady Windermere's Fan.*

In *Salomé* the fan is associated with all four main characters. The first association is with Salomé herself at the beginning of the play. When she emerges into the moonlight after rejecting Herod's sin-infested banquet, the young Syrian, who sees Salomé as innocent and dovelike, says: "The Princess has hidden her face behind her fan!" (page 585). The symbolism of this is clear: The fan is a veil covering Salomé's true nature. Interestingly, the fan obscures Salomé's nature only in the eyes of the young Syrian; the page of Salomé's mother Herodias knows what is behind the fan. The Syrian's youth and inexperience, then, are the real "fan" in this case. As he comes to realize the true Salomé, the fan imagery is dropped.

The imagery is picked up by Jokanaan in his attacks on Herodias. At one point, Jokanaan cries out from his cistern prison: "Bid her rise up from the bed of her abominations, from the bed of her incestuousness, that she may hear the words of him who prepareth the way of the Lord, that she may repent her of her iniquities. Though she will never repent, but will stick fast in her abominations; bid her come, for the fan of the Lord is in His hand" (588). This passage, like many others uttered by Jokanaan, has a double meaning. At the conscious level, Jokanaan is attacking Herodias, but unconsciously he is bidding her to come to him even though she will not repent: He wants her for himself (Nassaar 80-109).

The reference to the fan, though, is interesting. The fan is in Christ's hand and by extension Jokanaan's. It is a threefold symbol. Primarily it is aggressive, a weapon with which Jokanaan can strike Herodias much as Lady Windermere wished to strike Mrs. Erlynne. In the Gospels, Christ is referred to by John the Baptist as having a winnowing-fan in his hand, with which he will separate the wheat from the chaff and toss the latter into the fire (Matthew 3.12; Luke 3.17-18). Jokanaan's aggressive intentions towards Herodias are thus quite clear. An open fan can also be protective, serving to shield the pure and holy from moral evil. But the fan has a third, suppressed meaning. Jokanaan declares early in the play that his rod is broken. If closed, the fan can thus be seen as a phallic symbol, a substitute for the rod and an indication of Jokanaan's unconscious desire for Herodias.

The fan as weapon and sexual symbol soon finds its way into the hands of Herodias. She says, as Herod's guests discuss the coming of Christ:

"Ho! Ho! Miracles! I do not believe in miracles. I have seen too many." (*To the Page*): "My fan! [. . .] How these men weary me! They are ridiculous!" (*To the*

Page): "Well, my fan!" (*The Page gives her the fan.*) "You have a dreamer's look, you must not dream. It is only sick people who dream." (*She strikes the Page with her fan.*)

(page 595)

In Herodias's possession, the fan becomes a weapon against men. Just as Salomé pushes the young Syrian to commit suicide, so Herodias hits the Syrian's best friend, the page, asserting her power over him. The fan becomes a declaration of the superiority of women over men.

Finally, and most important, the fan demonstrates Herodias's power over Jokanaan. When Salomé asks for and receives the prophet Jokanaan's head at the end of the play, Herod hides his face in shock but "HARODIAS *smiles and fans herself*" (603). Just as the daughter took Jokanaan's head, the mother relieves him of the fan and makes it her own, thus symbolically beheading him in a minor leitmotif that parallels Salomé's actual taking of his head.

There is one last reference to fans that must be noted. Toward the end of the play, Herod desperately offers Salomé all the delights of aestheticism if only she will withdraw her request for Jokanaan's head. The aesthetic objects that so delighted Dorian Gray are rejected by Salomé, but among them are "four fans fashioned from the feathers of parrots" that had been sent to Herod by "the King of the Indies" (602). Earlier, Salomé had used a fan to hide her nature, but now she rejects the fans partly because she no longer wishes to hide her true self in any way. The thrust of the play is for Salomé to express her personality and to strip away all veils obscuring her real self.

Works Cited

Nassaar, Christopher S. *Into the Demon Universe: A Literary Exploration of Oscar Wilde.* New Haven: Yale UP, 1974.

Wilde, Oscar. *Salomé. Complete Works of Oscar Wilde.* 3rd Edition. Glasgow: Harper, 1994. 583-605.

David Wayne Thomas (essay date March 2000)

SOURCE: Thomas, David Wayne. "The 'Strange Music' of *Salomé*: Oscar Wilde's Rhetoric of Verbal Musicality." *Mosaic* (March 2000): 15-38.

[*In the following essay, Thomas investigates the function of verbal musicality in Wilde's* Salomé.]

Salomé:

Thy voice was a censer that scattered strange perfumes, and when I looked on thee I heard a strange music.

—Oscar Wilde, *Salomé*

In the closing moments of Oscar Wilde's drama *Salomé* (1893, 1894), the matter of verbal music finds its nearest approach to explicit mention. Having performed her dance of seven veils before the lecherous Herod, Salomé comes to reflect on her dancer's reward—a silver platter bearing the head of the prophet Iokanaan—and she speaks of a "strange music" that had attended, in her imagination, the living presence of the prophet. Alarmed by the new silence, she laments, "There is no sound. I hear nothing" (327-28).[1] Fled is that music, indeed, but I suggest that Salomé's final remarks, proffered in the absence of that music, only confirm a strange musicality that has informed the drama all along. In one sense, this claim has a simple historiographic justification: Wilde himself indicated the "recurring phrases of *Salomé,* that bind it together like a piece of music with recurring *motifs*" (*Letters* 590), and his numerous references in this vein clarify that his association of *Salomé* and verbal musicality is not merely a passing one (*Letters* 331, 475, 492). But to clarify what interest we might bring to this association of music and words, we need to find a richer basis than the fact of Wilde's own consistent affirmation. That basis lies in the formal implications of a verbal-musical connection. I argue that the idea of verbal music arises in Wilde's *Salomé* to illuminate the nature and limits of any will to critical interpretation. So even as this discussion aims to spotlight an aspect of Wilde's play that has received virtually no critical attention, it also aims to demonstrate the generality of theoretical provocation at hand in Wilde's literary practice.

There have been earnest efforts to comprehend music and words within a seamless unity, but Wilde was not one for earnest efforts of that sort, and I do not try to locate an authentic musicality in the words of *Salomé.* Instead, I suggest that Wilde's concern in his *Salomé* is to enact and also to destabilize the very idea of a verbal-musical conjunction, to evoke an array of interpretive cruxes brought out precisely through his work's equivocal aspiration toward the condition of music. The strangeness of the play's dramatic music—the very interest of this dramatic music—inheres in the unstable dynamism of the transpositional aspiration itself. In this respect, *Salomé*'s verbal music is not about the communion of words and music. Instead, it is about the attractions and the inevitable precariousness of formal correspondences, artistic transpositions, encoding and decoding. The action of *Salomé,* presided over by a reflective moon, engenders a staging of critical reflection as such, bringing manifold issues of identity and difference into a carnival of inverted imaging and shaky introspections. So the work implies a comment on the uncertain condition of interpretation. In Wilde's approach to the conjuring of verbal music, nothing succeeds like failure.

This redemptive approach to failed aspiration seems prescient in the light of the personal disasters that awaited him. In a letter of early June, 1897, written a few weeks after his release from a two-year imprisonment with hard labor for acts of gross indecency, Wilde reviews his literary career by invoking the terms of subjectivity, objectivity and aesthetic formalism that will organize this discussion:

> One can really, as I say in *Intentions,* be far more subjective in an *objective* form than in any other way. If I were asked of myself as a dramatist, I would say that my unique position was that I had taken the Drama, the most objective form known of art, and made it as personal a mode of expression as the Lyric or the Sonnet, while enriching the characterization of the stage, and enlarging—at any rate in the case of *Salomé*—its artistic horizon.
>
> (*Letters* 589)[2]

Wilde's letter encourages us to find in his works a reflection of the artist himself, an *objectified subjectivity.* His longtime friend and confidante Ada Leverson suggests what such objectification of the Wildean self might actually involve—at least, in the matter of *Salomé*—for she proposes that, beyond the drama's cosmetic influences from the works of Maeterlinck, Flaubert, and Huysmans, it is still more decisively Wildean how "*Salomé* expressed *himself* in his innate love of the gorgeous and bizarre" (110-11). It is not initially clear, however, what it means for Wilde to have loved the gorgeous and the bizarre, nor even what makes the gorgeous gorgeous, finally, or the bizarre, bizarre.

Critics routinely examine these questions with reference to Wilde's sexuality. In that light, Wilde's concern to be "subjective in an objective form" might seem to indicate a desire to advance homosexual representation within a philistine and hyper-conventionalist world that reserved its affirmation for the regular, upright, unambiguous, immanent, objective. For *fin-de-siècle* Victorians, as the investigations of Michel Foucault have suggested, the newly minted category of the "homosexual" functioned in some measure of antithesis to all of those normalizing rubrics—it was an ambiguously open secret, a matter of sexual inversion (or, soon, perversion), the affliction of an errant soul, housed mistakenly in the wrong body. In the context of a social debate so fundamentally informed by metaphors of rule and deviation, the arch-inverter Oscar Wilde often seems to us a subversive artist in encoding, a guerrilla tactician who baffled Victorian conservatism by fashioning "new discursive strategies to express concerns unvoiced within the dominant culture" (Cohen 806). His popular comedy *The Importance of Being Earnest,* ostensibly about connubial prospects and cucumber sandwiches, becomes in this critical light a study in representing the homosexual male through the very mechanisms of Victorian compulsory heterosexuality (Craft). *The Picture of Dorian Gray* becomes, in turn, a depiction of the Image as construction site of male-male desire, a dilation on artistic influence as seminal confluence (Cohen; Dellamora). And readings of *Salomé* tend to decipher a "secret or unspeakable subtext" (Showalter 152), revealing a "masked depiction of one man's prohibited longing for another" (Finney 65), with Salomé herself as Wilde's transvestic alter ego (Garber 339-45). These critical precedents—along with readings by Jonathan Dollimore, Lee Edelman, Eve Kosofsky Sedgwick and others—have served as models for negotiating the ironic necessity of taking Wilde's works in an "earnest" critical spirit.

Like all interpretive styles, however, strategies of decoding hazard their particular blindnesses. In criticism on Wilde, one problem lies in the narrowing effect brought about finally by any suggestion that his subversive encoding encompasses the breadth of his literary concerns. Even if Wilde's enthusiasm for a London high-life of social and sexual carousing is indubitable—he recalled in *De Profundis* his period of "feasting with panthers" (492)—none of his comments in letters or secondhand reports underwrites an assumption that his primary interest as a literary artist lay in creating esoteric representations of this aspect of his life. Far more regularly, he reveals a distaste for the essentially stabilizing and arithmetical commitments of all decoding, for, in the end, encoding and decoding remain but two expressions of a fundamental literalism. And as a grudging Henry James once noted, writing, it so happens, a couple of months after Wilde completed *Salomé*: "Everything Oscar does is a deliberate trap for the literalist" (253).

James's literalist is not merely an earthbound bore but a figure arrested in flight from certain truths of reflection. This view pertains, at least, whenever *reflection* signifies not pure reproduction but rather, as in *Salomé,* inversion, permutation, transposition. Not simply a text made up of reflections or images, *Salomé* is a text about them, and nowhere more so than in its strange musicality. But once we have broached that distinction between reflections and reflections on reflection—a distinction between a logic and a metalogic—we will do well to put an even finer point on it. I propose that *Salomé* is a text about that very distinction, about the slippage between a logic and a metalogic. A critical vantage point on the very juxtaposition of logic and metalogic opens up exactly the conceptual recursion that Wilde cultivated so adeptly. Fundamentally informed by such positionings, his most characteristic literary gestures exhibit an intricate species of doubleness, what I call here an equivocal enactment, that leaves behind merely oppositional or self-canceling paradoxes and enters instead into a playful and unreckonable tangling of interpretive hierarchies. Sustained reading complicates the sense that any procedure of decoding can be at all appropriate to Salomé, for her image energizes and maintains a critical contest between the enticements of decoding and those of indeterminacy.

To those already knowledgeable about Wilde, music will probably seem a feeble springboard into these highly general dimensions of his thinking, because of all the arts, music was without a doubt the least congenial to his temperament and intellectual range. Richard Ellmann claims that music was "always a closed book" to Wilde (27). An overview of the literary and critical writings sup-

ports Ellmann's characterization, for Wilde's references to music, although frequent, are generally lackadaisical and, at their most deliberate, rise only to the provocatively impressionistic. In "The Critic as Artist I," for example, Gilbert observes that Dvořák "writes passionate, curiously-colored things" (243). Hardly a high-water mark in Dvořák criticism, it must be admitted. And in the opening lines to *The Importance of Being Earnest,* Algernon casts aside tiresome notions of accuracy in piano playing: "[A]nyone can play accurately," he observes. "As far as piano is concerned, sentiment is my forte" (480).

But Wildean flippancies generally merit some thought, and Algernon's word *sentiment* in fact collapses together at least two distinct and even contrary indications—one, a suggestion of unarticulated feeling, a feeling beyond words but gathered somehow into music; another, a suggestion of articulate feeling, of feeling gathered precisely into words. The duplex term *sentiment* highlights a slippage embedded in the Wildean notion of musicality generally, because for Wilde art is inevitably a matter of articulation, even while music remains for him essentially a matter of inarticulation. In this scheme, therefore, the essence of music as an art form is deeply at odds with Wilde's own suppositions about art itself. So if *Salomé* is a musical-verbal drama, it can only be so as the bearer of a fundamental representational complication. For that reason, the consistently uninspiring quality of Wilde's musical acumen cannot amount to a critical disincentive for this essay, because *Salomé*'s "success" as verbal music is not the central issue. More pertinent are the interpretive issues forced on stage through the play's equivocally interartistic enactment. Even when it is possible to identify features of Wilde's *Salomé* that enter the terrain of verbal musicality—features that evoke the structural, even phenomenological aspect of music—Wilde's own biases bring him inevitably back to music not just as a structure but as a figure, not just as a self-sufficient formalism but as the signal art of opposition, difference and otherness.

To uncover that interpretive crossfire in the drama's verbal-musical enactment, it will be well to consider first the nature of the drama's musical gesture, and to hold at bay, for the time being, those complications to be located in that gesture. We need not review the practical and theoretical history of verbal musicality, as accessible overviews are readily available (e.g., Scher 155-66), and Wilde's highly unprofessional relation to music would make an earnest and rigorous consideration of musical phenomenology something of a non sequitur in any case. Perhaps it can suffice to recall the vitality and pervasiveness of the interartistic motion within the Romantic and post-Romantic periods. Debussy's musical setting of Mallarmé's poem *L'Apres-midi d'une faune* was as characteristic as Whistler's painted "nocturnes" and "preludes." Especially in the poetry of Mallarmé, the verbal imagery of music, even the attempt to suggest that the poem *is* music, would signal one of the most characteristic tendencies of the Symbolist movement in literature and provide the defining background of Wilde's *Salomé*. Apparently a part of the contemporary fascination with synesthesia—as in Baudelaire's sonnet "Correspondances," where, in "the ecstasies of sense," "[a]ll scents and sounds and colors meet as one" (*Flowers of Evil* 12)—the interartistic gestures weaves like a thread through nineteenth century literature. (Another Baudelaire poem might be said to have handed Wilde the very notion of "strange music": "*une étrange musique*" names the buzzing of flies around a decaying animal carcass in "Une Charogne" [*Flowers of Evil* 265].) From its earlier formulations by figures like Percy Shelley, for whom transpositional notions could suggest the integration of phenomenal reality and the perceiving mind into an imaginative Oneness, to its later manifestations in the Wagnerist *Gesamtkunstwerk* and French Symbolist discourse, 19th-century interest in these integrative aesthetic gestures reflects the rise and the transformational decline of Romanticism, broadly conceived. As M. H. Abrams observes in his influential *The Mirror and the Lamp*, the late 19th century marks the culmination of a period inclined to the coordination of verbal and musical effects in particular (88-94 and passim).

Wilde's *Salomé* evinces such transpositional inclinations in several ways. To begin, its one-act structure allows it a distinctly monological and formally integrated narrative texture, much like a lyric poem or a musical composition. Uniquely among his plays, Wilde's *Salomé* appears not to have been initially conceived as a staged work, according to Ellmann, nor was Wilde deeply committed to the notion that it could only find its fulfillment as a staged effort (344). In *Salomé*, neither changes of setting nor discrete soliloquies introduce the perspectival disjunctions or adjustments characteristic of many narrative forms, most notably the novel, in regard to which Bakhtin has argued that a fundamental dialogism, a heterogeneity of voices and discursive directions, provides the essential feature. Bakhtin himself proposes that poetic expression exhibits "a unity of style," an effect both of the organicism of its language and of the personalizing lyric persona, whereas the novel "makes of the internal stratification of language, of its social heteroglossia and the variety of individual voices in it, the prerequisite for authentic novelistic discourse" (264). Cultivating a highly unitary and "poetic" flavor, then, *Salomé* reaches toward musicality in that sense outlined in Lawrence Kramer's *Music and Poetry*, which attempts to forge an inclusive interpretive framework for musical and poetic signification. Kramer disputes the easy antitheses between music and poetry and proposes instead that they exhibit a reciprocal and to some extent invertible participation in the polar opposition of significant structure—music's strong point—and referential connotation—the hallmark of poetic expression (5-8). As poeticized expression, therefore, *Salomé* attains some of the verbal musicality that aestheticians have found to inhere in poetry generally.

Salomé also suggests a kind of musicality in its elaborately artificial, highly mannered patterning of dialogue. If architecture can be called frozen music, then perhaps *Salomé*'s architecturalized dialogue invites similar associations. Most of the drama's formal measuredness is conveyed through its numerous tripled addresses: Salomé's seductive speech to the Young Syrian, her extravagant encomium to Iokanaan, Herod's pleadings to her that she alter her fatal request, Herodias's derisive comments to the anguished Herod. Like music, then, the play imposes a stylized and even metronomic procession, marking out its extensions through time with an alienating independence from a more usual fluid and unconscious experience of time. Wilde's fairy tales also illustrate his pleasure in such deliberately languorous extensions, for their folkloric tripartite structures periodically eliminate narrative tactics of suspense and replace them with a sometimes enchanting, sometimes frustrating indifference to narrative progress. There Wilde co-opts the tripling tendency of traditional folkloric procedures, putting those structures in service to the aestheticizing delectations of an opulent, even self-indulgent imaging.

Finally, the drama's studied dialogue is congruent with Western forms of musical exposition, wherein elementary patterns are proposed and developed through progressive elaborations on initial ur-patterns or motifs. The incantational rhythms of the opening lines, for example, counterpoise regularizing effects of verbal and syntactical repetition with carefully alternating enlargements and constrictions, thereby conveying a sense both of interconnection and development:

THE YOUNG SYRIAN:

> How beautiful is the Princess Salomé tonight!

THE PAGE OF HERODIAS:

> Look at the moon. How strange the moon seems! She is like a woman rising from a tomb. She is like a dead woman. One might fancy she was looking for dead things.

THE YOUNG SYRIAN:

> She has a strange look. She is like a little princess who wears a yellow veil, and whose feet are of silver. She is like a princess who has little white doves for feet. One might fancy she was dancing.

THE PAGE:

> She is like a woman who is dead. She moves very slowly.

> (301)

Here already in these first lines one sees those deliberate "recurring phrases of *Salomé*" that Wilde had said would bind the drama into a cohesive, highly formalized plenitude, "like a piece of music." Indeed, *Salomé* finds its definitive "musical" stratagem precisely in the matter of repetition.

Evident in many respects throughout the work, repetition is crucially deployed in Salomé's refrain to the prophet Iokanaan: "I will kiss thy mouth, Iokanaan" (310-11). Like a verbal residuum, the word simmered down to a foundational sonorous materiality, Salomé's refrain becomes the essential indicator of her absorption in the image of the prophet. *In Beyond the Pleasure Principle,* Freud links the repetition compulsion with primary libidinal self-involvement, as well as with the tendency not to remember, arguing that the repetition compulsion takes place in lieu of full consciousness of the pastness of the past, in lieu of memory (12-14). Pursuing her own unprincipled pleasures, Salomé reveals her oblivion to history—to cultural memory, that is—in her initial unfamiliarity with the identity of the prophet Elias, whom even the common soldiers can identify as a Judean prophet who has perhaps been revived now in the person of Iokanaan (268). So while her chanted words signal her absorption in another, they also underline her involuted consciousness, her disengaged solipsism and self involvement. While repetition serves in many other literary contexts as a binding force, an integrative gesture lending consecutive moments a resonant affinity—consider Walt Whitman, for example—the repetitions in *Salomé* delineate as well the unfolding conflicts of the play, communicating with considerable economy the play's disassociated atmosphere, its perspectival contests, and its epistemological unease.

Through repetition, in fact, the drama's orderly tripartite architectures are subjected to a dramatic disintegration. Lavishly praising his black hair and, next, his white body, Salomé is rebuked in both events by Iokanaan. Finally she fixes on the image of his red mouth and, rejected a third time here, she breaks the pattern of her address, dwells at this point, and settles definitively into her resolve to have her pleasures with this prophet. While Iokanaan, the Young Syrian, the Page, and the others address her, resist her, and try variously to unseat her resolve, Salomé has now found her focus and will not be diverted. Nine times she repeats that she will kiss the prophet's mouth, and, indeed, this thought is all she has to say for an extended period. (We hear nothing else from her until well after the arrival on stage of Herod, Herodias, and the party guests.) Her retirement from any outward engagement is signaled, as well, by her utter indifference when the emotionally overtaxed Young Syrian kills himself in frustration over her disregard for him. It is well to note that the Young Syrian kills himself not upon first confronting Salomé's passion for the prophet, but upon hearing the *repetition* of Salomé's words—"I will kiss thy mouth, Iokanaan"—for that repetition forces on the Young Syrian, in its demonstration of Salomé's autonomous will, the collapse of his own narcissistic vision, just as Narcissus himself died upon the consummation of his encounter with the radical otherness of the reflecting pool.

Simultaneously a figure of speech and of the body, the mouth of Iokanaan bridges a chasm of conceptual and material realities. (His presence in the drama actually underlines diachronically the distinction between verbalized conceptions and material presences, for we first experience him as a bodiless voice from the well, and we see him in the end as a voiceless, inert head on the stage.)

The mouth—richly sensuous, an organ of tremendous intimacy, for Freud the original erotogenic zone—is here the origin, as well, of what Salomé calls "terrible" words (305), scandalous and portentous outpourings that have not only struck fear into Herod and plagued Herodias, but also possessed Salomé herself with a sense of the physicality or materiality of these words. His voice, she exclaims in the original French text, has made her "drunk": "*Ta voix m'enivre*" (26). Almost as if to underline a connection between such physicality and the effects of music, these French lines became in the English version, "Thy voice is as music to mine ear" (308).

The mouth of Iokanaan, when brought together with Salomé's own mouth, provides the drama's essential image of illicit, overflowing union, leaving the legend's typical centerpiece—the famous dance—to pale in comparison. It is not the dance, after all, but the moment of the kiss that Aubrey Beardsley depicted first in his illustration "*Je baisé ta bouche*" in the *Studio* of April, 1893. Wilde saw the unsolicited drawing and was inspired to invite Beardsley's illustrations for the 1894 English publication of *Salomé*; Beardsley contributed many more illustrations, including a revision of the first, now retitled "The Climax." Wilde's decision to create and to spotlight the kiss would be recalled and interpreted, too, by Yeats in his 1935 play *The King of the Great Clock Tower,* a late rendering of the Salomé theme wherein the severed head sings: "What marvel is / Where the dead and the living kiss?" (640). This meeting of life and death in that marvelous climax represents not simply an inert concept of death, of "nothingness" or "negation," as it were, but the confrontation of life with death. Arriving at this dizzying juxtaposition through a spiral of repetitions, Wilde's *Salomé* exemplifies Victorian dramatic literature's boldest and most persuasive illustration of the libidinal, thanatonic involvements that we commonly link to obsessive repetition, the bodily raptures and the suspending, desocializing trajectory of passionate objectifications.

As Roland Barthes has it, "to repeat excessively is to enter into loss, into the zero of the signified," a process which for Barthes indicates, in our culture, an "eccentricity, thrust toward various marginal regions of music" (41). Deliberately eccentric, definitively marginal, the musicality of Salomé's words to the prophet prefigures the threat that her eccentric music can usher forth in an apocalyptic confrontation with Iokanaan, that ambassador of the Word. Salomé is approaching her own crisis at this moment, however, for she herself is soon to be put to death at Herod's command. Toward the end of this discussion, it will come time to return once again to this final episode in order to see that Salomé, participating in this verbal-musical drama, participates as well in a catastrophe of verbal-musical assertion, a catastrophe in which she, like the music with which she has been aligned, falls prey to the retaliation of Herod's word. Among the several unveilings in Wilde's tale—and "unveiling" or "revelation" is the root sense of the term *apocalypse*—one finds the revelation that representations, essentially, are vital but disappointed bids for consummation, acts of frustrated grasping. In the Judean princess's desire to partake of the corporeal-verbal union figured by the prophet's mouth, one sees her narcissistic aspiration toward the condition of music, but one sees as well a reflection of that lack through which all such aspiration is constructed.

Wilde's version of verbal musicality is, therefore, an equivocal enactment, articulating the uncertain, paradoxical terrain of the Wildean pose. As Wilde plays at avant-garde artistic transpositions, he at the same time builds a critical vantage point in relation to those exploits. This procedure highlights a loopy logic intrinsic to the very impulse toward breaking down artistic boundaries, for just as agitation can take form only within a contextual orthodoxy, so too does *Salomé*'s verbal music depend finally on the vitality of a distinction between music and the word. To gain the image of Wilde that I advance here, it is crucial to see that the twin concepts of immediate engagement and mediating criticism form no opposition merely, but a sort of knot, a nexus; this knotting together of action and criticism presents what one might well call the most decisively "Wildean" mode of literary operation, even a Wildean conception of human consciousness.

Said Wilde once, "In art I am Platonic, not Aristotelian, tho' I wear my Plato with a difference" (Raymond and Ricketts 15). He surely deployed the word *difference* with less freight than we give it today, but his meaning appears to be much the same as our contemporary meanings: in his Platonism, as in most things, Wilde's operational mode is neither one of obedient consent nor of polemicizing opposition, but rather one of participation via a manifold, differential enactment. Although Wilde's remark is tied to an occasion—it reflects his decision to change details of time and place in *The Importance of Being Earnest*—this remark also shows a general truth about Wilde, illustrating his inveterate habit of taking upon himself a role or a label, although not quite in a spirit of accurate or correct representation. Likewise, Wilde's manner of anti-Romanticism was never simply a rejection of Romanticism, but a mode of enacting it, wearing it, "with a difference." Perhaps the most decisive paradox of Oscar Wilde emerges in this neatly paradoxical formulation: he was quite sincere in his posing.

So just as Ada Leverson could remark that Wilde's *Salomé* in some sense "expressed himself," we might add that the drama "sincerely poses" as music. If one cannot finally establish that *Salomé* is a musical-verbal production, and if one, likewise, cannot finally dispose of that notion, the ensuing critical undecidability is not finally a problem; it is simply a conundrum of the sort that Wilde would extol in perhaps his most characteristic quip: "A Truth in art is that whose contradictory is also true" ("The Truth of Masks" 432).

Because Wilde's many references to music are hardly of a serious kind, it would be little trouble to dismiss his gesture across art forms as a manner of escapist dabbling, just a facile artistic ploy. His invocations of musicality are not, however, merely outbursts of militant frivolity, for even in his most lighthearted or absurd references to the idea, he gives the idea of music a specific role to play in his narrative structures or characterization. That role is exhibited typically through his most characteristic poseurs. One of his epigrammatically inclined aristocrats, for example, Lord Goring of *An Ideal Husband,* declines a young Miss's invitation to enter the music room after it becomes clear that there might actually be music within; he stays away for the sake of continued conversation, much more to his tastes (400). And in *The Picture of Dorian Gray,* when one of Wilde's society ladies praises Wagner's music by noting that its high volume permits one to converse without worrying about listeners in neighboring boxes (81), Wilde is having his fun with Wagner, but managing as well to counterpoise music with what is, for him and many others, its perpetual opponent: language.

The contest of sound and sense is more consequentially figured in Dorian Gray himself, who plays the piano in both the second and the second-to-last chapters of Wilde's only novel. Dorian's quite proficient playing sets his unarticulated, unselfconscious expressiveness apart from the highly deliberate verbal intelligence of Lord Henry Wotton, a presence in each of these chapters. But throughout the novel, Wotton's voice is itself insistently described as musical, and it is precisely the musicality of his words that allows Wotton to affect Dorian so profoundly. Wotton's voice is then no mere vehicle of logos, but an indefinitely situated phenomenon, meaningful yet crucially elusive. This enigmatic quality becomes evident through Dorian's thoughts as he labors to fathom the insinuating power that Wotton's voice has for him:

> Music had stirred him [Dorian Gray] like that. Music had troubled him many times. But music was not articulate. It was not a new world, but rather another chaos that it created in us. Words! Mere words! How terrible they were! How clear, and vivid and cruel! One could not escape from them. And yet what a subtle magic there was in them!
>
> (62)

Through Dorian's reflections, Wilde fashions music as an alluring but chaotic anti-figure, alien to any structural articulation, even without rules. Recalling so originary a motion as that of a new world brought forth from chaos, Dorian finds that music, which simply creates "another chaos," does not bridge that divide, while the Word does begin to do so. One sees in this passage that Wotton's influence on Dorian's life is not, as is often supposed, a matter of introducing something wholly new to an innocent youth, but one of rendering sensible to him the chaotic force of an elusive form, figured as musicality, but now with a difference—or, as today's semiological vocabulary will allow, "with difference." Dorian's awakening is an effect of that musical form rendered articulate— "clear, and vivid and cruel"—and music becomes both an illuminating enchantment and, just as much, *l'art fatal.*

The structural complexity of the musical canon and fugue, to say nothing of myriad other musical forms, makes plain that Wilde's conception of music as an elusive and destabilizing chaos hardly provides the truth of the matter. But Wilde's shortcomings as a music theorist may better serve to fuel our thinking than to license deprecation. Let it instead be instructive that music, the least discursive of art forms, remains alien to the most avidly dialectical and verbal of literary intelligences. In the classic manner of an impressionist criticism, Wilde's thoughts on music tell us less about music than about his critical intelligence and concerns. His continual resort to an idea of music, despite his manifest lack of traditional musical acumen, signals just that much more clearly how music is for him something significant but crucially remote, an art that is essentially and actively *other*. Music in words will finally not be music at all, but will remain, quite simply, music in words—music figured, music represented.

Wilde's actual concern, it seems, is to conjure the structural characteristics of a loosely conceived musicality so as to render musicality itself into a figure within his literary texts. *Salomé*'s peculiar power among Wilde's works to make something of this figuring of music emerges directly from the extent to which he in fact attempted, his verbal biases notwithstanding, to play at realizing or consummating that figuration, rather than merely to cast a verbal glance toward it. More than in any of his other works, the musical words of *Salomé* assume a consequential significance not only as an idea but as an aesthetic enactment. Where his critical dialogues, his reviews, his fictional prose, dramas and his poems all quite regularly invoke the concept of music, *Salomé* goes uniquely far in the direction of actually proposing to be music, to evoke it.

To the extent that *Salomé*'s musicality then serves no longer as a topical reference merely, as a critical figure signifying the anti-figural, but instead becomes imported into the fabric of the literary work itself, the representational issues become refocused away from the propositional or conceptual understandings of the work and into the "body" of the work itself, into its form as it is apprehended sensorally. This notion of attending to the sensuous body, of forcing the materialization of a form, is a matter of thematic importance within the action of the play, where Salomé's and Herod's fascinations both highlight the disruptive allure of an idea's radical objectification in sensually "present" form. Already in the very formal quality of the dramatic dialogue, however, we can see or hear the *matter* of form urged implicitly. *Salomé*'s bid to be musical serves to underline an aspect of materiality in language, emphasizing the necessity of its aural and temporal paths of transmission. The word must come to us embodied. Thus the matter of *Salomé*'s form is not merely an abstract issue; it incorporates the *materiality* through which alone a linguistic or conceptual form becomes accessible to thought. The transposition across art forms is a defamiliarizing tactic, an aspiration toward unification, surely, but just as much a reminder that form and matter—

name and thing, concept and content—interdepend in a fruitful but perpetual suspense.

The essentially suspended quality of aspiration figures deeply in Walter Pater's "The School of Giorgione" (1877), an essential period essay that Wilde undoubtedly knew. (Stealing from it was his characteristic tribute: in "*L'Envoi*," Wilde's introduction to Rennell Rodd's 1882 collection of poems *Rose Leaf and Apple Blossom*, Pater's essay is an unmistakable source of ideas and phrasing [*Miscellanies* 30-41, esp. 31].) Today, the most often-quoted line in Pater's essay is typically given without context: "All art constantly aspires toward the condition of music" (106). Without doubt, Wilde's *Salomé* aspires toward the condition of music, but why it does so remains uncertain as yet, and it seems unlikely, at any rate, that one could see Wilde himself as aspiring to the condition of a composer. A closer-than-passing consideration of Pater's notion might help clarify matters.

The condition of music, for Pater, involves an impeccable harmony of form and subject, and the other arts aim at this condition perpetually: "For while in all other kinds of art it is possible to distinguish the matter from the form, and the understanding can always make this distinction, yet it is the constant effort of art to obliterate it" (106). For Pater and Wilde both, music consummates an intercourse between matter and form, and the etymological provenance of Pater's word *obliterate*—to go 'against the letter,' to 'erase' what is articulated—suggests how deeply this aspiration toward the unity of matter and form is affiliated with a longing to repress articulated difference, to elude the chains of an essentially linguistic operation of distinction and determination. Still more decisive than the Paterian concepts of condition and constancy, therefore, will be the concept of *aspiration*. Like *desire, aspiration* denotes a dynamic state, a differential structure of longing for what is not with the aspirant, for what the aspiring mind in itself finally is not. Where *condition* and *constancy* might then be understood in terms of a positive stability, *aspiration* must finally name a protracted tension, a longing in the context of its own definitive denial or frustration. For Pater, it seems, the "effort" of art is to obliterate the very distinction that music has in fact already obliterated. Pater's formulation therefore entails that music *qua* art form has no effort before it at all. Music figures here a phenomenal plenitude that all other arts lack.

In this view, the nonmusical arts are constitutionally invested with a radical negativity, so that any gesture toward musical-verbal transposition can only come into being with a foretaste of that gesture's inevitable undoing. All the nonmusical arts, that is, only aspire to the condition of music by virtue of the fact that they never really achieve that condition. For Pater, a truly fine painting will not be that miraculous—and impossible—work which somehow succeeds to the condition of music, but rather that work which most fully realizes its own longing after that music-like integration of medium and meaning. An idea's self-realization becomes, in this light, not a creation or a resuscitation of pre-original unities, but a thematizing of what deconstructionists following Derrida call "difference at the origin."

Perhaps it is no coincidence, then, that the sobering quality of negative determinations constitutes the almost forgotten theme of "The School of Giorgione," an essay which is not, after all, about music, nor even about all the arts together, but about how educated people like Pater might deal most fruitfully with the recent determinations by scrutinizing critics that many works once thought to be Giorgione's are, in truth, not by Giorgione at all. One sees Pater's sense of loss in such determination when he writes that recent criticism has "so freely *diminished* the number of [Giorgione's] authentic works" (115; emphasis mine). Of course, recent criticism had not changed their number in any sense but that of historical memory. Perhaps there lurks in Pater's wording no mere imprecision, however, but a truer truth. (The notion of a "true truth," *a "vraie vérité"* undetermined by trammeling fact, is Pater's refrain in this essay.) Perhaps historical memory is the decisive matter after all, and Pater's sadness is one more reverberation of the Victorian era's more general difficulties with several profound historical determinations, revelations that the world's larger history has become no longer what one might have thought it to be, once.

The revelations about Giorgione carry for Pater the flavor of an apocalypse—or the sense of an ending, in Frank Kermode's still useful formulation. The verbal gesture toward music can then be seen in light of this historical context, for here that gesture reaches toward that art in which a form will be splendidly apparent, even while it seems exempt from the linguistic tangles and disillusionments of reference and representation. Linda *Dowling's Language and Decadence in the Victorian Fin de Siècle* offers intelligent support for the notion that literary aestheticism and decadence were fundamentally expressions of linguistic crisis, and, indeed, Pater is among her focal figures. (Her investment in a Derridean speech/writing dichotomy leads her to pay less attention to Wilde, whom she casts as a devotee of the presences of speech over the radicalism of *écriture* [185-88 and passim].) Pater finds in music, it seems, an art of reassuring incontrovertibility, untroubled by the disillusionments of any Higher Criticism: music begins and ends in ways accessible to human experience; it unfolds in harmony; its dramatic conflicts are internal and finally neutral, rather than referential and differentiated. The condition of music, thus figured by Pater and Wilde, contrasts with nothing so much as with the condition of humanity. In human life, that is, the origin and consummation lie outside of experience, and the whole referential issue of realism and anti-realism—fundamental for Wilde's art, and not uniquely—cannot be neatly mooted or contained. With such a vision of music, a vision that aligns music with a nonbeing that enigmatically surrounds and defines human being, one might finally make the best sense of Wilde's lack of sympathy with it: inarticulate for him, music remains fascinating but fundamentally inhumane, not a dead art,

but an art as alienating, indisputable, and inevitably victorious as death. The little art of words is rounded with a sleep—a sleep of music, of consummation, of death.

When a consideration of musicality and words in **Salomé** brings one to invoke the concept of death, it is time to consider Herod. His final gesture is itself an invocation of death, terse, decisive, expressing a deliberate resolution: "Kill that woman" (329). With his kingly judgment, however, Herod enacts a different order of fatality than does Salomé, whose insistence on having the head of the prophet expresses her thralldom to an unreflective, proto-Freudian pleasure principle. Although the biblical tale and ensuing adaptations generally cast Salomé as the pawn of Herodias, who herself either detests the prophet for his insults or, occasionally, desires him, Wilde's drama makes a point of Salomé's autonomy: "It is not my mother's voice that I heed. It is for my own pleasure that I ask the head of Iokanaan on a silver charger" (323). Obliged to grant Salomé's appalling wish, Herod finds in the chain of his own word a revelation of the logic of his world. His lesson is a horror, and his retaliation constitutes Wilde's most consequential addition to the legend. (No prior rendering of the theme has Herod putting Salomé to death.) Herod's fatal command allows a closure which not only creates a dramatic final tableau, but also forces into stark representation the intimate relation between literary closure and death, between literary death and "literal" death.

Critics commonly figure death as the crucible of representation, the site ultimately of the formation, the dissolution, and the reconstitution of all ideas of order. It is well to note, however, that one merely *figures* death in this way. At times, of course, one resorts to the convenience of asserting what death "is," but this amounts to a sort of shorthand or even an obfuscation, for it is finally the distinction of the concept of death that it names something profoundly at odds with any instinct to empirical investigation. Intractable reality, utter enigma—the definitively impractical topic—death defines the organic circumstances of each life but frustrates any will one might have to know what death in itself really is. Thus any discourse on death necessitates some degree of Kantian-style critique, one which asks not what the thing itself is, but considers instead under what conceptual conditions, and employing what presuppositions, one finds oneself in a position to entertain the idea at all. All predications to death of quality and essence proceed from some originating conceptual framework, revealing the psychological and cultural structures of such frameworking. (Goodwin and Bronfen collect essays exploring this premise in diverse contexts.) Outfitted with the blindness and partiality essential to any "viewpoint," ideas of death entail the most fundamental versions of critical supplementary thinking, of interpretive criticism. Like the famous veils of Salomé, the figure of death does not make apparent what is really behind the figure, but instead highlights the mandate of consciousness to constructive interpretation, to penetrative investigation. Little surprise, then, that the provocation of an interpretive enigma provides the opening note of this drama. As one sees in the initial dialogue of the Young Syrian and the Page, some ideas will be approachable only through the most impressionistic and ultimately private metaphors: "Death/Salomé is like [. . .]"; "One might fancy Death/ the Moon to be."

Herod's own mode of symbolic investigation introduces a conceptual or interpretive dissonance, one might say, into the musical atmospherics generated by the symbolist-styled figures of Salomé, Iokanaan, the Young Syrian and the Page of Herodias. This disruption does not betoken Herod's lesser involvement with the drama's musicality; instead, it underlines his specifically oppositional function within the verbal music of the work. Together with Herodias, Herod serves as an antipodal—or, if you will, contrapuntal—figure against the musical words of Salomé and her satellites. Like ambassadors from a realist work, Herod and Herodias set into the drama a different order of speech, just as they set into action a different order of psychological conflict, more recognizably realistic and "natural" at the same time that it is patently self-deceiving. Far from being an anti-realistic text, then, *Salomé* formulates an allegory of the contested consciousness, conjoining, on the one hand, the characteristically truncated, prereflective psychologies of the contemporary symbolist drama and, on the other hand, an elaborated, presciently Freudian vision of the repressed consciousness. So the story leads decisively into the "real" world at the moment of Salomé's death at Herod's command: the unrepentantly passionate figures—Salomé, Iokanaan and the Young Syrian—have been closeted away, and the King is full in his powers, although he is now haunted by fear for those powers and privately tormented by their dismaying cost.

Herod's unrest, as well as his determination to act out against that unrest, illustrates a by-now familiar dynamism of ambivalence, where desire and passion are not so much negated as negotiated, redirected, subsumed. Perhaps as pointed an indication as any of Herod's essential modernity will be how fully he can seem to be Foucault's topic in the following passage from *A History of Sexuality,* where Foucault considers the seeming paradox of a culture in which prudery and the obsessive investigation of sexuality would cohabit so easily:

> [T]he learned discourse on sex that was pronounced in the nineteenth century was imbued with age-old delusions, but also with systematic blindnesses: a refusal to see and to understand; but further—and this is the crucial point—a refusal concerning the very thing that was brought to light and whose formulation was urgently solicited. For there can be no misunderstanding that is not based on a fundamental relation to truth. Evading this truth, barring access to it, masking it: these were so many local tactics which, as if by superimposition and through a last-minute detour, gave a paradoxical form to a fundamental petition to know. Choosing not to recognize was yet another vagary of the will to truth.

(55)

Herod's order to kill the virgin temptress—his own last-minute detour—might at first seem a heavy-handed, spiteful meting out of punishment, a sort of "crude but conventional kind of poetic justice," as one critic has it (Schweik 135). But when Herod proposes to refuse or blot out the very thing his urgent solicitations have brought to light, he is not merely exercising a commonplace sort of power, not merely flexing the muscle of brute authority; he is embarking on that path of determined blindnesses that Foucault—like Nietzsche, like Freud—would find to characterize a comprehensive model of "civilized" life, wherein the will to knowledge is intricated with, rather than opposed to, a will to mask such knowledge. The ensuing structure of thought and action acquires what Foucault calls a "paradoxical form"; such formations, famously, are Wilde's essential medium.

Another consideration militates against the notion that Herod's brute authority should be reckoned the final victor in this play: unlike all other characters here, Herod is compelled to a fundamental change of vision, a development of perspective. It has been suggested by Christopher Nassaar (101) and others that Herod, with his concluding command, in some sense puts an end to himself as well as to Salomé. More precisely, perhaps, one might propose that, in putting an end to Salomé, Herod effects a corresponding end to some aspect of his own world. Salomé thus gains against Herod a reciprocal, rather less crude poetic justice, for while he ushers her into death, she introduces him into a new consciousness of death, into an inescapable, unwelcome, utterly human predicament.

The play closes with a dead object, the now speechless head of Iokanaan, returning to Salomé on a silver charger. We are back where this analysis began, then, at the point where Salomé names the "strange music" of this occasion. Although this play constitutes Wilde's most decided vision of the literary aspiration toward the condition of music, he finally gives the stage over not so much to any ardent musicality as to an estranging verbal discourse about it. This distinction between *Salomé*'s musical enactment and the eponymous heroine's closing words about such enactment returns us to my earlier distinction between a logic and metalogic. W. J. T. Mitchell's *Iconology,* which examines ideological dimensions in the word/image nexus, suggests that such a metalogical distinction is called for within all comparative study in the arts. Mitchell urges that we attend to "the way we depict the act of picturing, imagine the activity of imagining, figure the practice of figuration" (5). His "hypericons" name those representations that seem designed both to represent and to render problematic the act of representing, and he cites such figures as Plato's cave in *The Republic,* Aristotle's wax tablet in *De Anima,* Wittgenstein's hieroglyphic, and the painting *Las Meninas* read by Foucault in *The Order of Things.* Each of these images, says Mitchell, is no mere figure, but a figure of figuration.

Wilde's *Salomé* is a sort of hypericon, then, given the divided and even conflicted representational mandate embedded in its aspiration to verbal musicality. The equivocal reflection of musicality through words might best be seen as a representation of that representational impasse. The final moments of this drama reveal Salomé at the threshold of a rupture, just as the play's action—set entirely on another sort of threshold, a terrace—dramatizes the notion of a transitional passageway, a crossroads. Salomé's approach toward the differential universe of language marks the imminent end of the drama itself, and the voice that was music now speaks about music:

> Ah! Iokanaan, Iokanaan, thou wert the man that I loved alone among men! All other men were hateful to me. But thou wert beautiful! Thy body was a column of ivory set upon feet of silver. It was a garden full of doves and lilies of silver. It was a tower of silver decked with shields of ivory. There was nothing in the world so white as thy body. There was nothing in the world so black as thy hair. There was nothing in the world so red as thy mouth. Thy voice was a censer that scattered strange perfumes, and when I looked on thee I heard a strange music.
>
> (328)

As she lavishes words on the decollated head of the prophet, Salomé provides what one might call, with appropriate irony, a "recapitulation" of the drama's progress: she rehearses pointedly that lengthy address she had earlier directed to the still-living Iokanaan, whose body, hair, and mouth had consecutively proved so engrossing. The conjunction of represented decapitation and literal recapitulation illuminates, if obliquely, what is perhaps the most vital condition of literary representation: the possibility, even the necessity, of accommodating an estranged presence with the coping benedictions of the Word. Her means of coping is to repeat what she has said before, but here is a repetition littered with crucial differences. Salomé's first address to Iokanaan resulted in a decided cessation, a *cutting off* of her discourse, which then devolved into a sheerly libidinal and disengaged repetition. Her final address introduces a break as well, but this time with a telling rhetorical difference. Before, Salomé's words to the living prophet had been cast in similes, but at this point (both in the French and the English texts) she replaces simile with metaphor. The body that was once figured through simile after simile—"Thy body is white, like the lilies of a field that the mower hath never mowed" (309)—has apparently undergone a sort of graduation ceremony in its decapitation, for her associative figures of speech no longer propose mere resemblance, but identity: "Thy body *was* a column of ivory set upon feet of silver" (emphasis mine). Her use of the past tense, however, suggests also that she is not simply mad, but is reconstructing the situation. The music has fallen silent, but with her fictions of metaphoric unity, Salomé begins to theorize the prophet in relation to herself, to fathom that he is utterly lost to her, even as she begins to recover what he in fact was to her. Salomé's words amount to an advance into rhetorical interpretation: she takes flight in *apostrophe,* in an address to a definitively absent presence.

At the fountainhead of a Western philosophy of reflections on presences, Plato notes that reading differs from living conversation in one crucial particular: when questioned by the reader, the written word maintains an austere silence (*Protagoras* 329a). This silence is the originating circumstance of interpretation, and Salomé, in this light, has been forced to encounter finally a paradigm of reading or interpreting itself. Like the silent page of Plato, the silenced head of Iokanaan is a provocation to discourse. Where Salomé's first tripartite address had culminated in her swerve into a drunken, disassociated repetition, a reduction or a simplification, her departure here marks her passage into heterogeneous associations: "Thy voice was a censer that scattered strange perfumes, and when I looked on thee I heard a strange music." (328). Transposing into one another scent, sound and sight—in the classic synesthetic manner—her words reflect in this final event not a regressive verbal deterioration, but an exorbitant blossoming, highlighting no less for her than for us the ruptured categories of perception that underlay her infatuation with Iokanaan. Smelling his voice, hearing his looks, Salomé makes clear finally that she was stunned by a figure who embodied the paradoxical breaching of the very boundaries conventionally demarcated by those sensory rubrics. Iokanaan's attractions, therefore, are not merely effects of his "natural" sensible image, but are somehow products of the unhinging heterology suggested to Salomé by that image.

Where an image no longer reflects an unproblematic reality but instead a precise and pointed incommensurability with reality, that image is no longer a representation simply but a representation of representation, a figure of figuration. Here, values of objective mimesis become confounded by the perspectival involvements of the subjective interpreter. As Michael Riffaterre has remarked, the conjunction of description and imagery in literary discourse is taken rather too often to indicate that imagery can be a decorative addition to description, providing a continued confirmation of the referential commitments of description, even though imagery's "primary purpose is not to offer a representation, but to dictate an interpretation" (125). One finds in the construction and interpretation of such figures a perpetual logic of recursion, an ongoing negotiation of subjective perception and its objective occasion. In staging that negotiation, Wilde's *Salomé* might be said to find its nearest approach to a thesis: this play of revelations or unveilings defines the very dialectics of desire and revelation, where the thing revealed is finally not a thing in itself, but a figure defined by the personal and the cultural structures of a desiring, interpretive consciousness.

That proposition amounts, in fact, to a paraphrase of a Wildean comment offered earlier in this essay: "One can really [. . .] be far more subjective in an objective form than in any other way." Salomé's passion for Iokanaan resembles Wilde's own enduring attraction to this drama, which Ada Leverson had said "expressed himself in his innate love of the gorgeous and bizarre." For Wilde, the gorgeous and the bizarre are not merely affronts to Victorian moral convention, but affronts as well to the schematizing, anatomizing impulses of representational thought as the Victorians would know it. The "strange music" of *Salomé*, in its turn, is not finally a music in any distinct or rigorous sense, but a figure of an instructive impasse embedded in verbal musicality. *Salomé* registers no mere attempt at a literary music appreciation. Instead, this "strange music" allows one more way in which Wilde can spotlight the definitively, perpetually unfulfilled aspirations of representation itself.

Notes

1. Quotations from Wilde's *Salomé* are drawn primarily from the first English edition, although I refer once to the original French version of the play. The authority of the English text merits some comment. Translated rather incompetently by Lord Alfred Douglas—Wilde mentions "the schoolboy faults" of that "attempted translation" (*Letters* 432)—*Salomé* was later polished up by Wilde to an indeterminate extent, and critics have differed considerably in assessing the final authority of the English version. In any event, the points that I develop do not depend substantially on the peculiarities of any given version, so the original English text seems the logical choice in an English discussion.

2. Wilde here echoes his remarks from several months earlier in the long prison letter *De Profundis* (466). His reference to *Intentions* seems to indicate a passage in "The Critic as Artist II," where Gilbert dilates upon the proposition that "the more objective a creation appears to be, the more subjective it really is" (281).

Works Cited

Abrams, M. H. *The Mirror and the Lamp: Romantic Theory and the Critical Tradition.* New York: Oxford UP, 1953.

Allen, Virginia M. *The Femme Fatale: Erotic Icon.* Troy: Whitson, 1983.

Bakhtin, M. M. *The Dialogic Imagination.* Ed. Michael Holquist. Trans. Caryl Emerson and Michael Holquist. Austin: U of Texas P, 1981.

Barthes, Roland. *The Pleasure of the Text.* Trans. Richard Miller. New York: Hill and Wang, 1975.

Baudelaire, Charles. *Flowers of Evil.* [*Les Fleurs du Mal.*] Eds. Marthiel and Jackson Matthews. Various Trans. New York: New Directions, 1989.

Cohen, Ed. "Writing Gone Wilde: Homoerotic Desire in the Closet of Representation." *PMLA* 102.5 (1987): 801-13.

Craft, Christopher. "Alias Bunbury: Desire and Termination in *The Importance of Being Earnest.*" *Representations* 31 (1990): 19-46.

Dellamora, Richard. "Representation and Homophobia in *The Picture of Dorian Gray.*" *Victorian Newsletter* 73 (1988): 28-31.

Dijkstra, Bram. *Idols of Perversity: Fantasies of Feminine Evil in Fin-de-Siècle Culture.* New York: Oxford UP, 1986.

Dollimore, Jonathan. "Different Desires: Subjectivity and Transgression in Wilde and Gide." *Textual Practice* 1.1 (1987): 48-67.

Dowling, Linda. *Language and Decadence in the Victorian Fin de Siècle.* Princeton: Princeton UP, 1986.

Edelman, Lee. "Homographesis." *The Yale Journal of Criticism* 3.1 (1989): 189-207.

Ellmann, Richard. *Oscar Wilde.* New York: Knopf, 1988.

Finney, Gail. *Women in Modern Drama: Freud, Feminism, and European Theater at the Turn of the Century.* Ithaca: Cornell UP, 1989.

Foucault, Michel. *An Introduction.* Trans. Robert Hurley. New York: Vintage, 1980. Vol. 1 of *A History of Sexuality.* 3 vols. 1978-86.

Freud, Sigmund. *Beyond the Pleasure Principle.* Trans. James Strachey. New York: Norton, 1961.

Garber, Marjorie. *Vested Interests: Cross-Dressing and Cultural Representation.* New York: Harper, 1993.

Goodwin, Sarah Webster, and Elizabeth Bronfen, eds. *Death and Representation.* Baltimore: Johns Hopkins UP, 1993.

James, Henry. *Henry James: Selected Letters.* Ed. Leon Edel. Cambridge: Harvard UP, 1987.

Kermode, Frank. *The Sense of an Ending: Studies in the Theory of Fiction.* Oxford: Oxford UP, 1967.

Kosofsky-Sedgwick, Eve. *Epistemology of the Closet.* Berkeley: U of California P, 1990.

Kramer, Lawrence. *Music and Poetry: The Nineteenth Century and After.* Berkeley: U of California P, 1984.

Leverson, Ada. "Reminiscences." Wyndham 103-23.

Mitchell, W. J. T. *Iconology: Image, Text, Ideology.* Chicago: U of Chicago P, 1986.

Murray, Isobel, ed. *Oscar Wilde.* The Oxford Authors. Oxford: Oxford UP, 1989.

Nassaar, Christopher S. *Into the Demon Universe: A Literary Exploration of Oscar Wilde.* New Haven: Yale UP, 1974.

Pater, Walter. "The School of Giorgione." *The Renaissance: Studies in Art and Poetry. The 1893 Text.* Ed. Donald Hill. Berkeley: U of California P, 1980. 102-22.

Raymond, Jean Paul, and Charles Ricketts. *Oscar Wilde: Recollections.* Bloomsbury, London: Nonesuch, 1932.

Riffaterre, Michael. "Descriptive Imagery." *Yale French Studies* 61 (1981): 107-25.

Scher, Steven Paul. *Verbal Music in German Literature.* New Haven: Yale UP, 1968.

Schweik, Robert. "Oscar Wilde's *Salomé,* the Salomé Theme in Late European Art, and a Problem of Method in Cultural History." *Twilight of Dawn: Studies in English Literature in Transition.* Ed. O. M. Brack, Jr. Tucson: U of Arizona P, 1987. 123-36.

Showalter, Elaine. *Sexual Anarchy: Gender and Culture at the Fin de Sciècle.* New York: Viking, 1990.

Wilde, Oscar. "The Critic as Artist I." Murray 241-66.

————. "The Critic as Artist II." Murray 267-97.

————. [*De Profundis.*] *The Letters of Oscar Wilde.* Ed. Rupert Hart-Davis. New York: Harcourt, 1962. 423-511.

————. *The First Collected Edition of the Works of Oscar Wilde.* Ed. Robert Ross. 15 vols. London: Methuen, 1908-1922. Rpt. London: Dawsons, 1969.

————. *The Importance of Being Earnest.* Murray 477-538.

————. *The Letters of Oscar Wilde.* Ed. Rupert Hart-Davis. New York: Harcourt, 1962.

————. *Miscellanies. First Collected Edition.* Vol. 14.

————. *The Picture of Dorian Gray.* Murray 47-214.

————. *Salomé.* Murray 299-329.

————. *Salomé Drame en un acte. First Collected Edition.* Vol. 2. 1-82.

————. "The Truth of Masks." *The Artist as Critic: Critical Writings of Oscar Wilde.* Ed. Richard Ellmann. Chicago: U of Chicago P, 1968. 408-32.

Wyndham, Violet. *The Sphinx and Her Circle: A Biographical Sketch of Ada Leverson, 1862-1933.* London: Deutsch, 1963.

Yeats, William Butler. *The King of the Great Clock Tower. The Collected Plays of W. B. Yeats.* 2nd ed. London: Macmillan, 1953. 631-42.

Christopher S. Nassaar and Nataly Shaheen (essay date spring 2001)

SOURCE: Nassaar, Christopher S., and Nataly Shaheen. "Wilde's *Salomé*." *Explicator* 59, no. 3 (spring 2001): 132-34.

[*In the following essay, Nassaar and Shaheen discuss stylistic and thematic aspects of* Salomé.]

Wilde's **Salomé** has a tripartite structure. The moon-goddess Cybele, Salomé, and Herodias, for instance, represent the same principle in a descending order and are opposed respectively by Jesus, Jokanaan, and the Nazarenes. Jokanaan is associated with three colors—white, black, and red; Salomé in wooing him approaches him three times. The language often repeats basic words and phrases in groups of three. One of the significant tripartite

associations of the play is Salomé's connection with mythic demonic creatures. In his attempt to dramatize Salomé as a symbol of pure evil, Wilde associates her with the vampire, the siren, and the werewolf.

The vampiric associations are made clear at the opening of the play, when the Young Syrian notes how pale Salomé is and the Page of Herodias says of her, "She is like a woman rising from a tomb. She is like a dead woman" (583). Symbolically she is dead and in search of a human to satisfy her raging desire for blood, like any vampire. She chooses Jokanaan, but his continuous rejection of her creates a tense and expectant atmosphere. Salomé claims Jokanaan's head, and in a moment of darkness, she kisses and bites the severed head, her ultimate coupling with the dead prophet. She has won him, but Wilde leaves us, not only with a woman who has killed a prophet, but also with a woman declaring: "Ah! I have kissed thy mouth, Jokanaan. I have kissed thy mouth. There was a bitter taste on thy lips. Was it the taste of blood . . . ? But perchance it is the taste of love" (605). The pause that comes after "taste of blood" is significant. Salomé has bitten her victim and has drawn blood. The teasing silence that comes before her announcement that this is "the taste of love" is a moment for the audience to comprehend the nature of the vampire in the princess.

Another association that Wilde draws in his depiction of Salomé is that of a siren. One of the most famous literary stories of sirens is that found in the *Odyssey,* but the nineteenth-century literary landscape is full of them.[1] Salomé seduces men and directly causes their death, be it physical or spiritual, although paradoxically it is she who is ensnared by the voice of Jokanaan. The play opens with the Young Syrian fascinated by the princess. He unwillingly gazes on her. He is incapable of looking away even after his friend, the Page of Herodias, warns him. He is aware that his attraction is unsuitable because of her lineage and his position in her stepfather's palace, but he is captive to his raging desire. He defies the Tetrarch in his wish to please the princess, but when she rejects him, he destroys himself like the shipwrecked victims of Homer's sirens.

Immediately after the captain's death, Herod walks onto the terrace, only to find himself lured by Salomé. Salomé rejects his advances until she realizes that only through him can she capture Jokanaan. She weaves her spell around Herod as she dances her erotic dance. He is completely captured, and she takes advantage of the situation. She asks of him the only thing that he dare not give her, the head of Jokanaan. The promise that she has extracted in the heat of his passion forces Herod to surrender to her power of seduction. He becomes the slave of her desire who loses his hold on reality as he watches her feasting on the prophet's head. Herod's death by a siren is not physical. He remains alive, but his mental and spiritual existence is demolished by Salomé.

Even Jokanaan, the man/prophet who resists her overtures, is not free of her spell. Salomé, using her charms on others, is the active agent in his death sentence. Sirens, like vampires, transgress rules of human sexuality. Wilde plays on all taboos in this play.

Another violation is Wilde's use of human transformation. He does not accept the traditional separation between man and beast. He introduces the image of a werewolf, another creature that lived in the late Victorian imagination.[2] Under the light of a full moon, Salomé undergoes a change in her personality as the play's action rises. The change happens gradually as she is introduced and as she wins over the Young Syrian, but then she quickly takes on the more demonic role of seductress. At the end of her erotic dance, Salomé unashamedly announces her bestiality. She needs to "devour" Jokanaan to survive. The mutation reiterates Wilde's belief that human beings are beasts with bestial needs. This shocking statement would not have left his Victorian audience unmoved. Wilde is poking fun at their dearly held beliefs in the near-divinity of humankind and in their supremacy over all of God's other creations. To be reduced to mere animals with a need to kill is an insult to an audience that thought of themselves as the masters and conquerors of the world. In **Salomé,** Wilde aims to shock by all means possible, presenting a view of human nature that is at once compelling and terrifying.

Notes

1. Dante Gabriel Rossetti, in his late poetry, is siren-haunted, as in "Troy Town," "The Orchard-Pit," and the "Body's Beauty" sonnet of *The House of Life.*

2. William Morris's references to werewolves in *The Volsung Saga* (1876) are one example of the late Victorian interest in werewolves, as is Clemence Housman's *The Werewolf* (1896).

Work Cited

Wilde, Oscar. *Salomé. Complete Works.* 3rd ed. Glasgow: Harper, 1994.

FURTHER READING

Biographies

Ellmann, Richard. *Oscar Wilde.* New York: Alfred A. Knopf, 1988, 680 p.

Highly acclaimed biographical study.

Winwar, Frances. *Oscar Wilde and the Yellow 'Nineties.* Garden City, NY: Blue Ribbon Books, 1940, 381 p.

Popular biography of Wilde.

Criticism

Chamberlin, J. E. *Ripe Was the Drowsy Hour: The Age of Oscar Wilde.* New York: The Seabury Press, 1977, 222 p.

Examines Wilde in the social and artistic contexts of his time.

Ellmann, Richard, ed. *Oscar Wilde: A Collection of Critical Essays.* Englewood Cliffs, NJ: Prentice-Hall, 1969, 180 p.

Critical essays and poetical tributes by W. B. Yeats, André Gide, Alfred Douglas, John Betjeman, Thomas Mann, and Jorge Luis Borges, among others.

Ericksen, Donald H. *Oscar Wilde.* Boston: Twayne Publishers, 1977, 175 p.

Discusses sources, plot, characterization, language, and critical reception of Wilde's best-known works.

Woodcock, George. *The Paradox of Oscar Wilde.* London: T. V. Boardman & Co., 1949, 239 p.

Explores the different perspectives of Wilde.

Additional coverage of Wilde's life and career is contained in the following sources published by the Gale Group: *British Writers,* **Vol. 5;** *Concise Dictionary of British Literary Biography 1890-1914;* *Contemporary Authors,* **Vols. 104, 119;** *Dictionary of Literary Biography,* **Vols. 10, 19, 34, 57, 141, 156, 190;** *DISCovering Authors; DISCovering Authors: British Edition; DISCovering Authors: Canadian Edition; DISCovering Authors Modules: Dramatists, Most-studied Authors,* **and** *Novelists; DISCovering Authors 3.0; Drama for Students,* **Vols. 4, 8, 9;** *Exploring Short Stories; Literature Resource Center; Reference Guide to English Literature; Reference Guide to Short Fiction; St. James Guide to Fantasy Writers; Short Story Criticism,* **Vol. 11;** *Short Stories for Students,* **Vol. 7;** *Something About the Author,* **Vol. 24;** *Supernatural Fiction Writers; Twayne's English Authors; Twentieth-Century Literary Criticism,* **Vols. 1, 8, 23, 41;** *World Literature and Its Times,* **Vol. 4;** *World Literature Criticism;* **and** *Writers for Children.*

How to Use This Index

Literary Criticism Series
Cumulative Author Index

Alta 1942- .... **CLC 19**
    See also CA 57-60

Alter, Robert B(ernard) 1935- .... **CLC 34**
    See also CA 49-52; CANR 1, 47, 100

Alther, Lisa 1944- .... **CLC 7, 41**
    See also BPFB 1; CA 65-68; CAAS 30;
    CANR 12, 30, 51; CN 7; CSW; GLL 2;
    MTCW 1

Althusser, L.
    See Althusser, Louis

Althusser, Louis 1918-1990 .... **CLC 106**
    See also CA 131; 132; CANR 102; DLB
    242

Altman, Robert 1925- .... **CLC 16, 116**
    See also CA 73-76; CANR 43

Alurista
    See Urista, Alberto H.
    See also DLB 82; HLCS 1

Alvarez, A(lfred) 1929- .... **CLC 5, 13**
    See also CA 1-4R; CANR 3, 33, 63, 101;
    CN 7; CP 7; DLB 14, 40

Alvarez, Alejandro Rodriguez 1903-1965
    See Casona, Alejandro
    See also CA 131; 93-96; HW 1

Alvarez, Julia 1950- .... **CLC 93; HLCS 1**
    See also AAYA 25; AMWS 7; CA 147;
    CANR 69, 101; DA3; MTCW 1; NFS 5,
    9; SATA 129; WLIT 1

Alvaro, Corrado 1896-1956 .... **TCLC 60**
    See also CA 163

Amado, Jorge 1912-2001 ... **CLC 13, 40, 106;
    HLC 1**
    See also CA 77-80; CANR 35, 74; DAM
    MULT, NOV; DLB 113; HW 2; LAW;
    LAWS 1; MTCW 1, 2; RGWL 2; WLIT 1

Ambler, Eric 1909-1998 .... **CLC 4, 6, 9**
    See also BRWS 4; CA 9-12R; 171; CANR
    7, 38, 74; CMW 4; CN 7; DLB 77; MSW;
    MTCW 1, 2

Ambrose, Stephen E(dward)
    1936- .... **CLC 145**
    See also CA 1-4R; CANR 3, 43, 57, 83,
    105; NCFS 2; SATA 40

Amichai, Yehuda 1924-2000 .. **CLC 9, 22, 57,
    116; PC 38**
    See also CA 85-88; 189; CANR 46, 60, 99;
    CWW 2; MTCW 1

Amichai, Yehudah
    See Amichai, Yehuda

Amiel, Henri Frederic 1821-1881 .... **NCLC 4**
    See also DLB 217

Amis, Kingsley (William)
    1922-1995 ...... **CLC 1, 2, 3, 5, 8, 13, 40,
    44, 129**
    See also AITN 2; BPFB 1; BRWS 2; CA
    9-12R; 150; CANR 8, 28, 54; CDBLB
    1945-1960; CN 7; CP 7; DA; DA3; DAB;
    DAC; DAM MST, NOV; DLB 15, 27,
    100, 139; DLBY 1996; HGG; INT
    CANR-8; MTCW 1, 2; RGEL 2; RGSF 2;
    SFW 4

Amis, Martin (Louis) 1949- .... **CLC 4, 9, 38,
    62, 101**
    See also BEST 90:3; BRWS 4; CA 65-68;
    CANR 8, 27, 54, 73, 95; CN 7; DA3;
    DLB 14, 194; INT CANR-27; MTCW 1

Ammons, A(rchie) R(andolph)
    1926-2001 ...... **CLC 2, 3, 5, 8, 9, 25, 57,
    108; PC 16**
    See also AITN 1; AMWS 7; CA 9-12R;
    193; CANR 6, 36, 51, 73, 107; CP 7;
    CSW; DAM POET; DLB 5, 165; MTCW
    1, 2; RGAL 4

Amo, Tauraatua i
    See Adams, Henry (Brooks)

Amory, Thomas 1691(?)-1788 .... **LC 48**
    See also DLB 39

Anand, Mulk Raj 1905- .... **CLC 23, 93**
    See also CA 65-68; CANR 32, 64; CN 7;
    DAM NOV; MTCW 1, 2; RGSF 2

Anatol
    See Schnitzler, Arthur

Anaximander c. 611B.C.-c.
    546B.C. .... **CMLC 22**

Anaya, Rudolfo A(lfonso) 1937- ...... **CLC 23,
    148; HLC 1**
    See also AAYA 20; BYA 13; CA 45-48;
    CAAS 4; CANR 1, 32, 51; CN 7; DAM
    MULT, NOV; DLB 82, 206; HW 1; LAIT
    4; MTCW 1, 2; NFS 12; RGAL 4; RGSF
    2; WLIT 1

Andersen, Hans Christian
    1805-1875 ... **NCLC 7, 79; SSC 6; WLC**
    See also CLR 6; DA; DA3; DAB; DAC;
    DAM MST, POP; EW 6; MAICYA 1;
    RGSF 2; RGWL 2; SATA 100; WCH;
    YABC 1

Anderson, C. Farley
    See Mencken, H(enry) L(ouis); Nathan,
    George Jean

Anderson, Jessica (Margaret) Queale
    1916- .... **CLC 37**
    See also CA 9-12R; CANR 4, 62; CN 7

Anderson, Jon (Victor) 1940- .... **CLC 9**
    See also CA 25-28R; CANR 20; DAM
    POET

Anderson, Lindsay (Gordon)
    1923-1994 .... **CLC 20**
    See also CA 125; 128; 146; CANR 77

Anderson, Maxwell 1888-1959 .... **TCLC 2**
    See also CA 105; 152; DAM DRAM; DLB
    7, 228; MTCW 2; RGAL 4

Anderson, Poul (William)
    1926-2001 .... **CLC 15**
    See also AAYA 5, 34; BPFB 1; BYA 6, 8,
    9; CA 1-4R; 181; 199; CAAE 181; CAAS
    2; CANR 2, 15, 34, 64; CLR 58; DLB 8;
    FANT; INT CANR-15; MTCW 1, 2;
    SATA 90; SATA-Brief 39; SATA-Essay
    106; SCFW 2; SFW 4; SUFW

Anderson, Robert (Woodruff)
    1917- .... **CLC 23**
    See also AITN 1; CA 21-24R; CANR 32;
    DAM DRAM; DLB 7; LAIT 5

Anderson, Roberta Joan
    See Mitchell, Joni

Anderson, Sherwood 1876-1941 ..... **TCLC 1,
    10, 24; SSC 1, 46; WLC**
    See also AAYA 30; AMW; BPFB 1; CA
    104; 121; CANR 61; CDALB 1917-1929;
    DA; DA3; DAB; DAC; DAM MST, NOV;
    DLB 4, 9, 86; DLBD 1; EXPS; GLL 2;
    MTCW 1, 2; NFS 4; RGAL 4; RGSF 2;
    SSFS 4, 10, 11

Andier, Pierre
    See Desnos, Robert

Andouard
    See Giraudoux, Jean(-Hippolyte)

Andrade, Carlos Drummond de ..... **CLC 18**
    See also Drummond de Andrade, Carlos
    See also RGWL 2

Andrade, Mario de .... **TCLC 43**
    See also de Andrade, Mario
    See also LAW; RGWL 2; WLIT 1

Andreae, Johann V(alentin)
    1586-1654 .... **LC 32**
    See also DLB 164

Andreas Capellanus fl. c. 1185- .... **CMLC 45**
    See also DLB 208

Andreas-Salome, Lou 1861-1937 ... **TCLC 56**
    See also CA 178; DLB 66

Andress, Lesley
    See Sanders, Lawrence

Andrewes, Lancelot 1555-1626 .... **LC 5**
    See also DLB 151, 172

Andrews, Cicily Fairfield
    See West, Rebecca

Andrews, Elton V.
    See Pohl, Frederik

Andreyev, Leonid (Nikolaevich)
    1871-1919 .... **TCLC 3**
    See also CA 104; 185

Andric, Ivo 1892-1975 .... **CLC 8; SSC 36**
    See also CA 81-84; 57-60; CANR 43, 60;
    CDWLB 4; DLB 147; EW 11; MTCW 1;
    RGSF 2; RGWL 2

Androvar
    See Prado (Calvo), Pedro

Angelique, Pierre
    See Bataille, Georges

Angell, Roger 1920- .... **CLC 26**
    See also CA 57-60; CANR 13, 44, 70; DLB
    171, 185

Angelou, Maya 1928- ..... **CLC 12, 35, 64, 77,
    155; BLC 1; PC 32; WLCS**
    See also AAYA 7, 20; AMWS 4; BPFB 1;
    BW 2, 3; BYA 2; CA 65-68; CANR 19,
    42, 65; CDALBS; CLR 53; CP 7; CPW;
    CSW; CWP; DA; DA3; DAB; DAC;
    DAM MST, MULT, POET; DLB 38;
    EXPN; EXPP; LAIT 4; MAICYAS 1;
    MAWW; MTCW 1, 2; NCFS 2; NFS 2;
    PFS 2, 3; RGAL 4; SATA 49; WYA; YAW

Angouleme, Marguerite d'
    See de Navarre, Marguerite

Anna Comnena 1083-1153 .... **CMLC 25**

Annensky, Innokenty (Fyodorovich)
    1856-1909 .... **TCLC 14**
    See also CA 110; 155

Annunzio, Gabriele d'
    See D'Annunzio, Gabriele

Anodos
    See Coleridge, Mary E(lizabeth)

Anon, Charles Robert
    See Pessoa, Fernando (Antonio Nogueira)

Anouilh, Jean (Marie Lucien Pierre)
    1910-1987 . **CLC 1, 3, 8, 13, 40, 50; DC
    8**
    See also CA 17-20R; 123; CANR 32; DAM
    DRAM; DFS 9, 10; EW 13; GFL 1789 to
    the Present; MTCW 1, 2; RGWL 2

Anthony, Florence
    See Ai

Anthony, John
    See Ciardi, John (Anthony)

Anthony, Peter
    See Shaffer, Anthony (Joshua); Shaffer,
    Peter (Levin)

Anthony, Piers 1934- .... **CLC 35**
    See also AAYA 11; BYA 7; CA 21-24R;
    CANR 28, 56, 73, 102; CPW; DAM POP;
    DLB 8; FANT; MAICYAS 1; MTCW 1,
    2; SAAS 22; SATA 84; SATA-Essay 129;
    SFW 4; SUFW; YAW

Anthony, Susan B(rownell)
    1820-1906 .... **TCLC 84**
    See also FW

Antoine, Marc
    See Proust, (Valentin-Louis-George-Eugene-
)Marcel

Antoninus, Brother
    See Everson, William (Oliver)

Antonioni, Michelangelo 1912- .... **CLC 20,
    144**
    See also CA 73-76; CANR 45, 77

Antschel, Paul 1920-1970
    See Celan, Paul
    See also CA 85-88; CANR 33, 61; MTCW
    1

Anwar, Chairil 1922-1949 .... **TCLC 22**
    See also CA 121

Anzaldua, Gloria (Evanjelina) 1942-
    See also CA 175; CSW; CWP; DLB 122;
    FW; HLCS 1; RGAL 4

Baudelaire, Charles 1821-1867 . **NCLC 6, 29, 55; PC 1; SSC 18; WLC**
See also DA; DA3; DAB; DAC; DAM MST, POET; DLB 217; EW 7; GFL 1789 to the Present; RGWL 2

Baudouin, Marcel
See Peguy, Charles (Pierre)

Baudouin, Pierre
See Peguy, Charles (Pierre)

Baudrillard, Jean 1929- .... **CLC 60**

Baum, L(yman) Frank 1856-1919 ... **TCLC 7**
See also CA 108; 133; CLR 15; CWRI 5; DLB 22; FANT; JRDA; MAICYA 1; MTCW 1, 2; NFS 13; RGAL 4; SATA 18, 100; WCH

Baum, Louis F.
See Baum, L(yman) Frank

Baumbach, Jonathan 1933- .... **CLC 6, 23**
See also CA 13-16R; CAAS 5; CANR 12, 66; CN 7; DLBY 1980; INT CANR-12; MTCW 1

Bausch, Richard (Carl) 1945- .... **CLC 51**
See also AMWS 7; CA 101; CAAS 14; CANR 43, 61, 87; CSW; DLB 130

Baxter, Charles (Morley) 1947- . **CLC 45, 78**
See also CA 57-60; CANR 40, 64, 104; CPW; DAM POP; DLB 130; MTCW 2

Baxter, George Owen
See Faust, Frederick (Schiller)

Baxter, James K(eir) 1926-1972 .... **CLC 14**
See also CA 77-80

Baxter, John
See Hunt, E(verette) Howard, (Jr.)

Bayer, Sylvia
See Glassco, John

Baynton, Barbara 1857-1929 .... **TCLC 57**
See also DLB 230; RGSF 2

Beagle, Peter S(oyer) 1939- .... **CLC 7, 104**
See also BPFB 1; BYA 9, 10; CA 9-12R; CANR 4, 51, 73; DA3; DLBY 1980; FANT; INT CANR-4; MTCW 1; SATA 60; SUFW; YAW

Bean, Normal
See Burroughs, Edgar Rice

Beard, Charles A(ustin)
1874-1948 .... **TCLC 15**
See also CA 115; 189; DLB 17; SATA 18

Beardsley, Aubrey 1872-1898 .... **NCLC 6**

Beattie, Ann 1947- ..... **CLC 8, 13, 18, 40, 63, 146; SSC 11**
See also AMWS 5; BEST 90:2; BPFB 1; CA 81-84; CANR 53, 73; CN 7; CPW; DA3; DAM NOV, POP; DLB 218; DLBY 1982; MTCW 1, 2; RGAL 4; RGSF 2; SSFS 9

Beattie, James 1735-1803 .... **NCLC 25**
See also DLB 109

Beauchamp, Kathleen Mansfield 1888-1923
See Mansfield, Katherine
See also CA 104; 134; DA; DA3; DAC; DAM MST; MTCW 2

Beaumarchais, Pierre-Augustin Caron de
1732-1799 .... **LC 61; DC 4**
See also DAM DRAM; EW 4; GFL Beginnings to 1789; RGWL 2

Beaumont, Francis 1584(?)-1616 .... **LC 33; DC 6**
See also BRW 2; CDBLB Before 1660; DLB 58

Beauvoir, Simone (Lucie Ernestine Marie Bertrand) de 1908-1986 .... **CLC 1, 2, 4, 8, 14, 31, 44, 50, 71, 124; SSC 35; WLC**
See also BPFB 1; CA 9-12R; 118; CANR 28, 61; DA; DA3; DAB; DAC; DAM MST, NOV; DLB 72; DLBY 1986; EW 12; FW; GFL 1789 to the Present; MTCW 1, 2; RGSF 2; RGWL 2

Becker, Carl (Lotus) 1873-1945 ..... **TCLC 63**
See also CA 157; DLB 17

Becker, Jurek 1937-1997 .... **CLC 7, 19**
See also CA 85-88; 157; CANR 60; CWW 2; DLB 75

Becker, Walter 1950- .... **CLC 26**

Beckett, Samuel (Barclay)
1906-1989 .. **CLC 1, 2, 3, 4, 6, 9, 10, 11, 14, 18, 29, 57, 59, 83; SSC 16; WLC**
See also BRWR 1; BRWS 1; CA 5-8R; 130; CANR 33, 61; CBD; CDBLB 1945-1960; DA; DA3; DAB; DAC; DAM DRAM, MST, NOV; DFS 2, 7; DLB 13, 15, 233; DLBY 1990; GFL 1789 to the Present; MTCW 1, 2; RGSF 2; RGWL 2; WLIT 4

Beckford, William 1760-1844 .... **NCLC 16**
See also BRW 3; DLB 39, 213; HGG; SUFW

Beckman, Gunnel 1910- .... **CLC 26**
See also CA 33-36R; CANR 15; CLR 25; MAICYA 1; SAAS 9; SATA 6

Becque, Henri 1837-1899 .... **NCLC 3**
See also CA 192; DLB 192; GFL 1789 to the Present

Becquer, Gustavo Adolfo
1836-1870 .... **NCLC 106; HLCS 1**
See also DAM MULT

Beddoes, Thomas Lovell
1803-1849 .... **NCLC 3; DC 15**
See also DLB 96

Bede c. 673-735 .... **CMLC 20**
See also DLB 146

Bedford, Donald F.
See Fearing, Kenneth (Flexner)

Beecher, Catharine Esther
1800-1878 .... **NCLC 30**
See also DLB 1, 243

Beecher, John 1904-1980 .... **CLC 6**
See also AITN 1; CA 5-8R; 105; CANR 8

Beer, Johann 1655-1700 .... **LC 5**
See also DLB 168

Beer, Patricia 1924- .... **CLC 58**
See also CA 61-64; 183; CANR 13, 46; CP 7; CWP; DLB 40; FW

Beerbohm, Max
See Beerbohm, (Henry) Max(imilian)

Beerbohm, (Henry) Max(imilian)
1872-1956 .... **TCLC 1, 24**
See also BRWS 2; CA 104; 154; CANR 79; DLB 34, 100; FANT

Beer-Hofmann, Richard
1866-1945 .... **TCLC 60**
See also CA 160; DLB 81

Beg, Shemus
See Stephens, James

Begiebing, Robert J(ohn) 1946- .... **CLC 70**
See also CA 122; CANR 40, 88

Behan, Brendan 1923-1964 ...... **CLC 1, 8, 11, 15, 79**
See also BRWS 2; CA 73-76; CANR 33; CBD; CDBLB 1945-1960; DAM DRAM; DFS 7; DLB 13, 233; MTCW 1, 2

Behn, Aphra 1640(?)-1689 .... **LC 1, 30, 42; DC 4; PC 13; WLC**
See also BRWS 3; DA; DA3; DAB; DAC; DAM DRAM, MST, NOV, POET; DLB 39, 80, 131; FW; WLIT 3

Behrman, S(amuel) N(athaniel)
1893-1973 .... **CLC 40**
See also CA 13-16; 45-48; CAD; CAP 1; DLB 7, 44; IDFW 3; RGAL 4

Belasco, David 1853-1931 .... **TCLC 3**
See also CA 104; 168; DLB 7; RGAL 4

Belcheva, Elisaveta Lyubomirova
1893-1991 .... **CLC 10**
See also Bagryana, Elisaveta

Beldone, Phil "Cheech"
See Ellison, Harlan (Jay)

Beleno
See Azuela, Mariano

Belinski, Vissarion Grigoryevich
1811-1848 .... **NCLC 5**
See also DLB 198

Belitt, Ben 1911- .... **CLC 22**
See also CA 13-16R; CAAS 4; CANR 7, 77; CP 7; DLB 5

Bell, Gertrude (Margaret Lowthian)
1868-1926 .... **TCLC 67**
See also CA 167; DLB 174

Bell, J. Freeman
See Zangwill, Israel

Bell, James Madison 1826-1902 ... **TCLC 43; BLC 1**
See also BW 1; CA 122; 124; DAM MULT; DLB 50

Bell, Madison Smartt 1957- ...... **CLC 41, 102**
See also AMWS 10; BPFB 1; CA 111, 183; CAAE 183; CANR 28, 54, 73; CN 7; CSW; DLB 218; MTCW 1

Bell, Marvin (Hartley) 1937- .... **CLC 8, 31**
See also CA 21-24R; CAAS 14; CANR 59, 102; CP 7; DAM POET; DLB 5; MTCW 1

Bell, W. L. D.
See Mencken, H(enry) L(ouis)

Bellamy, Atwood C.
See Mencken, H(enry) L(ouis)

Bellamy, Edward 1850-1898 ...... **NCLC 4, 86**
See also DLB 12; RGAL 4; SFW 4

Belli, Gioconda 1949-
See also CA 152; CWW 2; HLCS 1

Bellin, Edward J.
See Kuttner, Henry

Belloc, (Joseph) Hilaire (Pierre Sebastien Rene Swanton) 1870-1953 ...... **TCLC 7, 18; PC 24**
See also CA 106; 152; CWRI 5; DAM POET; DLB 19, 100, 141, 174; MTCW 1; SATA 112; WCH; YABC 1

Belloc, Joseph Peter Rene Hilaire
See Belloc, (Joseph) Hilaire (Pierre Sebastien Rene Swanton)

Belloc, Joseph Pierre Hilaire
See Belloc, (Joseph) Hilaire (Pierre Sebastien Rene Swanton)

Belloc, M. A.
See Lowndes, Marie Adelaide (Belloc)

Bellow, Saul 1915- . **CLC 1, 2, 3, 6, 8, 10, 13, 15, 25, 33, 34, 63, 79; SSC 14; WLC**
See also AITN 2; AMW; BEST 89:3; BPFB 1; CA 5-8R; CABS 1; CANR 29, 53, 95; CDALB 1941-1968; CN 7; DA; DA3; DAB; DAC; DAM MST, NOV, POP; DLB 2, 28; DLBD 3; DLBY 1982; MTCW 1, 2; NFS 4; RGAL 4; RGSF 2; SSFS 12

Belser, Reimond Karel Maria de 1929-
See Ruyslinck, Ward
See also CA 152

Bely, Andrey .... **TCLC 7; PC 11**
See also Bugayev, Boris Nikolayevich
See also EW 9; MTCW 1

Belyi, Andrei
See Bugayev, Boris Nikolayevich
See also RGWL 2

Benary, Margot
See Benary-Isbert, Margot

Benary-Isbert, Margot 1889-1979 .... **CLC 12**
See also CA 5-8R; 89-92; CANR 4, 72; CLR 12; MAICYA 1; SATA 2; SATA-Obit 21

Benavente (y Martinez), Jacinto
1866-1954 .... **TCLC 3; HLCS 1**
See also CA 106; 131; CANR 81; DAM DRAM, MULT; GLL 2; HW 1, 2; MTCW 1, 2

Bialik, Chaim Nachman
1873-1934 .... **TCLC 25**
See also CA 170

Bickerstaff, Isaac
See Swift, Jonathan

Bidart, Frank 1939- .... **CLC 33**
See also CA 140; CANR 106; CP 7

Bienek, Horst 1930- .... **CLC 7, 11**
See also CA 73-76; DLB 75

Bierce, Ambrose (Gwinett)
1842-1914(?) ..... **TCLC 1, 7, 44; SSC 9;**
WLC
See also AMW; BYA 11; CA 104; 139;
CANR 78; CDALB 1865-1917; DA;
DA3; DAC; DAM MST; DLB 11, 12, 23,
71, 74, 186; EXPS; HGG; LAIT 2; RGAL
4; RGSF 2; SSFS 9; SUFW

Biggers, Earl Derr 1884-1933 .... **TCLC 65**
See also CA 108; 153

Billings, Josh
See Shaw, Henry Wheeler

Billington, (Lady) Rachel (Mary)
1942- .... **CLC 43**
See also AITN 2; CA 33-36R; CANR 44;
CN 7

Binchy, Maeve 1940- .... **CLC 153**
See also BEST 90:1; BPFB 1; CA 127; 134;
CANR 50, 96; CN 7; CPW; DA3; DAM
POP; INT CA-134; MTCW 1; RHW

Binyon, T(imothy) J(ohn) 1936- .... **CLC 34**
See also CA 111; CANR 28

Bion 335B.C.-245B.C. .... **CMLC 39**

Bioy Casares, Adolfo 1914-1999 ... **CLC 4, 8,**
13, 88; HLC 1; SSC 17
See also Casares, Adolfo Bioy; Miranda,
Javier; Sacastru, Martin
See also CA 29-32R; 177; CANR 19, 43,
66; DAM MULT; DLB 113; HW 1, 2;
LAW; MTCW 1, 2

Birch, Allison .... **CLC 65**

Bird, Cordwainer
See Ellison, Harlan (Jay)

Bird, Robert Montgomery
1806-1854 .... **NCLC 1**
See also DLB 202; RGAL 4

Birkerts, Sven 1951- .... **CLC 116**
See also CA 128; 133, 176; CAAE 176;
CAAS 29; INT 133

Birney, (Alfred) Earle 1904-1995 .. **CLC 1, 4,**
6, 11
See also CA 1-4R; CANR 5, 20; CP 7;
DAC; DAM MST, POET; DLB 88;
MTCW 1; PFS 8; RGEL 2

Biruni, al 973-1048(?) .... **CMLC 28**

Bishop, Elizabeth 1911-1979 ..... **CLC 1, 4, 9,**
13, 15, 32; PC 3, 34
See also AMWS 1; CA 5-8R; 89-92; CABS
2; CANR 26, 61, 108; CDALB 1968-
1988; DA; DA3; DAC; DAM MST,
POET; DLB 5, 169; GLL 2; MAWW;
MTCW 1, 2; PAB; PFS 6, 12; RGAL 4;
SATA-Obit 24; WP

Bishop, John 1935- .... **CLC 10**
See also CA 105

Bishop, John Peale 1892-1944 ..... **TCLC 103**
See also CA 107; 155; DLB 4, 9, 45; RGAL
4

Bissett, Bill 1939- .... **CLC 18; PC 14**
See also CA 69-72; CAAS 19; CANR 15;
CCA 1; CP 7; DLB 53; MTCW 1

Bissoondath, Neil (Devindra)
1955- .... **CLC 120**
See also CA 136; CN 7; DAC

Bitov, Andrei (Georgievich) 1937- ... **CLC 57**
See also CA 142

Biyidi, Alexandre 1932-
See Beti, Mongo
See also BW 1, 3; CA 114; 124; CANR 81;
DA3; MTCW 1, 2

Bjarme, Brynjolf
See Ibsen, Henrik (Johan)

Bjoernson, Bjoernstjerne (Martinius)
1832-1910 .... **TCLC 7, 37**
See also CA 104

Black, Robert
See Holdstock, Robert P.

Blackburn, Paul 1926-1971 .... **CLC 9, 43**
See also CA 81-84; 33-36R; CANR 34;
DLB 16; DLBY 1981

Black Elk 1863-1950 .... **TCLC 33**
See also CA 144; DAM MULT; MTCW 1;
NNAL; WP

Black Hobart
See Sanders, (James) Ed(ward)

Blacklin, Malcolm
See Chambers, Aidan

Blackmore, R(ichard) D(oddridge)
1825-1900 .... **TCLC 27**
See also CA 120; DLB 18; RGEL 2

Blackmur, R(ichard) P(almer)
1904-1965 .... **CLC 2, 24**
See also AMWS 2; CA 11-12; 25-28R;
CANR 71; CAP 1; DLB 63

Black Tarantula
See Acker, Kathy

Blackwood, Algernon (Henry)
1869-1951 .... **TCLC 5**
See also CA 105; 150; DLB 153, 156, 178;
HGG; SUFW

Blackwood, Caroline 1931-1996 .... **CLC 6, 9,**
100
See also CA 85-88; 151; CANR 32, 61, 65;
CN 7; DLB 14, 207; HGG; MTCW 1

Blade, Alexander
See Hamilton, Edmond; Silverberg, Robert

Blaga, Lucian 1895-1961 .... **CLC 75**
See also CA 157; DLB 220

Blair, Eric (Arthur) 1903-1950
See Orwell, George
See also CA 104; 132; DA; DA3; DAB;
DAC; DAM MST, NOV; MTCW 1, 2;
SATA 29

Blair, Hugh 1718-1800 .... **NCLC 75**

Blais, Marie-Claire 1939- .... **CLC 2, 4, 6, 13,**
22
See also CA 21-24R; CAAS 4; CANR 38,
75, 93; DAC; DAM MST; DLB 53; FW;
MTCW 1, 2

Blaise, Clark 1940- .... **CLC 29**
See also AITN 2; CA 53-56; CAAS 3;
CANR 5, 66, 106; CN 7; DLB 53; RGSF
2

Blake, Fairley
See De Voto, Bernard (Augustine)

Blake, Nicholas
See Day Lewis, C(ecil)
See also DLB 77; MSW

Blake, William 1757-1827 .... **NCLC 13, 37,**
57; PC 12; WLC
See also BRW 3; BRWR 1; CDBLB 1789-
1832; CLR 52; DA; DA3; DAB; DAC;
DAM MST, POET; DLB 93, 163; EXPP;
MAICYA 1; PAB; PFS 2, 12; SATA 30;
WCH; WLIT 3; WP

Blanchot, Maurice 1907- .... **CLC 135**
See also CA 117; 144; DLB 72

Blasco Ibanez, Vicente 1867-1928 . **TCLC 12**
See also BPFB 1; CA 110; 131; CANR 81;
DA3; DAM NOV; EW 8; HW 1, 2;
MTCW 1

Blatty, William Peter 1928- .... **CLC 2**
See also CA 5-8R; CANR 9; DAM POP;
HGG

Bleeck, Oliver
See Thomas, Ross (Elmore)

Blessing, Lee 1949- .... **CLC 54**
See also CAD; CD 5

Blight, Rose
See Greer, Germaine

Blish, James (Benjamin) 1921-1975 . **CLC 14**
See also BPFB 1; CA 1-4R; 57-60; CANR
3; DLB 8; MTCW 1; SATA 66; SCFW 2;
SFW 4

Bliss, Reginald
See Wells, H(erbert) G(eorge)

Blixen, Karen (Christentze Dinesen)
1885-1962
See Dinesen, Isak
See also CA 25-28; CANR 22, 50; CAP 2;
DA3; DLB 214; MTCW 1, 2; SATA 44

Bloch, Robert (Albert) 1917-1994 .... **CLC 33**
See also AAYA 29; CA 5-8R; 179; 146;
CAAE 179; CAAS 20; CANR 5, 78;
DA3; DLB 44; HGG; INT CANR-5;
MTCW 1; SATA 12; SATA-Obit 82; SFW
4; SUFW

Blok, Alexander (Alexandrovich)
1880-1921 .... **TCLC 5; PC 21**
See also CA 104; 183; EW 9; RGWL 2

Blom, Jan
See Breytenbach, Breyten

Bloom, Harold 1930- .... **CLC 24, 103**
See also CA 13-16R; CANR 39, 75, 92;
DLB 67; MTCW 1; RGAL 4

Bloomfield, Aurelius
See Bourne, Randolph S(illiman)

Blount, Roy (Alton), Jr. 1941- .... **CLC 38**
See also CA 53-56; CANR 10, 28, 61;
CSW; INT CANR-28; MTCW 1, 2

Bloy, Leon 1846-1917 .... **TCLC 22**
See also CA 121; 183; DLB 123; GFL 1789
to the Present

Blume, Judy (Sussman) 1938- .... **CLC 12, 30**
See also AAYA 3, 26; BYA 1, 8, 12; CA 29-
32R; CANR 13, 37, 66; CLR 2, 15, 69;
CPW; DA3; DAM NOV, POP; DLB 52;
JRDA; MAICYA 1; MAICYAS 1; MTCW
1, 2; SATA 2, 31, 79; WYA; YAW

Blunden, Edmund (Charles)
1896-1974 .... **CLC 2, 56**
See also BRW 6; CA 17-18; 45-48; CANR
54; CAP 2; DLB 20, 100, 155; MTCW 1;
PAB

Bly, Robert (Elwood) 1926- .... **CLC 1, 2, 5,**
10, 15, 38, 128; PC 39
See also AMWS 4; CA 5-8R; CANR 41,
73; CP 7; DA3; DAM POET; DLB 5;
MTCW 1, 2; RGAL 4

Boas, Franz 1858-1942 .... **TCLC 56**
See also CA 115; 181

Bobette
See Simenon, Georges (Jacques Christian)

Boccaccio, Giovanni 1313-1375 ... **CMLC 13;**
SSC 10
See also EW 2; RGSF 2; RGWL 2

Bochco, Steven 1943- .... **CLC 35**
See also AAYA 11; CA 124; 138

Bodel, Jean 1167(?)-1210 .... **CMLC 28**

Bodenheim, Maxwell 1892-1954 .... **TCLC 44**
See also CA 110; 187; DLB 9, 45; RGAL 4

Bodker, Cecil 1927- .... **CLC 21**
See also CA 73-76; CANR 13, 44; CLR 23;
MAICYA 1; SATA 14

Boell, Heinrich (Theodor)
1917-1985 ..... **CLC 2, 3, 6, 9, 11, 15, 27,**
32, 72; SSC 23; WLC
See also Boll, Heinrich
See also CA 21-24R; 116; CANR 24; DA;
DA3; DAB; DAC; DAM MST, NOV;
DLB 69; DLBY 1985; MTCW 1, 2

Boerne, Alfred
See Doeblin, Alfred

Boethius c. 480-c. 524 .... **CMLC 15**
See also DLB 115; RGWL 2

Callimachus c. 305B.C.-c.
240B.C. .... **CMLC 18**
See also AW 1; DLB 176; RGWL 2
Calvin, Jean
See Calvin, John
See also GFL Beginnings to 1789
Calvin, John 1509-1564 .... **LC 37**
See also Calvin, Jean
Calvino, Italo 1923-1985 .... **CLC 5, 8, 11, 22,
33, 39, 73; SSC 3, 48**
See also CA 85-88; 116; CANR 23, 61;
DAM NOV; DLB 196; EW 13; MTCW 1,
2; RGSF 2; RGWL 2; SFW 4; SSFS 12
Cameron, Carey 1952- .... **CLC 59**
See also CA 135
Cameron, Peter 1959- .... **CLC 44**
See also CA 125; CANR 50; DLB 234;
GLL 2
Camoens, Luis Vaz de 1524(?)-1580
See also EW 2; HLCS 1
Camoes, Luis de 1524(?)-1580 .... **LC 62;
HLCS 1; PC 31**
See also RGWL 2
Campana, Dino 1885-1932 .... **TCLC 20**
See also CA 117; DLB 114
Campanella, Tommaso 1568-1639 .... **LC 32**
See also RGWL 2
Campbell, John W(ood, Jr.)
1910-1971 .... **CLC 32**
See also CA 21-22; 29-32R; CANR 34;
CAP 2; DLB 8; MTCW 1; SFW 4
Campbell, Joseph 1904-1987 .... **CLC 69**
See also AAYA 3; BEST 89:2; CA 1-4R;
124; CANR 3, 28, 61, 107; DA3; MTCW
1, 2
Campbell, Maria 1940- .... **CLC 85**
See also CA 102; CANR 54; CCA 1; DAC;
NNAL
Campbell, (John) Ramsey 1946- ..... **CLC 42;
SSC 19**
See also CA 57-60; CANR 7, 102; HGG;
INT CANR-7; SUFW
Campbell, (Ignatius) Roy (Dunnachie)
1901-1957 .... **TCLC 5**
See also AFW; CA 104; 155; DLB 20, 225;
MTCW 2; RGEL 2
Campbell, Thomas 1777-1844 .... **NCLC 19**
See also DLB 93, 144; RGEL 2
Campbell, Wilfred .... **TCLC 9**
See also Campbell, William
Campbell, William 1858(?)-1918
See Campbell, Wilfred
See also CA 106; DLB 92
Campion, Jane .... **CLC 95**
See also AAYA 33; CA 138; CANR 87
Camus, Albert 1913-1960 ...... **CLC 1, 2, 4, 9,
11, 14, 32, 63, 69, 124; DC 2; SSC 9;
WLC**
See also AAYA 36; AFW; BPFB 1; CA 89-
92; DA; DA3; DAB; DAC; DAM DRAM,
MST, NOV; DLB 72; EW 13; EXPN;
EXPS; GFL 1789 to the Present; MTCW
1, 2; NFS 6; RGSF 2; RGWL 2; SSFS 4
Canby, Vincent 1924-2000 .... **CLC 13**
See also CA 81-84; 191
Cancale
See Desnos, Robert
Canetti, Elias 1905-1994 .. **CLC 3, 14, 25, 75,
86**
See also CA 21-24R; 146; CANR 23, 61;
79; CDWLB 2; CWW 2; DA3; DLB 85,
124; EW 12; MTCW 1, 2; RGWL 2
Canfield, Dorothea F.
See Fisher, Dorothy (Frances) Canfield
Canfield, Dorothea Frances
See Fisher, Dorothy (Frances) Canfield
Canfield, Dorothy
See Fisher, Dorothy (Frances) Canfield

Canin, Ethan 1960- .... **CLC 55**
See also CA 131; 135
Cankar, Ivan 1876-1918 .... **TCLC 105**
See also CDWLB 4; DLB 147
Cannon, Curt
See Hunter, Evan
Cao, Lan 1961- .... **CLC 109**
See also CA 165
Cape, Judith
See Page, P(atricia) K(athleen)
See also CCA 1
Capek, Karel 1890-1938 .... **TCLC 6, 37; DC
1; SSC 36; WLC**
See also CA 104; 140; CDWLB 4; DA;
DA3; DAB; DAC; DAM DRAM, MST,
NOV; DFS 7, 11 !**; DLB 215; EW 10;
MTCW 1; RGSF 2; RGWL 2; SCFW 2;
SFW 4
Capote, Truman 1924-1984 . **CLC 1, 3, 8, 13,
19, 34, 38, 58; SSC 2, 47; WLC**
See also AMWS 3; BPFB 1; CA 5-8R; 113;
CANR 18, 62; CDALB 1941-1968; CPW;
DA; DA3; DAB; DAC; DAM MST, NOV,
POP; DLB 2, 185, 227; DLBY 1980,
1984; EXPS; GLL 1; LAIT 3; MTCW 1,
2; NCFS 2; RGAL 4; RGSF 2; SATA 91;
SSFS 2
Capra, Frank 1897-1991 .... **CLC 16**
See also CA 61-64; 135
Caputo, Philip 1941- .... **CLC 32**
See also CA 73-76; CANR 40; YAW
Caragiale, Ion Luca 1852-1912 ...... **TCLC 76**
See also CA 157
Card, Orson Scott 1951- .... **CLC 44, 47, 50**
See also AAYA 11, 42; BPFB 1; BYA 5, 8;
CA 102; CANR 27, 47, 73, 102, 106;
CPW; DA3; DAM POP; FANT; INT
CANR-27; MTCW 1, 2; NFS 5; SATA
83, 127; SCFW 2; SFW 4; YAW
Cardenal, Ernesto 1925- ... **CLC 31; HLC 1;
PC 22**
See also CA 49-52; CANR 2, 32, 66; CWW
2; DAM MULT, POET; HW 1, 2; LAWS
1; MTCW 1, 2; RGWL 2
Cardozo, Benjamin N(athan)
1870-1938 .... **TCLC 65**
See also CA 117; 164
Carducci, Giosue (Alessandro Giuseppe)
1835-1907 .... **TCLC 32**
See also CA 163; EW 7; RGWL 2
Carew, Thomas 1595(?)-1640 . **LC 13; PC 29**
See also BRW 2; DLB 126; PAB; RGEL 2
Carey, Ernestine Gilbreth 1908- ...... **CLC 17**
See also CA 5-8R; CANR 71; SATA 2
Carey, Peter 1943- .... **CLC 40, 55, 96**
See also CA 123; 127; CANR 53, 76; CN
7; INT CA-127; MTCW 1, 2; RGSF 2;
SATA 94
Carleton, William 1794-1869 .... **NCLC 3**
See also DLB 159; RGEL 2; RGSF 2
Carlisle, Henry (Coffin) 1926- .... **CLC 33**
See also CA 13-16R; CANR 15, 85
Carlsen, Chris
See Holdstock, Robert P.
Carlson, Ron(ald F.) 1947- .... **CLC 54**
See also CA 105; CAAE 189; CANR 27;
DLB 244
Carlyle, Thomas 1795-1881 ..... **NCLC 22, 70**
See also BRW 4; CDBLB 1789-1832; DA;
DAB; DAC; DAM MST; DLB 55, 144,
254; RGEL 2
Carman, (William) Bliss
1861-1929 .... **TCLC 7; PC 34**
See also CA 104; 152; DAC; DLB 92;
RGEL 2
Carnegie, Dale 1888-1955 .... **TCLC 53**
Carossa, Hans 1878-1956 .... **TCLC 48**
See also CA 170; DLB 66

Carpenter, Don(ald Richard)
1931-1995 .... **CLC 41**
See also CA 45-48; 149; CANR 1, 71
Carpenter, Edward 1844-1929 .... **TCLC 88**
See also CA 163; GLL 1
Carpentier (y Valmont), Alejo
1904-1980 . **CLC 8, 11, 38, 110; HLC 1;
SSC 35**
See also CA 65-68; 97-100; CANR 11, 70;
CDWLB 3; DAM MULT; DLB 113; HW
1, 2; LAW; RGSF 2; RGWL 2; WLIT 1
Carr, Caleb 1955(?)- .... **CLC 86**
See also CA 147; CANR 73; DA3
Carr, Emily 1871-1945 .... **TCLC 32**
See also CA 159; DLB 68; FW; GLL 2
Carr, John Dickson 1906-1977 .... **CLC 3**
See also Fairbairn, Roger
See also CA 49-52; 69-72; CANR 3, 33,
60; CMW 4; MSW; MTCW 1, 2
Carr, Philippa
See Hibbert, Eleanor Alice Burford
Carr, Virginia Spencer 1929- .... **CLC 34**
See also CA 61-64; DLB 111
Carrere, Emmanuel 1957- .... **CLC 89**
Carrier, Roch 1937- .... **CLC 13, 78**
See also CA 130; CANR 61; CCA 1; DAC;
DAM MST; DLB 53; SATA 105
Carroll, James P. 1943(?)- .... **CLC 38**
See also CA 81-84; CANR 73; MTCW 1
Carroll, Jim 1951- .... **CLC 35, 143**
See also AAYA 17; CA 45-48; CANR 42
Carroll, Lewis ... **NCLC 2, 53; PC 18; WLC**
See also Dodgson, Charles Lutwidge
See also AAYA 39; BRW 5; BYA 5, 13; CD-
BLB 1832-1890; CLR 2, 18; DLB 18,
163, 178; DLBY 1998; EXPN; EXPP;
FANT; JRDA; LAIT 1; NFS 7; PFS 11;
RGEL 2; SUFW; WCH
Carroll, Paul Vincent 1900-1968 ...... **CLC 10**
See also CA 9-12R; 25-28R; DLB 10;
RGEL 2
Carruth, Hayden 1921- ..... **CLC 4, 7, 10, 18,
84; PC 10**
See also CA 9-12R; CANR 4, 38, 59; CP 7;
DLB 5, 165; INT CANR-4; MTCW 1, 2;
SATA 47
Carson, Rachel Louise 1907-1964 .... **CLC 71**
See also AMWS 9; ANW; CA 77-80; CANR
35; DA3; DAM POP; FW; LAIT 4;
MTCW 1, 2; NCFS 1; SATA 23
Carter, Angela (Olive) 1940-1992 ...... **CLC 5,
41, 76; SSC 13**
See also BRWS 3; CA 53-56; 136; CANR
12, 36, 61, 106; DA3; DLB 14, 207;
EXPS; FANT; FW; MTCW 1, 2; RGSF 2;
SATA 66; SATA-Obit 70; SFW 4; SSFS
4, 12; WLIT 4
Carter, Nick
See Smith, Martin Cruz
Carver, Raymond 1938-1988 ..... **CLC 22, 36,
53, 55, 126; SSC 8, 51**
See also AMWS 3; BPFB 1; CA 33-36R;
126; CANR 17, 34, 61, 103; CPW; DA3;
DAM NOV; DLB 130; DLBY 1984,
1988; MTCW 1, 2; RGAL 4; RGSF 2;
SSFS 3, 6, 12, 13; TCWW 2
Cary, Elizabeth, Lady Falkland
1585-1639 .... **LC 30**
Cary, (Arthur) Joyce (Lunel)
1888-1957 .... **TCLC 1, 29**
See also BRW 7; CA 104; 164; CDBLB
1914-1945; DLB 15, 100; MTCW 2;
RGEL 2
Casanova de Seingalt, Giovanni Jacopo
1725-1798 .... **LC 13**
Casares, Adolfo Bioy
See Bioy Casares, Adolfo
See also RGSF 2

Casas, Bartolome de las 1474-1566
See Las Casas, Bartolome de
See also WLIT 1
Casely-Hayford, J(oseph) E(phraim)
1866-1903 .... **TCLC 24; BLC 1**
See also BW 2; CA 123; 152; DAM MULT
Casey, John (Dudley) 1939- .... **CLC 59**
See also BEST 90:2; CA 69-72; CANR 23, 100
Casey, Michael 1947- .... **CLC 2**
See also CA 65-68; DLB 5
Casey, Patrick
See Thurman, Wallace (Henry)
Casey, Warren (Peter) 1935-1988 .... **CLC 12**
See also CA 101; 127; INT 101
Casona, Alejandro .... **CLC 49**
See also Alvarez, Alejandro Rodriguez
Cassavetes, John 1929-1989 .... **CLC 20**
See also CA 85-88; 127; CANR 82
Cassian, Nina 1924- .... **PC 17**
See also CWP; CWW 2
Cassill, R(onald) V(erlin) 1919- ... **CLC 4, 23**
See also CA 9-12R; CAAS 1; CANR 7, 45; CN 7; DLB 6, 218
Cassiodorus, Flavius Magnus c. 490(?)-c.
583(?) .... **CMLC 43**
Cassirer, Ernst 1874-1945 .... **TCLC 61**
See also CA 157
Cassity, (Allen) Turner 1929- .... **CLC 6, 42**
See also CA 17-20R; CAAS 8; CANR 11; CSW; DLB 105
Castaneda, Carlos (Cesar Aranha)
1931(?)-1998 .... **CLC 12, 119**
See also CA 25-28R; CANR 32, 66, 105; DNFS 1; HW 1; MTCW 1
Castedo, Elena 1937- .... **CLC 65**
See also CA 132
Castedo-Ellerman, Elena
See Castedo, Elena
Castellanos, Rosario 1925-1974 .... **CLC 66;**
HLC 1; SSC 39
See also CA 131; 53-56; CANR 58; CD-WLB 3; DAM MULT; DLB 113; FW; HW 1; LAW; MTCW 1; RGSF 2; RGWL 2
Castelvetro, Lodovico 1505-1571 .... **LC 12**
Castiglione, Baldassare 1478-1529 ...... **LC 12**
See also Castiglione, Baldesar
See also RGWL 2
Castiglione, Baldesar
See Castiglione, Baldassare
See also EW 2
Castillo, Ana (Hernandez Del)
1953- .... **CLC 151**
See also AAYA 42; CA 131; CANR 51, 86; CWP; DLB 122, 227; DNFS 2; FW; HW 1
Castle, Robert
See Hamilton, Edmond
Castro (Ruz), Fidel 1926(?)-
See also CA 110; 129; CANR 81; DAM MULT; HLC 1; HW 2
Castro, Guillen de 1569-1631 .... **LC 19**
Castro, Rosalia de 1837-1885 .... **NCLC 3, 78**
See also DAM MULT
Cather, Willa (Sibert) 1873-1947 .... **TCLC 1,**
11, 31, 99; SSC 2, 50; WLC
See also AAYA 24; AMW; AMWR 1; BPFB 1; CA 104; 128; CDALB 1865-1917; DA; DA3; DAB; DAC; DAM MST, NOV; DLB 9, 54, 78, 256; DLBD 1; EXPN; EXPS; LAIT 3; MAWW; MTCW 1, 2; NFS 2; RGAL 4; RGSF 2; RHW; SATA 30; SSFS 2, 7; TCWW 2
Catherine II
See Catherine the Great
See also DLB 150
Catherine the Great 1729-1796 .... **LC 69**
See also Catherine II

Cato, Marcus Porcius
234B.C.-149B.C. .... **CMLC 21**
See also Cato the Elder
Cato the Elder
See Cato, Marcus Porcius
See also DLB 211
Catton, (Charles) Bruce 1899-1978 . **CLC 35**
See also AITN 1; CA 5-8R; 81-84; CANR 7, 74; DLB 17; SATA 2; SATA-Obit 24
Catullus c. 84B.C.-54B.C. .... **CMLC 18**
See also AW 2; CDWLB 1; DLB 211; RGWL 2
Cauldwell, Frank
See King, Francis (Henry)
Caunitz, William J. 1933-1996 .... **CLC 34**
See also BEST 89:3; CA 125; 130; 152; CANR 73; INT 130
Causley, Charles (Stanley) 1917- .... **CLC 7**
See also CA 9-12R; CANR 5, 35, 94; CLR 30; CWRI 5; DLB 27; MTCW 1; SATA 3, 66
Caute, (John) David 1936- .... **CLC 29**
See also CA 1-4R; CAAS 4; CANR 1, 33, 64; CBD; CD 5; CN 7; DAM NOV; DLB 14, 231
Cavafy, C(onstantine) P(eter) ... **TCLC 2, 7;**
PC 36
See also Kavafis, Konstantinos Petrou
See also CA 148; DA3; DAM POET; EW 8; MTCW 1; RGWL 2; WP
Cavallo, Evelyn
See Spark, Muriel (Sarah)
Cavanna, Betty .... **CLC 12**
See also Harrison, Elizabeth (Allen) Cavanna
See also JRDA; MAICYA 1; SAAS 4; SATA 1, 30
Cavendish, Margaret Lucas
1623-1673 .... **LC 30**
See also DLB 131, 252; RGEL 2
Caxton, William 1421(?)-1491(?) .... **LC 17**
See also DLB 170
Cayer, D. M.
See Duffy, Maureen
Cayrol, Jean 1911- .... **CLC 11**
See also CA 89-92; DLB 83
Cela, Camilo Jose 1916-2002 .... **CLC 4, 13,**
59, 122; HLC 1
See also BEST 90:2; CA 21-24R; CAAS 10; CANR 21, 32, 76; DAM MULT; DLBY 1989; EW 13; HW 1; MTCW 1, 2; RGSF 2; RGWL 2
Celan, Paul -1970 .... **CLC 10, 19, 53, 82; PC**
10
See also Antschel, Paul
See also CDWLB 2; DLB 69; RGWL 2
Celine, Louis-Ferdinand .. **CLC 1, 3, 4, 7, 9,**
15, 47, 124
See also Destouches, Louis-Ferdinand
See also DLB 72; EW 11; GFL 1789 to the Present; RGWL 2
Cellini, Benvenuto 1500-1571 .... **LC 7**
Cendrars, Blaise .... **CLC 18, 106**
See also Sauser-Hall, Frederic
See also DLB 258; GFL 1789 to the Present; RGWL 2; WP
Centlivre, Susanna 1669(?)-1723 .... **LC 65**
See also DLB 84; RGEL 2
Cernuda (y Bidon), Luis 1902-1963 . **CLC 54**
See also CA 131; 89-92; DAM POET; DLB 134; GLL 1; HW 1; RGWL 2
Cervantes, Lorna Dee 1954- .... **PC 35**
See also CA 131; CANR 80; CWP; DLB 82; EXPP; HLCS 1; HW 1

Cervantes (Saavedra), Miguel de
1547-1616 .... **LC 6, 23; HLCS; SSC 12;**
WLC
See also BYA 1, 14; DA; DAB; DAC; DAM MST, NOV; EW 2; LAIT 1; NFS 8; RGSF 2; RGWL 2
Cesaire, Aime (Fernand) 1913- . **CLC 19, 32,**
112; BLC 1; PC 25
See also BW 2, 3; CA 65-68; CANR 24, 43, 81; DA3; DAM MULT, POET; GFL 1789 to the Present; MTCW 1, 2; WP
Chabon, Michael 1963- .... **CLC 55, 149**
See also CA 139; CANR 57, 96
Chabrol, Claude 1930- .... **CLC 16**
See also CA 110
Challans, Mary 1905-1983
See Renault, Mary
See also CA 81-84; 111; CANR 74; DA3; MTCW 2; SATA 23; SATA-Obit 36
Challis, George
See Faust, Frederick (Schiller)
See also TCWW 2
Chambers, Aidan 1934- .... **CLC 35**
See also AAYA 27; CA 25-28R; CANR 12, 31, 58; JRDA; MAICYA 1; SAAS 12; SATA 1, 69, 108; WYA; YAW
Chambers, James 1948-
See Cliff, Jimmy
See also CA 124
Chambers, Jessie
See Lawrence, D(avid) H(erbert Richards)
See also GLL 1
Chambers, Robert W(illiam)
1865-1933 .... **TCLC 41**
See also CA 165; DLB 202; HGG; SATA 107; SUFW
Chamisso, Adelbert von
1781-1838 .... **NCLC 82**
See also DLB 90; RGWL 2; SUFW
Chandler, Raymond (Thornton)
1888-1959 .... **TCLC 1, 7; SSC 23**
See also AAYA 25; AMWS 4; BPFB 1; CA 104; 129; CANR 60, 107; CDALB 1929-1941; CMW 4; DA3; DLB 226, 253; DLBD 6; MSW; MTCW 1, 2; RGAL 4
Chang, Eileen 1921-1995 .... **SSC 28**
See also CA 166; CWW 2
Chang, Jung 1952- .... **CLC 71**
See also CA 142
Chang Ai-Ling
See Chang, Eileen
Channing, William Ellery
1780-1842 .... **NCLC 17**
See also DLB 1, 59, 235; RGAL 4
Chao, Patricia 1955- .... **CLC 119**
See also CA 163
Chaplin, Charles Spencer
1889-1977 .... **CLC 16**
See also Chaplin, Charlie
See also CA 81-84; 73-76
Chaplin, Charlie
See Chaplin, Charles Spencer
See also DLB 44
Chapman, George 1559(?)-1634 .... **LC 22**
See also BRW 1; DAM DRAM; DLB 62, 121; RGEL 2
Chapman, Graham 1941-1989 .... **CLC 21**
See also Monty Python
See also CA 116; 129; CANR 35, 95
Chapman, John Jay 1862-1933 .... **TCLC 7**
See also CA 104; 191
Chapman, Lee
See Bradley, Marion Zimmer
See also GLL 1
Chapman, Walker
See Silverberg, Robert

Coleridge, Samuel Taylor
1772-1834 . **NCLC 9, 54, 99; PC 11, 39; WLC**
See also BRW 4; BRWR 2; BYA 4; CD-BLB 1789-1832; DA; DA3; DAB; DAC; DAM MST, POET; DLB 93, 107; EXPP; PAB; PFS 4, 5; RGEL 2; WLIT 3; WP

Coleridge, Sara 1802-1852 .... **NCLC 31**
See also DLB 199

Coles, Don 1928- .... **CLC 46**
See also CA 115; CANR 38; CP 7

Coles, Robert (Martin) 1929- .... **CLC 108**
See also CA 45-48; CANR 3, 32, 66, 70; INT CANR-32; SATA 23

Colette, (Sidonie-Gabrielle)
1873-1954 .... **TCLC 1, 5, 16; SSC 10**
See also Willy, Colette
See also CA 104; 131; DA3; DAM NOV; DLB 65; EW 9; GFL 1789 to the Present; MTCW 1, 2; RGWL 2

Collett, (Jacobine) Camilla (Wergeland)
1813-1895 .... **NCLC 22**

Collier, Christopher 1930- .... **CLC 30**
See also AAYA 13; BYA 2; CA 33-36R; CANR 13, 33, 102; JRDA; MAICYA 1; SATA 16, 70; WYA; YAW 1

Collier, James Lincoln 1928- .... **CLC 30**
See also Williams, Charles
See also AAYA 13; BYA 2; CA 9-12R; CANR 4, 33, 60, 102; CLR 3; DAM POP; JRDA; MAICYA 1; SAAS 21; SATA 8, 70; WYA; YAW 1

Collier, Jeremy 1650-1726 .... **LC 6**

Collier, John 1901-1980 .... **SSC 19**
See also CA 65-68; 97-100; CANR 10; DLB 77, 255; FANT; SUFW

Collingwood, R(obin) G(eorge)
1889(?)-1943 .... **TCLC 67**
See also CA 117; 155

Collins, Hunt
See Hunter, Evan

Collins, Linda 1931- .... **CLC 44**
See also CA 125

Collins, (William) Wilkie
1824-1889 .... **NCLC 1, 18, 93**
See also BRWS 6; CDBLB 1832-1890; CMW 4; DLB 18, 70, 159; MSW; RGEL 2; RGSF 2; SUFW; WLIT 4

Collins, William 1721-1759 .... **LC 4, 40**
See also BRW 3; DAM POET; DLB 109; RGEL 2

Collodi, Carlo .... **NCLC 54**
See also Lorenzini, Carlo
See also CLR 5; WCH

Colman, George
See Glassco, John

Colonna, Vittoria 1492-1547 .... **LC 71**
See also RGWL 2

Colt, Winchester Remington
See Hubbard, L(afayette) Ron(ald)

Colter, Cyrus 1910-2002 .... **CLC 58**
See also BW 1; CA 65-68; CANR 10, 66; CN 7; DLB 33

Colton, James
See Hansen, Joseph
See also GLL 1

Colum, Padraic 1881-1972 .... **CLC 28**
See also BYA 4; CA 73-76; 33-36R; CANR 35; CLR 36; CWRI 5; DLB 19; MAICYA 1; MTCW 1; RGEL 2; SATA 15; WCH

Colvin, James
See Moorcock, Michael (John)

Colwin, Laurie (E.) 1944-1992 .... **CLC 5, 13, 23, 84**
See also CA 89-92; 139; CANR 20, 46; DLB 218; DLBY 1980; MTCW 1

Comfort, Alex(ander) 1920-2000 .... **CLC 7**
See also CA 1-4R; 190; CANR 1, 45; CP 7; DAM POP; MTCW 1

Comfort, Montgomery
See Campbell, (John) Ramsey

Compton-Burnett, I(vy)
1892(?)-1969 .... **CLC 1, 3, 10, 15, 34**
See also BRW 7; CA 1-4R; 25-28R; CANR 4; DAM NOV; DLB 36; MTCW 1; RGEL 2

Comstock, Anthony 1844-1915 ...... **TCLC 13**
See also CA 110; 169

Comte, Auguste 1798-1857 .... **NCLC 54**

Conan Doyle, Arthur
See Doyle, Sir Arthur Conan
See also BPFB 1; BYA 4, 5, 11

Conde (Abellan), Carmen 1901-1996
See also CA 177; DLB 108; HLCS 1; HW 2

Conde, Maryse 1937- ..... **CLC 52, 92; BLCS**
See also BW 2, 3; CA 110; CAAE 190; CANR 30, 53, 76; CWW 2; DAM MULT; MTCW 1

Condillac, Etienne Bonnot de
1714-1780 .... **LC 26**

Condon, Richard (Thomas)
1915-1996 .... **CLC 4, 6, 8, 10, 45, 100**
See also BEST 90:3; BPFB 1; CA 1-4R; 151; CAAS 1; CANR 2, 23; CMW 4; CN 7; DAM NOV; INT CANR-23; MTCW 1, 2

Confucius 551B.C.-479B.C. .... **CMLC 19; WLCS**
See also DA; DA3; DAB; DAC; DAM MST

Congreve, William 1670-1729 . **LC 5, 21; DC 2; WLC**
See also BRW 2; CDBLB 1660-1789; DA; DAB; DAC; DAM DRAM, MST, POET; DLB 39, 84; RGEL 2; WLIT 3

Connell, Evan S(helby), Jr. 1924- . **CLC 4, 6, 45**
See also AAYA 7; CA 1-4R; CAAS 2; CANR 2, 39, 76, 97; CN 7; DAM NOV; DLB 2; DLBY 1981; MTCW 1, 2

Connelly, Marc(us Cook) 1890-1980 . **CLC 7**
See also CA 85-88; 102; CANR 30; DFS 12; DLB 7; DLBY 1980; RGAL 4; SATA-Obit 25

Connor, Ralph .... **TCLC 31**
See also Gordon, Charles William
See also DLB 92; TCWW 2

Conrad, Joseph 1857-1924 .... **TCLC 1, 6, 13, 25, 43, 57; SSC 9; WLC**
See also AAYA 26; BPFB 1; BRW 6; BRWR 2; BYA 2; CA 104; 131; CANR 60; CDBLB 1890-1914; DA; DA3; DAB; DAC; DAM MST, NOV; DLB 10, 34, 98, 156; EXPN; EXPS; LAIT 2; MTCW 1, 2; NFS 2; RGEL 2; RGSF 2; SATA 27; SSFS 1, 12; WLIT 4

Conrad, Robert Arnold
See Hart, Moss

Conroy, (Donald) Pat(rick) 1945- ... **CLC 30, 74**
See also AAYA 8; AITN 1; BPFB 1; CA 85-88; CANR 24, 53; CPW; CSW; DA3; DAM NOV, POP; DLB 6; LAIT 5; MTCW 1, 2

Constant (de Rebecque), (Henri) Benjamin
1767-1830 .... **NCLC 6**
See also DLB 119; EW 4; GFL 1789 to the Present

Conway, Jill K(er) 1934- .... **CLC 152**
See also CA 130; CANR 94

Conybeare, Charles Augustus
See Eliot, T(homas) S(tearns)

Cook, Michael 1933-1994 .... **CLC 58**
See also CA 93-96; CANR 68; DLB 53

Cook, Robin 1940- .... **CLC 14**
See also AAYA 32; BEST 90:2; BPFB 1; CA 108; 111; CANR 41, 90; CPW; DA3; DAM POP; HGG; INT CA-111

Cook, Roy
See Silverberg, Robert

Cooke, Elizabeth 1948- .... **CLC 55**
See also CA 129

Cooke, John Esten 1830-1886 .... **NCLC 5**
See also DLB 3, 248; RGAL 4

Cooke, John Estes
See Baum, L(yman) Frank

Cooke, M. E.
See Creasey, John

Cooke, Margaret
See Creasey, John

Cooke, Rose Terry 1827-1892 ...... **NCLC 110**
See also DLB 12, 74

Cook-Lynn, Elizabeth 1930- .... **CLC 93**
See also CA 133; DAM MULT; DLB 175; NNAL

Cooney, Ray .... **CLC 62**
See also CBD

Cooper, Douglas 1960- .... **CLC 86**

Cooper, Henry St. John
See Creasey, John

Cooper, J(oan) California (?)- .... **CLC 56**
See also AAYA 12; BW 1; CA 125; CANR 55; DAM MULT; DLB 212

Cooper, James Fenimore
1789-1851 .... **NCLC 1, 27, 54**
See also AAYA 22; AMW; BPFB 1; CDALB 1640-1865; DA3; DLB 3, 183, 250, 254; LAIT 1; NFS 9; RGAL 4; SATA 19; WCH

Coover, Robert (Lowell) 1932- ...... **CLC 3, 7, 15, 32, 46, 87; SSC 15**
See also AMWS 5; BPFB 1; CA 45-48; CANR 3, 37, 58; CN 7; DAM NOV; DLB 2, 227; DLBY 1981; MTCW 1, 2; RGAL 4; RGSF 2

Copeland, Stewart (Armstrong)
1952- .... **CLC 26**

Copernicus, Nicolaus 1473-1543 .... **LC 45**

Coppard, A(lfred) E(dgar)
1878-1957 .... **TCLC 5; SSC 21**
See also CA 114; 167; DLB 162; HGG; RGEL 2; RGSF 2; SUFW; YABC 1

Coppee, Francois 1842-1908 .... **TCLC 25**
See also CA 170; DLB 217

Coppola, Francis Ford 1939- ... **CLC 16, 126**
See also AAYA 39; CA 77-80; CANR 40, 78; DLB 44

Corbiere, Tristan 1845-1875 .... **NCLC 43**
See also DLB 217; GFL 1789 to the Present

Corcoran, Barbara (Asenath)
1911- .... **CLC 17**
See also AAYA 14; CA 21-24R; CAAE 191; CAAS 2; CANR 11, 28, 48; CLR 50; DLB 52; JRDA; MAICYAS 1; RHW; SAAS 20; SATA 3, 77, 125

Cordelier, Maurice
See Giraudoux, Jean(-Hippolyte)

Corelli, Marie .... **TCLC 51**
See also Mackay, Mary
See also DLB 34, 156; RGEL 2; SUFW

Corman, Cid .... **CLC 9**
See also Corman, Sidney
See also CAAS 2; DLB 5, 193

Corman, Sidney 1924-
See Corman, Cid
See also CA 85-88; CANR 44; CP 7; DAM POET

Cormier, Robert (Edmund)
1925-2000 .... **CLC 12, 30**
See also AAYA 3, 19; BYA 1, 2, 6, 8, 9; CA 1-4R; CANR 5, 23, 76, 93; CDALB 1968-1988; CLR 12, 55; DA; DAB; DAC; DAM MST, NOV; DLB 52; EXPN; INT

CANR-23; JRDA; LAIT 5; MAICYA 1; MTCW 1, 2; NFS 2; SATA 10, 45, 83; SATA-Obit 122; WYA; YAW

Corn, Alfred (DeWitt III) 1943- .... **CLC 33**
See also CA 179; CAAE 179; CAAS 25; CANR 44; CP 7; CSW; DLB 120; DLBY 1980

Corneille, Pierre 1606-1684 .... **LC 28**
See also DAB; DLB; DAM MST; EW 3; GFL Beginnings to 1789; RGWL 2

Cornwell, David (John Moore)
1931- .... **CLC 9, 15**
See also le Carre, John
See also CA 5-8R; CANR 13, 33, 59, 107; DA3; DAM POP; MTCW 1, 2

Cornwell, Patricia (Daniels) 1956- . **CLC 155**
See also AAYA 16; BPFB 1; CA 134; CANR 53; CMW 4; CPW; CSW; DAM POP; MSW; MTCW 1

Corso, (Nunzio) Gregory 1930-2001 . **CLC 1, 11; PC 33**
See also CA 5-8R; 193; CANR 41, 76; CP 7; DA3; DLB 5, 16, 237; MTCW 1, 2; WP

Cortazar, Julio 1914-1984 ... **CLC 2, 3, 5, 10, 13, 15, 33, 34, 92; HLC 1; SSC 7**
See also BPFB 1; CA 21-24R; CANR 12, 32, 81; CDWLB 3; DA3; DAM MULT, NOV; DLB 113; EXPS; HW 1, 2; LAW; MTCW 1, 2; RGSF 2; RGWL 2; SSFS 3; WLIT 1

Cortes, Hernan 1485-1547 .... **LC 31**

Corvinus, Jakob
See Raabe, Wilhelm (Karl)

Corvo, Baron
See Rolfe, Frederick (William Serafino Austin Lewis Mary)
See also GLL 1; RGEL 2

Corwin, Cecil
See Kornbluth, C(yril) M.

Cosic, Dobrica 1921- .... **CLC 14**
See also CA 122; 138; CDWLB 4; CWW 2; DLB 181

Costain, Thomas B(ertram)
1885-1965 .... **CLC 30**
See also BYA 3; CA 5-8R; 25-28R; DLB 9; RHW

Costantini, Humberto 1924(?)-1987 . **CLC 49**
See also CA 131; 122; HW 1

Costello, Elvis 1955- .... **CLC 21**

Costenoble, Philostene 1898-1962
See Ghelderode, Michel de

Costenoble, Philostene 1898-1962
See Ghelderode, Michel de

Cotes, Cecil V.
See Duncan, Sara Jeannette

Cotter, Joseph Seamon Sr.
1861-1949 .... **TCLC 28; BLC 1**
See also BW 1; CA 124; DAM MULT; DLB 50

Couch, Arthur Thomas Quiller
See Quiller-Couch, Sir Arthur (Thomas)

Coulton, James
See Hansen, Joseph

Couperus, Louis (Marie Anne)
1863-1923 .... **TCLC 15**
See also CA 115; RGWL 2

Coupland, Douglas 1961- .... **CLC 85, 133**
See also AAYA 34; CA 142; CANR 57, 90; CCA 1; CPW; DAC; DAM POP

Court, Wesli
See Turco, Lewis (Putnam)

Courtenay, Bryce 1933- .... **CLC 59**
See also CA 138; CPW

Courtney, Robert
See Ellison, Harlan (Jay)

Cousteau, Jacques-Yves 1910-1997 .. **CLC 30**
See also CA 65-68; 159; CANR 15, 67; MTCW 1; SATA 38, 98

Coventry, Francis 1725-1754 .... **LC 46**

Cowan, Peter (Walkinshaw) 1914- .... **SSC 28**
See also CA 21-24R; CANR 9, 25, 50, 83; CN 7; RGSF 2

Coward, Noel (Peirce) 1899-1973 . **CLC 1, 9, 29, 51**
See also AITN 1; BRWS 2; CA 17-18; 41-44R; CANR 35; CAP 2; CDBLB 1914-1945; DA3; DAM DRAM; DFS 3, 6; DLB 10, 245; IDFW 3, 4; MTCW 1, 2; RGEL 2

Cowley, Abraham 1618-1667 .... **LC 43**
See also BRW 2; DLB 131, 151; PAB; RGEL 2

Cowley, Malcolm 1898-1989 .... **CLC 39**
See also AMWS 2; CA 5-8R; 128; CANR 3, 55; DLB 4, 48; DLBY 1981, 1989; MTCW 1, 2

Cowper, William 1731-1800 ..... **NCLC 8, 94; PC 40**
See also BRW 3; DA3; DAM POET; DLB 104, 109; RGEL 2

Cox, William Trevor 1928-
See Trevor, William
See also CA 9-12R; CANR 4, 37, 55, 76, 102; DAM NOV; INT CANR-37; MTCW 1, 2

Coyne, P. J.
See Masters, Hilary

Cozzens, James Gould 1903-1978 . **CLC 1, 4, 11, 92**
See also AMW; BPFB 1; CA 9-12R; 81-84; CANR 19; CDALB 1941-1968; DLB 9; DLBD 2; DLBY 1984, 1997; MTCW 1, 2; RGAL 4

Crabbe, George 1754-1832 .... **NCLC 26**
See also BRW 3; DLB 93; RGEL 2

Crace, Jim 1946- .... **CLC 157**
See also CA 128; 135; CANR 55, 70; CN 7; DLB 231; INT CA-135

Craddock, Charles Egbert
See Murfree, Mary Noailles

Craig, A. A.
See Anderson, Poul (William)

Craik, Mrs.
See Craik, Dinah Maria (Mulock)
See also RGEL 2

Craik, Dinah Maria (Mulock)
1826-1887 .... **NCLC 38**
See also Craik, Mrs.; Mulock, Dinah Maria
See also DLB 35, 163; MAICYA 1; SATA 34

Cram, Ralph Adams 1863-1942 ..... **TCLC 45**
See also CA 160

Crane, (Harold) Hart 1899-1932 .... **TCLC 2, 5, 80; PC 3; WLC**
See also AMW; CA 104; 127; CDALB 1917-1929; DA; DA3; DAB; DAC; DAM MST, POET; DLB 4, 48; MTCW 1, 2; RGAL 4

Crane, R(onald) S(almon)
1886-1967 .... **CLC 27**
See also CA 85-88; DLB 63

Crane, Stephen (Townley)
1871-1900 ...... **TCLC 11, 17, 32; SSC 7; WLC**
See also AAYA 21; AMW; BPFB 1; BYA 3; CA 109; 140; CANR 84; CDALB 1865-1917; DA; DA3; DAB; DAC; DAM MST, NOV, POET; DLB 12, 54, 78; EXPN; EXPS; LAIT 2; NFS 4; PFS 9; RGAL 4; RGSF 2; SSFS 4; WYA; YABC 2

Cranshaw, Stanley
See Fisher, Dorothy (Frances) Canfield

Crase, Douglas 1944- .... **CLC 58**
See also CA 106

Crashaw, Richard 1612(?)-1649 .... **LC 24**
See also BRW 2; DLB 126; PAB; RGEL 2

Craven, Margaret 1901-1980 .... **CLC 17**
See also BYA 2; CA 103; CCA 1; DAC; LAIT 5

Crawford, F(rancis) Marion
1854-1909 .... **TCLC 10**
See also CA 107; 168; DLB 71; HGG; RGAL 4; SUFW

Crawford, Isabella Valancy
1850-1887 .... **NCLC 12**
See also DLB 92; RGEL 2

Crayon, Geoffrey
See Irving, Washington

Creasey, John 1908-1973 .... **CLC 11**
See also Marric, J. J.
See also CA 5-8R; 41-44R; CANR 8, 59; CMW 4; DLB 77; MTCW 1

Crebillon, Claude Prosper Jolyot de (fils)
1707-1777 .... **LC 1, 28**
See also GFL Beginnings to 1789

Credo
See Creasey, John

Credo, Alvaro J. de
See Prado (Calvo), Pedro

Creeley, Robert (White) 1926- .. **CLC 1, 2, 4, 8, 11, 15, 36, 78**
See also AMWS 4; CA 1-4R; CAAS 10; CANR 23, 43, 89; CP 7; DA3; DAM POET; DLB 5, 16, 169; DLBD 17; MTCW 1, 2; RGAL 4; WP

Crevecoeur, Hector St. John de
See Crevecoeur, Michel Guillaume Jean de
See also ANW

Crevecoeur, Michel Guillaume Jean de
1735-1813 .... **NCLC 105**
See also Crevecoeur, Hector St. John de
See also AMWS 1; DLB 37

Crevel, Rene 1900-1935 .... **TCLC 112**
See also GLL 2

Crews, Harry (Eugene) 1935- ..... **CLC 6, 23, 49**
See also AITN 1; BPFB 1; CA 25-28R; CANR 20, 57; CN 7; CSW; DA3; DLB 6, 143, 185; MTCW 1, 2; RGAL 4

Crichton, (John) Michael 1942- .... **CLC 2, 6, 54, 90**
See also AAYA 10; AITN 2; BPFB 1; CA 25-28R; CANR 13, 40, 54, 76; CMW 4; CN 7; CPW; DA3; DAM NOV, POP; DLBY 1981; INT CANR-13; JRDA; MTCW 1, 2; SATA 9, 88; SFW 4; YAW

Crispin, Edmund .... **CLC 22**
See also Montgomery, (Robert) Bruce
See also DLB 87; MSW

Cristofer, Michael 1945(?)- .... **CLC 28**
See also CA 110; 152; CAD; CD 5; DAM DRAM; DLB 7

Croce, Benedetto 1866-1952 .... **TCLC 37**
See also CA 120; 155; EW 8

Crockett, David 1786-1836 .... **NCLC 8**
See also DLB 3, 11, 183, 248

Crockett, Davy
See Crockett, David

Crofts, Freeman Wills 1879-1957 .. **TCLC 55**
See also CA 115; 195; CMW 4; DLB 77; MSW

Croker, John Wilson 1780-1857 .... **NCLC 10**
See also DLB 110

Crommelynck, Fernand 1885-1970 .. **CLC 75**
See also CA 189; 89-92

Cromwell, Oliver 1599-1658 .... **LC 43**

Cronenberg, David 1943- .... **CLC 143**
See also CA 138; CCA 1

Cronin, A(rchibald) J(oseph)
1896-1981 .... **CLC 32**
See also BPFB 1; CA 1-4R; 102; CANR 5; DLB 191; SATA 47; SATA-Obit 25

Cross, Amanda
See Heilbrun, Carolyn G(old)
See also BPFB 1; CMW; CPW; MSW

Dobrolyubov, Nikolai Alexandrovich
1836-1861 .... **NCLC 5**

Dobson, Austin 1840-1921 .... **TCLC 79**
See also DLB 35, 144

Dobyns, Stephen 1941- .... **CLC 37**
See also CA 45-48; CANR 2, 18, 99; CMW
4; CP 7

Doctorow, E(dgar) L(aurence)
1931- .... **CLC 6, 11, 15, 18, 37, 44, 65,
113**
See also AAYA 22; AITN 2; AMWS 4;
BEST 89:3; BPFB 1; CA 45-48; CANR
2, 33, 51, 76, 97; CDALB 1968-1988; CN
7; CPW; DA3; DAM NOV, POP; DLB 2,
28, 173; DLBY 1980; LAIT 3; MTCW 1,
2; NFS 6; RGAL 4; RHW

Dodgson, Charles Lutwidge 1832-1898
See Carroll, Lewis
See also CLR 2; DA; DA3; DAB; DAC;
DAM MST, NOV, POET; MAICYA 1;
SATA 100; YABC 2

Dodson, Owen (Vincent)
1914-1983 .... **CLC 79; BLC 1**
See also BW 1; CA 65-68; 110; CANR 24;
DAM MULT; DLB 76

Doeblin, Alfred 1878-1957 .... **TCLC 13**
See also Doblin, Alfred
See also CA 110; 141; DLB 66

Doerr, Harriet 1910- .... **CLC 34**
See also CA 117; 122; CANR 47; INT 122

Domecq, H(onorio Bustos)
See Bioy Casares, Adolfo

Domecq, H(onorio) Bustos
See Bioy Casares, Adolfo; Borges, Jorge
Luis

Domini, Rey
See Lorde, Audre (Geraldine)
See also GLL 1

Dominique
See Proust, (Valentin-Louis-George-Eugene-
)Marcel

Don, A
See Stephen, Sir Leslie

Donaldson, Stephen R(eeder)
1947- .... **CLC 46, 138**
See also AAYA 36; BPFB 1; CA 89-92;
CANR 13, 55, 99; CPW; DAM POP;
FANT; INT CANR-13; SATA 121; SFW
4; SUFW

Donleavy, J(ames) P(atrick) 1926- .... **CLC 1,
4, 6, 10, 45**
See also AITN 2; BPFB 1; CA 9-12R;
CANR 24, 49, 62, 80; CBD; CD 5; CN 7;
DLB 6, 173; INT CANR-24; MTCW 1,
2; RGAL 4

Donne, John 1572-1631 ..... **LC 10, 24; PC 1;
WLC**
See also BRW 1; BRWR 2; CDBLB Before
1660; DA; DAB; DAC; DAM MST,
POET; DLB 121, 151; EXPP; PAB; PFS
2, 11; RGEL 2; WLIT 3; WP

Donnell, David 1939(?)- .... **CLC 34**
See also CA 197

Donoghue, P. S.
See Hunt, E(verette) Howard, (Jr.)

Donoso (Yanez), Jose 1924-1996 ... **CLC 4, 8,
11, 32, 99; HLC 1; SSC 34**
See also CA 81-84; 155; CANR 32, 73; CD-
WLB 3; DAM MULT; DLB 113; HW 1,
2; LAW; LAWS 1; MTCW 1, 2; RGSF 2;
WLIT 1

Donovan, John 1928-1992 .... **CLC 35**
See also AAYA 20; CA 97-100; 137; CLR
3; MAICYA 1; SATA 72; SATA-Brief 29;
YAW

Don Roberto
See Cunninghame Graham, Robert
(Gallnigad) Bontine

Doolittle, Hilda 1886-1961 . **CLC 3, 8, 14, 31,
34, 73; PC 5; WLC**
See also H. D.
See also AMWS 1; CA 97-100; CANR 35;
DA; DAC; DAM MST, POET; DLB 4,
45; FW; GLL 1; MAWW; MTCW 1, 2;
PFS 6; RGAL 4

Doppo, Kunikida .... **TCLC 99**
See also Kunikida Doppo

Dorfman, Ariel 1942- .... **CLC 48, 77; HLC 1**
See also CA 124; 130; CANR 67, 70; CWW
2; DAM MULT; DFS 4; HW 1, 2; INT
CA-130; WLIT 1

Dorn, Edward (Merton)
1929-1999 .... **CLC 10, 18**
See also CA 93-96; 187; CANR 42, 79; CP
7; DLB 5; INT 93-96; WP

Dor-Ner, Zvi .... **CLC 70**

Dorris, Michael (Anthony)
1945-1997 .... **CLC 109**
See also AAYA 20; BEST 90:1; BYA 12;
CA 102; 157; CANR 19, 46, 75; CLR 58;
DA3; DAM MULT, NOV; DLB 175;
LAIT 5; MTCW 2; NFS 3; NNAL; RGAL
4; SATA 75; SATA-Obit 94; TCWW 2;
YAW

Dorris, Michael A.
See Dorris, Michael (Anthony)

Dorsan, Luc
See Simenon, Georges (Jacques Christian)

Dorsange, Jean
See Simenon, Georges (Jacques Christian)

Dos Passos, John (Roderigo)
1896-1970 ... **CLC 1, 4, 8, 11, 15, 25, 34,
82; WLC**
See also AMW; BPFB 1; CA 1-4R; 29-32R;
CANR 3; CDALB 1929-1941; DA; DA3;
DAB; DAC; DAM MST, NOV; DLB 4,
9; DLBD 1, 15; DLBY 1996; MTCW 1,
2; RGAL 4

Dossage, Jean
See Simenon, Georges (Jacques Christian)

Dostoevsky, Fedor Mikhailovich
1821-1881 . **NCLC 2, 7, 21, 33, 43; SSC
2, 33, 44; WLC**
See also Dostoevsky, Fyodor
See also DLB; DA; DA3; DAB; DAC;
DAM MST, NOV; EW 7; EXPN; NFS 3,
8; RGSF 2; RGWL 2; SSFS 8

Dostoevsky, Fyodor
See Dostoevsky, Fedor Mikhailovich
See also DLB 238

Doughty, Charles M(ontagu)
1843-1926 .... **TCLC 27**
See also CA 115; 178; DLB 19, 57, 174

Douglas, Ellen .... **CLC 73**
See also Haxton, Josephine Ayres; William-
son, Ellen Douglas
See also CN 7; CSW

Douglas, Gavin 1475(?)-1522 .... **LC 20**
See also DLB 132; RGEL 2

Douglas, George
See Brown, George Douglas
See also RGEL 2

Douglas, Keith (Castellain)
1920-1944 .... **TCLC 40**
See also BRW 7; CA 160; DLB 27; PAB;
RGEL 2

Douglas, Leonard
See Bradbury, Ray (Douglas)

Douglas, Michael
See Crichton, (John) Michael

Douglas, (George) Norman
1868-1952 .... **TCLC 68**
See also BRW 6; CA 119; 157; DLB 34,
195; RGEL 2

Douglas, William
See Brown, George Douglas

Douglass, Frederick 1817(?)-1895 .. **NCLC 7,
55; BLC 1; WLC**
See also AFAW 1, 2; AMWS 3; CDALB
1640-1865; DA; DA3; DAC; DAM MST,
MULT; DLB 1, 43, 50, 79, 243; FW;
LAIT 2; NCFS 2; RGAL 4; SATA 29

Dourado, (Waldomiro Freitas) Autran
1926- .... **CLC 23, 60**
See also CA 25-28R; 179; CANR 34, 81;
DLB 145; HW 2

Dourado, Waldomiro Autran
See Dourado, (Waldomiro Freitas) Autran
See also CA 179

Dove, Rita (Frances) 1952- .... **CLC 50, 81;
BLCS; PC 6**
See also AMWS 4; BW 2; CA 109; CAAS
19; CANR 27, 42, 68, 76, 97; CDALBS;
CP 7; CSW; CWP; DA3; DAM MULT,
POET; DLB 120; EXPP; MTCW 1; PFS
1; RGAL 4

Doveglion
See Villa, Jose Garcia

Dowell, Coleman 1925-1985 .... **CLC 60**
See also CA 25-28R; 117; CANR 10; DLB
130; GLL 2

Dowson, Ernest (Christopher)
1867-1900 .... **TCLC 4**
See also CA 105; 150; DLB 19, 135; RGEL
2

Doyle, A. Conan
See Doyle, Sir Arthur Conan

Doyle, Sir Arthur Conan
1859-1930 .... **TCLC 7; SSC 12; WLC**
See also Conan Doyle, Arthur
See also AAYA 14; BRWS 2; CA 104; 122;
CDBLB 1890-1914; CMW 4; DA; DA3;
DAB; DAC; DAM MST, NOV; DLB 18,
70, 156, 178; EXPS; HGG; LAIT 2;
MSW; MTCW 1, 2; RGEL 2; RGSF 2;
RHW; SATA 24; SCFW 2; SFW 4; SSFS
2; WCH; WLIT 4; WYA; YAW

Doyle, Conan
See Doyle, Sir Arthur Conan

Doyle, John
See Graves, Robert (von Ranke)

Doyle, Roddy 1958(?)- .... **CLC 81**
See also AAYA 14; BRWS 5; CA 143;
CANR 73; CN 7; DA3; DLB 194

Doyle, Sir A. Conan
See Doyle, Sir Arthur Conan

Dr. A
See Asimov, Isaac; Silverstein, Alvin; Silverstein, Virginia B(arbara Opshelor)

Drabble, Margaret 1939- ...... **CLC 2, 3, 5, 8,
10, 22, 53, 129**
See also BRWS 4; CA 13-16R; CANR 18,
35, 63; CDBLB 1960 to Present; CN 7;
CPW; DA3; DAB; DAC; DAM MST,
NOV, POP; DLB 14, 155, 231; FW;
MTCW 1, 2; RGEL 2; SATA 48

Drapier, M. B.
See Swift, Jonathan

Drayham, James
See Mencken, H(enry) L(ouis)

Drayton, Michael 1563-1631 .... **LC 8**
See also DAM POET; DLB 121; RGEL 2

Dreadstone, Carl
See Campbell, (John) Ramsey

Dreiser, Theodore (Herman Albert)
1871-1945 .... **TCLC 10, 18, 35, 83; SSC
30; WLC**
See also AMW; CA 106; 132; CDALB
1865-1917; DA; DA3; DAC; DAM MST,
NOV; DLB 9, 12, 102, 137; DLBD 1;
LAIT 2; MTCW 1, 2; NFS 8; RGAL 4

Drexler, Rosalyn 1926- .... **CLC 2, 6**
See also CA 81-84; CAD; CANR 68; CD
5; CWD

Fairbairns, Zoe (Ann) 1948- .... **CLC 32**
See also CA 103; CANR 21, 85; CN 7

Fairman, Paul W. 1916-1977
See Queen, Ellery
See also CA 114; SFW 4

Falco, Gian
See Papini, Giovanni

Falconer, James
See Kirkup, James

Falconer, Kenneth
See Kornbluth, C(yril) M.

Falkland, Samuel
See Heijermans, Herman

Fallaci, Oriana 1930- .... **CLC 11, 110**
See also CA 77-80; CANR 15, 58; FW;
MTCW 1

Faludi, Susan 1959- .... **CLC 140**
See also CA 138; FW; MTCW 1

Faludy, George 1913- .... **CLC 42**
See also CA 21-24R

Faludy, Gyoergy
See Faludy, George

Fanon, Frantz 1925-1961 .... **CLC 74; BLC 2**
See also BW 1; CA 116; 89-92; DAM
MULT; WLIT 2

Fanshawe, Ann 1625-1680 .... **LC 11**

Fante, John (Thomas) 1911-1983 ..... **CLC 60**
See also CA 69-72; 109; CANR 23, 104;
DLB 130; DLBY 1983

Farah, Nuruddin 1945- .. **CLC 53, 137; BLC 2**
See also AFW; BW 2, 3; CA 106; CANR
81; CDWLB 3; CN 7; DAM MULT; DLB
125; WLIT 2

Fargue, Leon-Paul 1876(?)-1947 .... **TCLC 11**
See also CA 109

Farigoule, Louis
See Romains, Jules

Farina, Richard 1936(?)-1966 .... **CLC 9**
See also CA 81-84; 25-28R

Farley, Walter (Lorimer)
1915-1989 .... **CLC 17**
See also BYA 14; CA 17-20R; CANR 8,
29, 84; DLB 22; JRDA; MAICYA 1;
SATA 2, 43; YAW

Farmer, Philip Jose 1918- .... **CLC 1, 19**
See also AAYA 28; BPFB 1; CA 1-4R;
CANR 4, 35; DLB 8; MTCW 1; SATA
93; SCFW 2; SFW 4

Farquhar, George 1677-1707 .... **LC 21**
See also BRW 2; DAM DRAM; DLB 84;
RGEL 2

Farrell, J(ames) G(ordon)
1935-1979 .... **CLC 6**
See also CA 73-76; 89-92; CANR 36; DLB
14; MTCW 1; RGEL 2; RHW; WLIT 4

Farrell, James T(homas) 1904-1979 . **CLC 1,
4, 8, 11, 66; SSC 28**
See also AMW; BPFB 1; CA 5-8R; 89-92;
CANR 9, 61; DLB 4, 9, 86; DLBD 2;
MTCW 1, 2; RGAL 4

Farrell, Warren (Thomas) 1943- ...... **CLC 70**
See also CA 146

Farren, Richard J.
See Betjeman, John

Farren, Richard M.
See Betjeman, John

Fassbinder, Rainer Werner
1946-1982 .... **CLC 20**
See also CA 93-96; 106; CANR 31

Fast, Howard (Melvin) 1914- ... **CLC 23, 131**
See also AAYA 16; BPFB 1; CA 1-4R, 181;
CAAE 181; CAAS 18; CANR 1, 33, 54,
75, 98; CMW 4; CN 7; CPW; DAM NOV;
DLB 9; INT CANR-33; MTCW 1; RHW;
SATA 7; SATA-Essay 107; TCWW 2;
YAW

Faulcon, Robert
See Holdstock, Robert P.

Faulkner, William (Cuthbert)
1897-1962 .... **CLC 1, 3, 6, 8, 9, 11, 14,
18, 28, 52, 68; SSC 1, 35, 42; WLC**
See also AAYA 7; AMW; AMWR 1; BPFB
1; BYA 5; CA 81-84; CANR 33; CDALB
1929-1941; DA; DA3; DAB; DAC; DAM
MST, NOV; DLB 9, 11, 44, 102; DLBD
2; DLBY 1986, 1997; EXPN; EXPS;
LAIT 2; MTCW 1, 2; NFS 4, 8, 13;
RGAL 4; RGSF 2; SSFS 2, 5, 6, 12

Fauset, Jessie Redmon
1882(?)-1961 .... **CLC 19, 54; BLC 2**
See also AFAW 2; BW 1; CA 109; CANR
83; DAM MULT; DLB 51; FW; MAWW

Faust, Frederick (Schiller)
1892-1944(?) .... **TCLC 49**
See also Austin, Frank; Brand, Max; Challis, George; Dawson, Peter; Dexter, Martin; Evans, Evan; Frederick, John; Frost,
Frederick; Manning, David; Silver, Nicholas
See also CA 108; 152; DAM POP; DLB
256

Fawkes, Guy
See Benchley, Robert (Charles)

Fearing, Kenneth (Flexner)
1902-1961 .... **CLC 51**
See also CA 93-96; CANR 59; CMW 4;
DLB 9; RGAL 4

Fecamps, Elise
See Creasey, John

Federman, Raymond 1928- .... **CLC 6, 47**
See also CA 17-20R; CAAS 8; CANR 10,
43, 83, 108; CN 7; DLBY 1980

Federspiel, J(uerg) F. 1931- .... **CLC 42**
See also CA 146

Feiffer, Jules (Ralph) 1929- ...... **CLC 2, 8, 64**
See also AAYA 3; CA 17-20R; CAD; CANR
30, 59; CD 5; DAM DRAM; DLB 7, 44;
INT CANR-30; MTCW 1; SATA 8, 61,
111

Feige, Hermann Albert Otto Maximilian
See Traven, B.

Feinberg, David B. 1956-1994 .... **CLC 59**
See also CA 135; 147

Feinstein, Elaine 1930- .... **CLC 36**
See also CA 69-72; CAAS 1; CANR 31,
68; CN 7; CP 7; CWP; DLB 14, 40;
MTCW 1

Feke, Gilbert David .... **CLC 65**

Feldman, Irving (Mordecai) 1928- ..... **CLC 7**
See also CA 1-4R; CANR 1; CP 7; DLB
169

Felix-Tchicaya, Gerald
See Tchicaya, Gerald Felix

Fellini, Federico 1920-1993 .... **CLC 16, 85**
See also CA 65-68; 143; CANR 33

Felsen, Henry Gregor 1916-1995 ..... **CLC 17**
See also CA 1-4R; 180; CANR 1; SAAS 2;
SATA 1

Felski, Rita .... **CLC 65**

Fenno, Jack
See Calisher, Hortense

Fenollosa, Ernest (Francisco)
1853-1908 .... **TCLC 91**

Fenton, James Martin 1949- .... **CLC 32**
See also CA 102; CANR 108; CP 7; DLB
40; PFS 11

Ferber, Edna 1887-1968 .... **CLC 18, 93**
See also AITN 1; CA 5-8R; 25-28R; CANR
68, 105; DLB 9, 28, 86; MTCW 1, 2;
RGAL 4; RHW; SATA 7; TCWW 2

Ferdowsi, Abu'l Qasem 940-1020 . **CMLC 43**
See also RGWL 2

Ferguson, Helen
See Kavan, Anna

Ferguson, Niall 1964- .... **CLC 134**
See also CA 190

Ferguson, Samuel 1810-1886 .... **NCLC 33**
See also DLB 32; RGEL 2

Fergusson, Robert 1750-1774 .... **LC 29**
See also DLB 109; RGEL 2

Ferling, Lawrence
See Ferlinghetti, Lawrence (Monsanto)

Ferlinghetti, Lawrence (Monsanto)
1919(?)- ..... **CLC 2, 6, 10, 27, 111; PC 1**
See also CA 5-8R; CANR 3, 41, 73;
CDALB 1941-1968; CP 7; DA3; DAM
POET; DLB 5, 16; MTCW 1, 2; RGAL 4;
WP

Fern, Fanny
See Parton, Sara Payson Willis

Fernandez, Vicente Garcia Huidobro
See Huidobro Fernandez, Vicente Garcia

Fernandez-Armesto, Felipe .... **CLC 70**

Fernandez de Lizardi, Jose Joaquin
See Lizardi, Jose Joaquin Fernandez de

Ferre, Rosario 1942- ...... **CLC 139; HLCS 1;
SSC 36**
See also CA 131; CANR 55, 81; CWW 2;
DLB 145; HW 1, 2; LAWS 1; MTCW 1;
WLIT 1

Ferrer, Gabriel (Francisco Victor) Miro
See Miro (Ferrer), Gabriel (Francisco
Victor)

Ferrier, Susan (Edmonstone)
1782-1854 .... **NCLC 8**
See also DLB 116; RGEL 2

Ferrigno, Robert 1948(?)- .... **CLC 65**
See also CA 140

Ferron, Jacques 1921-1985 .... **CLC 94**
See also CA 117; 129; CCA 1; DAC; DLB
60

Feuchtwanger, Lion 1884-1958 .... **TCLC 3**
See also CA 104; 187; DLB 66

Feuillet, Octave 1821-1890 .... **NCLC 45**
See also DLB 192

Feydeau, Georges (Leon Jules Marie)
1862-1921 .... **TCLC 22**
See also CA 113; 152; CANR 84; DAM
DRAM; DLB 192; GFL 1789 to the
Present; RGWL 2

Fichte, Johann Gottlieb
1762-1814 .... **NCLC 62**
See also DLB 90

Ficino, Marsilio 1433-1499 .... **LC 12**

Fiedeler, Hans
See Doeblin, Alfred

Fiedler, Leslie A(aron) 1917- .. **CLC 4, 13, 24**
See also CA 9-12R; CANR 7, 63; CN 7;
DLB 28, 67; MTCW 1, 2; RGAL 4

Field, Andrew 1938- .... **CLC 44**
See also CA 97-100; CANR 25

Field, Eugene 1850-1895 .... **NCLC 3**
See also DLB 23, 42, 140; DLBD 13; MAI-
CYA 1; RGAL 4; SATA 16

Field, Gans T.
See Wellman, Manly Wade

Field, Michael 1915-1971 .... **TCLC 43**
See also CA 29-32R

Field, Peter
See Hobson, Laura Z(ametkin)
See also TCWW 2

Fielding, Helen 1959(?)- .... **CLC 146**
See also CA 172; DLB 231

Fielding, Henry 1707-1754 .. **LC 1, 46; WLC**
See also BRW 3; BRWR 1; CDBLB 1660-
1789; DA; DA3; DAB; DAC; DAM
DRAM, MST, NOV; DLB 39, 84, 101;
RGEL 2; WLIT 3

Fielding, Sarah 1710-1768 .... **LC 1, 44**
See also DLB 39; RGEL 2

Fields, W. C. 1880-1946 .... **TCLC 80**
See also DLB 44

Fierstein, Harvey (Forbes) 1954- ..... **CLC 33**
See also CA 123; 129; CAD; CD 5; CPW;
DA3; DAM DRAM, POP; DFS 6; GLL

Figes, Eva 1932- .... **CLC 31**
See also CA 53-56; CANR 4, 44, 83; CN 7;
DLB 14; FW

Finch, Anne 1661-1720 .... **LC 3; PC 21**
See also DLB 95

Finch, Robert (Duer Claydon)
1900-1995 .... **CLC 18**
See also CA 57-60; CANR 9, 24, 49; CP 7;
DLB 88

Findley, Timothy 1930- .... **CLC 27, 102**
See also CA 25-28R; CANR 12, 42, 69;
CCA 1; CN 7; DAC; DAM MST; DLB
53; FANT; RHW

Fink, William
See Mencken, H(enry) L(ouis)

Firbank, Louis 1942-
See Reed, Lou
See also CA 117

Firbank, (Arthur Annesley) Ronald
1886-1926 .... **TCLC 1**
See also BRWS 2; CA 104; 177; DLB 36;
RGEL 2

Fish, Stanley
See Fish, Stanley Eugene

Fish, Stanley E.
See Fish, Stanley Eugene

Fish, Stanley Eugene 1938- .... **CLC 142**
See also CA 112; 132; CANR 90; DLB 67

Fisher, Dorothy (Frances) Canfield
1879-1958 .... **TCLC 87**
See also CA 114; 136; CANR 80; CLR 71,;
CWRI 5; DLB 9, 102; MAICYA 1; YABC
1

Fisher, M(ary) F(rances) K(ennedy)
1908-1992 .... **CLC 76, 87**
See also CA 77-80; 138; CANR 44; MTCW
1

Fisher, Roy 1930- .... **CLC 25**
See also CA 81-84; CAAS 10; CANR 16;
CP 7; DLB 40

Fisher, Rudolph 1897-1934 .. **TCLC 11; BLC
2; SSC 25**
See also BW 1, 3; CA 107; 124; CANR 80;
DAM MULT; DLB 51, 102

Fisher, Vardis (Alvero) 1895-1968 ...... **CLC 7**
See also CA 5-8R; 25-28R; CANR 68; DLB
9, 206; RGAL 4; TCWW 2

Fiske, Tarleton
See Bloch, Robert (Albert)

Fitch, Clarke
See Sinclair, Upton (Beall)

Fitch, John IV
See Cormier, Robert (Edmund)

Fitzgerald, Captain Hugh
See Baum, L(yman) Frank

FitzGerald, Edward 1809-1883 .... **NCLC 9**
See also BRW 4; DLB 32; RGEL 2

Fitzgerald, F(rancis) Scott (Key)
1896-1940 . **TCLC 1, 6, 14, 28, 55; SSC
6, 31; WLC**
See also AAYA 24; AITN 1; AMW; AMWR
1; BPFB 1; CA 110; 123; CDALB 1917-
1929; DA; DA3; DAB; DAC; DAM MST,
NOV; DLB 4, 9, 86, 219; DLBD 1, 15,
16; DLBY 1981, 1996; EXPN; EXPS;
LAIT 3; MTCW 1, 2; NFS 2; RGAL 4;
RGSF 2; SSFS 4

Fitzgerald, Penelope 1916-2000 . **CLC 19, 51,
61, 143**
See also BRWS 5; CA 85-88; 190; CAAS
10; CANR 56, 86; CN 7; DLB 14, 194;
MTCW 2

Fitzgerald, Robert (Stuart)
1910-1985 .... **CLC 39**
See also CA 1-4R; 114; CANR 1; DLBY
1980

FitzGerald, Robert D(avid)
1902-1987 .... **CLC 19**
See also CA 17-20R; RGEL 2

Fitzgerald, Zelda (Sayre)
1900-1948 .... **TCLC 52**
See also AMWS 9; CA 117; 126; DLBY
1984

Flanagan, Thomas (James Bonner)
1923- .... **CLC 25, 52**
See also CA 108; CANR 55; CN 7; DLBY
1980; INT 108; MTCW 1; RHW

Flaubert, Gustave 1821-1880 .... **NCLC 2, 10,
19, 62, 66; SSC 11**
See also DA; DA3; DAB; DAC; DAM
MST, NOV; DLB 119; EW 7; EXPS; GFL
1789 to the Present; LAIT 2; RGSF 2;
RGWL 2; SSFS 6

Flavius Josephus
See Josephus, Flavius

Flecker, Herman Elroy
See Flecker, (Herman) James Elroy

Flecker, (Herman) James Elroy
1884-1915 .... **TCLC 43**
See also CA 109; 150; DLB 10, 19; RGEL
2

Fleming, Ian (Lancaster) 1908-1964 . **CLC 3,
30**
See also AAYA 26; BPFB 1; CA 5-8R;
CANR 59; CDBLB 1945-1960; CMW 4;
CPW; DA3; DAM POP; DLB 87, 201;
MSW; MTCW 1, 2; RGEL 2; SATA 9;
YAW

Fleming, Thomas (James) 1927- ...... **CLC 37**
See also CA 5-8R; CANR 10, 102; INT
CANR-10; SATA 8

Fletcher, John 1579-1625 .... **LC 33; DC 6**
See also BRW 2; CDBLB Before 1660;
DLB 58; RGEL 2

Fletcher, John Gould 1886-1950 .... **TCLC 35**
See also CA 107; 167; DLB 4, 45; RGAL 4

Fleur, Paul
See Pohl, Frederik

Flooglebuckle, Al
See Spiegelman, Art

Flora, Fletcher 1914-1969
See Queen, Ellery
See also CA 1-4R; CANR 3, 85

Flying Officer X
See Bates, H(erbert) E(rnest)

Fo, Dario 1926- .... **CLC 32, 109; DC 10**
See also CA 116; 128; CANR 68; CWW 2;
DA3; DAM DRAM; DLBY 1997; MTCW
1, 2

Fogarty, Jonathan Titulescu Esq.
See Farrell, James T(homas)

Follett, Ken(neth Martin) 1949- .... **CLC 18**
See also AAYA 6; BEST 89:4; BPFB 1; CA
81-84; CANR 13, 33, 54, 102; CMW 4;
CPW; DA3; DAM NOV, POP; DLB 87;
DLBY 1981; INT CANR-33; MTCW 1

Fontane, Theodor 1819-1898 .... **NCLC 26**
See also CDWLB 2; DLB 129; EW 6;
RGWL 2

Fontenot, Chester .... **CLC 65**

Foote, Horton 1916- .... **CLC 51, 91**
See also CA 73-76; CAD; CANR 34, 51;
CD 5; CSW; DA3; DAM DRAM; DLB
26; INT CANR-34

Foote, Mary Hallock 1847-1938 .. **TCLC 108**
See also DLB 186, 188, 202, 221

Foote, Shelby 1916- .... **CLC 75**
See also AAYA 40; CA 5-8R; CANR 3, 45,
74; CN 7; CPW; CSW; DA3; DAM NOV,
POP; DLB 2, 17; MTCW 2; RHW

Forbes, Esther 1891-1967 .... **CLC 12**
See also AAYA 17; BYA 2; CA 13-14; 25-
28R; CAP 1; CLR 27; DLB 22; JRDA;
MAICYA 1; RHW; SATA 2, 100; YAW

Forche, Carolyn (Louise) 1950- .... **CLC 25,
83, 86; PC 10**
See also CA 109; 117; CANR 50, 74; CP 7;
CWP; DA3; DAM POET; DLB 5, 193;
INT CA-117; MTCW 1; RGAL 4

Ford, Elbur
See Hibbert, Eleanor Alice Burford

Ford, Ford Madox 1873-1939 ... **TCLC 1, 15,
39, 57**
See also Chaucer, Daniel
See also BRW 6; CA 104; 132; CANR 74;
CDBLB 1914-1945; DA3; DAM NOV;
DLB 34, 98, 162; MTCW 1, 2; RGEL 2

Ford, Henry 1863-1947 .... **TCLC 73**
See also CA 115; 148

Ford, John 1586-1639 .... **LC 68; DC 8**
See also BRW 2; CDBLB Before 1660;
DA3; DAM DRAM; DFS 7; DLB 58;
IDTP; RGEL 2

Ford, John 1895-1973 .... **CLC 16**
See also CA 187; 45-48

Ford, Richard 1944- .... **CLC 46, 99**
See also AMWS 5; CA 69-72; CANR 11,
47, 86; CN 7; CSW; DLB 227; MTCW 1;
RGAL 4; RGSF 2

Ford, Webster
See Masters, Edgar Lee

Foreman, Richard 1937- .... **CLC 50**
See also CA 65-68; CAD; CANR 32, 63;
CD 5

Forester, C(ecil) S(cott) 1899-1966 ... **CLC 35**
See also CA 73-76; 25-28R; CANR 83;
DLB 191; RGEL 2; RHW; SATA 13

Forez
See Mauriac, Francois (Charles)

Forman, James Douglas 1932- .... **CLC 21**
See also AAYA 17; CA 9-12R; CANR 4,
19, 42; JRDA; MAICYA 1; SATA 8, 70;
YAW

Fornes, Maria Irene 1930- . **CLC 39, 61; DC
10; HLCS 1**
See also CA 25-28R; CAD; CANR 28, 81;
CD 5; CWD; DLB 7; HW 1, 2; INT
CANR-28; MTCW 1; RGAL 4

Forrest, Leon (Richard) 1937-1997 .. **CLC 4;
BLCS**
See also AFAW 2; BW 2; CA 89-92; 162;
CAAS 7; CANR 25, 52, 87; CN 7; DLB
33

Forster, E(dward) M(organ)
1879-1970 ...... **CLC 1, 2, 3, 4, 9, 10, 13,
15, 22, 45, 77; SSC 27; WLC**
See also AAYA 2, 37; BRW 6; BRWR 2;
CA 13-14; 25-28R; CANR 45; CAP 1;
CDBLB 1914-1945; DA; DA3; DAB;
DAC; DAM MST, NOV; DLB 34, 98,
162, 178, 195; DLBD 10; EXPN; LAIT
3; MTCW 1, 2; NCFS 1; NFS 3, 10, 11;
RGEL 2; RGSF 2; SATA 57; SUFW;
WLIT 4

Forster, John 1812-1876 .... **NCLC 11**
See also DLB 144, 184

Forster, Margaret 1938- .... **CLC 149**
See also CA 133; CANR 62; CN 7; DLB
155

Forsyth, Frederick 1938- .... **CLC 2, 5, 36**
See also BEST 89:4; CA 85-88; CANR 38,
62; CMW 4; CN 7; CPW; DAM NOV,
POP; DLB 87; MTCW 1, 2

Forten, Charlotte L. 1837-1914 .... **TCLC 16;
BLC 2**
See also Grimke, Charlotte L(ottie) Forten
See also DLB 50, 239

Foscolo, Ugo 1778-1827 .... **NCLC 8, 97**
See also EW 5

Fosse, Bob .... **CLC 20**
See also Fosse, Robert Louis

Fosse, Robert Louis 1927-1987
   See Fosse, Bob
   See also CA 110; 123
Foster, Hannah Webster
   1758-1840 .... NCLC 99
   See also DLB 37, 200; RGAL 4
Foster, Stephen Collins
   1826-1864 .... NCLC 26
   See also RGAL 4
Foucault, Michel 1926-1984 . CLC 31, 34, 69
   See also CA 105; 113; CANR 34; DLB 242;
   EW 13; GFL 1789 to the Present; GLL 1;
   MTCW 1, 2
**Fouque, Friedrich (Heinrich Karl) de la
   Motte** 1777-1843 .... NCLC 2
   See also DLB 90; RGWL 2; SUFW
Fourier, Charles 1772-1837 .... NCLC 51
Fournier, Henri Alban 1886-1914
   See Alain-Fournier
   See also CA 104; 179
Fournier, Pierre 1916- .... CLC 11
   See also Gascar, Pierre
   See also CA 89-92; CANR 16, 40
Fowles, John (Robert) 1926- . CLC 1, 2, 3, 4,
   6, 9, 10, 15, 33, 87; SSC 33
   See also BPFB 1; BRWS 1; CA 5-8R;
   CANR 25, 71, 103; CDBLB 1960 to
   Present; CN 7; DA3; DAB; DAC; DAM
   MST; DLB 14, 139, 207; HGG; MTCW
   1, 2; RGEL 2; RHW; SATA 22; WLIT 4
Fox, Paula 1923- .... CLC 2, 8, 121
   See also AAYA 3, 37; BYA 3, 8; CA 73-76;
   CANR 20, 36, 62, 105; CLR 1, 44; DLB
   52; JRDA; MAICYA 1; MTCW 1; NFS
   12; SATA 17, 60, 120; WYA; YAW
Fox, William Price (Jr.) 1926- .... CLC 22
   See also CA 17-20R; CAAS 19; CANR 11;
   CSW; DLB 2; DLBY 1981
Foxe, John 1517(?)-1587 .... LC 14
   See also DLB 132
Frame, Janet .. CLC 2, 3, 6, 22, 66, 96; SSC
   29
   See also Clutha, Janet Paterson Frame
   See also CN 7; CWP; RGEL 2; RGSF 2
France, Anatole .... TCLC 9
   See also Thibault, Jacques Anatole Francois
   See also DLB 123; GFL 1789 to the Present;
   MTCW 1; RGWL 2; SUFW
Francis, Claude .... CLC 50
   See also CA 192
Francis, Dick 1920- .... CLC 2, 22, 42, 102
   See also AAYA 5, 21; BEST 89:3; BPFB 1;
   CA 5-8R; CANR 9, 42, 68, 100; CDBLB
   1960 to Present; CMW 4; CN 7; DA3;
   DAM POP; DLB 87; INT CANR-9;
   MSW; MTCW 1, 2
Francis, Robert (Churchill)
   1901-1987 .... CLC 15; PC 34
   See also AMWS 9; CA 1-4R; 123; CANR
   1; EXPP; PFS 12
Francis, Lord Jeffrey
   See Jeffrey, Francis
   See also DLB 107
Frank, Anne(lies Marie)
   1929-1945 .... TCLC 17; WLC
   See also AAYA 12; BYA 1; CA 113; 133;
   CANR 68; DA; DA3; DAB; DAC; DAM
   MST; LAIT 4; MAICYAS 1; MTCW 1,
   2; NCFS 2; SATA 87; SATA-Brief 42;
   WYA; YAW
Frank, Bruno 1887-1945 .... TCLC 81
   See also CA 189; DLB 118
Frank, Elizabeth 1945- .... CLC 39
   See also CA 121; 126; CANR 78; INT 126
Frankl, Viktor E(mil) 1905-1997 ...... CLC 93
   See also CA 65-68; 161
Franklin, Benjamin
   See Hasek, Jaroslav (Matej Frantisek)

Franklin, Benjamin 1706-1790 .... LC 25;
   WLCS
   See also AMW; CDALB 1640-1865; DA;
   DA3; DAB; DAC; DAM MST; DLB 24,
   43, 73, 183; LAIT 1; RGAL 4; TUS
**Franklin, (Stella Maria Sarah) Miles
   (Lampe)** 1879-1954 .... TCLC 7
   See also CA 104; 164; DLB 230; FW;
   MTCW 2; RGEL 2; TWA
Fraser, George MacDonald 1925- ...... CLC 7
   See also CA 45-48, 180; CAAE 180; CANR
   2, 48, 74; MTCW 1; RHW
Fraser, Sylvia 1935- .... CLC 64
   See also CA 45-48; CANR 1, 16, 60; CCA
   1
Frayn, Michael 1933- .... CLC 3, 7, 31, 47
   See also BRWS 7; CA 5-8R; CANR 30, 69;
   CBD; CD 5; CN 7; DAM DRAM, NOV;
   DLB 13, 14, 194, 245; FANT; MTCW 1,
   2; SFW 4
Fraze, Candida (Merrill) 1945- .... CLC 50
   See also CA 126
Frazer, Andrew
   See Marlowe, Stephen
Frazer, J(ames) G(eorge)
   1854-1941 .... TCLC 32
   See also BRWS 3; CA 118
Frazer, Robert Caine
   See Creasey, John
Frazer, Sir James George
   See Frazer, J(ames) G(eorge)
Frazier, Charles 1950- .... CLC 109
   See also AAYA 34; CA 161; CSW
Frazier, Ian 1951- .... CLC 46
   See also CA 130; CANR 54, 93
Frederic, Harold 1856-1898 .... NCLC 10
   See also AMW; DLB 12, 23; DLBD 13;
   RGAL 4
Frederick, John
   See Faust, Frederick (Schiller)
   See also TCWW 2
Frederick the Great 1712-1786 .... LC 14
Fredro, Aleksander 1793-1876 .... NCLC 8
Freeling, Nicolas 1927- .... CLC 38
   See also CA 49-52; CAAS 12; CANR 1,
   17, 50, 84; CMW 4; CN 7; DLB 87
Freeman, Douglas Southall
   1886-1953 .... TCLC 11
   See also CA 109; 195; DLB 17; DLBD 17
Freeman, Judith 1946- .... CLC 55
   See also CA 148; DLB 256
Freeman, Mary E(leanor) Wilkins
   1852-1930 .... TCLC 9; SSC 1, 47
   See also CA 106; 177; DLB 12, 78, 221;
   EXPS; FW; HGG; MAWW; RGAL 4;
   RGSF 2; SSFS 4, 8; SUFW; TUS
Freeman, R(ichard) Austin
   1862-1943 .... TCLC 21
   See also CA 113; CANR 84; CMW 4; DLB
   70
French, Albert 1943- .... CLC 86
   See also BW 3; CA 167
French, Marilyn 1929- .... CLC 10, 18, 60
   See also BPFB 1; CA 69-72; CANR 3, 31;
   CN 7; CPW; DAM DRAM, NOV, POP;
   FW; INT CANR-31; MTCW 1, 2
French, Paul
   See Asimov, Isaac
Freneau, Philip Morin 1752-1832 .. NCLC 1,
   111
   See also AMWS 2; DLB 37, 43; RGAL 4
Freud, Sigmund 1856-1939 .... TCLC 52
   See also CA 115; 133; CANR 69; EW 8;
   MTCW 1, 2
Freytag, Gustav 1816-1895 .... NCLC 109
   See also DLB 129
Friedan, Betty (Naomi) 1921- .... CLC 74
   See also CA 65-68; CANR 18, 45, 74; DLB
   246; FW; MTCW 1, 2

Friedlander, Saul 1932- .... CLC 90
   See also CA 117; 130; CANR 72
Friedman, B(ernard) H(arper)
   1926- .... CLC 7
   See also CA 1-4R; CANR 3, 48
Friedman, Bruce Jay 1930- ...... CLC 3, 5, 56
   See also CA 9-12R; CAD; CANR 25, 52,
   101; CD 5; CN 7; DLB 2, 28, 244; INT
   CANR-25
Friel, Brian 1929- .... CLC 5, 42, 59, 115; DC
   8
   See also BRWS 5; CA 21-24R; CANR 33,
   69; CBD; CD 5; DFS 11; DLB 13; MTCW
   1; RGEL 2
Friis-Baastad, Babbis Ellinor
   1921-1970 .... CLC 12
   See also CA 17-20R; 134; SATA 7
Frisch, Max (Rudolf) 1911-1991 ... CLC 3, 9,
   14, 18, 32, 44
   See also CA 85-88; 134; CANR 32, 74; CD-
   WLB 2; DAM DRAM, NOV; DLB 69,
   124; EW 13; MTCW 1, 2; RGWL 2
Fromentin, Eugene (Samuel Auguste)
   1820-1876 .... NCLC 10
   See also DLB 123; GFL 1789 to the Present
Frost, Frederick
   See Faust, Frederick (Schiller)
   See also TCWW 2
Frost, Robert (Lee) 1874-1963 .. CLC 1, 3, 4,
   **9, 10, 13, 15, 26, 34, 44; PC 1, 39;
   WLC**
   See also AAYA 21; AMW; AMWR 1; CA
   89-92; CANR 33; CDALB 1917-1929;
   CLR 67; DA; DA3; DAB; DAC; DAM
   MST, POET; DLB 54; DLBD 7; EXPP;
   MTCW 1, 2; PAB; PFS 1, 2, 3, 4, 5, 6, 7,
   10, 13; RGAL 4; SATA 14; WP; WYA
Froude, James Anthony
   1818-1894 .... NCLC 43
   See also DLB 18, 57, 144
Froy, Herald
   See Waterhouse, Keith (Spencer)
Fry, Christopher 1907- .... CLC 2, 10, 14
   See also BRWS 3; CA 17-20R; CAAS 23;
   CANR 9, 30, 74; CBD; CD 5; CP 7; DAM
   DRAM; DLB 13; MTCW 1, 2; RGEL 2;
   SATA 66
Frye, (Herman) Northrop
   1912-1991 .... CLC 24, 70
   See also CA 5-8R; 133; CANR 8, 37; DLB
   67, 68, 246; MTCW 1, 2; RGAL 4
Fuchs, Daniel 1909-1993 .... CLC 8, 22
   See also CA 81-84; 142; CAAS 5; CANR
   40; DLB 9, 26, 28; DLBY 1993
Fuchs, Daniel 1934- .... CLC 34
   See also CA 37-40R; CANR 14, 48
Fuentes, Carlos 1928- .. CLC 3, 8, 10, 13, 22,
   41, 60, 113; HLC 1; SSC 24; WLC
   See also AAYA 4; AITN 2; BPFB 1; CA
   69-72; CANR 10, 32, 68, 104; CDWLB
   3; CWW 2; DA; DA3; DAB; DAC; DAM
   MST, MULT, NOV; DLB 113; DNFS 2;
   HW 1, 2; LAIT 3; LAW; LAWS 1;
   MTCW 1, 2; NFS 8; RGSF 2; RGWL 2;
   WLIT 1
Fuentes, Gregorio Lopez y
   See Lopez y Fuentes, Gregorio
Fuertes, Gloria 1918-1998 .... PC 27
   See also CA 178; 180; DLB 108; HW 2;
   SATA 115
Fugard, (Harold) Athol 1932- . CLC 5, 9, 14,
   25, 40, 80; DC 3
   See also AAYA 17; AFW; CA 85-88; CANR
   32, 54; CD 5; DAM DRAM; DFS 3, 6,
   10; DLB 225; DNFS 1, 2; MTCW 1;
   RGEL 2; WLIT 2
Fugard, Sheila 1932- .... CLC 48
   See also CA 125
Fukuyama, Francis 1952- .... CLC 131
   See also CA 140; CANR 72

Gregory, J. Dennis
See Williams, John A(lfred)

Grekova, I. .... **CLC 59**

Grendon, Stephen
See Derleth, August (William)

Grenville, Kate 1950- .... **CLC 61**
See also CA 118; CANR 53, 93

Grenville, Pelham
See Wodehouse, P(elham) G(renville)

Greve, Felix Paul (Berthold Friedrich)
1879-1948
See Grove, Frederick Philip
See also CA 104; 141, 175; CANR 79;
DAC; DAM MST

Grey, Zane 1872-1939 .... **TCLC 6**
See also BPFB 2; CA 104; 132; DA3; DAM
POP; DLB 9, 212; MTCW 1, 2; RGAL 4;
TCWW 2

Grieg, (Johan) Nordahl (Brun)
1902-1943 .... **TCLC 10**
See also CA 107; 189

Grieve, C(hristopher) M(urray)
1892-1978 .... **CLC 11, 19**
See also MacDiarmid, Hugh; Pteleon
See also CA 5-8R; 85-88; CANR 33, 107;
DAM POET; MTCW 1; RGEL 2

Griffin, Gerald 1803-1840 .... **NCLC 7**
See also DLB 159; RGEL 2

Griffin, John Howard 1920-1980 ..... **CLC 68**
See also AITN 1; CA 1-4R; 101; CANR 2

Griffin, Peter 1942- .... **CLC 39**
See also CA 136

Griffith, D(avid Lewelyn) W(ark)
1875(?)-1948 .... **TCLC 68**
See also CA 119; 150; CANR 80

Griffith, Lawrence
See Griffith, D(avid Lewelyn) W(ark)

Griffiths, Trevor 1935- .... **CLC 13, 52**
See also CA 97-100; CANR 45; CBD; CD
5; DLB 13, 245

Griggs, Sutton (Elbert)
1872-1930 .... **TCLC 77**
See also CA 123; 186; DLB 50

Grigson, Geoffrey (Edward Harvey)
1905-1985 .... **CLC 7, 39**
See also CA 25-28R; 118; CANR 20, 33;
DLB 27; MTCW 1, 2

Grillparzer, Franz 1791-1872 . **NCLC 1, 102;
DC 14; SSC 37**
See also CDWLB 2; DLB 133; EW 5;
RGWL 2

Grimble, Reverend Charles James
See Eliot, T(homas) S(tearns)

Grimke, Charlotte L(ottie) Forten
1837(?)-1914
See Forten, Charlotte L.
See also BW 1; CA 117; 124; DAM MULT,
POET

Grimm, Jacob Ludwig Karl
1785-1863 .... **NCLC 3, 77; SSC 36**
See also DLB 90; MAICYA 1; RGSF 2;
RGWL 2; SATA 22; WCH

Grimm, Wilhelm Karl 1786-1859 .. **NCLC 3,
77; SSC 36**
See also CDWLB 2; DLB 90; MAICYA 1;
RGSF 2; RGWL 2; SATA 22; WCH

**Grimmelshausen, Hans Jakob Christoffel
von**
See Grimmelshausen, Johann Jakob Christoffel von
See also RGWL 2

**Grimmelshausen, Johann Jakob Christoffel
von** 1621-1676 .... **LC 6**
See also Grimmelshausen, Hans Jakob
Christoffel von
See also CDWLB 2; DLB 168

Grindel, Eugene 1895-1952
See Eluard, Paul
See also CA 104; 193

Grisham, John 1955- .... **CLC 84**
See also AAYA 14; BPFB 2; CA 138;
CANR 47, 69; CMW 4; CN 7; CPW;
CSW; DA3; DAM POP; MSW; MTCW 2

Grossman, David 1954- .... **CLC 67**
See also CA 138; CWW 2

Grossman, Vasily (Semenovich)
1905-1964 .... **CLC 41**
See also CA 124; 130; MTCW 1

Grove, Frederick Philip .... **TCLC 4**
See also Greve, Felix Paul (Berthold
Friedrich)
See also DLB 92; RGEL 2

Grubb
See Crumb, R(obert)

Grumbach, Doris (Isaac) 1918- . **CLC 13, 22,
64**
See also CA 5-8R; CAAS 2; CANR 9, 42,
70; CN 7; INT CANR-9; MTCW 2

Grundtvig, Nicolai Frederik Severin
1783-1872 .... **NCLC 1**

Grunge
See Crumb, R(obert)

Grunwald, Lisa 1959- .... **CLC 44**
See also CA 120

Guare, John 1938- .... **CLC 8, 14, 29, 67**
See also CA 73-76; CAD; CANR 21, 69;
CD 5; DAM DRAM; DFS 8, 13; DLB 7,
249; MTCW 1, 2; RGAL 4

Gubar, Susan (David) 1944- .... **CLC 145**
See also CA 108; CANR 45, 70; FW;
MTCW 1; RGAL 4

Gudjonsson, Halldor Kiljan 1902-1998
See Laxness, Halldor
See also CA 103; 164; CWW 2

Guenter, Erich
See Eich, Guenter

Guest, Barbara 1920- .... **CLC 34**
See also CA 25-28R; CANR 11, 44, 84; CP
7; CWP; DLB 5, 193

Guest, Edgar A(lbert) 1881-1959 ... **TCLC 95**
See also CA 112; 168

Guest, Judith (Ann) 1936- .... **CLC 8, 30**
See also AAYA 7; CA 77-80; CANR 15,
75; DA3; DAM NOV, POP; EXPN; INT
CANR-15; LAIT 5; MTCW 1, 2; NFS 1

Guevara, Che .... **CLC 87; HLC 1**
See also Guevara (Serna), Ernesto

Guevara (Serna), Ernesto
1928-1967 .... **CLC 87; HLC 1**
See also Guevara, Che
See also CA 127; 111; CANR 56; DAM
MULT; HW 1

Guicciardini, Francesco 1483-1540 ..... **LC 49**

Guild, Nicholas M. 1944- .... **CLC 33**
See also CA 93-96

Guillemin, Jacques
See Sartre, Jean-Paul

Guillen, Jorge 1893-1984 . **CLC 11; HLCS 1;
PC 35**
See also CA 89-92; 112; DAM MULT,
POET; DLB 108; HW 1; RGWL 2

Guillen, Nicolas (Cristobal)
1902-1989 .... **CLC 48, 79; BLC 2; HLC
1; PC 23**
See also BW 2; CA 116; 125; 129; CANR
84; DAM MST, POET; HW 1;
LAW; RGWL 2; WP

Guillen y Alavarez, Jorge
See Guillen, Jorge

Guillevic, (Eugene) 1907-1997 .... **CLC 33**
See also CA 93-96; CWW 2

Guillois
See Desnos, Robert

Guillois, Valentin
See Desnos, Robert

Guimaraes Rosa, Joao
See Rosa, Joao Guimaraes
See also LAW

Guimaraes Rosa, Joao 1908-1967
See also CA 175; HLCS 2; LAW; RGSF 2;
RGWL 2

Guiney, Louise Imogen
1861-1920 .... **TCLC 41**
See also CA 160; DLB 54; RGAL 4

Guinizelli, Guido c. 1230-1276 ...... **CMLC 49**

Guiraldes, Ricardo (Guillermo)
1886-1927 .... **TCLC 39**
See also CA 131; HW 1; LAW; MTCW 1

Gumilev, Nikolai (Stepanovich)
1886-1921 .... **TCLC 60**
See also CA 165

Gunesekera, Romesh 1954- .... **CLC 91**
See also CA 159; CN 7

Gunn, Bill .... **CLC 5**
See also Gunn, William Harrison
See also DLB 38

Gunn, Thom(son William) 1929- .. **CLC 3, 6,
18, 32, 81; PC 26**
See also BRWS 4; CA 17-20R; CANR 9,
33; CDBLB 1960 to Present; CP 7; DAM
POET; DLB 27; INT CANR-33; MTCW
1; PFS 9; RGEL 2

Gunn, William Harrison 1934(?)-1989
See Gunn, Bill
See also AITN 1; BW 1, 3; CA 13-16R;
128; CANR 12, 25, 76

Gunn Allen, Paula
See Allen, Paula Gunn

Gunnars, Kristjana 1948- .... **CLC 69**
See also CA 113; CCA 1; CP 7; CWP; DLB
60

Gurdjieff, G(eorgei) I(vanovich)
1877(?)-1949 .... **TCLC 71**
See also CA 157

Gurganus, Allan 1947- .... **CLC 70**
See also BEST 90:1; CA 135; CN 7; CPW;
CSW; DAM POP; GLL 1

Gurney, A(lbert) R(amsdell), Jr.
1930- .... **CLC 32, 50, 54**
See also AMWS 5; CA 77-80; CAD; CANR
32, 64; CD 5; DAM DRAM

Gurney, Ivor (Bertie) 1890-1937 ... **TCLC 33**
See also BRW 6; CA 167; PAB; RGEL 2

Gurney, Peter
See Gurney, A(lbert) R(amsdell), Jr.

Guro, Elena 1877-1913 .... **TCLC 56**

Gustafson, James M(oody) 1925- ... **CLC 100**
See also CA 25-28R; CANR 37

Gustafson, Ralph (Barker)
1909-1995 .... **CLC 36**
See also CA 21-24R; CANR 8, 45, 84; CP
7; DLB 88; RGEL 2

Gut, Gom
See Simenon, Georges (Jacques Christian)

Guterson, David 1956- .... **CLC 91**
See also CA 132; CANR 73; MTCW 2;
NFS 13

Guthrie, A(lfred) B(ertram), Jr.
1901-1991 .... **CLC 23**
See also CA 57-60; 134; CANR 24; DLB 6,
212; SATA 62; SATA-Obit 67

Guthrie, Isobel
See Grieve, C(hristopher) M(urray)

Guthrie, Woodrow Wilson 1912-1967
See Guthrie, Woody
See also CA 113; 93-96

Guthrie, Woody .... **CLC 35**
See also Guthrie, Woodrow Wilson
See also LAIT 3

Gutierrez Najera, Manuel 1859-1895
See also HLCS 2; LAW

Guy, Rosa (Cuthbert) 1928- .... **CLC 26**
See also AAYA 4, 37; BW 2; CA 17-20R;
CANR 14, 34, 83; CLR 13; DLB 33;
DNFS 1; JRDA; MAICYA 1; SATA 14,
62, 122; YAW

Gwendolyn
See Bennett, (Enoch) Arnold

H. D. .... **CLC 3, 8, 14, 31, 34, 73; PC 5**
See also Doolittle, Hilda

H. de V.
See Buchan, John

Haavikko, Paavo Juhani 1931- .. **CLC 18, 34**
See also CA 106

Habbema, Koos
See Heijermans, Herman

Habermas, Juergen 1929- .... **CLC 104**
See also CA 109; CANR 85; DLB 242

Habermas, Jurgen
See Habermas, Juergen

Hacker, Marilyn 1942- . **CLC 5, 9, 23, 72, 91**
See also CA 77-80; CANR 68; CP 7; CWP;
DAM POET; DLB 120; FW; GLL 2

Haeckel, Ernst Heinrich (Philipp August)
1834-1919 .... **TCLC 83**
See also CA 157

Hafiz c. 1326-1389(?) .... **CMLC 34**
See also RGWL 2

Haggard, H(enry) Rider
1856-1925 .... **TCLC 11**
See also BRWS 3; BYA 4, 5; CA 108; 148;
DLB 70, 156, 174, 178; FANT; MTCW
2; RGEL 2; RHW; SATA 16; SCFW; SFW
4; SUFW; WLIT 4

Hagiosy, L.
See Larbaud, Valery (Nicolas)

Hagiwara, Sakutaro 1886-1942 .... **TCLC 60;
PC 18**
See also CA 154

Haig, Fenil
See Ford, Ford Madox

Haig-Brown, Roderick (Langmere)
1908-1976 .... **CLC 21**
See also CA 5-8R; 69-72; CANR 4, 38, 83;
CLR 31; CWRI 5; DLB 88; MAICYA 1;
SATA 12

Hailey, Arthur 1920- .... **CLC 5**
See also AITN 2; BEST 90:3; BPFB 2; CA
1-4R; CANR 2, 36, 75; CCA 1; CN 7;
CPW; DAM NOV, POP; DLB 88; DLBY
1982; MTCW 1, 2

Hailey, Elizabeth Forsythe 1938- ..... **CLC 40**
See also CA 93-96; CAAE 188; CAAS 1;
CANR 15, 48; INT CANR-15

Haines, John (Meade) 1924- .... **CLC 58**
See also CA 17-20R; CANR 13, 34; CSW;
DLB 5, 212

Hakluyt, Richard 1552-1616 .... **LC 31**
See also DLB 136; RGEL 2

Haldeman, Joe (William) 1943- .... **CLC 61**
See Graham, Robert
See also AAYA 38; CA 53-56, 179; CAAE
179; CAAS 25; CANR 6, 70, 72; DLB 8;
INT CANR-6; SCFW 2; SFW 4

Hale, Sarah Josepha (Buell)
1788-1879 .... **NCLC 75**
See also DLB 1, 42, 73, 243

Halevy, Elie 1870-1937 .... **TCLC 104**

Haley, Alex(ander Murray Palmer)
1921-1992 .... **CLC 8, 12, 76; BLC 2**
See also AAYA 26; BPFB 2; BW 2, 3; CA
77-80; 136; CANR 61; CDALBS; CPW;
CSW; DA; DA3; DAB; DAC; DAM MST,
MULT, POP; DLB 38; LAIT 5; MTCW
1, 2; NFS 9

Haliburton, Thomas Chandler
1796-1865 .... **NCLC 15**
See also DLB 11, 99; RGEL 2; RGSF 2

Hall, Donald (Andrew, Jr.) 1928- ...... **CLC 1,
13, 37, 59, 151**
See also CA 5-8R; CAAS 7; CANR 2, 44,
64, 106; CP 7; DAM POET; DLB 5;
MTCW 1; RGAL 4; SATA 23, 97

Hall, Frederic Sauser
See Sauser-Hall, Frederic

Hall, James
See Kuttner, Henry

Hall, James Norman 1887-1951 ..... **TCLC 23**
See also CA 123; 173; LAIT 1; RHW 1;
SATA 21

Hall, (Marguerite) Radclyffe
1880-1943 .... **TCLC 12**
See also BRWS 6; CA 110; 150; CANR 83;
DLB 191; MTCW 2; RGEL 2; RHW

Hall, Rodney 1935- .... **CLC 51**
See also CA 109; CANR 69; CN 7; CP 7

Hallam, Arthur Henry
1811-1833 .... **NCLC 110**
See also DLB 32

Halleck, Fitz-Greene 1790-1867 .... **NCLC 47**
See also DLB 3, 250; RGAL 4

Halliday, Michael
See Creasey, John

Halpern, Daniel 1945- .... **CLC 14**
See also CA 33-36R; CANR 93; CP 7

Hamburger, Michael (Peter Leopold)
1924- .... **CLC 5, 14**
See also CA 5-8R; CAAE 196; CAAS 4;
CANR 2, 47; CP 7; DLB 27

Hamill, Pete 1935- .... **CLC 10**
See also CA 25-28R; CANR 18, 71

Hamilton, Alexander
1755(?)-1804 .... **NCLC 49**
See also DLB 37

Hamilton, Clive
See Lewis, C(live) S(taples)

Hamilton, Edmond 1904-1977 .... **CLC 1**
See also CA 1-4R; CANR 3, 84; DLB 8;
SATA 118; SFW 4

Hamilton, Eugene (Jacob) Lee
See Lee-Hamilton, Eugene (Jacob)

Hamilton, Franklin
See Silverberg, Robert

Hamilton, Gail
See Corcoran, Barbara (Asenath)

Hamilton, Mollie
See Kaye, M(ary) M(argaret)

Hamilton, (Anthony Walter) Patrick
1904-1962 .... **CLC 51**
See also CA 176; 113; DLB 10, 191

Hamilton, Virginia (Esther)
1936-2002 .... **CLC 26**
See also AAYA 2, 21; BW 2, 3; BYA 1, 2,
8; CA 25-28R; CANR 20, 37, 73; CLR 1,
11, 40; DAM MULT; DLB 33, 52; DLBY
01; INT CANR-20; JRDA; LAIT 5; MAI-
CYA 1; MAICYAS 1; MTCW 1, 2; SATA
4, 56, 79, 123; WYA; YAW

Hammett, (Samuel) Dashiell
1894-1961 .... **CLC 3, 5, 10, 19, 47; SSC
17**
See also AITN 1; AMWS 4; BPFB 2; CA
81-84; CANR 42; CDALB 1929-1941;
CMW 4; DA3; DLB 226; DLBD 6; DLBY
1996; LAIT 3; MSW; MTCW 1, 2; RGAL
4; RGSF 2

Hammon, Jupiter 1720(?)-1800(?) . **NCLC 5;
BLC 2; PC 16**
See also DAM MULT, POET; DLB 31, 50

Hammond, Keith
See Kuttner, Henry

Hamner, Earl (Henry), Jr. 1923- ...... **CLC 12**
See also AITN 2; CA 73-76; DLB 6

Hampton, Christopher (James)
1946- .... **CLC 4**
See also CA 25-28R; CD 5; DLB 13;
MTCW 1

Hamsun, Knut .... **TCLC 2, 14, 49**
See also Pedersen, Knut
See also EW 8; RGWL 2

Handke, Peter 1942- .... **CLC 5, 8, 10, 15, 38,
134; DC 17**
See also CA 77-80; CANR 33, 75, 104;
CWW 2; DAM DRAM, NOV; DLB 85,
124; MTCW 1, 2

Handy, W(illiam) C(hristopher)
1873-1958 .... **TCLC 97**
See also BW 3; CA 121; 167

Hanley, James 1901-1985 ..... **CLC 3, 5, 8, 13**
See also CA 73-76; 117; CANR 36; CBD;
DLB 191; MTCW 1; RGEL 2

Hannah, Barry 1942- .... **CLC 23, 38, 90**
See also BPFB 2; CA 108; 110; CANR 43,
68; CN 7; CSW; DLB 6, 234; INT CA-
110; MTCW 1; RGSF 2

Hannon, Ezra
See Hunter, Evan

Hansberry, Lorraine (Vivian)
1930-1965 ... **CLC 17, 62; BLC 2; DC 2**
See also AAYA 25; AFAW 1, 2; AMWS 4;
BW 1, 3; CA 109; 25-28R; CABS 3;
CANR 58; CDALB 1941-1968; DA;
DA3; DAB; DAC; DAM DRAM, MST,
MULT; DFS 2; DLB 7, 38; FW; LAIT 4;
MTCW 1, 2; RGAL 4

Hansen, Joseph 1923- .... **CLC 38**
See also Brock, Rose; Colton, James
See also BPFB 2; CA 29-32R; CAAS 17;
CANR 16, 44, 66; CMW 4; DLB 226;
GLL 1; INT CANR-16

Hansen, Martin A(lfred)
1909-1955 .... **TCLC 32**
See also CA 167; DLB 214

Hansen and Philipson eds. .... **CLC 65**

Hanson, Kenneth O(stlin) 1922- .... **CLC 13**
See also CA 53-56; CANR 7

Hardwick, Elizabeth (Bruce) 1916- . **CLC 13**
See also AMWS 3; CA 5-8R; CANR 3, 32,
70, 100; CN 7; CSW; DA3; DAM NOV;
DLB 6; MAWW; MTCW 1, 2

Hardy, Thomas 1840-1928 .. **TCLC 4, 10, 18,
32, 48, 53, 72; PC 8; SSC 2; WLC**
See also BRW 6; BRWR 1; CA 104; 123;
CDBLB 1890-1914; DA; DA3; DAB;
DAC; DAM MST, NOV, POET; DLB 18,
19, 135; EXPN; EXPP; LAIT 2; MTCW
1, 2; NFS 3, 11; PFS 3, 4; RGEL 2; RGSF
2; WLIT 4

Hare, David 1947- .... **CLC 29, 58, 136**
See also BRWS 4; CA 97-100; CANR 39,
91; CBD; CD 5; DFS 4, 7; DLB 13;
MTCW 1

Harewood, John
See Van Druten, John (William)

Harford, Henry
See Hudson, W(illiam) H(enry)

Hargrave, Leonie
See Disch, Thomas M(ichael)

Harjo, Joy 1951- .... **CLC 83; PC 27**
See also CA 114; CANR 35, 67, 91; CP 7;
CWP; DAM MULT; DLB 120, 175;
MTCW 2; NNAL; RGAL 4

Harlan, Louis R(udolph) 1922- .... **CLC 34**
See also CA 21-24R; CANR 25, 55, 80

Harling, Robert 1951(?)- .... **CLC 53**
See also CA 147

Harmon, William (Ruth) 1938- .... **CLC 38**
See also CA 33-36R; CANR 14, 32, 35;
SATA 65

Harper, F. E. W.
See Harper, Frances Ellen Watkins

Harper, Frances E. W.
See Harper, Frances Ellen Watkins

Harper, Frances E. Watkins
See Harper, Frances Ellen Watkins

Harper, Frances Ellen
See Harper, Frances Ellen Watkins

Hebbel, Friedrich 1813-1863 .... **NCLC 43**
See also CDWLB 2; DAM DRAM; DLB 129; EW 6; RGWL 2

Hebert, Anne 1916-2000 .... **CLC 4, 13, 29**
See also CA 85-88; 187; CANR 69; CCA 1; CWP; CWW 2; DA3; DAC; DAM MST, POET; DLB 68; GFL 1789 to the Present; MTCW 1, 2

Hecht, Anthony (Evan) 1923- ...... **CLC 8, 13, 19**
See also AMWS 10; CA 9-12R; CANR 6, 108; CP 7; DAM POET; DLB 5, 169; PFS 6; WP

Hecht, Ben 1894-1964 .... **CLC 8**
See also CA 85-88; DFS 9; DLB 7, 9, 25, 26, 28, 86; FANT; IDFW 3, 4; RGAL 4; TCLC 101

Hedayat, Sadeq 1903-1951 .... **TCLC 21**
See also CA 120; RGSF 2

Hegel, Georg Wilhelm Friedrich 1770-1831 .... **NCLC 46**
See also DLB 90

Heidegger, Martin 1889-1976 .... **CLC 24**
See also CA 81-84; 65-68; CANR 34; MTCW 1, 2

Heidenstam, (Carl Gustaf) Verner von 1859-1940 .... **TCLC 5**
See also CA 104

Heifner, Jack 1946- .... **CLC 11**
See also CA 105; CANR 47

Heijermans, Herman 1864-1924 .... **TCLC 24**
See also CA 123

Heilbrun, Carolyn G(old) 1926- .... **CLC 25**
See also Cross, Amanda
See also CA 45-48; CANR 1, 28, 58, 94; FW

Hein, Christoph 1944- .... **CLC 154**
See also CA 158; CANR 108; CDWLB 2; CWW 2; DLB 124

Heine, Heinrich 1797-1856 .... **NCLC 4, 54; PC 25**
See also CDWLB 2; DLB 90; EW 5; RGWL 2

Heinemann, Larry (Curtiss) 1944- .. **CLC 50**
See also CA 110; CAAS 21; CANR 31, 81; DLBD 9; INT CANR-31

Heiney, Donald (William) 1921-1993
See Harris, MacDonald
See also CA 1-4R; 142; CANR 3, 58; FANT

Heinlein, Robert A(nson) 1907-1988 . **CLC 1, 3, 8, 14, 26, 55**
See also AAYA 17; BPFB 2; BYA 4, 13; CA 1-4R; 125; CANR 1, 20, 53; CLR 75; CPW; DA3; DAM POP; DLB 8; EXPS; JRDA; LAIT 5; MAICYA 1; MTCW 1, 2; RGAL 4; SATA 9, 69; SATA-Obit 56; SCFW; SFW 4; SSFS 7; YAW

Helforth, John
See Doolittle, Hilda

Hellenhofferu, Vojtech Kapristian z
See Hasek, Jaroslav (Matej Frantisek)

Heller, Joseph 1923-1999 . **CLC 1, 3, 5, 8, 11, 36, 63; WLC**
See also AAYA 24; AITN 1; AMWS 4; BPFB 2; BYA 1; CA 5-8R; 187; CABS 1; CANR 8, 42, 66; CN 7; CPW; DA; DA3; DAB; DAC; DAM MST, NOV, POP; DLB 2, 28, 227; DLBY 1980; EXPN; INT CANR-8; LAIT 4; MTCW 1, 2; NFS 1; RGAL 4; YAW

Hellman, Lillian (Florence) 1906-1984 .. **CLC 2, 4, 8, 14, 18, 34, 44, 52; DC 1**
See also AITN 1, 2; AMWS 1; CA 13-16R; 112; CAD; CANR 33; CWD; DA3; DAM DRAM; DFS 1, 3; DLB 7, 228; DLBY 1984; FW; LAIT 3; MAWW; MTCW 1, 2; RGAL 4; TCLC 119

Helprin, Mark 1947- .... **CLC 7, 10, 22, 32**
See also CA 81-84; CANR 47, 64; CDALBS; CPW; DA3; DAM NOV, POP; DLBY 1985; FANT; MTCW 1, 2

Helvetius, Claude-Adrien 1715-1771 .. **LC 26**

Helyar, Jane Penelope Josephine 1933-
See Poole, Josephine
See also CA 21-24R; CANR 10, 26; SATA 82

Hemans, Felicia 1793-1835 ...... **NCLC 29, 71**
See also DLB 96; RGEL 2

Hemingway, Ernest (Miller) 1899-1961 .... **CLC 1, 3, 6, 8, 10, 13, 19, 30, 34, 39, 41, 44, 50, 61, 80; SSC 1, 25, 36, 40; WLC**
See also AAYA 19; AMW; AMWR 1; BPFB 2; BYA 2, 3, 13; CA 77-80; CANR 34; CDALB 1917-1929; DA; DA3; DAB; DAC; DAM MST, NOV; DLB 4, 9, 102, 210; DLBD 1, 15, 16; DLBY 1981, 1987, 1996, 1998; EXPN; EXPS; LAIT 3, 4; MTCW 1, 2; NFS 1, 5, 6; RGAL 4; RGSF 2; SSFS 1, 6, 8, 9, 11; TCLC 115; WYA

Hempel, Amy 1951- .... **CLC 39**
See also CA 118; 137; CANR 70; DA3; DLB 218; EXPS; MTCW 2; SSFS 2

Henderson, F. C.
See Mencken, H(enry) L(ouis)

Henderson, Sylvia
See Ashton-Warner, Sylvia (Constance)

Henderson, Zenna (Chlarson) 1917-1983 .... **SSC 29**
See also CA 1-4R; 133; CANR 1, 84; DLB 8; SATA 5; SFW 4

Henkin, Joshua .... **CLC 119**
See also CA 161

Henley, Beth .... **CLC 23; DC 6, 14**
See also Henley, Elizabeth Becker
See also CABS 3; CAD; CD 5; CSW; CWD; DFS 2; DLBY 1986; FW

Henley, Elizabeth Becker 1952-
See Henley, Beth
See also CA 107; CANR 32, 73; DA3; DAM DRAM, MST; MTCW 1, 2

Henley, William Ernest 1849-1903 .. **TCLC 8**
See also CA 105; DLB 19; RGEL 2

Hennissart, Martha
See Lathen, Emma
See also CA 85-88; CANR 64

Henry VIII 1491-1547 .... **LC 10**
See also DLB 132

Henry, O. .... **TCLC 1, 19; SSC 5, 49; WLC**
See also Porter, William Sydney
See also AAYA 41; AMWS 2; EXPS; RGAL 4; RGSF 2; SSFS 2

Henry, Patrick 1736-1799 .... **LC 25**
See also LAIT 1

Henryson, Robert 1430(?)-1506(?) ...... **LC 20**
See also BRWS 7; DLB 146; RGEL 2

Henschke, Alfred
See Klabund

Hentoff, Nat(han Irving) 1925- .... **CLC 26**
See also AAYA 4, 42; BYA 6; CA 1-4R; CAAS 6; CANR 5, 25, 77; CLR 1, 52; INT CANR-25; JRDA; MAICYA 1; SATA 42, 69; SATA-Brief 27; WYA; YAW

Heppenstall, (John) Rayner 1911-1981 .... **CLC 10**
See also CA 1-4R; 103; CANR 29

Heraclitus c. 540B.C.-c. 450B.C. ... **CMLC 22**
See also DLB 176

Herbert, Frank (Patrick) 1920-1986 .... **CLC 12, 23, 35, 44, 85**
See also AAYA 21; BPFB 2; BYA 4, 14; CA 53-56; 118; CANR 5, 43; CDALBS; CPW; DAM POP; DLB 8; INT CANR-5; LAIT 5; MTCW 1, 2; SATA 9, 37; SATA-Obit 47; SCFW 2; SFW 4; YAW

Herbert, George 1593-1633 ...... **LC 24; PC 4**
See also BRW 2; BRWR 2; CDBLB Before 1660; DAB; DAM POET; DLB 126; EXPP; RGEL 2; WP

Herbert, Zbigniew 1924-1998 .... **CLC 9, 43**
See also CA 89-92; 169; CANR 36, 74; CD-WLB 4; CWW 2; DAM POET; DLB 232; MTCW 1

Herbst, Josephine (Frey) 1897-1969 .... **CLC 34**
See also CA 5-8R; 25-28R; DLB 9

Herder, Johann Gottfried von 1744-1803 .... **NCLC 8**
See also DLB 97; EW 4

Heredia, Jose Maria 1803-1839
See also HLCS 2; LAW

Hergesheimer, Joseph 1880-1954 ... **TCLC 11**
See also CA 109; 194; DLB 102, 9; RGAL 4

Herlihy, James Leo 1927-1993 .... **CLC 6**
See also CA 1-4R; 143; CAD; CANR 2

Hermogenes fl. c. 175- .... **CMLC 6**

Hernandez, Jose 1834-1886 .... **NCLC 17**
See also LAW; RGWL 2; WLIT 1

Herodotus c. 484B.C.-c. 420B.C. .. **CMLC 17**
See also AW 1; CDWLB 1; DLB 176; RGWL 2

Herrick, Robert 1591-1674 .... **LC 13; PC 9**
See also BRW 2; DA; DAB; DAC; DAM MST, POP; DLB 126; EXPP; PFS 13; RGAL 4; RGEL 2; WP

Herring, Guilles
See Somerville, Edith Oenone

Herriot, James .... **CLC 12**
See also Wight, James Alfred
See also AAYA 1; BPFB 2; CA 148; CANR 40; CPW; DAM POP; LAIT 3; MAIC-YAS 1; MTCW 2; SATA 86; YAW

Herris, Violet
See Hunt, Violet

Herrmann, Dorothy 1941- .... **CLC 44**
See also CA 107

Herrmann, Taffy
See Herrmann, Dorothy

Hersey, John (Richard) 1914-1993 .... **CLC 1, 2, 7, 9, 40, 81, 97**
See also AAYA 29; BPFB 2; CA 17-20R; 140; CANR 33; CDALBS; CPW; DAM POP; DLB 6, 185; MTCW 1, 2; SATA 25; SATA-Obit 76

Herzen, Aleksandr Ivanovich 1812-1870 .... **NCLC 10, 61**

Herzl, Theodor 1860-1904 .... **TCLC 36**
See also CA 168

Herzog, Werner 1942- .... **CLC 16**
See also CA 89-92

Hesiod c. 8th cent. B.C.- .... **CMLC 5**
See also AW 1; DLB 176; RGWL 2

Hesse, Hermann 1877-1962 ... **CLC 1, 2, 3, 6, 11, 17, 25, 69; SSC 9, 49; WLC**
See also AAYA 43; BPFB 2; CA 17-18; CAP 2; CDWLB 2; DA; DA3; DAB; DAC; DAM MST, NOV; DLB 66; EW 9; EXPN; LAIT 1; MTCW 1, 2; NFS 6; RGWL 2; SATA 50

Hewes, Cady
See De Voto, Bernard (Augustine)

Heyen, William 1940- .... **CLC 13, 18**
See also CA 33-36R; CAAS 9; CANR 98; CP 7; DLB 5

Heyerdahl, Thor 1914-2002 .... **CLC 26**
See also CA 5-8R; CANR 5, 22, 66, 73; LAIT 4; MTCW 1, 2; SATA 2, 52

Heym, Georg (Theodor Franz Arthur) 1887-1912 .... **TCLC 9**
See also CA 106; 181

Heym, Stefan 1913- .... **CLC 41**
See also CA 9-12R; CANR 4; CWW 2; DLB 69

Holland, Isabelle 1920- .... **CLC 21**
See also AAYA 11; CA 21-24R, 181; CAAE 181; CANR 10, 25, 47; CLR 57; CWRI 5; JRDA; LAIT 4; MAICYA 1; SATA 8, 70; SATA-Essay 103; WYA

Holland, Marcus
See Caldwell, (Janet Miriam) Taylor (Holland)

Hollander, John 1929- .... **CLC 2, 5, 8, 14**
See also CA 1-4R; CANR 1, 52; CP 7; DLB 5; SATA 13

Hollander, Paul
See Silverberg, Robert

Holleran, Andrew 1943(?)- .... **CLC 38**
See also Garber, Eric
See also CA 144; GLL 1

Holley, Marietta 1836(?)-1926 .... **TCLC 99**
See also CA 118; DLB 11

Hollinghurst, Alan 1954- .... **CLC 55, 91**
See also CA 114; CN 7; DLB 207; GLL 1

Hollis, Jim
See Summers, Hollis (Spurgeon, Jr.)

Holly, Buddy 1936-1959 .... **TCLC 65**

Holmes, Gordon
See Shiel, M(atthew) P(hipps)

Holmes, John
See Souster, (Holmes) Raymond

Holmes, John Clellon 1926-1988 ...... **CLC 56**
See also CA 9-12R; 125; CANR 4; DLB 16, 237

Holmes, Oliver Wendell, Jr.
1841-1935 .... **TCLC 77**
See also CA 114; 186

Holmes, Oliver Wendell
1809-1894 .... **NCLC 14, 81**
See also AMWS 1; CDALB 1640-1865; DLB 1, 189, 235; EXPP; RGAL 4; SATA 34

Holmes, Raymond
See Souster, (Holmes) Raymond

Holt, Victoria
See Hibbert, Eleanor Alice Burford
See also BPFB 2

Holub, Miroslav 1923-1998 .... **CLC 4**
See also CA 21-24R; 169; CANR 10; CD-WLB 4; CWW 2; DLB 232

Homer c. 8th cent. B.C.- .... **CMLC 1, 16; PC 23; WLCS**
See also AW 1; CDWLB 1; DA; DA3; DAB; DAC; DAM MST, POET; DLB 176; EFS 1; LAIT 1; RGWL 2; WP

Hongo, Garrett Kaoru 1951- .... **PC 23**
See also CA 133; CAAS 22; CP 7; DLB 120; EXPP; RGAL 4

Honig, Edwin 1919- .... **CLC 33**
See also CA 5-8R; CAAS 8; CANR 4, 45; CP 7; DLB 5

Hood, Hugh (John Blagdon) 1928- . **CLC 15, 28; SSC 42**
See also CA 49-52; CAAS 17; CANR 1, 33, 87; CN 7; DLB 53; RGSF 2

Hood, Thomas 1799-1845 .... **NCLC 16**
See also BRW 4; DLB 96; RGEL 2

Hooker, (Peter) Jeremy 1941- .... **CLC 43**
See also CA 77-80; CANR 22; CP 7; DLB 40

Hope, A(lec) D(erwent) 1907-2000 .... **CLC 3, 51**
See also BRWS 7; CA 21-24R; 188; CANR 33, 74; MTCW 1, 2; PFS 8; RGEL 2

Hope, Anthony 1863-1933 .... **TCLC 83**
See also CA 157; DLB 153, 156; RGEL 2; RHW

Hope, Brian
See Creasey, John

Hope, Christopher (David Tully)
1944- .... **CLC 52**
See also AFW; CA 106; CANR 47, 101; CN 7; DLB 225; SATA 62

Hopkins, Gerard Manley
1844-1889 .... **NCLC 17; PC 15; WLC**
See also BRW 5; BRWR 2; CDBLB 1890-1914; DA; DA3; DAB; DAC; DAM MST, POET; DLB 35, 57; EXPP; PAB; RGEL 2; WP

Hopkins, John (Richard) 1931-1998 .. **CLC 4**
See also CA 85-88; 169; CBD; CD 5

Hopkins, Pauline Elizabeth
1859-1930 .... **TCLC 28; BLC 2**
See also AFAW 2; BW 2, 3; CA 141; CANR 82; DAM MULT; DLB 50

Hopkinson, Francis 1737-1791 .... **LC 25**
See also DLB 31; RGAL 4

Hopley-Woolrich, Cornell George 1903-1968
See Woolrich, Cornell
See also CA 13-14; CANR 58; CAP 1; CMW 4; DLB 226; MTCW 2

Horace 65B.C.-8B.C. .... **CMLC 39**
See also AW 2; CDWLB 1; DLB 211; RGWL 2

Horatio
See Proust, (Valentin-Louis-George-Eugene-)Marcel

Horgan, Paul (George Vincent O'Shaughnessy) 1903-1995 .. **CLC 9, 53**
See also BPFB 2; CA 13-16R; 147; CANR 9, 35; DAM NOV; DLB 102, 212; DLBY 1985; INT CANR-9; MTCW 1, 2; SATA 13; SATA-Obit 84; TCWW 2

Horn, Peter
See Kuttner, Henry

Hornem, Horace Esq.
See Byron, George Gordon (Noel)

Horney, Karen (Clementine Theodore Danielsen) 1885-1952 .... **TCLC 71**
See also CA 114; 165; DLB 246; FW

Hornung, E(rnest) W(illiam)
1866-1921 .... **TCLC 59**
See also CA 108; 160; CMW 4; DLB 70

Horovitz, Israel (Arthur) 1939- .... **CLC 56**
See also CA 33-36R; CAD; CANR 46, 59; CD 5; DAM DRAM; DLB 7

Horton, George Moses
1797(?)-1883(?) .... **NCLC 87**
See also DLB 50

Horvath, Odon von 1901-1938 .... **TCLC 45**
See also von Horvath, Oedoen
See also CA 118; 194; DLB 85, 124; RGWL 2

Horvath, Oedoen von -1938
See Horvath, Odon von

Horwitz, Julius 1920-1986 .... **CLC 14**
See also CA 9-12R; 119; CANR 12

Hospital, Janette Turner 1942- .... **CLC 42, 145**
See also CA 108; CANR 48; CN 7; RGSF 2

Hostos, E. M. de
See Hostos (y Bonilla), Eugenio Maria de

Hostos, Eugenio M. de
See Hostos (y Bonilla), Eugenio Maria de

Hostos, Eugenio Maria
See Hostos (y Bonilla), Eugenio Maria de

Hostos (y Bonilla), Eugenio Maria de
1839-1903 .... **TCLC 24**
See also CA 123; 131; HW 1

Houdini
See Lovecraft, H(oward) P(hillips)

Hougan, Carolyn 1943- .... **CLC 34**
See also CA 139

Household, Geoffrey (Edward West)
1900-1988 .... **CLC 11**
See also CA 77-80; 126; CANR 58; CMW 4; DLB 87; SATA 14; SATA-Obit 59

Housman, A(lfred) E(dward)
1859-1936 ... **TCLC 1, 10; PC 2; WLCS**
See also BRW 6; CA 104; 125; DA; DA3; DAB; DAC; DAM MST, POET; DLB 19; EXPP; MTCW 1, 2; PAB; PFS 4, 7; RGEL 2; WP

Housman, Laurence 1865-1959 .... **TCLC 7**
See also CA 106; 155; DLB 10; FANT; RGEL 2; SATA 25

Howard, Elizabeth Jane 1923- ..... **CLC 7, 29**
See also CA 5-8R; CANR 8, 62; CN 7

Howard, Maureen 1930- .... **CLC 5, 14, 46, 151**
See also CA 53-56; CANR 31, 75; CN 7; DLBY 1983; INT CANR-31; MTCW 1, 2

Howard, Richard 1929- .... **CLC 7, 10, 47**
See also AITN 1; CA 85-88; CANR 25, 80; CP 7; DLB 5; INT CANR-25

Howard, Robert E(rvin)
1906-1936 .... **TCLC 8**
See also BPFB 2; BYA 5; CA 105; 157; FANT; SUFW

Howard, Warren F.
See Pohl, Frederik

Howe, Fanny (Quincy) 1940- .... **CLC 47**
See also CA 117; CAAE 187; CAAS 27; CANR 70; CP 7; CWP; SATA-Brief 52

Howe, Irving 1920-1993 .... **CLC 85**
See also AMWS 6; CA 9-12R; 141; CANR 21, 50; DLB 67; MTCW 1, 2

Howe, Julia Ward 1819-1910 .... **TCLC 21**
See also CA 117; 191; DLB 1, 189, 235; FW

Howe, Susan 1937- .... **CLC 72, 152**
See also AMWS 4; CA 160; CP 7; CWP; DLB 120; FW; RGAL 4

Howe, Tina 1937- .... **CLC 48**
See also CA 109; CAD; CD 5; CWD

Howell, James 1594(?)-1666 .... **LC 13**
See also DLB 151

Howells, W. D.
See Howells, William Dean

Howells, William D.
See Howells, William Dean

Howells, William Dean 1837-1920 .. **TCLC 7, 17, 41; SSC 36**
See also AMW; CA 104; 134; CDALB 1865-1917; DLB 12, 64, 74, 79, 189; MTCW 2; RGAL 4

Howes, Barbara 1914-1996 .... **CLC 15**
See also CA 9-12R; 151; CAAS 3; CANR 53; CP 7; SATA 5

Hrabal, Bohumil 1914-1997 .... **CLC 13, 67**
See also CA 106; 156; CAAS 12; CANR 57; CWW 2; DLB 232; RGSF 2

Hrotsvit of Gandersheim c. 935-c. 1000 .... **CMLC 29**
See also DLB 148

Hsi, Chu 1130-1200 .... **CMLC 42**

Hsun, Lu
See Lu Hsun

Hubbard, L(afayette) Ron(ald)
1911-1986 .... **CLC 43**
See also CA 77-80; 118; CANR 52; CPW; DA3; DAM POP; FANT; MTCW 2; SFW 4

Huch, Ricarda (Octavia)
1864-1947 .... **TCLC 13**
See also CA 111; 189; DLB 66

Huddle, David 1942- .... **CLC 49**
See also CA 57-60; CAAS 20; CANR 89; DLB 130

Hudson, Jeffrey
See Crichton, (John) Michael

Hudson, W(illiam) H(enry)
1841-1922 .... **TCLC 29**
See also CA 115; 190; DLB 98, 153, 174; RGEL 2; SATA 35

Ingram, Willis J.
See Harris, Mark

Innaurato, Albert (F.) 1948(?)- ... **CLC 21, 60**
See also CA 115; 122; CAD; CANR 78; CD 5; INT CA-122

Innes, Michael
See Stewart, J(ohn) I(nnes) M(ackintosh)
See also MSW

Innis, Harold Adams 1894-1952 .... **TCLC 77**
See also CA 181; DLB 88

Ionesco, Eugene 1912-1994 ... **CLC 1, 4, 6, 9, 11, 15, 41, 86; DC 12; WLC**
See also CA 9-12R; 144; CANR 55; CWW 2; DA; DA3; DAB; DAC; DAM DRAM, MST; DFS 4, 9; EW 13; GFL 1789 to the Present; MTCW 1, 2; RGWL 2; SATA 7; SATA-Obit 79

Iqbal, Muhammad 1877-1938 .... **TCLC 28**

Ireland, Patrick
See O'Doherty, Brian

Irenaeus St. 130- .... **CMLC 42**

Iron, Ralph
See Schreiner, Olive (Emilie Albertina)

Irving, John (Winslow) 1942- ... **CLC 13, 23, 38, 112**
See also AAYA 8; AMWS 6; BEST 89:3; BPFB 2; CA 25-28R; CANR 28, 73; CN 7; CPW; DA3; DAM NOV, POP; DLB 6; DLBY 1982; MTCW 1, 2; NFS 12; RGAL 4

Irving, Washington 1783-1859 . **NCLC 2, 19, 95; SSC 2, 37; WLC**
See also AMW; CDALB 1640-1865; DA; DA3; DAB; DAC; DAM MST; DLB 3, 11, 30, 59, 73, 74, 183, 186, 250, 254; EXPS; LAIT 1; RGAL 4; RGSF 2; SSFS 1, 8; SUFW; WCH; YABC 2

Irwin, P. K.
See Page, P(atricia) K(athleen)

Isaacs, Jorge Ricardo 1837-1895 ... **NCLC 70**
See also LAW

Isaacs, Susan 1943- .... **CLC 32**
See also BEST 89:1; BPFB 2; CA 89-92; CANR 20, 41, 65; CPW; DA3; DAM POP; INT CANR-20; MTCW 1, 2

Isherwood, Christopher (William Bradshaw) 1904-1986 ... **CLC 1, 9, 11, 14, 44**
See also BRW 7; CA 13-16R; 117; CANR 35, 97; DA3; DAM DRAM, NOV; DLB 15, 195; DLBY 1986; IDTP; MTCW 1, 2; RGAL 4; RGEL 2; WLIT 4

Ishiguro, Kazuo 1954- ... **CLC 27, 56, 59, 110**
See also BEST 90:2; BPFB 2; BRWS 4; CA 120; CANR 49, 95; CN 7; DA3; DAM NOV; DLB 194; MTCW 1, 2; NFS 13; WLIT 4

Ishikawa, Hakuin
See Ishikawa, Takuboku

Ishikawa, Takuboku 1886(?)-1912 .... **TCLC 15; PC 10**
See also CA 113; 153; DAM POET

Iskander, Fazil 1929- .... **CLC 47**
See also CA 102

Isler, Alan (David) 1934- .... **CLC 91**
See also CA 156; CANR 105

Ivan IV 1530-1584 .... **LC 17**

Ivanov, Vyacheslav Ivanovich 1866-1949 .... **TCLC 33**
See also CA 122

Ivask, Ivar Vidrik 1927-1992 .... **CLC 14**
See also CA 37-40R; 139; CANR 24

Ives, Morgan
See Bradley, Marion Zimmer
See also GLL 1

Izumi Shikibu c. 973-c. 1034 .... **CMLC 33**

J .... **CLC 8**
See also CA 33-36R; CANR 28, 67; CN 7; DLB 2, 28, 218; DLBY 1980

J. R. S.
See Gogarty, Oliver St. John

Jabran, Kahlil
See Gibran, Kahlil

Jabran, Khalil
See Gibran, Kahlil

Jackson, Daniel
See Wingrove, David (John)

Jackson, Helen Hunt 1830-1885 .... **NCLC 90**
See also DLB 42, 47, 186, 189; RGAL 4

Jackson, Jesse 1908-1983 .... **CLC 12**
See also BW 1; CA 25-28R; 109; CANR 27; CLR 28; CWRI 5; MAICYA 1; SATA 2, 29; SATA-Obit 48

Jackson, Laura (Riding) 1901-1991
See Riding, Laura
See also CA 65-68; 135; CANR 28, 89; DLB 48

Jackson, Sam
See Trumbo, Dalton

Jackson, Sara
See Wingrove, David (John)

Jackson, Shirley 1919-1965 . **CLC 11, 60, 87; SSC 9, 39; WLC**
See also AAYA 9; AMWS 9; BPFB 2; CA 1-4R; 25-28R; CANR 4, 52; CDALB 1941-1968; DA; DA3; DAC; DAM MST; DLB 6, 234; EXPS; HGG; LAIT 4; MTCW 2; RGAL 4; RGSF 2; SATA 2; SSFS 1; SUFW

Jacob, (Cyprien-)Max 1876-1944 .... **TCLC 6**
See also CA 104; 193; GFL 1789 to the Present; GLL 2; RGWL 2

Jacobs, Harriet A(nn) 1813(?)-1897 .... **NCLC 67**
See also AFAW 1, 2; DLB 239; FW; LAIT 2; RGAL 4

Jacobs, Jim 1942- .... **CLC 12**
See also CA 97-100; INT 97-100

Jacobs, W(illiam) W(ymark) 1863-1943 .... **TCLC 22**
See also CA 121; 167; DLB 135; EXPS; HGG; RGEL 2; RGSF 2; SSFS 2; SUFW

Jacobsen, Jens Peter 1847-1885 .... **NCLC 34**

Jacobsen, Josephine 1908- .... **CLC 48, 102**
See also CA 33-36R; CAAS 18; CANR 23, 48; CCA 1; CP 7; DLB 244

Jacobson, Dan 1929- .... **CLC 4, 14**
See also AFW; CA 1-4R; CANR 2, 25, 66; CN 7; DLB 14, 207, 225; MTCW 1; RGSF 2

Jacqueline
See Carpentier (y Valmont), Alejo

Jagger, Mick 1944- .... **CLC 17**

Jahiz, al- c. 780-c. 869 .... **CMLC 25**

Jakes, John (William) 1932- .... **CLC 29**
See also AAYA 32; BEST 89:4; BPFB 2; CA 57-60; CANR 10, 43, 66; CPW; CSW; DA3; DAM NOV, POP; DLBY 1983; FANT; INT CANR-10; MTCW 1, 2; RHW; SATA 62; SFW 4; TCWW 2

James I 1394-1437 .... **LC 20**
See also RGEL 2

James, Andrew
See Kirkup, James

James, C(yril) L(ionel) R(obert) 1901-1989 .... **CLC 33; BLCS**
See also BW 2; CA 117; 125; 128; CANR 62; DLB 125; MTCW 1

James, Daniel (Lewis) 1911-1988
See Santiago, Danny
See also CA 174; 125

James, Dynely
See Mayne, William (James Carter)

James, Henry Sr. 1811-1882 .... **NCLC 53**

James, Henry 1843-1916 ..... **TCLC 2, 11, 24, 40, 47, 64; SSC 8, 32, 47; WLC**
See also AMW; AMWR 1; BPFB 2; BRW 6; CA 104; 132; CDALB 1865-1917; DA; DA3; DAB; DAC; DAM MST, NOV; DLB 12, 71, 74, 189; DLBD 13; EXPS; HGG; LAIT 2; MTCW 1, 2; NFS 12; RGAL 4; RGEL 2; RGSF 2; SSFS 9; SUFW

James, M. R.
See James, Montague (Rhodes)
See also DLB 156, 201

James, Montague (Rhodes) 1862-1936 .... **TCLC 6; SSC 16**
See also James, M. R.
See also CA 104; HGG; RGEL 2; RGSF 2; SUFW

James, P. D. .... **CLC 18, 46, 122**
See also White, Phyllis Dorothy James
See also BEST 90:2; BPFB 2; BRWS 4; CDBLB 1960 to Present; DLB 87; DLBD 17; MSW

James, Philip
See Moorcock, Michael (John)

James, Samuel
See Stephens, James

James, Seumas
See Stephens, James

James, Stephen
See Stephens, James

James, William 1842-1910 .... **TCLC 15, 32**
See also AMW; CA 109; 193; RGAL 4

Jameson, Anna 1794-1860 .... **NCLC 43**
See also DLB 99, 166

Jameson, Fredric (R.) 1934- .... **CLC 142**
See also CA 196; DLB 67

Jami, Nur al-Din 'Abd al-Rahman 1414-1492 .... **LC 9**

Jammes, Francis 1868-1938 .... **TCLC 75**
See also CA 198; GFL 1789 to the Present

Jandl, Ernst 1925-2000 .... **CLC 34**

Janowitz, Tama 1957- .... **CLC 43, 145**
See also CA 106; CANR 52, 89; CN 7; CPW; DAM POP

Japrisot, Sebastien 1931- .... **CLC 90**
See also CMW 4

Jarrell, Randall 1914-1965 .... **CLC 1, 2, 6, 9, 13, 49**
See also AMW; BYA 5; CA 5-8R; 25-28R; CABS 2; CANR 6, 34; CDALB 1941-1968; CLR 6; CWRI 5; DAM POET; DLB 48, 52; EXPP; MAICYA 1; MTCW 1, 2; PAB; PFS 2; RGAL 4; SATA 7

Jarry, Alfred 1873-1907 .... **TCLC 2, 14; SSC 20**
See also CA 104; 153; DA3; DAM DRAM; DFS 8; DLB 192; EW 9; GFL 1789 to the Present; RGWL 2

Jawien, Andrzej
See John Paul II, Pope

Jaynes, Roderick
See Coen, Ethan

Jeake, Samuel, Jr.
See Aiken, Conrad (Potter)

Jean Paul 1763-1825 .... **NCLC 7**

Jefferies, (John) Richard 1848-1887 .... **NCLC 47**
See also DLB 98, 141; RGEL 2; SATA 16; SFW 4

Jeffers, (John) Robinson 1887-1962 .. **CLC 2, 3, 11, 15, 54; PC 17; WLC**
See also AMWS 2; CA 85-88; CANR 35; CDALB 1917-1929; DA; DAC; DAM MST, POET; DLB 45, 212; MTCW 1, 2; PAB; PFS 3, 4; RGAL 4

Jefferson, Janet
See Mencken, H(enry) L(ouis)

Kingsley, Charles 1819-1875 .... **NCLC 35**
See also CLR 77; DLB 21, 32, 163, 178, 190; FANT; MAICYAS 1; RGEL 2; WCH; YABC 2

Kingsley, Henry 1830-1876 .... **NCLC 107**
See also DLB 21, 230; RGEL 2

Kingsley, Sidney 1906-1995 .... **CLC 44**
See also CA 85-88; 147; CAD; DLB 7; RGAL 4

Kingsolver, Barbara 1955- . **CLC 55, 81, 130**
See also AAYA 15; AMWS 7; CA 129; 134; CANR 60, 96; CDALBS; CPW; CSW; DA3; DAM POP; DLB 206; INT CA-134; LAIT 5; MTCW 2; NFS 5, 10, 12; RGAL 4

Kingston, Maxine (Ting Ting) Hong 1940- .... **CLC 12, 19, 58, 121; AAL; WLCS**
See also AAYA 8; AMWS 5; BPFB 2; CA 69-72; CANR 13, 38, 74, 87; CDALBS; CN 7; DA3; DAM MULT, NOV; DLB 173, 212; DLBY 1980; FW; INT CANR-13; LAIT 5; MAWW; MTCW 1, 2; NFS 6; RGAL 4; SATA 53; SSFS 3

Kinnell, Galway 1927- ..... **CLC 1, 2, 3, 5, 13, 29, 129; PC 26**
See also AMWS 3; CA 9-12R; CANR 10, 34, 66; CP 7; DLB 5; DLBY 1987; INT CANR-34; MTCW 1, 2; PAB; PFS 9; RGAL 4; WP

Kinsella, Thomas 1928- .... **CLC 4, 19, 138**
See also BRWS 5; CA 17-20R; CANR 15; CP 7; DLB 27; MTCW 1, 2; RGEL 2

Kinsella, W(illiam) P(atrick) 1935- . **CLC 27, 43**
See also AAYA 7; BPFB 2; CA 97-100; CAAS 7; CANR 21, 35, 66, 75; CN 7; CPW; DAC; DAM NOV, POP; FANT; INT CANR-21; LAIT 5; MTCW 1, 2; RGSF 2

Kinsey, Alfred C(harles) 1894-1956 .... **TCLC 91**
See also CA 115; 170; MTCW 2

Kipling, (Joseph) Rudyard 1865-1936 .. **TCLC 8, 17; PC 3; SSC 5; WLC**
See also AAYA 32; BRW 6; BYA 4; CA 105; 120; CANR 33; CDBLB 1890-1914; CLR 39, 65; CWRI 5; DA; DA3; DAB; DAC; DAM MST, POET; DLB 19, 34, 141, 156; EXPS; FANT; LAIT 3; MAICYA 1; MTCW 1, 2; RGEL 2; RGSF 2; SATA 100; SFW 4; SSFS 8; SUFW; WCH; WLIT 4; YABC 2

Kirk, Russell (Amos) 1918-1994 .. **TCLC 119**
See also AITN 1; CA 1-4R; 145; CAAS 9; CANR 1, 20, 60; HGG; INT CANR-20; MTCW 1, 2

Kirkland, Caroline M. 1801-1864 . **NCLC 85**
See also DLB 3, 73, 74, 250, 254; DLBD 13

Kirkup, James 1918- .... **CLC 1**
See also CA 1-4R; CAAS 4; CANR 2; DLB 27; SATA 12

Kirkwood, James 1930(?)-1989 .... **CLC 9**
See also AITN 2; CA 1-4R; 128; CANR 6, 40; GLL 2

Kirshner, Sidney
See Kingsley, Sidney

Kis, Danilo 1935-1989 .... **CLC 57**
See also CA 109; 118; 129; CANR 61; CDWLB 4; DLB 181; MTCW 1; RGSF 2; RGWL 2

Kissinger, Henry A(lfred) 1923- ..... **CLC 137**
See also CA 1-4R; CANR 2, 33, 66; MTCW 1

Kivi, Aleksis 1834-1872 .... **NCLC 30**

Kizer, Carolyn (Ashley) 1925- ... **CLC 15, 39, 80**
See also CA 65-68; CAAS 5; CANR 24, 70; CP 7; CWP; DAM POET; DLB 5, 169; MTCW 2

Klabund 1890-1928 .... **TCLC 44**
See also CA 162; DLB 66

Klappert, Peter 1942- .... **CLC 57**
See also CA 33-36R; CSW; DLB 5

Klein, A(braham) M(oses) 1909-1972 .... **CLC 19**
See also CA 101; 37-40R; DAB; DAC; DAM MST; DLB 68; RGEL 2

Klein, Joe .... **CLC 154**
See also Klein, Joseph

Klein, Joseph 1946-
See Klein, Joe
See also CA 85-88; CANR 55

Klein, Norma 1938-1989 .... **CLC 30**
See also AAYA 2, 35; BPFB 2; BYA 6, 7, 8; CA 41-44R; 128; CANR 15, 37; CLR 2, 19; INT CANR-15; JRDA; MAICYA 1; SAAS 1; SATA 7, 57; WYA; YAW

Klein, T(heodore) E(ibon) D(onald) 1947- .... **CLC 34**
See also CA 119; CANR 44, 75; HGG

Kleist, Heinrich von 1777-1811 ...... **NCLC 2, 37; SSC 22**
See also CDWLB 2; DAM DRAM; DLB 90; EW 5; RGSF 2; RGWL 2

Klima, Ivan 1931- .... **CLC 56**
See also CA 25-28R; CANR 17, 50, 91; CDWLB 4; CWW 2; DAM NOV; DLB 232

Klimentov, Andrei Platonovich 1899-1951 .... **TCLC 14; SSC 42**
See also CA 108

Klinger, Friedrich Maximilian von 1752-1831 .... **NCLC 1**
See also DLB 94

Klingsor the Magician
See Hartmann, Sadakichi

Klopstock, Friedrich Gottlieb 1724-1803 .... **NCLC 11**
See also DLB 97; EW 4; RGWL 2

Knapp, Caroline 1959- .... **CLC 99**
See also CA 154

Knebel, Fletcher 1911-1993 .... **CLC 14**
See also AITN 1; CA 1-4R; 140; CAAS 3; CANR 1, 36; SATA 36; SATA-Obit 75

Knickerbocker, Diedrich
See Irving, Washington

Knight, Etheridge 1931-1991 . **CLC 40; BLC 2; PC 14**
See also BW 1, 3; CA 21-24R; 133; CANR 23, 82; DAM POET; DLB 41; MTCW 2; RGAL 4

Knight, Sarah Kemble 1666-1727 .... **LC 7**
See also DLB 24, 200

Knister, Raymond 1899-1932 .... **TCLC 56**
See also CA 186; DLB 68; RGEL 2

Knowles, John 1926-2001 ... **CLC 1, 4, 10, 26**
See also AAYA 10; BPFB 2; BYA 3; CA 17-20R; CANR 40, 74, 76; CDALB 1968-1988; CN 7; DA; DAC; DAM MST, NOV; DLB 6; EXPN; MTCW 1, 2; NFS 2; RGAL 4; SATA 8, 89; YAW

Knox, Calvin M.
See Silverberg, Robert

Knox, John c. 1505-1572 .... **LC 37**
See also DLB 132

Knye, Cassandra
See Disch, Thomas M(ichael)

Koch, C(hristopher) J(ohn) 1932- .... **CLC 42**
See also CA 127; CANR 84; CN 7

Koch, Christopher
See Koch, C(hristopher) J(ohn)

Koch, Kenneth 1925- .... **CLC 5, 8, 44**
See also CA 1-4R; CAD; CANR 6, 36, 57, 97; CD 5; CP 7; DAM POET; DLB 5; INT CANR-36; MTCW 2; SATA 65; WP

Kochanowski, Jan 1530-1584 .... **LC 10**
See also RGWL 2

Kock, Charles Paul de 1794-1871 . **NCLC 16**

Koda Rohan
See Koda Shigeyuki

Koda Rohan
See Koda Shigeyuki
See also DLB 180

Koda Shigeyuki 1867-1947 .... **TCLC 22**
See also Koda Rohan
See also CA 121; 183

Koestler, Arthur 1905-1983 ... **CLC 1, 3, 6, 8, 15, 33**
See also BRWS 1; CA 1-4R; 109; CANR 1, 33; CDBLB 1945-1960; DLBY 1983; MTCW 1, 2; RGEL 2

Kogawa, Joy Nozomi 1935- ...... **CLC 78, 129**
See also CA 101; CANR 19, 62; CN 7; CWP; DAC; DAM MST, MULT; FW; MTCW 2; NFS 3; SATA 99

Kohout, Pavel 1928- .... **CLC 13**
See also CA 45-48; CANR 3

Koizumi, Yakumo
See Hearn, (Patricio) Lafcadio (Tessima Carlos)

Kolmar, Gertrud 1894-1943 .... **TCLC 40**
See also CA 167

Komunyakaa, Yusef 1947- .... **CLC 86, 94; BLCS**
See also AFAW 2; CA 147; CANR 83; CP 7; CSW; DLB 120; PFS 5; RGAL 4

Konrad, George
See Konrad, Gyorgy
See also CWW 2

Konrad, Gyorgy 1933- .... **CLC 4, 10, 73**
See also Konrad, George
See also CA 85-88; CANR 97; CDWLB 4; CWW 2; DLB 232

Konwicki, Tadeusz 1926- .... **CLC 8, 28, 54, 117**
See also CA 101; CAAS 9; CANR 39, 59; CWW 2; DLB 232; IDFW 3; MTCW 1

Koontz, Dean R(ay) 1945- .... **CLC 78**
See also AAYA 9, 31; BEST 89:3, 90:2; CA 108; CANR 19, 36, 52, 95; CMW 4; CPW; DA3; DAM NOV, POP; HGG; MTCW 1; SATA 92; SFW 4; YAW

Kopernik, Mikolaj
See Copernicus, Nicolaus

Kopit, Arthur (Lee) 1937- ...... **CLC 1, 18, 33**
See also AITN 1; CA 81-84; CABS 3; CD 5; DAM DRAM; DFS 7; DLB 7; MTCW 1; RGAL 4

Kops, Bernard 1926- .... **CLC 4**
See also CA 5-8R; CANR 84; CBD; CN 7; CP 7; DLB 13

Kornbluth, C(yril) M. 1923-1958 .... **TCLC 8**
See also CA 105; 160; DLB 8; SFW 4

Korolenko, V. G.
See Korolenko, Vladimir Galaktionovich

Korolenko, Vladimir
See Korolenko, Vladimir Galaktionovich

Korolenko, Vladimir G.
See Korolenko, Vladimir Galaktionovich

Korolenko, Vladimir Galaktionovich 1853-1921 .... **TCLC 22**
See also CA 121

Korzybski, Alfred (Habdank Skarbek) 1879-1950 .... **TCLC 61**
See also CA 123; 160

Lukacs, George .... **CLC 24**
   See also Lukacs, Gyorgy (Szegeny von)
Lukacs, Gyorgy (Szegeny von) 1885-1971
   See Lukacs, George
   See also CA 101; 29-32R; CANR 62; CD-
      WLB 4; DLB 215, 242; EW 10; MTCW
      2
Luke, Peter (Ambrose Cyprian)
   1919-1995 .... **CLC 38**
   See also CA 81-84; 147; CANR 72; CBD;
      CD 5; DLB 13
Lunar, Dennis
   See Mungo, Raymond
Lurie, Alison 1926- .... **CLC 4, 5, 18, 39**
   See also BPFB 2; CA 1-4R; CANR 2, 17,
      50, 88; CN 7; DLB 2; MTCW 1; SATA
      46, 112
Lustig, Arnost 1926- .... **CLC 56**
   See also AAYA 3; CA 69-72; CANR 47,
      102; CWW 2; DLB 232; SATA 56
Luther, Martin 1483-1546 .... **LC 9, 37**
   See also CDWLB 2; DLB 179; EW 2;
      RGWL 2
Luxemburg, Rosa 1870(?)-1919 ..... **TCLC 63**
   See also CA 118
Luzi, Mario 1914- .... **CLC 13**
   See also CA 61-64; CANR 9, 70; CWW 2;
      DLB 128
L'vov, Arkady .... **CLC 59**
Lyly, John 1554(?)-1606 .... **LC 41; DC 7**
   See also BRW 1; DAM DRAM; DLB 62,
      167; RGEL 2
L'Ymagier
   See Gourmont, Remy(-Marie-Charles) de
Lynch, B. Suarez
   See Borges, Jorge Luis
Lynch, David (K.) 1946- .... **CLC 66**
   See also CA 124; 129
Lynch, James
   See Andreyev, Leonid (Nikolaevich)
Lyndsay, Sir David 1485-1555 .... **LC 20**
   See also RGEL 2
Lynn, Kenneth S(chuyler)
   1923-2001 .... **CLC 50**
   See also CA 1-4R; 196; CANR 3, 27, 65
Lynx
   See West, Rebecca
Lyons, Marcus
   See Blish, James (Benjamin)
Lyotard, Jean-Francois
   1924-1998 .... **TCLC 103**
   See also DLB 242
Lyre, Pinchbeck
   See Sassoon, Siegfried (Lorraine)
Lytle, Andrew (Nelson) 1902-1995 ... **CLC 22**
   See also CA 9-12R; 150; CANR 70; CN 7;
      CSW; DLB 6; DLBY 1995; RGAL 4;
      RHW
Lyttelton, George 1709-1773 .... **LC 10**
   See also RGEL 2
Lytton of Knebworth, Baron
   See Bulwer-Lytton, Edward (George Earle
      Lytton)

Maas, Peter 1929-2001 .... **CLC 29**
   See also CA 93-96; INT CA-93-96; MTCW
      2
Macaulay, Catherine 1731-1791 .... **LC 64**
   See also DLB 104
Macaulay, (Emilie) Rose
   1881(?)-1958 .... **TCLC 7, 44**
   See also CA 104; DLB 36; RGEL 2; RHW
Macaulay, Thomas Babington
   1800-1859 .... **NCLC 42**
   See also BRW 4; CDBLB 1832-1890; DLB
      32, 55; RGEL 2

MacBeth, George (Mann)
   1932-1992 .... **CLC 2, 5, 9**
   See also CA 25-28R; 136; CANR 61, 66;
      DLB 40; MTCW 1; PFS 8; SATA 4;
      SATA-Obit 70
MacCaig, Norman (Alexander)
   1910-1996 .... **CLC 36**
   See also BRWS 6; CA 9-12R; CANR 3, 34;
      CP 7; DAB; DAM POET; DLB 27; RGEL
      2
MacCarthy, Sir (Charles Otto) Desmond
   1877-1952 .... **TCLC 36**
   See also CA 167
MacDiarmid, Hugh .... **CLC 2, 4, 11, 19, 63;
      PC 9**
   See also Grieve, C(hristopher) M(urray)
   See also CDBLB 1945-1960; DLB 20;
      RGEL 2
MacDonald, Anson
   See Heinlein, Robert A(nson)
Macdonald, Cynthia 1928- .... **CLC 13, 19**
   See also CA 49-52; CANR 4, 44; DLB 105
MacDonald, George 1824-1905 .... **TCLC 9,
      113**
   See also BYA 5; CA 106; 137; CANR 80;
      CLR 67; DLB 18, 163, 178; FANT; MAI-
      CYA 1; RGEL 2; SATA 33, 100; SFW 4;
      SUFW; WCH
Macdonald, John
   See Millar, Kenneth
MacDonald, John D(ann)
   1916-1986 .... **CLC 3, 27, 44**
   See also BPFB 2; CA 1-4R; CANR 1,
      19, 60; CMW 4; CPW; DAM NOV, POP;
      DLB 8; DLBY 1986; MSW; MTCW 1, 2;
      SFW 4
Macdonald, John Ross
   See Millar, Kenneth
Macdonald, Ross ..... **CLC 1, 2, 3, 14, 34, 41**
   See also Millar, Kenneth
   See also AMWS 4; BPFB 2; DLBD 6;
      MSW; RGAL 4
MacDougal, John
   See Blish, James (Benjamin)
MacDougal, John
   See Blish, James (Benjamin)
MacDowell, John
   See Parks, Tim(othy Harold)
MacEwen, Gwendolyn (Margaret)
   1941-1987 .... **CLC 13, 55**
   See also CA 9-12R; 124; CANR 7, 22; DLB
      53, 251; SATA 50; SATA-Obit 55
Macha, Karel Hynek 1810-1846 .... **NCLC 46**
Machado (y Ruiz), Antonio
   1875-1939 .... **TCLC 3**
   See also CA 104; 174; DLB 108; EW 9;
      HW 2; RGWL 2
Machado de Assis, Joaquim Maria
   1839-1908 ..... **TCLC 10; BLC 2; HLCS
      2; SSC 24**
   See also CA 107; 153; CANR 91; LAW;
      RGSF 2; RGWL 2; WLIT 1
Machen, Arthur .... **TCLC 4; SSC 20**
   See also Jones, Arthur Llewellyn
   See also CA 179; DLB 156, 178; RGEL 2;
      SUFW
Machiavelli, Niccolo 1469-1527 ..... **LC 8, 36;
      DC 16; WLCS**
   See also DA; DAB; DAC; DAM MST; EW
      2; LAIT 1; NFS 9; RGWL 2
MacInnes, Colin 1914-1976 .... **CLC 4, 23**
   See also CA 69-72; 65-68; CANR 21; DLB
      14; MTCW 1, 2; RGEL 2; RHW
MacInnes, Helen (Clark)
   1907-1985 .... **CLC 27, 39**
   See also BPFB 2; CA 1-4R; 117; CANR 1,
      28, 58; CMW 4; CPW; DAM POP; DLB
      87; MSW; MTCW 1, 2; SATA 22; SATA-
      Obit 44

Mackay, Mary 1855-1924
   See Corelli, Marie
   See also CA 118; 177; FANT; RHW
Mackenzie, Compton (Edward Montague)
   1883-1972 .... **CLC 18**
   See also CA 21-22; 37-40R; CAP 2; DLB
      34, 100; RGEL 2; TCLC 116
Mackenzie, Henry 1745-1831 .... **NCLC 41**
   See also DLB 39; RGEL 2
Mackintosh, Elizabeth 1896(?)-1952
   See Tey, Josephine
   See also CA 110; CMW 4
MacLaren, James
   See Grieve, C(hristopher) M(urray)
Mac Laverty, Bernard 1942- .... **CLC 31**
   See also CA 116; 118; CANR 43, 88; CN
      7; INT CA-118; RGSF 2
MacLean, Alistair (Stuart)
   1922(?)-1987 .... **CLC 3, 13, 50, 63**
   See also CA 57-60; 121; CANR 28, 61;
      CMW 4; CPW; DAM POP; MTCW 1;
      SATA 23; SATA-Obit 50; TCWW 2
Maclean, Norman (Fitzroy)
   1902-1990 .... **CLC 78; SSC 13**
   See also CA 102; 132; CANR 49; CPW;
      DAM POP; DLB 206; TCWW 2
MacLeish, Archibald 1892-1982 ... **CLC 3, 8,
      14, 68**
   See also AMW; CA 9-12R; 106; CAD;
      CANR 33, 63; CDALBS; DAM POET;
      DLB 4, 7, 45; DLBY 1982; EXPP;
      MTCW 1, 2; PAB; PFS 5; RGAL 4
MacLennan, (John) Hugh
   1907-1990 .... **CLC 2, 14, 92**
   See also CA 5-8R; 142; CANR 33; DAC;
      DAM MST; DLB 68; MTCW 1, 2; RGEL
      2
MacLeod, Alistair 1936- .... **CLC 56**
   See also CA 123; CCA 1; DAC; DAM
      MST; DLB 60; MTCW 2; RGSF 2
Macleod, Fiona
   See Sharp, William
   See also RGEL 2; SUFW
MacNeice, (Frederick) Louis
   1907-1963 .... **CLC 1, 4, 10, 53**
   See also BRW 7; CA 85-88; CANR 61;
      DAB; DAM POET; DLB 10, 20; MTCW
      1, 2; RGEL 2
MacNeill, Dand
   See Fraser, George MacDonald
Macpherson, James 1736-1796 .... **LC 29**
   See also Ossian
   See also DLB 109; RGEL 2
Macpherson, (Jean) Jay 1931- .... **CLC 14**
   See also CA 5-8R; CANR 90; CP 7; CWP;
      DLB 53
Macrobius fl. 430- .... **CMLC 48**
MacShane, Frank 1927-1999 .... **CLC 39**
   See also CA 9-12R; 186; CANR 3, 33; DLB
      111
Macumber, Mari
   See Sandoz, Mari(e Susette)
Madach, Imre 1823-1864 .... **NCLC 19**
Madden, (Jerry) David 1933- .... **CLC 5, 15**
   See also CA 1-4R; CAAS 3; CANR 4, 45;
      CN 7; CSW; DLB 6; MTCW 1
Maddern, Al(an)
   See Ellison, Harlan (Jay)
Madhubuti, Haki R. 1942- . **CLC 6, 73; BLC
      2; PC 5**
   See also Lee, Don L.
   See also BW 2, 3; CA 73-76; CANR 24,
      51, 73; CP 7; CSW; DAM MULT, POET;
      DLB 5, 41; DLBD 8; MTCW 2; RGAL 4
Maepenn, Hugh
   See Kuttner, Henry
Maepenn, K. H.
   See Kuttner, Henry

Marie de l'Incarnation 1599-1672 ...... **LC 10**
Marier, Captain Victor
   See Griffith, D(avid Lewelyn) W(ark)
Mariner, Scott
   See Pohl, Frederik
Marinetti, Filippo Tommaso
   1876-1944 .... **TCLC 10**
   See also CA 107; DLB 114; EW 9
Marivaux, Pierre Carlet de Chamblain de
   1688-1763 .... **LC 4; DC 7**
   See also GFL Beginnings to 1789; RGWL
   2
Markandaya, Kamala .... **CLC 8, 38**
   See also Taylor, Kamala (Purnaiya)
   See also BYA 13; CN 7
Markfield, Wallace 1926- .... **CLC 8**
   See also CA 69-72; CAAS 3; CN 7; DLB
   2, 28
Markham, Edwin 1852-1940 .... **TCLC 47**
   See also CA 160; DLB 54, 186; RGAL 4
Markham, Robert
   See Amis, Kingsley (William)
Marks, J
   See Highwater, Jamake (Mamake)
Marks-Highwater, J
   See Highwater, Jamake (Mamake)
Markson, David M(errill) 1927- .... **CLC 67**
   See also CA 49-52; CANR 1, 91; CN 7
Marley, Bob .... **CLC 17**
   See also Marley, Robert Nesta
Marley, Robert Nesta 1945-1981
   See Marley, Bob
   See also CA 107; 103
Marlowe, Christopher 1564-1593 ...... **LC 22,**
   47; DC 1; WLC
   See also BRW 1; BRWR 1; CDBLB Before
   1660; DA; DA3; DAB; DAC; DAM
   DRAM, MST; DFS 1, 5, 13; DLB 62;
   EXPP; RGEL 2; WLIT 3
Marlowe, Stephen 1928- .... **CLC 70**
   See also Queen, Ellery
   See also CA 13-16R; CANR 6, 55; CMW
   4; SFW 4
Marmontel, Jean-Francois 1723-1799 .. **LC 2**
Marquand, John P(hillips)
   1893-1960 .... **CLC 2, 10**
   See also AMW; BPFB 2; CA 85-88; CANR
   73; CMW 4; DLB 9, 102; MTCW 2;
   RGAL 4
Marques, Rene 1919-1979 .. **CLC 96; HLC 2**
   See also CA 97-100; 85-88; CANR 78;
   DAM MULT; DLB 113; HW 1, 2; LAW;
   RGSF 2
Marquez, Gabriel (Jose) Garcia
   See Garcia Marquez, Gabriel (Jose)
Marquis, Don(ald Robert Perry)
   1878-1937 .... **TCLC 7**
   See also CA 104; 166; DLB 11, 25; RGAL
   4
Marric, J. J.
   See Creasey, John
   See also MSW
Marryat, Frederick 1792-1848 .... **NCLC 3**
   See also DLB 21, 163; RGEL 2; WCH
Marsden, James
   See Creasey, John
Marsh, Edward 1872-1953 .... **TCLC 99**
Marsh, (Edith) Ngaio 1899-1982 .. **CLC 7, 53**
   See also CA 9-12R; CANR 6, 58; CMW 4;
   CPW; DAM POP; DLB 77; MSW;
   MTCW 1, 2; RGEL 2
Marshall, Garry 1934- .... **CLC 17**
   See also AAYA 3; CA 111; SATA 60
Marshall, Paule 1929- .. **CLC 27, 72; BLC 3;**
   SSC 3
   See also AFAW 1, 2; BPFB 2; BW 2, 3;
   CA 77-80; CANR 25, 73; CN 7; DA3;
   DAM MULT; DLB 33, 157, 227; MTCW
   1, 2; RGAL 4

Marshallik
   See Zangwill, Israel
Marsten, Richard
   See Hunter, Evan
Marston, John 1576-1634 .... **LC 33**
   See also BRW 2; DAM DRAM; DLB 58,
   172; RGEL 2
Martha, Henry
   See Harris, Mark
Marti (y Perez), Jose (Julian)
   1853-1895 .... **NCLC 63; HLC 2**
   See also DAM MULT; HW 2; LAW; RGWL
   2; WLIT 1
Martial c. 40-c. 104 .... **CMLC 35; PC 10**
   See also AW 2; CDWLB 1; DLB 211;
   RGWL 2
Martin, Ken
   See Hubbard, L(afayette) Ron(ald)
Martin, Richard
   See Creasey, John
Martin, Steve 1945- .... **CLC 30**
   See also CA 97-100; CANR 30, 100;
   MTCW 1
Martin, Valerie 1948- .... **CLC 89**
   See also BEST 90:2; CA 85-88; CANR 49,
   89
Martin, Violet Florence
   1862-1915 .... **TCLC 51**
Martin, Webber
   See Silverberg, Robert
Martindale, Patrick Victor
   See White, Patrick (Victor Martindale)
Martin du Gard, Roger
   1881-1958 .... **TCLC 24**
   See also CA 118; CANR 94; DLB 65; GFL
   1789 to the Present; RGWL 2
Martineau, Harriet 1802-1876 .... **NCLC 26**
   See also DLB 21, 55, 159, 163, 166, 190;
   FW; RGEL 2; YABC 2
Martines, Julia
   See O'Faolain, Julia
Martinez, Enrique Gonzalez
   See Gonzalez Martinez, Enrique
Martinez, Jacinto Benavente y
   See Benavente (y Martinez), Jacinto
Martinez de la Rosa, Francisco de Paula
   1787-1862 .... **NCLC 102**
Martinez Ruiz, Jose 1873-1967
   See Azorin; Ruiz, Jose Martinez
   See also CA 93-96; HW 1
Martinez Sierra, Gregorio
   1881-1947 .... **TCLC 6**
   See also CA 115
Martinez Sierra, Maria (de la O'LeJarraga)
   1874-1974 .... **TCLC 6**
   See also CA 115
Martinsen, Martin
   See Follett, Ken(neth Martin)
Martinson, Harry (Edmund)
   1904-1978 .... **CLC 14**
   See also CA 77-80; CANR 34; DLB 259
Marut, Ret
   See Traven, B.
Marut, Robert
   See Traven, B.
Marvell, Andrew 1621-1678 .... **LC 4, 43; PC**
   10; WLC
   See also BRW 2; BRWR 2; CDBLB 1660-
   1789; DA; DAB; DAC; DAM MST,
   POET; DLB 131; EXPP; PFS 5; RGEL 2;
   WP
Marx, Karl (Heinrich) 1818-1883 . **NCLC 17**
   See also DLB 129
Masaoka, Shiki .... **TCLC 18**
   See also Masaoka, Tsunenori
Masaoka, Tsunenori 1867-1902
   See Masaoka, Shiki
   See also CA 117; 191

Masefield, John (Edward)
   1878-1967 .... **CLC 11, 47**
   See also CA 19-20; 25-28R; CANR 33;
   CAP 2; CDBLB 1890-1914; DAM POET;
   DLB 10, 19, 153, 160; EXPP; FANT;
   MTCW 1, 2; PFS 5; RGEL 2; SATA 19
Maso, Carole 19(?)- .... **CLC 44**
   See also CA 170; GLL 2; RGAL 4
Mason, Bobbie Ann 1940- ... **CLC 28, 43, 82,**
   154; SSC 4
   See also AAYA 5, 42; AMWS 8; BPFB 2;
   CA 53-56; CANR 11, 31, 58, 83;
   CDALBS; CN 7; CSW; DA3; DLB 173;
   DLBY 1987; EXPS; INT CANR-31;
   MTCW 1, 2; NFS 4; RGAL 4; RGSF 2;
   SSFS 3,8; YAW
Mason, Ernst
   See Pohl, Frederik
Mason, Hunni B.
   See Sternheim, (William Adolf) Carl
Mason, Lee W.
   See Malzberg, Barry N(athaniel)
Mason, Nick 1945- .... **CLC 35**
Mason, Tally
   See Derleth, August (William)
Mass, Anna .... **CLC 59**
Mass, William
   See Gibson, William
Massinger, Philip 1583-1640 .... **LC 70**
   See also DLB 58; RGEL 2
Master Lao
   See Lao Tzu
Masters, Edgar Lee 1868-1950 .... **TCLC 2,**
   25; PC 1, 36; WLCS
   See also AMWS 1; CA 104; 133; CDALB
   1865-1917; DA; DAC; DAM MST,
   POET; DLB 54; EXPP; MTCW 1, 2;
   RGAL 4; WP
Masters, Hilary 1928- .... **CLC 48**
   See also CA 25-28R; CANR 13, 47, 97; CN
   7; DLB 244
Mastrosimone, William 19(?)- .... **CLC 36**
   See also CA 186; CAD; CD 5
Mathe, Albert
   See Camus, Albert
Mather, Cotton 1663-1728 .... **LC 38**
   See also AMWS 2; CDALB 1640-1865;
   DLB 24, 30, 140; RGAL 4
Mather, Increase 1639-1723 .... **LC 38**
   See also DLB 24
Matheson, Richard (Burton) 1926- .. **CLC 37**
   See also AAYA 31; CA 97-100; CANR 88,
   99; DLB 8, 44; HGG; INT 97-100; SCFW
   2; SFW 4
Mathews, Harry 1930- .... **CLC 6, 52**
   See also CA 21-24R; CAAS 6; CANR 18,
   40, 98; CN 7
Mathews, John Joseph 1894-1979 .... **CLC 84**
   See also CA 19-20; 142; CANR 45; CAP 2;
   DAM MULT; DLB 175; NNAL
Mathias, Roland (Glyn) 1915- .... **CLC 45**
   See also CA 97-100; CANR 19, 41; CP 7;
   DLB 27
Matsuo Basho 1644-1694 .... **LC 62; PC 3**
   See also Basho, Matsuo
   See also DAM POET; PFS 2, 7
Mattheson, Rodney
   See Creasey, John
Matthews, (James) Brander
   1852-1929 .... **TCLC 95**
   See also DLB 71, 78; DLBD 13
Matthews, Greg 1949- .... **CLC 45**
   See also CA 135
Matthews, William (Procter III)
   1942-1997 .... **CLC 40**
   See also AMWS 9; CA 29-32R; 162; CAAS
   18; CANR 12, 57; CP 7; DLB 5
Matthias, John (Edward) 1941- .... **CLC 9**
   See also CA 33-36R; CANR 56; CP 7

Middleton, Christopher 1926- .... **CLC 13**
See also CA 13-16R; CANR 29, 54; CP 7;
DLB 40

Middleton, Richard (Barham)
1882-1911 .... **TCLC 56**
See also CA 187; DLB 156; HGG

Middleton, Stanley 1919- .... **CLC 7, 38**
See also CA 25-28R; CAAS 23; CANR 21,
46, 81; CN 7; DLB 14

Middleton, Thomas 1580-1627 .... **LC 33; DC 5**
See also BRW 2; DAM DRAM, MST; DLB
58; RGEL 2

Migueis, Jose Rodrigues 1901- .... **CLC 10**

Mikszath, Kalman 1847-1910 .... **TCLC 31**
See also CA 170

Miles, Jack .... **CLC 100**

Miles, Josephine (Louise)
1911-1985 .... **CLC 1, 2, 14, 34, 39**
See also CA 1-4R; 116; CANR 2, 55; DAM
POET; DLB 48

Militant
See Sandburg, Carl (August)

Mill, Harriet (Hardy) Taylor
1807-1858 .... **NCLC 102**
See also FW

Mill, John Stuart 1806-1873 .... **NCLC 11, 58**
See also CDBLB 1832-1890; DLB 55, 190;
FW 1; RGEL 2

Millar, Kenneth 1915-1983 .... **CLC 14**
See also Macdonald, Ross
See also CA 9-12R; 110; CANR 16, 63,
107; CMW 4; CPW; DA3; DAM POP;
DLB 2, 226; DLBD 6; DLBY 1983;
MTCW 1, 2

Millay, E. Vincent
See Millay, Edna St. Vincent

Millay, Edna St. Vincent
1892-1950 ... **TCLC 4, 49; PC 6; WLCS**
See also Boyd, Nancy
See also AMW; CA 104; 130; CDALB
1917-1929; DA; DA3; DAB; DAC; DAM
MST, POET; DLB 45, 249; EXPP;
MAWW; MTCW 1, 2; PAB; PFS 3;
RGAL 4; WP

Miller, Arthur 1915- ...... **CLC 1, 2, 6, 10, 15,
26, 47, 78; DC 1; WLC**
See also AAYA 15; AITN 1; AMW; CA
1-4R; CABS 3; CAD; CANR 2, 30, 54,
76; CD 5; CDALB 1941-1968; DA; DA3;
DAB; DAC; DAM DRAM, MST; DFS 1,
3; DLB 7; LAIT 4; MTCW 1, 2; RGAL
4; WYAS 1

Miller, Henry (Valentine)
1891-1980 .... **CLC 1, 2, 4, 9, 14, 43, 84;
WLC**
See also AMW; BPFB 2; CA 9-12R; 97-
100; CANR 33, 64; CDALB 1929-1941;
DA; DA3; DAB; DAC; DAM MST, NOV;
DLB 4, 9; DLBY 1980; MTCW 1, 2;
RGAL 4

Miller, Jason 1939(?)-2001 .... **CLC 2**
See also AITN 1; CA 73-76; 197; CAD;
DFS 12; DLB 7

Miller, Sue 1943- .... **CLC 44**
See also BEST 90:3; CA 139; CANR 59,
91; DA3; DAM POP; DLB 143

Miller, Walter M(ichael, Jr.)
1923-1996 .... **CLC 4, 30**
See also BPFB 2; CA 85-88; DLB 8; SCFW;
SFW 4

Millett, Kate 1934- .... **CLC 67**
See also AITN 1; CA 73-76; CANR 32, 53,
76; DA3; DLB 246; FW; GLL 1; MTCW
1, 2

Millhauser, Steven (Lewis) 1943- .... **CLC 21,
54, 109**
See also CA 110; 111; CANR 63; CN 7;
DA3; DLB 2; FANT; INT CA-111;
MTCW 2

Millin, Sarah Gertrude 1889-1968 ... **CLC 49**
See also CA 102; 93-96; DLB 225

Milne, A(lan) A(lexander)
1882-1956 .... **TCLC 6, 88**
See also BRWS 5; CA 104; 133; CLR 1,
26; CMW 4; CWRI 5; DA3; DAB; DAC;
DAM MST; DLB 10, 77, 100, 160; FANT;
MAICYA 1; MTCW 1, 2; RGEL 2; SATA
100; WCH; YABC 1

Milner, Ron(ald) 1938- .... **CLC 56; BLC 3**
See also AITN 1; BW 1; CA 73-76; CAD;
CANR 24, 81; CD 5; DAM MULT; DLB
38; MTCW 1

Milnes, Richard Monckton
1809-1885 .... **NCLC 61**
See also DLB 32, 184

Milosz, Czeslaw 1911- ...... **CLC 5, 11, 22, 31,
56, 82; PC 8; WLCS**
See also CA 81-84; CANR 23, 51, 91; CD-
WLB 4; CWW 2; DA3; DAM MST,
POET; DLB 215; EW 13; MTCW 1, 2;
RGWL 2

Milton, John 1608-1674 ..... **LC 9, 43; PC 19,
29; WLC**
See also BRW 2; BRWR 2; CDBLB 1660-
1789; DA; DA3; DAB; DAC; DAM MST,
POET; DLB 131, 151; EFS 1; EXPP;
LAIT 1; PAB; PFS 3; RGEL 2; WLIT 3;
WP

Min, Anchee 1957- .... **CLC 86**
See also CA 146; CANR 94

Minehaha, Cornelius
See Wedekind, (Benjamin) Frank(lin)

Miner, Valerie 1947- .... **CLC 40**
See also CA 97-100; CANR 59; FW; GLL
2

Minimo, Duca
See D'Annunzio, Gabriele

Minot, Susan 1956- .... **CLC 44**
See also AMWS 6; CA 134; CN 7

Minus, Ed 1938- .... **CLC 39**
See also CA 185

Miranda, Javier
See Bioy Casares, Adolfo
See also CWW 2

Miranda, Javier
See Bioy Casares, Adolfo

Mirbeau, Octave 1848-1917 .... **TCLC 55**
See also DLB 123, 192; GFL 1789 to the
Present

Miro (Ferrer), Gabriel (Francisco Victor)
1879-1930 .... **TCLC 5**
See also CA 104; 185

Misharin, Alexandr .... **CLC 59**

Mishima, Yukio ... **CLC 2, 4, 6, 9, 27; DC 1;
SSC 4**
See also Hiraoka, Kimitake
See also BPFB 2; DLB 182; GLL 1; MJW;
MTCW 2; RGSF 2; RGWL 2; SSFS 5, 12

Mistral, Frederic 1830-1914 .... **TCLC 51**
See also CA 122; GFL 1789 to the Present

Mistral, Gabriela
See Godoy Alcayaga, Lucila
See also DNFS 1; LAW; RGWL 2; WP

Mistry, Rohinton 1952- .... **CLC 71**
See also CA 141; CANR 86; CCA 1; CN 7;
DAC; SSFS 6

Mitchell, Clyde
See Ellison, Harlan (Jay); Silverberg, Robert

Mitchell, James Leslie 1901-1935
See Gibbon, Lewis Grassic
See also CA 104; 188; DLB 15

Mitchell, Joni 1943- .... **CLC 12**
See also CA 112; CCA 1

Mitchell, Joseph (Quincy)
1908-1996 .... **CLC 98**
See also CA 77-80; 152; CANR 69; CN 7;
CSW; DLB 185; DLBY 1996

Mitchell, Margaret (Munnerlyn)
1900-1949 .... **TCLC 11**
See also AAYA 23; BPFB 2; BYA 1; CA
109; 125; CANR 55, 94; CDALBS; DA3;
DAM NOV, POP; DLB 9; LAIT 2;
MTCW 1, 2; NFS 9; RGAL 4; RHW;
WYAS 1; YAW

Mitchell, Peggy
See Mitchell, Margaret (Munnerlyn)

Mitchell, S(ilas) Weir 1829-1914 .... **TCLC 36**
See also CA 165; DLB 202; RGAL 4

Mitchell, W(illiam) O(rmond)
1914-1998 .... **CLC 25**
See also CA 77-80; 165; CANR 15, 43; CN
7; DAC; DAM MST; DLB 88

Mitchell, William 1879-1936 .... **TCLC 81**

Mitford, Mary Russell 1787-1855 ... **NCLC 4**
See also DLB 110, 116; RGEL 2

Mitford, Nancy 1904-1973 .... **CLC 44**
See also CA 9-12R; DLB 191; RGEL 2

Miyamoto, (Chujo) Yuriko
1899-1951 .... **TCLC 37**
See also Miyamoto Yuriko
See also CA 170, 174

Miyamoto Yuriko
See Miyamoto, (Chujo) Yuriko
See also DLB 180

Miyazawa, Kenji 1896-1933 .... **TCLC 76**
See also CA 157

Mizoguchi, Kenji 1898-1956 .... **TCLC 72**
See also CA 167

Mo, Timothy (Peter) 1950(?)- ... **CLC 46, 134**
See also CA 117; CN 7; DLB 194; MTCW
1; WLIT 4

Modarressi, Taghi (M.) 1931-1997 ... **CLC 44**
See also CA 121; 134; INT 134

Modiano, Patrick (Jean) 1945- .... **CLC 18**
See also CA 85-88; CANR 17, 40; CWW
2; DLB 83

Mofolo, Thomas (Mokopu)
1875(?)-1948 .... **TCLC 22; BLC 3**
See also AFW; CA 121; 153; CANR 83;
DAM MULT; DLB 225; MTCW 2; WLIT
2

Mohr, Nicholasa 1938- .... **CLC 12; HLC 2**
See also AAYA 8; CA 49-52; CANR 1, 32,
64; CLR 22; DAM MULT; DLB 145; HW
1, 2; JRDA; LAIT 5; MAICYA 1; RGAL
4; SAAS 8; SATA 8, 97; SATA-Essay 113;
WYA; YAW

Mojtabai, A(nn) G(race) 1938- ..... **CLC 5, 9,
15, 29**
See also CA 85-88; CANR 88

Moliere 1622-1673 ..... **LC 10, 28, 64; DC 13;
WLC**
See also DA; DA3; DAB; DAC; DAM
DRAM, MST; DFS 13; EW 3; GFL Begin-
nings to 1789; RGWL 2

Molin, Charles
See Mayne, William (James Carter)

Molnar, Ferenc 1878-1952 .... **TCLC 20**
See also CA 109; 153; CANR 83; CDWLB
4; DAM DRAM; DLB 215; RGWL 2

Momaday, N(avarre) Scott 1934- ...... **CLC 2,
19, 85, 95; PC 25; WLCS**
See also AAYA 11; AMWS 4; ANW; BPFB
2; CA 25-28R; CANR 14, 34, 68;
CDALBS; CN 7; CPW; DA; DA3; DAB;
DAC; DAM MST, MULT, NOV, POP;
DLB 143, 175, 256; EXPP; INT CANR-
14; LAIT 4; MTCW 1, 2; NFS 10; NNAL;
PFS 2, 11; RGAL 4; SATA 48; SATA-
Brief 30; WP; YAW

Monette, Paul 1945-1995 .... **CLC 82**
See also AMWS 10; CA 139; 147; CN 7;
GLL 1

Monroe, Harriet 1860-1936 .... **TCLC 12**
See also CA 109; DLB 54, 91

Paige, Richard
See Koontz, Dean R(ay)

Paine, Thomas 1737-1809 .... **NCLC 62**
See also AMWS 1; CDALB 1640-1865;
DLB 31, 43, 73, 158; LAIT 1; RGAL 4;
RGEL 2

Palamas, Kostes 1859-1943 .... **TCLC 5**
See also CA 105; 190; RGWL 2

Palazzeschi, Aldo 1885-1974 .... **CLC 11**
See also CA 89-92; 53-56; DLB 114

Pales Matos, Luis 1898-1959
See Pales Matos, Luis
See also HLCS 2; HW 1; LAW

Paley, Grace 1922- .. **CLC 4, 6, 37, 140; SSC 8**
See also AMWS 6; CA 25-28R; CANR 13,
46, 74; CN 7; CPW; DA3; DAM POP;
DLB 28, 218; EXPS; FW; INT CANR-
13; MAWW; MTCW 1, 2; RGAL 4;
RGSF 2; SSFS 3

Palin, Michael (Edward) 1943- .... **CLC 21**
See also Monty Python
See also CA 107; CANR 35; SATA 67

Palliser, Charles 1947- .... **CLC 65**
See also CA 136; CANR 76; CN 7

Palma, Ricardo 1833-1919 .... **TCLC 29**
See also CA 168; LAW

Pancake, Breece Dexter 1952-1979
See Pancake, Breece D'J
See also CA 123; 109

Pancake, Breece D'J .... **CLC 29**
See also Pancake, Breece Dexter
See also DLB 130

Panchenko, Nikolai .... **CLC 59**

Pankhurst, Emmeline (Goulden)
1858-1928 .... **TCLC 100**
See also CA 116; FW

Panko, Rudy
See Gogol, Nikolai (Vasilyevich)

Papadiamantis, Alexandros
1851-1911 .... **TCLC 29**
See also CA 168

Papadiamantopoulos, Johannes 1856-1910
See Moreas, Jean
See also CA 117

Papini, Giovanni 1881-1956 .... **TCLC 22**
See also CA 121; 180

Paracelsus 1493-1541 .... **LC 14**
See also DLB 179

Parasol, Peter
See Stevens, Wallace

Pardo Bazan, Emilia 1851-1921 .... **SSC 30**
See also FW; RGSF 2; RGWL 2

Pareto, Vilfredo 1848-1923 .... **TCLC 69**
See also CA 175

Paretsky, Sara 1947- .... **CLC 135**
See also AAYA 30; BEST 90:3; CA 125;
129; CANR 59, 95; CMW 4; CPW; DA3;
DAM POP; INT CA-129; MSW; RGAL 4

Parfenie, Maria
See Codrescu, Andrei

Parini, Jay (Lee) 1948- .... **CLC 54, 133**
See also CA 97-100; CAAS 16; CANR 32,
87

Park, Jordan
See Kornbluth, C(yril) M.; Pohl, Frederik

Park, Robert E(zra) 1864-1944 ..... **TCLC 73**
See also CA 122; 165

Parker, Bert
See Ellison, Harlan (Jay)

Parker, Dorothy (Rothschild)
1893-1967 .. **CLC 15, 68; PC 28; SSC 2**
See also AMWS 9; CA 19-20; 25-28R; CAP
2; DA3; DAM POET; DLB 11, 45, 86;
EXPP; FW; MAWW; MTCW 1, 2; RGAL
4; RGSF 2

Parker, Robert B(rown) 1932- .... **CLC 27**
See also AAYA 28; BEST 89:4; BPFB 3;
CA 49-52; CANR 1, 26, 52, 89; CMW 4;
CPW; DAM NOV, POP; INT CANR-26;
MSW; MTCW 1

Parkin, Frank 1940- .... **CLC 43**
See also CA 147

Parkman, Francis, Jr. 1823-1893 .. **NCLC 12**
See also AMWS 2; DLB 1, 30, 183, 186,
235; RGAL 4

Parks, Gordon (Alexander Buchanan)
1912- .... **CLC 1, 16; BLC 3**
See also AAYA 36; AITN 2; BW 2, 3; CA
41-44R; CANR 26, 66; DA3; DAM
MULT; DLB 33; MTCW 2; SATA 8, 108

Parks, Tim(othy Harold) 1954- ...... **CLC 147**
See also CA 126; 131; CANR 77; DLB 231;
INT CA-131

Parmenides c. 515B.C.-c.
450B.C. .... **CMLC 22**
See also DLB 176

Parnell, Thomas 1679-1718 .... **LC 3**
See also DLB 95; RGEL 2

Parra, Nicanor 1914- ... **CLC 2, 102; HLC 2; PC 39**
See also CA 85-88; CANR 32; CWW 2;
DAM MULT; HW 1; LAW; MTCW 1

Parra Sanojo, Ana Teresa de la 1890-1936
See de la Parra, (Ana) Teresa (Sonojo)
See also HLCS 2; LAW

Parrish, Mary Frances
See Fisher, M(ary) F(rances) K(ennedy)

Parshchikov, Aleksei .... **CLC 59**

Parson, Professor
See Coleridge, Samuel Taylor

Parson Lot
See Kingsley, Charles

Parton, Sara Payson Willis
1811-1872 .... **NCLC 86**
See also DLB 43, 74, 239

Partridge, Anthony
See Oppenheim, E(dward) Phillips

Pascal, Blaise 1623-1662 .... **LC 35**
See also EW 3; GFL Beginnings to 1789;
RGWL 2

Pascoli, Giovanni 1855-1912 .... **TCLC 45**
See also CA 170; EW 7

Pasolini, Pier Paolo 1922-1975 .. **CLC 20, 37, 106; PC 17**
See also CA 93-96; 61-64; CANR 63; DLB
128, 177; MTCW 1; RGWL 2

Pasquini
See Silone, Ignazio

Pastan, Linda (Olenik) 1932- .... **CLC 27**
See also CA 61-64; CANR 18, 40, 61; CP
7; CSW; CWP; DAM POET; DLB 5; PFS
8

Pasternak, Boris (Leonidovich)
1890-1960 ...... **CLC 7, 10, 18, 63; PC 6; SSC 31; WLC**
See also BPFB 3; CA 127; 116; DA; DA3;
DAB; DAC; DAM MST, NOV, POET;
EW 10; MTCW 1, 2; RGSF 2; RGWL 2;
WP

Patchen, Kenneth 1911-1972 .... **CLC 1, 2, 18**
See also CA 1-4R; 33-36R; CANR 3, 35;
DAM POET; DLB 16, 48; MTCW 1;
RGAL 4

Pater, Walter (Horatio) 1839-1894 . **NCLC 7, 90**
See also BRW 5; CDBLB 1832-1890; DLB
57, 156; RGEL 2

Paterson, A(ndrew) B(arton)
1864-1941 .... **TCLC 32**
See also CA 155; DLB 230; RGEL 2; SATA
97

Paterson, Katherine (Womeldorf)
1932- .... **CLC 12, 30**
See also AAYA 1, 31; BYA 1, 2, 7; CA 21-
24R; CANR 28, 59; CLR 7, 50; CWRI 5;
DLB 52; JRDA; LAIT 4; MAICYA 1;
MAICYAS 1; MTCW 1; SATA 13, 53, 92;
WYA; YAW

Patmore, Coventry Kersey Dighton
1823-1896 .... **NCLC 9**
See also DLB 35, 98; RGEL 2

Paton, Alan (Stewart) 1903-1988 ...... **CLC 4, 10, 25, 55, 106; WLC**
See also AAYA 26; AFW; BPFB 3; BRWS
2; BYA 1; CA 13-16; 125; CANR 22;
CAP 1; DA; DA3; DAB; DAC; DAM
MST, NOV; DLB 225; DLBD 17; EXPN;
LAIT 4; MTCW 1, 2; NFS 3, 12; RGEL
2; SATA 11; SATA-Obit 56; WLIT 2

Paton Walsh, Gillian 1937- .... **CLC 35**
See also Paton Walsh, Jill; Walsh, Jill Paton
See also AAYA 11; CANR 38, 83; CLR 2,
65; DLB 161; JRDA; MAICYA 1; SAAS
3; SATA 4, 72, 109; YAW

Paton Walsh, Jill
See Paton Walsh, Gillian
See also BYA 1, 8

Patton, George S(mith), Jr.
1885-1945 .... **TCLC 79**
See also CA 189

Paulding, James Kirke 1778-1860 ... **NCLC 2**
See also DLB 3, 59, 74, 250; RGAL 4

Paulin, Thomas Neilson 1949-
See Paulin, Tom
See also CA 123; 128; CANR 98; CP 7

Paulin, Tom .... **CLC 37**
See also Paulin, Thomas Neilson
See also DLB 40

Pausanias c. 1st cent. - .... **CMLC 36**

Paustovsky, Konstantin (Georgievich)
1892-1968 .... **CLC 40**
See also CA 93-96; 25-28R

Pavese, Cesare 1908-1950 .. **TCLC 3; PC 13; SSC 19**
See also CA 104; 169; DLB 128, 177; EW
12; RGSF 2; RGWL 2

Pavic, Milorad 1929- .... **CLC 60**
See also CA 136; CDWLB 4; CWW 2; DLB
181

Pavlov, Ivan Petrovich 1849-1936 . **TCLC 91**
See also CA 118; 180

Payne, Alan
See Jakes, John (William)

Paz, Gil
See Lugones, Leopoldo

Paz, Octavio 1914-1998 . **CLC 3, 4, 6, 10, 19, 51, 65, 119; HLC 2; PC 1; WLC**
See also CA 73-76; 165; CANR 32, 65, 104;
CWW 2; DA; DA3; DAB; DAC; DAM
MST, MULT, POET; DLBY 1990, 1998;
DNFS 1; HW 1, 2; LAW; LAWS 1;
MTCW 1, 2; RGWL 2; SSFS 13; WLIT 1

p'Bitek, Okot 1931-1982 ..... **CLC 96; BLC 3**
See also AFW; BW 2, 3; CA 124; 107;
CANR 82; DAM MULT; DLB 125;
MTCW 1, 2; RGEL 2; WLIT 2

Peacock, Molly 1947- .... **CLC 60**
See also CA 103; CAAS 21; CANR 52, 84;
CP 7; CWP; DLB 120

Peacock, Thomas Love
1785-1866 .... **NCLC 22**
See also BRW 4; DLB 96, 116; RGEL 2;
RGSF 2

Peake, Mervyn 1911-1968 .... **CLC 7, 54**
See also CA 5-8R; 25-28R; CANR 3; DLB
15, 160, 255; FANT; MTCW 1; RGEL 2;
SATA 23; SFW 4

Redgrove, Peter (William) 1932- . CLC **6, 41**
See also BRWS 6; CA 1-4R; CANR 3, 39, 77; CP 7; DLB 40

Redmon, Anne .... CLC **22**
See also Nightingale, Anne Redmon
See also DLBY 1986

Reed, Eliot
See Ambler, Eric

Reed, Ishmael 1938- .. CLC **2, 3, 5, 6, 13, 32, 60; BLC 3**
See also AFAW 1, 2; AMWS 10; BPFB 3; BW 2, 3; CA 21-24R; CANR 25, 48, 74; CN 7; CP 7; CSW; DA3; DAM MULT; DLB 2, 5, 33, 169, 227; DLBD 8; MSW; MTCW 1, 2; PFS 6; RGAL 4; TCWW 2

Reed, John (Silas) 1887-1920 .... TCLC **9**
See also CA 106; 195

Reed, Lou .... CLC **21**
See also Firbank, Louis

Reese, Lizette Woodworth 1856-1935 . PC **29**
See also CA 180; DLB 54

Reeve, Clara 1729-1807 .... NCLC **19**
See also DLB 39; RGEL 2

Reich, Wilhelm 1897-1957 .... TCLC **57**
See also CA 199

Reid, Christopher (John) 1949- .... CLC **33**
See also CA 140; CANR 89; CP 7; DLB 40

Reid, Desmond
See Moorcock, Michael (John)

Reid Banks, Lynne 1929-
See Banks, Lynne Reid
See also CA 1-4R; CANR 6, 22, 38, 87; CLR 24; CN 7; JRDA; MAICYA 1; SATA 22, 75, 111; YAW

Reilly, William K.
See Creasey, John

Reiner, Max
See Caldwell, (Janet Miriam) Taylor (Holland)

Reis, Ricardo
See Pessoa, Fernando (Antonio Nogueira)

Remarque, Erich Maria 1898-1970 . CLC **21**
See also AAYA 27; BPFB 3; CA 77-80; 29-32R; CDWLB 2; DA; DA3; DAB; DAC; DAM MST, NOV; DLB 56; EXPN; LAIT 3; MTCW 1, 2; NFS 4; RGWL 2

Remington, Frederic 1861-1909 ..... TCLC **89**
See also CA 108; 169; DLB 12, 186, 188; SATA 41

Remizov, A.
See Remizov, Aleksei (Mikhailovich)

Remizov, A. M.
See Remizov, Aleksei (Mikhailovich)

Remizov, Aleksei (Mikhailovich) 1877-1957 .... TCLC **27**
See also CA 125; 133

Renan, Joseph Ernest 1823-1892 .. NCLC **26**
See also GFL 1789 to the Present

Renard, Jules 1864-1910 .... TCLC **17**
See also CA 117; GFL 1789 to the Present

Renault, Mary .... CLC **3, 11, 17**
See also Challans, Mary
See also BPFB 3; BYA 2; DLBY 1983; GLL 1; LAIT 1; MTCW 2; RGEL 2; RHW

Rendell, Ruth (Barbara) 1930- .. CLC **28, 48**
See also Vine, Barbara
See also BPFB 3; CA 109; CANR 32, 52, 74; CN 7; CPW; DAM POP; DLB 87; INT CANR-32; MSW; MTCW 1, 2

Renoir, Jean 1894-1979 .... CLC **20**
See also CA 129; 85-88

Resnais, Alain 1922- .... CLC **16**

Reverdy, Pierre 1889-1960 .... CLC **53**
See also CA 97-100; 89-92; GFL 1789 to the Present

Rexroth, Kenneth 1905-1982 .... CLC **1, 2, 6, 11, 22, 49, 112; PC 20**
See also CA 5-8R; 107; CANR 14, 34, 63; CDALB 1941-1968; DAM POET; DLB 16, 48, 165, 212; DLBY 1982; INT CANR-14; MTCW 1, 2; RGAL 4

Reyes, Alfonso 1889-1959 .. TCLC **33; HLCS 2**
See also CA 131; HW 1; LAW

Reyes y Basoalto, Ricardo Eliecer Neftali
See Neruda, Pablo

Reymont, Wladyslaw (Stanislaw) 1868(?)-1925 .... TCLC **5**
See also CA 104

Reynolds, Jonathan 1942- .... CLC **6, 38**
See also CA 65-68; CANR 28

Reynolds, Joshua 1723-1792 .... LC **15**
See also DLB 104

Reynolds, Michael S(hane) 1937-2000 .... CLC **44**
See also CA 65-68; 189; CANR 9, 89, 97

Reznikoff, Charles 1894-1976 .... CLC **9**
See also CA 33-36; 61-64; CAP 2; DLB 28, 45; WP

Rezzori (d'Arezzo), Gregor von 1914-1998 .... CLC **25**
See also CA 122; 136; 167

Rhine, Richard
See Silverstein, Alvin; Silverstein, Virginia B(arbara Opshelor)

Rhodes, Eugene Manlove 1869-1934 .... TCLC **53**
See also CA 198; DLB 256

R'hoone, Lord
See Balzac, Honore de

Rhys, Jean 1894(?)-1979 ...... CLC **2, 4, 6, 14, 19, 51, 124; SSC 21**
See also BRWS 2; CA 25-28R; 85-88; CANR 35, 62; CDBLB 1945-1960; CD-WLB 3; DA3; DAM NOV; DLB 36, 117, 162; DNFS 2; MTCW 1, 2; RGEL 2; RGSF 2; RHW

Ribeiro, Darcy 1922-1997 .... CLC **34**
See also CA 33-36R; 156

Ribeiro, Joao Ubaldo (Osorio Pimentel) 1941- .... CLC **10, 67**
See also CA 81-84

Ribman, Ronald (Burt) 1932- .... CLC **7**
See also CA 21-24R; CAD; CANR 46, 80; CD 5

Ricci, Nino 1959- .... CLC **70**
See also CA 137; CCA 1

Rice, Anne 1941- .... CLC **41, 128**
See also Rampling, Anne
See also AAYA 9; AMWS 7; BEST 89:2; BPFB 3; CA 65-68; CANR 12, 36, 53, 74, 100; CN 7; CPW; CSW; DA3; DAM POP; GLL 2; HGG; MTCW 2; YAW

Rice, Elmer (Leopold) 1892-1967 ...... CLC **7, 49**
See also CA 21-22; 25-28R; CAP 2; DAM DRAM; DFS 12; DLB 4, 7; MTCW 1, 2; RGAL 4

Rice, Tim(othy Miles Bindon) 1944- .... CLC **21**
See also CA 103; CANR 46; DFS 7

Rich, Adrienne (Cecile) 1929- ... CLC **3, 6, 7, 11, 18, 36, 73, 76, 125; PC 5**
See also AMWS 1; CA 9-12R; CANR 20, 53, 74; CDALBS; CP 7; CSW; CWP; DA3; DAM POET; DLB 5, 67; EXPP; FW; MAWW; MTCW 1, 2; PAB; RGAL 4; WP

Rich, Barbara
See Graves, Robert (von Ranke)

Rich, Robert
See Trumbo, Dalton

Richard, Keith .... CLC **17**
See also Richards, Keith

Richards, David Adams 1950- .... CLC **59**
See also CA 93-96; CANR 60; DAC; DLB 53

Richards, I(vor) A(rmstrong) 1893-1979 .... CLC **14, 24**
See also BRWS 2; CA 41-44R; 89-92; CANR 34, 74; DLB 27; MTCW 2; RGEL 2

Richards, Keith 1943-
See Richard, Keith
See also CA 107; CANR 77

Richardson, Anne
See Roiphe, Anne (Richardson)

Richardson, Dorothy Miller 1873-1957 .... TCLC **3**
See also CA 104; 192; DLB 36; FW; RGEL 2

Richardson (Robertson), Ethel Florence Lindesay 1870-1946
See Richardson, Henry Handel
See also CA 105; 190; DLB 230; RHW

Richardson, Henry Handel .... TCLC **4**
See also Richardson (Robertson), Ethel Florence Lindesay
See also DLB 197; RGEL 2; RGSF 2

Richardson, John 1796-1852 .... NCLC **55**
See also CCA 1; DAC; DLB 99

Richardson, Samuel 1689-1761 ...... LC **1, 44; WLC**
See also BRW 3; CDBLB 1660-1789; DA; DAB; DAC; DAM MST, NOV; DLB 39; RGEL 2; WLIT 3

Richler, Mordecai 1931-2001 .... CLC **3, 5, 9, 13, 18, 46, 70**
See also AITN 1; CA 65-68; CANR 31, 62; CCA 1; CLR 17; CWRI 5; DAC; DAM MST, NOV; DLB 53; MAICYA 1; MTCW 1, 2; RGEL 2; SATA 44, 98; SATA-Brief 27

Richter, Conrad (Michael) 1890-1968 .... CLC **30**
See also AAYA 21; BYA 2; CA 5-8R; 25-28R; CANR 23; DLB 9, 212; LAIT 1; MTCW 1, 2; RGAL 4; SATA 3; TCWW 2; YAW

Ricostranza, Tom
See Ellis, Trey

Riddell, Charlotte 1832-1906 .... TCLC **40**
See also Riddell, Mrs. J. H.
See also CA 165; DLB 156

Riddell, Mrs. J. H.
See Riddell, Charlotte
See also HGG; SUFW

Ridge, John Rollin 1827-1867 .... NCLC **82**
See also CA 144; DAM MULT; DLB 175; NNAL

Ridgeway, Jason
See Marlowe, Stephen

Ridgway, Keith 1965- .... CLC **119**
See also CA 172

Riding, Laura .... CLC **3, 7**
See also Jackson, Laura (Riding)
See also RGAL 4

Riefenstahl, Berta Helene Amalia 1902-
See Riefenstahl, Leni
See also CA 108

Riefenstahl, Leni .... CLC **16**
See also Riefenstahl, Berta Helene Amalia

Riffe, Ernest
See Bergman, (Ernst) Ingmar

Riggs, (Rolla) Lynn 1899-1954 .... TCLC **56**
See also CA 144; DAM MULT; DLB 175; NNAL

Riis, Jacob A(ugust) 1849-1914 ..... TCLC **80**
See also CA 113; 168; DLB 23

Riley, James Whitcomb 1849-1916 .... TCLC **51**
See also CA 118; 137; DAM POET; MAICYA 1; RGAL 4; SATA 17

Rosa, Joao Guimaraes 1908-1967 ... **CLC 23; HLCS 1**
See also Guimaraes Rosa, Joao
See also CA 89-92; DLB 113; WLIT 1

Rose, Wendy 1948- .... **CLC 85; PC 13**
See also CA 53-56; CANR 5, 51; CWP;
DAM MULT; DLB 175; NNAL; PFS 13;
RGAL 4; SATA 12

Rosen, R. D.
See Rosen, Richard (Dean)

Rosen, Richard (Dean) 1949- .... **CLC 39**
See also CA 77-80; CANR 62; CMW 4;
INT CANR-30

Rosenberg, Isaac 1890-1918 .... **TCLC 12**
See also BRW 6; CA 107; 188; DLB 20,
216; PAB; RGEL 2

Rosenblatt, Joe .... **CLC 15**
See also Rosenblatt, Joseph

Rosenblatt, Joseph 1933-
See Rosenblatt, Joe
See also CA 89-92; CP 7; INT 89-92

Rosenfeld, Samuel
See Tzara, Tristan

Rosenstock, Sami
See Tzara, Tristan

Rosenstock, Samuel
See Tzara, Tristan

Rosenthal, M(acha) L(ouis)
1917-1996 .... **CLC 28**
See also CA 1-4R; 152; CAAS 6; CANR 4,
51; CP 7; DLB 5; SATA 59

Ross, Barnaby
See Dannay, Frederic

Ross, Bernard L.
See Follett, Ken(neth Martin)

Ross, J. H.
See Lawrence, T(homas) E(dward)

Ross, John Hume
See Lawrence, T(homas) E(dward)

Ross, Martin 1862-1915
See Martin, Violet Florence
See also DLB 135; GLL 2; RGEL 2; RGSF
2

Ross, (James) Sinclair 1908-1996 ... **CLC 13; SSC 24**
See also CA 73-76; CANR 81; CN 7; DAC;
DAM MST; DLB 88; RGEL 2; RGSF 2;
TCWW 2

Rossetti, Christina (Georgina)
1830-1894 .... **NCLC 2, 50, 66; PC 7; WLC**
See also BRW 5; BYA 4; DA; DA3; DAB;
DAC; DAM MST, POET; DLB 35, 163,
240; EXPP; MAICYA 1; PFS 10, 14;
RGEL 2; SATA 20; WCH

Rossetti, Dante Gabriel 1828-1882 . **NCLC 4, 77; WLC**
See also BRW 5; CDBLB 1832-1890; DA;
DAB; DAC; DAM MST, POET; DLB 35;
EXPP; RGEL 2

Rossi, Cristina Peri
See Peri Rossi, Cristina

Rossner, Judith (Perelman) 1935- . **CLC 6, 9, 29**
See also AITN 2; BEST 90:3; BPFB 3; CA
17-20R; CANR 18, 51, 73; CN 7; DLB 6;
INT CANR-18; MTCW 1, 2

Rostand, Edmond (Eugene Alexis)
1868-1918 .... **TCLC 6, 37; DC 10**
See also CA 104; 126; DA; DA3; DAB;
DAC; DAM DRAM, MST; DFS 1; DLB
192; LAIT 1; MTCW 1; RGWL 2

Roth, Henry 1906-1995 ..... **CLC 2, 6, 11, 104**
See also AMWS 9; CA 11-12; 149; CANR
38, 63; CAP 1; CN 7; DA3; DLB 28;
MTCW 1, 2; RGAL 4

Roth, (Moses) Joseph 1894-1939 ... **TCLC 33**
See also CA 160; DLB 85; RGWL 2

Roth, Philip (Milton) 1933- ... **CLC 1, 2, 3, 4, 6, 9, 15, 22, 31, 47, 66, 86, 119; SSC 26; WLC**
See also AMWS 3; BEST 90:3; BPFB 3;
CA 1-4R; CANR 1, 22, 36, 55, 89;
CDALB 1968-1988; CN 7; CPW 1; DA;
DA3; DAB; DAC; DAM MST, NOV,
POP; DLB 2, 28, 173; DLBY 1982;
MTCW 1, 2; RGAL 4; RGSF 2; SSFS 12

Rothenberg, Jerome 1931- .... **CLC 6, 57**
See also CA 45-48; CANR 1, 106; CP 7;
DLB 5, 193

Rotter, Pat ed. .... **CLC 65**

Roumain, Jacques (Jean Baptiste)
1907-1944 .... **TCLC 19; BLC 3**
See also BW 1; CA 117; 125; DAM MULT

Rourke, Constance (Mayfield)
1885-1941 .... **TCLC 12**
See also CA 107; YABC 1

Rousseau, Jean-Baptiste 1671-1741 ...... **LC 9**

Rousseau, Jean-Jacques 1712-1778 .... **LC 14, 36; WLC**
See also DA; DA3; DAB; DAC; DAM
MST; EW 4; GFL Beginnings to 1789;
RGWL 2

Roussel, Raymond 1877-1933 .... **TCLC 20**
See also CA 117; GFL 1789 to the Present

Rovit, Earl (Herbert) 1927- .... **CLC 7**
See also CA 5-8R; CANR 12

Rowe, Elizabeth Singer 1674-1737 ..... **LC 44**
See also DLB 39, 95

Rowe, Nicholas 1674-1718 .... **LC 8**
See also DLB 84; RGEL 2

Rowlandson, Mary 1637(?)-1678 .... **LC 66**
See also DLB 24, 200; RGAL 4

Rowley, Ames Dorrance
See Lovecraft, H(oward) P(hillips)

Rowling, J(oanne) K(athleen)
1966(?)- .... **CLC 137**
See also AAYA 34; BYA 13, 14; CA 173;
CLR 66, 79; SATA 109

Rowson, Susanna Haswell
1762(?)-1824 .... **NCLC 5, 69**
See also DLB 37, 200; RGAL 4

Roy, Arundhati 1960(?)- .... **CLC 109**
See also CA 163; CANR 90; DLBY 1997

Roy, Gabrielle 1909-1983 .... **CLC 10, 14**
See also CA 53-56; 110; CANR 5, 61; CCA
1; DAB; DAC; DAM MST; DLB 68;
MTCW 1; RGWL 2; SATA 104

Royko, Mike 1932-1997 .... **CLC 109**
See also CA 89-92; 157; CANR 26; CPW

Rozanov, Vassili 1856-1919 .... **TCLC 104**

Rozewicz, Tadeusz 1921- ...... **CLC 9, 23, 139**
See also CA 108; CANR 36, 66; CWW 2;
DA3; DAM POET; DLB 232; MTCW 1,
2

Ruark, Gibbons 1941- .... **CLC 3**
See also CA 33-36R; CAAS 23; CANR 14,
31, 57; DLB 120

Rubens, Bernice (Ruth) 1923- .... **CLC 19, 31**
See also CA 25-28R; CANR 33, 65; CN 7;
DLB 14, 207; MTCW 1

Rubin, Harold
See Robbins, Harold

Rudkin, (James) David 1936- .... **CLC 14**
See also CA 89-92; CBD; CD 5; DLB 13

Rudnik, Raphael 1933- .... **CLC 7**
See also CA 29-32R

Ruffian, M.
See Hasek, Jaroslav (Matej Frantisek)

Ruiz, Jose Martinez .... **CLC 11**
See also Martinez Ruiz, Jose

Rukeyser, Muriel 1913-1980 . **CLC 6, 10, 15, 27; PC 12**
See also AMWS 6; CA 5-8R; 93-96; CANR
26, 60; DA3; DAM POET; DLB 48; FW;
GLL 2; MTCW 1, 2; PFS 10; RGAL 4;
SATA-Obit 22

Rule, Jane (Vance) 1931- .... **CLC 27**
See also CA 25-28R; CAAS 18; CANR 12,
87; CN 7; DLB 60; FW

Rulfo, Juan 1918-1986 .. **CLC 8, 80; HLC 2; SSC 25**
See also CA 85-88; 118; CANR 26; CD-
WLB 3; DAM MULT; DLB 113; HW 1,
2; LAW; MTCW 1, 2; RGSF 2; RGWL 2;
WLIT 1

Rumi, Jalal al-Din 1207-1273 .... **CMLC 20**
See also RGWL 2; WP

Runeberg, Johan 1804-1877 .... **NCLC 41**

Runyon, (Alfred) Damon
1884(?)-1946 .... **TCLC 10**
See also CA 107; 165; DLB 11, 86, 171;
MTCW 2; RGAL 4

Rush, Norman 1933- .... **CLC 44**
See also CA 121; 126; INT 126

Rushdie, (Ahmed) Salman 1947- .... **CLC 23, 31, 55, 100; WLCS**
See also BEST 89:3; BPFB 3; BRWS 4;
CA 108; 111; CANR 33, 56, 108; CN 7;
CPW 1; DA3; DAB; DAC; DAM MST,
NOV, POP; DLB 194; FANT; INT CA-
111; MTCW 1, 2; RGEL 2; RGSF 2;
WLIT 4

Rushforth, Peter (Scott) 1945- .... **CLC 19**
See also CA 101

Ruskin, John 1819-1900 .... **TCLC 63**
See also BRW 5; BYA 5; CA 114; 129; CD-
BLB 1832-1890; DLB 55, 163, 190;
RGEL 2; SATA 24; WCH

Russ, Joanna 1937- .... **CLC 15**
See also BPFB 3; CA 5-28R; CANR 11,
31, 65; CN 7; DLB 8; FW; GLL 1;
MTCW 1; SCFW 2; SFW 4

Russell, George William 1867-1935
See A.E.; Baker, Jean H.
See also CA 104; 153; CDBLB 1890-1914;
DAM POET; RGEL 2

Russell, Jeffrey Burton 1934- .... **CLC 70**
See also CA 25-28R; CANR 11, 28, 52

Russell, (Henry) Ken(neth Alfred)
1927- .... **CLC 16**
See also CA 105

Russell, William Martin 1947-
See Russell, Willy
See also CA 164; CANR 107

Russell, Willy .... **CLC 60**
See also Russell, William Martin
See also CBD; CD 5; DLB 233

Rutherford, Mark .... **TCLC 25**
See also White, William Hale
See also DLB 18; RGEL 2

Ruyslinck, Ward .... **CLC 14**
See also Belser, Reimond Karel Maria de

Ryan, Cornelius (John) 1920-1974 ..... **CLC 7**
See also CA 69-72; 53-56; CANR 38

Ryan, Michael 1946- .... **CLC 65**
See also CA 49-52; DLBY 1982

Ryan, Tim
See Dent, Lester

Rybakov, Anatoli (Naumovich)
1911-1998 .... **CLC 23, 53**
See also CA 126; 135; 172; SATA 79;
SATA-Obit 108

Ryder, Jonathan
See Ludlum, Robert

Ryga, George 1932-1987 .... **CLC 14**
See also CA 101; 124; CANR 43, 90; CCA
1; DAC; DAM MST; DLB 60

S. H.
See Hartmann, Sadakichi

S. S.
See Sassoon, Siegfried (Lorraine)

Saba, Umberto 1883-1957 .... **TCLC 33**
See also CA 144; CANR 79; DLB 114;
RGWL 2

Sarmiento, Felix Ruben Garcia
See Dario, Ruben
Saro-Wiwa, Ken(ule Beeson)
1941-1995 .... **CLC 114**
See also BW 2; CA 142; 150; CANR 60;
DLB 157
Saroyan, William 1908-1981 ... **CLC 1, 8, 10,**
29, 34, 56; SSC 21; WLC
See also CA 5-8R; 103; CAD; CANR 30;
CDALBS; DA; DA3; DAB; DAC; DAM
DRAM, MST, NOV; DLB 7, 9, 86; DLBY
1981; LAIT 4; MTCW 1, 2; RGAL 4;
RGSF 2; SATA 23; SATA-Obit 24
Sarraute, Nathalie 1900-1999 .... **CLC 1, 2, 4,**
8, 10, 31, 80
See also BPFB 3; CA 9-12R; 187; CANR
23, 66; CWW 2; DLB 83; EW 12; GFL
1789 to the Present; MTCW 1, 2; RGWL
2
Sarton, (Eleanor) May 1912-1995 ..... **CLC 4,**
14, 49, 91; PC 39
See also AMWS 8; CA 1-4R; 149; CANR
1, 34, 55; CN 7; CP 7; DAM POET; DLB
48; DLBY 1981; FW; INT CANR-34;
MTCW 1, 2; RGAL 4; SATA 36; SATA-
Obit 86; TCLC 120
Sartre, Jean-Paul 1905-1980 . **CLC 1, 4, 7, 9,**
13, 18, 24, 44, 50, 52; DC 3; SSC 32;
WLC
See also CA 9-12R; 97-100; CANR 21; DA;
DA3; DAB; DAC; DAM DRAM, MST,
NOV; DFS 5; DLB 72; EW 12; GFL 1789
to the Present; MTCW 1, 2; RGSF 2;
RGWL 2; SSFS 9
Sassoon, Siegfried (Lorraine)
1886-1967 .... **CLC 36, 130; PC 12**
See also BRW 6; CA 104; 25-28R; CANR
36; DAB; DAM MST, NOV, POET; DLB
20, 191; DLBD 18; MTCW 1, 2; PAB;
RGEL 2
Satterfield, Charles
See Pohl, Frederik
Satyremont
See Peret, Benjamin
Saul, John (W. III) 1942- .... **CLC 46**
See also AAYA 10; BEST 90:4; CA 81-84;
CANR 16, 40, 81; CPW; DAM NOV,
POP; HGG; SATA 98
Saunders, Caleb
See Heinlein, Robert A(nson)
Saura (Atares), Carlos 1932-1998 .... **CLC 20**
See also CA 114; 131; CANR 79; HW 1
Sauser-Hall, Frederic 1887-1961 ...... **CLC 18**
See Cendrars, Blaise
See also CA 102; 93-96; CANR 36, 62;
MTCW 1
Saussure, Ferdinand de
1857-1913 .... **TCLC 49**
See also DLB 242
Savage, Catharine
See Brosman, Catharine Savage
Savage, Thomas 1915- .... **CLC 40**
See also CA 126; 132; CAAS 15; CN 7;
INT 132; TCWW 2
Savan, Glenn (?)- .... **CLC 50**
Sayers, Dorothy L(eigh)
1893-1957 .... **TCLC 2, 15**
See also BPFB 3; BRWS 3; CA 104; 119;
CANR 60; CDBLB 1914-1945; CMW 4;
DAM POP; DLB 10, 36, 77, 100; MSW;
MTCW 1, 2; RGEL 2; SSFS 12
Sayers, Valerie 1952- .... **CLC 50, 122**
See also CA 134; CANR 61; CSW
Sayles, John (Thomas) 1950- . **CLC 7, 10, 14**
See also CA 57-60; CANR 41, 84; DLB 44
Scammell, Michael 1935- .... **CLC 34**
See also CA 156

Scannell, Vernon 1922- .... **CLC 49**
See also CA 5-8R; CANR 8, 24, 57; CP 7;
CWRI 5; DLB 27; SATA 59
Scarlett, Susan
See Streatfeild, (Mary) Noel
Scarron 1847-1910
See Mikszath, Kalman
Schaeffer, Susan Fromberg 1941- ..... **CLC 6,**
11, 22
See also CA 49-52; CANR 18, 65; CN 7;
DLB 28; MTCW 1, 2; SATA 22
Schama, Simon (Michael) 1945- ..... **CLC 150**
See also BEST 89:4; CA 105; CANR 39,
91
Schary, Jill
See Robinson, Jill
Schell, Jonathan 1943- .... **CLC 35**
See also CA 73-76; CANR 12
Schelling, Friedrich Wilhelm Joseph von
1775-1854 .... **NCLC 30**
See also DLB 90
Scherer, Jean-Marie Maurice 1920-
See Rohmer, Eric
See also CA 110
Schevill, James (Erwin) 1920- .... **CLC 7**
See also CA 5-8R; CAAS 12; CAD; CD 5
Schiller, Friedrich von
1759-1805 .... **NCLC 39, 69; DC 12**
See also CDWLB 2; DAM DRAM; DLB
94; EW 5; RGWL 2
Schisgal, Murray (Joseph) 1926- .... **CLC 6**
See also CA 21-24R; CAD; CANR 48, 86;
CD 5
Schlee, Ann 1934- .... **CLC 35**
See also CA 101; CANR 29, 88; SATA 44;
SATA-Brief 36
Schlegel, August Wilhelm von
1767-1845 .... **NCLC 15**
See also DLB 94; RGWL 2
Schlegel, Friedrich 1772-1829 .... **NCLC 45**
See also DLB 90; EW 5; RGWL 2
Schlegel, Johann Elias (von)
1719(?)-1749 .... **LC 5**
Schleiermacher, Friedrich
1768-1834 .... **NCLC 107**
See also DLB 90
Schlesinger, Arthur M(eier), Jr.
1917- .... **CLC 84**
See also AITN 1; CA 1-4R; CANR 1, 28,
58, 105; DLB 17; INT CANR-28; MTCW
1, 2; SATA 61
Schmidt, Arno (Otto) 1914-1979 ...... **CLC 56**
See also CA 128; 109; DLB 69
Schmitz, Aron Hector 1861-1928
See Svevo, Italo
See also CA 104; 122; MTCW 1
Schnackenberg, Gjertrud (Cecelia)
1953- .... **CLC 40**
See also CA 116; CANR 100; CP 7; CWP;
DLB 120; PFS 13
Schneider, Leonard Alfred 1925-1966
See Bruce, Lenny
See also CA 89-92
Schnitzler, Arthur 1862-1931 ... **TCLC 4; DC**
17; SSC 15
See also CA 104; CDWLB 2; DLB 81, 118;
EW 8; RGSF 2; RGWL 2
Schoenberg, Arnold Franz Walter
1874-1951 .... **TCLC 75**
See also CA 109; 188
Schonberg, Arnold
See Schoenberg, Arnold Franz Walter
Schopenhauer, Arthur 1788-1860 .. **NCLC 51**
See also DLB 90; EW 5
Schor, Sandra (M.) 1932(?)-1990 ..... **CLC 65**
See also CA 132
Schorer, Mark 1908-1977 .... **CLC 9**
See also CA 5-8R; 73-76; CANR 7; DLB
103

Schrader, Paul (Joseph) 1946- .... **CLC 26**
See also CA 37-40R; CANR 41; DLB 44
Schreiner, Olive (Emilie Albertina)
1855-1920 .... **TCLC 9**
See also AFW; BRWS 2; CA 105; 154;
DLB 18, 156, 190, 225; FW; RGEL 2;
WLIT 2
Schulberg, Budd (Wilson) 1914- .. **CLC 7, 48**
See also BPFB 3; CA 25-28R; CANR 19,
87; CN 7; DLB 6, 26, 28; DLBY 1981,
2001
Schulman, Arnold
See Trumbo, Dalton
Schulz, Bruno 1892-1942 .. **TCLC 5, 51; SSC**
13
See also CA 115; 123; CANR 86; CDWLB
4; DLB 215; MTCW 2; RGSF 2; RGWL
2
Schulz, Charles M(onroe)
1922-2000 .... **CLC 12**
See also AAYA 39; CA 9-12R; 187; CANR
6; INT CANR-6; SATA 10; SATA-Obit
118
Schumacher, E(rnst) F(riedrich)
1911-1977 .... **CLC 80**
See also CA 81-84; 73-76; CANR 34, 85
Schuyler, James Marcus 1923-1991 .. **CLC 5,**
23
See also CA 101; 134; DAM POET; DLB
5, 169; INT 101; WP
Schwartz, Delmore (David)
1913-1966 ... **CLC 2, 4, 10, 45, 87; PC 8**
See also AMWS 2; CA 17-18; 25-28R;
CANR 35; CAP 2; DLB 28, 48; MTCW
1, 2; PAB; RGAL 4
Schwartz, Ernst
See Ozu, Yasujiro
Schwartz, John Burnham 1965- .... **CLC 59**
See also CA 132
Schwartz, Lynne Sharon 1939- .... **CLC 31**
See also CA 103; CANR 44, 89; DLB 218;
MTCW 2
Schwartz, Muriel A.
See Eliot, T(homas) S(tearns)
Schwarz-Bart, Andre 1928- .... **CLC 2, 4**
See also CA 89-92
Schwarz-Bart, Simone 1938- . **CLC 7; BLCS**
See also BW 2; CA 97-100
Schwitters, Kurt (Hermann Edward Karl
Julius) 1887-1948 .... **TCLC 95**
See also CA 158
Schwob, Marcel (Mayer Andre)
1867-1905 .... **TCLC 20**
See also CA 117; 168; DLB 123; GFL 1789
to the Present
Sciascia, Leonardo 1921-1989 .. **CLC 8, 9, 41**
See also CA 85-88; 130; CANR 35; DLB
177; MTCW 1; RGWL 2
Scoppettone, Sandra 1936- .... **CLC 26**
See also Early, Jack
See also AAYA 11; BYA 8; CA 5-8R;
CANR 41, 73; GLL 1; MAICYAS 1;
SATA 9, 92; WYA; YAW
Scorsese, Martin 1942- .... **CLC 20, 89**
See also AAYA 38; CA 110; 114; CANR
46, 85
Scotland, Jay
See Jakes, John (William)
Scott, Duncan Campbell
1862-1947 .... **TCLC 6**
See also CA 104; 153; DAC; DLB 92;
RGEL 2
Scott, Evelyn 1893-1963 .... **CLC 43**
See also CA 104; 112; CANR 64; DLB 9,
48; RHW
Scott, F(rancis) R(eginald)
1899-1985 .... **CLC 22**
See also CA 101; 114; CANR 87; DLB 88;
INT CA-101; RGEL 2

Smith, Martin Cruz 1942- .... **CLC 25**
See also BEST 89:4; BPFB 3; CA 85-88; CANR 6, 23, 43, 65; CMW 4; CPW; DAM MULT, POP; HGG; INT CANR-23; MTCW 2; NNAL; RGAL 4

Smith, Mary-Ann Tirone 1944- .... **CLC 39**
See also CA 118; 136

Smith, Patti 1946- .... **CLC 12**
See also CA 93-96; CANR 63

Smith, Pauline (Urmson)
1882-1959 .... **TCLC 25**
See also DLB 225

Smith, Rosamond
See Oates, Joyce Carol

Smith, Sheila Kaye
See Kaye-Smith, Sheila

Smith, Stevie .... **CLC 3, 8, 25, 44; PC 12**
See also Smith, Florence Margaret
See also BRWS 2; DLB 20; MTCW 2; PAB; PFS 3; RGEL 2

Smith, Wilbur (Addison) 1933- .... **CLC 33**
See also CA 13-16R; CANR 7, 46, 66; CPW; MTCW 1, 2

Smith, William Jay 1918- .... **CLC 6**
See also CA 5-8R; CANR 44, 106; CP 7; CSW; CWRI 5; DLB 5; MAICYA 1; SAAS 22; SATA 2, 68

Smith, Woodrow Wilson
See Kuttner, Henry

Smolenskin, Peretz 1842-1885 .... **NCLC 30**

Smollett, Tobias (George) 1721-1771 ... **LC 2, 46**
See also BRW 3; CDBLB 1660-1789; DLB 39, 104; RGEL 2

Snodgrass, W(illiam) D(e Witt)
1926- .... **CLC 2, 6, 10, 18, 68**
See also AMWS 6; CA 1-4R; CANR 6, 36, 65, 85; CP 7; DAM POET; DLB 5; MTCW 1, 2; RGAL 4

Snow, C(harles) P(ercy) 1905-1980 ... **CLC 1, 4, 6, 9, 13, 19**
See also BRW 7; CA 5-8R; 101; CANR 28; CDBLB 1945-1960; DAM NOV; DLB 15, 77; DLBD 17; MTCW 1, 2; RGEL 2

Snow, Frances Compton
See Adams, Henry (Brooks)

Snyder, Gary (Sherman) 1930- . **CLC 1, 2, 5, 9, 32, 120; PC 21**
See also AMWS 8; ANW; CA 17-20R; CANR 30, 60; CP 7; DA3; DAM POET; DLB 5, 16, 165, 212, 237; MTCW 2; PFS 9; RGAL 4; WP

Snyder, Zilpha Keatley 1927- .... **CLC 17**
See also AAYA 15; BYA 1; CA 9-12R; CANR 38; CLR 31; JRDA; MAICYA 1; SAAS 2; SATA 1, 28, 75, 110; SATA-Essay 112; YAW

Soares, Bernardo
See Pessoa, Fernando (Antonio Nogueira)

Sobh, A.
See Shamlu, Ahmad

Sobol, Joshua .... **CLC 60**
See also CWW 2

Socrates 470B.C.-399B.C. .... **CMLC 27**

Soderberg, Hjalmar 1869-1941 ...... **TCLC 39**
See also DLB 259; RGSF 2

Soderbergh, Steven 1963- .... **CLC 154**

Sodergran, Edith (Irene)
See Soedergran, Edith (Irene)
See also DLB 259; EW 11; RGWL 2

Soedergran, Edith (Irene)
1892-1923 .... **TCLC 31**
See also Sodergran, Edith (Irene)

Softly, Edgar
See Lovecraft, H(oward) P(hillips)

Softly, Edward
See Lovecraft, H(oward) P(hillips)

Sokolov, Raymond 1941- .... **CLC 7**
See also CA 85-88

Sokolov, Sasha .... **CLC 59**

Solo, Jay
See Ellison, Harlan (Jay)

Sologub, Fyodor .... **TCLC 9**
See also Teternikov, Fyodor Kuzmich

Solomons, Ikey Esquir
See Thackeray, William Makepeace

Solomos, Dionysios 1798-1857 .... **NCLC 15**

Solwoska, Mara
See French, Marilyn

Solzhenitsyn, Aleksandr I(sayevich)
1918- .. **CLC 1, 2, 4, 7, 9, 10, 18, 26, 34, 78, 134; SSC 32; WLC**
See also AITN 1; BPFB 3; CA 69-72; CANR 40, 65; DA; DA3; DAB; DAC; DAM MST, NOV; EW 13; EXPS; LAIT 4; MTCW 1, 2; NFS 6; RGSF 2; RGWL 2; SSFS 9

Somers, Jane
See Lessing, Doris (May)

Somerville, Edith Oenone
1858-1949 .... **TCLC 51**
See also CA 196; DLB 135; RGEL 2; RGSF 2

Somerville & Ross
See Martin, Violet Florence; Somerville, Edith Oenone

Sommer, Scott 1951- .... **CLC 25**
See also CA 106

Sondheim, Stephen (Joshua) 1930- . **CLC 30, 39, 147**
See also AAYA 11; CA 103; CANR 47, 67; DAM DRAM; LAIT 4

Song, Cathy 1955- .... **PC 21**
See also AAL; CA 154; CWP; DLB 169; EXPP; FW; PFS 5

Sontag, Susan 1933- .... **CLC 1, 2, 10, 13, 31, 105**
See also AMWS 3; CA 17-20R; CANR 25, 51, 74, 97; CN 7; CPW; DA3; DAM POP; DLB 2, 67; MAWW; MTCW 1, 2; RGAL 4; RHW; SSFS 10

Sophocles 496(?)B.C.-406(?)B.C. .... **CMLC 2, 47, 51; DC 1; WLCS**
See also AW 1; CDWLB 1; DA; DA3; DAB; DAC; DAM DRAM, MST; DFS 1, 4, 8; DLB 176; LAIT 1; RGWL 2

Sordello 1189-1269 .... **CMLC 15**

Sorel, Georges 1847-1922 .... **TCLC 91**
See also CA 118; 188

Sorel, Julia
See Drexler, Rosalyn

Sorokin, Vladimir .... **CLC 59**

Sorrentino, Gilbert 1929- .. **CLC 3, 7, 14, 22, 40**
See also CA 77-80; CANR 14, 33; CN 7; CP 7; DLB 5, 173; DLBY 1980; INT CANR-14

Soseki
See Natsume, Soseki
See also MJW

Soto, Gary 1952- ... **CLC 32, 80; HLC 2; PC 28**
See also AAYA 10, 37; BYA 11; CA 119; 125; CANR 50, 74, 107; CLR 38; CP 7; DAM MULT; DLB 82; EXPP; HW 1, 2; INT CA-125; JRDA; MAICYAS 1; MTCW 2; PFS 7; RGAL 4; SATA 80, 120; WYA; YAW

Soupault, Philippe 1897-1990 .... **CLC 68**
See also CA 116; 147; 131; GFL 1789 to the Present

Souster, (Holmes) Raymond 1921- .... **CLC 5, 14**
See also CA 13-16R; CAAS 14; CANR 13, 29, 53; CP 7; DA3; DAC; DAM POET; DLB 88; RGEL 2; SATA 63

Southern, Terry 1924(?)-1995 .... **CLC 7**
See also BPFB 3; CA 1-4R; 150; CANR 1, 55, 107; CN 7; DLB 2; IDFW 3, 4

Southey, Robert 1774-1843 .... **NCLC 8, 97**
See also BRW 4; DLB 93, 107, 142; RGEL 2; SATA 54

Southworth, Emma Dorothy Eliza Nevitte
1819-1899 .... **NCLC 26**
See also DLB 239

Souza, Ernest
See Scott, Evelyn

Soyinka, Wole 1934- .... **CLC 3, 5, 14, 36, 44; BLC 3; DC 2; WLC**
See also AFW; BW 2, 3; CA 13-16R; CANR 27, 39, 82; CD 5; CDWLB 3; CN 7; CP 7; DA; DA3; DAB; DAC; DAM DRAM, MST, MULT; DFS 10; DLB 125; MTCW 1, 2; RGEL 2; WLIT 2

Spackman, W(illiam) M(ode)
1905-1990 .... **CLC 46**
See also CA 81-84; 132

Spacks, Barry (Bernard) 1931- .... **CLC 14**
See also CA 154; CANR 33; CP 7; DLB 105

Spanidou, Irini 1946- .... **CLC 44**
See also CA 185

Spark, Muriel (Sarah) 1918- ..... **CLC 2, 3, 5, 8, 13, 18, 40, 94; SSC 10**
See also BRWS 1; CA 5-8R; CANR 12, 36, 76, 89; CDBLB 1945-1960; CN 7; CP 7; DA3; DAB; DAC; DAM MST, NOV; DLB 15, 139; FW; INT CANR-12; LAIT 4; MTCW 1, 2; RGEL 2; WLIT 4; YAW

Spaulding, Douglas
See Bradbury, Ray (Douglas)

Spaulding, Leonard
See Bradbury, Ray (Douglas)

Spelman, Elizabeth .... **CLC 65**

Spence, J. A. D.
See Eliot, T(homas) S(tearns)

Spencer, Elizabeth 1921- .... **CLC 22**
See also CA 13-16R; CANR 32, 65, 87; CN 7; CSW; DLB 6, 218; MTCW 1; RGAL 4; SATA 14

Spencer, Leonard G.
See Silverberg, Robert

Spencer, Scott 1945- .... **CLC 30**
See also CA 113; CANR 51; DLBY 1986

Spender, Stephen (Harold)
1909-1995 .... **CLC 1, 2, 5, 10, 41, 91**
See also BRWS 2; CA 9-12R; 149; CANR 31, 54; CDBLB 1945-1960; CP 7; DA3; DAM POET; DLB 20; MTCW 1, 2; PAB; RGEL 2

Spengler, Oswald (Arnold Gottfried)
1880-1936 .... **TCLC 25**
See also CA 118; 189

Spenser, Edmund 1552(?)-1599 ..... **LC 5, 39; PC 8; WLC**
See also BRW 1; CDBLB Before 1660; DA; DA3; DAB; DAC; DAM MST, POET; DLB 167; EFS 2; EXPP; PAB; RGEL 2; WLIT 3; WP

Spicer, Jack 1925-1965 .... **CLC 8, 18, 72**
See also CA 85-88; DAM POET; DLB 5, 16, 193; GLL 1; WP

Spiegelman, Art 1948- .... **CLC 76**
See also AAYA 10; CA 125; CANR 41, 55, 74; MTCW 2; SATA 109; YAW

Spielberg, Peter 1929- .... **CLC 6**
See also CA 5-8R; CANR 4, 48; DLBY 1981

Spielberg, Steven 1947- .... **CLC 20**
See also AAYA 8, 24; CA 77-80; CANR 32; SATA 32

Spillane, Frank Morrison 1918-
See Spillane, Mickey
See also CA 25-28R; CANR 28, 63; DA3; MTCW 1, 2; SATA 66

Tsvetaeva (Efron), Marina (Ivanovna)
1892-1941 .... **TCLC 7, 35; PC 14**
See also CA 104; 128; CANR 73; EW 11;
MTCW 1, 2; RGWL 2

Tuck, Lily 1938- .... **CLC 70**
See also CA 139; CANR 90

Tu Fu 712-770 .... **PC 9**
See also Du Fu
See also DAM MULT; WP

Tunis, John R(oberts) 1889-1975 ..... **CLC 12**
See also BYA 1; CA 61-64; CANR 62; DLB
22, 171; JRDA; MAICYA 1; SATA 37;
SATA-Brief 30; YAW

Tuohy, Frank .... **CLC 37**
See also Tuohy, John Francis
See also DLB 14, 139

Tuohy, John Francis 1925-
See Tuohy, Frank
See also CA 5-8R; 178; CANR 3, 47; CN 7

Turco, Lewis (Putnam) 1934- ..... **CLC 11, 63**
See also CA 13-16R; CAAS 22; CANR 24,
51; CP 7; DLBY 1984

Turgenev, Ivan (Sergeevich)
1818-1883 .... **NCLC 21, 37; DC 7; SSC
7; WLC**
See also DA; DAB; DAC; DAM MST,
NOV; DFS 6; DLB 238; EW 6; RGSF 2;
RGWL 2

Turgot, Anne-Robert-Jacques
1727-1781 .... **LC 26**

Turner, Frederick 1943- .... **CLC 48**
See also CA 73-76; CAAS 10; CANR 12,
30, 56; DLB 40

Turton, James
See Crace, Jim

Tutu, Desmond M(pilo) 1931- .... **CLC 80;
BLC 3**
See also BW 1, 3; CA 125; CANR 67, 81;
DAM MULT

Tutuola, Amos 1920-1997 ...... **CLC 5, 14, 29;
BLC 3**
See also AFW; BW 2, 3; CA 9-12R; 159;
CANR 27, 66; CDWLB 3; CN 7; DA3;
DAM MULT; DLB 125; DNFS 2; MTCW
1, 2; RGEL 2; WLIT 2

Twain, Mark .... **TCLC 6, 12, 19, 36, 48, 59;
SSC 34; WLC**
See also Clemens, Samuel Langhorne
See also AAYA 20; AMW; BPFB 3; BYA 2,
3, 11, 14; CLR 58, 60, 66; DLB 11;
EXPN; EXPS; FANT; LAIT 2; NFS 1, 6;
RGAL 4; RGSF 2; SFW 4; SSFS 1, 7;
SUFW; WCH; WYA; YAW

Tyler, Anne 1941- . **CLC 7, 11, 18, 28, 44, 59,
103**
See also AAYA 18; AMWS 4; BEST 89:1;
BPFB 3; BYA 12; CA 9-12R; CANR 11,
33, 53; CDALBS; CN 7; CPW; CSW;
DAM NOV, POP; DLB 6, 143; DLBY
1982; EXPN; MAWW; MTCW 1, 2; NFS
2, 7, 10; RGAL 4; SATA 7, 90; YAW

Tyler, Royall 1757-1826 .... **NCLC 3**
See also DLB 37; RGAL 4

Tynan, Katharine 1861-1931 .... **TCLC 3**
See also CA 104; 167; DLB 153, 240; FW

Tyutchev, Fyodor 1803-1873 .... **NCLC 34**

Tzara, Tristan 1896-1963 ..... **CLC 47; PC 27**
See also CA 153; 89-92; DAM POET;
MTCW 2

Uhry, Alfred 1936- .... **CLC 55**
See also CA 127; 133; CAD; CD 5; CSW;
DA3; DAM DRAM, POP; DFS 11; INT
CA-133

Ulf, Haerved
See Strindberg, (Johan) August

Ulf, Harved
See Strindberg, (Johan) August

Ulibarri, Sabine R(eyes) 1919- .... **CLC 83;
HLCS 2**
See also CA 131; CANR 81; DAM MULT;
DLB 82; HW 1, 2; RGSF 2

Unamuno (y Jugo), Miguel de
1864-1936 . **TCLC 2, 9; HLC 2; SSC 11**
See also CA 104; 131; CANR 81; DAM
MULT, NOV; DLB 108; EW 8; HW 1, 2;
MTCW 1, 2; RGSF 2; RGWL 2

Undercliffe, Errol
See Campbell, (John) Ramsey

Underwood, Miles
See Glassco, John

Undset, Sigrid 1882-1949 ..... **TCLC 3; WLC**
See also CA 104; 129; DA; DA3; DAB;
DAC; DAM MST, NOV; EW 9; FW;
MTCW 1, 2; RGWL 2

Ungaretti, Giuseppe 1888-1970 ... **CLC 7, 11,
15**
See also CA 19-20; 25-28R; CAP 2; DLB
114; EW 10; RGWL 2

Unger, Douglas 1952- .... **CLC 34**
See also CA 130; CANR 94

Unsworth, Barry (Forster) 1930- .... **CLC 76,
127**
See also BRWS 7; CA 25-28R; CANR 30,
54; CN 7; DLB 194

Updike, John (Hoyer) 1932- . **CLC 1, 2, 3, 5,
7, 9, 13, 15, 23, 34, 43, 70, 139; SSC 13,
27; WLC**
See also AAYA 36; AMW; AMWR 1; BPFB
3; BYA 12; CA 1-4R; CABS 1; CANR 4,
33, 51, 94; CDALB 1968-1988; CN 7;
CP 7; CPW 1; DA; DA3; DAB; DAC;
DAM MST, NOV, POET, POP; DLB 2, 5,
143, 218, 227; DLBD 3; DLBY 1980,
1982, 1997; EXPP; HGG; MTCW 1, 2;
NFS 12; RGAL 4; RGSF 2; SSFS 3

Upshaw, Margaret Mitchell
See Mitchell, Margaret (Munnerlyn)

Upton, Mark
See Sanders, Lawrence

Upward, Allen 1863-1926 .... **TCLC 85**
See also CA 117; 187; DLB 36

Urdang, Constance (Henriette)
1922-1996 .... **CLC 47**
See also CA 21-24R; CANR 9, 24; CP 7;
CWP

Uriel, Henry
See Faust, Frederick (Schiller)

Uris, Leon (Marcus) 1924- .... **CLC 7, 32**
See also AITN 1, 2; BEST 89:2; BPFB 3;
CA 1-4R; CANR 1, 40, 65; CN 7; CPW
1; DA3; DAM NOV, POP; MTCW 1, 2;
SATA 49

Urista, Alberto H. 1947- .... **PC 34**
See also Alurista
See also CA 45-48, 182; CANR 2, 32;
HLCS 1; HW 1

Urmuz
See Codrescu, Andrei

Urquhart, Guy
See McAlmon, Robert (Menzies)

Urquhart, Jane 1949- .... **CLC 90**
See also CA 113; CANR 32, 68; CCA 1;
DAC

Usigli, Rodolfo 1905-1979
See also CA 131; HLCS 1; HW 1; LAW

Ustinov, Peter (Alexander) 1921- .... **CLC 1**
See also AITN 1; CA 13-16R; CANR 25,
51; CBD; CD 5; DLB 13; MTCW 2

U Tam'si, Gerald Felix Tchicaya
See Tchicaya, Gerald Felix

U Tam'si, Tchicaya
See Tchicaya, Gerald Felix

Vachss, Andrew (Henry) 1942- .... **CLC 106**
See also CA 118; CANR 44, 95; CMW 4

Vachss, Andrew H.
See Vachss, Andrew (Henry)

Vaculik, Ludvik 1926- .... **CLC 7**
See also CA 53-56; CANR 72; CWW 2;
DLB 232

Vaihinger, Hans 1852-1933 .... **TCLC 71**
See also CA 116; 166

Valdez, Luis (Miguel) 1940- ..... **CLC 84; DC
10; HLC 2**
See also CA 101; CAD; CANR 32, 81; CD
5; DAM MULT; DFS 5; DLB 122; HW
1; LAIT 4

Valenzuela, Luisa 1938- .... **CLC 31, 104;
HLCS 2; SSC 14**
See also CA 101; CANR 32, 65; CDWLB
3; CWW 2; DAM MULT; DLB 113; FW;
HW 1, 2; LAW; RGSF 2

Valera y Alcala-Galiano, Juan
1824-1905 .... **TCLC 10**
See also CA 106

Valery, (Ambroise) Paul (Toussaint Jules)
1871-1945 .... **TCLC 4, 15; PC 9**
See also CA 104; 122; DA3; DAM POET;
EW 8; GFL 1789 to the Present; MTCW
1, 2; RGWL 2

Valle-Inclan, Ramon (Maria) del
1866-1936 .... **TCLC 5; HLC 2**
See also CA 106; 153; CANR 80; DAM
MULT; DLB 134; EW 8; HW 2; RGSF 2;
RGWL 2

Vallejo, Antonio Buero
See Buero Vallejo, Antonio

Vallejo, Cesar (Abraham)
1892-1938 .... **TCLC 3, 56; HLC 2**
See also CA 105; 153; DAM MULT; HW
1; LAW; RGWL 2

Valles, Jules 1832-1885 .... **NCLC 71**
See also DLB 123; GFL 1789 to the Present

Vallette, Marguerite Eymery
1860-1953 .... **TCLC 67**
See also CA 182; DLB 123, 192

Valle Y Pena, Ramon del
See Valle-Inclan, Ramon (Maria) del

Van Ash, Cay 1918- .... **CLC 34**

Vanbrugh, Sir John 1664-1726 .... **LC 21**
See also BRW 2; DAM DRAM; DLB 80;
IDTP; RGEL 2

Van Campen, Karl
See Campbell, John W(ood, Jr.)

Vance, Gerald
See Silverberg, Robert

Vance, Jack .... **CLC 35**
See also Vance, John Holbrook
See also DLB 8; FANT; SCFW 2; SFW 4;
SUFW

Vance, John Holbrook 1916-
See Queen, Ellery; Vance, Jack
See also CA 29-32R; CANR 17, 65; CMW
4; MTCW 1

**Van Den Bogarde, Derek Jules Gaspard
Ulric Niven** 1921-1999 .... **CLC 14**
See also Bogarde, Dirk
See also CA 77-80; 179

Vandenburgh, Jane .... **CLC 59**
See also CA 168

Vanderhaeghe, Guy 1951- .... **CLC 41**
See also BPFB 3; CA 113; CANR 72

van der Post, Laurens (Jan)
1906-1996 .... **CLC 5**
See also AFW; CA 5-8R; 155; CANR 35;
CN 7; DLB 204; RGEL 2

van de Wetering, Janwillem 1931- ... **CLC 47**
See also CA 49-52; CANR 4, 62, 90; CMW
4

Van Dine, S. S. .... **TCLC 23**
See also Wright, Willard Huntington
See also MSW

Van Doren, Carl (Clinton)
1885-1950 .... **TCLC 18**
See also CA 111; 168

Warung, Price .... **TCLC 45**
  See also Astley, William
  See also DLB 230; RGEL 2
Warwick, Jarvis
  See Garner, Hugh
  See also CCA 1
Washington, Alex
  See Harris, Mark
Washington, Booker T(aliaferro)
  1856-1915 .... **TCLC 10; BLC 3**
  See also BW 1; CA 114; 125; DA3; DAM
  MULT; LAIT 2; RGAL 4; SATA 28
Washington, George 1732-1799 .... **LC 25**
  See also DLB 31
Wassermann, (Karl) Jakob
  1873-1934 .... **TCLC 6**
  See also CA 104; 163; DLB 66
Wasserstein, Wendy 1950- .. **CLC 32, 59, 90;**
  DC 4
  See also CA 121; 129; CABS 3; CAD;
  CANR 53, 75; CD 5; CWD; DA3; DAM
  DRAM; DFS 5; DLB 228; FW; INT CA-
  129; MTCW 2; SATA 94
Waterhouse, Keith (Spencer) 1929- . **CLC 47**
  See also CA 5-8R; CANR 38, 67; CBD;
  CN 7; DLB 13, 15; MTCW 1, 2
Waters, Frank (Joseph) 1902-1995 .. **CLC 88**
  See also CA 5-8R; 149; CAAS 13; CANR
  3, 18, 63; DLB 212; DLBY 1986; RGAL
  4; TCWW 2
Waters, Mary C. .... **CLC 70**
Waters, Roger 1944- .... **CLC 35**
Watkins, Frances Ellen
  See Harper, Frances Ellen Watkins
Watkins, Gerrold
  See Malzberg, Barry N(athaniel)
Watkins, Paul 1964- .... **CLC 55**
  See also CA 132; CANR 62, 98
Watkins, Vernon Phillips
  1906-1967 .... **CLC 43**
  See also CA 9-10; 25-28R; CAP 1; DLB
  20; RGEL 2
Watson, Irving S.
  See Mencken, H(enry) L(ouis)
Watson, John H.
  See Farmer, Philip Jose
Watson, Richard F.
  See Silverberg, Robert
Waugh, Auberon (Alexander)
  1939-2001 .... **CLC 7**
  See also CA 45-48; 192; CANR 6, 22, 92;
  DLB 14, 194
Waugh, Evelyn (Arthur St. John)
  1903-1966 .. **CLC 1, 3, 8, 13, 19, 27, 44,**
  107; SSC 41; WLC
  See also BPFB 3; BRW 7; CA 85-88; 25-
  28R; CANR 22; CDBLB 1914-1945; DA;
  DA3; DAB; DAC; DAM MST, NOV,
  POP; DLB 15, 162, 195; MTCW 1, 2;
  NFS 13; RGEL 2; RGSF 2; WLIT 4
Waugh, Harriet 1944- .... **CLC 6**
  See also CA 85-88; CANR 22
Ways, C. R.
  See Blount, Roy (Alton), Jr.
Waystaff, Simon
  See Swift, Jonathan
Webb, Beatrice (Martha Potter)
  1858-1943 .... **TCLC 22**
  See also CA 117; 162; DLB 190; FW
Webb, Charles (Richard) 1939- .... **CLC 7**
  See also CA 25-28R
Webb, James H(enry), Jr. 1946- ...... **CLC 22**
  See also CA 81-84
Webb, Mary Gladys (Meredith)
  1881-1927 .... **TCLC 24**
  See also CA 182; 123; DLB 34; FW
Webb, Mrs. Sidney
  See Webb, Beatrice (Martha Potter)

Webb, Phyllis 1927- .... **CLC 18**
  See also CA 104; CANR 23; CCA 1; CP 7;
  CWP; DLB 53
Webb, Sidney (James) 1859-1947 .. **TCLC 22**
  See also CA 117; 163; DLB 190
Webber, Andrew Lloyd .... **CLC 21**
  See also Lloyd Webber, Andrew
  See also DFS 7
Weber, Lenora Mattingly
  1895-1971 .... **CLC 12**
  See also CA 19-20; 29-32R; CAP 1; SATA
  2; SATA-Obit 26
Weber, Max 1864-1920 .... **TCLC 69**
  See also CA 109; 189
Webster, John 1580(?)-1634(?) .... **LC 33; DC**
  2; WLC
  See also BRW 2; CDBLB Before 1660; DA;
  DAB; DAC; DAM DRAM, MST; DLB
  58; IDTP; RGEL 2; WLIT 3
Webster, Noah 1758-1843 .... **NCLC 30**
  See also DLB 1, 37, 42, 43, 73, 243
Wedekind, (Benjamin) Frank(lin)
  1864-1918 .... **TCLC 7**
  See also CA 104; 153; CDWLB 2; DAM
  DRAM; DLB 118; EW 8; RGWL 2
Wehr, Demaris .... **CLC 65**
Weidman, Jerome 1913-1998 .... **CLC 7**
  See also AITN 2; CA 1-4R; 171; CAD;
  CANR 1; DLB 28
Weil, Simone (Adolphine)
  1909-1943 .... **TCLC 23**
  See also CA 117; 159; EW 12; FW; GFL
  1789 to the Present; MTCW 2
Weininger, Otto 1880-1903 .... **TCLC 84**
Weinstein, Nathan
  See West, Nathanael
Weinstein, Nathan von Wallenstein
  See West, Nathanael
Weir, Peter (Lindsay) 1944- .... **CLC 20**
  See also CA 113; 123
Weiss, Peter (Ulrich) 1916-1982 .. **CLC 3, 15,**
  51
  See also CA 45-48; 106; CANR 3; DAM
  DRAM; DFS 3; DLB 69, 124; RGWL 2
Weiss, Theodore (Russell) 1916- ... **CLC 3, 8,**
  14
  See also CA 9-12R; CAAE 189; CAAS 2;
  CANR 46, 94; CP 7; DLB 5
Welch, (Maurice) Denton
  1915-1948 .... **TCLC 22**
  See also CA 121; 148; RGEL 2
Welch, James 1940- .... **CLC 6, 14, 52**
  See also CA 85-88; CANR 42, 66, 107; CN
  7; CP 7; CPW; DAM MULT, POP; DLB
  175, 256; NNAL; RGAL 4; TCWW 2
Weldon, Fay 1931- . **CLC 6, 9, 11, 19, 36, 59,**
  122
  See also BRWS 4; CA 21-24R; CANR 16,
  46, 63, 97; CDBLB 1960 to Present; CN
  7; CPW; DAM POP; DLB 14, 194; FW;
  HGG; INT CANR-16; MTCW 1, 2; RGEL
  2; RGSF 2
Wellek, Rene 1903-1995 .... **CLC 28**
  See also CA 5-8R; 150; CAAS 7; CANR 8;
  DLB 63; INT CANR-8
Weller, Michael 1942- .... **CLC 10, 53**
  See also CA 85-88; CAD; CD 5
Weller, Paul 1958- .... **CLC 26**
Wellershoff, Dieter 1925- .... **CLC 46**
  See also CA 89-92; CANR 16, 37
Welles, (George) Orson 1915-1985 .. **CLC 20,**
  80
  See also AAYA 40; CA 93-96; 117
Wellman, John McDowell 1945-
  See Wellman, Mac
  See also CA 166; CD 5

Wellman, Mac .... **CLC 65**
  See also Wellman, John McDowell; Well-
  man, John McDowell
  See also CAD; RGAL 4
Wellman, Manly Wade 1903-1986 ... **CLC 49**
  See also CA 1-4R; 118; CANR 6, 16, 44;
  FANT; SATA 6; SATA-Obit 47; SFW 4;
  SUFW
Wells, Carolyn 1869(?)-1942 .... **TCLC 35**
  See also CA 113; 185; CMW 4; DLB 11
Wells, H(erbert) G(eorge)
  1866-1946 .... **TCLC 6, 12, 19; SSC 6;**
  WLC
  See also AAYA 18; BPFB 3; BRW 6; CA
  110; 121; CDBLB 1914-1945; CLR 64;
  DA; DA3; DAB; DAC; DAM MST, NOV;
  DLB 34, 70, 156, 178; EXPS; HGG;
  LAIT 3; MTCW 1, 2; RGEL 2; RGSF 2;
  SATA 20; SCFW; SFW 4; SSFS 3; SUFW;
  WCH; WLIT 4; YAW
Wells, Rosemary 1943- .... **CLC 12**
  See also AAYA 13; BYA 7, 8; CA 85-88;
  CANR 48; CLR 16, 69; CWRI 5; MAI-
  CYA 1; SAAS 1; SATA 18, 69, 114; YAW
Welsh, Irvine 1958- .... **CLC 144**
  See also CA 173
Welty, Eudora 1909-2001 .... **CLC 1, 2, 5, 14,**
  22, 33, 105; SSC 1, 27, 51; WLC
  See also AMW; AMWR 1; BPFB 3; CA
  9-12R; CABS 1; CANR 32, 65; CDALB
  1941-1968; CN 7; CSW; DA; DA3; DAB;
  DAC; DAM MST, NOV; DLB 2, 102,
  143; DLBD 12; DLBY 1987, 2001; EXPS;
  HGG; LAIT 3; MAWW; MTCW 1, 2;
  NFS 13; RGAL 4; RGSF 2; RHW; SSFS
  2, 10
Wen I-to 1899-1946 .... **TCLC 28**
Wentworth, Robert
  See Hamilton, Edmond
Werfel, Franz (Viktor) 1890-1945 ... **TCLC 8**
  See also CA 104; 161; DLB 81, 124;
  RGWL 2
Wergeland, Henrik Arnold
  1808-1845 .... **NCLC 5**
Wersba, Barbara 1932- .... **CLC 30**
  See also AAYA 2, 30; BYA 6, 12, 13; CA
  29-32R, 182; CAAE 182; CANR 16, 38;
  CLR 3, 78; DLB 52; JRDA; MAICYA 1;
  SAAS 2; SATA 1, 58; SATA-Essay 103;
  WYA; YAW
Wertmueller, Lina 1928- .... **CLC 16**
  See also CA 97-100; CANR 39, 78
Wescott, Glenway 1901-1987 .. **CLC 13; SSC**
  35
  See also CA 13-16R; 121; CANR 23, 70;
  DLB 4, 9, 102; RGAL 4
Wesker, Arnold 1932- .... **CLC 3, 5, 42**
  See also CA 1-4R; CAAS 7; CANR 1, 33;
  CBD; CD 5; CDBLB 1960 to Present;
  DAB; DAM DRAM; DLB 13; MTCW 1;
  RGEL 2
Wesley, Richard (Errol) 1945- .... **CLC 7**
  See also BW 1; CA 57-60; CAD; CANR
  27; CD 5; DLB 38
Wessel, Johan Herman 1742-1785 .... **LC 7**
West, Anthony (Panther)
  1914-1987 .... **CLC 50**
  See also CA 45-48; 124; CANR 3, 19; DLB
  15
West, C. P.
  See Wodehouse, P(elham) G(renville)
West, Cornel (Ronald) 1953- .... **CLC 134;**
  BLCS
  See also CA 144; CANR 91; DLB 246
West, Delno C(loyde), Jr. 1936- .... **CLC 70**
  See also CA 57-60
West, Dorothy 1907-1998 .... **TCLC 108**
  See also BW 2; CA 143; 169; DLB 76

West, (Mary) Jessamyn 1902-1984 ... **CLC 7, 17**
    See also CA 9-12R; 112; CANR 27; DLB 6; DLBY 1984; MTCW 1, 2; RHW; SATA-Obit 37; YAW

West, Morris L(anglo) 1916-1999 ..... **CLC 6, 33**
    See also BPFB 3; CA 5-8R; 187; CANR 24, 49, 64; CN 7; CPW; MTCW 1, 2

West, Nathanael 1903-1940 .... **TCLC 1, 14, 44; SSC 16**
    See also AMW; BPFB 3; CA 104; 125; CDALB 1929-1941; DA3; DLB 4, 9, 28; MTCW 1, 2; RGAL 4

West, Owen
    See Koontz, Dean R(ay)

West, Paul 1930- .... **CLC 7, 14, 96**
    See also CA 13-16R; CAAS 7; CANR 22, 53, 76, 89; CN 7; DLB 14; INT CANR-22; MTCW 2

West, Rebecca 1892-1983 ... **CLC 7, 9, 31, 50**
    See also BPFB 3; BRWS 3; CA 5-8R; 109; CANR 19; DLB 36; DLBY 1983; FW; MTCW 1, 2; RGEL 2

Westall, Robert (Atkinson)
    1929-1993 .... **CLC 17**
    See also AAYA 12; BYA 2, 6, 7, 8, 9; CA 69-72; 141; CANR 18, 68; CLR 13; FANT; JRDA; MAICYA 1; MAICYAS 1; SAAS 2; SATA 23, 69; SATA-Obit 75; WYA; YAW

Westermarck, Edward 1862-1939 . **TCLC 87**

Westlake, Donald E(dwin) 1933- . **CLC 7, 33**
    See also BPFB 3; CA 17-20R; CAAS 13; CANR 16, 44, 65, 94; CMW 4; CPW; DAM POP; INT CANR-16; MSW; MTCW 2

Westmacott, Mary
    See Christie, Agatha (Mary Clarissa)

Weston, Allen
    See Norton, Andre

Wetcheek, J. L.
    See Feuchtwanger, Lion

Wetering, Janwillem van de
    See van de Wetering, Janwillem

Wetherald, Agnes Ethelwyn
    1857-1940 .... **TCLC 81**
    See also DLB 99

Wetherell, Elizabeth
    See Warner, Susan (Bogert)

Whale, James 1889-1957 .... **TCLC 63**

Whalen, Philip 1923- .... **CLC 6, 29**
    See also CA 9-12R; CANR 5, 39; CP 7; DLB 16; WP

Wharton, Edith (Newbold Jones)
    1862-1937 ... **TCLC 3, 9, 27, 53; SSC 6; WLC**
    See also AAYA 25; AMW; AMWR 1; BPFB 3; CA 104; 132; CDALB 1865-1917; DA; DA3; DAB; DAC; DAM MST, NOV; DLB 4, 9, 12, 78, 189; DLBD 13; EXPS; HGG; LAIT 2, 3; MAWW; MTCW 1, 2; NFS 5, 11; RGAL 4; RGSF 2; RHW; SSFS 6, 7; SUFW

Wharton, James
    See Mencken, H(enry) L(ouis)

Wharton, William (a pseudonym) . **CLC 18, 37**
    See also CA 93-96; DLBY 1980; INT 93-96

Wheatley (Peters), Phillis
    1753(?)-1784 ... **LC 3, 50; BLC 3; PC 3; WLC**
    See also AFAW 1, 2; CDALB 1640-1865; DA; DA3; DAC; DAM MST, MULT, POET; DLB 31, 50; EXPP; PFS 13; RGAL 4

Wheelock, John Hall 1886-1978 .... **CLC 14**
    See also CA 13-16R; 77-80; CANR 14; DLB 45

White, Babington
    See Braddon, Mary Elizabeth

White, E(lwyn) B(rooks)
    1899-1985 .... **CLC 10, 34, 39**
    See also AITN 2; AMWS 1; CA 13-16R; 116; CANR 16, 37; CDALBS; CLR 1, 21; CPW; DA3; DAM POP; DLB 11, 22; FANT; MAICYA 1; MTCW 1, 2; RGAL 4; SATA 2, 29, 100; SATA-Obit 44

White, Edmund (Valentine III)
    1940- .... **CLC 27, 110**
    See also AAYA 7; CA 45-48; CANR 3, 19, 36, 62; CN 7; DA3; DAM POP; DLB 227; MTCW 1, 2

White, Hayden V. 1928- .... **CLC 148**
    See also CA 128; DLB 246

White, Patrick (Victor Martindale)
    1912-1990 ...... **CLC 3, 4, 5, 7, 9, 18, 65, 69; SSC 39**
    See also BRWS 1; CA 81-84; 132; CANR 43; MTCW 1; RGEL 2; RGSF 2; RHW

White, Phyllis Dorothy James 1920-
    See James, P. D.
    See also CA 21-24R; CANR 17, 43, 65; CMW 4; CN 7; CPW; DA3; DAM POP; MTCW 1, 2

White, T(erence) H(anbury)
    1906-1964 .... **CLC 30**
    See also AAYA 22; BPFB 3; BYA 4, 5; CA 73-76; CANR 37; DLB 160; FANT; JRDA; LAIT 1; MAICYA 1; RGEL 2; SATA 12; SUFW; YAW

White, Terence de Vere 1912-1994 ... **CLC 49**
    See also CA 49-52; 145; CANR 3

White, Walter
    See White, Walter F(rancis)

White, Walter F(rancis)
    1893-1955 .... **TCLC 15; BLC 3**
    See also BW 1; CA 115; 124; DAM MULT; DLB 51

White, William Hale 1831-1913
    See Rutherford, Mark
    See also CA 121; 189

Whitehead, Alfred North
    1861-1947 .... **TCLC 97**
    See also CA 117; 165; DLB 100

Whitehead, E(dward) A(nthony)
    1933- .... **CLC 5**
    See also CA 65-68; CANR 58; CD 5

Whitemore, Hugh (John) 1936- .... **CLC 37**
    See also CA 132; CANR 77; CBD; CD 5; INT CA-132

Whitman, Sarah Helen (Power)
    1803-1878 .... **NCLC 19**
    See also DLB 1, 243

Whitman, Walt(er) 1819-1892 .. **NCLC 4, 31, 81; PC 3; WLC**
    See also AAYA 42; AMW; AMWR 1; CDALB 1640-1865; DA; DA3; DAB; DAC; DAM MST, POET; DLB 3, 64, 224, 250; EXPP; LAIT 2; PAB; PFS 2, 3, 13; RGAL 4; SATA 20; WP; WYAS 1

Whitney, Phyllis A(yame) 1903- .... **CLC 42**
    See also AAYA 36; AITN 2; BEST 90:3; CA 1-4R; CANR 3, 25, 38, 60; CLR 59; CMW 4; CPW; DA3; DAM POP; JRDA; MAICYA 1; MTCW 2; RHW; SATA 1, 30; YAW

Whittemore, (Edward) Reed (Jr.)
    1919- .... **CLC 4**
    See also CA 9-12R; CAAS 8; CANR 4; CP 7; DLB 5

Whittier, John Greenleaf
    1807-1892 .... **NCLC 8, 59**
    See also AMWS 1; DLB 1, 243; RGAL 4

Whittlebot, Hernia
    See Coward, Noel (Peirce)

Wicker, Thomas Grey 1926-
    See Wicker, Tom
    See also CA 65-68; CANR 21, 46

Wicker, Tom .... **CLC 7**
    See also Wicker, Thomas Grey

Wideman, John Edgar 1941- ...... **CLC 5, 34, 36, 67, 122; BLC 3**
    See also AFAW 1, 2; AMWS 10; BPFB 4; BW 2, 3; CA 85-88; CANR 14, 42, 67; CN 7; DAM MULT; DLB 33, 143; MTCW 2; RGAL 4; RGSF 2; SSFS 6, 12

Wiebe, Rudy (Henry) 1934- .. **CLC 6, 11, 14, 138**
    See also CA 37-40R; CANR 42, 67; CN 7; DAC; DAM MST; DLB 60; RHW

Wieland, Christoph Martin
    1733-1813 .... **NCLC 17**
    See also DLB 97; EW 4; RGWL 2

Wiene, Robert 1881-1938 .... **TCLC 56**

Wieners, John 1934- .... **CLC 7**
    See also CA 13-16R; CP 7; DLB 16; WP

Wiesel, Elie(zer) 1928- .... **CLC 3, 5, 11, 37; WLCS**
    See also AAYA 7; AITN 1; CA 5-8R; CAAS 4; CANR 8, 40, 65; CDALBS; DA; DA3; DAB; DAC; DAM MST, NOV; DLB 83; DLBY 1987; INT CANR-8; LAIT 4; MTCW 1, 2; NFS 4; SATA 56; YAW

Wiggins, Marianne 1947- .... **CLC 57**
    See also BEST 89:3; CA 130; CANR 60

Wiggs, Susan .... **CLC 70**

Wight, James Alfred 1916-1995
    See Herriot, James
    See also CA 77-80; SATA 55; SATA-Brief 44

Wilbur, Richard (Purdy) 1921- ..... **CLC 3, 6, 9, 14, 53, 110**
    See also AMWS 3; CA 1-4R; CABS 2; CANR 2, 29, 76, 93; CDALBS; CP 7; DA; DAB; DAC; DAM MST, POET; DLB 5, 169; EXPP; INT CANR-29; MTCW 1, 2; PAB; PFS 11, 12; RGAL 4; SATA 9, 108; WP

Wild, Peter 1940- .... **CLC 14**
    See also CA 37-40R; CP 7; DLB 5

Wilde, Oscar (Fingal O'Flahertie Wills)
    1854(?)-1900 ..... **TCLC 1, 8, 23, 41; DC 17; SSC 11; WLC**
    See also BRW 5; BRWR 2; CA 104; 119; CDBLB 1890-1914; DA; DA3; DAB; DAC; DAM DRAM, MST, NOV; DFS 4, 8, 9; DLB 10, 19, 34, 57, 141, 156, 190; EXPS; FANT; RGEL 2; RGSF 2; SATA 24; SSFS 7; SUFW; TEA; WCH; WLIT 4

Wilder, Billy .... **CLC 20**
    See also Wilder, Samuel
    See also DLB 26

Wilder, Samuel 1906-2002
    See Wilder, Billy
    See also CA 89-92

Wilder, Stephen
    See Marlowe, Stephen

Wilder, Thornton (Niven)
    1897-1975 .. **CLC 1, 5, 6, 10, 15, 35, 82; DC 1; WLC**
    See also AAYA 29; AITN 2; AMW; CA 13-16R; 61-64; CAD; CANR 40; CDALBS; DA; DA3; DAB; DAC; DAM DRAM, MST, NOV; DFS 1, 4; DLB 4, 7, 9, 228; DLBY 1997; LAIT 3; MTCW 1, 2; RGAL 4; RHW; WYAS 1

Wilding, Michael 1942- ...... **CLC 73; SSC 50**
    See also CA 104; CANR 24, 49, 106; CN 7; RGSF 2

Wiley, Richard 1944- .... **CLC 44**
    See also CA 121; 129; CANR 71

Wilhelm, Kate .... **CLC 7**
    See also Wilhelm, Katie (Gertrude)
    See also AAYA 20; CAAS 5; DLB 8; INT CANR-17; SCFW 2

Literary Criticism Series
Cumulative Topic Index

This index lists all topic entries in Gale's *Classical and Medieval Literature Criticism, Contemporary Literary Criticism, Drama Criticism, Literature Criticism from 1400 to 1800, Nineteenth-Century Literature Criticism,* and *Twentieth-Century Literary Criticism.*

Topic Index

DC Cumulative Nationality Index

ALGERIAN

Camus, Albert **2**

AMERICAN

Albee, Edward (Franklin III) **11**
Baldwin, James (Arthur) **1**
Baraka, Amiri **6**
Brown, William Wells **1**
Bullins, Ed **6**
Chase, Mary (Coyle) **1**
Childress, Alice **4**
Chin, Frank (Chew Jr.) **7**
Elder, Lonne III **8**
Fornés, Mariá Irene **10**
Fuller, Charles (H. Jr.) **1**
Glaspell, Susan **10**
Gordone, Charles **8**
Gray, Spalding **7**
Hansberry, Lorraine (Vivian) **2**
Hellman, Lillian (Florence) **1**
Henley, Beth **6, 14**
Hughes, (James) Langston **3**
Hurston, Zora Neale **12**
Hwang, David Henry **4**
Kaufman, George S. **17**
Kennedy, Adrienne (Lita) **5**
Kramer, Larry **8**
Kushner, Tony **10**
Mamet, David (Alan) **4**
Mann, Emily **7**
Miller, Arthur **1**
Norman, Marsha **8**
Odets, Clifford **6**
Rabe, David (William) **16**
Shange, Ntozake **3**
Shepard, Sam **5**
Sheridan, Richard Brinsley **1**
Simon, (Marvin) Neil **14**
Terry, Megan **13**
Valdez, Luis (Miguel) **10**
Wasserstein, Wendy **4**
Wilder, Thornton (Niven) **1**
Williams, Tennessee **4**
Wilson, August **2**
Zindel, Paul **5**

AUSTRIAN

Bernhard, Thomas **14**
Grillparzer, Franz **14**
Handke, Peter **17**
Hofmannsthal, Hugo von **4**
Schnitzler, Arthur **17**

BARBADIAN

Kennedy, Adrienne (Lita) **5**

BELGIAN

Ghelderode, Michel de **15**

CUBAN

Fornés, Mariá Irene **10**

CZECH

Chapek, Karel **1**
Havel, Václav **6**

DUTCH

Bernhard, Thomas **14**

ENGLISH

Ayckbourn, Alan **13**
Beaumont, Francis **6**
Beddoes, Thomas Lovell **15**
Behn, Aphra **4**
Churchill, Caryl **5**
Congreve, William **2**
Dekker, Thomas **12**
Dryden, John **3**
Fletcher, John **6**
Ford, John **8**
Jonson, Ben(jamin) **4**
Kyd, Thomas **3**
Lyly, John **7**
Marlowe, Christopher **1**
Middleton, Thomas **5**
Orton, Joe **3**
Pinter, Harold **15**
Shaffer, Peter (Levin) **7**
Stoppard, Tom **6**
Webster, John **2**

FRENCH

Anouilh, Jean (Marie Lucien Pierre) **8**
Artaud, Antonin (Marie Joseph) **14**
Beaumarchais, Pierre-Augustin Caron de **4**
Camus, Albert **2**
Cocteau, Jean **17**
Dumas, Alexandre (fils) **1**
Ionesco, Eugène **12**
Marivaux, Pierre Carlet de Chamblain de **7**
Molière **13**
Perrault, Charles **12**
Rostand, Edmond (Eugene Alexis) **10**
Sartre, Jean-Paul **3**
Scribe, (Augustin) Eugène **5**

GERMAN

Brecht, (Eugen) Bertolt (Friedrich) **3**
Schiller, Friedrich von **12**

GREEK

Aeschylus **8**
Aristophanes **2**
Euripides **4**
Menander **3**
Sophocles **1**

IRISH

Friel, Brian **8**
Goldsmith, Oliver **8**
Joyce, James (Augustine Aloysius) **16**
O'Casey, Sean **12**
Sheridan, Richard Brinsley **1**
Synge, (Edmund) J(ohn) M(illington) **2**
Wilde, Oscar **17**

ITALIAN

Fo, Dario **10**
Machiavelli, Niccolò **16**
Pirandello, Luigi **5**
Plautus **6**

JAPANESE

Zeami **7**

NIGERIAN

Clark Bekedermo, J(ohnson) P(epper) **5**
Soyinka, Wole **2**

NORWEGIAN

Ibsen, Henrik (Johan) **2**

ROMAN

Plautus **6**
Seneca, Lucius Annaeus **5**
Terence **7**

ROMANIAN

Ionesco, Eugène **12**

RUSSIAN

Chekhov, Anton (Pavlovich) **9**
Gogol, Nikolai (Vasilyevich) **1**
Turgenev, Ivan (Sergeevich) **7**

SOUTH AFRICAN

Fugard, (Harold) Athol **3**

SPANISH

Calderón de la Barca, Pedro **3**
García Lorca, Federico **2**
Molina, Tirso de **13**

ST. LUCIAN

Walcott, Derek (Alton) **7**

DC-17 Title Index

ISBN 0-7876-5946-0

90000

9 780787 659462